GO!

with Microsoft®

Office 2003
Intermediate

GO!

with Microsoft®

Office 2003
Intermediate

**John Preston, Sally Preston,
Robert L. Ferrett, Linda Foster-Turpen,
Jeffrey M. Howard, and Alicia Vargas**

Shelley Gaskin, Series Editor

PEARSON

Prentice
Hall

Upper Saddle River, New Jersey

Library of Congress Cataloging-in-Publication Data

Go! with Microsoft Office 2003 : intermediate / John Preston ... [et al.].
  p. cm. — (Go! with Microsoft Office 2003)
Includes bibliographical references and index.
  ISBN 0-13-183850-4 (spiral edition : alk. paper) — ISBN 0-13-145116-2
(perfect bound : alk. paper)
  1. Microsoft Office 2. Business—Computer programs. I. Preston, John M. II. Series.
HF5548.4.M525G624 2004
005.5—dc22

2004002863

Vice President and Publisher: Natalie E. Anderson
Executive Acquisitions Editor: Jodi McPherson
Senior Marketing Manager: Emily Williams Knight
Marketing Assistant: Nicole Beaudry
Senior Project Manager, Editorial: Mike Ruel
Project Manager, Editorial: Jodi Bolognese
Senior Media Project Manager: Cathi Profitko
Editorial Assistant: Alana Meyers
Senior Managing Editor, Production: Gail Steier de Acevedo
Senior Project Manager, Production: Tim Tate
Manufacturing Buyer: Tim Tate
Design Manager: Maria Lange
Art Director: Pat Smythe
Cover Designer: Brian Salisbury
Cover Photo: Steve Bloom/Getty Images, Inc.
Interior Designer: Quorum Creative Services
Full Service Composition: Black Dot Group
Printer/Binder: Von Hoffmann Corporation
Cover Printer: Phoenix Color Corporation

Microsoft, Windows, PowerPoint, Outlook, FrontPage, Visual Basic, MSN, The
Microsoft Network, and/or other Microsoft products referenced herein are
either trademarks or registered trademarks of Microsoft Corporation in the
U.S.A. and other countries. Screen shots and icons reprinted with permission
from the Microsoft Corporation. This book is not sponsored or endorsed by or
affiliated with Microsoft Corporation.

Microsoft and the Microsoft Office Specialist logo are trademarks or registered
trademarks of Microsoft Corporation in the United States and/or other countries. Pearson Education is independent from Microsoft Corporation and not
affiliated with Microsoft in any manner. This text may be used in assisting
students to prepare for a Microsoft Office Specialist Exam. Neither Microsoft,
its designated review company, nor Pearson Education warrants that use of
this text will ensure passing the relevant exam.

10 9 8 7 6 5 4 3 2 1
ISBN 0-13-183850-4

We dedicate this book to our granddaughters, who bring us great joy and happiness: Clara and Siena & Alexis and Grace.

—John Preston, Sally Preston, and Robert L. Ferrett

I would like to dedicate this book to my awesome family. I want to thank my husband, Dave Alumbaugh, who always lets me be exactly who I am; my kids, Michael, Jordan, and Ceara, who give me hope and my drive for everything that I do; my mom, who never gives up; and my dad, who has been my light, my rock, and one of my best friends every day that I can remember. I love you all and . . . thanks for putting up with me.

—Linda Foster-Turpen

I would like to dedicate this book to my beautiful wife, Dawn, and to my 5 children, Jacquelynn, Allie, Savannah, Jeffrey, and Jaysen.

—Jeffrey M. Howard

This book is dedicated with all my love to my husband Vic, who makes everything possible; and to my children Victor, Phil, and Emmy, who are an unending source of inspiration and who make everything worthwhile.

—Alicia Vargas

This book is dedicated to my students, who inspire me every day, and to my husband, Fred Gaskin.

—Shelley Gaskin

What does this logo mean?

It means this courseware has been approved by the Microsoft® Office Specialist Program to be among the finest available for learning **Microsoft® Office Word 2003, Microsoft® Office Excel 2003, Microsoft® Office PowerPoint® 2003**, and **Microsoft® Office Access 2003**. It also means that upon completion of this courseware, you may be prepared to take an exam for Microsoft Office Specialist qualification.

What is a Microsoft Office Specialist?

A Microsoft Office Specialist is an individual who has passed exams for certifying his or her skills in one or more of the Microsoft Office desktop applications such as Microsoft Word, Microsoft Excel, Microsoft PowerPoint, Microsoft Outlook, Microsoft Access, or Microsoft Project. The Microsoft Office Specialist Program typically offers certification exams at the "Specialist" and "Expert" skill levels.* The Microsoft Office Specialist Program is the only program approved by Microsoft for testing proficiency in Microsoft Office desktop applications and Microsoft Project. This testing program can be a valuable asset in any job search or career advancement.

More Information:

To learn more about becoming a Microsoft Office Specialist, visit **www.microsoft.com/officespecialist**

To learn about other Microsoft Office Specialist approved courseware from Pearson Education, visit **www.prenhall.com/phit**

GO!
Series for Microsoft® Office System 2003

Series Editor: Shelley Gaskin

Office
Getting Started
Brief
Intermediate
Advanced

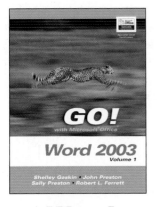

Word
Brief
Volume 1
Volume 2
Comprehensive

Access
Brief
Volume 1
Volume 2
Comprehensive

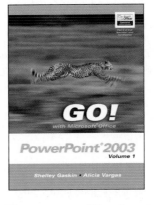

Excel
Brief
Volume 1
Volume 2
Comprehensive

PowerPoint
Brief
Volume 1
Volume 2
Comprehensive

GO! Series Reviewers

We would like to thank the following "Super Reviewers" for both their subject matter expertise and attention to detail from the instructors' perspective. Your time, effort, hard work, and diligence has helped us create the best books in the world. Prentice Hall and your author partners thank you:

Rocky Belcher	Sinclair CC
Judy Cameron	Spokane CC
Gail Cope	Sinclair CC
Larry Farrer	Guilford Tech CC
Janet Enck	Columbus State CC
Susan Fry	Boise State
Lewis Hall	Riverside CC
Jeff Howard	Finger Lakes CC
Jason Hu	Pasadena City College
Michele Hulett	Southwest Missouri State U.
Donna Madsen	Kirkwood CC
Cheryl Reindl-Johnson	Sinclair CC
Jan Spaar	Spokane CC
Mary Ann Zlotow	College of DuPage

We would also like to thank our valuable student reviewers who bring us vital input from those who will someday study from our books:

Nicholas J. Bene	Southwest Missouri State U.
Anup Jonathan	Southwest Missouri State U.
Kimber Miller	Pasadena City College
Kelly Moline	Southwest Missouri State U.
Adam Morris	Southwest Missouri State U.
Robert Murphy	Southwest Missouri State U.
Drucilla Owenby	Southwest Missouri State U.
Vince Withee	Southwest Missouri State U.

Finally, we have been lucky to have so many of you respond to review our chapter manuscripts. You have given us tremendous feedback and helped make a fantastic series. We could not have done it without you.

Abraham, Reni	Houston CC
Agatston, Ann	Agatston Consulting
Alejandro, Manuel	Southwest Texas Junior College
Ali, Farha	Lander University
Anik, Mazhar	Tiffin University
Armstrong, Gary	Shippensburg University
Bagui, Sikha	Univ. West Florida
Belton, Linda	Springfield Tech. Com College
Bennett, Judith	Sam Houston State University
Bishop, Frances	DeVry Institute- Alpharetta (ATL)
Branigan, Dave	DeVry University
Bray, Patricia	Allegany College of Maryland
Buehler, Lesley	Ohlone College
Buell, C	Central Oregon CC
Byars, Pat	Brookhaven College
Cacace, Rich	Pensacola Jr. College
Cadenhead, Charles	Brookhaven College
Calhoun, Ric	Gordon College
Carriker, Sandra	North Shore CC

Challa, Chandrashekar	Virginia State University
Chamlou, Afsaneh	NOVA Alexandria
Chapman, Pam	Wabaunsee CC
Christensen, Dan	Iowa Western CC
Conroy-Link, Janet	Holy Family College
Cosgrove, Janet	Northwestern CT Community Technical College
Cox, Rollie	Madison Area Technical College
Crawford, Hiram	Olive Harvey College
Danno, John	DeVry University/ Keller Graduate School
Davis, Phillip Md.	Del Mar College
Doroshow, Mike	Eastfield College
Douglas, Gretchen	SUNY Cortland
Driskel, Loretta	Niagara CC
Duckwiler, Carol	Wabaunsee CC
Duncan, Mimi	University of Missouri-St. Louis
Duvall, Annette	Albuquerque Technical Vocational Institute

Reviewers continues

Ecklund, Paula	Duke University	Menking, Rick	Hardin-Simmons University
Edmondson, Jeremy	Mount Pisgah School	Meredith, Mary	U. of Louisiana at Lafayette
Erickson, John	University of South Dakota	Mermelstein, Lisa	Baruch College
Falkenstein, Todd	Indiana University East	Metos, Linda	Salt Lake CC
Fite, Beverly	Amarillo College	Meurer, Daniel	University of Cincinnati
Foltz, Brian	East Carolina University	Monk, Ellen	University of Delaware
Friedrichsen, Lisa	Johnson County CC	Morris, Nancy	Hudson Valley CC
Fustos, Janos	Metro State	Nadas, Erika	Wright College
Gallup, Jeanette	Blinn College	Nadelman, Cindi	New England College
Gentry, Barb	Parkland College	Ncube, Cathy	University of West Florida
Gerace, Karin	St. Angela Merici School	Nicholls, Doreen	Mohawk Valley CC
Gerace, Tom	Tulane University	Orr, Claudia	New Mexico State University
Ghajar, Homa	Oklahoma State University	Otieno, Derek	DeVry University
Gifford, Steve	Northwest Iowa CC	Otton, Diana Hill	Chesapeake College
Gregoryk, Kerry	Virginia Commonwealth State University	Oxendale, Lucia	West Virginia Institute of Technology
Griggs, Debra	Bellevue CC	Paiano, Frank	Southwestern College
Grimm, Carol	Palm Beach CC	Proietti, Kathleen	Northern Essex CC
Helms, Liz	Columbus State CC	Pusins, Delores	HCCC
Hernandez, Leticia	TCI College of Technology	Reeves, Karen	High Point University
Hogan, Pat	Cape Fear CC	Rhue, Shelly	DeVry University
Horvath, Carrie	Albertus Magnus College	Richards, Karen	Maplewoods CC
Howard, Chris	DeVry University	Ross, Dianne	Univ. of Louisiana in Lafayette
Huckabay, Jamie	Austin CC	Rousseau, Mary	Broward CC
Hunt, Laura	Tulsa CC	Sams, Todd	University of Cincinnati
Jacob, Sherry	Jefferson CC	Sandoval, Everett	Reedley College
Jacobs, Duane	Salt Lake CC	Sardone, Nancy	Seton Hall University
Johnson, Kathy	Wright College	Scafide, Jean	Mississippi Gulf Coast CC
Jones, Stacey	Benedict College	Scheeren, Judy	Westmoreland County CC
Kasai, Susumu	Salt Lake CC	Schneider, Sol	Sam Houston State University
Keen, Debby	Univ. of Kentucky	Scroggins, Michael	Southwest Missouri State University
Kirk, Colleen	Mercy College		
Kliston, Linda	Broward CC	Sever, Suzanne	Northwest Arkansas CC
Kramer, Ed	Northern Virginia CC	Sheridan, Rick	California State University-Chico
Laird, Jeff	Northeast State CC	Sinha, Atin	Albany State University
Lange, David	Grand Valley State	Smith, T. Michael	Austin CC
LaPointe, Deb	Albuquerque TVI	Smith, Tammy	Tompkins Cortland CC
Lenhart, Sheryl	Terra CC	Stefanelli, Greg	Carroll CC
Letavec, Chris	University of Cincinnati	Steiner, Ester	New Mexico State University
Lightner, Renee	Broward CC	Sterling, Janet	Houston CC
Lindberg, Martha	Minnesota State University	Stroup, Tracey	Pasadena City College
Linge, Richard	Arizona Western College	Sullivan, Angela	Joliet Junior College
Loizeaux, Barbara	Westchester CC	Szurek, Joseph	University of Pittsburgh at Greensburg
Lopez, Don	Clovis- State Center CC District		
Low, Willy Hui	Joliet Junior College	Taylor, Michael	Seattle Central CC
Lowe, Rita	Harold Washington College	Thangiah, Sam	Slippery Rock University
Lucas, Vickie	Broward CC	Thompson-Sellers, Ingrid	Georgia Perimeter College
Lynam, Linda	Central Missouri State University	Tomasi, Erik	Baruch College
		Toreson, Karen	Shoreline CC
Machuca, Wayne	College of the Sequoias	Turgeon, Cheryl	Asnuntuck CC
Madison, Dana	Clarion University	Turpen, Linda	Albuquerque TVI
Maguire, Trish	Eastern New Mexico University	Upshaw, Susan	Del Mar College
Malkan, Rajiv	Montgomery College	Vargas, Tony	El Paso CC
Manning, David	Northern Kentucky University	Vicars, Mitzi	Hampton University
Marghitu, Daniela	Auburn University	Vitrano, Mary Ellen	Palm Beach CC
Marks, Suzanne	Bellevue CC	Wahila, Lori	Tompkins Cortland CC
Marquez, Juanita	El Centro College	Wavle, Sharon	Tompkins Cortland CC
Marucco, Toni	Lincoln Land CC	White, Bruce	Quinnipiac University
Mason, Lynn	Lubbock Christian University	Willer, Ann	Solano CC
Matutis, Audrone	Houston CC	Williams, Mark	Lane CC
McCannon, Melinda (Mindy)	Gordon College	Wimberly, Leanne	International Academy of Design and Technology
McClure, Darlean	College of Sequoias		
McCue, Stacy	Harrisburg Area CC	Worthington, Paula	NOVA Woodbridge
McEntire-Orbach, Teresa	Middlesex County College	Yauney, Annette	Herkimer CCC
McManus, Illyana	Grossmont College	Zavala, Ben	Webster Tech

About the Authors/Acknowledgments

About John Preston, Sally Preston, and Robert L. Ferrett

John Preston is an Associate Professor at Eastern Michigan University in the College of Technology, where he teaches microcomputer application courses at the undergraduate and graduate levels. He has been teaching, writing, and designing computer training courses since the advent of PCs and has authored and co-authored over 60 books on Microsoft Word, Excel, Access, and PowerPoint. He is a series editor for the *Learn 97*, *Learn 2000*, and *Learn XP* books. Two books on Microsoft Access that he co-authored with Robert Ferrett have been translated into Greek and Chinese. He has received grants from the Detroit Edison Institute and the Department of Energy to develop Web sites for energy education and alternative fuels. He has also developed one of the first Internet-based microcomputer applications courses at an accredited university. He has a BS from the University of Michigan in Physics, Mathematics, and Education and an MS from Eastern Michigan University in Physics Education. His doctoral studies were in Instructional Technology at Wayne State University.

Sally Preston is president of Preston & Associates, which provides software consulting and training. She teaches computing in a variety of settings, which provides her with ample opportunity to observe how people learn, what works best, and what challenges are present when learning a new software program. This diverse experience provides a complementary set of skills and knowledge that blends into her writing. Prior to writing for the *GO! series*, Sally was a co-author on the *Learn* series since its inception and has authored books for the *Essentials* and *Microsoft Office User Specialist (MOUS) Essentials* series. Sally has an MBA from Eastern Michigan University. When away from her computer, she is often found planting flowers in her garden.

Robert L. Ferrett recently retired as the director of the Center for Instructional Computing at Eastern Michigan University, where he provided computer training and support to faculty. He has authored or co-authored more than 60 books on Access, PowerPoint, Excel, Publisher, WordPerfect, and Word and was the editor of the *1994 ACM SIGUCCS Conference Proceedings*. He has been designing, developing, and delivering computer workshops for nearly two decades. Before writing for the *GO! series*, Bob was a series editor for the *Learn 97*, *Learn 2000*, and *Learn XP* books. He has a BA in Psychology, an MS in Geography, and an MS in Interdisciplinary Technology from Eastern Michigan University. His doctoral studies were in Instructional Technology at Wayne State University. For fun, Bob teaches a four-week Computers and Genealogy class and has written genealogy and local history books.

Acknowledgments from John Preston, Sally Preston, and Robert L. Ferrett

We would like to acknowledge the efforts of a fine team of editing professionals, with whom we have had the pleasure of working. Jodi McPherson, Jodi Bolognese, Mike Ruel, and Shelley Gaskin did a great job managing and coordinating this effort. We would also like to acknowledge the contributions of Tim Tate, Production Project Manager, and Emily Knight, Marketing Manager, as well as the many reviewers who gave invaluable criticism and suggestions.

About Linda Foster-Turpen

Linda Foster-Turpen is an instructor in Computer Information Systems at Albuquerque TVI in Albuquerque, New Mexico, where she teaches and has developed computer applications courses. Linda received her B.B.A. in Accounting as well as her M.B.A. in MIS and M.B.A. in Accounting from the University of New Mexico. She has developed new courses for her college including courses in Intranets/Extranets, Management Information Systems, and Distance Learning courses in introductory computer applications and Microsoft Access.

In addition to teaching and authoring, Linda likes to hike and backpack with her family. She lives in Corrales, New Mexico, with her husband Dave, her three children, Michael, Jordan, and Ceara, and their animals.

Acknowledgments from Linda Foster-Turpen

I would like to thank everyone at Prentice Hall (and beyond) who was involved with the production of this book. To my reviewers, your input and feedback were appreciated more than you could know. I would not want to write a book without you! To my technical editors, Jan Snyder and Mary Pascarella, thank you for your attention to detail and for your comments and suggestions during the writing of this book. A big thank you to Emily Knight in Marketing, Gail Steier de Acevedo and Tim Tate in Production, and Pat Smythe and Maria Lange in Design for your contributions. To the series editor, Shelley Gaskin, thank you for your wonderful vision for this book and the entire *GO! Series*. Your ideas and inspiration were the basis for this whole project from its inception. To the Editorial Project Manager, Mike Ruel, thanks for making sure all of my ducks were always in a row, and to the Executive Editor, Jodi McPherson, thank you for your faith and confidence in me from the beginning. A huge thanks to my students, you are the reason these books are written! I would also like to thank my colleagues at TVI for giving me a sounding board from which I could bounce ideas or just vent my frustrations. Any book takes a team of people, and I was most fortunate to have all of you on mine. I also want to thank God for . . . everything.

About Jeffrey M. Howard

Jeffrey M. Howard is a Computer Science instructor at Finger Lakes Community College, State University of New York, Canandiagua, N.Y. campus. He has been teaching for the last 15 years. He currently teaches Microsoft Applications (Word, Excel, PowerPoint, and Access), C++, Java, Assembly, and Engineering. Jeff also teaches Office and Concepts classes online through the SUNY Learning Network. He graduated from the University at Buffalo with a BA and MA in Mathematics.

When not working, Jeff tries to spend as much time as possible with his "beautiful and patient" wife, Dawn, and their children, Jacquelynn, Allie, Savannah, Jeffrey, and Jaysen.

Acknowledgments from Jeffrey M. Howard

I would like to thank my Executive Acquisitions Editor, Jodi McPherson, and Senior Project Manager, Mike Ruel, both at Prentice Hall. My special thanks also goes to Tim Tate, Senior Project Manager in Production.

I would also like to thank the Series Editor, Shelley Gaskin, who was a big help to me.

About Alicia Vargas

Alicia Vargas is a faculty member in Business Information Technology at Pasadena City College. She holds a master's and a bachelor's degree in Business Education from California State University, Los Angeles and has authored several textbooks and training manuals on Microsoft Word, Microsoft Excel, and Microsoft PowerPoint.

Acknowledgments from Alicia Vargas

There are many people at Prentice Hall whose dedication and commitment to educational excellence made this book possible. Among those people are Jan Snyder and Mary Pascarella, technical editors extraordinaire, whose work ensured the consistency and credibility of the manuscript; Tim Tate, Production Project Manager, and Emily Knight, Marketing Manager, whose work guaranteed the success of the final product; and Tracey Stroup, whose creative mind made many of the presentations possible. My thanks to all of you and your teams! I would also like to *especially* thank Mike Ruel, Editorial Project Manager, whose humor kept me on task and made the deadlines bearable; Shelley Gaskin, Series Editor, mentor, and friend, whose understanding of college students and their learning is the basis for this series; and Jodie McPherson, Executive Editor, whose energy and intelligence made the *GO! Series* a reality.

On a personal note, I would like to thank my parents, whose commitment to family and education became the foundation for who I am and what I do; and my family and friends whose support makes it all possible. Finally, and most importantly, I would like to thank my husband, Vic, and my three children, Victor, Phil, and Emmy. They keep me busy, they keep me laughing, but most of all, they just keep me! This one's for us!

About Shelley Gaskin

Shelley Gaskin, Series Editor, is a professor of business and computer technology at Pasadena City College in Pasadena, California. She holds a master's degree in business education from Northern Illinois University and a doctorate in adult and community education from Ball State University. Dr. Gaskin has 15 years of experience in the computer industry with several Fortune 500 companies and has developed and written training materials for custom systems applications in both the public and private sector. She is also the author of books on Microsoft Outlook and word processing.

Acknowledgments from Shelley Gaskin

Many talented individuals worked to produce this book, and I thank them for their continuous support. My Executive Acquisitions Editor, Jodi McPherson, gave me much latitude to experiment with new things. Editorial Project Manager Mike Ruel worked with me through each stage of writing and production. Emily Knight and the Prentice Hall Marketing team worked with me throughout this process to make sure both instructors and students are informed about the benefits of using this series. Also, very big thanks and appreciation goes to Prentice Halls' top-notch Production and Design team: Associate Director Product Development Melonie Salvati, Manager of Production Gail Steier de Acevedo, Senior Production Project Manager and Manufacturing Buyer Tim Tate, Design Manager Maria Lange, Art Director Pat Smythe, Interior Designer Quorum Creative Services, and Cover Designer Brian Salisbury.

Thanks to all!
Shelley Gaskin, Series Editor

Why I Wrote This Series

Dear Professor,

If you are like me, you are frantically busy trying to implement new course delivery methods (e.g., online) while also maintaining your regular campus schedule of classes and academic responsibilities. I developed this series for colleagues like you, who are long on commitment and expertise but short on time and assistance.

The primary goal of the **GO! Series**, aside from the obvious one of teaching **Microsoft® Office 2003** concepts and skills, is ease of implementation using any delivery method—traditional, self-paced, or online.

There are no lengthy passages of text; instead, bits of expository text are woven into the steps at the teachable moment. This is the point at which the student has a context within which he or she can understand the concept. A scenario-like approach is used in a manner that makes sense, but it does not attempt to have the student "pretend" to be someone else.

A key feature of this series is the use of Microsoft procedural syntax. That is, steps begin with where the action is to take place, followed by the action itself. This prevents the student from doing the right thing in the wrong place!

The *GO! Series* is written with all of your everyday classroom realities in mind. For example, in each project, the student is instructed to insert his or her name in a footer and to save the document with his or her name. Thus, unidentified printouts do not show up at the printer nor do unidentified documents get stored on the hard drives.

Finally, an overriding consideration is that the student is not always working in a classroom with a teacher. Students frequently work at home or in a lab staffed only with instructional aides. Thus, the instruction must be error-free, clearly written, and logically arranged.

My students enjoy learning the Microsoft Office software. The goal of the instruction in the *GO! Series* is to provide students with the skills to solve business problems using the computer as a tool, for both themselves and the organizations for which they might be employed.

Thank you for using the ***GO! Series for Microsoft® Office System 2003*** for your students.

Regards,

Shelley Gaskin, Series Editor

Preface

Philosophy

Our overall philosophy is ease of implementation for the instructor, whether instruction is via lecture, lab, online, or partially self-paced. Right from the start, the *GO! Series* was created with constant input from professors just like you. You've told us what works, how you teach, and what we can do to make your classroom time problem free, creative, and smooth running—to allow you to concentrate on not what you are teaching from but who you are teaching to—your students. We feel that we have succeeded with the *GO! Series*. Our aim is to make this instruction high quality in both content and presentation, and the classroom management aids complete—an instructor could begin teaching the course with only 15 minutes advance notice. An instructor could leave the classroom or computer lab; students would know exactly how to proceed in the text, know exactly what to produce to demonstrate mastery of the objectives, and feel that they had achieved success in their learning. Indeed, this philosophy is essential for real-world use in today's diverse educational environment.

How did we do it?

- All steps utilize **Microsoft Procedural Syntax**. The *GO! Series* puts students where they need to be, before instructing them what to do. For example, instead of instructing students to "Save the file," we go a few steps further and phrase the instruction as "On the **Menu** bar, click **File**, then select **Save As**."

- A unique teaching system (packaged together in one easy to use **Instructor's Edition** binder set) that enables you to teach anywhere you have to—online, lab, lecture, self-paced, and so forth. The supplements are designed to save you time:

  - *Expert Demonstration Document*—A new project that mirrors the learning objectives of the in-chapter project, with a full demonstration script for you to give a lecture overview quickly and clearly.

  - *Chapter Assignment Sheets*—A sheet listing all the assignments for the chapter. An instructor can quickly insert his or her name, course information, due dates, and points.

  - *Custom Assignment Tags*—These cutout tags include a brief list of common errors that students could make on each project, with check boxes so instructors don't have to keep writing the same error description over and over! These tags serve a dual purpose: The student can do a final check to make sure all the listed items are correct, and the instructor can check off the items that need to be corrected.

- **Highlighted Overlays**—These are printed and transparent overlays that the instructor lays over the student's assignment paper to see at a glance if the student changed what he or she needed to. Coupled with the Custom Assignment Tags, this creates a "grading and scoring system" that is easy for the instructor to implement.

- **Point Counted Chapter Production Test**—Working hand-in-hand with the Expert Demonstration Document, this is a final test for the student to demonstrate mastery of the objectives.

Goals of the GO! Series

The goals of the *GO! Series* are as follows:

- Make it *easy for the instructor to implement* in any instructional setting through high-quality content and instructional aids and provide the student with a valuable, interesting, important, satisfying, and clearly defined learning experience.

- Enable true diverse delivery for today's diverse audience. The *GO! Series* employs various instructional techniques that address the needs of all types of students in all types of delivery modes.

- Provide *turn-key implementation* in the following instructional settings:

    - Traditional computer classroom—Students experience a mix of lecture and lab.

    - Online instruction—Students complete instruction at a remote location and submit assignments to the instructor electronically—questions answered by instructor through electronic queries.

    - Partially self-paced, individualized instruction—Students meet with an instructor for part of the class, and complete part of the class in a lab setting.

    - Completely self-paced, individualized instruction—Students complete all instruction in an instructor-staffed lab setting.

    - Independent self-paced, individualized instruction—Students complete all instruction in a campus lab staffed with instructional aides.

- Teach—*to maximize the moment*. The *GO! Series* is based on the Teachable Moment Theory. There are no long passages of text; instead, concepts are woven into the steps at the teachable moment. Students always know what they need to do and where to do it.

Pedagogical Approach

The *GO! Series* uses an instructional system approach that incorporates three elements:

- *Steps are written in* **Microsoft Procedural Syntax**, which prevents the student from doing the right thing but in the wrong place. This makes it easy for the instructor to teach instead of untangle. It tells the student where to go first, then what to do. For example—"On the File Menu, click Properties."

- *Instructional strategies* including five new, unique ancillary pieces to support the instructor experience. The foundation of the instructional strategies is performance based instruction that is constructed in a manner that makes it *easy for the instructor* to demonstrate the content with the GO Series Expert Demonstration Document, guide the practice by using our many end-of-chapter projects with varying guidance levels, and assess the level of mastery with tools such as our Point Counted Production Test and Custom Assignment Tags.

- *A physical design* that makes it *easy for the instructor* to answer the question, "What do they have to do?" and makes it easy for the student to answer the question, "What do I have to do?" Most importantly, you told us what was needed in the design. We held several focus groups throughout the country where we showed **you** our design drafts and let you tell us what you thought of them. We revised our design based on your input to be functional and support the classroom experience. For example, you told us that a common problem is students not realizing where a project ends. So, we added an "END. You have completed the Project" at the close of every project.

Microsoft Procedural Syntax

Do you ever do something right but in the wrong place?

That's why we've written the *GO! Series* step text using Microsoft procedural syntax. That is, the student is informed where the action should take place before describing the action to take. For example, "On the menu bar, click File," versus "Click File on the menu bar." This prevents the student from doing the right thing in the wrong place. This means that step text usually begins with a preposition—a locator—rather than a verb. Other texts often misunderstand the theory of performance-based instruction and frequently attempt to begin steps with a verb. In fact, the objectives should begin with a verb, not the steps.

The use of Microsoft procedural syntax is one of the key reasons that the *GO! Series* eases the burden for the instructor. The instructor spends less time untangling students' unnecessary actions and more time assisting students with real questions. No longer will students become frustrated and say "But I did what it said!" only to discover that, indeed, they *did* do "what it said" but in the wrong place!

Chapter Organization—Color-Coded Projects

All of the chapters in every *GO! Series* book are organized around interesting projects. Within each chapter, all of the instructional activities will cluster around these projects without any long passages of text for the student to read. Thus, every instructional activity contributes to the completion of the project to which it is associated. Students learn skills to solve real business problems; they don't waste time learning every feature the software has. The end-of-chapter material consists of additional projects with varying levels of difficulty.

The chapters are based on the following basic hierarchy:

Project Name

Objective Name (begins with a verb)

Activity Name (begins with a gerund)

Numbered Steps (begins with a preposition or a verb using Microsoft Procedural Syntax.)

Project Name → **Project 1A Exploring Outlook 2003**

Objective Name → **Objective 1**
Start Outlook and Identify Outlook Window Elements

Activity Name → **Activity 1.1 Starting Outlook**

Numbered Steps → **1** On the Windows taskbar, click the Start button, determine from your instructor or lab coordinator where the Microsoft Office Outlook 2003 program is located on your system, and then click Microsoft Office Outlook 2003.

A project will have a number of objectives associated with it, and the objectives, in turn, will have one or more activities associated with them. Each activity will have a series of numbered steps. To further enhance understanding, each project, and its objectives and numbered steps, is color coded for fast, easy recognition.

In-Chapter Boxes and Elements

Within every chapter there are helpful boxes and in-line notes that aid the students in their mastery of the performance objectives. Plus, each box has a specific title—"Does Your Notes Button Look Different?" or "To Open the New Appointment Window." Our GO! Series Focus Groups told us to add box titles that indicate the information being covered in the box, and we listened!

Alert!

Does Your Notes Button Look Different?

The size of the monitor and screen resolution set on your computer controls the number of larger module buttons that appear at the bottom of the Navigation pane.

Alert! boxes do just that—they alert students to a common pitfall or spot where trouble may be encountered.

Another Way

To Open the New Appointment Window

You can create a new appointment window using one of the following techniques:

• On the menu bar, click File, point to New, and click Appointment.

• On the Calendar Standard toolbar, click the New Appointment button.

Another Way boxes explain simply "another way" of going about a task or shortcuts for saving time.

Note — Server Connection Dialog Box

If a message displays indicating that a connection to the server could not be established, click OK. Even without a mail server connection, you can still use the personal information management features of Outlook.

Notes highlight additional information pertaining to a task.

More Knowledge — Creating New Folders

A module does not have to be active in order to create new folders within it. From the Create New Folder text box, you can change the type of items that the new folder will contain and then select any location in which to place the new folder. Additionally, it is easy to move a folder created in one location to a different location.

More Knowledge is a more detailed look at a topic or task.

Organization of the GO! Series

The *GO! Series for Microsoft® Office System 2003* includes several different combinations of texts to best suit your needs.

- **Word, Excel, Access, and PowerPoint 2003** are available in the following editions:

    - **Brief:** Chapters 1–3 (1–4 for Word 2003)

    - **Volume 1:** Chapters 1–6
      ~ Microsoft Office Specialist Certification

    - **Volume 2:** Chapters 7–12 (7–8 for PowerPoint 2003)

    - **Comprehensive:** Chapters 1–12 (1–8 for PowerPoint 2003)
      ~ Microsoft Office Expert Certification for Word and Excel 2003.

- Additionally, the *GO! Series* is available in four combined **Office 2003** texts:

    - **Microsoft® Office 2003 Getting Started** contains the Windows XP Introduction and first chapter from each application (Word, Excel, Access, and PowerPoint).

    - **Microsoft® Office 2003 Brief** contains Chapters 1–3 of Excel, Access, and PowerPoint, and Chapters 1–4 of Word. Four additional supplementary "Getting Started" books are included (Internet Explorer, Computer Concepts, Windows XP, and Outlook 2003).

    - **Microsoft® Office 2003 Intermediate** contains Chapters 4–8 of Excel, Access, and PowerPoint, and Chapters 5–8 of Word.

    - **Microsoft® Office 2003 Advanced** version picks up where the Intermediate leaves off, covering advanced topics for the individual applications. This version contains Chapters 9–12 of Word, Excel, and Access.

Microsoft Office Specialist Certification

The *GO! Series* has been approved by Microsoft for use in preparing for the Microsoft Office Specialist exams. The Microsoft Office Specialist program is globally recognized as the standard for demonstrating desktop skills with the Microsoft Office System of business productivity applications (Microsoft Word, Microsoft Excel, Microsoft Access, Microsoft PowerPoint, and Microsoft Outlook). With Microsoft Office Specialist certification, thousands of people have demonstrated increased productivity and have proved their ability to utilize the advanced functionality of these Microsoft applications.

Instructor and Student Resources

Instructor's Resource Center and Instructor's Edition

The *GO! Series* was designed for you—instructors who are long on commitment and short on time. *We asked you how you use our books and supplements and how we can make it easier for you and save you valuable time.* We listened to what you told us and created this Instructor's Resource Center for you—different from anything you have ever had access to from other texts and publishers.

What is the Instructor's Edition?

1) Instructor's Edition

New from Prentice Hall, exclusively for the *GO! Series*, the Instructor's Edition contains the entire book, wrapped with vital margin notes—things like objectives, a list of the files needed for the chapter, teaching tips, Microsoft Office Specialist objectives covered, and MORE! Below is a sample of the many helpful elements in the Instructor's Edition.

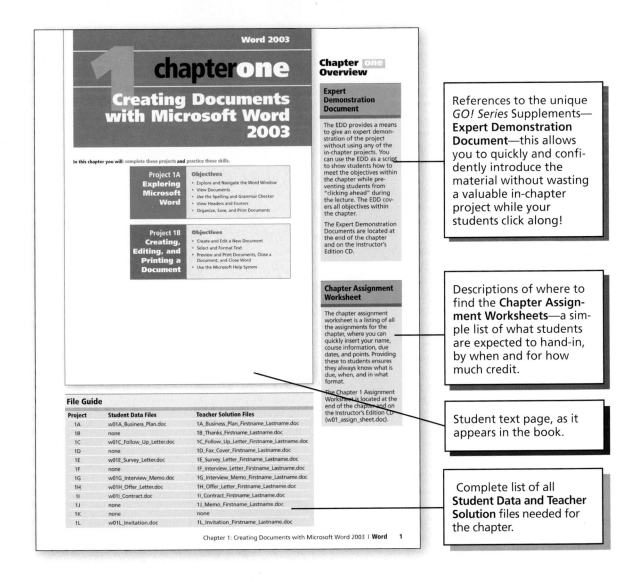

References to the unique *GO! Series* Supplements—**Expert Demonstration Document**—this allows you to quickly and confidently introduce the material without wasting a valuable in-chapter project while your students click along!

Descriptions of where to find the **Chapter Assignment Worksheets**—a simple list of what students are expected to hand-in, by when and for how much credit.

Student text page, as it appears in the book.

Complete list of all **Student Data and Teacher Solution** files needed for the chapter.

Reference to Prentice Hall's Companion Website for the *GO! Series*: **www.prenhall.com/go**

CW

www.prenhall.com/go

The Companion Website is an online training tool that includes personalization features for registered instructors. Data files are available here for download as well as access to additional quizzing exercises.

Each chapter also tells you where to find another unique *GO! Series* Supplement—the **Custom Assignment Tags**—use these in combination with the highlighted overlays to save you time! Simply check off what the students missed or if they completed all the tasks correctly.

Custom Assignment Tags

Custom Assignment Tags, which are meant to be cut out and attached to assignments, serve a dual purpose: the student can do a final check to make sure all the listed items are correct, and the instructor can quickly check off the items that need to be corrected and simply return the assignment.

The Chapter 1 Custom Assignment Tags are located at the end of the chapter and on the Instructor's Edition CD (w01_assign_tags.doc).

The Perfect Party

The Perfect Party store, owned by two partners, provides a wide variety of party accessories including invitations, favors, banners and flags, balloons, piñatas, etc. Party-planning services include both custom parties with pre-filled custom "goodie bags" and "parties in a box" that include everything needed to throw a theme party. Big sellers in this category are the Football and Luau themes. The owners are planning to open a second store and expand their party-planning services to include catering.

© Getty Images, Inc.

Getting Started with Microsoft Office Word 2003

Word processing is the most common program found on personal computers and one that almost everyone has a reason to use. When you learn word processing you are also learning skills and techniques that you need to work efficiently on a personal computer. Use Microsoft Word to do basic word processing tasks such as writing a memo, a report, or a letter. You can also use Word to do complex word processing tasks, including sophisticated tables, embedded graphics, and links to other documents and the Internet. Word is a program that you can learn gradually, adding more advanced skills one at a time.

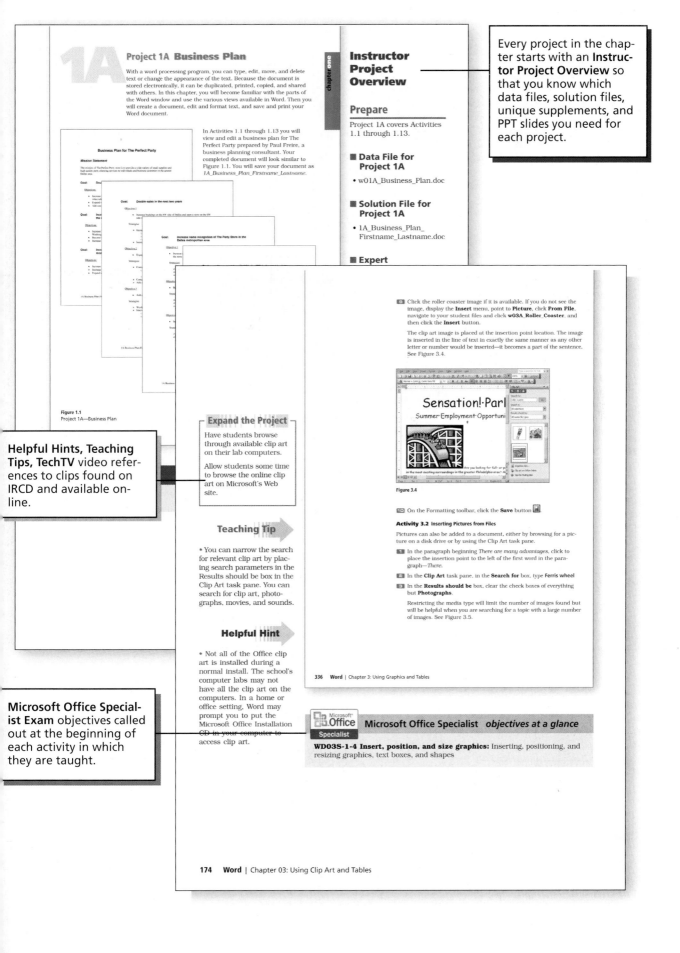

Every project in the chapter starts with an **Instructor Project Overview** so that you know which data files, solution files, unique supplements, and PPT slides you need for each project.

Helpful Hints, Teaching Tips, TechTV video references to clips found on IRCD and available online.

Microsoft Office Specialist Exam objectives called out at the beginning of each activity in which they are taught.

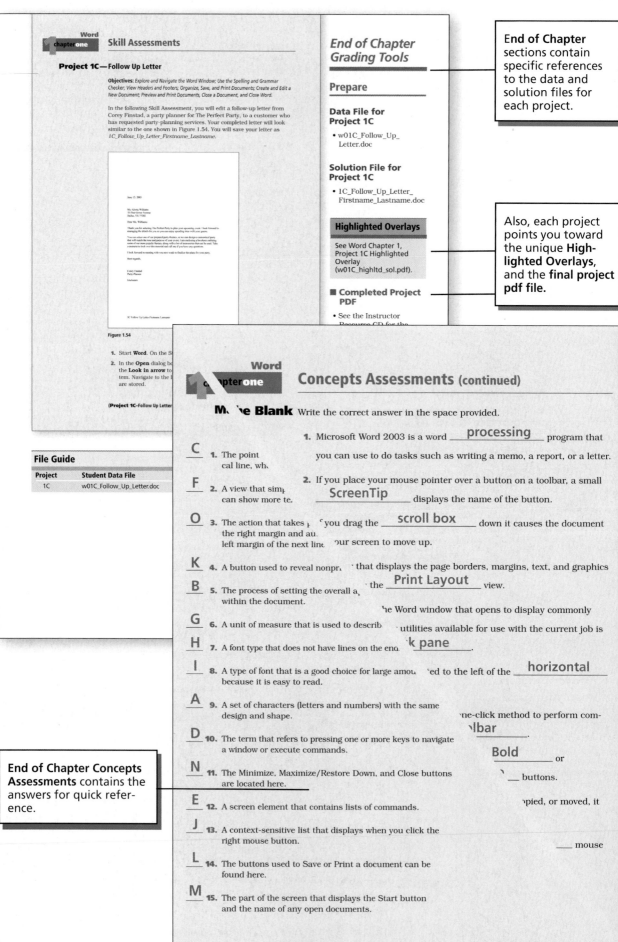

End of Chapter sections contain specific references to the data and solution files for each project.

Also, each project points you toward the unique **Highlighted Overlays**, and the **final project pdf file**.

End of Chapter Concepts Assessments contains the answers for quick reference.

Word

chapter one

Skill Assessments

Project 1C—Follow Up Letter

Objectives: *Explore and Navigate the Word Window; Use the Spelling and Grammar Checker; View Headers and Footers; Organize, Save, and Print Documents; Create and Edit a New Document; Preview and Print Documents, Close a Document, and Close Word.*

In the following Skill Assessment, you will edit a follow-up letter from Corey Finstad, a party planner for The Perfect Party, to a customer who has requested party-planning services. Your completed letter will look similar to the one shown in Figure 1.54. You will save your letter as *1C_Follow_Up_Letter_Firstname_Lastname.*

Figure 1.54

1. Start **Word**. On the S...
2. In the **Open** dialog b... the **Look in arrow** to ... tem. Navigate to the ... are stored.

(Project 1C-Follow Up Letter...

File Guide

Project	Student Data File
1C	w01C_Follow_Up_Letter.doc

End of Chapter Grading Tools

Prepare

Data File for Project 1C

- w01C_Follow_Up_Letter.doc

Solution File for Project 1C

- 1C_Follow_Up_Letter_Firstname_Lastname.doc

Highlighted Overlays

See Word Chapter 1, Project 1C Highlighted Overlay (w01C_highltd_sol.pdf).

■ **Completed Project PDF**

- See the Instructor Resource CD for the...

Word

chapter one

Concepts Assessments (continued)

Fill in the Blank Write the correct answer in the space provided.

1. Microsoft Word 2003 is a word _____**processing**_____ program that you can use to do tasks such as writing a memo, a report, or a letter.

2. If you place your mouse pointer over a button on a toolbar, a small _____**ScreenTip**_____ displays the name of the button.

3. The action that takes ... you drag the _____**scroll box**_____ down it causes the document the right margin and au... left margin of the next line ...ur screen to move up.

4. A button used to reveal nonpr... that displays the page borders, margins, text, and graphics ... the _____**Print Layout**_____ view.

5. The process of setting the overall a... within the document. ...he Word window that opens to display commonly

6. A unit of measure that is used to describ... utilities available for use with the current job is

7. A font type that does not have lines on the en... **k pane** _____.

8. A type of font that is a good choice for large amou... ed to the left of the _____**horizontal**_____ because it is easy to read.

9. A set of characters (letters and numbers) with the same design and shape. ...ne-click method to perform com-

10. The term that refers to pressing one or more keys to navigate a window or execute commands. ...lbar _____.

Bold _____ or

11. The Minimize, Maximize/Restore Down, and Close buttons are located here. ... _____ buttons.

12. A screen element that contains lists of commands. ...pied, or moved, it

13. A context-sensitive list that displays when you click the right mouse button. _____ mouse

14. The buttons used to Save or Print a document can be found here.

15. The part of the screen that displays the Start button and the name of any open documents.

Answer letters in left margin: C, F, O, K, B, G, H, I, A, D, N, E, J, L, M

Chapter summary pages contain links to Glossary and Key Terms, as well as information about Online Courses and Prentice Hall's Train and Assess Generation IT—online training and assessment.

Another supplement exclusive to the *GO! Series* is the **Point Counted Production Test.** Reminders are put on each chapter summary page, the printed documents are provided in the back of each chapter, and we also provide electronic versions in Word format on the IE CD-ROM for easy customization.

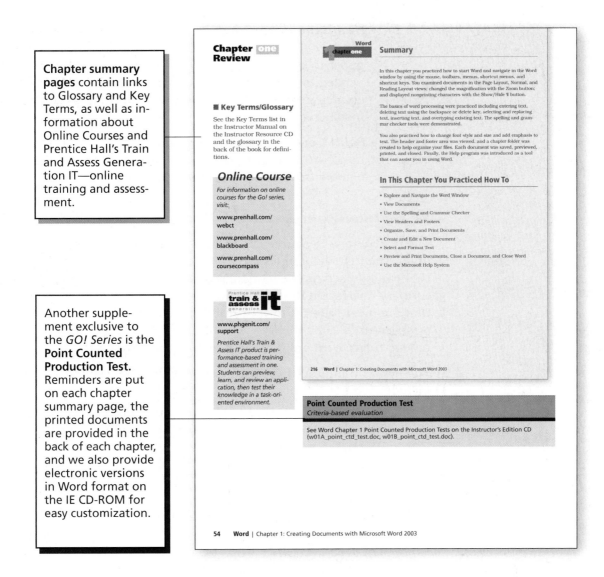

The Instructor's Edition also contains printed copies of these supplement materials *unique* to the *GO! Series*:

- *Expert Demonstration Document (EDD)*—A mirror image of each in-chapter project, accompanied by a brief script. The instructor can use it to give an expert demonstration of each objective that will be covered in the chapter, without having to use one of the chapter's projects. This EDD also prevents students from "working ahead during the presentation," as they do not have access to this document/project.

- *Chapter Assignment Sheets*—With a sheet listing all the assignments for the chapter, the instructor can quickly insert his or her name, course information, due dates, and points.

- *Custom Assignment Tags*—These cutout tags include a brief list of common errors that students could make on each project, with check boxes so instructors don't have to keep writing the same error description over and over! These tags serve a dual purpose: The student can do a final check to make sure all the listed items are correct, and the instructor can check off the items that need to be corrected.

- *Highlighted Overlays*—These are printed and transparent overlays that the instructor lays over the student's assignment paper to see at a glance if the student changed what he or she needed to. Coupled with the Custom Assignment Tags, this creates a "grading and scoring system" that is easy for the instructor to implement.

- *Point Counted Chapter Production Test*—Working hand-in-hand with the EDD, this is a final test for the student to demonstrate mastery of the objectives.

2) Enhanced Instructor's Resource CD-ROM

The Instructor's Resource CD-ROM is an interactive library of assets and links. The Instructor's Resource CD-ROM writes custom "index" pages that can be used as the foundation of a class presentation or online lecture. By navigating through the CD-ROM, you can collect the materials that are most relevant to your interests, edit them to create powerful class lectures, copy them to your own computer's hard drive, and/or upload them to an online course management system.

The new and improved Prentice Hall Instructor's Resource CD-ROM includes tools you expect from a Prentice Hall text:

- The Instructor's Manual in Word and PDF formats—includes solutions to all questions and exercises from the book and Companion Website

- Multiple, customizable PowerPoint slide presentations for each chapter

- Data and Solution Files

- Complete Test Bank

- Image library of all figures from the text

- TestGen Software with QuizMaster

  - TestGen is a test generator that lets you view and easily edit test bank questions, transfer them to tests, and print in a variety of formats suitable to your teaching situation. The program also offers many options for organizing and displaying test banks and tests. A built-in random number and text generator makes it ideal for creating multiple versions of tests that involve calculations and provides more possible test items than test bank questions. Powerful search and sort functions let you easily locate questions and arrange them in the order you prefer.

  - QuizMaster allows students to take tests created with TestGen on a local area network. The QuizMaster utility built into TestGen lets instructors view student records and print a variety of reports. Building tests is easy with TestGen, and exams can be easily uploaded into WebCT, Blackboard, and CourseCompass.

3) Instructor's Edition CD-ROM

The Instructor's Edition CD-ROM contains PDF versions of the Instructor's Edition as well as Word versions of the *GO! Series* unique supplements for easy instructor customization.

Training and Assessment— www2.phgenit.com/support

Prentice Hall offers performance-based training and assessment in one product—Train&Assess IT. The training component offers computer-based training that a student can use to preview, learn, and review Microsoft Office application skills. Web or CD-ROM delivered, Train IT offers interactive, multimedia, computer-based training to augment classroom learning. Built-in prescriptive testing suggests a study path based not only on student test results but also on the specific textbook chosen for the course.

The assessment component offers computer-based testing that shares the same user interface as Train IT and is used to evaluate a student's knowledge about specific topics in Word, Excel, Access, PowerPoint, Outlook, the Internet, and Computing Concepts. It does this in a task-oriented environment to demonstrate proficiency as well as comprehension of the topics by the students. More extensive than the testing in Train IT, Assess IT offers more administrative features for the instructor and additional questions for the student.

Assess IT also allows professors to test students out of a course, place students in appropriate courses, and evaluate skill sets.

OneKey—www.prenhall.com/onekey

OneKey lets you in to the best teaching and learning resources all in one place. OneKey for the *GO! Series* is all your students need for anywhere-anytime access to your course materials conveniently organized by textbook chapter to reinforce and apply what they've learned in class. OneKey is all you need to plan and administer your course. All your instructor resources are in one place to maximize your effectiveness and minimize your time and effort. OneKey for convenience, simplicity, and success... for you and your students.

Companion Website @ www.prenhall.com/go

This text is accompanied by a Companion Website at www.prenhall.com/go. Features of this new site include an interactive study guide, downloadable supplements, online end-of-chapter materials, additional practice projects, Web resource links, and technology updates and bonus chapters on the latest trends and hottest topics in information technology. All links to Web exercises will be constantly updated to ensure accuracy for students.

CourseCompass—www.coursecompass.com

 CourseCompass is a dynamic, interactive online course-management tool powered exclusively for Pearson Education by Blackboard. This exciting product allows you to teach market-leading Pearson Education content in an easy-to-use, customizable format.

Blackboard—www.prenhall.com/blackboard

 Prentice Hall's abundant online content, combined with Blackboard's popular tools and interface, result in robust Web-based courses that are easy to implement, manage, and use—taking your courses to new heights in student interaction and learning.

WebCT—www.prenhall.com/webct

 Course-management tools within WebCT include page tracking, progress tracking, class and student management, gradebook, communication, calendar, reporting tools, and more. Gold Level Customer Support, available exclusively to adopters of Prentice Hall courses, is provided free-of-charge on adoption and provides you with priority assistance, training discounts, and dedicated technical support.

TechTV—www.techtv.com

TechTV is the San Francisco-based cable network that showcases the smart, edgy, and unexpected side of technology. By telling stories through the prism of technology, TechTV provides programming that celebrates its viewers' passion, creativity, and lifestyle.

TechTV's programming falls into three categories:

1. **Help and Information**, with shows like *The Screen Savers*, TechTV's daily live variety show featuring everything from guest interviews and celebrities to product advice and demos; *Tech Live*, featuring the latest news on the industry's most important people, companies, products, and issues; and *Call for Help*, a live help and how-to show providing computing tips and live viewer questions.

2. **Cool Docs**, with shows like *The Tech Of...*, a series that goes behind the scenes of modern life and shows you the technology that makes things tick; *Performance*, an investigation into how technology and science are molding the perfect athlete; and *Future Fighting Machines*, a fascinating look at the technology and tactics of warfare.

3. **Outrageous Fun**, with shows like *X-Play*, exploring the latest and greatest in videogaming; and *Unscrewed* with Martin Sargent, a new late-night series showcasing the darker, funnier world of technology.

For more information, log onto www.techtv.com or contact your local cable or satellite provider to get TechTV in your area.

Visual Walk-Through

Project-based Instruction

Students do not practice features of the application; they create real projects that they will need in the real world. Projects are color coded for easy reference.

Projects are

named to reflect skills the student will be practicing, not vague project names.

Word 2003

1 chapterone

Creating Documents with Microsoft Word 2003

In this chapter you will: complete these projects and practice these skills.

Project 1A Exploring Microsoft Word	**Objectives** • Explore and Navigate the Word Window • View Documents • Use the Spelling and Grammar Checker • View Headers and Footers • Organize, Save, and Print Documents
Project 1B Creating, Editing, and Printing a Document	**Objectives** • Create and Edit a New Document • Select and Format Text • Preview and Print Documents, Close a Document, and Close Word • Use the Microsoft Help System

Learning Objectives

Objectives are clustered around projects. They help students to learn how to solve problems, not just learn software features.

The Greater Atlanta Job Fair

The Greater Atlanta Job Fair is a nonprofit organization that holds targeted job fairs in and around the greater Atlanta area several times each year. The fairs are widely marketed to companies nationwide and locally. The organization also presents an annual Atlanta Job Fair that draws over 2,000 employers in more than 70 industries and generally registers more than 5,000 candidates.

©Getty Images, Inc.

Getting Started with Outlook 2003

Do you sometimes find it a challenge to manage and complete all the tasks related to your job, family, and class work? Microsoft Office Outlook 2003 can help. Outlook 2003 is a personal information management program (also known as a PIM) that does two things: (1) it helps you get organized, and (2) it helps communicate with others efficiently. Successful people know that good organizational and communication skills are important. Outlook 2003 electronically stores and organizes appointments and due dates; names, addresses, and phone numbers; to do lists; and notes. Another major use of Outlook 2003 is its e-mail and fax capabilities, along with features with which you can manage group work such as the tasks assigned to a group of coworkers. In this introduction to Microsoft Office Outlook 2003, you will explore the modules available in Outlook and enter data into each module.

Each chapter

opens with a story that sets the stage for the projects the student will create, not force them to pretend to be someone or make up a scenario themselves.

Each chapter has

an introductory paragraph that briefs students on what is important.

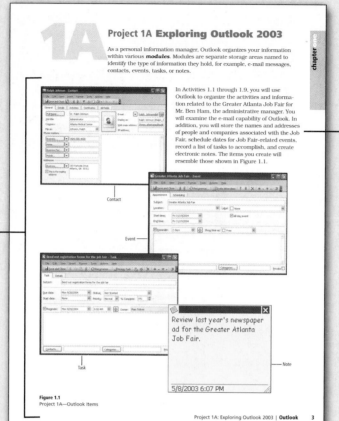

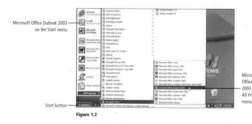

Steps

Color coded to the current project, easy to read, and not too many to confuse the student or too few to be meaningless.

Sequential Page Numbering

No more confusing letters and abbreviations.

End of Project Icon

All projects in the *GO! Series* have clearly identifiable end points, useful in self-paced or on-line environments.

Objective 5
Organize, Save, and Print Documents

In the same way that you use file folders to organize your paper documents, Windows uses a hierarchy of electronic folders to keep your electronic files organized. Check with your instructor or lab coordinator to see where you will be storing your documents (for example, on your own disk or on a network drive) and whether there is any suggested file folder arrangement. Throughout this textbook, you will be instructed to save your files using the file name followed by your first and last name. Check with your instructor to see if there is some other file naming arrangement for your course.

Activity 1.12 Creating Folders for Document Storage and Saving a Document

When you save a document file, the Windows operating system stores your document permanently on a storage medium—either a disk that you have inserted into the computer, the hard drive of your computer, or a network drive connected to your computer system. Changes that you make to existing documents, such as changing text or typing in new text, are not permanently saved until you perform a Save operation.

1 On the menu bar, click **File**, and then click **Save As**.

The Save As dialog box displays.

2 In the **Save As** dialog box, at the right edge of the **Save in** box, click the **Save in arrow** to view a list of the drives available to you as shown in Figure 1.30. The list of drives and folders will differ from the one shown.

Figure 1.30

Microsoft Procedural Syntax

All steps are written in Microsoft Procedural Syntax in order to put the student in the right place at the right time.

Activity 1.13 Printing a Document From the Toolbar

In Activity 1.13, you will print your document from the toolbar.

1 On the Standard toolbar, click the **Print** button .

One copy of your document prints on the default printer. A total of four pages will print, and your name and file name will print in the footer area of each page.

2 On your printed copy, notice that the formatting marks designating spaces, paragraphs, and tabs, do not print.

3 From the **File** menu, click **Exit**, saving any changes if prompted to do so.

Both the document and the Word program close.

Another Way

Printing a Document

There are two ways to print a document:

- On the Standard or Print Preview toolbar, click the Print button, which will print a single copy of the entire document on the default printer.
- From the File menu, click Print to display the Print dialog box, from which you can select a variety of different options, such as printing multiple copies, printing on a different printer, and printing some but not all pages.

End You have completed Project 1A

chapter **one**

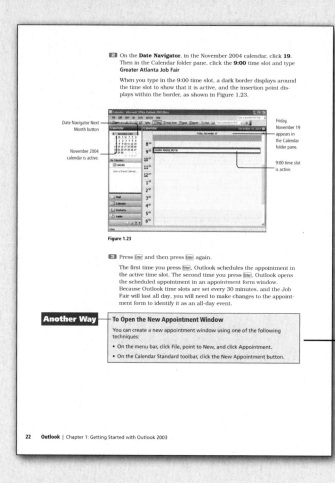

On the **Date Navigator**, in the November 2004 calendar, click **19**. Then in the Calendar folder pane, click the **9:00** time slot and type **Greater Atlanta Job Fair**

When you type in the 9:00 time slot, a dark border displays around the time slot to show that it is active, and the insertion point displays within the border, as shown in Figure 1.23.

Figure 1.23

Press Enter and then press Enter again.

The first time you press Enter, Outlook schedules the appointment in the active time slot. The second time you press Enter, Outlook opens the scheduled appointment in an appointment form window. Because Outlook time slots are set every 30 minutes, and the Job Fair will last all day, you will need to make changes to the appointment form to identify it as an all-day event.

Another Way — **To Open the New Appointment Window**

You can create a new appointment window using one of the following techniques:

• On the menu bar, click File, point to New, and click Appointment.

• On the Calendar Standard toolbar, click the New Appointment button.

Alert box
Draws students' attention to make sure they aren't getting too far off course.

Another Way box
Shows students other ways of doing tasks.

More Knowledge box
Expands on a topic by going deeper into the material.

Note box
Points out important items to remember.

End-of-Chapter Material
Take your pick... Skills Assessment, Performance Assessment, or Mastery Assessment. Real-world projects with high, medium, or low guidance levels.

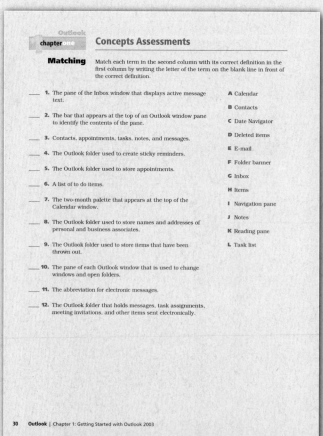

chapter one **Concepts Assessments**

Matching Match each term in the second column with its correct definition in the first column by writing the letter of the term on the blank line in front of the correct definition.

_____ **1.** The pane of the Inbox window that displays active message text.

_____ **2.** The bar that appears at the top of an Outlook window pane to identify the contents of the pane.

_____ **3.** Contacts, appointments, tasks, notes, and messages.

_____ **4.** The Outlook folder used to create sticky reminders.

_____ **5.** The Outlook folder used to store appointments.

_____ **6.** A list of to do items.

_____ **7.** The two-month palette that appears at the top of the Calendar window.

_____ **8.** The Outlook folder used to store names and addresses of personal and business associates.

_____ **9.** The Outlook folder used to store items that have been thrown out.

_____ **10.** The pane of each Outlook window that is used to change windows and open folders.

_____ **11.** The abbreviation for electronic messages.

_____ **12.** The Outlook folder that holds messages, task assignments, meeting invitations, and other items sent electronically.

A Calendar

B Contacts

C Date Navigator

D Deleted items

E E-mail

F Folder banner

G Inbox

H Items

I Navigation pane

J Notes

K Reading pane

L Task list

Objectives List

Each project in the GO! Series end-of-chapter section starts with a list of the objectives covered, in order to easily find the exercises you need to hone your skills.

Performance Assessments

Project 1D — Creating Folders for College Fairs

Objectives: *Start Outlook and Create Outlook Folders.*

The fairs for Mercer College and Georgia Tech have been set for April 2005. As a result, you need to create folders to hold vendor information for the fairs. When you have created the contact folders for these two fairs, your Contacts list will appear as in Figure 1.35.

Figure 1.35

1. Start Outlook, open the **Contacts** module, open the main **Contacts** folder, and on the menu bar, click **File**, point to **Folder**, and click **New Folder** to open the **Create New Folder** dialog box.

2. In the **Name** text box, type **Mercer College Fair 2005** ensure that **Contact Items** appears in the **Folder contains** text box, and click **OK**.

3. Repeat the procedures in Steps 1 and 2 to create another contacts folder named **Georgia Tech Fair 2005**

End You have completed Project 1D

End of Each Project Clearly Marked

Groups of steps that the student performs; the guided practice in order to master the learning objective.

On the Internet

In this section, students are directed to go out to the Internet for independent study.

On the Internet

Locating Friends on the Web

The World Wide Web not only stores information about companies. Web sites for bidding on items, and so forth, but it also contains telephone book information as well as e-mail addresses for many people—especially those who are students at universities! Search the Web for the colleges that three of your friends attend. After you locate the sites, search each university's e-mail directory for one of your friends. Then record these friends and their university e-mail addresses in your contacts list. Print a copy of each contact form as you create it.

GO! with Help

Training on Outlook

Microsoft Online has set up a series of training lessons at its online Web site. You can access Microsoft.com and review these training sessions directly from the Help menu in Outlook. In this project, you will work your way through the links on the Microsoft Web site to see what training topics they currently offer for Outlook. Log onto the required networks, connect to the Internet, and then follow these steps to complete the exercise.

1. If necessary, start Outlook. On the menu bar, click **Help** and then click **Office on Microsoft.com**.

   The Microsoft Office Online Web page opens in the default browser window.

2. On the left side of the Microsoft Office Online Web page, click the **Training** link.

   The Training Home Web page opens.

3. On the Training Home page, under Browse Training Courses, click **Outlook**.

   The Outlook Courses Web page opens.

4. On the Outlook Courses Web page list, click **Address your e-mail: Get it on the To line fast**.

   The Overview Web page displays information about the training session, identifies the goals of the session, and displays links for continuing the session. Navigation buttons appear in a grey bar toward the top of the Overview page for playing, pausing, and stopping the session. Yellow arrows appear above the navigation bar to advance to the next session page.

5. In the upper right side of the Overview page, on the gray navigation bar, click **Play**.

GO! with Help

A special section where students practice using the HELP feature of the Office application.

Contents in Brief

Table of Contents

Chapter 7 Working with Tables and Graphics 1403

Chapter 8 Using Word with Other Office Programs and Creating Mass Mailings 1483

Excel 2003

Access 2003

PowerPoint 2003

5

chapterfive

Using Charts, Special Effects, and Styles

In this chapter, you will: complete these projects **and** practice these skills.

Project 5A **Creating a Chart**	**Objectives** • Create a Chart with Microsoft Graph • Format a Chart • Add Special Text Effects
Project 5B **Creating and Using Styles**	**Objectives** • Use Existing Styles • Create and Modify New Styles • Modify the Document Window
Project 5C **Creating an Outline**	**Objective** • Create an Outline
Project 5D **Creating a Program Outline**	**Objective** • Create an Outline Using the Outline View and the Outlining Toolbar

University Medical Center

The University Medical Center (UMC) is a premier patient-care and research institution serving Orange Beach, Florida. To maintain UMC's sterling reputation, the Office of Public Affairs (OPA) actively promotes UMC's services, achievements, and professional staff. The OPA staff interacts with the media, writes press releases and announcements, prepares marketing materials, develops public awareness campaigns, maintains a speakers bureau, and conducts media training for physicians and researchers. The UMC will soon be announcing successful results of a clinical trial of a new surgical technique, so this announcement will be a high priority for the OPA staff for the next several weeks.

©Photosphere Images Ltd.

Making Professional Documents with Charts and Styles

Charts are visual representations of numeric data. Chart data is often easier to understand than textual data. Pie charts, which show the contributions of each piece to the whole, and column charts, which make comparisons among related numbers, are commonly used charts. Word features make it easy to design an effective chart.

Character, paragraph, and list styles provide a way to quickly apply formatting instructions to text. Character styles are applied to individual characters, paragraph styles are applied to entire paragraphs, and list styles are applied to bulleted or numbered lists. Word contains pre-defined styles, and you can also create your own styles.

Word also enables you to create and edit multiple-level outlines to organize an overview about a topic.

In this chapter, you will create and format charts. You will learn how to use existing styles and to create and modify new styles. Finally, you will create multilevel outlines.

Project 5A **Nutrition Flyer**

Graphical representation of numbers helps a reader understand the implications and trends in a visual manner that is easier to interpret than lists of numbers. Using the Microsoft Graph program, you can add attractive charts to documents and reports.

In Activities 5.1 through 5.8, you will edit a nutrition flyer for the University Medical Center Nutrition Unit. You will add a chart to the flyer showing the results of a nutrition survey and format the chart to make it visually appealing. You will also use special formatting features to give your flyer a professional look. Your completed document will look similar to Figure 5.1. You will save your document as *5A_Nutrition_Flyer_Firstname_Lastname.*

UNIVERSITY MEDICAL CENTER
Nutrition Notes

Where do you get your information?

Nutrition information is all around us. We get our nutrition information from a variety of people—doctors, nurses, nutritionists, cooks, parents, friends, neighbors, the lady in front of us in line at the grocery store, and many others. We also are bombarded with information on radio and television, the Internet, and in books and magazines. Everyone has an opinion on what's good for you, and more importantly, what's bad for you! With all of this available information, what source do we turn to when we really need good, reliable information?

Nutritionists at University Medical Center wondered the same thing. They conducted a survey of 1,000 randomly-chosen adults (18 and older) from the Orange Beach area. The overall results were not surprising:

Source of Nutrition Information

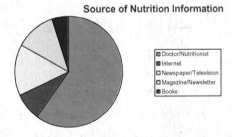

- Doctor/Nutritionist
- Internet
- Newspaper/Television
- Magazine/Newsletter
- Books

Two years ago, the last time the survey was done, only 2% of respondents reported that the Internet was their main source of information. This year, the number jumped to 8%, with younger people by far the most active in this category.

5A_Nutrition_Flyer_Firstname_Lastname

Figure 5.1
Project 5A—Nutrition Flyer

Objective 1
Create a Chart with Microsoft Graph

Charts are often used to make a set of numbers easier to understand. There are two ways to create a chart in Word using a built-in feature called *Microsoft Graph*. The easiest and most direct is to create a table with the data, and then create the chart directly from the table. You can also start Microsoft Graph and fill in the data in a table-like structure called a *datasheet*. There are 14 types of charts available in Word, each with a different purpose. The most commonly used are column, bar, pie, line, and area charts, as described in Figure 5.2.

Chart Types Available in Word	
Purpose of Chart	**Chart Type**
Show comparison among data	Column, Bar
Show proportion of parts to a whole	Pie
Show trends over time	Line, Area

Figure 5.2

Activity 5.1 Creating a Chart from a Word Table

1 On the Standard toolbar, click the **Open** button ▣. Navigate to the location where the student files for this textbook are stored. Locate **w05A_Nutrition_Flyer** and click once to select it. Then, in the lower right corner of the **Open** dialog box, click **Open**.

The w05A_Nutrition_Flyer file opens.

2 From the **File** menu, click **Save As**. In the **Save As** dialog box, navigate to the location where you are storing your files, creating a new folder for this chapter if you want to do so.

3 In the **File name** box, type **5A_Nutrition_Flyer_Firstname_Lastname** and then click **Save**.

4 Locate the table in the middle of the document, and then in the table, click anywhere to position the insertion point. From the **Table** menu, point to **Select**, and then click **Table**.

The table is selected, as shown in Figure 5.3. When creating a chart from a Word table, arrange the table so that the category labels form the first column and headings form the first row.

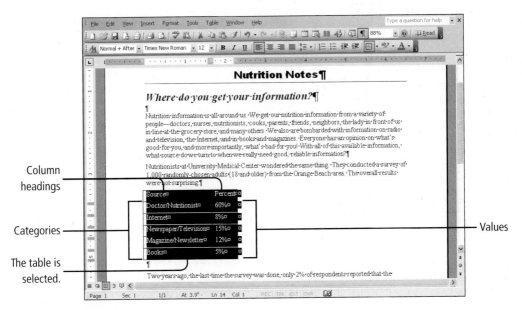

Column headings

Categories

The table is selected.

Values

Figure 5.3

5 From the **Insert** menu, point to **Picture**, and then click **Chart**.

The Microsoft Graph program displays a three-dimensional column chart surrounded by a slashed border and a Datasheet table. New toolbars also display.

Alert! — **If the Datasheet Disappears**

If you click outside the chart, the datasheet will disappear, and the chart will no longer be in edit mode. To return to edit mode, double-click the chart. If the datasheet still does not display, from the View menu, click Datasheet.

6 Look at Figure 5.4, and take a moment to become familiar with the parts of a chart with which you will be working.

The heading of the second column in the table—*Percent*—displays along the **category axis** (or x-axis). A **scale** of percentage values— from 0% to 60%—displays along the **value axis** (or y-axis). This scale is calculated by the Microsoft Graph program. The four categories from the first column are displayed in a **legend**, which relates the categories to the data in the chart. The chart graphic displays in the **plot area**; everything outside the plot area is the **chart area**. The table values have been copied to a datasheet, which is where future changes or additions to the data will be recorded. See Figure 5.4.

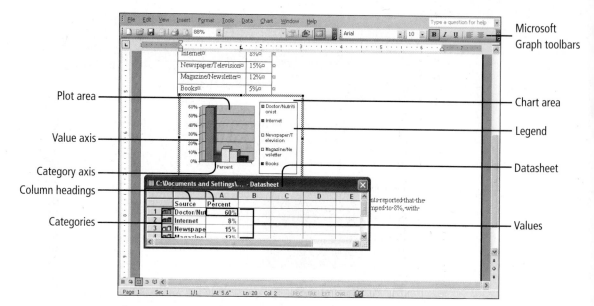

Plot area —
Value axis —
Category axis —
Column headings —
Categories —

Microsoft
Graph toolbars

Chart area
Legend
Datasheet
Values

Figure 5.4

7 On the Standard toolbar, click the **Save** button ![save icon].

Activity 5.2 Adding a Chart Title

Add a title to a chart to help the reader understand the topic of the chart's data.

1 From the **Chart** menu, click **Chart Options**. If necessary, in the **Chart Options** dialog box, click the **Titles tab**. Alternatively, right-click on the chart area and click Chart Options from the shortcut menu.

2 Click in the **Chart title** box and type **Source of Nutrition Information**

After a few seconds, the new title displays in the Preview area. See Figure 5.5.

New title ———

Preview area ———

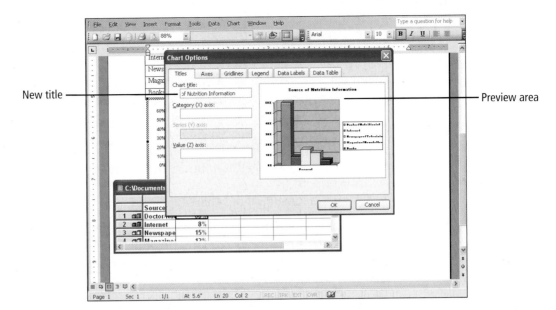

Figure 5.5

3 At the bottom of the **Chart Options** dialog box, click **OK**. Click in the datasheet to remove the selection box from the title.

The title is added to the chart, and the size of the chart area is reduced, as shown in Figure 5.6.

New chart title ———

Chart size is reduced.

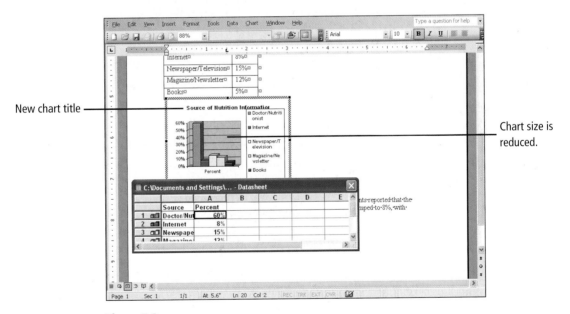

Figure 5.6

4 On the Standard toolbar, click the **Save** button 🖫.

Objective 2
Format a Chart

When you create a chart, it contains only the chart in default format and a legend. You can make changes to colors and backgrounds, change the size and page location of the chart, and add chart titles. Unless you have changed the default chart type, each new chart you create will be a **column chart**, which is used to compare data. Thus, if you need a pie chart or a line chart, you will need to change the chart type.

Activity 5.3 Changing the Chart Type

The purpose of a chart is to graphically depict one of three types of relationships—a comparison among data, the proportion of parts to a whole, or trends over time. The data in your chart shows the parts of a whole, which is most effectively illustrated using a **pie chart**.

1 Be sure that two toolbars display at the top of your screen. If only one toolbar row is displayed on your screen, at the right end of the Standard toolbar, click the **Toolbar Options** button ▐, and then click **Show Buttons on Two Rows**.

The Microsoft Graph Standard and Formatting toolbars are displayed in separate rows.

2 On the Standard toolbar, click the **Chart Type button arrow** 📈▾.

A menu of chart type buttons displays. See Figure 5.7.

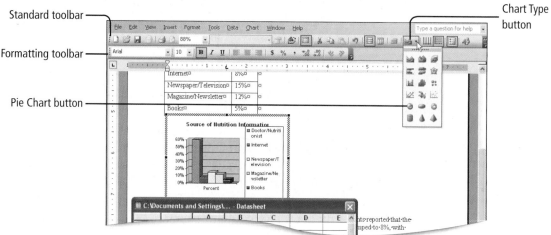

Figure 5.7

3 Move the pointer over the chart buttons and take a moment to look at the buttons and ScreenTips.

Notice that the buttons depict the type of chart with which they are associated.

4 From the **Chart Type** menu, click the **Pie Chart** button ●.

The chart changes into a pie chart, but only the first row of information is charted, as indicated by the icon in the datasheet. See Figure 5.8.

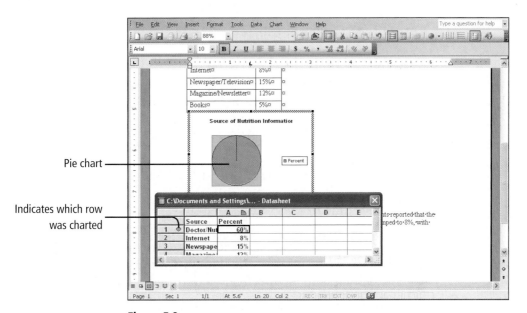

Pie chart

Indicates which row
was charted

Figure 5.8

More Knowledge — Two Ways of Displaying Chart Data

Charts can be displayed by row or by column. The difference can be very important. In a column chart, for example, changing the display from Rows to Columns switches the contents of the legend and the category (x) axis. In a pie chart this difference is particularly important. If you choose to display your data by rows, only the data in row 1 of the datasheet is displayed. If your data is in column format, you need to change the orientation of the chart to make the chart useful.

5 On the Standard toolbar, click the **By Column** button ⊞.

The chart displays all the data, and icons in each row of the datasheet show that a pie slice has been added for each row. All of the slices together add up to 100 percent. See Figure 5.9.

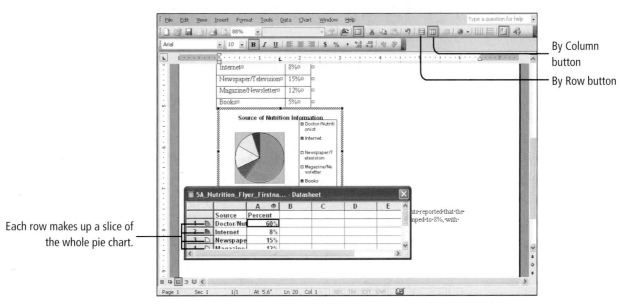

By Column
button

By Row button

Each row makes up a slice of
the whole pie chart.

Figure 5.9

6 On the Standard toolbar, click the **Save** button 🖫.

Activity 5.4 Formatting Chart Text

You can format any text on a chart, including the title, axis titles, and text in legends.

1 On the chart, click anywhere in the title *Source of Nutrition Information*.

A box with a gray border and sizing handles surrounds the title, indicating that the title is selected. You may have to click the title a second time to select it.

2 From the **Format** menu, click **Selected Chart Title**.

The Format Chart Title dialog box displays.

3 If necessary, on the **Format Chart Title** dialog box, click the **Font tab**.

Font options and a limited set of Effects are available in this dialog box.

4 Click the **Color arrow** to display the color palette, as shown in Figure 5.10.

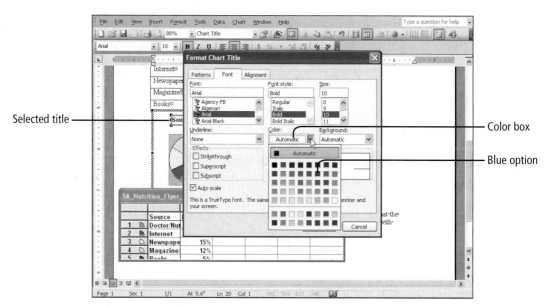

Figure 5.10

5 In the second row, click the sixth color—**Blue**—and then click **OK**.

The title is changed to blue. See Figure 5.11.

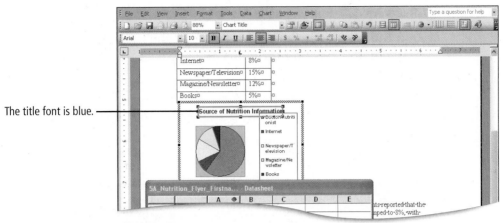

The title font is blue.

Figure 5.11

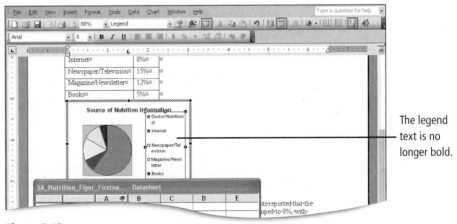

6 Click to select the legend. From the **Format** menu, click **Selected Legend**.

The Format Legend dialog box displays.

7 In the **Format Legend** dialog box, under **Font style**, click **Regular**, and then click **OK**.

The legend text changes from bold to regular, as shown in Figure 5.12.

The legend text is no longer bold.

Figure 5.12

8 On the datasheet, click in the title bar.

The Close button, which had been hidden while the datasheet was inactive, displays.

9 On the datasheet title bar, click the **Close** button ⊠.

The datasheet closes, but the chart remains active.

10 On the Standard toolbar, click the **Save** button 🔲.

Activity 5.5 Resizing and Centering a Chart

You can resize both the chart area and the individual chart elements. You can also position the chart on your page relative to the left and right margins.

1 With the chart selected, drag the handle in the middle of the right border to approximately **5 inches on the horizontal ruler**.

Notice that the selection box stretches as you drag to the right. See Figure 5.13.

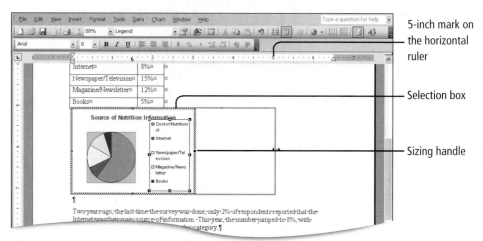

Figure 5.13

2 Release the mouse button.

Notice that the text in the legend has expanded to display the widest entry, although the title may still be cut off.

3 Move the pointer over the chart title and drag it to the right, near the edge of the chart box, as shown in Figure 5.14.

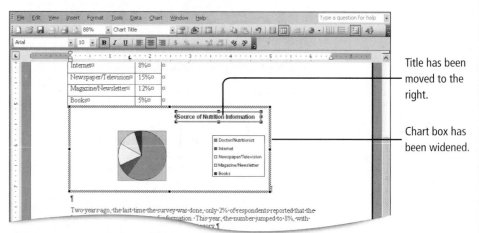

Figure 5.14

4 With the chart selected, drag the handle in the middle of the bottom border down to approximately **8 inches on the vertical ruler**.

The chart box is about 3 inches high. The legend and title size also increase, and the legend text may wrap.

5 Move the pointer to one of the corners of the plot area, which is the area used for the pie.

A ScreenTip displays identifying the plot area.

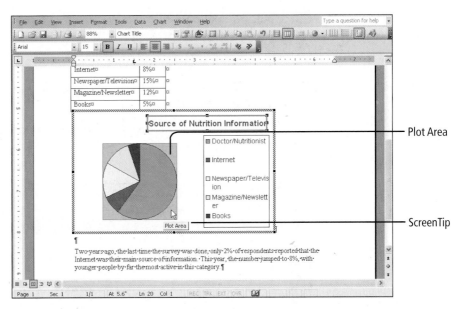

Plot Area

ScreenTip

Figure 5.15

6 Click once to select the plot area. Using the sizing handle in the lower right corner of the plot area, drag down and to the right until the chart is near the lower border of the chart box.

7 Using the sizing handle in the upper left corner of the plot area, drag up and to the left until the plot area is about 0.5 inch from the top border of the chart box.

Notice in Figure 5.16 that the legend text increases in size proportionally.

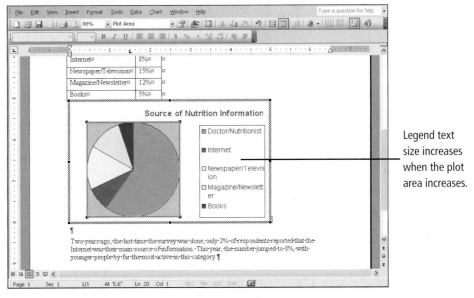

Legend text size increases when the plot area increases.

Figure 5.16

8 Click once on the legend. On the Formatting toolbar, click the **Font Size button arrow** ⌗10 ▾⌗, and then click **9**. If necessary, using the legend sizing handles, resize the legend box so that the text for each item displays on one line.

9 Click once on the plot area outside the pie. From the **Format** menu, click **Selected Plot Area**.

The Format Plot Area dialog box displays.

10 Under **Border**, click the **None** option button. Under **Area**, click the **None** option button.

This will remove the box and shading surrounding the pie. Compare your Format Plot Area dialog box with Figure 5.17.

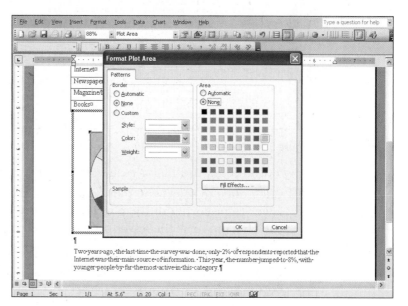

Figure 5.17

11 At the bottom of the **Format Plot Area** dialog box, click **OK**.

The plot area border and shading are removed.

12 Click in the document outside of the chart area to deselect the chart. Click once on the chart to select it. On the Formatting toolbar, click the **Center** button ▤.

The chart area is centered horizontally on the page, as shown in Figure 5.18.

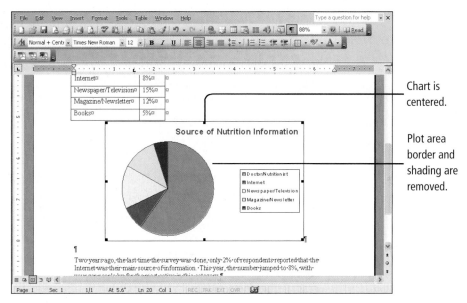

Chart is centered.

Plot area border and shading are removed.

Figure 5.18

13 In the table, click anywhere to position the insertion point. From the **Table** menu, point to **Delete**, and then click **Table**.

The table is removed, but the chart retains its data because the data is stored in the datasheet associated with the chart.

14 On the Standard toolbar, click the **Save** button 🔲.

Objective 3
Add Special Text Effects

Word provides a number of methods to format text in a distinctive manner. For example, magazines and books sometimes use a large first letter to begin the first paragraph of an article or chapter. This is referred to as a **drop cap**. The first letter can be three or four times taller than the rest of the text, which gives the text a finished look. Other distinctive text formatting is accomplished by adding a shadow effect, applying special underlining, or reducing the spacing between the letters.

Activity 5.6 Creating a Drop Cap

A drop cap gives text a professional look, but use it only once in an article or chapter.

1 Press Ctrl + Home to move to the top of the document. In the paragraph beginning *Nutrition information* select the letter *N* at the beginning of the paragraph.

2 From the **Format** menu, click **Drop Cap**.

The Drop Cap dialog box displays. Under Position, notice that the default is *None*, and there are two other options. The **Dropped** position enlarges the letter and places it into the text, as illustrated by the small example. The **In margin** position places the enlarged letter in the left margin. See Figure 5.19.

Drop cap default —

Selected letter —

Dropped option

In margin option

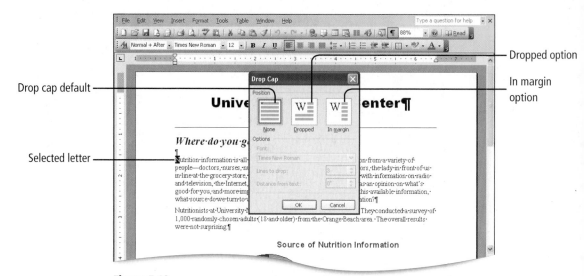

Figure 5.19

3 Under **Position**, click **Dropped**.

4 Under **Options**, click the **Lines to drop spin box up arrow** to change the line height of the drop cap to **4** lines.

Compare your Drop Cap dialog box with Figure 5.20.

Dropped position

Height (in lines) of drop cap

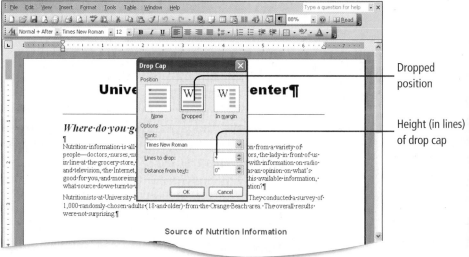

Figure 5.20

5 In the **Drop Cap** dialog box, click **OK**.

The drop cap is inserted in the text, and resize handles display around its border indicating that it is selected.

6 On the Formatting toolbar, click the **Font Color button arrow** , and from the displayed palette in the second row, click the sixth color—**Blue**.

The drop cap color changes to blue.

7 Click anywhere in the document to deselect the drop cap.

Compare your screen with Figure 5.21.

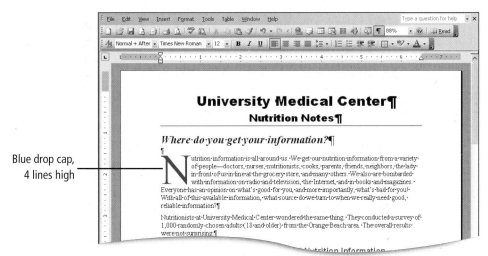

Blue drop cap, 4 lines high

Figure 5.21

8 On the Standard toolbar, click the **Save** button.

Activity 5.7 Adding a Shadow to a Title

Special text effects, such as shadows, are effective when used sparingly. Use the Font dialog box to add text effects and also to change several font characteristics at the same time.

1 Move to the top of the document. Move the pointer into the left margin to the left of the first line of text. When the pointer changes to a white arrow, click once to select the entire line.

2 From the **Format** menu, click **Font**.

The Font dialog box displays.

3 If necessary, at the top of the **Font** dialog box, click the **Font tab**.

In this dialog box, you can change many font characteristics, and a Preview window at the bottom of the dialog box will reflect the changes you make to the selected text. See Figure 5.22.

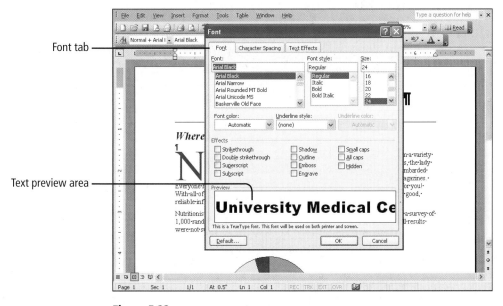

Font tab

Text preview area

Figure 5.22

4 In the **Font** dialog box, under **Font style**, click **Bold**.

Notice that the text in the preview box is shown in bold.

5 In the **Size** box, select **24** and type **32**

The 32-point font size is not an option in the Size list. If you want a font size that does not appear in the list, you can type it in the Size box.

6 Click the **Font color arrow**, and then in the second row, click **Blue**.

Blue is the sixth color in the second row. If you pause your mouse pointer over the colors, a ScreenTip displays the name of each color.

7 Under **Effects**, select the **Small caps** check box.

8 Under **Effects**, select the **Shadow** check box.

The changes to the text are reflected in the Preview box, as shown in Figure 5.23.

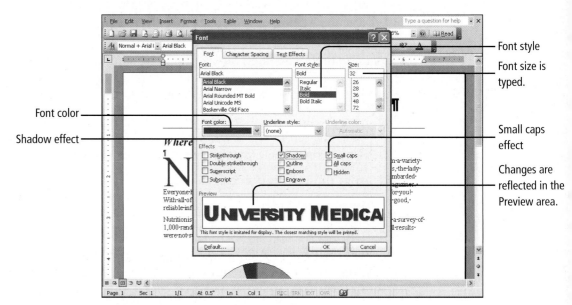

Figure 5.23

9 At the bottom of the **Font** dialog box, click **OK**, and then click anywhere to deselect the title and view the changes you have made. Compare your screen with Figure 5.24.

Figure 5.24

10 Move the pointer into the left margin to the left of the subtitle line, *Nutrition Notes*. When the pointer changes to a white arrow, drag down to select the subtitle, the divider line, and the heading *Where do you get your information?*

The second and third lines of the document are selected.

11 On the Formatting toolbar, click the **Font Color** button, which should have retained its previous usage of blue. If not, click the arrow on the right of the Font Color button and click the same color you used for the title and the drop cap. Click anywhere to deselect the text.

The top three lines of the document are blue, along with the drop cap and the title of the chart, as shown in Figure 5.25.

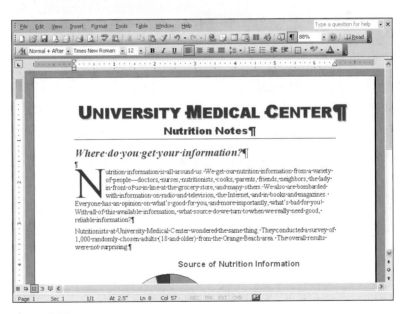

Figure 5.25

12 On the Standard toolbar, click the **Save** button.

Activity 5.8 Modifying Character Spacing

Increasing or decreasing font size changes the size of the letters and the spacing between the letters proportionally. You can make the text look denser by condensing (decreasing) the space between characters, which does not affect the font size. You can also expand (increase) the space between characters. This technique is useful to make text completely fill a page or to make text that is a little too long for a page or a text box fit precisely.

1 Move the pointer into the margin to the left of the paragraph beginning *Nutrition information*. When the pointer changes to a white arrow, drag down to select that paragraph and the next one.

When you use this method to select a paragraph containing a drop cap, the paragraph marker above the drop cap is also selected, as shown in Figure 5.26. Notice the spacing of the letters in the selected paragraphs.

Paragraph above the drop cap is selected.

Two paragraphs are selected.

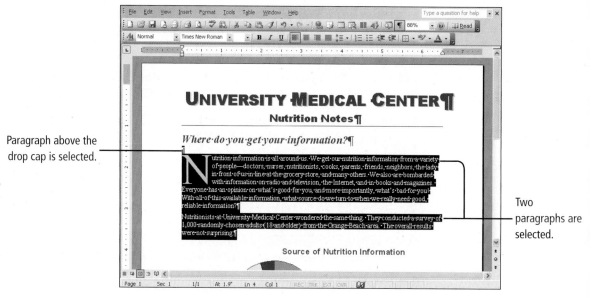

Figure 5.26

2 From the **Format** menu, click **Font**.

The Font dialog box displays.

3 At the top of the **Font** dialog box, click the **Character Spacing tab**.

In this dialog box you can adjust the scale, spacing, and position of characters, and a Preview window at the bottom of the dialog box will reflect changes made to the selected text.

4 Look at the Preview box and notice the spacing. Click the **Spacing arrow**. From the displayed list, point to **Condensed**, and then watch the Preview area as you click.

The *By* box to the right of the *Spacing* box displays *1 pt*. This means that the characters are moved 1 point closer together.

5 To the right of the **Spacing** box, click the **By spin box up arrow** to change the spacing to **0.3 pt**.

This will move the characters about a third of a point closer. Recall that a point is ½ of an inch. Compare your dialog box with Figure 5.27.

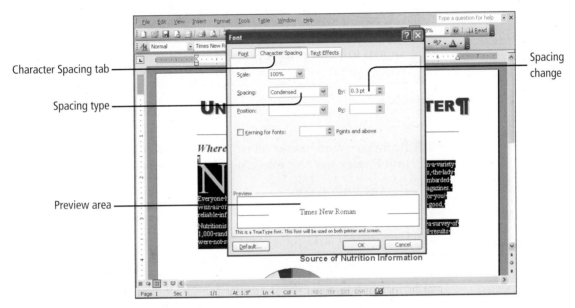

Character Spacing tab

Spacing type

Preview area

Spacing change

Figure 5.27

6 At the bottom of the **Font** dialog box, click **OK**. Click anywhere to deselect the text.

Notice how much the text is condensed. The first paragraph, which was seven lines long, is now six lines long, but the font size remains unchanged. Compare the selected text in Figure 5.26 to the text in Figure 5.28.

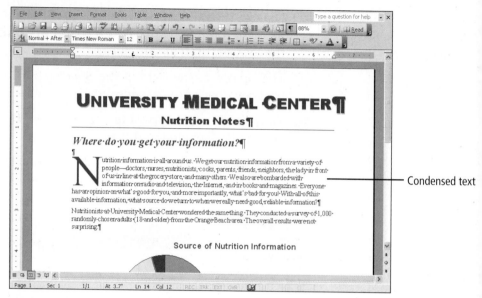

Condensed text

Figure 5.28

7 From the **View** menu, click **Header and Footer**. On the Header and Footer toolbar, click the **Switch Between Header and Footer** button.

8 On the **Header and Footer** toolbar, click the **Insert AutoText** button Insert AutoText ▾, and then click **Filename**.

The file name is inserted in the footer.

9 On the **Header and Footer** toolbar, click the **Close** button Close.

10 On the Standard toolbar, click the **Save** button.

11 On the Standard toolbar, click the **Print Preview** button. Take a moment to check your work. On the Print Preview toolbar, click the **Close Preview** button Close.

12 Make any necessary changes to your document. When you are satisfied, on the Standard toolbar, click the **Print** button. Close the document.

End You have completed Project 5A ——————————————

Project 5B Medical Records

Businesses often develop a uniform appearance for procedure and policy manuals that includes headings to help organize the material and make it easier for a user to find information. Microsoft Word includes a set of predefined styles with several heading levels, or you can create your own styles to use in your documents.

In Activities 5.9 through 5.17, you will edit a section of a medical center Policy and Procedure manual by applying new and existing styles. Your completed document will look similar to Figure 5.29. You will save your document as *5B_Medical_Records_Firstname_Lastname.*

Medical Center Policy and Procedure Manual

Topic: Official Medical Records

Policy and Procedure Manual Location: Section 1, Medical Center Administration

Section 1.4, Medical Records Policy and Procedure

Section 1.4.1, Integrated Central Medical Records System

I. Purpose:
   The purpose of this policy is to provide guidance to Medical Center physicians, both faculty and staff, in the development and maintenance of an integrated, central medic... documentation will be develope... receives assessment or treatmen... unit. All documentation will be s... This makes it a more efficient an... patient, and also better serves the...

II. Definitions:
   A. Integrated Medical Record – ... the documentation and diagno... and those received from othe...
   B. Centralized Medical Records... unique medical records of all... business functions.
   C. Official Medical Record – A... current centralized system an... system includes those medica... Family Practice Center, Pedia... Women's Center, Plastic Surg...
   D. Office/Shadow Records – Me... centralized medical records s... Official medical record.

III. Policy:
   It is the policy of Medical Cen... medical records system and to... order to support patient care.... functions of the organization acc...
   A. All original internal and exter... Medical Records to be assem... medical record.

5B_Medical_Records_Firstname_Lastna...

   B. Appropriately document the encounter within the patient's Official medical record.
   C. Discourage the creation or use of Office/Shadow medical records.

IV. Procedure:
   Whenever possible, the patient's Official medical record will be made available for each patient encounter with Medical Center physicians.
   A. All documentation should either occur directly within the Official medical record in accordance with applicable policies or should be forwarded to Medical Records after completed.
   B. Any external patient information received should be appropriately reviewed by the responsible provider and forwarded to Medical Records.

5B_Medical_Records_Firstname_Lastname

Figure 5.29
Project 5B—Medical Records

Objective 4
Use Existing Styles

A *template* is a model for documents of the same type, and it stores information that determines the basic structure for a document in Word. The template information includes document settings such as page layout, fonts, special formatting, and styles. A *style* is a group of formatting commands that Word stores with a specific name, which you can retrieve by name and apply to text. Unless you select a specific template, all new Word documents are based on the *Normal template*—stored in your computer as *Normal.dot*.

The Normal template contains a small set of built-in styles that you can use to format text with one action instead of three or four. The default settings for the Normal template include such formatting as Times New Roman font, font size of 12 pt., single spacing, left alignment, 1" top and bottom margins, and 1.25" left and right margins. Styles are added to text using either the Style button in the Formatting toolbar, or the Styles and Formatting task pane. There are four types of styles, as shown in Figure 5.30.

Word Style Types

Style Type	Purpose
Paragraph style	Controls the formatting of a paragraph, including line spacing, indents, alignment, tab stops, font type, and size.
Character style	Affects the selected text within a paragraph, including font style, font size, bold, italic, and underline.
Table style	Formats border type and style, shading, cell alignment, and fonts in a table.
List style	Formats font style, font size, alignment, and bullet or number characteristics in lists.

Figure 5.30

Activity 5.9 Displaying Styles

You can display the styles available for paragraphs on the left side of a document and show all of the available styles in a task pane on the right side of the document.

1 On the Standard toolbar, click the **Open** button 📖. Navigate to the location where the student files for this textbook are stored. Locate and open **w05B_Medical_Records**. Save the file as **5B_Medical_Records_Firstname_Lastname**

2 On the left edge of the horizontal scroll bar, click the **Normal View** button ≣.

The document changes to Normal View. Recall that Normal view gives you more area in which to type, but does not display graphics or the edges of the page. It also enables you to see the styles used for each paragraph. Page breaks are indicated by a dotted line.

3 From the **Tools** menu, click **Options**. Be sure the **View tab** is selected. See Figure 5.31.

View tab —

Style area width box

Normal View button —

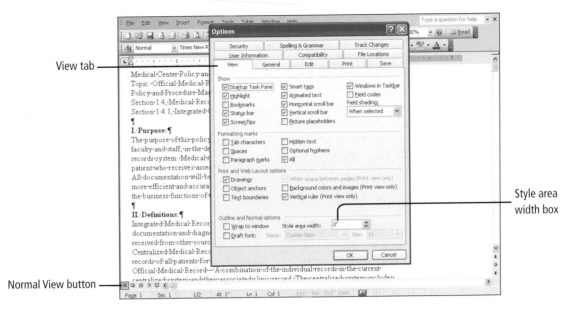

Figure 5.31

Note — Is Your Style Area Already On?

If the last person to use the computer left the style area on, you may see it when you switch to Normal View. If this is the case, perform Steps 6 and 7 to verify that your style area is the right size.

---

4 At the bottom of the **View tab**, under **Outline and Normal options**, click the **Style area width spin box up arrow** until the width is **0.6"**.

5 In the lower right corner, click **OK**.

A style area opens at the left side of the document, and the style name for each paragraph displays. All of the paragraphs in this document use the default Normal style, except the section headings, which use a style named *Subheading*—a style created for this chapter. See Figure 5.32.

Style area —

Subheading style —

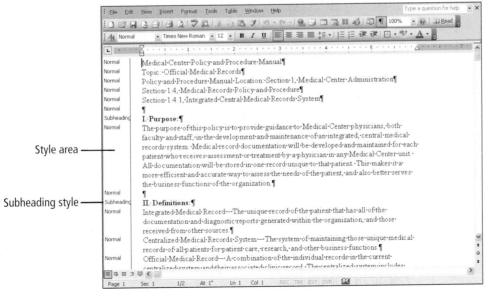

Figure 5.32

6 On the left side of the Formatting toolbar, click the **Styles and Formatting** button [44].

The Styles and Formatting task pane displays. The style of the paragraph that contains the insertion point is shown in the box at the top of this pane and is bordered in blue in the list of available styles.

7 If the right edge of the text is hidden behind the task pane, on the Standard toolbar, click the **Zoom button arrow** [100% ▾], and then click **Page Width**.

8 In your document, click to place the insertion point anywhere in the line that begins *II. Definitions*.

In the style area on the left, notice that this paragraph has the *Subheading* style applied. In the Styles and Formatting task pane, notice that the *Subheading* style is selected.

9 In the **Styles and Formatting** task pane, under **Pick formatting to apply**, examine the list of style names. If necessary, at the bottom of the **Styles and Formatting** task pane, in the **Show** box, click the arrow, and then click **Available formatting**.

The built-in styles, plus the *Subheading* style that was created for this chapter, are listed. See Figure 5.33.

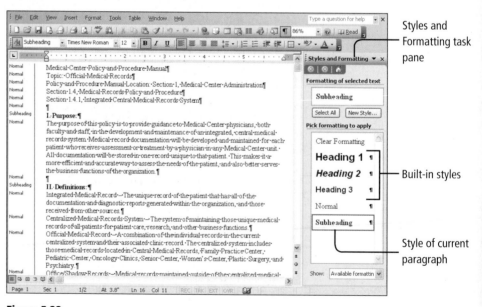

Styles and Formatting task pane

Built-in styles

Style of current paragraph

Figure 5.33

Note — Style Names Do Not Print

Although the style area looks like it is part of the document, it is not. It does not print, and there is no method to print the style names as shown on the screen.

10 On the Standard toolbar, click the **Save** button.

Activity 5.10 Working with Default Styles

Four styles are included with every document created with the Normal template, which is the default template in Word. The four styles include three heading styles and the Normal style. The Subheading style was created for this chapter. Your version of Word may display other styles that have been added to the default template.

1 At the top of the document, click to position the insertion point in the first line, which begins *Medical Center Policy*.

This is the document title. To apply a paragraph style, you need only position the insertion point somewhere in the paragraph—you do not need to select the entire paragraph.

2 In the **Styles and Formatting** task pane, under **Pick formatting to apply**, click **Heading 1**.

The Heading 1 style is applied to the title. The Heading 1 style includes a font size of 16 and bold font style. Notice that the *Heading 1* name in the Styles and Formatting task pane has the same character formatting—the style name also acts as a style preview, as shown in Figure 5.34.

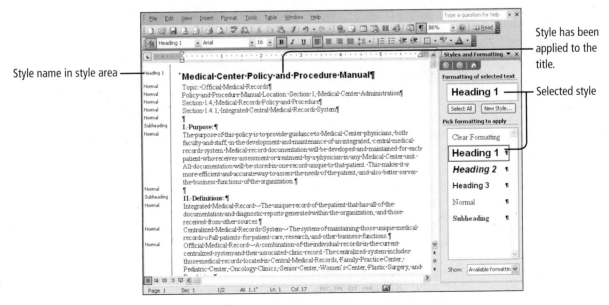

Style name in style area

Style has been applied to the title.

Selected style

Figure 5.34

3 Position the insertion point in the next line, beginning *Topic: Official*.

4 In the **Styles and Formatting** task pane, under **Pick formatting to apply**, click **Heading 2**.

The Heading 2 style includes a font size of 14, smaller than Heading 1, and bold and italic font style.

5 Position the insertion point in the next line, beginning *Policy and Procedure Manual*.

6 In the **Styles and Formatting** task pane, under **Pick formatting to apply**, click **Heading 3**.

The Heading 3 style includes font size of 13 and bold font style, as shown in Figure 5.35.

Heading 2 style —
Heading 3 style —

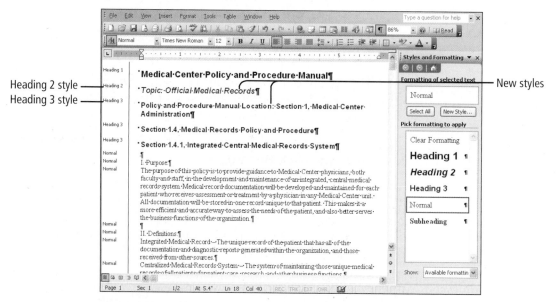

New styles

Figure 5.35

7 Move the pointer to the left of the line beginning *Section 1.4, Medical*. When the pointer changes to a white arrow, drag down to select that paragraph and the next one, beginning *Section 1.4.1, Integrated*.

8 In the **Styles and Formatting** task pane, under **Pick formatting to apply**, click **Heading 3**.

Notice that you can apply styles to more than one paragraph at a time.

9 Click to position the insertion point in the next line, beginning *I. Purpose*. In the **Styles and Formatting** task pane, under **Pick formatting to apply**, click **Heading 3**.

10 Click to position the insertion point in the line beginning *II. Definitions*. In the **Styles and Formatting** task pane, under **Pick formatting to apply**, click **Heading 3**.

11 On the Standard toolbar, click the **Save** button.

Activity 5.11 Clearing Styles

You can remove all formatting from a document or from selected text in a document, which removes any styles that were applied.

1 If necessary, position the insertion point in the line beginning *II. Definitions*.

2 In the **Styles and Formatting** task pane, under **Pick formatting to apply**, click **Clear Formatting**.

The Heading 3 style is removed, and the paragraph reverts to the Normal style. Notice that in task pane list, *Normal* is bordered.

3 Click to position the insertion point in the line beginning *I. Purpose*.

4 In the **Styles and Formatting** task pane, under **Pick formatting to apply**, click **Clear Formatting**.

The Heading 3 style is removed, and the paragraph reverts to the Normal style, as shown in Figure 5.36.

Paragraphs revert to Normal style.

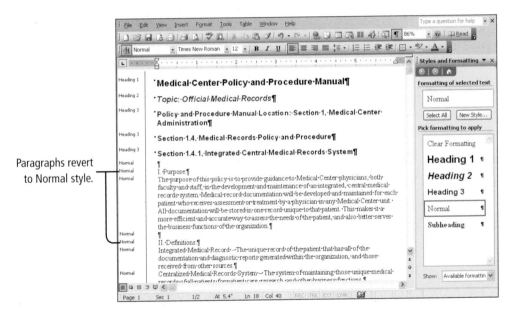

Figure 5.36

5 Move the pointer into the left margin to the left of the paragraph beginning *I. Purpose*. When the pointer changes to a white arrow, click once.

6 Move the pointer into the left margin to the left of the paragraph beginning *II. Definitions*. When the pointer changes to a white arrow, hold down [Ctrl] and click once.

Two nonadjacent paragraphs are selected, as shown in Figure 5.37.

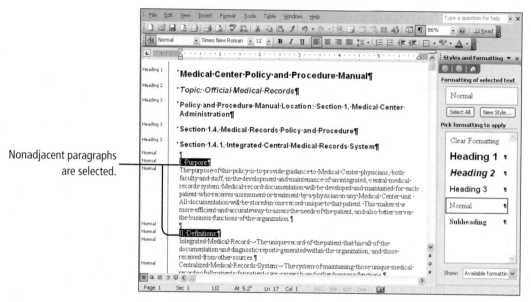

Nonadjacent paragraphs are selected.

Figure 5.37

7 In the **Styles and Formatting** task pane, under **Pick formatting to apply**, click **Subheading**.

The Subheading style is restored to both paragraphs.

8 On the Standard toolbar, click the **Save** button.

Objective 5
Create and Modify New Styles

By default, only a few styles are included with the Normal template, but you can create your own styles based on formats that you use often. For example, if you always type your name or company name in a distinctive manner (e.g., for example, bold, Verdana font, font size 14), you can create that as a style and apply it when needed. After you have created a style, you can modify it to suit your changing needs. One of the strengths of using styles is that it enables you to change all instances of a style throughout a document at the same time.

Activity 5.12 Creating and Applying Paragraph Styles

When you need to match special formatting guidelines to complete a document, you can use paragraph styles that will enable you to perform several formatting steps with a single click.

1 Move the pointer to the left of the line beginning *The purpose of this policy*. When the pointer changes to a white arrow, drag down to select the entire paragraph. Alternatively, you can double-click in the paragraph margin to select it.

2 On the Formatting toolbar, click the **Italic** button $\boxed{I}$.

3 From the **Format** menu, click **Paragraph**. If necessary, click the **Indents and Spacing tab**.

4 Under **General**, click the **Alignment arrow**, and then click **Justified**.

5 Under **Indentation**, click the **Left spin box up arrow** to set the left indent at **0.5"**.

6 Under **Indentation**, click the **Right spin box up arrow** to set the right indent at **0.5"**.

Compare your Paragraph dialog box with Figure 5.38.

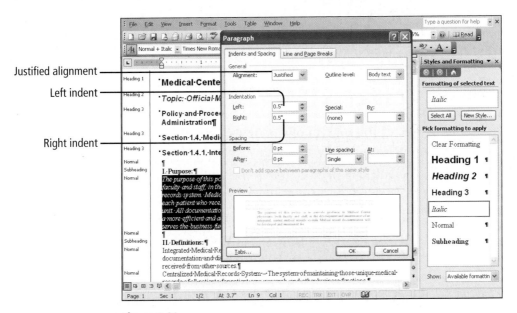

Justified alignment ——
Left indent ——
Right indent ——

Figure 5.38

7 At the bottom of the **Paragraph** dialog box, click **OK**.

The changes you made are reflected in the paragraph, and the paragraph remains selected.

8 With the paragraph still selected, in the **Styles and Formatting** task pane, under **Formatting of selected text**, click **New Style**.

The New Style dialog box displays.

9 In the **New Style** dialog box, under **Properties**, in the **Name** box, type **Intro**

A style formatting list displays under the preview window, as shown in Figure 5.39.

New style name ————
Selected paragraph ————

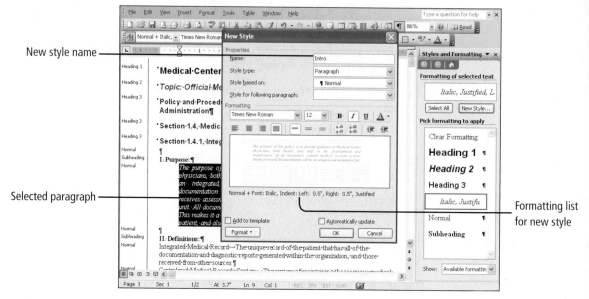

Formatting list
for new style

Figure 5.39

10 At the bottom of the **New Style** dialog box, click **OK**.

Even though you just created a style using the selected paragraph, you still need to apply the style. A temporary style displays the modifications you have made.

11 In the **Styles and Formatting** task pane, click the **Intro** style.

The new style is applied to the selected paragraph.

More Knowledge — Creating Styles Using the Style Box

There is a shortcut method to create styles using the Style box. Make the desired changes to a paragraph. In the Formatting toolbar, click once in the Style box. Type the name of the new style and press Enter. The new style is created and applied to the current paragraph. There are limitations to this method of creating styles. You can create only paragraph styles, and you have less control over the style than you have when creating a style in the New Style dialog box.

---

12 Scroll down and, near the end of the first page, click to place the insertion point in the paragraph beginning *It is the policy*. In the **Styles and Formatting** task pane, click the **Intro** style.

The paragraph changes to the new style, with both margins indented, the text justified, with italic font style. See Figure 5.40.

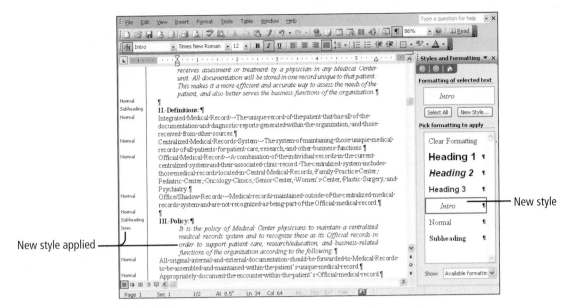

New style applied

New style

Figure 5.40

13 Scroll down and click to place the insertion point in the paragraph beginning *Whenever possible* near the end of the document. In the **Styles and Formatting** task pane, click the **Intro** style.

The paragraph changes to the new style.

14 On the Standard toolbar, click the **Save** button [img].

Activity 5.13 Creating and Applying List Styles

Styles can be created for lists and then applied to any text, which will change the text to match the list characteristics of the style.

1 Near the end of the document, move the pointer to the left of the line beginning *All documentation should*. When the pointer changes to a white arrow, drag down to select the last two paragraphs.

2 On the Formatting toolbar, click the **Numbering** button [img].

The two paragraphs are numbered.

3 From the **Format** menu, click **Bullets and Numbering**. In the displayed **Bullets and Numbering** dialog box, click the **Numbered tab**.

4 From the **Bullets and Numbering** dialog box, click the option with capital letters, as shown in Figure 5.41. If that option is not displayed, at the bottom of the Bullets and Numbering dialog box, click the Reset button.

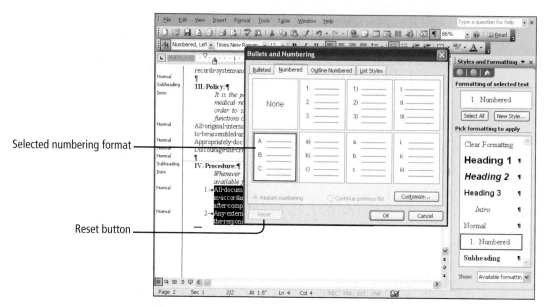

Selected numbering format —

Reset button —

Figure 5.41

5 At the bottom of the **Bullets and Numbering** dialog box, click **OK**.

The numbers change to letters.

6 From the Formatting toolbar, click the **Increase Indent** button 📇.

The selected list items are indented to the right.

7 In the **Styles and Formatting** task pane, under **Formatting of selected text**, click **New Style**.

The New Style dialog box displays.

8 In the **New Style** dialog box, under **Properties**, in the **Name** box, type **Points**

9 In the **New Style** dialog box, under **Properties**, click the **Style type arrow**, and then click **List**.

The list options display in the New Style dialog box, as shown in Figure 5.42.

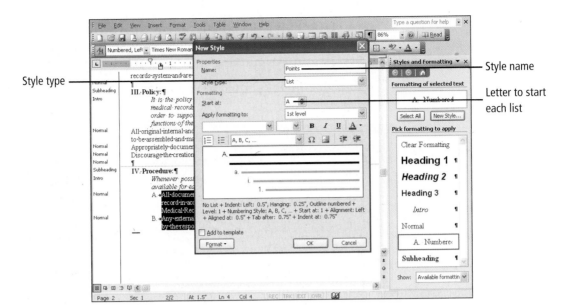

Style type

Style name

Letter to start each list

Figure 5.42

10 At the bottom of the **New Style** dialog box, click **OK**.

The list changes to the new style, and the new style name is displayed in the list of styles in the Styles and Formatting task pane. Notice in Figure 5.43 that the new list style also displays a small icon indicating the style type.

11 In the **Styles and Formatting** task pane, click the **Points** style.

Even though you just created a style using the selected paragraph, you still need to apply the style. When you apply a list style, the style displays in the Style box on the Formatting toolbar and in the Styles and Formatting task pane, but still displays Normal in the styles area. See Figure 5.43.

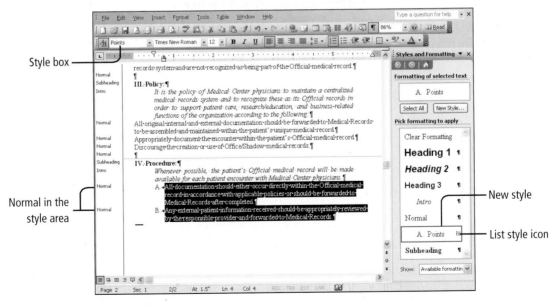

Style box

Normal in the style area

New style

List style icon

Figure 5.43

12 Scroll up in the document. In each paragraph containing text that uses the Normal style, position the insertion point, and then in the **Styles and Formatting** task pane, click the **Points** style.

Your document should look similar to Figure 5.44.

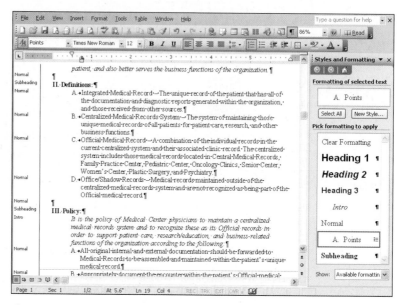

Figure 5.44

13 On the Standard toolbar, click the **Save** button ![save icon].

Activity 5.14 Creating and Applying Character Styles

Character styles are applied to selected text within a paragraph; they do not affect the formatting of the entire paragraph.

1 In the **Styles and Formatting** task pane, under **Formatting of selected text**, click **New Style**.

The New Style dialog box displays.

2 In the **New Style** dialog box, under **Properties**, in the **Name** box, type **Med Center**

3 Under **Properties**, click the **Style type arrow**, and then click **Character**.

Under Formatting, the character options display in the New Style dialog box.

4 In the **New Style** dialog box, under **Formatting**, locate the two boxes with arrows.

From the first box, you can select a font, and from the second box you can select a font size.

5 Click the **Font Size button arrow** and then click **14** points.

6 In the **New Style** dialog box, under **Formatting**, click the **Bold** button **B**.

7 In the **New Style** dialog box, under **Formatting**, click the **Font Color button arrow** A ▾, and in the third row, click the first color—**Red**. Compare your dialog box with Figure 5.45.

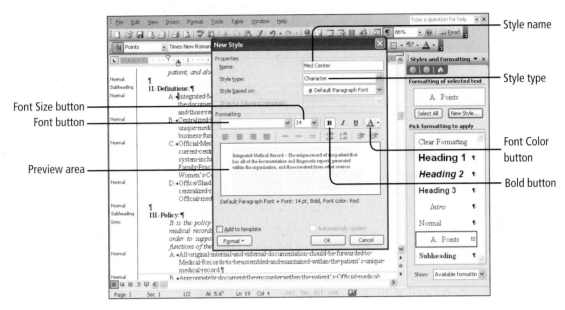

Figure 5.45

8 At the bottom of the **New Style** dialog box, click **OK**. Scroll to the top of the document.

The style is added to the Styles and Formatting task pane list, but the style has not been used to modify any text. Notice that the symbol on the right of the new style is a small *a*, which indicates a character style.

9 In the paragraph beginning *The purpose of this policy*, in the first sentence, select *Medical Center*.

10 In the **Styles and Formatting** task pane, click the **Med Center** style. Click on the text you just formatted to deselect the text.

The three formatting changes you made in the New Style dialog box are applied. See Figure 5.46.

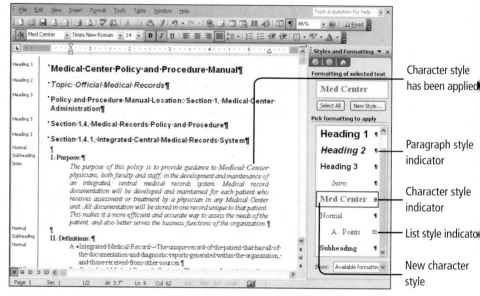

Character style has been applied

Paragraph style indicator

Character style indicator

List style indicator

New character style

Figure 5.46

11 In the same paragraph, in the fifth line, select **Medical Center**. In the **Styles and Formatting** task pane, click the **Med Center** style.

12 Locate *Medical Center* in the Intro style paragraphs following *III. Policy* and *IV. Procedure*, and apply the **Med Center** style to both, as shown in Figure 5.47.

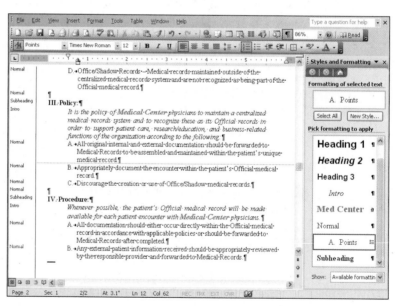

Figure 5.47

13 On the Standard toolbar, click the **Save** button.

Activity 5.15 Selecting and Modifying Styles

If you want to change a style, you can select all instances of the style, and then modify all of the paragraphs at once.

1 In the **Styles and Formatting** task pane, pause the mouse pointer over the **Subheading** paragraph style. Click the arrow on the right of the **Subheading** style.

A short menu displays, as shown in Figure 5.48. Here you can select, delete, or modify this style.

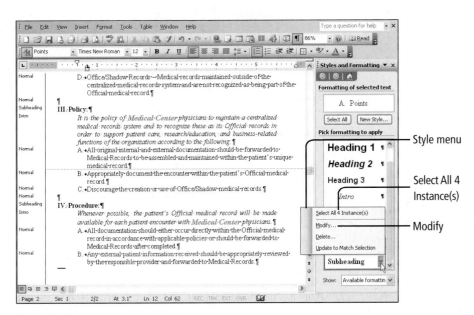

Figure 5.48

2 From the displayed menu, click **Select All 4 Instance(s)**.

All four of the Subheading style paragraphs are selected. While not required to change all of the paragraphs at once, selecting all of the instances helps you see where the style is used in the document.

3 Click the arrow on the right of the **Subheading** style again. From the displayed menu, click **Modify**.

The Modify Style dialog box displays.

4 In the **Modify Style** dialog box, under **Formatting**, click the **Italic** button *I*.

5 Near the bottom of the **Modify Style** dialog box, select the **Automatically update** check box.

The Automatically update feature enables you to change all of the paragraphs using the same style, and the style itself, by selecting and modifying only one paragraph. Compare your dialog box with Figure 5.49.

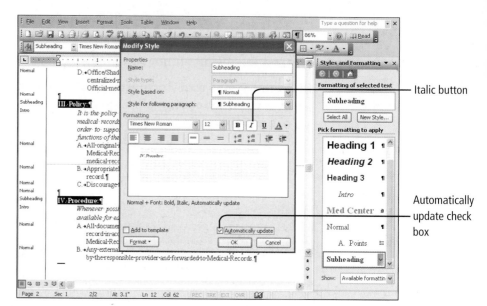

Italic button

Automatically update check box

Figure 5.49

6 At the bottom of the **Modify Style** dialog box, click **OK**.

All of the paragraphs using the Subheading style are changed, as shown in Figure 5.50.

Subheading style has been changed.

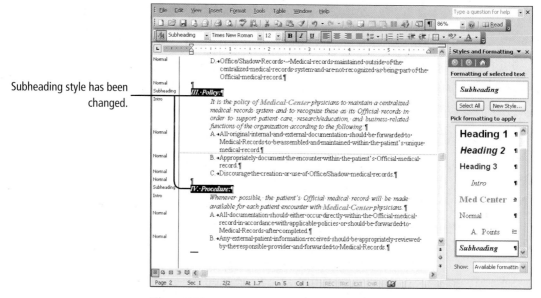

Figure 5.50

7 In the **Styles and Formatting** task pane, pause the mouse pointer over the **Med Center** character style. Click the arrow on the right of the **Med Center** style.

8 From the displayed menu, click **Modify**.

The Modify Style dialog box displays.

9 In the **Modify Style** dialog box, under **Formatting**, click the **Font Size button arrow**, and then click **12** points.

Compare your dialog box with Figure 5.51.

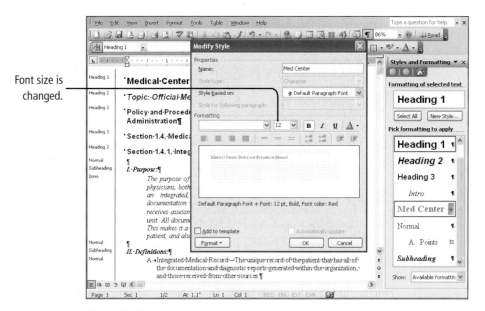

Font size is changed.

Figure 5.51

10 At the bottom of the **Modify Style** dialog box, click **OK**.

All of the text using the Med Center style is changed.

11 From the **Tools** menu, click **Options**. If necessary, click the **View tab**. Under **Outline and Normal options**, click the **Style area width spin box down arrow** until the style area width is **0"**. At the bottom of the **Options** dialog box, click **OK**. Alternatively, drag the vertical line on the right side of the style area to the left edge of the document window.

The style area on the left side of the screen closes.

12 On the Standard toolbar, click the **Save** button 📄.

Objective 6
Modify the Document Window

When you are working in Print Layout View, the gap between pages can take up a large portion of the screen, particularly when you are working on a laptop computer. You can minimize the gap between the pages so you can see more of your document, yet still maintain the visual advantage of seeing the edges of the paper. You can also split the window so that you can view two parts of a document at the same time. This is especially useful in long documents when you need to see pages at the beginning of the document and pages at the end of the document at the same time.

Activity 5.16 Hiding Spaces Between Pages

1 In the **Styles and Formatting** task pane, in the title bar, click the **Close** button ☒.

2 On the left edge of the horizontal scroll bar, click the **Print Layout View** button 📄. If necessary, set the Zoom to 100%.

The document changes to Print Layout View.

3 Scroll down until the break between the two pages is in view in the middle of your screen.

Notice how much of the screen is unused. You can see that a large portion of the screen contains blank white or gray space.

4 Move the pointer into the gray area between the two pages.

The pointer changes to a Hide White Spaces pointer, as shown in Figure 5.52.

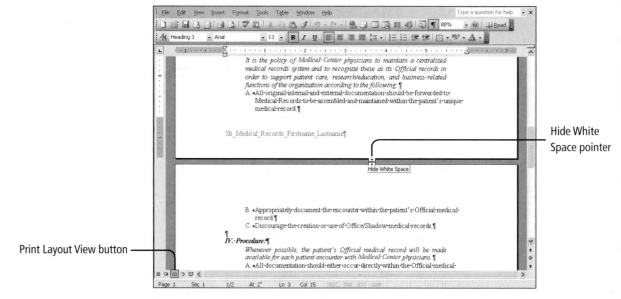

Figure 5.52

5 With the pointer positioned between the pages, click once.

Notice that the gap is closed, and the text appears to be on one continuous page, with a line showing the page breaks, as shown in Figure 5.53. Notice also that the footer area is hidden. The headers and footer areas are removed from the display, although both will still print.

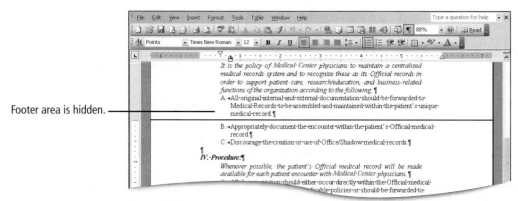

Figure 5.53

6 Move the pointer over the black line between the two pages and click.

The gap between the pages displays again.

Activity 5.17 Splitting the Window

1 At the top of the vertical scroll bar, above the arrow, locate the small gray bar, called a **split box**, and then move the pointer over the split box.

The pointer changes to a Resize Pointer, an up- and down-pointing arrow, as shown in Figure 5.54.

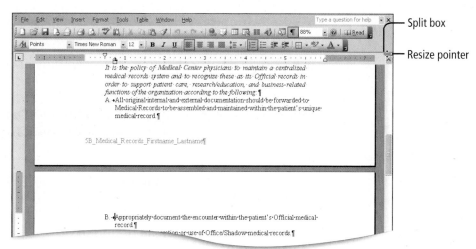

Split box

Resize pointer

Figure 5.54

2 With the Resize pointer displayed, drag about half way down the screen and release the mouse button.

The window splits in two, with a separate vertical and horizontal scroll bar for each portion of the window, as shown in Figure 5.55.

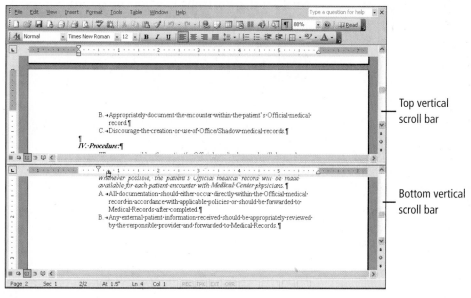

Top vertical scroll bar

Bottom vertical scroll bar

Figure 5.55

3 Use the top vertical scroll bar to scroll to the top of the document.

4 Use the bottom vertical scroll bar to scroll to the last section of the document, beginning with the *IV. Procedure* heading.

You can work on one part of the document while viewing another part, and you can cut or copy and paste between the two windows. If you are working in one window, you will need to click in the other window to make it active.

5 In the upper window, move the pointer slightly below the horizontal scroll bar until the Resize pointer displays.

6 Double-click or, alternatively, drag the bar to the top of the screen.

The second window is closed.

7 From the **View** menu, click **Header and Footer**. On the Header and Footer toolbar, click the **Switch Between Header and Footer** button 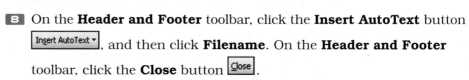.

8 On the **Header and Footer** toolbar, click the **Insert AutoText** button , and then click **Filename**. On the **Header and Footer** toolbar, click the **Close** button ⌊Close⌋.

9 On the Standard toolbar, click the **Save** button 🖫.

10 On the Standard toolbar, click the **Print Preview** button ⌊🔍⌋. Take a moment to check your work. On the Print Preview toolbar, click the **Close Preview** button ⌊Close⌋.

11 Make any necessary changes to your document, and then, on the Standard toolbar, click the **Print** button ⌊🖨⌋.

12 On the far right edge of the menu bar, click the **Close Window** button ⌊✕⌋.

End You have completed Project 5B ────────────────

Project 5C Policy Outline

Outlines can help you organize the content of a document and provide a structure for writing. Microsoft Word has a built-in outline format that can be applied to documents.

In Activities 5.18 through 5.19, you will create a multilevel outline for a portion of a medical center policy manual. The manual will have eight sections, but the outline you will create will be for the Medical Center Facilities and Services section. Your completed document will look similar to Figure 5.56. You will save your document as *5C_Policy_Outline_Firstname_Lastname.*

MEDICAL CENTER POLICY AND PROCEDURE MANUAL

I. MEDICAL CENTER ADMINISTRATION
II. FACULTY POLICIES
III. STAFF POLICIES
IV. MEDICAL CENTER FACILITIES AND SERVICES
    A. Equipment Center
       1. Equipment Center Overview
       2. Checkout Procedures
       3. Equipment Purchases
       4. Equipment Repair
    B. Medical Communications
       1. Medical Communications Overview
       2. Medical Illustration Policies and Procedures
       3. Waiver Procedures
    C. Medical Center Libraries
       1. Graduate Library Policy and Procedures
       2. Medical Library Policy and Procedures
    D. Space and Facilities
       1. Medical Center Space Inventory
       2. Storage in Corridors
       3. Vacated Space
       4. Environmental Services
       5. Facilities Maintenance
       6. Cleanup Procedures
V. FINANCIAL MANAGEMENT
VI. HUMAN RESOURCES
VII. SAFETY AND SECURITY
VIII. FORMS

5C_Policy_Outline_Firstname_Lastname

Figure 5.56
Project 5C—Policy Outline

Objective 7
Create an Outline

An *outline* is a list of topics for an oral or written report that visually indicates the order in which the information will be discussed, and the relationship of the topics to each other and to the total report. Outlines are used in planning situations to organize and rearrange information. The most basic outline is a numbered list, which has only one outline level. Word provides up to nine levels in an outline.

Activity 5.18 Creating a Multilevel Outline

The first step in creating an outline is to define the outline format.

1 On the Standard toolbar, click the **Open** button. Navigate to the location where the student files for this textbook are stored. Locate and open **w05C_Policy_Outline**. Save the file as **5C_Policy_Outline_Firstname_Lastname**

2 Click to position the insertion point to the left of the second line, which begins *Medical Center Administration*. Using the scroll bar, scroll down to the end of the document, hold down the Shift key, point to end of the last line, and then click again.

All of the text, with the exception of the title, is selected.

3 On the **Format** menu, click **Bullets and Numbering**. In the displayed **Bullets and Numbering** dialog box, click the **Outline Numbered tab**. Click the second option in the first row.

The Bullets and Numbering dialog box should look like Figure 5.57. If the second option in the first row does not match the figure, see Step 4.

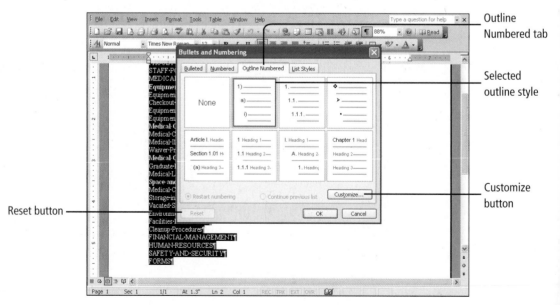

Figure 5.57

4️⃣ Locate the **Reset** button at the bottom of the **Bullets and Numbering** dialog box. If the **Reset** button is active (dark), click it, and then click **Yes** when prompted to restore the default settings. If the **Reset** button is light gray, the button is inactive.

If someone has adjusted the outline settings on your computer, it is a good idea to restore the outline default settings.

5️⃣ In the lower right corner of the **Bullets and Numbering** dialog box, click the **Customize** button.

The Customize Outline Numbered List dialog box displays. Under Number format, the Level starts at 1 by default. All formatting that you do will affect only the selected outline level.

6️⃣ Under **Number format**, in the **Number style** box, click the arrow, and then click **I, II, III** from the list. In the **Number format** box, place the insertion point to the right of the parenthesis mark and press Bksp. Type a period.

Notice the format displayed in the Preview area.

7️⃣ Under **Number format**, in the **Number position** box, click the arrow, and then click **Right** from the list. Under **Text position**, click the **Indent at spin box up arrow** to set the indent at **0.3"**.

In a formal outline, the Roman numerals should align on the decimal. These numbers need a little extra space to fit properly. Compare your Customize Outline Numbered List dialog box with Figure 5.58.

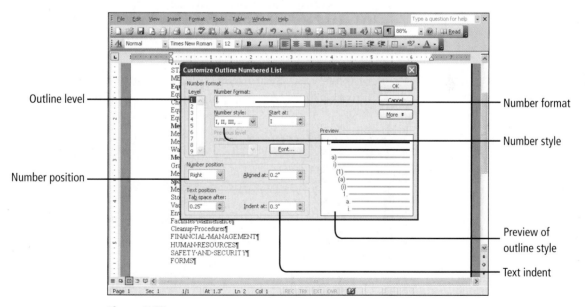

Figure 5.58

8 Under **Number format**, in the **Level** box, click **2**. In the **Number style** box, click the arrow, and then click **A, B, C** from the list. In the **Number format** box, place the insertion point to the right of the parenthesis mark and press Bksp. Type a period.

Compare your Customize Outline Numbered List dialog box with Figure 5.59.

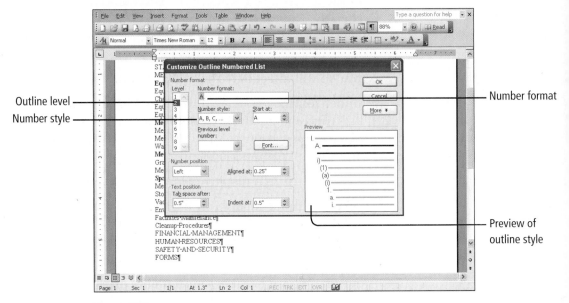

Outline level
Number style
Number format
Preview of outline style

Figure 5.59

9 Under **Number format**, in the **Level** box, click **3**. In the **Number style** box, click the arrow, and then click **1, 2, 3** from the list. In the **Number format** box, place the insertion point to the right of the parenthesis mark and press Bksp. Type a period.

Compare your Customize Outline Numbered List dialog box with Figure 5.60.

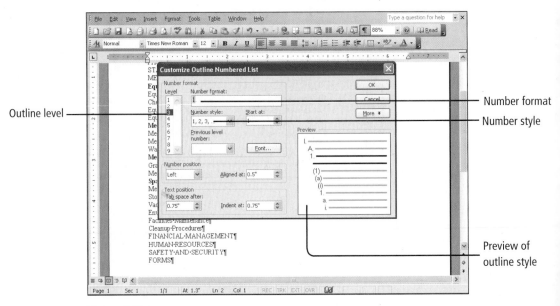

Outline level
Number format
Number style
Preview of outline style

Figure 5.60

10 In the upper right corner of the **Customize Outline Numbered List** dialog box, click **OK**. Hold down Ctrl and press Home.

The outline is created, but all items are at the top level—not visually indented to show different levels. See Figure 5.61.

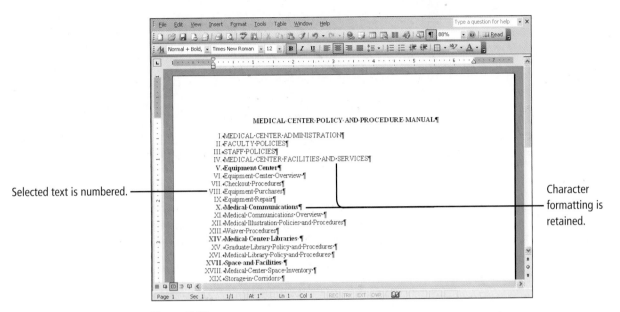

Selected text is numbered. ——————

Character formatting is retained.

Figure 5.61

11 On the Standard toolbar, click the **Save** button 🖫.

Activity 5.19 Setting Outline Levels

After you set up a list as a multilevel outline, you can use the Increase Indent and Decrease Indent buttons on the Formatting toolbar to change outline levels. In this activity, you will set the lines shown in all caps at outline Level 1, the entries shown in bold at outline Level 2, and the entries shown in Normal text at outline Level 3.

1 Click to position the insertion point anywhere in the paragraph beginning *V. Equipment Center*.

You do not need to select the entire paragraph to change the outline level.

2 On the Formatting toolbar, click the **Increase Indent** button 📝.

The line is indented 0.25 inch, and the number changes from *V* to *A*, a second-level outline entry. See Figure 5.62.

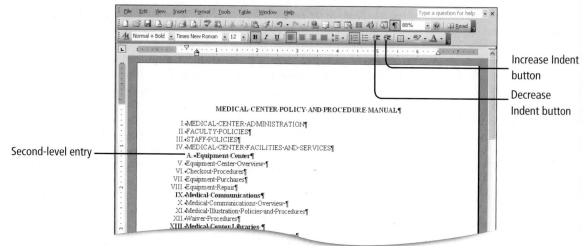

Figure 5.62

3. Move the pointer into the left margin to the left of the next line beginning *Equipment Center Overview*. When the pointer changes to a white arrow, drag down to select that paragraph and the next three.

Four lines are selected.

4. On the Formatting toolbar, click the **Increase Indent** button twice.

All four lines become third-level outline entries, as shown in Figure 5.63.

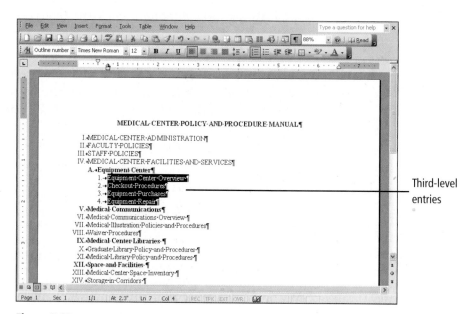

Figure 5.63

5. Continue setting outline levels for the remainder of the document. Recall that text in all caps retains its first-level setting, text in bold should be set at the second level, and normal text should be set at the third level. Use the **Increase Indent** button once on the bold text and twice on the normal text.

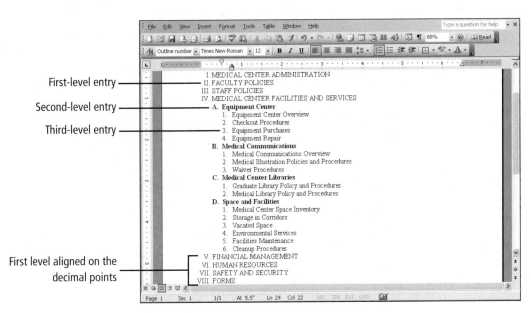

6 On the Standard toolbar, click the **Show/Hide** button ¶ to hide the nonprinting characters.

Compare your outline with Figure 5.64. Notice that the first-level entries align on the decimal points, not the left margin. This is the proper format of a formal outline.

First-level entry
Second-level entry
Third-level entry

First level aligned on the decimal points

Figure 5.64

7 On the Standard toolbar, click the **Show/Hide** button ¶ to display the nonprinting characters again. From the **View** menu, click **Header and Footer**. On the Header and Footer toolbar, click the **Switch Between Header and Footer** button.

8 On the **Header and Footer** toolbar, click the **Insert AutoText** button Insert AutoText ▾, and then click **Filename**. On the **Header and Footer** toolbar, click the **Close** button Close.

9 On the Standard toolbar, click the **Save** button.

10 On the Standard toolbar, click the **Print Preview** button. Take a moment to check your work. On the Print Preview toolbar, click the **Close Preview** button Close.

11 Make any necessary changes to your document, and then, on the Standard toolbar, click the **Print** button.

12 On the far right edge of the menu bar, click the **Close Window** button ×.

End You have completed Project 5C

Project 5D **Fitness**

The Outline View enables you to use the Outlining toolbar to quickly create an outline based on heading styles. This outline can be rearranged, and heading levels can be changed with the click of a button.

In Activities 5.20 through 5.21 you will use the Outline View and the Outlining toolbar to create an outline for a summer fitness program at the University Medical Center. You will format existing text using the Outline toolbar, and you will modify and rearrange the outline. Your completed document will look similar to Figure 5.65. You will save your document as *5D_Fitness_Program_Firstname_Lastname.*

Summer Sports and Fitness Program

The University Medical Center will off a full range of sports, fitness, and dance programs beginning after Memorial Day. The following programs are offered to all Medical Center staff and their families at no cost.

Sports

Competitive sports will be offered in the mornings this summer. Slots fill up very quickly, especially for golf and tennis.

Golf

All rounds will be played on the University golf course on Monday and Wednesday mornings, except the week of the tournament. All participants will play in foursomes. Tee times will be at 6 a.m., 8 a.m., and 10 a.m.

Tennis

Matches will be played on the tennis courts at the IM building. If demand is great enough, the courts behind Married Housing will also be available. Court times will be assigned in one hour blocks on Monday or Thursday mornings. Players need to specify whether they are interested in singles, doubles, or mixed

Rowing

There were not a lot of people interested in two- and this summer only kayak racing will be offered. The ti determined.

Fitness

Swimming

All swimming events will be held at the Natatorium t pool will be used most of the summer by the high sch Summer Quest program. Free swimming will be avai Swimmersize classes will be held at noon on Monday The number of fitness programs has been increased b sessions last summer.

Aerobics

The aerobics program has not been finalized.

Martial Arts

The martial arts program has not been finalized.

5D_Fitness_Firstname_Lastname

Kickboxing

Kickboxing has become extremely popular with young adults and additional classes will be considered. The classes are currently scheduled on Wednesday evening and Saturday morning.

Dance

Jazz and Tap

West Coast Swing

Ballroom Dance

5D_Fitness_Firstname_Lastname

Figure 5.65
Project 5D—Fitness

Objective 8
Create an Outline Using the Outline View and the Outlining Toolbar

When you display a document in Word's Outline View, Word treats each paragraph as a separate topic to which you can apply either Heading or Body Text styles. Word's built-in Heading 1 style represents the highest heading level, called Level 1, in an outline.

Activity 5.20 Creating an Outline Using the Outlining Toolbar

An outline created using the Outline View and the Outlining toolbar enables you to look at sections of a document, and move all of the text under a heading by clicking that heading.

1 On the Standard toolbar, click the **Open** button. Navigate to the location where the student files for this textbook are stored. Locate and open **w05D_Fitness**. Save the file as **5D_Fitness_Firstname_Lastname**

2 To the left of the horizontal scroll bar, click the **Outline View** button. To the left of the Formatting toolbar, click the **Styles and Formatting** button.

The document displays in Outline View. The Outlining toolbar displays under the Formatting toolbar and the Styles and Formatting task pane displays on the right of the screen.

3 Display the style area on the left of the screen by displaying the **Tools** menu, and then clicking **Options**. Click the **View tab**. Under **Outline and Normal options**, click the **Style area width spin box up arrow** until the style area width is **0.5"**. At the bottom of the **Options** dialog box, click **OK**.

In Outline View, each paragraph is considered a topic, and will be preceded by a symbol. If the paragraph does not have a Heading style, it is considered *body text*, and the symbol is a small box called a *topic marker*. Compare your screen with Figure 5.66.

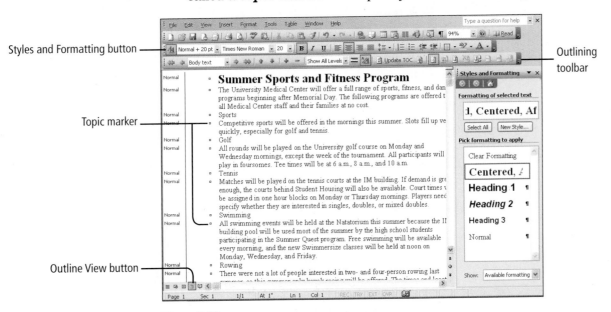

Styles and Formatting button —

Topic marker —

Outline View button —

Outlining toolbar

Figure 5.66

4 Click to position the insertion point in the fifth line of the document, which contains only the word *Sports*. In the Styles and Formatting task pane, under **Pick formatting to apply**, click **Heading 1**.

The paragraph changes to the Heading 1 style. The outline level, Level 1, displays in the Outline Level box. An open plus symbol, called an ***Expand button***, replaces the topic marker to the left of the paragraph, as shown in Figure 5.67. The expand button indicates that there is lower-level text associated with this heading, which in this instance is the remaining text in the document.

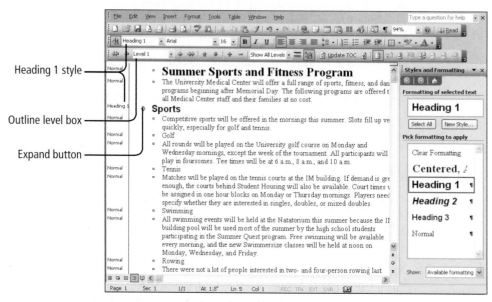

Heading 1 style
Outline level box
Expand button

Figure 5.67

5 Scroll down and click to position the insertion point in the line that contains only the word *Fitness*. Press F4—the Repeat key. Repeat this process to change the *Kickboxing* line to a **Heading 1** style. Alternatively, click the Heading 1 style in the Styles and Formatting task pane.

The F4 button repeats the immediately-preceding command, in this instance the application of the Heading 1 style.

6 Hold down Ctrl and press Home. Position the insertion point in the eighth line of the document, which contains only the word *Golf*.

Notice that this line currently uses the Normal style, and has a topic marker on the left.

7 On the Outlining toolbar, click the **Demote** button [→].

The paragraph changes to a Heading 2 style. The outline level is Level 2, as shown in Figure 5.68. All of the text following the word *Golf*, up to but not including the next heading, is also demoted and is treated as subordinate text to the *Golf* heading. The Demote and Promote buttons can be used to set the outline level of existing text, or you may find it faster to use the Styles and Formatting task pane along with the F4 key.

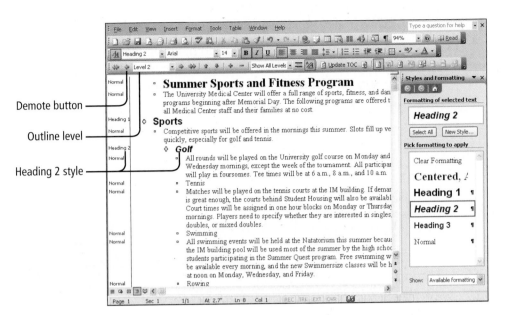

Demote button

Outline level

Heading 2 style

Figure 5.68

8 Click to position the insertion point in the line that contains only the word *Tennis*. In the **Styles and Formatting** task pane, under **Pick formatting to apply**, click **Heading 2**.

9 Scroll down and position the insertion point in the line that contains only the word *Swimming*. Press F4. Continue this process to the end of the document, changing *Rowing*, *Aerobics*, and *Martial Arts* to a **Heading 2** style. Hold down Ctrl and press Home.

Compare your document with Figure 5.69.

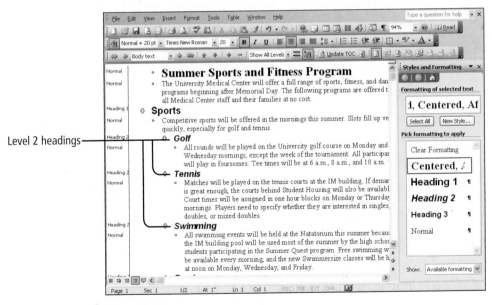

Level 2 headings

Figure 5.69

10 On the Standard toolbar, click the **Save** button 🖫.

Activity 5.21 Modifying an Outline in Outline View

In Outline View, you can change heading levels, rearrange headings in an existing outline, and show only the parts of the outline you want to see. You can also enter new text in the outline.

1 To the left of the *Swimming* heading, click the **Expand** button.

The heading, along with all of its subordinate text (and headings if there were any) are selected, as shown in Figure 5.70.

Move Down button —

Expand button —
Selected heading and subordinate material —

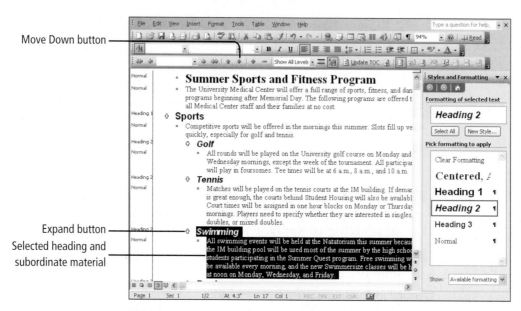

Figure 5.70

2 Scroll down until you can see the end of the document. On the Outlining toolbar, click the **Move Down** button.

The Swimming heading and the subordinate paragraph move down one topic (paragraph).

3 Click the **Move Down** button twice more.

The *Swimming* heading and related text are moved to the *Fitness* section, as shown in Figure 5.71.

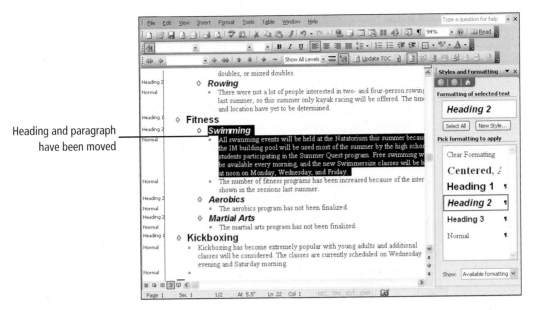

Heading and paragraph have been moved

Figure 5.71

4 Click to position the insertion point in the *Kickboxing* heading.

On the Outlining toolbar, click the **Demote** button.

The Kickboxing heading changes from a Heading 1 style to a Heading 2 style, and from Level 1 to Level 2. It is now subordinate to (a lower level than) the Fitness heading. See Figure 5.72.

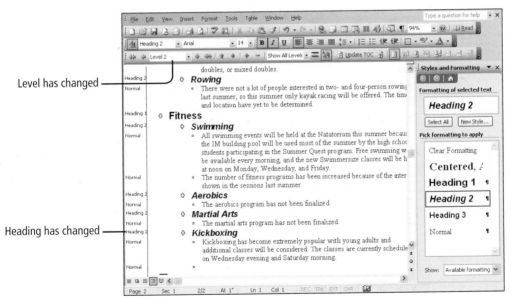

Level has changed

Heading has changed

Figure 5.72

5 Hold down [Ctrl] and press [Home]. Hold down [Ctrl] and press [A] to select the entire document. On the Outlining toolbar, click the **Show Level button arrow** Show All Levels ▾, and then click **Show Level 2**. Click anywhere to deselect the text.

Everything at Level 2 and higher is displayed, as shown in Figure 5.73. Headings underlined with wavy lines indicate that subordinate body text exists, but is currently hidden from view. In this manner, you can view the overall sections of your report (or presentation) without the clutter of the remaining text.

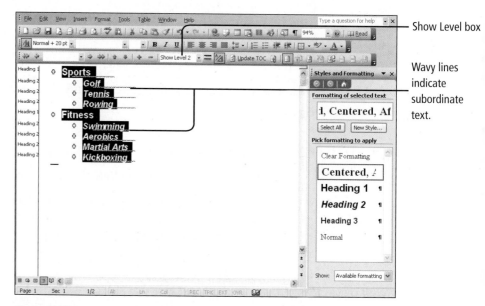

Figure 5.73

6 On the Outlining toolbar, click the **Show Level button arrow** Show Level 2 ▾, and then click **Show All Levels**.

The headings and body text are all displayed.

7 Near the top of the document, position the pointer over the **Expand** button to the left of the *Sports* heading. Double-click the **Expand** button.

All of the subordinate headings and text associated with the *Sports* heading are hidden—this is referred to as being **collapsed**. The Fitness heading is not affected. See Figure 5.74.

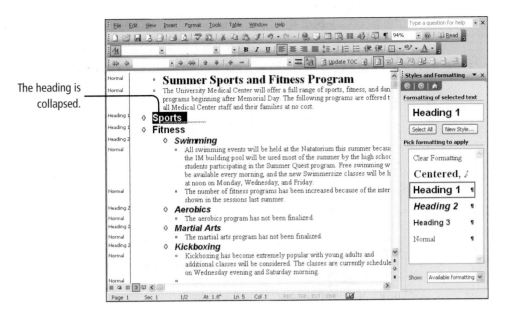

The heading is collapsed.

Figure 5.74

8 Press Ctrl + End to position the insertion point at the end of the last line of the document, and then press Enter. Click the **Promote** button twice. Type **Dance**

A new Level 1 heading is created.

9 Press Enter. Click the **Demote** button and type **Jazz and Tap**

A new Level 2 heading is created.

10 Press Enter and type **West Coast Swing** Press Enter again and type **Ballroom Dance**

The Dance heading now has three Level 2 headings under it. The Level 2 headings have no subordinate headings or text, indicated by a **Collapse button** to the left of each, as shown in Figure 5.75.

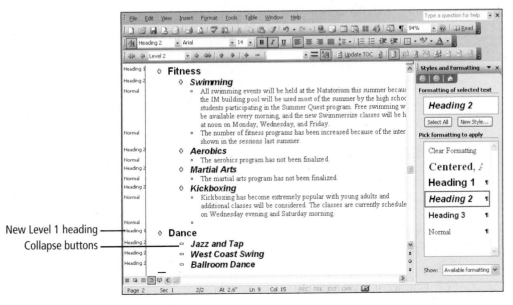

New Level 1 heading
Collapse buttons

Figure 5.75

11 To the left of the Formatting toolbar, click the **Styles and Formatting** button ![] to close the Styles and Formatting task bar. To the left of the horizontal scroll bar, click the **Print Layout View** button ![]. Hold down Ctrl and press Home.

Compare your document with Figure 5.76.

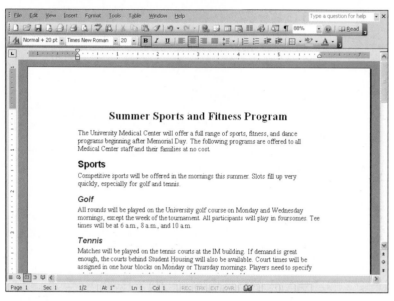

Figure 5.76

12 From the **View** menu, click **Header and Footer**. On the Header and Footer toolbar, click the **Switch Between Header and Footer** button ![].

13 On the **Header and Footer** toolbar, click the **Insert AutoText** button ![Insert AutoText ▾], and then click **Filename**.

The file name is inserted in the footer.

14 On the **Header and Footer** toolbar, click the **Close** button ![Close].

15 On the Standard toolbar, click the **Save** button ![].

16 On the Standard toolbar, click the **Print Preview** button ![]. Take a moment to check your work. On the Print Preview toolbar, click the **Close Preview** button ![Close].

17 Make any necessary changes to your document. When you are satisfied, on the Standard toolbar, click the **Print** button ![].

18 On the menu bar, click the **Close** button ![X], saving any changes.

End You have completed Project 5D ────────────────────────────

Summary

In this chapter, you used the Microsoft Graph program to create a chart from data displayed in a table. After the chart was created, you modified the elements of the chart by adding a title, changing the chart type, changing the font size and color and changing the size and placement of the chart in your document.

Some new character effects were demonstrated, including adding a drop cap to the first letter in the first paragraph of a document, adding a shadow effect to a title, and changing the character spacing in a paragraph.

Styles were introduced as a method to apply uniform formatting to long documents to achieve a consistent appearance. You practiced how to apply existing styles, set new styles, and modify styles for paragraph, character, and list style formats.

Techniques for modifying the Word window were demonstrated, including splitting a window so you can see the top and bottom of a document at the same time, and hiding the white space when you are in Print Layout view so that more text displays on the screen.

Finally, you practiced using a multilevel outline by modifying the outline format and applying it to text in a document. You also created an outline in the Outline View, and practiced changing ouline levels and moving blocks of text by move outline headings.

In This Chapter You Practiced How To

- Create a Chart with Microsoft Graph
- Format a Chart
- Add Special Text Effects
- Use Existing Styles
- Create and Modify New Styles
- Modify the Document Window
- Create an Outline
- Create an Outline Using the Outline View and the Outlining Toolbar

Matching   Match each term in the second column with its correct definition in the first column by writing the letter of the term on the blank line in front of the correct definition.

_____ **1.** A built-in feature of Word that is used to create charts.

_____ **2.** A type of chart that shows comparison among data.

_____ **3.** A type of chart that shows trends over time.

_____ **4.** A type of chart that shows the proportion of parts to the whole.

_____ **5.** A table-like structure that is part of the Microsoft Graph program in which you can enter the numbers used to create a chart.

_____ **6.** The chart element that relates the data displayed to the categories.

_____ **7.** The area on a chart where the graphic (pie or column) is placed, which can be resized by using sizing handles.

_____ **8.** A text effect that adds a silhouette behind the letters.

_____ **9.** A group of formatting commands that are stored with a specific name and can be retrieved and applied to text.

_____ **10.** A type of style that controls the font, font size, and font style applied to individual characters.

_____ **11.** The default Word template.

_____ **12.** A list of topics that visually indicates the order in which information in an oral or written report will be presented and the relationship of the topics to each other.

_____ **13.** The dialog box used to create an outline.

_____ **14.** In the Styles and Formatting task pane, the term that describes the items listed under _Pick formatting to apply_.

_____ **15.** An enlarged letter positioned at the beginning of text and displayed on several lines.

A Bullets and Numbering

B Character style

C Column

D Datasheet

E Drop cap

F Legend

G Line

H Microsoft Graph

I Normal

J Outline

K Pie

L Plot area

M Shadow

N Style

O Style names

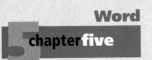
Fill in the Blank Write the correct answer in the space provided.

1. The data along the bottom of a chart displays in the

   _____ axis.

2. The numbers along the left side of a chart display in the

   _____ axis.

3. The numbers on the left side of a chart are called a(n)

   _____ because they display a range of numbers.

4. A large first letter used to begin the first paragraph in a chapter or

   article is known as a _____.

5. Increasing or decreasing the space between letters is accomplished

   by changing the _____ spacing.

6. The information that determines the basic structure and format

   of a document is known as a _____.

7. To change the line spacing, indents, alignment, and tab stops, you

   could change the _____ style.

8. A quick way to create a new style is to set the style, and then type

   a name in the _____ box.

9. An item in an outline can be moved to a lower level by clicking the

   _____ button.

10. In the Styles and Formatting task pane, you can click the arrow

    at the right end of a selected style and choose _____

    to change the style.

Project 5E—Service Area

Objectives: *Create a Chart with Microsoft Graph, Format a Chart, Add Special Text Effects, Use Existing Styles, Create and Modify New Styles, Modify the Document Window, and Create an Outline.*

In the following Skill Assessment, you will create and modify a pie chart that shows the geographic distribution of patients in the University Medical Center service area. Your completed document will look similar to the one shown in Figure 5.77. You will save your document as *5E_Service_Area_Firstname_Lastname.*

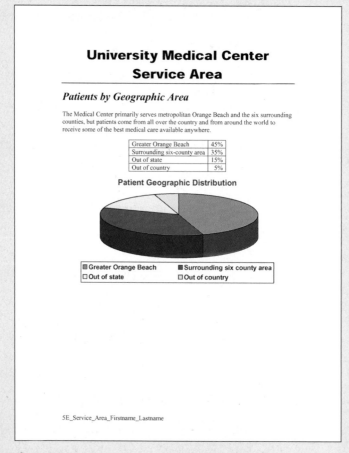

Figure 5.77

1. On the Standard toolbar, click the **Open** button. Navigate to the location where the student files for this textbook are stored. Locate and open **w05E_Service_Area**. Save the file as
   5E_Service_Area_Firstname_Lastname

2. In the table, click anywhere to position the insertion point in the table. From the **Table** menu, point to **Select**, and then click **Table**.

(Project 5E–Service Area continues on the next page)

(Project 5E–Service Area continued)

3. From the **Insert** menu, point to **Picture**, and then click **Chart**. The Microsoft Graph program displays and the data from the table displays in the datasheet.

4. Be sure that your Standard and Formatting toolbars are displayed on two rows. (If only one toolbar row is displayed on your screen, at the right end of the toolbar, click the Toolbar Options button, and then click Show Buttons on Two Rows.)

5. Click anywhere inside the **datasheet**, and then on the datasheet title bar, click the **Close** button. On the Chart toolbar, click the **By Column** button. Recall that the data must be displayed by column before you can change the default column chart into another type of chart.

6. On the Chart toolbar, click the **Chart Type arrow**, and then in the fifth row, click the second button—the **3-D Pie Chart**. Use the ScreenTip to help identify the chart type. The chart display changes to a pie chart. On the Standard toolbar, click the **Save** button.

7. From the **Chart** menu, click **Chart Options**. If necessary, in the Chart Options dialog box, click the Titles tab. Alternatively, right-click on the chart and click Chart Options from the shortcut menu. Click in the **Chart title** box, type **Patient Geographic Distribution** and then click **OK**.

8. Right-click the **Chart Title** and from the shortcut menu click **Format Chart Title**. In the **Format Chart Title** dialog box, click the **Font tab**. The font displayed is Arial, Bold, 10 pt. Click the **Color arrow**. From the displayed palette, in the second row, click the sixth color—**Blue**. Click **OK**.

9. Right-click the **Legend** and from the shortcut menu click **Format Legend**. In the **Format Legend** dialog box, click the **Placement tab**, and then click the **Bottom** option button. From this dialog box, you can move the legend to different areas on the chart. Click **OK**.

10. Drag the lower right sizing handle of the chart box down and to the right until the right edge of the chart area is at approximately **6 inches on the horizontal ruler** and the lower edge of the chart is at approximately **6 inches on the vertical ruler**.

11. Right-click in the **Plot Area**—the gray area behind the pie chart—and click **Format Plot Area** from the shortcut menu. Under **Border**, click **None**. Under **Area**, click **None**, and then click **OK**.

12. Click in the body of the document to close the Microsoft Graph program and return to the document window. Click on the chart once to select it, and then on the Formatting toolbar click the **Center** button to center the chart on the page. Compare your screen with Figure 5.77.

(Project 5E–Service Area continues on the next page)

(Project 5E–Service Area continued)

13. From the **View** menu, display the Header and Footer toolbar, switch to the footer, and then, on the Header and Footer toolbar, click **Insert AutoText**. From the displayed list, click **Filename**. Close the Header and Footer toolbar.

14. On the Standard toolbar, click the **Save** button, and then click the **Print Preview** button to see the document as it will print. Click the **Print** button, and then close the file, saving changes if prompted to do so.

 End **You have completed Project 5E** ━━━━━━━━━━━━━━━━━━━

Project 5F—Child Care

Objectives: *Add Special Text Effects, Create an Outline, and Modify the Document Window.*

In the following Skill Assessment, you will format a multilevel outline of the topics for a child care symposium that is being held by the University Medical Center. You will also add a drop cap to the title. Your completed document will look similar to the one shown in Figure 5.78. You will save your document as *5F_Child_Care_Firstname_Lastname.*

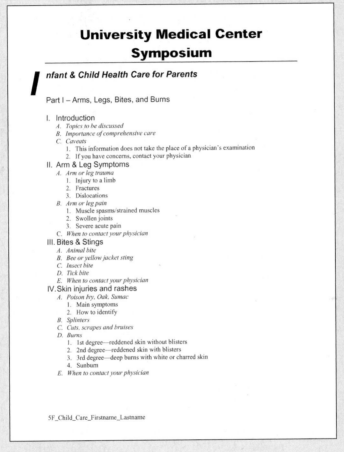

Figure 5.78

1. On the Standard toolbar, click the **Open** button. Navigate to the location where the student files for this textbook are stored. Locate and open **w05F_Child_Care**. Save the file as **5F_Child_Care_Firstname_Lastname**

2. Be sure the document is in **Print Layout View**. If necessary, change the Zoom setting to Page Width. Move the mouse pointer to the top edge of the document until you see the *Hide White Space* pointer, and then click. This will maximize your viewing area.

(Project 5F–Child Care continues on the next page)

(Project 5F–Child Care continued)

3. Notice that the lines in the body of the document are formatted in three ways—Arial 14 pt., Times New Roman italic 12 pt., and Times New Roman 12 pt. (no emphasis). Select the line *Infant & Child Health for Parents*. From the **Format** menu, click **Drop Cap**. In the **Drop Cap** dialog box, under **Position**, click **In margin**. Under **Options**, change the **Lines to drop** box to **2**, and then click **OK**.

4. Near the top of the document, click to position the insertion point to the left of *Introduction*. Use the scroll bar to view the end of the document, position the pointer to the right of the last word in the document, hold down [Shift], and then click to select all the text from *Introduction* to the end.

5. With the text still selected, on the **Format** menu, click **Bullets and Numbering**. If necessary, in the Bullets and Numbering dialog box, click the Outline Numbered tab. In the first row, click the second **Outline Numbered** box. At the bottom of the **Bullets and Numbering** dialog box, check to see if the **Reset** button is active (not gray), and if it is, click it, and then click **Yes** when prompted to restore the default settings.

6. In the lower right, click the **Customize** button. Under **Number format**, in the **Number style** box, click the arrow, and then click **I, II, III** from the list. In the **Number format** box, place the insertion point to the right of the parenthesis mark and press [Bksp]. Type a period. Under **Number format**, in the **Number position** box, click the arrow, and then click **Right** from the list. Under **Text position**, click the **Indent at spin box up arrow** to set the indent at **0.3"**. The first level of the outline format is set.

7. Under **Number format**, in the **Level** box, click **2**. In the **Number style** box, click the arrow, and then click **A, B, C** from the list. In the **Number format** box, place the insertion point to the right of the parenthesis mark and press [Bksp]. Type a period. The second level of the outline format is set.

8. Under **Number format**, in the **Level** box, click **3**. In the **Number style** box, click the arrow, and then click **1, 2, 3** from the list. In the **Number format** box, place the insertion point to the right of the parenthesis mark and press [Bksp]. Type a period. In the upper right corner of the **Customize Outline Numbered List** dialog box, click **OK**.

9. Hold down [Ctrl] and press [Home]. On the Standard toolbar, click the **Save** button. Click to position the insertion point to the left of the paragraph beginning *II. Topics to be discussed* and drag down to select the next two lines, ending with *IV. Caveats*. (The Roman numerals will not be selected.) On the Formatting toolbar, click the **Increase Indent** button. These items become A.–C. Recall that the Increase Indent button is used to move items in an outline to a lower level.

(Project 5F–Child Care continued)

10. Move the pointer into the selection area to the left of the paragraph that begins *II. This information* and select that line and the following line. On the Formatting toolbar, click the **Increase Indent** button twice. These two lines are changed to the third level in the outline and become 1.–2.

11. Locate and select the remaining lines displayed in Times New Roman 12 pt. italic and set them to outline level two. (Hint: Hold down and select each italic line.) Click Increase Indent once to get the result A. B. C. and so forth. Use the same technique to locate and select the remaining lines displayed in Times New Roman without emphasis, and then set them to outline level three (click Increase Indent twice to get the result 1. 2. 3. and so forth). Compare your document with Figure 5.78.

12. From the **View** menu, display the Header and Footer toolbar, switch to the footer and then, on the Header and Footer toolbar, click **Insert AutoText**. From the displayed list, click **Filename**. Close the Header and Footer toolbar.

13. On the Standard toolbar, click the **Save** button, and then click the **Print Preview** button to see the document as it will print. Click the **Print** button, and then close the file, saving changes if prompted to do so.

End **You have completed Project 5F** ————————————————

Project 5G — Art Program

Objectives: *Use Existing Styles and Create and Modify New Styles.*

In the following Skill Assessment, you will format an informational flyer about the University Medical Center arts program. You will use existing styles, create new styles, and modify a style. Your completed document will look similar to the one shown in Figure 5.79. You will save your document as *5G_Art_Program_Firstname_Lastname.*

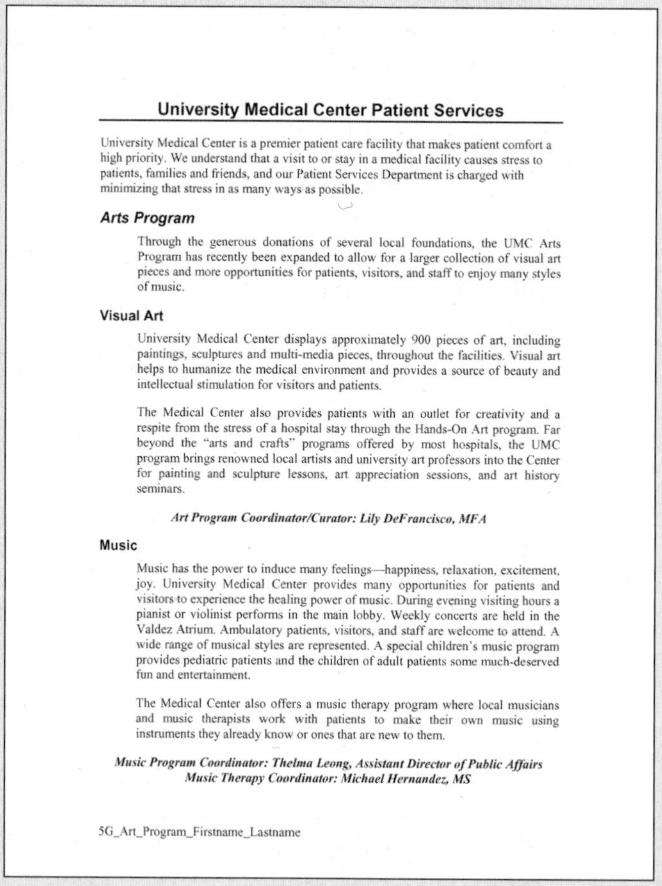

University Medical Center Patient Services

University Medical Center is a premier patient care facility that makes patient comfort a high priority. We understand that a visit to or stay in a medical facility causes stress to patients, families and friends, and our Patient Services Department is charged with minimizing that stress in as many ways as possible.

Arts Program

Through the generous donations of several local foundations, the UMC Arts Program has recently been expanded to allow for a larger collection of visual art pieces and more opportunities for patients, visitors, and staff to enjoy many styles of music.

Visual Art

University Medical Center displays approximately 900 pieces of art, including paintings, sculptures and multi-media pieces, throughout the facilities. Visual art helps to humanize the medical environment and provides a source of beauty and intellectual stimulation for visitors and patients.

The Medical Center also provides patients with an outlet for creativity and a respite from the stress of a hospital stay through the Hands-On Art program. Far beyond the "arts and crafts" programs offered by most hospitals, the UMC program brings renowned local artists and university art professors into the Center for painting and sculpture lessons, art appreciation sessions, and art history seminars.

Art Program Coordinator/Curator: Lily DeFrancisco, MFA

Music

Music has the power to induce many feelings—happiness, relaxation, excitement, joy. University Medical Center provides many opportunities for patients and visitors to experience the healing power of music. During evening visiting hours a pianist or violinist performs in the main lobby. Weekly concerts are held in the Valdez Atrium. Ambulatory patients, visitors, and staff are welcome to attend. A wide range of musical styles are represented. A special children's music program provides pediatric patients and the children of adult patients some much-deserved fun and entertainment.

The Medical Center also offers a music therapy program where local musicians and music therapists work with patients to make their own music using instruments they already know or ones that are new to them.

Music Program Coordinator: Thelma Leong, Assistant Director of Public Affairs
Music Therapy Coordinator: Michael Hernandez, MS

5G_Art_Program_Firstname_Lastname

Figure 5.79

1. On the Standard toolbar, click the **Open** button. Navigate to the location where the student files for this textbook are stored. Locate and open **w05G_Art_Program**. Save the file as **5G_Art_Program_Firstname_Lastname**

2. To the left of the horizontal scroll bar, click the **Normal View** button. From the **Tools** menu, click **Options**. Be sure the **View tab** is selected. At the bottom of the **View tab**, under **Outline and Normal options**, click the **Style area width spin box arrows** as necessary until the width is **0.6"**. Click **OK**.

(Project 5G–Art Program continues on the next page)

(Project 5G–Art Program continued)

3. On the left side of the Formatting toolbar, click the **Styles and Formatting** button. If the right edge of the text is hidden behind the task pane, on the Standard toolbar, click the Zoom button arrow, and then click Page Width.

4. Click anywhere in the first line, *University Medical Center Patient Services*. In the **Styles and Formatting** task pane, under **Pick formatting to apply**, click **Heading 1**. Click anywhere in the line *Arts Program*, and then click **Heading 2**. Click in the line *Visual Art*, and then click **Heading 3**. Scroll down the page, click in the line *Music*, and then click **Heading 3**. You have now completed applying existing heading styles to the major headings in this document.

5. Scroll to the top of the document, locate the paragraph beginning *Through the generous*, and then triple-click in the paragraph to select it. From the **Format** menu, click **Paragraph**. If necessary, click the **Indents and Spacing tab**. Under **General**, click the **Alignment arrow**, and then click **Justified**. Under **Indentation**, click the **Left spin box up arrow** to set the left indent at **0.5"**. Under **Spacing**, click the **Before spin box up arrow** to set the Before spacing to **6 pt**. Click the **After spin box up arrow** to set the After spacing to **12 pt**. Click **OK**.

6. With the paragraph still selected, in the **Styles and Formatting** task pane, under **Formatting of selected text**, click the **New Style** button. In the **New Style** dialog box, under **Properties**, in the **Name** box, type **Para** and then click **OK**. In the **Styles and Formatting** task pane, click the **Para** style. Recall that after you create a style, you must click it to apply the style to the selected paragraph.

7. Click in the first paragraph under *Visual Art* that begins *University Medical Center*, and then from the **Styles and Formatting** task pane, under **Pick formatting to apply**, click **Para**. Click in the next paragraph that begins *The Medical Center*, and then click **Para**. Scroll down until the paragraphs under the *Music* heading are displayed on your screen. Move the mouse pointer to the left margin until it changes to a white selection arrow, and then drag to select the first two paragraphs under *Music*, beginning with *Music has the power*. From the **Styles and Formatting** task pane, click **Para**.

8. Just above the *Music* heading, select the one-line paragraph that begins *Art Program Coordinator*. In the **Styles and Formatting** task pane, click the **New Style** button. In the displayed **New Style** dialog box, under **Properties**, in the **Name** box, type **Contact** In the **New Style** dialog box, under **Formatting**, click the **Bold** button, the **Italic** button, and the **Center** button. Click **OK**. In the **Styles and Formatting** task pane, click the **Contact** style to apply the style to the selected paragraph.

(Project 5G–Art Program continues on the next page)

(Project 5G–Art Program continued)

9. Scroll down and select the last two paragraphs in the document, beginning with *Music Program Coordinator*. From the **Styles and Formatting** task pane, click **Contact** to apply the style to the selected paragraphs.

10. Hold down Ctrl and press Home. Click in the heading at the top of the document—*University Medical Center Patient Services*. On the Formatting toolbar, click the **Center** button. From the **Format** menu, display the **Borders and Shading** dialog box, and if necessary, click the **Borders tab**. Under **Style**, be sure the single line at the top of the Style area is selected. Click the **Width arrow**, and then click **1½ pt**. In the **Preview** area, click the **bottom** of the graphic to apply the line under the paragraph. Click **OK**.

11. From the **Format** menu, display the **Paragraph** dialog box. Under **Spacing**, change the **After** box to **12 pt.**, and then click **OK**.

12. In the **Styles and Formatting** task pane, click the **New Style** button. Under **Properties**, in the **Name** box, type **Title 1** and then click **OK**. In the **Styles and Formatting** task pane, click **Title 1** to apply the style to the title at the top of the document.

13. On the **Styles and Formatting** task pane's title bar, click the **Close** button. From the **Tools** menu, click **Options**. On the **View tab**, under **Outline and Normal options**, in the **Style area width** box, select the number, type **0** and then click **OK**.

14. To the right of the horizontal scroll bar, click the **Print Layout View** button. Compare your document with Figure 5.79. From the **View** menu, display the Header and Footer toolbar, switch to the footer, and then, on the Header and Footer toolbar, click **Insert AutoText**. From the displayed list, click **Filename**. Close the Header and Footer toolbar.

15. On the Standard toolbar, click the **Save** button, and then click the **Print Preview** button to see the document as it will print. Click the **Print** button, and then close the Print Preview. Close the file, saving changes if prompted to do so.

 End **You have completed Project 5G** ——————————————

Project 5H — Daily Patients

Objectives: *Create a Chart with Microsoft Graph and Format a Chart.*

In the following Performance Assessment, you will create a column chart that shows the number of patients treated daily at University Medical Center by service provided. Your completed document will look similar to the one shown in Figure 5.80. You will save your document as *5H_Daily_Patients_Firstname_Lastname.*

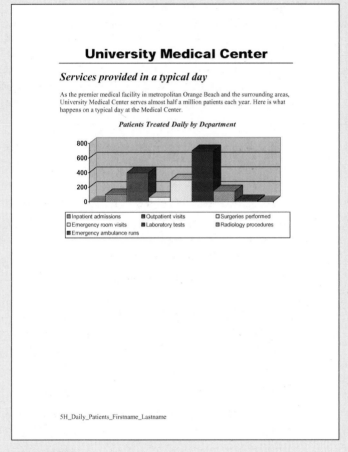

University Medical Center

Services provided in a typical day

As the premier medical facility in metropolitan Orange Beach and the surrounding areas, University Medical Center serves almost half a million patients each year. Here is what happens on a typical day at the Medical Center.

Patients Treated Daily by Department

5H_Daily_Patients_Firstname_Lastname

Figure 5.80

1. On the Standard toolbar, click the **Open** button. Navigate to the location where the student files for this textbook are stored. Locate and open **w05H_Daily_Patients**. Save the file as **5H_Daily_Patients_Firstname_Lastname**

2. Click anywhere in the table. Display the **Table** menu, point to **Select**, and then click **Table**. From the **Insert** menu, point to **Picture,** and then click **Chart**.

(Project 5H–Daily Patients continues on the next page)

(Project 5H–Daily Patients continued)

3. Be sure that two toolbar rows are displayed. If only one toolbar row is displayed on your screen, at the right end of the toolbar, click the Toolbar Options button, and then click Show Buttons on Two Rows.

4. Click in the **datasheet**, and then, on the datasheet title bar, click the **Close** button. Right-click in the white area of the chart, and then, from the shortcut menu, click **Chart Options**. Click the **Titles tab**. Click in the **Chart title** box, type **Patients Treated Daily by Department** and then click **OK**. On the Standard toolbar, click the **Save** button.

5. Scroll down so that you can see the 7-inch mark on the vertical ruler. Position the pointer over the right middle sizing handle on the outside border of the chart and drag to the right to approximately **6 inches on the horizontal ruler**. Point to the bottom middle sizing handle and drag down to approximately **6.5 inches on the vertical ruler**. Refer to Figure 5.80 as a guide.

6. Right-click the **Legend**, from the shortcut menu click **Format Legend**, and then click the **Font tab**. Change the **Size** box to **10** and the **Font style** box to **Regular**. Click the **Placement tab**, and then click **Bottom**. Click **OK**.

7. Right-click the **chart title**, and then, from the shortcut menu, click **Format Chart Title**. Click the **Font tab**. Under **Font**, scroll the list and click **Times New Roman**. Change the **Font style** box to **Bold Italic**, the **Size** box to **14**, and then click **OK**.

8. Click anywhere outside the selected chart to close the Microsoft Graph program and return to the document window. Click on the chart once to select it, and then, on the Formatting toolbar, click the **Center** button to center the chart on the page. Compare your screen with Figure 5.80.

9. Scroll as necessary to view the entire table, and then click in the table. From the **Table** menu, point to **Delete**, and then click **Table**. Recall that the data is now incorporated in the underlying datasheet that is represented by the chart—the table is no longer needed.

10. From the **View** menu, display the Header and Footer toolbar, switch to the footer, and then, on the Header and Footer toolbar, click **Insert AutoText**. From the displayed list, click **Filename**. Close the Header and Footer toolbar.

11. On the Standard toolbar, click the **Save** button, and then click the **Print Preview** button to see the document as it will print. Click the **Print** button, and then close the Print Preview. Close the file, saving changes if prompted to do so.

End You have completed Project 5H

Project 5I — Specialties

Objectives: *Add Special Text Effects, Create an Outline, and Modify the Document Window.*

In the following Performance Assessment, you will format the outline for an index of specialties available at University Medical Center. You will also apply a special text effect to the title. Your completed document will look similar to the one shown in Figure 5.81. You will save your document as *5I_Specialties_Firstname_Lastname.*

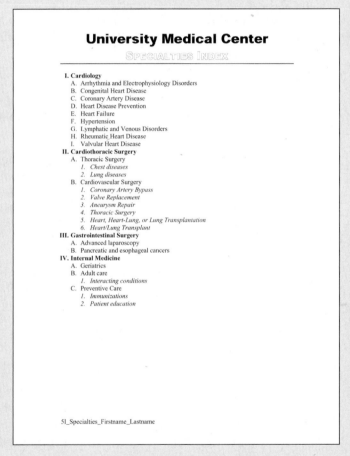

Figure 5.81

1. On the Standard toolbar, click the **Open** button. Navigate to the location where the student files for this textbook are stored. Locate and open **w05I_Specialties**. Save the file as **5I_Specialties_Firstname_Lastname**

2. Open the header. Select the line *Specialties Index.* From the **Format** menu, display the **Font** dialog box. Under **Effects**, select the **Outline** check box and the **Small caps** check box. Click the **Character Spacing tab**. Click the **Spacing By up spin arrow** to display **0.5 pt**. Click **OK**. Close the header.

(Project 5I–Specialties continues on the next page)

(Project 5I–Specialties continued)

3. If necessary, click the Print Layout button, and then change the **Zoom** setting to **Page Width**. Move the mouse pointer to the top edge of the document until you see the **Hide White Space** pointer, and then click. This will maximize your viewing area.

4. Click to position the insertion point to the left of *Cardiology*. Use the scroll bar to move to the end of the document, and, at the end of the last word, hold down Shift and click to select all but the title lines in the document.

5. From the **Format** menu, display the **Bullets and Numbering** dialog box, and then click the **Outline Numbered tab**. In the first row, click the second option. Check to see if the **Reset** button is active or grayed. If it is active, click it, and then click **Yes** to reset the selected outline format.

6. Click the **Customize** button. In the **Customize Outline Numbered List** dialog box, in the **Number style** box, display the list and click **I, II, III**. In the **Number format** box, replace the parenthesis mark with a period. Change the **Number position** box to **Right**. Under **Text position**, change the **Indent at** box to **0.3"**.

7. Under **Number format**, in the **Level** box, click **2**. In the **Number style** box, click **A, B, C** from the list. In the **Number format** box, replace the parenthesis mark with a period.

8. Under **Number format**, in the **Level** box, click **3**. In the **Number style** box, click **1, 2, 3** from the list. In the **Number format** box, replace the parenthesis mark with a period. Click **OK**.

9. Hold down Ctrl and press Home to move to the top of the document. Save your changes. Select the items labeled *II.* through *X.* and click the **Increase Indent** button. These items display as specialties under *Cardiology*.

10. Click anywhere in the line *Thoracic Surgery* and click the **Increase Indent** button. Select the next two lines—*III. Chest diseases* and *IV. Lung diseases*—which are formatted in italic. Click the **Increase Indent** button twice.

11. Continue to format the outline. Items that are not bold or italic are Level 2 items. Items formatted in italic are Level 3 items. (Hint: Use Ctrl to select multiple lines, and then apply the indent formatting.) Compare your document with Figure 5.81.

12. Display the **View** menu and click **Header and Footer**. Switch to the footer area, click the **Insert AutoText** button, and then click **Filename**. Close the Header and Footer toolbar.

(Project 5I–Specialties continues on the next page)

(Project 5I–Specialties continued)

13. Click the **Save** button, and then click the **Print Preview** button to see the document as it will print. Click the **Print** button, and then close the Print Preview. Close the file, saving changes if prompted to do so.

 End You have completed Project 5I

Project 5J — Annual Report

Objectives: *Use Existing Styles, Create and Modify New Styles, Create an Outline Using the Outline View and the Outlining Toolbar.*

In the following Performance Assessment, you will format a draft outline of the annual report for the University Medical Center Foundation by using and creating styles and creating an outline. Your completed document will look similar to the one shown in Figure 5.82. You will save your document as *5J_Annual_Report_Firstname_Lastname.*

> *ANNUAL REPORT, DRAFT OVERVIEW*
>
> ## University Medical Center Foundation
>
> **Introduction**
>
> **University Medical Center in the Community**
>
> This section will outline the programs and services UMC provides to the community. It will include a section of "quick facts" with statistics such as number of patients treated, number of procedures, etc.
>
> **How UMC Foundation Impacts the Center**
>
> This section will introduce the programs funded by the Foundation and how those programs serve the community.
>
> **Section I**
>
> **H. J. Worthington Hospice**
> - Overview of the purpose of the hospice and the care provided to terminally ill patients
> - Overview of operating expenses
> - Narrative overview
> - Pie chart showing department expenses as percentage of total
>
>   This section will include two quotes from patient family members on their experience with the hospice's programs and staff.
>
> **University Medical Center Health Careers Scholarship Fund**
> - Overview of why the scholarship was established
> - Amount of the scholarship
> - Overview of criteria for selection of recipient
> - Short description of the qualifications of past two years' recipients
> - Quotes from past two years' recipients
>
>   This section will include two quotes from recipients of University Medical Center scholarships.
>
> **University Medical Center Cancer Center Fund**
> - Overview of the Cancer Center
> - Founding date
> - Purpose
> - Overview including types of state-of-the-art treatments, number of patients treated, support programs
> - Overview operating expenses
> - Percentage of expenses funded by the Foundation
>
>   This section will include a quote from one of the Center's physicians regarding the state-of-the-art treatments available at the center.
>
> 5J_Annual_Report_Firstname_Lastname

Figure 5.82

(Project 5J–Annual Report continues on the next page)

(Project 5J–Annual Report continued)

1. On the Standard toolbar, click the **Open** button. Navigate to the location where the student files for this textbook are stored. Locate and open **w05J_Annual_Report**. Save the file as 5J_Annual_Report_Firstname_Lastname

2. To the left of the horizontal scroll bar, click the **Outline View** button. To the left of the Formatting toolbar, click the **Styles and Formatting** button. Set the Zoom to 100% if the text on the screen seems too large.

3. Display the style area on the left of the screen by displaying the **Tools** menu, and then clicking **Options**. Click the **View tab**. Under **Outline and Normal options**, click the **Style area width spin box up arrow** until the style area width is **0.5"**. At the bottom of the **Options** dialog box, click **OK**.

4. Click to position the insertion point in the second line of the document, which contains only the word *Introduction*. In the Styles and Formatting task pane, under **Pick formatting to apply**, click **Heading 1**.

5. Scroll down and click to position the insertion point in the line that contains only *Section I*. Press F4—the Repeat key. Alternatively, click the Heading 1 style in the Styles and Formatting task pane.

6. Position the insertion point in the third line of the document, which begins *How UMC Foundation*. On the Outlining toolbar, click the **Demote** button.

7. Position the insertion point in the line that begins *University Medical Center in the Community*. In the **Styles and Formatting** task pane, under **Pick formatting to apply**, click **Heading 2**.

8. Use the same procedure to apply a **Heading 2** style to the other three lines that use an italic font style. Hold down Ctrl and press Home.

9. To the left of the third line, which begins *How UMC Foundation*, click the **Expand** button.

10. On the Outlining toolbar, click the **Move Down** button twice.

11. On the Outlining toolbar, click the **Show Level button arrow**, and then click **Show Level 2**. Click anywhere to deselect the text. Only Level 1 and Level 2 headings display; the remaining text is hidden from view so that you can see only the Level 1 and 2 headings.

12. Click to position the insertion point in the line that begins *H. J. Worthington*. On the Outlining toolbar, click the **Expand** button to expand only that section of the document.

13. Near the top of the document, position the pointer over the **Expand** button to the left of the line that begins *How UMC Foundation*. Double-click the **Expand** button to expand that section. This is another way to expand the text under a single section.

(Project 5J–Annual Report continues on the next page)

(Project 5J–Annual Report continued)

14. On the Outlining toolbar, click the **Show Level button arrow**, and then click **Show All Levels**.

15. To the left of the horizontal scroll bar, click the **Print Layout View** button. To the left of the Formatting toolbar, click the **Styles and Formatting** button to close the Styles and Formatting task pane. Compare your document with Figure 5.82.

16. Display the **View** menu and click **Header and Footer**. Switch to the footer area, click the **Insert AutoText** button, and then click **Filename**. Close the Header and Footer toolbar.

17. Click the **Save** button, and then click the **Print Preview** button to see the document as it will print. Close the Print Preview. Click the **Print** button, and then close the file, saving changes if prompted to do so.

End You have completed Project 5J

Project 5K — Growth

Objectives: *Create a Chart with Microsoft Graph and Format a Chart.*

In the following Mastery Assessment, you will create a two-column chart for a University Medical Center report to show how staff levels have increased to keep up with the growing population of Orange Beach. Your completed document will look similar to the one shown in Figure 5.83. You will save your document as *5K_Growth_ Firstname_Lastname.*

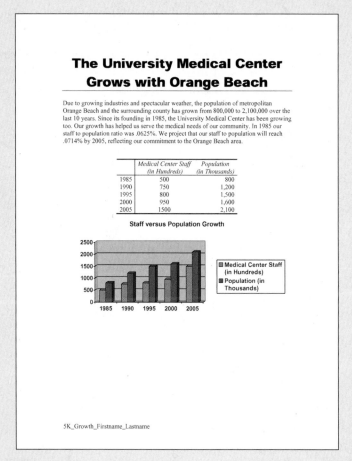

Figure 5.83

1. **Start** Word. From your student files, open **w05K_Growth**. Save the file with the name **5K_Growth_Firstname_Lastname** in the same location as your other files. In the same manner as you have done in previous documents, display the footer and insert the **AutoText** filename.

2. Select the entire table, display the **Insert** menu, point to **Picture**, and then click **Chart**. Close the datasheet. If necessary, click the Toolbar Options button, and then click Show Buttons on Two Rows to display both toolbars.

(Project 5K–Growth continues on the next page)

(Project 5K–Growth continued)

3. On the Chart toolbar, click the **By Column** button. To make a year-by-year comparison between staff and population, the data needs to be displayed by column.

4. Right-click in the white area of the chart, and then click **Chart Options**. In the **Chart title** box, type **Staff versus Population Growth** and then click **OK**.

5. Scroll so that you can view the 7-inch mark on the vertical ruler. Position the pointer over the right middle sizing handle of the chart and drag to approximately **6 inches on the horizontal ruler**. Point to the bottom middle sizing handle and drag down to approximately **7 inches on the vertical ruler**. Refer to Figure 5.83 as a guide.

6. Click in the body of the document to return to the document window. Click on the chart once to select it, and then, on the Formatting toolbar, click the **Center** button. Compare your screen with Figure 5.83.

7. Save the completed document. Preview the document, and then print it.

End **You have completed Project 5K**

Project 5L—Speakers

Objectives: *Add Special Text Effects, Modify the Document Window, Create an Outline, and Apply and Modify Styles.*

In the following Mastery Assessment, you will format a speaker directory for the University Medical Center. You will apply an outline format that uses styles, modify one of the styles, add a special text effect to the opening paragraph, and modify the document window as you work. Your completed document will look similar to the one shown in Figure 5.84. You will save your document as *5L_Speakers_Firstname_Lastname*.

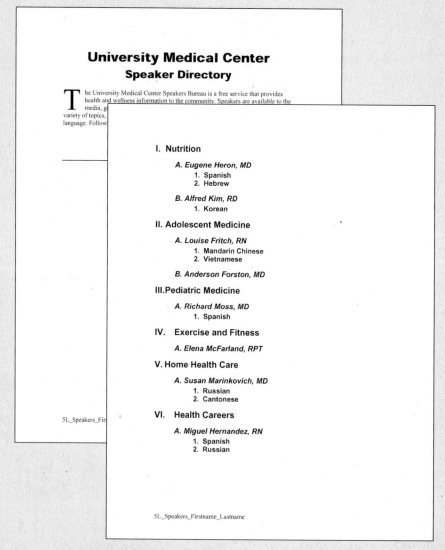

Figure 5.84

(Project 5L–Speakers continues on the next page)

(Project 5L–Speakers continued)

1. Start Word. From your student files, open **w05L_Speakers**. Save the file with the name **5L_Speakers_Firstname_Lastname** in the same location as your other files. In the same manner as you have done in previous documents, display the footer and insert the **AutoText** filename.

2. Position the insertion point in the paragraph beginning *The University Medical Center*. From the **Format** menu, open the **Drop Cap** dialog box, and then, under **Position**, click **Dropped**. Under **Options**, click the **Distance from text spin box up arrow** to add **0.1"** extra spacing between the drop cap and the text to its right. Click **OK**.

3. If necessary, change the Zoom setting to Page Width. Move the mouse pointer to the top edge of the document until you see the **Hide White Space** pointer, and then click.

4. Select the two paragraphs beginning *Ricardo*, which will include the phone number under his name. From the Formatting toolbar, change the selected lines to **14 pt.**, **Bold**, and **Italic**, and then **Center** the text.

5. Starting with *Nutrition*, select all of the remaining text through the end of the document. From the **Format** menu, display the **Bullets and Numbering** dialog box, and then click the **Outline Numbered tab**. In the second row, click the third option. Check to see if the **Reset** button is active or grayed. If active, click it to restore the original settings to this outline choice. This outline uses the I. A. 1. format you have practiced and combines it with the Heading 1, 2, 3, styles. Click **OK**.

6. Scroll up to view the result. A new page was created starting with *Nutrition*. Click in the paragraph that begins *II. Eugene Heron, MD* and click the **Increase Indent** button once. In this manner, the speakers need to be indented to Level 2. Listed under Dr. Heron are two languages—*II. Spanish* and *III. Hebrew*. Select these paragraphs and click the **Increase Indent** button twice. In this manner, the languages for each speaker need to be indented to Level 3. Continue down the page and indent the speaker names to Level 2 and the languages to Level 3. Compare your screen with Figure 5.84 to verify the outline levels.

7. On the Formatting toolbar, click the **Styles and Formatting** button. In the **Styles and Formatting** task pane, under **Pick formatting to apply**, scroll down the list, point to and then click the arrow to the right of **Heading 3**, and then click **Select All 10 Instance(s)**. Click the arrow again and click **Modify**. In the **Modify Style** dialog box, under **Formatting**, locate the second row of buttons. Point to the third button from the right to display the ScreenTip **Decrease Paragraph Spacing**. Click this button twice. Watch the preview window to see how the space before and after the example is decreased. Select the **Automatically Update** check box, and then click **OK**.

(Project 5L–Speakers continues on the next page)

(Project 5L–Speakers continued)

8. Scroll the page to see the results. Close the **Styles and Formatting** task pane. Position the pointer at the top edge of the document and click the **Show White Space** pointer. Compare your screen with Figure 5.84.

9. Save the completed document. Preview the document, and then print it.

 End You have completed Project 5L ——————————————

Project 5M — Outline

Objectives: *Add Special Text Effects, Use Existing Styles, and Create an Outline.*

Outlines can help you organize information when you are writing research papers for your classes. In this Problem Solving exercise, you will create your own outline for a research paper on a topic of your choice. You will also use some of the styles you have practiced and apply some special text effects. You will save your outline as *5M_Outline_Firstname_Lastname*.

1. Select a topic for your paper. It can be a paper for another class, something you are interested in researching, or a topic related to the use of computers.

2. Enter the title of your research paper and apply the **Heading 1** style. **Center** the heading.

3. Under the title, type **Outline** Apply the **Heading 2** style and **center** this subheading. Select the *Outline* subheading and, from the **Font** dialog box, apply the **Outline** effect. Click the **Character Spacing tab** and expand the spacing to **1.0"**. Press Enter to move to any empty line.

4. Open the **Bullets and Numbering** dialog box. Click the **Outline Numbered tab** and, as practiced in the chapter, set the outline Level 1 format to I. II. III., set the Level 2 format to A. B. C., and set the Level 3 format to 1. 2. 3. Click **OK**.

5. Write your outline, using the **Increase Indent** button to position topics at the second or third level of the outline as appropriate. Include at least four Level 1 headings, at least two Level 2 headings under each major topic, and two instances of Level 3 headings somewhere in the outline.

6. Proofread your outline and remove any spelling, grammar, or typographical errors. In the footer area and using the **AutoText** button, insert the **Filename**. Save the document.

7. Print the document, and then close the file, saving changes if prompted to do so.

End **You have completed Project 5M** ——————————————————————

Project 5N—Personal Styles

Objective: *Create and Modify New Styles.*

The University Medical Center is issuing a press release about an upcoming health information series. In this Problem Solving exercise you will create new styles and apply them to the press release that has been written announcing this program. You will save the article as *5N_Press Release.*

1. Locate and open **w05N_Press Release**. Save it as **5N_Press_Release_Firstname_Lastname** with your other files. As you have with previous files, display the footer area and insert the **AutoText** filename.

2. Display the **Styles and Formatting** task pane. If necessary, change the view to **Normal**. Use the **Options** dialog box to display the **Styles area** on the left side of the window.

3. Using the skills you have practiced in this chapter, create a paragraph style named **PR** that is all **caps**, **Arial Black**, **18 pt.** and apply it to *Press Release.*

4. Create another paragraph style using font and paragraph styles of your own choice and apply it to the article headline that begins *The New Health.* Name the style **News Headline**.

5. Create a character style that is **Bold**, **Italic**, and **Red** and name it **UMC** Apply the **UMC** character style to all occurrences of *University Medical Center* in the body of the document—but not in the article headline.

6. Save the document, print it, and then close the file.

End You have completed Project 5N ————————————

On the Internet

Downloading More Charting Tools

In this chapter you practiced using the Microsoft Graph program to create column charts, pie charts, and a line chart. There are other charting
tools available as downloads from the Microsoft online support site.

1. Be sure that you are connected to the Internet. Open Word and, in
   the **Type a question for help** box, type **chart types** and press Enter.

2. In the Search Results task pane, click **Timeline**. A Template window
   opens on your screen with a Timeline chart displayed. Click the **Next
   arrow** at the bottom of the window to browse through the 10 templates that are available.

3. Click the **Previous** button until the screen returns to the Timeline
   template.

4. If you are working in a lab, check to be sure you can download files.
   If it is permitted, click the **Download** button. The template displays
   with instructions telling you how to use the template.

5. Follow the instructions and practice using the Timeline chart template
   you downloaded. Fill in the timeline with significant events in your life
   over the course of the time displayed. Follow the instructions to
   replace dates on the timeline as needed.

6. When you are done, close the file without saving changes, and then
   close Word.

Styles in Word 2003 Help

Using styles can be very helpful if you need to format a large document. In this chapter you were introduced to the basics of how to create and apply styles. You can learn more about styles by reviewing some of the Word Help topics on the subject. One helpful technique when you are formatting a large document is to specify that one paragraph style follow another. For example, you may want a body text style to always follow a Heading 3 style.

1. Start Word. In the **Type a question for help** box, type **Styles**. Scroll through the list of topics that displays in the Search Results task pane.

2. From this list of help topics, click *Specify that one paragraph style follow another* and read the results. Print these instructions if you want.

3. In a blank document write two brief paragraphs. Format the first paragraph with a style of your choosing. Modify the style so it is followed by another specific paragraph style—not the Normal style. Using the Help instructions, update the style applied to the first paragraph to test the change. The style of the second paragraph should change if it was done correctly.

4. Review some of the other Help topics related to styles, printing any that interest you. Test some of the other instructions to learn more about applying styles.

5. Close the Help task pane, close your document without saving the changes, and then exit Word.

chaptersix

Working on a Group Project

In this chapter, you will: complete these projects **and** practice these skills.

Project 6A **Creating a Document from a Template**	**Objective** • Create a Document Using a Template
Project 6B **Preparing a Document for Distribution to Others**	**Objectives** • Review and Modify Document Properties • Use Comments in a Document • Track Changes in a Document
Project 6C **Comparing Different Versions of a Document**	**Objectives** • Circulate Documents for Review • Compare and Merge Documents

The Management Association of Pine Valley

The Management Association of Pine Valley is an employers' group providing legal services, training, human resources consulting, and organizational development to member companies. Members are small and mid-size companies with 1 to 1,000 employees. Although most services come from the association's staff of experts, some services are outsourced. The association will also assist its members in procuring needed services from other organizations.

Working on a Group Project

The process of creating documents is often a team effort. The people who need to review a document may be in the same office, in different cities, or even in different countries. After a document has been created, it is often necessary for several people to review it. Word includes several features that enable you to keep track of changes made to the original document and to add comments to the text. Changes made by others can be accepted or rejected by the document's author.

When no central network is available, documents can be distributed as attachments to email messages. If time is short and people are working on different copies of the same document, you can compare and merge them, using the Track Changes feature to accept or reject changes.

Project 6A Memo

Templates contain predefined document formats that can be used to save time and to create a consistent look for similar documents. Templates exist for resumes, memos, letters, reports, brochures, faxes, and several other document types.

In Activities 6.1 through 6.2, you will use a template to create a memo for a team working on an upcoming conference for The Management Association of Pine Valley. You will replace existing text and replace placeholder text used to reserve areas of the document for specific kinds of information. Your completed document will look similar to Figure 6.1. You will save your document as *6A_Memo_Firstname_Lastname*.

**The Management
Association of
Pine Valley**

Memo

To: David Rosenberg, Siena Madison

From: Deepa Patel, Director of Human Resource Counseling

CC: Satarkta Kalam, Director of Labor Relations Services

Date: August 19

Re: Document Reviews

We will be working on two documents this week to present as part of a package to our members at next month's Human Resources Conference. Bill Newson finished the first drafts before he left on vacation. I would like you to read them carefully and give me your opinions. You can edit the documents I send you, but be sure you turn on the Track Changes feature in Word. I will need your edits by Friday.

6A_Memo_Firstname_Lastname

Figure 6.1
Project 6A—Memo

Objective 1
Create a Document Using a Template

A **template** is a model for documents of the same type; it is a predefined structure that contains the basic document settings, such as fonts, margins, and available styles. Unless otherwise specified, every Word document is based on the default Normal template. A document template can also store document elements such as headers, greetings, text blocks, and company logos. Word provides document templates for memos, resumes, and other common business documents. Other templates can be built using **wizards**, which ask you for information about the type of document you want to create. Document templates use a .dot file extension.

Activity 6.1 Creating a Memo Using a Template

1 Start Microsoft Word. From the **File** menu, click **New**.

The New Document task pane opens, as shown in Figure 6.2. If another Word document is open, it still displays in the document window.

On my computer option —————————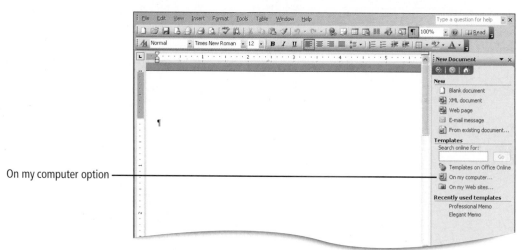

Figure 6.2

2 In the **New Document** task pane, under **Templates**, click **On my computer**.

The Templates dialog box displays. Notice the template categories displayed in the tabs at the top of the dialog box.

3 In the **Templates** dialog box, click the **Memos tab**, and then click the **Professional Memo** icon.

A preview of the memo displays in the Preview area. Under Create New, you have the option of creating a new document based on the Professional Memo template or of creating a new, customized template (document model) by modifying the existing template. See Figure 6.3.

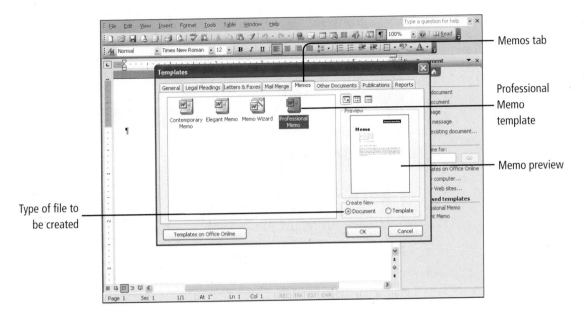

Type of file to be created

Memos tab

Professional Memo template

Memo preview

Figure 6.3

More Knowledge — Templates on the Web

If you are connected to the Internet, you can click the *Templates on Office Online* button at the bottom of the Templates dialog box. This will give you access to hundreds of available templates for Word, Excel, Access, and PowerPoint. The Word templates will display the Word icon that appears on the left side of the Word title bar. Available Word templates on the Web include a performance review, a net worth calculator, many styles of calendars, and even a timeline diagram.

4 At the bottom of the **Templates** dialog box, click **OK**. On the Standard toolbar, click the **Zoom button arrow** 100% ⋅, and then click **Page Width**.

The Professional Memo template displays, and the new document is unnamed. See Figure 6.4. The small black squares in the left margin are part of the template and display when paragraphs are formatted with a style that keeps paragraphs together rather than splitting them across pages. You need not be concerned with styles in this project.

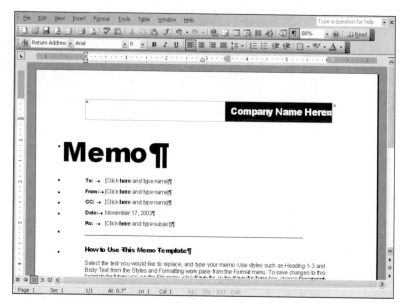

Figure 6.4

■5■ Be sure that you can see the nonprinting characters displayed on your screen. If necessary, on the Standard toolbar, click the Show/Hide ¶ button to display the formatting characters.

■6■ On the Standard toolbar, click the **Save** button . In the **Save As** dialog box, navigate to the location where you are storing your projects for this chapter, creating a new folder for Chapter 6 if you want to do so. In the **File name** box, type **6A_Memo_Firstname_Lastname** and then click **Save**.

Word saves the file as a document with a .doc extension, and the formatting is based on the template.

Activity 6.2 Replacing Placeholder Text and Customizing the Memo

Sample text and **_placeholder text_** display in a document created from a template. Placeholder text reserves space for the text you will insert; it looks like text, but cannot be edited—it can only be replaced. You will edit all or some of this text and replace it with your personalized content.

■1■ At the top of the document, select the title **Company Name Here**. Type **The Management Association of** and then press Shift + Enter. Type **Pine Valley** to complete the company name. On the Formatting toolbar, click the **Center** button .

Because this placeholder title is formatted as a one-row table with two cells, the title is centered in the table's cell. Recall that pressing Enter while holding down Shift creates a manual line break, but keeps all of the text in the same paragraph with the same paragraph formatting. See Figure 6.5.

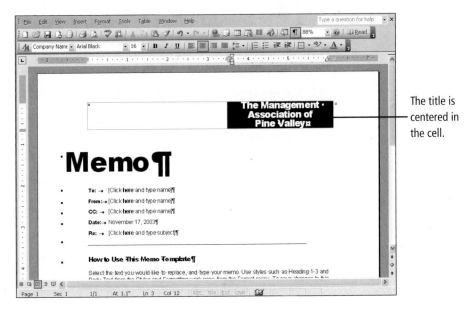

The title is centered in the cell.

Figure 6.5

2 In the **To** line, click **[Click here and type name]**.

Notice that a single click selects the entire placeholder text. Placeholder text cannot be edited and behaves more like a graphic than text. See Figure 6.6.

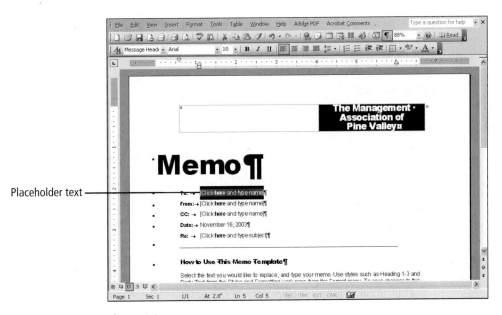

Placeholder text

Figure 6.6

3 Type **David Rosenberg, Siena Madison**

The text you typed replaces the placeholder text.

4 In the **From** line, click **[Click here and type name]**. Type **Deepa Patel, Director of Human Resource Consulting**

5 In the **CC** line, click **[Click here and type name]**. Type **Satarkta Kalam, Director of Labor Relations Services**

6 In the **Date** line, select the existing date and type **August 19**

This replaces the default date, which is the current date.

7 In the **Re** line, click **[Click here and type subject]**. Type **Document Reviews**

Compare your document with Figure 6.7. You can see that using a predefined memo template saves you time in creating the basic parts of a memo.

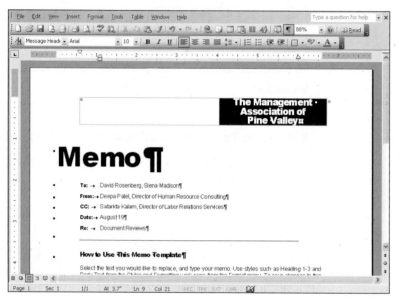

Figure 6.7

8 If necessary, scroll down to view the middle portion of the document. Select the line **How to Use This Memo Template** and press Delete.

9 Select the paragraph that begins *Select the text you would like*. Type

We will be working on two documents this week to present as part of a package to our members at next month's Human Resources Conference. Bill Newson finished the first drafts before he left on vacation. I would like you to read them carefully and give me your opinions. You can edit the documents I send you, but be sure you turn on the Track Changes feature in Word. I will need your edits by Friday.

Compare your memo with Figure 6.8.

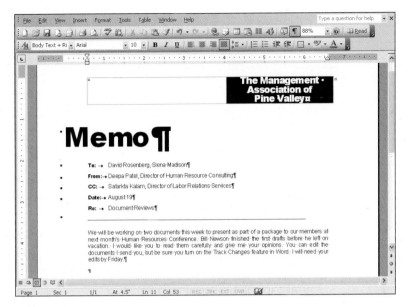

Figure 6.8

10 From the **View** menu, click **Header and Footer**. On the Header and Footer toolbar, click the **Switch Between Header and Footer** button 🔳.

11 Press ⌨Delete⌨ twice to remove the page number that was included as part of the template. On the **Header and Footer** toolbar, click the **Insert AutoText** button ⎹ Insert AutoText ▾⎸. Point to **Header/Footer** and click **Filename**.

The file name is inserted in the footer.

12 On the Header and Footer toolbar, click the **Close** button ⎹Close⎸.

13 On the Standard toolbar, click the **Save** button 💾.

14 On the Standard toolbar, click the **Print Preview** button 🔍. Take a moment to check your work. On the Print Preview toolbar, click the **Close Preview** button ⎹Close⎸.

15 Make any necessary changes to your document. When you are satisfied, on the Standard toolbar, click the **Print** button 🖨. Close the document, saving changes if you are prompted to do so.

End You have completed Project 6A ——————————————————

Project 6B Exit Interview

Microsoft Word records information about every document, such as document size, word count, date and time last edited, and author. This information is available to you from the Properties dialog box. When a document is edited by several people, changes and comments, along with the name of the person making each change or comment, can be displayed using the Track Changes feature.

In Activities 6.3 through 6.11, you will edit a draft document to be distributed to member businesses of The Management Association of Pine Valley, and you will look at the document summary. The draft document has been completed by one person; edits and comments have been added by another. You will make changes to the document and add more comments, and then you will accept or reject each of the changes. Your completed document will look similar to Figure 6.9. You will save your document as 6B_Exit_Interview_ Firstname_Lastname.

DRAFT: Exit Interviews – Voluntary Separation

Exit interviews with employees who are voluntarily leaving the organization are useful to determine why an employee has decided to leave and to find opportunities for improving the organization's overall employee relations.

When conducting an exit interview, the interviewer should be relaxed and open to encourage honest feedback. The employee should be treated with respect and given time to discuss concerns and ask questions.

Sample questions for an exit interview include:

- What did you like most about your job?
- What did you like least about your job?
- What made you decide to leave this job?
- Do you feel adequate training was provided for you to do your job?
- Do you think your supervisor treated you and others fairly and reasonably? explain.
- Were you given access to information for promotional opportunities within organization?
- Do you believe you were given honest consideration for promotion?
- Do you feel your contributions were appreciated by your supervisor, co-w organization?
- Did you have the appropriate tools (equipment and resources) to do your j
- Do you believe your salary matched the job you were doing?
- Were you satisfied with the employee benefits? (Ask for details if necessa
- Was the physical environment comfortable and did it allow for productivit
- Was the job presented to you realistically at the time you were hired?

The organization should have strict confidentiality rules in place. These processes explained to the employee so they feel comfortable speaking freely, especially reg negative feedback.

For the exit interview information to be useful to the organization, the information interviews should be analyzed and summarized at least annually. Compare the inf turnover statistics for a period of time to identify trends. Appropriate feedback sho supervisors and managers while protecting the identity of employees who gave th

6B_Exit_Interview_Firstname_Lastname

Filename:	6B_Exit_Interview_Firstname_Lastname.doc
Directory:	C:\Student
Template:	C:\Documents and Settings\Bob\Application Data\Microsoft\Templates\Normal.dot
Title:	DRAFT: Exit Interviews
Subject:	Student Name
Author:	Bill Newsom
Keywords:	Exit Interviews, Fall Conference
Comments:	Draft copy of the Exit Interviews handout for the Fall conference.
Creation Date:	9/5/2003 9:02:00 PM
Change Number:	10
Last Saved On:	9/5/2003 11:40:00 PM
Last Saved By:	Siena Madison
Total Editing Time:	133 Minutes
Last Printed On:	9/6/2003 2:38:00 AM

As of Last Complete Printing
    Number of Pages: 1 (approx.)
    Number of Words: 300 (approx.)
    Number of Characters: 1,713 (approx.)

Figure 6.9
Project 6B—Exit Interview

Objective 2
Review and Modify Document Properties

Document properties—recorded statistics and other related information, such as the date the document was created, the date it was last modified, where the file is stored, and the author's name—are updated each time the document is modified.

Additionally, you can add document summary information to the properties area. You can give the document a title or a subject, and you can add the name of the company for which the document was created. Keywords can be added, which can help when searching for a document in Windows. The document properties also can be printed.

Activity 6.3 Viewing the Summary

1 On the Standard toolbar, click the **Open** button . Navigate to the location where the student files for this textbook are stored. Locate and open **w06B_Exit_Interview**. Save the file as **6B_Exit_Interview_Firstname_Lastname**

2 On the Standard toolbar, click the **Zoom button arrow** 100%, and then click **Page Width**. If necessary, on the Standard toolbar, click the Show/Hide ¶ button ¶ to display formatting marks.

Alert!

Check Your Screen

Changes were made to this document and comments have been added. Your screen may display the changes, or they may be hidden. The Reviewing toolbar may or may not be displayed. If the changes are displayed, they may be shown as multicolored text and balloons in the right margin of the document or just multicolored text in the document. Do not be concerned about the arrangement of your screen or the toolbar configuration at this point.

3 From the **File** menu, click **Properties**. If necessary, click the General tab.

The document's Properties box displays, with the document name in the title bar. The General tab displays the type of document, file location, and file size. The creation date and date last modified also are displayed, as shown in Figure 6.10.

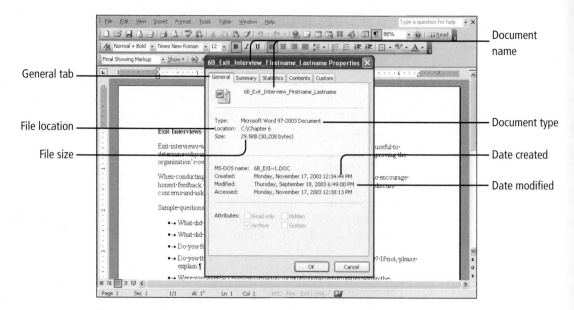

Document name

General tab

File location

File size

Document type

Date created

Date modified

Figure 6.10

4 In the **Properties** box, click the **Summary tab**.

The name in the Author box is the name of the person who originally registered the Office software, although the name can be changed at any time. The name in the Company box is the name of the last entry in that box; it will stay that way for each new document until it is modified. These two boxes are the only ones that are filled in automatically. See Figure 6.11.

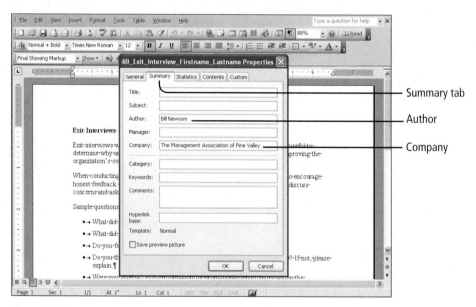

Summary tab

Author

Company

Figure 6.11

5 In the **Properties** box, click the **Statistics tab**.

The Statistics tab expands on the information in the General tab, displaying the last time the document was printed, how many revisions have been made to the document, and how many minutes the document has been open—referred to as *editing time*. Editing time is not an exact measurement of actual time on task, because the document may have been left open overnight with no editing, and the time would still be added to the total. Document statistics are also displayed. See Figure 6.12.

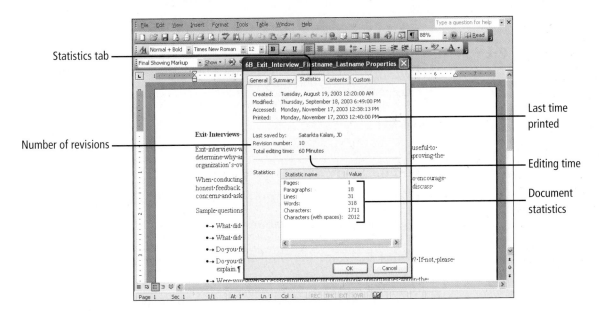

Statistics tab

Number of revisions

Last time printed

Editing time

Document statistics

Figure 6.12

Activity 6.4 Editing the Summary and Printing the Document Properties

Editing summary information and adding more information can make the document easier to find using the Windows search feature. It also enables you to make notes about the document for future reference.

1 In the **Properties** box, click the **Summary tab**.

2 On the **Summary** sheet, in the **Title** box, delete the existing text, and then type **DRAFT: Exit Interviews**

3 In the **Keywords** box, type **Exit Interviews, Fall Conference**

4 In the **Comments** box, type **Draft copy of the Exit Interviews handout for the Fall conference.**

Compare your screen with Figure 6.13.

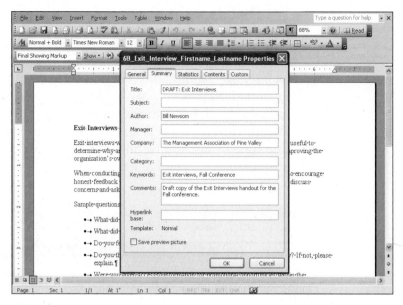

Figure 6.13

5 In the **Subject** box, type your name.

6 At the bottom of the **Properties** box, click **OK**.

7 On the Standard toolbar, click the **Save** button 📄.

Activity 6.5 Checking Word and Paragraph Counts

Some documents written for magazines or newsletters have word count or line count limits. Word enables you to open a toolbar that keeps track of the number of words, lines, and even characters in a document.

1 From the **Tools** menu, click **Word Count**.

The Word Count dialog box displays, as shown in Figure 6.14. These are the same statistics that were displayed in the Statistics sheet of the document's Properties box.

Show Toolbar button —————

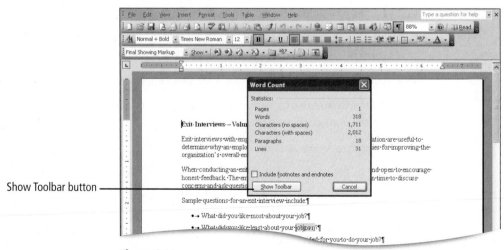

Figure 6.14

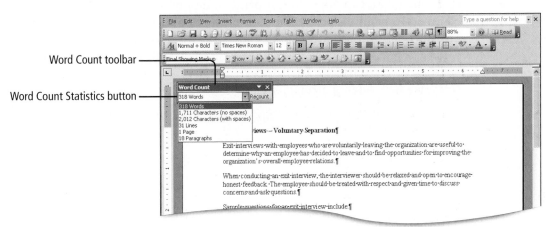

2 At the bottom of the **Word Count** dialog box, click **Show Toolbar**.

The Word Count toolbar displays.

3 At the bottom of the **Word Count** dialog box, click **Cancel**.

4 In the Word Count toolbar, click the **Word Count Statistics** button `<Click Recount to view>`.

The list of statistics displays, as shown in Figure 6.15. Notice the number of words in the document.

Word Count toolbar

Word Count Statistics button

Figure 6.15

5 Click to position the insertion point to the left of the first line of the document, beginning *Exit Interviews*, closing the displayed list. Type **DRAFT:** and then press Space.

Notice that the Word Count Statistics box displays *<Click Recount to view>*.

6 In the Word Count toolbar, click the **Recount** button `Recount`.

The Word Count Statistics box displays the new number of words—319—in the document.

7 Leave the Word Count toolbar open for the following activities. On the Standard toolbar, click the **Save** button.

Objective 3
Use Comments in a Document

A *comment* is a note that an author or reviewer adds to a document. Word displays the comment in either a balloon-type graphic in the margin of the document or in a reviewing pane at the bottom of the document. Comments are a good way to communicate when more than one person is involved in the editing process.

Comments are like sticky notes attached to the document—they can be seen and read, but they do not print. When more than one person adds comments, each person's comments are displayed in a different color. The author's initials are also displayed in the comment box. Comments can be edited, and more than one author can edit the same comment.

Activity 6.6 Adding a Comment

Comments can be added at a specific location in a document or to a selection of text.

1 From the **Tools** menu, click **Options**, and then click the **Track Changes tab**.

The Options dialog box displays. See Figure 6.16.

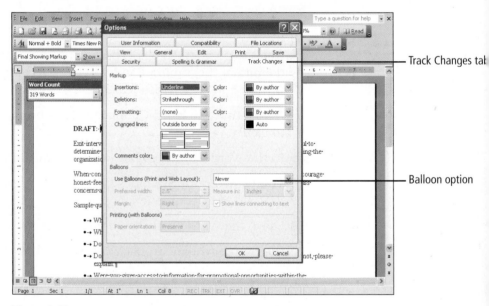

Figure 6.16

2 Under **Balloons**, click the **Use Balloons (Print and Web Layout) arrow**, and then click **Always**.

When the Track Changes feature is active, this action will cause Word to always display comments and deletions in the right margin in a balloon when the document is displayed in Print Layout or Web Layout views.

More Knowledge

In the Track Changes tab of the Options dialog box, you can change the width of the balloons. You can also set the balloons to display in the left margin.

3 In the **Options** dialog box, click the **User Information tab**.

4 Under **User information**, write down the current name and initials so that you can restore them when this project is completed. In the **Name** box type **Siena Madison** and in the **Initials** box type **SFM**

The name and initials will be used when comments are added and changes are made to the document. Compare your dialog box with Figure 6.17.

User Information tab

Name

Initials

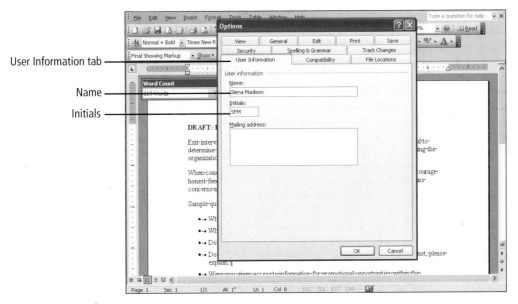

Figure 6.17

Note — Restoring Word Settings

When you are using a computer that is used by more than one person, and you make a change to Word settings, it is always good practice and common courtesy to restore the setting when you are finished.

5 Click **OK** to close the **Options** dialog box. From the **View** menu, point to **Toolbars**. Examine the list to see if the **Reviewing** toolbar is displayed (checked). If it is not checked, click it; if it is checked, click outside the menu to close it.

The Reviewing toolbar displays.

6 On the Standard toolbar, click the **Zoom button arrow** 100% ▾, and then click **Page Width**. Be sure that you are in **Print Layout** view, and if necessary, from the View menu, click Print Layout.

The window adjusts to make more space for the balloons. On small screens, such as those on laptop computers, the text may be almost too small to read.

7 Select the paragraph near the top of the document that begins *Sample questions*. If necessary, drag the Word Count toolbar away from the Reviewing toolbar. From the Reviewing toolbar, click the

Insert Comment button 🖼. Type **I think this list covers the necessary topics very well!**

The new comment displays in the right margin. The initials *SFM* appear at the beginning of the comment, followed by the number *1*, which means that this is the first comment in the document. See Figure 6.18.

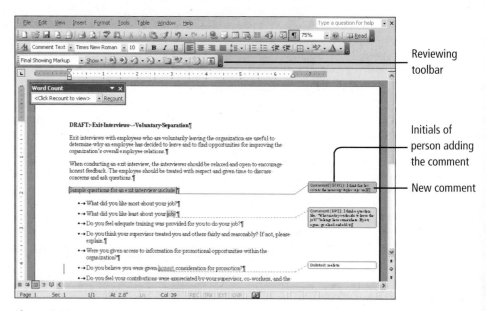

Figure 6.18

8 Click to position the insertion point at the end of the first (title) line of the document that begins *Draft Exit Interviews*. From the Reviewing toolbar, click the **Insert Comment** button. Type **Should there be a separate form for salaried vs. hourly employees?**

The last word of the line is highlighted, and the comment displays in the right margin. This comment is now *SFM1*, and the other comment you added changes to *SFM2*, as shown in Figure 6.19.

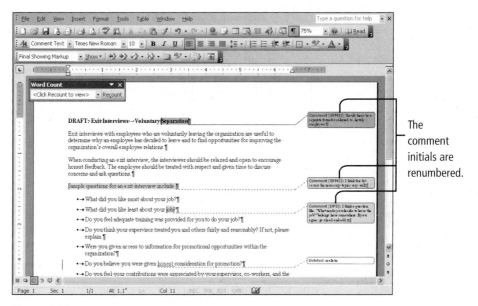

The comment initials are renumbered.

Figure 6.19

9 On the Standard toolbar, click the **Save** button.

Activity 6.7 Reading Comments Using the Reviewing Pane

You can view comments in a reviewing pane at the bottom of the screen as well as in balloons in the margin. The advantage to using the reviewing pane is that you can jump from comment to comment and read text that is sometimes too small to read in the margin.

1 On the Word Count toolbar, click the **Recount** button Recount.

Notice that the document word count has not changed. Comments do not affect document statistics.

2 On the Reviewing toolbar, click the **Reviewing Pane** button.

The reviewing pane displays at the bottom of the screen. The comment closest to the insertion point displays in the pane. The reviewing pane also includes the full name of the person who added the comment and the date and time of the comment, as shown in Figure 6.20.

Comments do not
affect word count.

Full name of the person
who added the comment

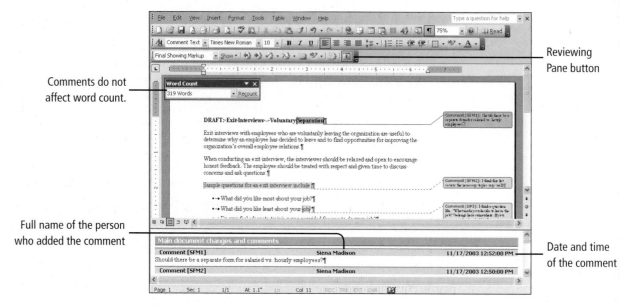

Reviewing
Pane button

Date and time
of the comment

Figure 6.20

3 In the upper window of your screen, use the vertical scroll bar to scroll down to the bottom of the document. Click to place the insertion point anywhere in the last paragraph, which has a comment attached.

The comment associated with this paragraph displays in the reviewing pane.

4 In the reviewing pane, use the small vertical scroll bar to scroll up. Click the comment labeled *SFM2*.

The upper window moves to display the selected comment so that the screen and reviewing pane comments match, as shown in Figure 6.21.

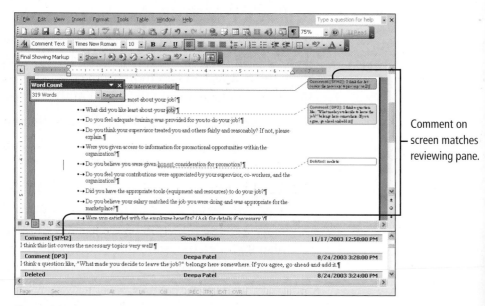

Comment on
screen matches
reviewing pane.

Figure 6.21

5 From the **View** menu, point to **Toolbars**, and then click **Word Count** to close the Word Count toolbar.

6 On the Standard toolbar, click the **Save** button 🖫.

Activity 6.8 Editing a Comment

Comments can be edited in the balloons or in the reviewing pane. You can also add a response to someone else's comment.

1 In the reviewing pane, in comment *DP3*, select the words *a question like*, press Delete, and then type **the following question:**

Be sure you remove the comma from the original text and add the colon to the end of the new text. Notice that the text is also changed in the balloon. Your reviewing pane should look like Figure 6.22.

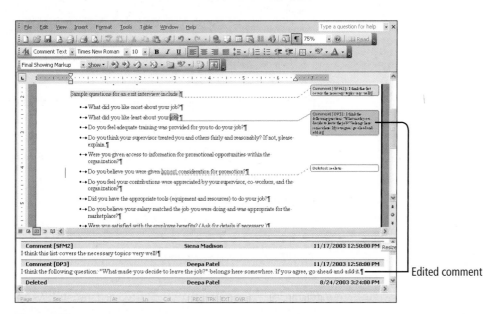

Figure 6.22

2 In the reviewing pane, in comment *DP3*, place the insertion point at the end of the comment and press Enter.

A second line is added to the comment made by another person.

3 In the reviewing pane, in the new line for comment *DP3*, type **I agree. Let's add this question. Siena**

Because the comment is being edited by someone other than the comment author, signing your name lets everyone know who responded to comment. See Figure 6.23.

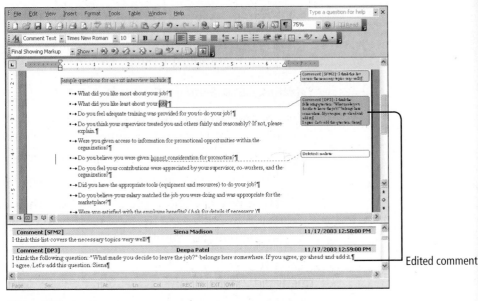

Edited comment

Figure 6.23

4 On the Reviewing toolbar, click the **Reviewing Pane** button.

The reviewing pane closes.

5 On the Standard toolbar, click the **Save** button.

Objective 4
Track Changes in a Document

The **Track Changes** feature in Word provides a visual indication of deletions, insertions, and formatting changes in a document. If the document is edited by more than one person, the changes are in different colors for each new reviewer. After the document has been reviewed by the appropriate individuals, the author can locate the changes and accept or reject the edits.

Activity 6.9 Turning on Track Changes

While viewing a document with the Track Changes feature active, the document can be displayed in final form, showing what the document would look like if all suggested changes were accepted. Comments are also hidden.

1 Hold down Ctrl and press Home.

The insertion point moves to the beginning of the document.

2 On the Reviewing toolbar, click the **Display for Review button arrow** Final Showing Markup and click **Final**.

All comments and marked changes are hidden, and the document displays as it will print if all of the changes are accepted. See Figure 6.24.

Display for Review button ——

Track Changes button

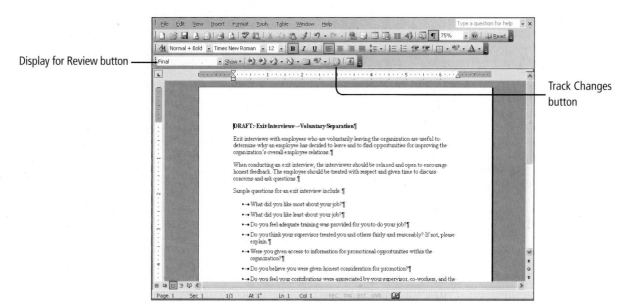

Figure 6.24

3 On the Reviewing toolbar, click the **Display for Review button arrow** `Final Showing Markup`, and then click **Final Showing Markup**.

All changes to the document, such as deletions, insertions, and formatting modifications are displayed. Comments also are displayed.

4 From the Reviewing toolbar, click the **Track Changes** button.

Track Changes is turned on, and any changes you make to the document will be visually indicated in the right margin and in the text. Notice that *TRK* is dark on the status bar.

5 Position the insertion point at the end of the second bullet point, beginning *What did you like least.* Press Enter.

A bullet point is added to the list, and a line displays to the left of the new line, indicating that a change has been made to the document at this location.

6 Type **What made you decide to leave this job?**

Notice that the inserted text is displayed with a different color and is underlined. The short vertical black line positioned in the left margin indicates the point at which a change has been made, but not what type of change. The type of change—formatting as a bullet point—is indicated in a balloon in the right margin.

7 Point to the new bullet point.

A ScreenTip displays, showing who made the change and when. See Figure 6.25.

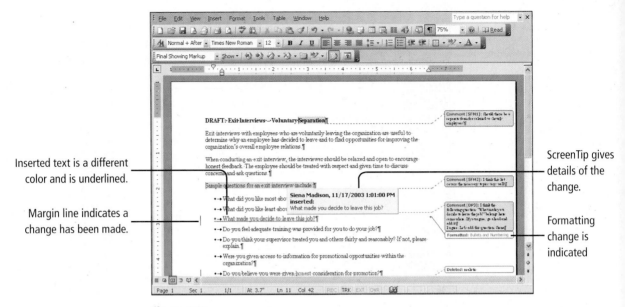

Inserted text is a different color and is underlined.

Margin line indicates a change has been made.

ScreenTip gives details of the change.

Formatting change is indicated

Figure 6.25

8 Scroll down and locate the bullet point beginning *Do you believe your salary.* Select *and was appropriate for the marketplace.* Do not select the question mark. Press Delete.

The selected text is deleted, and the deleted text is displayed in a balloon to the right of the line. A dotted line points to the location of the deleted text, as shown in Figure 6.26.

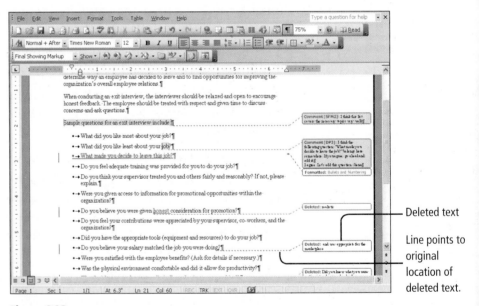

Deleted text

Line points to original location of deleted text.

Figure 6.26

9 On the Standard toolbar, click the **Save** button.

Activity 6.10 Locating Changes in a Document

You can locate changes and comments in the order they appear in the document, or you can display only comments and changes by selected reviewers.

1 Hold down [Ctrl] and press [Home] to move to the top of the document. On the Reviewing toolbar, click the **Next** button ⟶.

The insertion point moves to the first change or comment in the document. See Figure 6.27.

Next button ⟶

Comment is selected. ⟶

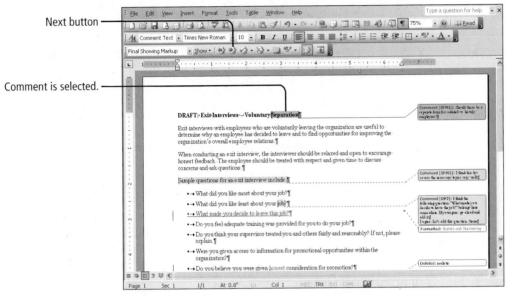

Figure 6.27

2 On the Reviewing toolbar, point to the **Next** button ⟶, and then watch your screen as you click the button five times.

The comments and changes are highlighted in the order they display in the document. The deletion of the word *realistic* is selected.

3 On the Reviewing toolbar, click the **Next** button ⟶ again.

The next comment or change is selected, in this case the insertion of the word *honest*. When the change was made, the word *realistic* was selected, and *honest* was typed to replace it. Deleting text and then inserting new text are treated as two separate changes to the document.

4 On the Reviewing toolbar, click the **Show button arrow** ⟶. Take a moment to study the available options.

You can display only comments, insertions and deletions, or formatting changes, or a combination of those changes. You can also display only the changes or comments by a specific reviewer.

5 In the **Show** menu, point to **Reviewers**.

A list of all of the reviewers who have made changes to the document displays, as shown in Figure 6.28.

Show button ———————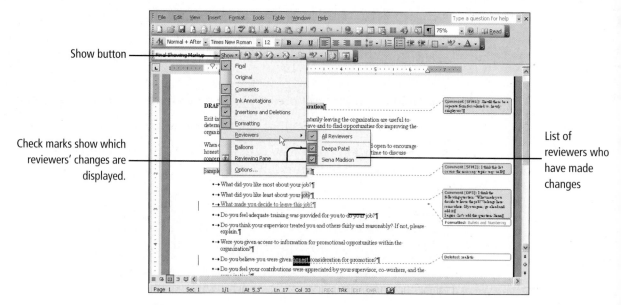

Check marks show which
reviewers' changes are
displayed.

List of
reviewers who
have made
changes

Figure 6.28

6 From the **Reviewers** list, click **Deepa Patel**.

This action hides Deepa Patel's comments. Because only two reviewers made changes to the document, only those of Siena Madison are now displayed in the document.

7 Click the **Show button arrow** again, and then point to **Reviewers**.

Notice that the check box for Deepa Patel is cleared, as shown in Figure 6.29.

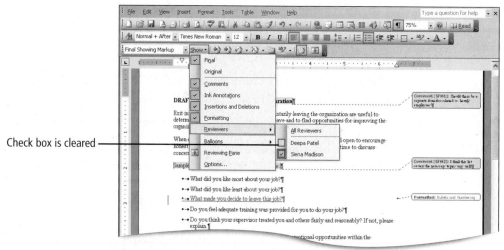

Check box is cleared ———————

Figure 6.29

8 From the **Reviewers** list, click **All Reviewers**.

All of the comments and changes are once again displayed.

9 On the **Reviewing** toolbar, click the **Track Changes** button.

The Track Changes feature is turned off. Notice that *TRK* is gray on the status bar. Changes made from this point on will not be marked, but existing changes and comments still display in the document.

10 On the Standard toolbar, click the **Save** button [icon].

Activity 6.11 Accepting or Rejecting Changes in a Document

When all of the reviewers have made their suggestions and added their comments, the author must decide which changes to accept and which to reject, and which comments to act on. Unlike changes, comments are not accepted or rejected. The author reads the comments, decides whether any action is necessary, and then removes them.

1 Hold down Ctrl and press Home to move to the top of the document. On the Reviewing toolbar, click the **Next** button [icon].

The insertion point moves to the first comment in the document, which is a comment that will not be acted on.

2 On the Reviewing toolbar, click the **Reject Change/Delete Comment** button [icon].

The comment is deleted, and the insertion point remains at the comment location, as shown in Figure 6.30.

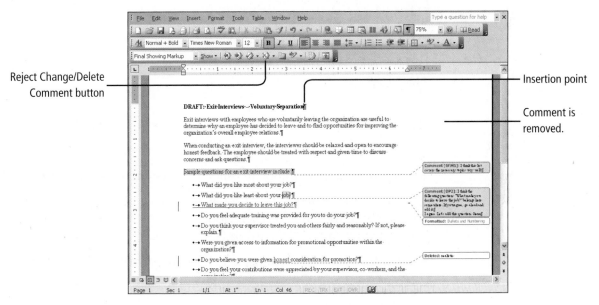

Reject Change/Delete Comment button

Insertion point

Comment is removed.

Figure 6.30

3 On the Reviewing toolbar, click the **Next** button [icon].

The next comment is selected. This comment requires no action and can be removed.

4 On the Reviewing toolbar, click the **Reject Change/Delete Comment** button [icon]. On the Reviewing toolbar, click the **Next** button [icon].

The next comment is selected. This comment has already been acted on when the third bullet point was added, so the comment can be removed.

5 On the Reviewing toolbar, click the **Reject Change/Delete Comment** button. On the Reviewing toolbar, click the **Next** button.

The inserted bullet point is highlighted.

6 On the Reviewing toolbar, click the **Accept Change** button.

The change is accepted, and the balloon is removed, as shown in Figure 6.31.

Accept Change button —

Change is accepted. —

Figure 6.31

7 On the Reviewing toolbar, click the **Next** button.

The deleted word *realistic* in its balloon is selected.

8 On the Reviewing toolbar, click the **Accept Change** button.

Recall that selecting and replacing text is actually two changes—a deletion and an insertion. Notice that the deletion has been accepted, but the insertion is still marked as a change.

9 On the Reviewing toolbar, click the **Next** button to select the insertion. On the Reviewing toolbar, click the **Accept Change** button.

The insertion is accepted.

10 On the Reviewing toolbar, click the **Accept Change button arrow**, and then click **Accept All Changes in Document**.

The remaining changes are accepted. The comment about the last paragraph is all that remains that requires action.

11 On the Reviewing toolbar, click the **Next** button. On the Reviewing toolbar, click the **Reject Change/Delete Comment** button.

The last comment is removed. Because there are no other changes or comments, the extra space in the right margin closes, as shown in Figure 6.32.

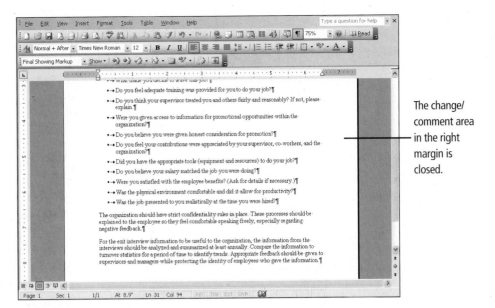

The change/comment area in the right margin is closed.

Figure 6.32

12 From the **Tools** menu, click **Options**, and then click the **User Information tab**. Restore the name and initials that you changed earlier. Click **OK**.

13 From the **View** menu, click **Header and Footer**. On the Header and Footer toolbar, click the **Switch Between Header and Footer** button.

14 On the **Header and Footer** toolbar, click the **Insert AutoText** button Insert AutoText ▾, and then click **Filename**.

The file name is inserted in the footer.

15 On the **Header and Footer** toolbar, click the **Close** button Close.

16 On the Standard toolbar, click the **Save** button.

17 From the **File** menu, click **Print**. Near the bottom of the **Print** dialog box, click the **Print what arrow**, and then click **Document properties**. Click **OK**.

All of the document properties are printed.

18 On the Standard toolbar, click the **Print Preview** button. Take a moment to check your work. On the Print Preview toolbar, click the **Close Preview** button Close.

19 Make any necessary changes to your document. When you are satisfied, on the Standard toolbar, click the **Print** button. Close the document, saving changes if you are prompted to do so.

End **You have completed Project 6B**

Project 6C Insurance

Documents on which several people collaborate often need to be saved in a universal format that can be edited by reviewers using different word processing programs and that can be attached to emails for review. When reviewed documents are returned, Word has a feature that enables you to compare and merge edited documents.

In Activities 6.12 through 6.15, you will edit an article about health care benefits for the newsletter of The Management Association of Pine Valley. You will save the document in a universal document format and send it to another member of the reviewing team. Then you will compare and merge two versions of the same document. Your completed document will look similar to Figure 6.33. You will save your document as *6C_Insurance_Firstname_Lastname*.

Health Insurance: Preparing for Open Enrollment

In the fall, many companies will be offering open enrollment for health insurance. If you want to make your open enrollment season a success, it is a good idea to do a little groundwork well in advance. This is especially true if you are offering a new, more cost-effective plan with the same company or a more beneficial policy with another company. It is even more important that employees clearly understand the benefits of a new policy (or policy options) that they are not going to like.

Communication is the key to successful—or at least non-acrimonious—changes in employee benefits. Unfortunately, it is the weak link in most companies, at a time when the costs and complexities of health insurance plans make communication even more important.

The following steps need to be implemented well before the open enrollment period begins:

1. Map out changes in the plans, and carefully examine how these changes will affect the employees.
2. Check with the insurance provider to see if any sample guides are available that might help you present the information most effectively.
3. Craft a message to the employees, explaining the differences in the new plan, focusing on the positive provisions. Try to anticipate potential problem areas and defuse them, if possible.
4. Discuss the message with the union or other employee representatives.
5. Send the message to the employees. This is often best done in the summer during the vacation season.
6. Provide regular follow-ups for additional general information and to answer concerns that have been voiced.

The messages need to be well crafted, presenting the information in a positive light. Don't oversell one plan or the other—a simple side-by-side comparison is far more effective, and can be designed to slightly favor a particular plan.

6C_Insurance_Firstname_Lastname

Figure 6.33
Project 6C—Insurance

Objective 5
Circulate Documents for Review

Documents created in Microsoft Word are saved in Microsoft's own format, which is indicated by the *.doc* extension on the document name. Some reviewers you work with may not be using Word, and their word processing program may not be able to read a Word document. You can save a Word document in **Rich Text Format (RTF)**, a universal document format that can be read by almost any word processing program. RTF files can be converted back to Word format when the editing process is complete. RTF documents use an *.rtf* extension.

Documents can be distributed as attachments to email messages. After the documents are returned from reviewers, they can be compared and merged.

Activity 6.12 Saving a Document in a Different Format

When you save a Word document as an RTF file, all but the most complex formatting is translated into a format usable by nearly all word processing programs.

1 On the Standard toolbar, click the **Open** button. Navigate to the location where the student files for this textbook are stored. Locate and open **w06C_Insurance**. Save the file as **6C_Insurance_Firstname_Lastname**

2 On the Standard toolbar, click the **Zoom button arrow** 100%, and then click **Page Width**. Be sure that the nonprinting format marks are displayed, and if necessary, on the Standard toolbar, click the Show/Hide ¶ button to display formatting marks.

3 From the **File** menu, click **Save As**.

The Save As dialog box displays.

4 At the bottom of the **Save As** dialog box, click the **Save as type arrow** and scroll down until you can see **Rich Text Format (*.rtf)**. See Figure 6.34. (The **.rtf* may or may not display, depending on your system setup.)

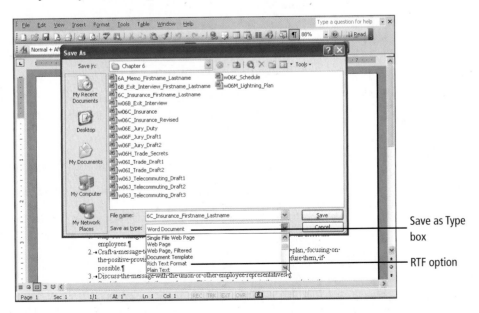

Figure 6.34

5 From the **Save as type** list, click **Rich Text Format (*.rtf)**.

Notice that the file name in the File name box changes to 6C_Insurance_Firstname_Lastname.rtf. The extension may or may not display.

6 At the bottom of the **Save As** dialog box, click **Save**.

The document is saved as an RTF document.

7 From the **File** menu, click **Close**. From the **File** menu, click **Open**. Move to the location of your student files. If necessary, in the Open toolbar, click the **Views button arrow** , and then click **Details** to view the **Type** column.

The Open dialog box displays, showing a list of your documents, including the RTF file you just saved. The document type is shown in the *Type* column. See Figure 6.35.

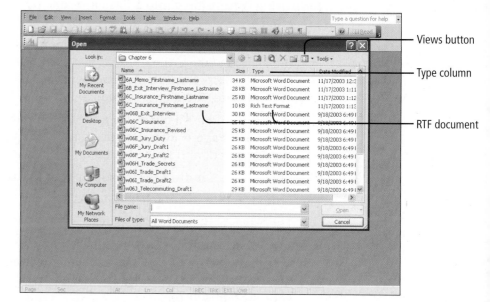

Figure 6.35

8 In the **Open** dialog box, click **6C_Insurance_Firstname_ Lastname.rtf**, and then click **Open**.

9 From the **View** menu, click **Header and Footer**. On the Header and Footer toolbar, click the **Switch Between Header and Footer** button .

10 On the **Header and Footer** toolbar, click the **Insert AutoText** button , and then click **Filename**.

The file name is inserted in the footer.

11 On the **Header and Footer** toolbar, click the **Close** button Close.

12 From the **File** menu, click **Save As**. At the bottom of the **Save As** dialog box, click the **Save as type arrow**, scroll, as necessary, and then click **Word Document (*.doc)**.

The file name changes back to 6C_Insurance_Firstname_Lastname.doc, if extensions are displayed.

13 At the bottom of the **Save As** dialog box, click **Save**.

A dialog box displays, indicating that a file of the same name already exists and asking what you want to do, as shown in Figure 6.36.

Replace existing file option ——

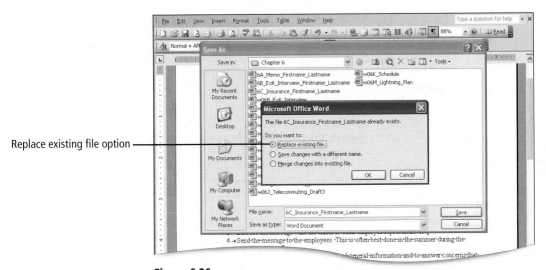

Figure 6.36

14 From the dialog box, click **OK** to replace the existing file.

This Word file that you modified replaces the original RTF version of the same file. If you are not sure what to do when you see this dialog box, you should save the document under a different name.

Activity 6.13 Attaching Documents to an Email Message

Documents can be attached to email messages and sent to others for them to review.

1 From the **File** menu, point to **Send To**.

The *Send To* submenu displays. From this menu, you can send an email, attach the current document to an email, or send a fax. See Figure 6.37.

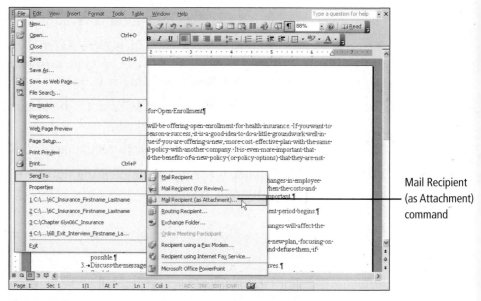

Mail Recipient
(as Attachment)
command

Figure 6.37

▣2 From the **Send To** menu, click **Mail Recipient (as Attachment)**.

After a few moments, an email window opens. The name of the document becomes the Subject text, and the name of the document also displays as the attachment name.

Alert! ── **Does Your Screen Differ?**

The appearance of your screen depends on various settings that your system administrator established when Office was installed and how the program has been used most recently. The email window may or may not be maximized, and the elements on the screen depend on the default email program on your computer. If you are using a non-Microsoft mail program, you may have to switch to the program yourself, or this feature may not work at all. Many organizations use Microsoft Outlook or Microsoft Outlook Express as their email program, but yours may differ. In this example, Outlook Express is the active email program.

▣3 Click within the white message area in the lower portion of the email window and type **David, Siena:** and press Enter.

▣4 Type **Please review this document and return it by Friday.**

▣5 In the top of the email window, in the **Subject** box, select the existing text and replace it with **Insurance document for your review**

▣6 In the **To** box, type **DRosenberg@mapv.org**

▣7 In the **Cc** box, type **SMadison@mapv.org**

This sends a copy of the email and attachment to Siena Madison. Compare your screen with Figure 6.38.

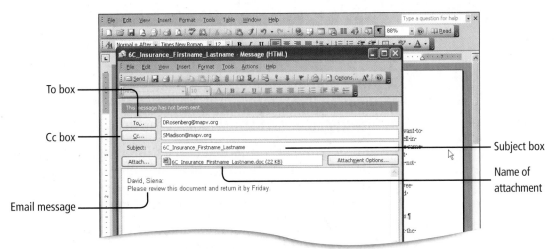

To box

Cc box

Email message

Subject box

Name of attachment

Figure 6.38

8 Because you may or may not have an appropriate email connection at this time, rather than clicking the Send button, display the **File** menu, and then click **Close**. Do not save your changes when prompted.

No email is sent, and your document redisplays.

Objective 6
Compare and Merge Documents

It is not always possible for reviewers to make their comments and edits on a single copy of a document, as you practiced in Project B. When more than one person makes changes to different *copies* of the same document, identifying all the changes can be challenging. Word has a feature that combines the Track Changes feature with a document comparison operation. When you compare two or more documents, the changes are identified, and the Reviewing toolbar is used to decide which changes to accept and which ones to reject. The changes can be stored in the open document, or the combined documents can be saved as a new document.

There are three ways to merge documents, as shown in the table in Figure 6.39.

Three Ways to Merge Reviewed Documents	
Type of Merge	**Results**
Merge	Differences in the documents are displayed as tracked changes in the unopened (baseline) document.
Merge into current document	Differences in the documents are displayed as tracked changes in the open document.
Merge into new document	Changes in both documents are merged into a new, third document, with differences shown as tracked changes.

Figure 6.39

Activity 6.14 Comparing and Merging Documents

To combine documents, you need one of the documents open and the other closed.

1 With your **6C_Insurance_Firstname_Lastname** document open, from the **Tools** menu, click **Compare and Merge Documents**.

The Compare and Merge Documents dialog box displays.

2 If necessary, at the bottom of the **Compare and Merge Documents** dialog box, clear the **Legal blackline** check box. Use the **Look in arrow** to navigate to the location where the student files for this textbook are stored. Locate and select **w06C_Insurance_Revised**.

3 At the bottom of the **Compare and Merge Documents** dialog box, click the **Merge button arrow**.

The three merge commands are listed.

4 From the **Merge** list, click **Merge into current document**.

The documents are compared and merged. The differences between the two documents are displayed as tracked changes in the open document, and the Reviewing toolbar opens. See Figure 6.40.

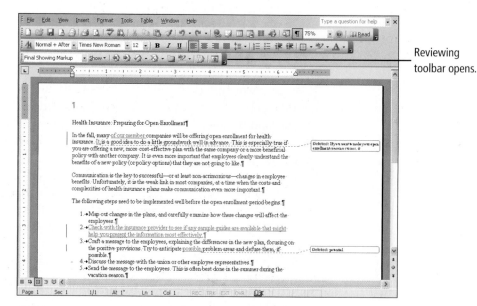

Figure 6.40

5 On the Standard toolbar, click the **Save** button.

Activity 6.15 Accepting and Rejecting Merge Changes

Once you have identified the differences between two documents, you need to decide which changes to accept and which to reject.

1 On the Reviewing toolbar, click the **Next** button.

The inserted text *of our member* is highlighted, as shown in Figure 6.41.

Reject Change/Delete
Comment button

Next button

Accept Change button

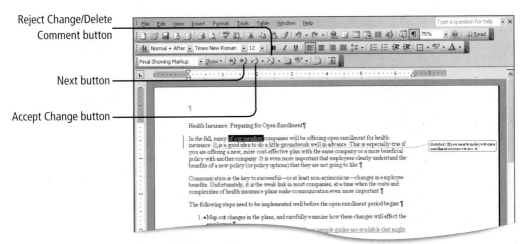

Figure 6.41

2 On the Reviewing toolbar, click the **Reject Change/Delete Comment** button.

The change is removed from the document.

3 On the Reviewing toolbar, click the **Next** button.

The phrase beginning *If you want to make* has been deleted, and the word *It* has been inserted.

4 On the Reviewing toolbar, click the **Reject Change/Delete Comment** button.

The inserted text is removed, but the deleted text has not been addressed yet.

5 On the Reviewing toolbar, click the **Next** button, and then click the **Reject Change/Delete Comment** button.

The deleted text is returned to the document.

6 Click the **Next** button, and then click the **Accept Change** button.

The numbered item is added to the document.

7 Click the **Next** button, and then click the **Reject Change/Delete Comment** button.

The inserted word *possible* is removed.

8 Click the **Next** button, and then click the **Reject Change/Delete Comment** button.

The deleted word *potential* is returned to the document. That was the last tracked change in the document, so the expanded right margin is replaced by the standard document margin, as shown in Figure 6.42.

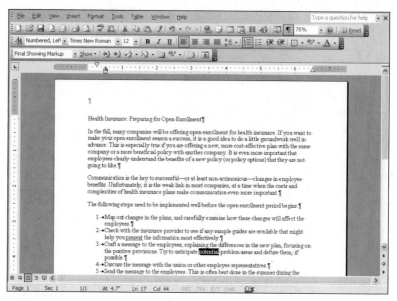

Figure 6.42

9 Click the **Next** button ▶▶ once more.

A change was found in the footer—one document had the footer, the other did not.

10 Click the **Accept Change** button ✅▾. On the **Header and Footer** toolbar, click the **Close** button Close .

The footer is kept in the document.

11 On the Standard toolbar, click the **Save** button 🖫.

12 On the Standard toolbar, click the **Print Preview** button 🔍. Take a moment to check your work. On the Print Preview toolbar, click the **Close Preview** button Close .

13 Make any necessary changes to your document. When you are satisfied, on the Standard toolbar, click the **Print** button 🖶. Close the document, saving changes if you are prompted to do so, and close Word.

End You have completed Project 6C

Summary

Businesses and organizations standardize document formats to give their printed materials a consistent look. Templates set up a document's structure, including page formatting, font, font size, margins, and indents. Templates are useful because they give all documents of a similar type the same look.

Business documents often are composed through a collaborative effort; that is, many individuals contribute text and ideas to the document. Word offers a number of collaboration tools. Document properties are statistics and document information that are stored with a document and can be used for document identification. These include the date the document was created and the date it was last modified. Summary information is also available and can include the document name, title, subject, and company. Information on the document category, keywords for document searches, and comments can also be added. Document statistics, such as word and line counts, enable you to keep within document guidelines.

When documents are exchanged between reviewers, comments can be added and edited, and changes can be tracked. Comments are identified by reviewer and can be added anywhere in the document, although they are not included in the final print version. The Track Changes option also enables the reader to see who made changes and exactly what changes were made. Once all of the comments have been added, and the changes by various reviewers are completed, the changes can be accepted or rejected, and the comments can be deleted.

While many companies provide a file server for quick access to group documents, it is often expedient to send document copies via email. Documents can be sent as attachments to email messages, and these documents can be compared and merged when the reviews are complete. Rich Text Format (RTF) is available if you need to send the document to someone using a word processor other than Microsoft Word.

In This Chapter You Practiced How To

- Create a Document Using a Template
- Review and Modify Document Properties
- Use Comments in a Document
- Track Changes in a Document
- Circulate Documents for Review
- Compare and Merge Documents

Matching

Match each term in the second column with its correct definition in the first column by writing the letter of the term on the blank line in front of the correct definition.

_____ 1. Statistics and related information about a document, including file size and location, author, title, and subject.

_____ 2. The template on which most documents are based; it contains the default Word document settings.

_____ 3. The document property that shows the title, author, company, subject, and keywords for a document.

_____ 4. A small, bordered shape in the right margin that displays a change or comment.

_____ 5. A toolbar that keeps track of document statistics.

_____ 6. A template set up with the elements necessary for a specific document type, such as a memo, resume, or letter.

_____ 7. An area at the bottom of the screen that displays comments and tracked changes.

_____ 8. A note attached to a document.

_____ 9. The process by which documents are compared and differences are displayed as tracked changes in the unopened (baseline) document.

_____ 10. The Word feature that enables you to see which reviewer made edits or added comments to a document.

_____ 11. A universal document format that can be read by nearly all word processing programs.

_____ 12. The command that compares two documents and creates a new document to display the differences.

_____ 13. Text in a document created using a template; this text can be replaced but not edited.

_____ 14. The toolbar button that highlights the first change or comment following the insertion point.

_____ 15. A step-by-step program that asks you questions and then sets up a document based on your answers.

A Balloon

B Comment

C Document properties

D Document template

E Merge

F Merge into new document

G Next button

H Normal template

I Placeholder text

J Reviewing pane

K RTF

L Summary

M Track Changes

N Wizard

O Word Count

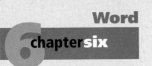

Concepts Assessments (continued)

Fill in the Blank Write the correct answer in the space provided.

1. Document template files have a(n) _____ extension.

2. The _____ toolbar enables you to track, accept or reject changes, and delete comments.

3. _____ text is selected with a single click.

4. Microsoft Word files use a(n) _____ extension, which may or may not display depending on your system setup.

5. Adding Keywords to the _____ tab of the Properties dialog box is useful when you use the Windows Search command.

6. In the Properties dialog box, the _____ tab displays a document's word and line count.

7. On the Reviewing toolbar, click the Display for Review button arrow, and then click _____ to hide tracked changes and comments.

8. Rich Text Format documents use a(n) _____ extension.

9. To attach an open document to an email message using Word, click the _____ command from the File menu.

10. When using Track Changes, balloons are displayed in the _____ margin.

Project 6D — Jury Duty Memo

Objective: *Create a Document Using a Template.*

In the following Skill Assessment, you will create a memo for The Management Association of Pine Valley. The memo will involve the review of a draft of a company policy regarding jury duty. Your completed document will look similar to the one shown in Figure 6.43. You will save your document as *6D_Jury_Duty_Memo_Firstname_Lastname*.

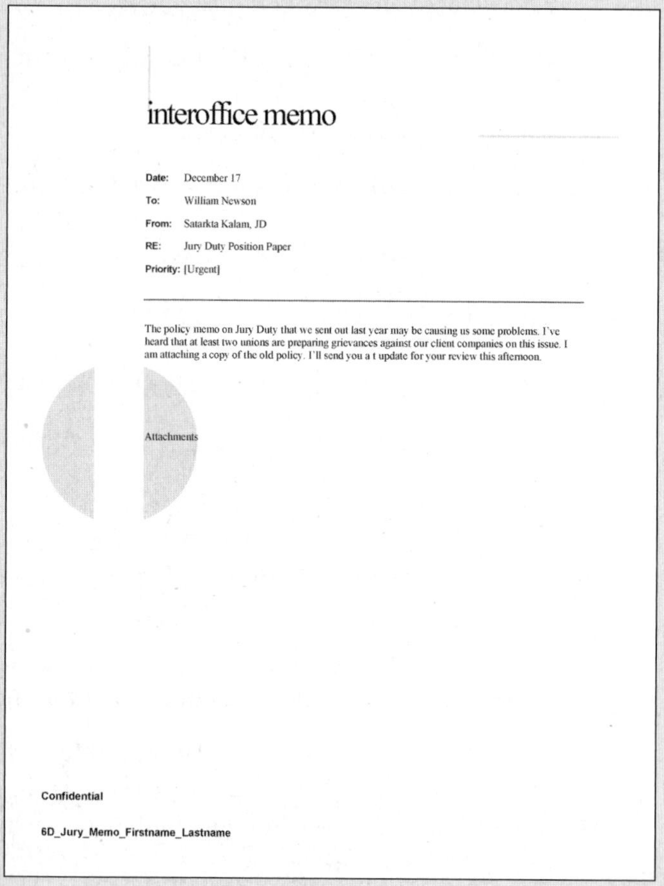

interoffice memo

Date: December 17
To: William Newson
From: Satarkta Kalam, JD
RE: Jury Duty Position Paper
Priority: [Urgent]

The policy memo on Jury Duty that we sent out last year may be causing us some problems. I've heard that at least two unions are preparing grievances against our client companies on this issue. I am attaching a copy of the old policy. I'll send you a t update for your review this afternoon.

Attachments

Confidential

6D_Jury_Memo_Firstname_Lastname

Figure 6.43

1. From the **File** menu, click **New**. In the **New Document** task pane, under **Templates**, click **On my computer**.

2. In the **Templates** dialog box, click the **Memos tab**, and then click the **Memo Wizard** icon. At the bottom of the **Templates** dialog box, click **OK**.

3. Examine the first **Memo Wizard** dialog box. Notice the sequence line on the left side, with the *Start* box highlighted in green. At the bottom of the dialog box, click **Next**.

(Project 6D – Jury Duty Memo continues on the next page)

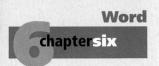

(Project 6D–Jury Duty Memo continued)

4. In the *Style* **Memo Wizard** dialog box, click the **Contemporary** option button. Click **Next**.

5. In the *Title* **Memo Wizard** dialog box, accept *Interoffice Memo* as the title text by clicking **Next**.

6. In the *Heading Fields* **Memo Wizard** dialog box, if necessary, click to select (place a check mark in) the **Priority** check box. In the first three text boxes, substitute the following text, and then click **Next**. (Note that if another student has recently completed this exercise on the computer at which you are seated, the information may already be filled in.)

Date: **December 17**
From: **Satarkta Kalam, JD**
Subject: **Jury Duty Position Paper**

7. In the *Recipient* **Memo Wizard** dialog box, in the **To** text box, type **William Newson** and then click **Next**.

8. In the *Closing Fields* **Memo Wizard** dialog box, if necessary, select the **Attachments** check box, and then click **Next**.

9. In the *Header/Footer* **Memo Wizard** dialog box, under **Which items would you like in the footer for all pages?**, if necessary, clear the **Date** and **Page Number** check boxes, and then click **Next**.

10. In the *Finish* **Memo Wizard** dialog box, click **Finish** to display the customized memo. If the **Office Assistant** displays, click **Cancel** to close it.

11. On the Standard toolbar, click the **Save** button. Navigate to the location where the student files for this textbook are stored. Save the file as **6D_Jury_Duty_Memo_Firstname_Lastname**

12. Select the entire line **Cc: [Click here and type names]** and press Delete.

13. Click **[Click here and type your memo text]**. Type the following:

The policy memo on Jury Duty that we sent out last year may be causing us some problems. I've heard that at least two unions are preparing grievances against our client companies on this issue. I am attaching a copy of the old policy. I'll send you a draft of a possible update for your review this afternoon.

14. From the **View** menu, click **Header and Footer**. On the Header and Footer toolbar, click the **Switch Between Header and Footer** button.

15. In the footer area, position the insertion point at the end of *Confidential*, and then press Enter. On the **Header and Footer** toolbar, click the **Insert AutoText** button, and then click **Filename**. Because of special formatting in the template, the file name overlaps the marked footer area; however, this will print properly.

(Project 6D – Jury Duty Memo continues on the next page)

(Project 6D–Jury Duty Memo continued)

16. On the **Header and Footer** toolbar, click the **Close** button.

17. On the Standard toolbar, click the **Save** button.

18. On the Standard toolbar, click the **Print Preview** button. Take a moment to check your work. On the Print Preview toolbar, click the **Close Preview** button.

19. Make any necessary changes to your document. When you are satisfied, on the Standard toolbar, click the **Print** button. Close the document, saving any changes.

End **You have completed Project 6D** ————————————

Project 6E — Jury Duty

Objectives: *Use Comments in a Document, Track Changes in a Document, and Compare and Merge Documents.*

In the following Skill Assessment, you will edit an employee leave policy for jury duty. You will work with the document summary. You will add comments, track changes, and then accept or reject the changes and remove the comments. Your completed document will look similar to the one shown in Figure 6.44. You will save your document as *6E_Jury_Duty_Firstname_Lastname*.

1. Start Word. On the Standard toolbar, click the **Open** button. Navigate to the location where the student files for this textbook are stored. Locate and open **w06E_Jury_Duty**. Save the file as **6E_Jury_Duty_Firstname_Lastname**

2. On the Standard toolbar, click the **Zoom button arrow**, and then click **Page Width**. If necessary, on the Standard toolbar, click the Show/Hide ¶ button to display formatting marks.

3. From the **Tools** menu, click **Options**, and then click the **Track Changes tab**. Under **Balloons**, click the **Use Balloons (Print and Web Layout) arrow**, and then click **Always**.

4. In the **Options** dialog box, click the **User Information tab**. Note the name and initials and restore them when Project 6F is completed. Under **User information**, in the **Name** box, type **Satarkta Kalam, JD** and in the **Initials** box, type **SK** Click **OK**.

5. From the **View** menu, point to **Toolbars** and if necessary, click **Reviewing** to activate the Reviewing toolbar.

(Project 6E–Jury Duty continues on the next page)

(Project 6E–Jury Duty continued)

Jury Duty – Employee Leave Policy
XYZ Corporation

XYZ Corporation encourages its employees to fulfill their civic responsibility by serving jury duty when required. The Company provides income protection for this time away from work by paying the difference between jury duty pay and your regular day's pay. Income protection is provided for a maximum of 5 work days; if additional time away is required due to jury obligations, income protection will be decided on a case-by-case basis.

All full-time and part-time employees are eligible under this policy.

In instances where the employee's lengthy absence from work would be detrimental to the Company, the Company may provide a letter for the employee to present to the Court requesting an excuse from or delay in jury duty requirements.

All employees who are called for jury duty are required to immediately notify their supervisor so that scheduling adjustments can be made.

Employees are required to present evidence of their jury duty attendance (usually a form provided by the Court) to their supervisor upon their return to work. The supervisor will provide the Court documentation to Payroll for processing.

Employees are required to return to work as the Court's schedule allows during jury duty and upon release by the Court.

All employee benefits and accruals such as vacation and sick leave will continue while the employee is on jury duty.

XYZ Corporation has the authority to change, modify, or approve exceptions to this policy at any time and without notice.

6E_Jury_Duty_Firstname_Lastname

Figure 6.44

6. Near the top of the document, locate the sentence that begins *The Company provides income protection*. Hold down Ctrl and click anywhere in the sentence to select it. From the Reviewing toolbar, click the **Insert Comment** button. Type **This phrase could cause trouble.**

7. In the lower portion of the page, select the sentence that begins *Employees are required to return to work*. From the Reviewing toolbar, click the **Insert Comment** button. Type **This is another controversial section.** On the Standard toolbar, click the **Save** button.

8. Hold down Ctrl and press Home. From the Reviewing toolbar, click the **Track Changes** button to turn the feature on. On the Reviewing toolbar, click the **Display for Review button arrow**, and then click **Final Showing Markup**. This will display the changes within the document.

(Project 6E–Jury Duty continues on the next page)

(Project 6E–Jury Duty continued)

9. In the paragraph that begins *In instances where the employee*, double-click *lengthy* and press Delete.

10. In the same paragraph, position the insertion point after *from* near the end of the paragraph. Press Space, and then type **or delay in**

11. In the paragraph that begins *All employees who are called*, select *who are* and press Delete.

12. On the **Reviewing** toolbar, click the **Track Changes** button to turn off Track Changes.

13. Hold down Ctrl and press Home to move to the top of the document. On the Reviewing toolbar, click the **Next** button.

14. On the Reviewing toolbar, click the **Reject Change/Delete Comment** button to delete the first comment.

15. On the Reviewing toolbar, click the **Next** button, and then click the **Accept Change** button to accept the insertion.

16. On the Reviewing toolbar, click the **Next** button, and then click the **Reject Change/Delete Comment** button to delete the second comment. Repeat this procedure to accept any changes and remove any other comments in the document.

17. From the **View** menu, click **Header and Footer**. On the Header and Footer toolbar, click the **Switch Between Header and Footer** button.

18. On the **Header and Footer** toolbar, click the **Insert AutoText** button, and then click **Filename**.

19. On the **Header and Footer** toolbar, click the **Close** button.

20. On the Standard toolbar, click the **Save** button.

21. On the Standard toolbar, click the **Print Preview** button. Take a moment to check your work. On the Print Preview toolbar, click the **Close Preview** button.

22. Make any necessary changes to your document. When you are satisfied, on the Standard toolbar, click the **Print** button.

23. From the **Tools** menu, click **Options**, and then click the **User Information tab**. Restore the name and initials that you changed earlier. Click **OK**. Close the file, saving any changes.

End You have completed Project 6E ————————————————————

Project 6F — Jury Final

Objectives: *Review and Modify Document Properties, Circulate Documents for Review, and Compare and Merge Documents.*

In the following Skill Assessment, you will finalize edits on two different drafts of the employee leave policy for jury duty. You will work with the document summary and print the summary. You will also compare, merge, and respond to tracked changes in the two draft documents to produce a final document. Your completed document will look similar to the one shown in Figure 6.45. You will save your document as *6F_Jury_Final_Firstname_Lastname.*

Jury Duty – Employee Leave Policy
XYZ Corporation

XYZ Corporation encourages its employees to fulfill their civic responsibility by serving jury duty when required. The Company provides income protection for this time away from work by paying the difference between jury duty pay and your regular day's pay. Income protection is provided for a maximum of 5 work days; if additional time away is required due to jury obligations, income protection will be decided on a case-by-case basis.

All full-time and part-time employees are eligible under this policy.

In instances where the employee's absence from work would be detrimental to the Company, the Company may provide a letter for the employee to present to the Court requesting an excuse from or delay in jury duty requirements.

All employees who are called for jury duty are required to immediately notify their supervisor so that scheduling adjustments can be made.

Employees are required to present evidence of their jury duty attendance (usually a form provided by the Court) to their supervisor upon their return to work. The supervisor will provide the Court documentation to Payroll for processing.

Employees are required to return to work as the Court's schedule allows during jury duty and upon release by the Court. Employees required to be in court for any part of a day will not be required to work the remainder of that day.

All employee benefits and accruals such as vacation and sick leave will continue while the employee is on jury duty.

XYZ Corporation has the authority to change, modify, or approve exceptions to this policy at any time and without notice.

Afternoon and night shift employees shall have the option of choosing to be excused from the shift either immediately before or immediately after the day of jury duty.

6F_Jury_Final_Firstname_Lastname

Figure 6.45

1. On the Standard toolbar, click the **Open** button. Navigate to the location where the student files for this textbook are stored. Locate and open **w06F_Jury_Draft1**. Save the file as **6F_Jury_Final_Firstname_Lastname**

2. On the Standard toolbar, click the **Zoom button arrow**, and then click **Page Width**. If necessary, to display formatting marks on the Standard toolbar, click the Show/Hide ¶ button.

(Project 6F–Jury Final continues on the next page)

(Project 6F–Jury Final continued)

3. From the **File** menu, click **Properties**. If necessary, click the **Summary tab**.

4. In the **Summary** sheet, in the **Author** box, type your name.

5. In the **Summary** sheet, type the following in the indicated boxes:

Title	**Jury Duty Final**
Keywords	**Jury, Leave**
Comments	**Final Draft of the Jury Duty policy statement document**
Company	**The Management Association of Pine Valley**

6. At the bottom of the **Properties** box, click **OK**. On the Standard toolbar, click the **Save** button.

7. From the **File** menu, click **Save As**. At the bottom of the **Save As** dialog box, click the **Save as type arrow**, scroll down, and then click **Rich Text Format**. At the bottom of the **Save As** dialog box, click **Save**.

8. From the **File** menu, click **Print**. Near the bottom of the **Print** dialog box, click the **Print what arrow**, and then click **Document properties**. Click **OK** to print the document properties. Notice that the document type is .rtf.

9. From the **File** menu, click **Close**. From the **File** menu, click **Open**. If necessary, move to the location of your student files. Check to see that the document type is visible, and if necessary, click the Views button arrow in the upper right corner of the dialog box, and then click Details. In the **Open** dialog box, click the *Word document* **6F_Jury_Final_Firstname_Lastname**, and then click **Open**.

10. From the **Tools** menu, click **Compare and Merge Documents**. In the displayed dialog box, navigate to the location where the student files for this textbook are stored. Locate and select **w06F_Jury_Draft2**.

11. At the bottom of the **Compare and Merge Documents** dialog box, click the **Merge button arrow**. If necessary, at the bottom of the **Compare and Merge Documents** dialog box, clear the **Legal blackline** check box. From the **Merge** list, click **Merge into current document**.

12. On the Standard toolbar, click the **Save** button.

13. On the Reviewing toolbar, click the **Next** button, and then click the **Accept Change** button to accept the deletion of *lengthy*.

14. On the Reviewing toolbar, click the **Next** button, and then click the **Accept Change** button to accept the insertion of the sentence beginning *Employees required to be in court.*

(Project 6F–Jury Final continues on the next page)

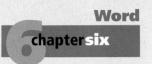
(Project 6F–Jury Final continued)

15. On the Reviewing toolbar, click the **Next** button, and then click the **Reject Change/Delete Comment** button to reject the deletion of *and without notice.*

16. On the Reviewing toolbar, click the **Next** button, and then click the **Accept Change** button to accept the addition of the paragraph beginning *Afternoon and night shift.*

17. On the Standard toolbar, click the **Save** button.

18. From the **View** menu, click **Header and Footer**. On the Header and Footer toolbar, click the **Switch Between Header and Footer** button. Click the **Insert AutoText** button, and then click **Filename**.

19. On the **Header and Footer** toolbar, click the **Close** button.

20. On the Standard toolbar, click the **Print Preview** button. Take a moment to check your work. On the Print Preview toolbar, click the **Close Preview** button. Make any necessary changes to your document. When you are satisfied, on the Standard toolbar, click the **Print** button.

21. If you are using your own computer and have it set up to use Word for email, from the **File** menu, point to **Send To**.

22. From the **Send To** menu, click **Mail Recipient (as Attachment)**. In the open area in the bottom part of the email window, type your name and press .

23. Type **Please review this document over the weekend and return it by Monday.**

24. In the top of the email window, in the **Subject** box, select the existing text and type **Jury Duty document**

25. In the **To** box, type your email address.

26. If you are sure you have an appropriate email configuration, click the **Send** button; otherwise, from the **File** menu, click **Close** and do not save your changes. If necessary, check your email to make sure the document arrived.

End **You have completed Project 6F** ——————————————

Project 6G — Trade Fax

Objectives: *Create a Document Using a Template and Circulate Documents for Review.*

In the following Performance Assessment, you will create a fax to a company about an enclosed trade secret and nondisclosure agreement. Your completed document will look similar to the one shown in Figure 6.46. You will save your document as *6G_Trade_Fax_Firstname_Lastname.*

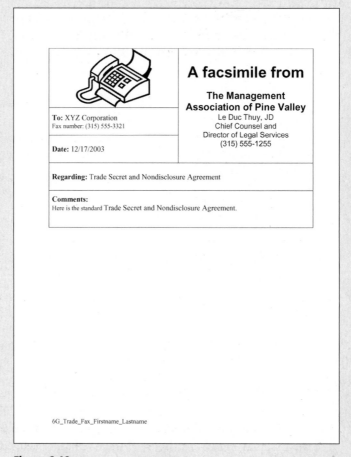

A facsimile from

**The Management
Association of Pine Valley**
Le Duc Thuy, JD
Chief Counsel and
Director of Legal Services
(315) 555-1255

To: XYZ Corporation
Fax number: (315) 555-3321

Date: 12/17/2003

Regarding: Trade Secret and Nondisclosure Agreement

Comments:
Here is the standard Trade Secret and Nondisclosure Agreement.

6G_Trade_Fax_Firstname_Lastname

Figure 6.46

1. From the **File** menu, click **New**. In the **New Document** task pane, under **Templates**, click **On my computer**.

2. In the **Templates** dialog box, click the **Letters & Faxes tab**, and then click the **Business Fax** icon. At the bottom of the **Templates** dialog box, click **OK**. If you do not have the same business fax template as the one displayed in Figure 6.46, use a similar one and adjust your responses accordingly.

(Project 6G–Trade Fax continues on the next page)

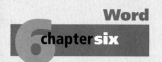
(Project 6G–Trade Fax continued)

3. Save the document as **6G_Trade_Fax_Firstname_Lastname**

4. Replace the **To** placeholder with **XYZ Corporation**

5. Place the insertion point after *Fax number* and type **(315) 555-3321**

6. Replace the **Business name** placeholder with **The Management Association of Pine Valley**

7. Replace the **Contact information** placeholder with the following:

   Le Duc Thuy, JD
   Chief Counsel and
   Director of Legal Services
   (315) 555-0155

8. Replace the **Regarding** placeholder with **Trade Secret and Nondisclosure Agreement**

9. In the **Comments** box, on the line below *Comments*, type **Here is the standard Trade Secret and Nondisclosure Agreement.**

10. Use **Insert AutoText** to insert the file name in a footer, and then close the footer.

11. On the Standard toolbar, click the **Save** button. Preview the document, and then print it.

12. Save and close the document.

 You have completed Project 6G ——————————————

Project 6H — Trade Secrets

Objectives: *Use Comments in a Document and Track Changes in a Document.*

In the following Performance Assessment, you will add comments and make changes to a trade secrets and nondisclosure agreement policy statement, and then you will accept or reject changes. Your completed document will look similar to the one shown in Figure 6.47. You will save your document as *6H_Trade_Secrets_Firstname_Lastname*.

1. On the Standard toolbar, click the **Open** button. Navigate to the location where the student files for this textbook are stored. Locate and open **w06H_Trade_Secrets**. This file contains comments and changes that have been made with the Track Changes feature turned on. Save the file as **6H_Trade_Secrets_Firstname_Lastname**

2. On the Standard toolbar, click the **Zoom button arrow**, and then click **Page Width**. If necessary, on the Standard toolbar, click the Show/Hide ¶ button to display formatting marks.

(Project 6H–Trade Secrets continues on the next page)

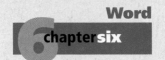
(Project 6H–Trade Secrets continued)

Trade Secret and Nondisclosure Agreement

This Agreement is entered into on this ___ day of _____, 20__ by and between _____ ("Company") and _____ ("Employee").

Whereas, 1) Company has agreed to hire Employee; 2) as part of his/her employment, Employee will learn confidential information and trade secrets belonging to the Company; 3) the dissemination of such confidential information and trade secrets to persons inside or outside of the Company who are not entitled to receive such information is harmful to the company.

Therefore, Employee agrees not to disclose to any such person any confidential information or trade secret, directly or indirectly, whether for compensation or no compensation, without the written consent of the Company.

If Employee is not sure whether information he/she has obtained falls under said definition, Employee shall treat that information as confidential unless Employee is informed otherwise by the Company.

Employee acknowledges that a violation of this Agreement will cause damage and harm to the Company that can include loss of competitive advantage, loss of revenue, and other harm not specifically outlined in this Agreement. Employee agrees that upon written notice from Company of a breach of this agreement that Employee will immediately cease all activities which are or are claimed to constitute said breach. Employee agrees that Company may request relief for damages incurred by any such breach.

This agreement remains in effect until released in writing by the Company and is not cancelled by the end of Employee's employment with the company.

The parties have executed this Agreement on the date written above.

[Company Name]

_____
By: [Signer's name]

_____
By: [Employee's Name]

This Agreement is enforced under the laws of _____ [name of state].

6H_Trade_Secrets_Firstname_Lastname

Figure 6.47

3. From the **Tools** menu, click **Options**, and then click the **Track Changes tab**. Turn on balloons for all tracked changes.

4. In the **Options** dialog box, click the **User Information tab**. Note the name and initials and restore them when Project 6I is completed. Under **User information**, in the **Name** box, type **David Rosenberg** and in the **Initials** box, type **DR**

5. Right-click on any toolbar and if necessary, click Reviewing to display the toolbar. Turn on **Track Changes** (the button will display as orange when the feature is turned on and as blue when the feature is turned off).

6. Select the title (the first line of the document). Change the font to **Arial Black** and the font size to **14**.

7. In the paragraph that begins *Therefore, Employee agrees*, position the insertion point after the space following the word *confidential*. Type **or proprietary** and press Space.

(Project 6H–Trade Secrets continues on the next page)

(Project 6H–Trade Secrets continued)

8. In the paragraph that begins *Employee acknowledges that a violation*, near the end of the paragraph, position the insertion after the space following the word *request*. Type **equitable** and press Space.

9. Save the document. Hold down Ctrl and press Home to move to the beginning of the document. On the Reviewing toolbar, click the **Next** button, and then click the **Accept Change** button to accept the formatting change to the title. Press the **Next** button again, and then click the **Accept Change** button to accept the deletion of *4*.

10. Move to the next change, an insertion of *3*, and accept it. Move to the next change, the insertion of *or proprietary*, and accept it.

11. Move to the next change and click the **Reject Change/Delete Comment** button to reject the deletion of the paragraph beginning *If Employee is not sure*.

12. Move to the next change. Accept the insertion of *equitable*. Leave the comment at the end of the document for the next reviewer to read. Turn off **Track Changes**.

13. Use **Insert AutoText** to insert the file name in a footer, and then close the footer. In the **Reviewing** toolbar, click the **Display for Review arrow** and click **Final** to show the document without the comment in the margin.

14. If you are not going to do Project 6I, from the **Tools** menu, click **Options**, and then click the **User Information tab**. Restore the name and initials that you changed earlier. Click **OK**.

15. Save the document. Preview and print the document. Close all documents, saving any changes.

End You have completed Project 6H ———————————————

Project 6I — Trade Final

Objectives: *Review and Modify Document Properties and Compare and Merge Documents.*

In the following Performance Assessment, you will change the document properties for a trade secrets and nondisclosure agreement policy statement, and then you will compare and merge two drafts of the same documents. Your completed document will look similar to the one shown in Figure 6.48. You will save your document as *6I_Trade_Final_Firstname_Lastname*.

1. On the Standard toolbar, click the **Open** button. Navigate to the location where the student files for this textbook are stored. Locate and open **w06I_Trade_Draft1**.

(Project 6I–Trade Final continues on the next page)

(Project 6I–Trade Final continued)

Trade Secret and Nondisclosure Agreement

This Agreement is entered into on this _____ day of _____, 20___ by and between _____ ("Company") and _____ ("Employee").

Whereas, 1) Company has agreed to hire Employee; 2) as part of his/her employment, Employee will learn confidential information and trade secrets belonging to the Company; 3) the dissemination of such confidential information and trade secrets to persons inside or outside of the Company who are not entitled to receive such information is harmful to the company.

Therefore, Employee agrees not to disclose to any such person any confidential information or trade secret, directly or indirectly, whether for compensation or no compensation, without the written consent of the Company.

If Employee is not sure whether information he/she has obtained falls under said definition, Employee shall treat that information as confidential unless Employee is informed otherwise by the Company.

Employee acknowledges that a violation of this Agreement will cause damage and harm to the Company that can include loss of competitive advantage, loss of revenue, and other harm not specifically outlined in this Agreement. Employee agrees that upon written notice from Company of a breach of this agreement that Employee will immediately cease all activities which are or are claimed to constitute said breach. Employee agrees that Company may request relief for damages incurred by any such breach.

This agreement remains in effect until released in writing by the Company and is not cancelled by the end of Employee's employment with the company.

The parties have executed this Agreement on the date written above.

[Insert Company Name]

_____
By: [Signer's name]

_____
By: [Employee's Name]

This Agreement is enforced under the laws of _____.
[Name of State]

6I_Trade_Final_Firstname_Lastname

Figure 6.48

2. From the **Tools** menu, click **Options**, and then click the **Track Changes tab**. Under **Balloons**, be sure the **Use Balloons (Print and Web Layout)** box indicates **Always**. If necessary, change the **Zoom** to **Page Width** and turn on the formatting characters.

3. From the **Tools** menu, click **Compare and Merge Documents**. Navigate to the location where the student files for this textbook are stored. Locate and select **w06I_Trade_Draft2**.

4. At the bottom of the **Compare and Merge Documents** dialog box, click the **Merge button arrow**. From the **Merge** list, click **Merge into new document**. All differences between the two versions are displayed in an unnamed document, leaving the original documents unchanged.

5. Save the new document on your screen as **6I_Trade_Final_Firstname_Lastname**

(Project 6I–Trade Final continues on the next page)

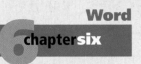

(Project 6I–Trade Final continued)

6. On the Reviewing toolbar, click the **Next** button. All of the changes appear to be selected, but this is an indication that the document margins have changed, as shown in the first balloon. Click the **Accept Change** button to accept the new margins.

7. Move to the next change, which is inserted underlines to make the black lines longer, and accept the change. Repeat the procedure for the other three line changes.

8. Move to the next change, in which the word *Insert* was inserted, and accept the change.

9. On the Reviewing toolbar, click the **Next** button, and then click the **Accept Change button arrow**. Click **Accept All Changes in Document** to accept the remainder of the changes. If necessary, delete any remaining comments.

10. Create a footer, use **Insert AutoText** to insert the file name, and then close the footer. Save the document.

11. From the **File** menu, click **Properties** and move to the **Summary** sheet, if necessary.

12. In the **Summary** sheet, type the following in the indicated boxes:

Author	**your name**
Title	**Trade Secrets Policy Statement**
Comments	**Final Draft of the Trade Secrets and Nondisclosure Agreement policy statement**
Company	**The Management Association of Pine Valley**

13. Save your work. Preview the document and print it if you are satisfied with the way it looks.

14. From the **Tools** menu, click **Options**, and then click the **User Information tab**. Restore the name and initials that you changed earlier. Click **OK**. Close all documents, saving any changes.

End You have completed Project 6I

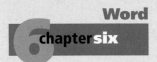
Project 6J — Telecommuting

Objectives: *Compare and Merge Documents and Review and Modify Document Properties.*

In the following Mastery Assessment, you will compare and merge three drafts of a proposed Telecommuting Policy for The Management Association of Pine Valley. To merge three documents, you compare and merge two of them, and then compare the third document to the merged document. Your completed document will look similar to the one shown in Figure 6.49. You will save your document as *6J_Telecommuting_Firstname_Lastname.*

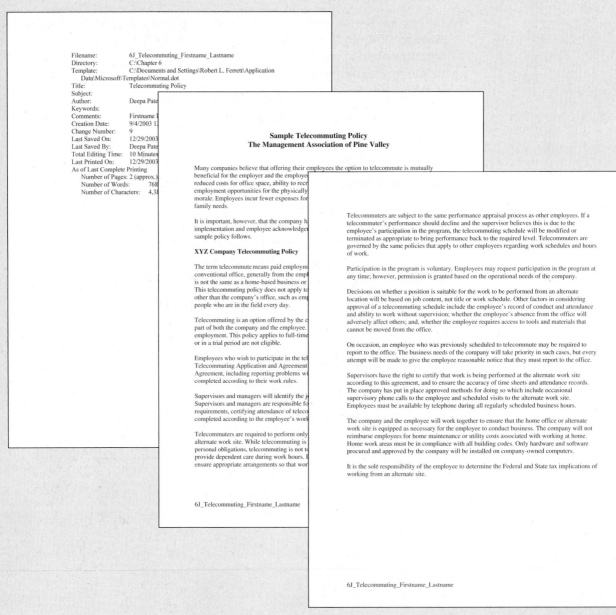

Figure 6.49

(Project 6J–Telecommuting continues on the next page)

(Project 6J–Telecommuting continued)

1. Start Word. From your student files, open **w06J_Telecommuting_ Draft1**. Save the file with the name **6J_Telecommuting_Firstname_ Lastname** in the same location as your other files from this textbook. In the same manner as you have done in previous documents, create a footer and insert the **AutoText** filename.

2. Compare and merge the document **w06J_Telecommuting_Draft2** into the current document. In the displayed box, be sure the first option— **Your document**—is selected, and then click **Continue with Merge**.

3. Accept changes until you reach the deletion of *means*. Reject the change from *means* to *is defined as*. Reject the deletion of the sentence that begins *It is the sole responsibility*. Accept all other changes and click Save.

4. Compare and merge the **w06J_Telecommuting_Draft3** document into the current document on your screen. Accept the default and click **Continue with Merge**. At the bottom of the document, reject the deletion of the sentence that begins *It is the sole responsibility*. Accept all other changes and save the document.

5. In the document summary, type **Telecommuting Policy** as the **Title**, **Deepa Patel** as the **Author**, and **The Management Association of Pine Valley** as the **Company**. Type your name in the **Comments** box.

6. Save the completed document. Preview and print the document, and then print the document properties. Save and close the document.

 You have completed Project 6J ————————————————————

Project 6K — Schedule

Objectives: *Use Comments in a Document, Track Changes in a Document, Review and Modify Document Properties, and Circulate Documents for Review.*

In the following Mastery Assessment, you will edit a document regarding training sessions and seminars that has already been edited extensively by a colleague. You will make changes, and then print the document displaying all of the changes and comments. Your completed document will look similar to the one shown in Figure 6.50. You will save your document as *6K_Schedule_Firstname_Lastname*.

1. Start Word. From your student files, open **w06K_Schedule**. Save the file with the name **6K_Schedule_Firstname_Lastname** in the same location as your other files. In the same manner as you have done in previous documents, display the footer and insert the **AutoText** filename.

(Project 6K–Schedule continues on the next page)

(Project 6K–Schedule continued)

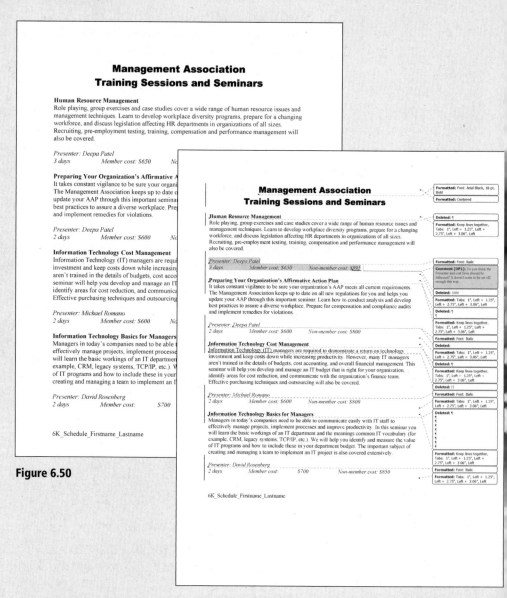

Figure 6.50

2. Turn on the Reviewing toolbar and, if necessary, turn on **Track Changes**. If necessary, turn on balloons for all tracked changes.

3. At the end of each Training Session description, the name of the Presenter is listed, followed in the next line by the date and cost. Go through the document and make all of these line pairs **Italic**. This will add additional tracked changes, but in a different color to identify you as a new reviewer.

(Project 6K–Schedule continues on the next page)

(Project 6K–Schedule continued)

4. In the middle of page 1, locate the first line following the *Information Technology Cost Management* heading, select *IT* (the first word in the sentence), and then replace it with **Information Technology (IT)**

5. Scroll down to examine the numerous changes to the document. To print these tracked changes, from the **Print** dialog box, click the **Print what** arrow, and then click **Document showing markup**. Under **Page range**, click the **Pages** option button, and then in the **Pages** box, type **1** so that only the first page prints. Click **OK**.

6. On the Reviewing toolbar, click the **Display for Review arrow**, and then click **Final** to see what the final document will look like. Print only the first page.

7. In the document summary, add your name and the current date to the **Comments** area. Change the **Title** to **Training Sessions and Seminars** and change the **Company** to **The Management Association of Pine Valley**

8. If your email system is set to do so, send the document as an email attachment to a friend or to yourself. Save your changes and close the document.

End **You have completed Project 6K** ——————————————

Project 6L — Resume

Objectives: *Create a Document Using a Template and Review and Modify Document Properties.*

Your resume is the first thing a prospective employer sees. Two things are important in an effective resume: the look of the document and the information about yourself. A professional-looking resume will give you a much better chance of having the potential employer take the time to read about your qualifications. In this project, you will create and save your resume as *6L_Resume_Firstname_Lastname*.

1. Create a new document using the **Professional Resume** template in the **Other Documents tab** of the **Templates** dialog box. Save the document as **6L_Resume_Firstname_Lastname**

2. At the top of the resume, enter your address and phone number as indicated by the placeholder text.

3. Write an objective for a job you are considering now or in the future after you have completed more education.

4. Replace the information in the various categories with your own information. If you have had only one job, delete the other job headings and their associated information.

5. Under *Education*, add any certificates or degrees you have. If you have not yet earned a certificate or degree, enter the expected date of certificate completion or graduation. Add any honors you have received, and/or your grade point average if it is above 3.0 on a 4.0 scale. Be sure you include your major, if you have one.

6. Add any interests where indicated, and then delete the *Tips* section, unless you have a category you would like to add (such as Public Service).

7. Go to the **Document Properties** dialog box and add your name in the **Author** box and the name of this document in the **Title** box. Type your college name for the **Company** name. In the **Comments** area, add the current date. Save your work and close the document. You might want to keep this file and update it whenever appropriate.

End **You have completed Project 6L** ────────────

Project 6M—Lightning

Objectives: *Use Comments in a Document and Review and Modify Document Properties.*

In this project, you will add and edit comments in a draft copy of a lightning action plan document. You will save the document as *6M_Lightning_Firstname_Lastname*.

1. Locate and open **w06M_Lightning**. Save it as **6M_Lightning_Firstname_Lastname** with your other files. As you have with previous files, display the footer area and insert the **AutoText** filename.

2. Turn on the **Reviewing** toolbar and open the **reviewing pane**.

3. Display the Properties sheet, write down the existing **User Information**, and then change the user information to your name and initials.

4. Look through the document and add two comments on any topic of your choice.

5. Respond to the comments of Satarkta Kalam as if you were a member of the team working on the document and knew the answers to his questions. Search the Web to find a site with information about lightning safety for outdoor workers and add a sentence about the site. Add a hyperlink to a word or phrase in the new sentence that will take the reader to the site you have found.

6. Restore the **User Information** to the original name and initials. Save the document, print it, and then close the file.

 End You have completed Project 6M ——————

On the Internet

Downloading a Template from the Office Web Site

In this chapter you created a professional-looking memo using a template that was stored on your computer. Many templates are installed with Microsoft Office, but one that is exactly right for your purpose may not be included. Microsoft has an Internet site that makes many additional templates available.

1. Be sure that you are connected to the Internet. Open Word. In the **New Document** task pane, under **Templates**, click **Templates on Office Online**.

2. On the Templates page of Microsoft Office Online, scroll down to see the categories of templates that are available to you. Click on some of the categories to see what you can download.

3. Click the **Back** button until the screen returns to the Template page.

4. Under the **Health Care and Wellness** category, click **Diet and Exercise**. Click one of the templates that looks interesting to you. Make sure you select one that has the Word icon to the left of the template name. This list also includes Excel, PowerPoint, and Access templates. Notice the template is previewed on the screen.

5. If you are working in a lab, check to make sure you can download files. If it is permitted, click the **Download Now** button. The template displays with instructions explaining how to use the template.

6. Follow the instructions and practice using the template you downloaded.

7. When you are done, close the file without saving changes and then close Word. Remember that even though you have not saved your changes, the template is now available on the computer.

Sending a Document for Review

In this chapter you practiced sending an email with a document attached. You can learn more about sending documents for review by examining some of the Word Help topics on the subject. Word includes a reviewing feature that makes the process much more interactive than attaching an email. When you send a document using the *Mail Recipient (for Review)* command instead of the *Mail Recipient (as Attachment)* command, the program keeps track of your messages, flags them, and turns on the Track Changes feature when the document is returned.

1. Start Word. In the **Type a Question for Help** box, type **mail for review** and press Enter.

2. Examine the list of topics that displays in the Search Results task pane. From this list of help topics, click **About sending a file for review** and read the results. At the top of the Help window, click the **Show All** button, and then print these instructions if you want.

3. In a blank document, write two brief paragraphs about how and when you might use email to work collaboratively on a document. In the Search Results pane, click **Send a document in e-mail**, and then click **Send a document for review**. Notice the restrictions on the email programs that will work for this procedure.

4. If you are using one of these email programs and have permission to do so, follow the instructions to create and send this document to a friend. In the email message, ask the friend to make several changes and send the message back.

5. When you get the message back, in the Search Results pane, click **End a review cycle**. Read the instructions. End the review cycle and respond to the tracked changes.

6. Close the Help window and the Help task pane, close your document without saving the changes, and exit Word.

7 chapterseven

Working with Tables and Graphics

In this chapter, you will: complete these projects **and** practice these skills.

Project 7A **Creating a Custom Table**	**Objectives** • Create and Apply a Custom Table Style • Format Cells in a Table
Project 7B **Applying Advanced Table Features**	**Objectives** • Modify Table Properties • Use Advanced Table Features
Project 7C **Creating a Complex Table**	**Objective** • Draw a Complex Table
Project 7D **Inserting Objects in a Document**	**Objectives** • Insert Objects in a Document • Modify an Image

Oceana Palm Grill

Oceana Palm Grill is a chain of 25 upscale, casual, full-service restaurants based in Austin, Texas. The company opened its first restaurant in 1975 and now operates 25 outlets in the Austin and Dallas areas. Plans call for 15 additional restaurants to be opened in North Carolina and Florida by 2008. These ambitious plans will require the company to bring in new investors, develop new menus, and recruit new employees, all while adhering to the company's strict quality guidelines and maintaining its reputation for excellent service.

© Getty Images, Inc.

Working with Tables and Graphics

To create consistent-looking tables, Word enables you to create custom table styles in the same way you create styles for characters, paragraphs, and lists. These styles control the structure of the table and the formatting of the text in the cells. Advanced table features enable you to use a vertical text orientation, to merge cells together to create more effective headings, and to align text in cells horizontally as well as vertically. You can also wrap text around a table. Text in cells can be sorted, and numbers can be added using formulas. Free-form tables can be created using an electronic pencil and eraser and other tools from the Tables and Borders toolbar.

Objects, such as tables from Excel and graphics from Web sites, can be imported into Word. With special formatting tools, you can rotate an object, resize it, and change the contrast and brightness.

7A

Project 7A **Grill Menu**

Styles are used to perform several formatting procedures at once. In this project, you will create and use a table style. You also will apply special formatting tools to modify text formatting in table cells.

In Activities 7.1 through 7.5, you will create a table style and apply it to a draft of a new lunch menu for the Oceana Palm Grill. You will align text in a cell both horizontally and vertically, change text direction in a cell, and merge cells. Your completed document will look similar to Figure 7.1. You will save your document as *7A_Grill_Menu_Firstname_Lastname.*

Proposed lunch menu, Orlando, Florida: Restaurant scheduled to open on October 5

Note: Prices below are for formatting purposes only. Final pricing to be determined.

Oceana Palm Grill
Lunch

Appetizers		
Blue Crab Chowder	$5.25
Made with a broth of tomato, basil, and lobster	
Roasted Fresh Artichoke	$4.50
Served with creamy dipping sauce	
Nicoise Salad	$12.95
Seared tuna in olive oil with citrus-pomegranate vinaigrette	
Caesar Salad	$8.95
With grated Reggiano Parmesan	
With grilled marinated chicken	$10.00
With grilled shrimp	$11.50

Main Courses

Herb Crusted Salmon	$12.95
Served with fresh vegetables, potatoes Anna, and a light lemon sauce	
Sautéed Gulf Shrimp	$15.50
Served over homemade linguini with roasted peppers and tomatoes and a bit of garlic	
Roasted Portabello Mushroom	$12.00
Served with ratatouille over fresh fettuccine	
Charbroiled Prime Burger	$10.50
Grilled to your specification with your choice of toppings and served with spiced fries and homemade mayonnaise	

Lunch menu is available from 11 a.m. until 2 p.m.

Executive Chef — Donna Rohan Kurian

7A_Grill_Menu_Firstname_Lastname

Figure 7.1
Project 7A—Grill Menu

Objective 1
Create and Apply a Custom Table Style

Recall that a *style* is a combination of formatting steps, such as font, font size, and indentation, that you name and store as a set. You can create a table style to use over and over again, giving your tables a consistent format. For example, the Oceana Palm Grill uses a Word table to create all of its menus. By developing a table style, each new menu can be formatted with the same distinctive style.

Activity 7.1 Creating a Table Style

When you create a table style, you can apply formats, such as borders, to the entire table, and you can add special formats to individual parts of the table, such as applying shading to specific rows and columns.

1 On the Standard toolbar, click the **Open** button. Navigate to the location where the student files for this textbook are stored. Locate and open **w07A_Grill_Menu**. Save the file as **7A_Grill_Menu_Firstname_ Lastname** creating a new folder for Chapter 7 if you want to do so.

2 On the Standard toolbar, click the **Zoom button arrow** `100%`, and then click **Page Width**. If necessary, on the Standard toolbar, click the Show/Hide ¶ button to show formatting marks.

3 From the **Format** menu, click **Styles and Formatting**.

The Styles and Formatting task pane opens.

4 At the top of the **Styles and Formatting** task pane, click **New Style**.

The New Style dialog box displays. See Figure 7.2.

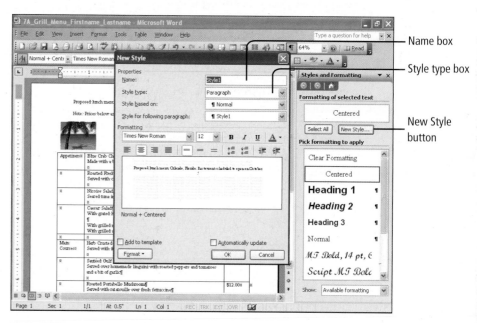

Figure 7.2

5 In the **New Style** dialog box, under **Properties**, in the **Name** box type **Oceana Grill** Click the **Style type arrow** and from the displayed list, click **Table**.

A sample table displays in the preview area. Under Formatting, notice that the default setting is to apply the formatting to the *Whole table*, as shown in Figure 7.3.

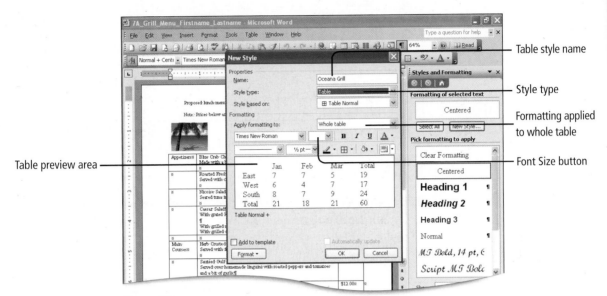

Figure 7.3

Table style name

Style type

Formatting applied to whole table

Font Size button

Table preview area

6 Under **Formatting**, be sure that **Whole table** is displayed in the **Apply formatting to** box, and immediately below the box, locate the small two-row toolbar in the **New Style** dialog box. Click the **Font button arrow** Times New Roman, scroll up or down as necessary, and then click **Comic Sans MS**. Click the **Font Size button arrow** 12 —the button will be blank—and then click **12**.

7 On the **New Style** dialog box toolbar, click the **Border button arrow**, and then click **No Border**.

The style is set to format an entire table with Comic Sans MS 12 point font and to remove all border lines. The new style settings display below the preview area. Compare your New Style dialog box with Figure 7.4.

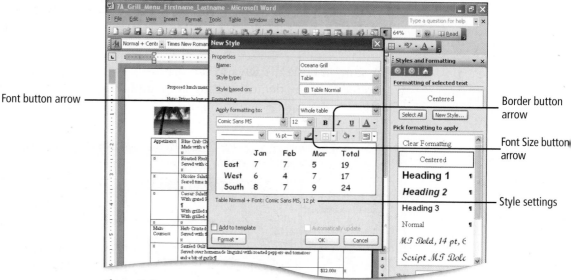

Font button arrow

Border button arrow

Font Size button arrow

Style settings

Figure 7.4

8 Under **Formatting**, click the **Apply formatting to arrow**, and then click **Left column**.

Any formatting changes you make at this point will affect only the left column of the table.

9 On the **New Style** dialog box toolbar, click the **Bold** button **B**, and then click the **Italic** button **I**.

10 On the **New Style** dialog box toolbar, click the **Shading Color button arrow**, and then in the first row, click the fourth color—**Gray-12.5%**.

When you use the new style, the left column of the table will be formatted with bold and italic text, and the column will be shaded in gray. A preview of the style displays in the preview area, as shown in Figure 7.5.

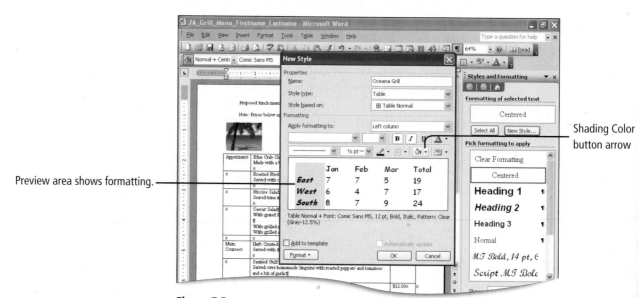

Preview area shows formatting.

Shading Color button arrow

Figure 7.5

11 Under **Formatting**, click the **Apply formatting to arrow**, and then click **Last row**.

Any formatting changes you make at this point will affect only the last row of the table.

12 On the **New Style** dialog box toolbar, click the **Italic** button I.

13 At the bottom of the **New Style** dialog box, click **OK**.

The style is saved with the document and displays in the Styles and Formatting task pane as a table style. A small boxed grid to the right of the style name *Oceana Grill* indicates that it is a table style, as shown in Figure 7.6.

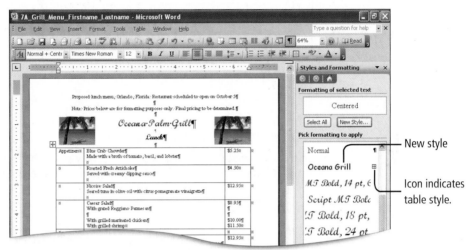

Figure 7.6

14 On the Standard toolbar, click the **Save** button 🖫.

Activity 7.2 Applying a Table Style

Applying a table style is a one-click process. After applying the style to your table, you can make further adjustments to the style.

1 Click anywhere in the menu table in the **7A_Grill_Menu_Firstname_Lastname** document.

You do not need to select the whole table to apply a table style; it is sufficient to position the insertion point somewhere in the table.

2 In the **Styles and Formatting** task pane, click the **Oceana Grill** style.

The formatting you created in the new table style is applied to the entire table, although the formatting to the last row will not be noticeable until text is entered. Light borders still display, but these are cell location indicators and will not print. See Figure 7.7.

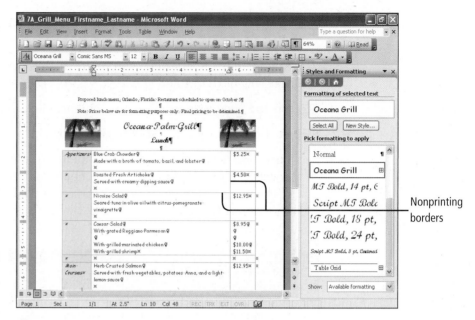

Nonprinting borders

Figure 7.7

3 On the Standard toolbar, click the **Print Preview** button. Examine the table to verify that the light borders will not print. When you are through, on the Print Preview toolbar, click the **Close Preview** button.

4 At the top of the table, move the pointer over the top edge of the middle column until it displays as a **black down arrow**, and then click once to select the column. Alternatively, click anywhere in the middle column and, from the Table menu, point to Select, and then click Column.

The middle column is selected.

5 On the Formatting toolbar, click the **Center** button.

Within each row, the text in the middle column is centered.

6 Use the technique you just practiced to select the right column of the table. On the Formatting toolbar, click the **Align Right** button.

Within each row, the text in the right column is aligned right. Because all of the menu prices use two decimal points, the numbers align appropriately.

7 On the Standard toolbar, click the **Print Preview** button 🔍. Compare your screen with Figure 7.8.

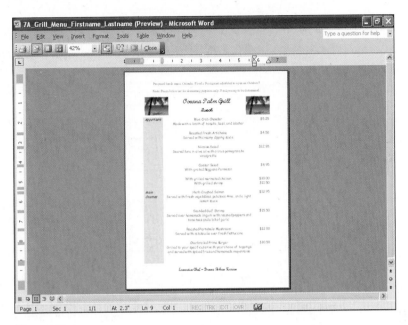

Figure 7.8

8 On the Print Preview toolbar, click the **Close Preview** button `Close`. On the title bar of the **Styles and Formatting** task pane, click the **Close** button ✖. On the Standard toolbar, click the **Save** button 💾.

Objective 2
Format Cells in a Table

You have practiced formatting text in the cells of a table using the same formatting features that are available for use with paragraph text. These include text formatting such as bold and italic and text alignment such as centering. There are some special formatting features available in tables that are not available for use with paragraph text. These include vertical alignment in a cell and changing text direction from horizontal to vertical. When you want text to span multiple columns or rows, a table feature enables you to merge cells.

Activity 7.3 Merging Cells

When you need a row or column heading to extend beyond one cell, merge adjacent cells. In this activity, you will use the Tables and Borders toolbar to merge cells. The Tables and Borders toolbar includes the buttons shown in Figure 7.9.

Tables and Borders Toolbar Buttons

Name	Button	Description
Draw Table		Creates a custom table.
Eraser		Removes lines or portions of lines in a table.
Line Style		Displays available line styles.
Line Weight		Displays available line weights.
Border Color		Displays border color choices.
Outside Border		Displays border styles.
Shading Color		Displays shading color choices.
Insert Table		Displays the Insert Table dialog box.
Merge Cells		Combines selected cells into one cell.
Split Cells		Divides the selected cell into smaller cells.
Align		Displays horizontal and vertical cell alignment choices.
Distribute Rows Evenly		Makes selected row heights uniform.
Distribute Columns Evenly		Makes selected column widths uniform.
Table AutoFormat		Displays the Table AutoFormat dialog box.
Change Text Direction		Changes horizontal text to vertical and vertical text to horizontal text.
Sort Ascending		Sorts selected cells in ascending (a to z) order.
Sort Descending		Sorts selected cells in descending (z to a) order.
AutoSum		Sums the numbers in the row to the left of, or the column above, the selected cell.

Figure 7.9

1 From the **View** menu, point to **Toolbars**, and then click **Tables and Borders**.

The Tables and Borders toolbar displays. The toolbar may be docked with the other toolbars or floating above the text.

2 Locate the upper left cell of the menu table, which contains *Appetizers*. Drag downward to select the first cell and the next three empty cells, as shown in Figure 7.10.

Selected cells ——

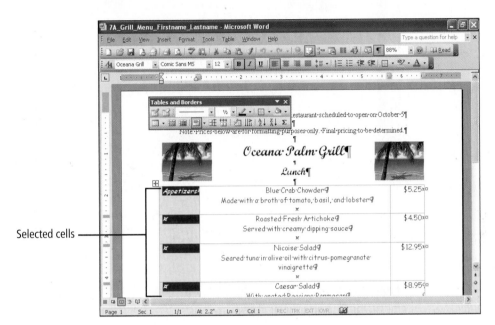

Figure 7.10

3 On the Tables and Borders toolbar, click the **Merge Cells** button ⊞.

The four cells are merged into one, as shown in Figure 7.11.

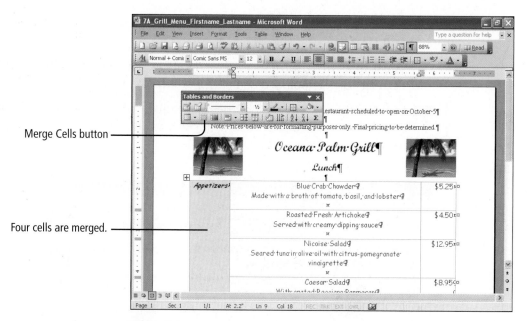

Merge Cells button

Four cells are merged.

Figure 7.11

4 Scroll down until you can see the last five rows of the table. Locate the *Main Courses* cell in the first column, and then drag downward to select that cell and the next three empty cells. Do not select the last cell in the column.

5 On the Tables and Borders toolbar, click the **Merge Cells** button.

The four cells are merged into one.

6 Move the pointer to the left of the last row of the table until it changes into a white arrow, and then click once to select the entire row. Alternatively, click in the first cell of the last row and drag to the right until all three cells are selected.

7 On the Tables and Borders toolbar, click the **Merge Cells** button.

The three cells are merged into one.

8 Click to position the insertion point in the last row of the table; the insertion point will blink at the right end. On the Formatting toolbar, click the **Center** button. Type **Lunch menu is available from 11 a.m. until 2 p.m.**

The text is centered across the bottom of the table. See Figure 7.12.

Note — Formatting Changes

Notice that the text you typed in the merged cell is bold and italic, and the cell is shaded, although you did not specify bold when you created the Oceana Grill table style. When you merge cells horizontally, the new cell retains the formatting of the leftmost cell. When you merge cells vertically, the new cell retains the formatting of the topmost cell.

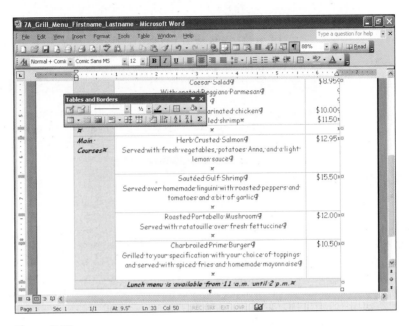

Figure 7.12

9 Move the pointer to the left of the last row of the table until it changes into a white arrow, and then click once to select the row. On the Formatting toolbar, click the **Bold** button **B** to deselect bold. On the Formatting toolbar, click the **Font Size button arrow** `12 ▾`, and then click **10**.

10 On the Standard toolbar, click the **Save** button.

Activity 7.4 Changing Text Direction

Word tables include a feature that enables you to change the text direction. This is effective for column titles that do not fit at the top of narrow columns or for row headings that cover multiple rows.

1 Click to position the insertion point anywhere in the words *Main Courses*.

2 In the Tables and Borders toolbar, click the **Change Text Direction** button ▥.

The text direction is changed to vertical, as shown in Figure 7.13.

Vertical text ───────

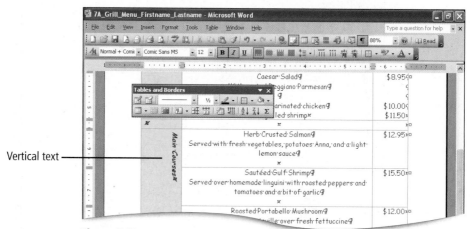

Figure 7.13

3 In the Tables and Borders toolbar, click the **Change Text Direction** button ▥ again.

The text remains vertical, but faces the other direction and moves to the lower portion of the cell.

4 In the Tables and Borders toolbar, click the **Change Text Direction** button ▥ again.

The text returns to horizontal. The Change Text Direction button is a three-way switch, moving among horizontal text and two vertical text orientations.

5 In the Tables and Borders toolbar, click the **Change Text Direction** button [ ] twice. Move the insertion point over the beginning of the word *Main*.

Notice that the text select pointer [I] is horizontal.

6 Drag upward to select **Main Courses**. On the Formatting toolbar, click the **Font Size button arrow** [12 ▼], and then click **28**.

The font size increases, as shown in Figure 7.14.

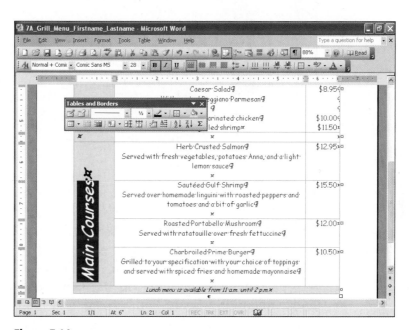

Figure 7.14

7 Scroll up and position the insertion point in the *Appetizers* cell. In the Tables and Borders toolbar, click the **Change Text Direction** button [ ] twice.

8 Move the pointer over the beginning of the word *Appetizers*. Drag up to select **Appetizers**. On the Formatting toolbar, click the **Font Size button arrow** [12 ▼], and then click **28**. Compare your screen with Figure 7.15.

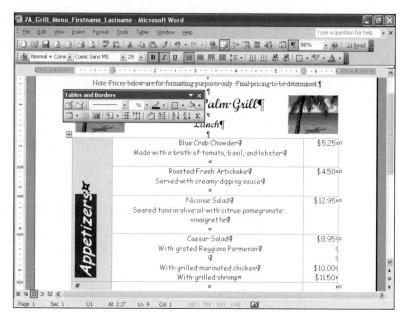

Figure 7.15

9 On the Standard toolbar, click the **Save** button ⊞.

Activity 7.5 Changing Text Position in a Cell

With paragraph text outside of a table, you are limited to horizontal alignment. In table cells, you can align text left, center, and right, as well as top, center, and bottom. You also can use all possible combinations of horizontal and vertical alignment, such as top left or bottom right.

1 Click to position the insertion point anywhere in the *Appetizers* cell.

2 On the Tables and Borders toolbar, click the **Align button arrow** ▤ ▾.

The nine possible alignment combinations are displayed, as shown in Figure 7.16.

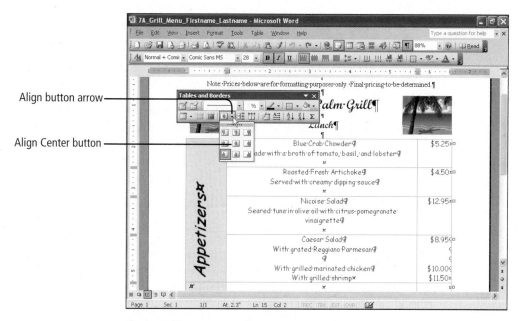

Align button arrow—

Align Center button—

Figure 7.16

3 In the second row, click the second alignment—**Align Center**.

The text is centered left-to-right and top-to-bottom, as shown in Figure 7.17.

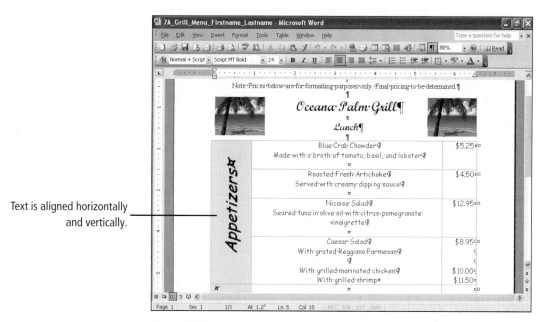

Text is aligned horizontally and vertically.

Figure 7.17

4 Scroll down and click to position the insertion point anywhere in the *Main Courses* cell. On the Tables and Borders toolbar, click the **Align button arrow** ▭▾ and from the displayed menu, click **Align Center**.

5 From the **View** menu, click **Header and Footer**. On the Header and Footer toolbar, click the **Switch Between Header and Footer** button ▣.

6 On the Header and Footer toolbar, click the **Insert AutoText** button `Insert AutoText ▾`, and then click **Filename**.

The file name is inserted in the footer.

7 On the Header and Footer toolbar, click the **Close** button `Close`. Right-click any toolbar, and from the displayed list, click **Tables and Borders** to turn off the display of the toolbar.

8 On the Standard toolbar, click the **Save** button ▣.

9 On the Standard toolbar, click the **Print Preview** button ▣. Take a moment to check your work. On the Print Preview toolbar, click the **Close Preview** button `Close`.

10 Make any necessary changes to your document. When you are satisfied, on the Standard toolbar, click the **Print** button ▣. Close the document, saving any changes.

End You have completed Project 7A ————————————————————

Project 7B **Teen Safety**

Word includes features to sort and summarize data in a table. Additionally, table properties can be adjusted to wrap text around a small table and to make text fit in a specified cell size.

In Activities 7.6 through 7.11, you will edit a memo about teen worker safety in Oceana Palm Grill restaurants. You will wrap text around a table and fit text in a cell. You will also sort information in a table, sum columns of numbers in a table, and add table captions. Your completed document will look similar to Figure 7.18. You will save your document as *7B_Teen_Safety_Firstname_Lastname.*

 Oceana Palm Grill

MEMO

To: Devin Washington, Vice President, Quality and Customer Service

From: Laura Mabry Hernandez, Vice President, Human Resources

Date: July 7

Subject: Teen Worker Safety in Our Restaurants

Table 1. Oceana Teen Injuries

Year	Teen Injuries
2000	47
2001	51
2002	39
2003	38

Approximately 15% of our current workforce is between 16 and 20 years old. As we expand into new geographic areas, that percentage is expected to increase. The Occupational Safety and Health Administration (OSHA) estimates that nationwide approximately 30% of food service employees are under 20 years old.

In the next few months, OSHA is expected to announce a new safety program for teen workers. In anticipation of this new program, I have put together some data about injuries. Table 1 shows injuries to our teenage employees from 2000-2003. Reported injuries to teenage restaurant workers in the eight-county area are shown in Table 2, although the data is by fiscal year (July through June) and does not directly match our company data.

Table 2. Teen Worker Injuries in Restaurants

	FY 99-00	FY 00-01	FY 01-02	FY 02-03
Burns	687	719	722	672
Cuts	478	515	574	617
Sprains	247	244	316	291
Fractures	29	31	19	40
Total	1,441	1,509	1,631	1,620

7B_Teen_Safety_Firstname_Lastname

Figure 7.18

Objective 3
Modify Table Properties

Tables have properties that can be adjusted. For example, from the Table Properties dialog box you can wrap text around small tables, set row height and column width, set vertical alignment in cells, and force text to fit in a specified column width.

Activity 7.6 Wrapping Text Around Tables

1 On the Standard toolbar, click the **Open** button 📷. Navigate to the location where the student files for this textbook are stored. Locate and open **w07B_Teen_Safety**. Save the file as **7B_Teen_Safety_ Firstname_Lastname** in the folder where you are storing your projects for this chapter.

2 On the Standard toolbar, click the **Zoom button arrow** 100% ▾, and then click **Page Width**. If necessary, on the Standard toolbar, click the Show/Hide ¶ button to show formatting marks.

3 Scroll down to display the small *Teen Injuries* table, and then click to position the insertion point anywhere in the table.

4 From the **Table** menu, click **Table Properties**, and then in the displayed **Table Properties** dialog box, click the **Table tab**.

The Table tab of the Table Properties dialog box displays, as shown in Figure 7.19.

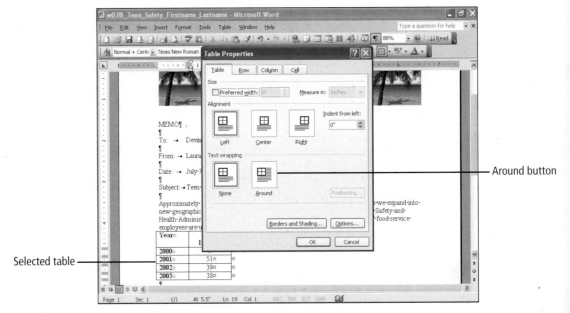

Figure 7.19

5 Under **Text wrapping**, click **Around**, and then click **OK**.

Text wraps around the right side of the table.

6 Move the pointer over the table.

The **_table move handle_** displays above the upper left corner of the table, as shown in Figure 7.20. Using the table move handle, you can move the table without first selecting it.

Move handle ———

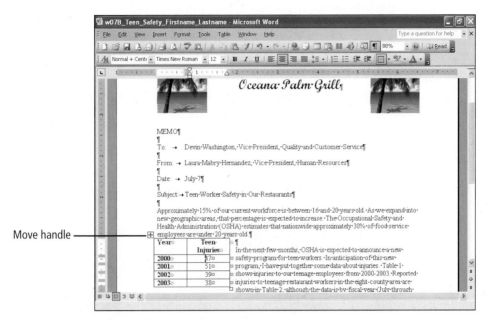

Figure 7.20

7 Point to the table move handle to display the move pointer ⊕, and then drag the table upward until the dotted box representing the table is even with the paragraph that begins *Approximately 15% of our current workforce.*

Compare your table with Figure 7.21.

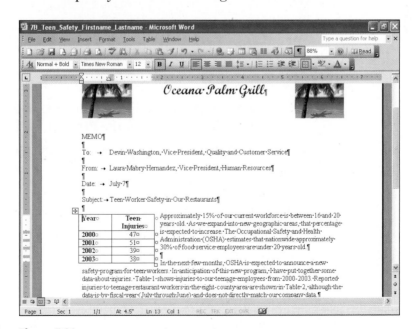

Figure 7.21

8 On the Standard toolbar, click the **Save** button 🖫.

Activity 7.7 Fitting Text in a Cell

If you want to squeeze a little more text into a cell or reduce two text lines to one, the text can be compressed to exactly the right size by using table properties.

1 In the *Teen Injuries* table, click to position the insertion point in the *Teen Injuries* cell.

Notice that the text in this cell wraps to a second line, but could almost fit on one line.

2 From the **Table** menu, click **Table Properties**, and then click the **Cell tab**.

The Cell tab of the Table Properties dialog box displays.

3 In the lower right corner, click **Options**.

The Cell Options dialog box displays, as shown in Figure 7.22.

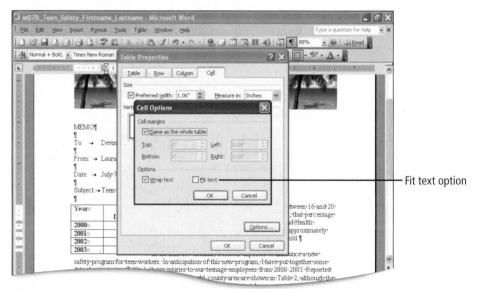
— Fit text option

Figure 7.22

4 In the **Cell Options** dialog box, under **Options**, clear the **Wrap text** check box, and then select the **Fit text** check box.

5 In the **Cell Options** dialog box, click **OK**. In the **Table Properties** dialog box, click **OK**.

The text is compressed to fit on one line, as shown in Figure 7.23. A light blue line under the text indicates that the Fit text feature has been used in this cell.

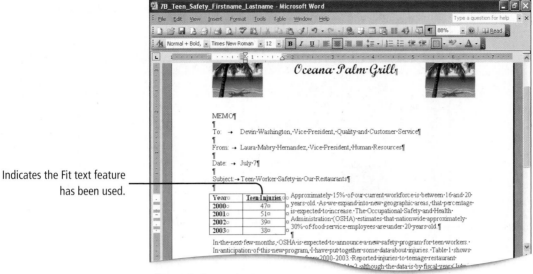

Indicates the Fit text feature has been used.

Figure 7.23

6 On the Standard toolbar, click the **Save** button ▣.

Objective 4
Use Advanced Table Features

Word tables have a few spreadsheet capabilities. For example, you can *sort*—organize in a particular order—the data in a table numerically or alphabetically in ascending or descending order on any of the columns. You also can use a limited group of formulas in a cell. These can be used to add a column or row or to calculate an average. Unlike a spreadsheet, however, if you change a number in a cell that is used in a formula, the formula must be recalculated manually.

Captions are titles that can be added to Word objects and are numbered sequentially as they are added. You can add a caption to each table in a document, which makes it easier to refer to the tables in the text.

Activity 7.8 Sorting Tables by Category

Tables can be sorted by category (column) either alphabetically or numerically. No matter which column you sort on, the rows remain intact.

1 In the second table, at the bottom of the document, click anywhere to position the insertion point.

The table does not need to be selected to perform a sort operation.

2 From the **Table** menu, click **Sort**.

The table is selected, and the Sort dialog box opens, as shown in Figure 7.24.

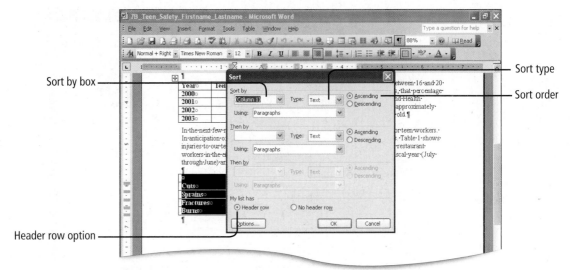

Sort by box

Sort type

Sort order

Header row option

Figure 7.24

3 At the bottom of the dialog box, under **My list has**, be sure the **Header row** option button is selected. At the top of the dialog box, under **Sort by**, notice that the sort will be performed based on the data in **Column 1**. Accept all of the other defaults and click **OK**.

The text is sorted in alphabetical order by type of injury—the data in Column 1. Although the order of the rows has been changed to alphabetic order, the data attached to each type of injury remains with its appropriate row. If you do not indicate that the table has a header (column title) row, the first cell will be sorted along with the other cells in the column.

4 From the **Table** menu, click **Sort** again. Click the **Sort by arrow**, and then click **FY 02-03**.

This will sort by the numbers in the last column.

5 Under **Sort by**, click the **Descending** option button.

This will sort the numbers from highest to lowest.

6 At the bottom of the **Sort** dialog box, click **OK**. Click anywhere in the document to deselect the table.

This process reordered the rows. They are no longer in alphabetic order by type of injury; rather, they are in numerical order based on the data for the fiscal year 2002–2003, from the highest number of injuries to the lowest. See Figure 7.25.

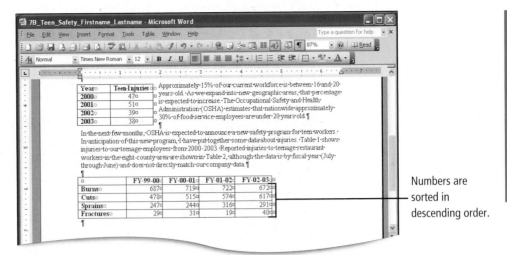

Figure 7.25

Numbers are sorted in descending order.

---

7 On the Standard toolbar, click the **Save** button.

Activity 7.9 Using Formulas in Tables

When you need to analyze numbers, it is best to use a spreadsheet program such as Microsoft Excel. However, when you need to do a simple calculation in Word, you can insert a formula in a table.

1 In the table at the bottom of the page, click in the last row to position the insertion point. From the **Table** menu, point to **Insert**, and then click **Rows Below**.

A new row is added to the table.

Another Way

To Add Rows to a Table

You can add a row to the bottom of a table by pressing the Tab key when the insertion point is in the lower-right cell of the table. Also, when one or more rows are selected, the Insert Table button in the Standard toolbar changes to an Insert Rows button, which will insert the same number of blank rows as the number of existing rows that are selected.

---

2 Click in the first cell of the new row, type **Total** and then press ⌨Tab to move to the second cell in the row.

3 From the **Table** menu, click **Formula**.

The Formula dialog box displays. The default formula is =SUM(ABOVE). This formula calculates the sum of the numbers in all of the cells above the current cell—up to the first empty cell or cell that contains text—and places the result in the current cell. You can specify a special number format—for example, the number of decimal places—and you can use the Paste function box to specify a function other than the sum.

4 Click the **Number format arrow** and from the displayed list, click **#,##0**.

This number format places a comma after every third digit and places a zero in empty cells. See Figure 7.26.

Default formula

Number format adds commas.

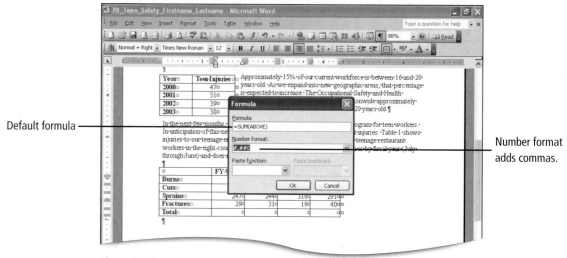

Figure 7.26

5 In the **Formula** dialog box, click **OK**.

The column is summed, and the total displays in the active cell. Notice that a comma has been added to the total. See Figure 7.27.

A comma has been added to the sum.

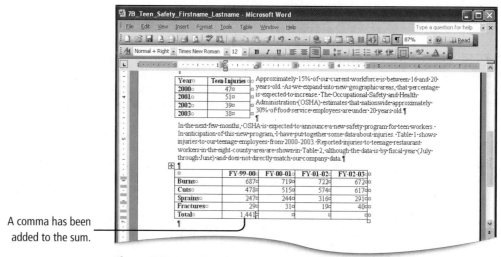

Figure 7.27

Alert!	**Be Careful with Column Headings**

If you are going to use formulas in a table, do not use numbers as column headings. In the column you just summed, a column heading such as *2000*, instead of a heading that began with text such as FY 99-00, would be included in the formula and the sum would have been in error by 2,000. Unlike an Excel spreadsheet, when using formulas, a Word table has no way to identify a numeric header as anything but a number.

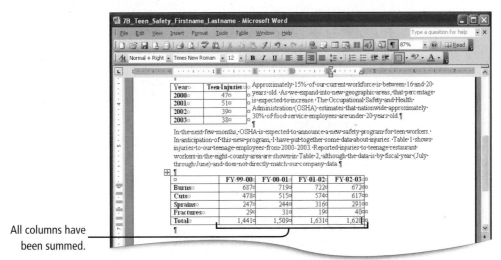

6 Repeat the procedure you used in Steps 3 through 5 to sum the other three columns of numbers. Compare your table with Figure 7.28.

All columns have been summed.

Figure 7.28

Note — Summing Multiple Rows

When you place a formula in a table, the default formula is =SUM(ABOVE), assuming there is a number in the cell above the selected cell. If there is a number in the cell to the left of the selected cell and no number in the cell above, the default is =SUM(LEFT). If you need to sum several rows, place formulas in the lower rows first. This will keep the cell above the selected cell empty so that the default choice is =SUM(LEFT) instead of =SUM(ABOVE). Also, do not leave a cell empty within a range if you want to sum the entire range. If there is no value, then enter a 0.

---

7 On the Standard toolbar, click the **Save** button.

Activity 7.10 Adding Captions to Tables

Captions make it easy to refer to a table or figure in a document that contains multiple objects.

1 Be sure the insertion point is still positioned somewhere in the lower table. From the **Insert** menu, point to **Reference**, and then click **Caption**.

The Caption dialog box displays. Because a table is selected, the default caption starts with *Table 1*. Word will assist you in numbering tables sequentially, as you will see as you progress through this activity.

2 Refer to Figure 7.29, and then after *Table 1* type a period, press Spacebar, and then type **Teen Worker Injuries in Restaurants**

Compare your Caption dialog box with Figure 7.29.

Table number ——

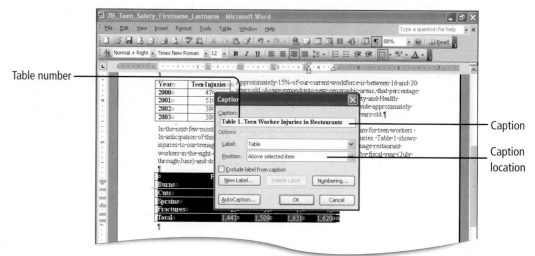

Caption

Caption location

Figure 7.29

3 At the bottom of the **Caption** dialog box, click **OK**.

The caption is added to the top of the table, as shown in Figure 7.30. A green, wavy line may also display under the *Table 1* text.

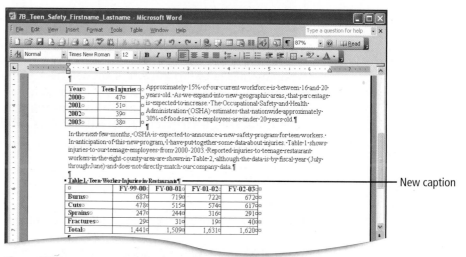

New caption

Figure 7.30

4 Position the insertion point anywhere in the upper table. From the **Insert** menu, point to **Reference**, and then click **Caption**.

Notice that the caption box displays *Table 1* because the selected table comes before the one to which you just added a caption. The bottom table will be renumbered as *Table 2* when you add the caption to the current table.

5 Under **Caption**, following *Table 1* type a period, press Spacebar, type **Oceana Teen Injuries** and then click **OK**.

The caption is added to the first table, and the second table is renumbered. See Figure 7.31.

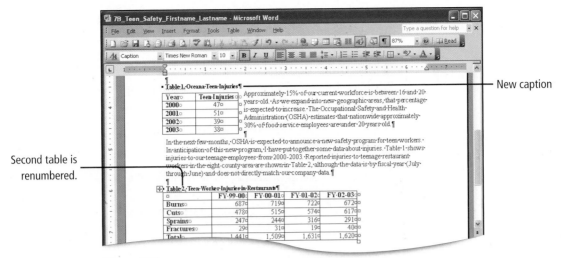

Second table is renumbered.

New caption

Figure 7.31

6 On the Standard toolbar, click the **Save** button.

Activity 7.11 Using the Toolbar to AutoFormat a Table

Recall that you can give your table a professional design by using any of the built-in table formats. This is quickly accomplished from the Table AutoFormat button on the Tables and Borders toolbar.

1 Click to position the insertion point anywhere in the lower table. If necessary, right-click any toolbar and click Tables and Borders.

The Tables and Borders toolbar displays.

2 On the Tables and Borders toolbar, click the **Table AutoFormat** button. In the **Table AutoFormat** dialog box, under **Table styles**, scroll down and click **Table Simple 3**.

A preview of the table displays in the Preview area. Compare your dialog box with Figure 7.32.

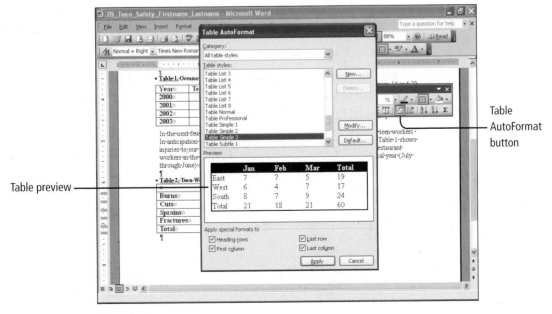

Table preview

Table AutoFormat button

Figure 7.32

3 At the bottom of the **Table AutoFormat** dialog box, click **Apply**.

The AutoFormat is applied to the table.

4 Use the procedure you practiced in Steps 2 and 3 to AutoFormat the other table using the **Table Simple 3** style. Close the Tables and Borders toolbar.

Compare your document with Figure 7.33.

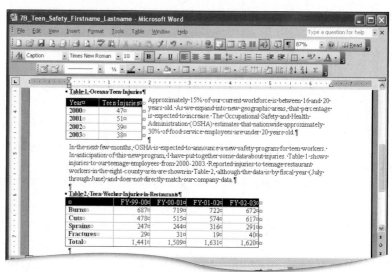

Figure 7.33

5 From the **View** menu, click **Header and Footer**. On the Header and Footer toolbar, click the **Switch Between Header and Footer** button.

6 On the Header and Footer toolbar, click the **Insert AutoText** button Insert AutoText ▾, and then click **Filename**.

The file name is inserted in the footer.

7 On the Header and Footer toolbar, click the **Close** button Close.

8 On the Standard toolbar, click the **Save** button.

9 On the Standard toolbar, click the **Print Preview** button. Take a moment to check your work. On the Print Preview toolbar, click the **Close Preview** button Close.

10 Make any necessary changes to your document. When you are satisfied, on the Standard toolbar, click the **Print** button. Close the document, saving any changes.

End You have completed Project 7B

Project 7C **Purchase Order**

When you create a table using the Insert Table button or the Insert command from the Table menu, the result is a table structure comprised of rows and columns of uniform size. Sometimes, however, you need the structure of a table coupled with the flexibility to form rows and columns of varying size and format. For example, a form, such as a purchase order, not only needs the structure of a table, but also needs to have some flexibility in the sizing and shading of cells and rows and in the alignment of text.

In Activities 7.12 through 7.15, you will create a purchase order for the Oceana Palm Grill. You will draw a table, add and erase lines, change column widths and row heights, and format the table. Your completed document will look similar to Figure 7.34. You will save your document as *7C_Purchase_Order_Firstname_Lastname.*

Oceana Palm Grill	P.O. Number	Vendor	Date	
	Quantity	Description	Unit Price	Total
	Authorization		Department	

7C_Purchase_Order_Firstname_Lastname

Figure 7.34

Objective 5
Draw a Complex Table

When you create a complex table using the Tables and Borders toolbar, you use an electronic pencil and eraser to sketch out the table shape you need. After the outline is created, you use the other buttons on the toolbar to refine the table format.

Activity 7.12 Drawing a Complex Table

When you use the Draw Table command, first draw the outside, rectangular border of the table.

1 Start Word. From the Standard toolbar, click the **New Blank Document** button 🗋. Save the file as **7C_Purchase_Order_Firstname_Lastname** in the folder where you are storing your projects for this chapter.

2 On the Standard toolbar, click the **Zoom button arrow** [100% ▾], and then click **75%**. If necessary, on the Standard toolbar, click the Show/Hide ¶ button to show formatting marks.

3 If the Tables and Borders toolbar is not displayed, right-click on any toolbar, and then click Tables and Borders.

The Tables and Borders toolbar displays, either floating on your screen or docked to the other toolbars.

4 On the Tables and Borders toolbar, click the **Draw Table** button 🗒, and then move the mouse pointer into the document area and notice the pencil shape of the pointer. On the Tables and Borders toolbar, click the **Line Style button arrow** [———— ▾] to display the list of line styles. Drag the scroll box down and click the style with two thin outside lines and a thick inside line.

5 Move the pointer into the document window and locate the vertical and horizontal rulers.

As you move the pointer within the document window, notice that faint dotted lines display in both the horizontal and vertical rulers. You will use these visual guides to determine the placement and dimensions of your table as you draw. Also notice that the Draw Table pointer looks like a pencil. See Figure 7.35.

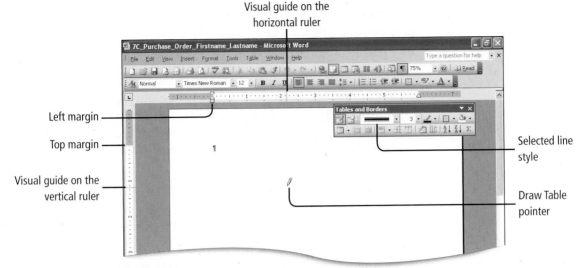

Visual guide on the horizontal ruler

Left margin

Top margin

Visual guide on the vertical ruler

Selected line style

Draw Table pointer

Figure 7.35

6 Move your pointer so that, in the **horizontal ruler**, the guide is positioned **0.5 inches to the *left* of the left margin**—in the shaded area. Then, move the pointer so that, in the **vertical ruler**, the guide is positioned **even with the top margin**. Refer to Figure 7.35 to locate the top margin in the horizontal ruler.

7 With your pointer positioned as described in Step 6, drag to the right to **6.5 inches on the horizontal ruler** (into the shaded area) and to **3.5 inches on the vertical ruler**. Release the mouse button. If you are not satisfied with your result, click the Undo button ⟲ ▾ and begin again.

You have created outside boundaries with dimensions of 3.5 inches high and 7 inches wide, as shown in Figure 7.36.

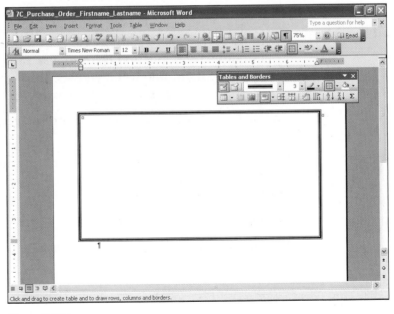

Figure 7.36

8 On the Standard toolbar, click the **Save** button ⊟.

Activity 7.13 Adding and Removing Table Lines

You can draw horizontal and vertical lines inside the table using the Draw Table pointer.

1 If necessary, click the **Draw Table** button ⬚ to activate the Draw Table pointer. Position the tip of the pencil pointer over the upper border of the table at **0.5 inch on the horizontal ruler**. Drag down, and when you see the dotted vertical line extending to the bottom table boundary, release the left mouse button.

A line in the same style as your border extends to the bottom table boundary. End-of-cell marks and the end-of-row mark indicate that you have created a Word table with a structure of two columns and one row. Compare your table with Figure 7.37.

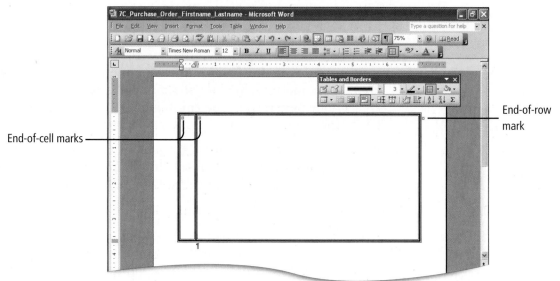

End-of-cell marks

End-of-row mark

Figure 7.37

2 With the **Draw Table** pointer still active, position the pointer on the right boundary of the first column at **1 inch on the vertical ruler**. Drag to the right, and when you see the dotted line extending to the right boundary, release the left mouse button.

A line in the same style as your border extends to the right table boundary.

3 Repeat this process to draw two more horizontal lines—one beginning at **2 inches on the vertical ruler** and one beginning at **3 inches on the vertical ruler**. If you are not satisfied with your result, click the **Undo** button ↩ and begin again.

Compare your table with Figure 7.38.

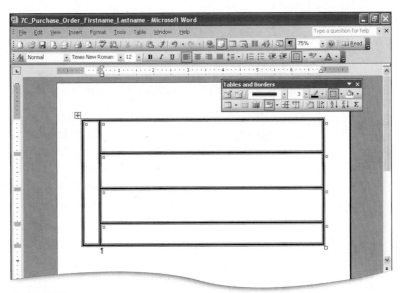

Figure 7.38

On the Tables and Borders toolbar, click the **Eraser** button .

The pointer becomes a small eraser.

Position the **Eraser** pointer on the second horizontal line within the table (not including the top border line), and then click the left mouse button.

The line is erased.

Position the pointer on the last horizontal line within the table (not including the bottom border line), and then click to erase it.

Compare your table with Figure 7.39.

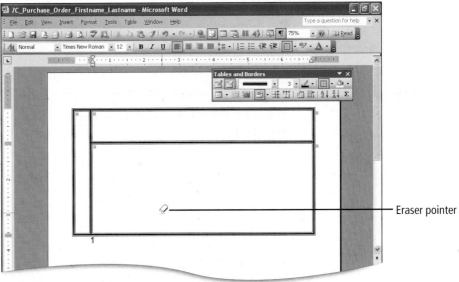

Eraser pointer

Figure 7.39

7 On the Tables and Borders toolbar, click the **Line Style arrow** [——— ▾], scroll up to the top of the list, and then click the first border style—a single solid line.

The Draw Table pointer becomes active.

8 In **Row 1**, **Column 2**, position your pencil pointer just below the top table border at approximately **2.5 inches on the horizontal ruler**. Drag down slightly, to the top border of the row below. In a similar manner, position your pencil pointer just below the top table border at approximately **4.5 inches on the horizontal ruler** and drag down slightly, to the top border of the row below.

Two vertical lines are added, as shown in Figure 7.40. You need not be positioned exactly at these measurements, because later you will use the Distribute Columns Evenly feature to set these measurements precisely.

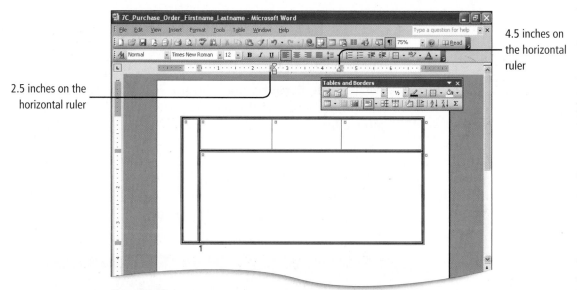

2.5 inches on the horizontal ruler

4.5 inches on the horizontal ruler

Figure 7.40

Alert! — **Accidentally Changing the Border**

If you select a different line style and then click directly on the border when attempting to draw a line in a table, you might change the line formatting of the border to the current line style selection. Click the Undo button and begin again.

9 In **Row 2**, position your pointer at the top edge of the row and draw three vertical lines to the bottom border at approximately **2 inches**, **3.75 inches**, and **5.5 inches on the horizontal ruler**.

10 In **Column 2**, position your pointer on the left border, and draw two horizontal lines extending to the right table boundary at approximately **0.5 inches** and **1.5 inches** on **the vertical ruler**.

11 On the Tables and Borders toolbar, click the **Line Style arrow** and click the first double-line border style. In **Column 2**, position your pointer on the left border at **3 inches on the vertical ruler** and draw a horizontal line extending to the right table boundary. Click the **Draw Table** button to return to the I-beam pointer.

Compare your table with Figure 7.41.

Single line at 0.5 inch on the vertical ruler

Single line at 1.5 inches on the vertical ruler

Double line at 3 inches on the vertical ruler

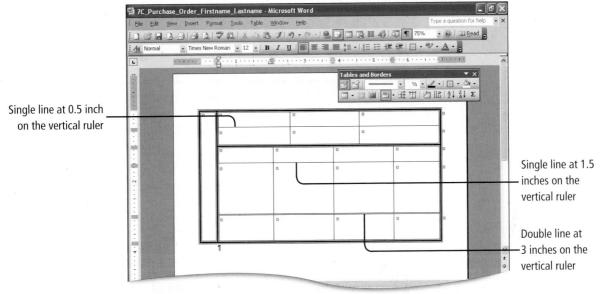

Figure 7.41

12 On the Standard toolbar, click the **Save** button.

Activity 7.14 Distributing Columns Evenly and Changing Text Direction

The ***Distribute Columns Evenly*** command formats columns so that their widths are equal within the boundaries that you select. A similar command—***Distribute Rows Evenly***—formats rows so that their heights are equal within the boundaries that you select.

1 Select, by dragging, the six cells that comprise **Columns 2**, **3**, and **4** in **Rows 1** and **2**.

2 On the Tables and Borders toolbar, click the **Distribute Columns Evenly** button.

The columns within the two rows are now equal in width and are evenly spaced, as shown in Figure 7.42.

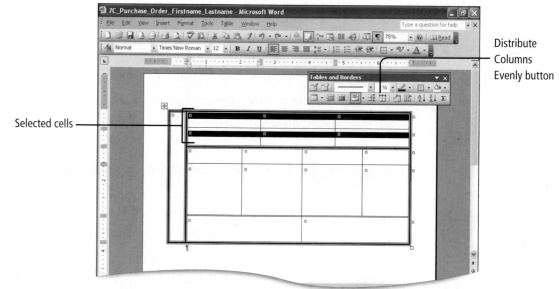

Distribute
Columns
Evenly button

Selected cells

Figure 7.42

3 On the Tables and Borders toolbar, click the **Eraser** button [icon]. In Row 5, use the **Eraser** pointer to erase the first and third single-line column borders.

4 On the Tables and Borders toolbar, click the **Eraser** button [icon] to deselect the Eraser and redisplay the pointer as an I-beam.

5 Click anywhere in the first column to position the insertion point to the left of its end-of-cell marker. On the Formatting toolbar, click the **Center** button [icon]. On the Tables and Borders toolbar, click the **Change Text Direction** button [icon] twice.

6 On the Formatting toolbar, click the **Bold** button [B]. Click the **Font Size arrow** and click **28**. Type **Oceana Palm Grill**

The text is displayed vertically, as shown in Figure 7.43.

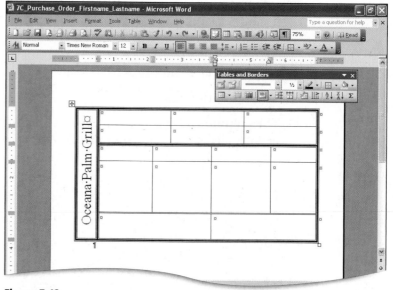

Figure 7.43

7 On the Standard toolbar, click the **Save** button .

Activity 7.15 Formatting a Complex Table

Table cells can be formatted to enhance the appearance of a table.

1 Move the pointer to the left of the first row of the table until it changes to a white arrow, and then click once.

The first row is selected—it includes the entire vertical column.

2 On the Tables and Borders toolbar, click the **Shading Color button arrow**, and then in the first row, click the fourth color—**Gray-12.5%**.

The selected cells are shaded.

3 In the third row, select the four cells. (Hint: Locate the end-of-row markers to help you locate the third row.) On the Tables and Borders toolbar, click the **Shading Color** button. Click anywhere in the document to deselect the cells.

The selected cells are shaded Gray 12.5%. Compare your table with Figure 7.44.

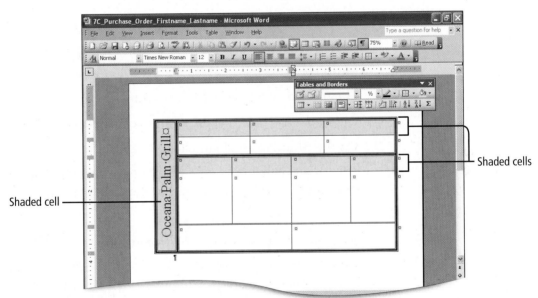

Figure 7.44

4 In the first row, click to position the insertion point in the second column. Type **P. O. Number** and press Tab. Type **Vendor** and press Tab. Type **Date**

5 In the third row, click to position the insertion point in the second column. Type **Quantity** and press Tab. Type **Description** and press Tab. Type **Unit Price** and press Tab. Type **Total**

6 In the fifth row, click to position the insertion point in the second column. Type **Authorization** and press Tab. Type **Department**

Compare your table with Figure 7.45.

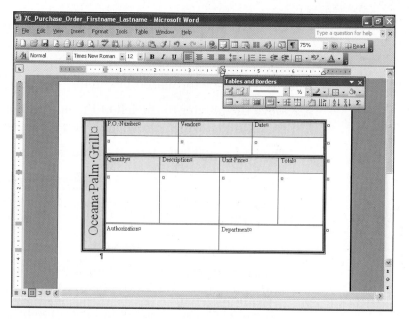

Figure 7.45

7 Close the Tables and Borders toolbar. From the **View** menu, click **Header and Footer**. On the Header and Footer toolbar, click the **Switch Between Header and Footer** button 🖃.

8 On the **Header and Footer** toolbar, click the **Insert AutoText** button `Insert AutoText ▾`, and then click **Filename**.

The file name is inserted in the footer.

9 On the Header and Footer toolbar, click the **Close** button `Close`.

10 On the Standard toolbar, click the **Save** button 🖫.

11 On the Standard toolbar, click the **Print Preview** button 🔍. Take a moment to check your work. On the Print Preview toolbar, click the **Close Preview** button `Close`.

12 Make any necessary changes to your document. When you are satisfied, on the Standard toolbar, click the **Print** button 🖨. Close the document, saving any changes, and close Word.

End You have completed Project 7C

Project 7D **Special Event**

An **object** is any type of graphic—for example, a line, a shape, a WordArt, a text box, an AutoShape, a clip art image, a picture, or an Excel chart— that can be inserted in a document. Objects can be moved and resized, and some can be rotated. You can use special tools to modify graphic images in a variety of ways.

In Activities 7.16 through 7.20, you will complete a memo regarding a proposed cheese tasting night at the Oceana Palm Grill. You will insert and modify objects and wrap text around the objects. You will also lighten an image and place it behind text. Your completed document will look similar to Figure 7.46. You will save your document as *7D_Special_Event_Firstname_Lastname.*

  Oceana Palm Grill

MEMO TO: Laura Mabry Hernandez, Seth Weddel, Duc Buy

FROM: Donna Rohan Kurian, Executive Chef

DATE: December 17

SUBJECT: Cheese Specials on Tuesdays

I have been thinking about emphasizing cheese in our menus, but I'm not sure how to proceed. I have been considering a trial run in one of the restaurants, probably North Austin. I would like to try a weekly event, probably on Tuesday evenings, where the focus is on a good selection of cheese.

I can envision two possibilities—a selection of cheese plates, or a cheese bar (or possibly both). The cheeses would have to be matched with compatible fruit and bread or crackers. They could be used as appetizers, or for desserts, as is common in Europe.

The cheese plates should be varied and diverse, using a mixture of hard and soft, sharp and mild, unusual and familiar.

I am really excited about this possible new feature for our restaurants. I think that it will catch on in this area if it is done right. It will mean that our employees will need to become familiar with the various cheeses and their characteristics. I have included a link to a USDA document that gives lots of information. You will need Adobe Acrobat Reader to read it. Take a look and let me know what you think of the idea.

7D_Special_Event_Firstname_Lastname

Figure 7.46

Objective 6
Insert Objects in a Document

Clip art images, pictures, and other graphic objects are frequently inserted into Word documents. Another type of object that can be inserted is a **PDF document**. A PDF, as it is usually called, is a document formatted in the Portable Document Format developed by Adobe Systems. The format is recognized as one of the standard document formats. PDF files can be opened on most computers, using most operating systems. All that is required is the **Adobe Acrobat Reader**, which can be downloaded from the Adobe Systems Web site at no charge. Most computers in college computer labs have this program installed. If you are working on your own computer, you will need Adobe Acrobat Reader to complete these activities.

Activity 7.16 Inserting Objects from Files

Some objects, when inserted into a Word document, do not display. Instead, an icon containing a link to the file displays. This is true when you insert a PDF.

1 On the Standard toolbar, click the **Open** button. Navigate to the location where the student files for this textbook are stored. Locate and open **w07D_Special_Event**. Save the file as **7D_Special_Event_Firstname_Lastname**

2 On the Standard toolbar, click the **Zoom button arrow** 100%, and then click **Page Width**. If necessary, on the Standard toolbar, click the Show/Hide ¶ button to show formatting marks.

3 Click to position the insertion point at the beginning of the paragraph that begins *I have been thinking*. From the **Insert** menu, click **Object**. In the displayed **Object** dialog box, click the **Create New tab**.

The Object dialog box displays, as shown in Figure 7.47.

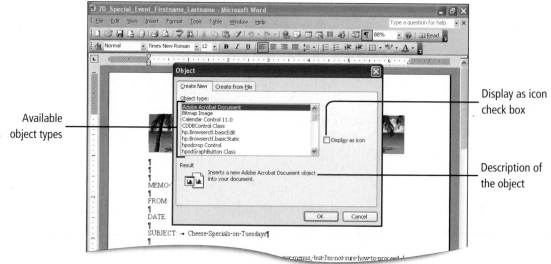

Available object types

Display as icon check box

Description of the object

Figure 7.47

4 Take a moment to scroll down and examine the types of objects that can be inserted into a Word document. When you are finished, under **Object type**, click **Adobe Acrobat Document**.

If the Adobe Acrobat Document Object Does Not Display

If the Adobe Acrobat Document option does not display in the Object type box, you will need to use the following procedure: In the Object dialog box, click the *Create from File* tab. Click the Browse button, locate the w07D_Cheese document in your student files, and then click Insert. Proceed to Step 5, ignoring references to PDF files.

5 In the **Object** dialog box, select the **Display as icon** check box, and then click **Change Icon**.

The Change Icon dialog box displays.

6 In the **Change Icon** dialog box, click the second icon, which displays *PDF* at the top. In the **Caption** box, select the text and type **USDA Cheese Information**

Compare your dialog box with Figure 7.48.

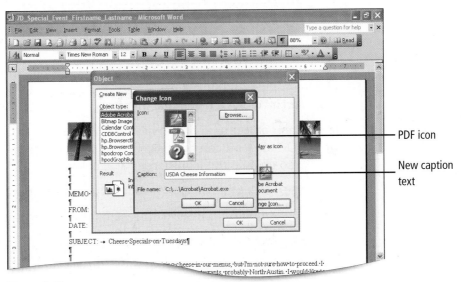

PDF icon

New caption text

Figure 7.48

7 In the **Change Icon** dialog box, click **OK**. In the **Object** dialog box, click **OK**.

The Open dialog box displays, with *Acrobat(*.pdf)* selected in the *Files of type* box. Adobe Acrobat files use a *.pdf* file extension. There may be a delay before the dialog box displays.

8 Navigate to the location where the student files for this textbook are stored. Locate and open **w07D_Cheese**.

The *How to Buy Cheese* PDF document opens in a separate window.

9 In the title bar of the new window, click the **Close** button ⊠.

The PDF file closes, and an icon is placed at the beginning of the paragraph. The icon is captioned *USDA Cheese Information*. See Figure 7.49. The PDF file is embedded in the Word document.

Adobe Acrobat icon ——

New icon label ——

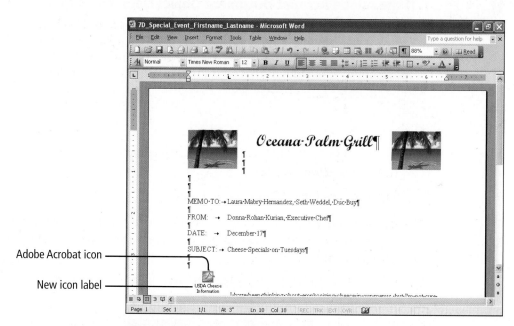

Figure 7.49

10 On the Standard toolbar, click the **Save** button 💾.

Activity 7.17 Modifying Objects

Each object type has a special set of features that can be modified. The PDF file icon can be resized, and you can wrap text around it. You can also change the icon border and color.

1 Click once on the **Acrobat Document icon** to select it.

An object border with resizing handles displays.

2 From the **Format** menu, click **Object**, and then click the **Layout tab**.

You can wrap text around a PDF icon in the same way that you wrap text around an image.

3 Under **Wrapping style**, click **Square**. Under **Horizontal alignment**, click the **Right** option button, and then click **OK**.

The paragraph text wraps around the icon, and it is aligned at the right, as shown in Figure 7.50. An anchor symbol in the left margin indicates that the object is connected to the paragraph with the anchor.

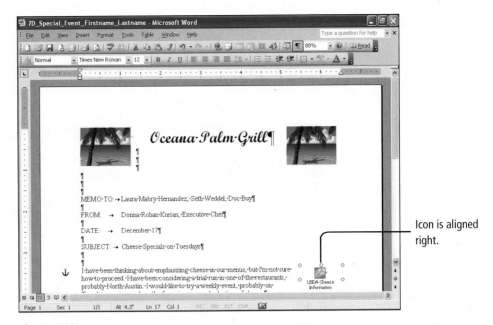

Icon is aligned right.

Figure 7.50

4 Right-click the icon, and then from the displayed shortcut menu, click **Format Object**. In the **Format Object** dialog box, click the **Colors and Lines tab**.

5 Under **Fill**, click the **Color arrow**. From the color palette, in the fourth row, click the third color—**Yellow**.

This will change the icon background to yellow.

6 Under **Line**, click the **Color arrow**. From the color palette, in the third row, click the first color—**Red**.

7 Under **Line**, click the **Weight up spin arrow** until the line weight is **1.5** pt.

Compare your Format Object dialog box with Figure 7.51.

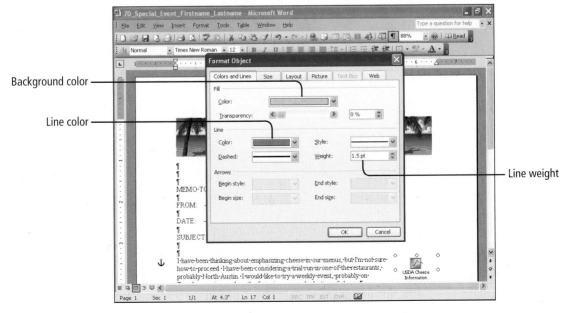

Background color

Line color

Line weight

Figure 7.51

8 At the bottom of the **Format Object** dialog box, click **OK**. Scroll up so you can see the entire icon.

The icon box displays with a red border with yellow fill, as shown in Figure 7.52.

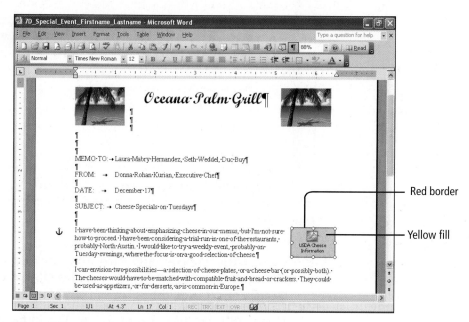

Figure 7.52

9 Double-click the icon.

The Adobe Acrobat window opens, and the PDF document displays.

10 If a task pane is open to the right of the document, click **Hide** to close it. Take a moment to scroll through the document. When you are finished, in the title bar of the **Adobe Acrobat** window, click the **Close** button ☒.

11 On the Standard toolbar, click the **Save** button 🖫.

Objective 7
Modify an Image

You can use many tools in Word to modify a clip art image or a picture. You can *crop* an image, which hides part of the picture without resizing it. Pictures often are cropped to focus attention on a particular area or to remove unwanted parts of the picture. You can *scale* an image, which resizes the image, while keeping the same proportions. You can change the *contrast* and *brightness* of an image. Contrast is the differentiation between light and dark. When you increase contrast, the darks get darker and the lights get lighter. When you decrease the contrast, the dark areas brighten and the light areas darken. Changing the brightness brightens or darkens the bright areas and the dark areas at the same time.

Activity 7.18 Cropping and Rotating Images

Unwanted or unnecessary parts of an image can be hidden by cropping, without affecting the rest of the image. The image can also be rotated to a more effective position.

1 Click to position the insertion point at the beginning of the paragraph that begins *I have been thinking*. From the **Insert** menu, point to **Picture**, and then click **From File**. Navigate to the location where the student files for this textbook are stored. Locate and insert **w07D_Cheese_Wedge**.

The cheese wedge image is placed at the insertion point.

2 Click to select the image and open the Picture toolbar. If the toolbar does not display, from the View menu, point to Toolbars, and then click Picture.

The Picture toolbar may be docked with other toolbars or may float, as shown in Figure 7.53.

3 On the Picture toolbar, click the **Crop** button 🔲. Move the **Crop pointer** to the handle in the lower left corner of the image. Drag up and to the right until the image border is just to the left of and slightly below the cheese wedge, as shown in Figure 7.53.

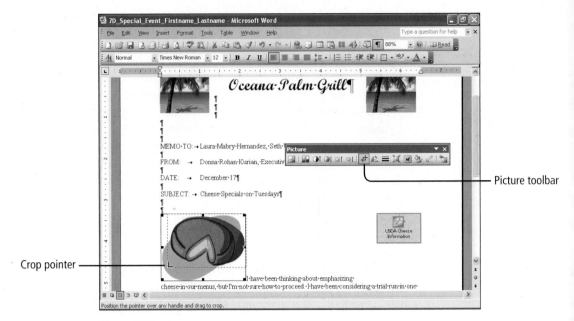

Crop pointer

Picture toolbar

Figure 7.53

4 Release the mouse button.

The image is cropped, and the paragraph adjusts to the new image size. Recall that at this point the image is part of the text, and a change in the image size results in adjustments in the word wrap in the remainder of the paragraph.

> **Note** — **Cropping Images**
>
> When you crop an image, part of the image is hidden, so the image size is reduced. The size of the remaining objects in the image, however, is not reduced. When you crop an image, you also can retrieve the cropped parts of the image by using the Crop pointer and dragging out to the former edges of the image.

5 On the Picture toolbar, click the **Rotate Left 90°** button .

The image is rotated 90° to the left, and a rotate handle is added, as shown in Figure 7.54. You can drag the **rotate handle** to rotate an image to any angle.

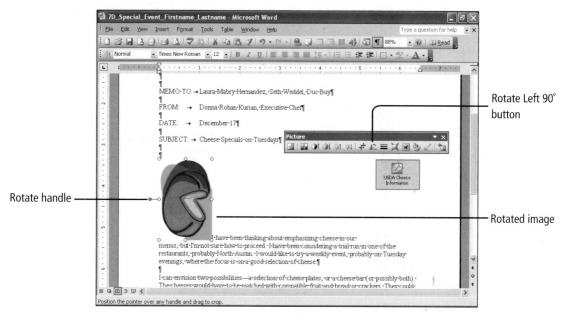

Rotate Left 90°
button

Rotate handle

Rotated image

Figure 7.54

Alert!

If the Rotate Handle Does Not Display

If you rotate the picture and the rotate handle does not display, right-click the image. From the shortcut menu, click Format Picture, and then click the Layout tab. Click Square, and then click OK. Your screens will look somewhat different than Figures 7.55 through 7.60.

6 On the Picture toolbar, click the **Rotate Left 90°** button three more times.

The image returns to its original orientation.

7 Move the pointer over the **rotate handle**. Using the ruler as a guide, drag the rotate handle to the left about 0.25 inches.

The image is rotated slightly. Compare your image with Figure 7.55.

Rotate handle ———

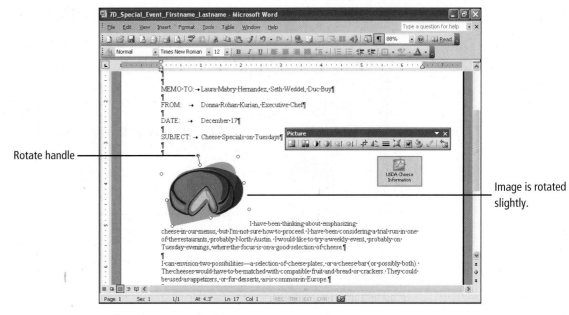

Image is rotated slightly.

Figure 7.55

8 On the Standard toolbar, click the **Save** button 🖫.

Activity 7.19 Scaling and Resizing Images

Images can be resized by dragging the resizing handles or by using the scaling feature in the Format Object dialog box.

1 Move the pointer over the sizing handle in the middle of the right border of the image. Drag to the right about 2 inches.

The image is distorted, as shown in Figure 7.56.

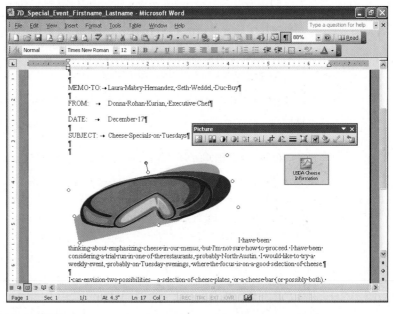

Figure 7.56

2 On the Standard toolbar, click the **Undo** button 🔄 ▾.

The image returns to its original size.

3 Right-click the image. From the shortcut menu, click **Format Picture**. From the **Format Picture** dialog box, click the **Size tab**.

4 Under **Scale**, confirm that the **Lock aspect ratio** and the **Relative to original picture size** check boxes are selected.

The **aspect ratio** is the proportional relationship of the height and width of an image. When manually resizing a picture, always drag a corner sizing handle to retain the aspect ratio of an image.

5 Under **Scale**, in the **Height** box, highlight **100%** and type **250**

The image will be 2.5 times as wide and high as it was originally. Compare your Format Picture dialog box with Figure 7.57. Your numbers may be slightly different.

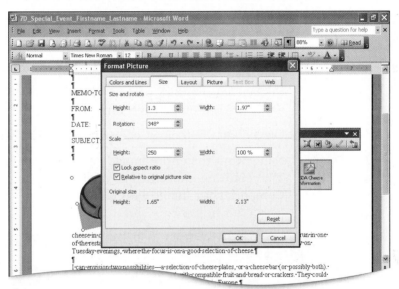

Figure 7.57

6 At the bottom of the **Format Picture** dialog box, click **OK**.

7 On the Standard toolbar, click the **Save** button 💾.

Activity 7.20 Controlling Image Contrast and Brightness

You can control the contrast and brightness of an image. Recall that when you increase contrast, the darks get darker and the lights get lighter, whereas changing the brightness brightens or darkens the bright areas and the dark areas at the same time.

1 Scroll up so that you can see the entire image. On the Picture toolbar, click the **Color** button 🖼️, and from the list, click **Grayscale**.

The image color is changed to grayscale. **Grayscale** displays colors as varying shades of gray, as shown in Figure 7.58.

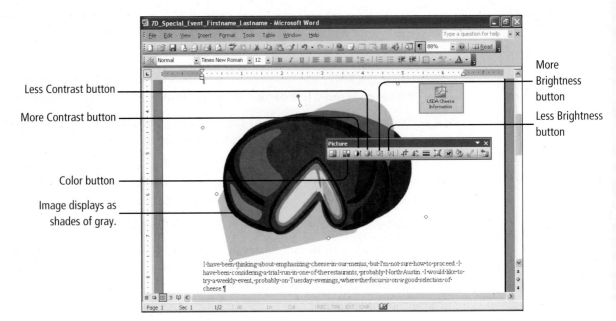

Less Contrast button

More Contrast button

Color button

Image displays as
shades of gray.

More
Brightness
button

Less Brightness
button

Figure 7.58

2 On the Picture toolbar, click the **Less Contrast** button 12 times.

Notice that the dark parts of the image are lightened, and the light areas are darkened each time you click the button.

3 On the Picture toolbar, click the **More Brightness** button 12 times.

Notice that the entire image lightens each time you click the button. The resulting image has a "washed out" look and is very light. Compare your image with Figure 7.59.

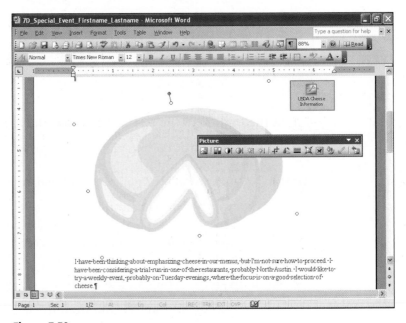

Figure 7.59

Another Way

To Use the Format Picture Dialog Box to Adjust Contrast and Brightness

You also can adjust the contrast and brightness of an image using the menu. Right-click the image and click Format Picture (or Format Object) on the shortcut menu. In the Format Picture dialog box, click the Picture tab. Under Image control, type the desired percentages in the Brightness and Contrast boxes. Images by default use 50% Brightness and 50% Contrast. In the image you just adjusted, the Brightness should be 86% and the Contrast 14%.

4 Right-click the image. From the shortcut menu, click **Format Picture**. In the **Format Picture** dialog box, click the **Layout tab**.

5 Under **Wrapping style**, click **Behind text**, and then click **OK**.

The image is placed behind the text, but the image is still a little too dark.

6 On the Picture toolbar, click the **More Brightness** button once.

The image is lightened slightly, and the text is easier to read.

7 Hold down Ctrl and press ↓ eight times, watching the image as you press the key.

Notice that the image is **nudged**—moved in small increments—down slightly each time you press the arrow key. This technique enables you to position an image exactly where you want it.

8 Hold down Ctrl and press → three times.

The image moves slightly to the right. See Figure 7.60. Use the nudge technique as necessary to move your image approximately as shown in Figure 7.60.

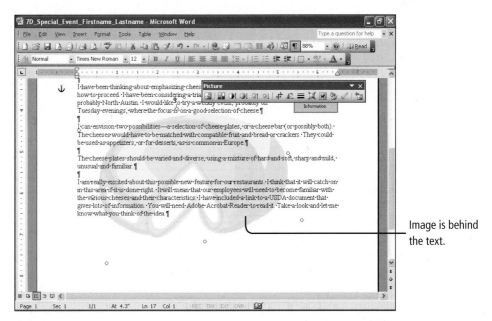

Image is behind the text.

Figure 7.60

9 From the **View** menu, click **Header and Footer**. On the Header and Footer toolbar, click the **Switch Between Header and Footer** button 🔲.

10 On the Header and Footer toolbar, click the **Insert AutoText** button Insert AutoText ▾ , and then click **Filename**.

The file name is inserted in the footer.

11 On the Header and Footer toolbar, click the **Close** button Close .

12 On the Standard toolbar, click the **Save** button 🔲.

13 On the Standard toolbar, click the **Print Preview** button 🔍. Take a moment to check your work. On the Print Preview toolbar, click the **Close Preview** button Close .

14 Make any necessary changes to your document. When you are satisfied, on the Standard toolbar, click the **Print** button 🖨. Close the document, saving changes if necessary, and close Word.

End You have completed Project 7D ─────────────────────

Summary

Tables are used for many purposes, and Word has advanced tools to enable you to present table data effectively and attractively. You can align text in cells horizontally (left, center, and right) and vertically (top, center, and bottom), giving you nine possible alignment combinations. When cell width is a concern, you can change the text direction from horizontal to vertical. Cells also can be merged horizontally or vertically to facilitate titles that extend beyond a cell's width or height.

If you create new tables often, you can standardize the look of your tables by creating a table style. Table styles enable you to format the whole table or just parts of a table, such as the left or right column or the top or bottom row. Once you have created a table style, a single click will result in the formatting changes saved in the style.

Sometimes you need the features of a table coupled with the flexibility to form rows and columns of varying size and format. The Draw Table command enables you to create a table with nonuniform rows and columns. When used with the other commands on the Tables and Borders toolbar, you can create a table with the exact specifications you need.

Clip art images and pictures can be modified using advanced formatting features. The contrast or brightness of an image can be modified to lighten or darken the whole image or to accentuate the difference between the light and dark areas. Color images can be changed to grayscale, which displays colors as shades of gray. You can crop an image to remove portions of the image without changing the size of the remaining image. An image can also be resized proportionally and rotated to any angle with precision.

In This Chapter You Practiced How To

- Create and Apply a Custom Table Style
- Format Cells in a Table
- Modify Table Properties
- Use Advanced Table Features
- Draw a Complex Table
- Insert Objects in a Document
- Modify an Image

Concepts Assessments

Matching   Match each term in the second column with its correct definition in the first column by writing the letter of the term on the blank line in front of the correct definition.

_____ **1.** A small circle on a selected image that can be dragged to change the angle of an image.

_____ **2.** The differentiation between light and dark parts of an image.

_____ **3.** The light-to-dark ratio of an image.

_____ **4.** A title that can be added to a table or figure.

_____ **5.** A free program that is used to open Portable Document Format (PDF) files.

_____ **6.** To resize an image, keeping the same image proportions.

_____ **7.** Displays all colors as shades of gray.

_____ **8.** Type of style that displays a small grid to the right of the style name in the Styles and Formatting task pane.

_____ **9.** To trim part of a picture or clip art image without resizing the image.

_____ **10.** Proportional relationship of the height and width of an image.

_____ **11.** A combination of formatting steps, such as font, font size, and indentation, that you name and store as a set.

_____ **12.** A small box that displays at the outside upper-left corner of a table that can be dragged to move the entire table to a different location in a document.

_____ **13.** The process of organizing data in a particular order.

_____ **14.** Any type of graphic—for example, a shape, a WordArt, an AutoShape, a clip art image, a picture, or an Excel chart— that can be inserted into a document.

_____ **15.** A document formatted in the Portable Document Format developed by Adobe Systems.

A Adobe Acrobat Reader

B Aspect ratio

C Brightness

D Caption

E Contrast

F Crop

G Grayscale

H Object

I PDF Document

J Rotate handle

K Scale

L Sort

M Style

N Table

O Table move handle

Fill in the Blank Write the correct answer in the space provided.

1. Text can be aligned in a cell both horizontally and

_____.

2. A(n) _____ enables you to sum numbers in a table row or column.

3. If you increase the contrast of an image, the dark areas are made darker, and the light areas are made _____.

4. Adobe Acrobat files use a(n) _____ extension.

5. If you decrease the brightness of an image, the dark areas are made darker, and the light areas are made _____.

6. You can create a table _____ to perform many formatting commands at one time.

7. A(n) _____ is used as a numbered title for a table and can be placed above or below the table.

8. PDF files can be read using Adobe Acrobat _____.

9. You can _____ on a column in a table to arrange the contents of the column in alphabetical or numerical order.

10. An object can be rotated to any angle by dragging the

_____.

Project 7E—Staff Schedule

Objectives: *Create and Apply a Custom Table Style, Format Cells in a Table, and Use Advanced Table Features.*

In the following Skill Assessment, you will edit a table in a document for the Oceana Palm Grill, which describes an employee schedule for the lunch hour of the grand opening of a new restaurant in the chain. Your completed document will look similar to the one shown in Figure 7.61. You will save your document as *7E_Staff_Schedule_Firstname_Lastname*.

Figure 7.61

1. On the Standard toolbar, click the **Open** button. Navigate to the location where the student files for this textbook are stored. Locate and open **w07E_Staff_Schedule**. Save the file as **7E_Staff_Schedule_Firstname_Lastname**

2. On the Standard toolbar, click the **Zoom button arrow**, and then click **Page Width**. If necessary, on the Standard toolbar, click the Show/Hide ¶ button to show formatting marks. Right-click on any toolbar, and then click **Tables and Borders** from the shortcut menu. The Tables and Borders toolbar displays.

(Project 7E–Staff Schedule continues on the next page)

(Project 7E–Staff Schedule continued)

3. From the **Format** menu, click **Styles and Formatting**. At the top of the **Styles and Formatting** task pane, click **New Style**. In the displayed **New Style** dialog box, under **Properties**, in the **Name** box, type **Schedule**

4. Click the **Style type arrow** and from the displayed list, click **Table**.

5. Under **Formatting**, with **Whole table** displayed in the **Apply formatting to** box, on the **New Style** dialog box toolbar, click the **Font button arrow**, scroll as necessary, and then click **Arial**. Click the **Font Size button arrow**, and then click **12**. Click the **Border button arrow**, and then click **All Borders**.

6. Under **Formatting**, with **Whole table** still displayed in the **Apply formatting to** box, at the lower left side of the dialog box, click the **Format arrow**, and from the displayed list click **Table Properties**. If necessary, click the **Table tab**. Under **Alignment**, click **Center**, and then click **OK**.

7. Under **Formatting**, click the **Apply formatting to arrow**, and then click **Even row stripes**, which will shade every other row. On the **New Style** dialog box toolbar, click the **Shading Color button arrow**, and then in the first row, click the third color—**Gray-10%**.

8. Under **Formatting**, click the **Apply formatting to arrow**, and then click **Right column** to set formats for the right column of the table. On the **New Style** dialog box toolbar, click the **Align button arrow**, and then click **Align Center Right**. At the bottom of the **New Style** dialog box, click **OK**. Your new style is created, but has not yet been applied.

9. Click anywhere in the table in your **7E_Staff_Schedule_Firstname_ Lastname** document. In the **Styles and Formatting** task pane, click the **Schedule** style. Close the **Styles and Formatting** task pane.

10. In the first row of the table, select the right three cells, beginning with *Last Name* and ending with *Hourly Rate*. On the Tables and Borders toolbar, click the **Change Text Direction** button. On the Tables and Borders toolbar, click the **Align button arrow**, and then click the **Center** button.

11. Move the pointer into the left margin area of the first row of the table until it turns into a white arrow, and then click once to select the row. From the Formatting toolbar, click the **Bold** button. From the **Table** menu, point to **Insert**, and then click **Rows Above**.

12. With the first row still selected, on the Tables and Borders toolbar, click the **Merge Cells** button. Type **Tentative Schedule**

13. Select the text *Tentative Schedule* that you just typed. On the Formatting toolbar, if necessary, click the **Center** button. On the Formatting toolbar, click the **Font Size arrow**, and then click **24**.

(Project 7E–Staff Schedule continues on the next page)

(Project 7E–Staff Schedule continued)

14. Move the pointer to the left of the third row of the table, beginning *Host*, until it turns into a white arrow. Drag down to select the third row through the last row of the table. Be sure that you do *not* select the ending paragraph marker outside of the table.

15. From the **Format** menu, click **Paragraph**, and then click the **Indents and Spacing tab**. Under **Spacing**, in the **After** box, click the **up spin arrow** to add **6 pt.** spacing after each row.

16. With the rows still selected, from the **Table** menu, click **Sort**. Be sure that under **My list has**, the **No Header row** option is selected, and that the **Sort by** box displays **Column 1**. Be sure the **Ascending** option button is selected.

17. Click the first **Then by arrow** and click **Column 2**. This action directs Word to sort on the first column, and then, when two or more items in the first column are the same, to sort on the second column.

18. At the bottom of the **Sort** dialog box, click **OK** to sort the table by Position and, within position, by Last Name. Within groups, where the Position name is the same, Word further sorts the rows by Last Name (Column 2). Compare your document with Figure 7.61.

19. From the **View** menu, click **Header and Footer**. On the Header and Footer toolbar, click the **Switch Between Header and Footer** button. On the **Header and Footer** toolbar, click the **Insert AutoText** button, and then click **Filename**. On the **Header and Footer** toolbar, click the **Close** button.

20. On the Standard toolbar, click the **Save** button. On the Standard toolbar, click the **Print Preview** button. Take a moment to check your work. On the Print Preview toolbar, click the **Close Preview** button.

21. Make any necessary changes to your document. When you are satisfied, on the Standard toolbar, click the **Print** button. Close the document, saving it if you are prompted to do so.

End You have completed Project 7E ——————————————————————

Project 7F—Investment

Objectives: *Create and Apply a Custom Table Style, Modify Table Properties, and Use Advanced Table Features.*

In the following Skill Assessment, you will edit a letter to a potential investor in which you will wrap text around two tables, create and apply a custom table style, add table captions, and use a formula to calculate average sales. Your completed document will look similar to the one shown in Figure 7.62. You will save your document as *7F_Investment_Firstname_Lastname*.

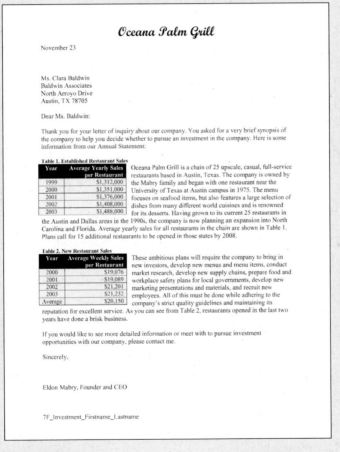

Figure 7.62

1. On the Standard toolbar, click the **Open** button. Navigate to the location where the student files for this textbook are stored. Locate and open **w07F_Investment**. Save the file as **7F_Investment_Firstname_Lastname**

(Project 7F–Investment continues on the next page)

(Project 7F–Investment continued)

2. On the Standard toolbar, click the **Zoom button arrow**, and then click **Page Width**. If necessary, on the Standard toolbar, click the Show/Hide ¶ button to show formatting marks. Right-click on any toolbar, and then from the shortcut menu, click **Tables and Borders** to display the Tables and Borders toolbar. Drag the toolbar so that it is not blocking your view or dock it to the other toolbars on your screen.

3. From the **Format** menu, click **Styles and Formatting**. At the top of the **Styles and Formatting** task pane, click **New Style**. In the displayed **New Style** dialog box, under **Properties**, in the **Name** box, type Investment

4. Click the **Style type arrow** and from the displayed list, click **Table**.

5. Under **Formatting**, be sure that **Whole table** displays in the **Apply formatting to** box. On the **New Style** dialog box toolbar, click the **Border button arrow**, and then click **All Borders**. Click the **Shading Color button arrow**, and then in the first row, click the second color—**Gray-5%**.

6. Under **Formatting**, click the **Apply formatting to** arrow and from the displayed list, click **Header row**. On the **New Style** dialog box toolbar, click the **Shading Color button arrow**, and then in the fourth row, click the first color—**Black**. On the **New Style** dialog box toolbar, click the **Bold** button.

7. At the bottom of the **New Style** dialog box, click **OK**. The new table style is created and listed in the Styles and Formatting task pane.

8. Click anywhere in the **Average Yearly Sales** table. In the **Styles and Formatting** task pane, click the **Investment** style. Click anywhere in the **Average Weekly Sales** table. In the **Styles and Formatting** task pane, click the **Investment** style.

9. Close the **Styles and Formatting** task pane. Right-click the **Average Yearly Sales** table, click **Table Properties**, and then click the **Table tab**. Under **Text wrapping**, click **Around**, and then click **OK**.

10. Right-click the **Average Weekly Sales** table, click **Table Properties**, and then click the **Table tab**. Under **Text wrapping**, click **Around**, and then click **OK**.

11. Position the insertion point anywhere in the **Average Weekly Sales** table. From the **Insert** menu, point to **Reference**, and then click **Caption**. Under **Caption**, at the insertion point type a period, press Spacebar, type New Restaurant Sales and then click **OK**.

12. Position the insertion point anywhere in the **Average Yearly Sales** table. From the **Insert** menu, point to **Reference**, and then click **Caption**. Under **Caption**, type a period, press Spacebar, type Established Restaurant Sales and then click **OK**.

(Project 7F–Investment continues on the next page)

(Project 7F–Investment continued)

13. Position the insertion point in the lower right cell of the **Average Weekly Sales** table and press Tab. In the left cell of the new row, type **Average** and then press Tab.

14. From the **Table** menu, click **Formula**. In the **Formula** dialog box, in the **Formula** box, select *SUM* and type **AVERAGE** The formula should indicate *=AVERAGE(ABOVE)*.

15. Click the **Number format arrow**, and then click **$#,##0.00;($#,##0.00)**. Delete everything from the first period on, so that the number format is *$#,##0* (without the period). This displays a number with a dollar sign and commas, but there is no preset formula for this format. Click **OK**. Compare your document with Figure 7.62.

16. From the **View** menu, click **Header and Footer**. On the Header and Footer toolbar, click the **Switch Between Header and Footer** button. On the Header and Footer toolbar, click the **Insert AutoText** button, and then click **Filename**. On the Header and Footer toolbar, click the **Close** button.

17. On the Standard toolbar, click the **Save** button.

18. On the Standard toolbar, click the **Print Preview** button. Take a moment to check your work. On the Print Preview toolbar, click the **Close Preview** button.

19. Make any necessary changes to your document. When you are satisfied, on the Standard toolbar, click the **Print** button. Close the document, saving it if you are prompted to do so.

End You have completed Project 7F ———————————

Project 7G — Gift Card

Objectives: *Insert Objects in a Document and Modify an Image.*

In the following Skill Assessment, you will edit a poster announcing gift cards available at the Oceana Palm Grill. You will insert a picture from a file and rotate it, change the contrast and brightness of the picture, send an image behind text, and enlarge a picture proportionally. Your completed document will look similar to the one shown in Figure 7.63. You will save your document as *7G_Gift_Card_Firstname_Lastname*.

1. On the Standard toolbar, click the **Open** button. Navigate to the location where the student files for this textbook are stored. Locate and open **w07G_Gift_Card**. Save the file as **7G_Gift_Card_Firstname_Lastname**

(Project 7G–Gift Card continues on the next page)

(Project 7G–Gift Card continued)

Oceana Palm Grill

Gift Cards

Give the gift they'll be sure to enjoy!

Graduation
Birthday
Anniversary
Thank you
Just because

Any occasion at all!

The Oceana Palm Grill Gift Card is the perfect choice

People who are hard to shop for will love our selection and quality!

Oceana Palm Grill Gift Cards are available at any of our locations
And can be purchased in any denomination

Oceana Palm Grill
Perfect for All Occasions!

7G_Gift_Card_Firstname_Lastname

Figure 7.63

2. On the Standard toolbar, click the **Zoom button arrow**, and then click **Page Width**. If necessary, on the Standard toolbar, click the Show/Hide ¶ button to display formatting marks.

3. Click to position the insertion point at the beginning of the line that begins *Give the gift*. From the **Insert** menu, point to **Picture**, and then click **From File**. Navigate to the location where the student files for this textbook are stored. Locate and select **w07G_Chef_Hat**, and then click **Insert**.

4. Click the **chef hat** image to select it. If necessary, display the Picture toolbar by right-clicking the image, and from the shortcut menu, clicking the Show Picture Toolbar. On the Picture toolbar, click the **Rotate Left 90°** button.

5. Drag the **Rotate** handle until the hat is tilted about 45° to the left. Refer to Figure 7.63.

6. On the Picture toolbar, click the **Less Contrast** button once, and then click the **More Brightness** button once.

(Project 7G–Gift Card continues on the next page)

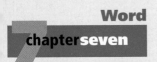
(Project 7G–Gift Card continued)

7. Right-click the image. From the shortcut menu, click **Format Picture**. In the displayed **Format Picture** dialog box, click the **Layout tab**. Under **Wrapping style**, click **Behind text**, and then click **OK**.

8. Right-click the image. From the shortcut menu, click **Format Picture**. From the **Format Picture** dialog box, click the **Size tab**. Under **Scale**, confirm that the **Lock aspect ratio** and the **Relative to original picture size** check boxes are selected.

9. Under **Scale**, in the **Height** box, select **100%**, type **125** and then click **OK**.

10. Select the five lines that begin *Graduation* and end *Just because*. From the Formatting toolbar, click the **Font Size arrow**, and then click **36** to increase the font size.

11. From the Standard toolbar, click the **Zoom button arrow**, and then click **Whole Page**. Drag the image as necessary to visually center it on the poster. Hold down [Ctrl] and press the arrow keys to nudge the image into its final position, as shown in Figure 7.63. Return to **Page Width** zoom.

12. From the **View** menu, click **Header and Footer**. On the Header and Footer toolbar, click the **Switch Between Header and Footer** button. On the Header and Footer toolbar, click the **Insert AutoText** button, and then click **Filename**. On the Header and Footer toolbar, click the **Close** button.

13. On the Standard toolbar, click the **Save** button. Then, on the Standard toolbar, click the **Print Preview** button. Take a moment to check your work. On the Print Preview toolbar, click the **Close Preview** button.

14. Make any necessary changes to your document. When you are satisfied, on the Standard toolbar, click the **Print** button. Close the document.

 End **You have completed Project 7G**

Project 7H—Safety Training

Objectives: *Create and Apply a Custom Table Style, Format Cells in a Table, Use Advanced Table Features, and Insert Objects in a Document.*

In the following Performance Assessment, you will edit a memo about safety training for teenage workers at the Oceana Palm Grill. You will sort a table, merge cells, and change text direction. You also will insert and modify an image. Your completed document will look similar to the one shown in Figure 7.64. You will save your document as *7H_Safety_Training_Firstname_Lastname.*

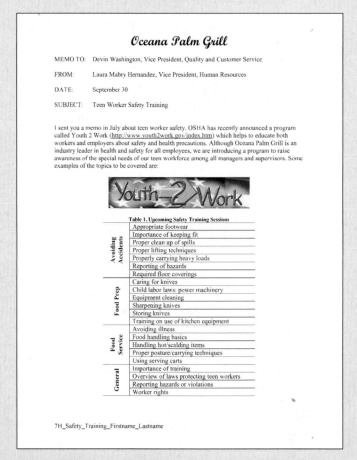

Figure 7.64

1. On the Standard toolbar, click the **Open** button. Navigate to the location where the student files for this textbook are stored. Locate and open **w07H_Safety_Training**. Save the file as **7H_Safety_Training_Firstname_Lastname**

(Project 7H—Safety Training continues on the next page)

(Project 7H–Safety Training continued)

2. Be sure that formatting marks are displayed and zoom to **Page Width**. Display the Tables and Borders toolbar. Scroll so that you can view the entire table in the middle of your screen. Click to position your insertion point somewhere in the table. From the **Table** menu, point to **Select**, and then click **Table**. On the Formatting toolbar, click the **Center** button.

3. From the **Table** menu, click **Sort**. Set the sort settings to sort first on **Column 1**, and **Then by Column 2**, both in **Ascending** order. Specify that the table has no header row, and then click **OK**.

4. In the first column, select all of the *Avoiding Accident* cells except the first one. Press Del. In the same manner, delete all but the first instance of *Food Prep*, *Food Service*, and *General*.

5. In the first column, select the *Avoiding Accident* cell and the blank cells under it (the top seven cells in the first column should be selected). On the Tables and Borders toolbar, click the **Merge Cells** button. In the same manner, merge *Food Prep*, *Food Service*, and *General* with the empty cells below them.

6. Move the pointer to the top of the first column until it turns to a black arrow, and then click to select the column. On the Tables and Borders toolbar, click the **Change Text Direction** button twice. On the Formatting toolbar, click the **Bold** button. On the Tables and Borders toolbar, click the **Align button arrow**, and then click the **Align Center** button.

7. From the **Table** menu, click **Table Properties**, and then click the **Column tab**. Under **Size**, change the **Preferred width** to **.7**

8. Click in the table to deselect all the rows. From the **Insert** menu, point to **Reference**, and then click **Caption**. Confirm that the Position is *Above selected item*. Under **Caption**, type a period and press Spacebar. Type **Upcoming Safety Training Sessions** and click **OK**. On the Formatting toolbar, click the **Center** button.

9. Click to position the insertion point in the blank line just above the caption. From the **Insert** menu, point to **Picture**, and then click **From File**. Navigate to the location where the student files for this textbook are stored. Locate and insert **w07H_Youth2Work**. From the Formatting toolbar, click the **Center** button. Press Enter to add a blank line after the graphic. Position the insertion point at the end of the paragraph before the graphic and press Enter.

10. Click anywhere in the table. From the **Table** menu, point to **Select**, and then click **Table**. From the **Format** menu, click **Borders and Shading**, and then click the **Borders tab**. In the Preview area, click to deselect the left and right borders. Click **OK**.

(Project 7H–Safety Training continues on the next page)

(Project 7H–Safety Training continued)

11. From the **View** menu, click **Header and Footer**. On the Header and Footer toolbar, click the **Switch Between Header and Footer** button. Click the **Insert AutoText** button, and then click **Filename**. On the **Header and Footer** toolbar, click the **Close** button.

12. On the Standard toolbar, click the **Save** button. Preview the document, and then print it. Close the document.

End You have completed Project 7H ————————————————

Project 7I — Travel Form

Objectives: *Format Cells in a Table, Use Advanced Table Features, Draw a Complex Table, and Insert Objects in a Document.*

In the following Performance Assessment, you will edit a travel form for the Oceana Palm Grill. You will use the Draw Table feature, insert an object, and format the table. Your completed document will look similar to the one shown in Figure 7.65. You will save your document as *7I_Travel_Form_Firstname_Lastname.*

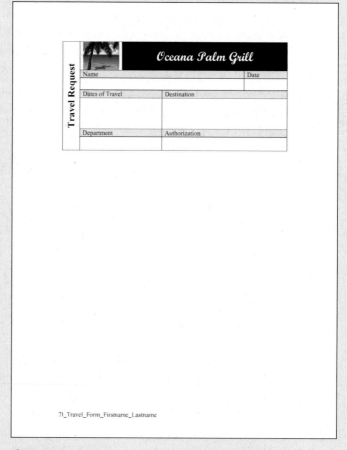

Figure 7.65

(Project 7I–Travel Form continues on the next page)

(Project 7I–Travel Form continued)

1. On the Standard toolbar, click the **Open** button. Navigate to the location where the student files for this textbook are stored. Locate and open **w07I_Travel_Form**. Save the file as 7I_Travel_Form_Firstname_Lastname

2. Right-click on the table, click **Table Properties**, and then click the **Table tab**. Under **Alignment**, click **Center**, and then click **OK**.

3. If necessary, display the Tables and Borders toolbar. On the Tables and Borders toolbar, click the **Eraser** button. Click the vertical line to the right of *Destination* to erase it. Erase the vertical line to the right of *Authorization*. Click the **Eraser** button to turn it off.

4. On the Tables and Borders toolbar, click the **Draw Table** button. Position the Draw Table pencil pointer on the upper left corner of the table. Drag to the left to **-0.5 inches on the horizontal ruler** (in the blue shaded area left of the table) and then down so the dotted line extends to the bottom of the table. This will add a narrow column to the left side of the table. Refer to Figure 7.65 for the size and location of the added table column. If you are not satisfied with your result, click the **Undo** button and begin again. Click the **Draw Table** button to turn it off.

5. On the Tables and Borders toolbar, click the **Change Text Direction** button twice. From the Formatting toolbar, click the **Bold** button. Click the **Font Size arrow** and click **16**. Click the **Font arrow**, and then click **Times New Roman**. Type Travel Request

6. On the Tables and Borders toolbar, click the **Draw Table** button. Move the Draw Table (pencil) pointer just under *Name*. Drag to the right until the dashed line touches the right table border. Repeat this procedure under *Dates of Travel* and *Department*. Refer to Figure 7.65. Click the **Draw Table** button to turn it off.

7. Click in the *Name* cell and drag to the right until the *Date* cell is also selected. On the Tables and Borders toolbar, click the **Shading Color button arrow**, and then in the first row, click the third button— **Gray-10%**. Repeat this procedure to shade the *Dates of Travel*, *Destination*, *Department*, and *Authorization* cells.

8. On the Tables and Borders toolbar, click the **Draw Table** button. Move the Draw Table (pencil) pointer to the top border of the table at **1.5 inches on the horizontal ruler**; drag down from the top border only to the bottom of the first row. This will create the cell in which you will insert the picture. Refer to Figure 7.65. Click the **Draw Table** button to turn it off.

(Project 7I–Travel Form continues on the next page)

(Project 7I–Travel Form continued)

9. Click to position the insertion point in the cell you just created (to the left of the *Oceana Palm Grill* cell). From the **Insert** menu, point to **Picture**, and then click **From File**. Locate and insert the **w07I_Grill_Logo** file. Click to select the image. Drag the lower right sizing handle up and to the left until the image is about 1 inch wide. Use the horizontal ruler as a guide.

10. Click to position the insertion point in the *Oceana Palm Grill* cell. On the Tables and Borders toolbar, click the **Shading Color button arrow**, and then in the fourth row, click the first button—**Black**. On the Tables and Borders toolbar, click the **Align button arrow**, and from the displayed palette, click the **Align Center** button. Click outside of the table to deselect. Compare your document with Figure 7.65.

11. From the **View** menu, click **Header and Footer**. On the Header and Footer toolbar, click the **Switch Between Header and Footer** button. Click the **Insert AutoText** button, and then click **Filename**. On the **Header and Footer** toolbar, click the **Close** button.

12. On the Standard toolbar, click the **Save** button. Preview the document, and then print it. Close the document.

End You have completed Project 7I ────────────────

Project 7J — Press Release

Objectives: *Create and Apply a Custom Table Style, Modify Table Properties, Use Advanced Table Features, Insert Objects in a Document, and Modify an Image.*

In the following Performance Assessment, you will edit a press release regarding the record growth of the Oceana Palm Grill. You will add a column of numbers in a table and insert and modify an image. Your completed document will look similar to the one shown in Figure 7.66. You will save your document as *7J_Press_Release_Firstname_Lastname.*

1. On the Standard toolbar, click the **Open** button . Navigate to the location where the student files for this textbook are stored. Locate and open **w07J_Press_Release**. Save the new document as 7J_Press_Release_Firstname_Lastname

2. Display the **Styles and Formatting** task pane and create a **New Style**. At the top of the **New Style** dialog box, in the **Name** box, type **Growth**

(Project 7J–Press Release continues on the next page)

(Project 7J–Press Release continued)

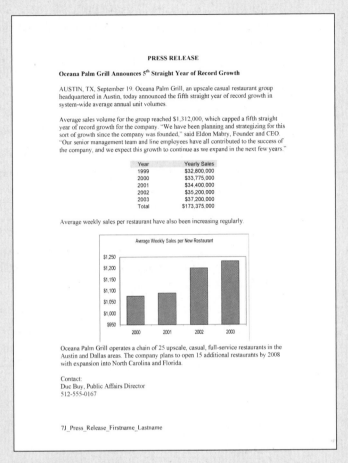

Figure 7.66

3. As the **Style type**, click **Table**. Under **Formatting**, click the **Apply formatting to arrow**, and then click **Header row**. On the **New Style** dialog box toolbar, click the **Bold** button. Click the **Border button arrow**, and then click **No Border**. Click the **Shading Color button arrow**, and then in the first row, click the third box—**Gray-10%**.

4. Under **Formatting**, click the **Apply formatting to arrow**, and then click **Left column**. On the **New Style** dialog box toolbar, click the **Align button arrow**, and then click **Align Center**. Click **OK**.

5. Position the insertion point in the table and click the **Growth** style. Close the task pane.

6. In the table, position the insertion point in the last row. From the **Table** menu, click **Insert**, and then click **Rows Below**. In the left cell of the new row, type **Total** and then press Tab.

7. From the **Table** menu, click **Formula**. In the **Number format** box, type **$#,##0** and then click **OK**.

(Project 7J–Press Release continues on the next page)

(Project 7J–Press Release continued)

8. Right-click on the table and click **Table Properties** from the shortcut menu. If necessary, click the **Table tab**. Under **Alignment**, click **Center**, and then click **OK**.

9. Click to position the insertion point in the blank line above the paragraph that begins *Oceana Palm Grill operates*.

10. From the **Insert** menu, point to **Picture**, and then click **From File**. From your student files, locate and insert **w07J_New_Locations**.

11. Click the chart to select it. Drag the middle sizing handle on the right border of the chart to the left approximately **1 inch**. Use the ruler as a guide. On the Formatting toolbar, click the **Center** button. Click to deselect the chart. Compare your document with Figure 7.66.

12. From the **View** menu, click **Header and Footer**. On the Header and Footer toolbar, click the **Switch Between Header and Footer** button. Click the **Insert AutoText** button, and then click **Filename**. On the **Header and Footer** toolbar, click the **Close** button.

13. On the Standard toolbar, click the **Save** button. Preview the document, and then print it. Close the document.

End You have completed Project 7J

Project 7K — Locations

Objectives: *Format Cells in a Table, Modify Table Properties, and Use Advanced Table Features.*

In the following Mastery Assessment, you will edit a table of possible Oceana Palm Grill locations in North Carolina. You will sort the data, modify the table structure, and format the table data. Your completed document will look similar to the one shown in Figure 7.67. You will save your document as *7K_Locations_Firstname_Lastname*.

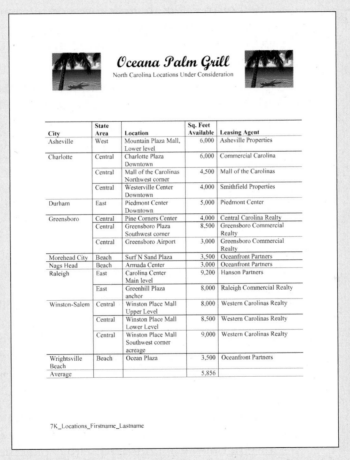

Figure 7.67

1. Locate and open **w07K_Locations**. Save the file as **7K_Locations_Firstname_Lastname** in the same location as your other files for this chapter. In the same manner as you have done in previous documents, display the footer and insert the **AutoText** filename.

2. **Sort** the table on the **City** column in ascending order, specifying that you have a header row in this table.

(Project 7K–Locations continues on the next page)

(Project 7K–Locations continued)

3. Display the Tables and Borders toolbar. In the first column of the table, delete the second and third instances of *Charlotte*. Select the *Charlotte* cell and the two empty cells below it. Merge the three cells.

4. Use the same technique to delete duplicate city names and merge the city name cells with the empty cells below them.

5. Select the top row of the table. Change the text to **Bold**. Align the first row text **Bottom Left**.

6. Add a row to the bottom of the table. In the left cell, type **Average** In the fourth cell of the new row, add a formula to show the average square footage of the possible restaurant locations. (Hint: Delete *SUM* and insert *AVERAGE*.) Select **#,##0** as the number format, to match the numbers above.

7. Select the table. Display the **Borders and Shading** dialog box and remove the left and right borders from the table.

8. Save the completed document. Preview and print the document.

End You have completed Project 7K

Project 7L — Regulations

Objectives: *Format Cells in a Table, Modify Table Properties, Use Advanced Table Features, Insert Objects in a Document, and Modify an Image.*

In the following Mastery Assessment, you will edit a memo regarding Oceana Palm Grill training sessions covering Texas Department of Health regulations. You will insert and modify graphics and create and modify a small table. Your completed document will look similar to the one shown in Figure 7.68. You will save your document as *7L_Regulations_Firstname_Lastname.*

1. From your student files, open **w07L_Regulations**. Save the file with the name **7L_Regulations_Firstname_Lastname** in the same location as your other files from this chapter. Display the footer and insert the **AutoText** filename.

2. Press + End to move to the end of the document. At this location, create a 4-row by 2-column table. Add the following text:

Date	Time
March 18	9 a.m.
March 18	3 p.m.
March 19	9 p.m.

(Project 7L–Regulations continues on the next page)

(Project 7L–Regulations continued)

MEMO

TO: Donna Rohan Kurian, Executive Chef

FROM: Devin Washington, VP Quality and Customer Service

DATE: March 4

SUBJECT: Texas Department of Health Regulations

As part of the health training for all Texas outlet kitchen and back-of-the-house employees, Oceana Palm Grill will be reinforcing compliance with all Department of Health regulations. The following background information from the Bureau of Food and Drug Safety (http://www.tdh.state.tx.us/bfds/retail/about.html) will be provided to all employees:

"The Texas Department of Health (TDH) began implementation of the state Retail Food Inspection Program after passage of Senate Bill 1421 during the 73rd legislative session. It was during this legislative session that the Retail Foods Division came into existence. The law requires TDH to permit and inspect retail food facilities in areas of the State where no local health authority currently regulates. Many establishments which had gone uninspected and unregulated for many years are now required to permit and to meet minimum food safety standards; as a result, the general public is provided a much greater degree of safety. Rules to implement the legislation were approved and adopted by the Texas Board of Health on May 20, 1994. The Retail Foods Division (RFD) is in the Bureau of Food and Drug Safety under the Associateship for Consumer Health Protection. The Division Director oversees two branches in the RFD, the Accreditation and Training Branch and the Field Operations and Enforcement Branch."

Your knowledge of government regulations and commitment to quality are a big part of Oceana Palm Grill's success. Your participation in this training initiative will help to assure that all our restaurants far exceed all minimum requirements and continue to provide our customers with the highest possible quality food and beverages. The training sessions dates and times are listed in the table on the right.

Date	Time
March 18	9 a.m.
March 18	3 p.m.
March 19	9 p.m.

7L_Regulations_Firstname_Lastname

Figure 7.68

3. Display the Tables and Borders toolbar. Select the table. Click the **Table AutoFormat** button. Under **Table styles**, click **Table Grid 8**. Be sure that special formatting is *not* applied to the last row or last column. From the **Table** menu, point to **AutoFit**, and then click **AutoFit to Contents**.

4. Change the table properties to wrap the text around the table. Use the table move handle to move the table to the right edge of the last paragraph, as shown in Figure 7.68.

5. Position the insertion point at the beginning of the paragraph that starts *The Texas Department*. From your student files, insert the **w07L_Texas** image.

6. Format the picture to wrap text **Tight** around the image. Change the **Scale** of the image to **125%** and be sure to retain the image proportions. Compare your document with Figure 7.68.

7. Save the completed document. Preview and print the document.

End You have completed Project 7L

Problem Solving

Project 7M — Employee

Objectives: *Insert Objects in a Document and Modify an Image.*

Good employees are critical to the success of a business. Employee of the Month awards help build team spirit and motivate individuals. In this project, you will complete an Employee of the Month announcement from Oceana Palm Grill. You will save your document as *7M_Employee_ Firstname_Lastname.*

1. Locate and open **w07M_Employee**. Save the document as **7M_Employee_Firstname_Lastname** and add the file name to the footer.

2. Type your name as indicated as Employee of the Month.

3. Type two short paragraphs about why you think you won the award. For example, helping to train new employees, helping out when the restaurant was short of staff, and so forth. Give yourself any job title you like, other than CEO or President, and make sure the text fits the job.

4. Have someone take your picture with a digital camera. Insert your picture in the document as indicated. Scale your picture, making the width **4 inches**. Put a border around the picture, make the border line at least **2 pt.**, and change the color of the border to **blue**.

5. Save the completed document. Preview and print the document.

End You have completed Project 7M ———————————————

Project 7N — Personal Styles

Objectives: *Format Cells in a Table, Modify Table Properties, Use Advanced Table Features, Insert Objects in a Document, and Modify an Image.*

The United States Department of Agriculture has set nutrition guidelines, including a food pyramid. The food pyramid suggests the relative proportions of different foods that should be eaten to maintain a healthy diet. They include a list showing the optimum number of servings per day for different types of food.

1. You will use a PDF file to find the data needed for this project. Go to My Computer. Locate and open **w07N_Food_Pyramid**, which is a PDF file. If you cannot open the PDF file, it means that Adobe Acrobat Reader is not installed on your computer. To obtain Adobe Acrobat Reader, go to www.adobe.com and follow instructions for downloading and installing the program. You will need to register with Adobe, but there is no charge to download the program, or any obligation by registering.

(Project 7N–Personal Styles continues on the next page)

(Project 7N–Personal Styles continued)

2. Scroll down until you find the list of the recommended number of servings of different foods. Print just the pages containing that information.

3. Create a new document and save the document as *7N_Food_Pyramid_Firstname_Lastname*. Add a brief introductory paragraph, and then create a two-column table, with food types in the first column and number of servings in the second column.

4. Look through the information you printed, find the column that is appropriate for you, and create a table of recommended servings.

5. Find a clip art image of food and insert it into your document.

6. Change the color of the image to grayscale and change the contrast and brightness so it is light enough to place behind your table.

7. Scale the image to about 5 inches wide. Format the image so that it appears behind the table.

8. Save your work. Preview and print the document, and then close the document.

End You have completed Project 7N ——————————————

On the Internet

Downloading a Template from the Office Web Site

In this chapter, you formatted and modified several tables. Tables are also used for many of the templates that are available on the Microsoft Office Web site. Once these templates are downloaded to your computer, you can use the same techniques you practiced in this chapter to modify them.

1. Be sure that you are connected to the Internet. Open Word, and from the **File** menu, click **New**. In the **New Document** task pane, under **Templates**, click **Templates on Office Online** (you may have to select Templates Homepage to get to Office Online).

2. On the **Templates** page of Microsoft Office Online, scroll down to see the categories of templates that are available to you. Click on some of the categories to see what you can download.

3. Click the **Back** button until the screen returns to the **Template** page.

4. Under the **Healthcare and Wellness** category, click **Diet and Exercise**. Click the **Food Diary** template.

5. If you are working in a college computer lab, check to be sure you can download files. If it is permitted, click the **Download Now** button. You may be asked to install the Microsoft Office **Template and Media Control** program. You will need to install this program if you have not already done so. The template displays.

6. Save the template as a Word document using a name of your choice. Modify the information in the Food Group column. Find an appropriate clip art image or picture and insert it. Resize the image, lighten it, and place it behind the table.

7. When you are done, save and close the file. The original template is still available on your computer.

Creating an Excel Chart in Word

In this chapter you practiced using the Insert menu to insert objects. In the Object dialog box, you had the choice of creating a new object or creating an object from a file. Among the new objects you can create in Word is an Excel chart.

1. Start Word. In the *Type a question for help* box, type **create Excel chart**

2. Examine the list of topics that displays in the **Search Results** task pane. From this list of help topics, click **Insert information by creating a linked object or embedded object**.

3. Locate and read the instructions for creating an embedded Excel chart in Word.

4. In a blank document, create a chart using the **Insert** menu command. You will need to switch between Excel worksheets in the Excel window in your document. You will add and edit your data in the **Sheet1** worksheet and format the chart in the **Chart1** worksheet. (Hint: To change the chart formatting, double-click on the chart element you want to change.)

5. Try using the various buttons on the Chart toolbar to see what you can do with an Excel chart.

6. Close the **Help** window and the **Help** task pane, close your document without saving the changes, and exit Word.

8 chaptereight

Using Word with Other Office Programs and Creating Mass Mailings

In this chapter, you will: complete these projects **and** practice these skills.

Project 8A **Embedding and Linking Objects**	**Objectives** • Embed Excel Charts and Data • Link to Excel Charts and PowerPoint Presentations

Project 8B **Using Mail Merge**	**Objectives** • Create Labels Using the Mail Merge Wizard • Create a Form Letter • Merge Letters with Records from the Data Source

The Greater Atlanta Job Fair

The Greater Atlanta Job Fair is a nonprofit organization supported by the Atlanta Chamber of Commerce and Atlanta City Colleges. The organization holds several targeted job fairs in the Atlanta area each year. Candidate registration is free and open to area residents and students enrolled in certificate or degree programs at any of the City Colleges. Employers pay a nominal fee to participate in the fairs. When candidates register for a fair, their resumes are scanned into an interactive, searchable database that is provided to the employers.

© Getty Images, Inc.

Working with Excel, Access, and PowerPoint

Microsoft Office 2003 is an integrated program, which means that individual Office programs are more useful by making use of the features of the other programs. Excel, the Office spreadsheet, is used frequently with Word. Excel data can be inserted as a Word table. Excel charts can be inserted as objects into Word documents, either as static (unchangeable) graphic objects or as dynamic objects that link back to the Excel program. In this arrangement, updates to the Excel data result in identical updates to the Word objects based on that data. PowerPoint presentations can be linked to a button in a Word document. Microsoft Access data can be inserted into Word tables, and Access reports can be exported into Word.

Creating form letters and labels is a common business task and one in which communication between programs is essential. For example, address information from Access databases, Excel lists, and Word tables can be inserted in Word to customize form letters and to create mailing labels.

Project 8A **Job Fair Overview**

Information from other Office programs can be inserted into Microsoft Word documents. This information includes data from Excel spreadsheets, data from Access tables, Excel charts, or PowerPoint slides. The information can be embedded in the document or linked to the source document.

In Activities 8.1 through 8.6, you will add Excel data and charts to a Word document for Yolanda Strickland, the assistant to the employer coordinator. The document will be sent to potential organization participants in the Greater Atlanta Job Fair. You will also insert a link to a PowerPoint presentation. Your completed document will look similar to Figure 8.1. You will save your document as *8A_Job_Fair_Overview_ Firstname_Lastname.*

MEMO TO: Michael Augustino, Executive Director

FROM: Yolanda Strickland

DATE: February 26

SUBJECT: Charts and Data for Form Letter

I am working on the draft of the mass mailing form letter we are going to send to area businesses at the end of the month. I have chosen some data that I think is appropriate to help sell our services. The first chart I have chosen is a breakdown of the representation by industry at the 2004 job fairs. I am considering the following pie chart:

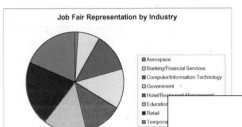

I think a table showing the attendance over a five year period wou... broken down by location and year. I do not have all of the inform... yet, but I should have those numbers by the end of the week. I ha... spreadsheet that I took the data from, so when you open this next... updated.

Job Fair Attendance

	2000	2001	2002
Atlanta	7,873	8,145	9,683
Decatur	4,580	4,879	5,105
East Point	2,520	2,641	2,598
Forest Park	1,580	2,109	1,988
Lawrenceville	1,938	2,325	2,542
Macon	4,687	4,873	4,998
North Atlanta	3,647	3,879	3,764
Total Attendance	28,825	30,852	32,680

8A_Job_Fair_Overview_Firstname_Lastname

I would also like to include a chart showing total attendance at all of the job fairs over the last five years. This chart is also incomplete, but should be ready next week. The chart will update automatically.

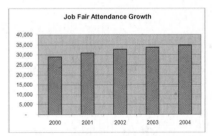

If you have any comments or questions, let me know. I would also appreciate your input on the charts and table I have selected. I have also created a PowerPoint presentation that we could put on our Web site and possibly use when talking to prospective businesses:

Greater Atlanta Job Fair

8A_Job_Fair_Overview_Firstname_Lastname

Figure 8.1
Project 8A—Job Fair Overview

Objective 1
Embed Excel Charts and Data

All Microsoft Office programs support **OLE**, which stands for **Object Linking and Embedding** and is pronounced *o-LAY*. OLE is a program-integration technology for sharing information between Office programs. Objects, for example, a table, chart, graphic, or other form of information created in one Office program—the **source file**—can be linked to or embedded in another Office program—the **destination file**.

To **embed** means to insert, using a format that you specify, information from a source file in one program into a destination file in another program. An embedded object maintains the characteristics of the original application, but is not tied to the original file. For example, the object's information in the destination file does not change if you modify the information in the source file.

Activity 8.1 Embedding an Excel Chart

Excel has a more sophisticated charting program than Word. When a complex chart is required within a Word document, it makes sense to develop the chart in Excel, and then embed it in your Word document.

1 Open Word. On the Standard toolbar, click the **Open** button. Navigate to the location where the student files for this textbook are stored. Locate and open **w08A_Job_Fair_Overview**. Save the file as **8A_Job_Fair_Overview_Firstname_Lastname** creating a new folder for this chapter if you want to do so.

2 On the Standard toolbar, click the **Zoom button arrow** 100% , and then click **Page Width**. If necessary, on the Standard toolbar, click the Show/Hide ¶ button to show formatting marks.

3 On the Windows taskbar, click the **Start** button start , navigate to the location of the Microsoft Office programs, and then open **Excel**.

On the Standard toolbar, click the **Open** button. Navigate to the location where the student files for this textbook are stored. Locate and open the **w08A_Job_Fair_Statistics** Excel file. Save the file as **8A_Job_Fair_Statistics_Firstname_Lastname** and save it in the same location as your **8A_Job_Fair_Overview** file.

4 At the bottom of the Excel screen, click the **Representation by Industry sheet tab** to display the second worksheet in the workbook.

The worksheet contains data and a ***chart***, which presents a graphical representation of the data. A ***worksheet*** is a grid pattern of rows and columns. The intersection of a row and a column is a ***cell***, similar to the structure of a Word table. An Excel workbook consists of one or more worksheets.

5 Click in a white area of the *Job Fair Representation by Industry* Excel chart to select it.

Sizing handles display around the border of the chart, and colored borders surround the data that is represented in the chart, as shown in Figure 8.2.

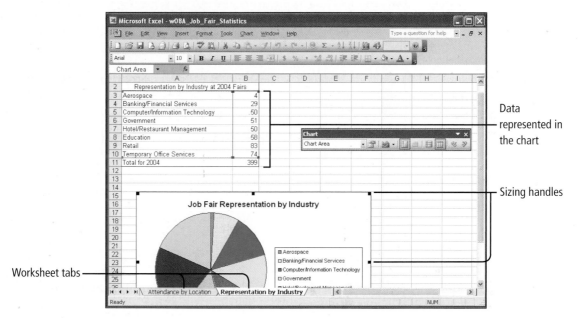

Figure 8.2

6 From the Standard toolbar, click the **Copy** button.

The Excel chart is copied to the Office Clipboard.

7 On the taskbar, click the Microsoft Word icon for your **8A_Job_Fair_Overview** file.

8 Locate the paragraph that begins *I am working* and click to position the insertion point in the second blank line below that paragraph. From the **Edit** menu, click **Paste Special**.

The Paste Special dialog box displays. The **Paste Special** command enables you to copy information from one location and paste it in another location using a different format, such as a Microsoft Excel Object, Picture, or Web format. Here you can paste the selected chart as an Excel Chart Object or as a Picture—as an embedded object. Or, if you click the Paste link option button, you can paste the selected chart as a linked object. See Figure 8.3.

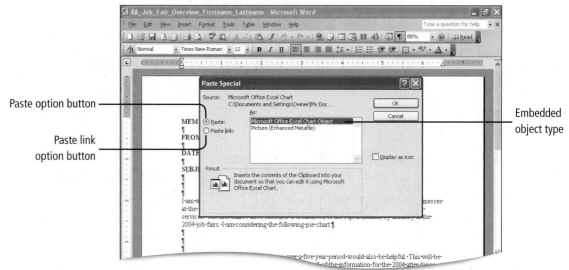

Paste option button

Paste link option button

Embedded object type

Figure 8.3

More Knowledge — Pasting an Excel Chart into a Word Document

The Paste Special command enables you to embed an Excel chart in a Word document in two ways. If you embed the chart as a picture, you will be able to use picture formatting commands, but will not be able to edit the chart data. If you embed the chart as an Excel object, you will be able to edit the chart using Excel commands, but you will not have access to the original Excel data. Additionally, changes to the original data in the Excel file will not be reflected in the Word document. If you click the Paste link option button and link, rather than embed, the Excel chart, you can go back to the original source file and make changes that will be reflected in the linked chart within your Word document.

9 In the **Paste Special** dialog box, click **OK** to accept the default option.

The chart is embedded at the insertion point location, as shown in Figure 8.4. As an embedded object, changes made to the original Excel file will not be reflected here in the Word document. The two charts are not tied to each other in any way.

Embedded chart ———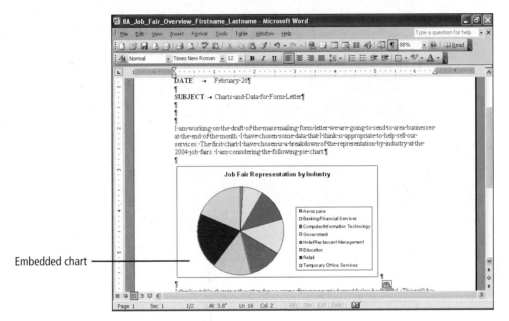

Figure 8.4

10 On the Standard toolbar, click the **Save** button.

Activity 8.2 Embedding Excel Data

Excel data—the rows and columns of information—can be embedded using the same procedure you used to embed a chart.

1 On the taskbar, click the Microsoft Excel icon for the **8A_Job_Fair_ Statistics** file. At the lower edge of the workbook, click the **Attendance by Location sheet tab**.

Excel data is stored in cells, which are labeled by column letter and row number. For example, the cell in the upper left corner of a worksheet is cell A1.

2 Move the pointer to cell **A1** and drag down and to the right to cell **F10**.

The data table is selected, as shown in Figure 8.5.

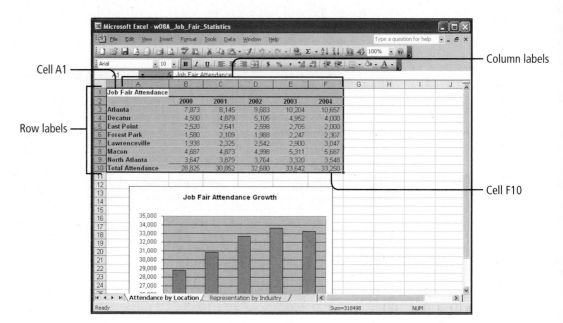

Figure 8.5

3 On the Standard toolbar, click the **Copy** button.

The selected cells are placed on the Office Clipboard.

4 On the taskbar, click the Microsoft Word icon for your **8A_Job_Fair_Overview** file. Locate the paragraph beginning *I think a table* and click to position the insertion point in the second blank line following that paragraph.

5 From the **Edit** menu, click **Paste Special**.

The Paste Special dialog box displays. Selecting cells of data, rather than a chart as you did in Activity 8.1, offers more formats with which the information can be embedded.

6 In the **Paste Special** dialog box, under **As**, click **Microsoft Office Excel Worksheet Object**, and then click **OK**.

The data table is embedded in the document, as shown in Figure 8.6.

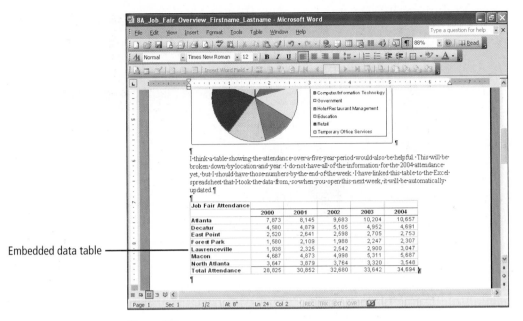

Embedded data table —

Figure 8.6

7 On the Standard toolbar, click the **Save** button [icon].

Activity 8.3 Editing Embedded Excel Charts and Data

When you use the Paste Special command to embed a chart or data from an Excel worksheet as Excel objects into your Word document, you can activate the Excel commands to edit the objects without leaving the Word program.

1 Scroll to position the colored pie chart, **Job Fair Representation by Industry**, in the center of your screen. Move your mouse pointer anywhere over the chart, right-click to display a shortcut menu, point to **Chart Object**, and then click **Edit**. Alternatively, double-click in the white area of the chart.

A slashed border surrounds the chart, and the worksheet tabs from the Excel file display at the bottom of the chart. Your chart number tab may display a different number. Excel buttons temporarily display in the toolbars, and Excel commands temporarily replace Word commands in the menus. The Chart toolbar may also display. See Figure 8.7.

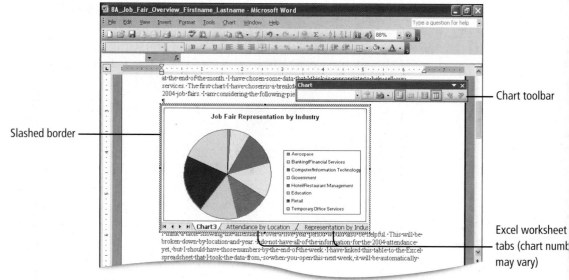

Chart toolbar

Slashed border

Excel worksheet tabs (chart numb may vary)

Figure 8.7

2 Click anywhere in the **pie graphic**.

A sizing handle displays on each of the pie wedges.

3 Click the **pale green pie wedge**.

Handles display around the pale green wedge only, indicating that it is selected. See Figure 8.8.

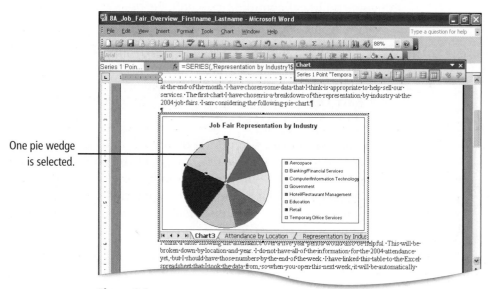

One pie wedge is selected.

Figure 8.8

4 Right-click the selected pie wedge and from the shortcut menu, click **Format Data Point**.

The Format Data Point dialog box displays.

5 Under **Area**, in the fourth row, click the fourth color—**Lime Green**.

Compare your Format Data Point dialog box with Figure 8.9.

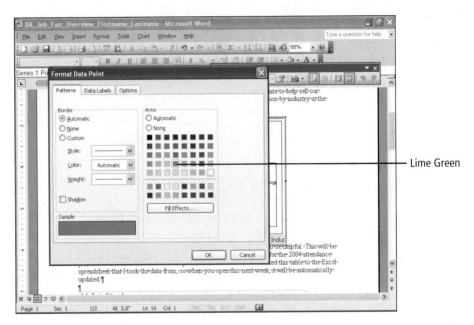

Lime Green

Figure 8.9

6 At the bottom of the **Format Data Point** dialog box, click **OK**. Click anywhere in the document to deselect the chart.

Notice that the color of the pie wedge changes to lime green, as does the related box in the legend. See Figure 8.10. When you deselect, the Excel program is closed and the toolbars and menus return to the Word commands. Although you were able to activate Excel commands and edit the chart while in Word, this action did not make any changes to the original Excel file. The original Excel file remains unchanged.

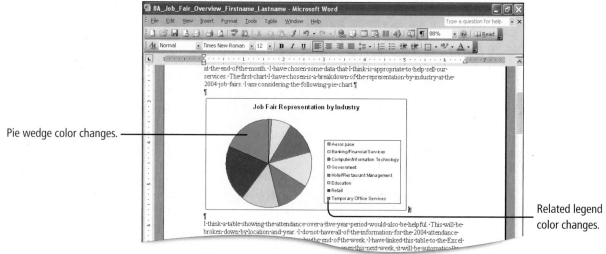

Pie wedge color changes. ————

Related legend color changes.

Figure 8.10

7 Scroll down and display the *Job Fair Attendance* data table in the center of your screen. Move your mouse pointer over the table, right-click, point to **Worksheet Object**, and then click **Edit**. Alternatively, double-click on the table.

A slashed border surrounds the data table, and the worksheet tabs from the Excel file display at the bottom of the table. Excel buttons temporarily display in the toolbars, and Excel commands temporarily replace Word commands in the menus.

8 At the intersection of **column F** and **row 4**, click cell **F4**, type **4691** and then press Enter.

The number changes, and the Total Attendance for 2004, in cell F10, is recalculated because cell F10 contains a formula that adds the numbers in the 2004 column. You do not need to type the comma—it is added by Excel.

9 Click cell **F5**, type **2753** and then press Enter.

10 Click anywhere in the document to deselect the data table.

Recall that these changes will not be reflected in the original Excel file. You can activate Excel commands to edit this table, but as an embedded Excel object, this table is no longer tied to the original Excel file. Compare your screen with Figure 8.11.

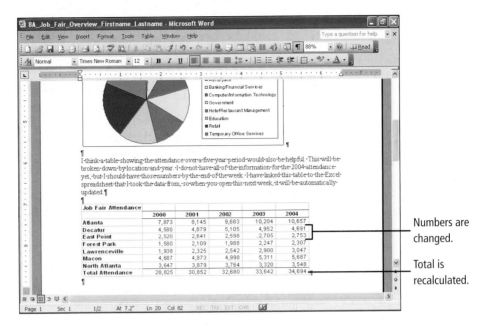

Figure 8.11

11 On the Standard toolbar, click the **Save** button.

Objective 2
Link to Excel Charts and PowerPoint Presentations

In Activities 8.1 through 8.3, you embedded an Excel chart and Excel data into a Word document. Although you were able to activate Excel commands to edit the Excel objects, the objects themselves were not tied to the original Excel file. For example, the changes you made to the 2004 attendance numbers in the Word document were not made to the original Excel spreadsheet from which the data originated.

If you want to make changes to Excel data and have the changes also made to the corresponding Excel object in a Word document, then you should **link**, rather than embed, the Excel object. To link means to insert information from a source file in one program into a destination file in another program, while maintaining a connection between the two.

Activity 8.4 Linking to an Excel Chart

A **linked object** is an object that maintains a direct connection to the source file. Linked data is stored in the source file (the Excel workbook); it is *not* stored in the destination file (the Word document). What you see in the Word document is only a representation of the Excel file. Unlike the embedded object, you cannot activate Excel commands while in Word, because the object is not a part of the actual Word document. Changes must be made by opening the source file (the original Excel workbook), after which the linked object in the destination file (the Word document) is also updated.

1 On the taskbar, click the Microsoft Excel icon for the **8A_Job_Fair_Statistics** file. Click the **Attendance by Location sheet tab** at the bottom of the worksheet.

2 Click in the white area of the chart once to select it. From the Standard toolbar, click the **Copy** button 🗐.

3 On the taskbar, click the Microsoft Word icon for your **8A_Job_Fair_Overview** file. Scroll to the second page, locate the paragraph beginning *I would also like to include*, and then click to position the insertion point in the second blank line following that paragraph.

4 From the **Edit** menu, click **Paste Special**.

The Paste Special dialog box displays.

5 In the **Paste Special** dialog box, click the **Paste link** option button.

Under *As*, notice that *Microsoft Office Excel Chart Object* is the only choice, as shown in Figure 8.12.

Paste link
option button

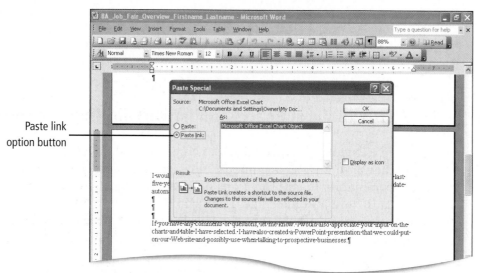

Figure 8.12

6 In the upper right corner of the **Paste Special** dialog box, click **OK**.

The chart is placed at the insertion point location.

7 On the Standard toolbar, click the **Save** button [image].

Activity 8.5 Modifying Charts Linked to Excel Data

Recall that a linked object behaves differently from an embedded object. To edit the linked object, you must do so from the source file; thus you cannot activate the Excel commands within Word, as you did for an embedded object. Linking is especially useful when the Word document will be maintained as an online document. In that manner, any changes to the Excel data will be reflected automatically in the online Word document that contains the linked object.

1 On the taskbar, click the Microsoft Excel icon for the **w08A_Job_Fair_Statistics** file.

2 Click cell **F4** to select it, type **4691** and then press Enter.

The number changes, and the Total Attendance for 2004 in cell F10 is recalculated because cell F10 contains a formula that adds the 2004 column.

3 Select cell **F5**, type **2753** and then press Enter.

The number changes, and the Total Attendance for 2004 is again recalculated. Because the chart in the worksheet is based on the data in the cells, it is also updated, as shown in Figure 8.13.

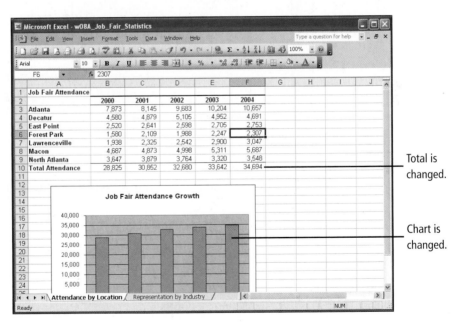

Total is changed.

Chart is changed.

Figure 8.13

4 From the **File** menu, click **Save**. Close Excel. If necessary, on the taskbar click the Microsoft Word icon for your *8A_Job_Fair_Overview* file. Look at the last column in the chart.

Although this is a linked object, and you have changed information in the source file, the linked object is not updated automatically because the destination file is open. Only closed files are updated automatically, because before a document is opened, Word checks for any links and updates them.

5 Right-click the **Job Fair Attendance Growth** chart and from the shortcut menu, click **Update Link**.

After a few seconds, the chart is updated to reflect the changes in the source file—the Excel worksheet. Compare your screen with Figure 8.14.

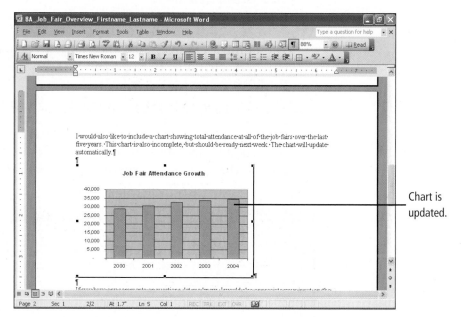

Chart is updated.

Figure 8.14

6 On the Standard toolbar, click the **Save** button.

Note — Updating Links

By default, Word updates any links in your document, provided the document is closed. Each time you open the document, Word checks whether any links have changed and updates them accordingly. This process can take a few minutes if your document has numerous links. If you make a change to the source file, and the destination file happens to be open, as you did in the previous activity, you will need to initiate the Update Link command manually.

Activity 8.6 Linking to a PowerPoint Presentation

Within a Word document, you can insert a link to a PowerPoint presentation. Because this memo will be sent by e-mail, in this activity you will insert a link to a PowerPoint presentation that the e-mail recipient can view by clicking on the link.

1 Hold down Ctrl and press End to move the insertion point to the end of the document.

2 From the **Insert** menu, click **Object**. In the **Object** dialog box, click the **Create from File tab**.

3 Click **Browse**, navigate to the location of your student files, and then click **w08A_Presentation**. Click **Insert**.

The file name displays in the *File name* box, as shown in Figure 8.15.

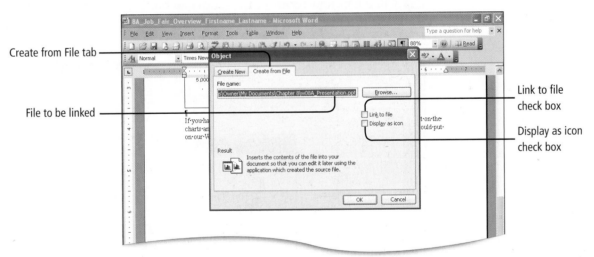

Create from File tab

File to be linked

Link to file check box

Display as icon check box

Figure 8.15

4 At the right side of the **Object** dialog box, select the **Link to file** check box and select the **Display as icon** check box.

A preview PowerPoint icon displays near the bottom of the Object dialog box. The default caption for the icon is the document name and location. A Change Icon button displays under the preview icon. See Figure 8.16.

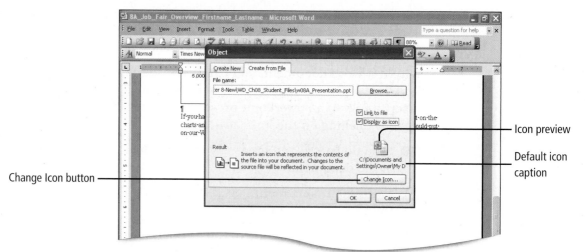

Change Icon button

Icon preview

Default icon caption

Figure 8.16

5 Click **Change Icon**. In the **Caption** box, select and delete the text. Type **Greater Atlanta Job Fair** as shown in Figure 8.17.

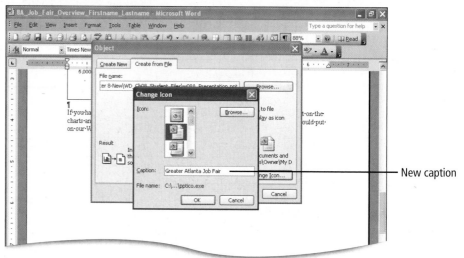

New caption

Figure 8.17

6 At the bottom of the **Change Icon** dialog box, click **OK**. At the bottom of the **Object** dialog box, click **OK**.

The icon is placed in line with the text in the last paragraph.

7 Right-click the new icon. From the shortcut menu, click **Format Object**. In the **Format Object** dialog box, click the **Layout tab**.

8 Under **Wrapping style**, click **Square**. At the bottom of the **Format Object** dialog box, click **OK**.

9 Drag the icon up and to the right until it is located at the right side of the last paragraph, as shown in Figure 8.18.

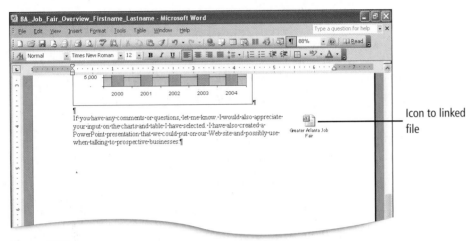

Icon to linked file

Figure 8.18

10 Double-click the icon.

The PowerPoint presentation opens, as shown in Figure 8.19.

Alert!

If the PowerPoint Presentation Does Not Run

If you do not have PowerPoint installed on your computer, you will get a message indicating that the associated program cannot be found. If this happens, click OK and move to Step 12.

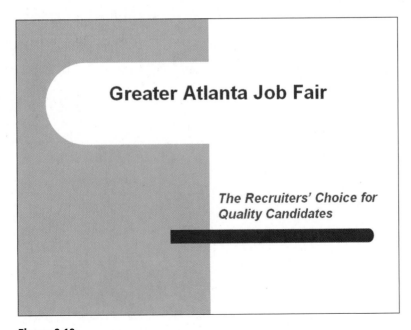

Figure 8.19

11 Click the left mouse button to advance through the presentation one slide at a time. When you reach the black slide, which indicates the end of the slide show, click once.

The PowerPoint presentation closes, and your Word document redisplays.

12 Press Ctrl + Home to move to the top of the document. Click the pie chart, and then on the Formatting toolbar, click the **Center** button ▤ to center the chart horizontally on the page. Select and then center horizontally the remaining two objects in the document.

13 From the **View** menu, click **Header and Footer**. On the Header and Footer toolbar, click the **Switch Between Header and Footer** button ▣. Click the **Insert AutoText** button Insert AutoText ▾, and then click **Filename**.

The file name is inserted in the footer.

14 On the Header and Footer toolbar, click the **Close** button Close. On the Standard toolbar, click the **Save** button 🖫.

15 On the Standard toolbar, click the **Print Preview** button 🔍. Use the PageDown and Page Up buttons to view both pages in Print Preview. Take a moment to check your work. On the Print Preview toolbar, click the **Close Preview** button Close.

16 Make any necessary changes to your document. When you are satisfied, on the Standard toolbar, click the **Print** button 🖨. Close the document, saving any changes.

End You have completed Project 8A ─────────────────────────

8B

Project 8B **Form Letter**

Form letters and mailing labels can be created quickly by merging names and addresses from a Word table, an Access database, or an Excel spreadsheet with a Word document. File folder labels, business cards, and index cards can be created in a similar manner.

In Activities 8.7 through 8.17, you will use a wizard to create and print a set of labels—from information in a Word table—suitable for printing on a sheet of blank mailing labels. You will save this document as *8B_Labels_ Firstname_Lastname*. You will also create a form letter that will be sent to individuals requesting information about the Greater Atlanta Job Fair. You will merge name and address data from an Access database with a letter in Word, and then preview and print one of the letters. Finally, you will customize another letter and print it. Your completed documents will look similar to Figure 8.20. You will save your letters as *8B_Form_Letter_ Firstname_Lastname* and *8B_Form_Letter2_ Firstname_Lastname*, and the label document as *8B_Labels_ Firstname_Lastname.*

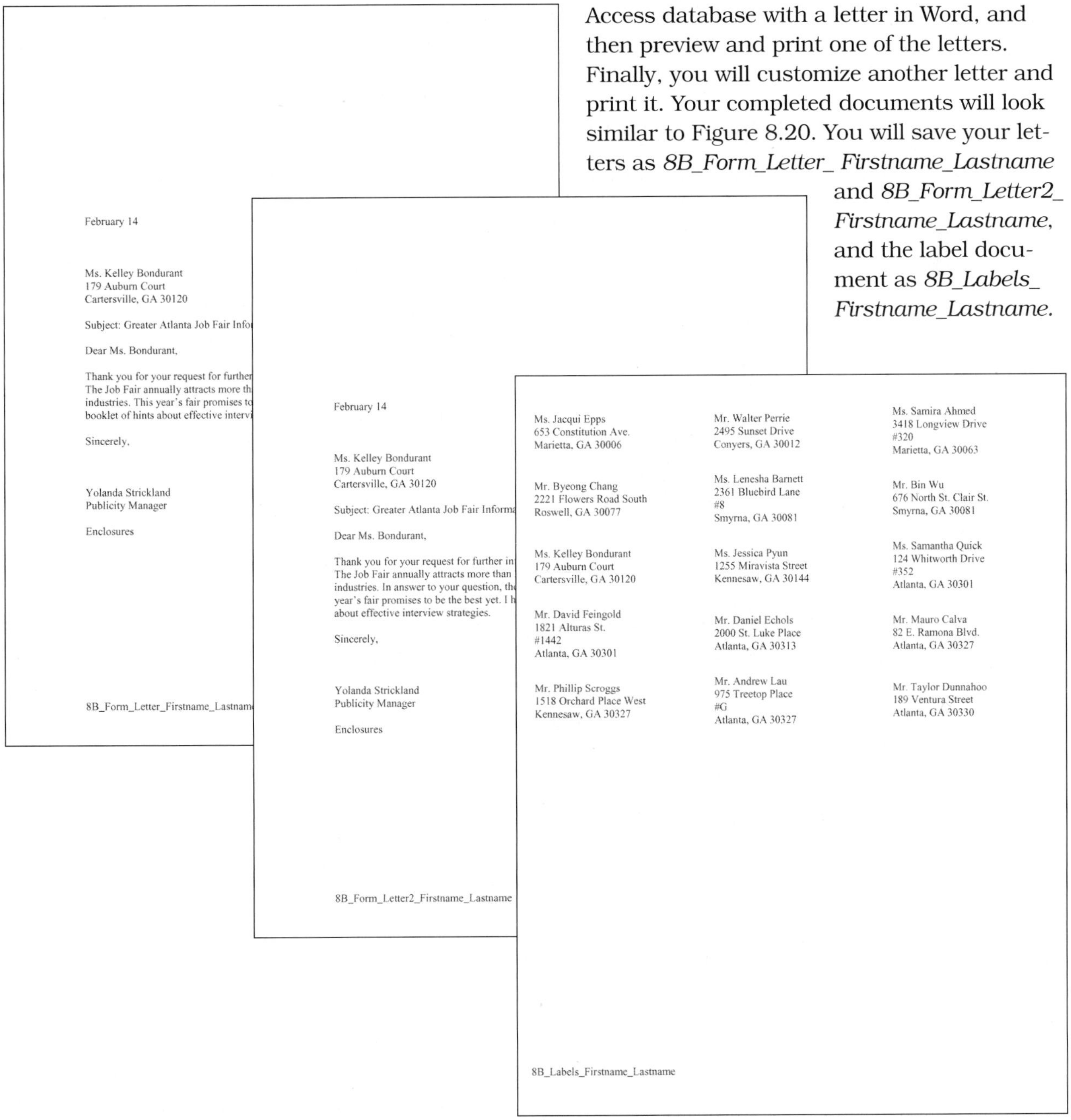
February 14

Ms. Kelley Bondurant
179 Auburn Court
Cartersville, GA 30120

Subject: Greater Atlanta Job Fair Info

Dear Ms. Bondurant,

Thank you for your request for further
The Job Fair annually attracts more th
industries. This year's fair promises t
booklet of hints about effective intervi

Sincerely,

Yolanda Strickland
Publicity Manager

Enclosures

8B_Form_Letter_Firstname_Lastnam

February 14

Ms. Kelley Bondurant
179 Auburn Court
Cartersville, GA 30120

Subject: Greater Atlanta Job Fair Informa

Dear Ms. Bondurant,

Thank you for your request for further in
The Job Fair annually attracts more than
industries. In answer to your question, th
year's fair promises to be the best yet. I h
about effective interview strategies.

Sincerely,

Yolanda Strickland
Publicity Manager

Enclosures

8B_Form_Letter2_Firstname_Lastname

Ms. Jacqui Epps 653 Constitution Ave. Marietta, GA 30006	Mr. Walter Perrie 2495 Sunset Drive Conyers, GA 30012	Ms. Samira Ahmed 3418 Longview Drive #320 Marietta, GA 30063
Mr. Byeong Chang 2221 Flowers Road South Roswell, GA 30077	Ms. Lenesha Barnett 2361 Bluebird Lane #8 Smyrna, GA 30081	Mr. Bin Wu 676 North St. Clair St. Smyrna, GA 30081
Ms. Kelley Bondurant 179 Auburn Court Cartersville, GA 30120	Ms. Jessica Pyun 1255 Miravista Street Kennesaw, GA 30144	Ms. Samantha Quick 124 Whitworth Drive #352 Atlanta, GA 30301
Mr. David Feingold 1821 Alturas St. #1442 Atlanta, GA 30301	Mr. Daniel Echols 2000 St. Luke Place Atlanta, GA 30313	Mr. Mauro Calva 82 E. Ramona Blvd. Atlanta, GA 30327
Mr. Phillip Scroggs 1518 Orchard Place West Kennesaw, GA 30327	Mr. Andrew Lau 975 Treetop Place #G Atlanta, GA 30327	Mr. Taylor Dunnahoo 189 Ventura Street Atlanta, GA 30330

8B_Labels_Firstname_Lastname

Figure 8.20

Objective 3
Create Labels Using the Mail Merge Wizard

Using Word's *mail merge* feature, labels are created by combining (merging) two documents—a *main document* and a *data source*. The main document starts out blank, and is formatted for a specific label size. The data source contains the names and addresses of the individuals to whom the letters or postcards are being sent. Names and addresses in a data source can be contained in a Word table, an Excel spreadsheet, or an Access database.

The easiest way to perform a Mail Merge is to use the Mail Merge Wizard. Recall that a wizard asks you questions and, based on your answers, walks you step by step through a process. Labels are used to address envelopes or postcards or to label disks, name badges, file folders, and so on. Sheets of precut labels can be purchased from office supply stores.

Activity 8.7 Adding an Address to a Word Address Table

Mail merge information can come from many sources, including Microsoft Word tables. These tables can be edited just like any other Word table.

1 Open Word. On the Standard toolbar, click the **Open** button. Navigate to the location where the student files for this textbook are stored. Locate and open **w08B_Job_Fair_Addresses**. Save the file as **8B_Job_Fair_Addresses_Firstname_Lastname**

2 On the Standard toolbar, click the **Zoom button arrow** 100%, and then click **Page Width**. If necessary, on the Standard toolbar, click the Show/Hide ¶ button to show formatting marks.

A table of addresses displays. The first row contains the column names. The remaining rows contain addresses. See Figure 8.21.

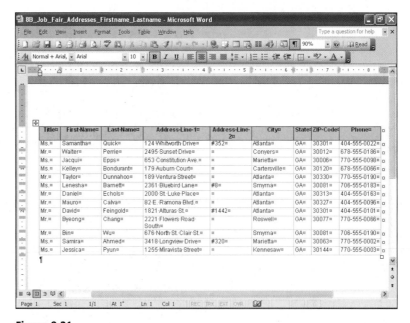

Figure 8.21

3 Click to position the insertion point in the last cell of the last row. Press Tab.

A new row is added to the table.

4 In the first cell of the new row, type **Mr.**

5 In the second cell of the new row, type **Phillip**

6 Type the following in the rest of the blank cells of the new row, leaving the Address Line 2 cell blank:

Scroggs

1518 Orchard Place West

[leave this cell blank]

Kennesaw

GA

30152

770-555-0005

Compare your table with Figure 8.22. The proper name *Scroggs* may display as a misspelled word on your system.

New name and address ——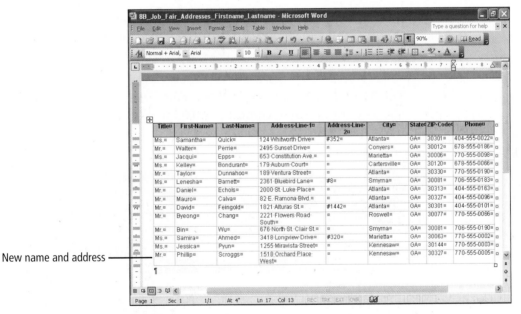

Figure 8.22

7 On the Standard toolbar, click the **Save** button. From the **File** menu, click **Close** to close the document.

Activity 8.8 Starting the Mail Merge Wizard to Set Up Labels

The label feature in Word contains the product numbers of the standard Avery label products as well as several other brands. Each product number is associated with a layout in Word's table format consisting of the height and width of the label. Because the product numbers predefine the label layout, the creation of labels is a simple and automated process. The first two steps in creating labels using the Mail Merge Wizard are identifying the label type and identifying the data source.

1 On the Standard toolbar, click the **New Blank Document** button. From the **Tools** menu, point to **Letters and Mailings**, and then click **Mail Merge**.

The Mail Merge task pane displays.

2 In the **Mail Merge** task pane, under **Select document type**, click the **Labels** option button. At the bottom of the task pane, click **Next: Starting document**.

Step 2 of 6 of the Mail Merge Wizard displays—identified at the bottom of the task pane.

3 In the middle of the task pane, under **Change document layout**, click **Label options**.

The Label Options dialog box displays.

4 In the **Label Options** dialog box, under **Label information**, click the **Label products arrow**, and then click **Avery standard**. Under **Product number**, scroll as necessary and click **5160 - Address**. See Figure 8.23.

The Avery 5160 address label is a commonly used label. The precut sheets contain three columns of 10 labels each—for a total of 30 labels per sheet.

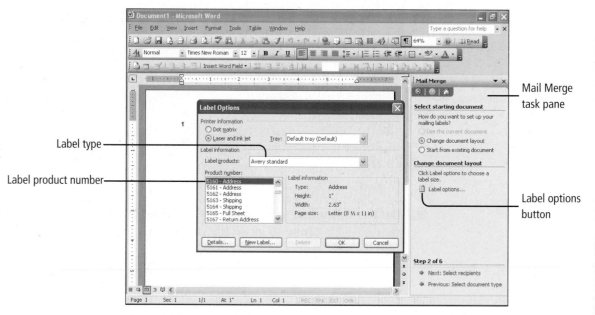

Figure 8.23

5 At the bottom of the **Label Options** dialog box, click **OK**.

The label document displays, showing the label outlines. Recall that label layouts result in a predefined Word table.

6 At the bottom of the **Mail Merge** task pane, click **Next: Select recipients**.

In Step 3 of the Mail Merge Wizard, you must identify the recipients—the data source. For your recipient data source, you can choose to use an existing list—for example, a list of names and addresses that you have in an Access database, an Excel spreadsheet, a Word table, or your Outlook contacts list. If you do not have an existing data source, you can type a new list at this point in the wizard.

Note — Creating a New Address List

When you select the *Type a new list* option, the data that you enter will be stored in a Microsoft Access table but can be edited using Word.

7 Be sure that the **Use an existing list** option button is selected, and then under **Use an existing list**, click **Browse**. Navigate to the folder where you are storing your projects for this chapter and click **8B_Job_Fair_Addresses_Firstname_Lastname**—the Word table you just edited—and then click **Open**.

The Mail Merge Recipients dialog box displays, as shown in Figure 8.24. In a database or Word address table, each row of information that contains data for one person is called a *record*. The column headings—for example, *Last Name* and *First Name*—are referred to as *fields*. A field describes the data in a record.

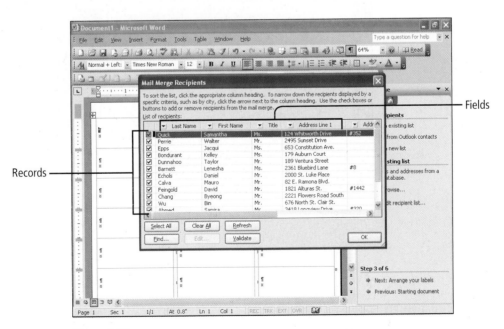

Figure 8.24

8 Use the scroll bar in the lower portion of the dialog box to scroll to the right, and then click the **ZIP Code** field column heading.

The records are sorted in numerical order by ZIP code, and the dialog box data window shifts back to display the first column.

9 At the bottom of the **Mail Merge Recipients** dialog box, click **OK**.

<<Next Record>> displays in each table cell.

10 On the Standard toolbar, click the **Save** button [image]. Navigate to the folder where you are storing your projects for this chapter, and in the **Save As** dialog box, type **8B_Labels_Firstname_Lastname** and then click **Save**.

Activity 8.9 Completing the Mail Merge Wizard

You can add or edit names and addresses while completing the Mail Merge Wizard. You can also match your column names with preset names used in Mail Merge.

1 In the **Mail Merge** task pane, under **Use an existing list**, click **Edit recipient list**.

The Mail Merge Recipients dialog box displays.

2 At the bottom of the **Mail Merge Recipients** dialog box, click **Edit**.

The Data Form dialog box displays, as shown in Figure 8.25. You can edit or delete the selected record, or use the same dialog box to add a new recipient.

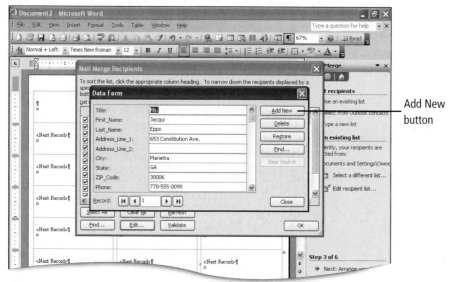

Figure 8.25

3 On the right side of the **Data Form** dialog box, click **Add New**.

The Data Form dialog box displays a new blank record.

4 In the Data Form dialog box, type the following, using the ⎡Tab⎤ key to move from field to field.

Title:	**Mr.**
First_Name:	**Andrew**
Last_Name:	**Lau**
Address_Line_1:	**975 Treetop Place**
Address_Line_2:	**#G**
City:	**Atlanta**
State:	**GA**
ZIP_Code:	**30327**
Phone:	**770-555-0008**

Compare your Data Form dialog box with Figure 8.26.

New mail merge recipient —————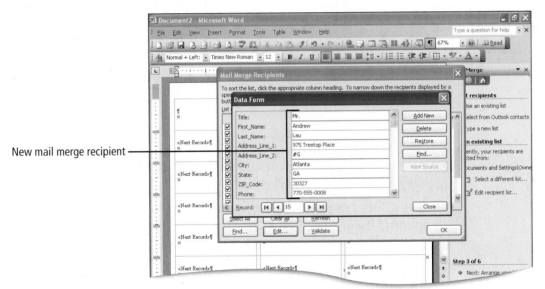

Figure 8.26

5 At the bottom of the **Data Form** dialog box, click **Close**. At the bottom of the **Mail Merge Recipients** dialog box, click **OK**. At the bottom of the **Mail Merge** task pane, click **Next: Arrange your labels**.

In Step 4 of 6 of the Mail Merge Wizard, Word provides various ways to arrange and add features to your labels. For example, you can add a **_Postal bar code_**, which applies a bar code based on the ZIP code so that the address can be scanned and sorted electronically by the U.S. Postal Service.

6 Under **Arrange your labels**, click **Address block**. In the **Insert Address Block** dialog box, under **Specify address elements**, examine the **Preview** area, and then clear the **Insert company name** check box.

This is a list of home addresses, so the organization name is not relevant. Notice that the label preview in the Preview box no longer displays a company. Compare your dialog box with Figure 8.27.

Insert company name check box

Address block preview

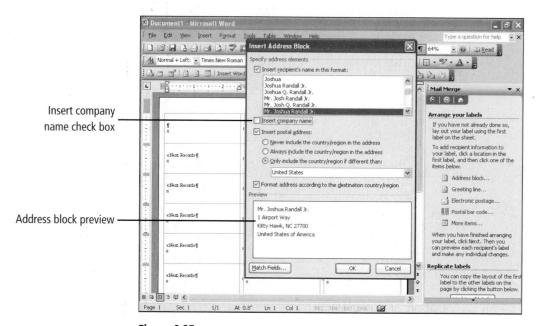

Figure 8.27

7 At the bottom of the **Insert Address Block** dialog box, click **Match Fields**. Scroll down and examine the dialog box.

If your field names are descriptive, the Mail Merge program will identify them correctly, as is the case with the information in the Required Information section, as shown in Figure 8.28. If you need to match a field, use the drop-down list to choose the correct field from your database or table.

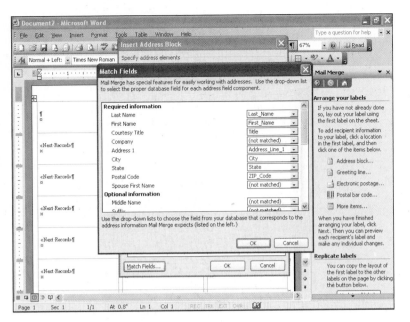

Figure 8.28

8 At the bottom of the **Match Fields** dialog box, click **OK**. At the bottom of the **Insert Address Block** dialog box, click **OK**.

The Address block is inserted in the first label space and is surrounded by double angle brackets. Only the *Address Block* field name is displayed, but this represents the address block you saw in the Preview area of the Insert Address Block dialog box.

9 In the task pane, under **Replicate labels**, click **Update all labels**.

An address block is inserted in each label space for each subsequent record.

10 At the bottom of the task pane, click **Next: Preview your labels**.

Step 5 of the Mail Merge Wizard task pane displays, and the labels are filled in with the information from the data source. Notice that the labels are sorted numerically by the ZIP Code field. The order of the labels is from left to right and then down to the next row, as shown in Figure 8.29. Notice also that in some cases, where there is an apartment or unit number, there are addresses on two lines. This is done automatically when the *Address Block* is inserted.

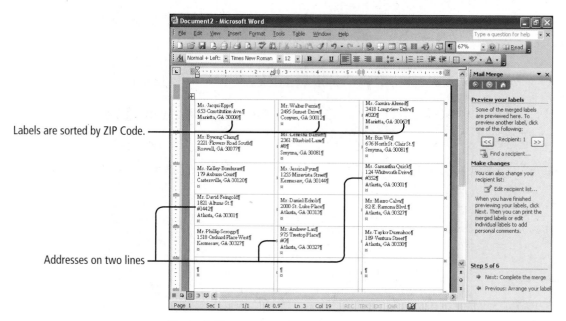

Labels are sorted by ZIP Code.

Addresses on two lines

Figure 8.29

More Knowledge — Previewing Your Labels

When the labels are large, the *Preview your labels* button enables you to scroll through your labels to examine them. This is particularly useful when you are using the Mail Merge Wizard to create letters. You can also use *Find a recipient* to locate a particular record.

11 At the bottom of the task pane, click **Next: Complete the merge**.

Step 6 of 6 of the Mail Merge task pane displays. At this point you can print or edit your labels.

12 On the Standard toolbar, click the **Save** button 🖫.

Activity 8.10 Editing Labels

Once the labels are created, you can edit individual labels when necessary.

1 In the first row of labels, locate the label for Ms. Samira Ahmed. Click to place the insertion point to the left of the apartment number—**#320**.

The label text is shaded in gray, but the insertion point is still visible.

2 Press Bksp twice.

The text is moved up to the end of the previous line.

3 Press Spacebar to add a space before the apartment number.

4 Repeat the procedure you used in Steps 1 through 3 to change the other four two-line addresses to one-line addresses.

Compare your labels to Figure 8.30.

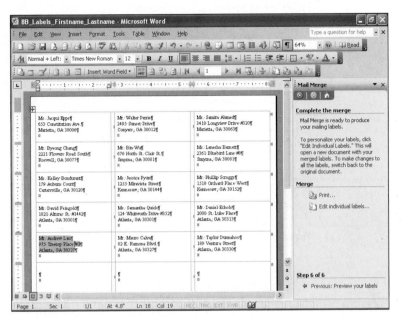

Figure 8.30

5 On the Standard toolbar, click the **Save** button.

More Knowledge — Delivery Addresses for Envelopes and Labels

For more information from the United States Postal Service about addressing envelopes and labels, go to **www.usps.com/businessmail101/welcome.htm** and click Addressing.

Activity 8.11 Previewing and Printing Labels

Before you print, it is always a good idea to preview your labels to be sure the information fits in the space reserved for each label.

1 On the Standard toolbar, click the **Print Preview** button.

2 Position the mouse pointer over the labels and click the **magnifying glass pointer**.

The labels are displayed at full size (100%), as shown in Figure 8.31.

Figure 8.31

3 On the Print Preview toolbar, click the **Close** button Close.

4 From the **View** menu, click **Header and Footer**. On the Header and Footer toolbar, click the **Switch Between Header and Footer** button. Click the **Insert AutoText** button Insert AutoText ▾, and then click **Filename**. On the Header and Footer toolbar, click the **Close** button Close.

The file name is inserted in the footer.

5 On the Standard toolbar, click the **Save** button.

6 In the **Mail Merge** task pane, under **Merge**, click **Print**. In the **Merge to Printer** dialog box, under **Print records**, click the **From** option button. In the **From** box, type **1** and in the **To** box, type **1**

This action will print only page 1. Adding a footer forced the last row of labels onto page 2, but because the labels on page 2 are empty, there is no need to print page 2.

7 In the **Merge to Printer** dialog box, click **OK**.

The Print dialog box displays.

8 At the bottom of the **Print** dialog box, click **OK** to print the labels. Close the document, saving any changes, and close Word.

The labels will print on whatever paper is in the printer. In this case, unless you have preformatted labels available, you will print your labels on a sheet of paper. This has the advantage of enabling you to proof the labels before you print them on more expensive label sheets.

Objective 4
Create a Form Letter

A *form letter* is a letter with standardized wording that can be sent to many different people. Each letter is customized to contain the name and address of the individual to whom the letter is being sent. The *salutation*, the part of the letter that begins *Dear*, and some information within the body of the letter also can be customized for each individual.

Using Word's mail merge feature, form letters are created by combining information from two documents—a main document and a data source. The main document contains the text and graphics that are the same for each version of the letter. This is called the *constant information*. The data source contains the information to be merged—for example, a list of names and addresses. This is called the *variable information* because it *varies* (differs) for each letter.

Activity 8.12 Setting Up a Form Letter

First, create the main document—the letter containing the constant information. You can create or locate an existing data source later.

1 In Word, display a new blank document, and if necessary, close the **Getting Started** task pane. On the Standard toolbar, click the **Zoom button arrow** 100% ⏷, and then click **Page Width**. If necessary, on the Standard toolbar, click the Show/Hide ¶ button to show formatting marks.

2 Right-click on any toolbar, and then click **Mail Merge**.

The Mail Merge toolbar displays, docked to the other toolbars at the top of your screen. Most of the buttons are gray because you have not yet begun the Mail Merge procedure.

3 Take a moment to point to each button on the Mail Merge toolbar and study the information in the table shown in Figure 8.32.

Mail Merge Toolbar Buttons

Name	Button	Description
Main document setup		Displays the Main Document Type dialog box, where you specify the document type, such as labels, letters, or envelopes.
Open Data Source		Displays the Select Data Source dialog box.
Mail Merge Recipients		Displays the Mail Merge Recipients dialog box, where you select or deselect recipients or edit or add names and addresses.
Insert Address Block		Displays the Insert Address Block dialog box, where you customize the data and format of the address block.
Insert Greeting Line		Displays the Greeting Block dialog box, where you customize the data and format the greeting line.
Insert Merge Fields		Displays the Insert Merge Field dialog box, showing the fields you can insert into the document.
Insert Word Field	Insert Word Field ▾	Displays a menu of built-in fields.
View Merged Data		Toggles between field names and values in the document.
Highlight Merge Fields		Highlights merged fields in the active document.
Match Fields		Displays the Match Fields dialog box, where you can match the fields in your database document with Mail Merge fields.
Propagate Labels		Enables you to create a single label, and then use the same data and format to create labels for the remaining records in a data source.
First Record		Displays the first merged record.
Previous Record		Displays the previous merged record.
Go to Record	1	Moves to a specific merged record.
Next Record		Displays the next merged record.
Last Record		Displays the last merged record.
Find Entry		Searches for a specific merged record.
Check for Errors		Checks for errors before printing the file.
Merge to New Document		Merges the source document and the data in a new document.
Merge to Printer		Merges the source document and the data and sends the resulting documents to the printer.
Merge to E-mail		Merges the source document and the data and sends the documents by e-mail.
Merge to Fax		Merges the source document and the data and sends the documents by fax.
Toolbar Options		Enables you to add or remove toolbar buttons.

Figure 8.32

4 On the Mail Merge toolbar, click the **Main document setup** button 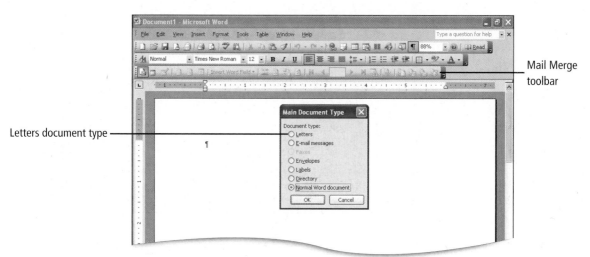.

The Main Document Type dialog box displays. See Figure 8.33.

Figure 8.33

5 Under **Document type**, click the **Letters** option button, and then click **OK**.

Because you are creating this document from the Mail Merge toolbar, you can type the constant information and then use Mail Merge commands directly from the Mail Merge toolbar.

6 Type **February 14** and then press Enter five times.

7 Type the following text, pressing Enter twice after the Subject line:

Subject: Greater Atlanta Job Fair Information

Thank you for your request for further information about the Greater Atlanta Job Fair. The Job Fair annually attracts more than 2,000 employers representing more than 70 industries. This year's fair promises to be the best yet. I have enclosed a brochure, and a booklet of hints about effective interview strategies.

8 Press Enter twice and type **Sincerely,**

9 Press Enter four times and type **Yolanda Strickland**

10 Press Enter and type **Publicity Manager**

11 Press Enter twice and type **Enclosures**

12 From the **File** menu, click **Page Setup**, and then click the **Layout tab**. Under **Page**, click the **Vertical alignment arrow**, and then click **Center**. Click **OK**.

Compare your screen with Figure 8.34.

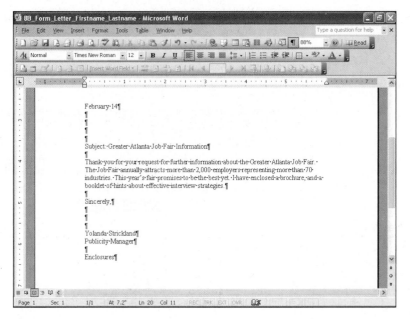

Figure 8.34

🔢 On the Standard toolbar, click the **Save** button 🖫. Navigate to the location in which you are storing your files for this chapter and save the file as **8B_Form_Letter_Firstname_Lastname**

Activity 8.13 Opening, Editing, and Sorting a Data Source

Word provides two ways to merge the data source with the main document—you can use the Mail Merge Wizard, as you did in earlier activities with mailing labels, or you can use the Mail Merge toolbar. Using the toolbar gives you more flexibility in setting up your form letter.

1️⃣ Near the left edge of the Mail Merge toolbar, click the **Open Data Source** button 🔲. Navigate to the location where the student files for this textbook are stored. If necessary, in the Select Data Source dialog box, click the Views button arrow, and then click Details. Locate and select the **Access file** named **w08B_Job_Fair_Addresses**. Be sure that the file has an icon with a key in it, rather than the Word icon that displays a *W*. Click **Open**.

This file is a Microsoft Access database, and it contains a table of names and addresses. Most of the buttons on the Mail Merge toolbar become active.

2️⃣ On the Mail Merge toolbar, click the **Mail Merge Recipients** button 🔳.

The Mail Merge Recipients dialog box displays a list of all of the names in the database table. Check marks to the left of each name indicate that the name currently is selected. See Figure 8.35.

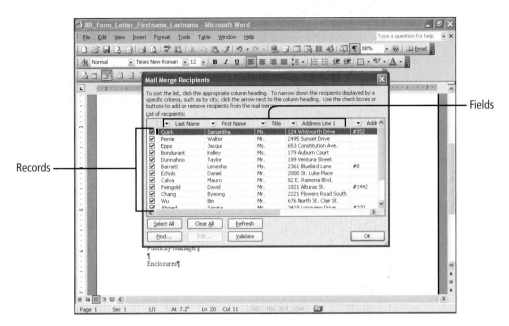

Records ⎯⎯⎯⎯⎯

Fields

Figure 8.35

3 Use the horizontal scroll bar to view all the fields included in the data table, and then scroll back to display the **Last Name** field.

You will not use all of these fields in the form letter.

4 Click the **Last Name** column heading.

The records are reordered so that they are in alphabetical order by Last Name. Mailing lists are usually sorted by either the last name or the ZIP code. When sorted by ZIP codes, reduced rates, called ***bulk mailing***, are available from the United States Postal Service.

5 Locate the record for **Feingold** and click to clear the check mark next to Feingold's record.

By clearing the check box, Mail Merge will not generate a form letter for this individual. See Figure 8.36.

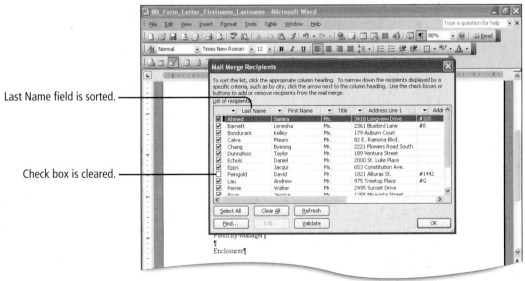

Last Name field is sorted. ⎯⎯⎯⎯

Check box is cleared. ⎯⎯⎯⎯

Figure 8.36

Editing and Adding Information to the Data Table

An Edit button on the Mail Merge Recipients dialog box enables you to edit the selected record. You can also click Edit, and then click the New Entry button to add new records to the data table. Modifying the records in, or adding records to, the database in a Mail Merge operation also modifies and adds records in the original database file. Thus, use caution if you are using a database that is used by others and remember that you are making permanent changes to the data source.

6 At the lower right corner of the **Mail Merge Recipients** dialog box, click **OK**.

7 On the Standard toolbar, click the **Save** button 🖫

Activity 8.14 Inserting Merge Fields

After you have created your main document—the letter—and identified your data source—the list of names and addresses—you are ready to insert **merge fields** into your main document. A merge field is a placeholder that you insert in the main document. For example, a specific merge field instructs Word to insert a city name that is stored in the City field of your data source. Merge fields are placed in the main document by displaying a field list, from which you can insert merge fields in any order.

1 Click to position the insertion point in the blank line just above the *Subject* line.

2 On the Mail Merge toolbar, click the **Insert Merge Fields** button 📄.

A list of available fields displays, as shown in Figure 8.37. These are the same fields you saw in the Mail Merge Recipients dialog box. The *Title* field is selected by default.

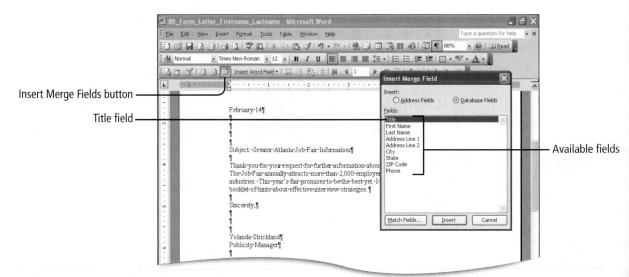

Figure 8.37

More Knowledge — Inserting an Address Block

You also can add a complete address by clicking the Insert Address Block button on the Mail Merge toolbar. If all of your street addresses use a single address field, this procedure works well. When you have multiple address fields, as you do in the Job Fair Address database, using the Address Block would require you to adjust those addresses after the merge.

3 With the **Title** field selected, at the bottom of the **Insert Merge Field** dialog box, click the **Insert** button.

The Title field is inserted into the document, surrounded by double angle brackets.

4 Under **Fields**, click the **First Name** field, and then click the **Insert** button. Repeat this procedure to insert the **Last Name** field.

Notice that there are no spaces between the fields. These will be added later. See Figure 8.38.

Inserted fields —

Double angle brackets indicate a merge field. —

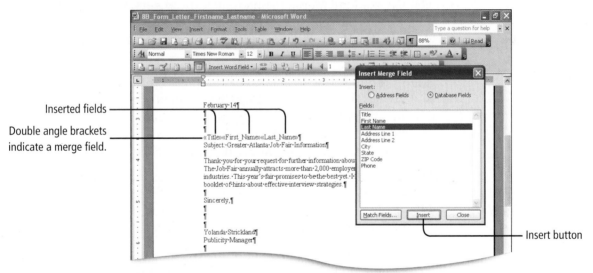

Insert button —

Figure 8.38

5 At the bottom of the **Insert Merge Field** dialog box, click the **Close** button. Press Enter. On the Mail Merge toolbar, click the **Insert Merge Fields** button 🔲 again.

6 Under **Fields**, click the **Address Line 1** field, and then click the **Insert** button. Repeat this procedure to insert the **Address Line 2** field.

7 Close the **Insert Merge Field** dialog box and press Enter. On the Mail Merge toolbar, click the **Insert Merge Fields** button 🔲 again.

8 Use the same procedure you used in Step 6 to add the **City**, **State**, and **ZIP Code** fields. Click the **Close** button. Press Enter.

Compare your document with Figure 8.39.

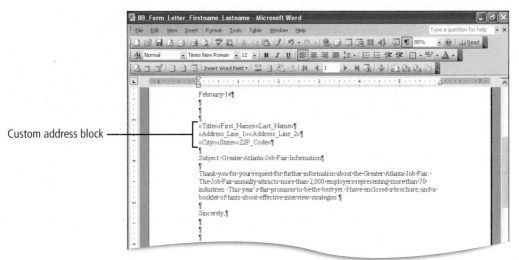

Custom address block

Figure 8.39

9 Click to place the insertion point at the end of the *Subject* line, and then press Enter twice. Type **Dear** and then press Spacebar.

10 On the Mail Merge toolbar, click the **Insert Merge Fields** button ▣. With **Title** selected, click **Insert** to insert the **Title** field. Click **Last Name**, and then click **Insert**. Click the **Close** button, and then type a comma.

11 In the first row of fields, click to position the insertion point between the **Title** field and the **First Name** field (<<First_Name>> will appear to be shaded). Press Spacebar. Repeat this procedure to insert a space between the **First Name** and **Last Name** fields and between the **Address Line 1** and **Address Line 2** fields.

12 In the third row of fields, click to position the insertion point between the **City** field and the **State** field. Type a comma, and then press Spacebar. Add a space between the **State** and **ZIP Code** fields. In the greeting line, add a space between the **Title** and **Last Name** fields.

The letter (main document) and the source data are now linked, although you still see only the field names, and not the names of the individuals in the source document. Compare your document with Figure 8.40.

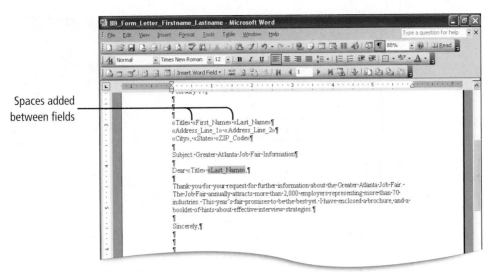

Spaces added between fields

Figure 8.40

13 On the Standard toolbar, click the **Save** button.

Objective 5
Merge Letters with Records from the Data Source

After the merge fields are added to the form letter—the main document—one letter for each person in the data source is created. You can preview the letters one at a time, print the letters directly from the Mail Merge document, or merge all of the letters into one Word document that you can edit. Merging the letters into one Word document is useful if you want to add customized information to individual letters.

Activity 8.15 Previewing Merged Data

Before you print your form letters, it is a good idea to scan them to verify that you have the result you intended, and to make any necessary adjustments.

1 On the Mail Merge toolbar, click the **Highlight Merge Fields** button.

Each of the merged fields is shaded in gray, enabling you to quickly examine each field that you have included, and the spacing and formatting within the fields. See Figure 8.41.

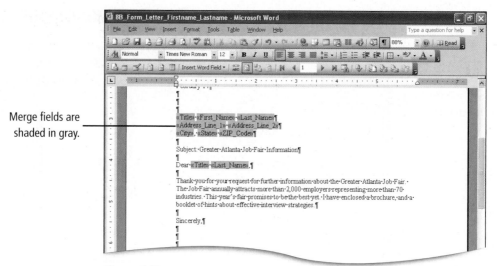

Merge fields are shaded in gray.

Figure 8.41

2 On the Mail Merge toolbar, click the **View Merged Data** button ⟪⟫.

The first form letter displays. The highlighted fields indicate the data taken from the first record in the sorted data source. See Figure 8.42.

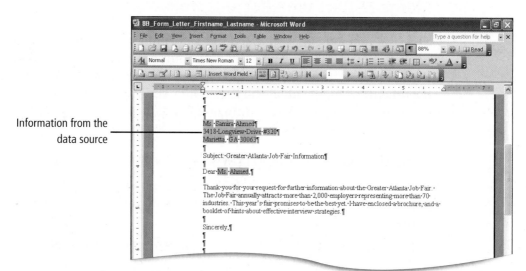

Information from the data source

Figure 8.42

3 On the Mail Merge toolbar, click the **Next Record** button ▶ several times to examine the address block of the form letters.

Notice that the letters are addressed in alphabetical order by Last Name.

4 On the Mail Merge toolbar, click the **Last Record** button ▶|, examine the last record, and then click the **First Record** button |◀.

5   On the Mail Merge toolbar, click the **Highlight Merge Fields** button 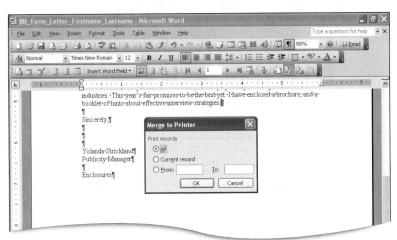 to deselect the field highlights. If the insertion point is in a field, and the field is gray, then click anywhere in the body of the document to deselect the field. On the Formatting toolbar, click the **Show/Hide ¶** button.

6   Using the **Next Record** button, scroll up or down through the letters with all of the formatting turned off to see what the final letters will look like. When you are through, on the Formatting toolbar, click the **Show/Hide ¶** button again to restore your view of the formatting marks.

7   On the Standard toolbar, click the **Save** button.

Activity 8.16   Printing Form Letters

You can print your form letters directly from your Mail Merge document.

1   On the Mail Merge toolbar, click the **First Record** button.

2   From the **View** menu, click **Header and Footer**. On the Header and Footer toolbar, click the **Switch Between Header and Footer** button. Click the **Insert AutoText** button, and then click **Filename**.

The file name is inserted in the footer of each letter.

3   On the Header and Footer toolbar, click the **Close** button.

4   On the Mail Merge toolbar, click the **Merge to Printer** button.

The Merge to Printer dialog box displays, as shown in Figure 8.43.

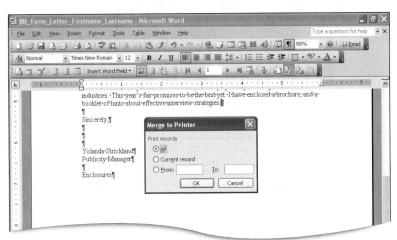

Figure 8.43

5 Under **Print records**, click the **From** option button. In the **From** box, type **1** and in the **To** box, type **2**

6 At the bottom of the **Merge to Printer** dialog box, click **OK**.

The Print dialog box displays.

7 At the bottom of the **Print** dialog box, click **OK**. The first two form letters will print.

8 On the Standard toolbar, click the **Save** button.

Activity 8.17 Merging Form Letters to a Word Document

If you need to customize the constant information—information in the main document—in the letters, you can merge all of the letters into one document and then edit only the letters you want to change. When you merge to a single document, a page break is inserted after each letter.

1 On the Mail Merge toolbar, click the **Merge to New Document** button.

The Merge to New Document dialog box displays, as shown in Figure 8.44.

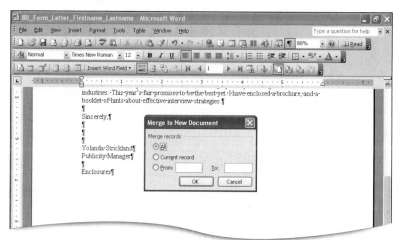

Figure 8.44

2 Under **Merge records**, click the **All** option button, and then click **OK**.

All 14 letters are combined into one document, with page breaks between the letters. In the status bar, notice that *1/14* displays, indicating a Word document of 14 pages.

3 At the bottom of the vertical scroll bar, click the **Select Browse Object** button , and then click the **Go To** button .

The Find and Replace dialog box displays. The Go To tab is selected by default, as shown in Figure 8.45.

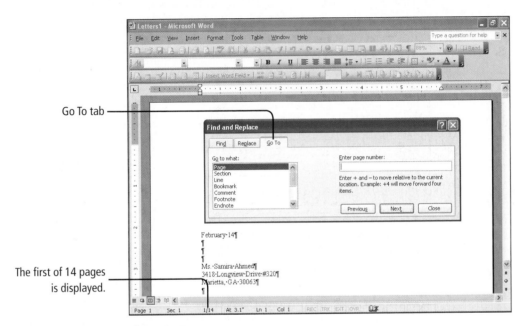

Go To tab

The first of 14 pages is displayed.

Figure 8.45

4 In the **Find and Replace** dialog box, under **Enter page number**, type **3** and then, at the bottom of the dialog box, click the **Go To** button.

The insertion point moves to page 3.

5 At the bottom of the **Find and Replace** dialog box, click **Close**.

6 In the paragraph beginning *Thank you for your request*, click to position the insertion point in the third line, just after the period following *industries*. Press [Spacebar] and type **In answer to your question, there will be 17 medical firms represented.**

Compare your letter with Figure 8.46.

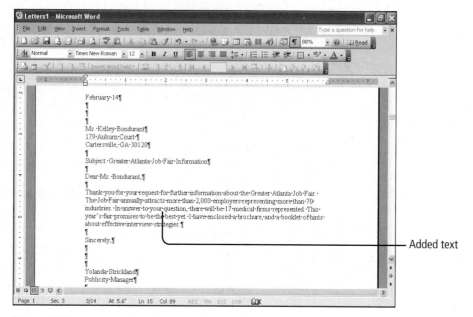

Figure 8.46

7 On the **File** menu, click **Save As**. In the **Save As** dialog box, navigate to the folder where you are storing your projects for this chapter and type **8B_Form_Letter2_Firstname_Lastname** and then click **Save**.

8 From the **File** menu, click **Print**. Under **Page range**, click in the **Pages** box, and then type **3** Click **OK** to print page 3, the third letter.

9 Close both documents, saving any changes, and then close Word.

End You have completed Project 8B

Summary

Microsoft Word documents can be integrated with other Office programs. It is common to combine a Word document with information in Excel and Access. Numbers and text from Access or Excel can be pasted into a Word document, where they become Word tables. You can use the Paste Special command to paste the data into the Word document, and then activate the source program's commands to edit the data while in Word. You also can paste the data and keep the link to the source program. When the data is edited in the source program, it can also be updated automatically in the Word document.

Charts from Excel can be pasted into Word documents and treated as images. As with data, the Paste Special command enables you to edit the Excel chart using the Excel program commands while viewing the document in Word. Excel charts can also be linked so that changes in the Excel spreadsheet are reflected in the Word document.

Links to other programs can be placed in Word documents in the form of icons. When you double-click on a linked icon, the program and program file open.

Word tables, Access databases, and Excel spreadsheets can be used to create customized form letters and labels, when the same basic letter must be sent to a number of different people. You can insert address information from Access databases and Excel lists in a Word document and customize each letter to contain the name and address of the individual to whom the letter is being sent. You can customize the text within the body of the letter. You can also customize the labels you create.

When creating a merge, the list of recipients is taken from a data source, which can be a Word table, an Excel spreadsheet, or an Access database. Within the data source, the columns of the table form the fields, and the rows of the table form the records. When the information in the data source document is merged with the text in the main document, one letter is generated for every record in the data source document.

In This Chapter You Practiced How To

- Embed Excel Charts and Data
- Link to Excel Charts and PowerPoint Presentations
- Create Labels Using the Mail Merge Wizard
- Create a Form Letter
- Merge Letters with Records from the Data Source

Matching

Match each term in the second column with its correct definition in the first column by writing the letter of the term on the blank line in front of the correct definition.

_____ **1.** To insert, using a format that you specify, information from a source file in one program, such as Excel, PowerPoint, or Access, into a destination file in another program, such as Word.

_____ **2.** All of the fields containing information about one person and stored in a row in a data table.

_____ **3.** In a mail merge for a form letter, the text and graphics that are the same from letter to letter.

_____ **4.** A letter with standardized wording that can be sent to many different people when merged with an address list.

_____ **5.** A Word feature that combines information from two documents—a main document and a data source—to create customized form letters or labels.

_____ **6.** In a mail merge, the information, such as name and address, that varies from letter to letter.

_____ **7.** In a mail merge, a placeholder inserted into the main document where information from the records in the data source will be placed.

_____ **8.** The process of arranging the information in a data source in alphabetical or numerical order by a specific field.

_____ **9.** An object that is created in a source file and inserted into a destination file, and which maintains a direct connection to the source file.

_____ **10.** The column headings in a data source—for example, *Last Name* and *First Name*.

_____ **11.** The acronym for Object Linking and Embedding, a term that refers to Microsoft's program-integration technology for sharing information between Office programs.

_____ **12.** Mail sorted by ZIP code that qualifies for reduced postage rates from the United States Postal Service.

_____ **13.** In a mail merge, the file that contains the information to be merged—for example, a list of names and addresses.

_____ **14.** An arrangement of black bars based on a ZIP code and added to an envelope or label so that the address can be scanned and sorted electronically by the United States Postal Service.

_____ **15.** In a mail merge, the document that contains the text and graphics that are the same for each version of the letter.

A Bulk mailing

B Constant information

C Data source

D Embed

E Fields

F Form letter

G Linked object

H Mail Merge

I Main document

J Merge field

K OLE

L Postal bar code

M Record

N Sort

O Variable information

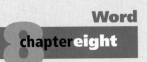
Fill in the Blank   Write the correct answer in the space provided.

1. To use mail merge, you need a main document and a(n)

   _____.

2. If you copy a range of cells from an Excel spreadsheet and then paste it into a Word document without using the Paste Special command, the result is a Word _____.

3. A linked object maintains a direct connection to the

   _____.

4. Microsoft Access is a(n) _____ program.

5. In a data table, click on the column heading to

   _____ the records by that field.

6. The _____ command allows you to copy information from one location and paste it in another location using a different format.

7. To create labels or form letters, use the Mail Merge toolbar or the Mail Merge _____, which walks you through the process step by step.

8. When you use the Paste Special command to _____ an Excel chart into a Word document, you can use Excel commands to edit the chart.

9. A row of data in a data table is referred to as a(n)

   _____.

10. If you want to make changes to Excel data and have the changes also made to the corresponding Excel object in a Word document, then you should _____, rather than embed, the Excel object.

Project 8C—Volunteers Letter

Objectives: *Embed Excel Charts and Data and Link to Excel Charts and PowerPoint Presentations.*

In the following Skill Assessment, you will embed an Excel chart into a letter to volunteers who will be working at the Greater Atlanta Job Fair. You also will insert a link to a PowerPoint presentation. Your completed document will look similar to the one shown in Figure 8.47. You will save your document as *8C_Volunteers_Letter_Firstname_Lastname*.

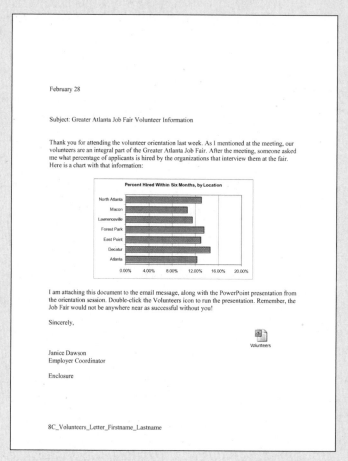

Figure 8.47

1. Start Word and on the Standard toolbar, click the **Open** button. Navigate to the location where the student files for this textbook are stored. Locate and open **w08C_Volunteers_Letter**. Save the file as **8C_Volunteers_Letter_Firstname_Lastname**

2. On the Standard toolbar, click the **Zoom button arrow**, and then click **Page Width**. If necessary, on the Standard toolbar, click the Show/Hide ¶ button to show formatting marks.

(Project 8C–Volunteers Letter continues on the next page)

(Project 8C–Volunteers Letter continued)

3. Click the **Start** button, locate the Excel program, and then start **Excel**. On the Standard toolbar, click the **Open** button. Navigate to the location where the student files for this textbook are stored. Locate and open the Excel file **w08C_Hiring_Results**.

4. Click in a white area of the bar chart entitled **Percent Hired Within Six Months, by Location** to select it. When the chart is selected, notice that in the cells above, the data represented in the chart is bordered. From the Standard toolbar, click the **Copy** button.

5. On the taskbar, click the Microsoft Word icon for your **8C_Volunteers_ Letter** file. Locate the paragraph that begins *I am attaching*, and then click to position the insertion point in the second blank line above that paragraph.

6. From the **Edit** menu, click **Paste Special**. In the displayed **Paste Special** dialog box, be sure the **Paste** option button is selected and that under **As**, **Microsoft Office Excel Chart Object** is selected. Click **OK**.

7. Click to select the chart. From the Formatting toolbar, click the **Center** button to center the chart horizontally.

8. Scroll down to view the lower half of the document on your screen. Click to position the insertion point at the end of the paragraph that begins *I am attaching*.

9. From the **Insert** menu, click **Object**. In the **Object** dialog box, click the **Create from File tab**.

10. Click **Browse**, navigate to the location of your student files, click to select the **w08C_Volunteers** PowerPoint presentation, and then click the **Insert** button. Select the **Link to file** check box and the **Display as icon** check box.

11. Click the **Change Icon** button. In the **Caption** box, select and delete the text. Type **Volunteers**

12. At the bottom of the **Change Icon** dialog box, click **OK**. At the bottom of the **Object** dialog box, click **OK**.

13. Right-click the new icon. From the shortcut menu, click **Format Object**. In the **Format Object** dialog box, click the **Layout tab**.

14. Under **Wrapping style**, click **Square**. At the bottom of the **Format Object** dialog box, click **OK**.

15. Drag the icon to an open area under the right side of the paragraph that begins *I am attaching*. The anchor should display to the left of the paragraph that begins *I am attaching*. Compare your document with Figure 8.47.

(Project 8C–Volunteers Letter continues on the next page)

(Project 8C–Volunteers Letter continued)

16. Double-click the new icon. Click the mouse button to advance through the presentation one slide at a time. When you reach a black slide, click once.

17. On the Standard toolbar, click the **Save** button. Use the taskbar to move to Excel and close the program. Do not save changes to the Excel file if prompted.

18. From the **View** menu, click **Header and Footer**. On the Header and Footer toolbar, click the **Switch Between Header and Footer** button. Click the **Insert AutoText** button, and then click **Filename**. On the Header and Footer toolbar, click the **Close** button. On the Standard toolbar, click the **Save** button.

19. On the Standard toolbar, click the **Print Preview** button. Take a moment to check your work. On the Print Preview toolbar, click the **Close Preview** button.

20. Make any necessary changes to your document. When you are satisfied, on the Standard toolbar, click the **Print** button. Close the document, saving your changes.

End You have completed Project 8C ─────────────────────

Project 8D — Volunteers Form Letter

Objectives: *Create a Form Letter and Merge Letters with Data from a Data Source.*

In the following Skill Assessment, you will use the Mail Merge Wizard to address letters to volunteers who will be working at the Greater Atlanta Job Fair. You will also use the Mail Merge toolbar to insert the name of the organization that the volunteer has been asked to assist, and then you will print the form letters. Your completed document will look similar to the one shown in Figure 8.48. You will save your document as *8D_Volunteers_Form_Letter_Firstname_Lastname.*

1. On the Standard toolbar, click the **Open** button. Navigate to the location where the student files for this textbook are stored. Locate and open **w08D_Volunteers_Form_Letter**. Save the file as **8D_Volunteers_Form_Letter_Firstname_Lastname**

2. On the Standard toolbar, click the **Zoom button arrow**, and then click **Page Width**. If necessary, on the Standard toolbar, click the Show/Hide ¶ button to show formatting marks.

(Project 8D–Volunteers Form Letter continues on the next page)

(Project 8D–Volunteers Form Letter continued)

February 28

Mary Martinez
3293 Nyland Ave.
Atlanta, GA 30327

Subject: Greater Atlanta Job Fair Volunteer Information
Your Assigned Organization: Atlanta Insurance Brokers

Thank you for attending the volunteer orientation last week. As I mentioned at the meeting, our volunteers are an integral part of the Greater Atlanta Job Fair. After the meeting, someone asked me what percentage of applicants is hired by the organizations that interview them at the fair. Here is a chart with that information:

The organization you have been assigned to work with is mentioned at the top of this letter. We have tried to find the best match between organization and volunteer whenever possible. As I mentioned after the meeting, the Job Fair would not be anywhere near as successful without you!

Sincerely,

Janice Dawson
Employer Coordinator

Enclosure

8D_Volunteers_Form_Letter_Firstname_Lastname

Figure 8.48

3. On the Windows taskbar, click the **Start** button, navigate to the location of the Microsoft Office programs, and then open **Excel**. On the Standard toolbar, click the **Open** button. Navigate to the location where the student files for this textbook are stored. Locate and open the Excel file **w08D_Volunteer_Help**. Examine the table, which will be used as the data source for a mail merge. Close Excel. Do not save changes if prompted.

4. Click to position the insertion point at the end of the first line—the line containing the date. Press Enter three times. From the **Tools** menu, point to **Letters and Mailings**, and then click **Mail Merge**. In the **Mail Merge** task pane, be sure the **Letters** option button is selected, and then at the bottom of the task pane, click **Next: Starting document**.

5. Under **Select starting document**, be sure the **Use the current document** option button is selected. At the bottom of the task pane, click **Next: Select recipients**.

(Project 8D–Volunteers Form Letter continues on the next page)

(Project 8D–Volunteers Form Letter continued)

6. Under **Use an existing list**, click **Browse**. Navigate to the location where the student files for this textbook are stored. Locate and click the **w08D_Volunteer Help** Excel file, and then click **Open**.

7. In the **Select Table** dialog box, **Volunteer_Help** is the only data table identified. Be sure the **First row of data contains column headers** check box is selected, and then click **OK**.

8. In the **Mail Merge Recipients** dialog box, click the **Last Name** column header to sort the recipient list by the last names of the volunteers.

9. Use the horizontal scroll bar in the **Mail Merge Recipients** dialog box to scroll to the right. Notice that there is a field for *Assigned Organization*. Recall that each volunteer will be assigned one organization to assist during the job fair. At the bottom of the **Mail Merge Recipients** dialog box, click **OK**. At the bottom of the task pane, click **Next: Write your letter**.

10. At the top of the task pane, under **Write your letter**, click **Address block**. In the **Insert Address Block** dialog box, under **Specify address elements**, clear the **Insert company name** check box because there is no company field associated with this data source. Click **OK**.

11. At the bottom of the **Mail Merge** task pane, click **Next: Preview your letters**. In the upper portion of the task pane, under **Preview your letters**, click the **Next Record (>>)** and **Previous Record (<<)** buttons as necessary to scroll through the letters and examine the address blocks. There are a total of 15 letters.

12. At the bottom of the task pane, click **Next: Complete the merge**. Close the **Mail Merge** task pane.

13. If necessary, display the Mail Merge toolbar.

14. Locate the line *Your Assigned Organization:* and click to position the insertion point following the space at the end of that line. On the Mail Merge toolbar, click the **Insert Merge Fields** button. (Display ScreenTips if you are not sure which button to click.)

15. In the **Insert Merge Field** dialog box, click **Assigned Organization**, and then click **Insert**. Notice that the field names are the column headings from the Excel table you examined. Click **Close** to close the dialog box. Notice that for the displayed letter, an Organization name is inserted. On the Standard toolbar, click the **Save** button. Compare your document with Figure 8.48.

16. On the Mail Merge toolbar, click the **Highlight Merge Fields** button so that you can view the areas that contain merged information. On the Mail Merge toolbar, click the **Next Record** button or **Previous Record** button to scroll through the letters. Examine the *Assigned Organization* field.

(Project 8D–Volunteers Form Letter continues on the next page)

(Project 8D–Volunteers Form Letter continued)

17. On the Mail Merge toolbar, click the **Highlight Merge Fields** button to deselect the field highlights. On the Formatting toolbar, click the **Show/Hide ¶** button.

18. Scroll through the letters with all of the formatting turned off to see what the final letters will look like. When you are through, on the Formatting toolbar, click the **Show/Hide ¶** button again to restore formatting marks.

19. From the **View** menu, click **Header and Footer**. On the Header and Footer toolbar, click the **Switch Between Header and Footer** button. Click the **Insert AutoText** button, and then click **Filename**. Click the **Close** button.

20. On the Mail Merge toolbar, click the **Merge to Printer** button. Under **Print records**, click the **From** option button. In the **From** box, type **1** and in the **To** box, type **2**

21. At the bottom of the **Merge to Printer** dialog box, click **OK**. At the bottom of the **Print** dialog box, click **OK**. The first two letters of the 15 will print. Close the document, and save your changes.

End **You have completed Project 8D** ————————————————

Project 8E—Volunteers Mailing Labels

Objective: *Create Labels Using the Mail Merge Wizard.*

In the following Skill Assessment, you will use the Mail Merge Wizard to create mailing labels for letters sent to volunteers who will be working at the Greater Atlanta Job Fair. Your completed document will look similar to the one shown in Figure 8.49. You will save your document as *8E_Volunteers_Mailing_Labels_Firstname_Lastname.*

1. Start Word and be sure a new blank document is displayed. From the **Tools** menu, point to **Letters and Mailings**, and then click **Mail Merge**.

2. In the **Mail Merge** task pane, under **Select document type**, click the **Labels** option button, and then at the bottom of the task pane, click **Next: Starting document**.

3. Under **Change document layout**, click **Label options**.

4. In the **Label Options** dialog box, under **Label information**, click the **Label products arrow** and then click **Avery standard**. Under **Product number**, scroll down the list and click **5160 - Address**.

5. At the bottom of the **Label Options** dialog box, click **OK**. The blank labels, formatted as a Word table, display. At the bottom of the task pane, click **Next: Select recipients**.

(Project 8E–Volunteers Mailing Labels continues on the next page)

(Project 8E–Volunteers Mailing Labels continued)

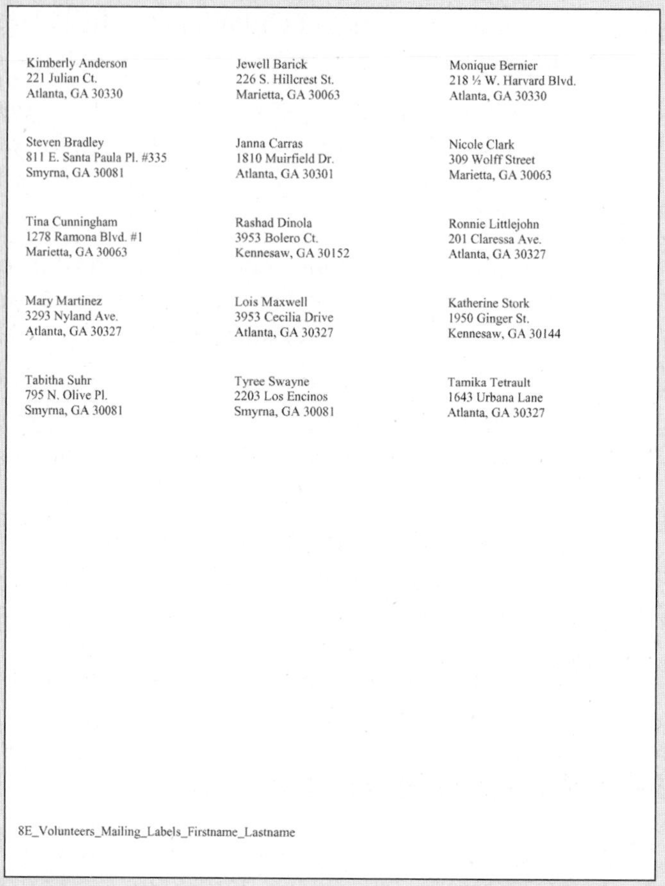

Kimberly Anderson 221 Julian Ct. Atlanta, GA 30330	Jewell Barick 226 S. Hillcrest St. Marietta, GA 30063	Monique Bernier 218 ½ W. Harvard Blvd. Atlanta, GA 30330
Steven Bradley 811 E. Santa Paula Pl. #335 Smyrna, GA 30081	Janna Carras 1810 Muirfield Dr. Atlanta, GA 30301	Nicole Clark 309 Wolff Street Marietta, GA 30063
Tina Cunningham 1278 Ramona Blvd. #1 Marietta, GA 30063	Rashad Dinola 3953 Bolero Ct. Kennesaw, GA 30152	Ronnie Littlejohn 201 Claressa Ave. Atlanta, GA 30327
Mary Martinez 3293 Nyland Ave. Atlanta, GA 30327	Lois Maxwell 3953 Cecilia Drive Atlanta, GA 30327	Katherine Stork 1950 Ginger St. Kennesaw, GA 30144
Tabitha Suhr 795 N. Olive Pl. Smyrna, GA 30081	Tyree Swayne 2203 Los Encinos Smyrna, GA 30081	Tamika Tetrault 1643 Urbana Lane Atlanta, GA 30327

8E_Volunteers_Mailing_Labels_Firstname_Lastname

Figure 8.49

6. Under **Use an existing list**, click **Browse**. Navigate to the location where the student files for this textbook are stored. Locate and click the Access file **w08E_Job_Fair_Addresses**, and then click **Open**. The **Select Table** dialog box displays, showing two data tables in the database. Click **Volunteer Help**, and then click **OK**.

7. Click the **Last Name** field column heading to sort the records alphabetically by last name, and then click **OK**. At the bottom of the task pane, click **Next: Arrange your labels**.

8. Under **Arrange your labels**, click **Address block**. In the **Insert Address Block** dialog box, under **Specify address elements**, clear the **Insert company name** check box. Click **OK**.

9. If necessary, scroll down in the task pane. Under **Replicate labels**, click **Update all labels**. At the bottom of the task pane, click **Next: Preview your labels**. Examine your labels. Compare your document with Figure 8.49.

(Project 8E–Volunteers Mailing Labels continues on the next page)

(Project 8E–Volunteers Mailing Labels continued)

10. Now that you have viewed the preview of the labels, at the bottom of the task pane, click **Next: Complete the merge**. Close the **Mail Merge** task pane.

11. On the **File** menu, click **Save As**. In the **Save As** dialog box, type 8E_Volunteers_Mailing_Labels_Firstname_Lastname and then click **Save**.

12. On the Standard toolbar, click the **Print Preview** button. Click the magnifying glass pointer in the middle of the labels. On the Print Preview toolbar, click the **Close** button.

13. From the **View** menu, click **Header and Footer**. On the Header and Footer toolbar, click the **Switch Between Header and Footer** button. Click the **Insert AutoText** button, and then click **Filename**. On the Header and Footer toolbar, click the **Close** button.

14. On the Standard toolbar, click the **Save** button.

15. In the Mail Merge toolbar, click the **Merge to Printer** button. Under **Print records**, click the **From** option button. In the **From** box, type **1** and in the **To** box, type **1** (Because page 2 contains no labels, it is not necessary to print it.)

16. At the bottom of the **Merge to Printer** dialog box, click **OK**. At the bottom of the **Print** dialog box, click **OK** to print the labels. Close the document, saving any changes.

 End You have completed Project 8E

Project 8F — Financial Information

Objectives: *Embed Excel Charts and Data and Link to Excel Charts and PowerPoint Presentations.*

In the following Performance Assessment, you will edit a memo about financial results from the Greater Atlanta Job Fair, one of the regional job fairs in the Greater Atlanta area. You will embed a table and link a chart. Your completed document will look similar to the one shown in Figure 8.50. You will save your document as *8F_Financial_Information_Firstname_Lastname*.

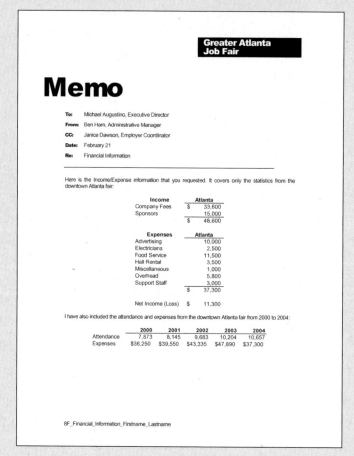

Figure 8.50

1. On the Standard toolbar, click the **Open** button. Navigate to the location where the student files for this textbook are stored. Locate and open **w08F_Financial_Information**. Save the file in your storage location as **8F_Financial_Information_Firstname_Lastname**

2. Start Excel, and then locate and open the **w08F_Atlanta_Information** Excel file. If necessary, click the **2004 Income sheet tab** at the bottom of the worksheet. Save the file in your storage location as **8F_Atlanta_Information_ Firstname_Lastname**

3. Click in cell **A3** and drag to the right one column and then down to cell **B18**. On the Standard toolbar, click the **Copy** button.

(Project 8F–Financial Information continues on the next page)

(Project 8F–Financial Information continued)

4. On the taskbar, click the Microsoft Word icon for your **8F_Financial_ Information** file. Locate the paragraph that begins *I have also included* and then click to position the insertion point in the second blank line above the paragraph.

5. From the **Edit** menu, click **Paste Special**. In the **Paste Special** dialog box, click the **Paste link** option button, and then click **Microsoft Office Excel Worksheet Object**. Click **OK** to paste the selected cells from the Excel worksheet into the Word document and to create a link to the source document.

6. Examine the *Expenses* and the *Net Income (Loss)* for Atlanta in the new table. Double-click the new table to return to the linked worksheet. Click cell **B13**. Type **1000** and press (Enter).

7. From the taskbar, switch back to your Word **8F_Financial_ Information** file. Right-click anywhere on the table and click **Update Link** from the shortcut menu. Notice that the *Miscellaneous* expense, the *Expenses* total, and the *Net Income (Loss)* are updated.

8. From the taskbar, navigate to the Excel spreadsheet and click on the **Atlanta Expenses sheet tab**. Click in cell **A3** and drag to the right through column F and then down to cell **F5**. On the Standard toolbar, click the **Copy** button.

9. Navigate back to your Word document. Click to position the insertion point in the last blank line of the document. From the **Edit** menu, click **Paste Special**. Be sure the **Paste** option button is selected and under **As**, click **Microsoft Office Excel Worksheet Object**. Click **OK**.

10. To edit the new table, double-click anywhere in the table to activate Excel. Click in the lower right cell—$36,800—press (Delete), and type **37300**

11. Click outside the table. Click the table to select it, and, on the Formatting toolbar, click the **Center** button. Center the other table in the same manner. Compare your document with Figure 8.50.

12. From the **View** menu, click **Header and Footer**. On the Header and Footer toolbar, click the **Switch Between Header and Footer** button. Click the **Insert AutoText** button, point to **Header/Footer**, and then click **Filename**. On the Header and Footer toolbar, click the **Close** button. On the Standard toolbar, click the **Save** button.

13. On the Standard toolbar, click the **Print Preview** button. Take a moment to check your work. On the Print Preview toolbar, click the **Close Preview** button.

14. Make any necessary changes to your document. When you are satisfied, on the Standard toolbar, click the **Print** button. Close the document, saving your changes.

End You have completed Project 8F

Project 8G — Confirmation Letter

Objectives: *Create a Form Letter and Merge Letters with Data from a Data Source.*

In the following Performance Assessment, you will use the Mail Merge Wizard to add an address block to a letter to the organizations that are participating in the Greater Atlanta Job Fair. Then you will use the Mail Merge toolbar to insert the number of booths ordered and the booth charges for each organization. You will also add a greeting line. Your completed document will look similar to the one shown in Figure 8.51. You will save your document as *8G_Confirmation_Letter_Firstname_Lastname.*

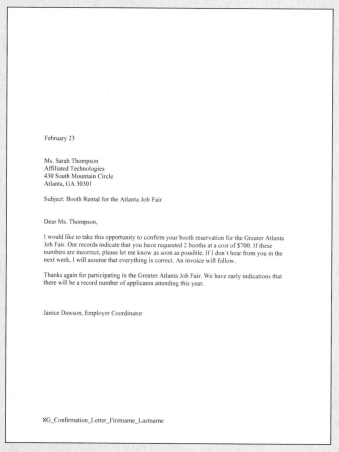

February 23

Ms. Sarah Thompson
Affiliated Technologies
430 South Mountain Circle
Atlanta, GA 30301

Subject: Booth Rental for the Atlanta Job Fair

Dear Ms. Thompson,

I would like to take this opportunity to confirm your booth reservation for the Greater Atlanta Job Fair. Our records indicate that you have requested 2 booths at a cost of $700. If these numbers are incorrect, please let me know as soon as possible. If I don't hear from you in the next week, I will assume that everything is correct. An invoice will follow.

Thanks again for participating in the Greater Atlanta Job Fair. We have early indications that there will be a record number of applicants attending this year.

Janice Dawson, Employer Coordinator

8G_Confirmation_Letter_Firstname_Lastname

Figure 8.51

1. On the Standard toolbar, click the **Open** button. Navigate to the location where the student files for this textbook are stored. Locate and open **w08G_Confirmation_Letter**. In your storage location, save the file as **8G_Confirmation_ Letter_Firstname_Lastname**

2. Click to position the insertion point at the end of the first line—the line containing the date. Press Enter three times.

(Project 8G–Confirmation Letter continues on the next page)

(Project 8G–Confirmation Letter continued)

3. From the **Tools** menu, point to **Letters and Mailings**, and then click **Mail Merge**. In the **Mail Merge** task pane, be sure the **Letters** option button is selected, and then at the bottom of the task pane, click **Next: Starting document**.

4. Be sure you are using the current document for the mail merge, and then click **Next: Select recipients**.

5. Under **Use an existing list**, click **Browse**. Navigate to the location where the student files for this textbook are stored. Locate and click the Access file **w08G_Job_Fair_Addresses**, and then click **Open**.

6. In the **Select Table** dialog box, click **Organization_Addresses**, and then click **OK**. Scroll to view the fields at the right of list, and notice that fields are included for both the number of Booths the organization has requested, and the Amount Due for booth rental. At the bottom of the **Mail Merge Recipients** dialog box, click **OK**. At the bottom of the task pane, click **Next: Write your letter**.

7. Under **Write your letter**, click **Address block**. Because there is a Company Name field, do not deselect the Insert Company Name check box. Click **OK**. At the bottom of the task pane, click **Next: Preview your letters**. In the task pane, click the **Next Record** and **Previous Record** buttons as necessary to scroll through the letters and examine the address blocks.

8. At the bottom of the task pane, click **Next: Complete the merge**. Close the **Mail Merge** task pane. If necessary, right-click any toolbar, and click Mail Merge to open the Mail Merge toolbar. Click the **View Merged Data** button to display the field names, rather than the recipient names.

9. Position the insertion point at the end of the *Subject* line and press Enter three times. Type **Dear** and then press Spacebar. On the Mail Merge toolbar, click the **Insert Merge Fields** button. In the **Insert Merge Fields** dialog box, click **Title**, and then click **Insert**. Use the same procedure to insert the **Lastname** field, and then click **Close**. Add a space between the title and last name and add a comma after the last name.

10. In the paragraph that begins *I would like*, click to position the insertion point just after the word *requested* and add a space. On the Mail Merge toolbar, click the **Insert Merge Fields** button, click the **Booths** field, and then click **Insert**. Close the **Insert Merge Field** dialog box.

11. At the end of the same sentence, position the insertion point before the period. Press Spacebar and type **$** On the Mail Merge toolbar, click the **Insert Merge Fields** button, click the **Amount Due** field, and then click **Insert**. Close the **Insert Merge Field** dialog box.

(Project 8G–Confirmation Letter continues on the next page)

Project 8G: Confirmation Letter | **Word** 1543

(Project 8G–Confirmation Letter continued)

12. On the Mail Merge toolbar, click the **Highlight Merge Fields** button. Click the **View Merged Data** button. Scroll through the form letters using the **Next Record** button and examine the inserted fields. Compare your document with Figure 8.51.

13. From the **File** menu, click **Page Setup**, and then click the **Layout tab**. Under **Page**, click the **Vertical alignment arrow**, and then click **Center**. Create a footer and insert the file name.

14. On the Mail Merge toolbar, click the **Merge to Printer** button. In the **From** box, type **1** and in the **To** box, type **2**

15. At the bottom of the **Merge to Printer** dialog box, click **OK**. At the bottom of the **Print** dialog box, click **OK**. The first two letters will print. Close the document and save any changes.

End You have completed Project 8G ————————————

Project 8H — Confirmation Labels

Objective: *Create Labels Using the Mail Merge Wizard.*

In the following Performance Assessment, you will use the Mail Merge Wizard to create a set of mailing labels for the organizations participating in the Greater Atlanta Job Fair. Because the addresses are long, and the name and title of the contact person and the organization will be included, you will need to use a large label. Your completed document will look similar to the one shown in Figure 8.52. You will save your document as *8H_Confirmation_Labels_Firstname_Lastname*.

1. Open Word and display a new blank document. From the **Tools** menu, point to **Letters and Mailings**, and then click **Mail Merge**. In the **Mail Merge** task pane, click the **Labels** option button, and then at the bottom of the task pane, click **Next: Starting document**.

2. Under **Change document layout**, click **Label options**. In the **Label Options** dialog box, under **Label information**, click the **Label products arrow**, and then click **Avery standard**. Under **Product number**, scroll down the list and click **5162 - Address**. Click **OK**, and then click **Next: Select recipients**.

3. Under **Use an existing list**, click **Browse**. Navigate to the location where the student files for this textbook are stored. Locate and click the Access file **w08H_Job_Fair_Addresses**, and then click **Open**. In the **Select Table** dialog box, click **Organization_Addresses**, and then click **OK**.

(Project 8H–Confirmation Labels continues on the next page)

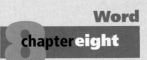

(Project 8H–Confirmation Labels continued)

Mr. Carson Fallacker
Director of Human Resources
A&G Consulting
107 Marguerite Drive South, Suite 15
Roswell, GA 30077

Ms. Sarah Thompson
Director of Recruiting
Affiliated Technologies
430 South Mountain Circle
Atlanta, GA 30301

Ms. Christa Jakabowski
Vice President, Administration
Atlanta Insurance Brokers
352 Piedmont Circle
Roswell, GA 30077

Mr. Sun Cho
Director, Professional Recruiting
Atlanta Veterans Medical Center
8553 Hunters Glen Blvd.
Atlanta, GA 30301

Mr. Lamar Caldwell
Director of Operations
Derrikson Brothers Construction
2215 Lake Park Drive
Marietta, GA 30063

Ms. Gail Bradley
Vice President Human Resources
DYCarlson Corp.
511 King Street
Smyrna, GA 30081

Mr. Shawn McFarland
Recruiting Representative
Georgia US Bank
980 Peachtree St., Suite 3200
Atlanta, GA 30313

Ms. Cianna Williams
Recruiting Representative
GR Data Storage
415 Technology Drive
Atlanta, GA 30330

Ms. Julie Lewis
HR Director
Olivare Corporation
2000 Delowe St., Suite 5
Atlanta, GA 30327

Mr. Brian Garcia
VP Administration
Southeast and Coastal Recycling Systems
698 Rosedale Circle SE, Suite 550
Kennesaw, GA 30144

Mr. Jared Simmons
HR Representative
Thinkanswer Technologies
898 Lakeview Drive
Conyers, GA 30012

Mr. Bilal Hadad
Medical Technology Recruiter
Underwood Medical Systems
1558 McVie Plaza Drive
Marietta, GA 30006

Mr. Nicholas Russo
Director of Human Resources
Verasound Energy
1 Verasound Way
Smyrna, GA 30080

Ms. Maya Brock
Office Manager
Wisener Heating & Air Conditioning
862 Ingleside Way, #315
Cartersville, GA 30120

8H_Confirmation_Labels_Firstname_Lastname

Figure 8.52

4. Scroll to the right, click the **Organization Name** field column heading to sort the records alphabetically by Organization Name, and then click **OK**. At the bottom of the task pane, click **Next: Arrange your labels**.

5. Under **Arrange your labels**, click **More items**. In the **Insert Merge Field** dialog box, under **Fields**, click **Title**, and then click **Insert**. Use the same procedure to add the **Firstname** and **Lastname** fields. Click **Close**. In the first label, add a space between each of the new fields. Click at the end of the new line and press Enter to create another label line.

6. Click **More items**. In the **Insert Merge Field** dialog box, under **Fields**, click **Job Title**. Click **Insert**, and then click **Close**. Press Enter to create another label line.

7. Click **Address block**. Under **Specify address elements**, clear the **Insert recipient's name in this format** check box, because you have already added a customized recipient's name.

(Project 8H–Confirmation Labels continues on the next page)

(Project 8H–Confirmation Labels continued)

8. Click the **Match Fields** button. Under **Required information**, click the **Company box arrow**, click **Organization Name**, and then click **OK**. Click **OK** to close the **Insert Address Block** dialog box.

9. Under **Replicate labels**, click **Update all labels**. At the bottom of the task pane, click **Next: Preview your labels**. Examine your labels.

10. At the bottom of the task pane, click **Next: Complete the merge**. Close the **Mail Merge** task pane. Compare your document with Figure 8.52.

11. On the **File** menu, click **Save As**. In the **Save As** dialog box, type **8H_Confirmation_Labels_Firstname_Lastname** and then click **Save**.

12. On the Standard toolbar, click the **Print Preview** button. Click the magnifying glass pointer in the middle of the labels. On the Print Preview toolbar, click the **Close** button.

13. Create a footer and add the file name. On the Standard toolbar, click the **Save** button.

14. In the Mail Merge toolbar, click the **Merge to Printer** button. In the **From** box, type **1** and in the **To** box, type **1**

15. At the bottom of the **Merge to Printer** dialog box, click **OK**. At the bottom of the **Print** dialog box, click **OK** to print the labels. Close the document.

End You have completed Project 8H

Project 8I—Cover Sheet

Objectives: *Create a Form Letter, Merge Letters with Records from the Data Source, and Create Labels Using the Mail Merge Wizard.*

In the following Mastery Assessment, you will use the Mail Merge Wizard to create file folder labels for the organizations participating in the Greater Atlanta Job Fair. You will also create a paper cover sheet for a file folder. Your completed document will look similar to the one shown in Figure 8.53. You will save your documents as *8I_Cover_Sheet_Firstname_Lastname* and *8I_Folder_Labels_Firstname_Lastname*.

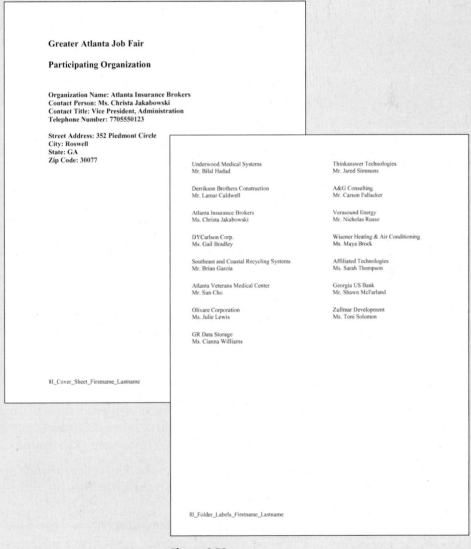

Figure 8.53

(Project 8I–Cover Sheet continues on the next page)

(Project 8I–Cover Sheet continued)

1. Start Word. From your student files, locate and open **w08I_Cover_ Sheet**. Save the file as **8I_Cover_Sheet_Firstname_Lastname** in the same location as your other files from this chapter. Create a footer and insert the **AutoText** filename.

2. Display the Mail Merge toolbar, if necessary. Click the **Open Data Source** button and open the Access file **w08I_Job_Fair_Addresses**. Select the **Organization_Addresses** table.

3. Click at the end of the line *Organization Name* and press Spacebar once following the colon. Click the **Insert Merge Fields** button, click **Organization Name**, click **Insert**, and then click **Close**. Using this technique, insert the Merge Fields for the remaining lines, using the **Title**, **Firstname**, and **Lastname** fields for the Contact Person. Be sure you add a space after the colons and a space between fields in the *Contact Person* line.

4. Beginning with the line *Organization Name*, select all of the text through the end of the page. Change the **Font Size** to **14 pt.** and apply **Bold**.

5. Click the **View Merged Data** button and scroll through the 15 records. Save your changes.

6. Preview and print the first two cover sheets, and then close the document.

7. In a new document, open the **Mail Merge Wizard**. Choose **Labels**, and then select the **5766 - File Folder** Avery label option.

8. Select recipients from the Access file **w08I_Job_Fair_Addresses** and select the **Organization_Addresses** table.

9. Under **Arrange your labels**, click **More items** and insert the **Organization Name**. Close the dialog box and move down one line. Click **More items** and add the three contact person fields—**Title**, **Firstname**, and **Lastname**. Add a space between the contact person fields. Click **Update all labels**.

10. Preview your labels, and then complete the merge. Compare your document with Figure 8.53. Save the document as **8I_Folder_Labels_Firstname_ Lastname**.

11. Print page 1 of 1 of the file folder labels. Close the document, saving any changes, and then close Word.

End **You have completed Project 8I**

Project 8J — Successful Applicants

Objectives: *Embed Excel Charts and Data and Link to Excel Charts and PowerPoint Presentations.*

In the following Mastery Assessment, you will edit a memo about the number of applicants hired per job fair location. You will embed a chart and link to a data table. Your completed document will look similar to the one shown in Figure 8.54. You will save your document as *8J_Successful_Applicants_Firstname_Lastname*.

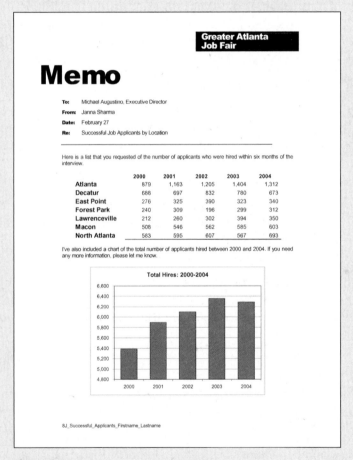

Figure 8.54

(**Project 8J**–Successful Applicants continues on the next page)

(Project 8J–Successful Applicants continued)

1. Start Word. From your student files, open **w08J_Successful_ Applicants**. Save the file with the name 8J_Successful_Applicants_ Firstname_Lastname in the same location as your other files from this chapter. Display the footer and insert the **AutoText** filename.

2. Start Excel and open the **w08J_Job_Fair_Hires** Excel file. Save the file as **8J_Job_Fair_Hires_Firstname_Lastname**

3. Select and then copy cells **A3** through **F10**. Be sure you do not include the *Total Hires* row.

4. Switch to Word and click in the blank line above the paragraph that begins *I've also included*. Then, use the **Paste Special** command to embed the Excel data as a **Microsoft Office Excel Worksheet Object**. Add a blank line after the new table.

5. Position the insertion point at the end of the last paragraph and press Enter twice.

6. Switch to Excel, select and copy the chart, and then return to Word. Use the **Paste Special** command to link the chart to the spreadsheet.

7. Switch to Excel. Examine the chart for the year 2004. Change cell **F10** from *593* to **693** and press Enter. Notice that the chart changes. Save your work and switch to Word. Right-click the chart and click **Update Link** from the shortcut menu. Notice the change in the chart.

8. In the table, locate and double-click the lower right cell—the one that you changed in the Excel worksheet. Change *593* to **693** in the selected cell. Notice that the changes are made in Excel, even though the table is in Word. Click outside the table.

9. Center both the table and the chart. Save your work. Preview and print the document. Compare your document with Figure 8.54. Close Word and Excel.

 You have completed Project 8J ——————————————

Project 8K — Index Cards

Objectives: *Create a Form Letter and Merge Letters with Data from the Data Source.*

For quick reference, many organizations use index cards. The organizers of the Greater Atlanta Job Fair use index cards for businesses and job seekers. You will create a set of index cards for the volunteers who work at the various fairs. These index cards are available in letter-size sheets with four cards to a sheet. You will save your document as *8K_Index_Cards_Firstname_Lastname.*

1. Start Word. Start the Mail Merge Wizard. Use **w08K_Job_Fair_Addresses** as the mail merge source.

2. Create labels based on the Avery **5315 - Note Card** label.

3. Set up the cards to show the last name, followed by a comma and space, and then the first name. Add the full address in a format of your choice. Be sure you include the phone number and the company with which the volunteer has been assigned to work.

4. Format the volunteer's name in a slightly larger font than the rest of the card and emphasize the name in a distinctive manner.

5. Save the completed document as **8K_Index_Cards_Firstname_Lastname**

6. Preview and print the first page of labels.

 You have completed Project 8K

Project 8L — Press Release

Objective: *Embed Excel Charts and Data.*

In this chapter, you practiced embedding Excel charts and data, and linking to PowerPoint presentations. There are other objects you can create and embed.

1. Create a new document and save the document as **8L_Press_Release_Firstname_Lastname** Add a brief introductory paragraph announcing the text of the new radio advertisement regarding the upcoming job fairs.

(Project 8L–Press Release continues on the next page)

(Project 8L–Press Release continued)

2. If you have access to a microphone, plug it in to the computer as instructed. From the **Insert** menu, click **Object**. In the **Object** dialog box, click the **Create New tab**, and under **Object type**, click **Wave Sound**. Select the **Display as icon** check box. (If you cannot record your voice, in the Object dialog box, click the Create from File tab, and browse to and select the **w08L_Press_Release** file that is included with your student files. Insert the object from a file the same way you embed an Excel chart from a file.) Display the sound as an icon.

3. In your textbook, turn to the second page of this chapter—the one that contains a picture depicting the Greater Atlanta Job Fair. Locate the paragraph to the left of the picture that begins *The Greater Atlanta Job Fair is a non-profit*. On the **Sound Object** dialog box, click the **Record** button (the button with the circle on it). Read the paragraph about the Greater Atlanta Job Fair into the microphone. When you are finished, click the **Stop** button (the button with the black rectangle on it).

4. Click the **Play** button (the button with the triangle pointing to the right) to listen to your announcement. If you are not satisfied, from the Sound Object File menu, click New and try again. When you are satisfied with your result, from the **Sound Object** dialog box **File** menu, click **Exit & Return**. Double-click your sound icon to listen to your recording.

5. Save your document and close Word.

 You have completed Project 8L

On the Internet

Downloading a Data Table from a Web Site

In this chapter you used data from Access and Excel in a Word document. Often, a table on the Web can also be inserted into a Word document as a Word table, after which it can be edited—unless the table on the Web site is a graphic.

1. Be sure that you are connected to the Internet. Open Word.

2. Go to a Web site that has data in a table format. The following sites might be useful, although you can use any site you like:

www.yahoo.com	Click the **Finance** icon at the top of the Yahoo window. Under **Market Summary**, click **Dow**. In the task pane, at the left side of the screen, click **Historical Prices**. In the **Prices** table, highlight the column headings and four or five rows of data.
www.spc.noaa.gov/ archive/tornadoes	Scroll down and click **Tables: (HTML format)**. Choose one of the tables and highlight the column headings and a few rows of data.

3. After you have selected the data, copy and then paste it into a Word document. Try changing information in the table cells. If the data is in table format, it can be edited. If it is text lined up to look like a table, it can be changed, but probably will need to be edited. If the table is an image, you will not be able to make any changes to the data.

4. When you are done, close the file without saving your changes.

Updating Links

In this chapter you practiced linking data in a Word document to data in a source document created in Excel or Access. The links can be updated regularly, as long as the source file remains in the same folder in which it was stored when the link was created. If the file is moved, however, you will not be able to use Word to reopen the link without taking steps to reconnect the link.

1. Start Word. In the *Type a question for help* box, type **update a link**

2. In the **Search Results** task bar, click **Reconnect a linked object**.

3. Read the instructions for reconnecting a link, and print these instructions.

4. Open your **8A_Job_Fair_Statistics** file. Scroll down and right-click the second chart. Click **Update Link** to be sure the link is still active.

5. In **My Computer**, move the **w08A_Job_Fair_Statistics** file to a different folder. Try to update the link to the chart again.

6. Use the Help information to reconnect the link. Open the Excel document and change one of the numbers in the 2004 column to change the total attendance for that year. Go back to the Word document and update the link again to confirm that the link has been reestablished.

7. Close the **Help** window and the **Help** task pane, close your document without saving the changes, and then exit Word. Move the **w08A_Job_Fair_Statistics** file back to its original folder. Because you did not save your changes to the Word document, the link to the original source document folder remains.

Excel 2003

4 chapterfour

Ranges and Functions

In this chapter, you will: complete these projects **and** practice these skills.

Project 4A **Creating and Using Named Ranges**	**Objectives** • Create Range Names • Use Range Names in a Formula

Project 4B **Using Statistical Functions**	**Objective** • Create Statistical Functions

Project 4C **Using Date and Financial Functions**	**Objective** • Create Date & Time and Financial Functions

Project 4D **Using Logical Functions and Controlling the Print Area**	**Objectives** • Create Logical Functions • Set and Clear a Print Area

Owens Family Builders

Owens Family Builders was founded in 1968 as Owens and Sons Builders; in 1980 the name was changed to reflect the extended family that had joined the business. Today the company has more than 300 employees, including 50 members of the Owens family.

Focusing on home building, the company is known for quality construction, innovative design, and customer service. Owens Family Builders has built more than 3,000 homes in the Orlando area and has also built many schools, shopping centers, and government buildings.

© Getty Images, Inc.

Ranges and Functions

In this chapter you will create range names and use them in a formula. You will also create statistical, date and time, financial, and logical functions. Finally, you will set and clear a print area.

Project 4A **Construction Costs**

In this project, you will work with groups of cells, referred to as ranges. You will name, modify, and delete ranges and use row and column labels to name ranges.

In Activities 4.1 through 4.5, you will edit a workbook created by Warren Owen, president of the Owens Custom Home division of Owens Family Builders, which details the construction costs for the past year by quarter. The two worksheets of your completed workbook will look similar to Figure 4.1. You will save the workbook as *4A_Construction_Costs_Firstname_Lastname.*

Owens Family Builders
Construction Costs by Quarter
Custom Home Division

		1st Qtr		2nd Qtr		3rd Qtr		4th Qtr
Land Acquisition	$	1,155,547	$	1,153,544	$	953,541	$	827,647
Surveying		14,867		18,463		9,683		5,385
Grading		136,548		152,529		127,527		145,527
Utilities		14,987		28,982		32,981		10,932
Roads		574,802		327,801		319,800		474,082
Concrete Supplies		129,510		127,014		128,532		125,432
Lumber Supplies		264,184		143,183		175,181		167,182
Electrical Supplies		112,806		94,803		72,836		62,854
Plumbing Supplies		92,187		134,928		61,987		53,187
Roof Tiles		64,436		42,956		58,867		52,329
Appliances		56,893		65,839		31,736		56,983
Decorating		9,432		12,345		14,874		21,984
Front Landscaping		16,389		19,384		48,567		37,482
Total by Quarter	$	2,642,588	$	2,321,771	$	2,036,112	$	2,041,006

4A_Construction_Costs_Firstname_Lastname

Owens Family Builders
Annual Construction Costs
Custom Home Division

Land Costs	$	6,485,175
Building Costs		2,164,394
Interior Costs		270,086
Front Landscaping		121,822
Total	$	9,041,477

4A_Construction_Costs_Firstname_Lastname

Figure 4.1
Project 4A—Construction Costs

Objective 1
Create Range Names

Recall that a range is a group of two or more cells that can be adjacent (touching one another) or nonadjacent (not touching one another). When you select a range of cells, all the cells in the range can, as a group, be formatted, moved, copied, or deleted. If the cells are adjacent, the range is referred to by the first and last cell in the range, for example, B3:B7. If the cells are nonadjacent, commas are used between each cell reference, for example B3, B7, B10. Another way to refer to a range of cells is by **range name**. A range name usually defines the purpose of the selected cells and provides a distinctive, easy-to-remember name.

Activity 4.1 Naming a Range

By assigning a name to a range of cells, you can use the name in a formula to refer to the group of cells. This makes it easier for you and others to understand the meaning of formulas in a worksheet. It also simplifies navigation in large worksheets because you can use the Go To command to move to a named range.

1 **Start** Excel. Click the **Open** button 📂, navigate to the student files that accompany this textbook, and then open the file **e04A_Construction_Costs**.

2 From the **File** menu, click **Save As**. In the **Save As** dialog box, navigate to the location where you are storing your projects for this chapter, creating a new folder for Chapter 4 if you want to do so. In the **File name** box, type **4A_Construction_Costs_Firstname_Lastname** and then click **Save** or press Enter.

3 Select the range **A1:E1**, and then click the **Merge and Center** button 🔳. Select the range **A2:E2**, and then press F4, the repeat key, to repeat the merge and center action. Repeat for the range **A3:E3**.

4 Click cell **B5**, type **1st Qtr** and then press Enter. Click cell **B5** again, and then drag the fill handle to the right through **E5** to create a series of four quarters. With the range **B5:E5** selected, on the Formatting toolbar, click the **Bold** button **B** and the **Align Right** button 📄.

5 Click cell **A18**, type **Total by Quarter** and then, in cell **B18**, use **AutoSum** Σ ▾ to create a total of the 1st Qtr costs. Copy the formula across through cell **E18**, and leave the range selected.

6 With the range **B18:E18** selected, hold down Ctrl and select the range **B6:E6**.

The two nonadjacent ranges are selected, as shown in Figure 4.2.

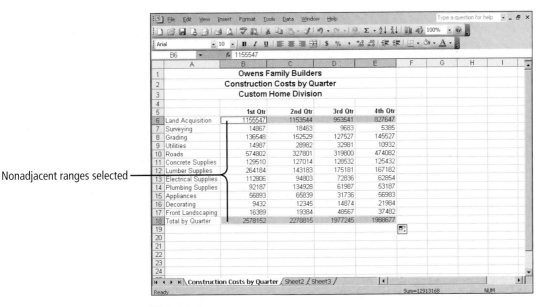

Nonadjacent ranges selected

Figure 4.2

7 On the Formatting toolbar, click the **Currency Style** button $, and then click the **Decrease Decimal** button two times. Select the range **B7:E17**. On the Formatting toolbar, click the **Comma Style** button , and then click the **Decrease Decimal** button two times.

8 Select the range **B6:E10**. To the right of the Formula Bar, click in the **Name Box**. The cell reference *B6* moves to the left edge of the box and is highlighted in blue. Type **Land_Costs** as shown in Figure 4.3, and then press Enter.

The name *Land_Costs* is assigned to the group of values in the range. These values represent the costs involved in getting land ready for construction. Excel has some rules for naming ranges, which are described in the table in Figure 4.4. Take a moment to study this information.

Name Box

Selected range

Figure 4.3

Rules for Naming a Range of Cells in Excel

Characteristic	Rule
Characters	The first character of the name must be a letter or an underscore (_). Although you can use a maximum of 255 characters, short, meaningful names are the most useful. Numbers can be part of a name, but symbols other than the underscore (_) or period (.) cannot.
Words	Names can be more than one word, but there cannot be spaces between the words. Use an underscore or a period as a separator in range names that have multiple words, for example, Land_Costs.
Cell references	Names cannot be the same as cell references, for example, A1.
Case	Names can contain uppercase and lowercase letters. Excel does not distinguish between uppercase and lowercase characters in range names. For example, if you have created the name *Land* and then create another name called *LAND* in the same workbook, the second name will replace the first one.

Figure 4.4

9 Select the range **B11:E13**. From the **Insert** menu, point to **Name**, and then click **Define**.

This is another method to name a range. The Define Name dialog box displays, as shown in Figure 4.5. Notice that in the large box under *Names in workbook*, the first range that you named, *Land_Costs*, is listed. At the bottom of the dialog box, the selected range, *B11:E13*, is indicated by absolute cell references—dollar signs. In the *Names in workbook* box, Excel suggests *Concrete_Supplies* as the name for this range, which is the text in the first cell to the left of the selected range.

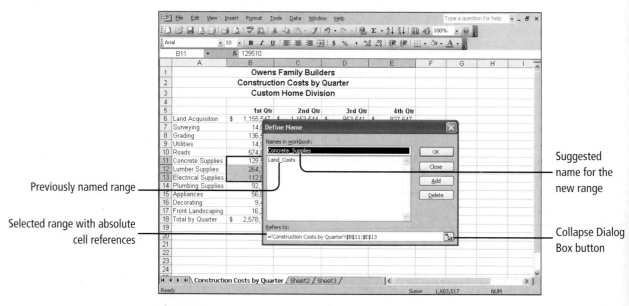

Previously named range

Selected range with absolute cell references

Suggested name for the new range

Collapse Dialog Box button

Figure 4.5

Note — Properties of Named Ranges

A range name is always absolute. If you insert rows, the range adjusts to the new cell address to represent the cells that were originally defined by the range name. Also, if you move the cells, the range name goes with them to the new location.

10 At the bottom of the dialog box, locate the **Refers to** box, as shown in Figure 4.5. Then, at the right edge of the **Refers to** box, point to and click the **Collapse Dialog Box** button.

The dialog box collapses (shrinks) so that only the *Refers to* box is visible, and the selected range is surrounded by a moving border, as shown in Figure 4.6. A Collapse dialog button temporarily shrinks a dialog box so that you have a larger view of the data in your worksheet while still being able to complete commands within the dialog box.

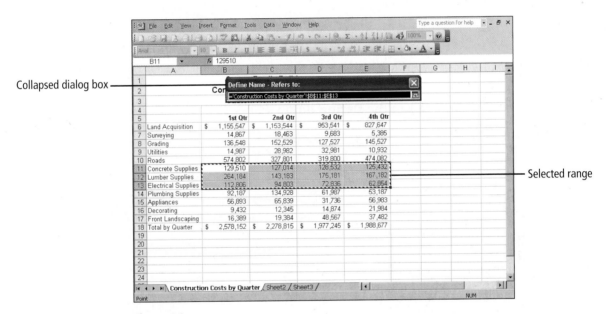

Collapsed dialog box

Selected range

Figure 4.6

11 If necessary, drag the collapsed dialog box by its title bar to the upper right of your screen so that it is not blocking the selection. Then, change the range selection by dragging to select the range **B11:E14**.

A moving border surrounds the new range, and the range, formatted with absolute cell references, displays in the *Refers to* box of the collapsed dialog box, as shown in Figure 4.7.

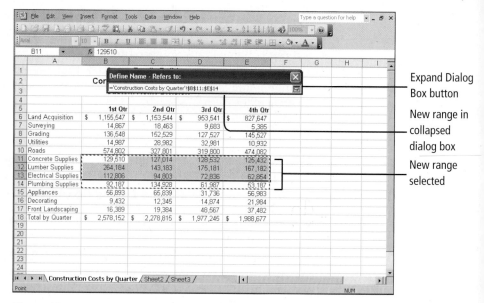

Figure 4.7

12 At the right edge of the collapsed dialog box, click the **Expand Dialog Box** button, as shown in Figure 4.7, to restore the dialog box to its original size.

13 In the **Define Name** dialog box, under **Names in workbook**, click in the box and delete the text *Concrete_Supplies*. Type **Supply_Costs** as shown in Figure 4.8.

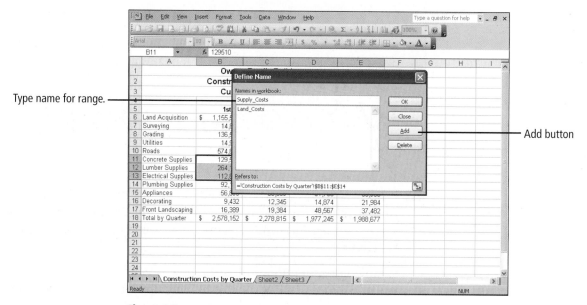

Figure 4.8

14 Click the **Add** button. The range name *Land_Costs* displays above the range name *Supply_Costs*. Click **OK** to close the dialog box and return to the worksheet. Click anywhere to cancel the selection.

15 Click the **Name Box arrow**.

The two range names that you have created display, in alphabetical order, as shown in Figure 4.9.

Name Box arrow

List of named ranges

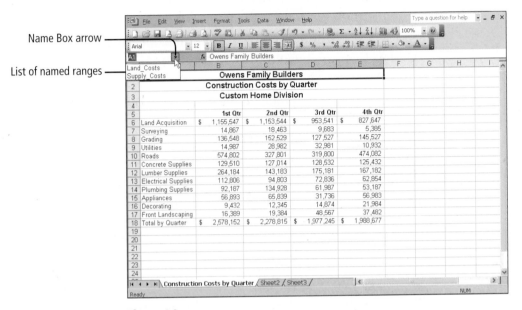

Figure 4.9

16 From the displayed list, click **Land_Costs** and notice that the range of values that make up land costs is highlighted, as shown in Figure 4.10.

Range name in Name Box

Selected range is highlighted.

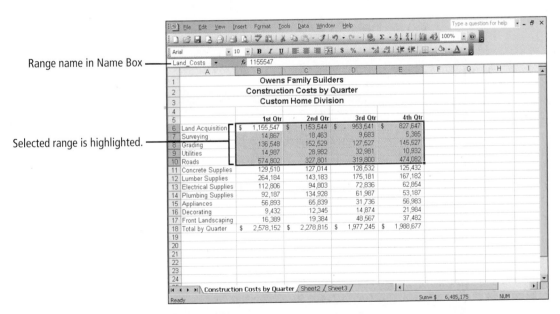

Figure 4.10

17 Click the **Name Box arrow** again, and on the displayed list, click **Supply_Costs**.

The range of values that make up Supply Costs is highlighted.

18 Select the range **B15:E16**. Click in the **Name Box**, type **Interior_Costs** and then press Enter to create the range name.

19 Click the heading for **row 15** to select the entire row. From the **Insert** menu, click **Rows**. A new **row 15** is inserted, and the remaining rows move down one row.

20 Click the **Name Box arrow**, and then click **Interior_Costs**. Notice that Excel highlights the correct range of cells, adjusting for the newly inserted row.

21 On the Standard toolbar, click the **Save** button 🖫.

Activity 4.2 Modifying a Range

In this activity you will modify the range named *Supply_Costs* to include new data, and then name the new range *Building_Costs*.

1 Click cell **A15**, type **Roof Tiles** and then press Tab. In cell **B15**, type **64436** and press Tab. In cell **C15**, type **42956** and press Tab. In cell **D15**, type **58867** and press Tab. In cell **E15**, type **52329** and press Enter.

The cells in the newly inserted row adopt the format (thousand comma separator) of the cells in the row above.

2 Hold down Ctrl and press F3, which is the keyboard shortcut for displaying the **Define Name** dialog box.

3 In the **Names in workbook** list, click **Supply_Costs**. At the bottom of the dialog box, click in the **Refers to** box and edit the reference, changing **E14** to **E15** as shown in Figure 4.11.

This action will include the *Roof Tiles* values in the named range.

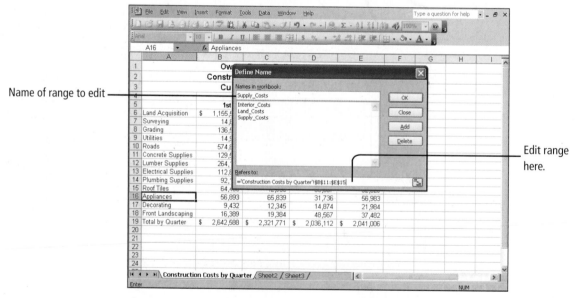

Figure 4.11

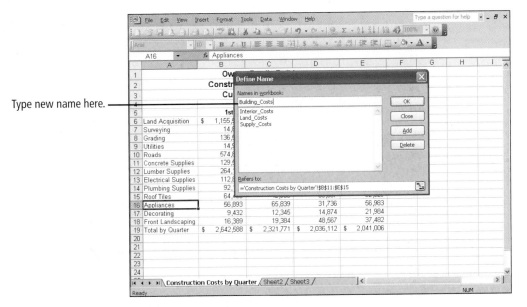

Type new name here. ———

Figure 4.12

4️⃣ Click the **Names in workbook** box, delete *Supply_Costs*, and then type **Building_Costs** as shown in Figure 4.12.

5️⃣ Click **OK** to close the dialog box. On the Standard toolbar, click **Save** 💾 to save the changes you have made to your workbook.

Activity 4.3 Deleting a Range Name

If you create a range name and decide that you no longer need it, you can easily delete the range name and its accompanying range reference. Deleting a range name does not modify the cell contents or formatting of the cells.

1️⃣ Click the **Name Box arrow**. Four named ranges display on the list. Click **Supply_Costs** and notice the range that is highlighted.

This was the range of cells and range name that you created before adding the data regarding Roof Tiles.

2️⃣ Click the **Name Box arrow** again, click **Building_Costs**, and notice that the updated range, including **Roof Tiles**, is highlighted.

3️⃣ To delete the range name *Supply_Costs*, which is no longer needed, display the **Insert** menu, point to **Name**, and then click **Define**.

4️⃣ In the displayed **Define Name** dialog box, under **Names in workbook**, click **Supply_Costs**, and then, on the right side of the dialog box, click the **Delete** button. Click **OK** to close the dialog box.

Deleting a range name does not delete any cells or any values. It only deletes the name that you have applied to a group of cells.

5️⃣ Click the **Name Box arrow**, and notice that only three ranges display and that they are arranged alphabetically.

6 On the Standard toolbar, click **Save** 🖫 to save the changes you have made to your workbook.

Activity 4.4 Using Row and Column Labels to Name a Range

You can use the Create command to use existing row or column labels as the name for a range of cells. This will save you the step of typing a name.

1 Select the range **A18:E18**. From the **Insert** menu, point to **Name**, and then click **Create**.

The Create Names dialog box displays, as shown in Figure 4.13. A check mark displays in the *Left column* check box, which indicates that Excel will use the contents of the cell in the leftmost column of the selection as the range name. Using this dialog box, instead of the Define Names dialog box, saves you the step of typing a name.

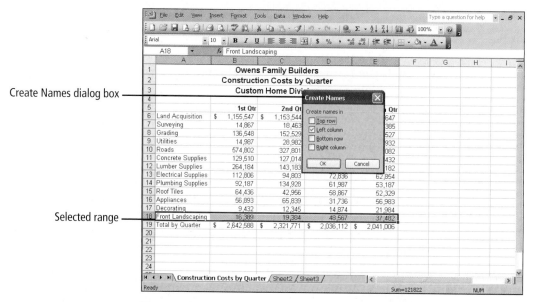

Create Names dialog box ⟶

Selected range ⟶

Figure 4.13

2 In the **Create Names** dialog box, click **OK**, and then click anywhere to cancel the selection.

3 Click the **Name Box arrow**, and then click the name **Front_Landscaping**. Notice that in the new range name, Excel inserted the underscore necessary to fill a blank space in the range name. Also notice that the actual range consists of only the numeric values, as shown in Figure 4.14.

This method is convenient for naming a range of cells without having to actually type a name—Excel uses the text of the first cell to the left of the selected range as the range name and then formats the name properly.

Range name formatted
properly by Excel

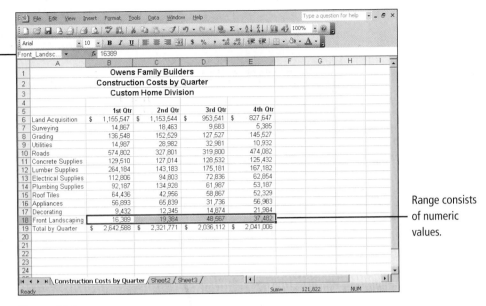

Range consists
of numeric
values.

Figure 4.14

◄4 On the Standard toolbar, click **Save** 🖫 to save the changes you have
made to your workbook.

Objective 2
Use Range Names in a Formula

After you establish a name for a range of cells, you can use the name in a
formula. The name can also be made available to other worksheets in the
same workbook or in worksheets in other workbooks, which is easier to
recall than having to remember and type the worksheet name and cell
reference. In Activity 4.5, you will use range names in formulas.

Activity 4.5 Creating Formulas Using Range Names

◄1 If necessary, **Open** 📂 your file **4A_Construction_Costs_
Firstname_Lastname**.

◄2 Click the **Sheet2** tab. Rename the sheet tab either by pointing to
and then double-clicking the Sheet2 tab or by pointing to and right-
clicking the Sheet2 tab, and then clicking Rename. Type **Annual
Costs** as the name for Sheet 2.

◄3 In cell **B5**, type **=sum(Land_Costs)** as shown in Figure 4.15, and
then press Enter.

Recall that SUM is a *function* (a formula already built by Excel) that
adds all the cells in a range. Thus, Excel sums all the cells in the range
you defined as *Land_Costs* on the first worksheet in the workbook and
then places the result in cell B5 of this worksheet. Your result should
be 6485175.

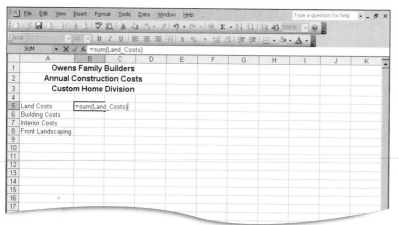

Figure 4.15

4 In cell **B6**, type **=sum(Building_Costs)** and press Enter.

You may type *sum* using lowercase letters; Excel will convert it to uppercase letters when you press Enter.

5 In cell **B7**, type **=sum(Interior_Costs)** and press Enter.

6 In cell **B8**, type **=sum(Front_Landscaping)** and press Enter.

7 In cell **A9**, type **Total** and then, in cell **B9**, use the **AutoSum** function button **Σ ▾** to compute the total annual costs.

Your result should be 9041477.

8 Format the range **B6:B8** using the **Comma Style** button **,** , and then click the **Decrease Decimal** button **.00 ▸.0** twice so that you have zero decimal places.

9 Click cell **B5**, hold down Ctrl, and then click cell **B9** to select the two nonadjacent cells. Format cells **B5** and **B9** using the **Currency Style** button **$** , and then click the **Decrease Decimal** button **.00 ▸.0** twice so that you have zero decimal places. Compare your worksheet with Figure 4.16.

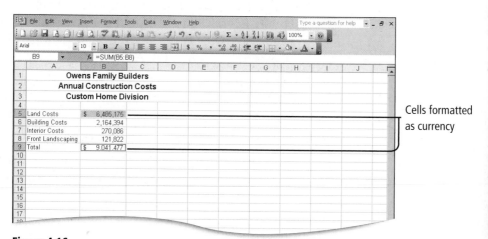

Cells formatted as currency

Figure 4.16

10 Click anywhere to deselect the cells. Right-click the **Annual Costs** sheet tab, and then click **Select All Sheets**.

Recall that by selecting all sheets, workbook formatting such as footers and page centering is applied to all sheets in the workbook.

Another Way ── **To Change Page Setup for Multiple Worksheets**

If you select two or more sheet tabs by holding down Ctrl, and then make changes in the Page Setup dialog box, the changes affect only the selected sheets—not all the sheets in the workbook.

---

11 From the **File** menu, click **Page Setup**. Click the **Margins tab**, and then, under **Center on page**, select the **Horizontally** check box. Click the **Header/Footer tab**, and then click **Custom Footer**. With the insertion point positioned in the **Left section**, on the dialog box toolbar click the **File name** button.

&[File] displays, as shown in Figure 4.17. This code will place the file name in the footer.

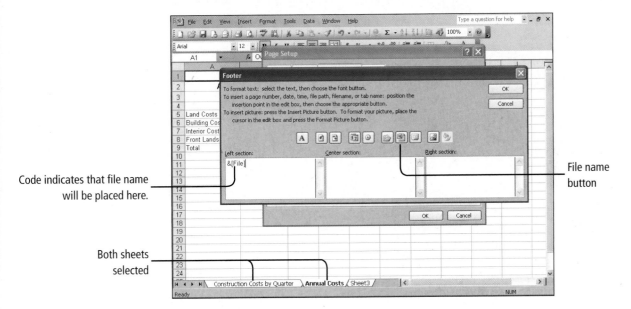

Code indicates that file name will be placed here.

Both sheets selected

Figure 4.17

12 Click **OK** twice to close the dialog boxes. On the Standard toolbar, click the **Print Preview** button 🔲. Because you have selected all sheets, both sheets can be viewed in Print Preview. Press (PageDown) to view the second worksheet, and then press (Page Up) to return to the print preview of the first worksheet. On the Print Preview toolbar, click the **Close** button.

13 **Save** 🔲 your file. From the **File** menu, click **Print**. Because the sheets are still grouped, both worksheets will print, and it is not necessary to click the *Entire Workbook* option button. Click **OK**.

14 Right-click the **Annual Costs** sheet tab, and then click **Ungroup Sheets**. Hold down (Ctrl) and press (`) to display the formulas. Display the **Page Setup** dialog box, click the **Page tab**, and under **Scaling**, click the **Fit to** option button. On the Standard toolbar, click the **Print** button 🖨 to print the formulas.

Recall that (`) is located below (Esc) on most keyboards. It is used with (Ctrl) to toggle between the worksheet numbers and the formulas.

15 Hold down (Ctrl) and press (`) again to redisplay the worksheet. Close the workbook, saving changes if prompted to do so.

End **You have completed Project 4A**

Project 4B **Projected Revenues**

In this project, you will use Excel functions—prebuilt formulas—to compute various statistics such as median, average, minimum, and maximum.

In Activities 4.6 through 4.10, you will edit a workbook created by John Zeidler, Chief Financial Officer for Owens Family Builders, which projects the various sources of revenue for the company over the next three years. Your completed worksheet will look similar to Figure 4.18. You will save your workbook as *4B_Projected_Revenues_Firstname_Lastname.*

Owens Family Builders
Statement of Projected Revenues Over Next Three Years

		YEAR 1		YEAR 2		YEAR 3
Revenue Income by Source						
Custom Homes	$	1,809,347	$	1,191,525	$	1,205,816
Office Buildings		3,200,567		3,789,000		3,978,654
Shopping Centers		2,509,879		3,567,890		2,908,397
Public Schools		4,567,890		5,400,678		4,900,567
Municipal Facilities		2,345,675		1,987,554		2,346,787
Roadways		5,467,890		6,789,003		7,567,909
Bridges		2,456,785		2,345,785		3,457,892
Design Fees		69,915		71,548		89,915
Construction Management Fees		2,543,256		2,456,734		2,765,889
Total Revenue by Source	$	24,971,204	$	27,599,717	$	29,221,826
Investment Earnings						
Investment Earnings	$	450,687	$	500,876	$	550,678
Total Investment Earnings						
Rental Income						
Office Rental Income	$	147,000	$	152,321	$	168,521
Total Rental Income						
Transfers from Other Funds						
Sale of Easements		213,557		251,246		198,354
Projected Insurance Excess Reserves		234,990		235,467		260,987
Total Transfers from Other Funds	$	448,547	$	486,713	$	459,341
Total Projected Revenue From All Sources	$	51,437,189	$	56,826,057	$	60,081,533

Summary Data

		YEAR 1		YEAR 2		YEAR 3
Median Revenue	$	2,509,879	$	2,456,734	$	2,908,397
Minimum Revenue	$	69,915	$	71,548	$	89,915
Maximum Revenue	$	5,467,890	$	6,789,003	$	7,567,909
Average Annual Income Over the Three-Year Period	$	56,114,926				
Number of Different Revenue Sources		9				

4B_Projected_Revenues_Firstname_Lastname

Figure 4.18
Project 4B—Projected Revenues

Objective 3
Create Statistical Functions

Recall that a cell can contain either a constant value (text, numbers, dates, and times) or a formula. Recall also that a function is a formula that has already been built for you by Excel. For example, Excel's SUM function adds a series of cell values. This function is used so frequently that it has a button on the Standard toolbar. You can sum a column of numbers by writing a formula to add the specific cells, or you can use the SUM function. Compare the following two formulas:

=A1+A2+A3+A4+A5+A6+A7+A8+A9+A10
=SUM(A1:A10)

Both formulas instruct Excel to add together the values in cells A1 through A10, and both give the same result. It is much easier, however, to type the shortened version. And that is what a function is—a short, predefined formula.

Activity 4.6 Using the Insert Function Command to Create the MEDIAN Function

Excel has defined many complex formulas that are regularly used in business. You have access to these functions (predefined formulas) from the Insert Function dialog box. You can display the Insert Function dialog box from the Insert menu or by clicking the Insert Function button—*fx*—to the left of the Formula Bar.

All functions begin with an equal sign (=), which indicates the beginning of a formula. The equal sign is followed by the ***function name***, for example, *SUM*, which indicates the type of calculation that will be performed. The function name is followed by a set of ***arguments***—the information that Excel needs to make the calculation—set off in parentheses. The proper format of typing the equal sign, the function name, and the arguments is referred to as the ***function syntax***.

1 **Start** Excel. Click the **Open** button , navigate to the student files that accompany this textbook, and open the file **e04B_Projected_Revenues**.

2 From the **File** menu, click **Save As**. In the **Save As** dialog box, navigate to the location where you are storing your projects for this chapter. In the **File name** box, type **4B_Projected_Revenues_Firstname_Lastname** and then click **Save** or press Enter.

3 Take a moment to familiarize yourself with the data in this worksheet, which lists the various sources of income projected over the next three years. Then, scroll down as necessary and click cell **B30**.

In this cell, you will use an Excel function to determine the *median* revenue in Year 1. Within a set of values, the median is the value below and above which there are an equal number of values. It is the value that falls in the middle of a ranked set of values.

4 From the **Insert** menu, click **Function**.

The Insert Function dialog box displays.

5 Under **Search for a function**, click the **Or select a category arrow** to display Excel's list of function categories as shown in Figure 4.19.

There are nine categories of functions, and within each, Excel has numerous predefined formulas. Three additional categories include *Most Recently Used*, which catalogs the functions you have used most recently so that they are easily located to use again; *All*, which lists all of Excel's predefined formulas in alphabetic order; and *User Defined*, which enables you to make up your own formulas and assign them a short function name.

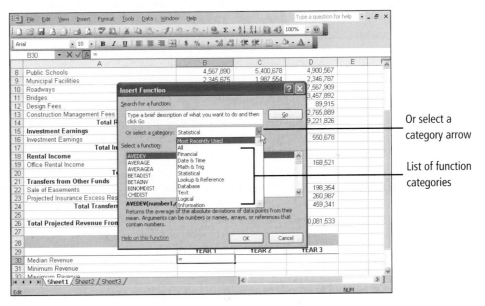

Figure 4.19

6 From the displayed list, click **Statistical**, and then, under **Select a function**, scroll down the alphabetic list and click **MEDIAN**.

Notice that at the bottom of the Insert Function dialog box, the function syntax and a brief description of the function display, as shown in Figure 4.20. This information is helpful in explaining what the formula will calculate.

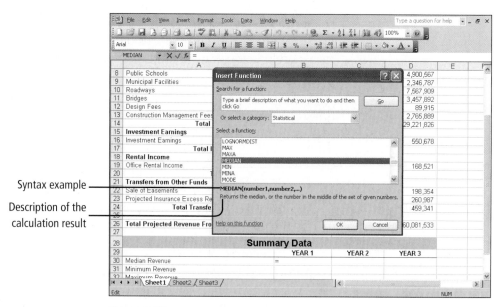

Syntax example

Description of the calculation result

Figure 4.20

7 Click **OK**.

The Function Arguments dialog box for the MEDIAN function displays, as shown in Figure 4.21.

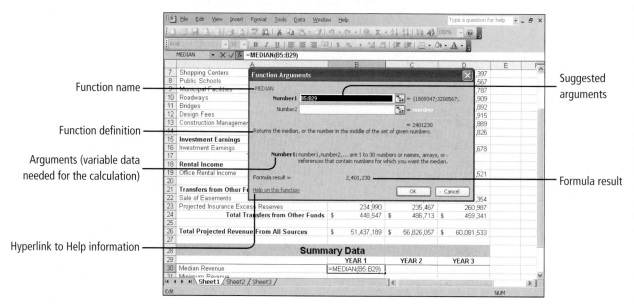

Function name

Function definition

Arguments (variable data needed for the calculation)

Hyperlink to Help information

Suggested arguments

Formula result

Figure 4.21

8 Take a moment to study Figure 4.21 to see each part of the **Function Arguments** dialog box.

9 Look at cell **B30** and notice that Excel will attempt to define a group of cells for the arguments—the information needed to perform the calculation. See Figure 4.21.

In this instance, this is not the group of cells among which you want to find the median.

10 In the **Function Arguments** dialog box, at the right edge of the **Number 1** box, click the **Collapse Dialog Box** button. Point to the blue title bar, and then drag the collapsed dialog box to the upper right corner of the screen, as shown in Figure 4.22.

The dialog box collapses (shrinks), leaving only the Number 1 box, and is moved off the worksheet area.

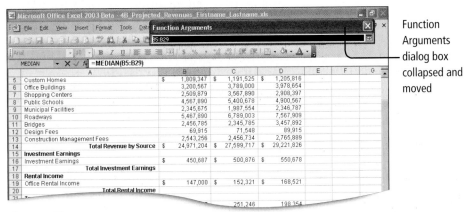

Function Arguments dialog box collapsed and moved

Figure 4.22

11 With the dialog box in the upper right corner of your screen, scroll the worksheet so that **rows 5 through 15** are visible, and then select the range **B5:B13**.

A moving border surrounds the cells, and the range displays as the argument—information needed for the calculation—in the Number1 box and in the Formula Bar. See Figure 4.23. The newly selected range also displays in the destination cell B30.

Formula displays in the Formula Bar.

Moving border surrounds selection.

Selected range becomes argument.

Formula in destination cell

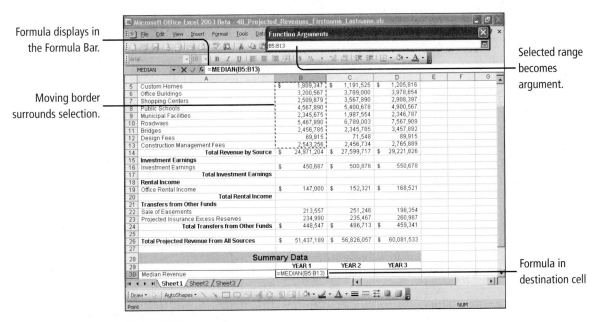

Figure 4.23

12 At the right edge of the collapsed dialog box, click the **Expand Dialog Box** button to redisplay the full dialog box.

Notice that the result of the formula—2,509,879—displays in the lower portion of the dialog box.

13 Click **OK**.

The result displays in cell B30. Look up at the Formula Bar and notice that the formula =MEDIAN(B5:B13) displays as the underlying formula. Excel looked at all the numbers in the group, ranked them in order of smallest to largest, and then determined which value fell in the middle of the group. This is how the mathematical median is calculated. When ranked in order from smallest to largest, half the values are below 2,509,879 and half the values are above 2,509,879.

14 With cell **B30** as the active cell, position your mouse pointer over the fill handle, and then drag to the right to copy the MEDIAN function to cells **C30** and **D30**. Compare your screen with Figure 4.24 and identify the function name and arguments in the formula displayed on the Formula Bar.

Excel copies the formula relative to the new locations. The median revenue income is 2,456,734 for Year 2 and 2,908,397 for Year 3.

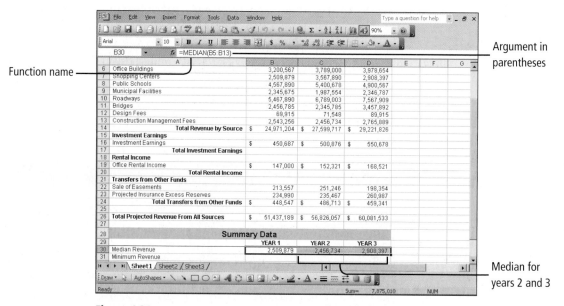

Figure 4.24

15 On the Standard toolbar, click the **Save** button.

Activity 4.7 Using the Insert Function Command to Create the MIN Function

1 Click cell **B31**. On the left edge of the **Formula Bar**, click the **Insert Function** button.

Recall that you can display the Insert Function dialog box either from the Insert menu or by clicking the Insert Function button on the Formula Bar.

2 Check that the **Statistical** category displays in the **Or select a category** box, and then, under **Select a function**, scroll down the alphabetic list and click **MIN**.

The MIN function—minimum—looks at a set of values and determines which value is the smallest. In determining the smallest value among a set of values, Excel does not consider any cells that contain text or logical values such as TRUE or FALSE.

3 Click **OK**.

The Function Arguments dialog box displays.

4 To get a clearer view of your worksheet, move your pointer into the **Function Arguments** dialog box, and then, at the right edge of the **Number1** box, click the **Collapse Dialog Box** button.

The dialog box collapses (shrinks), leaving only the Number1 box.

5 Scroll the worksheet so that **rows 5 through 15** are visible, and then select the range **B5:B13**.

A moving border surrounds the cells, and the range displays as the argument in the Number1 box and also in the Formula Bar, as shown in Figure 4.25.

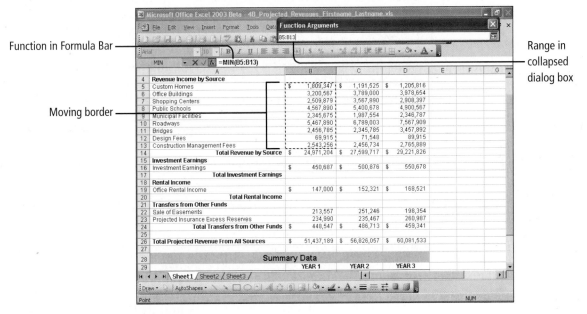

Function in Formula Bar

Range in collapsed dialog box

Moving border

Figure 4.25

6 At the right edge of the collapsed dialog box, click the **Expand Dialog Box** button to redisplay the full dialog box.

Notice that the result of the formula—69,915—displays in the lower portion of the dialog box.

7 Click **OK**.

The minimum (smallest) value within the selected range—69,915—displays in cell B31. In a short list such as this one, you could probably find the smallest value by looking through the list, but you can see that in a long list of values, Excel can quickly determine the smallest value.

8 With cell **B31** as the active cell, use the fill handle to copy the formula to cells **C31** and **D31**.

You can see that in each year, income from Design Fees is the smallest source of income.

9 On the Standard toolbar, click **Save** 🔲 to save the changes you have made to your workbook.

Another Way

To Enter Functions Without Using the Insert Function Dialog Box

Two other methods can be used.

You can get access to some of the most common functions by clicking the arrow on the AutoSum button found on the Standard toolbar. First, click in the cell where you want the results of the function to be displayed, click the AutoSum button arrow, and then choose the function from the displayed list. Verify that the default cell range is correct, or drag to adjust the range, and then press Enter to see the results. If the function you want is not displayed on the AutoSum button list, click the More Functions command at the end of the list to open the Insert Function dialog box.

Alternatively, if you know the function name and the syntax for the arguments, you can type the formula for the function directly in the destination cell. For example, to calculate the minimum, type =MIN(B5:B13), where B5:B13 is the range of cells you want evaluated.

Activity 4.8 Using the Insert Function Command to Create the MAX Function

1 Click cell **B32**. Using either the Insert menu or the Insert Function button to the left of the Formula Bar, display the **Insert Function** dialog box.

2 Be sure you are in the **Statistical** category. Scroll down the alphabetic list, click **MAX**, and then click **OK**.

The Function Arguments dialog box displays. The MAX function—maximum—looks at a set of values and determines which value is the largest. In determining the largest value among a set of values, Excel does not consider any cells that contain text or logical values such as TRUE or FALSE.

3 In the **Number1** box of the **Function Arguments** dialog box, notice that the box is highlighted, indicating that if you begin to type, your new keystrokes will replace any existing text. Type **b5:b13** as shown in Figure 4.26, and then click **OK**.

The result in cell B32 is 5,467,890. As you have practiced, you can insert arguments into the boxes of the Function Arguments dialog box by dragging to select a range of cells or by typing the cell reference for a range of cells.

Formula displays
in Formula Bar.

Cell range
entered

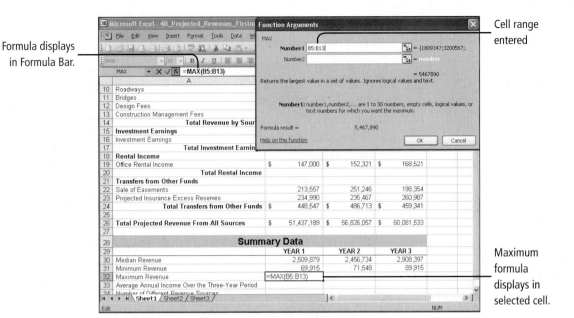

Maximum
formula
displays in
selected cell.

Figure 4.26

4 With cell **B32** as the active cell, copy the formula to cells **C32** and
D32. Compare your screen with Figure 4.27.

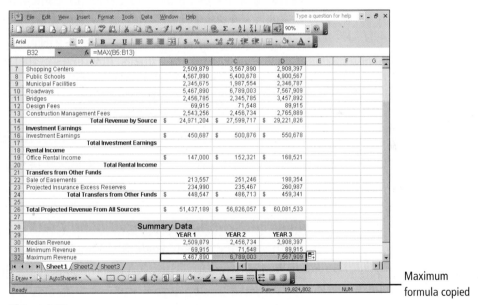

Maximum
formula copied

Figure 4.27

5 On the Standard toolbar, click **Save** 🖫 to save the changes you have
made to your workbook.

Activity 4.9 Using the Insert Function Command to Create the AVERAGE Function

In this activity, you will compute the average annual revenue from all sources over the three-year period. To compute this average value, you must add the total projected revenue for each of the three years, and then divide the total by 3. Of course, Excel has a function for computing an arithmetic average—all you have to do is define which cells to use in the calculation.

1 Click cell **B33**, and then display the **Insert Function** dialog box.

2 Be sure you are in the **Statistical** category, and then click the **AVERAGE** function.

3 Click **OK** to display the **Function Arguments** dialog box. If necessary, scroll so that **row 26** is visible.

4 Select the range **B26:D26**, and then click **OK**.

The result, 56,114,926, displays in cell B33. The projected revenue from all sources will average $56,114,926 in each year of the three-year period.

5 On the Standard toolbar, click **Save** 🖫 to save the changes you have made to your workbook.

Activity 4.10 Using the Insert Function Command to Create the COUNT Function

Within a range of selected cells, the COUNT function counts the number of cells that contain numbers. It ignores cells that contain text, logical values (such as TRUE or FALSE), or that are blank. In a short worksheet, it is easy to visually count the number of cells in a range, but in a large worksheet, this feature is very useful.

1 Click cell **B34** and display the **Insert Function** dialog box.

2 Check that you are in the **Statistical** category, click the **COUNT** function, and then click **OK**.

The Function Arguments dialog box displays.

3 In the **Value1** box, click to collapse the dialog box, and then scroll as necessary to view **rows 5 through 15**.

4 Select the range **B5:B13**. In the collapsed dialog box, click the **Expand Dialog Box** button to redisplay the full **Function Arguments** dialog box.

Notice that the result, 9, displays in the Function Arguments dialog box, as shown in Figure 4.28.

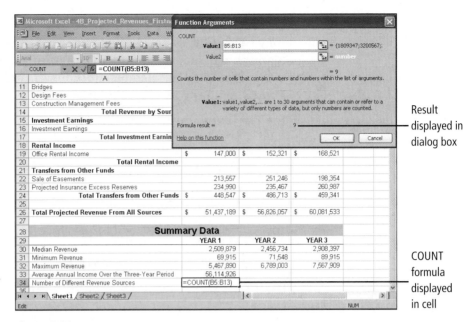

Figure 4.28

5 Click **OK** to display the result of the formula in the cell.

On a short worksheet like this, it would be easy to count the various revenue sources, but you can see that on a large worksheet, this formula would be quite useful.

6 Select the range **B30:D32**, hold down Ctrl, and then click cell **B33**.

On the Formatting toolbar, click the **Currency Style** button $, and then click the **Decrease Decimal** button twice. Click in a blank cell to cancel the selection, and then compare your worksheet with Figure 4.29.

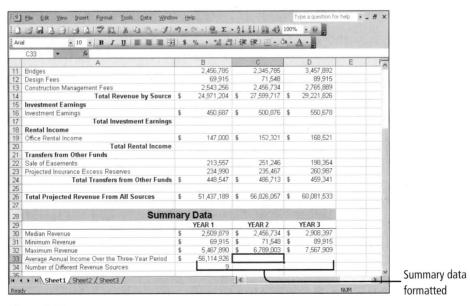

Figure 4.29

7 From the **File** menu, click **Page Setup**. Click the **Page tab**, and then, under **Orientation**, click the **Landscape** option button. Click the **Margins tab**, and then, under **Center on page**, select the **Horizontally** check box. Click the **Header/Footer tab**, and then click **Custom Footer**. With the insertion point positioned in the **Left section**, click the **File name** button. Click **OK** twice.

8 **Save** your file, and then click the **Print Preview** button.

On the Print Preview toolbar, click the **Print** button, and then click **OK**.

9 Hold down Ctrl and press ` to display the formulas. Click the **Print Preview** button.

The formulas expand the worksheet across two pages.

10 On the Print Preview toolbar, click **Setup**. In the **Page Setup** dialog box, click the **Page tab**. Under **Orientation**, be sure **Landscape** is selected. Under **Scaling**, click the **Fit to** option button, and then click **OK**.

The scaling option shrinks the font as necessary so that the formulas will display on one page, as shown in Figure 4.30.

Formulas display on one page.

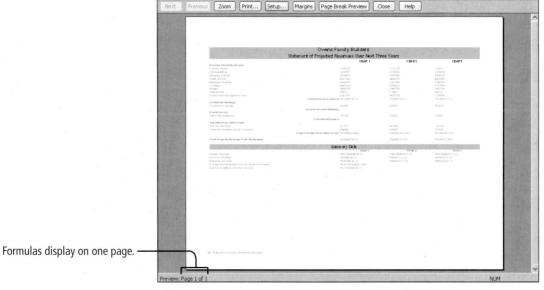

Figure 4.30

11 On the Print Preview toolbar, click **Print**, and then click **OK**.

12 Hold down Ctrl and press ` to redisplay the worksheet. Close the workbook, saving changes if prompted to do so.

End You have completed Project 4B

Project 4C New Benefits

In Project 4C you will use functions within the Date & Time, Financial, and Logical categories. Using these functions, you will compute monthly loan payments and annuity values.

In Activities 4.11 through 4.13, you will edit a workbook created by Juan Sanchez, Director of Employee Benefits for Owens Family Builders, which details the cost of a new plan to provide pick-up trucks for each of the 24 construction managers and also to provide an annuity benefit for the construction managers and construction crew members. An **_annuity_** is an investment that pays the beneficiary an amount of money in a lump sum or as a series of equal annual payments. The two worksheets of your workbook will look similar to Figure 4.31. You will name the workbook _4C_New_Benefits_Firstname_Lastname_.

Proposed Annuity Benefit
Construction Managers and Crew Members

	Number of Eligible Employees	Total Initial Purchase Cost	Annual Payment Cost	Total Cost for the Life of the Annuity
Managers	24	$ 360,000	$ 48,000	$1,080,000
Crew Members	75	$1,125,000	$150,000	$3,375,000
Total	99	$1,485,000	$198,000	$4,455,000
Average Return Rate	10%			
Contributing Years	15			
Annual Contribution	2000			
Initial Contribution per Employee	15000			
Computed on:	12/18/2003 13:12			
Annuity Value Per Employee at the End of 15 Years	$132,558.18			

4C_New_Benefits_Firstname_Lastname

Figure 4.31a
Project 4C—New Benefits
Proposed Annuity Benefit worksheet

Pick-up Truck Financing Proposal
9/24/2004

Item	24 Pick-up Trucks
Purchase Price	600000
Down Payment	60000
Loan Amount	540000
Rate	0.06
Term of Loan	3
Monthly Payment	($16,427.85)

4C_New_Benefits_Firstname_Lastname

Figure 4.31b Pick-up Truck Financing Proposal worksheet

Objective 4
Create Date & Time and Financial Functions

Excel assigns a serial value to a date and then uses that value to calculate the number of days between two dates. For example, in the period July 16, 2004, to July 31, 2004 (a typical payroll period), Excel looks at the serial numbers of the two dates and subtracts the smaller one from the larger one. Excel also has numerous functions for complex business calculations.

Activity 4.11 Applying the DATE and NOW Functions

The DATE function places, in the selected cell, a serial value that represents a particular day, month, and year. Excel has assigned the number 1 to the date January 1, 1900, and continues numbering the days consecutively. For example, January 1, 2008, has the serial value 39,448 because there are 39,448 days between the base date of January 1, 1900, and January 1, 2008.

1 **Start** Excel. Click the **Open** button ⬚, navigate to the student files that accompany this textbook, and open the file **e04C_New_Benefits**.

2 From the **File** menu, click **Save As**. In the **Save As** dialog box, navigate to the location where you are storing your projects for this chapter. In the **File name** box, type **4C_New_Benefits_Firstname_Lastname** and then click **Save** or press Enter.

3 Be sure that **Truck Financing** is the active sheet, and then click cell **A2**.

4 From the **Insert** menu, click **Function**. Click the **Or select a category arrow**, and from the displayed list, click **Date & Time**. Under **Select a function**, click **DATE**, and then click **OK**.

The Function Arguments dialog box displays with three different boxes for arguments—*Year*, *Month*, and *Day*.

5 Using the date September 24, 2004, type each argument—year first—as a number, as shown in Figure 4.32.

The formula =DATE(2004,9,24) displays in the cell and in the Formula Bar. Notice the number—38254—displayed in the dialog box as the serial value for this date.

Formula displayed

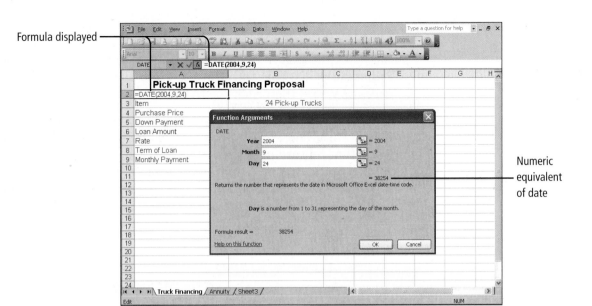

Numeric equivalent of date

Figure 4.32

6 Click **OK** to close the dialog box.

The date—9/24/2004—displays in cell A2.

Note — Does Your Date Display Leading Zeros?

Your date may display with leading zeros—09/24/2004. This is controlled by the date configuration set for your operating system and does not change the purpose or results of the date functions.

7 With cell **A2** as the active cell, display the **Format Cells** dialog box, and then click the **Number tab**. Under **Category**, click **General**, and then click **OK**.

The serial value of the date, 38254, displays. Recall that all cells have the General format by default; however, the DATE function applies the Date format to the cell. To view the sequential serial number that represents a particular date, you must reformat the cell to the General format.

8 On the Standard toolbar, click the **Undo** button to restore the cell format to Date and display the date.

9 Click the **Annuity** sheet tab, and then click cell **B11**. On the Formula Bar, click the **Insert Function** button [fx]. In the displayed **Insert Function** dialog box, with **Date & Time** as the category, scroll as necessary, and then click the **NOW** function. Click **OK**.

The Function Arguments dialog box displays, as shown in Figure 4.33. The NOW function places, in the selected cell, a serial value that represents today's date and the current time. This is a volatile function, that is, a function that is subject to change, because each time you open a workbook that contains the NOW function, the day, month, year, and time can be updated by gathering the date and time from your computer's internal calendar and clock.

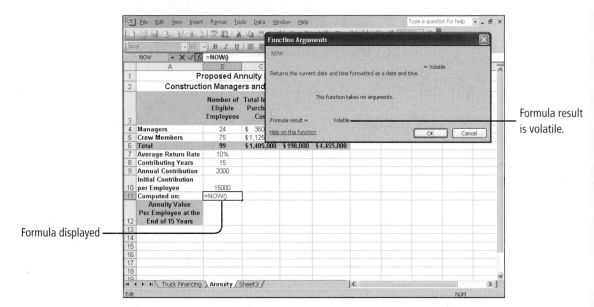

Formula result is volatile.

Formula displayed

Figure 4.33

Note — Working with the NOW Function

If you open a workbook containing the NOW function, you will be prompted to save your changes even if you do not perform any editing in the cells. This is because the NOW function will attempt to update the cell where it is used to the current date and time.

10 In the **Function Arguments** dialog box, notice that the NOW function has no arguments. The function captures the current date and time from your computer system's internal calendar and clock. Click **OK**.

The current date and time display in cell B11.

11 With cell **B11** as the active cell, display the **Format Cells** dialog box, and then, on the **Number tab**, click **General**. In the **Sample** area, notice that the serial value for the date and time is displayed. See Figure 4.34.

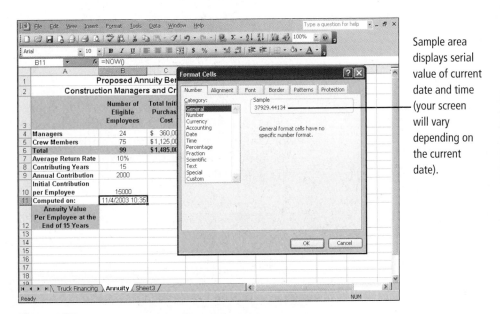

Sample area displays serial value of current date and time (your screen will vary depending on the current date).

Figure 4.34

12 In the lower right corner of the **Format Cells** dialog box, click **Cancel** so that the format of the cell is not changed from the Date format.

13 On the menu bar, click the **Save** button ![save icon].

Activity 4.12 Applying the Financial Function FV

The **FV** function calculates *future value*. Future value is the value of an investment at the end of a specified period of time, based on periodic, constant payments and a constant interest rate.

For example, Owens Family Builders wants to purchase an annuity for employees who have 10 or more years of service with the company. After an additional 15 years of service, this investment would provide each employee with a sum of money that would be paid as a lump sum or as a series of equal annual payments.

1 If necessary, click the **Annuity** sheet tab, and then click cell **B12**.

2 From the **Insert** menu, click **Function**. In the displayed **Insert Function** dialog box, click the **Or select a category arrow**, and then click **Financial**. Under **Select a function**, click **FV**.

Using this function, you will calculate the value of a $15,000 annuity at the end of 15 years, assuming that the company contributes $2,000 to each employee's annuity at the beginning of each year and that there is an average rate of return of 10 percent per year for each of the 15 remaining years.

3 At the bottom of the dialog box, locate the information in bold, which is the structure of the FV formula, and the descriptive information, as shown in Figure 4.35.

The FV function uses the structure *(rate, number of periods, payment, present value, type)*. You need not, of course, be concerned with the exact structure of the calculation because Excel has done that work for you by predefining the formula as a function. You need only supply the arguments (needed information) with which Excel should make the calculations.

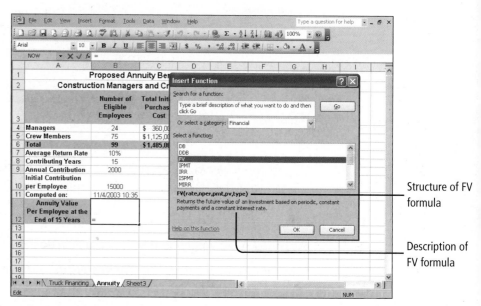

Figure 4.35

4 In the lower right corner, click **OK** to display the **Function Arguments** dialog box. If necessary, drag the dialog box to the right side of your screen. With the insertion point positioned in the **Rate** box, click cell **B7**, which contains the percentage rate of return per year.

B7 displays in the Rate box, cell B7 is surrounded by a moving border, and a definition and example of Rate is provided.

5 Press [Tab] to move the insertion point to the **Nper** box, and then click cell **B8**.

B8 displays in the Nper box, and cell B8 is surrounded by a moving border. **Nper** is the total number of payment periods—15—in the annuity investment.

6 Press [Tab] to move the insertion point to the **Pmt** box, type - (minus sign), and then click cell **B9**.

-B9 displays in the Pmt box, and cell B9 is surrounded by a moving border. **Pmt** represents the payment that will be made in each annual period. Because this amount will be paid out, it should be entered as a negative number.

7 Press [Tab] to move the insertion point to the **Pv** box, type - (minus sign), and then click cell **B10**.

-B10 displays in the Pv box, and cell B10 is surrounded by a moving border. **Pv** represents the present value—what the annuity is worth now—which is $15,000, the employee's initial contribution. This is also an amount that will be paid out. Thus, the value should be entered as a negative number.

8 Press [Tab] to move the insertion point to the **Type** box, and type **1**

Type represents the timing of the payment—whether it will be paid at the beginning of each period (indicated by a 1) or at the end of the period (indicated by a 0). Compare your Function Arguments dialog box with Figure 4.36.

Function formula displayed in Formula Bar

Arguments entered for FV function

Formula partially displayed in destination cell

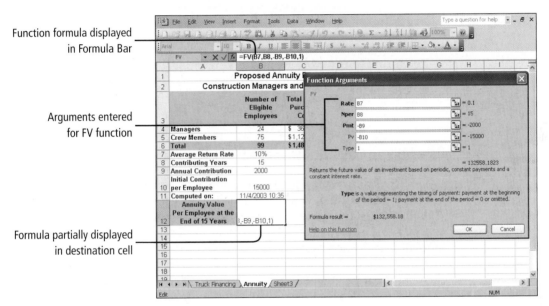

Figure 4.36

9 Notice that cell **B12** is the active cell and that the function formula is partially displayed in the cell. Move to the lower right corner of the **Function Arguments** dialog box, and then click **OK**.

The result, $132,558.18, displays in cell B12. At the end of 15 years, the annuity investment for each employee will be worth $132,558.18. Using Excel's FV function, you can see how quickly an investment of this type can add up.

10 On the Standard toolbar, click the **Save** button 🖫 to save the changes you have made to your workbook.

Activity 4.13 Applying the Financial Function PMT

The **PMT** function calculates the payment for a loan based on constant payments and a constant interest rate. The structure for the function is *PMT(rate, number of periods, present value, future value, type)*.

For example, Juan Sanchez wants to calculate the monthly payments the company will have to make to finance the purchase of 24 new pick-up trucks. The total cost of the trucks, less the down payment, is $540,000. Juan wants to finance this amount over three years at an annual interest rate of 6 percent.

1 Click the **Truck Financing** sheet tab, and then click cell **B9**.

2 From the **Insert** menu, click **Function** to display the **Insert Function** dialog box. Within the **Financial** category, scroll as necessary, and then click **PMT**. Click **OK** to display the **Function Arguments** dialog box for the PMT function. If necessary, drag the dialog box to the right of your screen.

To complete the PMT formula, you must first determine the total number of loan payment periods (months), which is 12 months × 3 years, or 36 months.

Note — Calculating a Monthly Payment

When borrowing money, the interest rate and term—length of the loan—is quoted in years. The payments on a loan, however, are usually made monthly. Therefore, the term, stated in years, and annual interest rate have to be changed to a monthly equivalent in order to calculate the monthly payment amount. This is done by dividing the interest rate by 12 to derive a monthly interest rate and multiplying the term by 12 to convert the number of years to the number of months (payment periods) for the term of the loan.

3 With your insertion point positioned in the **Rate** box, type **b7/12**

This will instruct Excel to divide the annual interest rate of 6 percent—0.06 in decimal notation—located in cell B7 by 12 (months), which will result in a monthly interest rate.

4 Press [Tab] to move the insertion point to the **Nper** box.

5 At the bottom of the dialog box, notice that *Nper* represents the number of payments for the loan (number of periods).

6 Click cell **B8**, and then type ***12** so that Excel converts the number of years in the loan to the total number of months.

Recall that this function is calculating a monthly payment. Thus, all values in the function must be expressed in months.

7 Press `Tab` to move your insertion point to the **Pv** box.

Pv represents the present value—the total value that a series of future payments is worth now.

8 Click cell **B6** to instruct Excel to use the value 540000 in cell **B6**. Compare your dialog box with Figure 4.37. Notice that the different parts of the PMT argument are separated by commas (,).

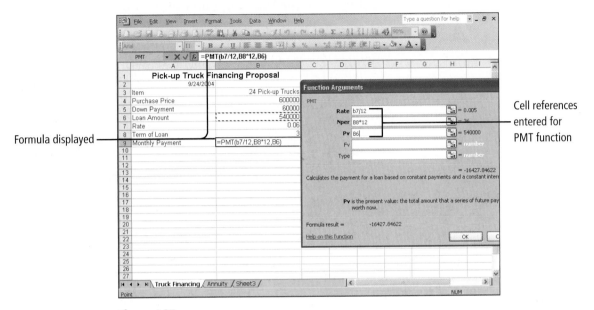

Formula displayed

Cell references entered for PMT function

Figure 4.37

9 Click **OK**.

The monthly payment amount, ($16,427.85), displays in cell B9. The amount is displayed in red and in parentheses to show that it is a negative number, a number that will be paid out.

10 On the **Truck Financing sheet tab**, right-click, and then click **Select All Sheets**. From the **File** menu, click **Page Setup**. Click the **Margins tab**, and then under **Center on page**, select the **Horizontally** check box.

11 Click the **Header/Footer tab**, and then click **Custom Footer**. With the insertion point positioned in the **Left section**, click the **File Name** button. Click **OK** twice.

12 On the Standard toolbar, click the **Save** button, and then click the **Print Preview** button. Because you have grouped the sheets, both worksheets can be viewed in Print Preview. On the Print Preview toolbar, click **Print**, and then click **OK**.

13 With the sheets still grouped, hold down Ctrl and press ⟨'⟩ to display the formulas. Click the **Print Preview** button 🔍 again. On the Print Preview toolbar, click **Next** three times to see the four formula pages.

Both worksheets display but are spread across four pages.

14 On the Print Preview toolbar, click **Setup**. In the **Page Setup** dialog box, click the **Page tab**. Under **Orientation**, click **Landscape**, under **Scaling**, click the **Fit to** option button, and then click **OK**.

The Annuity Benefit sheet displays on one page.

15 On the Print Preview toolbar, click the **Previous** button twice to see the first part of the Truck Financing page. On the Print Preview toolbar, click **Setup**. In the **Page Setup** dialog box, on the **Page tab**, click **Landscape**, and then click **OK**.

For this worksheet, the scaling option is not needed—the landscape orientation is sufficient to display the formulas on one page.

16 On the Print Preview toolbar, click **Print**, and then click **OK**. Hold down Ctrl and press ⟨'⟩ to redisplay the worksheet numbers. Close the workbook, saving changes if prompted to do so.

The formulas print for both worksheets.

End You have completed Project 4C ─────────────────────────

Project 4D **Office Payroll**

In Project 4D, you will use Excel's Logical functions, which apply a conditional test to determine whether a condition is true or false. You will also print a portion of a worksheet.

In Activities 4.14 through 4.15, you will edit a workbook created by Jennifer Owen, Payroll Manager, that lists the number of hours worked and the hourly pay rate of the administrative staff at Owens Family Builders. Your completed worksheet will look similar to Figure 4.38. You will name the workbook *4D_Admin_Payroll_Firstname_ Lastname.*

Administrative Office Payroll - Week of July 23					
Employee	Hours	Hourly Pay Rate	Regular Pay	Overtime Pay	Total Weekly Salary
Fong, B.	52	$35.50	$1,420.00	$639.00	$2,059.00
Owen-Hughes, M.	38	$22.50	$855.00	$0.00	$855.00
Freeman, M.	61	$22.50	$900.00	$708.75	$1,608.75
Daly, M.	58	$17.50	$700.00	$472.50	$1,172.50
Ensler, V.	36	$21.75	$783.00	$0.00	$783.00
Sobel, D.	47	$40.00	$1,600.00	$420.00	$2,020.00
Rhode, A.	42	$15.50	$620.00	$46.50	$666.50
Total Weekly Payroll					$9,164.75

4D_Admin_Payroll_Firstname_Lastname

Figure 4.38
Project 4D—Office Payroll

Objective 5
Create Logical Functions

Most of the functions that fall in the category of Logical functions use a **conditional test** to determine whether a specified condition is true or false. A conditional test is performed by using an equation to compare two values (or two functions or two formulas).

A conditional test must have at least one **logical operator**—a mathematical symbol that tests the relationship between the two elements of the conditional test. Take a moment to become familiar with the logical operator symbols in the table shown in Figure 4.39.

Logical Operators

Logical Operator Symbol	Definition
=	Equal to
>	Greater than
<	Less than
>=	Greater than or equal to
<=	Less than or equal to
<>	Not equal to

Figure 4.39

Activity 4.14 Applying the IF Function

The IF Logical function helps you make a decision about assigning a value to a cell dependent on a **logical test**. A logical test is any value or expression that can be evaluated as true or false. For example, *C8=100* is an expression that can be evaluated as true or false. If the value in cell C8 is equal to 100, the expression is true. If the value in cell C8 is not 100, the expression is false.

1 **Start** Excel. Click the **Open** button 🖼, navigate to the student files that accompany this textbook, and open the file **e04D_Admin_Payroll**. From the **File** menu, click **Save As**. In the **Save As** dialog box, navigate to the location where you are storing your projects for this chapter. In the **File name** box, type **4D_Admin_Payroll_Firstname_Lastname** and then click **Save** or press Enter.

2 From the **View** menu, click **Header and Footer**. Click the **Custom Footer** button. With the insertion point positioned in the **Left section**, click the **File Name** button 🔲. Click **OK** twice. Then, take a moment to familiarize yourself with the data in the workbook.

In this worksheet, you will use the IF function to determine whether or not an employee has earned any overtime pay. All hours over 40 worked in a week are paid as overtime, and the overtime hourly pay rate is one and a half times the regular hourly pay rate.

3 Click cell **D3**. On the Formula Bar, click the **Insert Function** button [fx] . In the displayed **Insert Function** dialog box, click the **Logical** category, and then, under **Select a function**, click **IF**. Click **OK**. If necessary, drag the dialog box to the right side of your screen.

The IF function determines whether a condition is met and returns one value if the condition is true and another value if the condition is false.

4 With the insertion point positioned in the **Logical_test** box, type **b3>40**

This directs Excel to look at the value in cell B3, the hours worked during the week, and then determine whether the value is greater than 40. This will determine whether or not the employee has worked any overtime hours during the week.

5 Press [Tab] to move the insertion point to the **Value_if_true** box, and then type **c3*40**

This directs Excel to multiply the value in cell C3 (the hourly pay rate) times 40 if the condition in the argument above is TRUE (greater than 40). Recall that the first 40 hours worked in any week are paid at the regular hourly rate.

6 Press [Tab] to move the insertion point to the **Value_if_false** box, and then type **b3*c3**

This directs Excel to multiply the value in cell B3 (the number of hours worked) times the value in cell C3 (the regular hourly pay rate for 40 or fewer hours worked). Compare your dialog box with Figure 4.40.

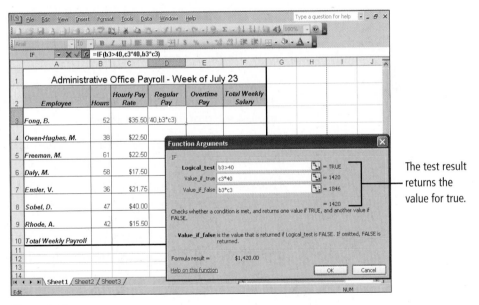

Figure 4.40

7 Click **OK**.

The result, $1,420.00, displays in cell D3. In this cell, the true value was returned because cell B3 is greater than 40.

8 Using the fill handle, copy the formula down through cell **D9**, and then compare your worksheet with Figure 4.41.

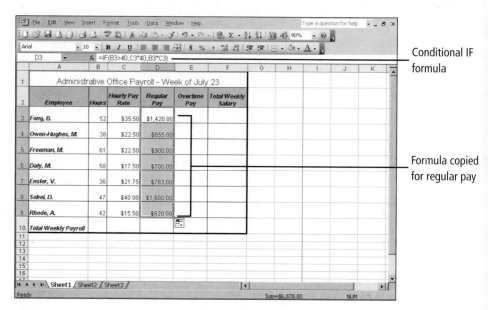

Conditional IF formula

Formula copied for regular pay

Figure 4.41

9 Click cell **E3**, and then display the **Insert Function** dialog box. Click the **IF** function, and then click **OK**.

10 In the **Logical_test** box, type **b3>40**

This directs Excel to look at the value in cell B3 and determine whether it is greater than 40, which will indicate whether or not the employee earned any overtime.

11 Press Tab to move to the **Value_if_true** box, and then type **(b3-40)*(1.5*c3)**

This directs Excel, provided that the logical test result is true, to subtract 40 from the value in cell B3, and then multiply the result times one and a half times the value in cell C3. More specifically, Excel calculates the number of hours worked over 40, and then multiplies that number by the overtime hourly rate—which is one and a half times the regular hourly rate.

More Knowledge — How Excel Performs Calculations

Order of Operations

When performing calculations, Excel follows a set of mathematical rules referred to as *order of operations*. Moving from left to right, it performs operations from the highest level to the lowest. First it applies negation (-), then percentage (%), then exponentiation (^), followed by division (/) or multiplication (*), and finally addition (+) or subtraction (-). You can override this order by the use of parentheses because any operations inside of parentheses are performed first. For example, substituting the values for cells B3—52—and C3—$35.50—in the formula in Step 11 results in (52-40)*(1.5*35.50). Performing the operations inside the parentheses first simplifies the equation to 12*53.25, or $639. If the parentheses are removed from this formula, the result would be different, and not the desired result. Parentheses play an important part in assuring that you get the correct results in your formulas.

12 Press Tab to move to the **Value_if_false** box, and type **0.00**

If the logical test is FALSE, the employee does not earn any overtime pay, and the result in this column should display as zero dollars.

13 Click **OK**.

The result, $639.00, displays in cell E3, which is the value 12 (number of hours over 40 worked) times the overtime hourly rate (1.5 × 35.50 = 53.25).

14 Using the fill handle, copy the formula down through cell **E9**, and then compare your worksheet with Figure 4.42.

By examining your worksheet, you can see that the employees who worked fewer than 40 hours per week (Owens-Hughes and Ensler) received no overtime pay.

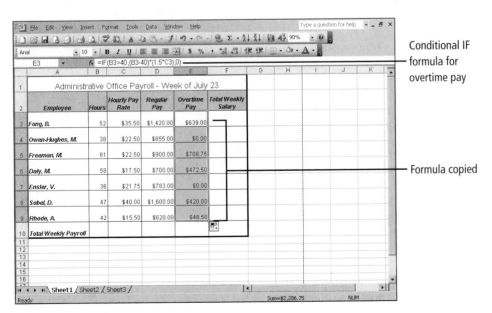

Figure 4.42

15 Click cell **F3**. On the Standard toolbar, click the **AutoSum** button ☒ ▾.

AutoSum proposes to add the values in cells B3:E3. To calculate the Total Weekly Salary, you need only add the Regular Pay to the Overtime Pay.

16 With the moving border displayed around the range **B3:E3**, select the range **D3:E3**, and then press ⏎. Click cell **F3** again, and then copy the formula down through cell **F9**. In cell **F10**, use the **AutoSum** button ☒ ▾ to compute the total weekly Administrative Office Payroll cost. Compare your screen with Figure 4.43.

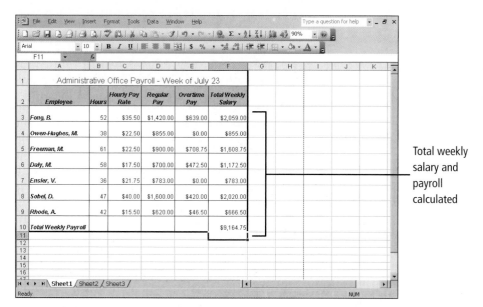

Total weekly salary and payroll calculated

Figure 4.43

17 From the **File** menu, click **Page Setup**, and then click the **Margins tab**. Under **Center on page**, select the **Horizontally** check box, and then click **OK**. On the Standard toolbar, click the **Save** button 🖫, and then click the **Print Preview** button 🔍 to view your worksheet as it will print.

18 On the Print Preview toolbar, click **Close**, and leave the workbook open for the next activity.

Objective 6
Set and Clear a Print Area

Sometimes you do not need to print an entire worksheet; rather, you need to print only a portion of a worksheet. If you need to print a worksheet portion only once, select the cells, and then, in the Print dialog box, click the Selection option button.

If, on the other hand, you are likely to print the same portion of a worksheet over and over again, you can save time by naming the area *Print_Area*. For example, Jennifer Owen frequently prints a list of the Administrative Office employees and the number of hours they have worked in a given week—without the accompanying salary information. After you have set a print area, you also need to know how to clear it when necessary.

Activity 4.15 Setting and Clearing the Print Area

1 If necessary, **Open** 🖼 your file **4D_Admin_Payroll**.

2 Select the range **A2:B9**. From the **File** menu, point to **Print Area**, and then click **Set Print Area**.

The selected area is surrounded by a dashed border.

Another Way

To Set the Print Area

On the menu bar, click File, click Page Setup, click the Sheet tab, and then type the range into the Print area box.

---

3 Click in any blank cell, and notice that a smaller dashed border continues to surround the area. As shown in Figure 4.44, click the **Name Box arrow**, and then click **Print_Area**.

The Print Area is selected and once again surrounded by a thin, dashed border.

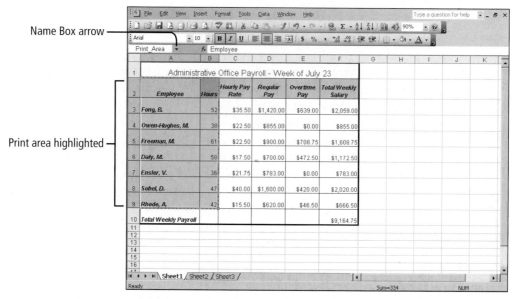

Name Box arrow

Print area highlighted

Figure 4.44

4 On the menu bar, click the **Print Preview** button. Notice that only the print area displays and will print. On the Print Preview toolbar, click the **Print** button, and then click **OK**.

5 To clear the Print Area, display the **File** menu, point to **Print Area**, and then click **Clear Print Area**. The print area is cleared.

6 On the Standard toolbar, click the **Save** button. Hold down Ctrl and press ˋ to display the formulas. Click the **Print Preview** button.

The formulas display across two pages.

7 On the Print Preview toolbar, click **Setup**. In the **Page Setup** dialog box, on the **Page tab**, click the **Landscape** and **Fit to** option buttons, and then click **OK**. On the Print Preview toolbar, click **Print**, and click **OK**.

8 Hold down Ctrl and press ˋ to redisplay the worksheet. Close the workbook, saving changes if prompted to do so. Close Excel.

End You have completed Project 4D

Summary

In this chapter, you created range names and used the names in a formula. By assigning a name to a range of cells, you can use the name in a formula. This makes it easier for you and other users of your worksheet to understand the meaning of the formula. Using a range name, you can also navigate to a specific section of a worksheet.

Naming ranges involves a few rules. The first character must be a letter, and you cannot use spaces. After you name ranges, you can modify or delete them. Modifying or deleting a range does not change the contents of the cells in the range.

In this chapter, you also worked with more of Excel's functions. A function is a predefined formula, and Excel provides many such formulas for use in complex calculations. When using the Date & Time functions, recall that Excel assigns a serial value to a date for the purpose of calculating the number of days between two dates. Using Statistical functions, you practiced calculating some of the most common statistical measures—average, median, minimum, maximum, and count.

Using Financial functions, you practiced calculating common financial transactions such as a future value and loan payments. Using Logical functions, you practiced performing conditional tests to determine whether a specified condition was true or false.

In This Chapter You Practiced How To

- Create Range Names
- Use Range Names in a Formula
- Create Statistical Functions
- Create Date & Time and Financial Functions
- Create Logical Functions
- Set and Clear a Print Area

Matching

Match each term in the second column with its correct definition in the first column by writing the letter of the term on the blank line in front of the correct definition.

_____ **1.** Within an Excel function, a value that represents the timing of the payment—whether it will be paid at the beginning of each period (indicated by a 1) or at the end of the period (indicated by a 0).

_____ **2.** The information that Excel uses to make the calculation within a function.

_____ **3.** A mathematical symbol that tests the relationship between the two elements of a conditional test, for example, greater than (>), less than (<), or equal (=).

_____ **4.** A specific name given to a range of cells, which can then be used to refer to the range in a function or formula.

_____ **5.** A test performed by using an equation to compare two values (or two functions or two formulas).

_____ **6.** An Excel function that calculates future value—the value of an investment at the end of a specified period of time—based on periodic, constant payments and a constant interest rate.

_____ **7.** Within a set of values, the value below and above which there are an equal number of values—the value that falls in the middle of a ranked set of values.

_____ **8.** A sum of money payable in a lump sum or as a series of equal annual payments.

_____ **9.** Within an Excel function, the value that represents what an annuity is worth now.

_____ **10.** Within an Excel function, the total number of payment periods in an annuity investment.

_____ **11.** A button within a dialog box that temporarily shrinks the dialog box so that you have a larger view of the data in your worksheet.

_____ **12.** Within an Excel function, the payment that will be made in each annual period.

_____ **13.** A formula that has already been built for you by Excel.

_____ **14.** A group of cells referred to by the first and last cell in the group, for example, B3:G7.

_____ **15.** The proper format of typing the equal sign, the function name, and the arguments when constructing a function.

A Annuity

B Arguments

C Collapse Dialog Box button

D Conditional test

E Function

F Function syntax

G FV

H Logical operator

I Median

J Nper

K Pmt

L Pv

M Range

N Range name

O Type

Fill in the Blank Write the correct answer in the space provided.

1. By assigning a _____ to a range of cells, it is easier for you and others to understand the meaning of formulas in a worksheet.

2. Assigning a name to a range of cells makes navigating a worksheet easier because you can use the _____ command to move to a named range.

3. The first character of a range name must be a(n) _____ or a(n) _____.

4. Range names can be more than one word; however, there can be no _____ between the words.

5. Deleting a range name does not modify or delete the cell _____ or _____ of the cells.

6. To view and get access to all of Excel's functions, display the _____ dialog box.

7. A function, like a formula, always begins with a(n) _____.

8. Excel has _____ different categories of functions, plus three additional categories: Most Recently Used, All, and User Defined.

9. Within a range of selected cells, the _____ function returns the number of cells that contain numbers.

10. Excel has assigned the serial value of 1 to the date _____.

11. The _____ function places, in the selected cell, a serial value that represents a particular day, month, and year.

(Fill in the Blank–continues on the next page)

Fill in the Blank–continued)

12. If you open a workbook containing the _____ function, when closing the workbook you will be prompted to save changes even if you did not perform any editing in the cells because the function attempts to update the cell in which it is used to contain the current date and time.

13. The symbol > is the logical operator that indicates _____.

14. The symbol < is the logical operator that indicates _____.

15. The symbols >= form the logical operator that indicates

_____.

Project 4E — Home Price

Objectives: *Create Range Names, Use Range Names in a Formula, and Create Statistical Functions.*

In the following Skill Assessment, you will calculate statistics regarding the prices of various new home plans that are built by the Owens Custom Homes division of Owens Family Builders. Your completed worksheet will look similar to Figure 4.45. You will save your workbook as *4E_Home_Price_Firstname_Lastname.*

Home Plans Available from Owen Custom Homes
In the Highlands Development (Standard Lot)

Home Plan Name	Plan Price	Number of Units Sold
The Santa Fe Model	$ 157,893	25
The Westwood Model	$ 146,523	23
The Windcrest Model	$ 233,329	16
The Orchard Model	$ 109,785	5
The Hazelton Model	$ 170,511	12
The Chestnut Model	$ 156,733	21
The Forester Model	$ 163,284	33
The Orlando Model	$ 352,178	26
The Orange Grove Model	$ 180,543	14
The Lakeside Model	$ 370,178	29
The Terrace Model	$ 278,889	15
AVERAGE Plan Price	$ 210,895	
MAXIMUM Plan Price	$ 370,178	
MINIMUM Plan Price	$ 109,785	
MEDIAN Plan Price	$ 170,511	
MAXIMUM Plan Sold		33
MINIMUM Plan Sold		5

4E_Home_Price_Firstname_Lastname

Figure 4.45

1. **Start** Excel. On the Standard toolbar, click the **Open** button, navigate to the student files that accompany this textbook, and open the file **e04E_Home_Price**.

2. From the **File** menu, click **Save As**. In the **Save As** dialog box, navigate to the location where you are storing your projects for this chapter. In the **File name** box, type **4E_Home_Price_Firstname_Lastname** and then click **Save** or press Enter.

(Project 4E–Home Price continues on the next page)

(Project 4E–Home Price continued)

3. Select the range **B3:B14**. You will use the column label in cell **B3** to create a range name for the price data. From the **Insert** menu, point to **Name**, and then click **Create**. In the **Create Names** dialog box, if necessary, click to place a check mark in the **Top row** check box. This will instruct Excel to use the label in the first row of the selection— **row 3**—as the name for the range you are creating. Click **OK**.

4. Select the range **C4:C14**. To create this range name, from the **Insert** menu, point to **Name**, and then click **Define**. In the **Names in workbook** box, type **Units** and then verify that in the **Refers to** box, the range =Sheet1!$C$4:$C$14 displays. Click **OK** to define the range name.

5. Click an empty cell to cancel the selection. Click the **Name Box arrow**, and from the displayed list, click **Plan_Price**. The range B4:B14 is selected. Click the **Name Box arrow** again, click **Units**, and be sure that the range C4:C14 is selected.

6. Click cell **B16**. From the **Insert** menu, click **Function**. Click the **Or select a category arrow**, and then from the displayed list, click **Statistical**. Under **Select a function**, click **AVERAGE**, and then click **OK** to display the **Function Arguments** dialog box.

   In the **Number1** box, type **Plan_Price** to indicate the range that Excel should average. Recall that you defined Plan_Price as the range B4:B14 and that it is acceptable to use a range name in a function or formula. Click **OK**. The result, $210,895, displays. Thus, the average price for a new home in this development is $210,895.

7. Click cell **B17**. To the left of the Formula Bar, click the **Insert Function** button. Under **Select a function**, scroll as necessary, and then click **MAX**. Click **OK**. In the displayed **Function Arguments** dialog box, in the **Number1** box, type **Plan_Price** to denote the range B4:B14 and to have Excel find the largest amount in that range. Click **OK**. The result, $370,178, displays, indicating that this is the most expensive plan in the development. Look at the list of numbers in the column labeled *Plan Price*. It is easy to determine visually, in this short list, that the largest (maximum) amount is $370,178, but in a longer worksheet, you can see that the MAX function is quite useful.

8. Click cell **B18**. Display the **Insert Function** dialog box, and then, in the **Statistical** category, scroll as necessary and click **MIN**. Click **OK** to display the **Function Arguments** dialog box. In the **Number1** box, type **Plan_Price** to denote the range B4:B14. Click **OK**. The result, $109,785, displays, indicating that this is the lowest-priced home plan in the development.

(Project 4E–Home Price continues on the next page)

(Project 4E–Home Price continued)

9. Click cell **B19**. Display the **Insert Function** dialog box, and then, in the **Statistical** category, scroll as necessary and click **MEDIAN**. Click **OK**, and then, in the **Number1** box, type **Plan_Price** Click **OK**. The result, $170,511, displays, indicating that half the plans are more expensive than $170,511, and half are less expensive.

10. Click cell **B17** and look at the Formula Bar. You can see that the pattern for inserting a function is the equal sign, the function abbreviation, and then the cells to be calculated enclosed in parentheses. In this case, the range of cells has been named. Click cell **B21** and type **=MAX(Units)** and notice that a blue border surrounds the range that you named *Units*. Press [Enter]. The result, 33, displays, indicating that the most popular model has sold 33 units.

11. Click cell **B22**. Using either the **Insert Function** dialog box, or by typing, insert the formula to find the minimum number of units—the least popular plan. Your result should be 5.

12. From the **File** menu, click **Page Setup**, and then click the **Margins tab**. Under **Center on page**, select the **Horizontally** check box. Click the **Header/Footer tab**, and then click **Custom Footer**. In the **Left section**, click the **File Name** button, and then click **OK** twice.

13. On the Standard toolbar, click the **Save** button, and then click the **Print Preview** button to view how your worksheet will print. On the Print Preview toolbar, click **Print**, and then click **OK**.

14. Hold down [Ctrl] and press [`] to display the formulas. Click the **Print Preview** button. On the Print Preview toolbar, click **Setup**. In the **Page Setup** dialog box, click the **Page tab**. Under **Scaling**, click the **Fit to** option button, and then click **OK**. On the Print Preview toolbar, click **Print**, and then click **OK**.

15. Hold down [Ctrl] and press [`] to display the worksheet. Close the workbook, saving changes if prompted to do so.

 You have completed Project 4E

Skill Assessments (continued)

Project 4F — Auto Purchase

Objective: *Create Financial Functions.*

In the following Skill Assessment, you will compute the payment for eight automobiles that Owens Family Builders is purchasing for the members of its sales staff. The purchase will be financed over a period of two years. Your completed worksheet will look similar to Figure 4.46. You will save your workbook as *4F_Auto_Purchase_Firstname_Lastname.*

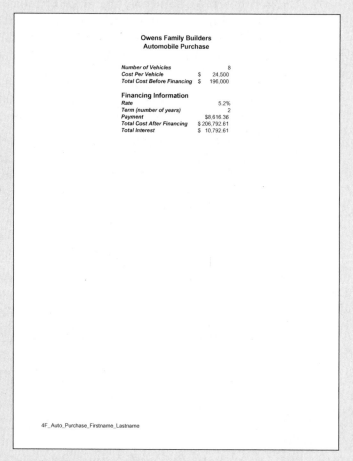

Figure 4.46

1. **Start** Excel. On the Standard toolbar, click the **Open** button, navigate to the student files that accompany this textbook, and open the file **e04F_Auto_Purchase**.

2. From the **File** menu, click **Save As**. In the **Save As** dialog box, navigate to the location where you are storing your projects for this chapter. In the **File name** box, type **4F_Auto_Purchase_Firstname_Lastname** and then click **Save** or press Enter.

(**Project 4F**–Auto Purchase continues on the next page)

(Project 4F–Auto Purchase continued)

3. Click cell **B7**. In this cell, you will compute the total purchase price for all eight vehicles. This calculation is the number of vehicles purchased multiplied by the cost per vehicle. Type or use the point-and-click method to enter the formula **=B5*B6** and then press Enter. The result, $196,000, displays. Notice that the cell adopted the format of the cell above it.

4. Click cell **B12**. The total purchase will be financed over two years at an interest rate of 5.2 percent. From the **Insert** menu, click **Function**. In the **Insert Function** dialog box, click the **Or select a category arrow**. From the displayed list, click **Financial**. Under **Select a function**, scroll as necessary, and then click **PMT**. Notice that this function calculates the payment for a loan based on constant payments and a constant interest rate.

5. Click **OK**. With your insertion point positioned in the **Rate** box, click cell **B10** to insert it in the **Rate** box, and then type **/12** This instructs Excel to divide the annual interest rate of 5.2 percent located in cell **B10** by 12 (months), which will result in a monthly interest rate. Press Tab to move the insertion point to the **Nper** box.

6. Nper is the total number of payments over the life of the loan. Click cell **B11** (number of years) to insert it into the **Nper** box, and then type ***12** to convert the number of years in the loan to the number of months. Recall that this function is calculating a monthly payment. Thus, all values in the function must be expressed in months. Press Tab to move the insertion point to the **Pv** box.

7. Pv represents the present value. Click cell **B7** to instruct Excel to use the *Total Cost Before Financing* as the present value. Click **OK** to compute the payment. The result, ($8,616.36), displays in red and in parentheses.

8. The payment displays as a negative number because it represents money paid out. In the Formula Bar, click to position the insertion point after the equal sign (=). Type **-** and then press Enter so that the result displays as a positive number.

9. To compute the total cost of the purchase and financing, you will construct a formula that multiplies the monthly payment by the total number of monthly payments. Click cell **B13**, type **=24*** and then click cell **B12**. Press Enter. The result, $206,792.61, displays.

10. To compute the total amount of interest that will paid over the life of the loan, you will construct a formula that subtracts the cost before financing from the total cost after financing. Click cell **B14**. Use either the point-and-click method or type to construct the formula as follows: **=B13-B7** The total amount of interest that will be paid is $10,792.61.

(Project 4F–Auto Purchase continues on the next page)

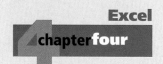

Skill Assessments (continued)

(Project 4F–Auto Purchase continued)

11. From the **File** menu, click **Page Setup**, and then click the **Margins tab**. Under **Center on page**, select the **Horizontally** check box. Click the **Header/Footer tab**, and then click **Custom Footer**. In the **Left section**, click the **File Name** button, and then click **OK** twice.

12. On the Standard toolbar, click the **Save** button, and then click the **Print Preview** button to view how your worksheet will print. On the Print Preview toolbar, click **Print**, and then click **OK**.

13. Hold down ⌃Ctrl and press ` to display the formulas. Click the **Print Preview** button. Verify that the formulas display on one page, and then, on the Print Preview toolbar, click **Print**. Click **OK**. Hold down ⌃Ctrl and press ` to redisplay the worksheet. Close the workbook, saving changes if prompted to do so.

End You have completed Project 4F ———————————————————

Project 4G — Bonus

Objectives: *Create Statistical Functions, Create Logical Functions, and Set and Clear a Print Area.*

In the following Skill Assessment, you will compute the average sale amount for the first quarter for sales associates in the Custom Home Division of Owens Family Builders. Using logical functions, you will also determine which associates qualify for a bonus. Your completed worksheet will look similar to Figure 4.47. You will save your workbook as *4G_Bonus_Firstname_Lastname.*

1. **Start** Excel. On the Standard toolbar, click the **Open** button, navigate to the student files that accompany this textbook, and then open the file **e04G_Bonus**.

2. From the **File** menu, click **Save As**. In the **Save As** dialog box, navigate to the location where you are storing your projects for this chapter. In the **File name** box, type **4G_Bonus_Firstname_Lastname** and then click **Save** or press Enter.

3. Click cell **E5**. In this cell, you will compute the average monthly sales amount for the sales associate in the first quarter. From the **Insert** menu, click **Function**. Click the **Or select a category arrow**, and from the displayed list, click **Statistical**. Under **Select a function**, click **AVERAGE**, and then click **OK**. The **Function Arguments** dialog box displays.

4. If necessary, drag the dialog box to the right so that you have a clear view of the data in the worksheet. In the **Number1** box, Excel has proposed the range B5:D5, which is the correct range that you want to average—the sales amounts for January, February, and March. Click **OK**. The result, $460,218.00, displays.

(Project 4G–Bonus continues on the next page)

(Project 4G–Bonus continued)

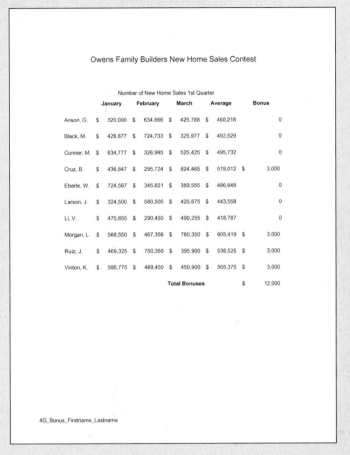

Owens Family Builders New Home Sales Contest

Number of New Home Sales 1st Quarter

		January		February		March		Average		Bonus
Anson, G.	$	320,000	$	634,866	$	425,788	$	460,218		0
Black, M.	$	426,877	$	724,733	$	325,977	$	492,529		0
Conner, M.	$	634,777	$	326,995	$	525,425	$	495,732		0
Cruz, B.	$	436,847	$	295,724	$	824,465	$	519,012	$	3,000
Eberle, W.	$	724,567	$	345,821	$	389,555	$	486,648		0
Larson, J.	$	324,500	$	580,500	$	425,675	$	443,558		0
Li, V.	$	475,655	$	290,450	$	490,255	$	418,787		0
Morgan, L.	$	568,550	$	467,356	$	780,350	$	605,419	$	3,000
Ruiz, J.	$	469,325	$	750,350	$	395,900	$	538,525	$	3,000
Vinton, K.	$	595,775	$	469,450	$	450,900	$	505,375	$	3,000
						Total Bonuses			$	12,000

4G_Bonus_Firstname_Lastname

Figure 4.47

5. Point to the fill handle so that the small black cross displays. Drag down to copy the formula through cell **E14**. With the range **E5:E14** selected, on the Formatting toolbar, click **Decrease Decimal** two times.

6. Sales associates who averaged $500,000 or more per month in sales over the three-month quarter qualify for a bonus of $3,000. You will use the Logical IF function to determine which associates will receive a bonus. Click cell **F5**. At the left edge of the Formula Bar, click the **Insert Function** button. Click the **Logical** category, click the **IF** function, and then click **OK**. The **Function Arguments** dialog box displays.

7. If necessary, drag the dialog box to the right of your screen so that you have a clear view of the data. With the insertion point in the **Logical_test** box, click cell **E5**, and then type **>=500000** This instructs Excel to determine if the value in cell **E5** is greater than or equal to 500000. Press (Tab).

(Project 4G–Bonus continues on the next page)

Skill Assessments (continued)

(Project 4G–Bonus continued)

8. With the insertion point in the **Value_if_true** box, type **3000** This instructs Excel to insert 3000 in the cell if the value in cell **E5** is greater than or equal to 500000. Press Tab.

9. With the insertion point in the **Value_if_false** box, type **0.00** This instructs Excel to insert 0.00 in the cell if the value in cell **E5** is not greater than or equal to 500000. Click **OK**. The result for sales associate Anson is zero.

10. Point to the fill handle, and then drag down through cell **F14**. You can see that four sales associates averaged over $500,000 per month and will receive a bonus. Select the range **F12:F14**, hold down Ctrl, and then click cell **F8**. With the four cells selected, click the **Currency Style** button, and then click the **Decrease Decimal** button twice.

11. Click cell **F15**, and then, on the Standard toolbar, click the **AutoSum** button. Verify that the range **F5:F14** is selected, and then press Enter to calculate the total bonuses paid to the sales associates. If necessary, format cell F15 using the Currency Style button, and then click Decrease Decimal two times.

12. From the **File** menu, click **Page Setup**, and then click the **Margins tab**. Under **Center on page**, select the **Horizontally** check box. Click the **Header/Footer tab**, and then click **Custom Footer**. In the **Left section**, click the **File Name** button, and then click **OK** twice.

13. To print only the sales figures, without the bonuses, select the range **A3:E14**. Then, from the **File** menu, point to **Print Area**, and click **Set Print Area**. On the menu bar, click the **Print Preview** button and verify that only the selected area displays. On the Print Preview toolbar, click **Print**, and then click **OK**.

14. From the **File** menu, point to **Print Area**, and then click **Clear Print Area**. Click any cell to cancel the selection.

15. On the Standard toolbar, click the **Save** button, and then click the **Print Preview** button to view how your worksheet will print. On the Print Preview toolbar, click **Print**, and then click **OK** to print the full worksheet.

16. Hold down Ctrl and press ` to display the formulas. Click the **Print Preview** button. On the Print Preview toolbar, click **Setup**. In the **Page Setup** dialog box, click the **Page tab**. Under **Orientation**, click **Landscape**, under **Scaling**, click the **Fit to** option button, and then click **OK**. On the Print Preview toolbar, click **Print**, and then click **OK**.

17. Hold down Ctrl and press ` to display the worksheet. Close the workbook, saving changes if prompted to do so.

End You have completed Project 4G

Performance Assessments

Project 4H — Survey

Objectives: *Create Range Names, Use Range Names in a Formula, Create Statistical Functions, and Set and Clear a Print Area.*

In the following Performance Assessment, you will calculate statistics regarding a survey conducted by the marketing department at Owens Family Builders. The survey polled residents in five adjacent neighborhoods about a proposal to construct a shopping area and adjoining park that would serve the residents of these neighborhoods. Your completed worksheet will look similar to Figure 4.48. You will save your workbook as *4H_Survey_Firstname_Lastname*.

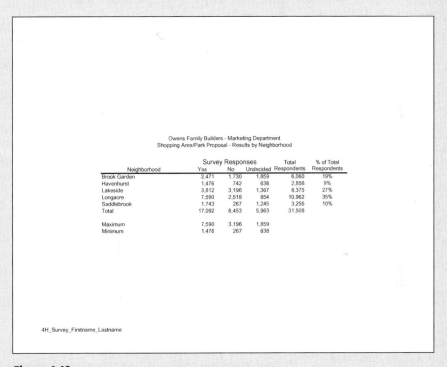

Owens Family Builders - Marketing Department
Shopping Area/Park Proposal - Results by Neighborhood

Neighborhood	Survey Responses			Total Respondents	% of Total Respondents
	Yes	No	Undecided		
Brook Garden	2,471	1,730	1,859	6,060	19%
Havenhurst	1,476	742	638	2,856	9%
Lakeside	3,812	3,196	1,367	8,375	27%
Longacre	7,590	2,518	854	10,962	35%
Saddlebrook	1,743	267	1,245	3,255	10%
Total	17,092	8,453	5,963	31,508	
Maximum	7,590	3,196	1,859		
Minimum	1,476	267	638		

4H_Survey_Firstname_Lastname

Figure 4.48

1. **Start** Excel. On the Standard toolbar, click the **Open** button, navigate to the student files that accompany this textbook, and then open the file **e04H_Survey**.

2. From the **File** menu, click **Save As**. In the **Save As** dialog box, navigate to the location where you are storing your projects for this chapter. In the **File name** box, type **4H_Survey_Firstname_Lastname** and then click **Save** or press Enter.

3. In cell **E6**, use the **AutoSum** button to calculate the Total Respondents from the Brook Garden neighborhood. Then, copy the formula down through cell **E10** to calculate the number of respondents from each of the remaining neighborhoods.

(Project 4H–Survey continues on the next page)

(**Project 4H**–Survey continued)

4. In cell **B11**, calculate the number of Yes respondents, and then copy the formula across through cell **E11**. Select the range **B6:E11** and apply **Comma Style** formatting with zero decimal places.

5. In cell **F6**, create a formula that calculates the percentage that the Brook Garden neighborhood represents out of the total respondents. To create this formula, divide the total respondents for the Brook Garden neighborhood by the total respondents in cell **E11**. (Hint: Make the reference to E11 absolute so that you can copy the formula down through the remaining neighborhoods. Recall that you can use the [F4] function key to make a cell reference absolute.) Copy the formula down through cell **F10**. With the range selected, apply **Percent Style** formatting with zero decimal places, and **Center** the percentages.

6. Select the range **B5:D10**. From the **Insert** menu, point to **Name**, and then click **Create**. In the **Create Names** dialog box, be sure the **Top row** check box is selected. Click **OK**. The label in the first row at the top of each column becomes the range name for each respective column.

7. Click the **Name Box arrow**, and verify that all three ranges were created using the column names. From the displayed list, click **Yes**, and verify that the range includes **B6:B10**. Repeat for the ranges named *No* and *Undecided*.

8. Click cell **B13**. Type **=MAX(Yes)** to instruct Excel to display the largest number within the *Yes* range of cells. Press [Enter]. In cells **C13** and **D13**, construct a similar formula to instruct Excel to display the largest number within the *No* range of cells and within the *Undecided* range of cells. In cells **B14:D14**, construct similar formulas using the **MIN** function. Format the range **B13:D14** using **Comma Style** and zero decimal places.

9. Change the **Page Orientation** to **Landscape**, and center the worksheet **Horizontally** and **Vertically** on the page. Create a custom footer and insert the file name in the **Left section**.

10. To print only the survey response information, select the range **A4:D11**. Then, from the **File** menu, point to **Print Area**, and click **Set Print Area**. On the menu bar, click the **Print Preview** button, and verify that only the selected area displays. On the Print Preview toolbar, click the **Print** button, and then click **OK**.

11. From the **File** menu, point to **Print Area**, and then click **Clear Print Area**. Click in any cell to cancel the selection.

12. On the Standard toolbar, click the **Save** button, and then click the **Print Preview** button to view how your worksheet will print. On the Print Preview toolbar, click **Print**, and then click **OK**.

(**Project 4H**–Survey continues on the next page)

(Project 4H–Survey continued)

13. Hold down Ctrl and press ` to display the formulas. Click the **Print Preview** button. On the Print Preview toolbar, click **Setup**. In the **Page Setup** dialog box, on the **Page tab**, click the **Landscape** and **Fit to** option buttons, and then click **OK**. On the Print Preview toolbar, click **Print**, and then click **OK**.

14. Hold down Ctrl and press ` to display the worksheet. Close the workbook, saving changes if prompted to do so.

 End You have completed Project 4H ———————————————

Project 4I—Annuity

Objective: *Create Date & Time and Financial Functions.*

In the following Performance Assessment, you will calculate the value of a $5,000 annuity at the end of 10 years, assuming that the company contributes $1,200 to the annuity at the beginning of each year and that the average rate of return is 8 percent per year for each of the 10 remaining years. Your completed worksheet will look similar to Figure 4.49. You will save your workbook as *4I_Annuity_Firstname_Lastname.*

1. **Start** Excel. On the Standard toolbar, click the **Open** button, navigate to the student files that accompany this textbook, and then open the file **e04I_Annuity**.

2. From the **File** menu, click **Save As**. In the **Save As** dialog box, navigate to the location where you are storing your projects for this chapter. In the **File name** box, type **4I_Annuity_Firstname_Lastname** and then click **Save** or press Enter.

3. Click cell **B18**. Display the **Insert Function** dialog box, select the **Financial** category, and then click the **FV** (future value) function. Click **OK**. If necessary, drag the **Function Arguments** dialog box to the right of your screen so that you have a clear view of the worksheet.

4. With the insertion point positioned in the **Rate** box, click the cell that contains the Average Return Rate of 8%. In the **Nper** box, click the cell that contains the number of Contributing Years. In the **Pmt** box, click the cell that contains the Annual Contribution amount. In the **Pv** box, click the cell that contains the Initial Contribution per Employee. In the **Type** box, type **1** to indicate that the payment into the annuity will be made at the beginning of each year. Click **OK** to calculate the future value of the annuity for each employee.

(Project 4I–Annuity continues on the next page)

(Project 4I–Annuity continued)

Owens Family Builders				
Employee Annuity Plan by Department				
	Total Eligible Employees	Total Initial Purchase Cost	Annual Payment Cost	Total Cost Life of the Annuity
Executives	6	$ 30,000	$ 7,200	$ 102,000
Managers	18	$ 90,000	$ 21,600	$ 306,000
Clerical	32	$ 160,000	$ 38,400	$ 544,000
Marketing	7	$ 35,000	$ 8,400	$ 119,000
Design	12	$ 60,000	$ 14,400	$ 204,000
Construction Mangement	12	$ 60,000	$ 14,400	$ 204,000
Security	15	$ 75,000	$ 18,000	$ 255,000
Total		$ 510,000	$ 122,400	$ 1,734,000

Computed On:	12/27/2003 7:43
Average Return Rate	8%
Contributing Years	10
Annual Contribution	$1,200
Initial Contribution per Employee	$5,000
Future Value of Annuity per Employee	$29,569.21

4I_Annuity_Firstname_Lastname

Figure 4.49

5. The result, ($29,569.21), displays as a negative number. To display a positive number, edit the formula so that a minus sign (-) is inserted between the equal sign (=) and the function name (FV).

6. In cell **C4**, create a formula that multiplies the number of Executives by the Initial Contribution per Employee, and make the reference to the Initial Contribution absolute. By doing so, you can copy the formula to other cells. Copy the formula down through cell **C10**. In cell **C11**, total the column.

7. In cell **D4**, create a formula that multiplies the number of Executives by the Annual Contribution, and make the reference to the Annual Contribution absolute. Copy the formula down through cell **D10**. In cell **D11**, total the column.

8. In cell **E4**, type **=(d4*b15)+c4** For each employee group, this formula instructs Excel to multiply the annual payment (cell **D4**) by the number of years (cell **B15**), and then add that figure to the initial payment (cell **C4**). Copy the formula down through cell **E10**. In cell **E11**, total the column.

(Project 4I–Annuity continues on the next page)

(Project 4I–Annuity continued)

9. Click cell **B13**, and then insert the **NOW** function from the **Date & Time** category. Recall that this function has no arguments; rather, it obtains the current date and time from your system's internal calendar and clock.

10. Display the **Page Setup** dialog box, and center the worksheet **Horizontally** on the page. Create a custom footer, and insert the file name in the **Left section**.

11. On the Standard toolbar, click the **Save** button, and then click the **Print Preview** button to view how your worksheet will print. On the Print Preview toolbar, click **Print**, and then click **OK**.

12. Hold down ⌘ Ctrl and press ｀ to display the formulas. Click the **Print Preview** button. On the Print Preview toolbar, click **Setup**. In the **Page Setup** dialog box, on the **Page tab**, click the **Landscape** and **Fit to** option buttons, and then click **OK**. On the Print Preview toolbar, click **Print**, and then click **OK**.

13. Hold down ⌘ Ctrl and press ｀ to display the worksheet. Close the workbook, saving changes if prompted to do so.

 End **You have completed Project 4I** ———————————

Project 4J — Prices

Objectives: *Create Range Names, Use Range Names in a Formula, and Create Statistical Functions.*

In the following Performance Assessment, you will calculate statistics regarding home prices in selected U.S. cities for Laura Owen Shafku, President of Owens Family Builders, who is interested in comparing the prices of homes in the Orlando area with those in other cities. Your completed worksheet will look similar to Figure 4.50. You will save your workbook as *4J_Prices_Firstname_Lastname*.

1. **Start** Excel. On the Standard toolbar, click the **Open** button, navigate to the student files that accompany this textbook, and then open the file **e04J_Prices**.

2. From the **File** menu, click **Save As**. In the **Save As** dialog box, navigate to the location where you are storing your projects for this chapter. In the **File name** box, type **4J_Prices_Firstname_Lastname** and then click **Save** or press Enter.

3. Select the range **B3:D41**. You will use the column labels in **row 3** to create range names for each year's data. From the **Insert** menu, point to **Name**, and then click **Create**. In the **Create Names** dialog box, be sure the **Top row** check box is selected. This will instruct Excel to use the labels in the top row of the selection as the range names. Click **OK**.

(Project 4J–Prices continues on the next page)

(Project 4J–Prices continued)

Average Home Prices In US Cities	In Thousands			Average Price
City	Year 2000	Year 2001	Year 2002	Over 3-Year Period
Albany/Schenectady/Troy, NY	111.1	121.6	130.5	121.1
Atlantic City, NJ	121.5	125.7	143.6	130.3
Austin/San Marcos, TX	142.8	152.0	156.5	150.4
Birmingham, AL	125.5	133.6	137.4	132.2
Boston, MA	314.2	356.6	405.0	358.6
Chattanooga, TN/GA	101.1	107.3	112.3	106.9
Cincinnati, OH/KY/IN	126.7	130.2	134.1	130.3
Dallas, TX	122.5	131.1	135.2	129.6
Daytona Beach, FL	85.3	93.7	108.3	95.8
Ft. Myers/Cape Coral, FL	97.6	121.1	133.6	117.4
Gainesville, FL	113.1	118.0	130.0	120.4
Greenville/Spartanburg, SC	118.1	124.5	125.3	122.6
Honolulu, HI	295.0	299.9	335.0	310.0
Indianapolis, IN	112.3	116.9	116.8	115.3
Lansing/East Lansing, MI	111.2	119.5	126.4	119.0
Madison, WI	153.6	162.5	177.0	164.4
Milwaukee, WI	140.7	149.4	173.8	154.6
New Orleans, LA	112.0	117.4	123.5	117.6
Monmouth/Ocean, NJ	179.0	208.6	251.7	213.1
Pensacola, FL	101.1	105.0	112.2	106.1
Philadelphia, PA/NJ	125.2	134.8	146.1	135.4
Pittsburgh, PA	93.6	97.8	101.5	97.6
Portland, OR	170.1	172.3	180.4	174.3
Raleigh/Durham, NC	158.4	168.2	172.2	166.3
Richmond/Petersburg, VA	129.8	133.3	142.3	135.1
Sacramento, CA	145.2	173.2	209.5	176.0
Salt Lake City/Ogden, UT	141.5	147.6	148.8	146.0
Sarasota, FL	132.0	168.1	176.2	158.8
Seattle, WA	230.1	245.4	254.0	243.2
Spokane, WA	104.2	108.0	108.7	107.0
Springfield, MA	120.4	127.4	139.8	129.2
Tacoma, WA	151.1	159.5	170.4	160.3
Tallahassee, FL	122.5	129.7	136.9	129.7
Tampa/St. Petersburg/Clearwater, FL	110.8	123.6	133.5	122.6
Topeka, KS	80.6	88.7	89.0	86.1
Tucson, AZ	120.5	128.8	146.4	131.9
Washington, DC/MD/VA	182.6	213.9	250.2	215.6
Worcester, MA	131.8	152.6	187.7	157.4
Average	137.8	149.1	162.2	149.7
Maximum	314.2	356.6	405.0	358.6
Minimum	80.6	88.7	89.0	86.1
Median	123.9	130.7	141.1	131.1
Average 2002 Price In Florida Cities	133.0			

4J_Prices_Firstname_Lastname

Figure 4.50

4. Click the **Name Box arrow,** and verify that the three ranges have been named.

5. Click cell **A12**, hold down Ctrl, and then click cell **D12**. Continue holding down Ctrl, and then click cell **A13**, and then cell **D13**. Continue holding down Ctrl, and then, in a similar manner, click each remaining city in the state of Florida **(FL)**, and then its **Year 2002** data. (There are seven cities in Florida.) With this nonadjacent range of cells selected, display the **Insert** menu, point to **Name**, and then click **Define**. Under **Names in workbook**, type FL_2002 The existing text is deleted. Click the **Add** button. The new range name is added to the list of named ranges. Click **OK** to close the dialog box, and then click anywhere to cancel the selection.

6. Click cell **E4**. For each city in the list, you will calculate the average home price over the three-year period. On the Standard toolbar, click the **AutoSum button arrow**, and then, from the displayed list, click

(Project 4J–Prices continues on the next page)

(Project 4J–Prices continued)

Average. Recall that you can select some of the more common functions using the AutoSum button. In cell **E4**, be sure Excel has proposed the correct range of cells to average—**B4:D4**—and then press Enter. Copy the formula down through cell **E41**.

7. Click cell **B43**. Type **=AVERAGE(Year_2000)** and notice that Excel borders the cells that comprise the range *Year_2000*. Press Enter. Format cell **B43** with one decimal place.

8. Click cell **C43**, display the **Insert Function** dialog box, display the **Statistical** category, click the **AVERAGE** function, and then click **OK**. In the **Number1** box, type **Year_2001** and then click **OK**. Format the cell with one decimal place. Look at the Formula Bar, and notice that the formula is the same format as the formula you typed in cell **B43**. You can either type functions or use the **Insert Function** dialog box to create them.

9. Using either the typing method or the dialog box method, calculate the Average statistic for Year 2002 in cell **D43** and the Average statistic for the 3-Year Period column in cell **E43**. (Hint: There is no defined range for the numbers in the 3-Year column. If you want, define and name the range. Otherwise, you will have to define the range in the dialog box by either dragging or typing; or you can type the function name into the cell, and then drag to select the range.) If necessary, format the cell with one decimal place.

10. For each of the four columns, compute the Maximum, Minimum, and Median statistics. Format the cells with one decimal place.

11. In cell **A48**, type **Average 2002 Price In Florida Cities** and then click cell **B48**. Type **=AVERAGE(FL_2002)** and notice that Excel borders the nonadjacent range that you defined. Press Enter. Format the cell with one decimal place.

12. Display the **Page Setup** menu, and center the worksheet **Horizontally** and **Vertically** on the page. Create a custom footer, and insert the file name in the **Left section**.

13. On the Standard toolbar, click the **Save** button, and then click the **Print Preview** button to view how your worksheet will print. On the Print Preview toolbar, click **Print**, and then click **OK**.

14. Hold down Ctrl and press ` to display the formulas. Click the **Print Preview** button. On the Print Preview toolbar, click **Setup**. In the **Page Setup** dialog box, on the **Page tab**, click the **Landscape** and **Fit to** option buttons, and then click **OK**. On the Print Preview toolbar, click **Print**, and then click **OK**.

15. Hold down Ctrl and press ` to redisplay the worksheet. Close the workbook, saving changes if prompted to do so.

End **You have completed Project 4J**

Mastery Assessments

Project 4K—Rates

Objectives: *Create Range Names, Use Range Names in a Formula, Create Statistical Functions, and Create Logical Functions.*

In the following Mastery Assessment, you will calculate water rates that will be applied to users in the new planned-development community recently completed by Owens Family Builders. This new, large community includes residential, commercial, and industrial buildings. Your completed worksheet will look similar to Figure 4.51. You will save your workbook as *4K_Rates_Firstname_Lastname*.

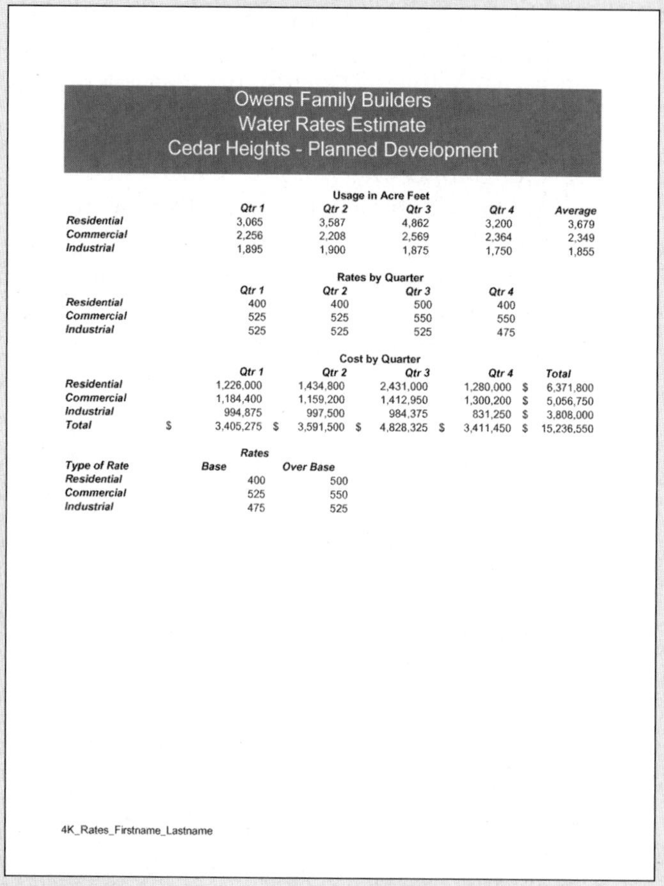

Owens Family Builders
Water Rates Estimate
Cedar Heights - Planned Development

Usage in Acre Feet	Qtr 1	Qtr 2	Qtr 3	Qtr 4	Average
Residential	3,065	3,587	4,862	3,200	3,679
Commercial	2,256	2,208	2,569	2,364	2,349
Industrial	1,895	1,900	1,875	1,750	1,855

Rates by Quarter	Qtr 1	Qtr 2	Qtr 3	Qtr 4
Residential	400	400	500	400
Commercial	525	525	550	550
Industrial	525	525	525	475

Cost by Quarter	Qtr 1	Qtr 2	Qtr 3	Qtr 4	Total
Residential	1,226,000	1,434,800	2,431,000	1,280,000	$ 6,371,800
Commercial	1,184,400	1,159,200	1,412,950	1,300,200	$ 5,056,750
Industrial	994,875	997,500	984,375	831,250	$ 3,808,000
Total	$ 3,405,275	$ 3,591,500	$ 4,828,325	$ 3,411,450	$ 15,236,550

Rates		
Type of Rate	Base	Over Base
Residential	400	500
Commercial	525	550
Industrial	475	525

4K_Rates_Firstname_Lastname

Figure 4.51

1. **Start** Excel. On the Standard toolbar, click the **Open** button, navigate to the student files that accompany this textbook, and then open the file **e04K_Rates**.

2. From the **File** menu, click **Save As**. In the **Save As** dialog box, navigate to the location where you are storing your projects for this chapter. In the **File name** box, type **4K_Rates_Firstname_Lastname** and then click **Save** or press Enter.

(Project 4K–Rates continues on the next page)

(Project 4K–Rates continued)

3. Click cell **B27**. From the **Insert** menu, point to **Name**, and then click **Define**. Under **Names in workbook**, delete *Residential*, type **Res_Base** and then click the **Add** button. Click **OK**.

4. Click cell **B28**, and then click the **Name Box**. Type **Comm_Base** and then press [Enter]. Click the **Name Box arrow** to view the two range names that you have created.

5. Using either the **Define Names** dialog box or the **Name Box**, name the following cells as indicated:

   B29   Ind_Base

   C27   Res_Over

   C28   Comm_Over

   C29   Ind_Over

6. Click the **Name Box arrow** and verify that you have six named ranges. In cell **F8**, use the **AVERAGE** function to calculate the average quarterly water usage for Residential users, and then copy the formula down for the Commercial and Industrial users.

7. Water rates are determined on a quarterly basis. Up to a certain level, the Base rate is used. If more water is used, the Over Base rate applies. Click cell **B14**, and insert the **IF** Logical function. Insert the arguments based on the following: If the Qtr 1 usage is less than or equal to the 4-quarter average usage, the rate is equal to the Res_Base rate. Otherwise, the rate is equal to the Res_Over rate. (Hint: For purposes of copying the formula across the quarters, cell **F8**, which contains the quarterly average, must be an absolute cell reference in the logical test portion of the argument. In the Value_if_true and Value_if_false portion of your function arguments, click the appropriate cells—the range names that you created will be inserted.) Copy the formula through cell **E14**.

8. Use the same type of IF function to determine the Commercial rates in cells **B15:E15** and the Industrial rates in cells **B16:E16**.

9. Click cell **B20**. Calculate the cost for residential customers in Qtr 1 by multiplying the Residential Qtr 1 rate (cell **B14**) times the Residential Qtr 1 usage (cell **B8**). Copy the formula over through the fourth quarter. Use the same technique to calculate the quarterly costs for the Commercial users in cells **B21:E21** and the Industrial customers in cells **B22:E22**. In cells **F20:F22**, use AutoSum to total the four quarters for each type of user. Format the range **F20:F23** using the **Currency Style** button and zero decimal places. Total the Cost by Quarter and total columns, beginning with cell **B23**, and apply the same format.

(Project 4K–Rates continues on the next page)

(Project 4K–Rates continued)

10. Display the **Page Setup** dialog box, and center the worksheet **Horizontally** on the page. Create a custom footer that contains the file name on the left.

11. Set a **Print Area** showing only the Cost by Quarter. **Print** the area, and then **Clear** the Print Area.

12. On the Standard toolbar, click the **Save** button, and then click the **Print Preview** button to view how your worksheet will print. On the Print Preview toolbar, click **Print**, and then click **OK**.

13. Display the formulas and AutoFit columns B:F so that the formulas are fully displayed on the worksheet. Click the **Print Preview** button, and then click **Setup**. In the **Page Setup** dialog box, click the **Landscape** and **Fit to** option buttons. On the Print Preview toolbar, click **Print**, and then click **OK**.

14. Hold down Ctrl and press ` to display the worksheet. Readjust the column widths, if necessary, to display all the figures. Close the workbook, saving changes if prompted to do so.

End You have completed Project 4K

Project 4L — Paving

Objectives: *Create Date & Time, Financial, and Logical Functions.*

In the following Mastery Assessment, you will calculate the payment and create an amortization schedule for three pieces of paving equipment being purchased by Owens Family Builders. Your completed worksheet will look similar to Figure 4.52. You will save your workbook as *4L_Paving_Firstname_Lastname.*

1. Start Excel. On the Standard toolbar, click the **Open** button, navigate to the student files that accompany this textbook, and then open the file **e04L_Paving**.

2. From the **File** menu, click **Save As**. In the **Save As** dialog box, navigate to the location where you are storing your projects for this chapter. In the **File name** box, type **4L_Paving_Firstname_Lastname** and then click **Save** or press Enter.

3. Click cell **B11**. The total purchase will be financed over three years at an interest rate of 4.2 percent. From the **Financial** category, insert the **PMT** function, and then click **OK** to display the **Function Arguments** dialog box.

(Project 4L–Paving continues on the next page)

(Project 4L–Paving continued)

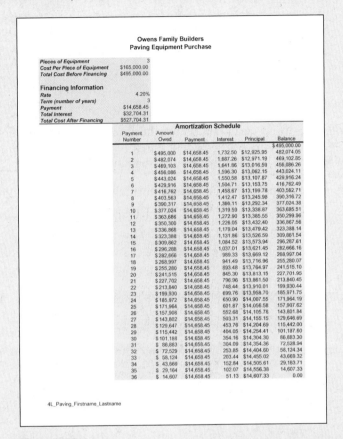

Owens Family Builders
Paving Equipment Purchase

Pieces of Equipment	3
Cost Per Piece of Equipment	$165,000.00
Total Cost Before Financing	$495,000.00

Financing Information

Rate	4.20%
Term (number of years)	3
Payment	$14,658.45
Total Interest	$32,704.31
Total Cost After Financing	$527,704.31

Amortization Schedule

Payment Number	Amount Owed	Payment	Interest	Principal	Balance
					$495,000.00
1	$495,000	$14,658.45	1,732.50	$12,925.95	482,074.05
2	$482,074	$14,658.45	1,687.26	$12,971.19	469,102.85
3	$469,103	$14,658.45	1,641.86	$13,016.59	456,086.26
4	$456,086	$14,658.45	1,596.30	$13,062.15	443,024.11
5	$443,024	$14,658.45	1,550.58	$13,107.87	429,916.24
6	$429,916	$14,658.45	1,504.71	$13,153.75	416,762.49
7	$416,762	$14,658.45	1,458.67	$13,199.78	403,562.71
8	$403,563	$14,658.45	1,412.47	$13,245.98	390,316.72
9	$390,317	$14,658.45	1,366.11	$13,292.34	377,024.38
10	$377,024	$14,658.45	1,319.59	$13,338.87	363,685.51
11	$363,686	$14,658.45	1,272.90	$13,385.55	350,299.96
12	$350,300	$14,658.45	1,226.05	$13,432.40	336,867.56
13	$336,868	$14,658.45	1,179.04	$13,479.42	323,388.14
14	$323,388	$14,658.45	1,131.86	$13,526.59	309,861.54
15	$309,862	$14,658.45	1,084.52	$13,573.94	296,287.61
16	$296,288	$14,658.45	1,037.01	$13,621.45	282,666.16
17	$282,666	$14,658.45	989.33	$13,669.12	268,997.04
18	$268,997	$14,658.45	941.49	$13,716.96	255,280.07
19	$255,280	$14,658.45	893.48	$13,764.97	241,515.10
20	$241,515	$14,658.45	845.30	$13,813.15	227,701.95
21	$227,702	$14,658.45	796.96	$13,861.50	213,840.45
22	$213,840	$14,658.45	748.44	$13,910.01	199,930.44
23	$199,930	$14,658.45	699.76	$13,958.70	185,971.75
24	$185,972	$14,658.45	650.90	$14,007.55	171,964.19
25	$171,964	$14,658.45	601.87	$14,056.58	157,907.62
26	$157,908	$14,658.45	552.68	$14,105.78	143,801.84
27	$143,802	$14,658.45	503.31	$14,155.15	129,646.69
28	$129,647	$14,658.45	453.76	$14,204.69	115,442.00
29	$115,442	$14,658.45	404.05	$14,254.41	101,187.60
30	$101,188	$14,658.45	354.16	$14,304.30	86,883.30
31	$ 86,883	$14,658.45	304.09	$14,354.36	72,528.94
32	$ 72,529	$14,658.45	253.85	$14,404.60	58,124.34
33	$ 58,124	$14,658.45	203.44	$14,455.02	43,669.32
34	$ 43,669	$14,658.45	152.84	$14,505.61	29,163.71
35	$ 29,164	$14,658.45	102.07	$14,556.38	14,607.33
36	$ 14,607	$14,658.45	51.13	$14,607.33	0.00

4L_Paving_Firstname_Lastname

Figure 4.52

4. If necessary, move the dialog box to the right of the screen. With your insertion point positioned in the **Rate** box, click cell **B9** to insert it in the **Rate** box, and then type **/12** This instructs Excel to divide the annual interest rate of 4.2 percent located in cell **B9** by 12 (months), which will result in a monthly interest rate. Press ⌨Tab to move the insertion point to the **Nper** box.

5. Click cell **B10** (number of years) to insert it in the **Nper** box, and then type ***12** to convert the number of years in the loan to the number of months. Press ⌨Tab to move the insertion point to the **Pv** box.

6. Click cell **B6** to instruct Excel to use the Total Cost Before Financing as the present value. Click **OK** to compute the payment. Widen the column as necessary. The result, ($14,658.45), displays in red.

7. In the Formula Bar, click to position the insertion point after the equal sign (=). Type **-** and then press ⌨Enter so that the result displays as a positive number.

8. To compute the total cost of the purchase and financing, you will construct a formula that multiplies the monthly payment by the total number of monthly payments. Click cell **B13**, type **=36*** and then click cell **B11**. Press ⌨Enter. The result, $527,704.31, displays.

(Project 4L–Paving continues on the next page)

(Project 4L–Paving continued)

9. In cell **B12**, compute the total amount of interest that will be paid over the life of the loan. Your result should be $32,704.31.

10. Click cell **B17**, type **1** and then press [Enter]. In cell **B18**, type **2** and then press [Enter]. Select both cells, and then point to the fill handle in cell **B18**. Drag down until the ScreenTip displays **36** (to the end of the yellow shading).

11. Click cell **G16**. Type **=b6** and then press [F4] so that the entry is absolute. Press [Enter]. Click cell **G16** again, and click the **Increase Decimal** button twice. This is the opening balance for the loan.

12. Click cell **C17**. The amount owed is the balance from the previous period. Type **=g16** and then press [Enter].

13. Click cell **D17**. Type **=b11** and then press [F4] so that the entry is absolute. Press [Enter]. This is the payment amount as computed using the PMT function.

14. Click cell **E17**. The interest for the period is equal to the monthly interest rate multiplied by the balance owed. Type **=** and then click cell **C17**. Type ***** and then click cell **B9**. Press the [F4] function key to make cell B9's entry absolute. Type **/12** so that the yearly rate is converted to a monthly rate. Press [Enter]. Your result should be 1,732.50.

15. Click cell **F17**. The amount applied to the loan principal is equal to the payment amount minus the interest amount. Type **=d17-e17** and then press [Enter].

16. Click cell **G17**. The new balance is equal to the previous balance minus the principal amount. Type **=g16-f17** and then press [Enter].

17. Select the range **C17:G17**, and then point to the fill handle in cell **G17**. Drag down to fill the formulas through the 36 payments. The Balance column should display zero for payment 36.

18. Display the **Page Setup** dialog box. Center the worksheet horizontally on the page. Create a custom footer with the file name in the **Left section**.

19. On the Standard toolbar, click the **Save** button, and then click the **Print Preview** button to view how your worksheet will print. On the Print Preview toolbar, click **Print**, and then click **OK**.

20. Display the formulas. Click the **Print Preview** button, and then click **Setup**. In the **Page Setup** dialog box, click the **Landscape** and **Fit to** option buttons, and then click **OK**. On the Print Preview toolbar, click **Print**, and then click **OK**.

21. Hold down [Ctrl] and press [`] to redisplay the worksheet. Close the workbook, saving changes if prompted to do so.

End You have completed Project 4L

Project 4M—Investments

Objectives: *Create Date & Time, Financial, and Logical Functions.*

John Zeidler, the Chief Financial Officer for Owens Family Builders, is considering two investment alternatives for the employee pension fund. In this project, you will complete a worksheet that will compare the two investments and determine which one will result in a better return. You will save the workbook as *4M_Investments_Firstname_Lastname.*

1. **Start** Excel. Locate and open the file **e04M_Investments**. Save the file using the name **4M_Investments_Firstname_Lastname**

2. In cell **B3**, enter the **NOW** function formula.

3. The Bond Fund requires an initial investment of $100,000 and annual payments of $1,000 for each employee over the next 10 years—the term of the investment. Based on past returns, Mr. Zeidler is estimating that the rate will be 7.5 percent on average. Enter the figures in the appropriate cells in the worksheet, and then, in cell **B9**, use the **FV** function to calculate the total value of the investment at the end of the term.

4. The Balanced Fund requires an initial investment of $250,000 and annual payments of $250,000 for the 10-year term of the investment. The estimated annual rate on this investment is 8 percent. Enter the figures in the appropriate cells in the worksheet, and then, in cell **C9**, use the **FV** function to calculate the ending value.

5. Format all the numbers in the worksheet appropriately.

6. In cell **B12**, use the IF function to display the name of the investment and the best investment return.

7. Center the worksheet horizontally on the page, and add a custom footer that displays the file name in the left section.

8. Save, and then print the worksheet. Display and print the formulas on one page.

End **You have completed Project 4M**

Problem Solving (continued)

Project 4N — Hours Worked

Objectives: *Create Statistical Functions, Create Date & Time and Financial Functions, and Create Logical Functions.*

Benefits for employees are granted after a certain length of employment. In this project, you will complete a worksheet for Juan Sanchez, Director of Employee Benefits, that calculates when benefits are due based on hire date. You will save the workbook as *4N_Benefits Earned_Firstname_ Lastname.*

1. **Start** Excel. Locate and open the file **e04N_Benefits_Earned**. Save the file using the name **4N_Benefits_Earned_Firstname_Lastname**

2. First, the hire date for each employee needs to be converted to a numeric equivalent. In **column C**, display the hire date for each employee as the numeric equivalent date.

3. Click cell **D4**, and enter **6/30/05** as the current date. Change this date to its numeric equivalent. Fill this number down through cell **D10**.

4. In cell **E4**, write a formula to determine the number of days the employee has been with the company. Fill this number through cell **E10**.

5. In cell **F4**, use the logical IF function to determine if the employee is eligible for health insurance. Evaluate whether the difference between the current date and the hire date—displayed in cell **E4**—is greater than or equal to the number in cell **C16**. Enter **Yes** in the true box and **No** in the false box. Copy this statement down **column F** to the other employees in the list.

6. In cell **G4**, write a similar statement to determine if the employee has met the requirement for life insurance shown in cell **C17**. In cell **H4**, write a statement to evaluate if the employee is eligible for Dental Insurance as shown in cell **C18**. Finally, in cell **I4** write a statement to evaluate if the employee is eligible for the Retirement program as shown in cell **C19**.

7. Fill all three formulas to the rest of the employees.

8. Open the **Page Setup** dialog box. Change the page orientation to landscape. Center the worksheet horizontally on the page, and add a custom footer that displays the file name in the left section.

9. Save, and then print the worksheet. Display and print the formulas on one page.

End You have completed Project 4N ───────────────

On the Internet

Researching the Cost of Financing a Home or Car

Several sites on the Internet can help you determine the cost of financing a home, car, boat, or other large purchase. Open your browser, and then use your favorite search engine, such as Google.com, to search for information about financing a house or a car. For keywords, enter **car loan** or **home loan** Pick one of the sites that result from the search. Many of these sites have a quick calculation to provide you with a payment estimate based on the amount borrowed and length of the loan. Click on the Loan Calculator button, and enter appropriate figures for the type of loan you are researching. After you see the results, check the figures provided by setting up a payment function in Excel. Open a new workbook, and enter each component used for the loan and the figures used in the Web site loan calculation. Use the PMT function to calculate the payment. Compare your results with the one provided by the Internet Web site.

GO! with Help

Special Column Formats

In this chapter, you practiced how to create IF functions. Use Excel Help to learn how to use text in an IF function.

1. From your student files, **Open** the worksheet **e04O_Help**.

2. In the **Type a question for help** box, type **How do I create an IF function?** and then press Enter. In the **Search Results** task pane, click **Create conditional formulas by using the If Function**. Read the topic to review the IF function. Under the Examples section of the Help window, notice that in the first example, text is included in the argument and that the text is enclosed in quotation marks. **Close** the Help window.

3. In cell **F5**, create an IF statement that uses text for the value_if_true and the value_if_false as follows: If the total of undecided respondents per district is greater than 30 percent of the total number of respondents per district, "Send Additional Information to Voters". Otherwise, "Additional Mailing Not Necessary". (Hint: In the **Logical test** box, type **D5>E5*.3** You do not need to type the quotation marks when you type the text in the **Value_if_true** and **Value_if_false** boxes because Excel will insert the quotation marks for you.) Copy the formula from cell **F5** through cell **F9**.

5

chapterfive

Creating Charts and Diagrams

In this chapter, you will: complete this project **and** practice these skills.

Project 5A **Charting Attendance by Location**	**Objectives** • Create a Column Chart • Modify a Column Chart • Print a Chart • Create and Modify a Line Chart • Create and Modify a 3-D Pie Chart • Create a Diagram • Organize and Format Worksheets

Greater Atlanta Job Fair

The Greater Atlanta Job Fair is a nonprofit organization supported by the Atlanta Chamber of Commerce and Atlanta City Colleges. The organization holds several targeted job fairs in the Atlanta area each year. Candidate registration is free and open to area residents and students enrolled in certificate or degree programs at any of the City Colleges. Employers pay a nominal fee to participate in the fairs. When candidates register for a fair, their resumes are scanned into an interactive, searchable database that is provided to the employers.

Creating Charts and Diagrams

A **chart** is a graphic representation of data in a worksheet. In many instances, data presented as a chart is easier to understand than a table of numbers. The most commonly used chart types are **column charts**, which are used to make comparisons among related numbers, **pie charts**, which show the contributions of each piece to the whole, and **line charts**, which show a trend over time. A chart can be placed on a separate sheet, called a **chart sheet**, or it can be **embedded** (placed within) the same worksheet as the data. You can also create diagrams using Excel. A **diagram** is a graphical illustration of a concept or relationship. When you have multiple worksheets in a workbook, it is helpful to name the sheets. You can also add color coding to the sheet tabs, add, delete, or hide sheets, or reposition sheets in the workbook.

Project 5A **Attendance**

Graphical representation of numbers helps a reader understand implications and trends in a visual manner that is easier to interpret than by reading the numbers alone. The Excel Chart Wizard helps you create a wide variety of charts that can be displayed either with the worksheet data or on a separate sheet. The Diagram Gallery provides six options for creating a diagram. In this chapter, you will create and modify each of these main chart types. You will also create a diagram and practice organizing worksheets.

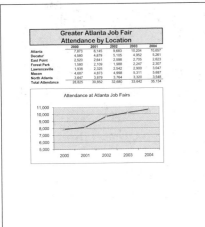

In Activities 5.1 through 5.28, you will create and modify column, pie, and line charts for the Greater Atlanta Job Fair that display attendance patterns at the fairs over a five-year period. You will examine the purpose of each chart type and practice selecting the data to display, using the Chart Wizard, and modifying and formatting various chart components. You will create a chart on a separate sheet and one that is embedded within the worksheet. You will also create a diagram to show the continuous process of holding job fairs. Finally, you will practice some techniques for organizing and formatting multiple worksheets. Your completed worksheets will look similar to Figure 5.1. You will save your workbook as *5A_Attendance_Firstname_Lastname.*

Embedded line chart

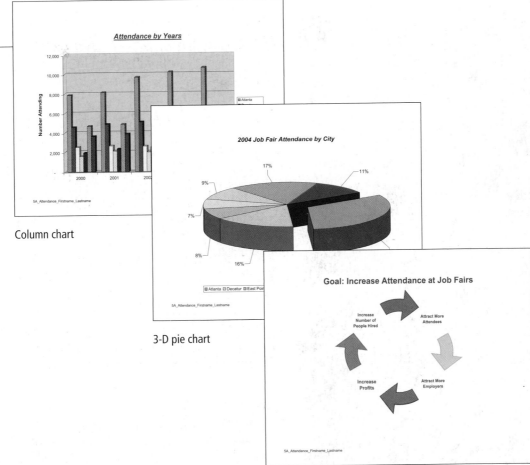

Column chart

3-D pie chart

Cycle diagram

Figure 5.1
Project 5A—Attendance

Objective 1
Create a Column Chart

Charts are used to make a set of numbers easier to understand. The type of chart used is determined by the data in your worksheet and the kind of relationship that you want your data to show. The Excel Chart Wizard makes it easy to create a variety of chart types. One of the most frequently used charts is the column chart, which compares groups of related numbers. A column chart presents the data in vertical columns. Groups of related numbers can also be represented in a bar chart, which uses horizontal bars instead of vertical columns.

Activity 5.1 Creating a 3-D Column Chart

To create a chart, first select the data you want to *plot*—represent graphically—and then access the **Chart Wizard**. The Chart Wizard is a feature that guides you, step by step, through the process of creating a chart.

1 **Start** Excel. On the Standard toolbar, click the **Open** button 📂. Navigate to the location where the student files for this textbook are stored. Locate and open the Excel file **e05A_Attendance**.

2 From the **File** menu, click **Save As**. In the **Save As** dialog box, navigate to the location in which you are storing your files, creating a new folder for this chapter if you want to do so.

3 In the **File name** box, type **5A_Attendance_Firstname_Lastname** and then click **Save**.

The data displayed shows the number of applicants who have attended job fairs held over the past five years at various locations in the greater Atlanta area.

4 Examine the data displayed in this worksheet. Locate the data that is identified in Figure 5.2.

When you create a chart, first decide whether you are going to plot the values representing totals or the values representing details. (You cannot plot both in the same chart.) In this example, you will select the details—the number of attendees at each location each year. To help the reader understand the chart, you will also select the *labels* for the data—the column and row headings that describe the values. In this spreadsheet, the labels will consist of the location names and the years.

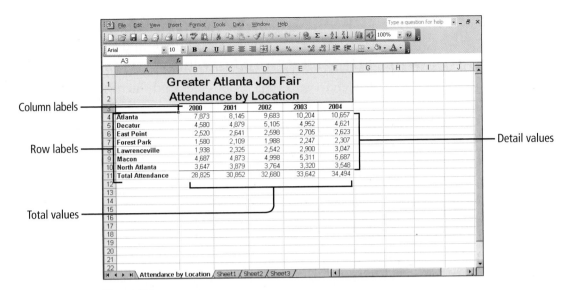

Column labels

Row labels

Detail values

Total values

Figure 5.2

5 Select the range **A3:F10**, and then, on the Standard toolbar, click the **Chart Wizard** button ▦. Alternatively, from the Insert menu, click Chart.

The Chart Wizard opens to the first step in the wizard with the Standard Types tab selected. The selected data is highlighted on the worksheet. In the first step of the wizard, you select the type of chart you want to use. On the left side of the Chart Wizard dialog box, you can select from among fourteen **standard chart types**—predefined chart designs. On the right side, you can choose the **chart sub-type**—variations of the selected standard chart type. The default chart is the clustered column chart. A description of the selected chart displays at the lower right of the dialog box. See Figure 5.3.

You can also use this dialog box to create a **custom chart**, which offers more advanced chart options and allows you to add your own features.

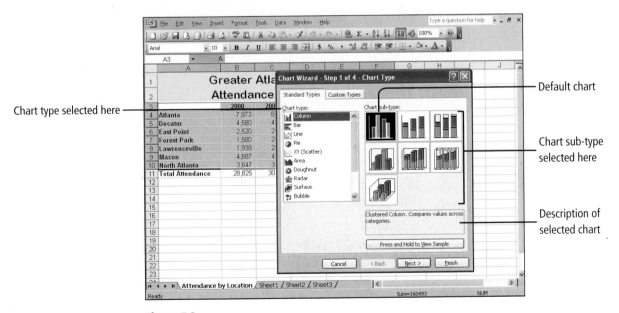

Chart type selected here

Default chart

Chart sub-type selected here

Description of selected chart

Figure 5.3

6 Be sure the **Standard Types tab** is selected. Under **Chart type**, be sure **Column** is selected, and then, under **Chart sub-type**, in the second row, click the first sub-type.

The chart sub-type is selected, and the description changes to *Clustered column with 3-D visual effect.*

7 On the lower right side of the dialog box, click the **Next** button.

In Step 2 of the Chart Wizard you can see a preview of the data as it will display in the chart. Notice that the Data range box displays the sheet name and the range of cells that are selected as an absolute value—recall that the $ symbol indicates an absolute reference, meaning the range will remain constant. See Figure 5.4.

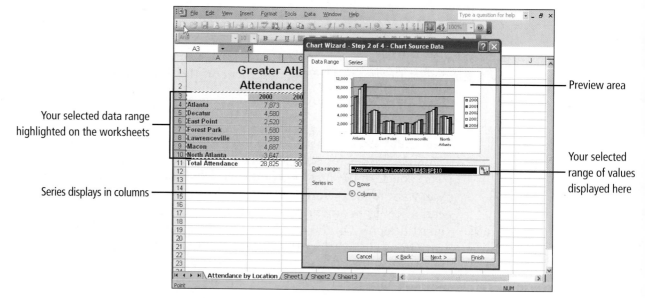

Figure 5.4

Note — Not All Data Labels Display

You may notice that not all of the location labels display along the lower edge of the preview window. This is because of the limited space in the dialog box. The labels will display when you view the finished chart, at which time you can adjust the label format as needed.

8 Verify that the **Data range** box displays =*'Attendance by Location'!$A$3:$F$10*, and then click the **Next** button to accept the settings in Step 2 and move to Step 3 in the Chart Wizard. Click the **Titles tab**.

In Step 3 of the wizard, you can add a title to the chart or to the **Category (X) axis**—the horizontal axis, or to the **Value (Z) axis**—the vertical axis along the left side of the chart. This shows the range of numbers needed to display the **data points**, the numeric values of the selected worksheet figures.

More Knowledge — Value (Y) Axis

Typically, the value axis in a chart is known as the y-axis. In this example, the value axis has been changed by the Chart Wizard to the z-axis because a 3-D chart sub-type was selected. If a two-dimensional chart were used, such as the default clustered column chart, the label for the vertical axis in the wizard would be Value (Y) axis.

9 In the **Chart title** box, click to position the insertion point, and then type **Attendance by Location**

After a moment, the title displays in the chart Preview area, and the chart area is resized. See Figure 5.5. Adjustments to the chart can be made after the chart is complete—the Preview area only gives you an idea of how the chart will display.

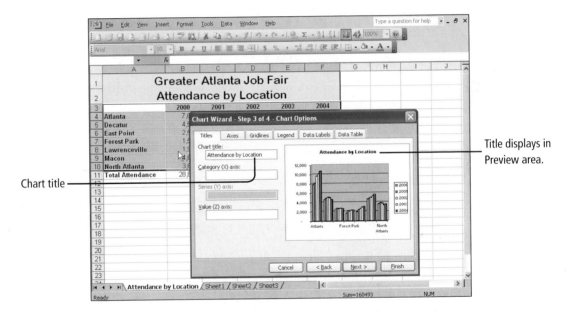

Figure 5.5

10 Click **Next**.

Step 4 of the Chart Wizard displays. Here you must decide the location of the chart. You can place the chart on a separate chart sheet in the workbook in which the chart fills the entire page or accept the default to display the chart as an object within the worksheet, which is an embedded chart. If you place the chart on a separate sheet, it's a good idea to rename the sheet to indicate the chart's location.

11 Click the **As new sheet** option button. In the **As new sheet** box, type **Attendance Chart**

The chart will be placed on a separate sheet named *Attendance Chart*. See Figure 5.6.

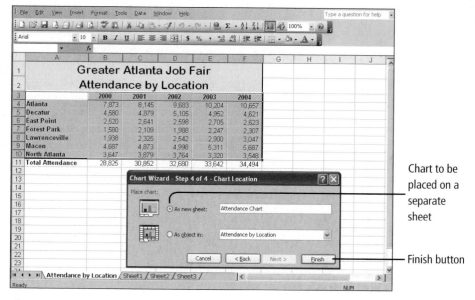

Figure 5.6

Chart to be placed on a separate sheet

Finish button

12 Click the **Finish** button.

The Chart Wizard dialog box closes, and the chart displays on a separate sheet. See Figure 5.7.

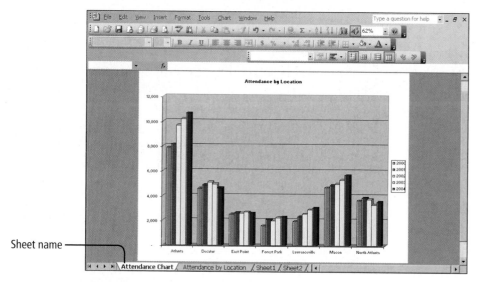

Sheet name

Figure 5.7

13 On the Standard toolbar, click the **Save** button 🖫.

Activity 5.2 Identifying Chart Elements

Before you can modify a chart, you need to be able to locate and identify different parts of the chart. **Chart objects** are the elements that make up a chart. As you move the mouse pointer around the chart, ScreenTips display to identify the name of different chart objects.

1 Point to the title at the top of the chart. A ScreenTip displays the name of the chart object—**Chart Title**—as shown in Figure 5.8. Move your mouse pointer around the chart and display the ScreenTip for each of the chart objects labeled in Figure 5.8. When the ScreenTip displays, click the chart object to select it.

Clicking a chart object is one way to select it. When a chart object is selected, **sizing handles** display at each corner of the chart object. Sizing handles, also known as **selection handles**, are the small boxes that surround a chart object to indicate that the object is selected and can be modified.

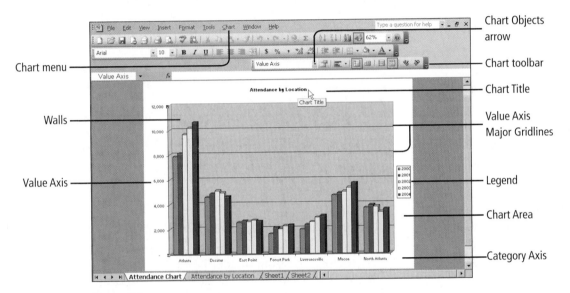

Figure 5.8

Note — Is It a Sizing Handle or a Selection Handle?

Sizing handles and selection handles look the same, and the terms are often used interchangeably. If a two-headed resize arrow—⬍ ⬌ ⬉—displays when you point to boxes surrounding an object, it is a sizing handle; otherwise, it is a selection handle. Some objects in a chart cannot be resized, such as the category axis or the value axis, but they can be selected and then reformatted.

---

2 A Chart menu and a Chart toolbar display when a chart is active. The Chart toolbar may be anchored under the Standard and Formatting toolbars or floating on your screen. Locate the Chart toolbar and point to each button to identify the button and display the ScreenTip name. The table in Figure 5.9 explains the purpose of each button. Take a moment to examine this information.

The Chart Toolbar

Button	Button Name	Description
	Chart Objects	Displays a list of chart objects. Clicking an object in the list selects the object.
	Format Selected Object	Opens the Format Selected Object dialog box. The ScreenTip displays the name of the selected object.
	Chart Type	Changes the chart type.
	Legend	Toggles the legend on and off.
	Data Table	Toggles the data table on and off.
	By Row	Displays the data series in rows.
	By Column	Displays the data series in columns.
	Angle Clockwise	Angles the selected text downward at a 45-degree angle.
	Angle Counterclockwise	Angles the selected text upward at a 45-degree angle.

Figure 5.9

Alert!

If the Chart Toolbar Does Not Display

The Chart toolbar should be displayed on your screen. If it is not, right-click any toolbar and from the displayed list, click Chart. The Chart toolbar may float on your screen or be anchored. To anchor the Chart toolbar, point to the title bar and drag it up under the second toolbar at the top of the screen. Release the mouse button.

3 The table in Figure 5.10 lists the objects that are typically found in a chart. Take a moment to study this information.

Excel Chart Objects

Object	Description
Chart area	The entire chart and all its elements.
Plot area	The area bounded by the category axis (x-axis) and the value axis (y-axis) that includes the data series.
Gridlines	Lines in the plot area that aid the eye in determining the plotted values.
Axis	A line that borders one side of the plot area, providing a frame of reference for measurement or comparison in a chart. For most charts, categories are plotted along the category axis, which is usually horizontal (the x-axis), and data values are plotted along the value axis, which is usually vertical (the y-axis).
Category axis	The horizontal axis (also called the x-axis) containing the data categories being plotted.
Value axis	The vertical axis (also called the y-axis) containing the numerical scale upon which the plotted data is based.
Data point	A single value from a worksheet cell.
Data marker	The graphic element that represents a single data point (a value that originates from a worksheet cell). Data markers with the same pattern represent one data series.
Data series	A group of related data points that are plotted in a chart. Each series in a chart has a unique color or pattern and is represented in the chart legend. You can plot one or more data series in a chart (except in a pie chart, which can contain only one data series).
Data label	A label that provides additional information about a data marker (a graphic element that represents a single data point or value that originates from a worksheet cell). Data labels can be applied to a single data marker, an entire data series, or all data markers in a chart. Depending on the chart type, data labels can show values, names of data series or categories, percentages, or a combination of these.
Legend	A small box that identifies the patterns or colors that are assigned to the data series or categories in a chart.
Tick marks	Small lines of measurement, similar to divisions on a ruler, that intersect an axis.
Tick mark labels	Identifying information for a tick mark generated from the cells on the worksheet used to create the chart.
Walls and floor	The areas surrounding a 3-D chart that give dimension and boundaries to the chart. Two walls and one floor are displayed within the plot area.

Figure 5.10

4 On the Chart toolbar, click the **Chart Objects arrow**, and then click on each item listed to locate the item on the chart.

The Chart Objects button is another way to select chart objects. While you are learning, this method is sometimes preferable.

5 Click the tallest column displayed for the **Atlanta** category.

All the columns representing the Series "2004" are selected—selection handles display at the corners of each column in the series—and a ScreenTip displays the value for the column you are pointing to. A *data series* is a group of related data—in this case, the attendees to all the job fairs that were held in 2004. Also notice that the Formula Bar displays the address for the selected data series. See Figure 5.11.

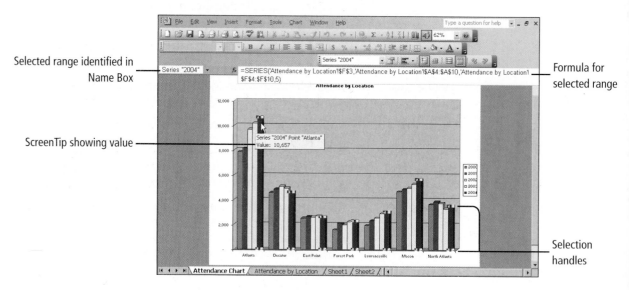

Figure 5.11

6 Locate the **Forest Park** category, and then click the shortest column displayed above the **Forest Park** category.

The selected series changes to those columns that represent the attendees at the job fairs in 2000. The Formula Bar and Name Box change and a new ScreenTip displays.

Objective 2
Modify a Column Chart

As you create a chart, you make choices about the data to include, the chart type, chart titles, and location. After the chart is created, you can change the chart type, change the way the data displays, add or change titles, select different colors, and modify the background, scale, or chart location.

Activity 5.3 Changing the Way the Data Displays

In the column chart you created, the attendance numbers are displayed along the value axis—the vertical axis—and the locations for each job fair are displayed along the category axis—the horizontal axis. The cells you select for a chart include the row and column labels from your worksheet. In a column or line chart, Excel selects whichever has *fewer* items—either the rows or the columns—and uses those labels to plot the data series, in this case, the years. After plotting the data series, Excel uses the remaining labels—in this example, the locations identified in the row headings—to create the labels on the category axis. A *legend*—the key that defines the colors used in the chart—identifies the data series, in this example, the years. A different color is used for each year in the data series. The chart, as currently displayed, compares the change in attendance year to year grouped by category location. You can change the chart to display the years on the category axis and the locations as the data series identified in the legend.

1 In the **Atlanta** category, click the second column, which is maroon in color.

All the columns with the same color are selected. The ScreenTip displays *Series "2001" Point "Atlanta" Value 8,145.*

2 Point to each of the other maroon columns that are selected and read the ScreenTip that displays.

The ScreenTip for each column identifies it as *Series "2001"*.

3 On the Chart toolbar, click the **By Row** button 📠.

The chart changes to display the locations as the data series. The locations are the row headings in the worksheet and are now identified in the legend. The years display as the category labels, as shown in Figure 5.12.

Note — Using the By Row and By Column Buttons

It is not necessary to select the columns or data series before clicking the By Row button or By Column button. In this instance, it is coincidental that columns are selected.

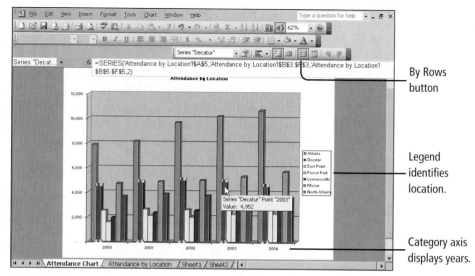

By Rows button

Legend identifies location.

Category axis displays years.

Figure 5.12

4 If necessary, click one of the maroon columns. Point to each maroon column and read the ScreenTip.

The ScreenTips for the maroon columns now identify this as the Decatur series.

5 Click outside the chart to cancel the selection of the columns. On the Standard toolbar, click the **Save** button.

More Knowledge — Changing the Range of Data in a Chart

After you have created a chart, you can adjust the range of data that is displayed in the chart. To do this, from the menu click Chart, Source Data. Edit the source address displayed in the Data Range box, or drag the data in the worksheet to adjust the range as needed.

Activity 5.4 Adding, Formatting, and Aligning Axis Titles

You can add new titles to a chart or modify existing titles. You can also change the format of the value and category axis labels.

1 From the menu bar, click **Chart**. From the displayed list, click **Chart Options**.

The Chart Options dialog box opens. Here you can change many different chart elements. The six tabs across the top of the dialog box—*Titles, Axes, Gridlines, Legend, Data Labels, Data Table*—identify the types of chart elements that can be modified.

2 If necessary, click the **Titles tab**.

3 Click in the **Value (Z) axis** box and type **Number Attending**

After a moment, the new title displays on the left side of the chart in the Preview area. See Figure 5.13.

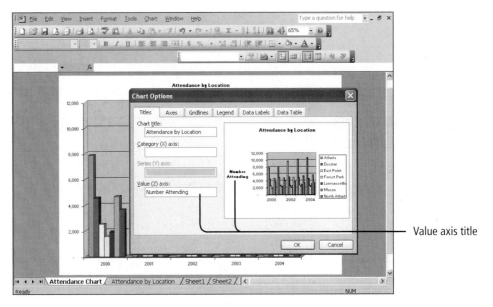

Value axis title

Figure 5.13

4 Click **OK**.

The dialog box closes, and the title is added to the left side of the chart. The axis title displays horizontally, but it would look better if aligned vertically.

5 Right-click the **Value Axis Title** you just added, and then, from the displayed shortcut menu, click **Format Axis Title**.

The Format Axis Title dialog box displays. Here you can change the format of the axis title, including the font, font size, style, or color, or the alignment of the text.

6 Click the **Font tab**, and then, in the list under the **Size** box, scroll as necessary and click **14**.

7 Click the **Alignment tab**. Under **Orientation**, drag the red diamond up to the top until the **Degrees** box displays **90**. See Figure 5.14.

The title alignment will change to 90 degrees.

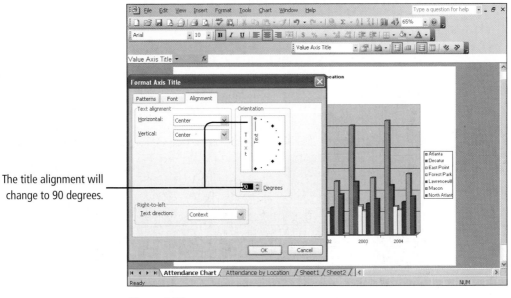

Figure 5.14

8 Click **OK**.

The dialog box closes. The orientation of the Value Axis Title is vertical, and the font size is increased to 14 pt.

9 On the Standard toolbar, click the **Save** button.

Another Way — **To Select Chart Objects**

You can use any of several methods to select and modify a chart object:

- Right-click the object and select the format option from the shortcut menu.

- Double-click the object, which opens the related format dialog box.

- On the Chart toolbar, click the Chart Objects arrow, from the displayed list click the chart object to select it, and then click the Format Object button.

Activity 5.5 Formatting Axis Labels

The labels along the value and category axes are the axis labels. These labels can be formatted in the same way as any other text.

1 On the left side of the chart, point to any number on the value axis. When the **Value Axis** ScreenTip displays, double-click to select the value axis and open the **Format Axis** dialog box.

In the Format Axis dialog box, you can change the patterns, scale, font, number format, and alignment of the axis labels.

2 Click the **Font tab**. Under **Size**, scroll as necessary, and then click **12**.

3 Click **OK**.

The dialog box closes. The value axis labels change to 12 pt.

4 On the Chart toolbar, click the **Chart Objects arrow** [_____] and, from the displayed list, click **Category Axis**.

The Category axis is selected, and selection handles display at each end of the category axis. See Figure 5.15.

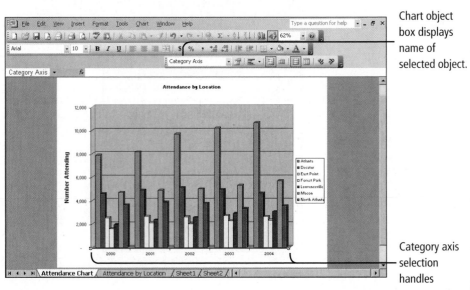

Chart object box displays name of selected object.

Category axis selection handles

Figure 5.15

5 On the Formatting toolbar, click the **Font Size arrow** 12 ▾ and, from the displayed list, click **12**.

The Category axis labels change to 12 pt. You can use the Formatting toolbar to format text on a chart in the same was as you do in the worksheet. If you want to change only the font, it is quicker to use the Formatting toolbar than the Format Axis dialog box.

6 On the Standard toolbar, click the **Save** button 🖫.

Activity 5.6 Formatting the Chart Title

1 Right-click the **Chart Title**—*Attendance by Location*—and then click **Format Chart Title**.

The Format Chart Title dialog box opens and displays the same formatting options as the Format Axis Title dialog box.

2 Click the **Font tab**. Under **Font style**, click **Bold Italic**. In the **Size** list, scroll as necessary, and then click **20**.

The Preview area displays the changes.

3 Click the **Color arrow**, and then, in the second row, click the sixth color—**Blue**.

4 Click the **Underline arrow**, and then click **Single**.

Compare your dialog box with Figure 5.16.

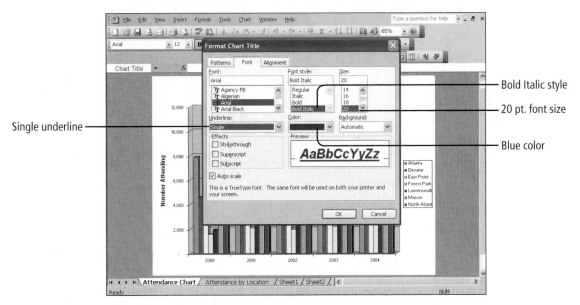

Figure 5.16

5 Click **OK**. Click in a white area of the chart to cancel the selection of the title and view your changes. On the Standard toolbar, click the **Save** button 🖫.

Activity 5.7 Editing the Chart Title

Because you have changed the data displayed in the chart in a manner that focuses on the attendance by year rather than the attendance by location, you should also change the chart title to reflect the data.

1 If necessary, click the **Chart Title**—*Attendance by Location*—to select it.

The title is selected, and a patterned box surrounds the title.

2 In the selected title, position the mouse pointer to the left of *Location*, and then click to place the insertion point.

To edit a title, click once to select the chart object, and then click a second time to position the insertion point in the title and change to editing mode.

3 Select *Location*, type **Years** and then click outside the title.

The title is changed to reflect the change in the data display. Compare your chart with Figure 5.17.

Chart title edited and formatted

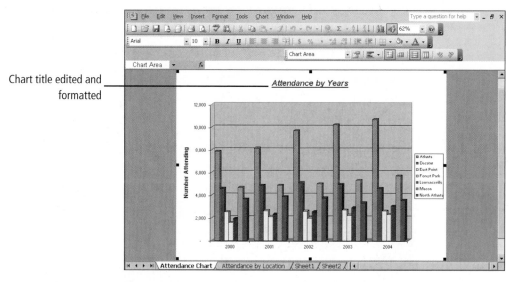

Figure 5.17

Activity 5.8 Editing Source Data

One of the characteristics of an Excel chart is that it reflects changes made to the underlying data.

1 Click anywhere in the white area of the chart. Then, in the **2004** column cluster, point to the second column—**Decatur**.

Notice that the Value for this column is 4,621.

2 Click the **Attendance by Location sheet tab** to move to the worksheet data.

3 Click cell **F5**, type **5261** and then press Enter.

The number of attendees at the 2004 Decatur Job Fair is updated.

4 Click the **Attendance Chart sheet tab**, and then point to the **Decatur** column for 2004.

The size of the column has expanded to reflect the change in data, and the new Value—5,261—displays in the ScreenTip. See Figure 5.18.

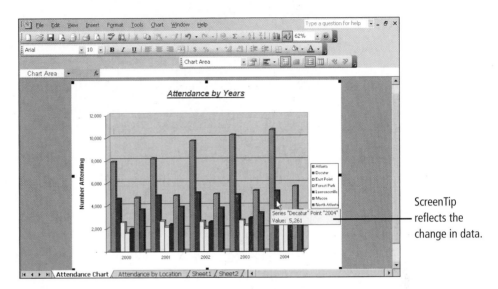

ScreenTip reflects the change in data.

Figure 5.18

5 On the Standard toolbar, click the **Save** button.

Objective 3
Print a Chart

Charts that are placed on their own sheet display in landscape orientation. If a chart is embedded with the worksheet, both the worksheet and chart print on the same page, and the orientation is controlled in the Page Setup dialog box.

Activity 5.9 Previewing and Printing a Chart

Before you print a chart, you should preview it.

1 With the *Attendance Chart* displayed, on the Standard toolbar click the **Print Preview** button.

2 From the Print Preview toolbar, click **Setup**, and then click the **Header/Footer tab**. Click the **Custom Footer** button. With the insertion point in the **Left section**, click the **File Name** button. Click **OK** twice.

The file name will print in the footer of the chart. Compare your screen with Figure 5.19.

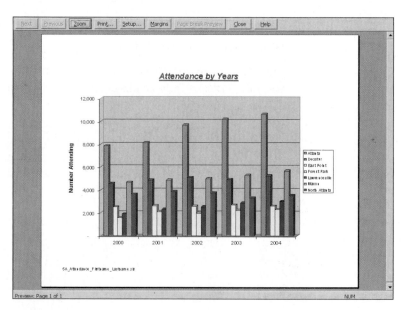

Figure 5.19

3 On the Print Preview toolbar, click the **Print** button . In the displayed **Print** dialog box, click **OK**.

The chart prints, and the Print Preview window closes.

4 On the Standard toolbar, click the **Save** button .

Objective 4
Create and Modify a Line Chart

Line charts are used to show trends over time. A line chart can consist of one line, such as the price of stock over time, or it can display more than one line to show a comparison of related numbers over time. For example, charts tracking stock or mutual fund performance often display the price of the mutual fund on one line and an industry standard for that particular type of fund on a different line.

Activity 5.10 Creating a Line Chart

In this activity, you will create a line chart showing the change in attendance at the Atlanta job fair over the five-year period covered by the worksheet.

1 With your **5A_Attendance_Firstname_Lastname** file open on your screen, click the **Attendance by Location sheet tab** to display the worksheet.

2 Select the range **A3:F4**, and then, on the Standard toolbar, click the **Chart Wizard** button .

The range is selected, and the Chart Wizard opens to Step 1 of the wizard. Cell A3 must be included in the selection, even though it is empty, because there must be the same number of cells in each row that is selected. The Chart Wizard will identify the first row as a category because of the empty first cell.

3 In the **Chart Wizard** dialog box, under **Chart type**, click **Line**.

The Chart sub-type area changes to display various styles of line charts, and the default line type—*Line with markers displayed at each data value*—is selected. See Figure 5.20.

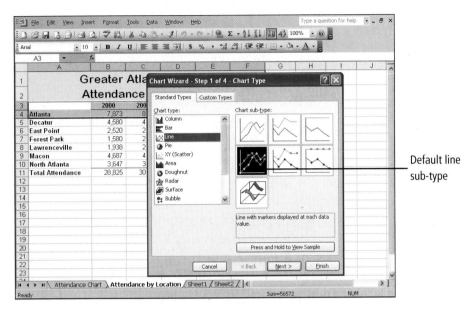

Default line sub-type

Figure 5.20

4 In the **Chart Wizard** dialog box, click the **Finish** button.

The dialog box closes, and the line chart displays on the worksheet. If you do not want to make any changes to the selected chart type and want it *embedded* in the worksheet—displayed on the same worksheet as the source data—you can skip Steps 2 through 4 of the wizard after you have selected the type of chart you want to create. See Figure 5.21.

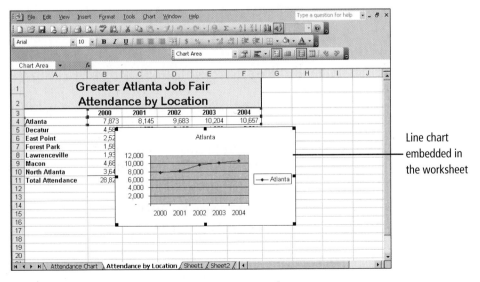

Line chart embedded in the worksheet

Figure 5.21

Activity 5.11 Moving and Resizing an Embedded Chart

When a chart is embedded in a worksheet it usually needs to be moved to a new location on the sheet, and often the size of the chart needs to be adjusted.

1 If necessary, click in the **Chart Area**—the white area surrounding the Plot Area—to select the chart.

Use the ScreenTip to help you identify the Chart Area. Recall that sizing handles display around the perimeter of the selected chart object—in this case the chart area.

2 Point to the **Chart Area**, and then drag the chart as shown in Figure 5.22 until the upper left corner of the chart is positioned at the upper left corner of cell **A13**.

A dotted outline displays to show the position of the chart as you move it.

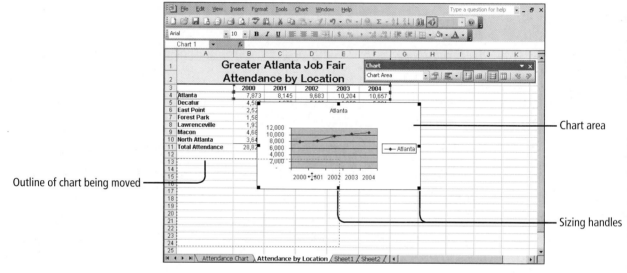

Figure 5.22

3 Release the mouse.

The chart is moved to a new location.

4 Scroll down as necessary to view **row 30**. Be sure the chart is selected. Move the pointer to the sizing handle in the lower right corner until the diagonal resize pointer ⬉ displays, as shown in Figure 5.23. Drag down and to the right until the lower right corner of the chart is positioned at the lower right corner of cell **F29**.

When you use the corner sizing handles to resize an object, the proportional dimensions—the relative height and width—are retained.

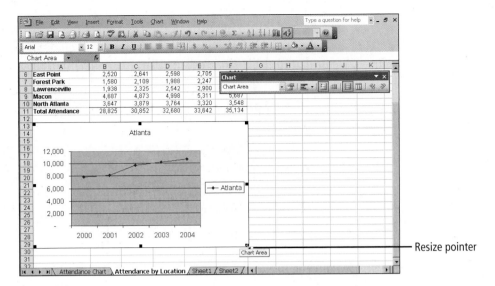

Figure 5.23

5 On the Standard toolbar, click the **Save** button ⊞.

More Knowledge — Using Snap to Grid

You can hold down [Alt] while you are moving or resizing an object to have the object align with the edge of the cell gridlines.

Activity 5.12 Deleting Legends and Changing Chart Titles

When you use the Chart Wizard to select the chart type, the resulting chart may have some elements that you want to delete or change. In the line chart, the title is *Atlanta*, and there is a legend that also indicates *Atlanta*. Because there is only one line of data, a legend is unnecessary, and the chart title can be made more specific.

1 In the embedded chart, click the **Legend**—*Atlanta*—to select it. Press [Delete].

The legend is removed from the chart, and the chart plot area expands.

2 Click the **Chart Title**—*Atlanta*. Click a second time to activate editing mode.

3 Select the title *Atlanta*, and then type **Attendance at Atlanta Job Fairs** to replace the selected text.

4 Click in the **Chart Area** to exit editing mode, and then click the new **Chart Title** to select it.

To format text in a chart, you can either select the text or select the chart object. In this instance, you are selecting the chart object so that you can change the font size.

5 On the Formatting toolbar, click the **Font Size arrow** 12 ▾, and then click **14**. Alternatively, right-click the Chart Title, click Format Chart Title, and use the displayed dialog box to change the font size.

The size of the title increases, and the plot area decreases slightly. Compare your chart with Figure 5.24.

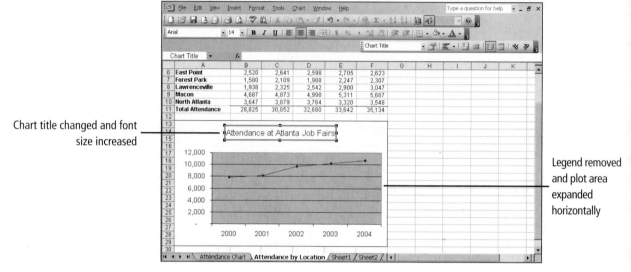

Chart title changed and font size increased

Legend removed and plot area expanded horizontally

Figure 5.24

6 On the Standard toolbar, click the **Save** button 💾.

Activity 5.13 Changing the Value Scale

In some cases, you will want to change the value *scale* on a chart to increase or decrease the variation among the numbers displayed. The scale is the range of numbers in the data series; the scale controls the minimum, maximum, and incremental values on the value axis. In the line chart, the attendance figures for Atlanta are all higher than 7,000, but the scale begins at zero, and the line occupies only the upper area of the chart.

1 On the left side of the line chart, point to the **Value Axis**, and when the ScreenTip displays, right-click. From the displayed shortcut menu, click **Format Axis**.

The Format Axis dialog box displays.

2 In the **Format Axis** dialog box, click the **Scale tab**.

Here you can change the beginning and ending numbers displayed on the chart and also change the unit by which the major gridlines display.

3 In the **Minimum** box, select the displayed number and type **5000** In the **Major unit** box, select the displayed number and type **1000** Compare your screen with Figure 5.25.

The Value Axis will start at 5000 with major gridlines at intervals of 1000. This will emphasize the change in attendance over the five years by starting the chart at a higher number and decreasing the interval for gridlines from 2000 to 1000. Notice that when you enter a number in one of the boxes, the check mark is removed. This indicates that the new number overrides the default settings.

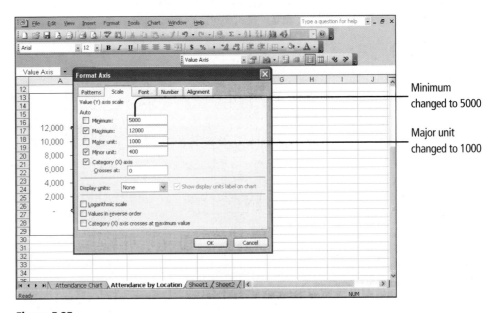

Minimum changed to 5000

Major unit changed to 1000

Figure 5.25

4 Click **OK**. On the Standard toolbar, click the **Save** button.

The dialog box closes, and the value axis on the chart changes to the new settings. See Figure 5.26.

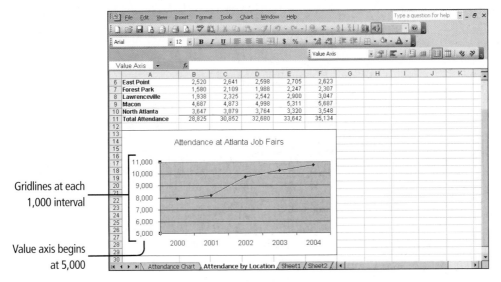

Gridlines at each 1,000 interval

Value axis begins at 5,000

Figure 5.26

Activity 5.14 Formatting the Plot Area and the Data Series

You can change the format of the Plot Area and the data series.

1 Right-click anywhere within the gray **Plot Area**, and then from the displayed shortcut menu, click **Format Plot Area**.

The Format Plot Area dialog box displays. Here you can change the border of the plot area or the background color.

2 Under **Area**, in the fifth row, click the fifth color—light turquoise.

The color displays in the Sample area. This is the same color shown in the title area on the worksheet. Compare your screen with Figure 5.27.

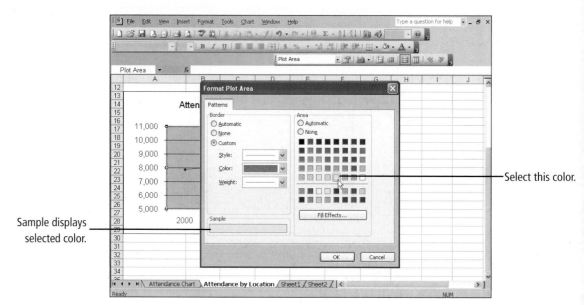

Sample displays selected color.

Select this color.

Figure 5.27

3 Click **OK**.

The background of the Plot Area changes to the selected color.

4 On the Chart toolbar, click the **Chart Objects arrow** [____], and then from the displayed list, click **Series "Atlanta"**.

The line on the chart representing the data series *Atlanta* is selected.

5 Click the **Format Data Series** button to display the **Format Data Series** dialog box. If necessary, click the **Patterns tab**.

Here you can change both the *data markers*—the indicators for a data point value, which on the line chart is represented by a diamond shape—or the line connecting the data markers.

6 Under **Line**, click the **Weight arrow**, and then click the third line in the displayed list. Click the **Color arrow**, and then, in the second row, click the sixth color—**Blue**.

7 Under **Marker**, click the **Style arrow**, and then, from the displayed list, click the **triangle**—the third symbol in the list. Click the **Foreground arrow** and, in the fourth row, click the third color— **Yellow**. Click the **Background arrow**, and then click **Yellow**. Compare your dialog box with Figure 5.28.

The foreground is the border color surrounding the symbol, and the background is the fill color in the middle of the symbol.

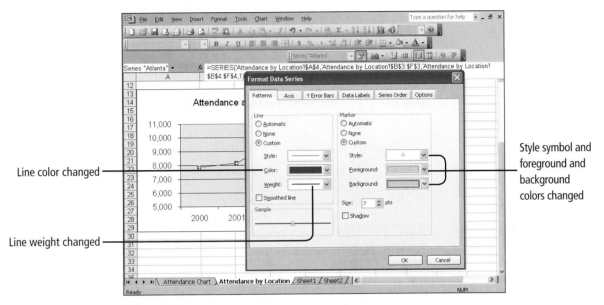

Line color changed

Line weight changed

Style symbol and foreground and background colors changed

Figure 5.28

8 Click **OK**. Click in any cell to cancel the selection of the chart.

The dialog box closes, and the data line and series markers change. See Figure 5.29.

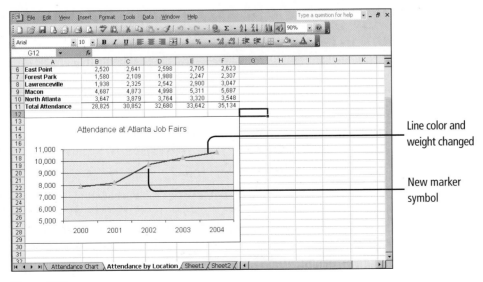

Line color and weight changed

New marker symbol

Figure 5.29

Activity 5.15 Printing a Worksheet with an Embedded Chart

1 Be sure the chart is not selected. On the Standard toolbar, click the **Print Preview** button 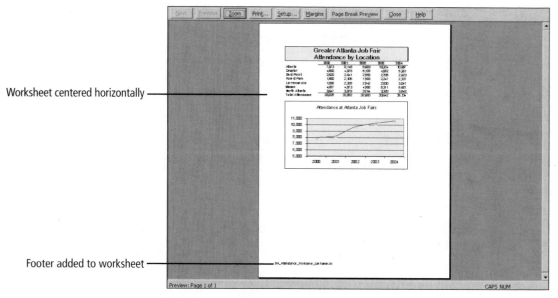.

The worksheet data and the chart display on a single page in the Print Preview window. You can see that the worksheet will look more professional if it is centered on the page.

2 On the Print Preview toolbar, click the **Setup** button. In the **Page Setup** dialog box, click the **Margins tab**.

The Page Setup dialog box displays the Margins tab.

3 In the lower part of the **Page Setup** dialog box, under **Center on page**, select the **Horizontally** check box.

4 Click the **Header/Footer tab**, and then click the **Custom Footer** button. With the insertion point in the **Left section**, click the **File Name** button. Click **OK** twice.

The file name will print in the footer. Compare your screen with Figure 5.30.

Worksheet centered horizontally ———————————

Footer added to worksheet ———————————

Figure 5.30

Note — The Worksheet Does Not Appear Exactly in the Center of the Page

If the right edge of the chart is touching the line between columns F and G, column G is included as part of the chart area, which causes the centering to appear to be slightly to the left of center. If this is a concern, you can use the right middle sizing handle to move the right edge of the chart off of the line between the columns.

5 On the **Print Preview** toolbar, click the **Print** button 🖨, and then click **OK**.

6 On the Standard toolbar, click the **Save** button 🖫.

Objective 5
Create and Modify a 3-D Pie Chart

Pie charts show the relationship of parts to a whole. For example, a pie chart can show contributions to income by products or services. It might also be used to show expenses by category to help understand and control expenses. It can be particularly useful when there are competitive goals among divisions or regions in a company.

Activity 5.16 Selecting Nonadjacent Data and Creating a Pie Chart

In this activity, you will create a pie chart to show how attendance at each individual city contributed to the overall attendance of the Job Fair in 2004. In the two previous charts, adjacent areas of the worksheet were selected for graphing. Sometimes you will need to select nonadjacent areas, such as the titles in one column or row and the totals in another.

1 With your **5A_Attendance** file open on your screen, be sure the **Attendance by Location** worksheet is displayed.

2 Scroll up if necessary, and then select the range **A4:A10**. Hold down Ctrl, and then select the range **F4:F10**.

Two nonadjacent data ranges are selected—the labels in column A and the numeric values in column F. See Figure 5.31.

Nonadjacent ranges selected —

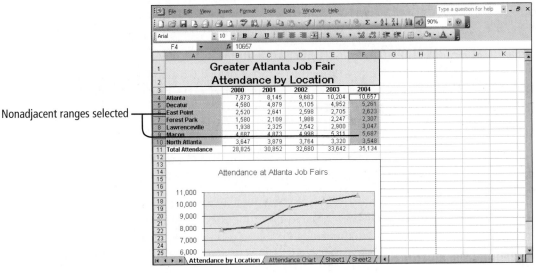

Figure 5.31

3 On the Standard toolbar, click the **Chart Wizard** button 📊.

The Chart Wizard opens with the default column chart selected.

4 In the **Chart Wizard** dialog box, under **Chart type**, click **Pie**.

Six pie chart sub-types display. The first one in the first row is selected as the default pie chart. See Figure 5.32.

Pie chart type selected —

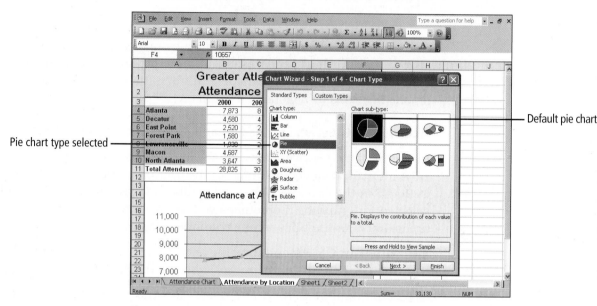

— Default pie chart

Figure 5.32

5 Click **Next**.

Step 2 of the Chart Wizard displays. In the worksheet, the selected data range is outlined by a moving border, and the pie sample displays in the Chart Wizard. No changes are needed in this step of the Chart Wizard.

6 Click **Next** to move to Step 3 of the Chart Wizard. Be sure the **Titles tab** is selected. Click in the **Chart title** box and type **2004 Job Fair Attendance by City**

After a moment, the chart title displays on the chart Preview area.

7 Click **Next** to move to Step 4 in the Chart Wizard. Click the **As new sheet** option button, and then type **2004 Attendance**

Recall that Step 4 of the Chart Wizard is used to determine whether you want the chart to be embedded within the worksheet or displayed on its own sheet. By entering a name in the *As new sheet* box, you are setting a name for the new worksheet that will be inserted in the workbook.

8 Click the **Finish** button to close the Chart Wizard. On the Standard toolbar, click the **Save** button 💾.

The pie chart displays on a separate sheet. Compare your screen with Figure 5.33.

Title added to chart ——

Worksheet named ——

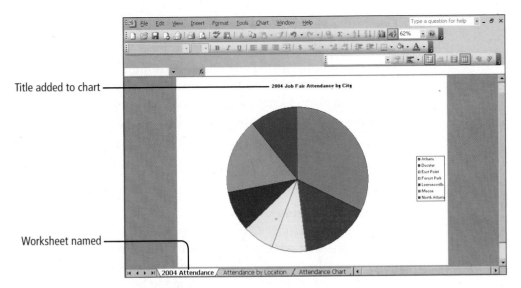

Figure 5.33

Activity 5.17 Changing Chart Type

After a chart is created, you can change the chart type from the Chart menu or by clicking the Chart Type button arrow on the Chart toolbar.

1 On the Chart toolbar, click the **Chart Type button arrow** .

A palette of chart types displays. Although not every available chart type in Excel displays on the palette, it provides a quick way to change chart types. A ScreenTip displays the name of the chart types as you point to each one. See Figure 5.34.

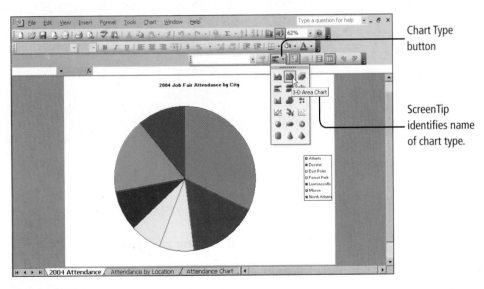

Chart Type button

ScreenTip identifies name of chart type.

Figure 5.34

2 From the displayed palette, in the second row, click the first chart type—**Bar Chart**.

The chart changes to a bar chart. Although you can see that the Atlanta location had the largest number of attendees in the year 2004, this chart is not as good a visual representation of how the attendance at each location contributed to the whole.

3 On the menu bar, click **Chart**, and then click **Chart Type**.

The Chart Type dialog box opens with the Bar chart type selected. Here you have access to the full range of the available charts in Excel.

4 Be sure the **Standard Types tab** is selected, and then under **Chart type** click **Pie**. Under **Chart sub-type**, in the first row click the second option—**Pie with a 3-D visual effect**. Notice the description in the lower right portion of the dialog box. Under the description, point to the **Press and Hold to View Sample** button, and hold down the left mouse button.

A sample of the new chart type displays. See Figure 5.35.

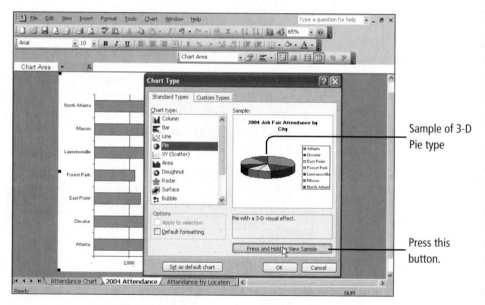

Sample of 3-D Pie type

Press this button.

Figure 5.35

5 Click **OK**. On the Standard toolbar, click the **Save** button.

Activity 5.18 Moving and Changing the Legend

The default location for a legend is the right side of the chart, but you can move the legend to another position.

1 On the right side of the chart, point to the legend, and when the **Legend** ScreenTip displays, right-click. From the displayed shortcut menu, click **Format Legend**.

The Format Legend dialog box displays. Here you can change the font of the legend text, the patterns—borders and background color of the legend box—or the placement of the legend.

2 Point to the **Format Legend** title bar and drag the dialog box to the left so that the legend is visible. Click the **Font tab**. Under **Size**, scroll as necessary and click **12**.

The Preview area displays the new font size, but the legend is not changed yet. It changes only after you click OK.

3 Click the **Placement tab**, and under **Placement**, click **Bottom**.

There are five options—Bottom, Corner, Top, Right, Left—for placement of the legend. Alternatively, you can drag the legend to a new location.

4 In the lower right side of the **Format Legend** dialog box, click **OK**.

The font size is increased, and the legend is placed at the lower edge of the chart, as shown in Figure 5.36. Because the legend was removed from the right side of the chart, the chart plot area expanded to the right.

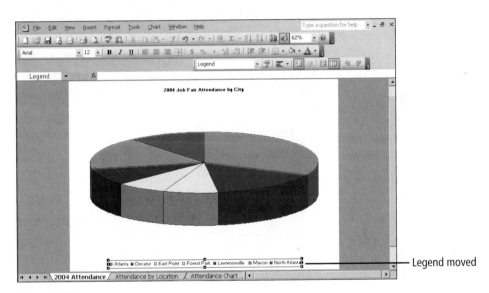

Legend moved

Figure 5.36

5 Click the **Chart Title** to select it. On the Formatting toolbar, click the **Font Size arrow** 12 ▾ , scroll as necessary, and then click **18**. On the same toolbar, click the **Italic** button *I*.

The font size is increased, and italic emphasis is added to the title.

6 On the Standard toolbar, click the **Save** button 🖫.

Activity 5.19 Adding and Formatting Data Labels

Data labels are labels that display the value, percentage, and/or category of each particular data point, which you recall is each single value in a worksheet that is plotted on the chart. The data point value is represented in the chart by a data marker such as a column, bar, line, or in this example, a pie piece.

1 From the **Chart** menu, click **Chart Options**.

The Chart Options dialog box displays.

2 In the **Chart Options** dialog box, click the **Data Labels tab**.

Data labels can contain one or more of the choices listed—Series name, Category name, Value, or Percentage. Labels can be used with any type of chart but are most often used with a pie chart.

3 Under **Label Contains**, select the **Value** and **Percentage** check boxes.

The preview window displays the chart with both labels. Sometimes it is difficult to determine whether the chart will look attractive and understandable until you look at the full-size chart. In the preview, the position of the value, followed by the percentage, looks like it could be confusing to a reader of your chart. See Figure 5.37.

Value and percentage data labels selected

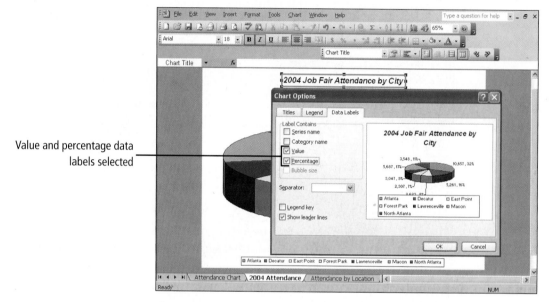

Figure 5.37

4 Click to clear the **Value** check box, and then click **OK**.

The data labels display next to each pie piece, indicating the percentage each pie slice represents of the entire pie. You can see that the data labels would be easier to read if they were larger and were moved away from the pie.

5 Point to any of the data labels and click.

Selection handles are displayed on each data label, indicating that all the labels are selected. Notice that the Formatting toolbar is active, which means it can be used to format the selected chart object.

6 On the Formatting toolbar, click the **Font Size arrow** $\boxed{12\ \blacktriangledown}$, and then, from the displayed list, click **14**.

The size of the labels increases, and the pie shrinks slightly.

7 On the chart, click the **11%** data label to select it. Point to the pat-terned outline around the label; when the pointer changes to a white arrow, drag up, away from the pie until the leader line displays, as shown in Figure 5.38.

A *leader line* is a line that connects the data label to its pie piece. You must drag the data label a minimum distance before the line will display.

Data label moved ———

Leader line connects data label to pie piece.

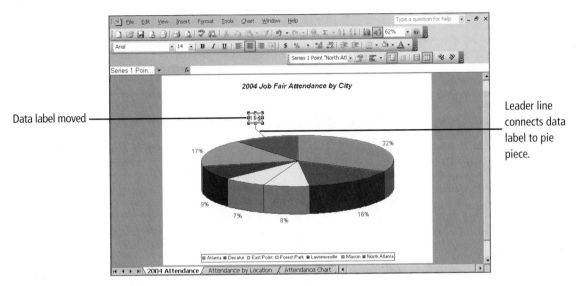

Figure 5.38

8 Click **17%** to select the data label, and then drag the label to the left, slightly away from the pie. Continue around the pie, dragging each data label away from the pie. Compare your screen with Figure 5.39.

The data labels are moved away from the pie, and leader lines display between each label and data marker.

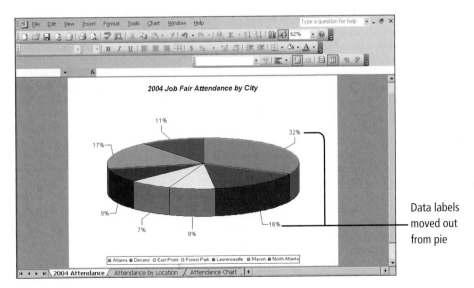

Data labels moved out from pie

Figure 5.39

9 On the Standard toolbar, click the **Save** button .

Activity 5.20 Formatting Chart Data Points

The colors used in column, bar, or pie charts can be changed, just as you changed the data markers for a line chart.

1 Point to the pie and click once to select it. Point to the pie piece labeled *9%*, which is the *Lawrenceville* data point, and click again to select only the **Lawrenceville** pie piece. See Figure 5.40.

Selection handles display around the Lawrenceville pie piece. To select a particular data point, click once to select the entire data series, in this instance the pie, and then click a second time on a specific data point to select it.

Pie piece selected ——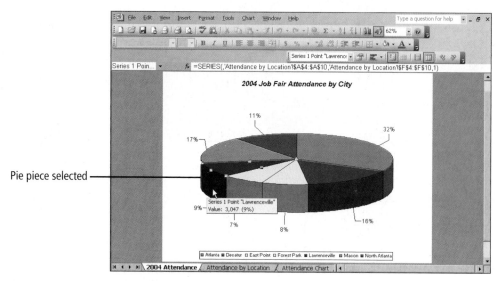

Figure 5.40

2 Right-click the selected pie piece, and from the displayed shortcut menu, click **Format Data Point**.

The Format Data Point dialog box opens. The color used for the selected pie piece displays in the Sample area and is pushed in—selected—under Area in the sixth row, fifth color. Notice that ScreenTips do not display to name the colors.

3 Point to the title bar of the dialog box and drag it to the upper right corner of your screen so that you can see the front half of the pie. Notice that the colors used in this chart are the colors in the sixth row under Area.

There are eight colors in each row, but only seven colors have been used in this chart.

4 In the **Format Data Point** dialog box, under **Area**, in row six, click the last color to change the color of the Lawrenceville data point to a lighter color.

The color displays in the Sample area.

5 In the lower right corner of the dialog box, click **OK**.

The color of the Lawrenceville pie piece changes, and the corresponding color in the legend also changes.

6 Point to the piece labeled *8%* for *East Point* and click to select that piece. Right-click the **East Point** piece, and from the displayed shortcut menu, click **Format Data Point**.

7 In the **Format Data Point** dialog box, under **Area**, in the fifth row, click the first color—**Rose**—and then click **OK**.

The color of the East Point pie piece changes, and the corresponding color in the legend also changes.

8 To the right of the *East Point* piece, double-click the piece labeled **16%—Decatur**. In the displayed dialog box, under **Area**, in the fourth row, click the second color—**Gold**—and then click **OK**.

The color of the *Decatur* piece changes, and the corresponding color in the legend also changes. Compare your screen with Figure 5.41.

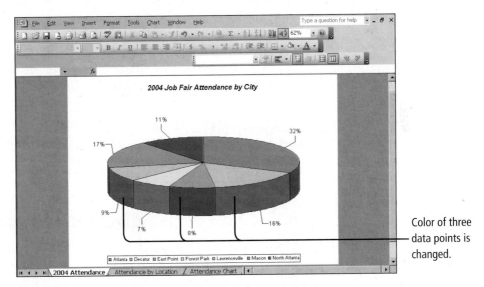

Color of three data points is changed.

Figure 5.41

9 On the Standard toolbar, click the **Save** button.

More Knowledge — Identifying Color Names

As you have experienced in this activity, not all the dialog boxes use ScreenTips to identify the names of colors. Fortunately, there is consistency of color placement among color palettes used in dialog boxes. To identify the name of a color, select some text, and then on the Formatting toolbar, click the Font Color arrow. Use the ScreenTips that display in this color palette to identify the names of the colors in other dialog boxes.

Activity 5.21 Adjusting the 3-D View Options

With a pie chart, you can change the orientation of the chart. For example, you can adjust the chart so that a different pie piece is moved toward the front of the chart for emphasis.

1 From the **Chart** menu, click **3-D View**.

The 3-D View dialog box opens. Using this dialog box you can rotate the chart and change the *elevation*—the angle at which a chart is tilted on the screen.

2 Under **Rotation**, click the **clockwise rotation** button—the one on the left—three times.

The rotation box changes to 30, and the graphic changes to show the effect. You can change the rotation by clicking either button to the right of the Rotation box. The button on the left rotates the pie clockwise—to the right—and the other button rotates the pie counterclockwise—to the left. You can also type a number in the rotation box if you have an idea of how much you want to rotate the pie. Each time you click one of the buttons, the rotation graphic and the rotation number change by 10 degrees. See Figure 5.42.

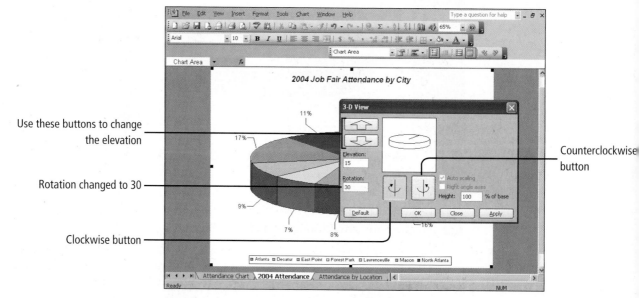

Use these buttons to change the elevation

Counterclockwise button

Rotation changed to 30

Clockwise button

Figure 5.42

3 In the **Rotation** box, select **30**, type **60** and then, in the lower right corner of the dialog box, click **Apply**. Drag the dialog box out of the way as needed so that you can see the pie.

The Rotation box changes to 60, and the chart is rotated. See Figure 5.43. In some dialog boxes, you can use the Apply button to see the effect of a change before you decide to make the change. To accept the change, you must click OK. If you close the dialog box without clicking OK, the change is not made to the chart.

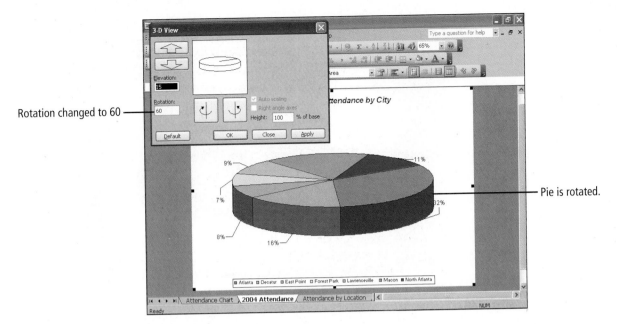

Rotation changed to 60

Pie is rotated.

Figure 5.43

4 In the **3-D View** dialog box, click **OK**. On the Standard toolbar, click the **Save** button 🔲.

The 60-degree rotation is accepted, and the dialog box closes. If the leader lines and data labels have moved, do not be concerned. You will adjust those in the next activity.

Activity 5.22 Exploding a Pie Chart

You can display all the pieces of a pie chart as separate pieces pulled away from the center of the pie; or you can selectively move a piece away from the pie. Pulling one or more pie pieces away from the pie is referred to as *exploding*.

1 Click the pie to select it, and then click the largest piece, labeled *32%*, which represents Atlanta.

Recall that to select a single data point, you first select the pie, and then select the specific data point—in this case, the Atlanta pie piece.

2 Point to the selected piece, and then drag it away from the pie as shown in Figure 5.44.

As you drag, an outline indicates the location of the pie piece.

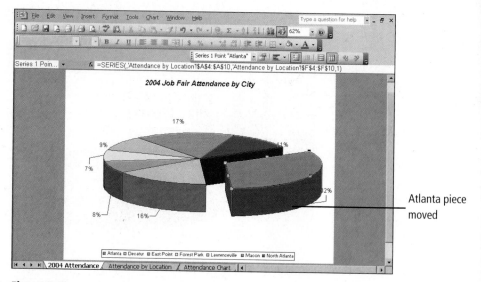

Atlanta piece moved

Figure 5.44

3 Using the technique you practiced in Activity 5.19, adjust any data labels that may have become disconnected or moved too far from their pie piece. Recall that you must first click any data label to select the group of labels, and then drag the individual label that needs to be adjusted. Be sure each data label has a leader line displayed.

4 From the **View** menu, click **Header/Footer**. Click **Custom Footer**. In the **Left section**, click the **File Name** button 🔲, and then click **OK** twice.

5 On the Standard toolbar, click the **Save** button 🔲, and then click the **Print Preview** button 🔍 to view the chart as it will print. On the Print Preview toolbar, click the **Print** button 🖨, and then click **OK**. Leave the workbook open for the next activity.

Objective 6
Create a Diagram

In addition to creating charts, Excel has six predefined diagrams that can be used to illustrate a concept or relationship. Unlike charts, **diagrams** do not depend on any underlying data in a worksheet; rather, they are graphical tools that help depict ideas or associations. For example, a diagram such as an organizational chart shows the reporting relationship among managers, supervisors, and employees. In the following activities, you will use the diagram program to create a cycle diagram to illustrate how the number of people hired through the job fairs increases the number of attendees, which, in turn, increases the number of employers who elect to have booths at the fairs.

Activity 5.23 Creating a Continuous Cycle Diagram

A cycle diagram illustrates a continuous process, which is a course of action that loops through the same cycle on an ongoing basis. The end result positively affects the beginning of the cycle.

1 To the left of the horizontal scroll bar, locate the **tab scrolling** buttons. Click the **right-most arrow** to move Sheet1 through Sheet3 into view, and then click the **Sheet1 tab**.

An empty worksheet, Sheet1, displays on your screen.

2 Click cell **A1** and type **Goal: Increase Attendance at Job Fairs** and then press Enter.

3 Click cell **A1** to select it. On the Formatting toolbar, click the **Font Size arrow** 12, scroll as necessary, and then click **24**. Click the **Bold** button **B**. Click the **Font Color arrow** **A** and in the second row, click the sixth color—**Blue**. Select the range **A1:J1**, and then click the **Merge and Center** button.

The title for your diagram is formatted.

4 From the **Insert** menu, click **Diagram**.

The Diagram Gallery dialog box opens, displaying six diagram types. See Figure 5.45.

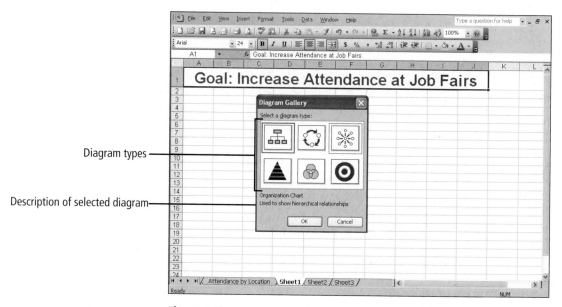

Diagram types

Description of selected diagram

Figure 5.45

5 Click on each diagram and read the description that explains the purpose of the diagram. Then, take a moment to examine the table in Figure 5.46.

Description of Diagrams

Diagram Name	What the Diagram Shows
Organization Chart	Hierarchical relationships
Cycle	A process with a continuous cycle
Radial	Relationships of a core element
Pyramid	Foundation-based relationships
Venn	Areas of overlap among elements
Target	Steps toward a goal

Figure 5.46

6 In the first row, click the second option—**Cycle Diagram**—and then click **OK**.

The cycle diagram graphic displays on the worksheet, and a text box on the right is selected ready for you to enter text. The Diagram toolbar floats on the screen. See Figure 5.47. The Diagram toolbar has commands that help you format and modify your diagram. You will use this toolbar in the next activity.

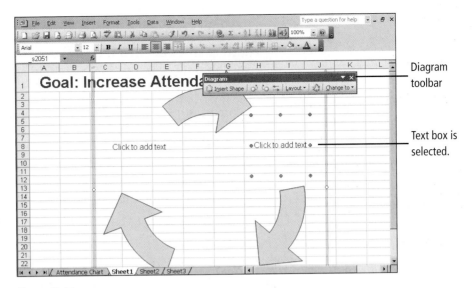

Figure 5.47

Diagram toolbar

Text box is selected.

7 Be sure the text box at the right of the diagram is selected, and then type **Attract More Attendees**

The text displays in the text box on the right side of the diagram. Notice that the text wraps to a second line.

8 Scroll as needed to display the text box at the bottom of the diagram. Click on the words **Click to add text** and type **Attract More Employers** On the left of the diagram, click on the words **Click to add text** and type **Increase Number of People Hired**

Text is added to the text boxes. The active text box is surrounded by a slashed border. Compare your diagram with Figure 5.48.

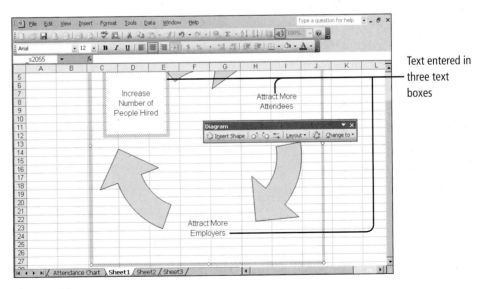

Figure 5.48

Text entered in three text boxes

9 On the left text box, click anywhere on the border.

The text box is selected, and circles display around the perimeter of the box. When the text box is selected in this manner, the text and text box can be formatted.

10 On the Formatting toolbar, click the **Bold** button **B**, and then click the **Font Color** button **A ·**.

The text font is changed to blue and bold. Recall that the Font Color button displays the last color selected, so when you click the Font Color button, the same blue that was used for the title is applied to the text box.

11 Use the technique you just practiced to change the font to blue and bold for the remaining two text boxes.

12 Point to the left outside edge of the diagram to display the four-way move pointer **⊕**, which displays with the white pointer arrow attached. Drag down and to the left to center the diagram under the title on the worksheet, as shown in Figure 5.49.

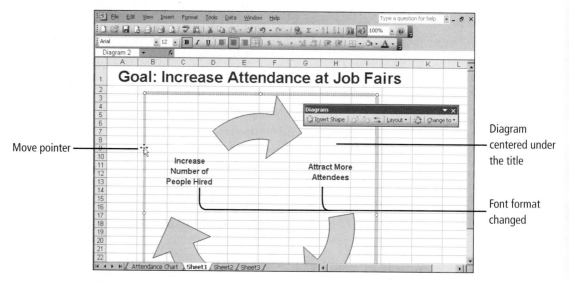

Figure 5.49

13 On the Standard toolbar, click the **Save** button **🖫**.

Activity 5.24 Inserting and Moving a Shape

If the diagram does not have enough shapes to illustrate the concept or display the relationship, you can add more shapes.

1 Point to the title bar of the Diagram toolbar and drag it to the top of your screen to anchor it under the other toolbars.

2 On the Diagram toolbar, click the **Insert Shape** button Insert Shape .

An arrow and text box are inserted in the upper left corner of the diagram.

3 Click the new text box and type **Increase Profits**

4 Click the patterned border surrounding the new text box. From the Formatting toolbar, change the font to **14** point, **Bold** with **Green** font color.

5 With the **Increase Profits** text box still selected, on the Diagram toolbar click the **Move Shape Backward** button .

The selected text box moves backward one position. To move a shape, first select it, and then click the Move Shape Forward or Move Shape Backward button. Each time you click one of these two directional buttons, the selected text box moves one position forward or back. Compare your diagram with Figure 5.50.

Shape inserted, formatted, and moved

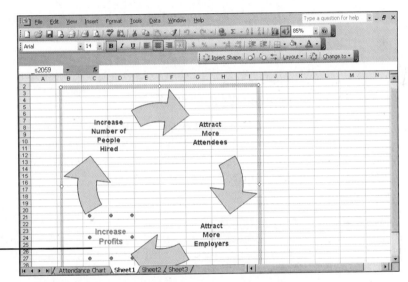

Figure 5.50

6 On the Standard toolbar, click the **Save** button .

Activity 5.25 Changing the Diagram Style

Excel offers a selection of preformatted styles that can be applied to a diagram.

1 On the Diagram toolbar, click the **Reverse Diagram** button .

The arrows reverse direction, and the boxes rotate counterclockwise one position. See Figure 5.51.

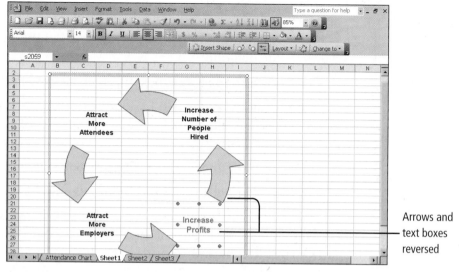

Arrows and text boxes reversed

Figure 5.51

2 On the Diagram toolbar, click the **Reverse Diagram** button ⬅ again to return the diagram to its original configuration.

3 On the Diagram toolbar, click the **AutoFormat** button 🖼.

The Diagram Style Gallery dialog box opens. Ten different styles can be used for this diagram.

4 In the **Diagram Style Gallery** dialog box, under **Select a Diagram Style**, click on each style to see the style displayed in the preview window. After reviewing the style selections, click **Primary Colors**. See Figure 5.52.

Primary Colors style selected

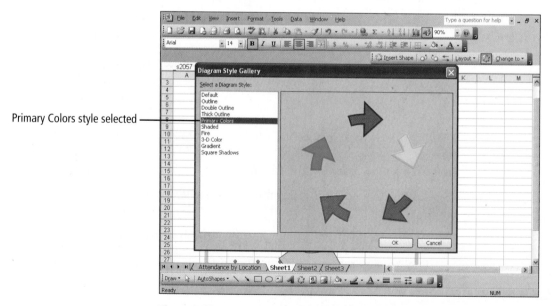

Figure 5.52

5 In the lower right corner of the dialog box, click **OK**.

The new style is applied to the diagram.

6 On the Standard toolbar, click the **Save** button 🖫.

7 From the **File** menu, click **Page Setup**. Click the **Page tab**, and then, under **Orientation**, click the **Landscape** option button. Click the **Margins tab**, and then, under **Center on page**, select the **Horizontally** check box. Click the **Header/Footer tab**, and then click **Custom Footer**. With the insertion point positioned in the **Left section**, click the **File Name** button 🔲. Click **OK** twice.

8 **Save** 🖫 your file, and then click the **Print Preview** button 🔍. On the Print Preview toolbar, click the **Print** button, and then click **OK**.

Objective 7
Organize and Format Worksheets

Worksheets can be deleted, inserted, and repositioned within a workbook. You have learned how to name a worksheet, but you can also add color to a sheet tab to help differentiate one from another. It is also possible to hide a worksheet within a workbook.

Activity 5.26 Inserting and Deleting Worksheets

1 Display the **Insert** menu, and then click **Worksheet**.

Sheet4 is inserted to the left of the Sheet1 tab, and Sheet4 becomes the active worksheet. Inserted worksheets are numbered consecutively.

Another Way ─ **Use the Shortcut Menu to Insert Worksheets**

You can also right-click a sheet tab and from the displayed shortcut menu, click Insert. From the displayed Insert dialog box, click the Worksheet icon and click OK to add a new worksheet.

---

2 Right-click the **Sheet4 tab**, and from the displayed shortcut menu, click Delete. Alternatively, from the Edit menu, click Delete Sheet.

Sheet4 is deleted. Because there was no data on this sheet, Excel does not warn you that you are about to delete a worksheet, nor can you click the Undo button.

3 Click the **Sheet2 tab**. In cell **A1**, type **September 2004** and press Enter.

Now that you have added text to this worksheet, you will be able to see what happens when you delete a sheet than contains data.

4 Hold down Ctrl and click the **Sheet3 tab** to select both Sheets 2 and 3. Display the **Edit** menu, and then click **Delete Sheet**.

A dialog box displays, warning you that data may exist in one or more of the selected sheets. This gives you a chance to change your mind and helps prevent you from inadvertently deleting active worksheets. See Figure 5.53.

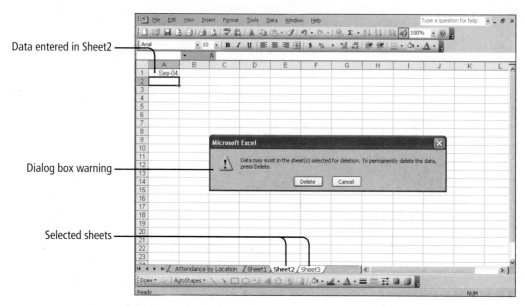

Data entered in Sheet2

Dialog box warning

Selected sheets

Figure 5.53

5 In the displayed dialog box, click **Delete**. Click the **Save** button 🖫.

Both sheets are deleted, and Sheet1 displays on the screen.

Activity 5.27 Formatting and Moving Worksheets

1 Double-click the **Sheet1 tab**, type **Attend Diagram** and then press Enter.

The name of the sheet is changed. Recall that you can double-click a sheet tab to change to the editing mode, or you can right-click the sheet tab and from the displayed shortcut menu click Rename, which also selects the sheet name and activates the editing mode.

2 Right-click the **Attend Diagram sheet tab** and, from the displayed shortcut menu, click **Tab Color**.

The Format Tab Color dialog box opens, as shown in Figure 5.54.

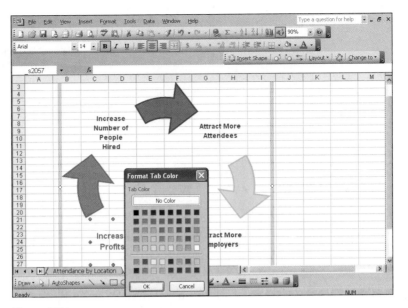

Figure 5.54

3 Under **Tab Color**, in the last row, click the second color—**Pink**—and then click **OK**.

The sheet tab displays a pink line under the sheet name.

4 If necessary, use the tab scrolling buttons to display the **Attendance by Location** sheet. Right-click the **Attendance by Location sheet tab**, and from the displayed list, click **Tab Color**. In the displayed **Format Tab Color** dialog box, in the fifth row, click the fifth color—**Light Turquoise**—to match the color used in this worksheet. Click **OK**.

5 Use the technique you just practiced to apply **Coral** to the **2004 Attendance sheet tab** and **Ocean Blue** to the **Attendance Chart sheet tab**. Both colors are in the sixth row of the color palette, the sixth and seventh colors, respectively.

Notice that the active sheet displays the sheet tab color as an underscore under the sheet name, and the inactive sheet tabs display the full color. If necessary, the color of the font changes to white to maintain a contrast with the color of the sheet tab. Refer to Figure 5.55.

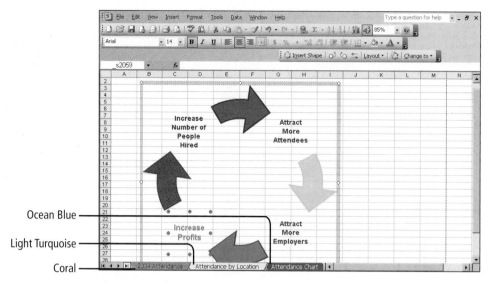

Ocean Blue

Light Turquoise

Coral

Figure 5.55

6 Click the **Attendance by Location tab** to make it the active sheet. On the **Attendance by Location tab**, click and hold down the left mouse button until a sheet icon displays. See Figure 5.56.

When you see the Sheet icon, you can drag to move the selected sheet to the left or right of the other sheet tabs.

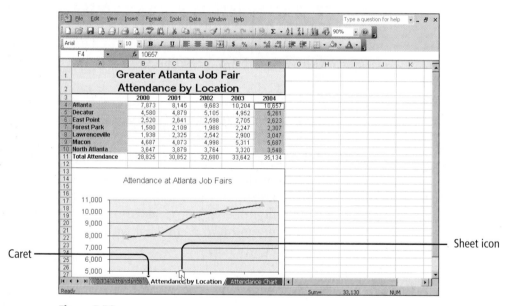

Caret

Sheet icon

Figure 5.56

7 Drag the **Attendance by Location sheet icon** to the left of the **2004 Attendance sheet tab**. Release the mouse.

As you move the sheet, notice the tiny triangle—called a **caret**—that indicates the location where the worksheet will be positioned.

8 On the Standard toolbar, click the **Save** button .

Activity 5.28 Hiding and Unhiding Worksheets

You can hide a worksheet in a workbook. For example, you may have a workbook of diagrams and charts that you want to share, but you do not want to include the worksheet data to discourage someone from changing the data, or you may not want to include all the diagrams or charts that are in the workbook.

1 If necessary, use the tab scrolling buttons to bring the **Attend Diagram** into view. Click the **Attend Diagram tab** to make it the active worksheet.

2 Display the **Format** menu, point to **Sheet**, and then click **Hide**.

The active worksheet—Attend Diagram—is hidden, and the chart worksheet displays on your screen.

3 Display the **Format** menu, point to **Sheet**, and click **Unhide**.

The Unhide dialog box displays, as shown in Figure 5.57, and under Unhide Sheet, the Attend Diagram sheet is listed.

Unhide dialog box lists hidden worksheet(s)

Attend Diagram worksheet tab not displayed

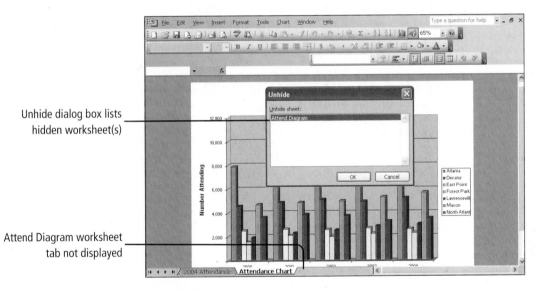

Figure 5.57

4 With the Attend Diagram sheet selected in the dialog box, click **OK** to return the sheet to view. Save your changes and close the workbook.

End You have completed Project 5A

Summary

The Excel charting feature provides a broad array of chart options for creating a graphical illustration of the numbers in a worksheet. In this chapter, the three main chart types were demonstrated: charts that show a relationship among data, charts that show trends over time, and charts that show the parts of a whole. You created and modified a column chart to show a comparison among related numbers, a line chart to display a trend over time, and a pie chart to show the contribution of parts to a whole. Within each chart type, you identified and modified various chart objects and created and formatted titles and labels.

Excel also offers six predefined diagram types. You created and modified a cycle diagram to practice working with some of the diagram features and options.

It is typical to have several worksheets in a workbook. To help you organize a workbook, you practiced inserting, deleting, moving, hiding, and unhiding worksheets. You also changed the tab color on the worksheets.

In This Chapter You Practiced How To

- Create a Column Chart
- Modify a Column Chart
- Print a Chart
- Create and Modify a Line Chart
- Create and Modify a 3-D Pie Chart
- Create a Diagram
- Organize and Format Worksheets

Matching

Match each term in the second column with its correct definition in the first column by writing the letter of the term on the blank line in front of the correct definition.

_____ **1.** A chart that is inserted into the same worksheet that contains the data used to create the chart.

_____ **2.** A type of chart that shows comparisons among data.

_____ **3.** A type of chart that uses lines to show a trend over time.

_____ **4.** A type of chart that shows the proportion of parts to the whole.

_____ **5.** A group of related data points.

_____ **6.** In a multicolumn chart, a key that identifies the data series by colors.

_____ **7.** A tool that walks you step by step through the process of creating a chart.

_____ **8.** A tool that is used to graphically illustrate a concept or relationship.

_____ **9.** The chart object that graphically represents the numbers in a worksheet.

_____ **10.** The range of numbers in the data series that controls the minimum, maximum, and incremental values on the value axis.

_____ **11.** Small boxes that surround an object or chart and that can be used to resize it.

_____ **12.** Variations on a main chart type.

_____ **13.** The default chart type that displays when you open the Chart Wizard.

_____ **14.** A single value in a worksheet represented by a data marker in a chart.

_____ **15.** A separate worksheet used to display an entire chart.

A Chart sheet

B Chart sub-type

C Chart Wizard

D Clustered column chart

E Column chart

F Data point

G Data series

H Diagram

I Embedded chart

J Legend

K Line chart

L Pie chart

M Plot area

N Scale

O Sizing handles

Fill in the Blank Write the correct answer in the space provided.

1. Elements that make up a chart are known as chart

   _____.

2. The numbers along the left side of a chart display in the

   _____ axis.

3. The graphic element, such as a column or pie slice, that represents a

   single data point is known as _____

   _____.

4. Text or numbers that provide additional information about a data

   marker, including values, percentages, data series, or categories are

   _____.

5. To create more advanced chart designs and incorporate your own

   features, you can click _____ types in the Chart

   Wizard.

6. The data along the bottom of a chart displays in the

   _____ axis.

7. The areas surrounding a 3-D chart that give dimension and bound-

   aries to the chart are the _____.

8. If you pull a pie piece away from the center of the pie, it is referred to

   as _____ the pie.

9. To reposition a sheet tab, _____ it to the left or right

   of the adjacent sheet tabs.

10. A diagram that is used to show hierarchical relationships is the

    _____.

Project 5B—Industry

Objectives: *Print a Chart, and Organize and Format Worksheets.*

Janice Dawson, the employer coordinator for the Greater Atlanta Job Fair, is responsible for attracting new employers to the fairs. She wants to know the percentage each industry group represents of the total number of employers attending the fairs and has gathered the data together in a worksheet. In the following Skill Assessment, you will create and modify a pie chart that shows the distribution of employers across several industry categories. Your completed chart will look similar to the one shown in Figure 5.58. You will save your workbook as *5B_Industry_Firstname_Lastname*.

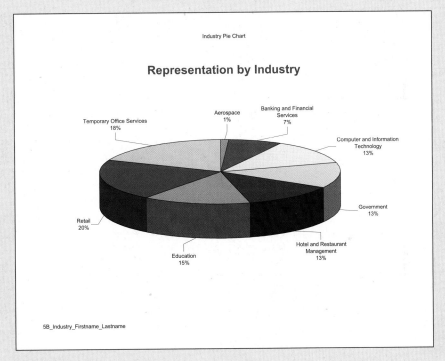

Figure 5.58

1. **Start** Excel. On the Standard toolbar, click the **Open** button. Navigate to the location where the student files for this textbook are stored. Locate and open **e05B_Industry**.

2. From the **File** menu, click **Save As**. In the **Save As** dialog box, use the **Save in arrow** to navigate to the location where you are storing your files for this chapter. In the **File name** box, type **5B_Industry_Firstname_Lastname** Click the **Save** button.

3. At the bottom of the worksheet, double-click the **Sheet1 tab**, type **2004 Industries** and then press Enter.

(Project 5B–Industry continues on the next page)

(Project 5B–Industry continued)

4. Right-click the **2004 Industries sheet tab**, and from the displayed shortcut menu, click **Tab Color**. In the displayed **Format Tab Color** dialog box, in the third row, click the first color—**Red**. Click **OK**.

5. Select the range **A3:B10**, and then, on the Standard toolbar, click the **Chart Wizard** button.

6. In Step 1 of the displayed **Chart Wizard** dialog box, under **Chart type**, click **Pie**, and then under **Chart sub-type**, in the first row click the second sub-type—**Pie with 3-D visual effect**. At the lower right of the dialog box, click **Next**.

7. In Step 2 of the **Chart Wizard**, verify that the **Data range** box displays =*'2004 Industries'!$A$3:$B$10*, and then click **Next**.

8. In Step 3 of the **Chart Wizard**, be sure the **Titles tab** is selected. Click the **Chart title** box, type **Representation by Industry** and then click **Next**.

9. In Step 4 of the **Chart Wizard**, delete the text in the **As new sheet** box, type **Industry Pie Chart** and then click **Finish**. On the Standard toolbar, click the **Save** button.

10. Right-click the **Legend** and from the displayed shortcut menu, click **Format Legend**. In the **Format Legend** dialog box, click the **Placement tab**, and then click **Bottom**. Click **OK**.

11. At the top of the chart, click the **Chart Title** to select it. From the Formatting toolbar, click the **Font Size arrow**, and click **22**. Click the **Font Color arrow**. From the displayed palette, in the sixth row, click the seventh color—**Ocean Blue**.

12. Display the **Chart** menu, and then click **Chart Options**. Click the **Data Labels tab**. Under **Label Contains**, select the **Category name** and **Percentage** check boxes. Be sure the **Show leader lines** check box is selected, and then click **OK**. The data labels are added, and the plot area of the pie shrinks.

13. Because you added the category names to the data labels, the legend is no longer needed. Right-click the **Legend**, and from the displayed shortcut menu, click **Clear** to remove the legend from the chart.

14. On the Chart toolbar, click the **Chart Objects arrow**. From the displayed list, click **Plot Area**. A patterned border displays around the plot area. Point to the sizing handle in the lower left corner of the plot area outline. When the pointer changes to a two-way resize arrow, drag down and to the left to increase the size of the plot area by approximately 1 to 2 inches. Point to the slashed border outline, and drag the enlarged plot area so that it is approximately centered under the title. Use Figure 5.58 as a reference.

(Project 5B–Industry continues on the next page)

(Project 5B–Industry continued)

15. Click any one of the data labels. Recall that if you click one data label, all the data labels are selected. On the Formatting toolbar, click the **Font Size arrow**, and then click **10**.

16. Click the data label **Temporary Office Services**, and drag it away from its pie piece so that a leader line displays. Recall that when a patterned border displays around an individual data label, the label can be moved. Continue around the pie and drag each label out from the pie until leader lines show between each label and its related pie slice.

17. Click the **2004 Industries sheet tab**, and hold down the mouse until the sheet icon displays. Drag the 2004 Industry sheet to the left of the **Industry Pie Chart sheet tab**. Click **Sheet2**, hold down , and click **Sheet3** to select both sheets. Right-click on one of the selected sheet tabs, and from the displayed shortcut menu, click **Delete** to remove the two empty sheets from the workbook.

18. Right-click the **Industry Pie Chart sheet tab**, and from the displayed shortcut menu, click **Tab Color**. In the **Format Tab Color** dialog box, in the sixth row, click the seventh color—**Ocean Blue**—and then click **OK**. Recall that ScreenTips do not display the color names in this dialog box, but this is the same color that was used earlier to format the chart title.

19. From the **View** menu, click **Header and Footer**. Click the **Custom Header** button. Click in the **Center section**, and then click the **Sheet Tab** button; the code $[Tab] displays in the Center section. Click **OK**. Click the **Custom Footer** button. With the insertion point positioned in the **Left section**, click the **File Name** button. Click **OK** twice.

20. On the Standard toolbar, click the **Save** button, and then click the **Print Preview** button to see how the worksheet will look when it prints. Compare your worksheet with Figure 5.58. Click the **Print** button, and then click **OK**. Close the file, saving changes if prompted to do so.

End **You have completed Project 5B**

Project 5C—Atlanta Results

Objectives: *Create and Modify a Line Chart, Print a Chart, and Organize and Format Worksheets.*

Ben Ham, the administrative manager for the Greater Atlanta Job Fair, tracks expenses and attendance for the fairs to determine the average cost per attendee. In the following Skill Assessment, you will create and format a line chart to show the trend in expenses at the Atlanta fair over the past five years. Your completed worksheet will look similar to the one shown in Figure 5.59. You will save your workbook as *5C_Atlanta_Results_Firstname_Lastname*.

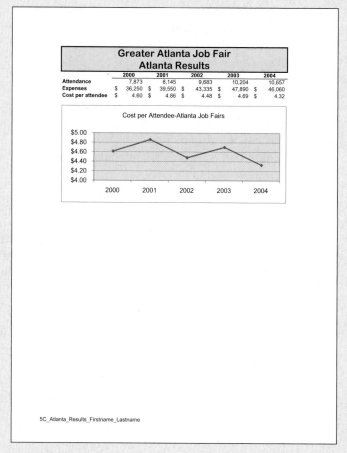

Figure 5.59

1. If necessary, **Start** Excel. On the Standard toolbar, click the **Open** button. Navigate to the location where the student files for this textbook are stored. Locate and open **e05C_Atlanta_Results**.

(Project 5C–Atlanta Results continues on the next page)

(Project 5C–Atlanta Results continued)

2. From the **File** menu, click **Save As**. In the **Save As** dialog box, use the **Save in arrow** to navigate to the location where you are storing your files for this chapter. In the **File name** box, type **5C_Atlanta_Results_Firstname_Lastname** Click the **Save** button.

3. In cell **A6**, type **Cost per attendee** and press Tab. Recall that a cell adopts the formatting of the cell above it. In cell **B6**, type **=b5/b4** and press Enter to calculate the cost per attendee for the 2000 fair. Click cell **B6** and use the fill handle to copy the formula to cells **C6:F6**. The cost per attendee is formatted as dollars, the same as the cells above.

4. Select the range **A3:F3**, hold down Ctrl, and select the range **A6:F6**. This selects the labels in **row 3** and the data to be charted in **row 6**. Recall that you must select the same number of cells in each row or column, even if one of the cells is empty. On the Standard toolbar, click the **Chart Wizard** button.

5. In Step 1 of the **Chart Wizard**, under **Chart type**, click **Line**. Under **Chart sub-type**, in the second row, click the first chart sub-type—*Line with markers displayed at each data value*. In the lower right corner of the Chart Wizard, click the **Next** button.

6. In Step 2 of the **Chart Wizard**, verify that the **Data range** box displays =*'Atlanta Results'!$A$3:$F$3,'Atlanta Results'!$A$6:$F$6*, and then click **Next**.

7. In Step 3 of the **Chart Wizard**, click the **Legend tab** and clear the **Show legend** check box. Recall that if there is only one line of data, a legend is not needed. Click **Next**.

8. In Step 4 of the **Chart Wizard**, be sure the **As object in** option is selected, and then click **Finish**. The chart displays on the worksheet.

9. Point to the **Chart Area** and drag the chart down and to the left. Position the upper left corner of the chart in the upper left corner of cell **A8**.

10. With the **Chart Area** selected, sizing handles display at the outside corners of the chart; point to the lower right corner. When a two-way resize arrow displays, drag as necessary to position the lower right corner of the chart aligned with the lower right corner of cell **F21**. The right edge of the chart aligns with the right edge of the data in the worksheet. On the Standard toolbar, click the **Save** button.

11. Click the **Chart Title** once to select it, and then click it a second time to place an insertion point in the title. Select the text, and then type **Cost per Attendee-Atlanta Job Fairs**

(Project 5C–Atlanta Results continues on the next page)

(Project 5C–Atlanta Results continued)

12. On the Chart toolbar, click the **Chart Objects arrow**, and from the displayed list click **Series "Cost per attendee"**. This selects the data series line on the plot area of the chart. On the **Chart** toolbar, click the **Format Data Series** button. Recall that the Format Selected Object button adopts the name of the selected object—in this instance, the data series.

13. In the **Format Data Series** dialog box, click the **Patterns tab** if necessary. Under **Line**, click the **Color arrow**, and then in third row, click the first color—**Red**. Click the **Weight arrow** and from the displayed list, click the third line. Under **Marker**, click the **Foreground arrow** and click **Red**; then click the **Background arrow** and click **Red**. Click **OK**. The data line and its marker change to red.

14. Right-click the **Plot Area**—the gray background—and from the displayed shortcut menu, click **Format Plot Area**. In the **Format Plot Area** dialog box, under **Area**, in the fifth row, click the fifth color—**Light Turquoise**, the same color that is used in the title of the worksheet. Click **OK**. Click in an empty cell to cancel the selection of the chart.

15. From the **File** menu, click **Page Setup**. Click the **Margins tab** and under **Center on page**, click **Horizontally**. Click the **Header/Footer tab**, and then click the **Custom Footer** button. With the insertion point positioned in the **Left section**, click the **File Name** button. Click **OK** twice.

16. Click to select the **Sheet1 tab**, hold down , and then click the **Sheet2 tab** and the **Sheet3** tab. With the three sheets selected, display the **Edit** menu, and then click **Delete Sheet**.

17. On the Standard toolbar, click the **Save** button, and then click the **Print Preview** button to see the worksheet as it will print. Compare your worksheet with Figure 5.59. Click the **Print** button, and then click **OK**. Close the file, saving changes if prompted to do so.

End You have completed Project 5C

Project 5D—Hires

Objectives: *Create a Line Chart, Change the Line Chart to a Column Chart, Modify a Column Chart, Print a Chart, and Organize and Format Worksheets.*

Janice Dawson, the employer coordinator for the Greater Atlanta Job Fair, tracks the number of people who get hired by an employer at each fair. In the following Skill Assessment, you will create and modify a chart to display the number of people hired at the fairs in the past five years. Your completed worksheet will look similar to the one shown in Figure 5.60. You will save your workbook as *5D_Hires__Firstname_Lastname*.

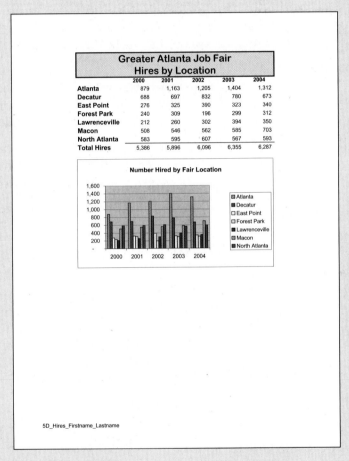

Greater Atlanta Job Fair Hires by Location					
	2000	**2001**	**2002**	**2003**	**2004**
Atlanta	879	1,163	1,205	1,404	1,312
Decatur	688	697	832	780	673
East Point	276	325	390	323	340
Forest Park	240	309	196	299	312
Lawrenceville	212	260	302	394	350
Macon	508	546	562	585	703
North Atlanta	583	595	607	567	593
Total Hires	5,386	5,896	6,096	6,355	6,287

5D_Hires_Firstname_Lastname

Figure 5.60

(Project 5D–Hires continues on the next page)

(Project 5D–Hires continued)

1. On the Standard toolbar, click the **Open** button. Navigate to the location where the student files for this textbook are stored. Locate and open **e05D_Hires**.

2. From the **File** menu, click **Save As**. In the **Save As** dialog box, use the **Save in arrow** to navigate to the location where you are storing your files for this chapter. In the **File name** box, type **5D_Hires_Firstname_Lastname** Click the **Save** button.

3. Select the range **A3:F10**. On the Standard toolbar, click the **Chart Wizard** button.

4. In Step 1 of the **Chart Wizard**, under **Chart type** click **Line**. Under **Chart sub-type**, in the second row, click the first option—**Line with markers displayed at each data value**. In the lower right corner of the Chart Wizard, click the **Next** button.

5. In Step 2 of the **Chart Wizard**, next to **Series in**, click the **Rows** option button. The preview changes to display the years on the category axis and the locations as the data series. Click **Next**.

6. In Step 3 of the **Chart Wizard**, click the **Titles tab**. Click the **Chart title** box and type **Number Hired by Fair Location** and then click **Next**.

7. In Step 4 of the **Chart Wizard**, be sure the **As object in** option is selected, and then click **Finish**. The chart displays on the worksheet.

8. Point to the **Chart Area** and drag the chart down and to the left. Position the upper left corner of the chart in the upper left corner of cell **A13**.

9. With the **Chart Area** selected, sizing handles display at the outside corners of the chart; point to the lower right corner. When a two-way resize arrow displays, drag as necessary until the lower right corner of the chart aligns with the lower right corner of cell **F28**. The right edge of the chart aligns with the right edge of the data in the worksheet. On the Standard toolbar, click the **Save** button.

10. On the Chart toolbar, click the **Chart Type button arrow**. From the displayed palette, in the third row, click the first chart—**Column Chart**. The chart type changes to columns grouped by year along the category axis.

(Project 5D–Hires continues on the next page)

(Project 5D–Hires continued)

11. On the Chart toolbar, click the **Chart Objects arrow**, and from the displayed list click **Value Axis**. On the Chart toolbar, click the **Format Axis** button. Recall that the Format Selected Object button takes on the name of the selected object—in this instance, Axis.

12. In the **Format Axis** dialog box, click the **Scale tab**. Under **Value (Y) axis scale**, select the value in the **Major unit** box and type **200** if necessary. Select the value in the **Minor unit** box and type **50** Click the **Font tab** and under **Size**, click **10**. In the lower right corner of the dialog box, click **OK**.

13. Double-click the **Legend**. In the displayed **Format Legend** dialog box, click the **Font tab**. Under **Size**, click **10**, and then click **OK**.

14. Click the **Chart Title**. On the Formatting toolbar, click the **Font Size arrow**, and then click **12**. Click the years on the **Category Axis**, on the Formatting toolbar click the **Font Size arrow**, and then click **10**. Click in an empty cell to cancel the selection of the chart.

15. Click cell **F9**, type **703** and then press Enter. The change is reflected in the chart for the Macon data series in 2004.

16. From the **File** menu, click **Page Setup**. Click the **Margins tab** and under **Center on page**, select **Horizontally**. Click the **Header/Footer tab**, and then click the **Custom Footer** button. With the insertion point positioned in the **Left section**, click the **File Name** button. Click **OK** twice.

17. Click to select the **Sheet1 tab**, hold down Ctrl, and then click the **Sheet2 tab** and the **Sheet3 tab**. With the three sheets selected, display the **Edit** menu, and then click **Delete Sheet**.

18. On the Standard toolbar, click the **Save** button, and then click the **Print Preview** button to see the worksheet as it will print. Compare your worksheet with Figure 5.60. Click the **Print** button, and then click **OK**. Close the file, saving changes if prompted to do so.

End You have completed Project 5D

Project 5E—Atlanta Expenses

Objectives: *Organize and Format Worksheets, Create and Modify a 3-D Pie Chart, and Print a Chart.*

Ben Ham, the administrative director for the Greater Atlanta Job Fair, has created a worksheet showing the income and expenses for the 2004 Atlanta Job Fair. In the following Performance Assessment, you will create a pie chart that shows the percentage that each expense represents out of the total for this fair. Your completed worksheet will look similar to the one shown in Figure 5.61. You will save your workbook as *5E_Atlanta_Expenses_Firstname_Lastname.*

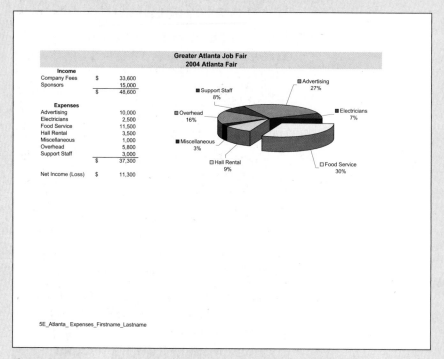

Figure 5.61

1. **Start** Excel. On the Standard toolbar, click the **Open** button. Navigate to the location where the student files for this textbook are stored. Locate and open **e05E_Atlanta_Expenses**.

2. From the **File** menu, click **Save As**. In the **Save As** dialog box, use the **Save in arrow** to navigate to the location where you are storing your files for this chapter. In the **File name** box, type **5E_Atlanta_Expenses_ Firstname_Lastname** Click the **Save** button.

3. Select the range **A9:B15**. On the Standard toolbar, click the **Chart Wizard** button. In Step 1 of the **Chart Wizard**, under **Chart type**, click **Pie**. Under **Chart sub-type**, in the first row, click the second option—**Pie with 3-D visual effect**. Click the **Finish** button. Recall that you can click **Finish** after you have selected the chart type, and then make modifications using the various charting tools.

(Project 5E–Atlanta Expenses continues on the next page)

(Project 5E–Atlanta Expenses continued)

4. Drag the chart to the right of the worksheet data, placing the left edge of the chart in the middle of **column C** and the top edge of the chart at the top of **row 3**. Using the lower right sizing handle, drag to expand the chart until the lower right corner of the chart is at the lower right corner of cell **K18**.

5. From the **Chart** menu, click **Chart Options**. In the **Chart Options** dialog box, click the **Legend tab** and clear the **Show legend** check box. Click the **Data Labels tab**, and under **Label Contains**, select the **Category name** and **Percentage** check boxes. On the lower left of the dialog box, click as needed to select both the **Legend key** check box and the **Show leader lines** check box. Click **OK** to close the dialog box.

6. From the **Chart** menu, click **3-D View**. In the **3-D View** dialog box, click the **counterclockwise rotation arrow**—the one on the right—three times, until the rotation box displays *330*. Click **OK**. On the Standard toolbar, click the **Save** button.

7. On the Chart toolbar, click the **Chart Objects arrow**, and then click **Plot Area**. A patterned border displays around the pie. Point to the lower left sizing handle and drag down and to the left to expand the plot area to align with the middle of **column E**. Use the upper right sizing handle to expand the plot area to align with the right edge of **column I**.

8. On the Chart toolbar, click the **Chart Objects arrow**, and then click **Series 1 Data Labels**. On the Formatting toolbar, click the **Font Size arrow**, and then click **10**.

9. Click the data label **Support Staff**. A patterned border displays around the label to indicate that it is selected. Drag the **Support Staff** label away from the pie slightly to display the leader line. Continue around the pie and drag each label out from the pie to display the leader line.

10. Click the pie, and then click the **Food Service** data marker—the yellow pie piece. Drag the **Food Service** slice away from the pie about 1/2 inch. Use Figure 5.61 as a reference.

11. Click cell **A1**. On the Formatting toolbar, click the **Merge and Center** button to unmerge this heading. Select cells **A1:K1**, and then click the **Merge and Center** button again to center the title over the worksheet and the chart. Repeat these actions to merge and center cell **A2** over cells **A2:K2**.

12. At the bottom of the worksheet, right-click the sheet tab **2004 Atlanta Fair**. From the shortcut menu, click **Tab Color**. In the **Format Tab Color** dialog box, in the third row, click the sixth color—**Light Blue**—and then click **OK**.

(Project 5E–Atlanta Expenses continues on the next page)

(Project 5E–Atlanta Expenses continued)

13. Click **Sheet1**, hold down [Shift] and click **Sheet3**. You can select a contiguous group of sheets using the [Shift] key. From the **Edit** menu, click **Delete Sheet**. The three empty sheets are deleted, and the 2004 Atlanta Fair sheet displays on your screen.

14. From the **File** menu, click **Page Setup**. Click the **Page tab**, and under **Orientation**, click **Landscape**. Click the **Header/Footer tab**, and then click the **Custom Footer** button. With the insertion point positioned in the **Left section**, click the **File Name** button. Click **OK** twice.

15. Right-click the white **Chart Area**. From the shortcut menu, click **Format Chart Area**. In the **Format Chart Area** dialog box, click the **Patterns tab**. Under **Border**, click **None**, and then click **OK**. The border surrounding the chart is removed.

16. On the Standard toolbar, click the **Save** button, and then click the **Print Preview** button to see the worksheet as it will print. Compare your worksheet with Figure 5.61. Click the **Print** button, and then click **OK**. Close the file, saving changes if prompted to do so.

End You have completed Project 5E

Project 5F—Communities

Objective: *Create a Diagram.*

Michael Augustino, executive director, has asked the marketing department for a diagram that shows all the locations where job fairs are held in the greater Atlanta area. In the following Performance Assessment, you will create a radial diagram. Your completed diagram will look similar to the one shown in Figure 5.62. You will save your workbook as *5F_Communities_Firstname_Lastname.*

1. Start Excel. In a new worksheet, in cell **A1** type **Communities We Serve** and press [Enter].

2. Select the range **A1:M1** and click the **Merge and Center** button. Change the **Font Size** to **24** pt., the **Font Color** to **Aqua**—the third row, fifth color of the **Font Color** palette—and then apply **Bold**.

3. On the Standard toolbar, click the **Save** button. In the **Save As** dialog box, navigate to the location where you are storing your files for this chapter. In the **File name** box, type **5F_Communities_Firstname_Lastname** and then click the **Save** button.

4. From the **Insert** menu, click **Diagram**. In the **Diagram Gallery** dialog box, in the first row, click the third diagram—**Radial Diagram**—and then click **OK**.

(Project 5F–Communities continues on the next page)

(Project 5F–Communities continued)

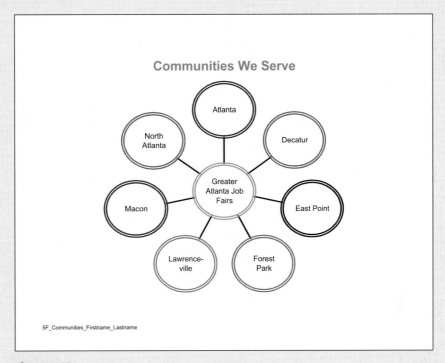

Figure 5.62

5. Point to the patterned border around the diagram. When the four-way **move pointer** displays, drag the diagram so that the top edge of the diagram outline is on the lower edge of **row 2** and the center sizing handle is positioned under the **column G** heading. If the Diagram toolbar is not docked at the top of your screen, drag it to a location where it is not blocking your view of the diagram.

6. Click in the circle at the top of the diagram, and type **Atlanta** Click in the center circle, and type **Greater Atlanta Job Fairs** The text wraps to three lines in the circle. Click in the circle on the lower left, and type **Macon** and in the circle on the lower right, type **Decatur**

7. On the Diagram toolbar, click the **Insert Shape** button. In the new circle, type **East Point** Click the **Insert Shape** button again and, in the new circle, type **Forest Park** Add another circle and type **Lawrenceville** and then add the last circle and type **North Atlanta** Seven total circles are around the perimeter. You will adjust the spacing of *Lawrenceville* later.

8. Alphabetically going clockwise, the *Macon* circle is out of order. Click the **Macon** circle, and then on the Diagram toolbar, click the **Move Shape Backward** button one time.

9. On the Diagram toolbar, click the **AutoFormat** button. From the **Diagram Style Gallery**, under **Select a Diagram Style**, click **Double Outline**, and then click **OK**.

(Project 5F–Communities continues on the next page)

(Project 5F–Communities continued)

10. Drag the right-middle sizing handle to the right edge of **column K**. Drag the left-middle sizing handle to the left edge of **column C**. Scroll down as needed, and use the lower-middle sizing handle and drag the outline to the top of **row 35**.

11. Lawrenceville does not fit on one line at this size font. Click between the *e* and *v* in *Lawrenceville* and type a hyphen so that *ville* wraps to a second line. Refer to Figure 5.62.

12. Click outside of the diagram so that it is not selected. From the **File** menu, click **Page Setup**. Click the **Page tab** and under **Orientation**, click **Landscape**. Click the **Margins tab** and under **Center on page**, click both **Horizontally** and **Vertically**. Click the **Header/Footer tab**, and then click the **Custom Footer** button. With the insertion point positioned in the **Left section**, click the **File Name** button. Click **OK** twice.

13. On the Standard toolbar, click the **Save** button, and then click the **Print Preview** button to see the worksheet as it will print. Compare your worksheet with Figure 5.63. Click the **Print** button, and then click **OK**. Close the file, saving changes if prompted to do so.

 You have completed Project 5F

Project 5G — 2004 Results

Objectives: *Create a Column Chart, Modify a Column Chart, Print a Chart, and Organize and Format Worksheets.*

Janice Dawson, employer coordinator, has gathered the figures for attendance and hires at the 2004 Job Fair and wants a chart to show the relative relationship of hires to attendance. In the following Performance Assessment, you will create a column chart and then change it to a bar chart. A bar chart is used for comparisons in a manner similar to a column chart, but the data is displayed in horizontal bars rather than in vertical columns. Your completed worksheet will look similar to the one shown in Figure 5.63. You will save your workbook as *5G_2004_Results_Firstname_Lastname.*

1. On the Standard toolbar, click the **Open** button. Navigate to the location where the student files for this textbook are stored. Locate and open **e05G_2004_Results**.

2. From the **File** menu, open the **Save As** dialog box. Navigate to the location where you are storing your files for this chapter. In the **File name** box, using your own name, type **5G_2004_Results_Firstname_Lastname** and then click the **Save** button.

(Project 5G–2004 Results continues on the next page)

(Project 5G–2004 Results continued)

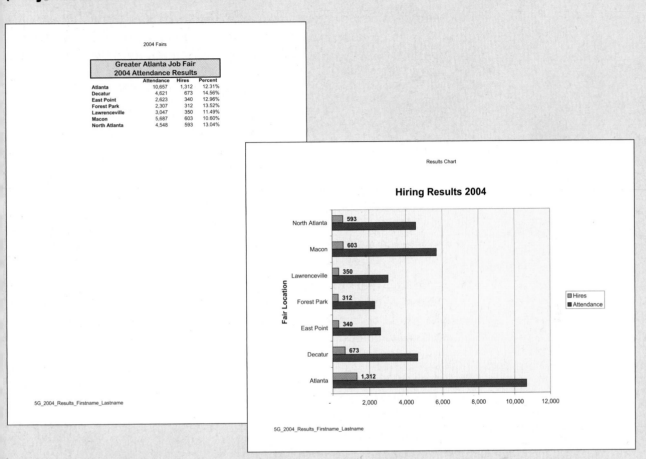

Figure 5.63

3. Select the range **A3:C10** and on the Standard toolbar, click the **Chart Wizard** button. With the **Column** Chart type selected, under **Chart sub-type**, in the first row click the second sub-type—**Stacked Column**—and then click **Next**.

4. In Step 2 of the **Chart Wizard**, click **Next**. In Step 3 of the **Chart Wizard**, click the **Titles tab**, and in the **Chart title** box, type Hiring Results 2004 In the **Category (X) axis** box, type Fair Location and then click **Next**.

5. In Step 4 of the **Chart Wizard**, be sure the **As object in** option button is selected, and then click **Finish**.

6. After a chart is created, you can change its location. Display the **Chart** menu and click **Location**. Click the **As new sheet** option button, and click **OK**.

7. Display the **Chart** menu, and click **Chart Type**. In the **Chart Type** dialog box, click **Bar**, and then under **Chart sub-type**, in the first row click the first sub-type—**Clustered Bar**. Click **OK**. The category axis displays along the left side of the chart and the value axis along the lower edge of the chart. On the Standard toolbar, click the **Save** button.

(Project 5G–2004 Results continues on the next page)

(Project 5G–2004 Results continued)

8. Double-click the category axis title **Fair Location**. In the **Format Axis Title** dialog box, click the **Alignment tab**. Under **Orientation**, drag the red diamond to the top of the diagram until **90** displays in the **Degrees** box. Alternatively, type **90** in the Degrees box. Click the **Font tab**, change the **Size** to **14**, and then click **OK**.

9. Click the **Category Axis** on the left side of the chart, and then, from the Formatting toolbar, change the **Font Size** to **12** pt. Click the **Value Axis** and change the **Font Size** to **12** pt. Change the **Font Size** for the **Chart Title** to **20** pt. and the **Legend** to **12** pt.

10. Double-click the **Plot Area**. In the **Format Plot Area** dialog box, under **Area**, in the sixth row, click the third color—**Ivory**—and then click **OK**. Double-click any of the blue bars to open the **Format Data Series** dialog box. Click the **Patterns tab**. Under **Area**, in the sixth row, click the seventh color—**Ocean Blue**—and then click **OK**.

11. From the Chart toolbar, click the **Chart Objects arrow**, click **Series "Hires"**, and then click the **Format Data Series** button. In the displayed dialog box, click the **Patterns tab**, and under **Area**, in the sixth row, click the sixth color—**Coral**. Click the **Data Labels tab**, and under **Label Contains**, select the **Value** check box. Click **OK**.

12. On the Chart toolbar, click the **Chart Objects arrow**, and then click **"Hires" Data Labels**. Using the Formatting toolbar, change the **Font Size** to **12** and click **Bold**.

13. Change the **Chart 1** sheet name to **Results Chart** Change the name of **Sheet1** to 2004 Fairs Select **Sheet2** and **Sheet3** and from the **Edit** menu, click **Delete Sheet**. Drag the **2004 Fairs** sheet to the left of the **Results Chart** sheet.

14. With the **2004 Fairs sheet tab** selected, display the **Page Setup** dialog box. Click the **Margins tab** and select the **Horizontally** check box. Click the **Header/Footer tab**, and then click the **Custom Header** button. In the **Center section**, insert the **Tab name**. Click the **Custom Footer** button. With the insertion point positioned in the **Left section**, click the **File Name** button. Click **OK** twice.

15. Click the Results Chart sheet tab. Create a **Custom Footer**, and in the **Left section**, insert the **File Name**.

16. On the Standard toolbar, click the **Save** button. Select both worksheets (use the Select All Sheets command), and then click the **Print Preview** button to see the worksheets as they will print. Compare your worksheets with Figure 5.63. Click the **Print** button, and then click **OK**. Close the file, saving changes if prompted to do so.

End You have completed Project 5G

Mastery Assessments

Project 5H — Profit

Objectives: *Create and Modify a Line Chart, Print a Chart, and Organize and Format Worksheets.*

Ben Ham, the administrative manager, has requested a chart showing the profit from each of the job fairs over the past five years. In the following Mastery Assessment, you will create and modify a line chart using multiple lines to show the trend in profit by fair. Your completed worksheets will look similar to Figure 5.64. You will save your workbook as *5H_Profit_Firstname_Lastname.*

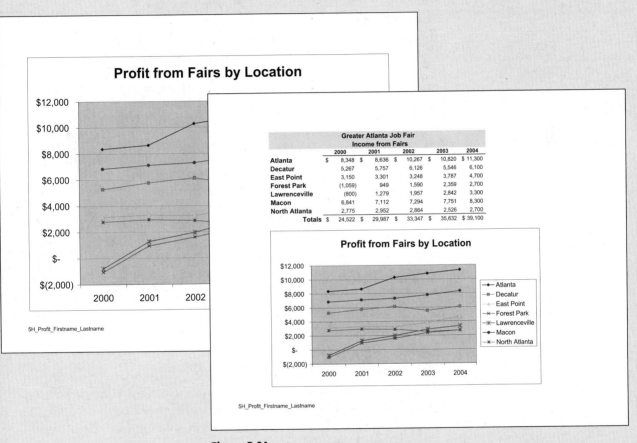

Figure 5.64

1. On the Standard toolbar, click the **Open** button. Navigate to the location where the student files for this textbook are stored. Locate and open **e05H_Profit**.

2. From the **File** menu, open the **Save As** dialog box. Navigate to the location where you are storing your files for this chapter. In the **File name** box, using your own information, type **5H_Profit_Firstname_Lastname** and then click the **Save** button.

3. Select the range **A3:F10**, and start the **Chart Wizard**. In Step 1 of the wizard, select a **Line chart** with markers displayed at each data value.

(Project 5H–Profit continues on the next page)

(Project 5H–Profit continued)

4. In Step 2, format the data range in **Rows**. In Step 3, insert **Profit from Fairs by Location** as the chart title. Display the chart as an object in the worksheet.

5. Position the upper left corner of the chart in cell **A13** and the lower right corner in cell **H33**. Save your work.

6. Change the **Font Size** of the **Chart Title** to **18** pt. If necessary, change the **Font Size** of the **Value Axis** to **12** pt., the **Category Axis** to **12** pt., and the **Legend** to **12** pt.

7. Click the **Value Axis** and open the **Format Axis** dialog box. Click the **Scale tab**, if necessary, select the **Category (X) axis** check box, and then, in the **Crosses at** box, type **-2000** Two of the figures in this chart had losses, so it is necessary to change the number for value (x) axis to cross the category (y) axis to a negative number. This also places the category titles under the plot area at the edge of the category axis.

8. Click the **North Atlanta** data line. On the Chart toolbar, click the **Format Data Series** button. Under **Line**, change the **Color** to **Orange**. Under **Marker**, click the **Style arrow**, and click the fifth option. Change the **Foreground** to **Green**. Click **OK**. Select the **Forest Park** data line and open the **Format Data Series** dialog box. Change the **Line** color to **Bright Green**, change the **Foreground Marker** color to **Blue**, and then click **OK**. Select the **Lawrenceville** data line and open the **Format Data Series** dialog box. Change the **Line** color to **Light Blue**, change the **Foreground Marker** color to **Red**, and then click **OK**.

9. With the chart selected, click the **Print Preview** button. On the Print Preview toolbar, click the **Setup** button. In the **Page Setup** dialog box, click the **Header/Footer tab**, and then click the **Custom Footer** button. With the insertion point positioned in the **Left section**, click the **File Name** button. Click **OK** twice. On the Print Preview toolbar, click the **Print** button, and then click **OK**.

10. Be sure the chart is not selected. Double-click the **Sheet1 tab**, type **Profit** and press Enter. Right-click the **Profit sheet tab** and click **Tab Color**. In the sixth row, click the second color—**Plum**. Select and delete **Sheet2** and **Sheet3**.

11. Be sure the chart is not selected, and then click the **Print Preview** button. The worksheet and chart will not print completely in portrait orientation. On the Print Preview toolbar, click the **Setup** button. Click the **Page tab**, and then click **Landscape**. Click the **Margins tab**, and then select the **Horizontally** check box. Click the **Header/Footer tab** and insert the **File Name** in the **Left section** of the footer. Click **OK** twice, and then click the **Print** button.

12. On the Standard toolbar, click the **Save** button and close the file.

End You have completed Project 5H

Project 5I—Expenses

Objectives: *Create a Column Chart, Modify a Column Chart, and Print a Chart.*

Executive Director Michael Augustino has requested a chart comparing direct expenses of the fairs. In the following Mastery Assessment, you will create a chart to compare the direct expenses for the fairs. Your completed worksheet will look similar to the one shown in Figure 5.65. You will save your workbook as *5I_Expenses_Firstname_Lastname*.

	Atlanta	Decatur	East Point	Forest Park	Lawrenceville	Macon	North Atlanta
		Greater Atlanta Job Fair					
		2004 Regional Expenses					
Advertising	10,000	3,000	2,500	2,000	2,500	3,500	2,500
Electricians	2,500	1,000	350	600	800	750	700
Food Service	11,500	4,000	3,000	2,500	2,800	3,250	3,500
Hall Rental	3,500	1,000	800	500	1,000	1,200	1,100
Miscellaneous	1,000	200	200	200	200	200	200
Overhead	5,800	1,200	1,200	1,200	1,200	1,200	1,200
Support Staff	3,000	500	500	500	500	500	500
$	37,300	$ 10,900	$ 8,550	$ 7,500	$ 9,000	$ 10,600	$ 9,700

5I_Expenses_Firstname_Lastname

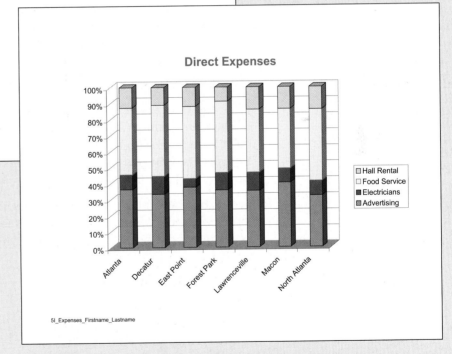

Figure 5.65

(Project 5I–Expenses continues on the next page)

(Project 5I–Expenses continued)

1. On the Standard toolbar, click the **Open** button. Navigate to the location where the student files for this textbook are stored. Locate and open **e05I_Expenses**.

2. From the **File** menu, open the **Save As** dialog box. Navigate to the location where you are storing your files for this chapter. In the **File name** box, using your own name, type **5H_Expenses_Firstname_Lastname** and then click the **Save** button.

3. Select the range **A3:H7** and start the **Chart Wizard**. This range accounts for the direct expenses for each fair. Create a **Column** chart using the **100% stacked column with a 3-D visual effect** chart type.

4. Accept the defaults in Step 2. In Step 3, insert **Direct Expenses** as the chart title. In Step 4, click the **As new sheet** option button. A 100% stacked chart lets you compare the relative expense category by location. This type of chart can be used in place of a pie chart when you want to compare parts of the whole—in this instance, direct expenses—across several categories—fair locations.

5. Change the font size of the chart title to **22** and the font color to **Red**. Change the font size of the value axis, the category axis, and the legend to **14**. Save your changes.

6. Click the **Category Axis**. On the Chart toolbar, click the **Angle Counterclockwise** button so that all the location names display.

7. Click the **Chart Objects arrow**, and then click **Walls**. Click the **Format Walls** button. Under **Area**, click **None**, and then click **OK**. The wall color is removed. Right-click the ivory **Food Service** series and click **Format Data Series**. Click the **Patterns tab** if necessary, and under **Border**, click the **Color arrow**, and then click **Red**. Click **OK**.

8. From the **View** menu, click **Header and Footer**. Create a custom footer with the file name in the **Left section**. Display the **Expenses** worksheet, and add a custom footer with the file name in the **Left section**.

9. In the **Expenses** worksheet, change cell **D5** to **350** and cell **E5** to **600** Save your changes.

10. Print both sheets. Close the workbook.

End You have completed Project 5I

Project 5J — Organization Chart

Objective: *Create a Diagram.*

The Greater Atlanta Job Fair has added a new department responsible for expanding to new markets in the southeastern United States. Executive Director Michael Augustino has drafted an outline for a new organizational structure and has requested that it be entered in the computer so that it can be distributed. In this Problem Solving exercise, you will use the diagram feature in Excel to create an organizational chart. You will save your workbook as *5J_Organizational_Chart_Firstname_Lastname*.

1. Open a new workbook. Use the **Diagram Gallery** to select the **Organizational Chart** diagram.

2. In the top box, type **Michael Augustino Executive Director**. The text will wrap within the box.

3. In the three subordinate boxes, enter the following names and titles:

   Janice Dawson Employer Coordinator

   Ben Ham Administrative Manager

   Derek Michaels Development Manager

4. Click the box containing **Janice Dawson**, and then click the **Insert Shape** button. In the new subordinate box, type **Yolanda Strickland**

5. Add a subordinate box to Ben Ham, and type **Janna Sharma** in the new box. Add a second subordinate box to Ben Ham, and type **Joseph Sorokin**

6. Save the file with your other files for this chapter as **5J_Organizational_Chart_Firstname_Lastname**

7. Use the resizing handles to expand the organizational chart area. Select the text in each box, and change the font to **14** pt. or the largest size that will fit in that box.

8. Click the **AutoFormat** button, and select a style of your choice. Adjust the font size as needed to ensure that the names and titles are fully displayed.

9. Enter an appropriate title in the first cell of the worksheet. Increase the font size to **20** pt., and center it over the organizational chart. In the footer area, in the left section insert the **File name**. Change the page orientation to **Landscape**.

10. Save your changes, print the worksheet, and then close the file.

 You have completed Project 5J ───────────────

Project 5K — Revenue

Objectives: *Create and Modify a 3-D Pie Chart, Print a Chart, and Organize and Manage Worksheets.*

The Greater Atlanta Job Fair needs a chart that will show the profit contribution of each of the fairs to the total revenue stream. In this Problem Solving exercise, you will create and modify a 3-D chart to display the amount and percentage each location has contributed to total revenues for 2004. You will save your workbook as *5K_Revenue_Firstname_Lastname*.

1. Locate and open the file **e5K_Revenue** Save it with your other files as **5K_Revenue_Firstname_Lastname**

2. Select the cells containing the location names, and using Ctrl, select the cells containing the net income (loss) figures for each location. (Hint: Do not include the row labels.)

3. Use the Chart Wizard to create a 3-D pie chart. Include an appropriate chart title, and save the chart on a separate sheet. Name the chart sheet **Revenue Distribution** and add a tab color of your choice. Name Sheet1 **2004 Results** and add a tab color.

4. Add data labels that include value and percentage. Drag the data labels away from the pie so that the leader lines display. Place the legend at the bottom of the chart. Increase the font size of the chart title to **20** pt., the data labels to **12** pt., and the legend to **12** pt.

5. Display the **3-D View** dialog box, and rotate the chart so that the largest piece is in the lower left (front) section of the pie. Pull this pie piece away from the pie and change its color to **Teal**. Change the two pieces on either side to a lighter color for contrast.

6. Add the file name to the left section of the footer for both the worksheets. Set the data worksheet to print in landscape orientation. Save your changes, and close the file.

End You have completed Project 5K

On the Internet

Graph Styles and Theory

In this chapter, you examined three basic types of charts. Understanding which type of chart to use to display the data appropriately takes some practice. Graph theory is a branch of mathematics that studies the use of graphs—charts in Excel terms. Some interesting Web sites are available to help you better understand different chart options and the type of data that can be illustrated graphically.

1. Open your browser, and in the address box type: **http://www.corda. com/examples/graph_styles**

2. Examine the different graph styles explained and illustrated on this Web site.

3. In the left panel, click **Examples**. The Corda examples Web page displays.

4. Under the **PopChart+OptiMap 5**, click **Weather Example**. This page shows several graph types used to display current weather conditions for a specific location.

5. Replace the displayed postal code with your postal code, and press Enter. Graphs related to the weather in your area are displayed. If necessary, scroll the page to see all the graphs.

6. Explore this Web site to discover some of the other uses for charts. When you are finished, close your browser.

Display Data on Two Scales

Sometimes you will have two data series where the range of numbers varies widely, such as population of a geographic area and the number in that population who are customers; or data types that are mixed, such as quantity and price. To display this type of information in a chart, you need two scales (values axes)—one on the left and one on the right.

1. **Start** Excel. In the **Type a question for help** box, type **Display data on two scales** Scroll through the list of topics that displays in the **Search Results** task pane.

2. From this list of help topics, click **Add a second axis** and read the results.

3. From the **Search Results** task pane, click the topic **About combination charts**. Read this topic, and then, at the top of the Microsoft Office Excel Help pane, click the **Print** button. Close the **Help** task panes.

4. Start a new worksheet. In range **A2:A11**, enter the years from 1996 through 2005. Select range **A2:A11** and use the **Format Cells** dialog box to format this range as **Text**, not numbers. (Note: Cell **A1** should be empty.)

5. In cell **B1**, type **Population** In cell **C1**, type **Customers** In range **B2:B11**, enter random numbers ranging from 1 million to 5 million. In range **C2:C11**, enter random numbers ranging from 10,000 to 100,000. Format the numbers with commas and no decimals.

6. Select the range **A1:C11** and click the **Chart Wizard** button. Click the **Custom Types tab** and select one of the two combination charts that uses two axes. If necessary, use the Help information to guide you through this process.

7. Complete the rest of the steps in the Chart Wizard to see your results.

8. Close the file without saving the results, and close Excel.

6

chaptersix

Working with Templates, Large Worksheets, and Other File Formats

In this chapter, you will: complete these projects **and** practice these skills.

Project 6A **Using Excel Templates**	**Objective** • Use Excel Templates
Project 6B **Working with Large Worksheets and Sharing Worksheets**	**Objectives** • Work with a Large Worksheet • Prepare a Worksheet to Share with Others
Project 6C **Using AutoFormats, Styles, Drawing Tools and the Research Feature**	**Objectives** • Enhance Worksheets with AutoFormats and Styles • Use Drawing Tools and Use the Research Feature
Project 6D **Using Goal Seek**	**Objective** • Use Goal Seek

Lake Michigan City College

Lake Michigan City College is located along the lakefront of Chicago—one of the country's most exciting cities. The college serves its large and diverse student body and makes positive contributions to the community through relevant curricula, partnerships with businesses and nonprofit organizations, and learning experiences that allow students to be full participants in the global community. The college offers three associate degrees in 20 academic areas, adult education programs, and continuing education offerings on campus, at satellite locations, and online.

© Getty Images, Inc.

Working with Templates, Large Worksheets, and Other File Formats

In this chapter, you will use an Excel template to report expenses, work with a large worksheet, save a worksheet as a Web page, and save worksheets in other file formats for easy transportation of data. You will practice creating and applying styles to a worksheet and use the AutoFormat feature to format a worksheet. You will add drawing objects to a worksheet and insert text using the Research feature. Finally, you will use the Goal Seek function to determine the interest rate necessary to reach a desired investment goal.

Project 6A **Expense Report**

Excel offers several predefined templates that can be used for common financial reports such as an expense report, time card, balance sheet, sales invoice, or purchase order.

Clarence Krasnow, Director of Resource Development, needs to submit his expense report for the month of September, which must include the advance he received to cover expenses related to a conference he attended in Denver. In Activity 6.1, you will open and complete an Excel template for reporting expenses. Your completed worksheet will look similar to Figure 6.1. You will save your workbook as *6A_Expense_Report_ Firstname_Lastname.*

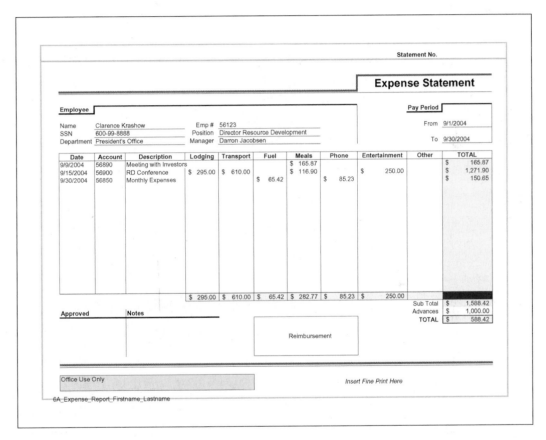

Figure 6.1
Project 6A—Expense Report

Objective 1
Use Excel Templates

A ***template*** is a workbook used as a pattern for creating other workbooks. Excel has several templates that you can use as the basis for creating common financial forms such as expense reports, time cards, and balance sheets. Templates are preformatted and have built-in formulas for performing calculations based on the data that you enter. The cells that contain the formulas are ***locked***, which prevents you from changing the formulas in the template.

Activity 6.1 Using an Excel Template

To open an Excel template, click the New command on the File menu. Alternatively, on the Getting Started task pane, click *Create a new workbook*, which will display the New Workbook task pane. From the New Workbook task pane, you can locate templates that are already on your computer or locate additional templates from the Web.

1 Start Excel. On the menu bar, click **File**, and then from the displayed list, click **New**.

The New Workbook task pane displays. From this task pane, you can locate templates from your computer or from the Web.

2 In the **New Workbook** task pane, under **Templates**, click **On my computer**. In the displayed **Templates** dialog box, click the **Spreadsheet Solutions tab**.

Several template options are available, as shown in Figure 6.2. The templates that display on your screen may not match the figure exactly.

Template options —

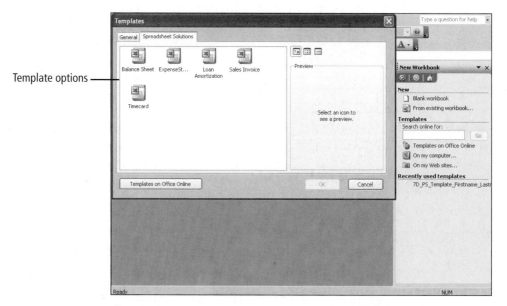

Figure 6.2

3 From the displayed templates, click **ExpenseStatement**, and then click **OK**.

The Expense Statement workbook opens at 85% zoom.

4 Change the zoom if necessary so that you can see the entire width of the worksheet on the screen, and then examine the form.

This template is used to report expenses. Notice that there is a bordered rectangle in the space next to *Name*. This is the active cell and the position at which you will begin entering data. Column labels are included in the body of the form—*Date, Description, Lodging,* and so forth. The ivory shaded areas contain formulas for calculating totals, and the cells there are locked so that you cannot enter anything in these areas or accidentally delete the formulas. See Figure 6.3.

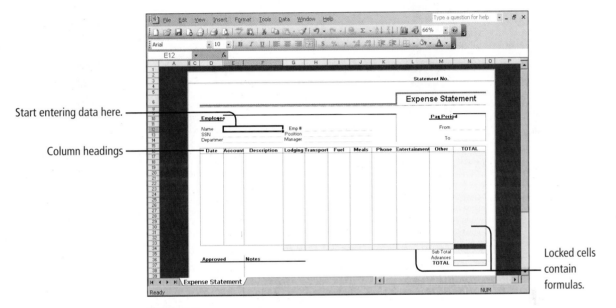

Start entering data here.

Column headings

Locked cells contain formulas.

Figure 6.3

5 Type **Clarence Krasnow** and press Tab.

The employee name is entered and the next *field*—a predefined area for a specific type of data—becomes the active cell. In this field, you will enter the employee number. In a form like this expense statement, categories of information are designated as fields, such as name, employee number, and social security number. Fields are useful because the information in a field can be gathered together in a database or used to create a report of all employees who have completed an expense report in a particular reporting period.

6 In the **Emp #** field, type **56123** and then press [Tab] to move to the **From**—beginning date—field. Notice the ScreenTip that displays with a message to tell you what information belongs in this field, as shown in Figure 6.4.

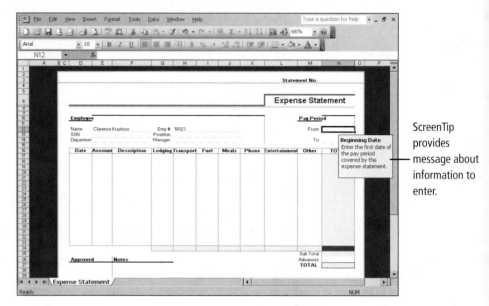

ScreenTip provides message about information to enter.

Figure 6.4

7 Type **9/1/04** and press [Tab] to move to the next field. In the **SSN** (Social Security Number) field, type **600-99-8888** and then press [Tab] to move to the **Position** field. Continue entering the data in the upper portion of the form as shown in the list that follows. If you make an error, hold down [Shift] and press [Tab] to move back one field at a time.

Position	**Director Resource Development**
Department	**President's Office**
Manager	**Darron Jacobsen**
To	**9/30/04**

The data for the upper portion of the form is complete.

8 If necessary, press [Tab] to move to the active cell under *Date.* Enter the information that follows. As you enter information for the expenses, not all categories or fields will be completed for each date. Press [Tab] as necessary to skip empty fields.

Date	Account	Description	Lodging	Transport	Fuel	Meals	Phone	Entertainment	Other
9/9/2004	56890	Meeting with Investors				165.87			
9/15/2004	56900	RD Conference	295.00	610.00		116.90		250.00	
9/30/2004	56850	Monthly Expenses			65.42		85.23		

Notice that as you enter monetary values, the ivory shaded areas at the right and end of the columns display the totals of the columns or rows. Compare your screen with Figure 6.5.

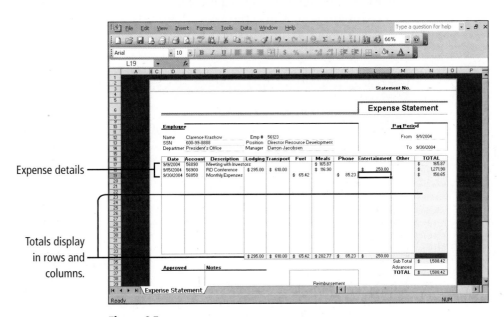

Expense details

Totals display in rows and columns.

Figure 6.5

9. From the **File** menu, click **Save As**. In the **Save As** dialog box, use the **Save in arrow** to navigate to the location where you are storing your files for this chapter, creating a new folder for Chapter 6 if you want to do so. In the **File name** box, delete the existing text and type **6A_Expense_Report_Firstname_Lastname** Click the **Save** button.

10. Try to click a cell in the ivory shaded areas on the Expense Statement report.

Notice that you cannot make any cell in the shaded areas the active cell. The cells are locked and may not be selected, thus protecting the formulas in these cells.

11 In the lower right side of the form, click in the white area to the right of *Advances*, read the displayed ScreenTip, type **1000** and then press [Enter]. Click in an empty white cell to close the ScreenTip that blocks the view of the total area.

The total amount is adjusted to reflect the advance that was given to this employee prior to the trip to the RD Conference. You can see that Krasnow needs to be reimbursed $588.42 for expenses.

12 From the **View** menu, click **Header and Footer**. Click the **Custom Footer** button. With the insertion point positioned in the **Left section**, click the **File name** button. Click **OK** twice.

13 On the Standard toolbar, click the **Save** button, and then click the **Print Preview** button to see the worksheet as it will print. Compare your worksheet with Figure 6.6. Click **Print**, and then click **OK**. Close the file, saving changes if prompted to do so.

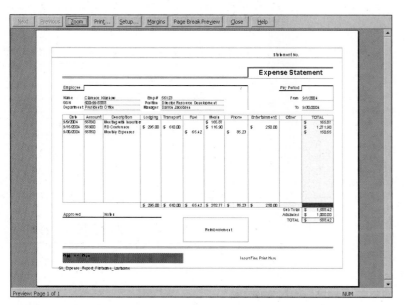

Figure 6.6

End You have completed Project 6A

Project 6B **Class Schedule**

Worksheets are often wider and longer than a single screen can display. Techniques for navigating in a large worksheet are necessary to help locate and update information. When worksheets are shared with other people, it is sometimes necessary to save the files in different formats to accommodate the needs of others.

When you work with large worksheets, you can use various techniques to help you navigate the worksheet and quickly find the information you need. For example, you can sort specific rows, columns, or ranges of cells in a different order or look only at specific information. You can also view two worksheets at the same time. Samantha Pruett, coordinator of the computer courses for the Business division, needs to update some records and determine which classes still need instructors for the fall semester. In Activities 6.2 through 6.16, you will work with a large worksheet that lists the class schedule for the Business Office Systems and Computer Information Systems departments at Lake Michigan City College. Your completed worksheets will look similar to Figure 6.7. You will save your workbook as *6B_Class_Schedule_Firstname_Lastname.*

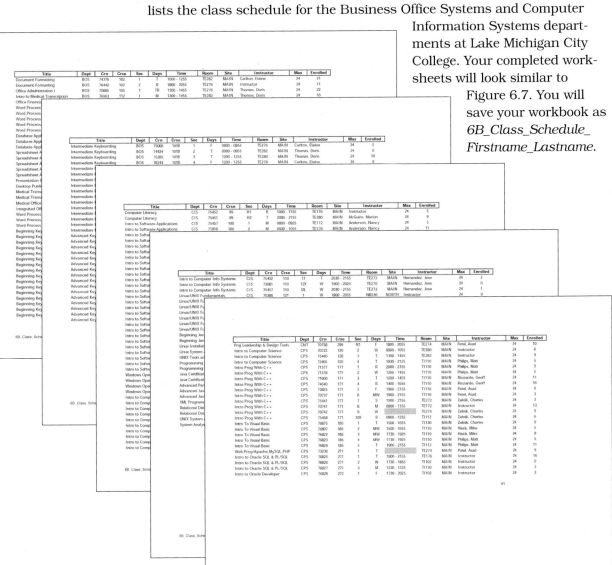

Figure 6.7
Project 6B—Class Schedule

Objective 2
Work with a Large Worksheet

You cannot view all the columns and rows of a large worksheet on your screen at one time. Therefore, Excel provides features that help you control what is displayed on the screen and navigate the worksheet to locate information quickly. For example, you can hide columns, sort information by rows and columns, and *filter* the data—limit the data displayed to match a stated condition. The *Freeze Panes* command is especially useful because it sets the column and row headings so that they remain on the screen while you scroll up and down the rows and across the columns. Finally, the Find and Replace command locates information anywhere in your worksheet.

Activity 6.2 Freezing and Unfreezing Panes

In a large worksheet, if you scroll down more than 30 rows or scroll across beyond column O (the exact row number and column letter varies, depending upon your screen resolution), you will no longer see row 1 or column A, where identifying information about the data is usually typed. Viewing cells that have no identifying row or column headings makes it practically impossible to work with data in any meaningful way. Fortunately, the Freeze Panes command allows you to select one or more rows or columns and freeze (lock) them into place. The locked rows and columns become separate *panes*. A pane is a portion of a worksheet window bounded by and separated from other portions by vertical or horizontal bars.

1 Start Excel. On the Standard toolbar, click the **Open** button ⬚. Navigate to the location where the student files for this textbook are stored. Locate and open the file **e06B_Class_Schedule**.

2 From the **File** menu, click **Save As**. In the **Save As** dialog box, use the **Save in arrow** to navigate to the location where you are storing your files for this chapter. In the **File name** box, type **6B_Class_Schedule_ Firstname_Lastname** Click the **Save** button. Scroll through the worksheet to examine the data.

The worksheet lists the computer courses that are available for the fall semester at Lake Michigan City College. See Figure 6.8.

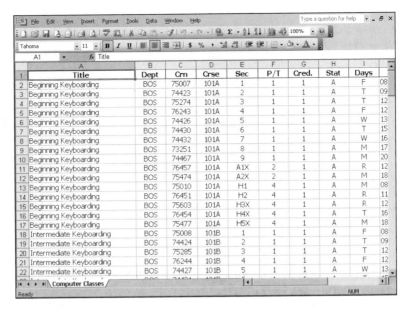

Figure 6.8

Note — Does Your Screen Look Different?

The amount of data that is displayed on your screen may be different than that shown in the figure. This is because of a difference in the resolution setting on your monitor. For newer monitors, the typical resolution setting is 1024×768 or higher. The figures in this book are shown at a resolution of 800×600, which displays fewer rows and columns at the same zoom setting.

3 Hold down Ctrl and press End to move to the last entry in the worksheet, cell **O170**. Notice that the column headings at the top and the course descriptions on the left are no longer in view, as shown in Figure 6.9.

You can see that working with data that has no identifying row and column headings makes it almost impossible to determine meaningful information from the displayed data.

Column headings do not display.

Course titles do not display.

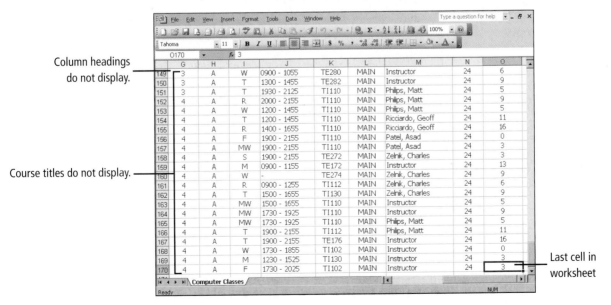

Last cell in worksheet

Figure 6.9

4 Hold down Ctrl and press Home to move to cell **A1** at the upper left corner of the worksheet.

5 Click cell **B2**. From the **Window** menu, click **Freeze Panes**.

A line displays along the right border of column A and across the lower border of row 1. All the row(s) above the selected cell and all the column(s) to the left of the selected cell are frozen on the screen and will remain on the screen when you scroll through the worksheet.

6 Hold down Ctrl and press End to move to the last entry in the worksheet. Notice that the column headings display in **row 1** and the course titles display in **column A** on the left, as shown in Figure 6.10.

Column headings display.

Course titles display.

Lines separate frozen row and column headings.

Last cell in worksheet

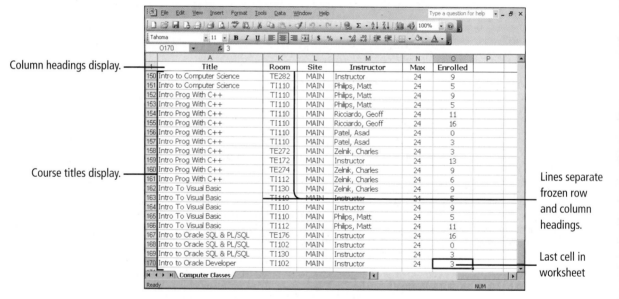

Figure 6.10

7 Hold down Ctrl and press Home again to move back to cell **B2**, the location of the Freeze Panes command, which now functions as the home cell for the worksheet. At the bottom of the window, on the horizontal scroll bar, click the **right scroll arrow** three times.

Columns B, C, and D scroll off the screen to the left, but the identifying information in column A still displays.

8 In the lower right corner of the window, click the **down scroll arrow** five times.

Rows 2 through 6 scroll off the screen, but the identifying information in row 1 still displays.

9 Display the **Window** menu and notice that the Freeze Panes command has changed to *Unfreeze Panes*. Click **Window** again to close the menu without removing the Freeze Panes command.

The Freeze Panes command is a toggle switch that is used to activate or deactivate the command.

Activity 6.3 Finding and Replacing Information

The *Find* command can search for and locate specific data each time it occurs in your worksheet. Excel finds the data you specify and moves the active cell to its location. The *Replace* command finds specific data and then replaces it with data that you specify. You can instruct Excel to stop at each cell containing the data to be replaced, at which point you can decide whether or not to make the replacement. Alternatively, you can instruct Excel to replace all occurrences without waiting for your input. In a worksheet that is too big to reliably scan visually, the Find and Replace commands help you confirm that you have found all instances of specific data. In this activity, you will use the Find and Replace commands to change all occurrences of the course number for the Windows Operating System class from 117 to 107.

1 Press Ctrl + Home to return to the top of the worksheet. Be sure cell **B2** (the home cell in the unfrozen portion of the worksheet) is the active cell. From the **Edit** menu, click **Find**. Alternatively, press Ctrl + F as the keyboard shortcut.

The Find and Replace dialog box displays. Here you can locate specific information and search the worksheet by row or column to find matching text.

2 In the **Find what** box, type **117** and then click **Find Next**. The first occurrence of *117* is located, and cell **D119** becomes the active cell. If necessary, click the title bar of the **Find and Replace** dialog box and drag it out of the way so that you can see cell **D119**.

You can see that the Find command is useful if you are looking for a specific piece of data in a large worksheet.

3 In the **Find and Replace** dialog box, click the **Replace tab**.

The dialog box expands, and the *Replace with* box displays.

4 In the **Replace with** box, type **107** and then click **Replace**.

The first occurrence of *117* is replaced with *107*, and the next occurrence of *117* is located, as shown in Figure 6.11.

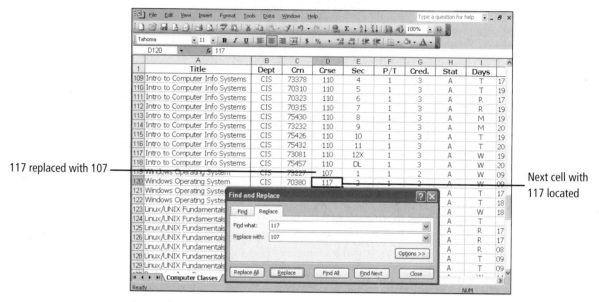

117 replaced with 107

Next cell with 117 located

Figure 6.11

5 In the **Find and Replace** dialog box, click **Replace All**.

A message box displays indicating that three instances of *117* have been found and replaced with *107*.

6 Click **OK** to acknowledge the message. In the **Find what** box, select **117**, and type **Applebee** In the **Replace with** box, select **107** and type **Applebee-Meyers** and then click **Find Next**.

The first occurrence of *Applebee* is located in cell M12. Before data can be replaced, you must first initiate the Find command.

7 Click **Replace All**.

A message box displays indicating that Excel has made eight replacements. Notice in cell M17 that the comma and first name of this instructor remain as part of the text in this cell. See Figure 6.12. Excel finds the data even if it is only part of a cell's contents.

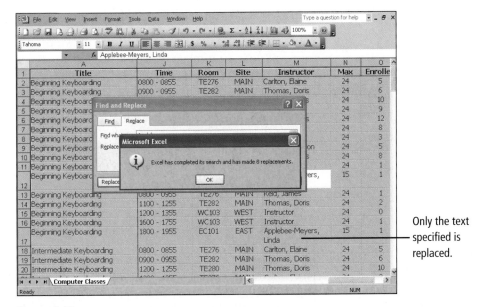

Only the text specified is replaced.

Figure 6.12

8 Click **OK** to acknowledge the message box, and then click **Close** in the **Find and Replace** dialog box.

The rows containing Applebee-Meyers expand, and the name wraps to a second line.

9 In the **column heading area**, drag the right border of **column M** to a width of **180 pixels**. Click the **Select All** box in the upper left corner of the worksheet (to the left of **column A** and above **row 1**). With the entire worksheet selected, display the **Format** menu, point to **Row**, and then click **AutoFit**.

The *Instructor* column expands to display the names without wrapping, and the rows readjust to the same height.

10 Press Ctrl + Home to cancel the selection of the worksheet and move to cell **B2**, the home cell in the unfrozen portion of the worksheet. On the Standard toolbar, click the **Save** button.

More Knowledge — Find and Replace Options

The Options button in the Find and Replace dialog box enables you to control the Find operation by defining specific characteristics. For example, you can specify a format for data that is bold and italic, and Excel will locate only cells that have that formatting. Or, you can match the case—uppercase or lower-case letters—or match only the entire content of cells. You can also search an entire workbook so that all matching cells are located throughout the entire workbook rather than on only a single worksheet.

Because Excel finds and replaces part of the content of a cell, it is important to be cautious when using the Replace All button so that you do not replace data unintentionally. If the number of changes seems too high, you can always click the Undo button, and then review each replacement before agreeing to the change.

Activity 6.4 Using the Go To Command

You can use the Go To command to move quickly to a specific cell or range of cells in a large worksheet. The Go To command can also be used to move to cells that have special characteristics, for example, to cells that are blank or to cells that contain constants (as opposed to formulas).

1 From the **Edit** menu, click **Go To**. Alternatively, press Ctrl + G to use the keyboard shortcut.

The Go To dialog box displays.

2 At the bottom of the **Go To** dialog box, click **Special**.

The Go To Special dialog box displays. You can use this dialog box to move to cells that contain the various special options listed. See Figure 6.13.

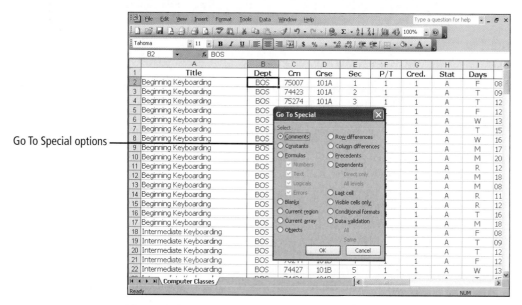

Go To Special options ——

Figure 6.13

3 In the first column, click the **Blanks** option button, and then click **OK**.

The blank cells in the *active area* of the worksheet are located, and the first blank cell displays on the screen as the active cell. The active area is the area of the worksheet that contains data or has contained data—it does not include any empty cells that have not been used in this worksheet. Cell J124 is missing the time for a Linux/UNIX class held on Tuesday.

4 On the Formatting toolbar, click the **Fill Color (Yellow)** button.

The missing information needs to be researched before a time can be entered, and the yellow fill color will help locate this cell later, when you have determined the correct time for the class.

5 Scroll down the screen and locate the other two cells identified as blank—**J148** and **J160**.

When you initiated the Go To command for Blank cells, Excel located and selected all blank cells in the active area. Thus, the formatting you applied to the first blank cell, yellow fill, was applied to all the selected cells. See Figure 6.14.

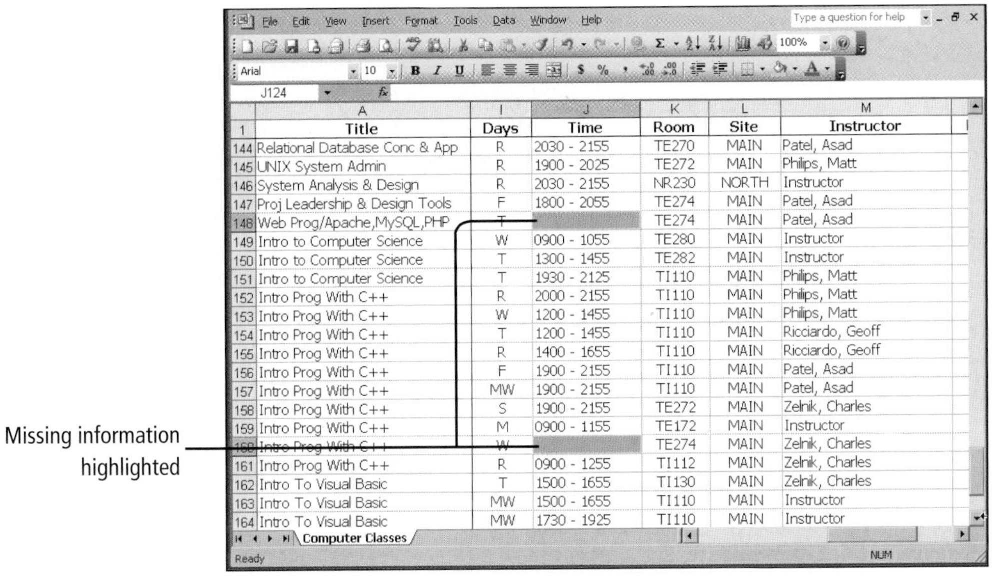

Missing information highlighted

Figure 6.14

6 On the Standard toolbar, click the **Save** button.

Activity 6.5 Using the COUNTIF Function

The **COUNTIF** function counts the number of cells within a range that meet a certain condition. For example, in this worksheet, Samantha Pruett needs to determine how many classes have not been assigned to a specific faculty member. When a class is unassigned, the word *Instructor* displays in column M—the Instructor column.

1 Press Ctrl + End to move to the end of the active area in the worksheet, and then scroll as necessary to click in cell **M172**.

In this cell you are going to use the COUNTIF function to construct a formula that will count the number of times the word *Instructor* occurs in column M. The title of the column, *Instructor*, displays in cell M1. Thus, the range used in the formula will start with cell M2.

2 On the Formula Bar, click the **Insert Function** button to display the **Insert Function** dialog box. Click the **Or select a category arrow** and click **Statistical**. Under **Select a function**, scroll as necessary and click **COUNTIF**. Compare your screen with Figure 6.15.

The COUNTIF function has two arguments—the range of cells to be evaluated and the **criteria**—the conditions on which cells will be evaluated.

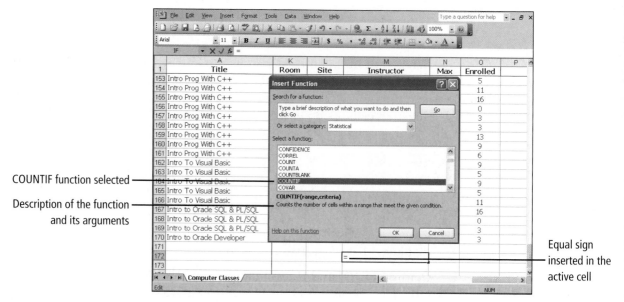

COUNTIF function selected ⎯

Description of the function ⎯
and its arguments

Equal sign
inserted in the
active cell

Figure 6.15

3 Click **OK**.

The Function Arguments dialog box displays.

4 In the **Range** box, type **m2:m170** and in the **Criteria** box, type **Instructor**
Compare your screen with Figure 6.16.

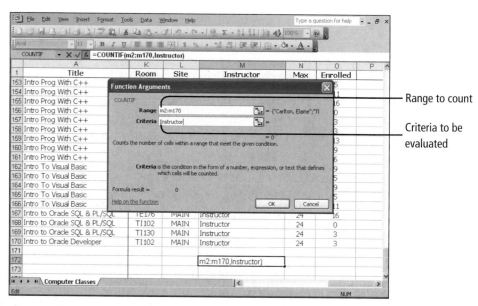

Range to count

Criteria to be
evaluated

Figure 6.16

5 Click **OK**.

The result—*47*—displays in cell M172. This is the number of classes
that, as yet, have no specific instructor assigned.

6 On the Standard toolbar, click the **Save** button ⊞.

Activity 6.6 Hiding and Unhiding Columns

In the next three activities, you will assign some classes to specific instructors. In a large worksheet, it is easier to work if you hide columns that are not necessary for the immediate task. You may also need to hide columns or rows to control the data that will print or to remove confidential information from view. For example, if you wanted to create a summary report, you could hide the columns between the row headings and the totals column, and the hidden columns would not display on the printed worksheet, resulting in a summary report.

1 Press [Ctrl] + [Home]. Scroll as necessary to view **columns F**, **G**, and **H** on your screen, and then select **columns F:H**.

2 From the **Format** menu, point to **Column**, and then, from the displayed list, click **Hide**.

Columns F, G, and H are hidden from view. Notice that the column labels skip from E to I, as shown in Figure 6.17. A dark line displays between columns E and I to indicate that columns from this location are hidden from view. After you click in another cell, however, this line will not be visible.

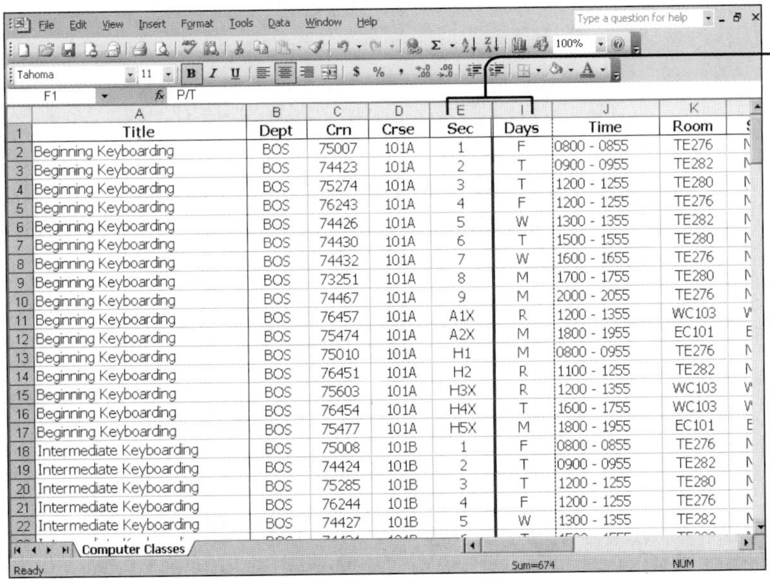

Column labels F, G, and H are hidden from view.

Figure 6.17

3 Select **columns E:I**.

To redisplay hidden columns, first select the columns on either side of the hidden columns, in this instance, columns E and I. Look for column or row headings that are missing letters or numbers in the sequence to determine whether a worksheet contains any hidden columns or rows.

4 From the **Format** menu, point to **Column**, and then click **Unhide**.

Columns F, G, and H redisplay.

5 Select **columns F**, **G**, and **H** again; right-click the selected columns and, from the shortcut menu, click **Hide**.

Columns F, G, and H are again hidden from view. You can also use the shortcut menu to hide or unhide selected columns or rows.

Activity 6.7 Arranging Workbooks and Splitting Worksheets

If you need to refer to information in one workbook while you have another workbook open, instead of jumping back and forth between the two workbooks, you can arrange the window to display sheets from more than one workbook. This is accomplished by using the Arrange command. Additionally, you can view separate parts of the same worksheet on your screen by using the Split command. This command helps you split the window into two or more panes.

1 With your **6B_Class_Schedule** workbook on the screen, on the Standard toolbar, click the **Open** button [icon]. Navigate to the location where the student files for this textbook are stored. Locate and open the file **e06B_Requests**.

The *Requests* file opens, and the *Class Schedule* file is no longer visible on your screen. You will use the Requests file to find instructors to assign to unassigned classes based on requests that instructors have made. This worksheet shows a list of instructors who have sent in requests for classes they would like to teach. It is not necessary to save this file using a different name because you will not be making any changes to it.

2 Display the **Window** menu and, at the bottom of the list, click your **6B_Class_Schedule** file to make it the active worksheet.

You can use the Window menu to select which worksheet is currently displayed. Alternatively, click the Excel file name icon displayed in the taskbar at the bottom of your screen.

3 From the **Window** menu, click **Arrange**.

The Arrange Windows dialog box displays. See Figure 6.18. This dialog box is used to control how two or more worksheets from multiple workbooks are arranged on the screen.

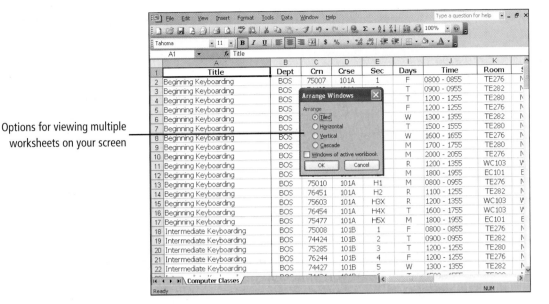

Options for viewing multiple worksheets on your screen

Figure 6.18

4 Click **Horizontal**, and then click **OK**.

The screen is split horizontally, and the *Requests* worksheet displays below the *Class Schedule* worksheet. The active window displays scroll bars, and its title bar displays in a darker shade of blue. See Figure 6.19.

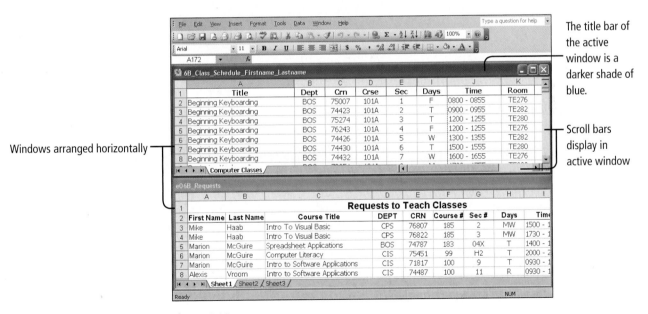

The title bar of the active window is a darker shade of blue.

Scroll bars display in active window

Windows arranged horizontally

Figure 6.19

5 If necessary, click the title bar of the **Class Schedule** worksheet to make it the active worksheet. From the **Window** menu, click **Unfreeze Panes**.

The Freeze Panes command is removed from the *Class Schedule* worksheet. When multiple worksheets are open on the screen, you must select the worksheet you want to activate before you choose a command. To activate a worksheet, click on the worksheet or click the worksheet's title bar.

6 With the **Class Schedule** worksheet active, press Ctrl + End to move to the end of the active area of the worksheet, scroll to view **column A**, and then click cell **A172**. On the vertical scroll bar, click the **down scroll arrow** twice so that you can see several empty rows.

You are going to split this window horizontally at row 172 so that you can view cell M172, which displays the number of classes that still need to have instructors assigned.

7 From the **Window** menu, click **Split**. Scroll to the right to display cell **M172**.

A gray horizontal bar displays at the top of row 172, as shown in Figure 6.20. Notice that there are two vertical scroll bars in the Class Schedule worksheet, one in each of the two worksheet parts displayed in this window.

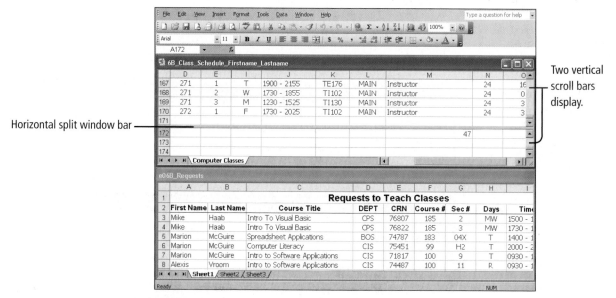

Figure 6.20

8 In the **Class Schedule** worksheet, scroll to the left. Above the split bar, click in any cell in **column C**. Press Ctrl + F to display the **Find and Replace** dialog box.

Column C lists the CRN—Course Registration Number—for each class. This is a unique number that identifies each class. You will use this information to locate the classes that need to be filled.

9 Look at the first request in the **Requests** worksheet, which is from Mr. Haab to teach Intro to Visual Basic. The CRN for this course is 76807. In the **Find what** box, type **76807** so that you can locate the course in the Class Schedule.

10 Click **Find Next**.

CRN 76807 is located in cell C163 of the Class Schedule worksheet.

11 Drag the **Find and Replace** dialog box out of the way—to the upper left of your screen. Verify that the information for this class in **row 163** of the **Class Schedule** worksheet matches the information listed in **row 3** of the **Requests** worksheet.

12 In the **Class Schedule** worksheet, scroll to the right, click in cell **M163**, type **Haab, Mike** to delete *Instructor*, and assign the class to Mr. Haab. Press Enter.

The class is assigned to Mr. Haab, and the total number of classes that still need to be assigned changes to 46. Compare your screen with Figure 6.21.

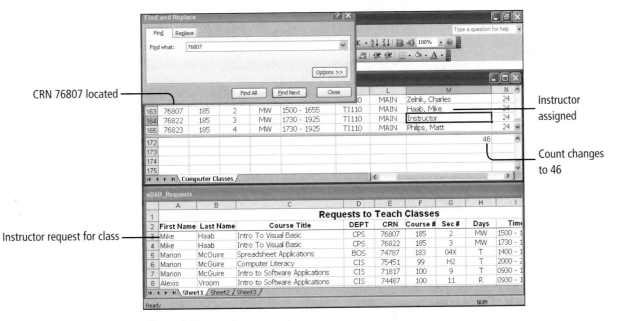

Figure 6.21

13 In the **Requests** worksheet, look at **row 4** and notice that the next class that Mr. Haab requested to teach is also a Visual Basic class—CRN 76822.

This class is listed in the next row of the Class Schedule worksheet—row 164.

14 In the **Class Schedule** worksheet, verify that the course in **row 164** is the same class—CRN 76822. In cell **M164**, type **Haab, Mike** and when his name displays in the cell, press Enter to accept the AutoComplete suggestion.

The second class is assigned, and the total number of classes that needs to be assigned changes to 45.

15 In the **Find and Replace** dialog box, in the **Find what** box, type **74787** (the next requested CRN), and then click **Find Next**.

CRN 74787 in cell C66 is selected. This is the class that displays in row 5 of the Requests worksheet. Marion McGuire has requested to teach this class.

16 Click cell **M66**, type **McGuire, Marion** and then press [Enter].

17 Continue to use the **Find and Replace** dialog box to locate the next three **CRNs** listed in the **Request** worksheet, and enter the appropriate instructor name for each class in **column M** of the **Class Schedule** worksheet.

After you have entered instructors for all six requests, there are 41 classes remaining that need to have instructors assigned.

18 Click **Close** in the **Find and Replace** dialog box. Click the **Requests** worksheet to make it active, and then click its **Close** button ☒.

19 From the **Window** menu, click **Remove Split**. On the **Class Schedule** title bar, click the **Maximize** button 🔲 to restore the size of the worksheet to its full size.

The worksheet expands again to fill the window.

20 On the Standard toolbar, click the **Save** button 💾 to save the changes to the **Class Schedule** worksheet.

Activity 6.8 Sorting a Worksheet

You can sort data in a worksheet based on the data in a row or a column. For example, in the Class Schedule worksheet, you could sort the data by the number of students enrolled (column N) from the lowest to the highest number. You could further sort in this manner within each department (column B). To sort a worksheet by a single column, you can use the Sort Ascending or Sort Descending buttons located on the Standard toolbar. To sort on more than one column, use the Sort dialog box.

1 Press [Ctrl] + [Home] to move to cell **A1**. Scroll down the worksheet and notice that the data is currently sorted first on **column B**—alphabetic by department. Within each department, the data is further sorted numerically on **column D—Crse**. Within each Crse group, the data is further sorted by **column E—Sec**.

The departments listed are BOS, CIS, CNT, and CPS. The course numbers are in *ascending* order—from the lowest number to the highest—within the department. Within each course number, the classes are sorted by section number—Sec. All the BOS courses are listed, and then all the CIS courses are listed, followed by CNT and CPS courses.

2 Scroll back to the top of the worksheet. From the **Data** menu, click **Sort**.

All the worksheet data in the active area is selected, and the Sort dialog box displays. From the Sort dialog box, you can sort on up to three columns of data.

3 Click the **Sort by arrow** and from the displayed list, click **Enrolled**. Be sure the **Ascending** option button is selected. Compare your **Sort** dialog box with the one shown in Figure 6.22.

This action will sort the data based on the numbers in column O— the enrollment number—with courses having the lowest enrollment listed first.

Worksheet will be sorted by number of students enrolled.

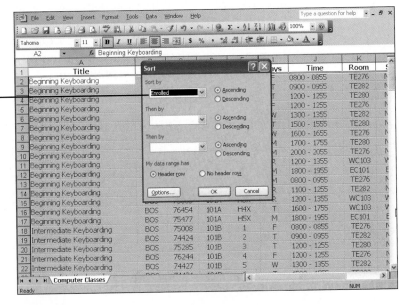

Figure 6.22

4 In the **Sort** dialog box, click **OK**. Scroll to the right so that you can see **column O**—Enrolled.

The data is sorted. The classes that have zero enrollments are listed first, as shown in Figure 6.23.

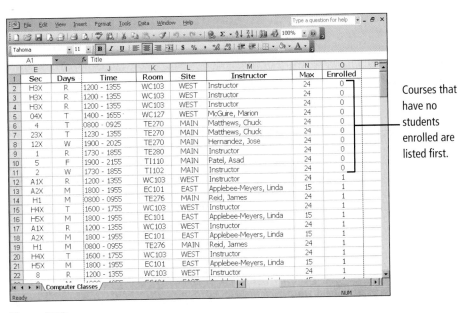

Courses that have no students enrolled are listed first.

Figure 6.23

5 From the **Data** menu, click **Sort**. Click the **Sort by arrow**, and then click **Days**. Click the first **Then by arrow** and then, from the displayed list, click **Time**. Click the second **Then by arrow** and then, from the displayed list, click **Room**. Be sure the **Ascending** option button is selected for all three sorts. Be sure the **Header row** option button is selected. See Figure 6.24.

The first row of the data is identified as a header row because it is a label for the content in each column. This sort will help determine whether there are any conflicts with room assignments. The data will first be sorted alphabetically by the *Days* field, which is known as the ***major*** sort, then by *Time*, and then by *Room*. The second and third sorts are known as ***minor*** sorts.

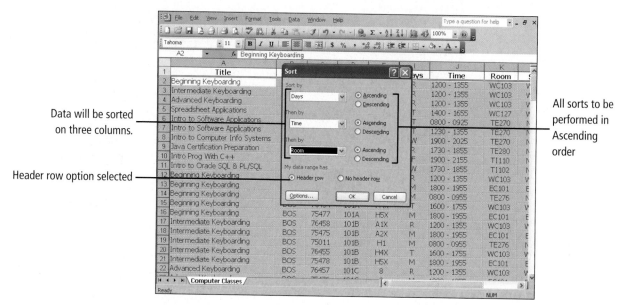

Data will be sorted on three columns.

Header row option selected

All sorts to be performed in Ascending order

Figure 6.24

6 In the **Sort** dialog box, click **OK**. Compare your screen with Figure 6.25.

The data is sorted. Because the days are sorted alphabetically, F (for *Friday*) is listed first, and then the times for the Friday classes are sorted in ascending order. Within the Friday group, the classes are further sorted from the earliest to the latest. Within each time period, the data is further sorted by room.

Keyboarding classes on Friday —

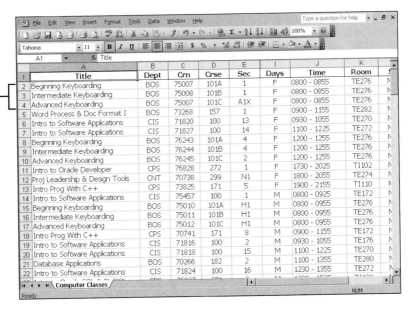

Figure 6.25

7 Examine the sorted data. Notice that the first three classes listed are on *Friday*, at *8:00*, in room *TE276*, with *Elaine Carlton* as the instructor.

These are all keyboarding classes, and the instructor teaches the three levels of keyboarding at the same time.

8 Scroll down until **rows 50** and **51** are in view. Notice that two *Visual Basic* classes are scheduled on *MW* at *17:30—5:30—*in room *TE110* with two different instructors listed.

This is a conflict of classroom assignment that will need to be resolved. Sorting data can help you identify such problems.

9 Press (Ctrl) + (Home) to make cell **A1** active again. From the **Data** menu, click **Sort**. Click the **Sort by arrow** and then, from the displayed list, click **Dept**. Click the first **Then by arrow** and click **Crse**. Click the second **Then by arrow**, click **Sec**, and then click **OK**.

The data is resorted. The sort is not identical to the original pattern, however, because Excel first sorts the course numbers that contain only numbers, and then sorts the course numbers that include letters, such as 101A, 101B, and 101C.

Activity 6.9 Using AutoFilter to Limit the Data Displayed

Another technique you can use when you are working with a large worksheet is to *filter*—limit the data displayed to match a specific condition.

1 If necessary, press (Ctrl) + (Home) to return to cell **A1**. From the **Data** menu, point to **Filter**, and then, from the displayed list, click **AutoFilter**.

Filter arrows are displayed next to each column heading, as shown in Figure 6.26.

Filter arrows —

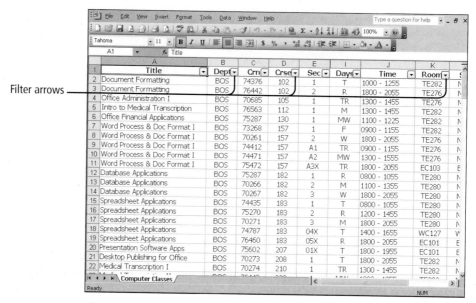

Figure 6.26

2 In the **Instructor** column—**column M**—click the **Filter arrow**.

The list displays the names of the instructors assigned to classes. At the top of the list you can choose to display *All*, the *Top 10*, or a *Custom* list.

3 From the displayed list, click **Hernandez, Jose**.

Four classes are listed for Mr. Hernandez, as shown in Figure 6.27. Only the matching rows are displayed; all the other rows are hidden. The row numbers displayed on the left are the rows where this information is found. The color of the Filter arrow changes to indicate that a filter is applied.

4 In the **Instructor** column—**column M**—click the **Filter arrow**, scroll to the top of the list, and then click **All**.

All the rows display.

Row location of matching information

Active filter arrow displays in blue

Only the matching data displays.

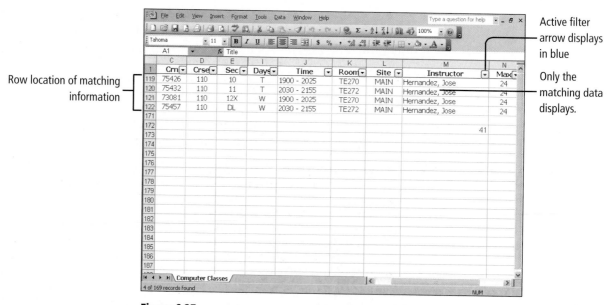

Figure 6.27

5 In the **Dept** column—**column B**—click the **Filter arrow**, and then click **CPS**. In the **Crse** column—**column D**—click the **Filter arrow**, and then click **171**.

Only the CPS course 171 displays. In this manner, you can apply filters to multiple columns.

6 In **column B**, click the **Filter arrow**, and then click **All**. In **column D**, click the **Filter arrow**, and then click **All**. Alternatively, display the Data menu, point to Filter, and then click Show All.

All the records redisplay.

7 From the **Data** menu, point to **Filter**, and then click **AutoFilter**.

The filter arrows are removed. The AutoFilter command is a toggle command—click it once to turn it on, click it again to turn it off.

8 On the Standard toolbar, click the **Save** button.

Objective 3
Prepare a Worksheet to Share with Others

You can share a worksheet with others by printing and distributing paper copies, sending it electronically, or displaying it as a Web page. Other people with whom you share the worksheet may not have the Excel program or may need it in a different format. You can save an Excel file as a text file or as a *comma separated value (CSV)* file, which inserts a comma between the data in each cell in a row and eliminates the boxed cell structure entirely. This format can be read by other programs that work with data, including most database programs. You can also add a *hyperlink* to a worksheet, which, when clicked, takes you to another location in the worksheet, to another file, or to a Web page on the Internet or on your organization's intranet. In the following activities, you will prepare the Course Schedule worksheet to share with faculty and to post to the college Web site. To prepare this schedule, you will need to refer to another workbook that shows instructor contact information.

Activity 6.10 Previewing and Modifying Page Breaks

Before you print a large worksheet, preview it to see where the pages will break across the columns and rows. You can move the page breaks to a column or row that groups the data logically, and you can change the orientation between portrait and landscape if you want to display more rows on the page (portrait) or more columns on the page (landscape). You can also *scale* the data to force the worksheet into a selected number of pages.

1 With your **Class Schedule** worksheet displayed, press Ctrl + Home to return to cell **A1**. On the Standard toolbar, click the **Print Preview** button. On the Print Preview toolbar, click the **Next** button seven times to view the eight pages required to print this worksheet.

As you view each page, notice that pages 5 through 8 display the time, room, site, and instructor related to the first four pages of the printout. The printed worksheet would be easier to read if all the information related to a class were on the same page.

2 From the Print Preview toolbar, click **Page Break Preview**. If the **Welcome to Page Break Preview** dialog box displays, close it.

The Page Break Preview window displays. Blue dashed lines show where the page breaks are in the current setup for this worksheet. Compare your screen with Figure 6.28.

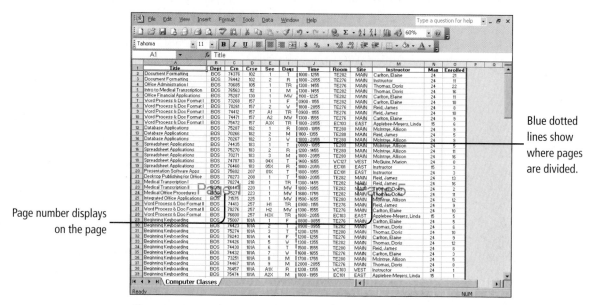

Blue dotted lines show where pages are divided.

Page number displays on the page

Figure 6.28

Note — A Dialog Box May Display

A Welcome to Page Break Preview dialog box may display with a message informing you that page breaks can be adjusted by clicking and dragging the breaks with your mouse. If this box displays, click OK to close it.

3 Scroll down to view the other pages and see where the page breaks are indicated. From the **View** menu, click **Normal** to redisplay the worksheet.

The Page Break view closes, and the Worksheet returns to the screen. When you are looking at the page breaks, the worksheet displays in a different view. When you close this view, the normal worksheet window returns—not the Print Preview window. Dashed lines display at the page break locations on the worksheet.

4 From the **File** menu, click **Page Setup**. On the **Page tab**, under **Orientation**, click **Landscape**. Under **Scaling**, click the **Fit to** option button. Be sure *1* displays in the **page(s) wide by** box, and then type **4** in the **tall** box.

The worksheet will print horizontally across the page with the time, room, site, and instructor information on the same row as the related class information.

5 Click the **Header/Footer tab**. Click **Custom Footer** and with the insertion point in the **Left section**, click the **File Name** button 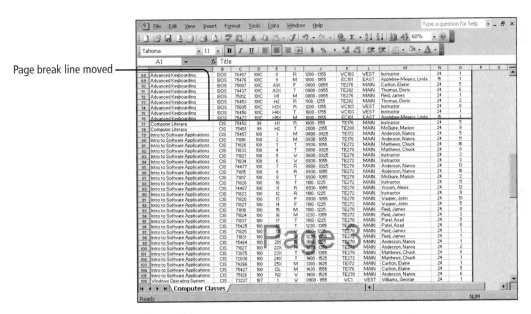. Click **OK** twice.

6 On the Standard toolbar, click the **Print Preview** button.

The Print Preview window displays. Notice in the lower left corner that the worksheet has been reduced to four pages. Each complete row of data will fit on one page.

7 On the Print Preview toolbar, click **Page Break Preview**. If necessary, click **OK** to close the **Welcome to Page Break Preview** dialog box. Scroll down to display the page break between **Page 2** and **Page 3**.

The page break needs to be adjusted so that a break occurs between the BOS courses and the CIS courses so that separate printouts can be sent to the BOS and CIS department heads.

8 Point to the horizontal page break line between **Page 2** and **Page 3**.

When the vertical resize pointer displays, drag the line up between **row 76** and **row 77**. Compare your screen with Figure 6.29.

Page break line moved

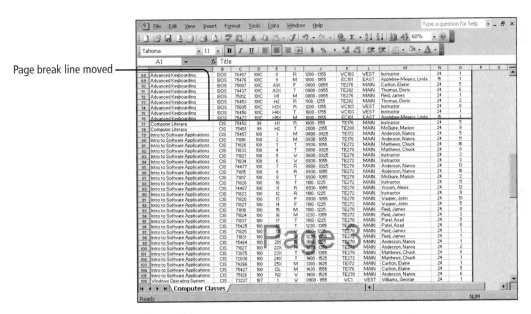

Figure 6.29

9 Scroll down to see the page break line between **Page 4** and **Page 5**. Drag the line up to break the page between **row 146** and **row 147**, which is the end of the CIS section.

10 On the Standard toolbar, click the **Print Preview** button. Click **Next** four times to scroll through the five pages that will print.

The BOS, CIS, and CNT/CPS courses will print on separate pages.

11 On the Print Preview toolbar, click **Normal View**. On the Standard toolbar, click the **Save** button.

Activity 6.11 Repeating Column or Row Headings

When a large worksheet is printed on several pages, you will usually want to repeat the column headings and, if necessary, the row headings on each page.

1 On the Standard toolbar, click the **Print Preview** button. On the Print Preview toolbar, click **Next** several times to view the pages.

Notice that the column headings display only on Page 1 and on none of the remaining pages. Repeating the column headings on each page will make it easier to understand and read the information on the printed pages.

2 On the Print Preview toolbar, click **Close**. From the **File** menu, click **Page Setup**. In the **Page Setup** dialog box, click the **Sheet tab**.

Here you can select rows to repeat at the top of each page or columns to repeat at the left of each page. To have access to this printing command, you must display the Page Setup dialog box from the Page Setup command on the File menu. It is not available from the Setup button on the Print Preview toolbar.

3 Under **Print titles**, click in the **Rows to repeat at top** box, and then, in the worksheet, click cell **A1**.

A moving border surrounds row 1, and the mouse pointer displays as a black select row arrow. The absolute reference $1:$1 displays in the Rows to repeat at top box. See Figure 6.30.

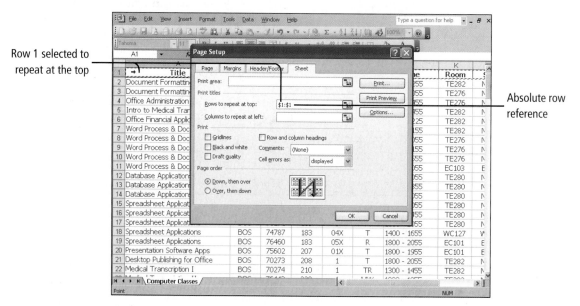

Row 1 selected to repeat at the top

Absolute row reference

Figure 6.30

More Knowledge — Using Expand and Collapse Boxes

On the Sheet tab of the Page Setup dialog box, the *Rows to repeat at top* box and the *Columns to repeat at left* box have the expand and collapse characteristic that you used previously in the function dialog boxes. Boxes that have this feature display a collapse arrow at the right side of the box that is used to collapse the larger dialog box so that you can see more of the worksheet. The destination box you are working with remains on the screen, and the arrow at the right end of the box changes to an expand arrow. This makes it easier to drag the reference area you want included in the box. After you select the reference area, click the expand arrow at the end of the collapsed box to redisplay the full dialog box and continue with the next action.

4 Click **OK**.

The Page Setup dialog box closes.

5 Press Ctrl + G to display the **Go To** box. In the **Go To** box, under **Reference**, type **k172** and press Enter.

You can use the Go To box to move to a specific cell on the worksheet. A label needs to be added to identify the number that displays in cell M172.

6 In cell **K172**, type **Unassigned classes:** and press Enter.

7 On the Standard toolbar, click the **Save** button, and then click the **Print Preview** button. On the Print Preview toolbar, click **Next**.

The second page displays, and the column headings from row 1 display at the top, as shown in Figure 6.31.

Column headings display on page 2.

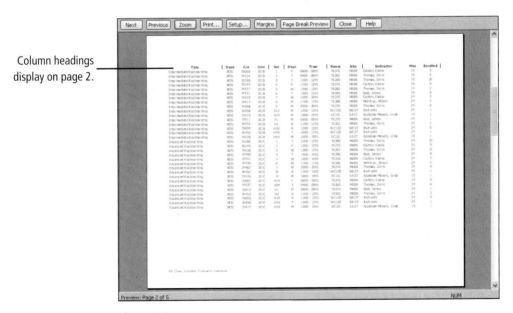

Figure 6.31

8 Click **Next** to view the remaining pages of the worksheet, and notice the column headings on each page and the label at the end of the worksheet to identify the number of unassigned classes. Verify that the page breaks are still located between each department and make any adjustments that may be necessary. On the Print Preview toolbar, click **Print**, and then click **OK**. Save your changes.

The five pages of the worksheet print.

Activity 6.12 Inserting a Hyperlink in a Worksheet

Recall that a hyperlink is colored and underlined text that you click to go to a file, a location in a file, a Web page on the World Wide Web, or a Web page on your organization's intranet. Hyperlinks can be attached to text or to graphics. In this activity, you will add a hyperlink that will open a file that contains the instructors' names, phone numbers, office locations, and email addresses.

1 Press [Ctrl] + [Home] to move to cell **A1**. Scroll to the right and click cell **M1**. On the Standard toolbar, click the **Insert Hyperlink** button [icon]. Alternatively, display the Insert menu and click Hyperlink.

The Insert Hyperlink dialog box displays.

2 On the **Link to** bar, if necessary, click **Existing File or Web Page**. Click the **Look in arrow** and navigate to the location where the student files for this textbook are stored. Click the **e06B_Faculty** file to select it.

The selected file contains the faculty phone numbers, office locations, and email addresses.

3 In the upper right corner of the **Insert Hyperlink** dialog box, click the **ScreenTip** button.

The Set Hyperlink ScreenTip dialog box displays.

4 In the **ScreenTip text** box, type **Click here for contact information**

When you point to the hyperlink on the worksheet, this is the text of the ScreenTip that will display. Compare your dialog box with the one shown in Figure 6.32.

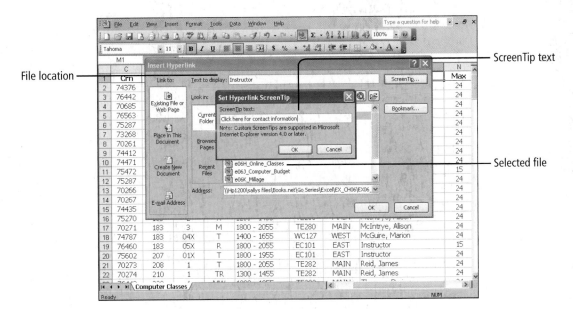

File location

ScreenTip text

Selected file

Figure 6.32

5 Click **OK** in the **Set Hyperlink ScreenTip** dialog box, and then click **OK** in the **Insert Hyperlink** dialog box.

The Instructor column heading is blue and underlined, indicating a hyperlink.

6 Point to the **Instructor hyperlink** and read the ScreenTip that displays.

When you point to the hyperlink, the Link Select mouse pointer displays 🖑 and the ScreenTip text you entered displays, as shown in Figure 6.33.

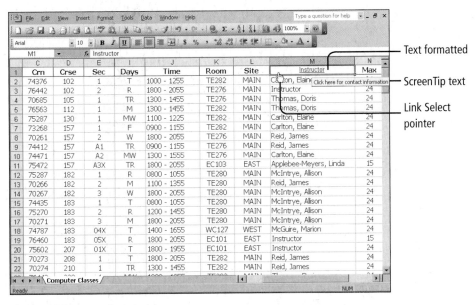

Text formatted

ScreenTip text

Link Select pointer

Figure 6.33

7 Click the **Instructor hyperlink**.

The Faculty file opens and displays the contact information for each faculty member, as shown in Figure 6.34. Additionally, the Web toolbar displays.

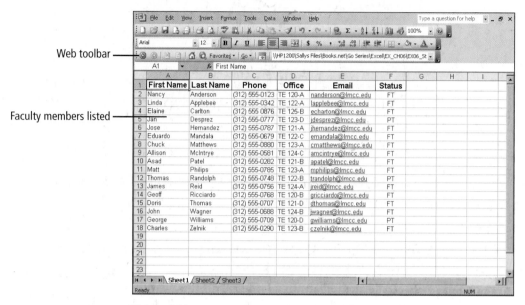

Web toolbar ————

Faculty members listed ————

Figure 6.34

8 On the Web toolbar, click the **Back** button.

The Class Schedule returns to the screen. The Instructor link changes color to indicate that it has been selected at least once.

9 On the Standard toolbar, click the **Save** button.

Activity 6.13 Modifying a Hyperlink

If the file to which the hyperlink refers is moved or renamed or a Web page to which a hyperlink refers gets a new address, the hyperlink needs to be modified to reflect the change.

1 On the Web toolbar, click the **Forward** button.

The Faculty worksheet displays.

2 From the **File** menu, click **Save As**. In the **Save As** dialog box, use the **Look in arrow** to navigate to the location where you are saving your files. In the **File name** box, type **6B_Faculty_Firstname_Lastname** and then click **Save**.

The file is saved in a new location with a new name.

3 To the right of the **Type a question for help** box, click the small **Close Window** button to close the Faculty file.

The Class Schedule file displays on your screen.

4 Right-click cell **M1**—the Instructor hyperlink—and from the displayed list, click **Edit Hyperlink**.

The Edit Hyperlink dialog box displays. The layout of this dialog box is the same as the Insert Hyperlink dialog box.

5 Click the **Look in arrow** and navigate to the location where you are saving the files for this chapter. Locate and select your file **6B_Faculty_Firstname_Lastname**.

6 Click **OK**. In cell **M1**, click the hyperlinked text—**Instructor**.

Your *6B_Faculty_Firstname_Lastname* file displays on your screen. The hyperlink has been changed to the new file and new file location.

7 Click the small **Close Window** button ⊠ to close the Faculty file.

The Class Schedule worksheet redisplays on your screen.

Activity 6.14 Viewing and Saving a Worksheet as a Web Page

Before you save a worksheet as a Web page, it is a good idea to view it as a Web page to see how it will display.

1 Display the **File** menu, and then click **Web Page Preview**.

Your browser program (Internet Explorer or other browser program) opens, and the worksheet displays in the browser, as shown in Figure 6.35. (Depending on your browser setup and screen resolution, your screen may vary somewhat from the figure.)

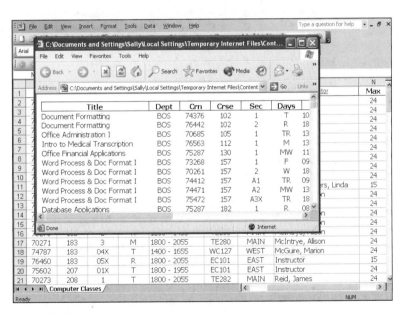

Figure 6.35

2 On the browser title bar, click the **Close** button ⊠.

3 From the **File** menu, click **Save as Web Page**. The **Save As** dialog box opens. At the lower edge of the dialog box, be sure the **Save as type** box displays **Web Page**.

4 If necessary, click the **Save in arrow** and navigate to the location where you are saving your files for this chapter. You will not see your other files, because only files with the type *Web Page* will be visible.

5 In the lower portion of the dialog box, click the **Change Title** button.

The Set Page Title dialog box displays. The text that you type here will become the title of the Web page when it is displayed.

6 In the **Set Page Title** dialog box, in the **Page title** box, type **Business Division Computer Courses (Firstname Lastname)** using your own name as part of the page title. Compare your screen with Figure 6.36.

Location where file will be saved

Page title

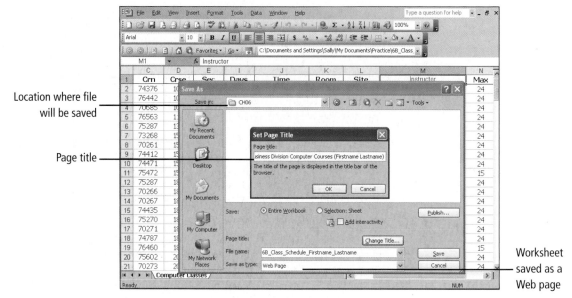

Worksheet saved as a Web page

Figure 6.36

7 In the **Set Page Title** dialog box, click **OK**. In the **Save As** dialog box, click **Save**.

The Save As dialog box closes.

8 On the right side of the blue Excel title bar, click the **Minimize** button ⬜ to minimize the Excel program to a button on your taskbar. Start your browser program (Internet Explorer or other browser program). From the menu bar, click **File**, and then click **Open**. In the **Open** dialog box, click the **Browse** button.

A dialog box displays, similar to the Open dialog box in Excel. Depending on the style of the displayed dialog box, you can click the Browse button or use the Look in arrow to navigate to the file folder location, and then select the file you want to open.

9 Click the **Browse** button or the **Look in arrow**, and then navigate to the location where you have saved the files for this chapter. Click the HTML file **6B_Class_Schedule_Firstname_Lastname**, and then click **Open**.

The name of the file you selected displays in the Open dialog box.

10 In the **Open** dialog box, click **OK**.

The Class Schedule file opens in your browser. The browser title bar displays the text you typed in the Set Page Title dialog box—Business Division Computer Courses. The file name may display .htm at the end, which is the extension that is given to files that are saved as Web pages. Compare your screen with Figure 6.37.

Page title —

File address —

Extension of .htm indicates Web page

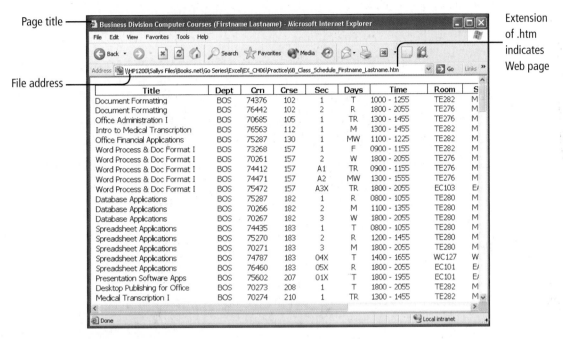

Figure 6.37

11 From the **File** menu, click **Page Setup**. In the **Page Setup** dialog box, change the Orientation to **Landscape**, and then click **OK**.

12 From the **File** menu, click **Print**. In the **Print** dialog box, change the page range from **All** to **1**, and then click **Print**.

The first page of the Class Schedule Web page prints. Depending on your printer, several of the columns on the right do not print. Do not be concerned about this; Web pages are meant to be viewed, not printed.

13 On the browser title bar, click the **Close** button ☒. On your taskbar, click the **6B_Class_Schedule** icon that displays to restore the Excel program and redisplay the worksheet.

The browser closes, and the Class Schedule worksheet displays on your screen.

Activity 6.15 Saving a Worksheet as a Comma Separated Values File

You can save an Excel worksheet as a comma separated value (CSV) file, which saves the contents of the cells by placing commas between them and an end-of-paragraph mark at the end of each row. This type of file can be readily exchanged with various database programs, in which it is referred to as a **comma delimited file**.

1 Be sure your **6B_Class_Schedule_Firstname_Lastname** file is open. From the menu bar, click **File**, and then click **Save As**.

The Save As dialog box opens.

2 If necessary, use the **Save in arrow** to navigate to the location where you are saving your files for this chapter. In the **File name** box type **6B_Schedule_CSV_Firstname_Lastname**

3 At the bottom of the **Save As** dialog box, click the **Save as type arrow**. Scroll through the displayed list and click **CSV (Comma delimited)**.

The Save as type box enables you to save files in different formats. Compare your dialog box with Figure 6.38. Your other files no longer display, because only CSV type files are displayed.

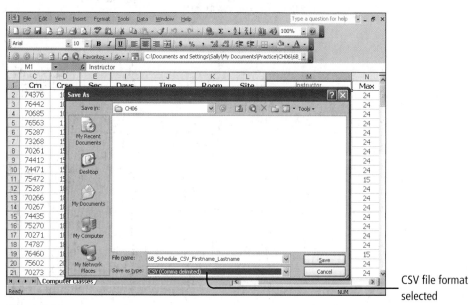

CSV file format selected

Figure 6.38

4 Click **Save**.

A dialog box displays to inform you that some features of the file may not be compatible with the CSV format. Features such as merged cells and formatting are lost. You can save the file and leave out incompatible features by clicking *Yes*, preserve the file in an Excel format by clicking *No*, or see what might be lost by clicking *Help*. See Figure 6.39.

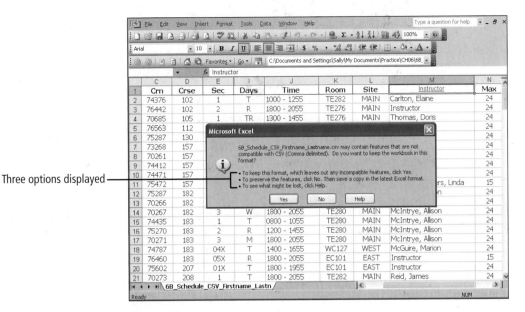

Three options displayed

Figure 6.39

Alert!

A Different Warning

You may see a different warning message about the selected format not supporting a workbook that has multiple sheets. Click OK to save the active worksheet and acknowledge the warning.

5 Click **Yes** to keep the CSV format.

The file is saved in the new format. The new file name displays in the title bar. If file extensions—the three letters that identify the type of files—are displayed on your computer, you will also see *.csv* after the file name.

6 Close your **6B_Schedule_CSV** file. Click **Yes** to save changes, and then click **Yes** to acknowledge the warning message.

Activity 6.16 Saving an Excel File as a Text File

1 On the Standard toolbar, click the **Open** button 📂. Navigate to the location where you are saving your files and open your Excel file (not the Web page file) **6B_Faculty_Firstname_Lastname**. (The file type shown at the bottom of the dialog box controls which types of files display here.)

2 From the **File** menu, click **Save As**. In the **Save As** dialog box, if necessary, use the **Save in arrow** to navigate to the location where you are saving your files for this chapter. In the **File name** box, type **6B_Faculty_TXT_Firstname_Lastname**

3 At the bottom of the **Save As** dialog box, click the **Save as type arrow**. Scroll through the displayed list and click **Text (Tab delimited)**.

A *tab delimited* text file is similar to a comma separated values file except that a tab character, rather than a comma, is used to separate the cell contents in the rows. Database programs can also read this type of data format easily.

4 Click **Save**.

A message box displays, advising you that the selected file type does not support workbooks that contain multiple sheets.

5 Click **OK**.

A second warning box displays, advising you that the file may contain features that are not compatible with the Text file format.

6 Click **Yes** to keep the format.

The new file name displays on the title bar.

7 Close the file. Click **Yes** to save the changes, click **OK**, and then click **Yes** to acknowledge the warning messages.

8 **Start** Microsoft Word. On the Standard toolbar, click the **Open** button.

9 In the **Open** dialog box, use the **Look in arrow** to navigate to the location where you are storing your files for this chapter.

10 At the bottom of the **Open** dialog box, click the **Files of type arrow** and, from the displayed list, click **Text Files**.

The *6B_Faculty_TXT_Firstname_Lastname* file displays on the list.

11 Click the **6B_Faculty_TXT_Firstname_Lastname** file to select it, and then click **Open**.

The file opens with tab characters inserted between each cell's data. Each row is treated as a paragraph. See Figure 6.40.

Tabs display between the data.

Paragraph marks indicate the end of a row of data.

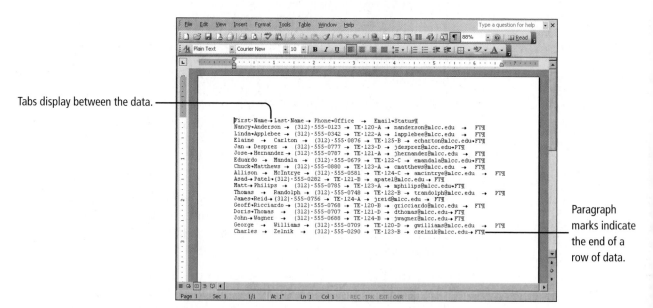

Figure 6.40

12 From the **View** menu, display the Header and Footer toolbar, and then click the **Switch Between Header and Footer** button 🖼. With the insertion point on the left side of the footer, on the Header and Footer toolbar, click the **Insert AutoText** button, and then click **Filename**.

13 Close the Header and Footer toolbar. On the Standard toolbar, click the **Print** button to print the one-page text file.

14 Close your **6B_Faculty_TXT** file, saving the changes when prompted to do so. If necessary, click **Yes** to acknowledge the warning message.

15 On the Word Standard toolbar, click the **Open** button 🖼. At the lower edge of the displayed **Open** dialog box, click the **Files of type arrow** and, from the displayed list, click **All Word Documents**. In the dialog box's title bar, click the **Close** button ✖. Close Word.

16 In the Excel program, click **View**, point to **Toolbars**, and then click **Web** to close the Web toolbar. Then, from the **File** menu, click **Open**, and at the bottom of the dialog box, click the **Files of type arrow** and click **Microsoft Office Excel Files**. Close Excel.

More Knowledge — Using a Tab Delimited Text File

After a file has been saved as a text file, it can be converted from tab delimited text to a Word table. Word has a *Convert Text to Table* command that can easily convert a tabbed file into a table. A table displays in a row and column format, like an Excel spreadsheet.

End You have completed Project 6B ——————————————

Project 6C Programming Classes

Excel has several more tools for improving the visual appeal of your worksheet. You can format a worksheet by using the AutoFormat command or by creating your own styles. You can add graphic elements to a worksheet such as circles, rectangles, arrows, and text boxes. The Research tool can help you locate information that is related to your worksheet content.

In Activities 6.17 through 6.20, you will use AutoFormat, styles, drawing tools, and research tools to format a worksheet for the Computer Science and Computer Systems Information departments. Your completed worksheets will look similar to Figure 6.41. You will save your workbook as *6C_Programming_Classes_Firstname_Lastname.*

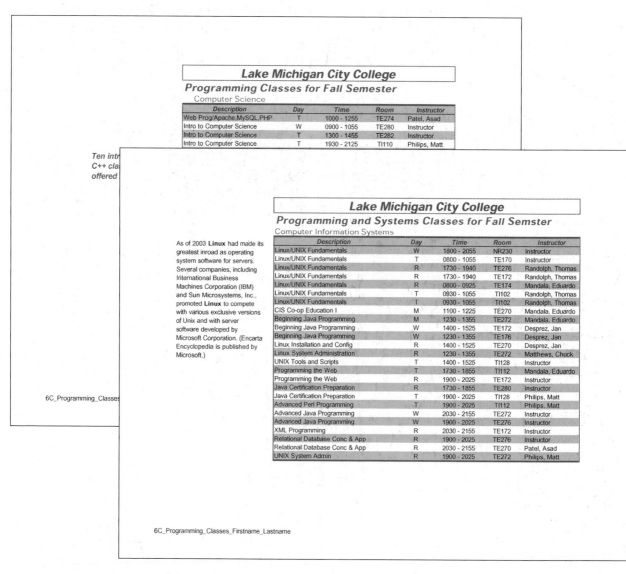

Figure 6.41
Project 6C—Programming Classes

Objective 4
Enhance Worksheets with AutoFormats and Styles

In addition to formatting cells from the Formatting toolbar and the Format Cells dialog box, you can also use the **AutoFormat** command. The AutoFormat feature provides a selection of predefined formats that can be applied to cells on a worksheet. Another alternative is to create your own **styles**, which are formats that you design and save and which can then be applied to cells in multiple worksheets or other workbooks.

Activity 6.17 Applying an AutoFormat

1 Start Excel. On the Standard toolbar, click the **Open** button. Navigate to the location where the student files for this textbook are stored. Locate and open the file **e06C_Programming_Classes**.

2 From the **File** menu, click **Save As**. In the **Save As** dialog box, use the **Save in arrow** to navigate to the location where you are storing your files for this chapter. In the **File name** box, type **6C_Programming_Classes_Firstname_Lastname** and then click the **Save** button.

This worksheet lists the programming courses that are available for the fall semester through the Computer Science department. Notice that the workbook contains two worksheets, one named CPS and the other, CIS.

3 On the **CPS** sheet, make cell **A1** the active cell. Display the **Insert** menu, and then click **Rows**. In the new cell **A1**, type **Lake Michigan City College** and press Enter.

4 Click the **CIS tab**. With the insertion point in cell **A1**, display the **Insert** menu, and then click **Rows**. In the new cell **A1**, type **Lake Michigan City College** and press Enter.

5 Click the **CPS tab**. Select the range **A4:E27**. From the **Format** menu, click **AutoFormat**.

The AutoFormat dialog box opens and displays predefined formats.

6 Scroll down the list, locate and then click the **List 1** AutoFormat.

This format applies gray to alternate lines, which helps lead the eye across a row of information. See Figure 6.42.

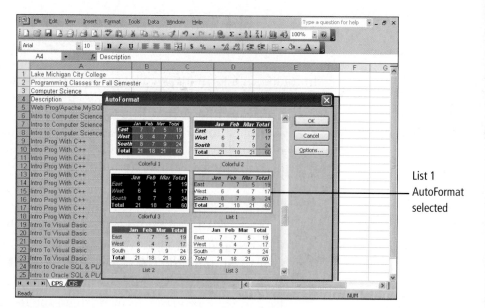

Figure 6.42

List 1
AutoFormat
selected

7 Click **OK**, and then click in any empty cell to view the results.

The format is applied to the selected cells.

8 Select columns **B**, **C**, and **D** and then, on the Formatting toolbar, click the **Center** button ▣. With the three columns selected, widen **columns B**, **C**, and **D** to **12 (89 pixels)**. Click in any empty cell and compare your screen with Figure 6.43.

Columns widened
and data centered

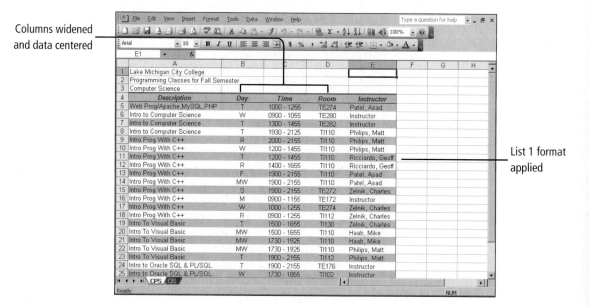

List 1 format
applied

Figure 6.43

9 Click the **CIS tab**. Select cells **A4:E29**. From the **Format** menu, click **AutoFormat**. In the **AutoFormat** dialog box, click **List 1**, and then click **OK**. **Center** columns **B**, **C**, and **D**, and then widen **columns B, C,** and **D** to **12 (89 pixels)**.

10 On the Standard toolbar, click the **Save** button.

Activity 6.18 Creating Styles

1 Click the **CPS tab** and click cell **A1**. From the **Format** menu, click **Style**.

The Style dialog box opens and displays the name and formats of the current style—*Normal*—that is applied to this cell. The ***Normal*** style is the default style that is applied to new worksheets. It includes Arial 10 pt. font and the other formats listed in the dialog box, as shown in Figure 6.44.

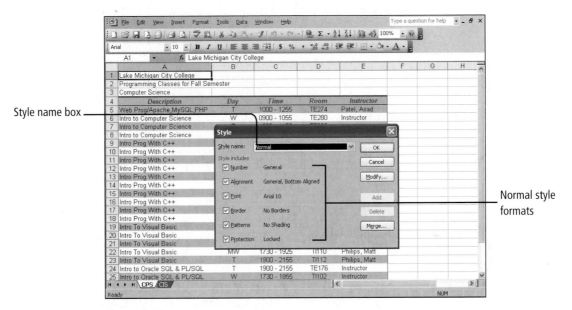

Style name box

Normal style formats

Figure 6.44

2 In the **Style name** box, type **LMCC** and then click the **Modify** button.

The Format Cells dialog box opens. Here you can define the format for your LMCC style.

3 Click the **Font tab**. Under **Font**, click **Tahoma**, under **Font style**, click **Bold Italic**, and under **Size**, click **18**. Click the **Color arrow** and then, in the second row, click the fifth color—**Teal**.

4 Click the **Border tab**. In the lower right corner of the dialog box, click the **Color arrow** and in the second row, click the fifth color—**Teal**. Under **Presets**, click **Outline**.

An outline displays in the Border area.

5 Click **OK**.

The Format Cells dialog box closes. The Style dialog box shows the selections you have made. Compare your dialog box with the one in Figure 6.45.

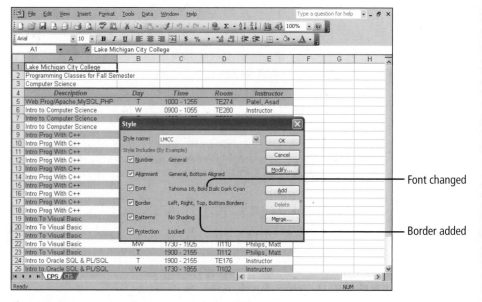

Figure 6.45

6 Click the **Add** button.

After you define the style, you must click Add to retain the selections you have made.

7 Click **OK**.

The Style is applied to cell A1.

8 Click cell **A2**. On the Formatting toolbar, change the **Font** to **Arial Rounded MT Bold** and change the **Font Size** to **16**. Click the **Font Color arrow** and then, in the fourth row, click the seventh color—**Plum**.

Now that you have set the formats you want, you can open the Style dialog and name this style. This is another way to create a style.

9 From the **Format** menu, click **Style**. In the **Style** dialog box, in the **Style name** box, type **Title** Notice that, after you assign a name, the font formats you have chosen are displayed under **Style Includes**, as shown in Figure 6.46.

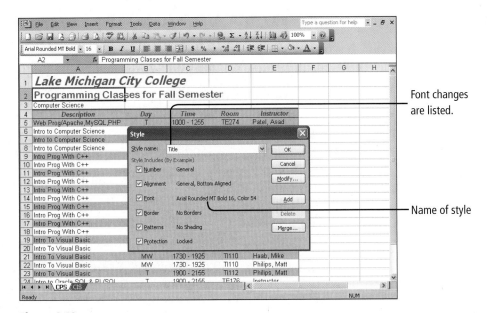

Font changes are listed.

Name of style

Figure 6.46

10 Click **Add**, and then click **OK**.

The style is applied to the selected cell, and the dialog box closes.

11 Click cell **A3**. Use one of the two methods you just practiced to create a style for this cell named **Department** Use **12** pt. **Arial Rounded MT Bold** font, **Plum** font color, and **Center** alignment. Compare your results with Figure 6.47.

Your three created styles applied to the three title lines

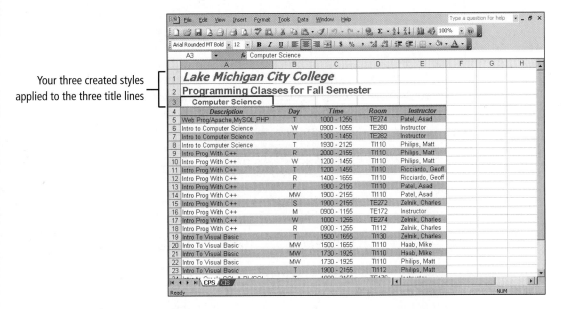

Figure 6.47

12 On the Standard toolbar, click the **Save** button .

Activity 6.19 Applying Styles to Other Worksheets

1 Click the **CIS tab**, and then click cell **A1**.

2 Display the **Format** menu, and then click **Style**.

The Style dialog box opens with the Normal style listed in the Style name box.

3 Click the **Style name arrow**, from the displayed list click **LMCC**, and then click **OK**.

The LMCC style is applied to cell A1. The styles you created in Activity 6.18 are available to use with other worksheets in this workbook.

4 Click cell **A2**. Display the **Format** menu and click **Style**. In the **Style** dialog box, click the **Style name arrow**, click **Title**, and then click **OK**.

5 Click cell **A3** and from the **Style** dialog box, apply the **Department** style. Widen **column A** to **35.00 (250 pixels)**. Save your work and click in any empty cell.

The three styles you created for the CPS worksheet have been applied to the CIS worksheet. Compare your screen with Figure 6.48.

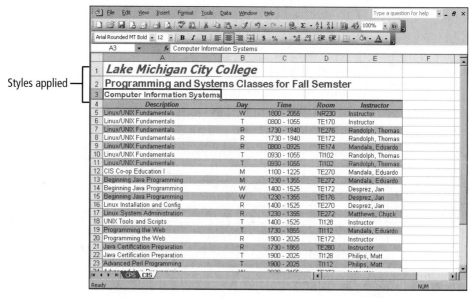

Figure 6.48

More Knowledge — Using Styles in Other Workbooks

Styles you create in one workbook are not automatically available for use in other workbooks. However, if you create styles in one workbook, you can merge the styles with other workbooks. Open the workbook that contains the styles, and then open the workbook where you want to use the styles. In the workbook where you want to add the styles, open the Styles dialog box and click the Merge button. A Merge Styles dialog box displays and lists the open workbook containing the styles. Select the workbook containing the styles, and then click OK. The styles are available for you to use in the new workbook.

Activity 6.20 Modifying Styles

After you create a style, you can alter it and the changes will be reflected in any cell that uses that style. In the following activity, you will change the Title style to bold italic. The border used in the LMCC style needs to be adjusted so that it covers the full length of the cells where the Lake Michigan Community College title displays.

1 Be sure the **CIS** worksheet is displayed. Click cell **A2**. From the **Format** menu, display the **Style** dialog box.

The Style dialog box opens with the Title style selected.

2 In the **Style** dialog box, click the **Modify** button.

The Format Cells dialog box displays.

3 Click the **Font tab**, under **Font style** click **Bold Italic**, and then click **OK**.

In the Style dialog box, the font for the Title style is changed to include Bold Italic. See Figure 6.49. Notice that the font in cell A2 has not yet been changed to Bold Italic.

Change in style not displayed in text

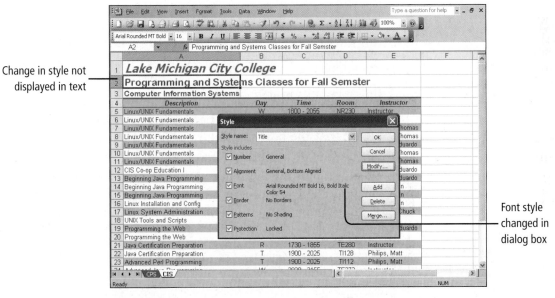

Font style changed in dialog box

Figure 6.49

4 Click **OK**.

The Style dialog box closes, and the font in cell A2 changes to Bold Italic. The change in style is applied only after the Style dialog box is closed.

5 Select cells **A1:E1** and then, on the Formatting toolbar, click the **Merge and Center** button ⊞. Click in any empty cell and notice that the Teal border no longer displays around the cell.

Because you cannot initiate the Merge and Center cells command from the Format Cells dialog box, you must make that formatting change before displaying the Style dialog box for the purpose of changing the style.

6 Click the **CPS tab**. Notice that the font for the Title in cell **A2** has changed to Bold Italic.

In most cases, changes to a style are updated to any cell in the workbook that uses that style.

7 Select **A1:E1** and then, on the Formatting toolbar, click the **Merge and Center** button ⊞. Display the **Format** menu and click **Style**.

The Style dialog box opens with the LMCC style listed in the Style name box. The Alignment needs to be changed to Center.

8 In the **Style** dialog box, click the **Modify** button. In the **Format Cells** dialog box, click the **Alignment tab**, under **Text alignment**, click the **Horizontal arrow**, and then click **Center**.

The text will be centered over the merged cell range, and the border displays over the merged cell area.

9 Click **OK** twice to close both dialog boxes.

10 Click the **CIS tab**. Click in any empty cell and notice that the border does not display around cell **A1**, even though a change was made to the LMCC format.

11 Click cell **A1**. Display the **Style** dialog box. Notice that the **Alignment** specifies **Horizontal Center, Bottom Aligned**.

12 Click **OK**. Click in any empty cell. On the Standard toolbar, click the **Save** button 🖫.

The style is reapplied. You need to reapply the style to the merged cell so that the border displays around the entire merged area. Compare your screen with Figure 6.50.

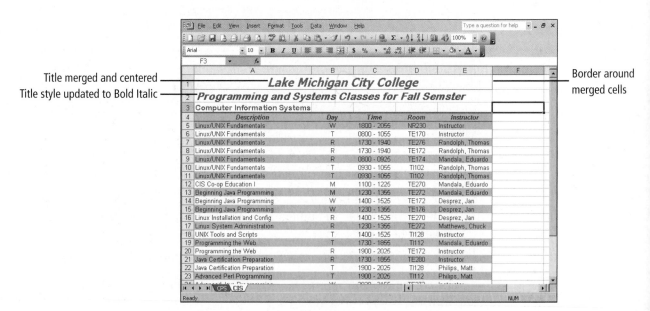

Title merged and centered —
Title style updated to Bold Italic —

Border around merged cells

Figure 6.50

Objective 5
Use Drawing Tools and Use the Research Feature

Drawing objects are shapes such as lines, arrows, rectangles, and circles that can be added to a worksheet and are especially useful to provide a place to document information or to draw attention to a particular cell or area of a worksheet. Additionally, the **Research** feature can be used to look up relevant information that can be placed within a drawing object. A button on the Standard toolbar opens the Research task pane, which provides an assortment of research tools such as a dictionary, thesaurus, encyclopedia, or other reference tools using the MSN Learning and Research Web site.

Activity 6.21 Using Drawing Tools

Drawing tools are objects such as lines, arrows, rectangles, and circles that can be added to a worksheet. The most common use in Excel is to add a *text box* for explanatory information related to the worksheet. A text box is a container into which you can type or insert text. Because a text box is a drawing object, it is not constrained by the dimension of a cell. You can resize, move, and format drawing objects.

1 Click the **CPS tab**, and then click anywhere in **column A**. From the **Insert** menu, click **Columns**.

An empty column is inserted to the left, and the remaining columns move to the right.

2 Widen **column A** to **30.00 (215 pixels)**. If the Drawing toolbar is not already displayed at the bottom of your screen, right-click on one of the toolbars and, from the displayed list, click Drawing. Alternatively, on the Standard toolbar, click the Drawing button.

The Drawing toolbar opens. On most systems, the Drawing toolbar docks at the lower edge of the window. See Figure 6.51.

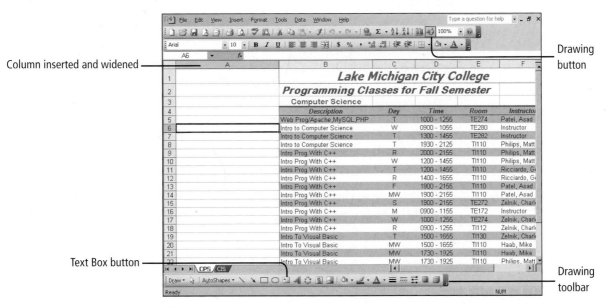

Figure 6.51

On the Drawing toolbar, click the **Text Box** button <span></span> and move the mouse pointer into the screen to the left side of cell **A9**.

The mouse pointer changes to a crosshair.

Look at Figure 6.52 to visualize how your box will be drawn, and then position the cross portion of the pointer at the upper boundary of cell **A9**, not quite at the left boundary. Drag down and to the right to the upper boundary of **row 14** and almost to the right boundary of **column A**.

As you draw, the mouse pointer changes shape slightly. When you release the mouse button, the text box displays with a slashed border and the insertion point inside the box, as shown in Figure 6.52. If you are not satisfied with your result, click the slashed border to display a pattern of dots, press Delete, click the Text Box button, and begin again.

Text box positioned in column A ———

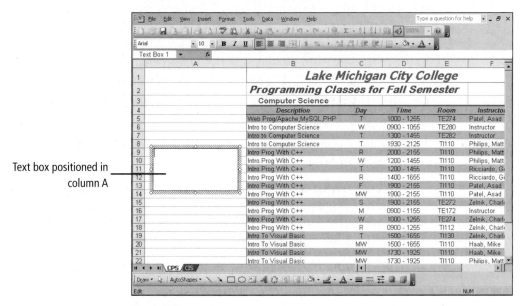

Figure 6.52

Inside the text box, type **Ten introductory C++ classes will be offered in the fall.**

Click the edge of the text box to display a pattern of dots.

To modify the text in a text box, you can either drag to select the text or display the pattern of dots. Displaying the pattern of dots acts to select all the text and the text box itself (although the text is not visibly selected) for the purpose of changing its format.

On the Formatting toolbar, change the **Font Size** to **12** pt., add **Bold** and **Italic** for emphasis, and then change the **Font Color** to **Plum**.

8 On the Drawing toolbar, click the **Line Color button arrow** . At the top of the displayed palette, click **No Line**. Click in any empty cell.

The font is formatted to match the spreadsheet format, and the line around the text box is removed. Compare your screen with Figure 6.53.

Text box font formatted ——

Perimeter line removed from text box

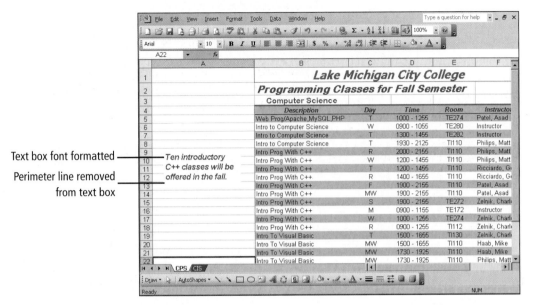

Figure 6.53

9 Look at Figure 6.54 to visualize how your arrow will be drawn. On the Drawing toolbar, click the **Arrow** button . Move the mouse pointer into the text box, to the right of the word *fall*, and then drag from the text box to the left edge of cell **B14**. If you are not satisfied with your result, press Delete, click the Arrow button, and begin again.

An arrow is drawn on the screen pointing to the C++ class offerings for this fall. Two small circles at either end indicate that the arrow object is selected. See Figure 6.54 to verify the placement of your arrow.

10 With the arrow still selected, on the Drawing toolbar, click the **Arrow Style** button . From the displayed list, point to the arrows to see the ScreenTips, and then locate and click **Arrow Style 9**. Click in any empty cell to cancel the selection and view the arrow's changed shape.

11 Click the arrow to select it, click the **Line Color button arrow** , and in the fourth row, click the seventh color—**Plum**. Compare your screen with Figure 6.54.

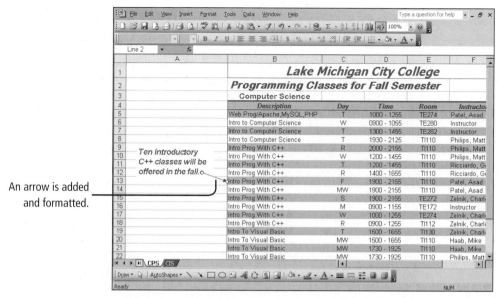

An arrow is added and formatted.

Figure 6.54

⒓ On the Standard toolbar, click the **Save** button 🖫.

Activity 6.22 Locating and Inserting Supporting Information

The Research tool can help you locate information related to topics or words in your worksheet.

◼ Click the **CIS tab**, and then click anywhere in **column A**. From the **Insert** menu, click **Columns**. Widen the new **column A** to **30.00 (215 pixels)**.

An empty column is inserted and widened to the left of the data.

◼ On the Drawing toolbar, click the **Text Box** button 🔲. Using the technique you practiced, in **column A**, draw a text box extending from cell **A4** to cell **A10**. If your computer is not connected to the Internet, read the Alert box following Step 4 and complete the instructions. Otherwise, continue with Step 3.

◼ On the Standard toolbar, click the **Research** button 🔍.

The Research task pane opens on the right of the window.

◼ In the **Search for** box, type **Linux** and then click the **All Reference Books arrow**. From the displayed list, click **Encarta Encyclopedia: English (North America)**.

The Research feature searches the designated reference and locates information and articles related to Linux. See Figure 6.55.

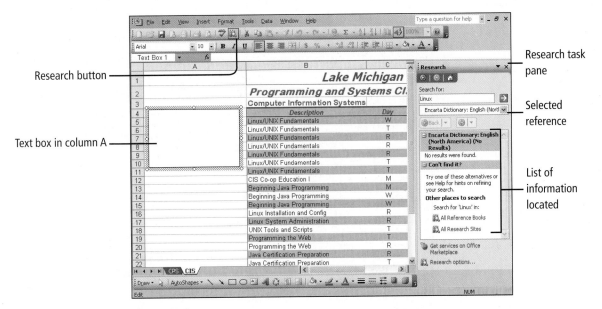

Research button

Text box in column A

Research task pane

Selected reference

List of information located

Figure 6.55

Alert!

If Your Computer Is Not Connected to the Internet

If your computer is not connected to the Internet, you will see a message box indicating that Excel cannot complete the operation. To continue with this activity, start Microsoft Word. On the Standard toolbar, click the Open button. In the folder that contains the files for this chapter, locate and open the Word File e06C_Linux. Use the techniques you have practiced in previous chapters to copy the text, and then close Word. On your Excel worksheet, click inside the text box and then, on the Formatting toolbar, click the Paste button. Continue the exercise at Step 9.

■5 Scroll through the list. Locate the reference to *Open Source Software article* and click the **Article—Encarta Encyclopedia** hyperlink.

The task pane moves to the left side of the screen, and the MSN Learning and Research window opens to the Open Source Software article.

■6 Scroll through the article and locate the paragraph beginning *As of 2003 Linux*. Starting at that point, drag to select the lines through the end of the parenthetical reference—ending *published by Microsoft.)* See Figure 6.56.

Research task pane —

Selected reference —

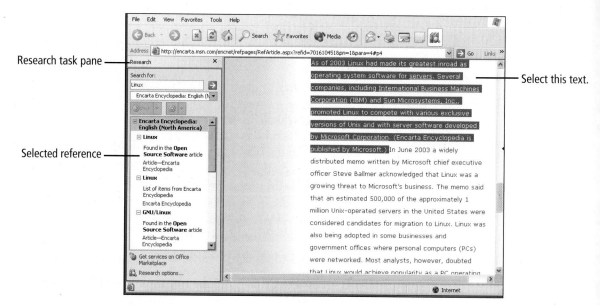

Select this text.

Figure 6.56

7 Press [Ctrl] + [C] to copy the selected text. Alternatively, from the Edit menu, click Copy. **Close** [X] the MSN Learning & Research window.

8 In **column A**, click in the text box, and then press [Ctrl] + [V] to paste the copied text. Alternatively, on the Standard toolbar, click the Paste button [🗎 ▼].

The reference to the Linux program displays in the text box.

9 On the lower edge of the text box, drag the middle sizing handle down until the entire reference is displayed. Compare your screen with Figure 6.57.

Reference displayed in text box —

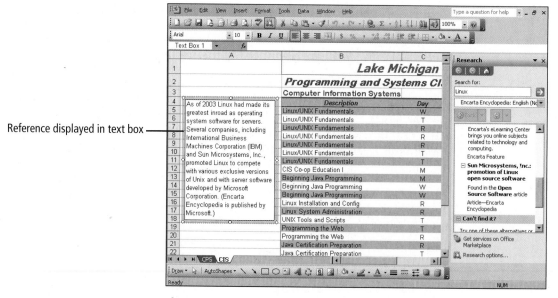

Figure 6.57

10 **Close** ☒ the **Research** task pane if it is still displayed. In the text box, in the first line, double-click the word **Linux**, and then click the **Bold** button **B**. Repeat this action to apply bold to the second occurrence of *Linux* in the article. On the Drawing toolbar, click the **Line Color button arrow** and at the top of the list, click **No Line** to remove the line from around the text box.

11 Select both worksheets. (Hint: Use the **Select All Sheets** command or the Ctrl key.) From the **File** menu, display the **Page Setup** dialog box. On the **Page tab**, click **Landscape**. On the **Margins tab**, under **Center on page**, select the **Horizontally** check box. On the **Header/Footer tab**, open the **Custom Footer** and, with the insertion point in the **Left section**, insert the **File Name**. Click **OK** twice.

12 On the Standard toolbar, click the **Save** button 🖫, and then click the **Print Preview** button 🔍. Scroll to view both worksheets, and then click **Print**. Click **OK** to print, and then close the workbook.

End You have completed Project 6C ——————————————————————

Project 6D **Pension**

Goal Seek is one of the Excel what-if analysis tools that can help you answer questions and plan for the future.

In Activity 6.23 you will use Goal Seek to determine the interest rate that is required to meet the investment goal for a pension fund investment. You will save your file as *6D_Pension_Firstname_Lastname.* Your completed worksheet will look similar to Figure 6.58.

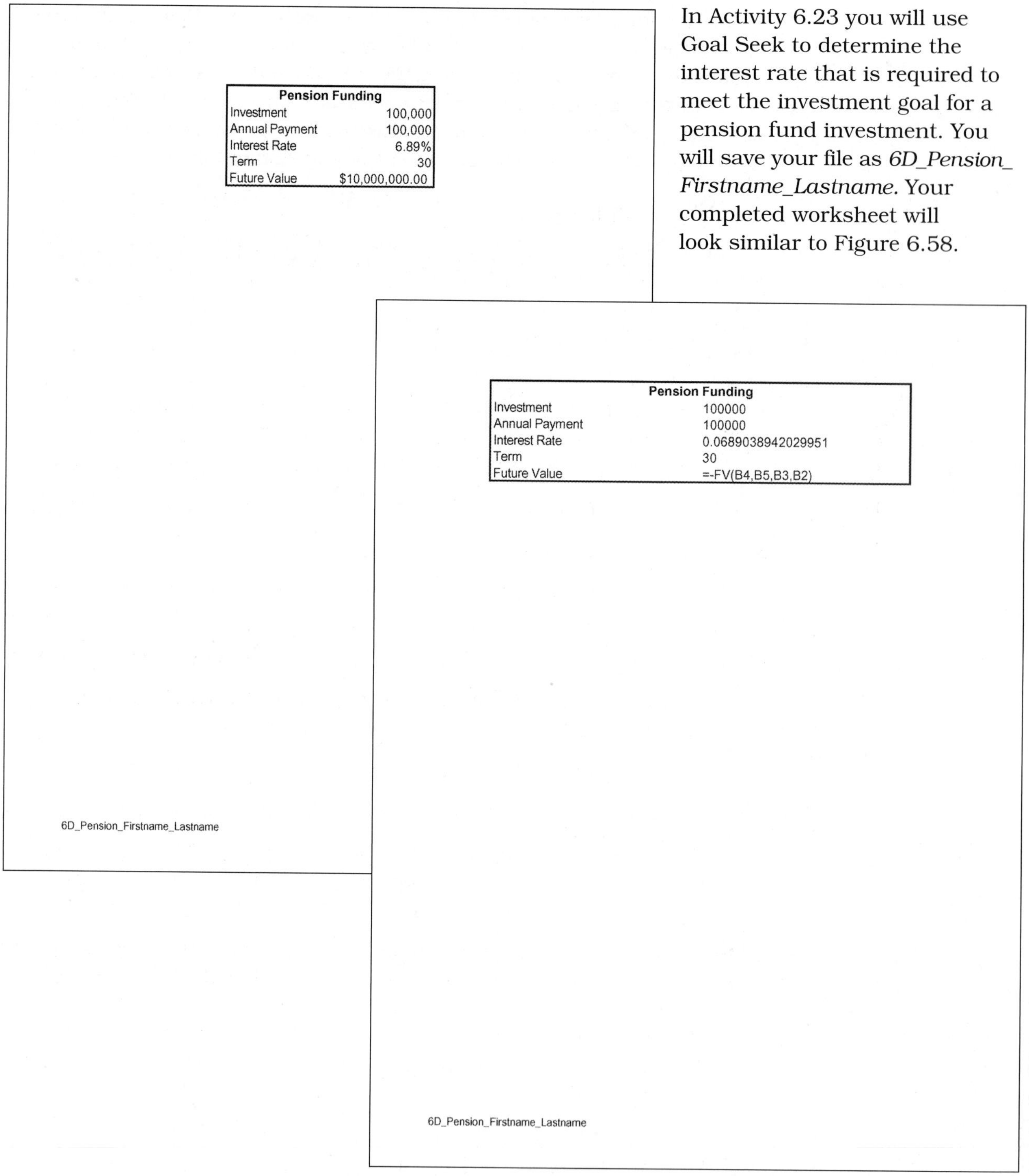

Pension Funding	
Investment	100,000
Annual Payment	100,000
Interest Rate	6.89%
Term	30
Future Value	$10,000,000.00

6D_Pension_Firstname_Lastname

Pension Funding	
Investment	100000
Annual Payment	100000
Interest Rate	0.0689038942029951
Term	30
Future Value	=-FV(B4,B5,B3,B2)

6D_Pension_Firstname_Lastname

Figure 6.58
Project 6D—Pension

Objective 6
Use Goal Seek

Goal Seek is a what-if analysis tool that can help you answer questions. Goal Seek is useful when you know the desired result of a formula but not the input value the formula needs to determine the result. For example, if you need to borrow money to buy a car but can only afford a payment of $200 a month, Goal Seek can help you answer the question, "How much can I borrow?" In the following activity, you will determine, for David Hanna, Vice President of Finance, the minimum interest rate required to meet the fund goal for a new investment for the employee pension fund. Mr. Hanna knows the amount of money that will be invested annually and the total amount that will be needed at the end of the term.

Activity 6.23 Using Goal Seek

1 Start Excel if necessary. On the Standard toolbar, click the **Open** button. Navigate to the location where the student files for this textbook are stored. Locate and open the file **e06D_Pension**.

2 Be sure only the Standard and Formatting toolbars are displayed. Close any other toolbars. From the **File** menu, click **Save As**. In the **Save As** dialog box, use the **Save in arrow** to navigate to the location where you are storing your files for this chapter. In the **File name** box, type **6D_Pension_Firstname_Lastname** Click the **Save** button.

This worksheet displays the figures for a pension fund investment.

3 In cell **B4**, type **6%** and press Enter.

This is an estimate of the interest rate to use in the Future Value formula.

4 Click cell **B6**. On the Formula Bar, click the **Insert Function** button [fx]. In the **Insert Function** dialog box, click the **Or select a category arrow**, and then click **Financial**.

The Financial functions display in the Select a function box.

5 In the **Select a function** box, click **FV**, and then click **OK**.

The Function Arguments dialog box displays. Recall that you used this function in an earlier chapter to determine the value of an annuity.

6 In the **Function Arguments** dialog box, click the **Rate** box, and then click cell **B4**—the estimated interest rate. Click the **Nper** box, and then click cell **B5**—the term of the investment. Click the **Pmt** box, and then click cell **B3**—the annual payments—and, finally, click the **Pv** box and click cell **B2**—the initial amount invested. Compare your screen with Figure 6.59.

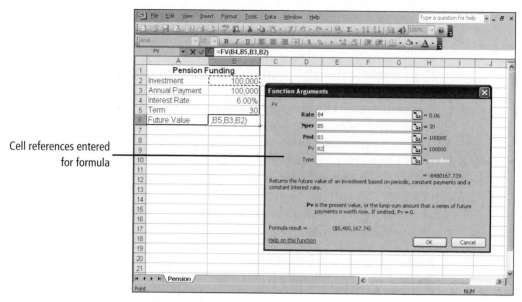

Cell references entered for formula

Figure 6.59

7 Click **OK**.

The Function Argument dialog box closes and the result—($8,480,167.74)—displays in cell B6.

The result displays as a negative number because these are funds that are paid out.

8 Click cell **B6** if necessary and, in the Formula Bar, edit the formula to place a minus sign after the equal sign. Verify that the formula displays as =-FV(B4,B5,B3,B2) and press Enter.

The results displays as a positive number—$8,480,167.74.

9 Make **B6** the active cell and then, from the **Tools** menu, click **Goal Seek**.

The Goal Seek dialog box opens, and B6 displays in the *Set cell* box. This is the cell in which you want to set the value to a specific amount—$10,000,000.

10 In the **Goal Seek** dialog box, click the **To value** box and type **10,000,000**—ten million.

This is the amount that you want the pension to be worth after the 30-year term. When you enter a number in this box, it is not necessary to use commas.

11 Click the **By changing cell** box, and then click cell **B4**—the interest rate.

The interest rate is the variable you are trying to find. Notice that the reference in the *By changing cell* box is absolute. Compare your screen with Figure 6.60.

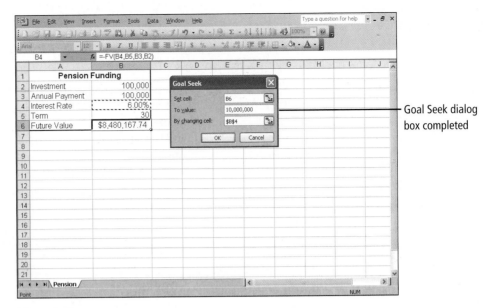

Goal Seek dialog box completed

Figure 6.60

12 Click **OK**.

The Goal Seek Status dialog box opens, stating that it found a solution. The Future Value in cell B6 displays $10,000,000.00, and the interest rate in cell B4 displays as 6.89%. This answers the question: "At what interest rate must I invest $100,000 to have the total value of the pension fund equal $10,000,000 after 30 years?"

13 In the **Goal Seek Status** dialog box, click **OK**.

The new numbers display in the worksheet.

14 From the **File** menu, display the **Page Setup** dialog box. On the **Margins tab**, under **Center on page**, select the **Horizontally** check box. On the **Header/Footer tab**, create a **Custom Footer** and place the **File Name** in the **Left section**. Click **OK** twice.

15 Save your file, and then print it. Press Ctrl + ` to display the formula. Print the formula page, and then press Ctrl + ` to return the page to the worksheet figures. After printing the file, close the file, saving changes if prompted to do so.

End You have completed Project 6D ⸻⸻⸻⸻⸻

Summary

Excel offers several template worksheets that you can use for common financial tasks such as completing an expense report, time card, sales invoice, or purchase order. These preformatted forms are quick and easy to use because they use a fill-in-the-blank approach. The formulas are prewritten in locked cells so that the user does not need to know how to use Excel to produce a report that has the appropriate totals. In Project 6A, you were introduced to templates when you completed an expense report.

Project 6B focused on several techniques for working with large worksheets. These included using the Freeze Panes command to keep column and row headings in place while scrolling the rest of the window; using the Find and Replace dialog box to locate and change information; using the Go To function to locate blank cells; and using the COUNTIF function to determine the number of cells that matched a certain condition. You hid columns to control what was displayed on the worksheet, and you practiced splitting the screen so that you could see two nonadjacent parts of the worksheet at the same time and scroll each area separately. The Arrange Workbooks feature was used so that you could view two worksheets from different workbooks at the same time. Finally, you used the Sort command to control the order of the data and the AutoFilter command to restrict the data that was displayed to only those rows that matched specific criteria.

Additional tools were introduced for sharing a large worksheet with others. You practiced how to repeat the column and row headings on each page and control the break between pages so that the data printed in a logical and organized manner. A hyperlink was inserted to another workbook to provide quick reference to contact information. You viewed and saved a worksheet as a Web Page, as a comma separated value file, and as a text file.

In Project 6C, the AutoFormat feature was introduced, and you practiced creating, applying, and modifying styles. Drawing tools were introduced, and you added a text box and an arrow to insert related comments on the worksheet. The Research tool was used to locate related information, and then you added that text to a text box.

Finally, in Project 6D, you used Goal Seek to determine the interest rate required to meet a specific funding goal for a pension investment.

In This Chapter You Practiced How To

- Use Excel Templates
- Work with a Large Worksheet
- Prepare a Worksheet to Share with Others
- Enhance Worksheets with AutoFormats and Styles
- Use Drawing Tools and Use the Research Feature
- Use Goal Seek

Matching

Match each term in the second column with its correct definition in the first column by writing the letter of the term on the blank line in front of the correct definition.

_____ 1. A function that enables you to determine the number of cells in a range that meet a specified condition.

_____ 2. The drawing object that is used most frequently to type comments or related information.

_____ 3. The file type that is used when you want to save an Excel file with tabs between each cell in a row.

_____ 4. A command that gives you a choice of predesigned formats that can be applied to a group of cells.

_____ 5. The default style that is applied to new workbooks.

_____ 6. The name for the group of objects such as lines, arrows, rectangles, and circles that can be added to a worksheet.

_____ 7. The what-if analysis tool that finds the input needed in one cell in order to determine the desired result in another cell.

_____ 8. The file type that is used when you need to save an Excel file so that there is a comma between each cell and a paragraph return at the end of each row.

_____ 9. A tool that can be used to help locate information related to the data in your worksheet.

_____ 10. The command that is used when you need to view multiple worksheets on your screen at the same time.

_____ 11. Predesigned and preformatted financial forms that have built-in formulas for calculating totals based on the data that is entered.

_____ 12. Colored and underlined text or a graphic that you click to go to a file, a location in a file, a Web page on the World Wide Web, or a Web page on your organization's intranet.

_____ 13. The command that is used to set the column and row headings so that they remain on the screen while you scroll to other parts of the worksheet.

_____ 14. Categories of information organized in columns.

_____ 15. The term used for a condition on which cells are evaluated, for the purpose of displaying only those rows that meet that condition.

A Arrange

B AutoFormat

C Comma separated value (CSV)

D COUNTIF

E Criteria

F Drawing objects

G Fields

H Freeze Panes

I Goal Seek

J Hyperlink

K Normal

L Research

M Templates

N Text Box

O Text (tab delimited)

Fill in the Blank Write the correct answer in the space provided.

1. In the Sort dialog box, if you want to sort the selected column in alphabetical order, click the _____ option button.

2. Some cells in a template are _____ to prevent the user from entering data in that cell or accidentally overwriting formulas.

3. When sorting data, the first sort is known as the _____ sort.

4. If the rows or the columns are locked so that they do not scroll, it is known as _____.

5. If you want to sort numerical data from the highest value to the lowest, choose _____.

6. When sorting on multiple columns, the second or third sort is known as a _____ sort.

7. When printing a large worksheet, you can change the rows or columns that print on each page by using the _____ view.

8. When printing a large worksheet, you can select rows or columns to repeat on each page using the _____ dialog box.

9. To be able to view and scroll two different areas on a worksheet at the same time, use the _____ _____ command.

10. To limit the data displayed to only those records that match a stated condition, use the _____ command.

Project 6E — Loan

Objectives: *Use Excel Templates, Work with a Large Worksheet, and Prepare a Worksheet to Share with Others.*

David Hanna, Vice President of Finance, is considering different financing options for the purchase of new equipment for the college. He has requested a spreadsheet calculating the loan payment and an amortization schedule as one of three financing options he is considering. In this project, you will use the Excel Loan Amortization template to calculate the payment and related amortization schedule. Your completed worksheet will look similar to the one shown in Figure 6.61. You will save your workbook as *6E_Loan_Firstname_Lastname.*

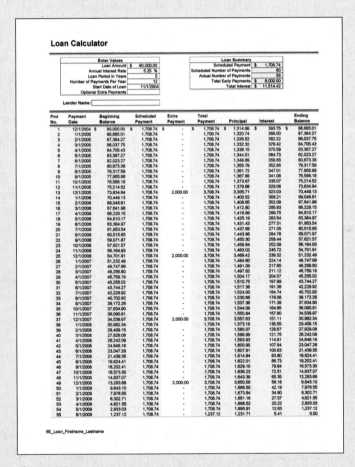

Figure 6.61

1. **Start** Excel. On the menu bar, click **File** and, from the displayed list, click **New**. In the **New Workbook** task pane, under **Templates**, click **On my computer**. In the displayed **Templates** dialog box, click the **Spreadsheet Solutions tab**. Click the **Loan Amortization** icon, and then click **OK**.

(Project 6E–Loan continues on the next page)

(Project 6E–Loan continued)

2. In the displayed **Loan Amortization** worksheet, in cell **D6** type **90,000** and then press [Enter]. Recall that templates are preformatted, and the value you entered displays in currency format with two decimals.

3. The active cell moves to cell **D7**—the Annual Interest Rate. Type **.0525** and press [Enter]. Recall that interest rates are usually entered in decimal format but display as percentages—5.25%.

4. The active cell moves to cell **D8**—the length or term of the loan in years. Type **5** and press [Enter].

5. In the **Number of Payments Per Year** cell—**D9**—type **12** and then press [Enter]. In the **Start Date** cell—**D10**—type **11/1/2004** and then press [Enter].

   The loan payment is calculated to be *$1,708.74*, and the interest paid for the term of the loan is *$12,524.31*. The amortization schedule is completed. A ScreenTip displays that describes how to use the Extra Payment option.

6. On the Standard toolbar, click the **Save** button. Save the file in your folder for this chapter with the name **6E_Loan_Firstname_Lastname**

7. Mr. Hanna thinks the college will be able to make additional payments of $2,000 at the end of each year of the loan—payment numbers 13, 25, 37, and 49. Click cell **E18**. From the **Window** menu, click **Freeze Panes**. Recall that freezing panes makes it easier to scroll the window and still see the identifying row or column titles.

8. Scroll down and click cell **E30**, type **2000** and press [Enter].

   The additional payment at the beginning of the second year of the loan—payment 13—is recorded, and the worksheet recalculates. *$2000* displays in cell H9—*Total Early Payments*.

9. Scroll down, click cell **E42**, type **2000** and then press [Enter]. The worksheet is recalculated, and the early payment total displays $4,000.00. Continue in this manner and enter an extra payment of $2,000 in cells **E54** and **E66**. Notice that the *Actual Number of Payments* shows as 55, the *Total Early Payments* as $8,000.00, and the *Total Interest* is reduced to *$11,514.42*.

10. From the **Window** menu, click **Unfreeze Panes**. From the **View** menu, click **Header and Footer**. Add the file name to the **Custom Footer** as you have in the past. Click the **Save** button.

11. Display the **File** menu and click **Web Page Preview**.

(Project 6E–Loan continues on the next page)

Skill Assessments (continued)

(Project 6E–Loan continued)

12. In the browser window, display the **File** menu and click **Save As**. Use the **Save in arrow** to navigate to the folder where you are saving your files for this chapter. In the **File name** box, be sure *6E_Loan_ Firstname_Lastname* displays. In the **Save as type** box, be sure **Web Page, complete (*.htm;*.html)** displays, and then click **Save**.

The file is saved as a Web page so that Mr. Hanna can view it using the college intranet.

13. Close the browser. From the **File** menu, display the **Page Setup** dialog box and, on the **Page tab**, under **Scaling**, click the **Fit to** option button. Be sure to fit to 1 page. In the **Page Setup** dialog box, click the **Print Preview** button and then, on the Print Preview toolbar, click the **Print** button and click **OK**.

14. Close the file, saving changes if prompted to do so.

End You have completed Project 6E

Project 6F — Degrees

Objectives: *Prepare a Worksheet to Share with Others and Enhance Worksheets with AutoFormats and Styles.*

Henry Sabaj, Vice President of Academic Affairs, wants to review the programs offered by departments and their related degrees. In this exercise, you will work with a large spreadsheet and create and apply styles. Your completed file will look similar to the one shown in Figure 6.62. You will save your workbook as *6F_Degrees_Firstname_Lastname*.

1. On the Standard toolbar, click the **Open** button. Navigate to the location where the student files for this textbook are stored. Locate and open the file **e06F_Degrees**.

2. From the **File** menu, click **Save As**. In the **Save As** dialog box, use the **Save in arrow** to navigate to the location where you are storing your files for this chapter. In the **File name** box, type **6F_Degrees_Firstname_Lastname** Click the **Save** button.

3. Click cell **A2**. From the Formatting toolbar, click the **Font arrow**, and then click **Tahoma**. Click the **Font Size arrow**, and then click **16**. Click the **Bold** button and the **Center** button. Click the **Font Color arrow** and in the second row, click the fifth color—**Teal**.

(Project 6F–Degrees continues on the next page)

(Project 6F–Degrees continued)

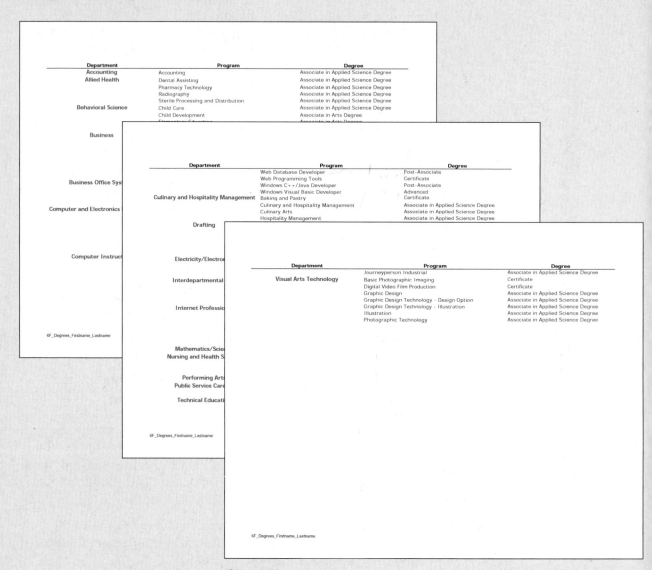

Figure 6.62

4. From the **Format** menu, click **Style**. In the **Style** dialog box, in the **Style name** box, type **Dept** Examine the changes to the **Style** dialog box to be sure it displays the choices you made in the previous step. (You may notice the font color displays Dark Cyan instead of Teal. The correct color has been selected, so do not be concerned about this naming difference.) Click **OK**.

5. Click cell **A3**, hold down Ctrl, and then click cells **A7** and **A11**. From the **Format** menu, click **Style**. Click the **Style name arrow**, click **Dept**, and then click **OK**.

The font size is likely too large for the longer department names and thus should be modified before it is applied to the rest of the worksheet.

(Project 6F–Degrees continues on the next page)

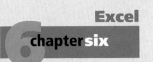
(Project 6F–Degrees continued)

6. Click cell **A11**, display the **Format** menu, and click **Style**. Be sure that *Dept* displays in the **Style name** box, and then click the **Modify** button. In the **Format Cells** dialog box, click the **Font tab**, and then change the **Size** to 14. Click **OK** twice.

All the cells that have been formatted using the Dept style are changed to a smaller font.

7. Hold down Ctrl and continue down the **Department** column to select the cells that contain department names. Next, use the **Style** dialog box to apply the **Dept** style to the cells that display a department name.

8. From the **File** menu, click **Page Setup**. On the **Page tab**, click **Landscape**. Under **Scaling**, click the **Fit to** option button, and then change the **tall** box to **3**. Click the **Header/Footer tab** and add the file name to the custom footer as you have in the past. Click the **Sheet tab** and, under **Print titles**, click in the **Rows to repeat at top** box, and then click the **row 1 heading** to select **row 1** to repeat at the top of each printed page. Click the **Print Preview** button. Scroll through the pages to see how they will display when printed.

9. On the Print Preview toolbar, click **Print**. Click **OK** in the **Print** dialog box. On the Standard toolbar, click the **Save** button, and then close your file.

End You have completed Project 6F

Project 6G—Enrollment

Objectives: *Enhance Worksheets with AutoFormats and Styles, Use Drawing Tools and Use the Research Feature, and Use Goal Seek.*

Joyce Walker-MacKinney, President of Lake Michigan City College, has a goal to grow student enrollment to 20,000 in the next ten years. She wants to know what the target student population should be in each intervening year and the rate of growth that is needed to achieve this goal. In this exercise you will use Goal Seek to answer these questions. Your completed worksheet will look similar to the one shown in Figure 6.63. You will save your workbook as *6G_Enrollment_Firstname_Lastname*.

1. Open a new, blank worksheet. In cell **A1**, type **Lake Michigan City College** and in cell **A2**, type **Enrollment Projection**

2. On the Standard toolbar, click the **Save** button. In the **Save As** dialog box, navigate to the location where you are storing your files for this chapter. In the **File name** box, type **6G_Enrollment_Firstname_Lastname** and then click **Save**.

(Project 6G–Enrollment continues on the next page)

(Project 6G–Enrollment continued)

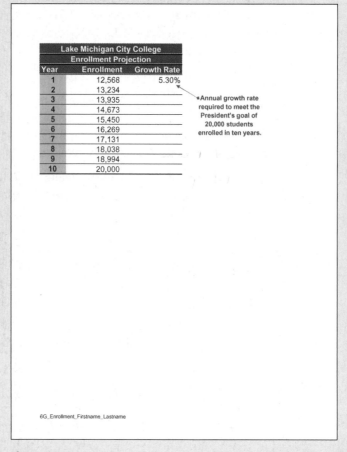

Figure 6.63

3. In cell **A3**, type **Year** and in cell **B3**, type **Enrollment** and in cell **C3**, type **Growth Rate**

4. In cell **A4**, type **1** and in cell **A5**, type **2** Select the range **A4:A5**, point to the fill handle in the corner of **A5**, and drag down to create the series 1 through 10.

5. In cell **B4**, type **12568** and press Enter. This is the current student enrollment. Click cell **B4**, on the Formatting toolbar click the **Comma Style** button, and then click the **Decrease Decimal** button twice.

(Project 6G–Enrollment continues on the next page)

(Project 6G–Enrollment continued)

6. In cell **B5**, type **=b4*(1+c4)** and press Enter. This formula multiplies the previous year's enrollment—cell **B4**—by 1 plus the growth rate that will display in cell **C4**. The absolute cell reference is applied to cell **C4** so that you can copy the formula to years 3 through 10 and maintain cell **C4** in the formula. The growth rate will be calculated when you use Goal Seek. Click cell **B5** and, using the fill handle, copy the formula to cells **B6:B13**. Because there is no value yet in cell C4, all the numbers display as *12568*. With the cells selected, on the Formatting toolbar, click the **Comma Style** button, and then click the **Decrease Decimal** button twice.

   The results—*12,568*—display in cells B6:B13. The result for each year displays the same number until the growth rate factor is determined using Goal Seek.

7. Click cell **B13**. In this cell, you want to set the value equal to the desired enrollment of 20,000. With cell **B13** the active cell, display the **Tools** menu and click **Goal Seek**. In the **Goal Seek** dialog box, be sure that *B13* displays in the **Set cell** box. In the **To value** box, type **20,000** and then press Tab. In the **By changing cell** box, type **c4** which is the cell you have designated to display the growth rate. Click **OK**.

   Goal Seek calculates the growth rate to be 0.052975. The dialog box shows that Goal Seek found an answer that results in 20,000 students enrolled in year 10.

8. In the **Goal Seek Status** dialog box, click **OK**. Click cell **C4** and format it as a percentage with two decimals so that it displays as *5.30%*. Save your changes.

9. Select the range **A3:C13**. From the **Format** menu, display the **AutoFormat** dialog box. Click the **Classic 2** format and click **OK**. Select the range **A1:C13** and change the **Font Size** to **14** pt. Widen **column A** to **65 pixels** and **columns B** and **C** to **145 pixels**.

10. Click cell **A3**. On the Formatting toolbar, double-click the **Format Painter** button, and then click cell **A1** and cell **A2**. Click the **Format Painter** button to turn it off. Recall that the Format Painter can be used to apply formats from one cell to another. Only the first part of the text in these cells may display. This will be corrected in the next step.

11. Select **A1:C1** and, from the Formatting toolbar, click the **Merge and Center** button. Repeat this action to merge and center cells **A2:C2**.

(Project 6G–Enrollment continues on the next page)

(Project 6G–Enrollment continued)

12. If necessary, on the Standard toolbar, click the Drawing button to display the Drawing toolbar. On the Drawing toolbar, click the **Text Box** button. Look at Figure 6.63 to visualize the location of the text box. Starting in the middle of the upper boundary of cell **D6**, drag down and to the right, to the lower-right corner of cell **F10**. In the text box you just created, type **Annual growth rate required to meet the President's goal of 20,000 students enrolled in ten years**.

13. Click the edge of the text box to display a pattern of dots indicating that it is selected. On the Formatting toolbar, change the **Font Size** to **12**, change the **Font Color** to **Plum**, change the alignment to **Center**, and apply **Bold**. On the Drawing toolbar, click the **Line Color button arrow**, and then click **No Line**. Recall that this removes the line from the border of the text box. Adjust the size of the text box so that the text displays on five lines.

14. On the Drawing toolbar, click the **Arrow** button. Draw an arrow from the text box to cell **C4** as shown in Figure 6.63. With the arrow selected, on the Drawing toolbar, click the **Line Color button arrow**, and then click **Plum**. Click the **Arrow Style** button, and then click **Arrow Style 8**.

15. Display the **Header and Footer** dialog box and add the file name to the custom footer as you have previously. From the **Page Setup** dialog box, center the worksheet horizontally on the page. Save your changes, and then click the **Print Preview** button to see the worksheet as it will print. Compare your worksheet with Figure 6.63. Print the file, and then close it.

 You have completed Project 6G

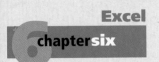
Project 6H—Online Classes

Objectives: *Work with a Large Worksheet and Enhance Worksheets with AutoFormats and Styles.*

The Academic Affairs office is promoting its increased offering of online classes. A worksheet has been developed listing the classes, but it needs to be formatted to make it more visually appealing. In this project, you will use the AutoFormat feature and create styles to apply to the worksheet. You will also update a name change. Your completed worksheet will look similar to the one shown in Figure 6.64. You will save your workbook as *6H_Online_Classes_Firstname_Lastname*.

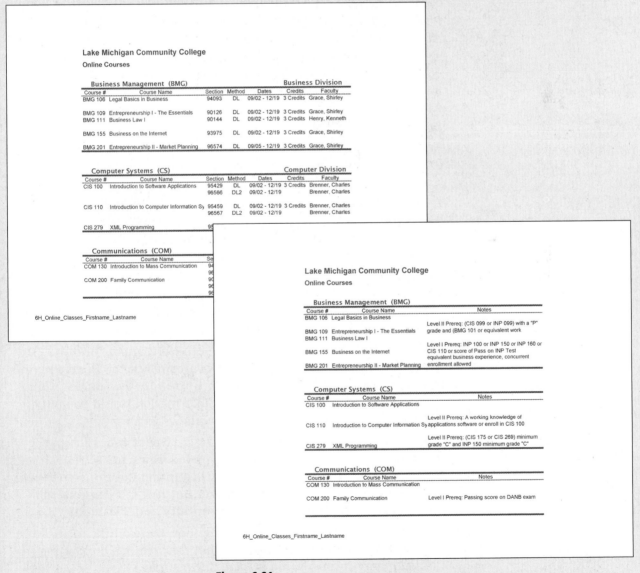

Figure 6.64

(Project 6H–Online Classes continues on the next page)

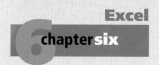
(Project 6H–Online Classes continued)

1. Start Excel. On the Standard toolbar, click the **Open** button. Navigate to the location where the student files for this textbook are stored. Locate and open the file **e06H_Online_Classes**. Save the file in your folder with the name 6H_Online_Classes_Firstname_Lastname

2. Click cell **A4**. Change the **Font** to **Lucida Sans**, the **Font Size** to **12 pt.**, and the **Font Color** to **Violet**. From the **Format** menu, open the **Style** dialog box. In the **Style name** box, type **Program** click **Add**, and then click **OK**.

3. Click cell **F4**. Open the **Style** dialog box, click the **Style name arrow**, click **Program**, and then click **OK**. Apply the **Program** style to the Program and Division titles in **rows 13** and **22** (Hint: Hold down Ctrl to select all the cells, and then apply the style to the multiple selection.)

4. Select the range **A5:H10**. Display the **Format** menu and click **AutoFormat**. Click the **Accounting 2** AutoFormat and then, at the right side of the dialog box, click the **Options** button. At the bottom of the dialog box, under **Formats to apply**, clear the check boxes for **Number, Alignment** and **Width/Height** This area of the **AutoFormat** dialog box enables you to customize the selected AutoFormat. Click **OK**.

5. Apply the same AutoFormat to the range **A14:H19** and **A23:H28**. (Hint: You cannot apply AutoFormat to multiple selections.)

6. Select cells **A1:A2**—the title lines. Click the **Font Color** button to apply the **Violet** color. Select **row 2** and increase its height to **27 pt. (36 pixels)**. Click cell **A2** and display the **Format Cells** dialog box. On the **Alignment tab**, under **Text alignment**, click the **Vertical arrow**, and then click **Center**. Click **OK**.

7. Click cell **A1**. Press Ctrl + F to open the **Find** dialog box. In the **Find what** box, type **Goetze** Click the **Replace tab** and, in the **Replace with** box, type **Rhoades** Click **Find Next**, and then click **Replace**. Replace all occurrences of Goetze with the new name.

8. From the **File** menu, open the **Page Setup** dialog box. Add the **File Name** to the **Left section** of the footer area. Click the **Print Preview** button. Click the **Next** button to view each of the two pages. Notice that as currently set up, each row of information would be split on two pages. **Close** the Print Preview window.

9. Display the **Page Setup** dialog box. On the **Sheet tab**, click in the **Rows to repeat at top** box, and then select **rows 1:2** so that the title rows repeat at the top of each page. Click in the **Columns to repeat at left** box, and then select **columns A:B**. Click the **Margins tab**, and center the worksheet both **Horizontally** and **Vertically.**

10. Click the **Print Preview** button. Verify that the two title lines display at the top of each page and that the columns containing the Course # and Course Name display on each page.

11. Save, print, and then close the file.

 End You have completed Project 6H

Project 6I—Timecard

Objectives: *Use Excel Templates, Work with a Large Worksheet, and Prepare a Worksheet to Share with Others.*

In this project, you will complete the Excel Timecard template to report the hours that Mary Adair, an hourly employee at the college, has worked for the past two weeks. You will also save the file as a CSV file so it can be uploaded to a database program. Your timecard template and CSV file will look similar to the ones shown in Figure 6.65. You will save your workbook as *6I_Timecard_Firstname_Lastname*.

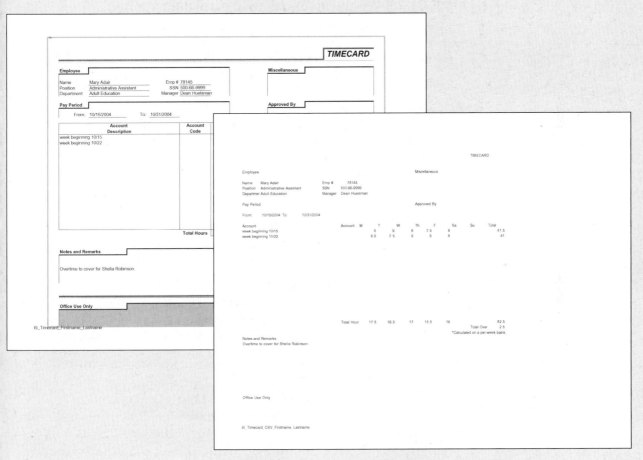

Figure 6.65

1. Start Excel. From the **File** menu, click **New**. In the **New Workbook** task pane, under **Templates**, click **On my computer**. In the **Templates** dialog box, click the **Spreadsheet Solutions tab**, click **Timecard**, and then click **OK**.

(Project 6I–Timecard continues on the next page)

(Project 6I–Timecard continued)

2. In the **Name** box, type **Mary Adair** In the **Emp** # box, type **78145** Enter the remainder of the employee information in the appropriate areas as follows:

Position	**Administrative Assistant**
SSN	**500-66-9999**
Department	**Adult Education**
Manager	**Dean Huelsman**

3. In the **From** field, type **10/15/2004** and, in the **To** field, type **10/31/2004** In the time card area, enter the following:

Account Description	M	T	W	Th	F
week beginning 10/15	9	9	8	7.50	8
week beginning 10/22	8.5	7.5	9	8	8

4. Display the **Page Setup** dialog box, click the **Header/Footer tab**, create a **Custom Footer**, and in the **Left section**, insert the **File Name**. Save the file in your folder for this chapter with the name **6I_Timecard_Firstname_Lastname**

5. In the *Notes and Remarks* area, type **Overtime to cover for Shelia Robinson**

6. On the Standard toolbar, click the **Save** button, and then click the **Print Preview** button to see the worksheet as it will print. Compare your worksheet with Figure 6.65. Click the **Print** button.

7. From the **File** menu, click **Save As**. In the **Save As** dialog box, change the **Save as type** box to **CSV (Comma Delimited)**. Change the **File name** to **6I_Timecard_CSV_Firstname_Lastname** Click **Save**, and then click **Yes** to acknowledge the information message.

8. Close the file, saving your changes and acknowledging any messages. Click the **Open** button. In the **Open** dialog box, change the **Files of type** box to display *All Files*. Locate and open the **6I_Timecard_CSV_Firstname_Lastname** file. It displays in Excel without the template formatting. Widen **columns E** and **G** to display all the cells. Select **columns A**, **B**, and **C** and, from the **Format** menu, point to **Column**, and then click **Hide**.

9. Click the **Print Preview** button. Open the **Page Setup** dialog box and add a custom footer with the file name as you have in the past. On the **Page tab**, click the **Fit to** option button and **Landscape** orientation. Print the file.

10. Save the changes and close the file, acknowledging the message boxes if they display. Click **Yes** to save the changes to the file.

End You have completed Project 6I

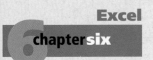
Performance Assessments (continued)

Project 6J—Computer Budget

Objectives: *Prepare a Worksheet to Share with Others, Enhance Worksheets with AutoFormats and Styles, Use Drawing Tools and Use the Research Feature, and Use Goal Seek.*

The price of computers has continued to drop over the years, so either the college budget for this item can be reduced or more computers and software can be purchased for the same amount of money each year. In this project, you will use Goal Seek to prepare a projection for Margaret Young, the Information Technology Director, for the cost of replacing computers based on past price reductions. Your completed worksheet will look similar to the one shown in Figure 6.66. You will save your workbook as *6J_Computer_Budget_Firstname_Lastname*.

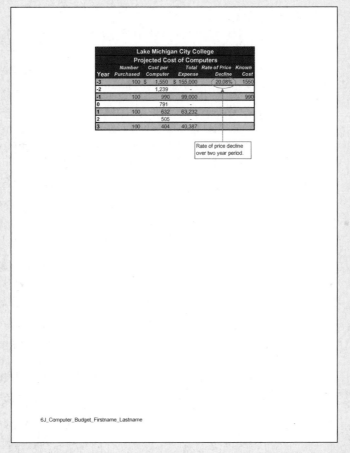

Figure 6.66

(Project 6J–Computer Budget continues on the next page)

(Project 6J–Computer Budget continued)

1. On the Standard toolbar, click the **Open** button. Navigate to the location where the student files for this textbook are stored. Locate and open the file **e06J_Computer_Budget**.

2. Open the **Save As** dialog box. Save the file in the folder with the other files for this chapter, using the name **6G_Computer_Budget_ Firstname_Lastname** Display the **Header and Footer** dialog box and add the file name to the custom footer as you have previously done.

3. Rather than showing specific years, the year column displays negative numbers for previous years, zero for the current year, and positive numbers for future years. Click cell **D4** and enter a formula that calculates the total expense for the computers purchased three years ago. Copy the formula to cells **D5:D10**. Zeros will display in these cells until the cost per computer is calculated.

4. In cell **C5**, type **=c4*(1-e4)** and press Enter. Copy this formula to cells **C6:C10**. This is the formula to calculate the rate of decline in computer prices, where the value in *E4* (not yet calculated) will be a rate of decline in price.

5. Click cell **C6** and display the **Goal Seek** dialog box. In the **To value** box, type **990** which is the known cost of computers last year. In the **By changing cell** box, type **e4** and then press Enter. The result shows a rate of decline of approximately *0.2008* in cell **E4**. Click **OK**.

6. Format cell **E4** as a percentage with two decimals. Format cells **C5:D10** using the **Comma Style** with no decimals. Format cells **C4:D4** using the **Currency Style** and no decimals. Save your changes.

7. Select the range **A3:F10**. Display the **AutoFormat** dialog box and apply the **Classic 3** style. Select cells **A6:F6**, press Ctrl, and select cells **A8:F8** and **A10:F10**. On the Formatting toolbar, click the **Fill Color arrow**, and then click **Gray 25%**.

8. Click cell **A3**, and then double-click the **Format Painter** button. Click cells **A1** and **A2**. **Merge and Center** the title in cell **A1** over cells **A1:F1**. Do the same for the title in cell **A2**.

9. On the Drawing toolbar, click the **Text Box** button, and then draw a box from the lower left corner of cell **D12** to the lower right side of cell **F14**. In the text box, type **Rate of price decline over two year period** Click the edge of the box to display a pattern of dots, click the **Font Color arrow**, and then click **Dark Blue**. This matches the font color used in the AutoFormat style that has been applied. Adjust the size of the text box as needed to display the text on two lines in an open space under the formatted area in **column E**.

(Project 6J–Computer Budget continues on the next page)

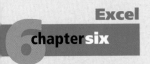
(Project 6J—Computer Budget continued)

10. On the Drawing toolbar, click the **Oval** button. Position the crosshair pointer above and to the left of cell **E4**. Drag down and to the right to draw a white oval over the number in cell **E4**. With the white oval selected, on the Drawing toolbar, click the **Fill Color arrow** and, at the top of the color palette, click **No Fill**. Click the **Line Color arrow** and click **Red**.

11. On the Drawing toolbar, click the **Arrow** button and draw an arrow from the text box to the number in cell **E4**. Click the **Line Color** button and apply **Red** to the arrow.

12. Display the **Page Setup** dialog box and center the page **Horizontally**.

13. On the Standard toolbar, click the **Save** button, and then click the **Print Preview** button. Compare your worksheet with Figure 6.66. Print the worksheet, and then close the file.

 End You have completed Project 6J ———————————————

Project 6K — Millage

Objectives: *Use Drawing Tools and Use the Research Feature and Use Goal Seek.*

Lake Michigan City College is partially funded by taxes assessed on property owners in the county. The current rate of 3.84 mills per $1,000 value in property will drop to 2.34 mills three years from now. Expenses are rising at an average of 7 percent a year. David Hanna, Vice-President of Finance, needs to determine how many mills to request in the next election cycle to continue the support of the college. In this project, you will determine how many mills (the fraction 1/1000 frequently used as a measurement of tax on property values) are needed to keep the college from going into a deficit. Your completed worksheet will look similar to the one shown in Figure 6.67. You will save your workbook as *6K_Millage_Firstname_Lastname*.

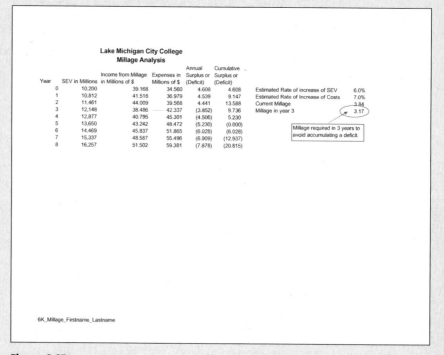

Figure 6.67

1. On the Standard toolbar, click the **Open** button. Navigate to the location where the student files for this textbook are stored. Locate and open the file **e06K_Millage**.

2. From the **File** menu, open the **Save As** dialog box. Navigate to the location where you are storing your files for this chapter. Save the file with the name **6K_Millage_Firstname_Lastname**

3. In cell **B5**, type **=b4*(1+i4)** to determine the rate of increase in property values. Copy the formula to cells **B6:B12**. Compare your worksheet with Figure 6.67 to verify the results for this range.

(Project 6K–Millage continues on the next page)

Mastery Assessments (continued)

(Project 6K–Millage continued)

4. In cell **C4**, type **=b4*i6/1000** This is the current value of taxable property in the county—cell **B4**—times the current mills—cell **I6**. The amount is divided by 1000 because millages are assessed on each thousand dollars of property value. Fill this formula to cells **C5** and **C6**. In cell **C7**, type **=b7*i7/1000** The millage drops in three years to 2.34 mills as listed in cell **I7**; therefore, the income from millage will drop to $28.427 million as calculated in this cell. Copy this formula to cells **C8:C12**. Compare your results with those shown in Figure 6.68.

5. In cell **D5**, type **=d4*(1+i5)** Expenses at the college are going up every year at a rate of 7 percent, as shown in cell **I5**. This formula calculates the estimated expenses based on this rate of increase. Fill this formula to cells **D6:D12**. Compare your results with those shown in Figure 6.68.

6. In cell **E4**, calculate the surplus or deficit by subtracting the expense from the income. Copy this formula to cells **E5:E12**.The college will have a shortfall (deficit) of $13.910 million in year 3. In 8 years, the deficit will be $21.339 million.

7. In cell **F4**, type **=e4** which is the surplus for year 0. In cell **F5**, write a formula to add the current year's surplus in cell **E5** to the previous year's surplus in **F4**. Fill this formula to cells **F6:F12**.

   The cumulative amount changes to a deficit of (0.322) in year 3 when the millage drops from 3.84 to 2.84. The total cumulative deficit in year 8 is (90,975). Millage for the college is voted on in the general election every three years, which is due to take place two years from year zero. Hanna needs to know how many mills to request to ensure that the college does not go into deficit and to keep it in a positive cash flow for at least three years after the vote. Compare your results with those in Figure 6.68.

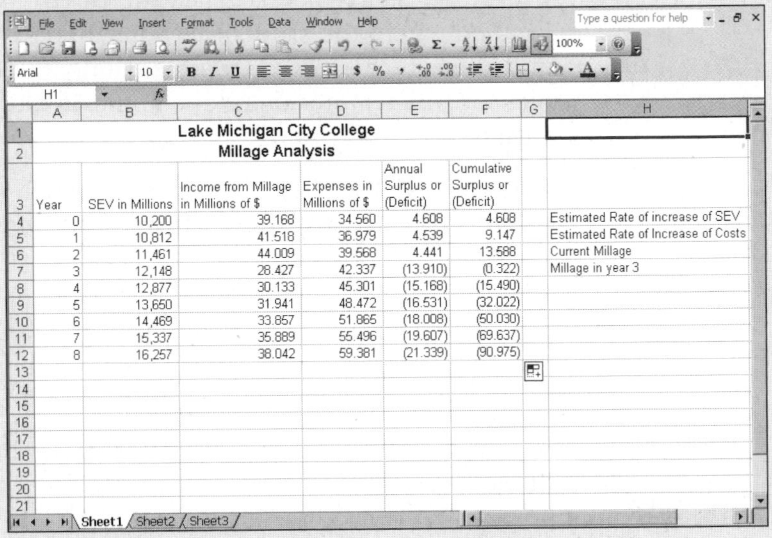

Year	SEV in Millions	Income from Millage in Millions of $	Expenses in Millions of $	Annual Surplus or (Deficit)	Cumulative Surplus or (Deficit)		
0	10,200	39.168	34.560	4.608	4.608		Estimated Rate of increase of SEV
1	10,812	41.518	36.979	4.539	9.147		Estimated Rate of Increase of Costs
2	11,461	44.009	39.568	4.441	13.588		Current Millage
3	12,148	28.427	42.337	(13.910)	(0.322)		Millage in year 3
4	12,877	30.133	45.301	(15.168)	(15.490)		
5	13,650	31.941	48.472	(16.531)	(32.022)		
6	14,469	33.857	51.865	(18.008)	(50.030)		
7	15,337	35.889	55.496	(19.607)	(69.637)		
8	16,257	38.042	59.381	(21.339)	(90.975)		

Figure 6.68

(Project 6K–Millage continues on the next page)

(Project 6K–Millage continued)

8. Click cell **F9**. You want the deficit at this point to be zero. Display the **Goal Seek** dialog box. Type **0** in the **To value** box. Click the **By changing cell** box and click cell **I7**. Click **OK**. The new millage needs to total 3.17.

9. Draw a text box from the middle of cell **H9** to the upper right boundary of cell **I11** and type **Millage required in 3 years to avoid accumulating a deficit**. Draw an **Arrow** from the text box to the number in **F9**. Draw an oval over **F9**. Change the **Fill Color** of the oval to **No Fill** and change the **Line Color** of the oval and the arrow to **Green**. Compare your screen with Figure 6.67.

10. Display the **Page Setup** dialog box. Change the orientation to **Landscape**. On the **Header/Footer tab**, add the file name as you have previously done. Save your changes. **Print** the file.

End You have completed Project 6K ──────────────

Project 6L — Organizations

Objectives: *Work with a Large Worksheet, Prepare a Worksheet to Share with Others, and Enhance Worksheets with AutoFormats and Styles.*

James Smith, Vice President of Student Affairs, has requested an updated listing of all the student organizations on campus. In the following Mastery Assessment, you will work with a large worksheet listing the student organizations. You will reorganize the information and apply styles. Your completed worksheet will look similar to the one shown in Figure 6.69. You will save your workbook as *6L_Organizations_Firstname_Lastname*.

1. On the Standard toolbar, click the **Open** button. Navigate to the location where the student files for this textbook are stored. Locate and open the file **e06L_Organizations**. Save the file with your other files for this chapter using the name **6L_Organizations_Firstname_Lastname**

2. Click cell **A3** and then, from the **Data** menu, click **Sort**. Sort in **Ascending** order by **Name of Organization**.

(Project 6L–Organizations continues on the next page)

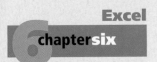
(Project 6L–Organizations continued)

Lake Michigan City College Student Organizations

Name of Organization	Sponsor	Contact
A.C.E. ACTION COMMUNITY EDUCATION	Student Affairs Office	Fredia Lot, flot@lmcc.org
ARTISTS CLUB	Art Department	Robert Kelly rkelly@lmcc.org
BUSINESS PROFESSIONAL ASSOCIATION	Business Education Department	Doris Thomas
CHESS CLUB	Math Department	Rachel Orkey rorkey@lmcc.org
CRIMINAL JUSTICE CLUB	Policy Academy	Judy McDaniels
DANCE CLUB	Theater Department	Nancy Andrews nandrews@lmcc.org
DENTAL ASSISTANTS CLUB	Health and Human Services Dept	
DRAMA CLUB	Theater Department	Alisha Weber
EUCLIDEANS	Math Department	Robert Donalson rdon@lmcc.org
FRENCH CLUB	Foreign Lanuage Dept	Kim Sneely ksneely@lmcc.org
FRENCH CLUB (BEGINNERS)	Foreign Language D	
GEOLOGY CLUB	Geography Departm	
GERMAN LANGUAGE AND CULTURE CLUB (GLACC)	Foreign Language D	
HUNGARIAN-AMERICAN FILM CLUB	Theater Department	
I.S.A. (INTERNATIONAL STUDENT ASSOCIATION)	Student Affairs Offic	
INTERNET PROFESSIONAL CLUB	Internet Professiona	
LMCC DIGITIZERS (Digital photography club)	Art Department	
LMCC PRIDE	Student Affairs Offic	
MAGIC THE GATHERING GAMING CLUB	Computer Departm	
PHI THETA KAPPA	Student Affairs Offic	
RADIOGRAPHY	Health and Human	
SOCIETY FOR CREATIVE ANACHRONISM	Student Affairs Offic	
SPANISH CLUB	Foreign Lanuage D	
STUDENT ADVOCACY CLUB	Student Affairs Offic	
STUDENT GOVERNMENT ASSOCIATION	Student Affairs Offic	
STUDENT NURSING CLUB	Health and Human	

6L_Organizations_Firstname_Lastname

Lake Michigan City College Student Organizations

Name of Organization	Contact Number	Meeting Day	Meeting Place
A.C.E. ACTION COMMUNITY EDUCATION	555-3565	Tue 3:00 - 4:30 pm	LA 236
ARTISTS CLUB	555-2408	Tue 5:00 - 9:00 pm	LA 371
BUSINESS PROFESSIONAL ASSOCIATION	555-5111		
CHESS CLUB	555-3500	Tue 1230 - 230 pm, Thur 5:00-7:00 pm	Food Court
CRIMINAL JUSTICE CLUB	555-0880	Tue 11:45 am - 1:00 pm	Mini Theatre, SCB
DANCE CLUB	555-3378	Wed 8:30 - 9:30 pm, Sat 10:00 am - Noon	Dance Studio, MLB
DENTAL ASSISTANTS CLUB	555-0672		
DRAMA CLUB			
EUCLIDEANS	555-0321	Mon 7:00 - 9:00 PM	BEB 120
FRENCH CLUB		Fri 1:30 - 3:00 pm (French 2)	Campus Book Store
FRENCH CLUB (BEGINNERS)		Fri 3:00 - 4:30 pm (French 1)	Campus Book Store
GEOLOGY CLUB	555-3582		
GERMAN LANGUAGE AND CULTURE CLUB (GLACC)	555-8567	Wed 3:30 - 4:30 pm	Mini theatre, SCB
HUNGARIAN-AMERICAN FILM CLUB	555-9870	Sun 6:00 - 9:00 pm	LA 175
I.S.A. (INTERNATIONAL STUDENT ASSOCIATION)	555-5128		
INTERNET PROFESSIONAL CLUB	555-3089		
LMCC DIGITIZERS (Digital photography club)			
LMCC PRIDE		Fri 5:30 - 7:00 pm	LA 175
MAGIC THE GATHERING GAMING CLUB			
PHI THETA KAPPA	555-3691		
RADIOGRAPHY	555-5119		
SOCIETY FOR CREATIVE ANACHRONISM	555-5215		
SPANISH CLUB	555-8567	Thu twice a month, 3:30-4:30 pm	LA 374
STUDENT ADVOCACY CLUB	555-3500		
STUDENT GOVERNMENT ASSOCIATION			
STUDENT NURSING CLUB	555-5015		

6L_Organizations_Firstname_Lastname

Figure 6.69

3. With cell **A3** as the active cell, from the **Data** menu display the **AutoFilter arrows** on the column labels in **row 3**. In **column B**, click the **Sponsor filter arrow**, and then click **Foreign Language Dept**. Change the **Contact** and **Contact Number** for the *German Language and Culture Club* to **Rochelle Gray** the same as shown for the *Spanish Club*. (Hint: You will need to scroll over to view **column A** to determine the row for the German Language Club. Use copy and paste.) Display all the rows again. (Hint: From the **Data** menu, point to **Filter** and click **Show All**.)

4. Use the **AutoFilter** to display only those records that are missing a **Contact Number**. (Hint: Click **Blanks** from the bottom of the list.) You should see seven clubs that list no Contact Number.

(Project 6L–Organizations continues on the next page)

Mastery Assessments (continued)

(Project 6L–Organizations continued)

5. Display all the rows again and turn off the **AutoFilter** feature. Click cell **A3**. Change the alignment to **Center**, change the **Font Color** to **Blue**, change the **Font** to **Comic Sans MS**, **14** pt. **Italic** and **Bold**. Open the **Style** dialog box and name this style **Heading** Click **Add**, and then click **OK**. Select the remaining headings in **row 3** and apply the style you created. Adjust the width of **column D** to accommodate the new heading style.

6. Click cell **A4**. Create a new style that includes **Comic Sans MS 12** pt. Name the style **Organization** and then apply it to the all the other organization names in **column A**.

7. The worksheet is too wide to print on one page and still be legible. Remove the **Merge and Center** from **row 1** so that you can select **column A** to repeat. (Hint: Click cell **A1** and click the **Merge and Center** button.) Display the **Sheet tab** of the **Page Setup** dialog box, set **row 3** to **repeat at the top** of the page, and then set **column A** to **repeat at the left** of every page. Change the scaling to **75% of normal size**.

8. Display the **Header/Footer tab** and add the file name to the **Left section** of the footer area. Save the file, view the **Print Preview**, and then print.

 End You have completed Project 6L ————————————————————

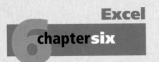
Problem Solving

Project 6M — Early Payoff

Objectives: *Use Excel Templates and Use Goal Seek.*

Goal Seek is a powerful tool that can help you answer questions concerning your own finances. Use the Loan Amortization template to set up a loan for a 30-year mortgage at a 6 percent interest rate. Pick a loan amount that would make sense for your circumstances. After the loan payment is calculated and the amortization schedule is complete, use Goal Seek to determine an Optional Extra Payment—cell D11—that would result in paying off the loan five years early. (Hint: You need to set cell H8 equal to 300.) Add a footer to the worksheet and save the file as *6M_Early_Payoff_ Firstname_Lastname.*

End You have completed Project 6M

Project 6N — Registration

Objectives: *Prepare a Worksheet to Share with Others, Enhance Worksheets with AutoFormats and Styles, Use Drawing Tools and Use the Research Feature.*

Lake Michigan City College recently implemented an online registration process. James Smith, Vice-President of Student Affairs, wants a graphic flow chart created to show the registration process using this new method. In this project, you will use the drawing tools to create a flow chart that illustrates the steps involved in registration. You will save your workbook as *6N_Registration_Firstname_Lastname.*

1. Open a blank worksheet. Add a footer in the usual location and save the file as **6N_Registration_Firstname_Lastname**

2. Add the Lake Michigan City College title to the top of the worksheet. Add a title in **row 2** that identifies the purpose of the worksheet.

3. Remove the gridlines from the worksheet. Use drawing tools to illustrate the registration process. Explore the shapes that are included in the **AutoShapes** button. Use the registration process that is followed at your school as your example. Draw arrows between each box and label appropriately.

4. Use the buttons on the Drawing toolbar to change the fill color, line color, and text color of the drawing objects.

5. Preview the worksheet and be sure it is evenly spaced and will print on one page. Print the file.

6. Save your changes and close the file.

End You have completed Project 6N

On the Internet

Exploring Microsoft Office Online Templates

In this chapter, you worked with the templates that are installed as part of the Excel 2003 program. Other templates are available from the Microsoft Web site.

1. Start Excel. Click **File**, **New**. In the **New Workbook** task pane, click the **Templates on Office Online** link.

2. In the **Microsoft Office Online Web** site, examine some of the templates that are listed in the **Quick links** pane.

3. Explore other parts of the Web site and open the templates that are of interest to you. Try downloading a template and using it.

4. When you are finished, close your browser.

GO! with Help

Merging Styles with Another Workbook

In this chapter you created, applied, and modified styles. You also used styles in multiple worksheets. Importing styles to another workbook was discussed in a More Knowledge box in Activity 6.19. Styles create a uniformity of appearance and help to create an organizational identity. In addition to merging styles from another workbook, you can also save styles to use in any new workbook. This is particularly useful if you want to create a style to be used in all departments in an organization. If the styles are saved, they can be easily moved to multiple computers for use by staff members in all areas of the organization.

1. Start Excel. In the **Type a question for help** box, type **Styles**

2. From the list of related help topics, click **Save styles to use in new workbooks**.

3. Read the instructions for this topic. Print the instructions if you want.

4. Open one of the files from this chapter that used styles, such as Project 6C.

5. Follow the procedure in the Help topic to save the styles from the Project as an .xlt file.

6. Open a new workbook and click the **File**, **New** command to see the available templates.

7. Select the template file you saved that contains the sample styles, and then use the styles in the new workbook.

8. Close the file without saving the results and close Excel.

7 chapterseven

Creating Templates, Using Lookup Functions, Validating Data, and Auditing Worksheets

In this chapter, you will: complete these projects **and** practice these skills.

Project 7A **Creating Your Own Templates**	**Objectives** • Create a Workbook Template • Edit a Template • Protect a Worksheet • Create a Worksheet Based on a Template
Project 7B **Referencing Information and Validating Entries**	**Objectives** • Use Lookup Functions • Validate Data • Use Conditional Formats
Project 7C **Using the Formula Auditing Toolbar**	**Objective** • Audit a Worksheet

El Cuero Specialty Wares

El Cuero de Mexico is a Mexico City-based manufacturer of high quality small leather goods for men and women. Its products include wallets, belts, handbags, key chains, and travel bags. The company distributes its products to department and specialty stores in the United States and Canada through its San Diego-based subsidiary, El Cuero Specialty Wares. Plans are currently under-way for a new marketing campaign focusing on several new lines that will be introduced next year.

© Getty Images, Inc.

Creating Templates, Using Lookup Functions, Validating Data, and Auditing Worksheets

Excel has built-in templates that can be used for common worksheet functions, but you can also create your own templates. In this chapter, you will create a template and insert a company logo on the template. You will protect the template to ensure that formulas and other informa-tion are not inadvertently changed. Once the template is protected, future users cannot enter new data into the protected cells. After you have protected and saved the template, you will create a new worksheet based on the template. On this worksheet, you will enter data to verify that the template performs as planned. Also in this chap-ter, you will use the lookup functions to locate information that is needed in a form. Then you will create a validation list to ensure that only accurate data is entered. You will apply a conditional format to hide error messages. Finally, in this chapter you will use Excel's auditing features to help you understand the construction of formulas in a worksheet, and locate and correct any errors.

Project 7A **Purchase Order**

Creating a template to use in a company gives you the opportunity to both design a template that will fit the company's needs and to personalize a template by adding a company logo.

El Cuero Specialty Wares ships its products to department and specialty stores. To improve its inventory control system, the company is creating a new set of forms. These forms must be easy to complete and reduce errors in the inventory control process. They must also provide a uniform image for the company.

In Activities 7.1 through 7.9, you will create a template for a purchase order form, which will include the company's logo. You will protect the purchase order template to ensure that totals for items ordered are calculated accurately. Your completed worksheet will look similar to Figure 7.1. You will save your workbook as *7A_Purchase_Order_Firstname_Lastname.*

El Cuero Specialty Wares

2900 Pacific Avenue
San Diego, CA 92108
Phone 619.555.0177

Order Date:	13-Oct-04
Order Number:	23
Purchase Order:	A-3421

Ship To:

Name	Joan Miller
Company	McKenzie Stewart
Address	5684 Palisades Blvd.
City, State, Postal code	Los Angeles, CA 90044
Phone	323.555.0230

Item Number	Description	Quantity	Unit Price	Total
W-TF	Tri-fold Wallet	12	7.00	$ 84.00
W-BF	Bi-fold Wallet	24	5.50	132.00
W-MC	Money clip	24	2.00	48.00
				-
				-
				-
				-
				-
				-
				-
				-
				-
				-
				-
				-
				-
				-
				-
			Order Total:	$ 264.00

Purchase Order

7A_Purchase_Order_Firstname_Lastname

Figure 7.1
Project 7A—Purchase Order

Objective 1
Create a Workbook Template

Recall that Excel has predesigned **templates**—workbooks that can be used as a pattern for creating other workbooks. Excel templates consist of financial forms to record expenses, time worked, balance sheet items, and other common financial reports. You can also create your own templates.

There are two reasons for creating templates for commonly used forms in an organization—**standardization** and **protection**. Standardization means that all forms created within the organization will have a uniform appearance; the data will always be organized in the same manner. Protection means that individuals entering data cannot change areas of the worksheet that are protected, and thus cannot alter important formulas and formats built in to the template.

Activity 7.1 Entering Template Text

To create a template, start with a blank worksheet; enter the text, formatting, and formulas needed for the specific worksheet function, and then save the file as a template. Saving a worksheet as a template adds the extension .xlt to the file name. In this activity, you will open a worksheet already begun for the purpose of creating a purchase order template, and then you will enter the remaining text, formatting, and formulas.

1 Start Excel. Click the **Open** button 🖼. In the **Open** dialog box, use the **Look in arrow** to navigate to the location where the student files for this textbook are stored on your computer. Locate and open the **e07A_Purchase_Order** file.

The name and address for El Cuero Specialty Wares have been entered in the worksheet.

2 Click cell **B6** and type **Order Date:** and then press Enter.

After the text is entered, cell B7 becomes the active cell.

3 In cell **B7** type **Order Number:** press Enter to move to cell **B8**, type **Purchase Order:** and then press Enter again.

4 Click cell **A10**. Type **Ship To:** and press Tab to move to cell **B10**. Type **Name** and then press ↓. In cell **B11** type **Company** and press Enter, in cell **B12** type **Address** and press Enter, in cell **B13** type **City, State, Postal code** and press Enter, and then in cell **B14** type **Phone** and press Enter again.

The labels for the purchase order heading are entered. Compare your screen with Figure 7.2.

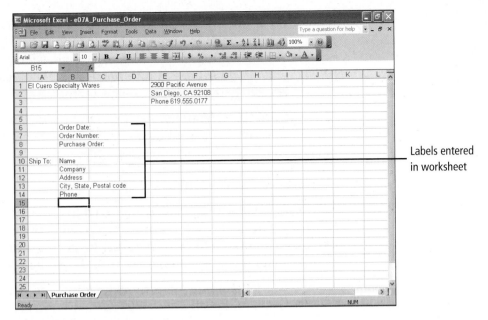

**Labels entered
in worksheet**

Figure 7.2

5 Click cell **B16**. Type **Item Number** and press ⎯Tab⎯ to move to cell **C16**.
Continuing across row 16, in cell **C16** type **Description** and press ⎯Tab⎯,
in cell **D16** type **Quantity** and press ⎯Tab⎯, in cell **E16** type **Unit Price**
and press ⎯Tab⎯, and in cell **F16** type **Total** and press ⎯Enter⎯.

The column headings are added to the purchase order. Compare
your screen with Figure 7.3.

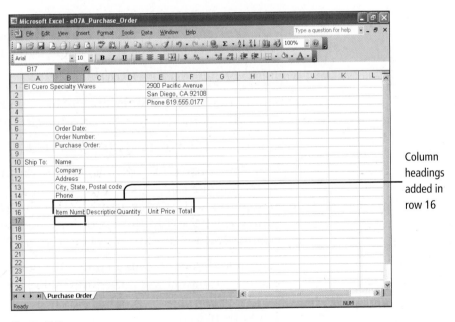

**Column
headings
added in
row 16**

Figure 7.3

6 From the **File** menu, click **Save As**. In the **Save As** dialog box, use the **Save in arrow** to navigate to the folder where you are storing your files, creating a new folder for this chapter if you want to do so. In the **File name** box, using your own name, type **7A_Purchase_Order_Firstname_Lastname** and then click **Save**.

Until the format and design of the purchase order are complete, you will save your work as a normal worksheet. When it is complete, you will save it as a template file.

Activity 7.2 Formatting a Template

After the basic text has been entered in a template, you can format it. One of the goals in designing a template is to make it easy for others to complete. It should be obvious to the person completing the form what information is needed and where it should be placed.

1 To the left of the **column A heading** and above the **row 1 heading**, locate and click the **Select All** button to select all the rows and columns in the worksheet. On the Formatting toolbar, click the **Font button arrow** Arial , and then click **Comic Sans MS**. Click in any cell in the worksheet to deselect.

2 Widen **column B** to **110 pixels**. Select the range **B6:B14**, and on the Formatting toolbar click the **Align Right** button .

3 Widen **column C** to **200 pixels**. Select **columns D:F** and widen to **75 pixels**. Select the range **D16:F16**, and on the Formatting toolbar click the **Align Right** button .

4 Select the range **C6:C8**. Display the **Format** menu and click **Cells**. In the **Format Cells** dialog box, click the **Border tab**. Under **Line**, from the **Style** list, click the first line in the first column—the dotted line. Click the **Color arrow**, and then in the first row, click the second color—**Brown**. Under **Border**, click the **Top Border** button, the **Middle Border** button, and the **Bottom Border** button. Click **OK**. With the range **C6:C8** still selected, on the Formatting toolbar, click the **Align Right** button .

5 Select the range **C11:C14**. Display the **Format Cells** dialog box. On the **Border tab**, in the **Style** list, click the first line in the first column. Click the **Color arrow**, and then click **Brown**. Under **Border**, click the **Top Border** button, the **Middle Border** button and the **Bottom Border** button, and then click **OK**.

Inserting borders on cells in a template creates lines as a place to record information when the form is filled out. This provides a good visual cue to the person filling out the form as to where information should be placed.

6 Select the range **B16:F40**. Right-click the selected area and click **Format Cells**. On the **Border tab**, under **Presets**, click the **Outline** button and the **Inside** button, and then click **OK**.

A grid of columns and rows is applied, which is helpful to those individuals completing the form.

7 Select the range **B16:F16**, hold down ⌈Ctrl⌉ and select the range **F17:F40**. On the Formatting toolbar, click the **Fill Color button arrow** ▥▾. In the displayed palette, in the last row, click the third color—**Light Yellow**. Click anywhere to deselect.

The selected color is applied to the column headings and to the column that will contain the formulas for the template.

8 On the Standard toolbar, click the **Print Preview** button ▣ to view the form as it will print. Compare your screen with Figure 7.4.

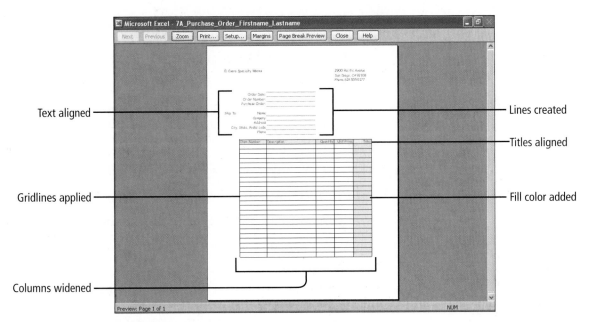

Figure 7.4

9 On the Print Preview toolbar, click **Close**. On the Standard toolbar, click the **Save** button ▣.

A dotted line on the worksheet indicates where the first page would end if the worksheet were printed as it is currently set up.

Activity 7.3 Entering Template Formulas

After the text is entered and formatted in your template, add formulas to the cells where you want the result of the calculations to display. In this activity, you will create a formula in the Total column to determine the dollar value for the quantity of each item ordered, and then create another formula to sum the Total column.

1 In cell **F17** type **=d17*e17** and press Enter.

A value of 0 displays in cell F17. However, when the person entering information into the worksheet types the Quantity in cell D17 and the Unit Price in cell E17, the formula will multiply the two values to calculate a total for the item that was ordered.

2 Use the fill handle to copy the formula in cell **F17** down through cell **F39**.

3 Click cell **F40**. On the Standard toolbar, click the **AutoSum** button ⌊Σ ▾⌋. Be sure the range that is displayed in the formula is *F17:F39*, and then press Enter.

4 Select the range **E17:E39**. On the Formatting toolbar, click the **Comma Style** button ⌊,⌋.

The Comma Style is applied; thus, when values are typed into the form, they will display with two decimals and commas in the appropriate locations.

5 Click cell **F17**, hold down Ctrl, and then click cell **F40**. On the Formatting toolbar, click the **Currency Style** button ⌊$⌋. Select the range **F18:F39**, and then click the **Comma Style** button ⌊,⌋.

Formats are applied to the totals column, and the zero in each cell changes to a hyphen.

6 Select the range **D40:E40**. Display the **Format Cells** dialog box. On the **Alignment tab**, under **Text control**, select the **Merge cells** check box, and then click **OK**. Type **Order Total:** and press Enter. Click cell **D40** again, and on the Formatting toolbar, click the **Align Right** button ⌊≣⌋.

A label is added and formatted to identify the total for the entire order.

7 Select the range **B40:C40**. Display the **Format Cells** dialog box and click the **Border tab**. In the **Border** preview area, click the **left, middle, and bottom** lines to remove them from the preview. Be sure the right and top lines remain in the preview area, and then click **OK**.

8 On the Standard toolbar, click the **Print Preview** button ![icon]. Compare your screen with Figure 7.5.

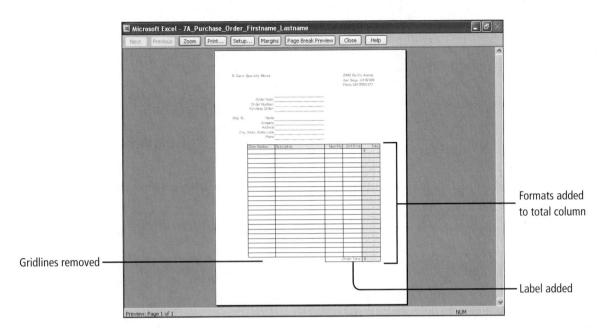

Formats added to total column

Gridlines removed

Label added

Figure 7.5

9 On the Print Preview toolbar, click **Close**. On the Standard toolbar, click the **Save** ![icon] button.

Activity 7.4 Saving a File as a Template

After you complete the formatting and design of a worksheet that you would like to use over and over again, save it as a template file. When saved as a template file, the .xlt file extension is added to the file name instead of .xls. Additionally, the file is saved in a specific Templates folder on the hard drive of your computer, or the network location where the Excel software resides. This makes the template available to other users who have access to the same folder. When the template is opened, a new *copy* of the worksheet opens, thus preserving the original template for future use. *You must complete the remainder of this project using the same computer, to ensure that you can access the file you are about to save on the computer's hard drive.*

1 From the **File** menu, click **Save As**. At the bottom of the **Save As** dialog box, click the **Save as type arrow**, and then from the displayed list, click **Template**.

Note that the *Save in* box immediately changes to display the Templates folder.

Is the Templates Folder Blocked?

If you are working in a college computer lab, your college may have placed restrictions on saving files to the Templates folder. Saving to the Templates folder makes the template available to anyone at this computer when they display the File menu, click New, and then click the General Templates tab. If you cannot store to the Templates folder, you can still save and use the template. The difference is that it will be available only to you. If you are unable to save your template in the Templates folder, navigate to the location where you are storing your files for this chapter, and save it there.

2 Click the **Save in arrow** to display the path to the Templates folder. Compare your screen with Figure 7.6. If the path to the templates folder is different from what is shown in Figure 7.6, write down the path—the folders that are listed in the displayed list—so you can locate the template on this computer later.

The Templates folder contains the files that are available in the Templates dialog box. The usual path is C:/Documents and Settings/name of computer owner/Application Data/Microsoft/Templates.

Path to Templates folder —

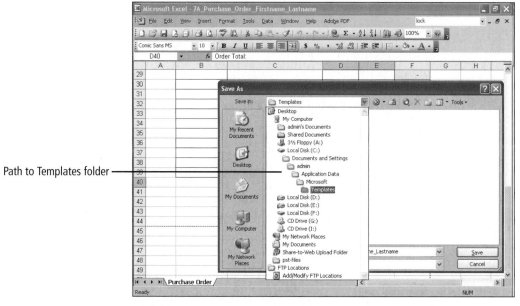

Figure 7.6

3 In the **File name** box, change the **File name** to 7A_PO_Template_ **Firstname_Lastname** and then click **Save**. If you are unable to save in the Templates folder, go to the next step.

4 Whether or not you were able to save your template in the Templates folder, you should still save a copy in your own storage location. Display the **File** menu and click **Save As** again. In the **Save As** dialog box, change the **Save as type** to **Template**, if necessary. Click the **Save in arrow** and navigate to the location where you are storing your other files for this chapter. Be sure the **File name** displays **7A_PO_Template_Firstname_Lastname** and then click **Save**. (If you previously saved to this location, click *Yes* to overwrite the original.)

A copy of the template is saved with your other files.

5 Close the template.

Objective 2
Edit a Template

After a template is created, others who have access to it can open it from the Templates dialog box, which creates a new copy in the format of a normal workbook—not a template. If you discover that you need to make changes to the template, you must specifically open it as a template—from the folder in which the template is stored.

Activity 7.5 Inserting and Modifying an Image

In the following activity, you will add a logo to the template and a label to identify its purpose.

1 On the Standard toolbar, click the **Open** button. Use the **Look in arrow** to navigate to the **Templates** folder on your computer. The default path is **C:/Documents and Settings/name of computer owner/Application Data/Microsoft/Templates**. Alternatively, use the path noted in Step 2 of the previous activity. If you were not able to save your template in the Templates folder, open the template from your storage location.

Templates that have been saved on this computer are shown in the displayed folder.

Alert!

Looking for Your Template?

Even if you were able to save your template to the computer's Templates folder, you may not be able to navigate to it in the Open dialog box. One of the options in the Windows File Manager program is to hide certain files. If that option has been selected on the computer you are using, you will not be able to see the Application Data folder. If you cannot locate the Application Data folder, navigate to your folder instead, and open the template from your storage location.

2 Select your **7A_PO_Template**, and then click **Open**.

If the file extensions are displayed on your computer, you will see the .xlt extension at the end of the file name in the title bar.

3 Click cell **A1** and press Delete to remove the company name. From the **Insert** menu, point to **Picture**, and then click **From File**.

4 In the displayed **Insert Picture** dialog box, click the **Look in arrow** and navigate to the folder where the student files that accompany this textbook are stored. Select the **e07A_Logo** file, and then click **Insert**.

The El Cuero logo is inserted in the upper left corner of the worksheet. Circles display on the sides and corners of the image—similar to the resizing handles that display on objects in a chart. The resizing handles indicate that the object is selected and can be formatted, moved, or resized. The Picture toolbar may display on the screen as a floating toolbar when the object is selected. See Figure 7.7.

Logo inserted —

Handles
— indicate image
is selected.

— Picture toolbar

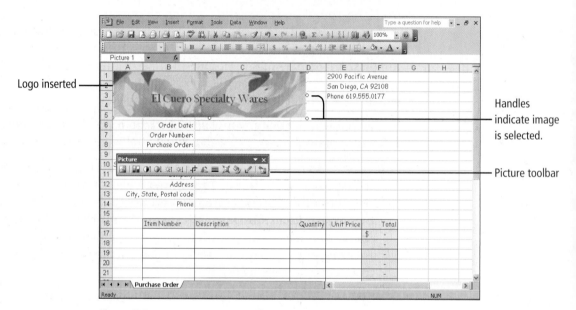

Figure 7.7

5 If necessary, display the Picture toolbar by right-clicking on any toolbar and clicking Picture. Move your mouse pointer over each button on the Picture toolbar to display the ScreenTip, and then take a moment to study the table in Figure 7.8.

Picture Toolbar

Button	ScreenTip	Description
	Insert Picture From File	Displays the Insert Picture dialog box.
	Color	Displays a list of options ranging from full color to black and white. Choices include Automatic—the original color of the image, Grayscale—shades of gray, Black & White, or *Washout*—a faded image that can be placed in the background, sometimes called a *watermark*.
	More Contrast	Makes the darks darker and the lights lighter.
	Less Contrast	Lessens the division between dark and light, blurring the image.
	More Brightness	Increases the lightness of the image.
	Less Brightness	Reduces the brightness of the image.
	Crop	Reduces the size of the image without changing the proportions of the image. Functionally, it hides parts of the image that you do not want included.
	Rotate Left 90°	Rotates the image 90 degrees to the left each time it is clicked.
	Line Style	Displays a menu of lines that can be applied to the borders of an image.
	Compress Pictures	Displays the Compress Pictures dialog box, which enables you to reduce the file size of an image—the amount of space required to store the image on your computer.
	Format Picture	Displays the Format Picture dialog box.
	Set Transparent Color	Used to make a color on an image transparent. Click the button, and then click the area you want to change to transparent.
	Reset Picture	Restores an image to its original settings.

Figure 7.8

6 On the Picture toolbar, click the **Crop** button ![crop icon], and then move the mouse pointer near the right outer edge of the logo.

The mouse pointer displays as an arrow attached to the crop icon and **crop handles** display at the corners and sides of the image. See Figure 7.9. When you **crop** an image, you hide part of the image without changing the overall proportion of the image. Using this tool, you can cut away unwanted parts of an image. If you change your mind, you can drag the crop tool in the opposite direction to restore the hidden portion. When you move the crop tool over a side crop handle, it takes a different shape.

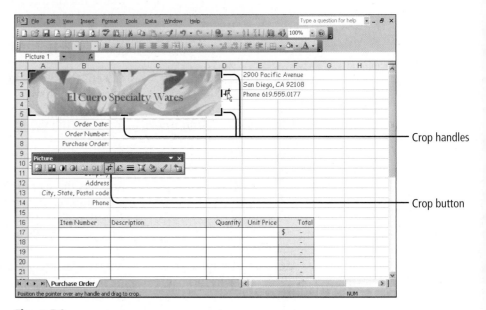

Figure 7.9

7 Position the **Crop** tool over the right middle crop handle and drag to the left until the right edge of the image is at the right edge of column **C**. Position the **Crop** tool over the left middle crop handle, and drag to the right until the left edge of the image is in the middle of column **A**. Compare your screen with Figure 7.10.

The image is cropped from both the right and left sides.

Left edge cropped to the middle of column A

Right edge aligns with column C.

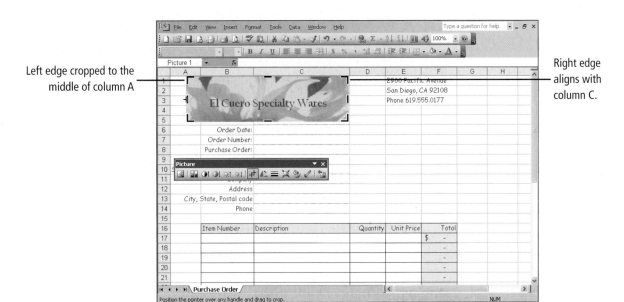

Figure 7.10

8 On the Picture toolbar, click the **Crop** button [icon] to turn off the crop tool. Move the mouse pointer over the image. When the four-way arrow displays, drag the image to the left to position it in the upper left corner of the worksheet.

The Crop button is a toggle button—click it once to turn it on, click it again to turn it off.

9 On the Picture toolbar, click the **Less Contrast** button [icon] four times.

The contrast in the image is reduced and it is more difficult to read the company name. You can control the contrast by using the Less Contrast and More Contrast buttons.

10 On the Picture toolbar, click the **More Contrast** button [icon] four times to return the contrast to its previous condition.

11 On the Picture toolbar, click the **More Brightness** button [icon] three times.

The background image is brighter and the company name is now easier to read. The More Brightness and Less Brightness buttons control image brightness.

12 On the Standard toolbar, click the **Save** button [icon]. Compare your screen with Figure 7.11.

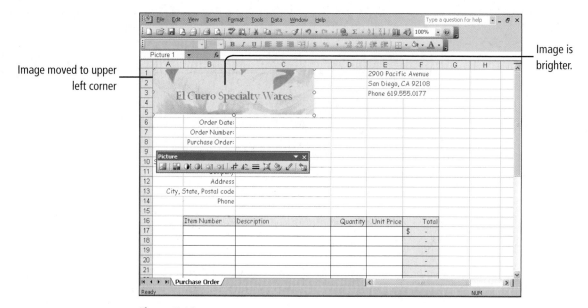

Image moved to upper left corner

Image is brighter.

Figure 7.11

Activity 7.6 Inserting and Modifying a WordArt Image

WordArt is a feature that transforms text into a stylized image that you can use to create a distinctive logo or heading. Because WordArt is a graphical object, it can be moved and resized. In addition, you can change its shape and color. In this activity, you will create and modify a vertical WordArt heading and place it at the left side of the purchase order grid.

1 Click cell **A16**. Display the **Insert** menu, point to **Picture**, and then click **WordArt**.

The WordArt Gallery dialog box opens and displays a palette of WordArt styles. To create a WordArt graphic, the first step is to select the style you want to use. After the image is created, you can modify it using the WordArt toolbar. See Figure 7.12.

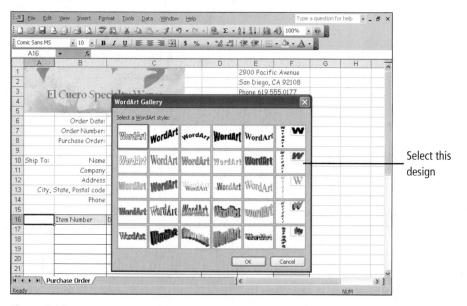

Select this design

Figure 7.12

Another Way — **To Open the WordArt Gallery**

If the Drawing toolbar is displayed on your screen (usually at the bottom of the Excel window), you can click the Insert WordArt button to open the WordArt Gallery dialog box.

2 In the **WordArt Gallery** dialog box, in the second row, click the sixth (last) WordArt style, and then click **OK**.

The Edit WordArt Text dialog box opens. Here you type the text you want to display as a WordArt image. You can also change the font style or size and apply bold or italic for emphasis.

3 In the **Edit WordArt Text** dialog box, type **Purchase Order** and then within the dialog box, click the **Font arrow**. From the displayed list, scroll up or down as necessary and click **Comic Sans MS**, and then click **OK**.

The WordArt image floats on your screen—not in cell A16—and the WordArt toolbar also displays on your screen. Sizing handles display around the outside of the WordArt, and a green *rotation handle* displays on the right side of the image. See Figure 7.13. Use the rotation handle to rotate an image in various directions.

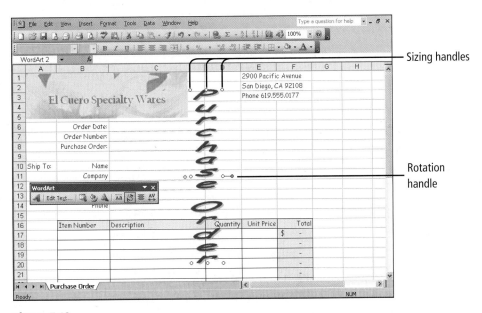

Figure 7.13

4 If necessary, drag the WordArt toolbar out of the way so that the WordArt image is fully visible. Move the mouse pointer over the green **rotation handle**.

The mouse pointer changes to the shape of a rotate arrow as shown in Figure 7.14. The *adjustment handle* displays at the left of the image, and can be used to adjust the appearance, but not the size, of a WordArt or AutoShape. For example, you can slant or angle the WordArt text. The effect of this feature varies depending on the WordArt shape.

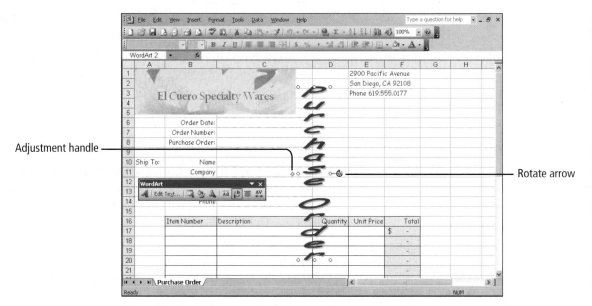

Figure 7.14

5 Drag downward until the WordArt image is approximately at a 45-degree angle—this need not be precise.

As you drag the image, dashed lines display to show the position where the image will be placed when you release the mouse button. You can use the rotation handle to revolve the image 360 degrees.

6 On the Standard toolbar, click the **Undo** button to return the image to its original orientation.

7 Move your mouse pointer over each button on the WordArt toolbar to display the ScreenTip, and then take a moment to study the table in Figure 7.15, which includes a description of each button on the WordArt toolbar.

WordArt Toolbar Buttons

Button	ScreenTip	Description
[icon]	Insert WordArt	Opens the WordArt Gallery dialog box so you can create a new WordArt image.
Edit Text...	Edit Text	Opens the Edit WordArt Text dialog box so you can change the text, font, font size, or emphasis.
[icon]	WordArt Gallery	Opens the WordArt Gallery dialog box so you can change the WordArt style for the current WordArt image.
[icon]	Format WordArt	Opens the Format WordArt dialog box so you can change the color, size, and other properties of the WordArt image.
[icon]	WordArt Shape	Displays a palette of shapes that can be applied to the WordArt image.
[icon]	WordArt Same Letter Heights	Changes the letters to fit in the same vertical space. Lowercase letters are enlarged to be the same height as uppercase letters, and letters with *font descenders* (the lower parts of letters, such as y and p that extend slightly below the line of text) are moved up to fit in the same space. The button turns this feature on and off.
[icon]	WordArt Vertical Text	Changes the orientation of the WordArt to a vertical display so the letters are stacked on top of each other. The button turns this feature on and off.
[icon]	WordArt Alignment	Displays a list of alignment options that can be used to change the alignment of the WordArt object when alignment is applicable.
[icon]	WordArt Character Spacing	Displays a list of spacing options, which controls the space between the letters of a WordArt object.

Figure 7.15

8 Point to the **WordArt** image. When the four-way arrow displays, drag the WordArt image to **column A** so the top of the image aligns with the top of cell **A16**. Scroll if necessary so you can see cell **A39**. Point to the center resize handle at the lower edge of the WordArt image and drag down so the end of the image aligns at the lower edge of cell **A39**. Compare your screen with Figure 7.16.

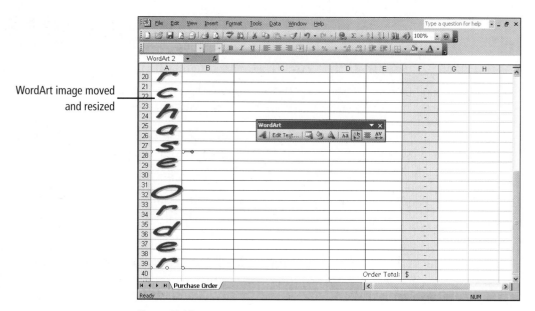

WordArt image moved and resized

Figure 7.16

---

9 On the WordArt toolbar, click the **Format WordArt** button. In the displayed **Format WordArt** dialog box, click the **Colors and Lines tab**.

From the Format WordArt dialog box, you can change the fill or line color of the image.

10 Under **Fill**, drag the **Transparency** scroll box to the right until **75%** displays in the Transparency ratio box. Alternatively, type 75 in the Transparency ratio box, or click the up spin arrow until 75% displays. See Figure 7.17.

The Transparency ratio changes the clearness of the color that is displayed.

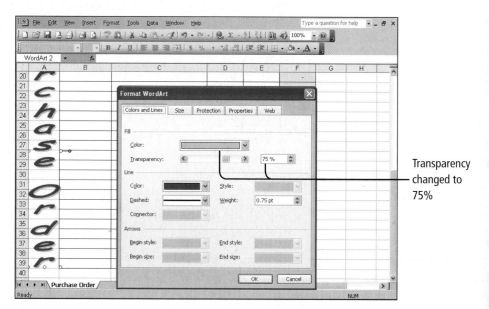

Transparency changed to 75%

Figure 7.17

11 Click **OK** to apply the transparency setting to the WordArt image. Click in any empty cell. On the Standard toolbar, click the **Save** button 🔲.

Objective 3
Protect a Worksheet

When the template design is complete, you can enable the protection of the worksheet. Protection prevents anyone from altering the formulas or changing other template components. By default, all cells in Excel are **locked**—data cannot be typed into them—but the locked feature is disabled until you protect the worksheet. After protection is enabled, the locked cells cannot be changed. Of course, you will want to designate some cells to be **unlocked**, so that individuals completing your form can type in their data.

The process of designating which cells should be unlocked and then protecting the worksheet is a two-step procedure. First, you designate which cells should be unlocked (the cells into which others can enter data). Second, you enable protection of the worksheet, which enforces the locked condition of all the other cells. You may add an optional **password** to prevent someone from disabling the worksheet protection. The password can be any combination of numbers, letters, or symbols up to 15 characters long. The password should be shared only with people who have permission to change the template.

Activity 7.7 Protecting a Worksheet

1 On your **7A_PO_Template** file, select the range **C6:C8**, hold down Ctrl and select **C10:C14** and **B17:E39**.

The selected cells are the ones that should *not* be locked when protection is applied. These are the cells into which people will type their data. Recall that when you apply protection, all cells will be locked, unless you specifically designate some to remain unlocked.

2 From the **Format** menu, click **Cells**. In the **Format Cells** dialog box, click the **Protection tab**, and then clear the check mark from the **Locked** check box.

In this manner, before you apply protection to a worksheet, you can remove the locked feature from the cells you want the user to be able to access. See Figure 7.18.

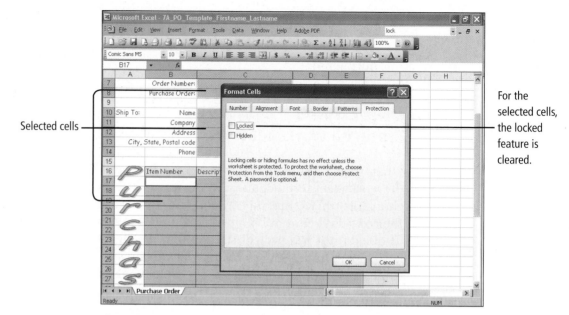

Selected cells

For the selected cells, the locked feature is cleared.

Figure 7.18

3 Click **OK**. From the **Tools** menu, point to **Protection**, and then click **Protect Sheet**.

The Protect Sheet dialog box opens. Under *Allow all users of this worksheet to*, the *Select locked cells* and *Select unlocked cells* check boxes are selected by default. The *Select locked cells* option allows the user to click the locked cells and view the formulas, but because the cells are locked, they cannot change the content or format of the locked cells. If you deselect this option, the user cannot view or even click in a locked cell. You can see that, because the check boxes are not selected, users cannot format cell columns or rows; nor can they insert or delete columns, rows, or hyperlinks.

4 Leave the first two check boxes selected. At the top of the dialog box, be sure the **Protect worksheet and contents of locked cells** check box is selected. In the **Password to unprotect sheet** box type **GO!Series**

The password does not display; rather, bullets display as placeholders for each letter or character that is typed. See Figure 7.19. Passwords are case sensitive, therefore, *go!series* is different from *GO!Series*.

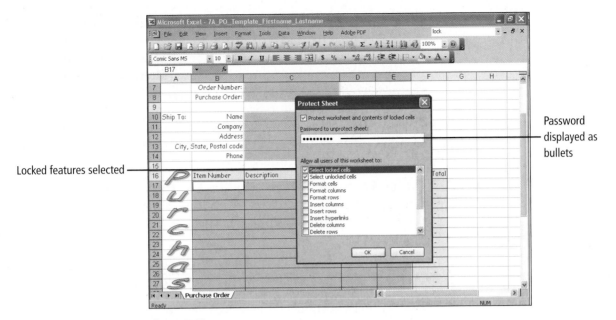

Locked features selected

Password displayed as bullets

Figure 7.19

5 Click **OK**. In the displayed **Confirm Password** dialog box, type **GO!Series** to confirm the password, and then click **OK**.

The dialog boxes close.

6 Click in any cell in the **Total** column, type **123** and observe what happens.

The number is not entered; instead a message informs you that the cell you are trying to change is protected.

7 Click **OK** to acknowledge the message. Click cell **D17**, type **10** and press Tab, type **7** and press Enter.

The numbers are recorded and the formulas in cells F17 and F40 calculate and display the results—$70.00.

8 On the Standard toolbar, click the **Undo** button twice to remove the two numbers that you typed, and then click the **Save** button.

You have tested your template, and it is protected and saved.

9 From the **View** menu, display the **Header and Footer tab** of the **Page Setup** dialog box. Click the **Custom Footer** button and add the **File name** to the **Left section** of the footer. Click **OK** twice to close the **Footer** and **Page Setup** dialog boxes.

10 Press Ctrl + Home.

Cell A1 is selected. It is a good idea to make cell A1 the active cell before saving your template to ensure that when the template is opened, the user will see the upper left portion of the worksheet.

chapter**seven**

11 From the **File** menu, click **Save As**. In the **Save As** dialog box, if necessary, use the **Save in arrow** to navigate to the templates folder. Recall that the path is **C:/Documents and Settings/name of computer owner/Application Data/Microsoft/Templates**. Save the protected template as **7A_PO_Template_Firstname_Lastname**. Click **Yes**, if prompted to override the existing file by this name. Repeat the process and save the file a second time in your storage location for this chapter. This ensures that a copy of the protected template is saved in your folder.

12 On the Standard toolbar, click the **Print Preview** button [icon] to see how the worksheet will look when it is printed. On the Print Preview toolbar click **Print**. Close the template, saving your changes if prompted to do so.

More Knowledge — Protecting Workbooks

In addition to protecting a single worksheet, you can also protect an entire workbook. From the Tools menu, point to Protection, and then click Protect Workbook. In the Protect Workbook dialog box, you can prevent alteration to the structure of the workbook and lock the position of the workbook window. You can also assign a password.

Objective 4
Create a Worksheet Based on a Template

After the template is protected and saved in the Templates folder, it is ready for use. Anyone with access to the Templates folder can open it, which opens a *new copy* of the template as a worksheet. Then the user can enter information in the unlocked cells and save it as a new file. Templates can be provided to coworkers by storing them on a company intranet, or they can be made available to customers through a Web site.

Activity 7.8 Using a Customized Template

1 If necessary, start Excel. From the **File** menu, click **New**. In the **New Workbook** task pane, under **Templates** click the **On my computer** link. In the displayed **Templates** dialog box, click the **General tab**.

Your 7A_PO Template is listed.

Alert!

Your Template Isn't Listed?
If you were unable to save your template to the computer's Templates folder, navigate to the folder where you are storing the files for this chapter to open your template.

2 Click your **7A_PO_Template** and click **OK**.

A new copy of the template opens—as a workbook, not as a template—and displays a *1* at the end of the file name in the title bar. The *1* indicates that this is a new workbook. If the file extensions are set to display on your computer, you will see .xls at the end of the file name.

3 Click cell **C6** and type **October 13, 2004** and press Enter, type **23** and press Enter, type **A-3421** and then press Enter twice to move to cell **C10**.

The date and purchase order numbers are entered.

4 Starting in cell **C10**, enter the company information as follows:

Name	**Joan Miller**
Company	**McKenzie Stewart**
Address	**5684 Palisades Blvd.**
City, State, Postal code	**Los Angeles, CA 90044**
Phone	**323.555.0230**

and then press Tab to move to the next unlocked cell.

The company information is entered and B17 is the active cell. Pressing Tab moves the active cell to the next cell that is unlocked.

5 In cell **B17** type **W-TF** and press Tab, type **Tri-fold Wallet** and press Tab, type **12** and press Tab, then type **7**

The first item ordered is entered.

6 Press Tab to return to the beginning of the next row. Complete the order by entering the following two items:

W-BF	**Bi-fold Wallet**	**24**	**5.5**
W-MC	**Money clip**	**24**	**2**

and then press Tab to move to the next unlocked cell.

The order is complete. Compare your screen with Figure 7.20.

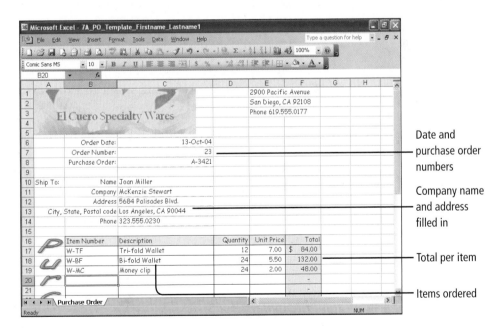

Figure 7.20

7 On the Standard toolbar, click the **Save** button ⊟.

The Save As dialog box opens. When the template was opened, Excel opened a new unsaved workbook, as indicated by *1* at the end of the name. In this manner, the person filling in the form is required to save the file as a new workbook, and the original template file is preserved to be used again as needed.

8 In the **Save As** dialog box, use the **Save in arrow** to navigate to the folder where you are storing your files for this chapter. In the **File name** box, type **7A_Purchase_Order_Firstname_Lastname** and then click **Save**. Click **Yes** to replace the existing file.

The file you used while you were developing the template is overwritten with this data file.

9 On the Standard toolbar, click the **Print Preview** button 🔍 to see how the worksheet will look when it is printed. On the Print Preview toolbar, click **Print**, and then click **OK**. Close the file, saving changes if prompted to do so.

Activity 7.9 Removing Worksheet Protection and Deleting a Template

If you need to make changes to a template after it is protected, you first need to remove the protection.

1 From the Standard toolbar, click the **Open** button 📂. Use the **Look in arrow** to navigate to the **Templates** folder on your computer (or, to your own folder if you were unable to store your template on the computer system). Recall that the default path is **C:/Documents and Settings/name of computer owner/Application Data/ Microsoft/Templates**. A template file has a small gold bar at the top of its icon, which differentiates it as a template, and not a workbook. Select your **7A_PO_Template** and click **Open**.

The template file stored in your computer's template folder displays on your screen.

2 Display the **Tools** menu, point to **Protection**, and then click **Unprotect Sheet**.

The Unprotect Sheet dialog box displays. Here you type the password that you assigned to this sheet.

3 In the **Password** box, type **GO!Series** and then click **OK** to remove the protection.

4 Click cell **F17**. Type **10** and press Enter. Click cell **F17** again.

The figure is displayed as $10.00, and 10 shows in the Formula bar. This demonstrates that you have removed the protection and can overwrite the formula that was in this cell.

5 On the Standard toolbar, click **Undo** to clear the number and return the formula to cell **F17**. From the **File** menu, click **Close**. Do *not* save changes when prompted to do so.

Next you will remove the template from this computer so that it is not available to the next person who might use the computer. If you were unable to save the template in the computer's Templates folder, you do not need to complete the next two steps.

6 On the Standard toolbar, click **Open**. In the **Open** dialog box, use the **Look in arrow** to navigate to the **Templates** folder if necessary. Click your **7A_PO_Template** file to select it, and then on the Open toolbar, click the **Delete** button.

The Confirm File Delete dialog box displays. Here you confirm that you want to delete the selected file. It is a good idea to check that you have selected the correct file to delete before clicking Yes. Note that the file will be sent to the recycle bin. See Figure 7.21.

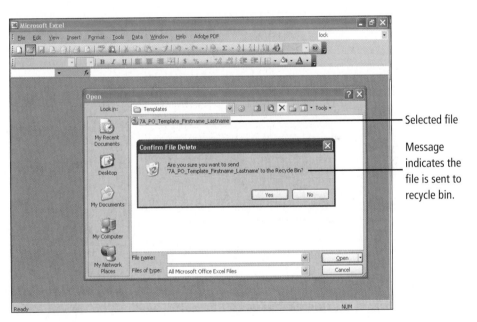

Selected file

Message indicates the file is sent to recycle bin.

Figure 7.21

7 In the **Confirm File Delete** dialog box, click **Yes** to confirm the deletion. Close the **Open** dialog box.

End You have completed Project 7A

7B Project 7B Phone Orders

Excel has several functions to look up information that is located in another part of the workbook. You can also create a list of acceptable data that can be entered in a cell. Formatting can be applied to a cell, based on a specified condition.

You can enhance a worksheet by adding lookup references and data lists, which will speed the completion of the workbook and improve the accuracy of the data. These functions are useful with a template, or in any situation where the same information must be referenced over and over again. The CFO at El Cuero Specialty Wares, Adriana Ramos, wants to speed the process of taking phone orders by developing a worksheet for order takers that automatically fills in product descriptions and prices.

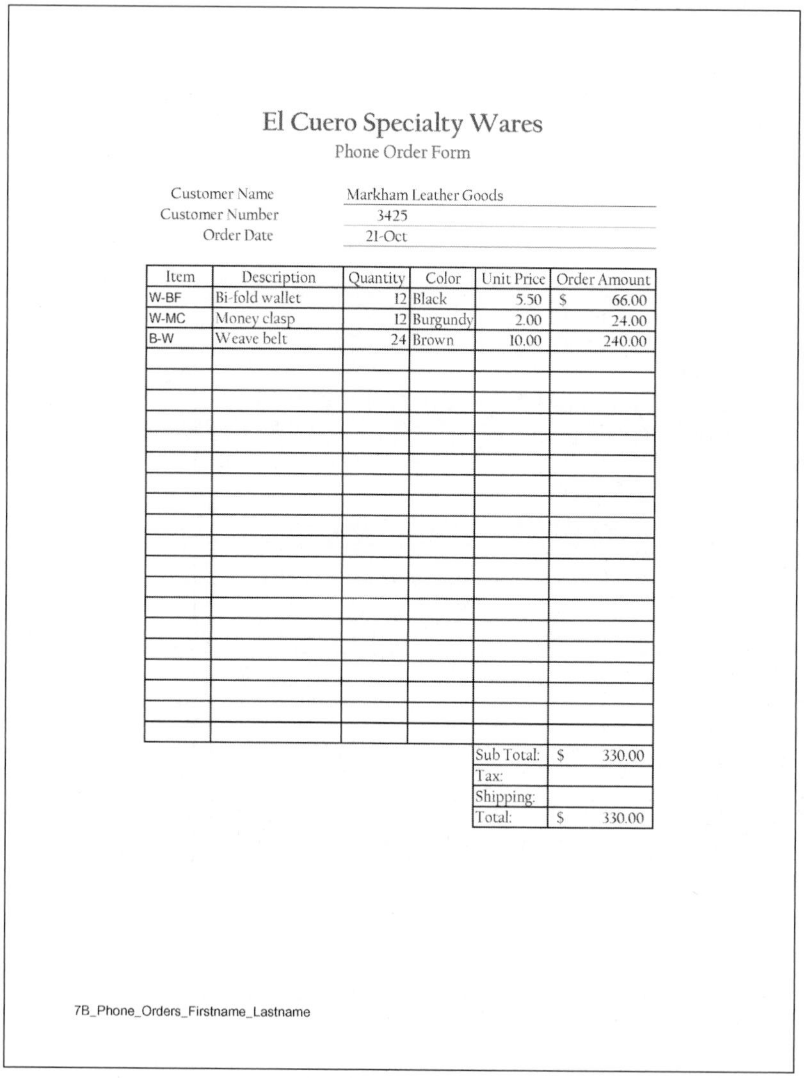

In Activities 7.10 through 7.15 you will enhance the Phone Orders form used at El Cuero Specialty Wares by inserting lookup functions to locate the product description and price, and a list box to locate a valid product code. You will improve the look of the worksheet by applying a conditional format to the totals column. Your completed worksheet will look similar to Figure 7.22. You will save your workbook as *7B_Phone_Order_Firstname_Lastname*.

El Cuero Specialty Wares
Phone Order Form

Customer Name   Markham Leather Goods
Customer Number   3425
Order Date   21-Oct

Item	Description	Quantity	Color	Unit Price	Order Amount
W-BF	Bi-fold wallet	12	Black	5.50	$ 66.00
W-MC	Money clasp	12	Burgundy	2.00	24.00
B-W	Weave belt	24	Brown	10.00	240.00

Sub Total:	$ 330.00
Tax:	
Shipping:	
Total:	$ 330.00

7B_Phone_Orders_Firstname_Lastname

Figure 7.22
Project 7B—Phone Order

Objective 5
Use Lookup Functions

When you type a value in a cell, Excel has the ability to look in a defined range of cells, called a **table array**, in another part of the workbook to find a corresponding value. For example, you can have a two-column range of cells containing names and phone numbers and define it as a table array. Then, you can type a name and have Excel fill in the phone number by looking it up in the table array. The **VLOOKUP** function looks up values in a table array that are arranged vertically in a column. The **HLOOKUP** function looks up values in a table array that are arranged horizontally in a row. Either lookup function can look up text or numbers. There is one requirement for the lookup functions to work properly; that is, the data in the table array must be sorted in ascending order.

Activity 7.10 Creating a Lookup Table

The first step in using a lookup function is to create or define a range of cell data that will serve as the table array. In the El Cuero Phone Order form, after an Item Number is entered on the form, the description of the item should display automatically in the Description column. To accomplish this, you will define a table array that includes the item number in one column and a description of the item in the second column.

1 Start Excel. On the Standard toolbar, click the **Open** button. Navigate to the folder where the student files for this textbook are stored. Locate and open **e07B_Phone_Orders**.

2 From the **File** menu, click **Save As**. In the **Save As** dialog box, use the **Save in arrow** to navigate to the location where you are storing your files for this chapter. In the **File name** box, type **7B_Phone_Orders_Firstname_Lastname** Click the **Save** button.

This worksheet is used to take orders from customers over the phone. See Figure 7.23.

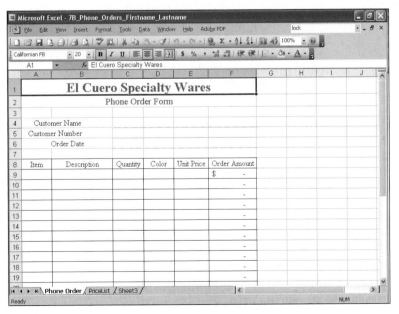

Figure 7.23

3 Click the **Price List sheet tab**.

On the Price List sheet, the Style Code, Description, and Unit Price are recorded. Before this list can be used to look up information, it must be sorted in ascending order by Style Code—the column that will be used to look up the matching information.

4 Select the range **A4:C11**. From the **Data** menu, click **Sort**. In the **Sort** dialog box, verify that the **Sort by** box displays **Style Code** and that the **Ascending** option button is selected.

Because the Header row option button is selected, the range to be sorted does not include the selected cells in row 4. Compare your screen with Figure 7.24.

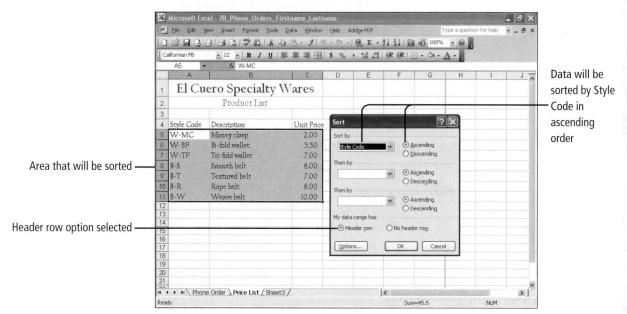

Figure 7.24

5 Click **OK**.

The data is sorted alphabetically by Style Code; B-R is first in the list and W-TF is last.

6 On the Standard toolbar, click the **Save** button.

Activity 7.11 Using the VLOOKUP Function

The VLOOKUP function looks up values in a table array that are arranged vertically. The arguments for this function are (Lookup_value,Table_array,Col_index_num) where Lookup value is the cell that contains the value that is to be looked up in the table array; Table array is the defined range of cells that contains the data that is to be looked up; and the column index number is the column number (1, 2, 3, 4, and so on) in the table array that contains the result you want to retrieve from the table.

1 Click the **Phone Order sheet tab**. In cell **A9** type **W-BF** and press Tab.

2 With cell **B9** as the active cell, display the **Insert** menu, and then click **Function**. Alternatively, click the Insert Function button located to the left of the Formula Bar.

The Insert Function dialog box displays.

3 Click the **Or select a category arrow**, and then from the displayed list, click **Lookup & Reference**. In the **Select a function** box, scroll to the end of the list, click **VLOOKUP**, and then click **OK**.

The VLOOKUP Function Arguments dialog box displays.

4 With the insertion point in the **Lookup_value** box, click cell **A9**.

Cell A9 contains the value for which you want to look up a description.

5 Click in the **Table_array** box, and then click the **Price List sheet tab**. On the **Price List** sheet, select the range **A4:B11**, and then press F4.

This range (table array) includes the value that will be looked up (W-BF), and the corresponding value to be displayed (Bi-fold wallet). By pressing F4, the absolute cell reference is applied to the table array so that the formula can be copied to the remainder of the column in the Phone Order sheet.

6 Click in the **Col_index_num** box and type **2**

The description for the selected item is found in column 2 of the table. Compare your screen with Figure 7.25.

Arguments entered in Function Arguments dialog box ———

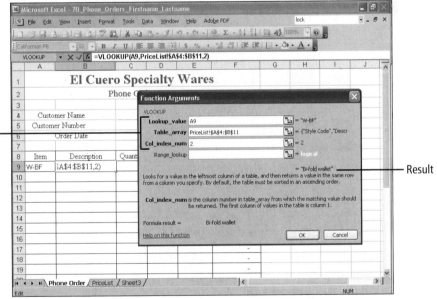

Result

Figure 7.25

7 Click **OK**.

The description for the first item displays in cell B9.

8 Press Tab, type **12** and press Tab, type **Black** and press Tab, type **5.5** and then press Enter.

The first ordered item is complete.

9 Click cell **B9** where the VLOOKUP formula is, point to the fill handle in the lower right corner of the cell, and then drag to fill the VLOOKUP formula down through cell **B30**.

The #N/A error notation displays in the cells where you copied the formula. The reason for the error is that a value is not available to the formula; values have not yet been entered in column A. Later in this project, you will apply a conditional format to hide the error message so that it will not be distracting to those who complete the order sheet. Compare your screen with Figure 7.26.

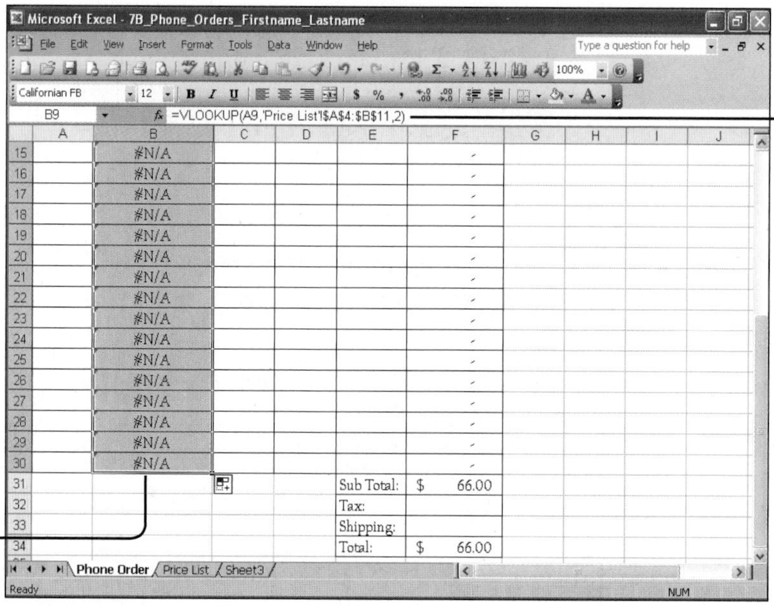

Figure 7.26

10 On the Standard toolbar, click the **Save** button.

Activity 7.12 Using the Paste Special Function to Create a Horizontal Lookup List

You can look up information in a table array that is arranged vertically, as you did in the last activity, or in a table array that is arranged horizontally. To reverse the data displayed in rows with the information displayed in columns, you can use one of several Paste Special features. **Paste Special** is an Excel command that enables you to paste just one particular characteristic of a cell, reverse rows and columns, or paste the results of a formula rather than the formula itself.

In this activity, you will use Paste Special to create a horizontal table array, and then in the following activity, you will use the horizontal table array to look up the Unit Price for items entered into the worksheet.

1 Click the **Price List sheet tab**. Select the range **A4:A11**, hold down Ctrl and select the range **C4:C11**, and then on the Standard toolbar, click the **Copy** button.

Recall that Ctrl can be used to select nonadjacent cell ranges.

2 Click cell **E4**, and then on the Standard toolbar, click the **Paste** button ⬛▾.

The Style Code list and the Unit Prices are copied to columns E and F.

3 With the range **E4:F11** still selected, click the **Copy** button ⬛ again. If the Clipboard task pane opens, close it. Click cell **D13**. From the **Edit** menu, click **Paste Special**.

The Paste Special dialog box opens as shown in Figure 7.27. In the top part of this dialog box, you can choose to paste different characteristics of the copied cells, such as the formulas, the formatting, the values only, or the column width. Under Operation, you can choose a mathematical operation to perform with a copied cell. At the bottom of the dialog box there are two check boxes—Skip blanks and Transpose. *Transpose* switches copied data between columns and rows.

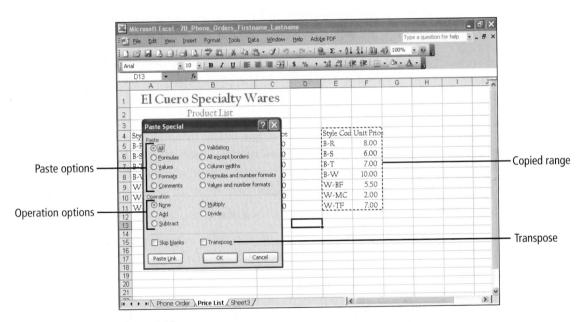

Figure 7.27

4 In the **Paste Special** dialog box, select the **Transpose** check box, and then click **OK**. Click in any empty cell. Press Esc to remove the moving border from around the copied cell range.

The data is displayed horizontally in rows 13 and 14, starting in cell D13.

5 On the Standard toolbar, click the **Save** button ⬛.

Activity 7.13 Using the HLOOKUP Function

The HLOOKUP function works like the VLOOKUP function, except the table array is displayed horizontally. In this activity, you will use the horizontal table array to look up the Unit Price for items entered into the worksheet.

1 Click the **Phone Order sheet tab** and click cell **E9**. From the **Insert** menu, click **Function**. Alternatively, click the Insert Function button to the left of the Formula Bar.

The Insert Function dialog box opens.

2 Be sure **Lookup & Reference** displays in the **Or select a category** box. In the **Select a function** box, scroll as necessary, click **HLOOKUP**, and then click **OK**.

The HLOOKUP Function Arguments dialog box displays.

3 With the insertion point in the **Lookup_value** box, click cell **A9**.

Cell A9 contains the Item number for which you want to look up the Unit Price in the horizontal table array.

4 Click in the **Table_array** box, and then click the **Price List sheet tab**. On the **Price List sheet**, move the dialog box as necessary and select the range **D13:K14**, and then press F4 to make the range reference absolute.

This range includes the value to be looked up—Item—and the result—Unit Price—the price which will display in column E. Recall that the absolute reference is applied so that the formula can be copied to the remainder of column E on the Phone Order sheet.

5 Click in the **Row_index_num** box and type **2**

The price for the selected item is found in row 2 of the table array. Compare your screen with Figure 7.28.

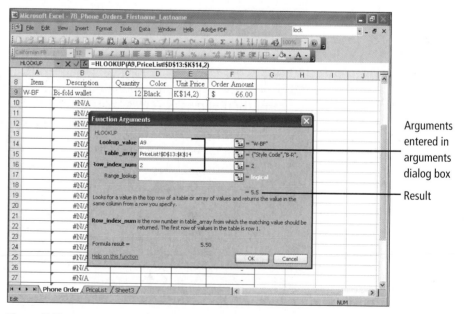

Figure 7.28

6 Click **OK**.

The Unit Price for the first item is located in the table array (defined range of cells) and displays in cell E9.

7 With cell **E9** as the active cell, point to the fill handle in the lower right corner of the cell and drag to copy the HLOOKUP function down through cell **E30**.

The #N/A error notation displays in the cells where you copied the formula and in column F. This means that a value is not yet available to the formula. The notation displays in both columns because values have not yet been entered in column A. Later in this project, you will apply a conditional format to hide this notation so that it does not distract the person filling in the form. Compare your screen with Figure 7.29.

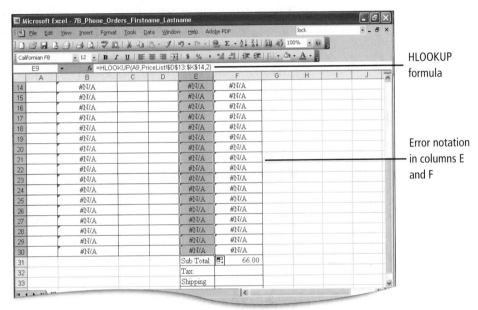

Figure 7.29

8 Click cell **A10**, type **W-MC** and press [Tab] twice.

Excel looks up the description in the vertical table array on the Price List sheet, and then displays the result in cell B10.

9 In cell **C10**, type **12** and press [Tab], type **Burgundy** and then press [Enter].

Excel looks up the price in the horizontal table array on the Price List sheet, and then displays the result in cell E10. The second item is ordered. You can see that after data is entered in the row, the error notations no longer display. You can also see that using lookup lists speeds the process and improves the accuracy in completing the order form.

10 On the Standard toolbar, click the **Save** button 🖫.

Objective 6
Validate Data

Another technique to improve accuracy in completing worksheets is a **validation list**—a list of values that are acceptable for a group of cells. Only values on the list are valid; any value not on the list is considered invalid. For example, in the Phone Order sheet, it would be useful if the Item number could be looked up from a list so that only valid style codes are entered. In the Data Validation dialog box, you can restrict the type of data entered into a cell by choosing from among Any Value, Whole Number, Decimal, List, Date, Time, Text Length, and Custom.

Activity 7.14 Creating a Validation List

When using a specific list of valid values, the list of valid values must either be on the same worksheet as the destination cell, or if in another worksheet, the cell range must be named. In this activity you will create a named range for the Style Codes, and then create a validation list for column A of the Phone Order worksheet.

1 If necessary, open your **7B_Phone_Orders_Firstname_Lastname** workbook. Click the **Price List sheet tab**. Select cells **A4:A11**, display the **Insert** menu, point to **Name**, and then click **Create**.

Recall that the Create Name command can be used to create a named range when one of the selected cells can be used as the range name.

2 In the **Create Names** dialog box be sure the **Top row** check box is selected, and then click **OK**.

Style_Code is designated as the range name for the selected cells. Recall that Excel replaces spaces with an underscore when it creates a range name.

3 Click the **Phone Order sheet tab**. Select cells **A9:A30**.

Before you set the validation requirement, you must first select the cells that you want to restrict to only valid entries from the list.

4 From the **Data** menu, click **Validation**. Be sure the **Settings tab** is selected.

The Data Validation dialog box displays.

5 In the **Data Validation** dialog box, click the **Allow arrow**, and then click **List**.

A Source box displays as the third box in the Data Validation dialog box. Here you select or type the source data.

6 Click to position the insertion point in the **Source** box and type **=Style_Code** and then compare your screen with Figure 7.30.

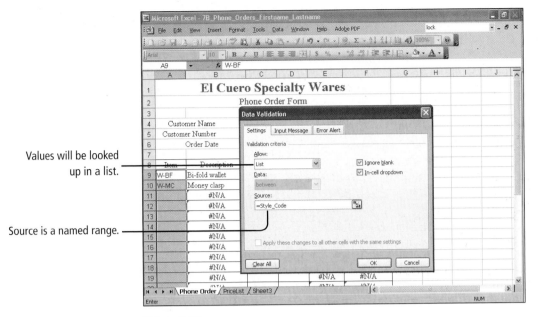

Values will be looked up in a list.

Source is a named range.

Figure 7.30

More Knowledge — Creating Validation Messages

In the Data Validation dialog box, you can use the Input Message tab to create a ScreenTip that will display when the cell is selected. The message can be an instruction that tells the user what to do. You can also use the Error Alert tab to create a warning message that displays if invalid data is entered in the cell.

7 Click **OK**. Click cell **A11**.

A list arrow displays at the right side of this cell.

8 In cell **A11**, click the list arrow to display the list, and then click **B-W**.

The Style Code is selected from the list and the Item, Description, and Unit Price cells are filled in for row 11.

9 Press [Tab] twice, type **24** and press [Tab], type **Brown** and then press [Enter] to return to the beginning of the next row. Compare your screen with Figure 7.31.

You can see that when taking orders by phone, it will speed the process if all of the necessary information can be filled in automatically. Furthermore, accuracy will be improved if item numbers are restricted to only valid data.

Order completed using a validation list.

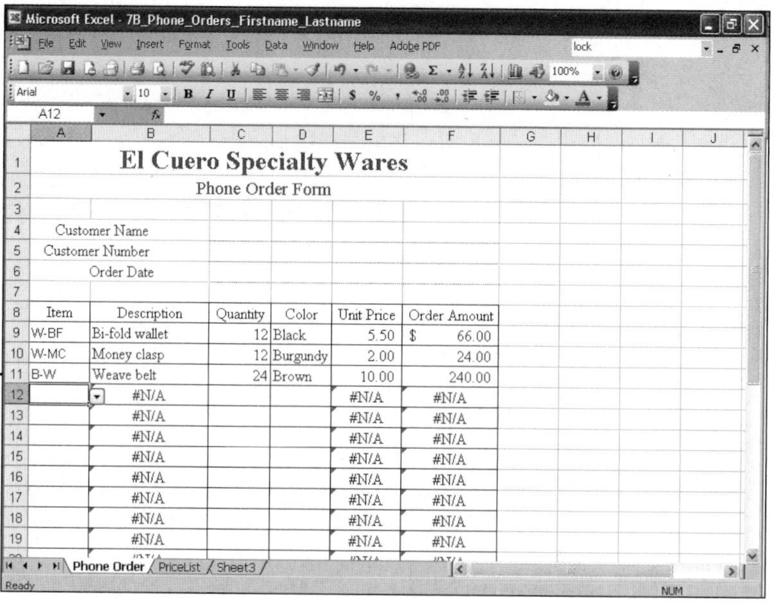

Figure 7.31

10 In cell **A12**, type **G-W** and press Tab.

An error message displays indicating that you entered a value that is not valid; that is, it is not on the validation list you created. Restricting the values that an order taker can enter will greatly improve the accuracy of orders.

11 In the displayed error message, click **Cancel**, and then on the Standard toolbar, click the **Save** button ⊟.

Objective 7
Use Conditional Formats

A **Conditional Format** is any format, such as cell shading or font color, that Excel automatically applies to cells if a specified condition is true. For example, if you want to draw attention to values that are unreasonably large, you can do the following: create a condition statement to define the value's limits; then apply a format, such as a different font color or background color to those cells that exceed the condition. In the Phone Order worksheet, you will apply a conditional format to hide the #NA error code.

Activity 7.15 Applying a Conditional Format

Recall that on the Phone Orders worksheet, formulas are in place so that when an Item number is entered, the Description and Unit Price are automatically filled in. Because not all of the formulas have values, error messages display. When order takers use the Phone Order worksheet, it would be distracting to see the columns of error messages displayed. In this activity, you will use conditional formatting to prevent the error notation from displaying, while leaving the formula intact.

1 Select cells **B12:B30**.

This is the first range of cells that displays the #NA error code. If you were preparing this worksheet as a template, you would select all of the cells in the Item column, but because you have already entered orders in the first three rows, the conditional format does not need to be applied to the first three cells.

2 From the **Format** menu, click **Conditional Formatting**.

The Conditional Formatting dialog box opens. Here you set the condition to which you want to apply a different format.

3 Under **Condition 1**, click the **Cell Value Is arrow**, and then click **Formula Is**.

The dialog box changes and a box displays to the right of the Formula Is statement so that you can set a specific condition or formula.

4 Press [Tab] to move to the box to the right of the Formula Is box. Type **=ISNA(B12)**

ISNA is one of nine IS functions that Excel uses to test for a type of value. This is a logical test that returns TRUE if the condition or value in the cell matches the condition that is being tested, and FALSE if that condition does not exist. In this case, the value that is being tested is the #*NA* error notation—which stands for value *not available*. This error notation displays when Excel is unable to compute a result because one of the values in a formula is missing. The syntax is ISNA(value) where value is the cell that is being tested—in this case, cell B12. Thus, the function asks the question, "Is NA present in cell B12?"

5 In the dialog box, click the **Format** button. In the **Format Cells** dialog box, click the **Color arrow**, and then in the fifth row, click the last color—**White**.

The result of this action will be that if the condition is true—the NA notation is present—then Excel will apply the white color to the cell. This will hide the notation by making it the same color as the cell background. Compare your screen with Figure 7.32.

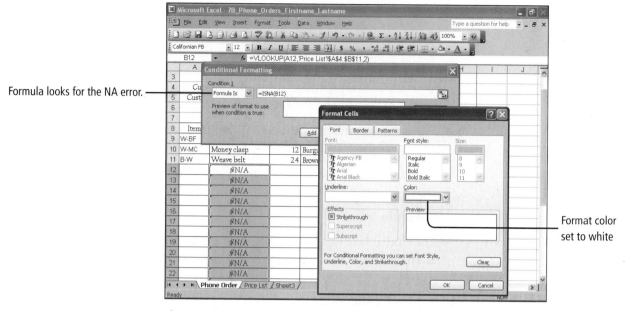

Formula looks for the NA error.

Format color set to white

Figure 7.32

Note — You Must Choose White

You have to specifically click the color *White* in the color palette, even though the color box appears to be white. When the Format Cells dialog box displays, the font color box is blank, no color is selected, which makes it appear to be white.

6 Click **OK** twice to close both dialog boxes.

The format is applied. The white font color displays in the cells when they are selected. See Figure 7.33.

Cells formatted to display the error code in white

Figure 7.33

7 Click an empty cell to deselect, and note that the cells in column B no longer show the notation, although it is still there.

Hiding the error code until actual data fills the cells will be much less distracting for the order taker.

8 Select cells **E12:E30**, and then from the **Format** menu, click **Conditional Formatting**. Change the first box to **Formula Is**. In the second box type **=ISNA(E12)** and then click the **Format** button. In the **Format Cells** dialog box, change the **Font color** to **White**. Click **OK** twice.

The #NA error code is hidden in column E.

9 Repeat this procedure to hide the #NA error code in the affected cells in **column F**.

After you have hidden the error notation, the triangle indicators still display in the upper left corner of the cells with the #NA error.

10 Click any cell with a green triangle, and then point to the **Trace Error** button.

The ScreenTip indicates that a value is not yet available, which, of course, is the case until the order taker enters data.

Note — Hiding Green Triangles

You can hide the green triangles so they do not display on the screen. Doing so, however, disables error checking from the software, not just from the worksheet that is currently open.

11 Starting in cell **C4**, type the following customer information:

Markham Leather Goods
3425
10/21

12 On the Standard toolbar, click the **Save** button 🖫. From the **File** menu, click **Page Setup** and click the **Header/Footer tab**. In the **Left section** of the **Custom footer**, insert the **File name**. On the **Margins tab**, select the **Horizontally** check box if necessary, and then click **Print Preview**. On the Print Preview toolbar, click the **Print** button, and then click **OK**.

13 Close the file, saving changes if prompted to do so.

End **You have completed Project 7B** ————————————————

Project 7C Sales Income

Using Excel's Formula Auditing toolbar, you can review a worksheet to locate errors, circle invalid data, and trace formulas.

Adriana Ramos, CFO of El Cuero Specialty Wares, has several interns working in her department. One of the interns is new to Excel and is having difficulty with errors on the sales income worksheet.

In Activities 7.16 through 7.20 you will use the Formula Auditing toolbar to review the sales income worksheet and resolve the errors. Your completed worksheet will look similar to Figure 7.34. You will save your workbook as *7C_Sales_Income_Firstname_Lastname*.

El Cuero Specialty Wares
Sales Income

Sales	January	February	March	April	May	June	Totals
Belts	$ 168,975	$ 154,893	$ 170,987	$ 173,689	$ 185,602	$ 198,006	$ 1,052,152
Handbags	275,863	186,541	286,548	346,075	358,700	402,800	$ 1,856,527
Key Chains	98,756	78,520	87,546	90,547	79,841	81,479	$ 516,689
Travel Bags	369,526	345,872	366,912	347,844	352,726	389,630	$ 2,172,510
Wallets	235,680	198,500	205,680	268,425	278,000	255,450	$ 1,441,735
Total Sales	$ 1,148,800	$ 964,326	$ 1,117,673	$ 1,226,580	$ 1,254,869	$ 1,327,365	$ 7,039,613
Expenses							
Cost of Goods	646,925	571,024	659,336	708,700	722,020	770,950	4,078,955
Overhead	60,000	60,000	60,000	60,000	60,000	60,000	360,000
Salaries	93,440	84,216	91,884	97,329	98,743	102,368	567,981
Marketing	57,440	48,216	55,884	61,329	62,743	66,368	351,981
Administration	22,976	19,287	22,353	24,532	25,097	26,547	140,792
Total Expenses	$ 880,781	$ 782,743	$ 889,457	$ 951,890	$ 968,604	$ 1,026,234	$ 5,499,709
Gross Profit/Loss	$ 268,019	$ 181,583	$ 228,216	$ 274,690	$ 286,265	$ 301,131	$ 1,539,904
Percent increase		-48%	20%	17%	4%	5%	
Marketing Percent	5%						
Admin Percent	2%						

7C_Sales_Income_Firstname_Lastname

Figure 7.34
Project 7C—Sales Income

Objective 8
Audit a Worksheet

Auditing is the process of examining a worksheet for errors in formulas. In complex worksheets, you can use the Formula Auditing toolbar to show relationships between cells and formulas, and ensure that formulas are logical and correct.

The Formula Auditing toolbar can also help you resolve error messages. Although sometimes it is appropriate to hide the error message, at other times error notations can indicate a problem that needs to be corrected.

In addition to error notations, you will also encounter triangle indicators that display in the corners of cells. The green triangle in the upper left corner of a cell indicates that the formula in the cell is suspect for some reason. Typically this is because the formula does not match the formulas in the cells next to it, or because it does not include all of the adjacent cells.

Activity 7.16 Tracing Formula Precedents

Tracing formulas helps you to understand the relationships among cells in a worksheet. As an auditing tool, it is a quick way to ensure that the formulas are correctly constructed.

1 Start Excel if necessary. On the Standard toolbar, click the **Open** button [image]. Navigate to the folder where the student files for this textbook are stored. Locate and open **e07C_Sales_Income**.

2 From the **File** menu, display the **Save As** dialog box. Navigate to the location where you are storing your files for this chapter. In the **File name** box, type **7C_Sales_Income_Firstname_Lastname** Click the **Save** button.

The worksheet shows the income and expenses related to sales for the first six months of the year. Several error notations are present (#VALUE!, #REF!, #NAME?), and green triangles display in the upper left corners of several cells. Two of the columns are too narrow to display the data and display pound signs—####. See Figure 7.35.

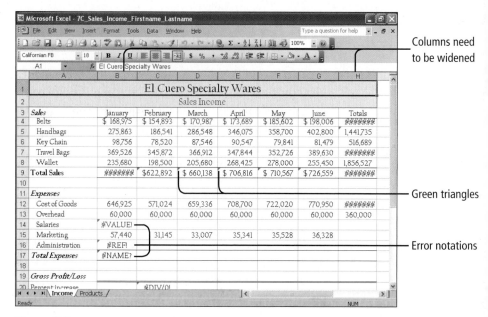

Figure 7.35

3 From the **Tools** menu, display the **Options** dialog box. Click the **Error Checking tab**. If necessary, under **Settings** select the **Enable background error checking** check box, and then click **OK**.

The error checking is enabled to help you resolve errors that are displayed in this worksheet.

4 Examine the table in Figure 7.36 to see a list of common error notations and their meanings.

Error Notations Defined

Error Notation	Meaning	Possible Cause
#DIV/0!	Cannot divide by zero	A formula refers to a blank cell for the divisor.
#NAME?	Does not recognize a name you used in a formula	A function or a named range may be misspelled.
#VALUE!	Cannot use a text field in a formula	A formula refers to a cell that contains a text value rather than a numeric value or a formula.
#REF!	Cannot locate the reference	A cell that is referenced in a formula may have been deleted or moved.
#N/A	No value is available	A formula is referring to an empty cell.
#NUM!	Invalid argument in a worksheet function	An unacceptable argument may have been used in a function.
#NULL!	No common cells	A space was entered between two ranges in a formula to indicate an intersection, but the ranges have no common cells.

Figure 7.36

5 Position the mouse pointer on the line between the **column B** and **C** headings and double-click to AutoFit the width of **column B**. Do the same to AutoFit **column H**.

Columns B and H are widened so that all of their data can display.

6 Click cell **C9**, point to the displayed **Trace Error button**, and read the **ScreenTip** that displays.

The ScreenTip indicates that adjacent cells containing numbers are not included in the formula. It is possible that the formula purposely consists of a group of cells that excludes some of the cells adjacent to it. However, because that is not as common as including all of the cells that are adjacent to one another, Excel flags this as a potential error. Recall that a green triangle displays in the upper left of a cell that Excel detects as having a potential error, and selecting the cell displays the Trace Error button.

7 Leave cell **C9** selected. From the **View** menu, point to **Toolbars**, and then click **Formula Auditing**. Move your mouse pointer over each button in the toolbar and view the ScreenTip to identify the name of each button. Take a moment to review the description of each button in the table in Figure 7.37.

Formula Auditing Toolbar Buttons

Button	ScreenTip	Description
	Error Checking	Locates and identifies errors, and opens a Help window that provides assistance in resolving errors.
	Trace Precedents	Displays arrows pointing to the cells that are used in the formula contained in the selected cells.
	Remove Precedent Arrows	Removes displayed precedent arrows.
	Trace Dependents	Displays arrows pointing to cells where the selected cell is used.
	Remove Dependent Arrows	Removes displayed dependent arrows.
	Remove All Arrows	Removes all auditing arrows that are displayed on the screen.
	Trace Error	In a cell that displays an error notation, displays arrows to show the cells that are referenced in the cell that contains the error.
	New Comment	Adds a comment to a cell on a worksheet.
	Circle Invalid Data	Compares cell entry to its validation list, and then circles any cells that do not meet the validation criteria.
	Clear Validation Circles	Removes validation circles from the worksheet.
	Show Watch Window	Opens the Watch Window toolbar. The Watch Window places the selected cell in a separate window where it can be watched as changes are made to the worksheet.
	Evaluate Formula	Opens the Evaluate Formula window, which can be used to examine the components of complex formulas.

Figure 7.37

8 On the Formula Auditing toolbar, click the **Trace Precedents** button 📑.

Precedents are cells that are referred to by a formula in another cell. Here, the precedent cells are bordered in blue. A blue arrow, called a *tracer arrow*, displays from cell C6:C8, pointing to the selected cell C9. A tracer arrow shows the relationship between the active cell and its related cells. Tracer arrows are blue when pointing from a cell that provides data to another cell. Because this total should include *all* of the product sales for February, this is indeed an error in the formula— the formula should include cells C4:C8. By tracing the precedents, you can see that two cells were mistakenly left out of the formula.

9 To the left of cell **C9**, click the **Trace Error** button to display a list of error checking options.

You can use the Trace Error button to help resolve errors in formulas. See Figure 7.38.

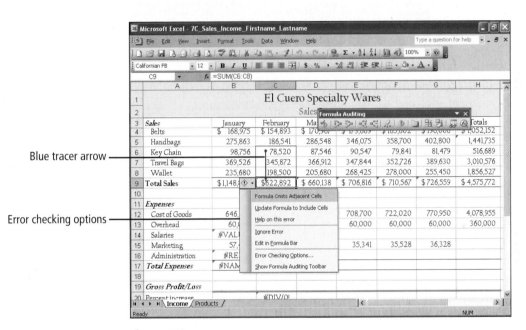

Blue tracer arrow

Error checking options

Figure 7.38

10 From the displayed list, click **Update Formula to Include Cells**, and then look at the formula in the **Formula Bar**.

The formula is updated to include cells C4:C8 and the green triangle is removed from the cell.

11 Click cell **D9**. Point to the **Trace Error** button and read the **ScreenTip**.

The same error exists in cell D9—not all adjacent cells in the column were included in the formula. This error also exists in cells E9:G9. You can click in each cell and use the Trace Error button's error checking options list to correct each formula, or, you can use the fill handle to copy the corrected formula to the remaining cells.

Click cell **C9** and use the fill handle to copy the corrected formula to cells **D9:G9**. AutoFit **columns D** through **G** to widen them to fit the contents.

All the green triangles are removed from this section.

Click cell **H5**, point to the displayed **Trace Error** button, and read the **ScreenTip**.

The formula in this cell is not the same as the formula in the other cells in this area of the worksheet.

On the Formula Auditing toolbar, click the **Trace Precedents** button.

A blue tracer arrow displays from cell B8, and the range B8:G8 is bordered in blue. This indicates that the formula in cell H5 is summing the values in row 8 rather than the values in row 5. See Figure 7.39.

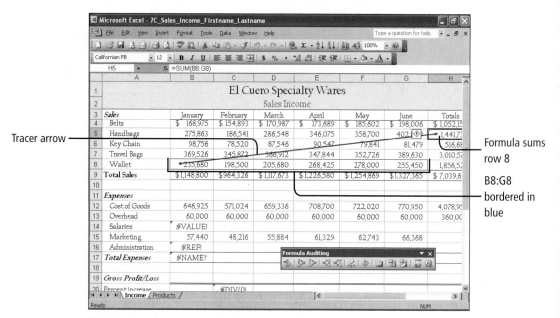

Tracer arrow

Formula sums row 8

B8:G8 bordered in blue

Figure 7.39

To the left of cell **H5**, click the **Trace Error** button to display the list of error checking options, click **Copy Formula from Above**, and then look at the **Formula Bar** to verify that the formula is summing the monthly totals in **row 5**.

The blue tracer arrow is removed and the formula is corrected—it now sums row 5.

16 Click cell **H4**. On the Formula Auditing toolbar, click the **Trace Precedents** button 🔳. To verify the remaining formulas in **column H**, click each of the remaining cells—**H5** through **H8**—and then click the **Trace Precedent** button 🔳 while each cell is selected.

Cells H7 and H8 display blue tracer arrows that are inconsistent with the other formulas in this column. However, green triangle indicators do not display in either of these cells. When auditing a worksheet, you cannot rely on the error notations and triangle indicators alone. To ensure the accuracy of a worksheet you should use the tracer arrows to verify that all of the formulas are logical and correct. Compare your screen with Figure 7.40.

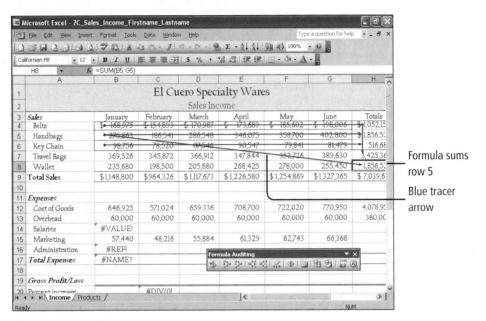

Formula sums row 5

Blue tracer arrow

Figure 7.40

17 On the Formula Auditing toolbar, click the **Remove All Arrows** button 🔳. Click cell **H6** and use the fill handle to copy the formula in this cell down to cells **H7** through **H8**.

18 On the Standard toolbar, click the **Save** button 🔳.

Activity 7.17 Tracing Dependents

1 Click cell **B14**, which displays the error #*VALUE!*. To the left of the cell, point to the **Trace Error** button and read the ScreenTip.

This formula is trying to use a cell that is the wrong data type—a cell that does not contain a number.

2 On the Formula Auditing toolbar, click the **Trace Precedents** button 🔳.

A blue tracer arrow indicates that cell B3 is included in the formula. Because cell B3 contains text—*January*—and not a number, no mathematical calculation can be made. The salaries should be calculated as 5 percent of Total Sales, plus the constant amount of 36,000.

3 On the Formula Auditing toolbar, click the **Trace Dependents** button [icon].

Dependents are cells that contain formulas that refer to other cells—they depend on the values of other cells to display a result. A red tracer arrow displays showing that the formula in cell B17 depends on the result of the formula in cell B14. Tracer arrows are red if a cell contains an error value, such as #VALUE!. See Figure 7.41.

Blue tracer arrow (pointing from a cell that provides data to another cell)

Red tracer arrow (cell contains an error value)

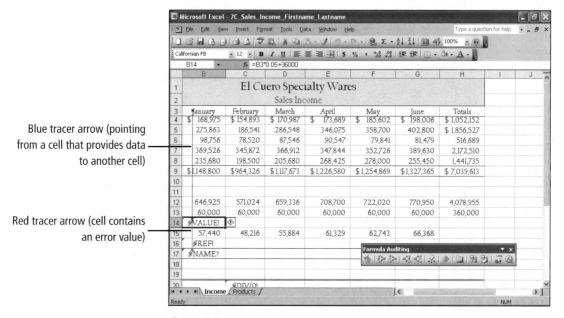

Figure 7.41

4 Click the displayed **Trace Error** button to display the list of error checking options. From the displayed list, click **Show Calculation Steps**.

The Evaluate Formula dialog box opens and displays the formula as ="January"*0.05+36000. January is not a number, nor is it a range name that refers to a group of numbers; thus, it cannot be used in a mathematical formula. At the bottom of the dialog box, Excel indicates that the next evaluation will result in an error.

5 In the dialog box, click **Evaluate**.

The formula displayed in the **Evaluation** box displays =*#Value!+36000*. You can use this box to evaluate each step of the formula. With complex formulas, this can be helpful in examining each piece of a formula to see where the error has occurred.

6 Click the **Close** button to close the **Evaluate Formula** dialog box. With cell **B14** still the active cell, click in the Formula Bar and edit as necessary to change the cell referenced in the formula to **B9**, and then press ⏎ Enter.

The error is removed and the result—93,440—displays in cell B14.

7 Use the fill handle to copy the corrected formula in cell **B14** across the row to cells **C14:G14**.

8 Click cell **B9**. On the Formula Auditing toolbar, click the **Trace Dependents** button ⊞.

Blue tracer arrows display in two directions—across row 9 to cell H9, and down column B to cells B14, B15, and B16. Each cell where an arrowhead displays indicates a dependent relationship. See Figure 7.42.

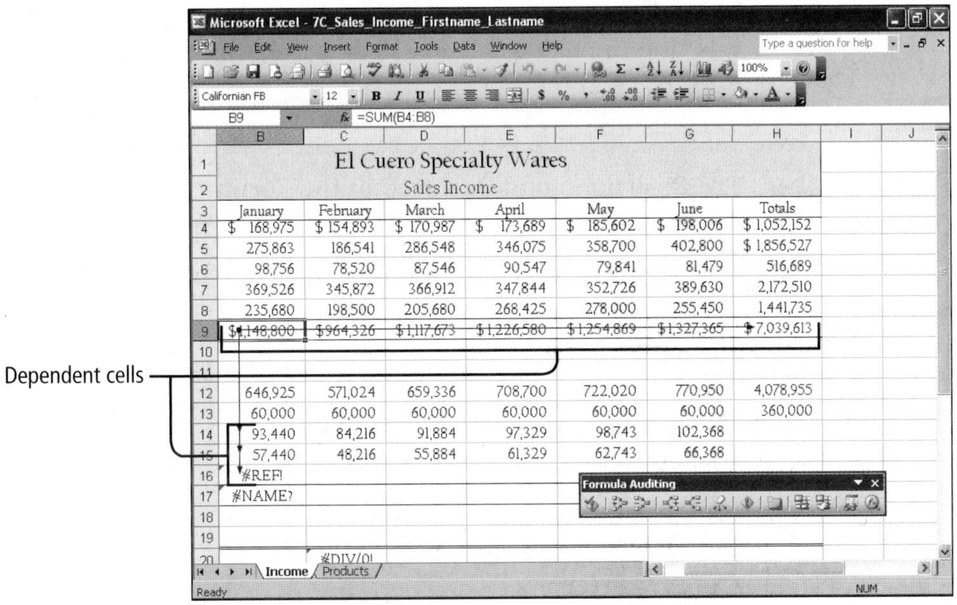

Figure 7.42

9 On the Formula Auditing toolbar, click the **Remove Dependent Arrows** button ⊞.

The arrows are removed from the screen.

10 On the Standard toolbar, click the **Save** button 🖫.

Activity 7.18 Tracing Formula Errors

Another tool you can use to help locate and resolve an error is Trace Error from the Formula Auditing toolbar. Use this command when a cell contains an error notation such as #Value!, #Ref!, #Name?, or #Div/0!.

1 Click cell **B16**, point to the displayed **Trace Error** button and read the **ScreenTip**.

The error message indicates that a cell that was referenced in the formula has been moved or deleted, or the function is causing an invalid reference error. In other words, Excel does not know where to look to get the value that should be used in the formula.

2 On the Formula Auditing toolbar, click the **Trace Error** button ⬦ twice.

The first time you click the Trace Error button, a precedent arrow is drawn from cell B9. The second time you click the button, an arrow is drawn between cells B9 and B4 and the cell range B4:B8 is bordered in blue. The blue border indicates that this range of cells is used in the formula in cell B9, which sums the values in the column.

3 Click in cell **A24**. Type **Admin Percent** and press [Tab], and then type **2%**

The percent used to calculate administrative expenses was moved or deleted from the worksheet, so you must re-enter the value. That way, it can be referenced in the formula in cell B16.

4 Click **B16**. Click the displayed **Trace Error** button to display the list of error checking options, and then click **Edit in Formula Bar**.

The insertion point is placed in the Formula Bar so that you can edit the formula.

5 Delete **#Ref!**. Type **b24** and press [F4] to make the cell reference absolute. Press [Enter].

The error notation in cell B16 is replaced with 22,976. The corrected formula needs to be copied across row 16, and it needs to use an absolute reference. That way, the 2 percent Admin Percent will be applied to the sales figure for each month.

6 Click cell **B16** and use the fill handle to copy the formula across the row to cells **C16:G16**.

7 On the Standard toolbar, click the **Save** button 🖫. Compare your screen with Figure 7.43.

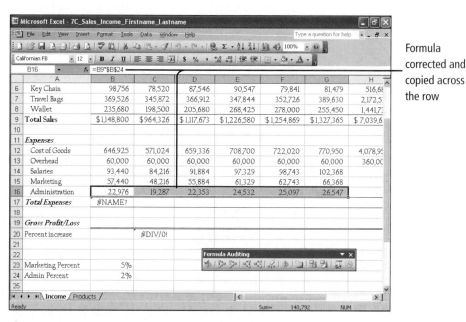

Formula corrected and copied across the row

Figure 7.43

Activity 7.19 Using Error Checking

Another command that can be used to locate and resolve errors is Error Checking. Clicking this button on the Formula Auditing toolbar opens the Error Checking dialog box, which provides an explanation about the error and enables you to move from one error to the next. Thus, you can review all of the errors on a worksheet.

1 Click cell **A1**. On the Formula Auditing toolbar, click the **Error Checking** button.

The Error Checking dialog box opens and cell B17 becomes the active cell. This is the first error that was located by the Error Checking program.

2 On the right side of the **Error Checking** dialog box, click **Help on this error**.

The Microsoft Office Excel Help window opens to the *Correct a #NAME? error* page. An explanation for this error is provided along with a list of possible causes and solutions.

3 Review the list of possible causes, and then click **Misspelling the name**.

The solution suggests that you correct the spelling or insert the correct function into the formula as shown in Figure 7.44. In this example, the function SUM was misspelled as *Sume*. The list of causes and solutions helps you identify problems that would result in the error notation.

Misspelled function —

List of possible causes and solutions

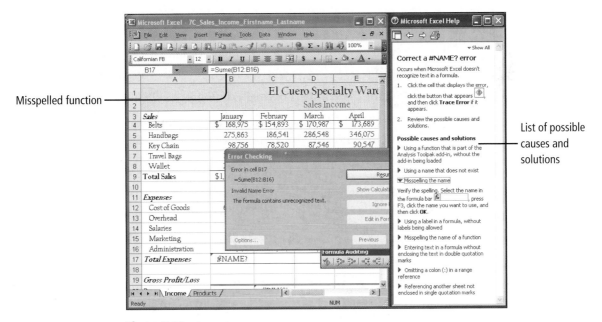

Figure 7.44

4 Close the **Help** window. In the **Error Checking** dialog box, click the **Resume** button.

The #NAME! error is highlighted again. You can fix this error now, or continue reviewing the worksheet for other errors.

5 In the **Error Checking** dialog box, click the **Edit in Formula Bar** button.

The insertion point is placed in the Formula Bar at the end of the formula.

6 Correct the function from *Sume* to **Sum** and press [Enter].

The error notation is removed and $880,781 displays in cell B17.

7 In the **Error Checking** dialog box, click **Resume**.

The next error is found in cell C20 where the error notation *#DIV/0!* is displayed. The Error Checking dialog box provides an explanation of this error—a formula or function is trying to divide by zero, or an empty cell.

8 Click the **Show Calculation Steps** button.

The Evaluate Formula dialog box opens. In the Evaluation box, *0/0* displays.

9 In the **Evaluate Formula** dialog box, click **Evaluate**.

The Evaluation box displays the error *#DIV/0!* and the Evaluate button changes to Restart.

10 Click **Restart**.

The formula (C19-B19)/C19 displays; the first C19 is underlined. The underline indicates that this is the part of the formula that is being evaluated. Each time you click the Evaluate button, it moves to the next cell reference or value in the formula.

11 In the **Evaluate Formula** dialog box, click the **Step In** button.

A second box displays, which normally displays the value in the referenced cell. In this case, the cell that is referenced is empty, as indicated in the message in the lower part of the dialog box. See Figure 7.45. In a complex formula, this dialog box can help you examine and understand each part of the formula and identify exactly where the error is located.

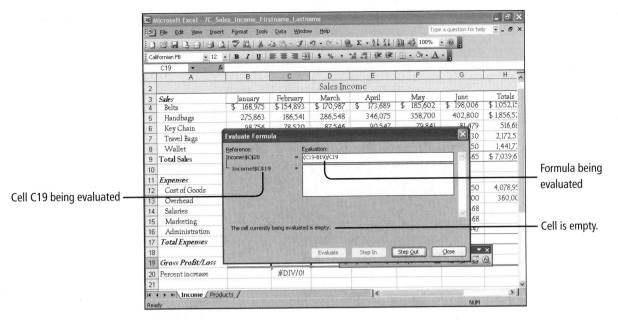

Cell C19 being evaluated —

Formula being evaluated

Cell is empty.

Figure 7.45

12 Click the **Step Out** button.

The cell evaluation box closes and the underline moves to the next cell in the formula—**B19**—which you can visually verify is empty by looking at the worksheet. To remove this error, you must complete the remainder of the worksheet.

13 Close the **Evaluate Formula** dialog box. In the **Error Checking** dialog box, click **Next**.

A message box displays stating that the error checking is complete for the entire sheet.

14 Click **OK**.

Both the message box and the Error Checking dialog box close.

15 Click cell **H13** and use the fill handle to copy this formula down to cells **H14:H16**. Click cell **B17** and use the fill handle to copy this formula across to cells **C17:H17**. Widen any columns, if necessary, to display all of the data.

The formulas in the rows and columns are completed.

16 Click cell **B19** and type **=b9-b17** Press [Enter], and then copy the formula across to cells **C19:H19**.

The profit or loss for each month is calculated. Notice that the #DIV/0! error in cell C20 is removed, but the formatting of the cell needs to be changed from dollars to percent.

17 Click cell **C20**, and on the Formatting toolbar click the **Percent Style** button ![percent]. Copy the formula across to cells **D20:G20**.

This formula calculates the percent change in profit, month to month. The percent in February, –48%, is negative because sales in February were lower than sales in January. Compare your screen with Figure 7.46.

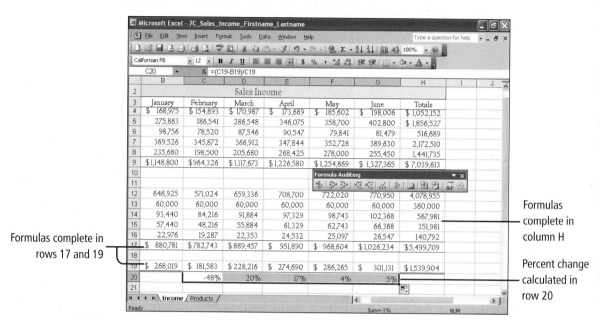

Figure 7.46

18 On the Standard toolbar, click the **Save** button ![save].

Activity 7.20 Circling Invalid Data

If validation lists are used in a worksheet, you can use the Formula Auditing toolbar to check the worksheet to be sure only valid values— ones from the list—have been entered on the worksheet.

1 Click the **Products sheet tab**.

A list of products included in each category is displayed on this sheet.

2 Click the **Name Box arrow**, and then click **Items**, which is the only range name that shows in the list box.

The named range in row 2 is highlighted. See Figure 7.47.

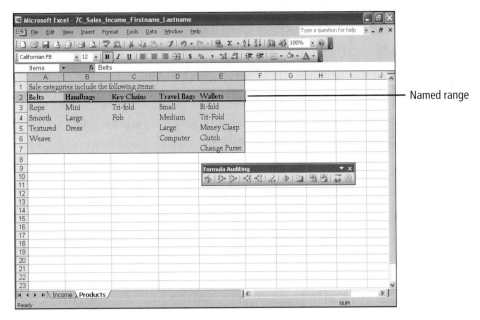

Figure 7.47

Named range

Click the **Income sheet tab**. On the Formula Auditing toolbar, click the **Circle Invalid Data** button [icon].

Red circles display around Key Chain and Wallet as shown in Figure 7.48.

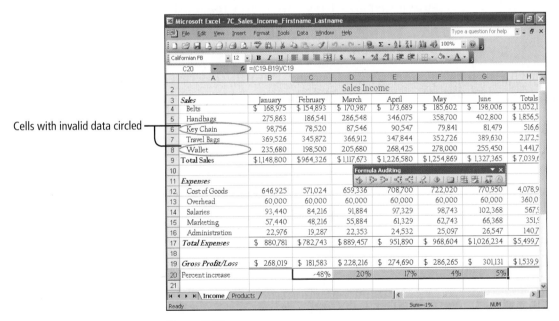

Cells with invalid data circled

Figure 7.48

4 Click cell **A6** and click the arrow at the right side of the cell.

The validation list displays.

5 From the displayed list, click **Key Chains**.

The item is corrected but the red circle is not removed.

6 Click cell **A8**, click the arrow, and then from the displayed list, click **Wallets**.

7 On the Formula Auditing toolbar, click the **Clear Validation Circles** button ⊞.

The circles are removed.

8 Click the **Circle Invalid Data** button ⊞ again. Close the Formula Auditing toolbar.

No circles are applied, which confirms that the data is now valid.

9 From the **File** menu, display the **Page Setup** dialog box. On the **Header/Footer tab**, open the **Custom Footer** and in the **Left section**, insert the **File name** in the footer. On the **Page tab**, click **Landscape**. On the **Margins tab**, center the page **Horizontally**. Click the **Print Preview** button. On the Print Preview toolbar, click the **Print** button, and then click **OK**.

10 On the Standard toolbar, click the **Save** button ⊟. Press Ctrl + ` to display the formulas. From the **File** menu, display the **Page Setup** dialog box. On the **Page tab**, click the **Fit to** option button and be sure it displays 1 page wide by 1 tall, and then click **Print**.

11 Press Ctrl + ` to display the worksheet figures, and then close the workbook. Save the changes you have made.

End You have completed Project 7C ————————————————————

Summary

In Excel, you can create templates for a variety of financial statements. Workbooks saved as template files can be made available to others over a network, or in the Templates dialog box on each computer. Templates offer two advantages—*standardization* and *protection*. By creating templates, you establish a standard and uniform set of reports or forms that can be used throughout an organization. By applying protection, required formulas are designed into the form, and cells on the worksheet can be locked; this prevents someone from changing the design or structure of the template.

Another advantage is that Excel templates are easy to use. Even someone unfamiliar with Excel can open a template as a workbook, enter data, and then print or save the file—all without having to construct formulas. Furthermore, Excel templates—with their built-in formulas—can improve the accuracy of record keeping. Excel's lookup and reference features can also make reports and forms more accurate. You practiced creating a vertical lookup—VLOOKUP—function and a horizontal—HLOOKUP—function, which are two of the lookup functions that are available in Excel. You also practiced adding data validation criteria to cells for the purpose of ensuring that only suitable entries were made in the selected cells.

Excel displays error notations when a formula cannot be calculated for lack of appropriate values. Although most of the time these notations offer useful advice and information, sometimes they occur because data has not yet been entered into the cells that are used in the formulas. When this happens, you can use Conditional Formatting to hide the error notation.

You can also audit a worksheet to look for inconsistencies, to diagnose problems, or to correct errors. The Formula Auditing toolbar can be used to identify the cells that are used in a formula, to locate and resolve errors, and to understand the construction of complex formulas.

In This Chapter You Practiced How To

- Create a Workbook Template
- Edit a Template
- Protect a Worksheet
- Create a Worksheet Based on a Template
- Use Lookup Functions
- Validate Data
- Use Conditional Formats
- Audit a Worksheet

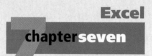
Concepts Assessments

Matching   Match each term in the second column with its correct definition in the first column by writing the letter of the term on the blank line in front of the correct definition.

_____ **1.** A function that enables you to look up values in a vertical list.

_____ **2.** A feature that can be used to create a stylized image out of text.

_____ **3.** A combination of characters that are applied to a file to prevent others from gaining access or changing the file.

_____ **4.** Formatting characteristics that are applied to cells when the value in the cell meets a specified condition.

_____ **5.** The action that makes cells accessible to others in a protected worksheet.

_____ **6.** A list of values that is acceptable for a group of cells.

_____ **7.** A function that enables you to look up values that are displayed horizontally in a row.

_____ **8.** An Excel tool with which you can transpose the row and column organization of cells.

_____ **9.** A worksheet condition that is enabled to make cells inaccessible unless they have been specifically unlocked.

_____ **10.** The act of reducing the size of an image by hiding part of it, which has the effect of cutting away unwanted parts of an image.

_____ **11.** A color condition that creates a faded image that can be placed in the background of a worksheet.

_____ **12.** An auditing tool that helps to verify the validity of lists used in a worksheet.

_____ **13.** The dialog box used to select a WordArt style.

_____ **14.** The formula that is used to identify the _not available_ error notation.

_____ **15.** An auditing button that is used to locate and identify errors and that provides assistance in resolving errors.

A =ISNA

B Circle Invalid Data

C Conditional format

D Crop

E Error Checking

F HLOOKUP

G Password

H Paste Special

I Protection

J Unlocking

K Validation list

L VLOOKUP

M Washout

N WordArt

O WordArt Gallery

Fill in the Blank Write the correct answer in the space provided.

1. When you use the Trace Precedents button, you are looking for cells that are used in _____.

2. When you click the Crop tool, brackets display around the selected image, which are known as _____.

3. When you create a template, the template file is saved with a(n) _____ file extension.

4. If you want to reverse the column and row arrangement of cells, select _____ in the Paste Special dialog box.

5. By default, all cells in a workbook are _____.

6. In the Protect Sheet dialog box, the _____ check box enables the user to click in locked cells and view the formulas, but not change the cell contents.

7. When you create a password, _____ display in the Set Password dialog box rather than the characters that are typed.

8. To change an image to a black and white or grayscale image, use the _____ button on the Format Picture toolbar.

9. To restore an image to its original settings, use the _____ button on the Picture toolbar.

10. To change the position of an image so that its orientation on the page is at a different angle, use the _____ that displays around the edge of the image.

Project 7D — Income Statement Template

Objectives: *Create a Workbook Template, Edit a Template, Protect a Worksheet, and Create a Worksheet Based on a Template.*

Adriana Ramos, CFO for El Cuero Specialty Wares, wants to create a set of templates that can be used for basic financial reporting. In this project, you will open a template that has been started, edit the template, protect the worksheet, and then reopen the file and create a worksheet based on your template. Your completed worksheet will look similar to the one shown in Figure 7.49. You will save your template as *7D_IS_Template_Firstname_Lastname* and your workbook as *7D_Income_Statement_Firstname_Lastname.*

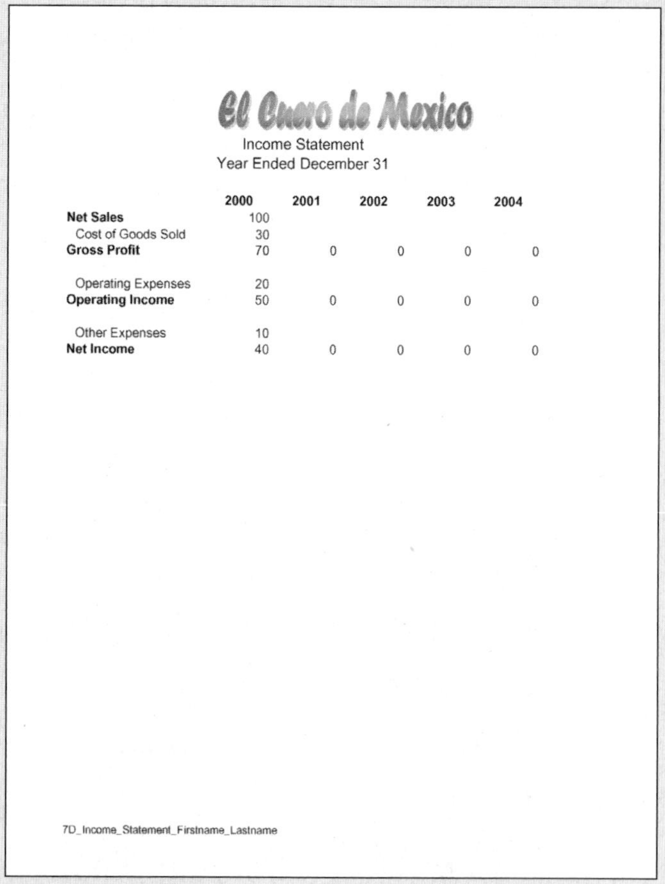

El Cuero de Mexico

Income Statement
Year Ended December 31

	2000	2001	2002	2003	2004
Net Sales	100				
Cost of Goods Sold	30				
Gross Profit	70	0	0	0	0
Operating Expenses	20				
Operating Income	50	0	0	0	0
Other Expenses	10				
Net Income	40	0	0	0	0

7D_Income_Statement_Firstname_Lastname

Figure 7.49

(Project 7D–Income Statement Template continues on the next page)

(Project 7D–Income Statement Template continued)**

1. On the Standard toolbar, click the **Open** button. Navigate to the location where the student files for this textbook are stored. Locate and open the template file **e07D_Income_Statement**. From the **File** menu, click **Save As**. In the **Save As** dialog box, navigate to the location where you are storing your files for this chapter. In the **File name** box, type 7D_IS_Template_Firstname_Lastname Be sure the **Save as type** box is set to **Template**. Click the **Save** button.

2. Click the **Select All** button in the upper left corner of the worksheet—between the row headings and the column headings—and then change the **Font Size** to **12**. Click cell **A1**. AutoFit column **A**. Display the **Insert** menu, point to **Picture**, and then click **WordArt**. In the **WordArt Gallery** dialog box, in the third row, click the first WordArt style, and then click **OK**.

3. In the **Edit WordArt Text** dialog box, type **El Cuero de Mexico** In the dialog box, click the **Font arrow**, scroll the displayed list and click **Forte**; click the **Size arrow**, and then click **28**. Click **OK**. Move the mouse pointer over the **WordArt** image until the 4-way move arrow displays. Drag the WordArt to the top of the worksheet spanning columns **B:E**.

4. Click cell **A4**, type **Income Statement** and press [Enter]. Select the range **A4:F4** and click the **Merge and Center** button. Click cell **A5**, type **Year Ended December 31** and then **Merge and Center** over the range **A5:F5**. Select cells **A4:A5** and change the **Font Size** to **14**. Click cell **A6**, display the **Insert** menu, and then click **Rows**.

5. Click Cell **B10**, type **=b8-b9** and then press [Enter]. This formula calculates the Gross Profit from Sales—Net Sales – Cost of Goods Sold. Copy the formula from **B10** across through cells **C10:F10**. Click cell **B13**, type **=b10-b12** and then press [Enter]. This formula calculates the Operating Income from Sales—Gross Profit from Sales – Operating Expenses. Copy this formula across the row to cells **C13:F13**.

6. Click cell **B16**, type **=b13-b15**, press [Enter], and then copy the formula across the row to cells **C16:F16**. This formula calculates the Net Income—Operating Income – Other Expenses—for the company.

7. **Save** your changes. Select the range **B8:F9**, hold down [Ctrl] and select **B12:F12**, and **B15:F15**. Display the **Format** menu, click **Cells**, and then click the **Protection tab**. Clear the check mark from the **Locked** check box, and then click **OK**. After protection is applied to the worksheet, users of the template will be able to enter data only into the cells you have marked to be left unlocked.

(Project 7D–Income Statement Template continues on the next page)**

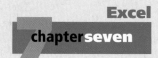

(Project 7D–Income Statement Template continued)

8. Display the **Tools** menu, point to **Protection**, and then click **Protect Sheet**. In the **Protect Sheet** dialog box, in the **Password to unprotect sheet** box, type **GO!Series** and then click **OK**. In the **Confirm Password** dialog box, type **GO!Series** again, and click **OK**. All cells that you did not mark as unlocked are now locked, and a password is also applied to the worksheet.

9. From the **View** menu, display the **Header and Footer tab** of the **Page Setup** dialog box. In the **Custom Footer**, add the **File name** to the **Left Section** of the footer. Click the **Margins tab**, and then center the worksheet **Horizontally** on the page. On the Standard toolbar, click the **Save** button.

10. From the **File** menu, click **Save As**. Navigate to your student folder. Change the **File name** box to 7D_Income_Statement_Firstname_ Lastname. Change the **Save as type** box to **Microsoft Office Excel Workbook**, and then click **Save**. This creates a new workbook using the template file.

11. To test the worksheet, click cell **B8**, type **100** and click **B9**, type **30** and click **B12**, type **20** and click **B15**, type **10** and press Enter. The results of the formulas display in cells B10 (*70*), B13 (*50*), and B16 (*40*).

12. On the Standard toolbar, click the **Save** button, and then click the **Print Preview** button. On the Print Preview toolbar click **Print**. In the **Print** dialog box, click **OK**.

13. Hold down Ctrl and press ` to display the formulas. From the **File** menu display the **Page Setup** dialog box. On the **Page tab** select **Landscape** and **Fit to** 1 page. Click the **Print Preview** button to be sure the formulas will print on one page. Click **Print** and then click **OK**. Press Ctrl and ` to redisplay the worksheet and then close the file.

End **You have completed Project 7D**

Project 7E — Packing Slip

Objectives: *Use Lookup Functions, Validate Data, and Use Conditional Formats.*

El Cuero de Mexico needs a packing slip to use as part of its inventory control system. In Project 7E, you will add features to a worksheet that can be used as a packing slip. Your completed worksheet will look similar to the one shown in Figure 7.50. You will save your workbook as *7E_Packing_Slip_Firstname_Lastname.*

El Cuero Specialty Wares
Packing Slip

Customer Name:
Order Number:
Order Date:

Item	Description	Color	Size	Quantity Ordered	Quantity Shipped	Comments
0501	Money clasp	Black	M 38	15	10	Item on back order

Ship Date:
Order Completed By:

7E_Packing_Slip_Firstname_Lastname   Last Modified: 11/17/2003

Figure 7.50

(Project 7E–Packing Slip continues on the next page)

(Project 7E–Packing Slip continued)

1. Start Excel. On the Standard toolbar, click the **Open** button and navigate to the location where the student files for this textbook are stored. Locate and open **e07E_Packing_Slip**. From the **File** menu, click **Save As**. Using your own name, save the file in your folder as **7E_Packing_Slip_Firstname_Lastname**

2. Display the **View** menu and click **Header and Footer**. Create a **Custom Footer** in the **Left section** containing the **File name**. In the **Right section**, type **Last modified:** and press Spacebar, and then click the **Date** button. Click **OK** to close both dialog boxes.

3. Click cell **B9**. To the left of the Formula Bar, click the **Insert Function** button. In the **Insert Function** dialog box, click the **Or select a category arrow**, and then click **Lookup & Reference**. Under **Select a function**, scroll as necessary and click **VLOOKUP**. Click **OK**.

4. In the **Function Arguments** dialog box, in the **Lookup_value** box, type **a9** This is the cell that will contain the value you want to look up. Click the **Table_array** box and at the right end of the box, click the **Collapse** button to temporarily shrink the dialog box. Click the **Product List sheet tab**, select the range **A5:B27**, and press F4 to apply an absolute reference. This defines the table array where Excel will look up the value. In the **Function Arguments** dialog box, at the right end of the box, click the **Expand** button. In the **Col_index_num** box, type **2** which directs Excel to look up the value in the second column of the defined table array. Click **OK** to close the dialog box. Recall that #N/A displays because A9 is currently empty, and thus the formula has no data to work with. Fill the formula from **B9** down to **B30**.

5. Select the range **A9:A30**. Display the **Format** menu and click **Cells**. Click the **Number tab**, under **Category** click **Text**, and then click **OK**. On the Product List worksheet, the Style Codes used in the table array were formatted as text because they are identifiers and not numbers to be used in calculations. Therefore, the Item column on the Packing Slip worksheet also needs to be formatted as text. Click cell **A9**, type **0501** and then press Tab to verify that the lookup function works. *Money clasp* displays in cell **B9**. Click **Undo**.

6. Click the **Product List sheet tab**. Select the range **A4:A27**. From the **Insert** menu, point to **Name**, and then click **Create**. In the **Create Names** dialog box, be sure that **Top row** is selected, and then click **OK**. Recall that you can create a range name by using the column or row heading for a range of cells.

(Project 7E–Packing Slip continues on the next page)

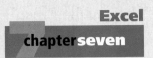
(Project 7E–Packing Slip continued)

7. Click the **Packing Slip sheet tab**. Click cell **A9**. Display the **Data** menu and click **Validation**. In the **Data Validation** dialog box, click the **Allow arrow**, and then click **List**. In the **Source** box type **=Style_Code** and then click **OK**. Use the fill handle to copy the validation criteria to cells **A10:A30**. In cell **A9**, click the list arrow, and then click **0501** to verify that the list works and that *Money clasp* displays in cell **B9**. Click **Undo** to remove your test data.

8. Select cells **F9:F30**. Display the **Format** menu and click **Conditional Formatting**. In the **Conditional Formatting** dialog box, be sure the **Condition 1 box** displays **Cell Value Is**. In the second box, click the arrow, and then click **less than**. Click in the third box, type **e9**

9. In the **Conditional Formatting** dialog box, click the **Format** button. In the **Format Cells** dialog box, under **Font style**, click **Bold**. Click the **Color arrow**, and in the third row, click the first color—**Red**. Click **OK** to close both dialog boxes. Click outside of the selection to deselect. If the Quantity Shipped in cell F9 is *less than* the quantity ordered in cell E9, the cell will turn red. This gives a visual indication that a back order situation exists—additional merchandise needs to be shipped to complete the order.

10. Click cell **A9**. Click the arrow, and then click **0501**. Press Tab twice to move to the **Color** column. Click the arrow, and then click **Black**. Press Tab, click the arrow in cell **D9**, and then click **M-38**. Press Tab, type **15** and press Tab. Type **10** and press Tab. In cell **G9** type **Item on back order** and then press Enter. The Quantity Shipped figure—10— displays in red, because it is less than the Quantity Ordered. This is another useful way to apply the Conditional Formatting feature.

11. Select the range **B10:B30**. From the **Format** menu, click **Conditional Formatting**. Under **Condition 1**, click the arrow, and then click **Formula Is**. Press Tab, type **=ISNA(B10)** and then click the **Format** button. On the **Font tab**, click the **Color arrow**, and in the fifth row, click the last color—**White**. Click **OK** twice, and then click in an empty cell to deselect. This action will apply a white font to the cell if the #NA error notation is present. Thus, if no data is present, the cell will appear to be blank.

12. On the Standard toolbar, click the **Save** button, and then click the **Print Preview** button to see how the worksheet will look when it is printed. On the Print Preview toolbar, click the **Print** button, and then click **OK**. Close the file and close Excel, saving changes if prompted to do so.

End **You have completed Project 7E**

Project 7F—Fixed Assets

Objective: *Audit a Worksheet.*

In this project, you will audit the Schedule of Changes in the General Fixed Assets worksheet for Adriana Ramos, CFO of El Cuero Specialty Wares, to verify that the formulas are logical and accurate. Your completed worksheet will look similar to the one shown in Figure 7.51. You will save your workbook as *7F_Fixed_Assets_Firstname_Lastname*.

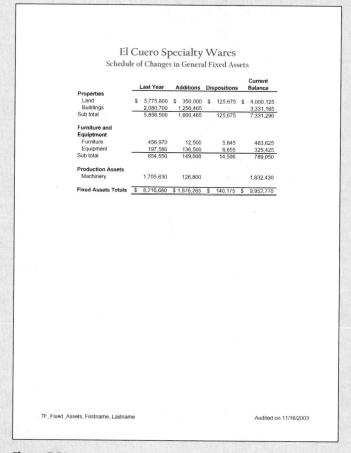

El Cuero Specialty Wares
Schedule of Changes in General Fixed Assets

	Last Year	Additions	Dispositions	Current Balance
Properties				
Land	$ 3,775,800	$ 350,000	$ 125,675	$ 4,000,125
Buildings	2,080,700	1,250,465		3,331,165
Sub total	5,856,500	1,600,465	125,675	7,331,290
Furniture and Equiptment				
Furniture	456,970	12,500	5,845	463,625
Equipment	197,580	136,500	8,655	325,425
Sub total	654,550	149,000	14,500	789,050
Production Assets				
Machinery	1,705,630	126,800	-	1,832,430
Fixed Assets Totals	$ 8,216,680	$ 1,876,265	$ 140,175	$ 9,952,770

7F_Fixed_Assets_Firstname_Lastname   Audited on 11/16/2003

Figure 7.51

(Project 7F–Fixed Assets continues on the next page)

(Project 7F–Fixed Assets continued)

1. On the Standard toolbar, click the **Open** button. Navigate to the location where the student files for this textbook are stored. Locate and open **e07F_Fixed_Assets**. From the **File** menu, click **Save As**. In the **Save As** dialog box, navigate to the location where you are storing your files for this chapter. In the **File name** box, type **7F_Fixed_Assets_Firstname_Lastname** Click the **Save** button.

2. Right-click on one of the toolbars, and then from the shortcut menu, click **Formula Auditing** to display the Formula Auditing toolbar. Drag the toolbar to the right of your screen, or dock it to the other toolbars. Take a moment to examine the worksheet to become familiar with its data and purpose.

3. Click cell **E6**, and then on the Formula Auditing toolbar, click the **Trace Precedents** button. Recall that precedents are cells that are referred to by a formula in another cell. The displayed tracer arrow shows that the formula in cell E6 uses cells *B6, C6,* and *D6*. Along the tracer arrow, blue dots indicate the cells used in the formula.

4. Look at the Formula Bar and review the formula. The previous year's value is listed in cell B6, acquisitions in cell C6 are added to cell B6, and land that has been disposed of in cell D6 is subtracted. This is a logical and accurate formula to determine the current value of an asset.

5. Click cell **E7** and click the **Trace Precedents** button. Verify that the same formula, with appropriate cell references, is used as in cell E6. Click cell **E8** and click the **Trace Precedents** button. This cell sums the column as suggested by the row heading *Sub total.* This is a logical and accurate formula to sum Land and Buildings to derive a value for Properties. On the Formula Auditing toolbar, click the **Remove all Arrows** button.

6. Click cell **E11**, and then look at the formula on the Formula Bar to view the calculation being performed. Then, on the Formula Auditing toolbar, click the **Evaluate Formula** button. Under **Evaluation**, the formula displays. Watch the **Evaluation** area, and as you watch, click **Evaluate** five times to see the formula as it is calculated. When the evaluation is concluded, the result—*463,625*—displays in the dialog box. The Evaluate button changes to the Restart button. Click the **Restart** button to display the original formula, and then close the dialog box. This is a good way to see the actual numbers being calculated in a formula.

7. Click cell **B11** and click the **Trace Dependents** button to see which cells depend on the value in **B11**. Recall that dependents are cells that contain formulas that refer to other cells. Thus, the formulas in cells *E11, B13,* and *B18* depend on the value in B11.

(Project 7F–Fixed Assets continues on the next page)

(Project 7F–Fixed Assets continued)

8. Click cell **B18** and click the **Trace Precedents** button. The blue border surrounding cells *B6:B16* indicates that all of the cells in this column are precedent cells; that is, each cell is used in the formula displayed in cell B18.

9. The formula in cell B18 is not logical or correct—it adds all of the values instead of adding the subtotals. In the Formula Bar, correct this formula to **=b8+b13+b16** and press Enter. The result should be $8,216,680. Click the **Remove All Arrows** button, select **B18** again, and then click the **Trace Precedents** button. The three cells that are summed have a blue dot within the tracer arrow. As you audit a worksheet, click the Remove All Arrows button as necessary so that you can get a clear view of each trace arrow's path.

10. Click cell **C18** and click the **Trace Precedents** button. The same error occurs in this formula; that is, all of the values were added instead of only the subtotals. Correct the formula in the Formula Bar to **=c8+c13+c16** and press Enter. Select **C18** and click **Trace Precedents** again. In the displayed blue tracer arrow, blue dots display in the cells included in the formula—in the same pattern as B18.

11. Click cell **D18**, click **Trace Precedents**, and then examine the formula. In the Formula Bar, correct the formula to **=d8+d13+d16** and trace the precedents again. Compare the pattern of the tracer arrow to the other two. (It is a good idea to include D16 even though it is empty in case data is entered in D16 in the future.) Examine and trace precedents for the formula in **E18**. The correct total in cell **E18** should be $9,952,770.

12. From the **View** menu, display the **Header/Footer tab** of the **Page Setup** dialog box. Add a **Custom Footer** with the **File name** in the **Left section**. In the **Right section** of the footer type **Audited on** and press Spacebar, and then click the **Date** button. Click the **Margins tab**, and then center the worksheet **Horizontally** on the page. Click the **Print Preview** button to see how the worksheet will look when printed.

13. Tracer arrows, unless removed, will print. Return to the worksheet and click the **Remove All Arrows** button. **Print** the worksheet and close the Formula Auditing toolbar. On the Standard toolbar, click the **Save** button, and then close your file.

End You have completed Project 7F

Performance Assessments

Project 7G — Invoice Template

Objectives: *Create a Workbook Template, Edit a Template, Protect a Worksheet, and Create a Worksheet Based on a Template.*

El Cuero Specialty Wares needs an invoice for its inventory control system. In this project, you will create an invoice template, edit the template, protect it, and then create a worksheet based on the template. Your completed worksheet will look similar to the one shown in Figure 7.52. You will save your workbook as *7G_Invoice_Template_Firstname_Lastname*.

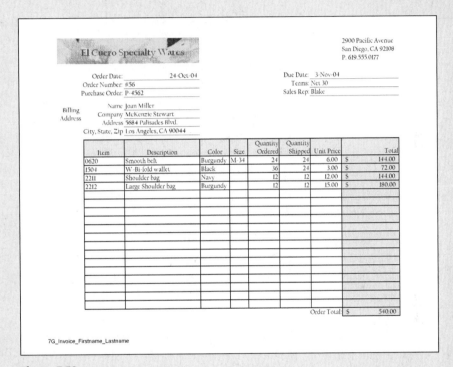

Figure 7.52

1. Start Excel. On the Standard toolbar, click the **Open** button. Navigate to the location where the student files for this textbook are stored. Locate and open **e07G_Invoice**.

2. Hold down Ctrl and select the ranges **C5:C7, C9:C12, B15:B32, D15:H32,** and **H5:H7**. Display the **Format Cells** dialog box, and on the **Protection tab**, clear the **Locked** check box. When you add protection to the worksheet, users will be able to enter information only into the cells you have left unlocked. From the **Tools** menu, open the **Protect Sheet** dialog box and enter **GO!Series** as the password.

(Project 7G–Invoice Template continues on the next page)

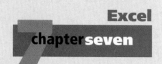

Performance Assessments (continued)

(Project 7G–Invoice Template continued)

3. Display the **Save As** dialog box, navigate to your folder for this chapter, change the **Save as type** box to **Template**, and save the file in your folder as 7G_Invoice_Template_Firstname_Lastname

4. To make further changes to your template, from the **Tools** menu, open the **Unprotect Sheet** dialog box and type **GO!Series** to remove the worksheet protection.

5. Click cell **A1**. From the **Insert** menu, point to **Picture**, and then click **From File**. In the **Insert Picture** dialog box, navigate to the location where the student files for this textbook are stored. Click **e07G_Logo** and click **Insert**.

6. On the Picture toolbar, click the **Crop** button. Drag the **top center crop handle** down to the lower boundary of **row 1**, drag the **right center crop handle** to the middle of **column D**, drag the **left center crop handle** to the middle of **column A**, and then drag the **bottom center crop handle** up to the lower boundary of **row 4**. Click the **Crop** button to deselect it, and then drag the cropped image to the upper left corner of cell **A1**. Click the **More Brightness** button three times. Click in any empty cell to deselect the image.

7. Widen **column D** to **70 pixels** to accommodate the longest color name, which is Burgundy.

8. Display the **Header/Footer tab** of the **Page Setup** dialog box, display the **Custom Footer**, and insert the **File name** in the **Left section**. Center the worksheet **Horizontally** on the page. From the **Tools** menu, open the **Protect Sheet** dialog box and type **GO!Series** as the password. **Save** your changes and close the file.

9. On the Standard toolbar, click the **Open** button. Navigate to your folder and open your **7G_Invoice_Template** file. **Save As** a **Microsoft Office Excel Workbook** in your folder with the name 7G_Invoice_Firstname_Lastname

10. In the appropriate cells, enter the following data, using ⟨Tab⟩ to move from cell to cell:

Order Date:	**October 24, 2004**	Due Date:	**November 3, 2004**
Order Number:	**#56**	Terms:	**Net 30**
Purchase Order:	**P-4562**	Sales Rep:	**Blake**
Name	**Joan Miller**		
Company	**McKenzie Stewart**		
Address	**5684 Palisades Blvd.**		
City, State, Zip	**Los Angeles, CA 90044**		

(Project 7G–Invoice Template continues on the next page)

Performance Assessments (continued)

(Project 7G–Invoice Template continued)

11. In the body of the invoice, use the list arrows that are built into the worksheet to help you complete the following information.

Item	Description	Color	Size	Quantity Ordered	Quantity Shipped	Unit Price
0620	Smooth belt	Burgundy	M-34	24	24	6.00
1504	W-Bi-fold wallet	Black		36	24	3.00
2211	Shoulder bag	Navy		12	12	12.00
2212	Large shoulder bag	Burgundy		12	12	15.00

The invoice total displays $540.00.

12. Save your changes. Click the **Print Preview** button. Compare your worksheet to Figure 7.52. Print the worksheet, and then save your file. Close the file, and then close Excel.

End You have completed Project 7G ———————————————————

Project 7H — Evaluations

Objectives: *Use Lookup Functions and Validate Data.*

El Cuero Specialty Wares has created a worksheet to use for job performance evaluations. Supervisors assign point values to job performance, and the total points that result are used to determine a job rating and a salary increase percentage range. In this project, you will open the worksheet, add lookup functions, and validate data. Your worksheet will look similar to the one shown in Figure 7.53. You will save your workbook as *7H_Evaluations_Firstname_Lastname*.

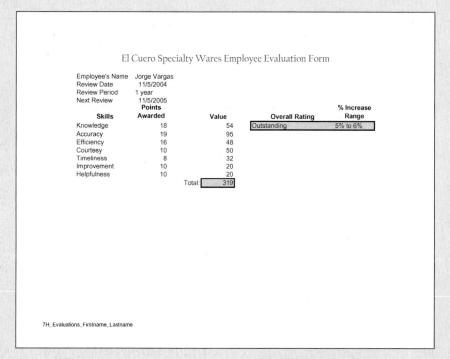

Figure 7.53

1. Start Excel. On the Standard toolbar, click the **Open** button. Navigate to the location where the student files for this textbook are stored. Locate and open the file **e07H_Evaluations**. Save the file in your folder using the name **7H_Evaluations_Firstname_Lastname**

2. Select the range **A2:D2** and click the **Copy** button. Click cell **A3**, display the **Edit** menu, and click **Paste Special**. In the **Paste Special** dialog box, select the **Transpose** check box, and then click **OK**. The cells are transposed from a row arrangement to a column arrangement. Select the range **A2:D2** again and press ⌐Delete⌐. AutoFit **column A**.

(Project 7H–Evaluations continues on the next page)

(Project 7H–Evaluations continued)

3. Click cell **B8** and observe the ScreenTip that displays. Cells B8:B10 contain a validation rule, which includes an input message and an error alert message. Click cell **B9**, display the **Data** menu, and then click **Validation**. In the displayed **Data Validation** dialog box, examine the data validation criteria on the **Settings tab**, and then examine the **Input Message tab** and the **Error Alert tab**. Close the dialog box.

4. Select the range **B11:B14** and display the **Data Validation** dialog box. On the **Settings tab**, set **Validation criteria** to **Allow** a **Decimal** with **Data between** a **Minimum** of **0** and a **Maximum** of **10**—the maximum points awarded to these job skill categories. Click the **Input Message tab**. In the **Title** box type **Points Allowed** and in the **Input message** box type **Enter a number between 0 and 10 based on your evaluation of this employee's courtesy** Click the **Error Alert tab**. Change the **Style** box to **Information**. In the **Error message** box, type **Number must be between 0 and 10** This error alert will display if the supervisor attempts to enter a number outside of the specified range. Click **OK**.

5. When you selected the range B11:B14 and created the validation criteria and the input message, the message you typed will display for each job skill. Because each skill is different, you must edit the message slightly to reflect the skill that is being evaluated. Click cell **B12**, display the **Data Validation** dialog box, click the **Input Message tab**, and edit the **Input message** by changing *courtesy* to **timeliness** Click **OK**, and then edit the input message for cells **B13** and **B14** in a similar manner.

6. Click cell **F8** and display the **Insert Function** dialog box. From the **Lookup & Reference** category, select the **VLOOKUP** function. In the **Function Arguments** dialog box, in the **Lookup_value** box, type **d15** and press F4 to create an absolute reference to this cell. Click the **Table_array** box, and then click the **Collapse** button to temporarily shrink the dialog box. Click the **Increase Grid sheet tab**. In this worksheet, select the range **F5:H9** and press F4 to create an absolute reference to this range of cells. Click the **Expand** button to restore the dialog box. In the **Col_index_num** box, type **2** to refer to the second column, and then click **OK**. The rating *Needs Improvement* displays because the current value in cell D15 is zero.

7. Copy the formula in cell **F8** to cell **G8**. Click cell **G8** and, in the Formula Bar, edit the formula so the column index is **3** instead of 2. Press Enter. The **Percent Increase Range** displays *0% to 1%*.

(Project 7H–Evaluations continues on the next page)

(Project 7H–Evaluations continued)

8. Click the **Print Preview** button. Open the **Page Setup** dialog box and add a **Custom Footer** with the **File name** in the **Left section**. On the **Page tab**, click **Landscape**, and on the **Margins tab**, center the page **Horizontally**.

9. Beginning in cell **B3**, enter the following information in the worksheet:

Employee Name	**Jorge Vargas**
Review Date	**11/5/04**
Review Period	**1 year**
Next Review	**11/5/05**
Knowledge	**18**
Accuracy	**19**
Efficiency	**16**
Courtesy	**10**
Timeliness	**8**
Improvement	**10**
Helpfulness	**10**

10. Weighted values, based on the data in the Increase Grid worksheet, display in column D. A total of *319* displays in cell D15, the overall rating changes to *Outstanding*, and the % Increase Range changes to *5% to 6%*. Compare your screen with Figure 7.53. **Save** the changes. **Print** the file, and then close it.

End You have completed Project 7H ————————————————

Project 7I — Salary Audit

Objectives: *Use Conditional Formats and Audit a Worksheet.*

El Cuero de Mexico is implementing a new employee review system. The pay grade and rate for employees must be audited to ensure that employees are properly classified and that their salary falls within the pay range for their pay grade. You will review a worksheet using validation criteria, a lookup function, and auditing tools to determine if each employee is in a valid pay grade and matching salary range. You will also use skills that you have practiced in previous chapters. Your completed worksheet will look similar to the one shown in Figure 7.54. You will save your workbook as *7I_Salary_Audit_Firstname_Lastname.*

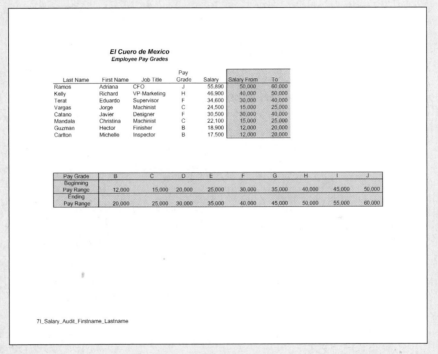

Figure 7.54

1. On the Standard toolbar, click the **Open** button. Navigate to the location where the student files for this textbook are stored. Locate and open **e07I_Salary_Audit**. Take a moment to examine the data in the worksheet.

2. Open the **Save As** dialog box. Save the file in the folder with the other projects for this chapter with the name **7I_Salary_Audit_ Firstname_Lastname** Create a **Custom Footer**, and in the **Left section**, add the **File name**.

(Project 7I–Salary Audit continues on the next page)

(Project 7I–Salary Audit continued)

3. Click cell **E5**. Display the **Conditional Formatting** dialog box. Be sure the first box displays **Cell Value Is**. In the second box, click the arrow, and then click **not between**. Click the third box and type **=f5**—the lower end of the salary range. Click the fourth box, and then type **=g5**—the upper end of the salary range. Be sure the two boxes with the cell references do *not* show an absolute value reference. If they do, click in each box, and then press F4 twice to remove both the column and the row absolute value indicator ($). Click the **Format** button and set the **Font style** to **Bold**. Click the **Patterns tab**, and under **Cell shading**, in the fifth row click the third color—**Light Yellow**. Click **OK** to close both dialog boxes.

4. Click cell **E5**. On the Standard toolbar, click the **Format Painter** button. Select the range **E6:E12** to apply the conditional format from cell E5 to these cells. Click in any blank cell. Note that three cells display the yellow conditional format because the salaries do not fall within the pay grade range.

5. Now that salary errors have been identified, they need to be corrected. Display the Formula Auditing toolbar, and then click the **Circle Invalid Data** button. Note that cell D12 is circled. Pay Grade *A* is invalid. The starting pay grade should be B. Change the pay grade in the cell that is circled to **B** The circle is removed, and the #N/A error notations in cells F12 and G12 are cleared.

6. Click cell **F5**, and then click the **Trace Precedents** button. Tracer arrows are drawn from the first cell in the green Pay Grade table, and the three rows of the Pay Grade table are bordered in blue. Click cell **G5** and click the **Trace Precedents** button. Another set of tracer arrows displays. The salary in cell E5 exceeds the pay range for Pay Grade I. Remove the arrows and change the Pay Grade for Adriana Ramos to **J** which is her correct Pay Grade. The yellow conditional format is removed.

7. Follow the same procedure to review the other two exceptions for the pay grade and range. After checking with the Human Resources department, it is determined that the following corrections should be made: For *Richard Kelly*, change the Pay Grade to **H** and for *Javier Catano* change the Salary to **30,500** Close the Formula Auditing toolbar.

8. Display the **Print Preview** window. Click the **Setup** button, be sure that **Landscape** is selected, and then center the page **Horizontally**. **Save** your changes. Select the range **A1:E12**, display the **Print** dialog box, and under **Print what**, click the **Selection** option button to print only the selected range. Click **OK**. Close the worksheet and close Excel.

End You have completed Project 7I

Project 7J — Sales Projection

Objective: *Audit a Worksheet.*

El Cuero de Mexico is in the process of projecting sales for the next year. You will review the worksheet using features on the Formula Auditing toolbar and visual inspection to find and correct several types of errors. Your completed worksheet will look similar to the one shown in Figure 7.55. You will save your workbook as *7J_Sales_Projection_Firstname_Lastname*.

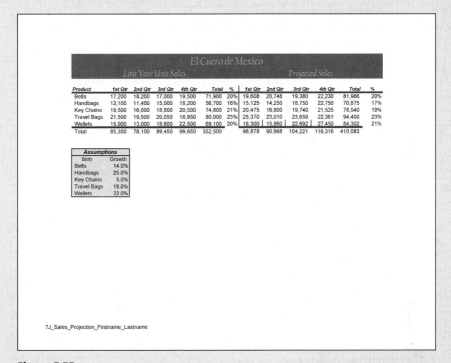

Figure 7.55

1. On the Standard toolbar, click the **Open** button. Navigate to the location where the student files for this textbook are stored. Locate and open **e07J_Sales_Projection**, and then read the displayed error message. Click **OK**.

2. If the Microsoft Help window displays, close it. If the Circular Reference toolbar displays, close it. Save the file in your folder using the name **7J_Sales_Projection_Firstname_Lastname**

(Project 7J–Sales Projection continues on the next page)

(Project 7J–Sales Projection continued)

3. Display the Formula Auditing toolbar. Click the **Error Checking** button. The first error located is an inconsistent formula in cell **I6**. The formulas in row 6 show last year's sales figures for Handbags and next year's projected sales figures for Handbags. Notice that the formula contains a reference to the growth rate for *Belts* in cell B15; it should refer to the growth rate for *Handbags* in cell B16. This formula is inconsistent with the other formulas in row 6. Edit the formula so that it computes the projected growth for Handbags in the second quarter by editing the formula in the Formula Bar to change $B$15 to **$B$16**

4. Click the **Resume** button. The next error is located in cell **M7**. Cell M7 displays the #DIV/0 error message in the cell and a green triangle in the corner indicating that a potential error exists. The Error Checking dialog box indicates that this is an error caused by attempting to divide by zero. This formula is also inconsistent with the other formulas in the column. Click **Next** to display the next message in the Error Checking box regarding the formula in cell M7. Click **Copy Formula from Above**. Notice the formula now references cell **L10** like the other formulas in this column, and the error messages is removed. Click **OK** to acknowledge the dialog box message that the error check is complete.

5. Error Checking alone cannot find all potential errors in a worksheet. It is still necessary to examine the worksheet and look for errors that the person who developed the workbook might have made. Note that the total in cell **L10** displays a dash instead of a number. Click cell **L10**. The formula in cell L10 sums the range of cells from L5 through L10. When a formula includes its own cell location in the range, it is called a **circular reference**. Edit the formula in cell **L10** to sum the values from L5:L9. The result should be 394,881.

6. Further visual examination reveals that the projected sales numbers for Wallets, the range H9:L9, are identical to the sales figures for last year. They should be higher by 22 percent, according to the projected assumption in cell B19. Click **H9**, and then on the Formula Auditing toolbar, click **Trace Precedents**. Note that the formula in **H9** refers to cell B20—an empty cell—instead of the growth factor for Wallets in B19. Edit this formula so that it refers to **$B$19** and then fill the formula to the right to cells **I9:K9**. The result in L9 should be 84,302.

7. Compare your screen to Figure 7.55 and resolve any other discrepancies. The total in cell **L10** should be 410,083. Create a **Custom Footer**, and in the **Left section**, add the **File name**. Change the orientation to **Landscape**, and center the worksheet **Horizontally**. **Save** your changes and print the file.

End You have completed Project 7J

Project 7K — Balance Sheet

Objectives: *Create a Workbook Template, Edit a Template, Protect a Worksheet, and Create a Worksheet Based on a Template.*

Adriana Ramos, CFO for El Cuero de Mexico, would like a template developed for the balance sheet summary report that needs to be prepared each month. In the following Mastery Assessment, you will complete a template by adding the necessary formulas and formatting. You will protect the template, and then base a worksheet on the template for the month-end report. Your completed worksheet will look similar to the one shown in Figure 7.56. You will save your workbook as *7K_Balance_Sheet_Firstname_Lastname*.

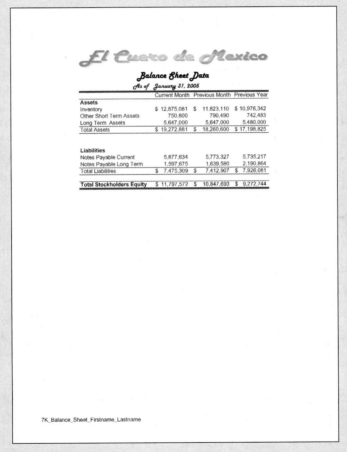

Figure 7.56

(Project 7K–Balance Sheet continues on the next page)

(Project 7K–Balance Sheet continued)

1. On the Standard toolbar, click the **Open** button. Navigate to the location where the student files for this textbook are stored. Locate and open the template file **e07K_Balance_Sheet**. In the folder where you are saving your projects for this chapter, save the file as a *template* using the name **7K_BalSheet_Template_Firstname_Lastname**

2. This template has protection applied. From the **Tools** menu, open the **Unprotect Sheet** dialog box and type **GO!Series** to remove the protection.

3. Click cell **A3** and press Delete. Select the range **B4:F4** and press Delete. In cell **B4**, type **Current Month** and in cell **C4**, type **Previous Month** and in cell **D4**, type **Previous Year** Select columns **B:D** and AutoFit, and then click anywhere to deselect the columns.

4. Open the **WordArt Gallery** and in the third row, click the first design. In the **Edit WordArt Text** dialog box, type **El Cuero de Mexico** Change the **Font** to **Harlow Solid Italic**, change the font **Size** to **24**, and then click **OK**. Select **row 1**, right-click, and then display the **Row Height** dialog box. Change the row height to **42**. Click cell **A1**, press Delete, and then move the **WordArt** image so that its left edge is at the left boundary of cell **A1**. Drag the right center sizing handle of the WordArt to the right boundary of cell **D1** to center it over columns **A** through **D**. Be sure the WordArt image does not touch the right border of column D.

5. **Merge and Center** the title in **A2** over cells **A2:D2**, and then change the font to **Harlow Solid Italic** and the font size to **16**. In cell **A3** type **As of** and then press Enter. Select **A3** again, and then right align the text and change the font to **Harlow Solid Italic** and the font size to **12**. Select the range **B3:C3**, display the **Format Cells** dialog box, click the **Alignment tab**, and under **Text control**, select the **Merge cells** check box. Click the **Font tab** and change the font to **Harlow Solid Italic** and the font size to **12**. Click the **Number tab** and select the **Date** category to display as **March 14, 2001**. Click **OK**. On the Formatting toolbar, click the **Align Left** button.

6. In cell **B9**, create a formula to sum the assets that will be listed in cells **B6:B8**. Copy the formula to cells **C9:D9**. Until data is entered, no totals display; you will see only 012875081.

7. In cell **B15**, create a formula to sum the liabilities that will be listed in cells **B13:B14**, and then copy the formula across the row to cells **C15:D15**.

8. In cell **B17**, use the point and click method to create a formula that calculates Total Assets minus Total Liabilities, and then copy the formula across the row to cells **C17:D17**.

(Project 7K–Balance Sheet continues on the next page)

(Project 7K–Balance Sheet continued)

9. Select the range **A4:D17**. From the **Format** menu, display the **AutoFormat** dialog box. Apply the **Accounting 2** style and click **OK**. Select the range **B6:D17** and click the **Decrease Decimal** button twice.

10. Display the **Page Setup** dialog box. Center the worksheet **Horizontally**, and then create a **Custom Footer** with the **File name** in the **Left section**.

11. Click cell **B3**. Hold down Ctrl and select **B6:D8** and **B13:D14**, which will be the cells in which users of the template will be able to enter data. To unlock these cells, display the **Format Cells** dialog box and on the **Protection tab**, clear the **Locked** check box. Click cell **A1**. From the **Tools** menu, display the **Protect Sheet** dialog box. Enter **GO!Series** as the password. **Save** the changes and close the template.

12. Open the template you just saved, display the **Save As** dialog box, change the **Save as type** box to **Microsoft Excel Workbook** and in your chapter folder, save as 7K_Balance_Sheet_Firstname_Lastname In cell **B3**, type **January 31, 2005** and, using the Tab key to move from cell to cell, enter the following data in the balance sheet. (Hint: You need not type the commas, because the format applied will enter them for you. Thus, it will be easy to use the numeric keypad on your keyboard.)

	Current Month	Previous Month	Previous Year
Inventory	12,875,081	11,823,110	10,976,342
Other Short Term Assets	750,800	790,490	742,483
Long Term Assets	5,647,000	5,647,000	5,480,000
Notes Payable Current	5,877,634	5,773,327	5,735,217
Notes Payable Long Term	1,597,675	1,639,580	2,190,864

13. The total displayed in cell **B17** should be *$11,797,572*. Save the worksheet and print it. Close the file.

End You have completed Project 7K

Project 7L — Expense Report

Objectives: *Create a Workbook Template, Protect a Worksheet, Create a Worksheet Based on a Template, Use Lookup Functions, Validate Data, and Use Conditional Formats.*

El Cuero de Mexico needs to create an expense report template. Based on the skills you have practiced, create an expense report template. Include an area for the employee's name, employee number, and department. Create columns for the following: date the expense was incurred, description of the expense, and an account number to which the expense will be charged. Include various expense categories such as transportation, lodging, meals, fuel, phone, seminars, and miscellaneous. Create a validation list for the account to charge (develop a list of account numbers of your choice) based on the expense category. Create the list on a second worksheet. In the transportation column, use a lookup function to look up the account to charge when an entry displays in this category. At the right side of the worksheet, create a totals column; sum the rows and the columns. Use conditional formatting to hide any #NA error messages that might display. Add the file name to the left section of the footer. Unlock the appropriate cells so that the expense report can be used, and then protect the worksheet. Save the file as a template with the name **7L_ExRp_Template_Lastname_Firstname** Open the template from the template folder and complete the report by using at least two rows of entries to verify that the formulas work as you had intended. Save the file as **7L_Expense_Report_Firstname_Lastname**

End You have completed Project 7L ——————————————————

Project 7M — Grades

Objective: *Use Lookup Functions.*

The lookup function is a useful tool to determine your grades in classes as you go through a semester. In this project, you will create a worksheet to track your grades for this and other classes. You will save your workbook as *7M_Grades_Firstname_Lastname.*

1. Open a blank worksheet. Add the file name to the left section of the footer, and save the file as **7M_Grades_Firstname_Lastname**

2. Set up a worksheet that lists the assignments for your class in column A and the point values that are allocated to each assignment in column B.

3. In column C, enter the points you have earned for each assignment. At the top of column D, type **Grade**

4. Beginning in column F, create a table array that displays the point and grade scale provided in your course syllabus, or other course material. Typically 90 percent or higher is an A, 80–89 percent is a B, and so forth. In the table array, enter scores on the left and the grade on the right. For each grade, enter the lowest value that is needed to achieve that grade. Sort the grading table so that the lowest grade is at the top of the table, and the highest grade is at the end of the table.

5. In column D, create a VLOOKUP to look up the equivalent letter grade for each assignment. Copy the formula down the column as necessary to complete the grading for the assignments listed.

6. Save your changes and close the file.

End You have completed Project 7M ———————————————

Using Templates from Microsoft Office Online

In this chapter, you created templates and practiced adding protection to worksheets. By now, you should know the value of protecting worksheets and be comfortable using the Formula Auditing toolbar. Next, you will examine the construction of formulas in templates by exploring a template from the Microsoft Web site.

1. Start Excel. From the **File** menu, click **New**. In the **New Workbook** task pane, click the **Templates on Office Online** link.

2. In the **Microsoft Office Online** Web site, under **Finance and Accounting**, click **Personal Finance**.

3. Examine the list of templates that are available to you, and then choose one to download.

4. Download one of the personal finance templates. Test the form to see if it is protected. Examine the formulas that have been used to make the form function. Open the Formula Auditing toolbar, and use it to see how the cells are interrelated.

5. Complete the form by using figures that are appropriate to the type of form you selected.

6. When you are finished, close your browser and close Excel.

GO! with Help

Discovering More About Lookup & Reference Functions

In this chapter you used the VLOOKUP and HLOOKUP functions to look up information that was contained in a list on another worksheet. Under the Lookup & Reference function category, there are several other methods that can be used to look up information.

1. Start Excel. In the **Type a question for help** box, type **Lookup & Reference**

2. From the list of related help topics, click **Look up values in a range**.

3. Click the **Show All** link and read through the examples in this topic.

4. There are several worksheet examples that can be copied from the Help page into a worksheet. This will allow you to examine the results of the lookup function. Follow the instructions provided in the Help topic to copy two or more of the lookup function examples into a worksheet so you can see the results of the formula.

5. Practice setting up an Index table, and creating an Index lookup function similar to the examples you examined.

6. Close the file without saving the results, and then close Excel.

8 chaptereight

Using Database Capabilities in Excel

In this chapter, you will: complete these projects **and** practice these skills.

Project 8A **Creating a Database in Excel**	**Objectives** • Import Data into Excel • Sort Data • Manage Data Using a Data Form

Project 8B **Filtering Information in an Excel Database**	**Objectives** • Use AutoFilter • Analyze Data with Excel Database Tools

Project 8C **Using Excel Database Functions**	**Objective** • Use Database Functions

The University Medical Center

The University Medical Center (UMC) is a premier patient-care and research institution serving the metropolitan area of Orange Beach, Florida. UMC enhances the health and well-being of the community through collaborative research and innovations in patient care, medications, and procedures. The center is renowned for its state-of-the-art cancer program and its South-central Florida Cardiovascular Center. The pediatrics wing specializes in the care of high-risk newborns.

© Getty Images, Inc.

Using Database Capabilities in Excel

Excel tracks and manages financial and numerical data and can also be used for simple databases. **Data** refers to facts about people, events, things, or ideas. A **database** is a collection of data related to a particular topic or purpose. Data that has been organized in a useful manner is referred to as **information**. An example of information at the University Medical Center is the list of employees who work in various departments or who work various shifts.

In this chapter, you will use Excel's database capabilities to organize data in a way that is useful. The skills you will practice include importing data into Excel from another source; organizing and sorting data; and entering, changing, and finding data using a form. You will also practice limiting data to display records that meet one or more specific conditions. You will add subtotals, and you will group and outline data. Finally, you will use database functions to summarize information.

Project 8A **Nurses**

To create a database in Excel, you can enter data using a form—or you can import information from another source. After the data is entered, you can change the order of the information, sort on one or more columns, and manage the information by using a data form.

The University Medical Center needs to keep track of many groups of people including patients, employees, and suppliers.

In Activities 8.1 through 8.7, you will import data about medical center nurses into Excel, and then reorganize and sort the information in a variety of useful ways. You will use a form to enter, find, and change data in the database. Your completed worksheet will look similar to Figure 8.1. You will save your workbook as *8A_Nurses_Firstname_Lastname*.

Nurse Records

Emp #	First Name	Last Name	Department	Address 1	Address 2	City	State	Postal Code	Phone
1	Tien	Vo	Geriatrics	5206 Wood Forest Drive		Miami	FL	33143	305-555-0100
2	Hirohiko	Hatano	General Surgery	2001 S. Freemont Ave.		Miami	FL	33145	305-555-0022
3	Tae Hong	Park	Neurology	1109 E. 17th St.	#200	Miami	FL	33174	305-555-0078
4	Josephine	Carreno	Radiology	476 Sundance Trail		Coral Springs	FL	33075	954-555-0010
5	Lydia	Van der Meer	Radiology	9801 E Okaloosa Ave	#D	Hialeah	FL	33013	305-555-0045
6	Tessa	Wilcox	Obstetrics	3222 E. 31st Ave.		Winter Park	FL	32790	407-555-0090
7	Vassily	Sokolov	Geriatrics	568 Baywater Dr.	#A	Coral Springs	FL	33077	954-555-0023
8	Sarah	Martin	Cardiology	5017 Springwood Dr.		Hialeah	FL	33010	305-555-0054
9	Yvonne	Garcia	Psychiatry	12003 Berkeley Square Ave.	#1650	Coral Springs	FL	33065	954-555-0045
10	Renee	Halperin	Obstetrics	9352 Tudor St.		Miami	FL	33150	305-555-0054
11	Mattie	Martin	Cardiology	518 Freedom Plaza Circle	#100	Miami	FL	33150	305-555-0034
12	Joann	Gibson	Pediatrics	782 Honors Drive		Miami	FL	33145	305-555-0766
13	Cecilia	Jefferson	Pediatrics	1520 E. Woodlawn Ave.		Coral Springs	FL	33077	954-555-0854
14	Donald	Fisher	Cardiology	6036 S. Macdill St.		Miami	FL	33145	305-555-0079
15	Pedro	Diaz	General Surgery	2764 E. 51st Ave.	#10	Hialeah	FL	33013	305-555-0073
16	Cherese	Wong	Neurology	2105 Bellmere Parkway		Winter Park	FL	32790	407-555-0037
17	Dylan	Young	Psychiatry	1808 N. Newport Ave.	#1210	Winter Park	FL	32790	407-555-0164
18	Gayle	Hansen	Radiology	3328 W. Van Buren Dr.		Miami	FL	33143	305-555-0145
19	Isidro	Stanley	Pediatrics	16 E. Chestnut St.		Coral Springs	FL	33065	954-555-0122
20	Robert	Wilcox	Obstetrics	8813 Fountain Ave.		Miami	FL	33174	305-555-0006
21	Phil	Lovell	Cardiology	2357 Pebble Beach	#184	Miami	FL	33143	305-555-0223
23	Patricia	McIntyre	Geriatrics	1613 Glen Harbor		Winter Park	FL	32790	407-555-0123

8A_Nurses_Firstname_Lastname

Figure 8.1
Project 8A—Nurses

Objective 1
Import Data into Excel

A database is organized in a format of horizontal rows and vertical columns—just like an Excel worksheet. Each horizontal row stores all of the data about one database item and is referred to as a *record*. Each vertical column stores information that describes the record and is referred to as a *field*. Information stored in a format of rows and columns is referred to as a *table*. Records can be typed into an Excel worksheet or imported from another original source such as Microsoft Access. In this project, you will use Excel's database tools to organize the names and addresses for a group of nurses at University Medical Center.

Activity 8.1 Importing Information into Excel from External Sources

Data is often stored in other computer programs. Rather than re-entering the data, you can import it from its original source. The source can be a database file, a Word table, a Web source, or another Excel workbook.

1 Start Excel. Close the **Getting Started** task pane. Click in cell **A3**. From the **Data** menu, point to **Import External Data**, and then click **Import Data**.

The Select Data Source dialog box opens. By default, the Look in box displays *My Data Sources*—a special folder in Windows where data sources may be stored.

2 Use the **Look in arrow** to navigate to the folder where the student files for this chapter are stored. Click the Access file **e08A_Nurses**. At the bottom of the dialog box, note that the *Files of type* box displays *All Data Sources*.

Microsoft Access is a database program used to manage database files. In this manner, you can import data from Access or from other database programs.

3 With the **e08A_Nurses** file selected, click the **Open** button. Alternatively, press Enter.

The Import Data dialog box displays, indicating that the table will be imported into the existing worksheet in cell A3—the active cell.

4 Click **OK**.

The table of nurses is imported into Excel, and you may see the External Data toolbar displayed on your screen. The field names display in row 3 and the records display in rows 4 to 23. Compare your screen with Figure 8.2.

Field names in row 3 ——

Records display in
rows 4 to 23.

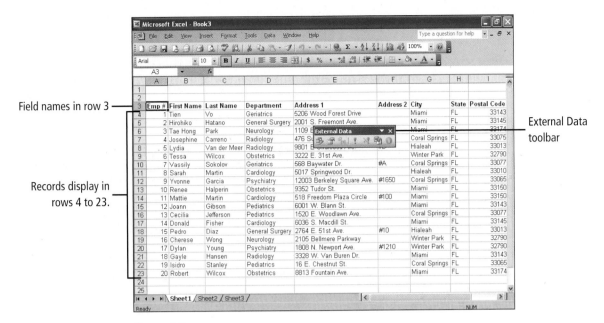

External Data
toolbar

Figure 8.2

5 If the External Data toolbar displays, close it. Select **column I**, and then on the Formatting toolbar, click the **Center** button [image].

The postal codes in column I are centered to provide visual separation from the phone numbers. In this manner, you can format data in a table to improve its readability.

Note — Displaying the External Data Toolbar

If the External Data toolbar has been closed previously, it may not open on your screen. As with any toolbar, you can display the External Data toolbar by right-clicking in any open toolbar at the top of the screen, and then from the displayed list, clicking External Data.

6 In cell **A1** type **Nurse Records** and then press Enter. Click cell **A1**, apply **Bold**, and then change the **Font Size** to **14** pt.

This forms a title for your database table.

Alert!

Avoid Placing Text Adjacent to a Database Table

If you place a title or other text in the row immediately above the table, Excel may interpret it as a column label. It is a good practice to leave the rows and columns adjacent to the table empty so that Excel can identify the boundaries of the table.

7 From the **File** menu, click **Save As**. In the **Save As** dialog box, use the **Save in arrow** to navigate to the folder where you are storing your files, creating a new folder for this chapter if you want to do so. In the **File name** box, type **8A_Nurses_Firstname_Lastname** and then click **Save**.

More Knowledge — Importing Data from a Word Table

Data in a Word table can also be imported into an Excel worksheet; however, the method for doing so is different from importing an Access database. First, be sure the information is displayed in a Word table. Then, place field names in the first row of the table and records in subsequent rows. Select the Word table and copy it. Open the Excel workbook into which you want to import the Word table, click in the cell where you want the data to begin, and then click the Paste button. The table will display in Excel and you can use Excel's database features to manipulate the data.

Objective 2
Sort Data

Data displayed in a database table can be sorted by one or more columns. For a simple sort on a single column, use the Sort Ascending or Sort Descending buttons on the Standard toolbar. For sorts on multiple columns, use the Data Sort dialog box.

Activity 8.2 Changing the Order of Information

Recall that a database is organized in a format of rows and columns referred to as a table. This format is also referred to as a *list*. When sorting information in a table, be sure there are no empty rows or columns. Also, be sure that the active cell is within the table data so that Excel will recognize the row and column boundaries of the data that you want to sort. In the following activity, you will sort the list of nurse employees.

1 In the table of data, click any cell in **column D**—the *Department* field.

To sort on a single column, the active cell can be any one of the cells containing data in the column.

2 On the Standard toolbar, click the **Sort Ascending** button.

The records (rows) in the table are sorted in alphabetical order by the Department field. The record for *Sarah Martin* in the Cardiology department displays as the first record.

3 On the Standard toolbar, click the **Undo** button.

The data is returned to its original order—sorted by the *Emp* # field. In addition, the range A4:J23, the records in the table, is selected.

4 In the table range, click any cell in **column G**—the *City* field. On the Standard toolbar, click the **Sort Descending** button ![Z/A down arrow].

The records are sorted in reverse alphabetical order by the City field. The record for Tessa Wilcox, who lives in Winter Park, displays as the first record in the table. See Figure 8.3.

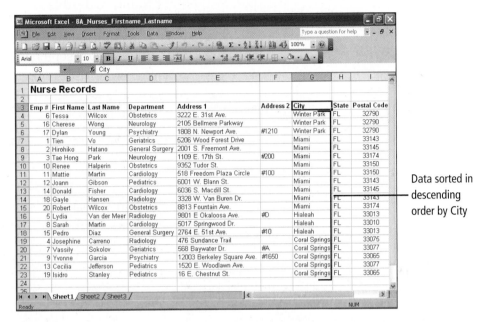

Data sorted in descending order by City

Figure 8.3

5 On the Standard toolbar, click the **Save** button ![save icon].

Activity 8.3 Sorting on Multiple Columns

To sort the records on more than one column, use the Data menu to open the Sort dialog box. Here you can sort on up to three columns at once, in ascending or descending order.

1 Click cell **A3**. On the menu bar click **Data**, and then click **Sort**.

The records are selected and the Sort dialog box displays. Note that *City* displays in the first Sort by box, because it was the last column used for sorting.

2 Click the **Sort by arrow**, and from the displayed list, click **Department**. To the immediate right, click the **Ascending** option button.

The Descending option button was selected because the last sort—by *City*—was in descending order.

3 Click the first **Then by arrow** and from the displayed list, click **Last Name**. Notice that the **Ascending** option button is selected by default.

4 Click the second **Then by arrow** and click **First Name**. Be sure the **Ascending** option button is selected. Note that under **My data range has**, the **Header row** option button is selected.

The records will be sorted first by the Department field—this is known as the ***major*** or ***primary*** sort. Within departments of the same name, the records will be further sorted by the Last Name field and then by the First Name field—this is known as the ***minor*** or ***secondary*** sort. Because you have indicated that the data range includes a header row, the first row of field names will not be interpreted as a record. Compare your screen with Figure 8.4.

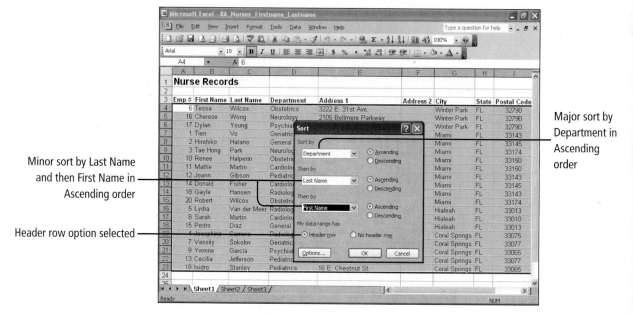

Minor sort by Last Name and then First Name in Ascending order

Header row option selected

Major sort by Department in Ascending order

Figure 8.4

5 Click **OK**.

The Sort dialog box closes, and the data is sorted as directed.

6 Locate the records for *Emp #11*, Mattie Martin and *Emp #8*, Sarah Martin.

Note that the records are sorted first by Department. Then within Departments, the records are sorted by Last Name. Within the Cardiology department, two employees have the same last name, so the records are further sorted by the First Name field. The same is true of the two employees with identical last names in the Obstetrics department. Robert Wilcox is sorted ahead of Tessa Wilcox. See Figure 8.5.

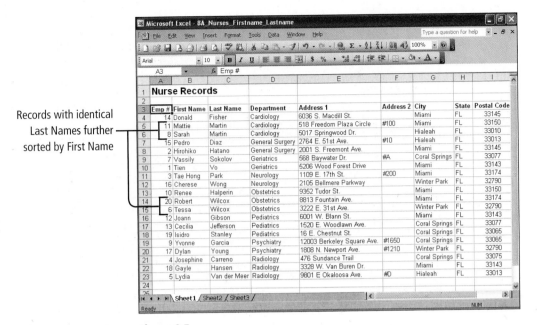

Records with identical Last Names further sorted by First Name

Figure 8.5

Activity 8.4 Undoing the Effects of a Sort

There are two ways to undo the effect of a sort. One is to use the Undo button. The other approach is to resort the data on the original sort field or fields.

1 On the Standard toolbar, click the **Undo** button.

The effect of the sort is undone, and the table is resorted in reverse alphabetic order by City.

Alert!

If You Save Your Workbook After Sorting

If you save your workbook after you have completed a sort, the Undo button will not be available to you to undo the sort. If you saved the workbook at the end of the previous activity, skip to Step 2 to continue.

2 From the **Data** menu, click **Sort**.

3 Click the **Sort by arrow** and click **Emp #**. If necessary, click the **Ascending** button.

4 Click the first **Then by arrow** and click **(none)**. Repeat this action to clear the field from the second **Then by** box. Compare your screen with Figure 8.6.

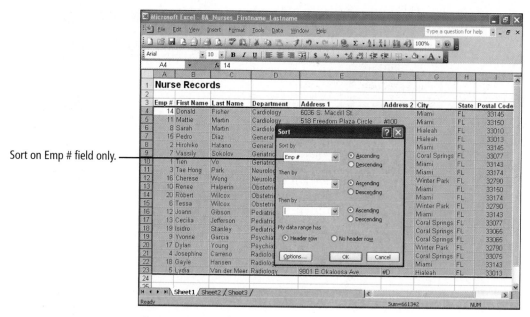

Sort on Emp # field only.

Figure 8.6

5 Click **OK**.

The records are resorted by the *Emp #* field.

6 On the Standard toolbar, click the **Save** button ![save].

Objective 3
Manage Data Using a Data Form

When working with a database, you will need to add new records, find existing records, and update or change existing records. These are all common database activities that need to be performed quickly and easily. With a small database, these activities can be performed directly in the table of data. However, if you work with a large number of records, it is helpful to create a *form*, which is based on the data entered in the worksheet.

Activity 8.5 Entering Data Using a Data Form

1 Double-click the **Sheet 1 tab**, type **Nurse Records** and then press Enter to name the sheet.

2 Click in any cell in the table of data. Display the **Data** menu, and then click **Form**.

A *Nurse Records* form displays with the field names of your table listed on the left and white data entry boxes on the right. The field information for the first record in the table is displayed in the form. Excel creates this dialog box based on the data in your table. It displays the name on the worksheet tab as the name of the form. See Figure 8.7. The buttons on the right are used to add or delete records, navigate among existing records, or locate records that meet specific conditions.

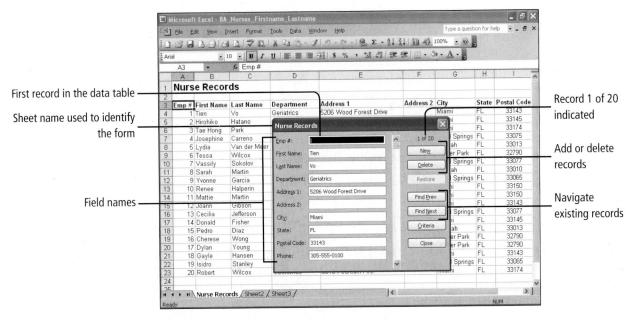

First record in the data table

Sheet name used to identify the form

Field names

Record 1 of 20 indicated

Add or delete records

Navigate existing records

Figure 8.7

3 In the **Nurse Records** form, click the **New** button.

The data entry boxes are cleared and are ready to receive a new record.

4 Type the information shown below, pressing Tab to move from field to field.

Emp #	23
First Name	**Patricia**
Last Name	**McIntyre**
Department	**Geriatrics**
Address 1	**1613 Glen Harbor**
Address 2	
City	**Winter Park**
State	**FL**
Postal Code	**32790**
Phone	**407-555-0123**

Alert! ── **If You Press Enter by Mistake**

If you press the ⌨Enter key rather than the ⌨Tab key, the form will move forward to the next record, which in this case is a blank record. To return to the record you were entering, click the *Find Prev* button. This returns to the previous record, in this case, the record for *Emp #23*.

5 On the **Nurse Records** form, click the **Close** button.

The form is closed and the record displays at the end of the table of data.

Alert! ── **If You Use the Close Button on the Form's Title Bar**

Clicking the Close button at the end of the form adds the record to the database list and closes the Nurse Record form. However, if you use the Close button on the title bar of the form, it cancels the data that has been entered in the form, and the record is not added to the list.

6 From the **Data** menu, click **Form**, and then click **New**. Enter the next new record as follows:

Emp #	**21**
First Name	**Phil**
Last Name	**Lovell**
Department	**Cardiology**
Address 1	**2357 Pebble Beach**
Address 2	**#184**
City	**Miami**
State	**FL**
Postal Code	**33143**
Phone	**305-555-0223**

7 On the **Nurse Records** form, click **Close**.

The record is added to the end of the table. Note that it is not automatically sorted in the table by *Emp #*, which is the field on which the table is currently sorted. New records do not have to be added in numerical order by Emp #, nor do all numbers in a sequence necessarily need to be used for Emp #. Compare your screen with Figure 8.8.

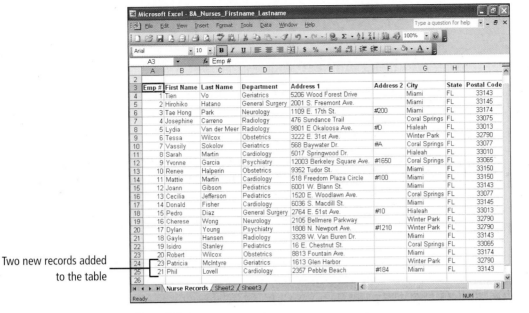
Two new records added to the table

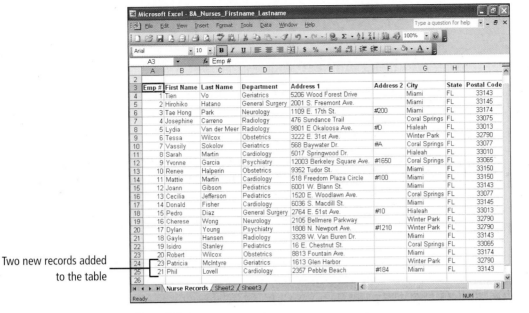

Figure 8.8

8 On the Standard toolbar, click the **Save** button 🖫.

Activity 8.6 Finding Data Using a Data Form

If you need to make changes to a record in a data table, you must first locate the record. In a large database, this is easily accomplished using the Form dialog box.

1 Click cell **A4** to move the active cell to the beginning of the database table. From the **Data** menu, click **Form**. In the displayed **Nurse Records** form, click the **Criteria** button.

The data boxes are cleared and *Criteria* displays above the buttons on the right side of the dialog box. Anything you type in one of the white data boxes becomes a search *criteria*—a value or condition that must be matched. Excel will search the records for the value you enter in the field.

2 Click the **City** box, type **Hialeah** and then click **Find Next**.

The record for *Emp # 5*, Lydia Van der Meer, displays in the form. This is the first record in the table that matches the criterion of *Hialeah* as the City. At the top right of the dialog box, note that 5 *of 22* is indicated. Lydia is the fifth record out of a total of 22.

3 Click the **Find Next** button.

The next record in the table that meets the criterion of *Hialeah*— Sarah Martin—displays.

4 Click **Find Next** again.

The record for Pedro Diaz displays.

5 Click **Find Next** again.

The record displayed does not change, which indicates that no further records in the table meet the criterion—nurses living in *Hialeah*.

6 Click the **Criteria** button.

Hialeah still displays in the City field. Before you begin a new search, you need to clear the previous criteria from the data boxes.

7 Select **Hialeah** and press Delete to clear this value from the **City** box. Click the **Last Name** box, type **Martin** and then click **Find Next**.

The record for Pedro Diaz returns to the screen, even though the last name does not match the criterion—Martin. In a database table, the *Find Next* button searches forward, and the *Find Prev* button searches backward, from the previous location. In the table of data, there is no record for Martin that follows the record for Pedro Diaz, which was the last displayed record. See Figure 8.9.

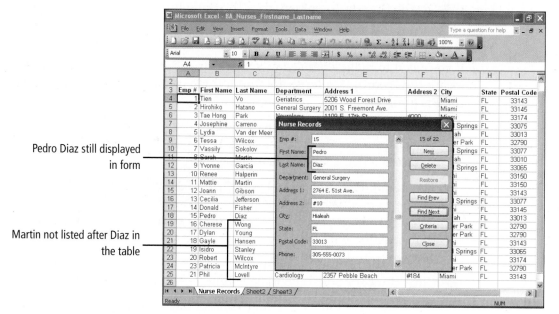

Pedro Diaz still displayed in form

Martin not listed after Diaz in the table

Figure 8.9

8 Click the **Find Prev** button.

The record for *Emp #11*, Mattie Martin, displays.

9 Click the **Find Prev** button again.

The record for *Emp #8*, Sarah Martin, displays.

10 Click the **Find Prev** button again, and then click the **Find Next** button twice to confirm that there are only two records with the last name *Martin*. Close the **Nurse Records** form.

Closing the form clears the criteria. A new search will start from the beginning of the table.

11 Open the **Nurse Records** form and click the **Criteria** button. In the **Department** data box, type **Cardiology** and in the **City** box type **Miami** Click the **Find Next** button.

The record for *Emp #11*, Mattie Martin, is located. This employee meets both criteria specified—*Cardiology* and *Miami*.

12 Click the **Find Next** button until you have located all of the records of nurses who work in Cardiology and live in Miami.

You should locate a total of 3 records.

13 Close the **Nurse Records** form.

Activity 8.7 Editing a Record Using a Data Form

So far you have used the data form to enter new records and find existing records. You can also use the data form to edit existing records. First, use the data form to locate the record that needs to be changed, and then make changes directly in the form. When you close the form, the changes will display in the data table.

1 From the **Data** menu, click **Form** to display the **Nurse Records** form. Click the **Criteria** button, and then in the **Emp #** box, type **12** and press Enter.

The record for Joann Gibson displays.

2 Change the address for Joann to the following:

782 Honors Drive

Miami FL 33145

3 On the right side of the form, click the **Close** button, and then in the table, verify that the address for *Emp #12* is changed.

Compare your screen with Figure 8.10.

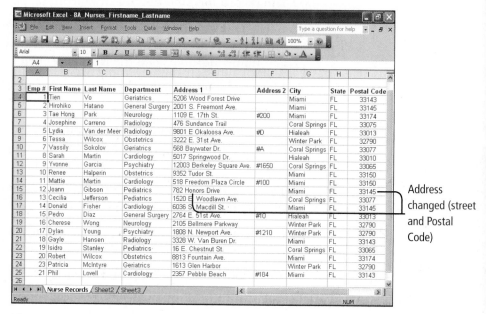

Address changed (street and Postal Code)

Figure 8.10

4 In the data table, click anywhere in the **Emp #** column, and then click the **Sort Ascending** button 🔼.

This sorts the new records that were added by *Emp #* with the rest of the table. As yet, there is no Emp #22.

5 From the **File** menu, display the **Page Setup** dialog box, and then click the **Header/Footer tab**. Create a **Custom Footer** and add the **File name** to the **Left section**. Click the **Page tab**, and then select **Landscape**. Click the **Print Preview** button. On the Print Preview toolbar, click **Print**, and then click **OK** to print the worksheet.

6 On the Standard toolbar, click the **Save** button 💾, and then close the workbook.

End You have completed Project 8A

Project 8B Department Nurses

One purpose of a database is to create information. Excel offers several methods to help you locate information, analyze records, add subtotals, and group and outline information.

When you work with a large number of records, you may need to manipulate the database to answer specific questions. For example, how many people work in the pediatric department, or who has nurse practitioner credentials? To answer such questions, use ***AutoFilter***, which limits the records that display in a data table by adding filters to one or more fields. Or you can create an ***Advanced Filter***, which limits the records that display based on comparison criteria. You can also add subtotals to a worksheet based on groups.

In Activities 8.8 through 8.16, you will work with another set of records for the nurses at the University Medical Center. Each record includes the department, classification, salary, and shift. Your completed worksheets will look similar to Figure 8.11. You will save your workbook as *8B_Dept_Nurses_Firstname_Lastname*.

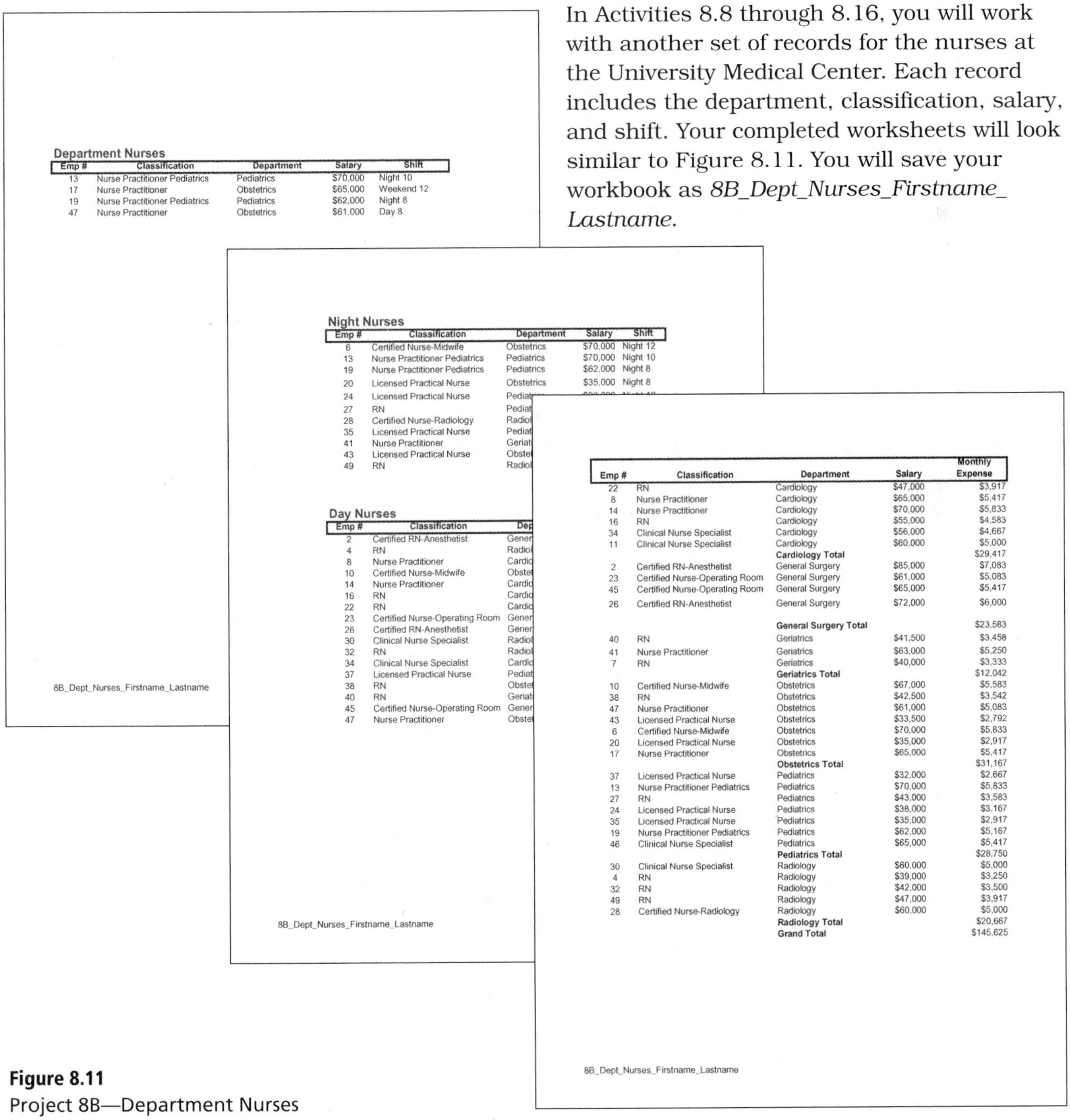

Department Nurses

Emp #	Classification	Department	Salary	Shift
13	Nurse Practitioner Pediatrics	Pediatrics	$70,000	Night 10
17	Nurse Practitioner	Obstetrics	$65,000	Weekend 12
19	Nurse Practitioner Pediatrics	Pediatrics	$62,000	Night 8
47	Nurse Practitioner	Obstetrics	$61,000	Day 8

8B_Dept_Nurses_Firstname_Lastname

Night Nurses

Emp #	Classification	Department	Salary	Shift
6	Certified Nurse-Midwife	Obstetrics	$70,000	Night 12
13	Nurse Practitioner Pediatrics	Pediatrics	$70,000	Night 10
19	Nurse Practitioner Pediatrics	Pediatrics	$62,000	Night 8
20	Licensed Practical Nurse	Obstetrics	$35,000	Night 8
24	Licensed Practical Nurse	Pediat		
27	RN	Pediat		
28	Certified Nurse-Radiology	Radiol		
35	Licensed Practical Nurse	Pediat		
41	Nurse Practitioner	Geriat		
43	Licensed Practical Nurse	Obste		
49	RN	Radiol		

Day Nurses

Emp #	Classification	Dep
2	Certified RN-Anesthetist	Gener
4	RN	Radiol
8	Nurse Practitioner	Cardic
10	Certified Nurse-Midwife	Obste
14	Nurse Practitioner	Cardic
16	RN	Cardic
22	RN	Cardic
23	Certified Nurse-Operating Room	Gener
26	Certified RN-Anesthetist	Gener
30	Clinical Nurse Specialist	Radiol
32	RN	Radiol
34	Clinical Nurse Specialist	Cardic
37	Licensed Practical Nurse	Pediat
38	RN	Obste
40	RN	Geriat
45	Certified Nurse-Operating Room	Gener
47	Nurse Practitioner	Obste

8B_Dept_Nurses_Firstname_Lastname

Emp #	Classification	Department	Salary	Monthly Expense
22	RN	Cardiology	$47,000	$3,917
8	Nurse Practitioner	Cardiology	$65,000	$5,417
14	Nurse Practitioner	Cardiology	$70,000	$5,833
16	RN	Cardiology	$55,000	$4,583
34	Clinical Nurse Specialist	Cardiology	$56,000	$4,667
11	Clinical Nurse Specialist	Cardiology	$60,000	$5,000
		Cardiology Total		$29,417
2	Certified RN-Anesthetist	General Surgery	$85,000	$7,083
23	Certified Nurse-Operating Room	General Surgery	$61,000	$5,083
45	Certified Nurse-Operating Room	General Surgery	$65,000	$5,417
26	Certified RN-Anesthetist	General Surgery	$72,000	$6,000
		General Surgery Total		$23,583
40	RN	Geriatrics	$41,500	$3,458
41	Nurse Practitioner	Geriatrics	$63,000	$5,250
7	RN	Geriatrics	$40,000	$3,333
		Geriatrics Total		$12,042
10	Certified Nurse-Midwife	Obstetrics	$67,000	$5,583
38	RN	Obstetrics	$42,500	$3,542
47	Nurse Practitioner	Obstetrics	$61,000	$5,083
43	Licensed Practical Nurse	Obstetrics	$33,500	$2,792
6	Certified Nurse-Midwife	Obstetrics	$70,000	$5,833
20	Licensed Practical Nurse	Obstetrics	$35,000	$2,917
17	Nurse Practitioner	Obstetrics	$65,000	$5,417
		Obstetrics Total		$31,167
37	Licensed Practical Nurse	Pediatrics	$32,000	$2,667
13	Nurse Practitioner Pediatrics	Pediatrics	$70,000	$5,833
27	RN	Pediatrics	$43,000	$3,583
24	Licensed Practical Nurse	Pediatrics	$38,000	$3,167
35	Licensed Practical Nurse	Pediatrics	$35,000	$2,917
19	Nurse Practitioner Pediatrics	Pediatrics	$62,000	$5,167
46	Clinical Nurse Specialist	Pediatrics	$65,000	$5,417
		Pediatrics Total		$28,750
30	Clinical Nurse Specialist	Radiology	$60,000	$5,000
4	RN	Radiology	$39,000	$3,250
32	RN	Radiology	$42,000	$3,500
49	RN	Radiology	$47,000	$3,917
28	Certified Nurse-Radiology	Radiology	$60,000	$5,000
		Radiology Total		$20,667
		Grand Total		$145,625

8B_Dept_Nurses_Firstname_Lastname

Figure 8.11
Project 8B—Department Nurses

Objective 4
Use AutoFilter

A *filtered* range displays only the records that meet the *criteria*—conditions that you specify to limit which records are included in the resulting set of records. AutoFilter assists in filtering a range by placing AutoFilter arrows to the right of column labels from which you can display a list of possible filters. Applying a filter is similar to using the Criteria button on the Data Form, but instead of seeing only one record that matches the criteria, you see all of the records that match the condition specified. Filters can be applied to more than one field.

Activity 8.8 Displaying Data Using AutoFilter

Applying a filter to a table of data enables you to isolate records that meet a particular condition. In this activity, you will filter the records to view only those nurses who work one of the day shifts.

1 Start Excel. On the Standard toolbar, click the **Open** button. Navigate to the folder where the student files for this textbook are stored. Locate and open **e08B_Dept_Nurses**.

2 From the **File** menu, click **Save As**. In the **Save As** dialog box, use the **Save in arrow** to navigate to the location where you are storing your files for this chapter. In the **File name** box, type **8B_Dept_Nurses_Firstname_Lastname** Click the **Save** button.

This worksheet lists the Emp #, Classification, Department, Salary, and Shift of nurses at the hospital. The empty rows at the top of the worksheet will be used later to query the database. See Figure 8.12.

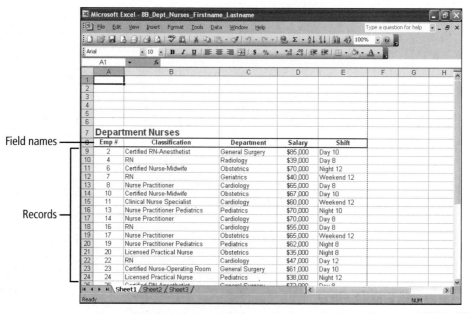

Figure 8.12

3 From the **File** menu, display the **Page Setup** dialog box, and then click the **Header/Footer tab**. Create a **Custom Footer**, and add the **File name** to the **Left section**.

4 Click cell **A10** to place the active cell in the data table.

A cell in the database must be active before you can filter the data.

5 From the **Data** menu, point to **Filter**, and then click **AutoFilter**.

Arrows display to the right of each of the column labels that comprise the field names.

6 In cell **E8**, click the **Shift arrow**, and from the displayed list, click **Day 10**.

The records for the nurses who work the *Day 10* shift are displayed. Note that there are gaps in the row numbers at the left of the window indicating that not all records are displayed—only those that meet the Day 10 condition. The number of records that match the criteria is indicated in the status bar. Compare your screen with Figure 8.13.

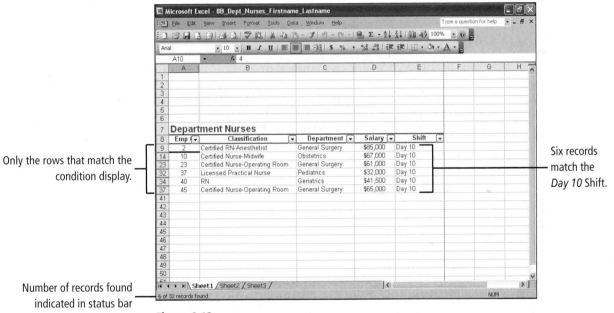

Only the rows that match the condition display.

Six records match the *Day 10* Shift.

Number of records found indicated in status bar

Figure 8.13

More Knowledge — Guidelines for Formatting Database Tables

Observe these guidelines when you create a database to ensure that you can manipulate the data. First, distinguish the field name headings by using a font style and formatting that is different from the data. Use borders to create a visual separation of the field names from the data. Avoid empty rows or columns in the data table. Place only one data table on a worksheet. Place critical information above or below the table—rather than to the side of the table, so that important information is not hidden when the data is filtered. Finally, avoid typing extra spaces at the beginning or end of data in a cell; this will affect the sorting and filtering of your data.

Activity 8.9 Displaying Data Using Multiple AutoFilter Criteria

You can filter on more than one field.

1 In cell **C8**, click the **Department arrow**, and then from the displayed list click **General Surgery**.

The records for the three nurses who work the *Day 10* shift in *General Surgery* display.

2 In cell **B8**, click the **Classification arrow**, and then from the displayed list click **Certified Nurse-Operating Room**.

Emp #23 and *#45* are classified as *Certified Nurse-Operating Room* and work in *General Surgery* and also work the *Day 10* shift.

3 From the **Data** menu, point to **Filter** and click **Show All**.

All of the records in the data table are redisplayed, and the AutoFilter arrows continue to display next to each column label.

4 In cell **C8**, click the **Department arrow**, and then click **Radiology**.

5 In cell **B8**, click the **Classification arrow**, and then click **RN**.

6 In cell **E8**, click the **Shift arrow**, and then click **Day 8**.

Two records—*Emp #4* and *Emp #32*—meet these three conditions. Compare your screen with Figure 8.14.

Two RNs work in Radiology during the *Day 8* shift.

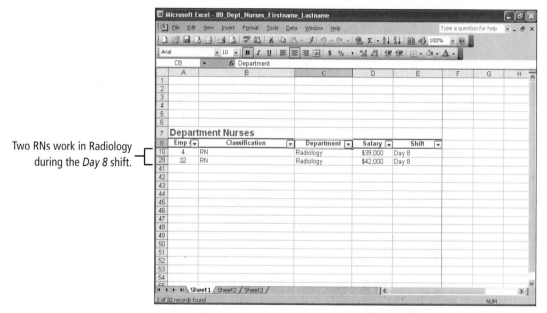

Figure 8.14

7 On the **Data** menu, point to **Filter**, and then click **Show All**.

Activity 8.10 Creating a Custom AutoFilter

AutoFilter offers you the option of creating a custom filter. With a custom filter, you can use **comparison operators**. Comparison operators are the equal sign (=), the greater than sign (>), or the less than sign (<) used singly or in combinations, to compare two values. When two values are compared using these operators, the result is a logical value of either TRUE or FALSE.

1 In cell **C8**, click the **Department arrow**, and then click **(Custom...)**.

In the displayed Custom AutoFilter dialog box, you can create a **compound filter**—a filter that uses more than one condition—and one that uses comparison operators.

2 Under **Department**, in the first box click the arrow to display the list, and then click **equals**. In the box to the right, display the list, and then click **Obstetrics**.

The first filter limits the list to nurses in the *Obstetrics* department.

3 Click the **Or** option button, and then for the second filter, display **equals** in the box on the left and **Pediatrics** in the box on the right.

Compare your screen with Figure 8.15.

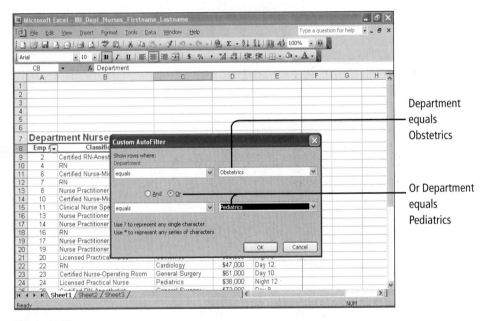

Figure 8.15

4 Click **OK**.

Nurses assigned to either Obstetrics or Pediatrics are displayed.

5 In cell **B8**, click the **Classification arrow**, and from the displayed list click **(Custom...)**.

6 In the **Custom AutoFilter** dialog box, under **Classification**, in the first box click the arrow to display the list. Scroll as necessary and click **contains**. Display the list for the box on the right. Note that two of the categories include the word *Practitioner*. Type **Practitioner** in the box.

This will filter the records to display only those nurses with a classification that contains the word *Practitioner*.

7 Click **OK**.

Four nurses meet the conditions of working in Obstetrics or Pediatrics and are classified as Nurse Practitioners. Compare your screen with Figure 8.16.

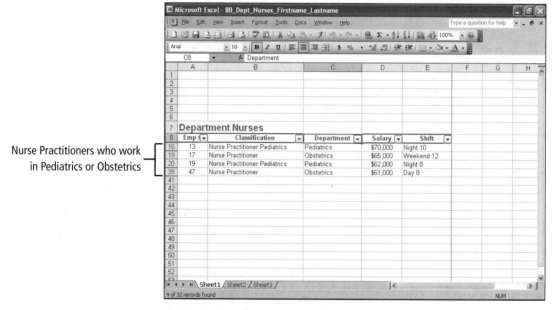

Nurse Practitioners who work in Pediatrics or Obstetrics

Figure 8.16

8 On the Standard toolbar, click the **Print** button.

Activity 8.11 Removing the AutoFilter

The AutoFilter is like a toggle button; you can turn it on and off.

1 From the **Data** menu, point to **Filter**, and then click **AutoFilter**.

AutoFilter is turned off, and the records in the database are redisplayed. The AutoFilter arrows are removed from the field headings.

2 On the Standard toolbar, click the **Save** button.

Leave the worksheet open for the next activity.

Objective 5
Analyze Data with Excel Database Tools

To create meaningful information from a database, you need to analyze the data. Sorting and filtering are useful techniques to analyze data. Other techniques for analyzing data include placing calculated fields in a database, using advanced filter techniques, and adding subtotals based on groupings of the data. The goal is to manipulate the data so that you can *query* the database. To query is to ask a question. For example, you can query the database to find the answer to the question, "What is the average salary for nurses in each department?"

Activity 8.12 Creating Criteria Using an Advanced Filter

AutoFilter limits the display of records based on filters you apply to one or more fields. With an *Advanced Filter*, you can specify criteria in one part of the worksheet and then have matching records display either in the table or in another part of the worksheet.

1 With your **8B_Dept_Nurses** file open, select the range **A7:E8**, and then on the Standard toolbar, click the **Copy** button .

The first step in creating an Advanced Filter is to set up a *criteria range* on your worksheet. This is an area on your worksheet where the criteria for the filter will be defined. It is placed above or below the data and consists of three rows—a title row, column labels that are the same as the data table, and at least one blank row. It must be separated from the table by at least one blank row. You will create your criteria range by copying the title and field names and then pasting them into the empty rows at the top of the worksheet.

2 Click cell **A2**, and then on the Standard toolbar, click the **Paste** button . Click cell **A2**, type **Criteria Range** and then press Enter.

By copying the titles and field names from the table, you also copy the formatting that has been applied. See Figure 8.17.

Criteria range created at the top of the worksheet —

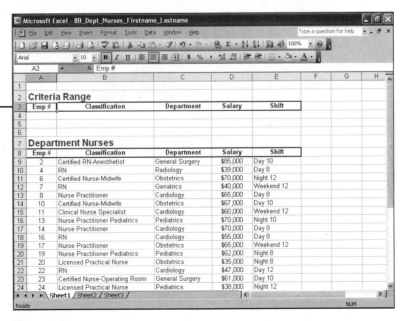

Figure 8.17

3 Select the range **A3:E4**. Click the **Name Box**, type **Criteria** and then press [Enter].

By naming the range *Criteria*, the reference for the range will automatically display in the Criteria range box when the Advanced Filter is applied. The defined area includes the field names and one empty row where the limiting criteria will be placed. It does not include the title *Criteria Range*.

4 Select the range **A8:E40**. Click in the **Name Box**, type **Database** and then press [Enter].

By naming the range *Database*, the reference will automatically display in the List range box when the Advanced Filter is applied.

5 Click cell **D4** and type **>=60000** and then press [Enter].

This creates a criterion using a comparison operator to look for salary values that are greater than or equal to 60,000. Do not include a comma when you type this value, because the comma is a cell format, not part of the value.

6 Click cell **A8**. From the **Data** menu, point to **Filter**, and then click **Advanced Filter**.

The Advanced Filter dialog box displays, and a moving border surrounds the range of data. This dialog box is used to define the database area or List range, the Criteria range, and the area where the results should display. Under *Action*, you can choose to display the results in the table—in-place—or copy the results to another location. Note that the *List range* is correctly identified as cells A8:E40, and the *Criteria range* is identified as cells A3:E4. Both ranges use an absolute reference. The filter results will display *in-place*—in the table. See Figure 8.18.

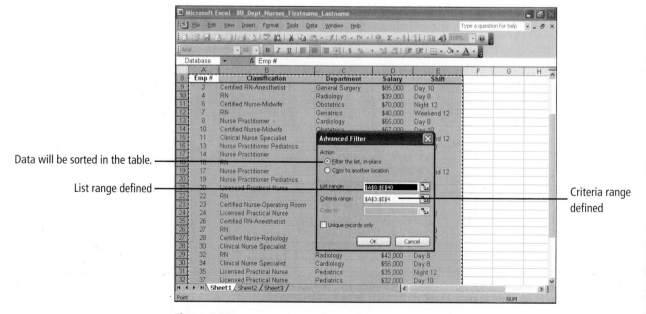

Data will be sorted in the table.

List range defined

Criteria range defined

Figure 8.18

7 Click **OK**.

The records displayed in the table show only those nurses whose salary is $60,000 or more. Compare your screen with Figure 8.19. The row numbers for the records included display in blue.

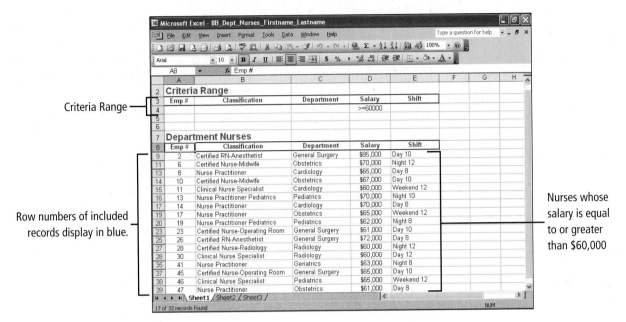

Criteria Range

Row numbers of included records display in blue.

Nurses whose salary is equal to or greater than $60,000

Figure 8.19

8 Click cell **B4**, type **Certified*** and then press Enter.

The asterisk (*) is a *wildcard*. It is used to search a field when you are uncertain of the exact value or when you want to widen the search to include more records. In this example, the use of a wildcard enables you to include all nurses whose classification begins with the word *Certified*. The wildcard directs Excel to find *Certified* and anything that might follow it. The criterion in the Salary field still applies. The use of two criteria on the same row is known as a *compound criteria*—both conditions must be met for the records to be included in the results.

9 Click cell **A8**. From the **Data** menu, point to **Filter**, and then click **Advanced Filter**. Verify that the database range is correctly identified in the **List range** box and that the **Criteria range** still indicates *$A$3:$E$4*. Click **OK**.

The certified nurses whose salary is $60,000 or more are listed in the table. Compare your screen with Figure 8.20.

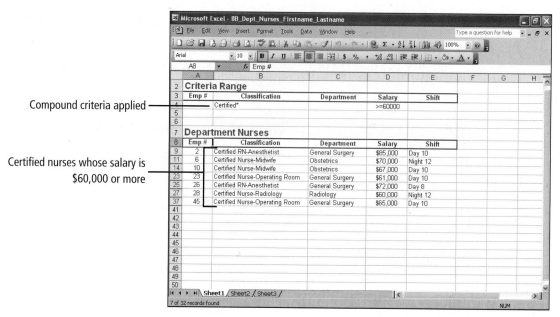

Compound criteria applied ——

Certified nurses whose salary is $60,000 or more ——

Figure 8.20

10 From the **Data** menu, point to **Filter**, and then click **Show All**.

All of the records are displayed, and the Advanced Filter is removed.

More Knowledge — Using Wildcards

A wildcard can help you locate information when you are uncertain how the information might be displayed in your records. The placement of the asterisk in relationship to the known value determines the result. If it is placed first, the variable will be in the beginning of the string of characters. For example, in a list of names if you used *son as the criteria, it will look for any name that ends in son. The results might display Peterson, Michelson, and Samuelson. If the asterisk is at the end of the known value in the criteria, then the variable will be at the end. You can also include the asterisk wildcard at the beginning and at the end of a known value.

A question mark (?) can also be used as part of your search criteria. Each question mark used in the criteria represents a single position or character that is unknown in a group of specified values. Searching for m?n would, for example, find min, men, and man; whereas searching for m??d would, for example, find mind, mend, mold.

Activity 8.13 Extracting Data to a New Area on the Worksheet

From the Advanced Filter dialog box, you can place filtered results in another area on your worksheet. This area is defined by Excel as an *Extract* area. Using this technique you can extract—pull out—different sets of data for comparison purposes.

1 Select the range **A2:E3** and on the Standard toolbar, click the **Copy** button [icon]. Click cell **G2** and on the Standard toolbar, click the **Paste** button [icon]. Click cell **G2**, type **Night Nurses** and then press Enter.

The format and content of the criteria is copied and modified to create an extract area. It is labeled *Night Nurses*—the records for the night nurses will be placed in this area.

2 Select the range **G3:K4**, in the **Name Box** type **Extract** and then press Enter. Widen **column H** to **27.00** (194 pixels) and **column I** to **14** (103 pixels). Select **row 3**, right-click over the selected row, click **Row Height**, and in the **Row Height** box type **13.5** and click **OK**.

The Extract area is defined, and this range will display automatically in the *Copy to* box of the Advanced Filter dialog box. The word *Extract* is used because it is recognized by Excel as the location to place the results of an advanced filter.

3 Click cell **B4** and press Delete to remove the Classification criteria. Click cell **D4** and press Delete to remove the Salary criteria. Click cell **E4**, type **Night*** and then press Enter.

A new criterion is defined to locate the nurses who work the night shift. Recall that the use of an asterisk will find all nurses whose shift begins with the word *Night*.

4 Click in cell **A8** to place the active cell in the database table. From the **Data** menu, display the **Advanced Filter** dialog box.

5 In the displayed dialog box, under **Action**, select the **Copy to another location** option button. Verify that in the **Copy to** box, the absolute reference to the Extract area—*$G$3:$K$4*—displays. Compare your screen with Figure 8.21.

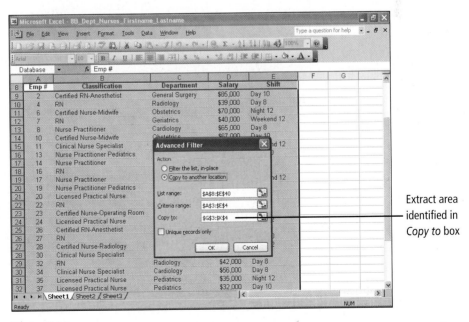

Extract area identified in *Copy to* box

Figure 8.21

6 Click **OK**.

A message indicates that the destination range is not large enough to accommodate all copied rows. Because you cannot know how many records will be found to match the criteria, you include one empty row when you define the Extract Range. The data that has been located by the Advanced Filter requires more than one row to display all of the records. Therefore, this message advises you that it will take more than one row to copy the records.

7 Click **Yes** to continue copying the rows.

Beginning in cell G4, the first record that meets the criterion displays.

8 Scroll as necessary to see the results in columns G through K.

Eleven records meet the criterion and are copied to the extract area on your worksheet. Rather than reformatting the table to display the requested records, Excel places the requested information in the Extract area. See Figure 8.22.

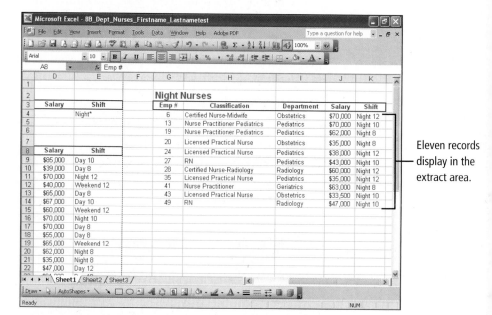

Figure 8.22

9 Select the range **G2:K3**, and then on the Standard toolbar, click the **Copy** button ▣. Click cell **G18**, and then on the Standard toolbar, click the **Paste** button ▣ ▾. Click cell **G18**, type **Day Nurses** and then press Enter.

A second extract area is identified and will be used for comparison purposes. You will modify the criteria, and then change the *Copy to* location in the Advanced Filter dialog box.

10 Click cell **E4**, type **Day*** and then press Enter.

11 Click cell **A8**. From the **Data** menu, display the **Advanced Filter** dialog box.

12 In the displayed dialog box, under **Action**, select the **Copy to another location** option button.

13 In the **Copy to** box, select the displayed range and press ⌈Delete⌋. In the **Copy to** box, click the **Collapse dialog box** button to temporarily shrink the dialog box. Select the range **G19:K20**, and then in the collapsed dialog box, click the **Expand dialog box** button. Compare your dialog box with Figure 8.23.

You can specify a new range where you want to place the results; you do not have to use the area that was previously defined as the extract area. After you have redefined the extract area, Excel will assign the name *Extract* to that area.

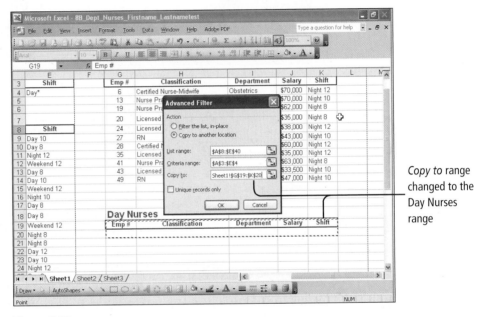

Figure 8.23

14 Click **OK**, and then in the displayed message box click **Yes** to copy the rest of the records. Scroll as needed to display the records extracted for the night and day shift nurses. Seventeen records meet the criterion for Day Nurses.

With an Advanced Filter, you have to count the number of records in the result yourself, unlike the AutoFilter, which displays the number of matching records in the status bar.

15 Select the range **G2:K36**. From the **File** menu, click **Print**. In the **Print** dialog box, under **Print what**, click **Selection**, and then in the lower left corner, click the **Preview** button. On the Print Preview toolbar, click the **Setup** button, and then center the data **Horizontally**. Click **OK**.

The list of Night Nurses and Day Nurses displays in the Preview window. Compare your screen with Figure 8.24.

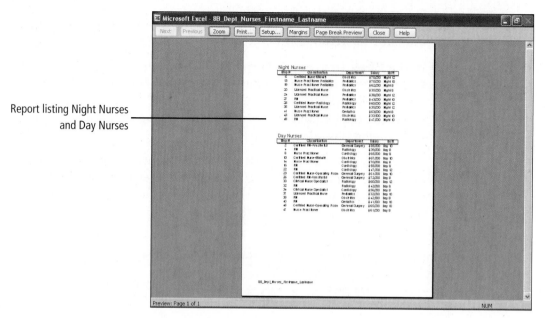

Report listing Night Nurses
and Day Nurses

Figure 8.24

16 On the Print Preview toolbar, click **Print**. On the Standard toolbar, click **Save** 🔲.

Activity 8.14 Using Subtotals

Data in an Excel database can be summarized by adding subtotals to the table. Fields with numerical or financial data can be summed or averaged. You can count fields that contain text values to determine how many records are in a group. You can also perform various statistical functions, such as finding the minimum or maximum value in a group. The first step in adding subtotals is to sort the data by the field for which you want to create a subtotal.

1 Click in cell **E9** to place the active cell in the **Shift** column of the database table. On the Standard toolbar, click the **Sort Ascending** button 🔳.

Recall that the active cell needs to be somewhere in the column on which you want to sort the data. The data in this column is text; it is sorted alphabetically and not numerically. The numbers are treated as text characters; therefore, the 1 in 10 comes before 8, and Day 10 and Day 12 display before Day 8.

2 From the **Data** menu, click **Subtotals**.

The displayed Subtotal dialog box is used to summarize data. In the first box, you can select the field by which you want to summarize the data. This selection directs Excel to create a group for each change in value in that field. In the second box, you can select the function you want to use. In the third area, you can select the field that you want to subtotal. In this table, the only numerical field is the Salary field. The check boxes at the end of the table control how the summary information will display.

3 In the **Subtotal** dialog box, in the **At each change in** box, display the list and click **Shift**. In the **Use function** box, display the list and click **Count**. In the **Add subtotal to** list, scroll the list and be sure only the **Shift** check box is selected. Compare your screen with Figure 8.25.

This will create subtotals by Shift to count the number of nurses who work each of the seven shifts.

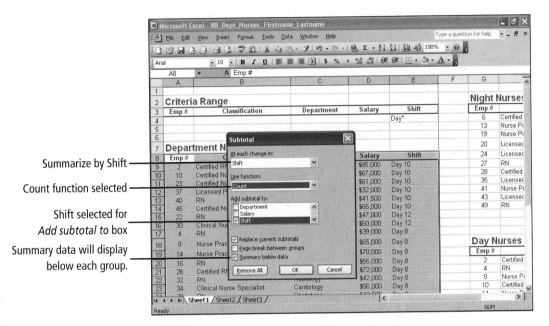

Summarize by Shift ——

Count function selected ——

Shift selected for
Add subtotal to box ——

Summary data will display
below each group. ——

Figure 8.25

4 Click **OK**. Widen column **D** to **13.00** (96 pixels).

Subtotals display at the end of each change in shift. Rows are inserted to display the number of nurses who work each shift. At the left side of the data table, Excel displays a gray bar with a visual *outline*. If you summarize data with formulas that contain functions, such as the COUNT or SUM function, Excel automatically outlines the data. The outline has three levels, and the outline details display on your screen. Later in this project, you will work with the outline. See Figure 8.26.

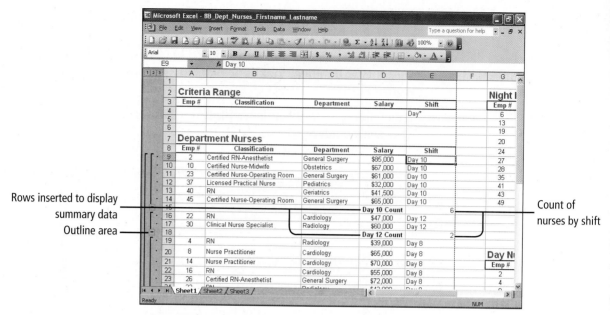

Rows inserted to display summary data

Outline area

Count of nurses by shift

Figure 8.26

5️⃣ From the **Data** menu, click **Subtotals**. In the lower left corner of the displayed dialog box, click the **Remove All** button.

Before you can create the next subtotal, you must remove existing subtotals and resort the data.

Activity 8.15 Adding a Calculated Field to a Database

A database table can contain values, calculations, or functions. In this activity, you will calculate monthly salary expenses by department. First you will add a field that will calculate the monthly salary for each nurse, and then you will use *Subtotals* to determine the monthly departmental expense for nursing.

1️⃣ Click cell **C9**, and then on the Standard toolbar, click the **Sort Ascending** button 🔼.

The records in the database table are resorted by the Department field.

2️⃣ Click cell **E9**, and then from the **Insert** menu, click **Columns**.

A column is inserted between the Salary and the Shift columns.

3️⃣ In cell **E8**, type **Monthly Expense** and then press ⏎.

A field name is added to the column and adopts the same formatting used in the other cells in the field name row.

4️⃣ In cell **E9**, type **=d9/12** press ⏎, and then copy the formula down to cell **E40**. With the range still selected, on the Formatting toolbar click the **Align Right** button ▤.

This formula calculates the monthly salary for each nurse; the numbers are right aligned.

5️⃣ Click anywhere in the data table. From the **Data** menu, click **Subtotals**. In the displayed dialog box, in the **At each change in** box, display the list and then click **Department**. In the **Use function** box, display the list and click **Sum**. Under **Add subtotal to**, scroll the list and be sure only the **Monthly Expense** check box is selected. Compare your dialog box with Figure 8.27.

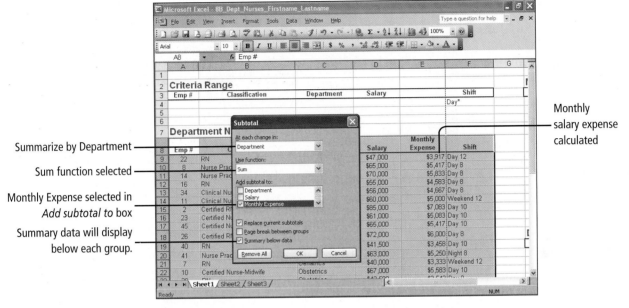

Summarize by Department

Sum function selected

Monthly Expense selected in *Add subtotal to* box

Summary data will display below each group.

Monthly salary expense calculated

Figure 8.27

6️⃣ Click **OK**. AutoFit **column C** to display the summary titles for each total row.

The data is grouped by Department. Subtotals for the Monthly Expense are displayed at the end of each department grouping. The gray outline displays at the left side of the table. In the next activity, you will practice using the outline.

7️⃣ On the Standard toolbar, click the **Save** button 🖫.

Activity 8.16 Grouping and Outlining Data

When you summarize data in a table with formulas that contain functions, such as the SUBTOTAL function to add subtotals, Excel automatically adds an outline. This gray bar along the left side of the worksheet lets you show and hide levels of detail with a single mouse click. For example, you can show details with the totals, which is the default view. Or, you can show only the summary totals or only the grand total. The buttons at the top of the outline area can be used to expand or collapse the outline.

1️⃣ With your **8B_Dept_Nurses** worksheet open, examine Figure 8.28 and locate on your screen the parts of the outline that are identified in the figure. If you do not see the outline symbols, from the Tools menu, click Options, click the View tab, and then under Window options, select the Outline symbols check box.

Outline level buttons —

Level bars —

Hide detail buttons —

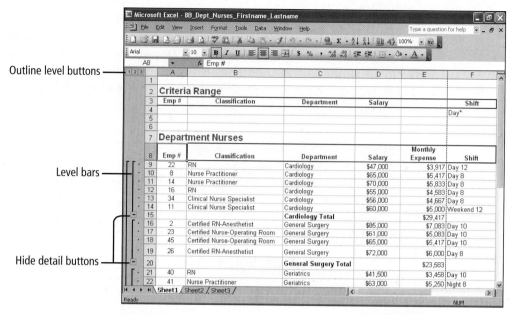

Figure 8.28

2 To the left of **row 15**, click the **Hide detail** button.

The ***detail data***—the individual records—for the Cardiology department is hidden and only the summary total for the Cardiology department displays.

3 To the left of **row 20**, click the **Hide detail** button.

The detail data for the General Surgery department is hidden and only the summary total for the General Surgery department displays. See Figure 8.29.

Details for Cardiology and General Surgery are hidden.

Figure 8.29

4 At the top of the outline area, click the **Level 2** button to hide all Level 3 details, and display only the Level 2 summary information, and the Level 1 Grand Total. See Figure 8.30.

Clicking the Level 2 button displays only the summary totals.

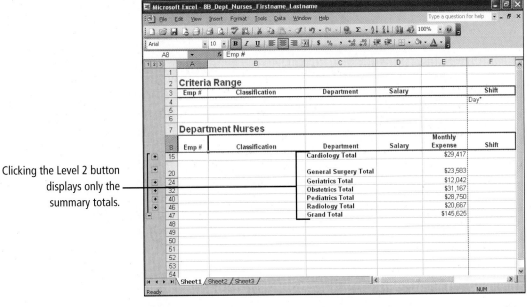

Figure 8.30

5 At the top of the outline area, click the **Level 1** button to display only the Grand Total. If necessary, click cell **E47** and format to currency with no decimals.

The total may need to be formatted separately.

6 At the top of the outline area, click the **Level 3** button to display all of the detail information again.

7 Click cell **E8**. Display the **Format Cells** dialog box and click the **Border tab**. Be sure the **Color** displays **Blue**, and then in the **Border** area, click the **Right** border to add a border on the right edge of this cell. Click **OK**.

8 Select the range **A7:E47**. From the **File** menu, click **Print**. In the displayed dialog box, under **Print what**, click the **Selection** option button. Click the **Preview** button and verify that the range will print on one page. On the Print Preview toolbar, click **Print**.

9 On the Standard toolbar, click **Save** ■. Close the file, and then close Excel.

More Knowledge — Outlining a Worksheet

A horizontal outline bar can be created for data that is summarized by row, rather than summarized by column as it was in this activity. In addition, if the data is not organized so that Excel can outline it automatically, you can create an outline manually. This is accomplished from the Settings dialog box—from the Data menu, point to Group and Outline, and then click Settings.

End You have completed Project 8B

Project 8C Pediatric Nurses

Excel has several functions that are database specific. These functions are similar to other Excel functions, but they are designed to manipulate and analyze data that is organized in a database structure.

In Activities 8.17 through 8.20, you will practice using database functions to analyze data. The data is contained in a worksheet that lists the nurses who are scheduled to work on Monday in the pediatric wing of the hospital. Your completed worksheet will look similar to Figure 8.31. You will save your workbook as *8C_Pediatric_Nurses_Firstname_Lastname*.

Monday Shift
Pediatric Nurses

Emp Num	Shift Code	Status	Hours per Shift	Hourly Wage	Wage per Shift
12	1	Nurse Practitioner	8	33.65	269.20
18	3	LPN	8	19.00	152.00
20	3	Nurse Supervisor	0	25.60	-
25	1	RN	8	22.38	179.04
26	5	LPN	12	17.50	210.00
27	5	RN	12	20.40	244.80
28	2	LPN	0	17.80	-
29	3	RN	8	21.25	170.00
30	6	Nurse Supervisor	12	28.20	338.40
31	1	RN	8	21.45	171.60
32	2	LPN	8	17.40	139.20
33	4	RN	8	22.00	176.00
34	6	RN	12	18.75	225.00
35	5	LPN	12	18.50	222.00
36	5	RN	0	19.75	-
37	1	LPN	0	17.90	-
39	1	LPN	8	18.75	150.00
40	3	RN	0	19.80	-
41	4	LPN	8	19.55	156.40
42	1	RN	0	29.50	-
43	6	LPN	12	18.62	223.44
44	5	Nurse Supervisor	12	27.25	327.00
48	2	RN	8	19.60	156.80

Average Hourly Wage for LPNs $ 18.34

Status
LPN

Wage per Shift for RNs $ 1,323.24

Status	Hours per Shift
RN	>0

Count Day Shift (Code 1, 3, 5)   10

Shift Code	Hours per Shift
1	>0
3	>0
5	>0

Day-Nurse Supervisor   44

Shift Code	Status	Hours per Shift
1	Nurse Supervisor	>0
3	Nurse Supervisor	>0
5	Nurse Supervisor	>0

8C_Pediatric_Nurses_Firstname_Lastname

Figure 8.31
Project 8C—Pediatric Nurses

Objective 6
Use Database Functions

Recall that functions are predefined formulas that perform calculations by using specific values, called arguments. Database functions are identified by the letter D—each function starts with a D, for example, DSUM, DAVERAGE, DCOUNT. The initial D identifies to Excel that a database range will be used in the formula, rather than a single column or row of numbers.

Activity 8.17 Using the DAVERAGE Database Function

The *syntax*—arrangement of elements—for the majority of database functions is: DFunction Name(database, field, criteria), where *database* identifies the range of cells where the data is displayed, *field* is the field name that is to be considered, and *criteria* is the range of cells where the search criteria has been defined. The criteria is defined in a separate area on the worksheet, similar to the criteria range in an *Advanced Filter*. In this activity, you will use the DAVERAGE function to determine the average hourly wage for LPNs (Licensed Practical Nurses) in the pediatric wing of the hospital.

1 Start Excel. On the Standard toolbar, click the **Open** button 📷. Navigate to the folder where the student files for this textbook are stored. Locate and open **e08C_Pediatric_Nurses**.

2 From the **File** menu, click **Save As**. In the **Save As** dialog box, use the **Save in arrow** to navigate to the location where you are storing your files for this chapter. In the **File name** box, type **8C_Pediatric_Nurses_Firstname_Lastname** Click the **Save** button.

This worksheet lists the Emp Num, Shift Code, Status, Hours per Shift, Hourly Wage, and Wage per Shift for pediatric nurses who work on Mondays. The Wage per Shift field contains a formula that multiplies the Hours per Shift in column D by the Hourly Wage in column E. The number in the Shift Code field is a code for the shift; the codes are described in the shaded table in cells H3:I9. Not all nurses work on Mondays; thus, some rows indicate 0 hours per shift. See Figure 8.32.

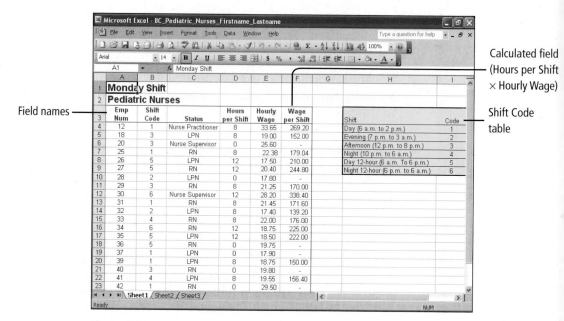

Calculated field
(Hours per Shift
× Hourly Wage)

Field names

Shift Code
table

Figure 8.32

3 Display the **Page Setup** dialog box and click the **Header/Footer tab**. Create a **Custom Footer** and in the **Left section**, add the **File name**.

4 Right-click any cell in **column A**, and from the shortcut menu click **Insert**. In the displayed **Insert** dialog box, click **Entire column**, and then click **OK**.

A new column is inserted to the left, and the data shifts to the right to column B.

5 In cell **A28**, type **Average Hourly Wage for LPNs** and press Tab. Widen **column A** to **26** (187 pixels).

Average Hourly Wage for LPNs will form the label for the function you will enter.

6 **Copy** cell **D3**, and then **Paste** it in cell **D28**.

Cell D28 will form the first cell in the criteria range for the DAVERAGE function, which must consist of at least two vertical cells. The top cell is the field name that is to be searched, and the cell immediately below it is the criteria the function will use in the search.

7 In cell **D29**, type **LPN** and press Tab.

The value—LPN—is the search criterion.

8 Click cell **B28**, and then to the left of the Formula Bar, click the **Insert Function** button [fx]. Alternatively, from the Insert menu, click Function.

Recall that you use the Insert Function dialog box to locate the function you want to use.

9 Click the **Or select a category arrow**, and from the displayed list, click **Database**. In the **Select a function** box, click **DAVERAGE**, and then click **OK**.

The Function Arguments dialog box for DAVERAGE displays. See Figure 8.33.

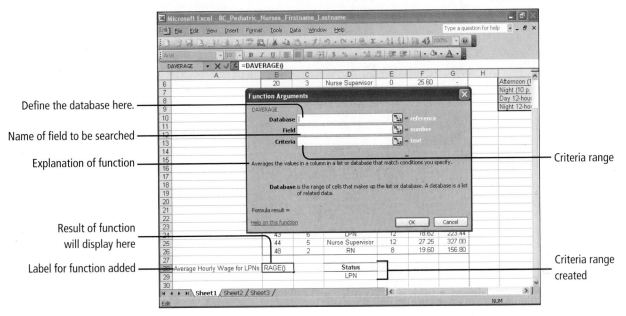

Define the database here.

Name of field to be searched

Explanation of function

Result of function will display here

Label for function added

Criteria range

Criteria range created

Figure 8.33

10 In the **Database** box, click the **Collapse dialog box** button, and then select the range **B3:G26**. Then, in the collapsed dialog box, click the **Expand dialog box** button.

The database range is defined and displays in the first argument box.

11 In the **Field** box, type **Hourly Wage** and press Tab.

The field or column to be averaged in the database is identified and the insertion point moves to the Criteria box. Note that Excel adds quotation marks around the Field name, which identifies it as a string of characters to use in the search.

12 With the insertion point in the **Criteria** box, select the range **D28:D29**—the criteria range that was previously defined.

The two cells in the criteria range will limit the average calculation to use only those records where *Status* is equal to *LPN*. Compare your screen with the dialog box in Figure 8.34.

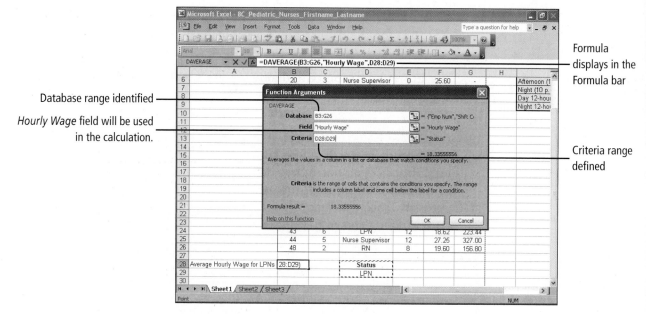

Database range identified

Hourly Wage field will be used in the calculation.

Formula displays in the Formula bar

Criteria range defined

Figure 8.34

13 Click **OK**. Format cell **B28** to **Currency Style**.

The result—$18.34—displays in cell B28. This is the average hourly wage for LPNs who work in the Pediatric wing of the hospital on Mondays.

14 On the Standard toolbar, click the **Save** button 🖫.

Activity 8.18 Using the DSUM Database Function

The DSUM function will sum a column of values in a database that is limited by criteria set for one or more cells. In this activity, you will sum the *Wage per Shift* for RNs who work in the Pediatric wing on Mondays.

1 In cell **A31**, type **Wage per Shift for RNs** and press Tab.

2 Select the range **D3:E3** and on the Standard toolbar, click the **Copy** button 🗐. Click cell **D31**, and then on the Standard toolbar, click the **Paste** button 🗐 ▾.

3 In cell **D32**, type **RN** and press Tab. In cell **E32**, type **>0** and then press Enter.

The *Status* will be limited to RN, and the *Hours per Shift* to those RNs who worked a number of hours greater than zero. This is a compound criteria—both conditions must be met for the record to be included in the calculation.

4 Click cell **B31**, and then type **=dsum(** to begin the formula for the DSUM function.

Recall that you can type the function arguments directly into the cell instead of using the *Function Arguments* dialog box. A ScreenTip displays listing the parts of the argument that need to be included. This guides you through the process of entering all of the arguments necessary for this function. See Figure 8.35.

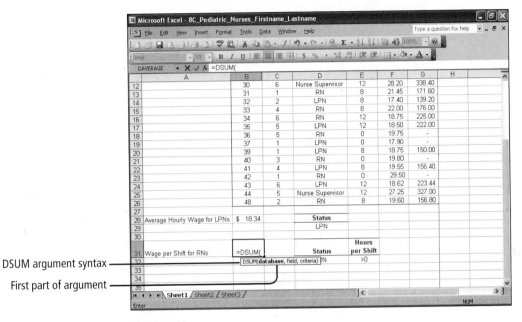

DSUM argument syntax —

First part of argument —

Figure 8.35

5 Select the range **B3:G26**, and then type **,** (a comma).

The database range is defined, and the *field* argument displays in bold. See Figure 8.36.

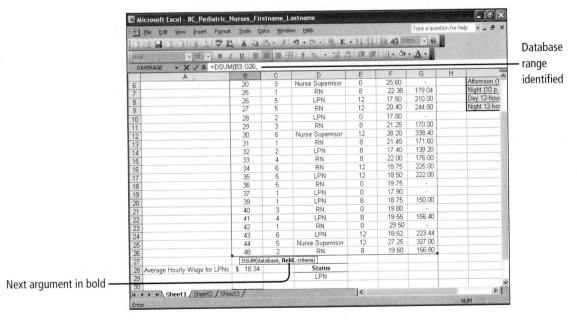

Database range identified

Next argument in bold —

Figure 8.36

6 Type **"Wage per Shift",** to enter the second part of the argument. Be sure to include the comma. You can look at the Formula Bar to see your typing and correct as necessary.

The field that you want to sum is the *Wage per Shift* field, so the field name is entered as the second argument. The quotation marks define this as a string of characters; it must match the field name exactly. The comma separates this argument from the next argument.

7 Type **d31:e32** and then press [Enter].

The criteria range is entered. Excel automatically adds a closing parenthesis. The final result of the formula—1323.24—displays in cell B31. The total cost to pay all the RNs who work in the Pediatric wing on Mondays is $1,323.24.

8 Click cell **B31**, on the Formatting toolbar click the **Currency Style** button $, and then widen **column B** slightly to display the figure. Examine the parts of the DSUM function on the Formula Bar. Compare your screen with Figure 8.37.

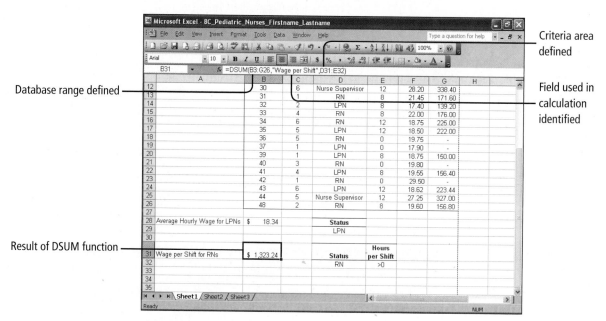

Figure 8.37

9 On the Standard toolbar, click the **Save** button.

Activity 8.19 Using DCOUNT

The DCOUNT function is similar to the COUNT function. Within a database list, it counts the number of occurrences of a specified condition—criterion. In this activity, you will count the number of nurses who work the day shift.

1 In cell **A34**, type **Count Day Shift (Code 1, 3, 5)** and press [Tab].

This forms the label for the function. Three shifts include daytime hours—Shift codes 1, 3, and 5—so all three will be included in the criteria range.

2 Click cell **C3**, hold down Ctrl, and click cell **E3**. On the Standard toolbar, click the **Copy** button. Click cell **D34**, and then on the Standard toolbar, click the **Paste** button.

3 In cell **D35**, type **1** and press Tab, type **>0** and press Enter.

The Shift Code value for the first daytime shift—1—is entered. To meet the conditions of this compound criteria, a nurse must be assigned to Shift 1 and work greater than zero hours.

4 In cell **D36**, type **3** and press Tab. In cell **E36**, type **>0** and press Enter.

The code for the second daytime shift is entered and functions as an *OR* criteria. Excel evaluates the criteria in row 35 and then will consider the criteria in row 36. If a record meets either condition it will be included in the calculation.

5 In cell **D37**, type **5** and press Tab. In cell **E37**, type **>0** and press Enter.

The code for the third daytime shift is entered; this also functions as an *OR* criteria. Thus, the calculation will count the number of nurses who worked more than zero hours in one of the three day shifts, whether it is Shift Code 1, 3, or 5.

6 Click cell **B34**. To the left of the Formula Bar, click the **Insert Function** button.

The Insert Function dialog box displays.

7 Click the **Or select a category arrow**, and then click **Database**. In the **Select a function** box, click **DCOUNT**, and then click **OK**.

The Function Arguments dialog box for DCOUNT displays.

8 In the **Database** box, click the **Collapse dialog box** button. Move the collapsed box to the lower portion of the screen. Scroll as necessary, and then select the range **B3:G26**. In the collapsed dialog box, click the **Expand dialog box** button.

The database range is defined and displays in the first argument box.

9 In the **Field** box, type **Emp Num** and then press Tab.

The *Emp Num* field will be counted.

10 In the **Criteria** box, click the **Collapse dialog box** button, scroll as necessary, and then select the range **D34:E37**—the criteria area that was previously defined. In the collapsed dialog box, click the **Expand dialog box** button.

The criteria area is defined. Compare your dialog box with Figure 8.38.

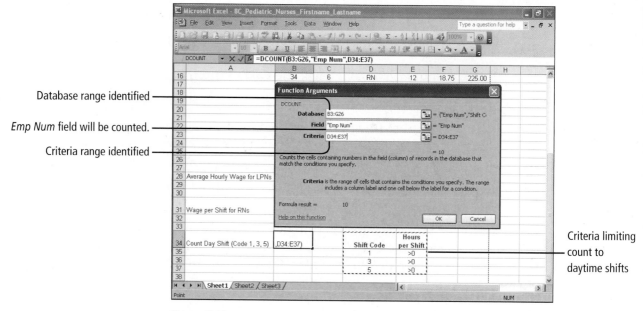

On the left side of the figure:
- Database range identified
- *Emp Num* field will be counted.
- Criteria range identified

On the right side of the figure:
- Criteria limiting count to daytime shifts

Figure 8.38

11 Click **OK**.

The result—10—displays in cell B34. This is the number of nurses assigned to work the day shift in the pediatric wing of the hospital on Mondays.

12 On the Standard toolbar, click the **Save** button.

Activity 8.20 Using DGET

The DGET function extracts from your data table a single record that matches the conditions you specify. If more than one record matches the conditions, DGET returns the #NUM! error code. If no record matches the conditions, DGET returns the #VALUE! error code.

1 In cell **A39**, type **Day-Nurse Supervisor** and press Tab.

This forms the label for the function, which will determine the employee number for the day shift nurse supervisor.

2 Copy the range **C3:E3**, and then paste it in cell **D39**. Widen **column E** to **15** (110 pixels).

3 In cell **D40**, type **1** and press Tab. In cell **E40**, type **Nurse Supervisor** and press Tab. In cell **F40**, type **>0** and then press Enter.

This criteria will search for an employee working Shift 1 with the status of *Nurse Supervisor*. There is only one supervisor assigned to the day shift—the DGET function extracts a single record that matches the conditions you specify.

4 In cell **D41**, type **3** and press Tab. In cell **E41**, type **Nurse Supervisor** and press Tab. In cell **F41**, type **>0** and press Enter.

5 Create a third criteria beginning in cell **D42** for a Nurse Supervisor who may be scheduled to Shift 5—the third daytime shift option.

The criteria for Shifts 3 and 5 is entered in rows 41 and 42.

6. Click cell **B39**, and display the **Insert Function** dialog box.

7. Be sure the **Or select a category** box displays **Database**. In the **Select a function** box, click **DGET**, and then click **OK**.

The Function Arguments box for DGET displays.

8. In the **Database box**, click the **Collapse dialog box** button, scroll as necessary, and then select the range **B3:G26**. In the collapsed dialog box, click the **Expand dialog box** button.

The database range is defined and displays in the first argument box.

9. In the **Field** box, type **Emp Num** and then press Tab.

Excel will *get*—locate—the *Emp Num* of the nurse who meets the criteria.

10. In the **Criteria** box, click the **Collapse dialog box** button, scroll as necessary, and then select the range **D39:F42**. In the collapsed box, click the **Expand dialog box** button.

The criteria range is defined. Compare your dialog box with Figure 8.39.

Database range identified —

Emp Num will be identified —

Criteria area identified —

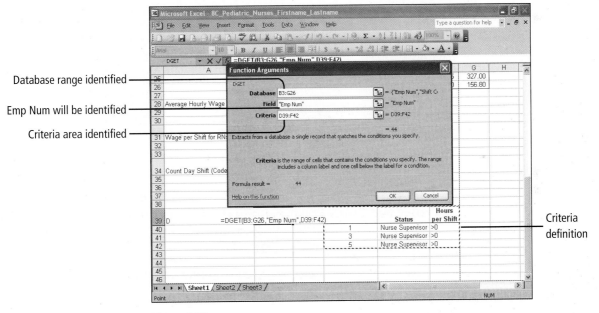

Criteria definition

Figure 8.39

11. Click **OK**.

The result—44—displays in cell B39. This is the *Employee Number* of the Nurse Supervisor assigned to work the day shift on Monday in the pediatric wing of the hospital.

12. On the Standard toolbar, click the **Print Preview** button. On the Print Preview toolbar, click the **Page Break Preview** button.

Recall that you can adjust a page break by using the *Page Break Preview*.

13 If the **Welcome** dialog box displays, click **OK**. Then drag the vertical break line from the right edge of **column F** to the right edge of **column G**.

Changing the vertical page break will enable you to print everything except the Shift Code table on the first page.

14 On the Standard toolbar, click the **Print Preview** button again to ensure that the database table and the results of the four database functions will print on one page. Compare your screen with Figure 8.40.

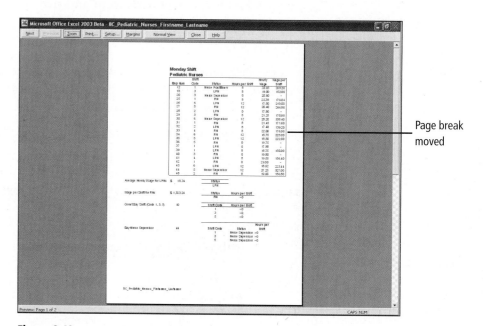

Page break moved

Figure 8.40

15 On the Print Preview toolbar, click the **Normal View** button to close the Page Break Preview. From the **File** menu click **Print**. In the **Print** dialog box, under **Print range**, in the **From** box type **1** and then in the **To** box type **1**. Click **OK**.

16 On the Standard toolbar, click the **Save** button . Close the workbook, and then close Excel.

End You have completed Project 8C

Summary

In this chapter, you used Excel to manage records that are typically found in a database. Data refers to facts about people, events, things, or ideas. A database is a collection of data related to a particular topic or purpose. Data organized in a useful manner is called information. A database is organized in a column and row structure often referred to as a table.

The first row in a database table contains the field names, and each subsequent row contains records. A record is all of the related information about a single person, event, or thing. A field is a category of information that describes the records. Each column contains a category of information.

To populate a database with records, you can enter records one at a time using a form that is based on the field names that have been defined in the database. You can also import data using the *Import External Data* command found on the Data menu. Most of the commands that are used with a database are found on the Data menu. You practiced sorting records using the *Sort Ascending* and *Sort Descending* buttons found on the Standard toolbar; by using the Sort dialog box, you can sort up to three fields. You practiced using the *Data Form* to update records and add new records.

To view only the records that meet certain conditions, you can use AutoFilter, a customized AutoFilter or the Advanced Filter. With AutoFilter, the records displayed must match the conditions set on one or more fields. A customized AutoFilter allows you to add comparison criteria on multiple fields, and the Advanced Filter enables you to list the records that match the criteria in a different area of the worksheet known as the *extract area*.

Database records can be subtotaled based on groups of data. You created subtotals for a database and practiced using the outline to display and hide detail information about the database.

Finally, you practiced using database functions to perform calculations on a database range that was limited by conditions that you defined in another area of the worksheet.

In This Chapter You Practiced How To

- Import Data into Excel
- Sort Data
- Manage Data Using a Data Form
- Use AutoFilter
- Analyze Data with Excel Database Tools
- Use Database Functions

Matching Match each term in the second column with its correct definition in the first column by writing the letter of the term on the blank line in front of the correct definition.

_____ **1.** A database function that locates one record in a database that meets a set of conditions.

_____ **2.** A database function that determines how many records match one or more conditions.

_____ **3.** The symbol inserted in a criterion to determine if a value is greater than a specific amount.

_____ **4.** The term used for conditions that must be matched for the record to be included in the search results.

_____ **5.** All of the related information about a single person, thing, idea, or event that displays in a row in a database.

_____ **6.** A command that assists in filtering a range by placing arrows to the right of column labels from which you can display a list of possible fields. Also provides a quick way to limit records based on values that must be matched in one or more columns.

_____ **7.** The database function that finds a total of values in one column based on criteria that are applied to other fields in a database.

_____ **8.** The asterisk character (*) used to search a field when you are uncertain of the exact value or when you want to widen the search to include more records.

_____ **9.** A form created by Excel based on the field names in the database and used to enter, change, or locate a record.

_____ **10.** A category of data that describes records and that displays in a column in a database.

_____ **11.** The equal sign (=), the greater than sign (>), or the less than sign (<) used singly or in combinations to compare two values.

_____ **12.** A collection of data related to a particular topic or purpose.

_____ **13.** Data that has been organized in a useful manner.

_____ **14.** Information stored in a format of rows and columns.

_____ **15.** A range that displays only the records that meet the criteria.

A >

B AutoFilter

C Comparison operators

D Criteria

E Data form

F Database

G DCOUNT

H DGET

I DSUM

J Field

K Filtered range

L Information

M Record

N Table

O Wildcard

Fill in the Blank Write the correct answer in the space provided.

1. Column headings in a database in Excel are referred to as

   _____.

2. Bringing data in from an external data source is known as

   _____.

3. The first field that is used for sorting in the Sort dialog box is

   known as the _____ sort key.

4. In Excel, a database may be referred to as a _____ or

   a _____.

5. To sort on a field in alphabetical order, click the

   _____ button.

6. To sort on multiple fields, use the Sort command found on the

   _____ menu.

7. Symbols such as > or < are two examples of symbols that are

   known as _____.

8. When more than one criteria must be met, it is known as a

   _____ criteria.

9. If criteria are listed in more than one row in a database

   function, the criteria on the second or third row are known

   as _____ criteria.

10. When you use Advanced Filter, you can elect to have the results

    displayed in a different part of the worksheet known as the

    _____ area.

Project 8D — Facilities

Objectives: *Import Data into Excel, Sort Data, Manage Data Using a Data Form, and Use AutoFilter.*

Gerald Hernandez, Facilities Manager at the University Medical Center, wants to set up a database in Excel to manage the records of his staff. In this project, you will import data from Access, sort the records, and manage the records by using a data form. Your completed worksheet will look similar to the one shown in Figure 8.41. You will save your workbook as *8D_Facilities_Firstname_Lastname*.

Facilities Staff Records

Classification	Last Name	First Name	Address1	Address2	City	State	Postal Code	Phone	Emp Num
Facilities Service	Bryant	Jeffery	1501 Bahia Dr.		Coral Springs	FL	33077	954-555-0000	24
Facilities Service	Carrasco	Tomas	1315 Sand Creek Way	#1650	Hialeah	FL	33013	305-555-0002	11
Facilities Service	Carter	Ted	20 S. 75th Ave.	#B	Hialeah	FL	33013	954-555-0076	30
Facilities Service	Holcomb	Tyrone	3266 Osprey Links Dr.	#15	Hialeah	FL	33010	305-555-0010	17
Facilities Service	Mauer	Vince	98510 Glen Cove Cir.		Coral Springs	FL	33075	954-555-0005	20
Maintenance	Miller	Anthony	3650 Gatlin Ave.		Ft. Lauderdale	FL	33330	754-555-0001	14
Facilities Service	Shoenfeld	Edward	4210 Chalfont St.		Hialeah	FL	33010	305-555-0104	28
Maintenance	De La Hoya	Naomi	1042 Mancha Real Dr.		Winter Park	FL	32790	407-555-0103	27
Maintenance	Feinberg	Sid	8 Tropic Bay Ct.		Miami	FL	33150	305-555-0033	22
Maintenance	Martinez	Enrique	252 Conway St.		Ft. Lauderdale	FL	33345	754-555-0007	23
Maintenance	Vogan	Corey	4180 Robala Dr. East		Ft. Lauderdale	FL	33394	754-555-0008	21
Maintenance	Weber	Harry	1057 Kislin Pl.		Miami	FL	33150	305-555-0030	19
Facilities Service	Mayfield	James	1243 Egret Drive		Ft. Lauderdale	FL	33345	754-555-0110	30

8D_Facilities_Firstname_Lastname

Figure 8.41

(Project 8D–Facilities continues on the next page)

(Project 8D–Facilities continued)

1. Start Excel. Close the **Getting Started** task pane. Click cell **A3**. From the **Data** menu, point to **Import External Data**, and then click **Import Data**.

2. Use the **Look in** box to navigate to the folder where the student files for this chapter are stored. Be sure that the **Files of type** box displays *All Data Sources*. Click the Access file **e08D_Facilities** and click the **Open** button.

3. In dialog box that displays, click **OK** to import the data to cell A3 of the existing worksheet.

4. In cell **A2**, type **Facilities Staff Records** and then press Enter. Select cell **A2** and format it as **Bold**, and change the **Font Size** to **14** pt. Select the range **A3:J3**. On the Formatting toolbar, click the **Borders button arrow**, and then click the **Outside Borders** button. Select **column H**—*Postal Code*—and on the Formatting toolbar, click the **Center** button.

5. Display the **Page Setup** dialog box, and then click the **Header/Footer tab**. Create a **Custom Footer**, and in the **Left section**, add the **File name**. From the **File** menu, click **Save As**. In the **Save As** dialog box, use the **Save in arrow** to navigate to the folder where you are storing your files. In the **File name** box, type 8D_Facilities_Firstname_Lastname and then click **Save**.

6. Examine the table, and note that it is currently sorted by the last field displayed—*Emp Num*. Click in cell **A3**. From the **Data** menu, click **Sort**. In the **Sort** dialog box, click the **Sort by arrow**, and from the displayed list click **Classification**. Click the first **Then by arrow**, and then click **Last Name**. Click the second **Then by arrow**, and then click **First Name**. Be sure the **Ascending** option button is selected for all three sorts and that the **Header row** option button is selected. Click **OK**.

7. Double-click the **Sheet 1 tab** and type **Facilities Staff** to rename the sheet. Click cell **A3**. From the **Data** menu, click **Form**. In the displayed **Facilities Staff** form, click the **Criteria** button. In the **Last Name** box type **Miller** and then click **Find Next**. The record for Anthony Miller displays in the form.

8. In the **Classification** box, select **Facilities Service**, type **Maintenance** and then press Enter. The classification for Anthony Miller is changed to *Maintenance*, and the change also takes place in the data table in the worksheet. The next record in the table—*Shoenfeld*—displays in the form.

(Project 8D–Facilities continues on the next page)

(Project 8D—Facilities continued)

9. In the **Facilities Staff** form, click the **New** button. Enter the new record shown below, using the ⌜Tab⌟ key to move from field to field.

Classification	**Facilities Service**
Last Name	**Mayfield**
First Name	**James**
Address1	**1243 Egret Drive**
Address2	
City	**Ft. Lauderdale**
State	**FL**
Postal Code	**33345**
Phone	**754-555-0110**
Emp Num	**30**

10. Click the **Close** button to add the record and close the form. From the **Data** menu, point to **Filter**, and then click **AutoFilter**. In cell **A3**, click the **Classification arrow**, and then click **(Custom...)**. In the **Custom AutoFilter** dialog box, under **Classification**, be sure **equals** displays. In the box to the right, display the list, and then click **Facilities Service**. Click the **OR** button. In the next set of boxes, display **equals** in the left box, and **Maintenance** in the right box. Click **OK**.

11. From the **File** menu, click **Page Setup**. In the **Page Setup** dialog box, click the **Page tab**, and then click **Landscape**. Click the **Margins tab**, and center the worksheet **Horizontally** on the page. Click the **Print Preview** button, and then compare your screen with Figure 8.41. Click the **Print** button, and then click **OK** to print the worksheet.

12. On the Standard toolbar, click the **Save** button, and then close the file.

End You have completed Project 8D

Project 8E — Schedule

Objectives: *Sort Data and Analyze Data with Excel Database Tools.*

In this project, you will use the sorting and subtotal capabilities of Excel to analyze schedules for the housekeeping staff. This information is needed for efficient scheduling and to ensure adequate coverage. Typically, five to six people are scheduled during the day and afternoon shifts, and two people are scheduled during the night shift. Your completed worksheet will look similar to the one shown in Figure 8.42. You will save your workbook as *8E_Schedule_Firstname_Lastname.*

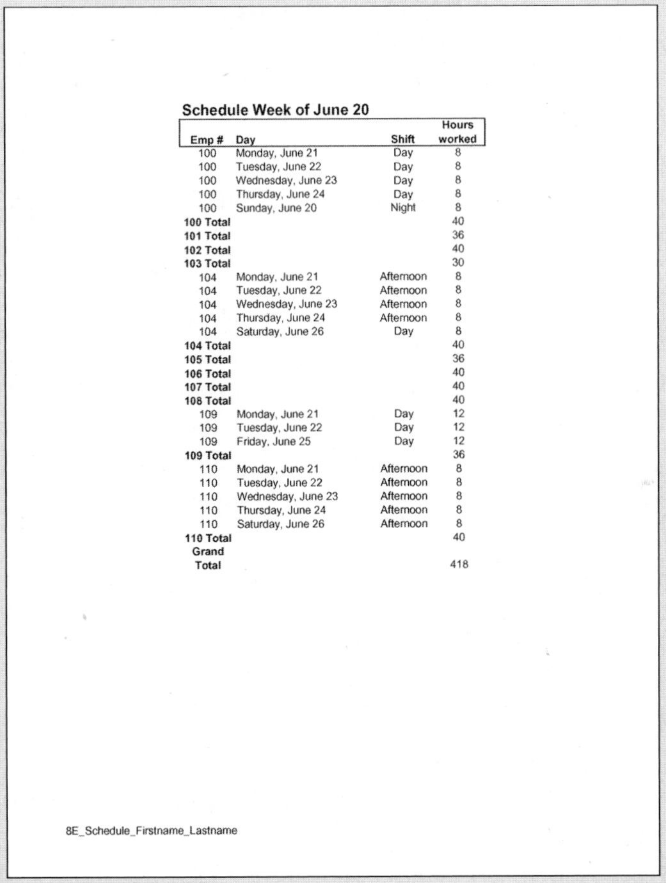

Schedule Week of June 20

Emp #	Day	Shift	Hours worked
100	Monday, June 21	Day	8
100	Tuesday, June 22	Day	8
100	Wednesday, June 23	Day	8
100	Thursday, June 24	Day	8
100	Sunday, June 20	Night	8
100 Total			40
101 Total			36
102 Total			40
103 Total			30
104	Monday, June 21	Afternoon	8
104	Tuesday, June 22	Afternoon	8
104	Wednesday, June 23	Afternoon	8
104	Thursday, June 24	Afternoon	8
104	Saturday, June 26	Day	8
104 Total			40
105 Total			36
106 Total			40
107 Total			40
108 Total			40
109	Monday, June 21	Day	12
109	Tuesday, June 22	Day	12
109	Friday, June 25	Day	12
109 Total			36
110	Monday, June 21	Afternoon	8
110	Tuesday, June 22	Afternoon	8
110	Wednesday, June 23	Afternoon	8
110	Thursday, June 24	Afternoon	8
110	Saturday, June 26	Afternoon	8
110 Total			40
Grand Total			418

8E_Schedule_Firstname_Lastname

Figure 8.42

(Project 8E–Schedule continues on the next page)

(Project 8E–Schedule continued)

1. Start Excel. On the Standard toolbar, click the **Open** button and navigate to the location where the student files for this textbook are stored. Locate and open **e08E_Schedule**.

2. Display the **Page Setup** dialog box and click the **Header/Footer tab**. Create a **Custom Footer**, and in the **Left section**, add the **File name**. From the **File** menu, click **Save As**. In the **Save As** dialog box, use the **Save in arrow** to navigate to the folder where you are storing your files for this chapter. In the **File name** box, type **8E_Schedule_Firstname_Lastname** and then click **Save**.

3. Click cell **A3**. From the **Data** menu, click **Sort**. In the displayed dialog box, click the **Sort by arrow**, and then click **Day**. Click the first **Then by arrow**, and then click **Shift**. Click the second **Then by arrow**, and then click **Emp #**. Be sure the **Ascending** option button is selected for all three sorts and that the **Header row** option button is selected. Click **OK**.

The data is sorted starting on Sunday, June 20—*Day*. Within the same day, the data is further sorted alphabetically by *Shift*. Within the same day and shift, the data is further sorted by *Emp #*.

4. From the **Data** menu, click **Subtotals**. In the **Subtotal** dialog box, click the **At each change in arrow**, and then click **Day**. Click the **Use function arrow**, and then click **Sum**. Under **Add subtotal to**, be sure only the **Hours worked** check box is selected. Click **OK**. A subtotal of the number of hours worked each day by all employees is added to the worksheet, and the gray outline bar is added to the left side of the workbook.

5. In the outline area to the left of the worksheet, click the **Level 2 button** at the top of the outline. Recall that you can collapse the details and display only the subtotals by group. The total hours worked each day for all shifts is displayed. It ranges from 42 hours on Sunday to 84 hours on Friday.

6. Display the **Page Setup** dialog box, and center the worksheet **Horizontally** on the page. Click the **Print** button, and then click **OK**. Now you have a copy of the total hours scheduled by day of the week.

7. From the **Data** menu, click **Subtotals**, and then at the bottom of the displayed dialog box, click **Remove All**. Recall that subtotals need to be removed before you start a new subtotal process.

8. Click cell **A3**, and from the **Data** menu click **Sort**. In the **Sort** dialog box, click the **Sort by arrow** and click **Emp #**. Click the first **Then by arrow**, and then click **Shift**. Click the second **Then by arrow**, and click **(none)**. Be sure both sorts will be in **Ascending** order, and then click **OK**.

(Project 8E–Schedule continues on the next page)

(Project 8E–Schedule continued)

9. From the **Data** menu, click **Subtotals**. In the **Subtotal** dialog box, click the **At each change in arrow**, and then click **Emp #**. Click the **Use Function arrow**, and then click **Sum**. Under **Add subtotal to**, be sure only the **Hours worked** check box is selected. Click **OK**.

10. At the top of the outline area, click the **Level 2** button. You can see that four employees are scheduled to work over 40 hours during the week—*Emp* # 100, 104, 109, and 110. At the top of the outline area, click the **Level 3** button to redisplay all of the rows.

11. To adjust the schedule, some of the employee's hours will be decreased. Select **row 8**, and then from the **Edit** menu, click **Delete**. The record for *Emp* # 100 to work on Friday has been deleted, and the hours for this employee are adjusted to 40.

12. Follow the same procedure to delete the hours for the employees listed below.

Emp #	Day	Shift	Hours
104	Friday, June 25	Afternoon	8
109	Wednesday, June 23	Afternoon	12
110	Friday, June 25	Afternoon	8

13. Click the **collapse** button next to the employee total for employee numbers *101, 102, 103, 105, 106, 107,* and *108*—everyone except the employees whose hours were changed. Compare your screen with Figure 8.42.

14. On the Standard toolbar, click the **Save** button, and then click the **Print Preview** button to see how the worksheet will look when it is printed. On the Print Preview toolbar, click the **Print** button, and then click **OK**. Close the file, and then close Excel, saving changes if prompted to do so.

End You have completed Project 8E

Project 8F — Facilities Pay

Objective: *Use Database Functions.*

In this project, you will use a worksheet that contains payroll information for the facilities staff. You will calculate the average pay and count how many employees have worked for the hospital for over five years. Your completed worksheet will look similar to the one shown in Figure 8.43. You will save your workbook as *8F_Facilities_Pay_Firstname_Lastname*.

Facilities Payroll Data

Emp #	Hourly Rate	Classification	Hire Date	Supervisor	Shift
10	$ 12.00	Housekeeping	6/22/2000	Juarez	Night
11	$ 13.50	Facilities Service	10/15/2002	Johnson	Day
12	$ 12.00	Housekeeping	5/5/2000	Juarez	Day
13	$ 11.25	Housekeeping	5/12/2002	Juarez	Afternoon
14	$ 14.00	Facilities Service	8/12/1999	Johnson	Afternoon
15	$ 13.00	Laundry	1/15/2000	Juarez	Day
16	$ 11.00	Housekeeping	1/18/2002	Juarez	Afternoon
17	$ 15.50	Facilities Service	3/8/2003	Johnson	Night
18	$ 11.50	Housekeeping	6/1/1995	Juarez	Day
19	$ 15.00	Maintenance	12/31/1999	Ackerman	Night
20	$ 13.00	Facilities Service	11/1/2003	Johnson	Night
21	$ 18.00	Maintenance	7/21/1998	Ackerman	Day
22	$ 18.00	Maintenance	2/15/2002	Ackerman	Night
23	$ 11.00	Maintenance	4/22/1996	Ackerman	Day
24	$ 13.25	Facilities Service	9/7/1998	Johnson	Day
25	$ 11.25	Housekeeping	3/4/2000	Juarez	Night
26	$ 11.00	Laundry	5/23/2003	Juarez	Day
27	$ 10.50	Maintenance	8/1/1998	Ackerman	Afternoon
28	$ 15.00	Facilities Service	5/12/2002	Johnson	Afternoon
29	$ 11.00	Laundry	7/11/2003	Juarez	Day
30	$ 15.50	Facilities Service	7/3/1998	Johnson	Day

Average hourly wage for Housekeeping		Classification
	$ 11.50	Housekeeping

Number of employees hired prior to 1/1/99		Hire Date
	6	<1/1/99

8F_Facilities_Pay_Firstname_Lastname

Figure 8.43

1. On the Standard toolbar, click the **Open** button. Navigate to the location where the student files for this textbook are stored. Locate and open **e08F_Facilities_Pay**. From the **File** menu, click **Save As**. In the **Save As** dialog box, navigate to the location where you are storing your files for this chapter. In the **File name** box, type **8F_Facilities_Pay_Firstname_Lastname** Click the **Save** button.

(**Project 8F–Facilities Pay** continues on the next page)

(Project 8F–Facilities Pay continued)

2. In cell **A26**, type **Average hourly wage for Housekeeping** and then press Enter. In cell **E26**, type **Classification** and in cell **E27** type **Housekeeping**

This will form the criteria range, which must be arranged vertically with the field name you want to examine in one cell and the condition in the cell below the field name.

3. Click cell **C27**. To the left of the Formula Bar, click the **Insert Function** button. Click the **Or select a category arrow** and click **Database**. Under **Select a function**, click **DAVERAGE**, and then click **OK**.

4. In the **Database** box, click the **Collapse dialog box** button, and then select the range **A3:F24**. In the collapsed dialog box, click the **Expand dialog box** button. In the **Field** box, type **Hourly Rate** and press Tab. With the **Criteria** box active, select the range **E26:E27**—the criteria range that was previously defined. Click **OK**. With cell **C27** as the active cell, on the Formatting toolbar, click the **Currency Style** button.

The result—*$11.50*—is the average hourly rate for employees with the classification of *Housekeeping*.

5. In cell **A29**, type **Number of employees hired prior to 1/1/99** and press Tab four times. In cell **E29**, type **Hire Date** and then in cell **E30** type **<1/1/99**

You can use a comparison operator with a date to locate dates that are before—less than—or after—greater than—the target date.

6. Click cell **C30** and display the **Insert Function** dialog box. In the **Database** category, under **Select a function**, click **DCOUNT**, and then click **OK**.

7. In the **Database** box, click the **Collapse dialog box** button, and then select the range **A3:F24**. Expand the dialog box. In the **Field** box, type **Emp #** and then press Tab. With the **Criteria** box active, select the range **E29:E30**—the criteria range that was previously defined. Click **OK**.

The result—*6*—is the number of employees hired prior to January 1, 1999.

8. Display the **Page Setup** dialog box and click the **Header/Footer tab**. Create a **Custom Footer**, and in the **Left section**, add the **File name**. Center the worksheet **Horizontally** on the page. Click the **Print Preview** button to see how the worksheet will display when printed. Compare your worksheet with Figure 8.43. **Print** the worksheet.

9. On the Standard toolbar, click the **Save** button, and then close your file.

End You have completed Project 8F

Project 8G—Physicians

Objectives: *Import Data into Excel, Sort Data, Manage Data Using a Data Form, and Use AutoFilter.*

In this project, you will import records into Excel for physicians who have volunteered to be part of an outreach program that will establish satellite clinics in various communities. You will also sort, update, and filter the records. Your completed worksheet will look similar to the one shown in Figure 8.44. You will save your workbook as *8G_Physicians_Firstname_Lastname*.

Physician Volunteers

Phy Num	First Name	Last Name	Dept	Addr1	Addr2	City	State	Postal Code	Phone
PHY129	Deepa	Subramani	Geriatrics	1516 NW 67th St.	#1560	Miami	FL	33143	305-555-0111
PHY641	Vivian	Marsh	Pediatrics	3920 Casa Aloma Way		Miami	FL	33150	305-555-0123
PHY539	Sharon	Brougher	Pediatrics	2314 Highland Lake Road		Miami	FL	33145	305-555-0109

8G_Physicians_Firstname_Lastname

Figure 8.44

1. Open a new blank worksheet, and click cell **A3**. From the **Data** menu, point to **Import External Data**, click **Import Data**, and display the **Select Data Source** dialog box. Use the **Look in** box to navigate to the folder where the student files for this chapter are stored. Click the Access file **e08G_Physicians**, and then click the **Open** button. In the **Import Data** dialog box, click **OK** to import the data beginning in cell A3 of the existing worksheet.

2. In cell **A2**, type **Physician Volunteers** and then press `Enter`. Select cell **A2**, apply **Bold**, change the **Font Size** to **14**, and then change the **Font Color** to **Plum**. Select the range **A3:J3**, and then change the **Font Color** to **Plum**. Display the **Format Cells** dialog box, click the **Border tab**, change the **Line Color** to **Plum**, and then add an **Outline** border. Click cell **I3**, and then change *Zip* to **Postal Code** Widen the column to display the title, and then center the postal codes in the column.

(Project 8G–Physicians continues on the next page)

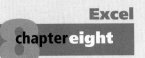
(Project 8G–Physicians continued)

3. From the **Page Setup** dialog box, create a **Custom Footer**, and then in the **Left section**, add the **File name**. From the **File** menu, click **Save As**. Navigate to the folder where you are storing your files and save the file as **8G_Physicians_Firstname_Lastname**

4. Click anywhere in the data. From the **Data** menu, display the **Sort** dialog box. Sort by **Dept**, and then by **Last Name**. Click **OK**.

5. Rename the **Sheet 1 tab** as **Volunteers** and then click cell **A3**. From the **Data** menu, click **Form**. In the displayed **Volunteers** form, click the **Criteria** button. In the **Dept** box, type **Pediatrics** and then click **Find Next**. Click **Find Next** again as needed to determine how many doctors from Pediatrics have volunteered—two.

6. Click the **New** button, and then add the following record:

Phy Num	**PHY539**
First Name	**Sharon**
Last Name	**Brougher**
Dept	**Pediatrics**
Addr1	**2314 Highland Lake Road**
Addr2	
City	**Miami**
State	**FL**
Postal Code	**33145**
Phone	**305-555-0109**

   Click the **Close** button at the bottom of the form. There are now three volunteers from Pediatrics.

7. From the **Data** menu, display the **AutoFilter arrows**. In cell **G3**, click the **City arrow**, and then click **Miami**. In cell **D3**, click the **Dept arrow**, and then click **(Custom...)**. In the **Custom AutoFilter** dialog box, create a filter that will match—**equals—Geriatrics Or Pediatrics**. Click **OK**. (Hint: You must use both sets of boxes and click the *OR* operator.) Three records meet the criteria.

8. From the **File** menu, click **Page Setup**. In the **Page Setup** dialog box, click the **Page tab**, and then click **Landscape**. Click the **Print Preview** button, and then compare your screen with Figure 8.44. Click the **Print** button, and then click **OK** to print the worksheet.

9. On the Standard toolbar, click the **Save** button, and then close the file.

End You have completed Project 8G ——————

Project 8H—Activity

Objectives: *Sort Data and Analyze Data with Excel Database Tools.*

In this project, you will use a worksheet that shows the number of patients seen by each physician and the average number of hours spent with each patient. The hours are indicated as a decimal unit that represents a portion of an hour. This information is used for various efficiency studies, allocation of resources, and tracking trends. Your completed worksheet will look similar to the one shown in Figure 8.45. You will save your workbook as *8H_Activity_Firstname_Lastname.*

Criteria Range

Physican Number	Dept	Number of Patients Seen	Average Hrs/ Patient	Total Patient Hours
		>=200	<=.50	

June Patient Activity

Physican Number	Dept	Number of Patients Seen	Average Hrs/ Patient	Total Patient Hours
PHY533	Cardiology	230	0.63	143.75
PHY148	Cardiology	200	0.75	150.00
PHY541	Cardiology	120	1.00	120.00
	Cardiology Total	550		413.75
PHY889	General Surgery	100	1.25	125.00
PHY130	General Surgery	80	1.50	120.00
	General Surgery Total	180		245.00
PHY545	Geriatrics	476	0.28	130.90
PHY353	Geriatrics	475	0.29	136.56
PHY129	Geriatrics	240	0.50	120.00
	Geriatrics Total	1191		387.46
PHY156	Obstetrics	230	0.63	143.75
PHY335	Obstetrics	230	0.57	129.95
PHY451	Obstetrics	200	0.75	150.00
	Obstetrics Total	660		423.70
PHY539	Pediatrics	300	0.33	99.00
PHY146	Pediatrics	290	0.55	159.50
PHY641	Pediatrics	240	0.60	144.00
	Pediatrics Total	830		402.50
PHY342	Radiology	460	0.28	126.50
PHY145	Radiology	450	0.30	135.00
	Radiology Total	910		261.50
	Grand Total	4321		2133.91

Extract

Physican Number	Dept	Number of Patients Seen	Average Hrs/ Patient	Total Patient Hours
PHY545	Geriatrics	476	0.28	130.90
PHY353	Geriatrics	475	0.29	136.56
PHY129	Geriatrics	240	0.50	120.00
PHY539	Pediatrics	300	0.33	99.00
PHY342	Radiology	460	0.28	126.50
PHY145	Radiology	450	0.30	135.00

8H_Activity_Firstname_Lastname

Figure 8.45

1. Start Excel. On the Standard toolbar, click the **Open** button. Navigate to the location where the student files for this textbook are stored. Locate and open the file **e08H_Activity**. Save the file in your folder using the name **8H_Activity_Firstname_Lastname**

2. Take a moment to examine the worksheet. Column D represents the portion of an hour that is spent with each patient on average. For example, PHY129 spends, on average, 0.50 of an hour or 30 minutes with each patient.

(Project 8H–Activity continues on the next page)

(Project 8H–Activity continued)

3. Click cell **E7**, and then type **Total Patient Hours** Click cell **D7**, click the **Format Painter** button, and then click cell **E7**. Click cell **E8** and use the point-and-click method to create a formula that multiplies the number of patients seen by the average hours per patient; **=C8*D8** Copy the formula down the column to cell **E23**. From the **Format Cells** dialog box, format the results in this column to the **Number** format with **2 decimals**.

4. Select the range **A7:E23**. In the **Name Box**, type **Database** and then press Enter. Click cell **A7**, and from the **Data** menu, display the **Sort** dialog box. Sort by **Dept** in **Ascending** order, and then by **Number of Patients Seen** in **Descending** order. The result is that within each department, the table is sorted by *Number of Patients Seen*; the physician who has seen the most patients is listed first.

5. Select the range **A6:E7**, click the **Copy** button, click cell **A1**, and then click the **Paste** button. Click cell **A1**, and then type **Criteria Range** Select the range **A2:E3**, in the **Name Box** type **Criteria** and then press Enter.

6. In cell **C3** type **>=200** and in cell **D3** type **<=0.50** Click in the database table. From the **Data** menu, point to **Filter**, and then click **Advanced Filter**. In the **Advanced Filter** dialog box, in the **List range** box, verify that the database range—**A7:E23**—is correctly displayed. In the **Criteria range** box, be sure the criteria range—**A2:E3**—is correctly displayed, and then click **OK**. Your result is a list of physicians who, during the month of June, saw 200 or more patients and averaged one half-hour (0.50) or less per patient.

7. **Copy** the range **A1:E2**, and then **Paste** it in cell **A25**. Click cell **A25**, and then type **Extract** Select the range **A26:E27**, and in the **Name Box**, type **Extract** and press Enter. Click cell **A7**, display the **Data** menu, point to **Filter**, and then click **Show All** to redisplay the records before applying the next filter.

8. From the **Data** menu, display the **Advanced Filter** dialog box again. Select the **Copy to another location** option button. Verify that the **Copy to** box displays the **Extract** range—**A26:E27**—and then click **OK**. In the message box, click **Yes** to complete the copy. Within the *Extract* area, a list of physicians who have seen 200 or more patients, and whose average time spent with a patient is less than or equal to one-half hour, displays. In this format, you still have the complete database displayed above.

(Project 8H–Activity continues on the next page)

(Project 8H–Activity continued)

9. Be sure cell **A7** is the active cell. From the **Data** menu, click **Subtotals**. In the **Subtotal** dialog box, click the **At each change in arrow**, and then click **Dept**. Click the **Use function arrow**, and then click **Sum**. Under **Add subtotal to**, be sure the **Number of Patients Seen** and **Total Patient Hours** check boxes are selected. Click **OK**. The total number of patients seen and the total number of patient contact hours per department displays, and the outline area is created. Widen **column B** if necessary to fully display the total labels.

10. From the **Page Setup** dialog box, create a **Custom Footer**, and in the **Left section**, add the **File name**. On the **Margins tab**, center the page **Horizontally**. Click the **Print Preview** button to verify that the worksheet will print on one page. Compare your screen with Figure 8.45.

11. **Print** the worksheet, **Save** the changes, and then close your file.

End You have completed Project 8H ——————————————

Project 8I — Billing

Objectives: *Analyze Data with Excel Database Tools and Use Database Functions.*

In this project, you will work with a Billing Per Patient worksheet to analyze the data using the database functions. Your completed worksheet will look similar to the one shown in Figure 8.46. You will save your project as *8I_Billing_Firstname_Lastname.*

1. On the Standard toolbar, click the **Open** button. Navigate to the location where the student files for this textbook are stored. Locate and open **e08I_Billing**. Take a moment to examine the data in the worksheet. A *Standard Billing Unit* represents a portion of an hour and is displayed as a decimal. Therefore, 0.50 is one-half hour or 30 minutes. If the *Average Units Spent with Patients* is 1.0, the physician is matching the standard billing unit, in terms of time, that has been set for his or her particular medical specialty.

2. Open the **Save As** dialog box. Save the file in the folder with the other projects for this chapter with the name **8I_Billing_Firstname_Lastname** Display the **Page Setup** dialog box, create a **Custom Footer**, and in the **Left section**, add the **File name**.

3. In cell **G3**, type **Billing Based on Standard Units** and then press ⏎. In cell **G4**, write a formula that multiplies the **Standard Billing Unit Per Patient (hrs)**—C4—times the **Physician's Rate per Billing Unit**—E4—times the **Number of Patients per Day**—F4. Copy the formula down through cell **G19**.

(Project 8I–Billing continues on the next page)

(Project 8I–Billing continued)

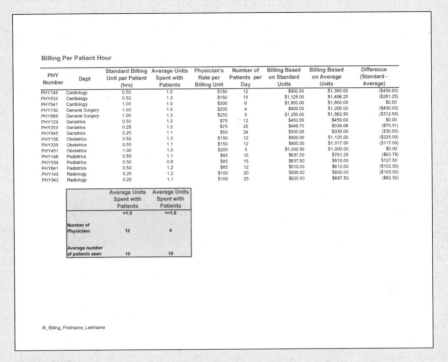

PHY Number	Dept	Standard Billing Unit per Patient (hrs)	Average Units Spent with Patients	Physician's Rate per Billing Unit	Number of Patients per Day	Billing Based on Standard Units	Billing Based on Average Units	Difference (Standard - Average)
PHY148	Cardiology	0.50	1.5	$150	12	$900.00	$1,350.00	($450.00)
PHY533	Cardiology	0.50	1.3	$150	15	$1,125.00	$1,406.25	($281.25)
PHY541	Cardiology	1.00	1.0	$300	6	$1,800.00	$1,800.00	$0.00
PHY130	General Surgery	1.00	1.5	$200	4	$800.00	$1,200.00	($400.00)
PHY889	General Surgery	1.00	1.3	$250	5	$1,250.00	$1,562.50	($312.50)
PHY129	Geriatrics	0.50	1.0	$75	12	$450.00	$450.00	$0.00
PHY353	Geriatrics	0.25	1.2	$75	25	$468.75	$539.06	($70.31)
PHY545	Geriatrics	0.25	1.1	$50	24	$300.00	$330.00	($30.00)
PHY156	Obstetrics	0.50	1.3	$150	12	$900.00	$1,125.00	($225.00)
PHY335	Obstetrics	0.50	1.1	$150	12	$900.00	$1,017.00	($117.00)
PHY451	Obstetrics	1.00	1.0	$200	5	$1,000.00	$1,000.00	$0.00
PHY146	Pediatrics	0.50	1.1	$85	15	$637.50	$701.25	($63.75)
PHY539	Pediatrics	0.50	0.8	$85	15	$637.50	$510.00	$127.50
PHY641	Pediatrics	0.50	1.2	$85	12	$510.00	$612.00	($102.00)
PHY145	Radiology	0.25	1.2	$100	20	$500.00	$600.00	($100.00)
PHY342	Radiology	0.25	1.1	$100	25	$625.00	$687.50	($62.50)

	Average Units Spent with Patients	Average Units Spent with Patients
	>1.0	<=1.0
Number of Physicians	12	4
Average number of patients seen	15	10

8I_Billing_Firstname_Lastname

Figure 8.46

4. In cell **H3**, type **Billing Based on Average Units** and then press Enter. In cell **H4**, write a formula to calculate the **Billing Based on Standard Units** times the **Average Units Spent with Patients**. This is the amount that it is costing the hospital, based on the billing rate and the average amount of time spent with patients. Copy the formula down the column to cell **H19**.

5. In cell **I3**, type **Difference (Standard - Average)** and then press Enter. In cell **I4**, calculate the difference between the figures in **column G** and **column H**, and then copy the formula down to cell **I19**. In most cases, the amount will display as a negative number because most doctors at the medical center are spending more time with patients than the standard that has been set. Therefore, it is costing the hospital more to serve patients than can be billed to the insurance companies, based on insurance industry standards.

6. With the range **I4:I19** still selected, display the **Format Cells** dialog box. Click the **Number tab**, and then click **Currency**. Under **Negative numbers**, click the third option—display negative numbers in parentheses. Be sure that *2* displays in the **Decimal places** box and that *$* displays in the **Symbol** box. Click **OK**. Click cell **F3**, and then on the Formatting toolbar, click the **Format Painter** button. Select the range **G3:I3** to copy the border format from cell F3 to these new column titles.

(Project 8I–Billing continues on the next page)

Performance Assessments (continued)

(Project 8I–Billing continued)

7. Sort the data table in alphabetical order by **Dept**. In cell **B24**, type **Number of Physicians** and in cell **B26**, type **Average number of patients seen** Select cells **B24** and **B26**, display the **Format Cells** dialog box, and on the **Alignment tab**, select the **Wrap text** check box. Apply **Bold** to both cells.

8. Copy cell **D3**, and then paste it in cell **C21** and in cell **D21**. In cell **C22**, type >1.0 and in cell **D22**, type <=1.0 Click cell **C24**, and then display the **Insert Function** dialog box. In the **Database** category, click **DCOUNTA**. This function is similar to the DCOUNT function, but it can count text fields rather than numeric fields. In the **Function Arguments** dialog box, in the **Database** box, click the **Collapse dialog box** button, and then select the range **A3:I19**. In the **Field** box, type "PHY Number" In the **Criteria** box, select the range **C21:C22**, and then click **OK**. The result—*12*—displays in the cell. This is the number of physicians who averaged 1 unit of billable time or more with each patient.

9. In cell **D24**, follow the same procedure to count the number of physicians who spent less than or equal to 1 unit of time with each patient on average. (Hint: Use the same database range and Field, but change the Criteria to cells D21:D22.) The result—*4*—displays in the cell.

10. Click cell **C26**, and then display the **Insert Function** dialog box. In the **Database** category, click **DAVERAGE**. In the **Function Arguments** dialog box, in the **Database** box, select the range **A3:I19**. In the **Field** box, click cell **F3**—you can use the cell address for the field you want to use in the calculation. In the **Criteria** box, select the range **C21:C22**, and then click **OK**. Format the result—*15*—as a **Number** with no decimals. In cell **D26**, repeat this process to calculate the average number of patients seen by doctors who spend the standard amount of time or less with each patient. Format the result as a number with no decimals. (Hint: Copy the formula from cell C26 and adjust the ranges as needed.)

11. Click cell **C21**, click the **Format Painter** button, and then click cell **B21**. Select the range **C22:D26**, and on the Formatting toolbar, click the **Center** button and the **Bold** button. Select the range **B21:D26**, display the **Fill Color** palette, and then click **Light Turquoise**. Display the **Format Cells** dialog box, and then click the **Border tab**. Be sure that the **Color** displays **Plum**. Under Presets, click **Outline** to add a border around the selected area.

12. Display the **Print Preview** window. Click the **Setup** button, change the **Orientation** to **Landscape**, and then click the **Fit to 1 page wide by 1 page tall** option button. Preview the worksheet, and then compare it with Figure 8.46. Print the worksheet, save your changes, and then close the file.

End You have completed Project 8I

Mastery Assessments

Project 8J — Staffing

Objectives: *Import Data into Excel, Sort Data, Manage Data Using a Form, Use AutoFilter, and Analyze Data with Excel Database Tools.*

So far you have worked with separate lists of the personnel records for the University Medical Center. In this project, you will work with a larger set of records. You will open a worksheet and import additional data into the worksheet. Then you will sort the data, add new records, and add subtotals by department. Your completed worksheet will look similar to the one shown in Figure 8.47. You will save your workbook as *8J_Staffing_Firstname_Lastname.*

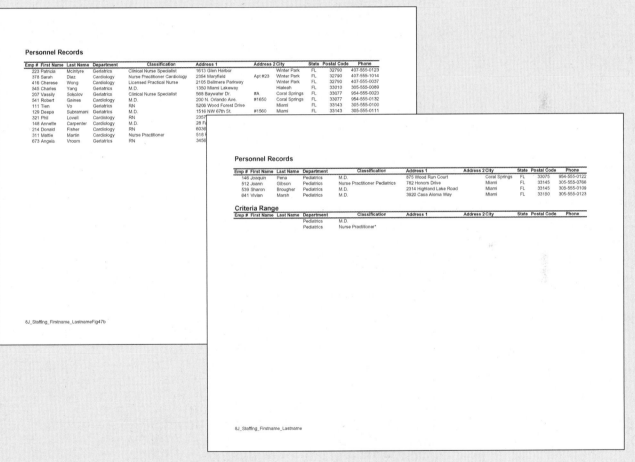

Figure 8.47

1. On the Standard toolbar, click the **Open** button. Navigate to the location where the student files for this textbook are stored. Locate and open **e08J_Staffing**. Create a **Custom Footer** and add the **File name** to the **Left section**. Save the file in your folder using the name **8J_Staffing_Firstname_Lastname**

(Project 8J–Staffing continues on the next page)

(Project 8J–Staffing continued)

2. Click cell **A42**. From the **Data** menu, point to **Import External Data**, click **Import Data**, and display the **Select Data Source** dialog box. From your student files, locate the **8J_Facilities_Staff** Access file, and then import the file beginning in cell **A42**.

3. Click cell **A4**, and then from the **Window** menu click **Freeze Panes**. Scroll down to display row **42** and verify that the categories for the imported data are correctly placed in each column. Select row **42**, and then from the **Edit** menu, click **Delete** to remove this row of field names. From the **Window** menu, click **Unfreeze Panes**.

4. Select **columns C:E** and AutoFit the selection to fully display the content of each column. **Sort** the records by **Emp #**.

5. From the **Data** menu, display the **Form** and use the **Criteria** button to locate the record for *Sarah Martin*. Change her information as follows:

First Name	Sarah
Last Name	Diaz
Address 1	2354 Maryfield
Address 2	Apt #23
City	Winter Park
State	FL
Postal Code	32790
Phone	407-555-1014

6. Use the data form to add the following new record:

Emp #	673
First Name	Angela
Last Name	Vroom
Department	Geriatrics
Classification	RN
Address 1	3456 Barnstown Trail
Address 2	
City	Miami
State	FL
Postal Code	33150
Phone	305-555-0233

(Project 8J–Staffing continues on the next page)

(Project 8J–Staffing continued)

7. Display the **AutoFilter** arrows. In cell **D3**, click the **Department arrow**, and then create a **Custom AutoFilter** to display the records for staff members in either **Geriatrics Or Cardiology**. **Sort** the resulting list by **Postal Code** in **Ascending** order. Print this list in **Landscape** on one page. This list will be used to send information to these employees about an upcoming seminar. Remove the AutoFilter.

8. Select the database range—**A3:K63**—and in the **Name Box**, type **Database** In cell **A65**, type **Criteria Range** and then format cell **A65** to **14** pt., and apply **Bold**. Copy the range **A3:K3**, and then paste it in cell **A66**. Name the range **A66:K67** as **Criteria** In cell **D67** type **Pediatrics** and in cell **E67** type **M.D.** In cell **D68** type **Pediatrics** and in cell **E67** type **Nurse Practitioner*** Using the wildcard will display any Nurse Practitioner who has a further designation.

9. Click in the data table, and then display the **Advanced Filter** dialog box. Verify that the **List range** correctly displays the database. Adjust the **Criteria range** to include row **68**. Click **OK**. The result will display four records—all the MDs and Nurse Practitioners who work in the Pediatrics department. Compare your screen with Figure 8.47. Print the results in landscape on one page.

10. Save the file and close it.

 End You have completed Project 8J ─────────────────────

Project 8K — Office Staff

Objective: *Analyze Data with Excel Database Tools.*

The office staff at the University Medical Center is paid either on an hourly rate or they are salaried. In this project, you have a worksheet listing staff members and their related payroll information. You will subtotal and outline the worksheet. Your completed worksheet will look similar to the one shown in Figure 8.48. You will save your workbook as *8K_Office_Staff_Firstname_Lastname.*

1. On the Standard toolbar, click the **Open** button. Navigate to the location where the student files for this textbook are stored. Locate and open the file **e08K_Office_Staff**. In the folder where you are saving your projects for this chapter, save the file using the name **8K_Office_Staff_Firstname_Lastname**

(Project 8K–Office Staff continues on the next page)

(Project 8K–Office Staff continued)

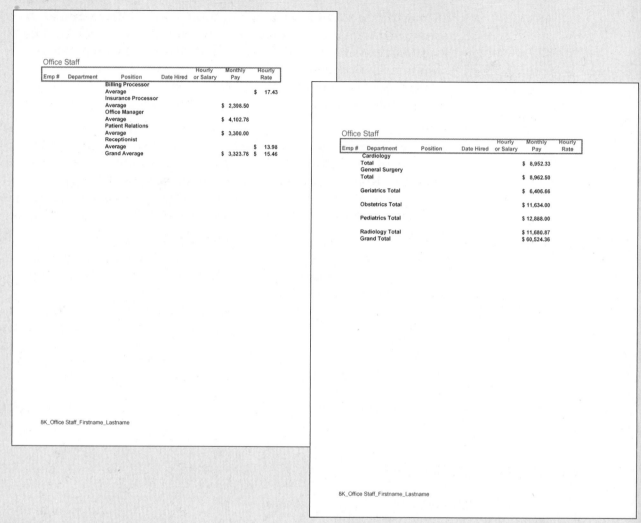

Figure 8.48

2. Sort the data alphabetically by **Position**. From the **Data** menu, display the **Subtotal** dialog box, and at each change in **Position**, **Average** the **Monthly Pay** and the **Hourly Rate**.

3. Hold down Ctrl, and then select all of the cells that display the *#DIV/0!* error notation. Then from the **Edit** menu, point to **Clear** and click **Contents** to remove the error notation. Excel attempted to average these cells even though they did not contain any values.

4. Click in any cell to deselect. Hold down Ctrl, and then select all the averages displayed in **columns F** and **G**, including the **Grand Averages** in **row 29**, and then click **Bold** and **Currency Style**.

(Project 8K–Office Staff continues on the next page)

(Project 8K – Office Staff continued)

5. In the displayed gray outline bar at the left, click the **Level 2** button to collapse the details and display only the averages. Display the **Page Setup** dialog box, and then click the **Header/Footer tab**. Create a **Custom Footer**, and in the **Left section**, add the **File name**. **Print** this report on one page. At the top of the outline bar, click the **Level 3** button to redisplay all of the records. Click in cell **A3**, display the **Subtotal** dialog box, and remove the subtotals.

6. In the **Monthly Pay** column, for those employees who have an hourly rate (the cell is empty), write a formula that calculates their monthly income by multiplying the **Hourly Rate** times **160** The results should display in the *Monthly Pay* column to the left of the *Hourly Rate* column.

7. **Sort** the database alphabetically by **Department**. Create a new set of subtotals, and at each change in **Department**, **Sum** only the **Monthly Pay**. Be sure to clear the check mark next to **Hourly Rate** in the **Subtotal** dialog box.

8. In **column F**, format the totals in **Bold**, and then format them as **Currency Style**. AutoFit **column F** to display the totals.

9. Use the outline **Level 2** to display only the **Department** subtotals and the **Grand Total**. The **Grand Total** displayed in cell **F30** should be *$60,524.36*. **Print** the report.

10. Save the worksheet, and then close the file.

 You have completed Project 8K ——————————

Project 8L — Appointments

Objectives: *Import Data into Excel, Sort Data, Use AutoFilter, Analyze Data with Excel Database Tools, and Use Database Functions.*

Each physician's office at the University Medical Center schedules patient appointments. In this project, you will import a schedule of appointments and use the skills you have practiced in this chapter to sort, update, and extract the data. The goal is to give each physician in the Pediatrics department a list of patients they need to see on Thursday morning. You will save the file as *8L_Appointments_Firstname_Lastname.*

1. Open a new blank worksheet. Click cell **A3**, and then import the Access file **e08L_Appointments**. Save the file as **8L_Apointments_Firstname_Lastname**

2. In cell **A1**, add the title **Pediatric Appointments** and format it appropriately. Select the data in **column E—Time**—and use the **Format Cells** dialog box to change the format for **Time** to a **1:30 PM** format.

3. Click cell **A3**, and then **Sort** the file by **Physician**, and then by **Date**, and then by **Time** of appointment.

4. Use the skills you have practiced in this chapter to extract three reports, one for each physician that lists the appointments they have scheduled for the morning of Thursday, June 24. Be sure the appointments are listed separately for each doctor and are in order by time.

5. Display the **Page Setup** dialog box and click the **Header/Footer tab**. Create a **Custom Footer**, and in the **Left section**, add the **File name**. **Print** the reports. Save the file, and then close it.

 You have completed Project 8L ——————————

Project 8M — Contact List

Objectives: *Sort Data, Manage Data Using a Data Form, and Use AutoFilter.*

Now that you are familiar with using Excel as a database tool, you can set up your own database of contact information. In this project, you will create a database for the names, addresses, and phone numbers of your family, friends, and associates. You will save your workbook as *8M_Contacts_Firstname_Lastname.*

1. Open a blank worksheet. Add the **File name** to the footer in the usual location, and save the file as **8M_Contacts_Firstname_Lastname**

(Project 8M–Contact List continues on the next page)

(Project 8M–Contact List continued)

2. Enter a title for your worksheet in cell **A1**. Starting in cell **A3**, enter field names across **row 3** for each category of information you want to include. You may want to include an email field, mobile phone, work phone, or other contact methods. Include a field that classifies the relationship, such as family, friend, associate. You may want to include a birthday date.

3. Select the range of your titles and name this range **Database** Name the sheet **Contacts** From the **Data** menu, display the **Form** and use it to enter 10 to 15 records.

4. Sort the records in alphabetical order by last name, and then by first name.

5. Display the **AutoFilter arrows**, and filter the records to display only **family** members.

6. Save your changes, and then close the file.

 End **You have completed Project 8M** ————————————

On the Internet

Importing Data Using a Web Query

In this chapter, you imported data from external sources by using *Import Data*. You can also import information that may be on a Web site by using *New Web Query*. This command is designed specifically to import data displayed in a table on a Web site. *Microsoft Help* has an online demonstration of how this type of import command works. To complete this *Help* exercise, you need to be connected to the Internet and have your computer's speakers turned on.

1. Start Excel. In the **Type a question for help** box, type **Import**

2. From the list of related *Help* topics, scroll as necessary and click **Demo: Import financial data from the Web**.

3. On the displayed Microsoft Office Assistant Web page, click the **Show All** button. This provides a written description and text of the demo.

4. Click the **Watch the demo!** button. It may take a few minutes for the demonstration to download.

5. When the Microsoft logo appears, close the Web page, and then close the Microsoft Office Assistant page.

6. After the file is imported, close the worksheet without saving.

Using Database Functions

In this chapter, you have practiced four of the database functions, DAVERAGE, DSUM, DCOUNT, and DGET. There are many other functions that can be used with a database such as DMAX, DMIN, or DSTDEV.

1. Start Excel. In the **Type a question for help** box, type **database functions**

2. From the list of related help topics, click one of the database functions that display.

3. In the upper right corner of the displayed *Help* topic, click the **Show All** button, and then **Maximize** the window. This reveals a sample database and the definitions and syntax for all of the database functions.

4. Copy the database sample, switch to your open Excel spreadsheet, and then paste the sample database.

5. In the sample database that you copied to your worksheet, practice at least three new database functions. Use the instructions and examples in the Help window to guide you as you practice using other functions.

6. After you have completed your practice, close Help, and then close the worksheet without saving it.

4 chapterfour

Customizing Tables, Data Access Pages, and Converting a Database

In this chapter, you will: complete these projects **and** practice these skills.

Project 4A
Restricting Data in a Table

Objectives

- Customize a Field
- Specify a Field Format
- Create Input Masks Using the Input Mask Wizard
- Create Input Masks Using the Input Mask Properties Box
- Specify a Required Field
- Validate Data Entry

Project 4B
Finding Data in a Table

Objectives

- Create a Lookup Wizard Field
- Find a Record
- Display Specific Records

Project 4C
Creating Data Access Pages and Converting a Database

Objectives

- Create and Use a Data Access Page
- Convert a Database from a Previous Version of Access

Jefferson Country Inn

About 2 hours outside Washington, DC, the Jefferson Country Inn is located in Charlottesville, Virginia. The Inn's proximity to Washington, DC, and Richmond, VA, make it a popular weekend getaway for locals and a convenient base for out-of-town vacationers. The Inn offers 12 rooms, all individually decorated. A fresh country breakfast and afternoon tea are included each day.

Meeting rooms offering the latest high-tech amenities like high-speed Internet connections have made the Inn an increasingly popular location for day-long meetings and events.

© Getty Images, Inc.

Customizing Tables, Data Access Pages, and Converting a Database

Access provides tools for customizing tables and improving data accuracy and data entry. In this chapter, you will use information from the Jefferson Country Inn to find specific information in a table without using a query, apply special formatting to records that meet specified conditions, and discover how Access can create Web pages containing table data. You will customize the fields in a table, create a data access page, and convert a database that was created in an older version of Access to the current version of Microsoft Access.

Project 4A Jefferson Inn Employees

You have practiced creating fields and indicating the type of data that could be entered by specifying the field's data type, for example, Text, Currency, or Number. This sets restrictions on the data entered in the field. You can further restrict the data by modifying the field's **properties**. A field's property determines its content and appearance. Restrict data in fields to keep the database organized, and also to help eliminate errors during the data entry process. You can also set a specific field size and create a default value for a field.

In Activities 4.1 through 4.10, you will modify the properties and customize the fields in a table that stores information about the Jefferson Country Inn. Specifically, you will add features to the tables that will help to accomplish two things: reduce errors in the data and make data entry easier. Your completed table will look similar to Figure 4.1. You will save your database as *4A_Jefferson_Inn_Employees_Firstname_Lastname*.

Jefferson Employees Firstname Lastname   10/25/2003

ID #	First Name	Last Name	Picture	Email	Address	City	State	Zip	Phone	Hire Date
0005	Rita	Doggett	Package	rdoggett@jeffinn.com	32S57 Seminole Trail	Rivanna	VA	22911-	434-555-0163	6/15/2003
0015	Beng	Ho	Package	bho@jeffinn.com	896 W. Emmett St.	Charlottesville	VA	22911-	434-555-0096	8/28/2000
0112	Wyatt	Beazley	Package	wbeazley@jeffinn.com	79 Fontaine Ave.	Charlottesville	VA	22910-	434-555-0183	8/31/2001
0120	Kent	Greenway	Package	kgreenway@jeffinn.com	66 Earlysville Rd.	Earlysville	VA	22936-	434-555-0047	3/21/2001
0205	Alvaro	Gutierrez	Package	agutierrez@jeffinn.com	25 Old Ivy	Charlottesville	VA	22910-	434-555-0098	1/2/2002
0215	Eva	Acree	Package	eacree@jeffinn.com	88 Arch Ave., #3	Waynesboro	VA	22980-	540-555-0038	6/15/2002
0301	Debra	Wildy	Package	dwildy@jeffinn.com	3210 Lew Dewitt Blvd.	Waynesboro	VA	22980-	540-555-0066	1/15/2003
0305	Luiza	Flores	Package	lflores@jeffinn.com	115 N. Augusta St., # 625	Staunton	VA	22407-	540-555-0002	6/15/2003
0306	Gracie	Steptoe	Package	gsteptoe@jeffinn.com	325 D S. Augusta St.	Staunton	VA	24401-	540-555-0122	1/15/2003
0307	David	Lim	Package	dlim@jeffinn.com	1829 W. Main St.	Waynesboro	VA	22980-	540-555-0101	6/15/2003
0405	Shelby	Rincon		srincon@jeffinn.com	63 W. Eden	Rivanna	VA	22911-	434-555-2736	5/6/1998
9810	Carol	Charles	Package	ccharles@jeffinn.com	6622 Garden St.	Charlottesville	VA	22909-	434-555-0022	5/5/1998
9812	Ruby	Benjamin	Package	rbenjamin@jeffinn.com	38 Thomas Jefferson Pkwy.	Charlottesville	VA	22909-	434-555-0186	6/8/1998
9910	Edwin	Sharp	Package	esharp@jeffinn.com	16 W. Market	Charlottesville	VA	22909-	434-555-0674	1/15/2003
9916	Lorraine	Hairston	Package	lhairston@jeffinn.com	457 Hollymeade Dr.	Charlottesville	VA	22909-	434-555-0159	7/21/1999

Page 1

Figure 4.1
Project 4A—Jefferson Inn Employees

Objective 1
Customize a Field

Activity 4.1 Changing a Data Type

In this activity you will change some of the data types for fields in the Jefferson Employees table to restrict the data entered and to make it more useful.

1 Using the skills you practiced earlier, create a new folder named Chapter 4 in the location where you will be storing your projects for this chapter. Locate the file **a04A_Jefferson_Inn_Employees** from your student files and copy and paste the file to the Chapter 4 folder you created. Remove the Read-only property from the file and rename the file as **4A_Jefferson_Inn_Employees_Firstname_Lastname** Start Access and open the database you just renamed.

2 On the Objects bar, click **Tables** if necessary, right-click the **Jefferson Employees** table, and then click **Rename**.

3 In the box that displays, and using your own information, type **Jefferson Employees Firstname Lastname** and then press Enter.

The table is renamed to include your name.

4 Open your **Jefferson Employees** table in **Datasheet view** and examine the data in the table. In particular, notice that the data in the Email column is employee Email addresses. Currently, this data is not formatted as hyperlinks; they will not open a Web page nor invoke an e-mail program when clicked.

The Jefferson Employees table contains information about the employees at Jefferson Country Inn, including an employee ID#, First Name, Last Name, Email, Address, and Hire Date information.

5 Switch to **Design view**.

6 In the **Email** row, click in the **Data Type** column, and then click the **downward-pointing arrow** that displays. See Figure 4.2.

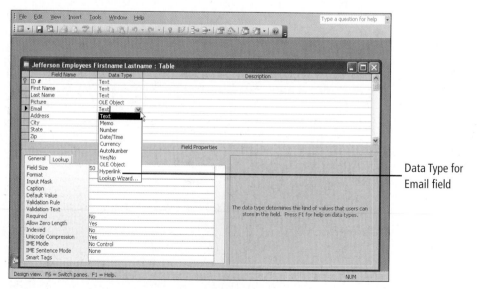

Data Type for Email field

Figure 4.2

7 From the displayed list of data types, click **Hyperlink**.

A Hyperlink field stores a hyperlink address. Selecting the Hyperlink data type will convert the data in the field to a Web hyperlink provided the data is in a recognizable hyperlink format. This Email field contains data entered in a format suitable for hyperlinks, for example, rdoggett@jeffinn.com.

8 Switch to **Datasheet view** and save the table when prompted. Examine the data in the Email column and notice that the data displays as hyperlinked Email addresses.

The text is a different color and underlined. Additionally, the Link

Select pointer displays when the mouse pointer is paused over one of the Email addresses. See Figure 4.3. Restricting data with a Hyperlink data type reduces errors in the table by ensuring that items like Email addresses have the proper format.

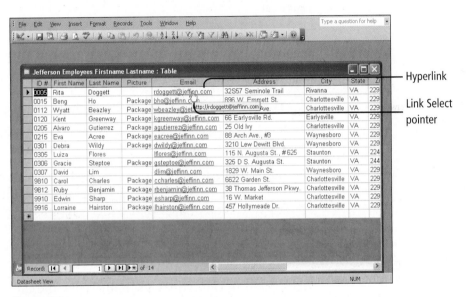

Figure 4.3

9 Switch to **Design view**. Under **Data Type**, scroll down as necessary, click in the **Hire Date** row, and then click the **downward-pointing arrow** that displays.

10 From the displayed list of data types, click **Date/Time**.

11 Switch to **Datasheet view**, save the table when prompted, and then examine the data in the **Hire Date** column.

Although the data in this column does not display differently than it did with the data type of *Text*, now there is a difference in the way the data will be interpreted when new data is entered.

12 In the first record—**Rita Doggett**—scroll as necessary to view the **Hire Date** field, delete the existing text, type **2222** and then press Enter.

The error message shown in Figure 4.4 displays, indicating that the value entered is not valid for this field. Restricting data with the Date/Time data type reduces errors in the table by ensuring that only entries that are entered as a date format are accepted.

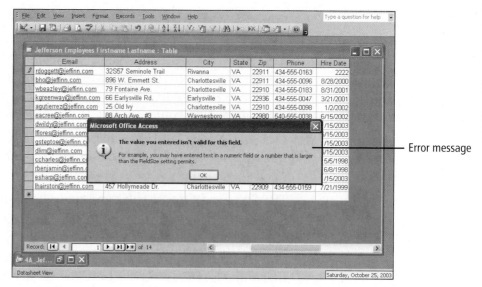
Error message

Figure 4.4

13 In the displayed message box, click **OK**, and then on the Table Datasheet toolbar, click the **Undo** button ![undo] twice.

The original date of 6/15/2003 displays in the field.

14 Switch to **Design view**. Notice the Data Type for the **Picture** field is *OLE Object.*

OLE stands for Object Linking and Embedding. Linking and embedding are the two methods by which external items can be contained in an Access database. **Embedded** objects are placed into the database object. **Linked** objects have only a link in the database object to the address or location of the external item, such as a picture or Word document. Thus, linked objects do not reside directly in the database.

15 Switch to **Datasheet view** and save the table if necessary. In the **Picture** column for **Kent Greenway's** record, point to and then double-click **Package**. See Figure 4.5. Alternatively, right-click, point to Package Object, and then click Activate Contents.

A program such as Windows Picture and Fax Viewer opens and a photo of Kent Greenway, an employee at Jefferson Inn, displays. A data type of OLE is suitable for this field because it allows database users to view pictures of the employees at Jefferson Country Inn. Three employees do not yet have pictures in their records.

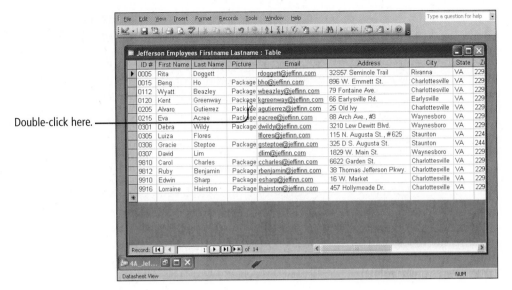

Double-click here.

Figure 4.5

16 On the title bar of the window where the picture displays, click the **Close** button ⊠. In the first record, the one for **Rita Doggett**, click in the **Picture** field, and then right-click to display the shortcut menu.

17 On the displayed shortcut menu, click **Insert Object**.

The dialog box to insert an object displays. OLE objects can be sounds, graphics, movies, documents, spreadsheets, or other objects that can be created within a Windows-based application. From this dialog box, you can create a new object or insert an existing object, assuming you know the location of the object.

18 On the left side of the dialog box, click the **Create from File** option button. Under **File**, click the **Browse** button, and then navigate to the location where the student files that accompany this textbook are stored. Double-click the file **a04A_RitaDoggett**, and then in the displayed dialog box, click **OK**.

After a few seconds, *Package* displays in the Picture field for Rita Doggett.

19 In the **Picture** field for **Rita Doggett**, double-click the word **Package**.

A photo of this employee displays.

20 On the title bar of the window where the picture displays, click the **Close** button ⊠.

21 Using the techniques you have just practiced to insert an object into a field, insert the picture files for the two remaining employees who do not yet have their pictures in the table—**Luiza Flores** and **David Lim**.

Every record now has an associated picture file for each employee. Take a moment to study the table in Figure 4.6, which describes the data types available in Access.

Data Types Supported by Access

Data Type	Description
Text	Text data including numbers that do not require calculations. Can be up to 255 characters in length.
Memo	Text data. Use for longer text fields; up to 65,536 characters.
Number	Numeric data that may be used in calculations.
Date/Time	Dates and/or times.
Currency	Currency or monetary values; dollar sign and two decimal places inserted by default.
AutoNumber	Numeric data in either sequential numbering in increments of 1 or random ID numbers.
Yes/No	True or False values.
OLE Object	OLE objects such as Word documents, Excel worksheets, and graphic files.
Hyperlink	Hyperlinks; either URLs or UNC paths.
Lookup Wizard	Not an actual data type, but listed under Data Types. Allows you to select a value for a field from another table or a list of values.

Figure 4.6

22 Switch to **Design view** for the next activity.

Activity 4.2 Changing a Field Size

In this activity, you will set a field size to restrict the size of the data that can be entered in a field.

1 In the upper portion of the table window, in the **Field Name** column, click anywhere in the **State** field. In the lower area of the screen, under **Field Properties**, notice that the field size is set to 255 characters, which is the default field size. See Figure 4.7.

The Field Properties area displays the properties—specifications—for a selected field.

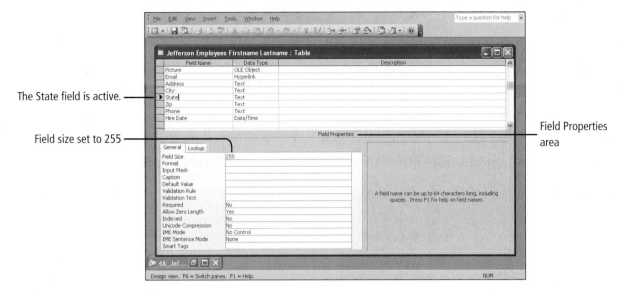

The State field is active.

Field size set to 255

Field Properties area

Figure 4.7

2 Under **Field Properties**, click in the **Field Size** box, select the existing text of **255**, and then type **2**

The Field Size property limits the number of characters that can be entered in a field and can be set for data types of Text, Number, and AutoNumber. The Field Size property can be set to any number between 0 and 255.

3 Switch to **Datasheet view** and save your changes.

Access displays a message as shown in Figure 4.8, indicating that some data may be lost because of the change in the field size.

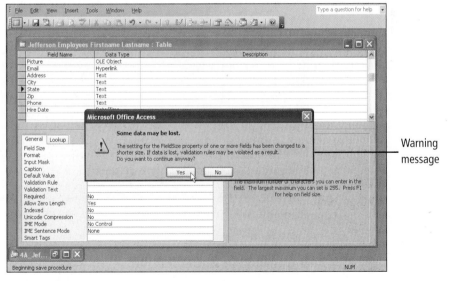

Warning message

Figure 4.8

4 In the displayed warning message box, click **Yes**. In the record for **Wyatt Beazley**, under the **State** column, select the existing text, and then try to type **Virginia**

Access will not allow more than two characters in this field because of the limitations you set in the field properties. Specifying a field size prevents a user from entering some types of invalid data, such as an entry that is too long.

5 Enter **VA** for the **State** field for **Wyatt Beazley**.

Activity 4.3 Entering a Default Value

Most employees who work for Jefferson Country Inn live in Virginia. Specifying a default value for this field will save time in data entry.

1 Switch to **Design view**. In the upper portion of the Table window, click in the **State** field if necessary to make it the active field.

2 Under **Field Properties**, in the **Default Value** box, type **VA** See Figure 4.9.

Notice to the right that a description of this field property displays. Also, to the right of the Default Value box, a small button with three dots, called the **Build button**, displays. The Build button displays after you click in a field property box so you can further define the property. You will use the Build button in a field property in a later activity.

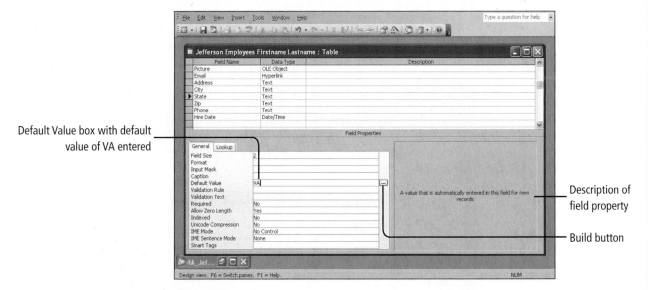

Default Value box with default value of VA entered

Description of field property

Build button

Figure 4.9

3 Switch to **Datasheet view** and save. Notice under the last record, in the **State** column, a value of VA is already entered, ready for the next record.

Specifying a default value for a field saves data entry time and also reduces the possibility of typographical errors.

4 Switch to **Design view**. Under **Field Properties**, notice that quotation marks surround *VA*.

Quotation marks indicate that the entry will be treated as a string. For further information on strings, see the discussion in Chapter 3 or refer to Access Help.

Objective 2
Specify a Field Format

Specifying a field format allows you to affect how data in a field will display. For example, the date 9-10-67 can be displayed as September 10, 1967, or 10-Sept-67, or 09-10-1967. Access allows you to choose the format to display data in a field.

Activity 4.4 Specifying a Field Format

In this activity, you will specify a date format for the Hire Date field that will affect how the date in this field displays.

1 In the upper portion of the Table window, click in the **Hire Date** field to make it the active field. Under **Field Properties**, click in the **Format** box, and then click the **downward-pointing arrow** that displays. See Figure 4.10.

A list of available formats for the Date/Time data type displays.

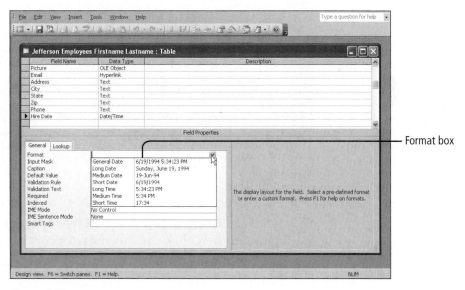

Figure 4.10

2 From the list of available formats, click **Long Date**.

The Property Update Options smart tag 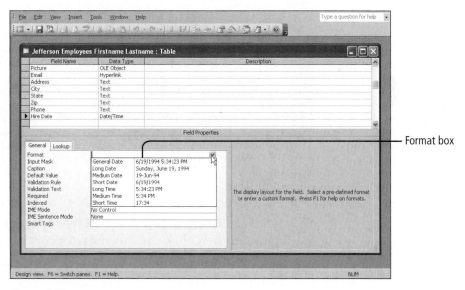 displays.

◾3 Switch to the **Datasheet view**, saving your changes. If necessary, use the horizontal scroll bar to scroll to the right so you can view the **Hire Date** field, and then adjust the column width so the entire contents of the **Hire Date** field display.

◾4 Notice the additional information—day of the week, month spelled, year in four digits—that displays in the **Hire Date** field as a result of the specified Date format. See Figure 4.11.

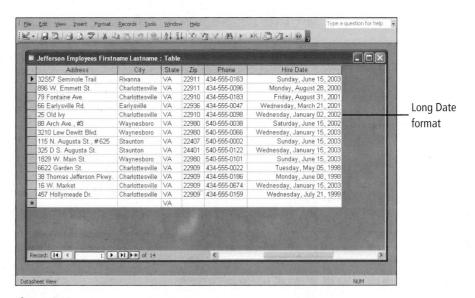

Long Date format

Figure 4.11

◾5 Switch to **Design view**. Under **Field Properties**, click in the **Format** box, and then click the **downward-pointing arrow**.

◾6 From the list of available formats, click **Medium Date**, and then switch to the **Datasheet view**, saving your changes.

◾7 If necessary, scroll to the right to view the **Hire Date** field and notice the display of the dates. See Figure 4.12.

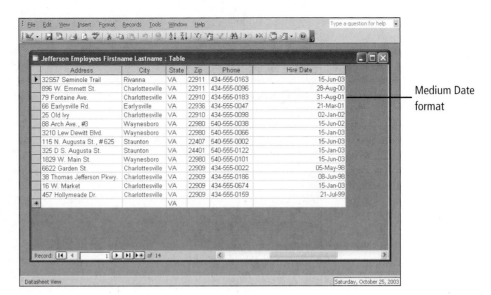

Medium Date
format

Figure 4.12

8 Double-click the column border to the right of the **Hire Date** field to adjust the column width to accommodate the widest entry.

9 Using the technique you just practiced, switch to **Design view**, change the format of the **Hire Date** field to **Short Date**, and then leave your table open in **Design view** for the next activity.

Objective 3
Create Input Masks Using the Input Mask Wizard

An *input mask* is a field property that determines the data that can be entered, how the data displays, and how the data is stored. There are two methods of adding an input mask to your table—using the Input Mask Wizard or using the Input Mask properties box.

Activity 4.5 Creating Input Masks Using the Input Mask Wizard

Regardless of which method you use for creating an input mask, the wizard or the properties box, an input mask displays a template for the data that is being entered, and it will not permit the entry of data that does not fit the template. Because postal zip codes require at least five digits, in this activity, you will create an input mask for the zip field that will require the entry of at least five digits.

1 In the upper portion of the Table window, click in the **Zip** field to make it the active field. Under **Field Properties**, click in the **Input Mask** box, and then click the **Build** button that displays. See Figure 4.13. If prompted, save the table.

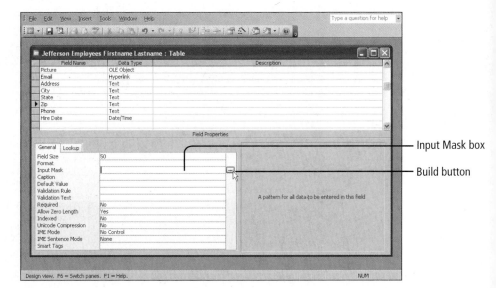

Figure 4.13

The Input Mask Wizard starts. The Input Mask Wizard allows you to create an input mask using one of several standard masks that Access has already built for you—such as Phone Number, Social Security Number, and Zip Code—for text and data fields.

2 In the first screen of the Input Mask Wizard, under **Input Mask**, click **Zip Code**, as shown in Figure 4.14. Click **Next**.

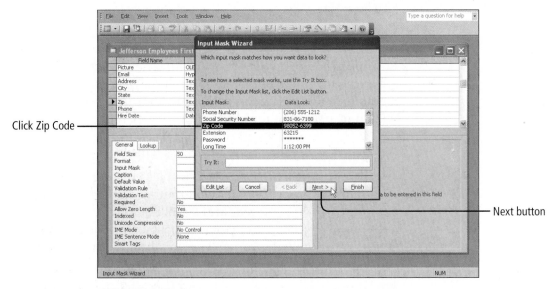

Figure 4.14

3 In the next screen of the wizard, notice the entry to the right of **Input Mask**.

A *0* indicates a required digit, and a *9* indicates an optional digit or space. The hyphen in between is a character that Access will insert in the specified place. See Figure 4.15. Most zip codes (postal codes) follow the format of five digits followed by a hyphen (-) and four optional digits.

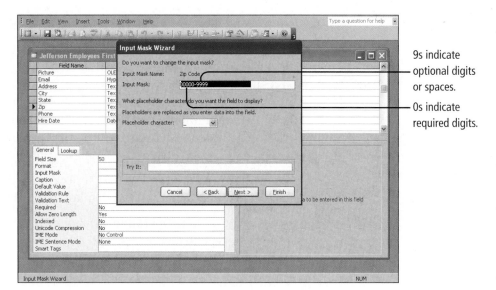

9s indicate
optional digits
or spaces.

0s indicate
required digits.

Figure 4.15

■ Leave all the settings at their defaults and click **Next**.

■ The third screen of the wizard asks how you want to store the data. Be sure that the **Without the symbols in the mask, like this** option button is selected, as shown in Figure 4.16. Click **Next**.

This third screen allows you to specify whether you want to store the data with the symbols, which takes up more space in the database, or without the symbols to save some space.

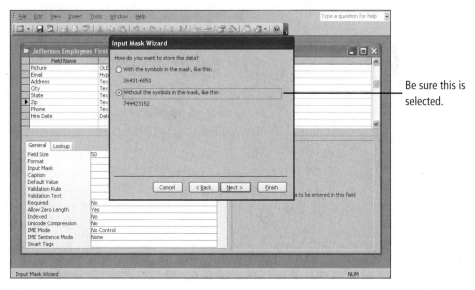

Be sure this is
selected.

Figure 4.16

6 In the final screen of the wizard, click **Finish**.

The wizard closes and Access displays the mask in the **Input Mask** box. Notice the 0s indicating the required digits for the postal code and the 9s that represent optional digits or spaces. The semicolons that follow separate the mask into three sections. This mask, however, has data only in the first section, the one containing the 0s and 9s. The other two sections are optional and not needed at this time.

7 Switch to **Datasheet view**, save the table, and scroll to the right to view the **Zip** field. Widen the **Zip** field if necessary to see the contents of the field. Notice the hyphens that display to the right of the five digits.

8 In the record for **Rita Doggett**, under **Zip**, delete the existing text and try to type **aaaaa** Access will not allow a letter entry because the input mask you just created requires numbers only in this field.

9 In the **Zip** field for Rita Doggett, type **22911**

10 Switch to **Design view** for the next activity.

Objective 4
Create Input Masks Using the Input Mask Properties Box

In addition to using the wizard, input masks can also be created directly in the Input Mask box. The advantage in doing this is that you can customize the mask for a particular field.

Activity 4.6 Specifying Uppercase and Lowercase Text

In this activity, you will use the **Input Mask Properties** box to create a mask that will ensure that an entry begins with a capital letter and that the remaining text in the field displays in lowercase letters.

1 With your **Jefferson Employees** table displayed in **Design view**, click in the **First Name** field to make it the active field.

2 Under **Field Properties**, in the **Input Mask** box, type **>L<??????????????** (There are 15 question marks.) See Figure 4.17.

The greater than (>) sign converts any text following it to uppercase. The *L* indicates that a letter (not a number) is required (first names begin with a letter), the less than (<) sign converts any text following it to lowercase, and the question marks (?) indicate optional letters.

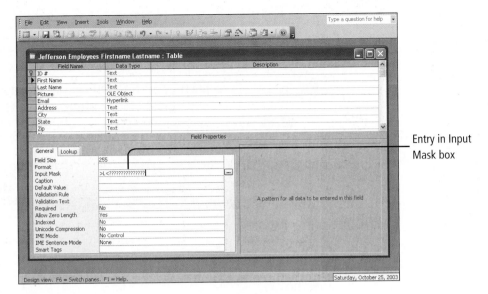

Entry in Input
Mask box

Figure 4.17

3 In the upper portion of the Table window, click in the **Last Name** field to make it the active field.

4 Under **Field Properties**, in the **Input Mask** box, type **>L<???????????????** (There are 15 question marks.)

5 In the upper portion of the Table window, click in the **City** field to make it the active field.

6 Under **Field Properties**, in the **Input Mask** box, type **>L<??????????????????** (There are 18 question marks to allow for longer city names.)

7 Switch to **Datasheet view** and save. Type the following information as the next record in the table being careful *not* to capitalize the first letter of the First Name, Last Name, and City fields, so that you can see how Access handles such errors. Because you set the **State** field to always display *VA*, you do not have to enter the state. There is no picture file available for this employee.

ID #	**0405**
First Name	**shelby**
Last Name	**rincon**
Picture	
Email	**srincon@jeffinn.com**
Address	**63 W. Eden**
City	**rivanna**
State	
Zip	**22911**
Phone	**434-555-2736**
Hire Date	**5/6/1998**

As you typed in the data, Access capitalized the first letter in the First Name, Last Name, and City fields. Additionally, Access entered a value of VA in the State field from the default value you gave it in an earlier activity.

8 Switch to **Design view** for the next activity.

Activity 4.7 Specifying Numeric Input Masks

In this activity, you will create an input mask that will require four digits in the ID # field in the Employee table.

1 In the upper portion of the Table window, click in the **ID #** field to make it the active field. Under **Field Properties**, click in the **Input Mask** box, and then type **0000** See Figure 4.18.

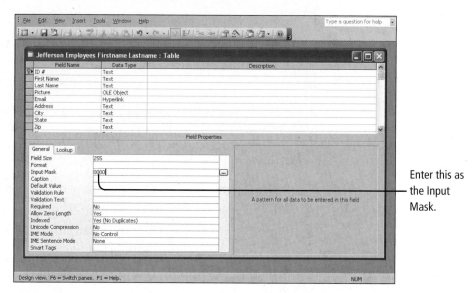

Enter this as the Input Mask.

Figure 4.18

More Knowledge — Do I Use Input Masks or Field Formats?

Input masks affect how data looks and is stored.

The characters that are used in input masks are similar to the ones you used earlier in the chapter when you specified a field format. The difference between specifying a field format and creating an input mask is that input masks affect how data looks and how it is stored. Field formats affect only how the data looks.

2 Switch to **Datasheet view** and save the table when prompted. Under the last record, click at the beginning of the **ID #** field.

Notice that Access has inserted a template that is four spaces long.

3 In the **ID #** field for this new record, try to type **abcd**

Access will not allow this entry because the input mask requires four digits and will not allow letters.

4 In the **ID #** field type **9999** and then click the **row selector** for this record. See Figure 4.19.

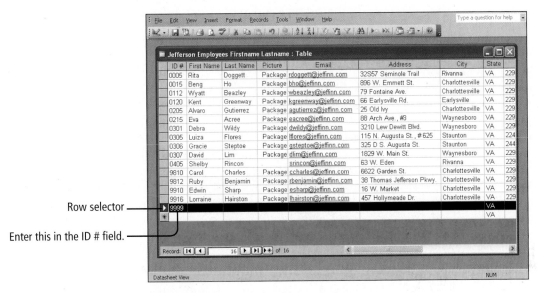

Row selector ——

Enter this in the ID # field. ——

Figure 4.19

5 Press Delete to delete this record, and then click **Yes**.

Because the ID # is the primary key in this table and a primary key field cannot be blank, Access requires that you type in an entry before you can delete the record. Custom input masks can be created to match your field requirements using the characters shown in the table in Figure 4.20. Use this table as a reference.

Another Way ——

Removing a Record

Use the Escape key

You can use Esc to remove a record you are currently entering. Upon creating a new record, pressing Esc once will remove the entry in the current field. Pressing Esc two times will remove the entire record.

Most Common Input Mask Characters

Character	Description
0	Required digit (0 through 9).
9	Optional digit or space.
#	Optional digit or space; blank positions are converted to spaces; plus and minus signs are allowed.
L	Required letter (A through Z).
?	Optional letter (A through Z).
A	Required letter or digit.
a	Optional letter or digit.
&	Required character (any kind) or a space.
C	Optional character (any kind) or a space.
<	All characters that follow are converted to lowercase.
>	All characters that follow are converted to uppercase.
!	Characters typed into the mask fill it from left to right. The exclamation point can be included anywhere in the input mask.
\	Character that follows is displayed as a literal character.
Password	Creates a password entry box where any character that is typed is stored as the character entered but displays as an *.

Figure 4.20

6 Switch to **Design view** for the next activity.

Objective 5
Specify a Required Field

Recall that if a table has a field designated as the primary key, an entry for this field is required; it cannot be left empty. You can set this requirement on other fields, and you may find it necessary to make an entry required for a field that is not the primary key. For example, in the following activity, you will specify that the employee name fields cannot be left empty for an employee at Jefferson Country Inn.

Activity 4.8 Specifying a Required Field

1 In the upper portion of the Table window, click in the **First Name** field to make it the active field. Under **Field Properties**, click in the **Required** box, and then click the **downward-pointing arrow** that displays. See Figure 4.21.

Only Yes and No appear in the list that displays.

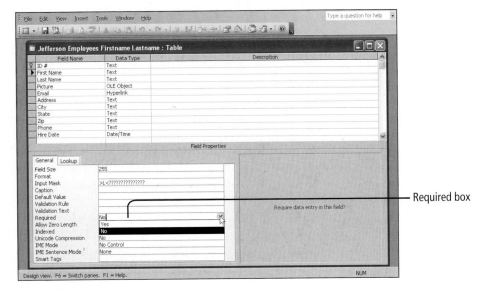

Required box

Figure 4.21

2 Click **Yes**.

Clicking Yes in the Required box will require a user to enter a first name for each record.

3 In the upper portion of the Table window, click in the **Last Name** field to make it the active field. In the **Field Properties** section, click in the **Required** box, and then click the **downward-pointing arrow** that displays.

4 Click **Yes**.

This action will require the person typing data into the database to enter a last name for each record.

5 Switch to **Datasheet view**, saving your changes when prompted. In the warning message that displays, click **Yes**. See Figure 4.22.

Access displays a message warning you that data integrity rules have been changed and asks you if you want the existing data to be tested with the new rules.

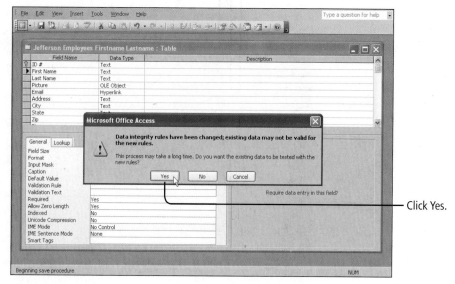

Click Yes.

Figure 4.22

6 Switch to **Design view** for the next activity.

Objective 6
Validate Data Entry

You can further restrict data entry by adding a validation rule to a field in your table. A **validation rule** is an expression that precisely defines the information that will be accepted in a field. An **expression** is a combination of functions, field values, constants, and operators that brings about a result. In the following activity, you will create a validation rule to restrict entries in the Hire Date field of your table.

Activity 4.9 Using the Expression Builder to Create Validation Rules

1 In the upper portion of the Table window, click in the **Hire Date** field to make it the active field. Under **Field Properties**, click in the **Validation Rule** box, and then click the **Build** button that displays. See Figure 4.23.

The **Expression Builder** dialog box displays. The Expression Builder is a feature used to create formulas (expressions) in query criteria, form and report properties, and table validation rules.

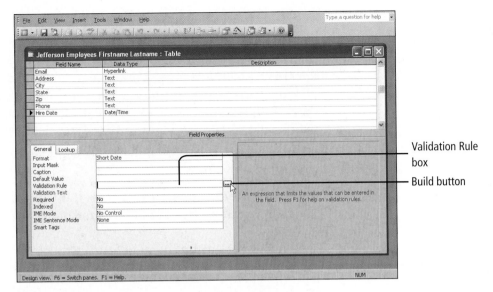

Validation Rule box

Build button

Figure 4.23

2 In the upper white area of the **Expression Builder** dialog box type **>=1/1/1998**

Jefferson Country Inn began operations on January 1, 1998; therefore, no hire dates should be prior to this one.

Another Way ── **Using the Expression Builder**

Type expressions or use the existing toolbar buttons

When creating an expression in the Expression Builder, you can either type in the entire expression, or, on the small toolbar within the dialog box, click an existing button, such as the > button, to insert the characters you need in your expression.

3 In the **Expression Builder** dialog box, click **OK**, and then switch to **Datasheet view**, saving your changes. Click **Yes** in the warning message.

4 In the **Hire Date** field for **Luiza Flores**, change the year to **1997** and then press Tab.

A message displays that the value you entered violates a validation rule set for this field.

5 In the message box, click **OK**, change the year back to **2003** for **Luiza Flores**, and then press Tab.

Access allows this entry because the validation rule you set is not violated.

6 Switch to **Design view** for the next activity.

Activity 4.10 Creating Validation Text

Setting a validation rule will prevent the entry of data that may violate the rule; but, what if the person entering the data is unaware of the rule? For this reason, it is a good practice to add *validation text* that will display the correct format in the event someone attempts to enter invalid data. In this activity, you will add validation text to accompany the validation rule you created for the **Hire Date** field.

1 In the upper portion of the Table window, be sure the **Hire Date** field is the active field.

2 Under **Field Properties**, click in the **Validation Text** box, and then type **Year must be 1998 or later** as shown in Figure 4.24.

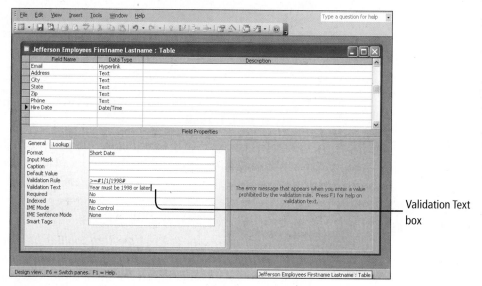

Figure 4.24

3 Switch to **Datasheet view** and save changes to the table. In the **Hire Date** field for **Rita Doggett**, change the year to **1997** and press Tab.

A message displays with the validation text you created for the Hire Date validation rule.

4 Click **OK**, and then click the **Undo** button two times.

5 From the **File** menu, click **Page Setup**. Click the **Margins** tab, and change the **Left** margin to **0.5** and change the **Right** margin to **0.5**. Click the **Page tab**, and under **Orientation**, click the **Landscape** button. Click **OK**.

6 Print the Jefferson Employees table. Close the table, save changes, close the database, and then close Access.

End You have completed Project 4A ——————————

Project 4B **Jefferson Inn Guests**

People sometimes spell things differently. To represent the state of Colorado, someone creating a mailing list might use *CO, Colo.,* or *Colorado*. These different spellings may not confuse the person who is looking at a printout of the mailing list because most people would understand that each of those three spellings indicates the state of Colorado. A computer, however, interprets data literally. For example, if you queried Access to create a mailing list of guests of Jefferson Country Inn from CO, it would not include those from Colo. or Colorado.

In Activities 4.11 through 4.15, you will create a Lookup Wizard field and practice skills that will assist you in finding data in the Guests table for Jefferson Country Inn. Additionally, you will apply conditional formatting to a field in the Guests table. Your completed table will look similar to Figure 4.25. You will save the database as *4B_Jefferson_Inn_Guests_ Firstname_Lastname.*

Guests Firstname Lastname   10/26/2003

Visit Date	Nights	First Name	Last Name	# in Party	Address	City	State	Zip	Phone
6/15/2003	2	Brandon	Smith	2	2745 Sherwin Ave.	Washington	DC	20017	202-555-0110
5/25/2003	2	Catrina	Johnson	3	3532 Preble St.	Richmond	VA	23222	804-555-0178
5/23/2003	2	Bill	Kukielka	2	1357 Nathan Lane, #D	Charlottesville	VA	22907	434-555-0098
7/21/2003	3	Zachary	Juras	2	15 Aspen Blvd.	Denver	CO	80202	303-555-0122
6/18/2003	1	Elaine	Broderick	1	1611 Lakehurst	Chicago	IL	60611	312-555-0129
5/15/2003	2	Julio	Ferrer	4	892 Cactus Ave.	Scottsdale	AZ	85259	480-555-0199
5/15/2003	1	Kelvin	McNeely	3	5188 S. University St.	Simi Valley	CA	93065	805-555-0154
6/15/2003	1	Theodora	Lanham	2	1849 Burleson Ave.	Naples	FL	34102	239-555-0173
6/15/2003	1	Ethan	Stowe	2	288 S. Orange Grove Blvd. #23	Orlando	FL	32825	407-555-0192
7/21/2003	3	Javier	Nye	2	2 West California St.	Clovis	CA	93613	559-555-0148
5/1/2003	4	Sharon	Cousins	1	333 S. Washington Blvd. #1215	Washington	DC	20011	240-555-0126
5/2/2003	4	Neel	Singh	4	76 Chesapeake Way	Baltimore	MD	21224	410-555-0182
5/30/2003	2	Leane	Wang	3	2444 Cortez Way	Richmond	VA	23222	804-555-0002
6/1/2003	3	Sacha	Federov	4	3318 Allegheny Court	Charlotte	NC	28210	704-555-0107
6/10/2003	4	Sirvat	Torosian	2	7982 Paseo Margarita	Austin	TX	78710	512-555-0082
5/12/2003	1	Brandon	Smith	1	9315 Orchard Ave.	Albuquerque	NM	87110	505-555-2749

Page 1

Figure 4.25
Project 4B—Jefferson Inn Guests

Objective 7
Create a Lookup Wizard Field

Creating a Lookup field restricts the data entered in a field because the person entering the data must choose from a predefined list. A **Lookup field** allows you to create and then display a list of values from a field in another table.

Activity 4.11 Creating a Lookup Wizard Field

In this activity you will create a Lookup Wizard field for the State field in the Guests table at Jefferson Country Inn.

1 Locate the file **a04B_Jefferson_Inn_Guests** from your student files and copy and paste the file to your Chapter 4 folder. Remove the Read-only property from the file and rename the file as **4B_Jefferson_Inn_Guests_Firstname_Lastname** Start Access and open the database you just renamed.

2 On the Objects bar, click **Tables** if necessary, right-click the **Jefferson Guests** table, and then click **Rename**.

3 In the box that displays and using your own information, type **Guests Firstname Lastname** and then press [Enter].

4 Open your **Guests** table in **Datasheet view**. Examine the fields and records in the table and notice that the last four records do not have entries for the **State** field.

These entries could be typed, but to ensure consistent entries for items in the State field, a Lookup field will be more efficient.

5 Switch to **Design view**. In the upper portion of the Table window, in the **Data Type** column, click in the **State** field under **Data Type**, and then click the **downward-pointing arrow** that displays.

6 From the list of data types, click **Lookup Wizard**. See Figure 4.26.

The Lookup Wizard starts.

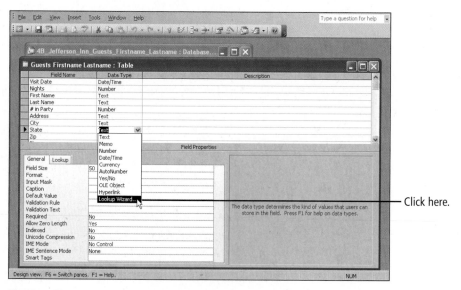

Figure 4.26

7 In the first screen of the wizard, be sure *I want the lookup column to look up the value in a table or query.* is selected.

The first screen of the Lookup Wizard allows you to choose whether you want Access to find the information from another table or whether you would like to type the information yourself.

8 Click **Next**. In the next screen of the wizard, under *Which table or query should provide the values for your lookup column?*, click **Table: States** as shown in Figure 4.27, and then click **Next**.

This database contains a table called States that includes the information you need for this field.

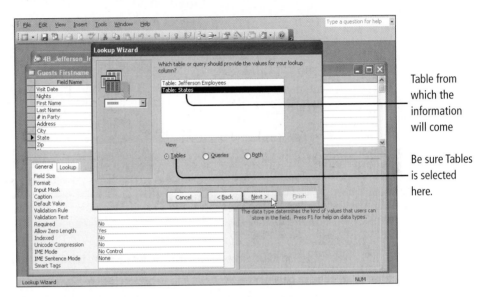

Table from which the information will come

Be sure Tables is selected here.

Figure 4.27

9 In the next screen, under **Available Fields**, click **Abbreviation**, and then click the **One Field** button ![button] to move the **Abbreviation** field under **Selected Fields**. Click **Next**.

10 In the **1** box, click the **downward-pointing arrow**, and then click **Abbreviation**. Leave the order as **Ascending**.

This screen allows you to choose a Sort order for the data in this field.

11 Click **Next**, and then at the next screen, click **Next** again.

12 Under *What label would you like for your lookup column?*, leave the default of **State**, and then click the **Finish** button.

13 Click **Yes** to save the table, and then switch to **Datasheet view**.

14 In the record for **Leane Wang**, under **State**, click once.

A downward-pointing arrow displays.

15 Click the **downward-pointing arrow**. From the list of states, scroll down, and then click **VA**, as shown in Figure 4.28.

VA displays in the State field for Leane Wang.

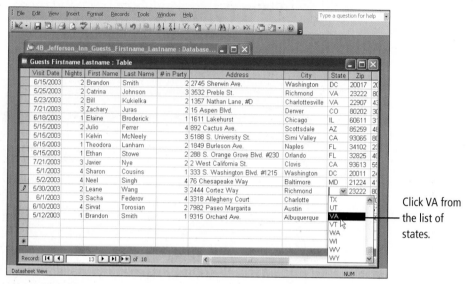

Figure 4.28

16 In the record of **Sacha Federov**, under **State**, click once, and then click the **downward-pointing arrow**.

17 From the list of states, click **NC**.

18 Repeat this technique to add **TX** as the state for **Sirvat Torosian** and **NM** as the state for **Brandon Smith**.

19 Stay in **Datasheet view** for the next activity.

Objective 8
Find a Record

Queries can locate information, but for a quick search to simply locate a record in a table, for example, the record of a specific guest, use the Find button on the Table Datasheet toolbar. Performing a search using this method is similar to using Find and Replace in other Microsoft Office applications.

Activity 4.12 Finding a Record by Searching a Single Field

In this activity you will use the Find button to locate a specific guest in the Guests table for Jefferson Country Inn.

1 In the **Datasheet view** of your **Guests** table, click anywhere in the **Last Name** column.

To search for a record using the Find button, you must first select the field where you want Access to look for your information.

2 On the Table Datasheet toolbar, click the **Find** button 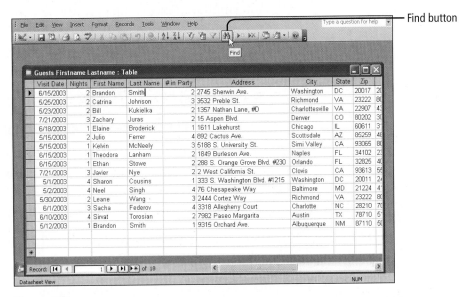.
See Figure 4.29.

The Find and Replace dialog box displays.

— Find button

Figure 4.29

3 In the **Find What** box, type **nye** and then click **Find Next**.

Access has located the record with *nye* as a last name as indicated by
the highlighted last name and the row selector. See Figure 4.30.

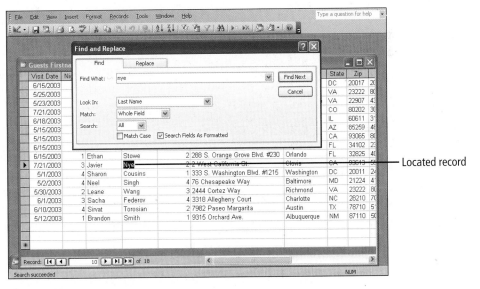

— Located record

Figure 4.30

4 If necessary, move the **Find and Replace** dialog box out of your way by clicking and dragging its title bar up and to the right so you can view the record Access has located.

This method is particularly useful to quickly locate a record and view the information. For example, at the Jefferson Inn, employees might want to quickly find information such as a guest reservation.

5 In the **Find and Replace** dialog box, click **Cancel** to close the dialog box.

6 Leave your table open in **Datasheet view** for the next activity.

Activity 4.13 Finding a Record by Searching the Table

It is faster to search for a particular record by having Access search only one field, as you just practiced in the last activity. However, you can perform a search and have Access search all the fields in the table.

1 Click anywhere in the first record of the table, and then on the Table Datasheet toolbar, click the **Find** button ⚲.

The Find and Replace dialog box displays.

2 In the **Find What** box, type **Washington**

3 In the **Look In** box, click the **arrow**, and then from the displayed list, click **Guests Firstname Lastname: Table**.

Searching the entire table is useful if you do not know in what field the information is located.

4 In the **Match** box, click the **arrow**, and then from the displayed list, click **Any Part of Field**.

Clicking Any Part of Field directs Access to locate an instance of *Washington* even if it is not the entire entry in a field.

5 Click **Find Next**.

Access locates the record for Brandon Smith, who lives in the City of *Washington*.

6 Click **Find Next**.

Access locates the record for Sharon Cousins, who has *Washington* in her address.

7 Click **Find Next**.

Access highlights *Washington* in the City field for Sharon Cousins.

8 Click **Find Next**.

A message displays indicating that the searching of the records is finished. Access displays a message indicating that the item was not found. This means that after it found the three occurrences, it did not find any more.

9 Click **OK**, and then click **Cancel** in the **Find and Replace** dialog box.

10 Leave the table open in **Datasheet view** for the next activity.

Objective 9
Display Specific Records

Sorting records organizes a table in a logical manner; but viewing the entire table can be difficult. To locate and display only the records you would like to see, you can create a filter. You can apply a simple filter while viewing a table (or form). Creating a filter to quickly view desired information while hiding unwanted records is quicker than creating a query, but it does not allow you to specify criteria as precisely as a query does.

Activity 4.14 Displaying Specific Records Using Filter By Selection

In this activity, you will create a Filter By Selection to locate those records that have *VA* as the state. **Filter By Selection** allows you to locate records based on data in a field.

1 In the **Datasheet view** of your **Guests** table, in the **State** column, click in the record for **Catrina Johnson**. (For this example, you could click in any record where the state is VA.)

2 On the Table Datasheet toolbar, click the **Filter By Selection** button. See Figure 4.31.

Three records display; each has VA in the State field.

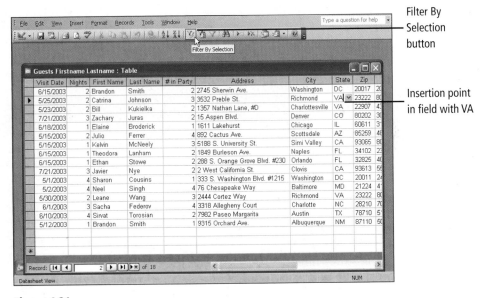

Figure 4.31

Note — Filter By Selection

Unmatched fields are not deleted.

When you filter a table, the records that do not match are not deleted from your table; they are only hidden from view.

3 On the Table Datasheet toolbar, click the **Remove Filter** button ⟨Y⟩. See Figure 4.32.

The filter is removed and all the records display.

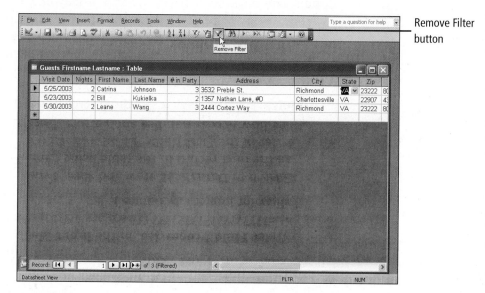

Figure 4.32

4 In the **Last Name** column, in the record for **Ethan Stowe**, select the **S** in *Stowe*. See Figure 4.33.

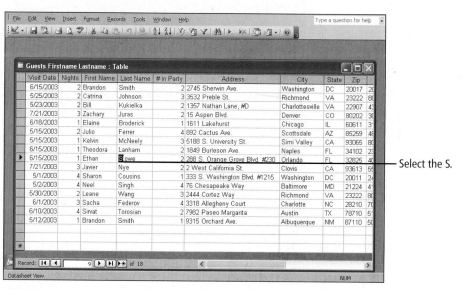

Figure 4.33

5 On the Table Datasheet toolbar, click the **Filter By Selection** button ⟨▽⟩.

Four records display; each has a last name beginning with S.

6 On the Table Datasheet toolbar, click the **Remove Filter** button ▽.

The filter is removed and all the records display.

7 Leave your table open in **Datasheet view** for the next activity.

Activity 4.15 Displaying Specific Records Using Filter By Form

Suppose you are looking for information based on more than one field in a table. For example, you may need to find a guest at Jefferson Inn whose name, you think, begins with a K and you think he or she is from Virginia. For a search such as this, you could not use Filter By Selection; instead you would use **Filter By Form**. This is a technique for filtering data that uses a version of the current form or datasheet with empty fields in which you can type the values that you want the filtered records to contain.

1 On the Table Datasheet toolbar, click **Filter By Form** 🖳.
See Figure 4.34.

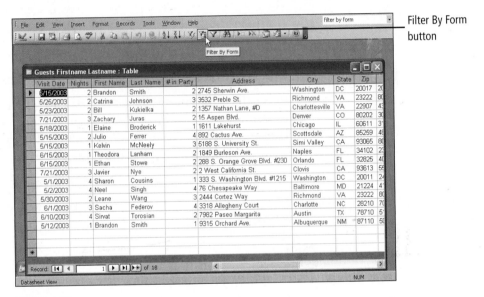

Filter By Form button

Figure 4.34

2 In the **Last Name** column, delete any existing text and then type **k***

The asterisk (*) is a wildcard that serves as a placeholder for any number of characters.

3 Click in the **State** column, click the **arrow** that displays, scroll down to the bottom of the list, and then click **VA**. See Figure 4.35.

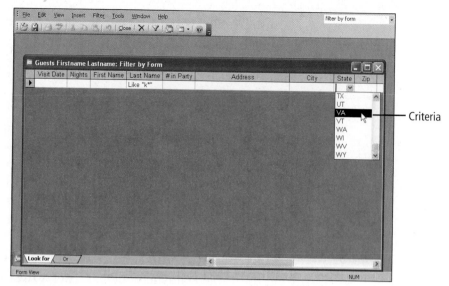

Criteria

Figure 4.35

4 On the Table Datasheet toolbar, click the **Apply Filter** button ▽.
The record for Bill Kukielka in VA displays.

5 On the Table Datasheet toolbar, click the **Remove Filter** button ▽.

6 From the **File** menu, click **Page Setup**. Click the **Margins tab**, and
then change the **Left** and **Right** margins to **0.5**. Be sure the **Print
Headings** check box is selected. Click the **Page tab**, and under
Orientation, click the **Landscape** option button. Click **OK**. On the
Standard toolbar, click the **Print** button 🖨.

7 Close the table, click **Yes** if prompted to save any changes, close the
database, and then close Access.

End You have completed Project 4B ━━━━━━━━━━━━━━━━━━━━━━━

Pages, the fifth object on the Objects bar, enables you to view information contained in a database from the Internet or a company intranet. An *intranet* is a privately owned Web-based network used by companies and organizations to share information by using Web technology, but without publishing their private information on the public Internet. Access pages are viewed by users through a *browser*—a program such as Microsoft Internet Explorer—that enables you to view Web pages.

In Activities 4.16 through 4.18, you will create a data access page for Jefferson Country Inn so guests can view listings of books, videos, and DVDs that are available for them to check out from the Inn's library. Your data access page will look like Figure 4.36. You will save the database as *4C_Jefferson_Inn_Library_Firstname_Lastname*. Additionally, in Activity 4.19, you will convert a database containing older records for the Inn from a previous version of Access to the current version.

Firstname Lastname Jefferson Library   Page 1 of 1

Firstname Lastname Library Page

ID#:   B1
Title: Around the World in 80 Days
Media: Book
Quantity: 1

| ◄◄ ◄ | Jefferson Library 1 of 16 | ► ►◄ ►◄ ►X ▧ ᵍ ⅍ ᴢ↓ ᴢ↑ ᵥ ᵧ ▨ |

accdp://138758864/   10/26/2003

Figure 4.36
Project 4C—Jefferson Inn Library

Objective 10
Create and Use a Data Access Page

Activity 4.16 Creating a Data Access Page

In this activity you will create a data access page so that guests of the Jefferson Country Inn can view a list of library items that are available to check out from the Jefferson Inn's library.

■ Locate the file **a04C_Jefferson_Inn_Library** from your student files and copy and paste the file to the Chapter 4 folder you created. Remove the Read-only property from the file and rename the file as **4C_Jefferson_Inn_Library_Firstname_Lastname** Start Access and open the database you just renamed.

■ Open the **Jefferson Library** table in **Datasheet view** and examine the records in the table.

The table contains a list of items such as books, CDs, DVDs, and videos that guests of Jefferson Country Inn can check out from the Inn's library.

■ **Close** the table.

■ On the Objects bar, click **Pages**.

Three command icons for creating or editing data access pages display.

■ In the Database window, double-click **Create data access page by using wizard**.

The Page Wizard begins and is similar to other wizards you have used in Access to create a new object.

■ Under **Tables/Queries** verify that **Table: Jefferson Library** displays. This is the table that contains the information to display in the data access page.

■ To the right of the list of available fields, click the **All Fields** button [>>]. See Figure 4.37.

All of the fields from the Jefferson Library table will be used in the corresponding data access page.

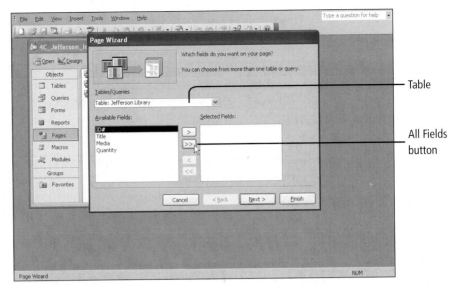

Table

All Fields
button

Figure 4.37

8 Click **Next**. Under **Do you want to add any grouping levels?**, accept the default ID# and click **Next** again.

9 On the page regarding sort order, click **Next**.

10 Under **What title do you want for your page?**, and using your own information, type the title as shown in Figure 4.38.

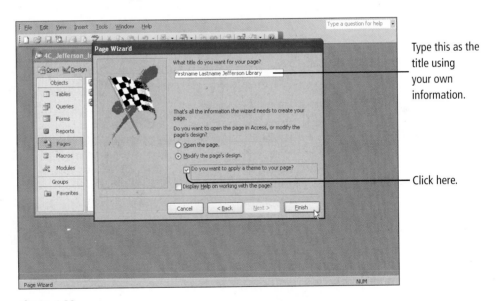

Type this as the
title using
your own
information.

Click here.

Figure 4.38

11 In the same screen where you added the title, select (click to place a check mark in) the *Do you want to apply a theme to your page?* check box, and then click **Finish**. See Figure 4.38.

The page is created and the Theme dialog box displays.

12 Under **Choose a Theme**, click **Iris**, and then click **OK**.

The data access page displays in Design view with the theme you selected. This view of a data access page is similar to the Design view of a form or report.

13 Maximize the data access page. If necessary, close the Field List task pane and the Toolbox toolbar.

14 At the top of the page, click anywhere in the area *Click here and type title text*. Then, using your own information, type **Firstname Lastname Library Page** as the name of the page.

The page title displays across the top of the page. See Figure 4.39.

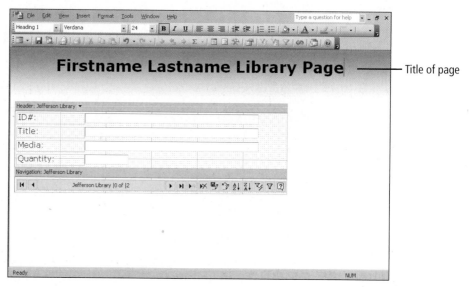

Figure 4.39

15 To the right of the *Type a question for help* box, locate the small **Close Window** button ⊠ and click it to close the data access page. Click **Yes** to save changes to the design of *data access page 'Page1'*.

The Save As Data Access Page dialog box displays.

16 In the **Save As Data Access Page** dialog box, verify that the location where the page will be saved is your Chapter 4 folder and the file name is as shown in Figure 4.40, with your own information.

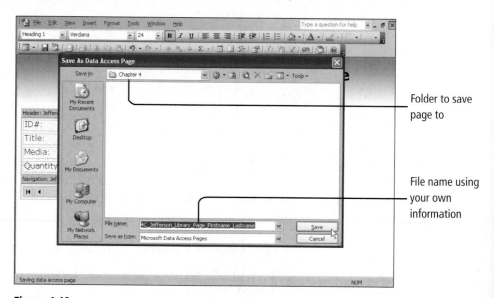

Figure 4.40

17 Click **Save**, and then click **OK** in the message that displays.

You are not using a UNC path for this page; therefore, it is OK to click OK. A shortcut to your data access page displays in the Database window, indicated by the small icon with a curved arrow.

18 Click the **Restore Window** button 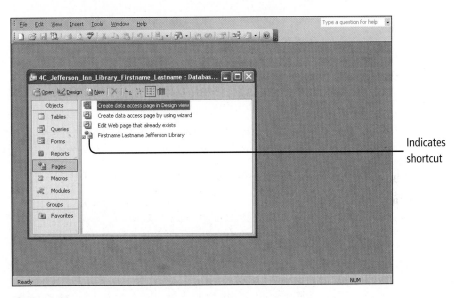 to restore the Database window to its original size.

19 Leave the database open for the next activity.

Activity 4.17 Viewing the Data Access Page with a Browser

Data access pages can be viewed directly in Access or in browser software.

1 On the Objects bar, be sure that **Pages** is selected. In the Database window, double-click the **shortcut** to your **Jefferson Library Page**. See Figure 4.41.

The page opens in Page view. Data access pages are not contained in the database itself. Rather, a shortcut to the page displays in the Database window and the actual page is stored in another location as specified when the page was created.

Indicates shortcut

Figure 4.41

2 On the Page View toolbar, click the **Design View** button .

The page displays in Design view. Use Design view to make changes to the layout of the page.

3 On the Page Design toolbar, click the **Page View** button .

The page redisplays in Page view. Page view is useful to see how the page will display in the browser without actually connecting to the Internet or the organization's intranet. You can think of this as a Web page preview.

4 In the lower portion of the data access page, locate the **Navigation bar**, as shown in Figure 4.42.

The navigation buttons in a data access page function in the same manner as the navigation buttons in a table or form.

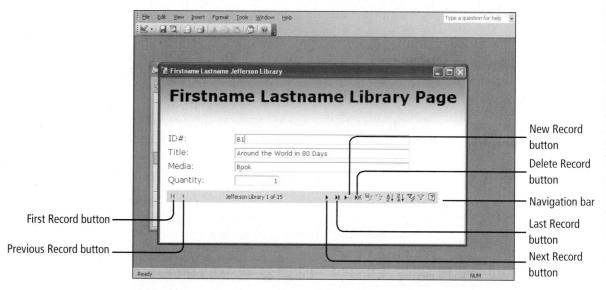

Figure 4.42

5 Practice clicking the various navigation buttons and view the records that display.

6 On the Page View toolbar, click the **View button arrow** ⬇️, and then from the list of views, click **Web Page Preview**. See Figure 4.43.

The page opens in the default browser.

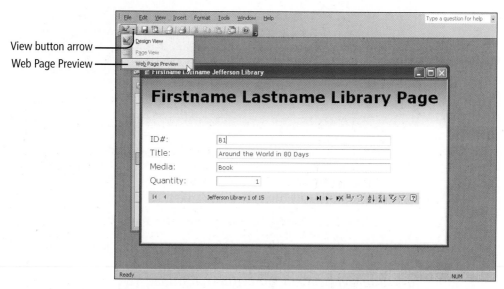

Figure 4.43

7 Examine the page and notice that it looks like it did in Page view.

The page will function in Web Page Preview as it did in Page view.

8 If necessary, click to position the insertion point in the **ID#** field. On the Navigation bar, click the **Sort Ascending** button.

The records are sorted alphabetically by ID#; the first record displays.

9 On the Navigation bar, click the **Sort Descending** button.

The records are sorted in reverse alphabetical order; the last record displays.

10 Use the navigation buttons to navigate to the record titled *Big Band Jazz*, and then click in the **Media** field so the insertion point is blinking in the field.

11 On the **Navigation bar**, click the **Filter by Selection** button.

Five records are filtered and each has a Media of CD, as shown on the Navigation bar. See Figure 4.44.

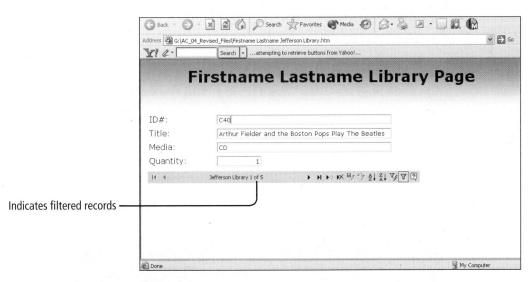

Indicates filtered records ——

Figure 4.44

12 Click the **Next Record** button to view the next CD in the table.

You can see that the Filter by Selection feature is useful to display only specific records.

13 On the **Navigation bar**, click the **Filter Toggle Button** located to the right of the Filter by Selection button.

The filter is removed and the Navigation bar indicates 15 records.

14 Leave the data access page open in Web Page Preview for the next activity.

Activity 4.18 Using a Data Access Page

1 On the **Navigation bar**, click the **New** button.

Data access pages can be used to add records to the data in a table.

2 Complete the information in the fields, as shown in Figure 4.45.

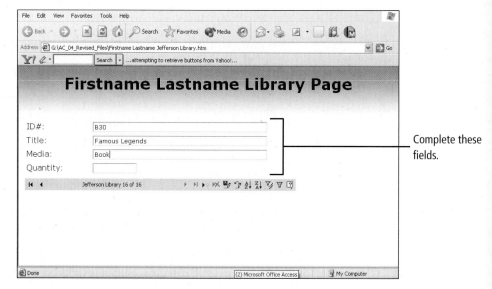

Figure 4.45

Complete these fields.

---

3 After you have filled in the information, on the **Navigation bar**, click the **Save** button 💾 .

The record is saved as part of the table.

4 **Close** ✖ the Web Page Preview, and then **close** ✖ the data access page. On the Objects bar, click **Tables**, and then open the **Jefferson Library** table.

The record you entered in the data access page displays in the table. See Figure 4.46.

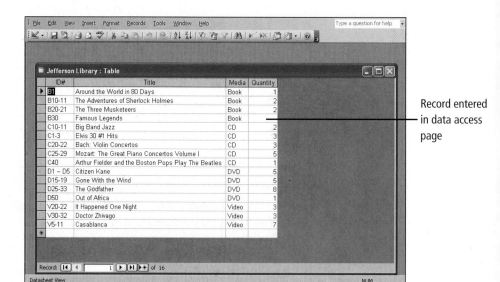

Figure 4.46

Record entered in data access page

5 **Close** ☒ the table.

6 On the Objects bar, click **Pages**, open the **Jefferson Library** data access page, and then print it.

7 Close the page, close the database, and then close Access.

Objective 11
Convert a Database from a Previous Version of Access

As you work with Access, occasionally you will likely need to convert a database created in a prior version of Access to the current version. Perhaps the company you work for created all of its databases in Access 97 (or Access 2000) and now they would like to use the information in those databases in Microsoft Access 2003. To achieve full functionality of the latest version of Access, those older databases will need to be converted to the new version.

Activity 4.19 Converting a Database from a Previous Version of Access

1 Locate the file **a04C_Jefferson_Suppliers1999** from your student files and copy and paste the file to the Chapter 4 folder you created. Remove the Read-only property from the file.

2 Start Access and open this database.

You will see the message in Figure 4.47 indicating that this database was created in an earlier version of Access and you will not be able to make changes to it.

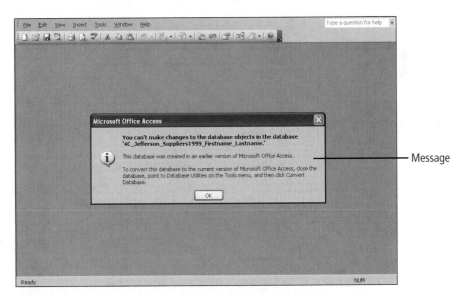

Figure 4.47

3 Click **OK**.

The database opens.

4 Drag the right edge of the Database window to view the full name in the title bar. Notice that it indicates that this database is in Access 97 file format. See Figure 4.48.

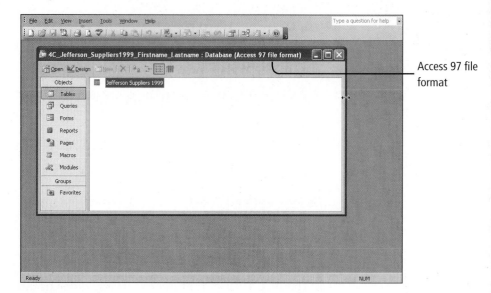

Access 97 file format

Figure 4.48

5 From the **Tools** menu, point to **Database Utilities**, point to **Convert Database**, and then click **To Access 2002 – 2003 File Format**.

The Convert Database Into dialog box displays.

6 Click the **Save in arrow**, and then navigate to the Chapter 4 folder where you are saving your projects for this chapter.

7 In the **File name** box, select the existing text and, using your own information, type **4C_Jefferson_Converted_Suppliers_Firstname_ Lastname** and then click **Save**.

Access displays a message that after you have converted the database, you can no longer share information with Access 2000 users or Access 97 users.

8 Click **OK**.

The old database remains open in the Database window.

9 Close the **a04C_Jefferson_Suppliers1999** database.

Access remains open.

10 On the Database toolbar, click the **Open** button and, if necessary, navigate to the location where you just saved the converted database (your Chapter 4 folder).

11 Double-click your **4C_Jefferson _Converted_Suppliers** file.

12 The converted database opens. Drag the right edge of the database window to see the full name in the title bar.

Notice in the title bar of the database window that the Access 2002-2003 File Format displays.

13 Close the database, and then close Access.

End You have completed Project 4C

Summary

Using Microsoft Access 2003 you can set several properties that enable you to limit the data that users can enter into a database. In this chapter you practiced customizing fields by using several data types, such as Hyperlink and OLE. Additionally, you practiced specifying formats such as date formats. You created an input mask to control data entry and added a validation rule that allows a user to enter only data that meets certain criteria. You constructed a lookup field that allows the user to select data from another table.

In this chapter you also practiced locating specific data directly from a table by using several tools. You used the Find button to search either one field or the entire table for a particular entry. The Filter By Selection and Filter By Form methods are useful for locating records in a table.

Data access pages are a new database object you created in this chapter that allow you to view information contained in a table from either the Internet or a company intranet using a browser. You created a data access page, observed the page in Design view, Page view, and Web Page Preview. You practiced using the data access page to add a new record to its corresponding table.

Finally, you practiced converting a database created in an earlier version of Access to the current version of Access.

In This Chapter You Practiced How To

- Customize a Field
- Specify a Field Format
- Create Input Masks Using the Input Mask Wizard
- Create Input Masks Using the Input Mask Properties Box
- Specify a Required Field
- Validate Data Entry
- Create a Lookup Wizard Field
- Find a Record
- Display Specific Records
- Create and Use a Data Access Page
- Convert a Database from a Previous Version of Access

Matching   Match each term in the second column with its correct definition in the first column by writing the letter of the term on the blank line in front of the correct definition.

_____ **1.** The feature that allows you to locate records based on data in more than one field.

_____ **2.** The field property that determines the data that can be entered, how the data displays, and how the data is stored.

_____ **3.** A feature that allows you to display a list of values from a field in another table in order to restrict data entry.

_____ **4.** The data type that allows you to insert graphics, spreadsheets, and other objects in a table.

_____ **5.** The text that displays if a user attempts to enter data in a field that violates a validation rule.

_____ **6.** A program such as Internet Explorer that enables you to view Web pages.

_____ **7.** A feature of Access that is used to create formulas in query criteria, form and report properties, and table validation rules.

_____ **8.** Allows you to locate records based on data in one field.

_____ **9.** When working with OLE fields, these objects are actually placed into the database object.

_____ **10.** A privately owned network that uses Web technology to share information within an organization.

_____ **11.** When working with OLE fields, these objects are not contained in the database; only their address or location is contained in the database.

_____ **12.** Expression that defines the information that will be accepted in a field.

_____ **13.** The database object that allows users to manipulate data in a database via the Internet.

_____ **14.** A combination of functions, field values, constants, and operators that brings about a result.

_____ **15.** The field setting that determines the content and appearance of that field.

A Browser

B Embedded

C Expression

D Expression Builder

E Filter By Form

F Filter By Selection

G Input Mask

H Intranet

I Linked

J Lookup field

K OLE

L Pages

M Property

N Validation rule

O Validation text

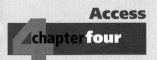
Fill in the Blank Write the correct answer in the space provided.

1. One method of keeping a database organized and useful is to

    _____, or limit, the data that can be entered in the

    database.

2. The data type that allows the entry of additional text, up to 65,536

    characters, is _____.

3. The data type that permits the entry of a URL is _____.

4. If a field will have the same entry most of the time, you can assign a

    _____ to the field to save data entry time and ensure

    consistency.

5. In an input mask, the _____ sign causes the letters

    that follow to be capitalized.

6. The lower portion of the table window is called the

    _____.

7. After a filter has been applied to a table, in order to view all the

    records in the table, you must _____ the filter.

8. The view of a data access page that displays the page in a browser is

    the _____.

9. To gain full functionality of an older database, you must

    _____ the database to the most current version

    of Access.

10. Commands for Database Utilities, which contain the option to convert

    a database, are located on the _____ menu.

Project 4D — Guests1

Objectives: *Customize a Field, Specify a Field Format, and Create Input Masks Using the Input Mask Wizard.*

In the following Skill Assessment, you will customize fields in the database and create an input mask for a field using the wizard. This database is used by the Jefferson Country Inn to store information about the guests that stay at the Inn. Your completed table will look like the one shown in Figure 4.49. You will rename and save the database as *4D_Guests1_Firstname_Lastname.*

Jefferson Guests Firstname Lastname   10/26/2003

Visit Date	Nights	First Name	Last Name	# in Party	Address	City	State	Zip	Phone
6/15/2003	2	Brandon	Smith	2	2745 Sherwin Ave.	Washington	DC	20017	202-555-0110
5/25/2003	2	Catrina	Johnson	3	3532 Preble St.	Richmond	VA	23222	804-555-0178
5/23/2003	2	Bill	Kukielka	2	1357 Nathan Lane, #D	Charlottesville	VA	22907	434-555-0098
7/21/2003	3	Zachary	Juras	2	15 Aspen Blvd.	Denver	CO	80202	303-555-0122
6/18/2003	1	Elaine	Broderick	1	1611 Lakehurst	Chicago	IL	60611	312-555-0129
5/15/2003	2	Julio	Ferrer	4	892 Cactus Ave.	Scottsdale	AZ	85259	480-555-0199
5/15/2003	1	Kelvin	McNeely	3	5188 S. University St.	Simi valley	CA	93065	805-555-0154
6/15/2003	1	Theodora	Lanham	2	1849 Burleson Ave.	Naples	FL	34102	239-555-0173
6/15/2003	1	Ethan	Stowe	2	288 S. Orange Grove Blvd. #23	Orlando	FL	32825	407-555-0192
7/21/2003	3	Javier	Nye	2	2 West California St.	Clovis	CA	93613	559-555-0148
5/1/2003	4	Sharon	Cousins	1	333 S. Washington Blvd. #1215	Washington	DC	20011	240-555-0126
5/2/2003	4	Neel	Singh	4	76 Chesapeake Way	Baltimore	MD	21224	410-555-0182
5/30/2003	2	Leane	Wang	3	2444 Cortez Way	Richmond	VA	23222	804-555-0002
6/1/2003	3	Sacha	Federov	4	3318 Allegheny Court	Charlotte	NC	28210	704-555-0107
6/10/2003	4	Sirvat	Torosian	2	7982 Paseo Margarita	Austin	TX	78710	512-555-0082
5/12/2003	1	Brandon	Smith	1	9315 Orchard Ave.	Albuquerque	NM	87110	505-555-2749
9/6/2003	2	Devon	Albrey	2	306 Skyward	Sedona	AZ	86339	(928) 555-444

Page 1

Figure 4.49

1. Locate the file **a04D_Guests1** from your student files and copy and paste the file to the Chapter 4 folder where you are storing your projects for this chapter. Remove the Read-only property from the file and rename the file as **4D_Guests1_Firstname_Lastname** Start Access and open the database you just renamed.

2. On the Objects bar, click **Tables** if necessary, right-click the **Jefferson Guests** table, and then click **Rename**.

3. In the box that displays and using your own information, type **Jefferson Guests Firstname Lastname** and then press Enter.

4. Open your **Jefferson Guests** table in **Datasheet view** and examine the data in the table. Switch to **Design view**. In the upper portion of the Table window, click in the **# in Party** field to make it the active field.

(Project 4D–Guests1 continues on the next page)

(Project 4D–Guests1 continued)

5. Under **Field Properties**, in the **Default Value** box, type **2**

6. Switch to **Datasheet view** and save the table. Notice under the last record, in the **# in Party** column, a value of 2 is already entered, ready for the next record. Specifying a default value for a field saves data entry time and also reduces the possibility of typographical errors.

7. Switch to **Design view** and click in the **City** field to make it the active field. Under **Field Properties**, in the **Input Mask** box, type **>L<????????????????????** (There are 20 question marks.) The greater than (>) sign forces the following text to display in uppercase. The L requires a letter entry (first names begin with a letter), the less than (<) sign forces the following text to display in lowercase, and the question mark (?) allows either a letter or no letter to be entered.

8. Click in the **Visit Date** field to make it the active field. Under **Field Properties**, click in the **Format** box, click the **arrow**, and from the list of date formats, click **Short Date**.

9. Switch to **Datasheet view** and save the table. Click in the first column of the last row of the table. Type the following information as the next record in the table paying careful attention not to capitalize the first letter of the **City** field. Notice that you do not have to type in an entry for the **# in Party** field. Note: Do not enter a phone number for this record. You will do that in a later step.

Visit Date	**9/6/2003**
Nights	**2**
First Name	**Devon**
Last Name	**Albrey**
# in Party	**2**
Address	**306 Skyward**
City	**sedona**
State	**AZ**
Zip	**86339**
Phone	

As you typed in the data, Access capitalized the first letter in the City field. Additionally, Access entered a value of 2 in the # in Party field from the default value you defined.

10. Switch to **Design view** and in the upper portion of the Table window, click in the **Phone** field to make it the active field. Under **Field Properties**, click in the **Input Mask** box, and then click the **Build** button that displays.

11. In the first screen of the Input Mask Wizard, click **Phone Number**, if necessary, and then click **Next**.

(Project 4D–Guests1 continues on the next page)

(Project 4D—Guests1 continued)

12. Leave all the default settings and click **Next**.

13. On the third screen of the wizard that asks you how you want to store the data, be sure *Without the symbols in the mask, like this* is selected, and then click **Next**.

14. In the final screen of the wizard click **Finish**. Access creates an input mask for a typical phone number.

15. Switch to **Datasheet view**, save, and if necessary, scroll to the right to view the **Phone** field. In the last record, click in the **Phone** field and notice the parentheses and hyphen that display.

16. Click in the **Zip** field for this record, press [Tab], and then type **9285554444** as the phone number. Press [Tab], and then scroll to the right to view the entry. Now that you have defined the field as a phone number, Access inserts the parentheses and hyphens commonly used as the format for a phone number. You did not have to type them.

17. From the **File** menu, click **Page Setup**. Click the **Page tab**, and then under **Orientation**, click the **Landscape** option button. Click **OK**, and then click **Print** to print the Guests table. Close the database and then close Access.

End You have completed Project 4D

Project 4E — Guests2

Objectives: *Specify a Required Field, Validate Data Entry, and Create a Lookup Wizard Field.*

In the following Skill Assessment, you will add a required field and create validation rules and text for fields in the Guests table for Jefferson Country Inn. Additionally, you will add a Lookup field to the table. The table will look similar to the one shown in Figure 4.50. You will save your database as *4E_Guests2_Firstname_Lastname*.

1. Locate the file **a04E_Guests2** from your student files and copy and paste the file to the Chapter 4 folder where you are storing your projects for this chapter. Remove the Read-only property from the file and rename the file as **4E_Guests2_Firstname_Lastname** Start Access and open the database you just renamed.

2. On the Objects bar, click **Tables** if necessary, right-click the **Jefferson Guests** table, and then click **Rename**.

3. In the box that displays and using your own information, type **Guests2 Firstname Lastname** and then press [Enter].

(Project 4E—Guests2 continues on the next page)

(Project 4E–Guests2 continued)

Visit Date	Nights	First Name	Last Name	# in Party	Address	City	State	Zip	Phone
					Guests2 Firstname Lastname				10/26/2003
6/15/2003	2	Brandon	Smith	2	2745 Sherwin Ave.	Washington	DC	20017	202-555-0110
5/25/2003	2	Catrina	Johnson	3	3532 Preble St.	Richmond	VA	23222	804-555-0178
5/23/2003	2	Bill	Kukielka	2	1357 Nathan Lane, #D	Charlottesville	VA	22907	434-555-0098
7/21/2003	3	Zachary	Juras	2	15 Aspen Blvd.	Denver	CO	80202	303-555-0122
6/18/2003	1	Elaine	Broderick	1	1611 Lakehurst	Chicago	IL	60611	312-555-0129
5/15/2003	2	Julio	Ferrer	4	892 Cactus Ave.	Scottsdale	AZ	85259	480-555-0199
5/15/2003	1	Kelvin	McNeely	3	5188 S. University St.	Simi Valley	CA	93065	805-555-0154
6/15/2003	1	Theodora	Lanham	2	1849 Burleson Ave.	Naples	FL	34102	239-555-0173
6/15/2003	1	Ethan	Stowe	2	288 S. Orange Grove Blvd. #23	Orlando	FL	32825	407-555-0192
7/21/2003	3	Javier	Nye	2	2 West California St.	Clovis	CA	93613	559-555-0148
5/1/2003	4	Sharon	Cousins	1	333 S. Washington Blvd. #1215	Washington	DC	20011	240-555-0126
5/2/2003	7	Neel	Singh	4	76 Chesapeake Way	Baltimore	MD	21224	410-555-0182
5/30/2003	2	Leane	Wang	3	2444 Cortez Way	Richmond	VA	23222	804-555-0002
6/1/2003	3	Sacha	Federov	4	3318 Allegheny Court	Charlotte	NC	28210	704-555-0107
6/10/2003	4	Sirvat	Torosian	2	7982 Paseo Margarita	Austin	TX	78710	512-555-0082
5/12/2003	1	Brandon	Smith	1	9315 Orchard Ave.	Albuquerque	NM	87110	505-555-2749

Page 1

Figure 4.50

4. Open your **Guests2** table in **Datasheet view** and examine the data in the table.

5. Switch to **Design view**. In the upper portion of the Table window, click in the **Visit Date** field to make it the active field. Under **Field Properties**, click in the **Required** box, click the **arrow**, and then click **Yes**. Clicking Yes in the Required box will require the person entering the data to enter a visit date for each record.

6. In the upper portion of the Table window, click in the **Last Name** field to make it the active field. Under **Field Properties**, click in the **Required** box, click the **arrow**, and then click **Yes**.

7. In the upper portion of the Table window, click in the **# in Party** field to make it the active field. Under **Field Properties**, click in the **Validation Rule** box, and then click the **Build** button that displays.

8. In the upper white area of the Expression Builder, type **>0** The entry in the **# in Party** field should be greater than zero. In the **Expression Builder** dialog box, click **OK**.

9. Verify that the **# in Party** is still the active field and under **Field Properties**, in the **Validation Text** box, click, and then type **The number of people in the party must be greater than 0**

(Project 4E–Guests2 continues on the next page)

(Project 4E–Guests2 continued)

10. In the upper portion of the Table window, in the **Nights** field, click in the **Data Type** column, and then click the **arrow**. From the list of data types, click **Lookup Wizard**.

11. In the first screen of the wizard, be sure *I want the lookup column to look up the value in a table or query* option button is selected. The first screen of the Lookup Wizard allows you to choose whether you want Access to find the information from another table or whether you would like to type in the information yourself.

12. Click **Next**. In the next screen of the wizard, under **Which table or query should provide the values for your lookup column?**, verify that **Table: Nights** is selected, and then click **Next**.

13. In the next screen, under **Available Fields**, click **# of Nights** if necessary, and then click the **One Field** button to move the **# of Nights** field under **Selected Fields**. Click **Next**.

14. In the **1** box, click the **arrow**, and then click **# of Nights**. Leave the order as **Ascending**. Click **Next**, and then at the next screen, click **Next** again.

15. Under **What label would you like for your lookup column?**, accept the default of **Nights**, and then click the **Finish** button. Click **Yes** to save the table, and click **Yes** in any messages that display.

16. Switch to **Datasheet view** and save the table if prompted. In the **Visit Date** field for **Elaine Broderick**, delete the date, and then press [Tab]. A message displays that this field cannot be empty.

17. In the message box, click **OK**, change the date back to **6/18/2003** for **Elaine Broderick**, and then press [Tab].

18. Click in the **Nights** field for **Neel Singh**, and then click the **downward-pointing arrow** that displays. From the list that displays, click **7** to change the number of nights for this record.

19. Click in the **# in Party** field for **Zachary Juras**, delete the existing text, type **0** and then press [Tab]. A message displays indicating that the number in the party must be greater than 0.

20. Click **OK**, and then type **2** to change the **# in Party** back to its original entry.

21. From the **File** menu, click **Page Setup**. Click the **Page tab**, click **Landscape**, and then click **OK**. On the toolbar, click the **Print** button to print the Guests table. Close the table, close the database, and then close Access.

End **You have completed Project 4E**

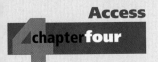
Project 4F — Employees

Objectives: *Find a Record, Display Specific Records, and Create and Use a Data Access Page.*

In the following Skill Assessment, you will practice finding specific records in the Employees table for Jefferson Country Inn. Additionally, you will create a data access page for the database and then convert a database created in an older version of Access to the current version. Your completed database objects will look similar to the ones shown in Figure 4.51. You will save the database as *4F_Employees_Firstname_Lastname* in the folder designated for this chapter.

Jefferson Employees Firstname Lastname   10/26/2003

ID #	First name	Last name	Email	Address	City	State	Zip	Phone	Hire Date
9812	Ruby	Benjamin	rbenjamin@jeffinn.com	38 Thomas Jefferson Pkwy.	Charlottesville	VA	22909	434-555-0186	6/8/1998
0112	Wyatt	Beazley	wbeazley@jeffinn.com	79 Fontaine Ave.		Charlottesville	VA	22910	434-555-0183	8/31/2001

Page 1

Firstname Lastname 4F Employees   Page 1 of 1

Firstname Lastname
Employees Page

ID #:	9810
First name:	Carol
Last name:	Charles
Email:	ccharles@jeffinn.com
Address:	6622 Garden St.
City:	Charlottesville
State:	VA
Zip:	22909
Phone:	434-555-0022
Hire Date:	5/5/1998

Jefferson Employees Firstname Lastname 1 of 14

accdp://136711504/   10/26/2003

Figure 4.51

(Project 4F–Employees continues on the next page)

(Project 4F–Employees continued)

1. Locate the file **a04F_Employees** from your student files and copy and paste the file to the Chapter 4 folder where you are storing your assignments for this chapter. Remove the Read-only property from the file and rename the file as **4F_Employees_Firstname_Lastname** Start Access and open the database you just renamed.

2. On the Objects bar, click **Tables** if necessary, right-click the **Jefferson Employees** table, and then click **Rename**.

3. In the box that displays and using your own information, type **4F Employees Firstname Lastname** and then press Enter.

4. Open your **Employees** table in **Datasheet view** and examine the data in the table.

5. Click anywhere in the **City** column. To search for a record using the **Find** button, you must first select the field where you want Access to look for the information.

6. On the **Table Datasheet** toolbar, click the **Find** button. In the **Find What** box, type **Waynesboro** and then click **Find Next**. Move the dialog box as necessary, and notice that Access locates a record with Waynesboro as the City, as indicated by the highlighted City and the row selector.

7. In the **Find and Replace** dialog box, click **Find Next** (move the **Find and Replace** dialog box out of your way if necessary). Access locates another record with a City of Waynesboro.

8. In the **Find and Replace** dialog box, click **Find Next** two more times. Access displays a message that it has finished searching the records and the search item was not found. Click **OK**, and then in the **Find and Replace** dialog box, click **Cancel** to close the dialog box.

9. In the **Zip** column, click in the record for **Beng Ho**. On the Table Datasheet toolbar, click the **Filter By Selection** button. Three records display; each has a Zip of 22910, the same as the Zip for Beng Ho.

10. On the **Table Datasheet** toolbar, click the **Remove Filter** button.

11. In the **Last name** column, in the record for **Wyatt Beazley**, select the **B** in *Beazley*. On the Table Datasheet toolbar, click the **Filter By Selection** button. Two records display, each with a Last name beginning with the letter B.

12. From the **File** menu, display the **Page Setup** dialog box, click **Page**, click **Landscape**, and then click **OK**. On the **Table Datasheet** toolbar, click the **Print** button.

(Project 4F–Employees continues on the next page)

(Project 4F – Employees continued)

13. On the **Table Datasheet** toolbar, click the **Remove Filter** button. Close the table and save your changes.

14. On the Objects bar, click **Pages** and in the Database window, double-click **Create data access page by using wizard**.

15. Under **Tables/Queries** verify that *Table: 4F Employees Firstname Lastname* displays—this is the table that contains the information to display in the data access page. To the right of the list of available fields, click the **All Fields** button.

16. Click **Next** and in the following screen, under *Do you want to add any grouping levels?*, click **Next** again.

17. In the next screen click **Next**. Under **What title do you want for your page?**, and using your own information, type **4F_Employees_Page_Firstname Lastname** In this same screen, select *Do you want to apply a theme to your page?* check box, and then click **Finish**.

18. In the displayed **Theme** dialog box, under **Choose a Theme**, click **Axis**, and then click **OK**.

19. If necessary, close the task pane and any floating toolbars. Click anywhere in *Click here and type title text*, and using your own information, type **Firstname Lastname** and then press Enter. Then type **Employees Page** If necessary, select the text you just typed and format it as bold, 24 point, to match your name.

20. **Close** the data access page and click **Yes** to save changes to the design of *data access page 'Page1.'* In the **Save As** dialog box, verify that the location where the page will be saved is your Chapter 4 folder and the file name is *4F_Employees_Page_Firstname_Lastname*. Click **Save**, and then click **OK** in the message that displays. A shortcut to the data access page displays in the database window.

21. In the Database window, double-click the data access page you just created. On the Page View toolbar, click the **Print** button.

22. Close the page, close the database, and then close Access.

End You have completed Project 4F

Project 4G—Library1

Objectives: *Customize a Field, Specify a Field Format, Specify a Required Field, and Validate Data Entry.*

In the following Performance Assessment, you will customize the fields in the Library database for Jefferson Country Inn. The Inn uses the database to store information about library items that are available for guests to use. Your completed table will look like the one shown in Figure 4.52. You will save your database as *4G_Library1_Firstname_Lastname*.

Library1 Firstname Lastname   10/26/2003

ID#	Title	Media	Quantity	Placed on Shelf
B1	Around the World in 80 Days	Book	1	01-Jun-02
B10-11	The Adventures of Sherlock Holmes	Book	2	10-Jun-02
B20-21	The Three Musketeers	Book	2	20-May-02
C10-11	Big Band Jazz	CD	2	14-Apr-02
C1-3	Elvis 30 #1 Hits	CD	3	14-Apr-02
C20-22	Bach: Violin Concertos	CD	3	25-Apr-02
C25-29	Mozart: The Great Piano Concertos Volume I	CD	5	28-May-02
C40	Arthur Fielder and the Boston Pops Play The Beatles	CD	1	01-Jul-02
D1 – D5	Citizen Kane	DVD	5	15-May-02
D15-19	Gone With the Wind	DVD	5	23-Jun-02
D25-33	The Godfather	DVD	8	21-Jul-02
D50	Out of Africa	DVD	1	12-Aug-02
V20-22	It Happened One Night	Video	3	12-Aug-02
V30-32	Doctor Zhivago	Video	3	23-May-02
V5-11	Casablanca	Video	7	23-May-02

Page 1

Figure 4.52

1. Locate the file **a04G_Library1** from your student files and copy and paste the file to the Chapter 4 folder where you are storing your assignments for this chapter. Remove the Read-only property from the file and rename the file as **4G_Library1_Firstname_Lastname** Start Access and open the database you just renamed.

2. On the Objects bar, click **Tables** if necessary, right-click the **Jefferson Library** table, and then rename the table as **Library1 Firstname Lastname**

(Project 4G–Library1 continues on the next page)

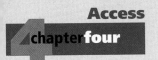
(Project 4G–Library1 continued)

3. Open your **Library1** table in **Datasheet view**, examine the data in the table, and then switch to **Design view**.

4. Click anywhere in the **Media** field. Under **Field Properties**, notice the default **Field Size** of **255**. Change the field size for the **Media** field to **7**

5. Click in the **Placed on Shelf** field name to make it the active field, and then under **Field Properties**, in the **Format** box, change the format to **Medium Date**.

6. Click in the **Title** field to make it the active field, and then under **Field Properties**, in the **Required** box, click **Yes**.

7. Click in the **Placed on Shelf** field to make it the active field, and then under **Field Properties**, in the **Validation Rule** box, open the **Expression Builder**. Type **>4/1/02** Close the **Expression Builder** dialog box.

8. Verify that the **Placed on Shelf** field is still the active field and in the **Validation Text** box, type **The Date must be later than 4/1/02**

9. Switch to **Datasheet view**, save changes, and accept any warnings that display.

10. Print the **Library** table. Close the table. Close the database, and then close Access.

 End You have completed Project 4G ——————————

Project 4H—Library2

Objectives: *Create Input Masks Using the Input Mask Wizard, Create a Lookup Wizard Field, and Find a Record.*

In the following Performance Assessment, you will create an input mask and a lookup field for the Library database at Jefferson Country Inn. Additionally, you will locate specific records within the Library table. Your completed table will look similar to Figure 4.53. You will rename the database as *4H_Library2_Firstname_Lastname*.

1. Locate the file **a04H_Library2** from your student files and copy and paste the file to the Chapter 4 folder where you are storing your assignments for this chapter. Remove the Read-only property from the file and rename the file as **4H_Library2_Firstname_Lastname** Start Access and open the database you just renamed.

(Project 4H–Library2 continues on the next page)

(Project 4H–Library2 continued)

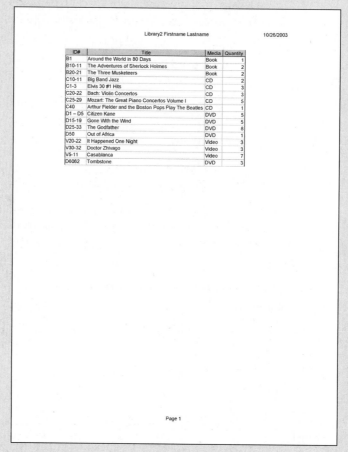

Library2 Firstname Lastname   10/26/2003

ID#	Title	Media	Quantity
B1	Around the World in 80 Days	Book	1
B10-11	The Adventures of Sherlock Holmes	Book	2
B20-21	The Three Musketeers	Book	2
C10-11	Big Band Jazz	CD	2
C1-3	Elvis 30 #1 Hits	CD	3
C20-22	Bach: Violin Concertos	CD	3
C25-29	Mozart: The Great Piano Concertos Volume I	CD	5
C40	Arthur Fielder and the Boston Pops Play The Beatles	CD	1
D1 – D5	Citizen Kane	DVD	5
D15-19	Gone With the Wind	DVD	5
D25-33	The Godfather	DVD	8
D50	Out of Africa	DVD	1
V20-22	It Happened One Night	Video	3
V30-32	Doctor Zhivago	Video	3
V5-11	Casablanca	Video	7
D6062	Tombstone	DVD	3

Page 1

Figure 4.53

2. On the Objects bar, click **Tables** if necessary, right-click the **Jefferson Library** table, and then rename the table as **Library2 Firstname Lastname**

3. Open your **Library2** table in **Datasheet view**, examine the data in the table, and then switch to **Design view**.

4. Click in the **ID#** field to make it the active field, and then in the **Input Mask** box, type **L0aaaaa** (be sure to type a zero, not the upper-case O).

5. In the **Quantity** field under **Data Type**, change the data type to **Lookup Wizard**. Specify that you want to look up the values in a table or query.

6. In the next screen of the wizard, verify that **Table: Quantity** is selected, and then click **Next**. In the next screen, click **Number List** if necessary, and then move the **Number List** field under **Selected Fields**, and then click **Next**.

(Project 4H–Library2 continues on the next page)

(Project 4H–Library2 continued)

7. Specify that the **sort** order is by **Number List**, **Ascending**. Click **Next** two more times. Accept the default label, click the **Finish** button, and then save the table.

8. Switch to **Datasheet view**. Verify that the specifications that you created for this table have taken effect by adding the following record to the table:

ID#	Title	Media	Quantity
D6062	Tombstone	DVD	3

9. Click anywhere in the **Quantity** column. Click the **Find** button. In the **Find What** box, type **1** and then click **Find Next**. Access has located a record with a Quantity of 1. Click **Find Next** again. Access locates another record with a Quantity of 1. Continue this until Access notifies you that it has finished searching the records. Click **OK** and then close the **Find and Replace** dialog box.

10. Print the Library table. Close the table. Close the database, and then close Access.

End You have completed Project 4H ──────────────

Project 4I—Recipes

Objectives: *Display Specific Records, Create and Use a Data Access Page, and Convert a Database from a Previous Version of Access.*

In the following Performance Assessment, you will practice filtering a table in the Recipes database for Jefferson Country Inn. In addition, you will create a data access page for the Recipes table. Finally, you will convert a database from an older version of Access to the current version. Your completed database objects will look similar to the ones shown in Figure 4.54. You will save your database as *4I_Recipes_Firstname_Lastname.*

1. Locate the file **a04I_Recipes** from your student files and copy and paste the file to the Chapter 4 folder where you are storing your assignments for this chapter. Remove the Read-only property from the file and rename the file as **4I_Recipes_Firstname_Lastname** Start Access and open the database you just renamed.

2. On the Objects bar, click **Tables** if necessary, right-click the **Jefferson Dishes** table, and then rename the table as **Jefferson Dishes Firstname Lastname**

3. Open your **Jefferson Dishes** table in **Datasheet view** and examine the data in the table.

(Project 4I–Recipes continues on the next page)

(Project 4I–Recipes continued)

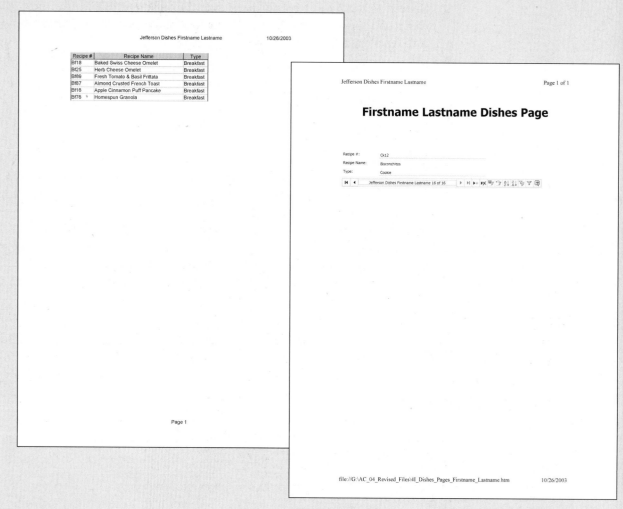

Figure 4.54

4. On the Table Datasheet toolbar, click **Filter By Form**. In the **Type** column, click the **downward-pointing arrow**, and then click **Breakfast**. On the Table Datasheet toolbar, click the **Apply Filter** button.

5. Print the filtered table. On the Table Datasheet toolbar, click the **Remove Filter** button. Close the table and save changes.

6. On the Objects bar, click **Pages**, and then create a data access page by using the wizard. Base the page on your **Jefferson Dishes** table, include all fields from the table, and then accept all remaining defaults in the wizard. In the page's **Design view**, add a title as follows: **Firstname Lastname Dishes Page**

(Project 4I–Recipes continues on the next page)

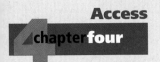
(Project 4I–Recipes continued)

7. Switch to the **Web Page Preview**, save your changes and name the file **4I_Dishes_Page_Firstname Lastname** and then add the following record by using the Web Page Preview:

Recipe #	Recipe Name	Type
Ck12	**Bisconchitos**	**Cookie**

8. Save the new record, and then with the new record displayed in the Web Page Preview, print the page.

9. Close the Web Page Preview, and then close any remaining windows in the database. Close the database, and then close Access.

10. Locate the file **a04I_Expenses2000** from your student files and copy and paste the file to the Chapter 4 folder you created. Remove the Read-only property from the file.

11. Start Access and open the database you just copied. From the **Tools** menu, point to **Database Utilities**, point to **Convert Database**, and then click **To Access 2002 – 2003 File Format**.

12. In the **Save in** box, navigate to the Chapter 4 folder where you are saving your projects for this chapter and in the **File name** box, select the existing text and type **4I_Converted_Expenses_Firstname_Lastname** and then click **Save**. Click **OK** in the warning message.

13. Close the database, and then close Access.

End You have completed Project 4I

Project 4J—Inventory

Objectives: *Customize a Field, Specify a Field Format, Create Input Masks Using the Input Mask Wizard, Specify a Required Field, Validate Data Entry, Create a Lookup Wizard Field, and Find a Record.*

In the following Mastery Assessment, you will customize a table for the Jefferson Country Inn. Your completed table will look similar to the one shown in Figure 4.55. You will save your database as *4J_Inventory_Firstname_Lastname.*

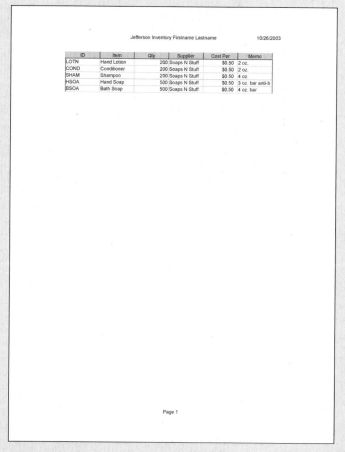

Figure 4.55

1. Locate the file **a04J_Inventory** from your student files and copy and paste the file to the Chapter 4 folder where you are storing your projects for this chapter. Remove the Read-only property from the file and rename the file as **4J_Inventory_Firstname_Lastname** Start Access and open the database you just renamed.

2. Rename the **Jefferson Inventory** table as **Jefferson Inventory Firstname Lastname**

(**Project 4J–Inventory continues on the next page**)

(Project 4J–Inventory continued)

3. Open your **Jefferson Inventory** table in **Datasheet view**, examine the data in the table, and then switch to **Design view** and make the following changes to the table:

Make the **Supplier** field required.

Change the data type for the **Memo** field to **Memo**.

Change the data type for the **Cost Per** field to **Currency**.

Change the data type for the **Qty** field to **Number**.

Add an input mask for the **ID** field that requires four capital letters (Hint: >LLLL)

Create a validation rule for the **Qty** field to ensure that the quantity is greater than or equal to 0.

Add validation text to support the validation rule you just created.

Add a lookup field between the **Supplier** field and the **Supplier List** table.

4. Create a **Filter By Selection** to locate the records that have **Soaps N Stuff** as the **Supplier**. Print the filtered table, and then remove the filter.

5. Close the table. Close the database, and then close Access.

 End You have completed Project 4J ─────────────

Project 4K — Guests Web Page

Objectives: *Display Specific Records and Create and Use a Data Access Page.*

In the following Mastery Assessment, you will create a data access page for the Jefferson Country Inn. Your completed page will look similar to the one shown in Figure 4.56. You will rename the database as *4K_Guests_Web_Page_Firstname_Lastname*.

1. Locate the file **a04K_Guests_Web_Page** from your student files and copy and paste the file to the Chapter 4 folder where you are storing your projects for this chapter. Remove the Read-only property from the file and rename the file as **4K_Guests_Web_Page_Firstname_ Lastname** Start Access and open the database you just renamed.

2. Rename the **Jefferson Guests** table as **4K Jefferson Guests Firstname Lastname** and then open your **Jefferson Guests** table and examine the data in the table.

(Project 4K–Guests Web Page continues on the next page**)**

(Project 4K–Guests Web Page continued)

4K Jefferson Guests Firstname Lastname   Page 1 of 1

Firstname Lastname Guests

Visit Date: 6/15/2003
Nights: 2
First Name: Brandon
Last Name: Smith
in Party: 2
Address: 2745 Sherwin Ave.
City: Washington
State: DC
Zip: 20017
Phone: 202-555-0110

file://G:\AC_04_Revised_Files\4K_Guests_Firstname_Lastname.htm   10/26/2003

Figure 4.56

3. Close the table, and then create a data access page by using the wizard based on the information in your **Jefferson Guests** table. Include all of the fields from the table, and then accept all remaining defaults in the wizard until the last screen, and then apply the Papyrus theme to the page.

4. Add a title to the page, using your own information, that reads **Firstname Lastname Guests**

5. From the File menu, display the **Web Page Preview**, save the page as **4K_Guests_Firstname_Lastname** and then print the page.

6. Close the Web Page Preview, close the data access page, close the database, and then close Access.

End You have completed Project 4K

Project 4L — Suppliers

Objectives: *Customize a Field, Specify a Field Format, Create Input Masks Using the Input Mask Wizard, Specify a Required Field, and Create a Lookup Wizard Field.*

1. Locate the file **a04L_Suppliers** from your student files and copy and paste the file to the Chapter 4 folder where you are storing your assignments for this chapter. Remove the Read-only property from the file and rename the file as **4L_Suppliers_Firstname_Lastname** Start Access and open the database you just renamed.

2. Rename the Suppliers table as **4L_Suppliers_Firstname Lastname**

3. Using the skills you have practiced in this chapter, customize the fields in the table where appropriate. You should change data types, add input masks, require fields, and create a lookup field for the **Name** field.

4. Make a list of the changes you have made to the table, and then print your table.

 You have completed Project 4L ——————————

Project 4M — Jefferson Meeting Rooms

Objective: *Create and Use a Data Access Page.*

The owners of Jefferson Country Inn would like a Web page that contains information about their guest rooms. Guest rooms at the Jefferson Inn are named after the flowers and trees that Thomas Jefferson grew in his gardens at Monticello. Copy the student file a04M_Guest_Rooms to your storage location, clear the Read-only property, rename it **4M_Guest_Rooms_Firstname_Lastname** and then open the database.

Create a data access page from the Jefferson Guest Rooms table in this database. Include a theme of your choice and an appropriate title for the Web page. Save all files to the folder where you are storing your projects for this chapter.

 You have completed Project 4M ——————————

On the Internet

How Do Databases and Web Applications Relate?

The power of the Internet combined with the strengths of database applications has changed the way businesses manage their information.

Go online and perform a search to identify the relationship between databases and Web applications.

GO! with Help

Viewing Information About Data Types

Working with data types is an important part of working with Access databases. In this exercise, you will view information about data types in Access.

1. Start Access. In the **Type a question for help** box, type **data types** then press Enter.

2. In the displayed **Search Results** task pane, click the result **Field data types available in Access (MDB)**. Maximize the displayed window, and at the top of the window, click **Show All**. Scroll through and read about data types in Access.

3. If you want, print a copy of the information by clicking the **Print** button at the top of the window.

4. Close the Microsoft Office Access Help window, and then close Access.

5

chapterfive

Building and Maintaining a Relational Database

In this chapter, you will: complete these projects **and** practice these skills.

Project 5A **Building a Relational Database**	**Objectives** • Index Fields in a Table • View Relationships in a Database • Establish Relationships Between Tables • Create a Query from Joined Tables

Project 5B **Maintaining a Relational Database**	**Objectives** • Identify and Correct Design Errors in Tables • Protect and Maintain a Database

Southland Gardens

With gardening booming as a hobby, Southland Media, a TV production company headquartered in Irvine, California, saw a need for practical and entertaining information on the subject.

"Southland Gardens" was developed especially for the year-round gardeners in Southern California. The show features experts on vegetable and flower gardening, landscape design, projects for kids, and tours of historical and notable gardens. The company also offers a companion Web site where viewers can get more information about show segments, purchase supplies, and e-mail guests of the show.

Building and Maintaining a Relational Database

Access databases are relational databases—the tables in a database can relate, or connect, to other tables through common fields. Advantages of relational databases are a reduction in data redundancy and improved data accuracy. Access includes features to establish relationships between tables. Additionally, Access includes many features to help you maintain and protect your databases, such as checking for duplicate data and adding security features to a database.

Project 5A **Southland Gardens**

Access allows you to create relational databases where relationships can be established between tables that have related information. Relational databases reduce data redundancy and promote data accuracy and data integrity. Data redundancy occurs when the same data is stored in more than one location.

In Activities 5.1 through 5.8, you will create indexes and establish relationships for the tables in the database for Southland Gardens. Additionally, you will create a query from joined tables. Your relationships window will look similar to Figure 5.1. You will save your database as *5A_SouthlandGardens_Firstname_Lastname.*

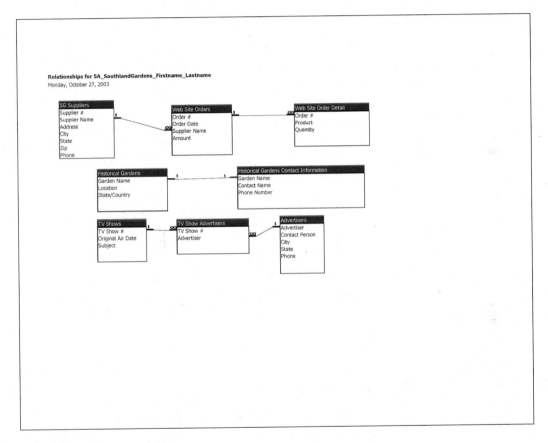

Figure 5.1
Project 5A—Southland Gardens

Objective 1
Index Fields in a Table

You have practiced setting primary keys and sorting fields in database objects. Adding a primary key to a field automatically creates an *index* for that field. An index is a special list that is created in Access to speed up searches and sorting—like the index at the back of a book. The index is visible only to Access, and not to you, but it helps Access find items much faster. Indexes can be added to fields that are not set as a primary key. Additionally, indexes can be created for multiple fields in a table.

Activity 5.1 Indexing Fields Without Duplicates

When you add an index to a field, you have the option of allowing duplicate values in that field or not allowing them. When a primary key is created, the field is always indexed without duplicates because primary keys, by their definition, cannot contain duplicate values. You can, however, add an index without duplicates to a field that is not the primary key. In this activity you will add an index to a field that will not allow duplicates.

1 Using the skills you practiced earlier, create a new folder named Chapter 5 in the location where you will be storing your projects for this chapter. Locate the file **a05A_SouthlandGardens** from your student files and copy and paste the file to the Chapter 5 folder you created. Remove the Read-only property from the file and rename the file as **5A_SouthlandGardens_Firstname_Lastname** Start Access and open the database you just renamed.

2 Open the **TV Shows** table in **Datasheet view** and examine the data in the table.

3 Switch to **Design view** and click once in the **Original Air Date** field to make it the active field.

4 Under **Field Properties**, click once in the **Indexed** box, and then click the **downward-pointing arrow** that displays. See Figure 5.2.

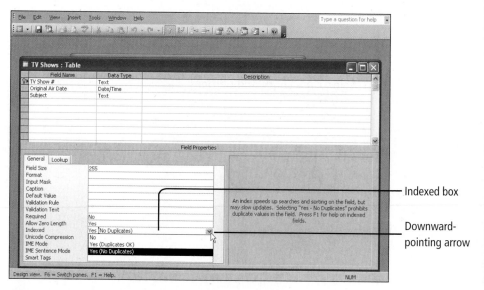

Figure 5.2

5 From the displayed list, click **Yes (No Duplicates)**.

By adding an index without duplicates to the Original Air Date field, you are assured that Access will add an index to speed searching and sorting and not allow duplicate data in this field. Each TV show for Southland Gardens has only one original air date. Recall that in large Access tables, adding an index to one or more fields will speed your searches.

6 Close the **TV Shows** table and save changes when prompted.

Activity 5.2 Indexing Fields with Duplicates

You can also create an index for a field where duplicate data *is* appropriate. For example, you may want to create an index for a Last Name field to speed searching and sorting on this field. Such a field, of course, frequently contains duplicate last names. In this activity you will add an index to a field that will allow duplicates.

1 Open the **SG Employees** table and switch to **Design view**.

2 Click once in the **Last Name** field to make it the active field.

3 Under **Field Properties**, click once in the **Indexed** box, and then click the **downward-pointing arrow** that displays.

4 From the displayed list, click **Yes (Duplicates OK)**.

By adding an index to a field and allowing duplicates, you create faster searches and sorts on this field, while still allowing duplicate data.

5 Close the **SG Employees** table and save changes when prompted.

Another Way

Displaying Indexes

Display the Indexes Dialog Box

Display the Indexes dialog box by clicking the Indexes button while in Design view. A list of indexes for the table will display.

Objective 2
View Relationships in a Database

A database created using Microsoft Access 2003 is a ***relational database***, which is a database that can contain multiple tables that are related (or connected) to each other by common fields. Typically, data about an item is stored only once in a relational database thus reducing or eliminating redundant data. Relational databases store data about different topics in different tables and allow you to connect the data together in a meaningful way. ***Flat file databases*** store different types of information in one table and usually contain data about one particular item in multiple places. This creates redundant information and increases the likelihood of data entry errors.

Activity 5.3 Viewing Relationships in a Database

The connection between two fields in separate tables within a relational database is called a ***relationship***. Relationships between tables allow you to bring related information together. For example, Southland Gardens sells various garden tools on their companion Web site. Thus, the database for Southland Gardens includes a Web Site Orders table that lists the Order #, Order Date, Supplier, and the Amount of the Order. There is also a Web Site Order Detail table that lists the individual items in each order. The Order # field exists in both tables, thus relating the two tables to each other.

1 Open the **Web Site Orders** table in **Datasheet view**. Examine the data in the table.

2 At the left side of the table, notice the column containing ***expand indicators*** (plus signs) next to the Order # for each record. See Figure 5.3.

Expand indicators —

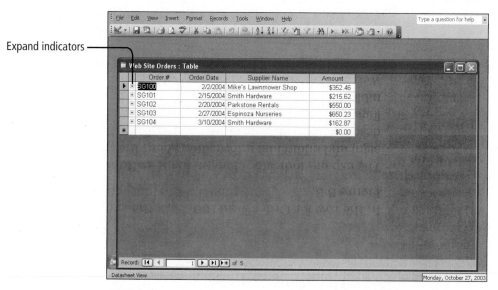

Figure 5.3

3 In the row for Order # **SG100**, click the **expand indicator**. See Figure 5.3.

The expand indicator changes to the ***collapse indicator*** (a minus sign) and additional information about the order—the product description and the quantity ordered for each product—displays. See Figure 5.4. This information is gathered from the Web Site Order Detail table, because a relationship has been created between a field in the Web Site Orders table and a field in the Web Site Order Detail table.

Collapse indicator ——

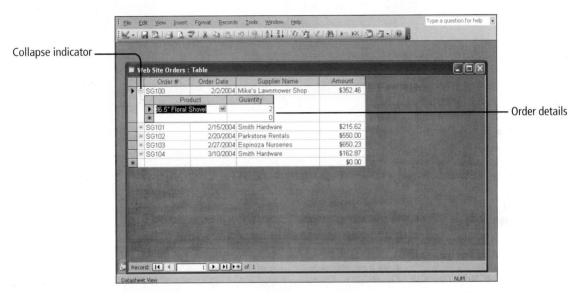

Order details

Figure 5.4

4 Click the **collapse indicator** (minus sign) for this record.

The details of the order are removed from view.

5 In the row for Order # **SG101**, click the **expand indicator**.

The order details for this order display indicating that three products—12' Hose, Border Rake, and Front Tine Rototiller— were included in this order.

6 Click the **collapse indicator** for this record.

7 Close the **Web Site Orders** table and open the **Web Site Order Detail** table in **Datasheet view**.

8 Examine the data in this table and notice the order information for the orders **SG100** and **SG101**. This information matches the information that displayed in the Web Site Orders table. Close the **Web Site Order Detail** table.

9 On the Database toolbar, click the **Relationships** button 🔲. See Figure 5.5.

The ***Relationships window*** displays. Here you can view, create, and modify relationships between tables and also between queries. Currently, four tables display in the Relationships window.

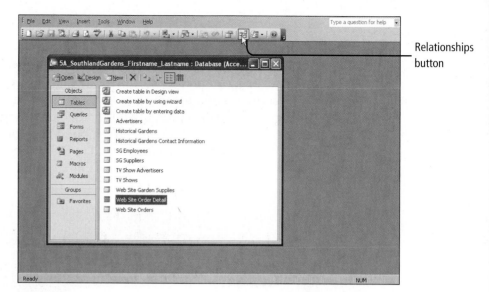

Relationships button

Figure 5.5

10 Position the pointer over the right edge of the **Web Site Order Detail** table, and then with the double arrow displayed, drag the right edge of the **Web Site Order Detail** table to the right until the entire title of the table is displayed. See Figure 5.6.

Use this technique to display the content of a table in the Relationships window. The sides and lower corners of a table in the Relationships window can be manipulated in a manner similar to that for any other window in the Windows operating system.

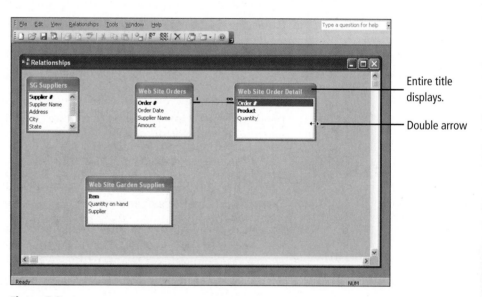

Entire title displays.

Double arrow

Figure 5.6

11 On the Relationship toolbar, click the **Show All Relationships** button ▦.

Any existing relationships between tables are displayed. Currently there is one established relationship—the relationship between the Web Site Orders table and the Web Site Order Detail table. Because of this relationship, you were able to expand an order in the Web Site Orders table to see data contained within the Web Site Order Detail table. See Figure 5.7.

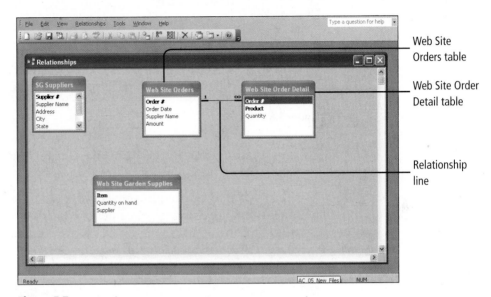

Web Site Orders table

Web Site Order Detail table

Relationship line

Figure 5.7

12 Locate the line connecting the two tables.

The line connecting the two tables is the **Relationship line**. There is a *1* next to the Web Site Orders table and an infinity (∞) sign next to the Web Site Order Detail table. This indicates a **one-to-many relationship** between these tables. One-to-many relationships occur when one record in the first table (the Web Site Orders table) corresponds to many records in the second table (the Web Site Order Detail table).

13 In the Relationships window, drag the title bar of the **Web Site Order Detail** table to the right about 0.5 of an inch. The exact distance need not be precise.

The line connecting the two tables stretches and moves. The tables that display in the Relationships window can be moved by dragging their title bars without breaking the line that indicates existing relationships.

14 In the Relationships window, locate the **Web Site Garden Supplies** table, and if necessary, move and expand the table so its list of fields is in full view. See Figure 5.8.

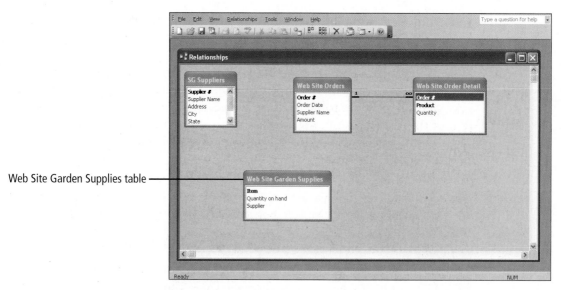

Web Site Garden Supplies table —

Figure 5.8

15 Point to any field in the **Web Site Garden Supplies** table and right-click. From the shortcut menu that displays, click **Hide Table**.

The Web Site Garden Supplies table is removed from view in the Relationships window. This action does not delete the table; it simply allows more space to view and create relationships among tables, and removes from view those tables whose relationships you are not concerned with at this time.

16 In each of the table windows, notice the fields that are in bold text. See Figure 5.9.

Bold text indicates the primary key for the table. Recall that the primary key in a table serves as a unique identifier for each record in a table.

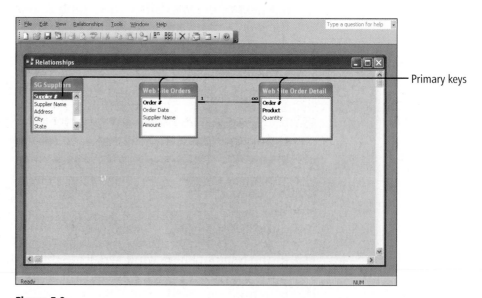

— Primary keys

Figure 5.9

17 Keep the Relationships window open for the next activity.

Objective 3
Establish Relationships Between Tables

Relationships between tables allow you to relate the information in one table to the information in another table, as you saw between the Web Site Orders table and the Web Site Order Detail table. Three types of relationships are possible: one-to-many, one-to-one, and many-to-many. When two tables are related, or *linked*, a ***foreign key*** is created in the second table. A foreign key is the field in the second table that identifies the linked records. In the example of the Web Site Orders table and the Web Site Order Detail table, the Order # field is the primary key in the Web Site Orders table and the foreign key in the Web Site Order Detail table.

Activity 5.4 Establishing a One-to-Many Relationship and Enforcing Referential Integrity

In the previous activity, the relationship between the Web Site Orders table and the Web Site Order Detail table was a ***one-to-many*** relationship, which can be indicated as *1:∞*. This means that for each record in the Web Site Orders table, there can be many records in the Web Site Order Detail table—one order, many products in the order. However, for each record in the Web Site Order Detail table, there can be only one record in the Web Site Orders table—each product ordered is associated with only one order. One-to-many relationships are the most common type of relationship between two database tables. In this activity, you will establish a one-to-many relationship between the SG Suppliers table and the Web Site Orders table.

1 Be sure the Relationships window is open.

2 Locate the **SG Suppliers** table, point to the **Supplier Name** field in that table, and click so that it is highlighted. Drag the highlighted name to the **Web Site Orders** table, positioning your pointer directly over the **Supplier Name** field in the **Web Site Orders** table, and then release the mouse button. See Figure 5.10.

The Edit Relationships dialog box displays. See Figure 5.11.

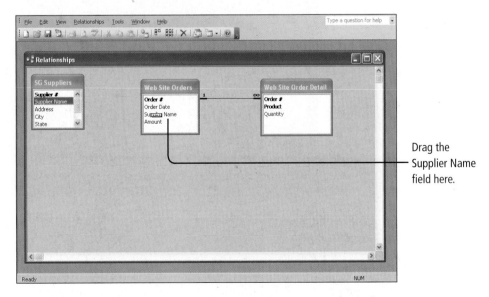

Drag the Supplier Name field here.

Figure 5.10

Edit Relationships dialog box —

Supplier Name from SG
Suppliers table

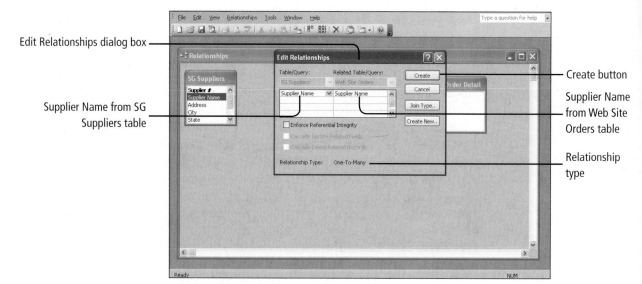

— Create button

Supplier Name
— from Web Site
Orders table

Relationship
type

Figure 5.11

3 In the **Edit Relationships** dialog box, notice that *Supplier Name* is
indicated in both columns—from both the **SG Suppliers** table and
the **Web Site Orders** table. Refer to Figure 5.11.

4 At the bottom of the **Edit Relationships** dialog box, to the right of
Relationship Type, notice that *One-To-Many* displays.

5 In the **Edit Relationships** dialog box, click **Create**. See Figure 5.11.

A relationship line is drawn between the Supplier Name fields in
both the SG Suppliers table and the Web Site Orders table. See
Figure 5.12.

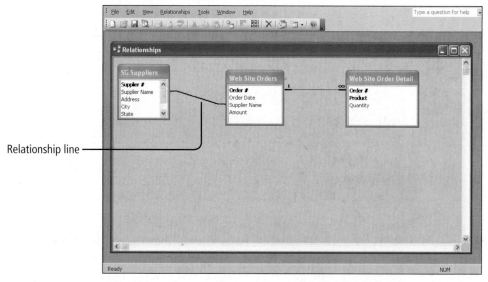

Relationship line —

Figure 5.12

6 Examine the line and notice that there is no one-to-many indication
as there is in the existing relationship between the Web Site Orders
table and the Web Site Order Detail table.

7 Right-click on the **relationship line** that you just created, and from the displayed shortcut menu, click **Edit Relationship**.

The Edit Relationships window displays. Alternatively, you can double-click the Relationship line to display the Edit Relationships dialog box.

8 In the Edit Relationships window, select (click to place a check mark in) the **Enforce Referential Integrity** check box. See Figure 5.13.

Referential integrity is a set of rules that Access uses to ensure that the data between related fields is valid. Enforcing referential integrity between the two Supplier Name fields ensures that no supplier name can exist in the Web Site Orders table unless that supplier name is a valid supplier name in the SG Suppliers table.

Enforce Referential Integrity check box

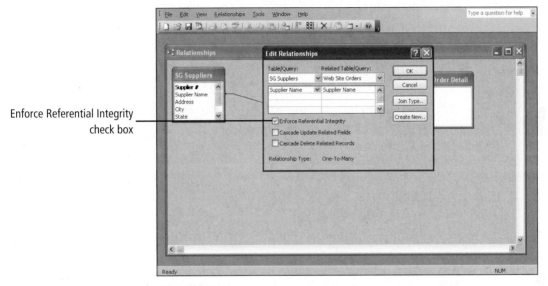

Figure 5.13

9 Click **OK**.

The relationship line now indicates a one-to-many relationship.

10 Right-click the **relationship line** between the **Supplier Name** fields again, and then click **Edit Relationship** to display the **Edit Relationships** dialog box.

11 In the lower portion of the **Edit Relationships** dialog box, select the **Cascade Update Related Fields** check box.

When the Cascade Update Related Fields check box is selected, any changes you make to the primary key in the first table—the SG Suppliers table—will automatically update the foreign key in the second table—the Web Site Orders table. For example, if a supplier changes the name of his or her company, changing the name in the SG Suppliers table will automatically change the supplier's name in the Web Site Orders table too.

12 Select the **Cascade Delete Related Records** check box.

The result of this action will be that when a record with a primary key is deleted, the matching foreign key record(s) will be deleted in the related table. There can be more than one record deleted in the related table.

> ## Note — Cascade
>
> The word *cascade* refers to things arranged in a series so that action on one produces an action on the next.

13 In the upper right corner of the dialog box, click **OK**. Leave the Relationships window open for the next activity.

Activity 5.5 Printing the Relationships Window

Printing the Relationships window creates a report that displays the relationships for the database. You can save this report for future reference.

1 With the Relationships window open, display the **File** menu, and then click **Print Relationships**.

Access displays a report with a header *Relationships for* and the database name.

2 From the **File** menu, display the **Page Setup** dialog box, change the **Page Orientation** to **Landscape**, and then click **OK**. On the Print Preview toolbar, click the **Print** button.

The Relationships report prints.

3 **Close** the Relationships report and click **Yes** when prompted to save your changes to the report. Verify that the default name for the report is **Relationships for 5A SouthlandGardens Firstname Lastname** and click **OK** to save the report.

4 **Close** the Relationships window. In the Database window, on the Objects bar, click **Reports**, and then verify that the Relationships report you created is listed. Leave the database open for the next activity.

Activity 5.6 Establishing a One-to-One Relationship

One-to-one relationships require that for every record in one table, there can be only one matching record in the other table. This kind of relationship is much less common than one-to-many relationships.

1 On the Objects bar, click **Tables**, open the **Historical Gardens** table in **Datasheet view**, and then examine the data in the table.

Recall that the Southland Gardens TV show frequently features famous historical gardens.

2 **Close** ⊠ the **Historical Gardens** table, open the **Historical Gardens Contact Information** table in **Datasheet view**, and then examine the data in the table.

These two tables both contain the Garden Name field. This table contains the name and phone number of the person to contact regarding a particular historical garden.

3 **Close** ⊠ the **Historical Gardens Contact Information** table, and then on the Database toolbar, click the **Relationships** button 🖼.

4 In the gray area of the displayed Relationships window, right-click to display a shortcut menu. See Figure 5.14.

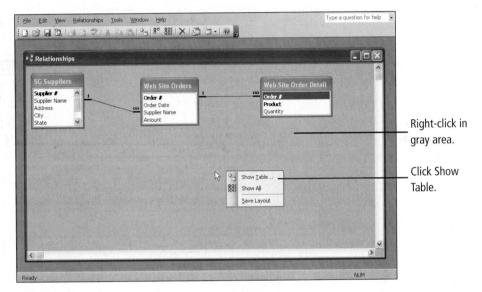

Right-click in gray area.

Click Show Table.

Figure 5.14

5 From the shortcut menu, click **Show Table**. Refer to Figure 5.14.

The Show Table dialog box displays.

Another Way ┤ **Displaying Tables in the Relationships Window**

Alternatively, you can click the Show Table button on the Relationships toolbar.

---

6 In the **Show Table** dialog box, click **Historical Gardens**, and then click **Add**. Alternatively, you can double-click a table to add it to the Relationships window.

7 In the **Show Table** dialog box, double-click the **Historical Gardens Contact Information** table to add it to the Relationships window, and then click **Close**.

The Historical Gardens table and the Historical Gardens Contact Information table have been added to the Relationships window.

8 Move and resize the table windows in the Relationships window to match, approximately, Figure 5.15.

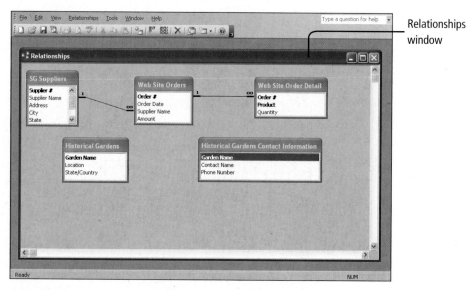

Figure 5.15

9 In the **Historical Gardens** table, point to the **Garden Name** field, and then drag and drop it on top of the **Garden Name** field in the **Historical Gardens Contact Information** table.

The Edit Relationships dialog box displays.

10 In the lower portion of the **Edit Relationships** dialog box, notice that the **Relationship Type** is *One-To-One*.

For each record in the Historical Gardens table, there is only one record in the Historical Gardens Contact Information table.

More Knowledge — One-to-One Relationships

How do you know it should be a one-to-one relationship?

How do you know if you should create a one-to-one relationship? If you could add the data from the second table to the first table without creating redundant records, then a one-to-one relationship can exist between the two tables.

11 In the **Edit Relationships** dialog box, select the **Enforce Referential Integrity** check box, select the **Cascade Update Related Fields** check box, select the **Cascade Delete Related Records** check box, and then click **Create**. Leave the Relationships window open for the next activity.

A relationship line between the Historical Gardens table and the Historical Gardens Contact Information table indicates a one-to-one relationship. See Figure 5.16.

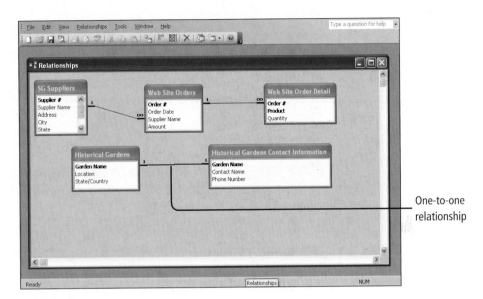

One-to-one relationship

Figure 5.16

Activity 5.7 Establishing a Many-to-Many Relationship

Another relationship, although not a common one, is the ***many-to-many relationship***. Many-to-many relationships involve two tables that each have a one-to-many relationship to a third table, called a ***junction table***. The primary keys of the junction table are composed of the primary keys of each of the other tables. For example, in the Southland Gardens database, each episode of the TV show (TV Shows table) can have many advertisers (Advertisers table) and each advertiser can appear on many shows.

1 Right-click in a gray area of the Relationships window, and then from the shortcut menu, click **Show Table**. From the **Show Table** dialog box, add the **TV Shows** table, the **TV Show Advertisers** table, and the **Advertisers** table to the Relationships window. Close the **Show Table** dialog box.

The TV Shows table contains information about Southland Garden TV shows that have aired. The Advertisers table contains the name and address and contact information for the sponsors that pay Southland to show their ads on a TV show. The TV Show Advertisers table contains a list of the aired shows and the advertisers who had an ad on each show.

2 Move and resize the tables in the Relationships window to match Figure 5.17.

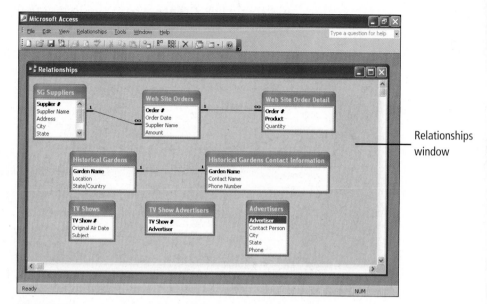

Figure 5.17

3 In the **TV Shows** table, point to the **TV Show #** field, and then drag and drop it on top of the **TV Show #** field in the **TV Show Advertisers** table.

4 In the **Edit Relationships** dialog box, select the **Enforce Referential Integrity** check box, the **Cascade Update Related Fields** check box, and the **Cascade Delete Related Records** check box, and then click **Create**.

5 In the **TV Show Advertisers** table, point to the **Advertiser** field, and then drag and drop it on top of the **Advertiser** field in the **Advertisers** table.

6 In the **Edit Relationships** dialog box, select the **Enforce Referential Integrity** check box, the **Cascade Update Related Fields** check box, and the **Cascade Delete Related Records** check box, and then click **Create**.

7 Examine the Relationships window. Notice the one-to-many relationships you established. These one-to-many relationships create a many-to-many relationship. See Figure 5.18.

By creating the one-to-many relationship between the TV Shows table and the TV Show Advertisers table, and then creating another one-to-many relationship between the Advertisers table and the TV Show Advertisers table, you created a many-to-many relationship between the TV Shows table and the Advertisers table, with the TV Show Advertisers table serving as the junction table.

In both the TV Shows table and the TV Show Advertisers table, the primary key is the TV Show # field. The primary keys of the junction table—the TV Show Advertisers table—is a combination of the two primary keys of the other two tables. You can see that in the TV Show Advertisers table, both fields are in bold, indicating that they are primary keys.

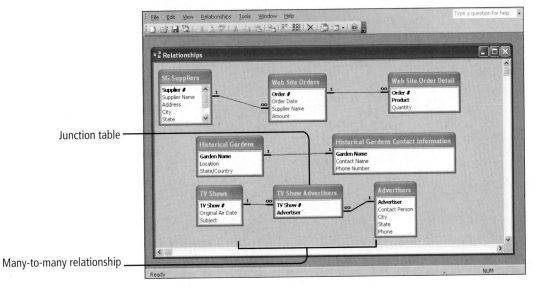

Junction table

Many-to-many relationship

Figure 5.18

Note — Deleting a Relationship

To delete an existing relationship between tables, right-click the Relationship line and then click Delete.

---

8 From the **File** menu, click **Print Relationships**. Display the **File** menu again, click **Page Setup**, and on the **Page tab**, click **Landscape**. Click **OK**. Click the **Print** button 🖨 to print the Relationships report.

9 **Close** ☒ the Relationships report and click **Yes** to save the changes to the design of the report. In the **Save As** dialog box, save the report as **Relationships for 5A SouthlandGardens Firstname Lastname** (delete *1* from the end of the proposed name), click **OK**, and then click **Yes** to replace the existing report.

10 Close the Relationships window. Leave the database open for the next activity.

Objective 4
Create a Query from Joined Tables

When a query is created from related tables, the relationships between the tables automatically display in the query design grid.

Activity 5.8 Creating a Query from Joined Tables

In this activity, you will create a query that will display the orders for a particular supplier.

1 On the Objects bar, click **Queries**, and then double-click **Create query in Design view**.

2 In the **Show Table** dialog box, double-click the **SG Suppliers**, **Web Site Orders**, and **Web Site Order Detail** tables to add them to the table area, and then click **Close**. As shown in Figure 5.19, enlarge the upper portion of the window by dragging the upper edge of the title bar, and enlarge each of the table windows to get a complete view of each table's name and list of fields.

The tables are added to the table area of the query window, and their relationship lines display.

3 In the **SG Suppliers** table, double-click **Supplier Name** to add the field to the design grid.

4 In the **Web Site Orders** table, double-click **Order #** to add the field to the design grid.

5 In the **Web Site Order Detail** table, add the **Product** and **Quantity** fields to the design grid.

6 In the design grid, under **Supplier Name**, in the **Criteria** row, type **Smith Hardware** and then click the **Run** button ![Run button]. See Figure 5.19.

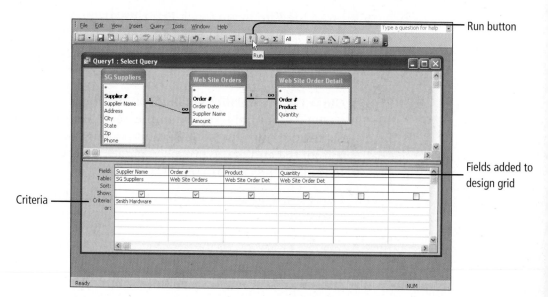

Figure 5.19

7 Examine the query results. Smith Hardware is one of the suppliers that supplies items that are offered for sale on Southland Gardens' companion Web site. See Figure 5.20.

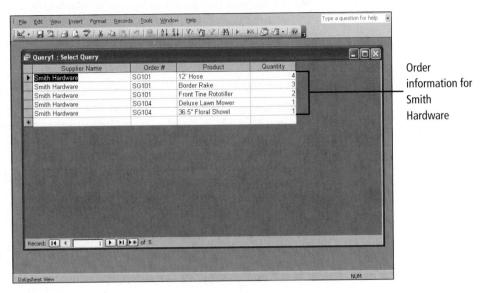

Order information for Smith Hardware

Figure 5.20

8 Close the query, click **Yes** to save it, and then, using your own information, save the query as **Smith Hardware Query Firstname Lastname**

9 Close the database, and then close Access.

End You have completed Project 5A ────────────────────

Project 5B **Southland Gardens Maintenance**

You have practiced using Access features that help to reduce or eliminate errors and redundant information. It is impossible to eliminate all errors and redundancy, but there are Access tools to assist with identifying, or getting rid of, unnecessary data.

In Activities 5.9 through 5.16, you will practice skills that will enable you to maintain and protect the relational database for Southland Gardens. Your completed printouts will look similar to Figure 5.21. You will save the database as *5B_SouthlandGardens_Maintenance_Firstname_Lastname.*

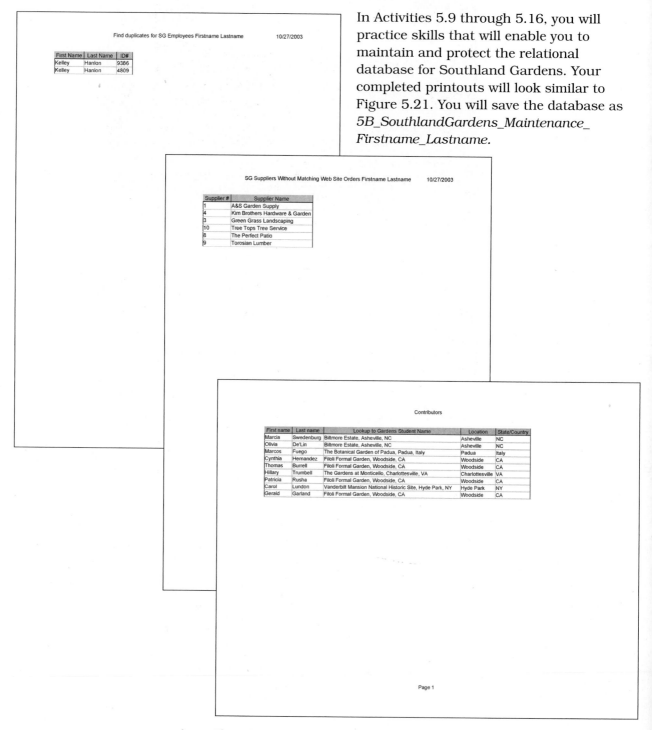

Figure 5.21
Project 5B—Southland Gardens Maintenance

Objective 5
Identify and Correct Design Errors in Tables

Activity 5.9 Finding Duplicate Records

Even when a table contains a primary key, it is still possible to have duplicate records in a table. For example, the same employee could be entered into a table twice but with different ID#s. In this activity, you will use the Find Duplicates Query Wizard to create a query that will locate duplicate records in a table for Southland Gardens.

1 Locate the file **a05B_SouthlandGardens_Maintenance** from your student files, and then copy and paste the file to the Chapter 5 folder you created earlier. Remove the Read-only property from the file and rename the file as **5B_SouthlandGardens_Maintenance_Firstname_ Lastname** Start Access and open the database you just renamed.

2 On the Database toolbar, click the **New Object button arrow** 🔳▾. From the list that displays, click **Query** as shown in Figure 5.22.

The New Query dialog box displays a list of query types.

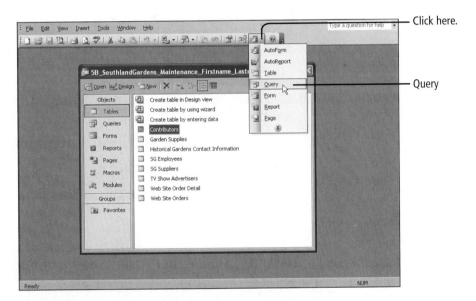

Figure 5.22

3 From the list of query types, click **Find Duplicates Query Wizard** as shown in Figure 5.23, and then click **OK**.

The Find Duplicates Query Wizard starts.

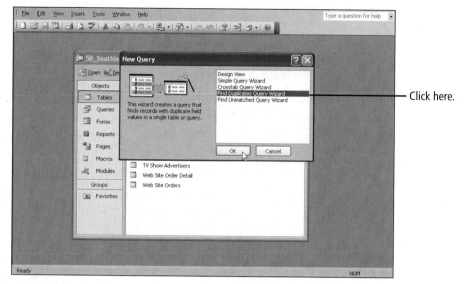

Figure 5.23

4 From the list of tables, click **Table: SG Employees**, and then click **Next**.

5 In the screen that indicates *Which fields might contain duplicate information?*, click **First Name**, and then click the **One Field** button ![image].

6 Click **Last Name**, click the **One Field** button ![image], and then click **Next**.

7 Read the information at the top of this screen, click the **ID#** field, and then click the **One Field** button ![image]. See Figure 5.24.

The field that you select in this screen will display in the query results.

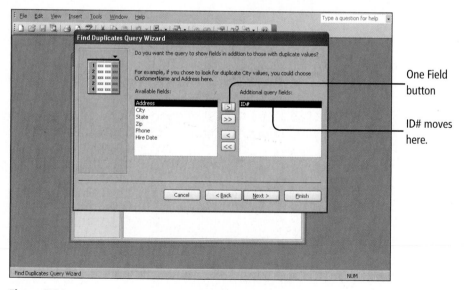

Figure 5.24

8 Click **Next** and in this final screen of the wizard, using your own information, add your name to the default query name so the name of the query is **Find duplicates for SG Employees Firstname Lastname** and then click **Finish**.

The query results display with two records that have the same first name and last name, *Kelley Hanlon*, but with different ID#s.

9 Print the query, and then close the query. Leave the database open for the next activity.

Access has limitations on what it can determine for you. In this instance, further investigation would be necessary to determine if this is one employee that was entered into the database twice with different ID#s, or if this is two different employees with the same name.

Activity 5.10 Finding Unmatched Records

You can use the Find Unmatched Query Wizard to create a query that will locate unmatched records in related tables. For example, in the SG Suppliers table, you could locate individual suppliers with whom no orders have been placed and then delete them from the table. It makes sense to delete unneeded records.

1 On the Database toolbar, click the **New Object button arrow** . From the list that displays, click **Query**.

The New Query dialog box displays a list of query types.

2 From the list of query types, click **Find Unmatched Query Wizard**, and then click **OK**.

The Find Unmatched Query Wizard starts. The first screen of the wizard asks you to identify the first table in which you want Access to compare records.

3 From the list of tables, click **Table: SG Suppliers**, and then click **Next**.

The next screen of the wizard displays. Here you identify the table that you would like Access to compare to the first table for the purpose of locating unmatched records.

4 From the list of tables, click **Table: Web Site Orders**, and then click **Next**.

The next screen of the wizard asks you to identify which field is in both tables.

5 From the list of fields, click **Supplier Name** in both lists, click the **double-headed arrow** button, and then compare your dialog box with Figure 5.25.

At the bottom of the dialog box, Access indicates that the matching fields are Supplier Name.

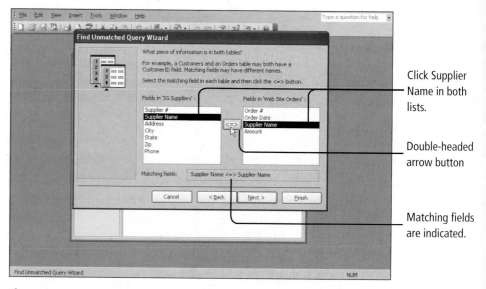

Click Supplier
Name in both
lists.

Double-headed
arrow button

Matching fields
are indicated.

Figure 5.25

6 Click **Next**. In this screen of the wizard, click **Supplier #**, and then click the **One Field** button ⊡.

7 Click **Supplier Name**, click the **One Field** button ⊡, and then click **Next**.

8 In the last screen of the wizard, using your own information, add your name to the default query name so the name of the query is **SG Suppliers Without Matching Web Site Orders Firstname Lastname** and then click **Finish**.

The query results display six supplier names with whom no orders have been placed. See Figure 5.26.

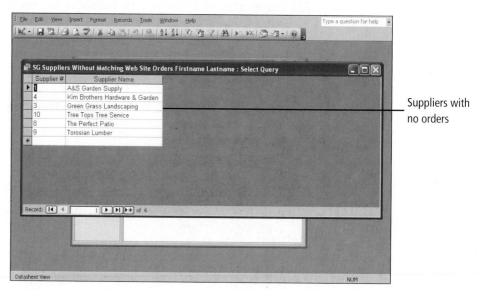

Suppliers with
no orders

Figure 5.26

9 Print the query, and then close the query. Leave the database open for the next activity.

Activity 5.11 Examining Tables to Check for Design Errors

A challenging task for new database users is to build accurate tables using an efficient design and without typographical errors and redundant fields. Access analyzing features examine a table or database and look for errors in the table or the database design. In this activity, you will use the Table Analyzer to check for design errors in a table.

In this database, if a featured historical garden is fortunate enough to have a contributing sponsor—someone who donates funds to the garden—the sponsor receives mention on the TV episode that features the garden. The information about contributing sponsors is contained in the Contributors table.

1 Be sure your database is open from the previous activity.

2 On the menu bar, click **Tools**, point to **Analyze**, and then click **Table**.

The first two screens of the Table Analyzer wizard are introductory explanatory screens that describe how the Table Analyzer functions and provide examples for you.

3 Read the information in the first screen, and then click **Next**.

4 Read the information in the second screen, and then click **Next**.

The third screen of the wizard asks you to identify which table contains fields with values that are repeated in many records.

5 From the list of tables, click **Contributors** as shown in Figure 5.27. Click **Next**.

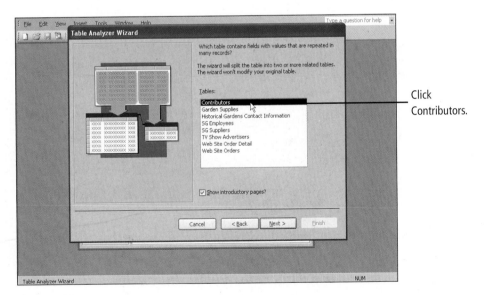

Figure 5.27

6 In this screen of the wizard, verify that the **Yes, let the wizard decide** option button is selected, and then click **Next**.

7 In this screen of the wizard, examine the suggestion that Access makes, which is to split the **Contributors** table. See Figure 5.28.

Access suggests splitting the Contributors table into two tables—one table that will list the Contributors and a lookup field to another table that lists the Garden information that pertains to each contributor.

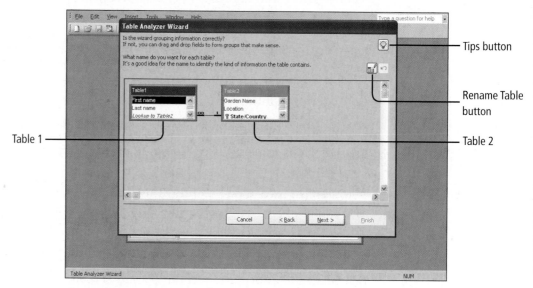

Figure 5.28

8 In the upper right corner of the wizard screen, click the **Tips** button. Refer to Figure 5.28.

A list of helpful tips for splitting these tables displays. See Figure 5.29.

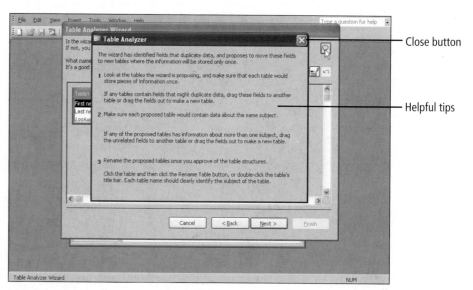

Figure 5.29

9 Read these important tips carefully; they will assist in your understanding of good database design. When you are finished, click the **Close** button ⊠ in the Table Analyzer window that lists these tips.

10 Click the **title bar** of **Table1** so that it is selected, and then in the upper right corner, click the **Rename Table** button. Refer to Figure 5.28.

11 In the dialog box that displays, and using your own information, type **Garden Contributors Firstname Lastname** and then click **OK**.

12 Click the title bar of **Table2** to select it, and then click the **Rename Table** button.

13 In the dialog box, and using your own information, type **Gardens Firstname Lastname** and then click **OK**.

14 Click **Next**.

The next screen of the wizard displays as shown in Figure 5.30.

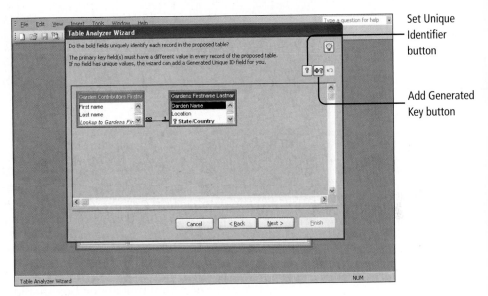

Figure 5.30

15 In this screen, in the **Gardens** table on the right, click the **Garden Name** field, and then click the **Set Unique Identifier** button. Refer to Figure 5.30.

The primary key for this table is changed to Garden Name. Garden Name is a unique field in this table.

16 Click **Next**, and in this final screen of the wizard, accept the default settings, and then click **Finish**.

A Help topic on the Table Analyzer may display, and a Select Query displays based on the information you entered in the wizard.

17 Examine the information in the displayed Help window, and print this window if you would like to use the information for future reference. Then click the Help window's **Close** button ☒.

18 Print the Contributors query, and then close the query. On the Objects bar, click **Tables**.

Access created a Contributors query that contains the information from the old Contributors table and a Lookup field. The database window displays with the names of the two tables Access created and the word OLD attached to the old Contributors table. See Figure 5.31. Leave the database open for the next activity.

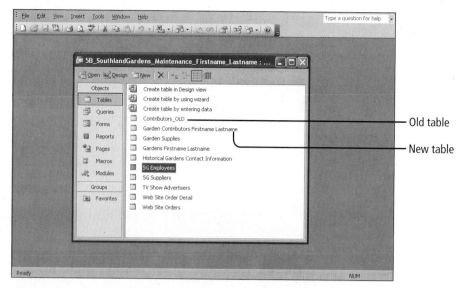

Old table

New table

Figure 5.31

Activity 5.12 Testing the Design of a Database

The Performance Analyzer feature examines the objects in a database and makes recommendations to *optimize* (improve performance by increasing efficiency) the database. In this activity, you will use the Performance Analyzer to test the design of the database for Southland Gardens.

1 On the menu bar, click **Tools**, point to **Analyze**, and then click **Performance**.

The Performance Analyzer dialog box displays.

2 Click the **Tables tab** if necessary. Notice that a list of all the tables in the database displays. On the right side, click **Select All**. See Figure 5.32.

A small check mark displays to the left of each table name, indicating that the Performance Analyzer will examine all of the table objects in the database.

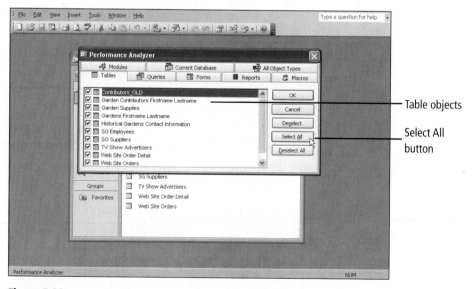

Table objects

Select All button

Figure 5.32

3 Click **OK**.

Access displays suggestions for increasing the efficiency of this database. Access categorizes the results of the Performance Analyzer into three categories: Recommendation, Suggestion, and Idea. The Fixed category within the Key area will display next to a suggestion if you choose to have Access optimize the suggestion and implement the recommendation. See the Key area in Figure 5.33. The Performance Analyzer found three items for which it suggests ideas as shown in Figure 5.33.

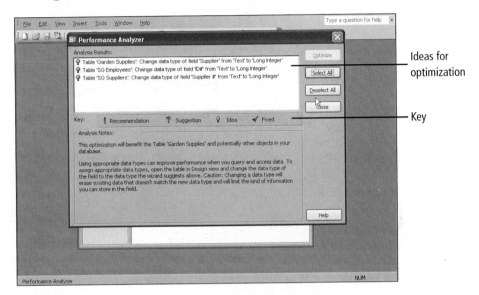

Ideas for optimization

Key

Figure 5.33

4 Click the **Close** button ⊠ to close the Performance Analyzer.

Your database will function properly without implementing any of these ideas. However, in large databases, you will likely want to implement Recommendations. To do so, you would click on the Recommendation you would like to implement, and then click the Optimize button.

5 Close the database, and then close Access.

Objective 6
Protect and Maintain a Database

Controlling who has access to your database is part of protecting and maintaining a database. Frequently, databases contain sensitive data that should only be accessed by authorized users. For example, think of the database of student grades at your college. Access has several features that allow you to control who can open a database, and within various Access features, control different degrees of security.

Activity 5.13 Protecting a Database with a Password

Protecting database files with a password is a common method for protecting a database from unauthorized users. When trying to open a file that is password protected, the user is prompted to enter the password in order to gain access to the file. In this activity, you will create a password for your database.

1 Locate the file **a05B_Password** from your student files and copy and paste the file to the Chapter 5 folder you created earlier. Remove the Read-only property from the file and rename the file as **5B_Password_ Firstname_Lastname** Start Access and open the database you just renamed.

2 On the **Tools** menu, point to **Security**, and then click **Set Database Password**.

A message displays indicating that you need to open the database for *exclusive use*. Exclusive use means that nobody else can have the database open at that time.

3 Click **OK**, and then close the database.

4 On the **File** menu, click **Open**, and then navigate to the location where you are storing your projects for this chapter.

5 Click your **5B_Password** file (the one that you just renamed) once, and then in the lower right corner, locate the **Open button arrow** and click it to display a menu. See Figure 5.34.

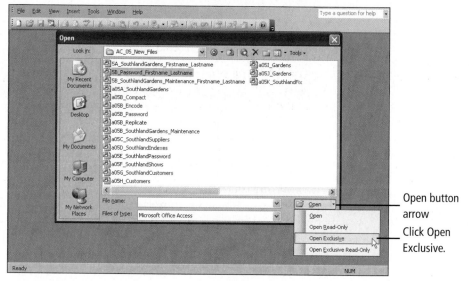

Figure 5.34

6 From the displayed menu, click **Open Exclusive**. When the database opens, display the **Tools** menu, point to **Security**, and then click **Set Database Password**.

The Set Database Password dialog box displays as shown in Figure 5.35.

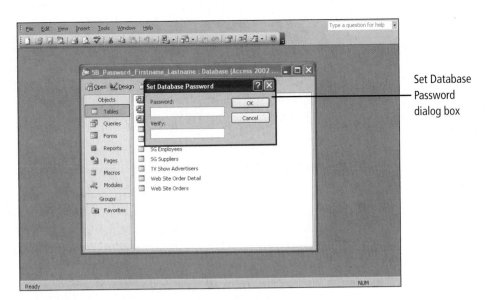

Set Database Password dialog box

Figure 5.35

7 In the **Password** box, type **Bstudent007** (as you type, only * characters display) and press Tab.

The insertion point moves to the Verify box.

Note — Passwords display as *****

When you type a password in the Password box, each character that you type will display as an asterisk (*). This ensures that someone looking over your shoulder at your screen cannot learn your password as you type it.

8 In the **Verify** box, type **Bstudent007** and then click **OK** to assign the password to the database.

When creating a password, you must enter the password twice to ensure that you entered it correctly.

Note — Passwords are case sensitive

Passwords in Access are case sensitive, meaning that Access will interpret *B* differently than *b*. Take care when typing a password to only capitalize letters that were initially entered as uppercase letters.

9 Close the database, and then reopen it.

The Password Required dialog box displays.

10 Under **Enter database password** type **student** and then click **OK**.

Access warns you that the password is not valid.

11 Click **OK** to close the message, and then type the correct password that you created, **Bstudent007** and then click **OK**.

The database opens.

12 Close the database.

Note — Removing a Password from Your Database

To remove a password from a database, open the database with the password. Then, on the Tools menu, point to Security and click Unset Database Password. Type the password that you have added to the database, and then press [Enter]. The password is removed.

Activity 5.14 Encoding and Decoding a Database

Sometimes security measures are not enough to keep unwanted users from viewing the information in your databases. A database created with Microsoft Access is a **binary** file, which means that it is constructed of mostly unreadable characters. If an Access database is opened in a word processor, Microsoft Word for example, the file will appear to most people to be completely unreadable. If, however, you continue looking through the file, you will notice some readable characters as shown in Figure 5.36.

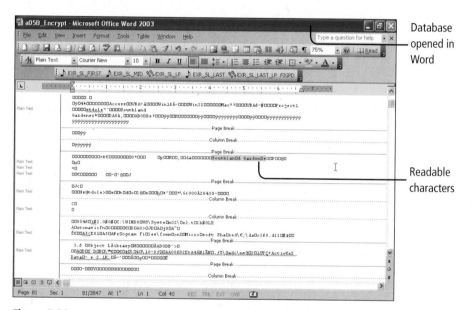

Database opened in Word

Readable characters

Figure 5.36

1 Locate the file **a05B_Encode** from your student files and copy and paste the file to the Chapter 5 folder you created earlier. Remove the Read-only property from the file and rename the file as **5B_Encode_ Firstname_Lastname** Start Access and open the database you just renamed.

2 From the **Tools** menu, point to **Security**, and then click **Encode/Decode Database**.

The Encode Database As dialog box displays. To prevent unauthorized users from opening your database in a word processing program and scanning the file for information, you can **encode** the database. Encoding a file scrambles the file so it is unreadable.

3 Use the **Save in** arrow to navigate to the folder where you are storing your projects for this chapter, and then in the **File name** box, delete the existing text and type **5B_Southland_Encode_Firstname_Lastname** as the file you want to create, and then click **Save**.

Access creates an encoded version of the database in the location you specified but leaves the original database open.

4 **Close** ⊠ the **5B_Encode** database (you can leave Access open) and then open a word processing program such as Microsoft Word or Notepad.

5 In the word processing program, open the encoded file you just created. You will likely need to click the **Files of type arrow**, and then click **All Files**. In the dialog box that displays, click **OK**.

The original database file was difficult to read in a word processor (see Figure 5.36), but the encoded version is even more difficult to read. The file that displays in the word processing program will be many pages long (approximately 3850 pages!). Encoding a file does not prevent a user from opening the file in Access or provide any password protection. Encoding a file prevents someone who does not have a copy of Access from being able to read the data in the file.

6 Close the word processing program.

7 Start Access, if necessary, and then open your **5B_Southland_Encode** database.

The encoded database looks like the original. You can tell the files apart by the different file names you specified. In this example your original file was the 5B_Encode_Firstname_Lastname file and the file name you specified for the encoded file was 5B_Southland_Encode_Firstname_Lastname. When working with an encoded file in Access, you may notice that some tasks take longer to complete.

8 Close the **5B_Southland_Encode** database but leave Access open. On the **Tools** menu, point to **Security** and click **Encode/Decode Database**.

9 In the **Encode/Decode Database** dialog box, browse to the folder where you are storing your projects for this chapter, click the **5B_Southland_Encode** file with your name in it, and then click **OK**.

The Decode Database As dialog box opens.

10 In the **File name** box, using your own information, type **5B_Southland_Decode_Firstname_Lastname** and then click **Save**.

Decoding a database unscrambles it back to the format the database was originally.

11 Close Access.

Activity 5.15 Compacting and Repairing Database Files

After you work with a database for a period of time, the file may become quite large. Even if you delete objects from the database, Access does not really delete them; it only *marks* them for deletion. As a consequence, database files can grow quite large even though the data in the file appears to be small. **Compacting** a database will remove these deleted objects from the database.

1 Locate the file **a05B_Compact** from your student files and copy and paste the file to the Chapter 5 folder you created earlier. Remove the Read-only property from the file and rename the file as **5B_Compact_Firstname_Lastname**

Before you compact a database, you should create a backup of the database. You have done this by copying the database to your folder.

2 Start Access, but do not open the database yet. On the **Tools** menu, point to **Database Utilities**, and then click **Compact and Repair Database**.

The Database to Compact From dialog box opens.

3 Navigate to the folder where you are storing your projects for this chapter, and then click your file **5B_Compact_Firstname_Lastname** file to select it. With the file still selected, in the lower right corner of the dialog box, click **Compact**.

4 In the displayed **Compact Database Into** dialog box, click the **5B_Compact_Firstname_Lastname** file with your name, and then click **Save**.

Because you are saving the compacted database using the same name, Access displays the message shown in Figure 5.37.

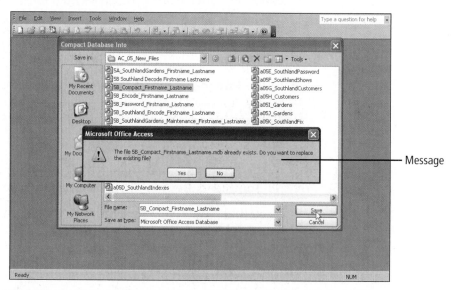

Figure 5.37

5 Click **Yes**.

The Access window displays. You will not see a visual indication of compacting, but compacting has taken place.

Activity 5.16 Making Backup Copies of a Database and Replicating a Database

It is common to have individuals seated at different computers working on the same database. This will create several different versions of the same database. In order to bring the different versions into one, cohesive version, the database should be replicated. *Replicating* a database is the process of creating copies, or *replicas*, of the database so that multiple users can edit the database.

1 Locate the file **a05B_Replicate** from your student files and copy and paste the file to the Chapter 5 folder you created earlier. Remove the Read-only property from the file and rename the file as **5B_Replicate_ Firstname_Lastname** Start Access and open the database you just renamed.

2 On the **Tools** menu, point to **Replication**, and then click **Create Replica**.

The message in Figure 5.38 displays. When you click Yes, the 5B Replicate database becomes the *Design Master*. The Design Master is a copy of the original database and is the only database in the *replica set* to which you can make structural changes—such as adding new tables or adding new fields to existing tables. The replica set consists of the Design Master and any replicas, or copies, that you create.

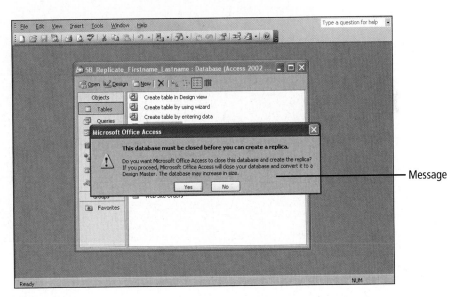

Figure 5.38

3 Click **Yes**.

After a moment, another message displays, recommending that you create a backup copy of the file.

4 Click **Yes**.

The Location of New Replica dialog box displays. See Figure 5.39.

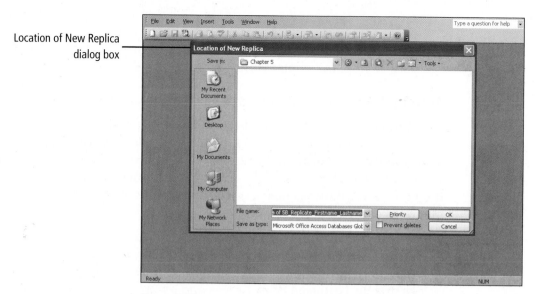

Figure 5.39

5 If necessary, navigate to the location where you are storing your projects for this chapter, keep the default file name, and then click **OK**.

The new Design Master database displays along with a message box similar to the one shown in Figure 5.40.

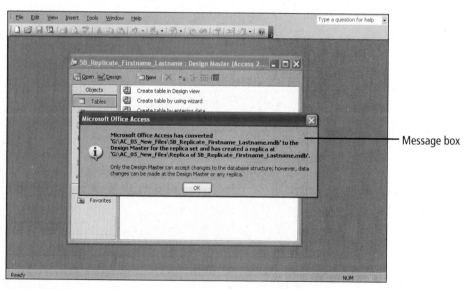

Message box

Figure 5.40

6 In the message box, click **OK**.

The Database window displays and indicates *Design Master*. See Figure 5.41.

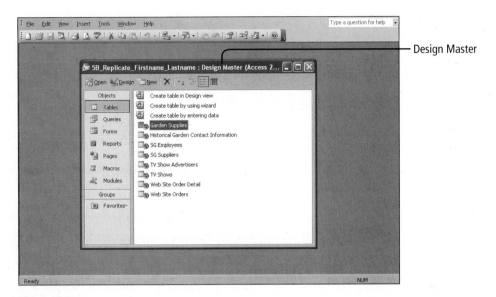
— Design Master

Figure 5.41

7 Close the Design Master database, and then close Access.

Replicating a database and managing the replicas is a complex process. The steps above showed you how to replicate a database. To learn more about this process, refer to the replication topic in Access Help.

End **You have completed Project 5B**

Summary

In this chapter you practiced techniques for building and maintaining a relational database. You created indexes to speed searching and sorting on fields. Additionally, you practiced viewing the relationships in a database and created three types of relationships: one-to-many, one-to-one, and many-to-many. Relationships in a database help to reduce data redundancy and increase data accuracy. You also created a query from tables that were joined.

Additionally, you practiced techniques for maintaining a database by identifying and correcting tables and using the Find Duplicates Query Wizard and the Find Unmatched Query Wizard. You used features of Access that analyzed both the database and tables within the database.

You practiced applying various security measures to a database, including password protection, and encoding and decoding a database. You practiced compacting a database by using the Compact and Repair feature of Access. Finally, you practiced replicating a database.

In This Chapter You Practiced How To

- Index Fields in a Table

- View Relationships in a Database

- Establish Relationships Between Tables

- Create a Query from Joined Tables

- Identify and Correct Design Errors in Tables

- Protect and Maintain a Database

Matching Match each term in the second column with its correct definition in the first column by writing the letter of the term on the blank line in front of the correct definition.

_____ **1.** A special list that is created in Access to speed up searches and sorting.

_____ **2.** A type of database that can contain two or more tables that are related (connected) to each other by common fields.

_____ **3.** The third table in a many-to-many relationship.

_____ **4.** An association among tables in which a record in Table A can have many matching records in Table B, and a record in Table B can have many matching records in Table A—made possible by defining one-to-one relationships to a third table.

_____ **5.** A database type that stores different types of information in one table—usually contains data about one particular item in multiple places.

_____ **6.** The method used to locate records that do not have corresponding records in a related table.

_____ **7.** Copies of a database that are distributed to multiple users for editing.

_____ **8.** An association between two tables in which each record in Table A can have only one matching record in Table B, and each record in Table B can have only one matching record in Table A.

_____ **9.** The type of file created with Microsoft Access that is composed mostly of unreadable characters.

_____ **10.** A set of rules that Access uses to ensure that the data between related fields is valid.

_____ **11.** An association between two tables in which a record in Table A can have many matching records in Table B, but a record in Table B has only one matching record in Table A.

_____ **12.** Between two linked tables, the field in the second table that identifies the linked records.

_____ **13.** A process that removes deleted objects from a database and thus increases available space.

_____ **14.** The Design Master and any replicas of a database.

_____ **15.** Opening a database in a manner where no other users can open the database at the same time.

A Binary

B Compacting

C Exclusive use

D Find Unmatched Query Wizard

E Flat file database

F Foreign key

G Index

H Junction table

I Many-to-many relationship

J One-to-many relationship

K One-to-one relationship

L Referential integrity

M Relational database

N Replicas

O Replica set

Fill in the Blank   Write the correct answer in the space provided.

1. The line that Access draws to indicate a link between fields is the

   _____.

2. The connection between fields in a relational database is called a(n)

   _____.

3. The option when creating relationships that will cause Access to
   automatically change the data in a linked table to reflect a change in
   the first table is called _____.

4. _____ is the manner in which a database must first
   be opened in order to set a password for the database.

5. _____ a file, or scrambling it so that it is unreadable,
   will prevent users who do not have a copy of Access from opening a
   database and gathering information contained in the database.

6. Creating copies of a database so multiple users can edit the database is called _____.

7. The option when creating relationships that will cause Access to
   delete a record in a linked table if it is deleted in the first table is
   called _____.

8. The window where you can view, create, and modify relationships
   between tables and queries is the _____ window.

9. The process of updating and merging replicas with the Design
   Master is called _____.

10. Unscrambling a database that has been previously scrambled is
    called _____.

Project 5C—Southland Suppliers

Objectives: *View Relationships in a Database, Establish Relationships Between Tables, and Create a Query from Joined Tables.*

In the following Skill Assessment, you will view and create relationships for the Southland Suppliers database. Additionally, you will create a query from the joined tables that will identify the supplies that Southland Gardens features and sells on its Web site from Parkstone Rentals. Your completed query will look similar to the one shown in Figure 5.42. Your completed Relationships report will look similar to the one shown in Figure 5.42. You will rename and save the database as *5C_SouthlandSuppliers_Firstname_Lastname*.

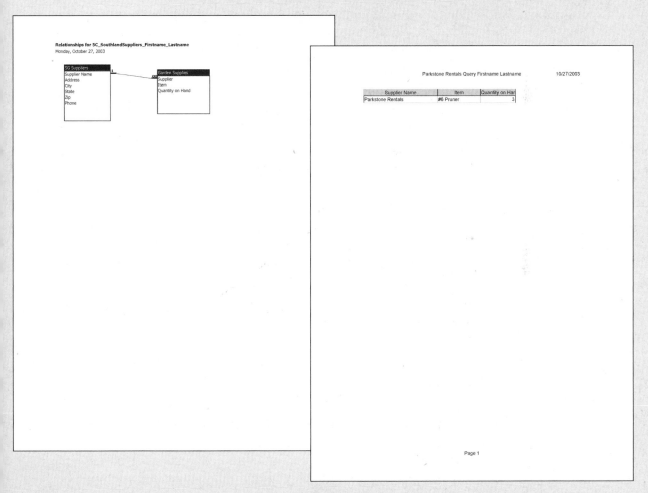

Figure 5.42

1. Locate the file **a05C_SouthlandSuppliers** from your student files and copy and paste the file to the Chapter 5 folder where you are storing your projects for this chapter. Remove the Read-only property from the file and rename the file as **5C_SouthlandSuppliers_Firstname_Lastname** Start Access and open the database you just renamed.

(Project 5C–Southland Suppliers continues on the next page)

(Project 5C–Southland Suppliers continued)

2. Open the **SG Suppliers** table in **Datasheet view** and examine the data in the table. Close the **SG Suppliers** table, and then open the **Garden Supplies** table in **Datasheet view** and examine the data in the table.

3. Close the **Garden Supplies** table. On the Database toolbar, click the **Relationships** button.

4. Right-click in the gray area of the Relationships window, and from the displayed shortcut menu, click **Show Table**.

5. In the **Show Table** dialog box, click **SG Suppliers**, click **Add**, click **Garden Supplies**, click **Add**, and then click **Close**.

6. Move and enlarge the tables so that you can see the entire title of the tables and all of the fields in the table. In the **SG Suppliers** table, point to the **Supplier Name** field, and then drag and drop it on top of the **Supplier** field in the **Garden Supplies** table.

7. In the **Edit Relationships** dialog box, select the **Enforce Referential Integrity** check box, select both the **Cascade Update Related Fields** and **Cascade Delete Related Records** check boxes, and then click **Create**.

8. With the Relationships window open, display the **File** menu, and then click **Print Relationships**. On the Print Preview toolbar, click the **Print** button.

9. Close the Relationships report and click **Yes** when prompted to save your changes to the report. Click **OK** to save the report using the default report name. Close the Relationships window, and then in the Database window, on the Objects bar, click **Reports**. Verify that the **Relationships** report you created is listed.

10. On the Objects bar, click **Queries**, and then double-click **Create query in Design view**.

11. In the **Show Table** dialog box, double-click the **SG Suppliers** and **Garden Supplies** tables to add them to the table area, and then click **Close**.

12. If necessary, enlarge the parts of the Select Query window and the tables so that you can see the entire title bar of each table and all the fields in each table. In the **SG Suppliers** table, double-click **Supplier Name** to add the field to the design grid. In the **Garden Supplies** table, double-click **Item** and **Quantity on Hand** to add the two fields to the design grid.

13. Under **Supplier Name**, in the **Criteria** row, type **Parkstone Rentals** and then on the toolbar click the **Run** button.

The query results display one item from Parkstone Rentals.

(Project 5C–Southland Suppliers continues on the next page)

(Project 5C–Southland Suppliers continued)

14. Close the query, click **Yes** to save it, and then, using your own information, save it as **Parkstone Rentals Query Firstname Lastname** Print the query.

15. Close the database, and then close Access.

End You have completed Project 5C ───────────────────

Project 5D — Southland Indexes

Objectives: *Index Fields in a Table, and Identify and Correct Design Errors in Tables.*

In the following Skill Assessment, you will create an index for the Historical Gardens table in the Southland Gardens database. Additionally, you will create a query that will locate duplicate records in the Customers table. The query will look similar to the one shown in Figure 5.43. You will save your database as *5D_SouthlandIndexes_Firstname_Lastname.*

Find duplicates for Customers Firstname Lastname — 10/27/2003

Last Name	First Name
Dinkel	Virginia
Dinkel	Virginia
Hines	Frank
Hines	Frank

Page 1

Figure 5.43

(Project 5D–Southland Indexes continues on the next page)

(Project 5D–Southland Indexes continued)

1. Locate the file **a05D_SouthlandIndexes** from your student files and copy and paste the file to the Chapter 5 folder where you are storing your projects for this chapter. Remove the Read-only property from the file and rename the file as **5D_SouthlandIndexes_Firstname_Lastname** Start Access and open the database you just renamed.

2. Open the **Historical Gardens** table in **Datasheet view** and examine the data in the table.

3. Switch to **Design view** and click once in the **Location** field to make it the active field.

4. Under **Field Properties**, click once in the **Indexed** box, click the **arrow**, and from the displayed list, click **Yes (Duplicates OK)**. This creates an index that will not only speed searches and sorting on this field, but will also allow duplicate entries in the field.

5. Close the **Historical Gardens** table and save changes when prompted.

6. On the Database toolbar, click the **New Object button arrow**, and from the displayed list, click **Query**.

7. In the displayed **New Query** dialog box, from the list of query types, click **Find Duplicates Query Wizard**, and then click **OK**.

8. In the first Wizard screen, from the list of tables, click **Table: Customers**, and then click **Next**.

9. In this screen, which indicates *Which fields might contain duplicate information?*, click **Last Name**, click the **One Field** button, and then click **Next**.

10. In this screen, which indicates *Do you want the query to show fields in addition to those with duplicate values?*, click the **First Name** field, and then click the **One Field** button. Click **Next**.

11. In this final screen of the wizard, using your own information, add your name to the default query name so the name of the query is **Find duplicates for Customers Firstname Lastname** and then click **Finish**.

    Query results display with two duplicate records that have the same First Name and Last Name, *Virginia Dinkel* and *Frank Hines*. Further investigation at this point would be necessary to determine if the duplicates for Virginia Dinkel and Frank Hines were truly employees entered into the table twice with different ID#s, or if each Virginia Dinkel and each Frank Hines is a different person.

12. Print and then close the query. Close the database, and then close Access.

 End You have completed Project 5D ——————————————

Project 5E — Southland Password

Objectives: *Identify and Correct Design Errors in Tables and Protect and Maintain a Database.*

In the following Skill Assessment, you will add a password for the Southland Gardens database. Additionally, you will create a query to find unmatched records in the Web Site Orders table for Southland Gardens. Your completed query will look similar to the one shown in Figure 5.44. You will save the database as *5E_SouthlandPassword_Firstname_ Lastname* in the folder designated for this chapter.

Figure 5.44

1. Locate the file **a05E_SouthlandPassword** from your student files and copy and paste the file to the Chapter 5 folder you created earlier. Remove the Read-only property from the file and rename the file as **5E_SouthlandPassword_Firstname_Lastname** Start Access but DO NOT OPEN THE DATABASE you just renamed.

(Project 5E–Southland Password continues on the next page)

(Project 5E–Southland Password continued)

2. Be sure that no databases are open. On the **File** menu, click **Open**, and then navigate to the location where you are storing your projects for this chapter.

3. Click your **5E_SouthlandPassword_Firstname_Lastname** file once to select it. In the lower right corner, locate and then click the **Open button arrow**, and from the displayed list, click **Open Exclusive**. Recall that opening a database for Exclusive use will ensure that no one else can open the database at this time.

4. On the **Tools** menu, point to **Security**, and then click **Set Database Password**.

5. In the **Password** box, type **Keyboard2** and press ⟨Tab⟩.

6. In the **Verify** box, type **Keyboard2** and then click **OK** to assign the password to the database. Close the database, and then reopen it.

7. Type the correct password you created, **Keyboard2** and then click **OK**.

8. On the Database toolbar, click the **New Object button arrow**. From the displayed list, click **Query**.

9. In the **New Query** dialog box, from the list of query types, click **Find Unmatched Query Wizard**, and then click **OK**.

10. In the screen that indicates *Which table or query contains records you want in the query results?*, from the list of tables, click **Table: Web Site Order Detail**, and then click **Next**.

11. In the screen that indicates *Which table or query contains the related records?*, click **Table: Web Site Orders**, and then click **Next**.

12. In the screen that indicates *What piece of information is in both tables?*, from the list of fields, click **Order #** in both lists, and then click the **double-headed arrow** button. The matching fields are indicated in the lower portion of the dialog box. Click **Next**.

13. In the screen that indicates *What fields do you want to see in the query results?*, click the **All Fields** button to move all three fields to the **Selected fields** list, and then click **Next**.

14. In the last screen of the wizard, using your own information, delete the existing text and type **Order Detail Without Matching Orders Firstname Lastname** and then click **Finish**.

The query results display one unmatched record, that with an Order # of SG103.

15. Print the query. Close the query, close the database, and then close Access.

End You have completed Project 5E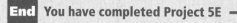

Project 5F — Southland TV Shows

Objectives: *Index Fields in a Table and Create a Query from Joined Tables.*

In the following Performance Assessment, you will create an index in a table and create a query to find unmatched records for Southland Gardens. Your completed table will look similar to the one shown in Figure 5.45. You will save your database as *5F_SouthlandTV_Shows_Firstname_Lastname.*

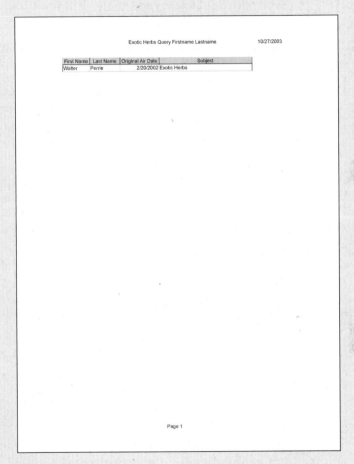

First Name	Last Name	Original Air Date	Subject
Walter	Perrie	2/20/2002	Exotic Herbs

Exotic Herbs Query Firstname Lastname   10/27/2003

Page 1

Figure 5.45

1. Locate the file **a05F_SouthlandTV_Shows** from your student files and copy and paste the file to the Chapter 5 folder you created earlier. Remove the Read-only property from the file and rename the file as **5F_SouthlandTV_Shows_Firstname_Lastname** Start Access and open the database you just renamed.

2. Open the **TV Shows** table and examine the data in the table.

3. Switch to **Design view**, click once in the **Producer** field, and then under **Field Properties**, click once in the **Indexed** box. Click the **arrow**, and from the displayed list, click **Yes (Duplicates OK)**.

(Project 5F–Southland TV Shows continues on the next page)

(Project 5F–Southland TV Shows continued)

4. Close the **TV Shows** table and save changes when prompted.

5. On the Objects bar, click **Queries**, and then double-click **Create query in Design view**.

6. Add both tables to the Select Query window, and then click **Close**. Adjust the size of the window and tables as necessary.

7. From the **SG Employees** table, add the **First Name** and **Last Name** to the design grid.

8. From the **TV Shows** table, add the **Original Air Date** and **Subject** fields to the design grid.

9. Under **Subject**, in the **Criteria** row, type **Exotic Herbs** and then click the **Run** button. In the query result, one record that has a subject of Exotic Herbs displays, indicating that one show had a subject of Exotic Herbs.

10. Close the query, click **Yes** to save it, and then, using your own information, save it as **Exotic Herbs Query Firstname Lastname**

11. Print the Exotic Herbs query. Close the database, and then close Access.

 End You have completed Project 5F

Project 5G — Customers

Objectives: *View Relationships in a Database and Establish Relationships Between Tables.*

In the following Performance Assessment, you will establish one-to-many relationships and view those relationships for Southland Gardens. Your relationships report will look similar to Figure 5.46. You will rename the database as *5G_SouthlandCustomers_Firstname_Lastname*.

1. Locate the file **a05G_SouthlandCustomers** from your student files and copy and paste the file to the Chapter 5 folder you created earlier. Remove the Read-only property from the file and rename the file as **5G_SouthlandCustomers_Firstname_Lastname** Start Access and open the database you just renamed.

2. Open the **Customers** table in **Datasheet view**. Examine the data in the table.

3. Close the **Customers** table, and then open the remaining tables in the database and view the data in them. Close all the tables.

4. On the Database toolbar, click the **Relationships** button.

(Project 5G–Customers continues on the next page)

(Project 5G–Customers continued)

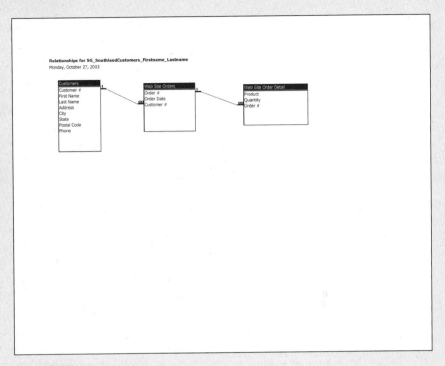

Figure 5.46

5. Right-click in the gray area, click **Show Table**, and then add the **Customers**, **Web Site Orders**, and **Web Site Order Detail** tables to the Relationships window. Resize and move the tables as necessary so that you can view the title bar and complete field list for each table.

6. In the **Customers** table, point to the **Customer #** field, and then drag and drop it on top of the **Customer #** field in the **Web Site Orders** table.

7. In the displayed **Edit Relationships** dialog box, select the **Enforce Referential Integrity** check box, and then click **Create**. A one-to-many relationship is created.

8. In the **Web Site Orders** table, point to the **Order #** field, and then drag and drop it on top of the **Order #** field in the **Web Site Order Detail** table.

9. In the **Edit Relationships** dialog box, select the **Enforce Referential Integrity** check box, and then click **Create**. A one-to-many relationship is created.

10. With the Relationships window open, display the **File** menu, and then click **Print Relationships**. Display the **Page Setup** dialog box and change the page orientation to **Landscape**. On the Print Preview toolbar, click the **Print** button.

(Project 5G–Customers continues on the next page)

(Project 5G–Customers continued)

11. Close the Relationships report and click **Yes** when prompted to save your changes to the report. Using your own information, save the report as **Relationships for 5G_SouthlandCustomers_Firstname Lastname**

12. Close the Relationships window, close the database, and then close Access.

 End **You have completed Project 5G**

Project 5H—Customer Web Site Orders

Objectives: *Identify and Correct Design Errors in Tables and Protect and Maintain a Database.*

In the following Performance Assessment, you will attempt to establish a relationship in a database but will find that you first need to use an Access feature to identify and correct errors in a table. You will correct the errors by locating unmatched records between tables. After locating the unmatched records, you will delete the unmatched records and then establish the relationship. Your completed Relationships report and query results will look similar to the ones shown in Figure 5.47. Additionally, you will encode a database for security purposes. You will save your database as *5H_Customers_Firstname_Lastname*.

1. Locate the file **a05H_Customers** from your student files and copy and paste the file to the Chapter 5 folder you created earlier. Remove the Read-only property from the file and rename the file as **5H_Customers_Firstname_Lastname** Start Access and open the database you just renamed.

2. Open the Relationships window and add the **Web Site Orders** table and the **Web Site Order Detail** table. Move and size the tables so that you can see the entire table title and all the fields. In the **Web Site Orders** table, point to the **Order #** field, and then drag and drop it on the **Order #** field in the **Web Site Order Detail** table. In the **Edit Relationships** dialog box, select the **Enforce Referential Integrity** check box, and then click **Create**. Access displays a message stating referential integrity cannot be enforced.

3. In the message box, click **OK**, close the **Edit Relationships** dialog box, and then close the Relationships window. Click **Yes** to save changes to the layout of the Relationships window.

4. On the Database toolbar, click the **New Object button arrow**. From the displayed list, click **Query**, and from the list of query types, click **Find Unmatched Query Wizard**. Click **OK**.

(Project 5H–Customer Web Site Orders continues on the next page)

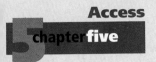

(Project 5H–Customer Web Site Orders continued)

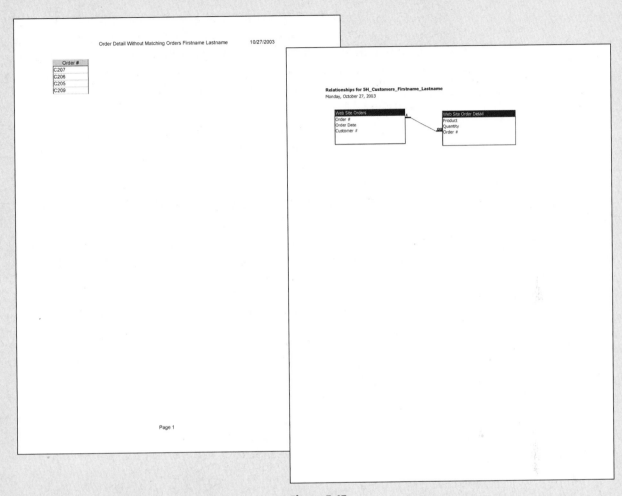

Figure 5.47

5. From the list of tables, click **Table: Web Site Order Detail** and then click **Next**. In this screen, from the list of tables, click **Table: Web Site Orders**, and then click **Next**.

6. From the list of fields, click **Order #** in both lists and then click the **double-headed arrow** button. Click **Next**. Under **Available fields**, click **Order #**, click the **One Field** button, and then click **Next**.

7. In the last screen of the wizard, using your own information, name the query **Order Detail Without Matching Orders Firstname Lastname** and then click **Finish**.

8. Print the query results, and then close the query window.

9. Open the **Web Site Order Detail** table in **Datasheet view**, and then, using your printed query as a reference, delete the records that have the same Order # as in the query results—Order #s **C205**, **C206**, **C207**, and **C209**. Close the table and save if prompted.

(Project 5H–Customer Web Site Orders continues on the next page)

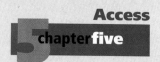
(Project 5H–Customer Web Site Orders continued)

10. Open the Relationships window and create a one-to-many relationship between the **Order #** field in the **Web Site Orders** table and **Order #** field in the **Web Site Order Detail** table. Select the **Enforce Referential Integrity** check box. Print the Relationships report. Close the report and save it as **Relationships for 5H_Customers Firstname_Lastname** Close the Relationships window.

11. On the **Tools** menu, point to **Security**, and then click **Encode/Decode Database**. In the **Encode Database As** dialog box, use the **Save in arrow** to navigate to the folder where you are storing your projects for this chapter and then, in the **File name** box, type **5H_Customer_Encode_Firstname_Lastname** as the file you want to create. Click **Save**.

12. Close the 5H_Customers database and then open the encoded file in a word processing program. View the file, and then close the word processing program. Close Access.

End You have completed Project 5H ————————————————

Project 5I — Gardens

Objectives: *Index Fields in a Table, View Relationships in a Database, Establish Relationships Between Tables, and Identify and Correct Design Errors in Tables.*

In the following Mastery Assessment, you will perform several operations on the Garden database for Southland Gardens to help improve data accuracy and data integrity. You will also create an index to speed searching and sorting. Your printed Relationships report will look similar to the one shown in Figure 5.48. You will save your database as *5I_Gardens_Firstname_Lastname.*

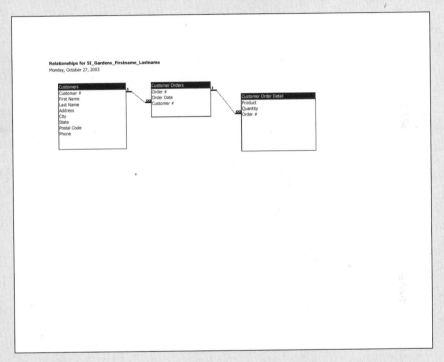

Figure 5.48

1. Locate the file **a05I_Gardens** from your student files and copy and paste the file to the Chapter 5 folder where you are storing your projects for this chapter. Remove the Read-only property from the file and rename the file as **5I_Gardens_Firstname_Lastname** Start Access and open the database you just renamed.

2. In the **States** table, create an index that will not allow duplicate records in the **Abbreviation** field.

3. Create a one-to-many relationship between the **Customers** table and the **Customer Orders** table using the **Customer #** field and enforce referential integrity. Select both the **Cascade Update Related Fields** and **Cascade Delete Related Records** check boxes.

(Project 5I–Gardens continues on the next page)

(Project 5I–Gardens continued)

4. Create a one-to-many relationship between the **Customer Orders** table and the **Customer Order Detail** table using the **Order #** field and enforce referential integrity. You will not be able to enforce referential integrity in this relationship because there are unmatched records between the tables. To correct this, create a query using the **Find Unmatched Query Wizard** to locate the unmatched records between the **Customer Order Detail** table and the **Customer Orders** table. In the query, specify the **Customer Order Detail** table first. Use the **Order #** field as the piece of information that is in both tables. Specify the **Order #** field to display in the query result. Save the query with the default name. Make a note of the Order #s displayed in the query result.

5. Delete any unmatched records from the **Customer Order Detail** table that were displayed in the unmatched records query result you just created, and then establish the relationship between the **Customer Orders** and **Customer Order Detail** table and enforce referential integrity. Select both the **Cascade Update Related Fields** and **Cascade Delete Related Records** check boxes.

6. Change the page orientation of the Relationships report to **Landscape**, print the Relationships report, and be sure your name is in the report name. Close the Relationships report, saving any changes. Close the database and then close Access.

End You have completed Project 5I

Project 5J — Compact Gardens

Objectives: *Create a Query from Joined Tables and Protect and Maintain a Database.*

In the following Mastery Assessment, you will create a query from joined tables. Your completed query will look similar to the one shown in Figure 5.49. Additionally, you will compact the database. You will rename the database as *5J_Gardens_Firstname_Lastname*.

1. Locate the file **a05J_Gardens** from your student files and copy and paste the file to the Chapter 5 folder where you are storing your projects for this chapter. Remove the Read-only property from the file and rename the file as **5J_Gardens_Firstname_Lastname** Start Access and open the database you just renamed.

2. Create a query that will locate all of the customers in the **Customers** table that have a **Customer Representative** with an **ID#** of **1637**. In your query results, include the **ID#** field from the **SG Employees** table and the **Customer #**, **First Name**, and **Last Name** fields from the **Customers** table.

(Project 5J–Compact Gardens continues on the next page)

(Project 5J–Compact Gardens continued)

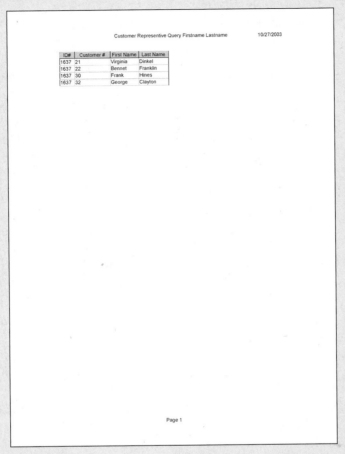

Figure 5.49

3. Save the query as **Customer Representative Query Firstname Lastname** and then print the query.

4. Close the **5J Gardens** database. Compact the **5J_Gardens** database. Save the compacted file as **5J_Gardens_Compacted_Firstname_Lastname** and then close Access.

 You have completed Project 5J ————————————————————

Project 5K — Historical Contacts

Objective: *Create a Query Using the Simple Query Wizard.*

The Simple Query Wizard will not limit data, but it will retrieve data. It is ideal, for example, to create a simple phone list of the contacts in a database.

1. Locate the file **a05K_Historical_Gardens** from your student files and copy and paste the file to the Chapter 5 folder where you are storing your assignments for this chapter. Remove the Read-only property from the file and rename the file as **5K_Historical_Gardens_Firstname_ Lastname** Start Access and open the database you just renamed.

2. On the Objects bar, click **Queries**, and then on the Database window toolbar, click **New**. From the displayed list, click **Simple Query Wizard**, and then click **OK**. In the first screen of the Wizard, under **Tables/Queries**, click the arrow, and from the displayed list, click **Table: Historical Gardens Contact Information**. Use the **One Field** button to add the fields **Contact Name** and **Phone Number**, and then click **Next**.

3. Type **Gardens Phone List Firstname Lastname** as the title for the query, and then click **Finish**. Print the query, close the database, and then close Access.

 End **You have completed Project 5K** ————————

Project 5L — SG Income

Objective: *Create and Modify a Crosstab Query.*

Sales of products on the TV show's companion Web site have been growing. The owners of Southland Gardens would like to compare income from each product by state. A special type of query, called a crosstab query, can calculate a sum, average, count, or other type of total for data that is grouped by two types of information—in this case by product and by state. The products will be listed down the left side of the query result, and the states will be listed across the top. Recall that you can run a query based on an existing query. A query containing the product, state, and amount has already been created.

1. Locate the file **a05L_SG_Income** from your student files and copy and paste the file to the Chapter 5 folder where you are storing your assignments for this chapter. Remove the Read-only property from the file and rename the file as **5L_SG_Income_Firstname_Lastname** Start Access and open the database you just renamed.

(Project 5L–SG Income continues on the next page)

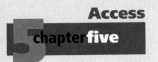

(Project 5L–SG Income continued)

2. On the Objects bar, click **Queries**, and then on the Database window toolbar, click **New**. From the displayed list, click **Crosstab Query Wizard**, and then click **OK**. Under **View**, click the **Queries** option button. At the top of the dialog box, click **Query: Customers Query**, and then click **Next**.

3. Here you select which fields' values (you can pick more than one field) that you want to use as row headings. Under **Available Fields**, click **Product**, and then click the **One Field** button to move this field to the **Selected Fields** list. Click **Next**. Here you select which field's values (you can pick only one field) that you want to use as column headings. Click **StateOrProvince**, and then click **Next**.

4. Here you decide what number you want calculated for each column and row intersection. Under **Fields**, click **Amount**. Under **Functions**, click **Sum**. Click **Next**. Under **What do you want to name your query?**, type **Crosstab Firstname Lastname** and then click **Finish**. Change the **Page Setup** to **Landscape**, and then print your crosstab query. Close the query, close the database, and close Access.

End You have completed Project 5L

On the Internet

Databases and Normalization

The power of relational databases depends on the relationships that are established between the tables in the database. The process of identifying and eliminating the problems associated with data redundancy and a lack of data integrity is called normalization.

Go online and perform a search to learn more about databases and normalization.

GO! with Help

Exporting Data from Access

You can export data from Access to other Microsoft Office 2003 programs. For example, information in a table can be exported into an Excel spreadsheet.

1. Start Access. In the **Type a question for help** box, type **export data** and then press [Enter].

2. In the displayed **Search Results** task pane, click the result **Export data or database objects**. Maximize the displayed window. Locate and then click the link **To a Microsoft Excel or other spreadsheet**. Then, click **Save an object's output as a Microsoft Excel file.** Print the Help information. Close the Help window.

3. Open any of the databases that you used in this chapter and, using the printed information, export one of the tables to an Excel spreadsheet. Save the spreadsheet in your chapter folder with a name of your choice.

4. Close the database, and then close Access.

chaptersix

Advanced Forms and Subforms

In this chapter, you will: complete these projects **and** practice these skills.

Project 6A **Customizing a Form**	**Objectives**
	• Add Fields to a Form
	• Use Toolbar Buttons to Enhance a Form
	• Use Form Control Properties
	• Make a Form User-Friendly

Project 6B **Creating a Form and Subform**	**Objectives**
	• Create a Form in Design View
	• Create a Subform

The Perfect Party

The Perfect Party store, owned by two partners, provides a wide variety of party accessories including invitations, favors, banners and flags, balloons, piñatas, etc. Party planning services include both custom parties with prefilled custom "goodie bags" and "parties in a box" that include everything needed to throw a theme party. Big sellers in this category are the Football and Luau themes. The owners are planning to open a second store and expand their party planning services to include catering.

© Getty Images, Inc.

Advanced Forms and Subforms

Access forms provide you with a way to enter, edit, and display data. You have created forms by using an AutoForm and by using the Form Wizard. Forms can also be created directly in Design view. Access provides tools with which you can enhance the visual appeal of forms, for example, by adding color, backgrounds, borders, user instructions, and ControlTips to the form. In this chapter, you will use advanced techniques to customize forms in Access.

Forms can be used to manipulate data from multiple tables if a relationship exists between the tables. You have practiced creating relationships between tables and have seen that information from multiple objects can be presented in one object, such as a query that located data from multiple tables. Similarly, you can use a form to view information from multiple tables when a one-to-many relationship exists between the tables; this is accomplished by using a form and a subform. A form that is embedded within another form (the main form) is called a *subform*. Subforms are used to view, enter, and edit detailed information that is related to the data in the main form. In this chapter, you will create a subform.

Project 6A New Customers

The Perfect Party uses forms in Access to enter data about their customers into a database. Forms can be customized by adding font colors, backgrounds, borders, and visual cues. Customizing a form in this manner makes the form easier to use for the person who is entering the data.

In Activities 6.1 through 6.10, you will modify and enhance the form that The Perfect Party uses to gather data about new customers. Additionally, you will customize the form using many of the features Access provides to make forms easy to use. Your completed form will look similar to Figure 6.1.

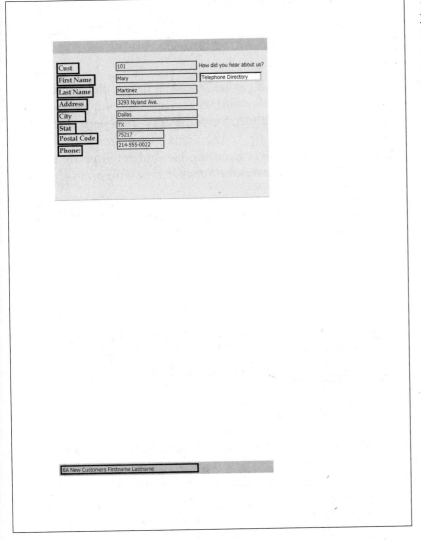

Figure 6.1
Project 6A—New Customers

Objective 1
Add Fields to a Form

Using either AutoForm or the Form Wizard, you have practiced creating a form in which you included all of the fields from the underlying table in the form. Fields can also be added to the form after the form is created.

Activity 6.1 Adding Fields to a Form

In this activity, you will add two fields to the Customer Information form, which is used to enter customer information into The Perfect Party customer database.

1 Using the skills you practiced earlier, create a new folder named Chapter 6 in the location where you will be storing your projects for this chapter. Locate the file **a06A_PerfectParty** from your student files and copy and paste the file to the Chapter 6 folder you created. Remove the Read-only property from the file and rename the file as **6A_PerfectParty_Firstname_Lastname** Start Access and open the database you just renamed.

2 On the Objects bar, click **Forms**. Open the **Customer Information** form in **Form view** and examine the layout and fields in the form.

The underlying table for the Customer Information form is the PP Customers table. This form is **bound**—linked to—the PP Customers table. The PP Customers table is the **record source** for the Customer Information form. Between two bound objects, the record source is the object from which the actual data comes.

3 Switch to **Design view** and maximize the window. View the controls in the form, and then resize the right edge of the form to approximately **4.5 inches on the horizontal ruler** and the bottom edge to approximately **3 inches on the vertical ruler**. See Figure 6.2. This will give you more space to work with the form.

Recall that the Design view of a form displays **text box controls**—where the actual data from the corresponding table is displayed—and **label controls**—the field names from the corresponding table. See Figure 6.2. Each text box is bound (linked to) a specific field in the table. A **control** is a graphical user interface object, such as a text box, a check box, scroll bar, or command button, which provides user control for a program.

Label controls ——— 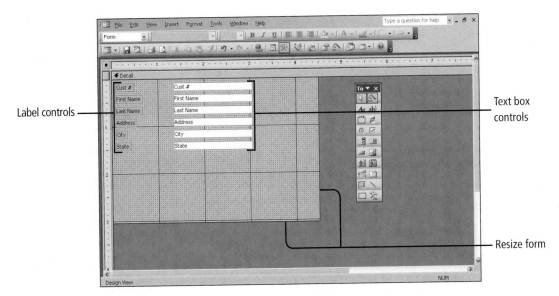 ——— Text box controls

——— Resize form

Figure 6.2

4 From the **View** menu, click **Page Header/Footer**. If necessary, display the Toolbox toolbar, and then click the **Label** button [Aa]. In the **Page Footer section**, draw a label control as shown in Figure 6.3, and then, using your own information, type **6A New Customers Firstname Lastname**

5 If necessary, on the Form Design toolbar, click the **Field List** button [▦] to display the field list. Alternatively, display the View menu, and then click Field List.

The field list displays a list of the fields from the corresponding table—PP Customers.

6 Point to the lower edge of the field list, drag to expand the list so that you can view all the field names, and then drag the list to the right side of your screen. In the **Field List**, click the **Postal Code** field, and then drag it into the **Detail section** of the form, positioning the small white box attached to your mouse pointer directly under the left edge of the white **State** text box control. Compare your screen with Figure 6.3. If you are not satisfied with your result, click **Undo** and begin again. Notice that the point at which you drop the small box attached to the pointer is where the white text box control will be created, and the label control will be positioned to the left.

The Postal Code control is added to the Customer Information form.

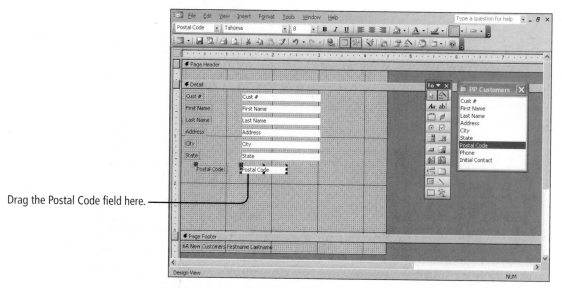

Drag the Postal Code field here.

Figure 6.3

Note — Positioning the Fields You Add to a Form

Position the field where you want the text box control to be

When adding fields to a form in Design view by dragging from the Field List, the position is determined by the text box control. Drag and drop the field from the field list in the location where you want the text box control to be and the label control will be positioned to the left of the text box control. Then, select the label control, display the pointing hand pointer, and adjust its position as desired.

7 Point to the large selection handle in the upper left corner of the **Postal Code label control** until the pointing hand mouse pointer displays. Then, using the techniques you have practiced in previous chapters, adjust the position of the **Postal Code label control** and text box control as shown in Figure 6.4. (Hint: Recall that you can use the arrow keys on your keyboard to nudge the controls in small increments.)

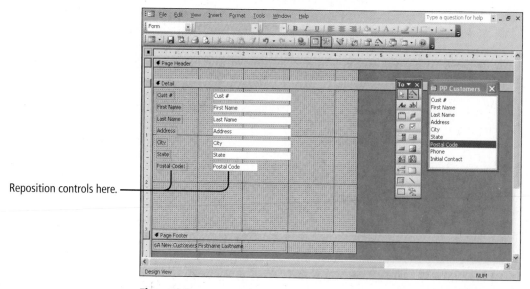

Reposition controls here.

Figure 6.4

8 Use the technique you just practiced to add the **Phone** field to the **Customer Information** form, and then adjust the position of the controls, as shown in Figure 6.5.

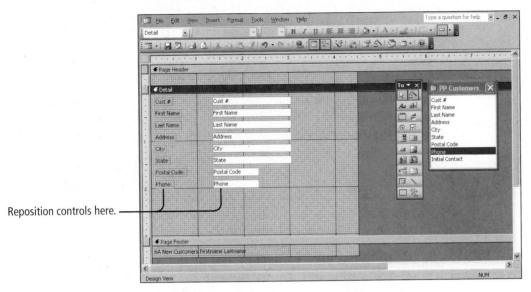

Reposition controls here. ——

Figure 6.5

9 Save the form and switch to **Form view** to view the changes to the form.

10 Switch to **Design view** and leave the **Customer Information** form open in Design view for the next activity.

Objective 2
Use Toolbar Buttons to Enhance a Form

Many of the Access features for enhancing the appearance of a form are available from the Formatting toolbar. For example, from the Formatting toolbar, you can modify font colors that make the form more attractive.

Activity 6.2 Modifying Font Color

In this activity, you will modify the font color in the fields for the Customer Information form.

1 With the **Customer Information** form open in Design view, click once in the **Cust # label control**. See Figure 6.6.

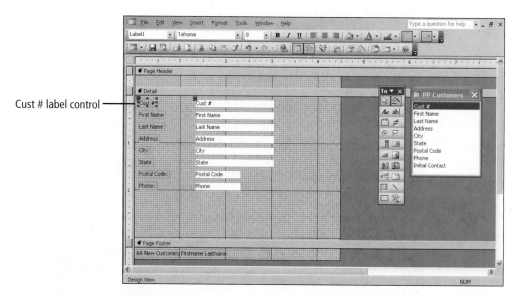

Cust # label control

Figure 6.6

2 On the Formatting toolbar, click the **Font/Fore Color button arrow** 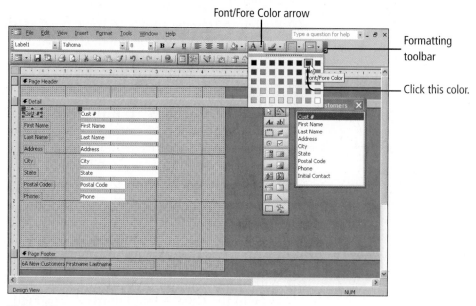, and from the color palette, in the first row, click the seventh color—**dark blue**. See Figure 6.7.

The color of the text changes from black to blue.

Font/Fore Color arrow

Formatting toolbar

Click this color.

Figure 6.7

3 Hold down Shift and click each of the remaining label controls to select them. On the Formatting toolbar, click the **Font/Fore Color** button. Notice that you do not need to display the color palette—the button retains the color most recently used.

Another Way — **To Select Controls on a Form**

Use the rulers!

Controls on a form can be selected by using either the horizontal ruler or the vertical ruler in Design view. Clicking on a location on the horizontal ruler will select all of the controls on the form that are located directly beneath the location on the ruler where you clicked. Clicking a location on the vertical ruler will select the controls that are located directly to the right in the form.

4 Deselect the label controls, and then switch to **Form view** to view the changes to the form. See Figure 6.8.

Font color in labels changed to blue

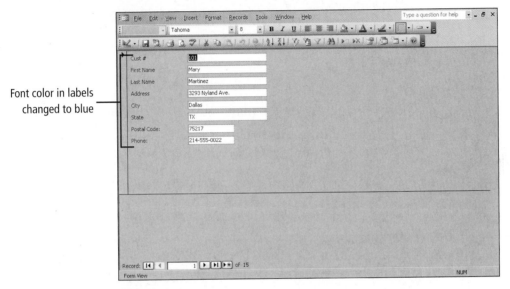

Figure 6.8

5 Switch to **Design view** and leave the form open in Design view for the next activity.

Activity 6.3 Adding a Background Color to a Form

Color can also be added to the background of a form. In this activity, you will modify the background color for the Customer Information form.

1 With the **Customer Information** form open in Design view, locate the **Section Selector** for the **Detail** section, as shown in Figure 6.9.

Section selectors are used to select entire sections of a form to perform section-level operations, such as adding background colors.

2 Click once on the **Section Selector** for the **Detail** section. See Figure 6.9.

The darkened bar, as shown in Figure 6.9, indicates that the entire Detail section of the form is selected.

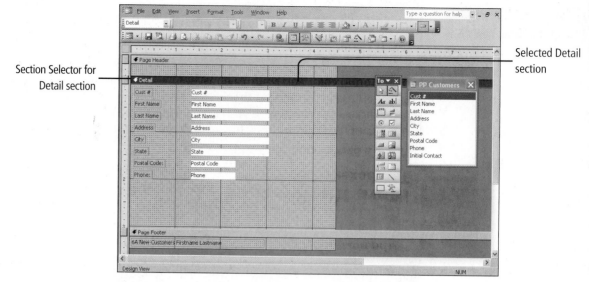

Section Selector for
Detail section

Selected Detail
section

Figure 6.9

3 On the Formatting Toolbar, click the **Fill/Back Color button arrow**
🪣▾, and from the displayed palette, in the fifth row, click the second color—**pale peach**. See Figure 6.10.

The background color for the form changes to a peach color.

Fill/Back Color arrow

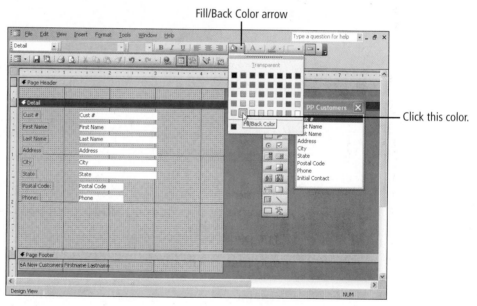

Click this color.

Figure 6.10

4 Switch to **Form view** and view the background color that has been added to the form.

5 Switch to **Design view**, display the **Fill/Back Color** palette again, and then in the fifth row, click the third color—**pale yellow**.

The background color for the form changes to yellow.

6 Save the form, and then switch to **Form view** and view the background color for the form. See Figure 6.11.

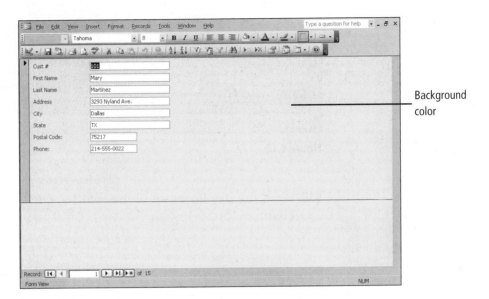

Figure 6.11

7 Switch to **Design view** and leave the form open in Design view for the next activity.

More Knowledge — Adding a Background Color to Text boxes

Apply a background color to a text box

Background colors can also be added to the background of text box controls. First, click the text box control to which you want to add a background color. Then, on the Formatting toolbar, click the Fill/Back Color arrow, and click the background color you want to apply.

Activity 6.4 Applying a Border to a Control in a Form

In this activity, you will add a border to controls in the Customer Information form.

1 With the **Customer Information** form open in Design view, click once in the **Cust # label control**.

2 On the Formatting toolbar, click the **Line/Border Width button arrow** [ ]. See Figure 6.12.

Line/Border Width arrow

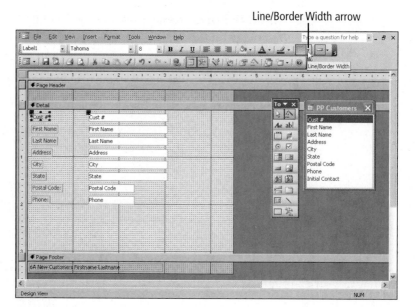

Figure 6.12

3 From the displayed set of line widths, click **3** 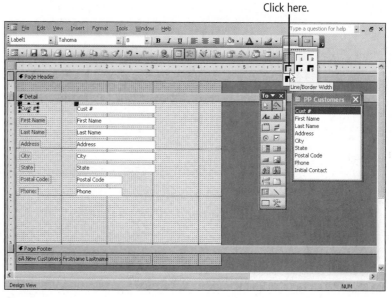 as shown in Figure 6.13.

Click here.

Figure 6.13

4 Switch to **Form view** and view the border that surrounds the **Cust # label**.

This border is too wide to be visually appealing on this form.

5 Switch to **Design View**, be sure the **Cust # control** is still selected, and then change the **Line/Border Width** to **2**.

6 On the **Edit** menu, click **Select All** to select all of the controls on the form, and then apply a **Line/Border Width** of **2** to all of the controls. You need only click the button, because it has retained its most recent selection of 2. See Figure 6.14.

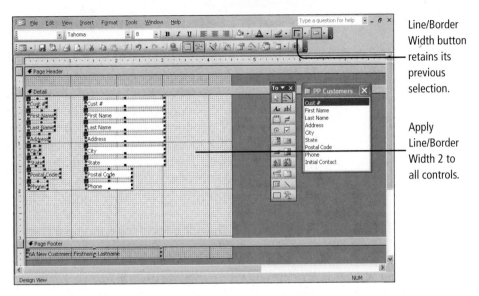

Line/Border Width button retains its previous selection.

Apply Line/Border Width 2 to all controls.

Figure 6.14

More Knowledge — Applying Formats

Use the Format Painter

Once you apply formatting to a control, you can apply the same formatting to a control by using the Format Painter located on the Formatting toolbar. Select the control that has the formatting that you want to apply to other controls, click the Format Painter button on the Formatting toolbar, and then click the control to which you want the formatting applied.

7 Deselect the controls, save the form, and then switch to **Form view** and view the changes made to the form. See Figure 6.15.

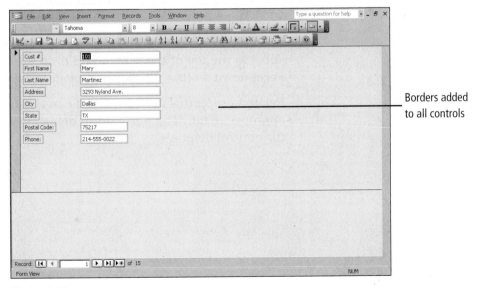

Borders added to all controls

Figure 6.15

8 Switch to **Design view** and leave the form open in Design view for the next activity.

Objective 3
Use Form Control Properties

There are multiple methods you can use to modify a form's appearance. Each control on a form has ***properties***—characteristics that determine not only the appearance, but also the structure and behavior of the control, as well as the characteristics of the text or data it contains. You can view a control's properties on its associated ***property sheet***. The color and border width of a control are examples of control properties. They can be changed from the Formatting toolbar, as you did in the previous activity, and are also available in each control's associated property sheet, along with numerous other control properties.

Activity 6.5 Changing Text Properties on a Form Using the Property Sheet

In this activity, you will modify text properties for the Customer Information form using the property sheet associated with a control.

1 With the **Customer Information** form open in Design view, click once in the **Cust # label control**.

2 On the Form Design toolbar, click the **Properties** button 🖾 to display the property sheet.

The property sheet for the Cust # label control displays. Both the title bar and the box at the top of the property sheet indicate *Label1*.

Another Way

To Display the Property Sheet

Click the Properties button

You can also display a control's property sheet by right-clicking a control, and then clicking Properties from the shortcut menu. Alternatively, you can double-click the control.

3 Click the **Format tab**, and then, if necessary, move the property sheet to the top of the screen and drag the lower edge of the property sheet down so that all properties can be viewed. See Figure 6.16.

Related properties for the control can be displayed by clicking on the appropriate tab. The Format tab displays properties related to how the control displays.

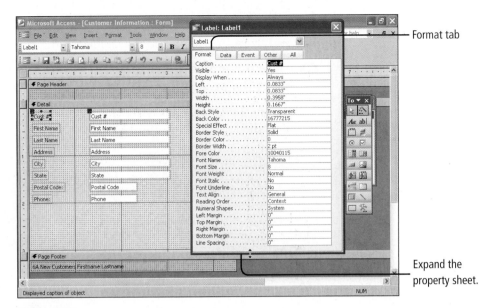

Format tab

Expand the property sheet.

Figure 6.16

4 About halfway down the list, locate and click in the **Font Name** box, and then click the **down arrow** that displays. See Figure 6.17.

A list of available fonts displays.

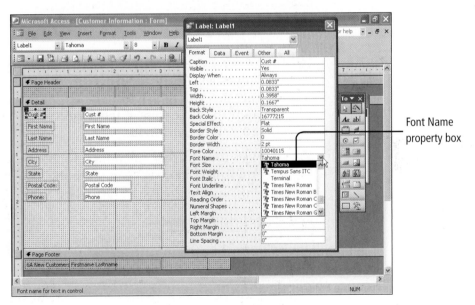

Font Name property box

Figure 6.17

5 From the list of available fonts, scroll as necessary, and then click **Book Antiqua**.

6 Click in the **Font Size** box, click the **down arrow** that displays, and from the list of font sizes, click **10**.

7 Click in the **Font Weight** box, click the **down arrow** that displays, and from the displayed list, click **Bold**.

8 Close the property sheet by clicking the **Close** button ☒ in the title bar of the property sheet.

9 Resize the **Cust # label control** to accommodate the increased font size and weight. See Figure 6.18.

Resize ——

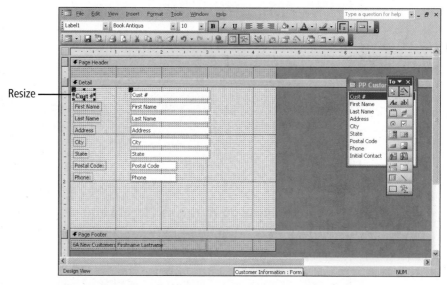

Figure 6.18

10 Hold down Shift and select all the remaining label controls. Display the Properties sheet, and then use the techniques you just practiced to apply the same modifications to the remaining label controls as you applied to the **Cust # label control** (**Book Antiqua** font, font size **10**, font weight **Bold**).

11 Deselect the controls and adjust each control slightly to accommodate the enlarged text. Then, save the form and switch to **Form view** to view the changes to the form. See Figure 6.19.

Text modifications ——

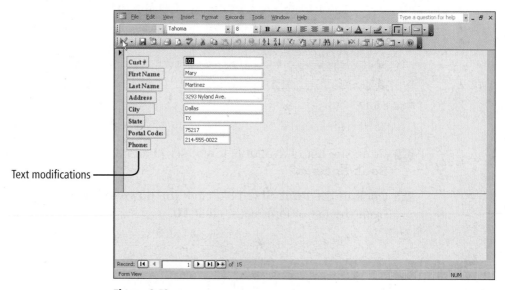

Figure 6.19

12 Switch to **Design view** and leave the form open in Design view for the next activity.

Activity 6.6 Refining Additional Properties on a Form Using the Properties Box

In this activity, you will modify more properties for the Customer Information form using the property sheet.

1 With the **Customer Information** form open in Design view, click the **Cust # text box control**, display the **Properties sheet**, click once in the **Back Style** box, and then click the **down arrow** that displays. See Figure 6.20.

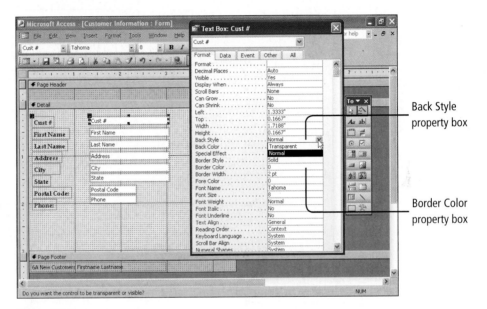

Back Style property box

Border Color property box

Figure 6.20

2 Click **Transparent**.

The background of the control is now transparent and will allow the background color of the form to show through.

3 Click once in the **Border Width** box, click the **down arrow**, and in the list of widths, click **1 pt**.

4 Click once in the **Border Color** box, click the **Build** button (the button with the three small dots), and from the displayed **Color** dialog box, in the third row, click the seventh color—**burgundy**. Compare your property sheet with Figure 6.21, and then click **OK**.

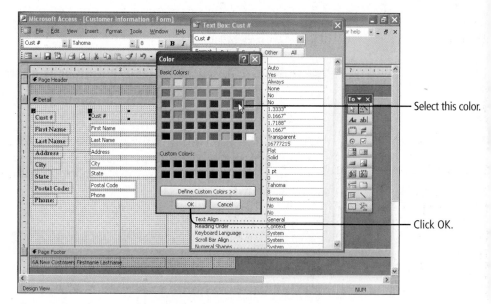

Figure 6.21

5 Without closing the property sheet, hold down Shift and select the remaining text box controls on the form. See Figure 6.22.

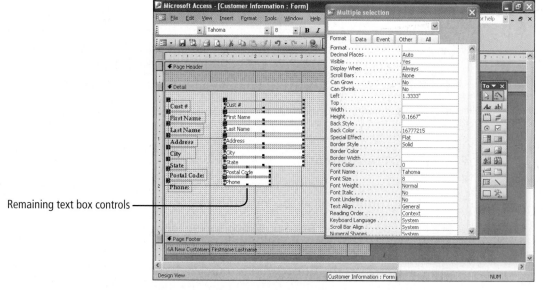

Figure 6.22

6 To the remaining text box controls, apply the same **Back Style**, **Border Width**, and **Border Color** as you applied to the **Cust # text box control**.

7 Close the property sheet, save the form, deselect the controls, and then switch to **Form view** to view the changes you have made to the form. See Figure 6.23.

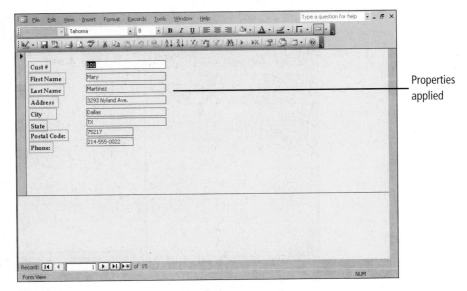

Properties applied

Figure 6.23

━━━

8 Switch to **Design view** and leave the form open in Design view for the next activity.

Objective 4
Make a Form User-Friendly

To make Access forms easy to use, you can also add instructions for a user that display on the status bar while data is being entered and custom ControlTips that display within the form. Additionally, you can change the *tab order* of the fields on a form and add controls such as a *combo box* to a form. Tab order refers to the order in which fields are selected when the ⎡Tab⎤ key is pressed—the order does not necessarily have to be in the exact order that the controls display on the screen. A combo box allows the person entering data into the form to either type the information or choose information from a predefined list.

Activity 6.7 Adding Instructions to the Status Bar of a Form

One way to make data entry easier is to provide instructions relating to the field that will display on the *status bar*. The status bar is the horizontal bar at the bottom of the screen directly above the taskbar. Its function is to display information about the current condition of the program, such as the status of items in the window and the progress of the current task, or information about the selected item. In this activity, you will use features of Access to add user instructions to the status bar in the Customer Information form.

1 With the **Customer Information** form open in Design view, click the **First Name text box control** to select it, and then click the **Properties** button to display the property sheet.

2 In the Properties sheet, click the **Other tab**. See Figure 6.24.

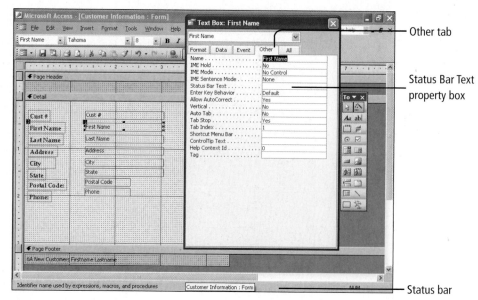

Other tab

Status Bar Text
property box

Figure 6.24

Status bar

3 In the **Status Bar Text** box, type **Enter customer's First Name**

4 Click in the **Last Name text box control** to select it.

5 In the property sheet, in the **Status Bar Text** box, type **Enter customer's Last Name**

6 Close the Properties sheet, switch to **Form view**, click once in the **First Name** field in the form, and view the status bar. See Figure 6.25.

The instructions that you specified display in the status bar.

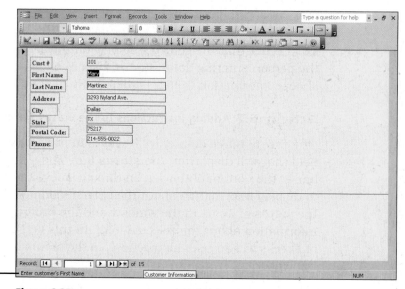

Instructions in status bar

Figure 6.25

7 Click in the **Last Name** field and view the instruction that displays in the status bar.

8 Switch to **Design view** and leave the form open in Design view for the next activity.

Activity 6.8 Creating Custom ControlTips

Another way to make a form easier to use is to add custom **ControlTips** that display when a user pauses the mouse pointer over a control in a form. A ControlTip, similar to a Windows ScreenTip, temporarily displays descriptive text while the mouse pointer is paused over the control. This method is somewhat limited, because most users use the Tab key to move from field to field, and thus do not see the ControlTip. However, adding ControlTips is a useful technique, particularly in a training situation when a user is new to the data entry form.

1 With the **Customer Information** form open in Design view, click the **Cust # label control** to select it.

2 Display the **Properties sheet** and click the **Other tab**.

3 In the **ControlTip Text** box, type **Customer #** as shown in Figure 6.26.

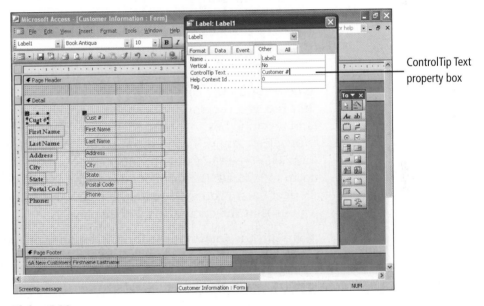

ControlTip Text property box

Figure 6.26

4 Without closing the Properties sheet, click the **Address label control** once to select it.

5 In the **Properties sheet**, in the **ControlTip Text** box, type **Customer Address**

6 Close the **Properties sheet**, save the form, switch to **Form view**, and position your mouse pointer over the **Cust # label**. See Figure 6.27.

The ControlTip you specified displays.

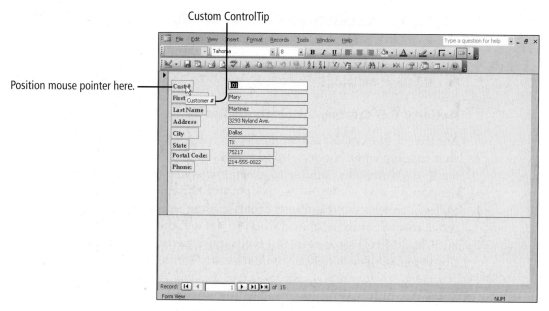

Custom ControlTip

Position mouse pointer here.

Figure 6.27

7 Switch to **Design view** and leave the form open in Design view for the next activity.

Activity 6.9 Adding a Combo Box to a Form

A **combo box** is another control that can be added to a form. A combo box combines the features of a text box and a list box—you can either type text into the control or choose a selection from a predefined list. A **list box** is a control that displays a scrollable list of selections. You can add a combo box to a form to display a list of values from which a user can select. The values in a combo box can either come from a table or the user can type the value. In this activity, you will add a combo box to the form to indicate the form of advertising that brought the customer to The Perfect Party. You will create the list that the user will see by typing the values that the combo box will display.

1 With the **Customer Information** form open in Design view, if necessary, click the Toolbox button ![icon] to display the Toolbox toolbar.

2 On the Toolbox toolbar, click the **Combo Box** button ![icon], and then position your mouse pointer in the form as shown in Figure 6.28.

Toolbox button
on the toolbar

Position your
mouse pointer
here.

Combo Box
button

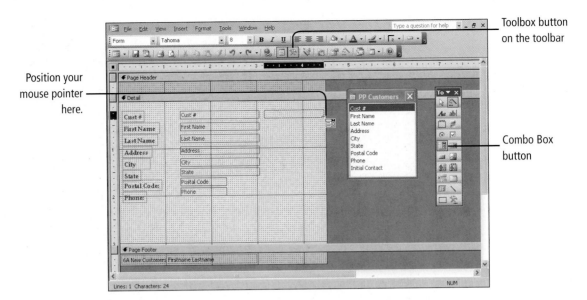

Figure 6.28

3 Draw a rectangle as shown in Figure 6.29, and then release the mouse button.

The Combo Box Wizard displays.

Draw a
rectangle.

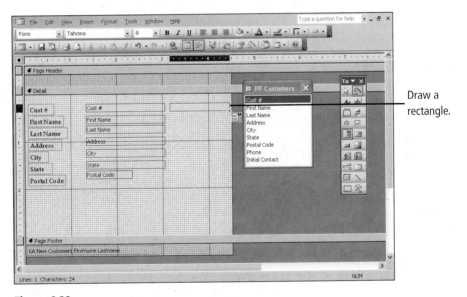

Figure 6.29

4 In the first screen of the wizard, click the **I will type in the values that I want** option button, and then click **Next**.

5 In this screen of the wizard, click under **Col1**, type **Telephone Directory** and then widen the column slightly so that you can see your typing as shown in Figure 6.30.

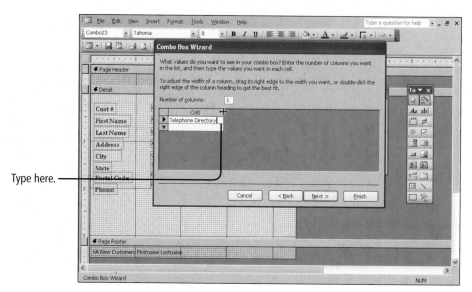

Type here.

Figure 6.30

6 Press ⌷Tab⌷ and type **Internet**

7 Press ⌷Tab⌷ and type **Newspaper Ad**

8 Press ⌷Tab⌷ and type **Friend**

9 Press ⌷Tab⌷ and type **Other** as shown in Figure 6.31, and then click **Next**.

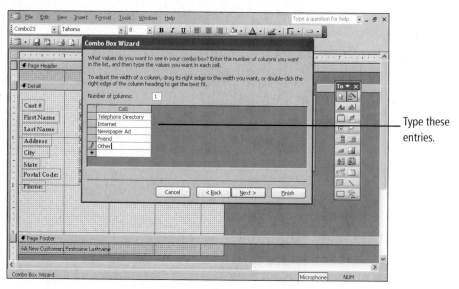

Type these entries.

Figure 6.31

10 In this screen, be sure that the **Remember the value for later use** option button is selected.

This screen allows you to choose how you want Access to store the values you typed for the combo box.

11 Click **Next**, and in this screen of the wizard, under *What label would you like for your combo box?*, type **How did you hear about us?** and then click **Finish**.

12 Reposition the control below its label control as shown in Figure 6.32 (move the white box down and the label control to the right). This control is an ***unbound*** object, meaning that the data in this field is not derived from data that is contained in a table; rather, the data is derived from the list you created within the wizard.

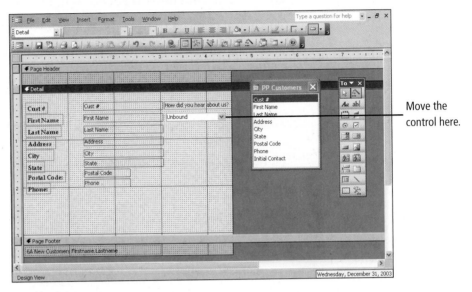

Move the control here.

Figure 6.32

13 Be sure the white **combo box text box control** you added is selected, and then click the **Properties** button 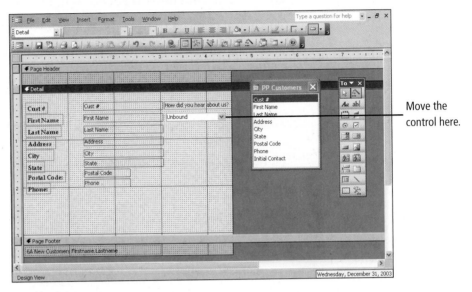 to display the Properties sheet.

14 Click the **Data tab** and then in the **Control Source** box, click the **down arrow**. See Figure 6.33.

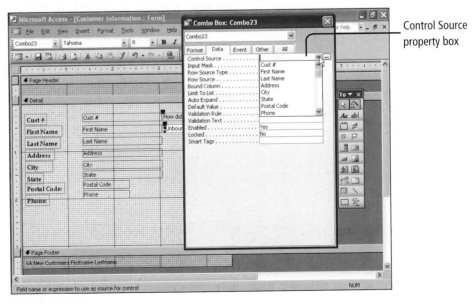

Control Source property box

Figure 6.33

15 From the displayed list, scroll down and click **Initial Contact**.

Specifying this field as the control source will insert the information entered in the combo box into the Initial Contact field for this customer in the PP Customers table. In this manner, the table will be updated with the information about how the customer learned about The Perfect Party.

16 Close the **Properties sheet**, switch to **Form view**, and while viewing the record for Cust # 101, click the **down arrow** that displays in the **combo box control** you added to the form.

The list of choices that you specified displays.

17 Click **Telephone Directory** as shown in Figure 6.34.

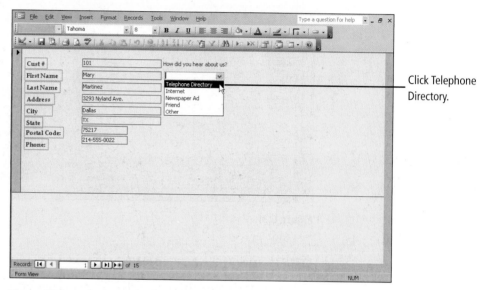

Figure 6.34

18 Close the form, save your changes, and open the **PP Customers** table in Datasheet View. Locate the information for Cust # 101, and notice that under Initial Contact, the new information has been inserted.

19 Close the **PP Customers** table.

Activity 6.10 Changing the Tab Order on a Form

You can customize the order in which you enter data on a form by customizing the tab order on a form. Tab order refers to the order in which the fields will be selected each time the Tab key is pressed.

1 Open the **Customer Information** form in **Form view**, and watch the form as you press Tab eight times.

Notice that the insertion point moves from field to field starting with the Cust # and ending with the combo box control.

2 Switch to **Design view**, display the **View** menu, and then click **Tab Order**. Alternatively, right-click the control and click Tab Order from the displayed shortcut menu.

The Tab Order dialog box displays.

3 Click the **selector** that is to the left of the **Combo** field. See Figure 6.35. (Note: You will see a number, such as *19*, next to your combo box. This is a number automatically assigned by Access and will differ from the number shown in the figure, depending on what controls have been created previously on your computer.)

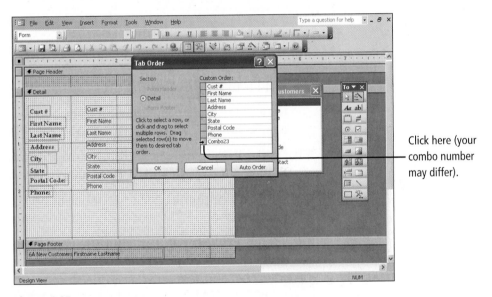

Click here (your combo number may differ).

Figure 6.35

4 Drag this field up under the **Cust #** field, as shown in Figure 6.36, and then click **OK**.

The order of fields that displays in this list is the order in which fields will be selected as the Tab key is pressed.

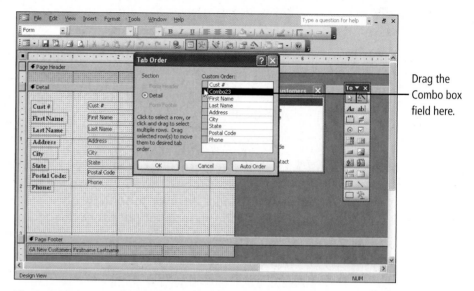

Figure 6.36

5 Switch to **Form view** and press Tab.

Notice that the insertion point moves from the Cust # field to the combo box, because this is the tab order you specified.

6 On the **File** menu, click **Print**. In the **Print** dialog box, under **Print Range**, click the **Selected Record(s)** option button, and then click **OK**.

The form containing record #101 will print, with your name in the page footer.

7 Close the form and save your changes. Close the database and close Access.

End You have completed Project 6A

Project 6B **Existing Customers**

As you have seen and practiced, forms can be created using a variety of methods. Another method by which a form can be created is by creating the form entirely in Design view.

In Activities 6.11 through 6.15, you will create a form in Design view and then modify the form. Additionally, you will add a subform to an existing form. Your completed form will look similar to Figure 6.37.

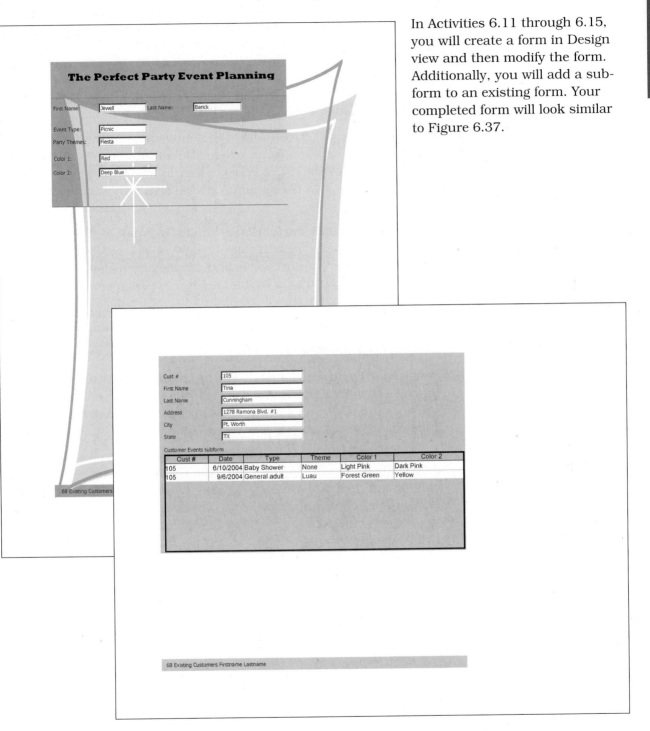

Figure 6.37
Project 6B—Existing Customers

Objective 5
Create a Form in Design View

Usually when you create a form, you will use either AutoForm or the Form Wizard and then modify the form in Design view to suit your needs. When the selections in AutoForm or the Form Wizard do not provide a good match with the specifications for your form, you can create a form entirely in Design view. Creating a form in Design view is a common technique when additional controls, such as combo boxes or subforms, need to be added to the form.

Activity 6.11 Creating a Form in Design View

In this activity, you will create a form that customers of The Perfect Party fill out when they are planning an event. The information in this form will assist the employees at The Perfect Party in helping customers choose party supplies for their event. You will create the form entirely in Design view.

1 Locate the file **a06B_PerfectParty** from your student files and copy and paste the file to the Chapter 6 folder you created. Remove the Read-only property from the file and rename the file as **6B_PerfectParty_Firstname_Lastname** Start Access and open the database you just renamed.

2 On the Objects bar, click **Forms**, and then on the database window toolbar, click the **New** button .

3 In the **New Form** dialog box, from the list of methods to create a form, be sure **Design View** is selected. Next to *Choose the table or query where the object's data comes from*, click the **down arrow**, and then click **Event Choices**. See Figure 6.38.

Event Choices is a query in this database. Forms can be based on either tables or queries. You will create this form using fields that exist in multiple tables. When creating a form in Design View where the data will come from multiple tables, it is easier to use a query as the record source for the form because the tables were already specified in the query.

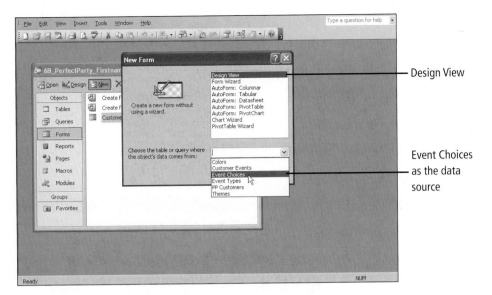

Design View

Event Choices
as the data
source

Figure 6.38

4 Click **OK**.

A blank form displays in Design view and the field list for the Event Choices query displays. Additionally, the Toolbox toolbar displays floating on your screen. See Figure 6.39.

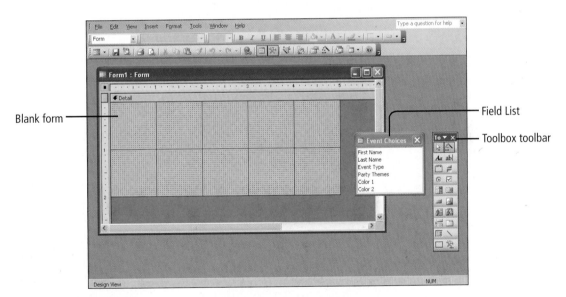

Blank form

Field List

Toolbox toolbar

Figure 6.39

5 Display the **File** menu, click **Save As** and then, in the **Save As** dialog box, under **Save Form 'Form 1' To** type **Event Planning** Click **OK**.

The name displays in the title bar of the form.

6 Using the techniques you practiced in Project 6A, add the fields from the field list to the form and reposition them approximately as shown in Figure 6.40. (Hint: Align the left edge of the small white box attached to the pointer, which represents the white label control, with the vertical grid line. Use Ctrl plus the arrow keys to move in small increments.)

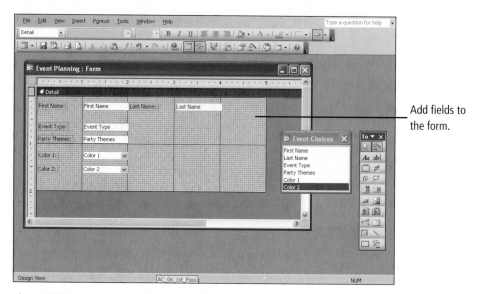

Add fields to the form.

Figure 6.40

7 Click the **Color 1 text box control**, hold down Shift, and then click the **Color 2 text box control**.

Both controls are selected.

8 Resize the controls by dragging a right center sizing handle to approximately **2.25 inches on the horizontal ruler**, so that they display as shown in Figure 6.41.

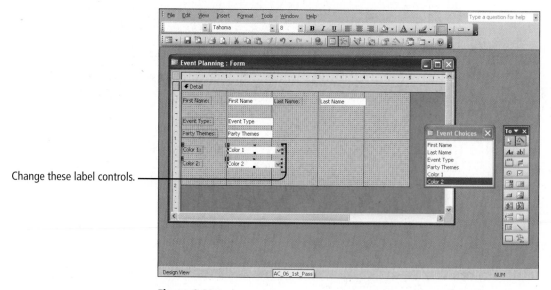

Change these label controls.

Figure 6.41

9 Deselect the controls.

10 Using the technique you practiced in Project 6A, click the **Section Selector** for the **Detail section**, click the **Fill/Back Color button arrow** 🎨▾, and in the fifth row, click the seventh color—**lavender**.

11 On the Form Design toolbar, click the **Save** button 💾 to save the form.

12 Leave the form open in Design view for the next activity.

Activity 6.12 Specifying a Picture Background

Forms can be customized to reflect the intention of the designer, whether it be fun, serious, or professional. In this activity, you will add a picture to the background of the form.

1 Be sure your **Event Planning** form is open in **Design view**, and locate the **Form selector** as shown in Figure 6.42.

The **Form selector** is the box where the rulers meet, in the upper left corner of a form in Design view. Use the Form selector to perform form-level operations, such as selecting the form.

Form selector —

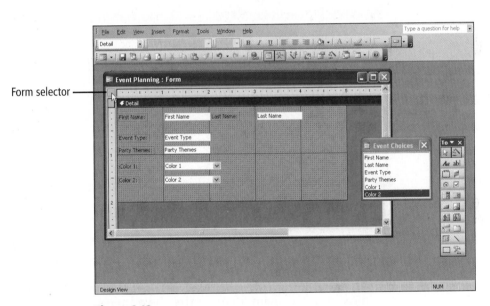

Figure 6.42

Another Way ┤ **To Select the Entire Form**

Use the Edit menu

Another way to select the entire form is to display the Edit menu and then click Select Form.

---

2 Double-click the **Form selector**.

The Properties sheet for the form displays.

3 Click the **Format tab**, click in the **Picture** box, and then click the **Build** button (the button with the three small dots).

4 In the displayed **Insert Picture** dialog box, navigate to the location where your student files are stored, and then double-click the file **a06B_ppbackground**.

The ppbackground graphic displays in the background of the form. (In this file name, *pp* stands for Perfect Party.)

5 Click in the **Picture Size Mode** box, click the **down arrow**, and then click **Stretch**.

The Stretch mode sizes the picture to fit the Form window.

6 **Close** X the Properties sheet, **Save** 🖫 the form, switch to **Form view**, and then view the changes you have made to the form.

More Knowledge — Other Picture Properties

Picture Type, Picture Alignment, Picture Tiling

From the property sheet, you can modify additional properties related to a graphic inserted into the form. Picture Type allows you to choose whether the picture will be embedded or linked. Picture Alignment allows you to modify the alignment of the picture. If you want the picture to be repeated across the form's background, choose the Yes option for Picture Tiling.

7 Switch to **Design view** and leave the form open for the next activity.

Activity 6.13 Adding a Title to the Form

A title on a form informs the user about the purpose of a form. In this activity, you will add a title to the Event Planning form.

1 Be sure your **Event Planning** form is open in **Design view**, maximize the form, display the **View** menu, and then click **Form Header/Footer**.

Form Header and Footer sections display in the form.

2 Expand the **Form Header section** down to approximately **0.5 inches on the vertical ruler** by positioning your pointer on the horizontal line between the **Form Header section** and the **Detail section** until the pointer changes to a large double arrow, then drag downward to approximately **0.5 inch on the vertical ruler**. (Hint: Drag past the 0.5 inch mark to view it, and then drag up again for precise positioning.)

3 If necessary, display the Toolbox, and then on the Toolbox toolbar, click the **Label** button 🗛. Draw a label control in the **Form Header section** as shown in Figure 6.43.

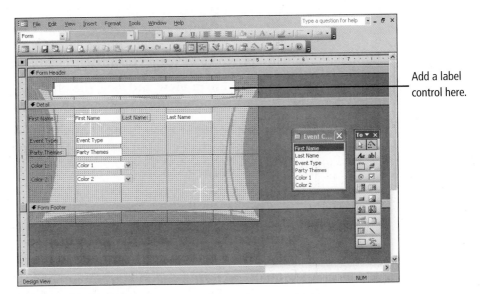

Add a label control here.

Figure 6.43

4 In the label box, type **The Perfect Party Event Planning**

5 Click in a blank area of the form to deselect the **Form Header label control**, and then click it again to select it.

6 On the Formatting toolbar, click the **Center** button ▤.

The text in the label control is centered horizontally within the label.

7 With the label still selected, change the font for the text in the label to **Rockwell Extra Bold**, and then change the font size to **16**.

8 If necessary, drag the left and right center resize handles to accommodate the text, and then compare your screen with Figure 6.44.

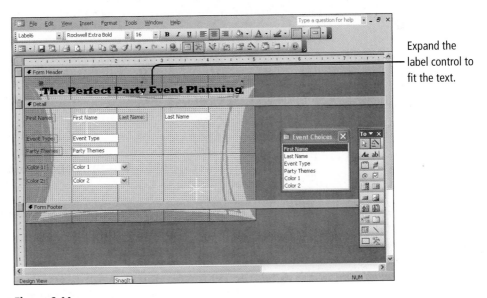

Expand the label control to fit the text.

Figure 6.44

9 Display the **View** menu, and then click **Page Header/Footer**. Add a label control in the **Page Footer section** and, using your own information, type **6B Existing Customers Firstname Lastname**

10 Switch to **Form view** and view the changes you have made to the form. Navigate to record **6**, the record for Jewell Barick.

11 On the **File** menu, click **Print**. In the **Print** dialog box, under **Print Range**, click the **Selected Record(s)** option button, and then click **OK**.

12 Close the form and save your changes.

Objective 6
Create a Subform

A **subform** is a form contained within another form. The form that contains the subform is the **main form**. Subforms are especially useful when you want to display data between two tables that have a one-to-many relationship. To create a form that will display data from two tables, a relationship must exist between the tables. The main form contains the data that is the *one* side of the relationship and the subform contains the data that is the *many* side of the relationship.

Activity 6.14 Creating a Subform

The Customer Information form you modified in Project 6A contains contact information about customers of The Perfect Party. The owners of The Perfect Party want to view the information in the Customer Information form and, at the same time, view information about the events that each customer has coordinated through The Perfect Party. This is accomplished by creating a subform within a main form. In this activity, you will add a subform that contains information about customer events to the main form—the Customer Information form.

1 Open the **Customer Information** form in **Design view**. If necessary, close the **Field List**.

2 **Maximize** the form if necessary, and then expand the width of the form to **6.5 inches on the horizontal ruler**.

Expanding the form will provide space for you to place the subform.

3 From the **View** menu, add the **Page Header/Footer sections** to your form. Then, create a label in the **Page Footer** and type **6B Existing Customers Firstname Lastname**

4 In the **Toolbox**, locate the **Subform/Subreport** button 🖼️.

Recall that the Toolbox contains controls that can be added to database objects.

5 Click the **Subform/Subreport** button 🖼️, draw a control in the lower part of the form as shown in Figure 6.45, and then release the mouse button.

The SubForm Wizard displays.

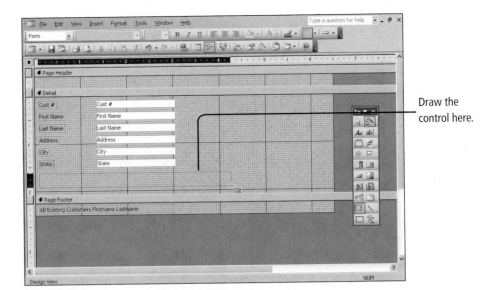

Draw the
control here.

Figure 6.45

6 In the first screen of the wizard, accept the default selection *Use existing Tables and Queries* by clicking **Next**.

7 Under **Table/Queries**, click the **down arrow**, and then click **Table: Customer Events**.

The Customer Events table contains the information that will display in the subform.

8 Click the **All Fields** button $\boxed{>>}$, and then click **Next**.

Clicking the All Fields button will cause all of the fields in the Customer Events table to display in the subform.

9 This screen allows you to define which fields link the main form to the subform. In other words, this is where you choose which field(s) are common to both tables. Be sure that the **Choose from a list** option button is selected, and then click **Next**.

10 In the final screen of the wizard, accept the default subform name and click **Finish**.

A subform is created in the Customer Information form. The form may display much smaller than it did before you created the subform.

11 **Maximize** the form, close the **Field List**, and close the **Toolbox**. The subform will display too small to be useful; therefore, expand the subform by dragging the right edge of the subform to **6.5 inches on the horizontal ruler**. Then, if necessary, hold down Ctrl and click ↓ ten to twelve times to nudge the subform down so that the subform label control is not touching the **State control**.

12 Switch to **Form view** and view the subform.

The record with Cust # 101 displays in the main form and below the main form, notice the subform that displays any events that are related to this customer. See Figure 6.46.

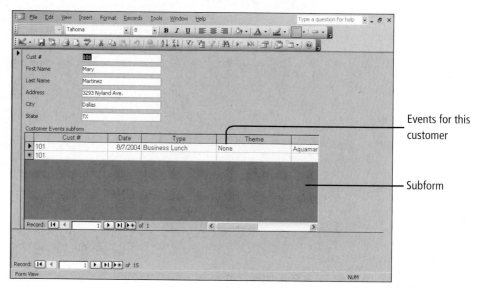

Figure 6.46

13 Leave the form open in **Form view** for the next activity.

Activity 6.15 Adding Records Using the Subform

Records that are added in a subform will also be added to and display in the corresponding table. In this activity, you will add a record using the subform in the Customer Information form, and that will update information in the Customer Events table.

1 Be sure your **Customer Information** form is open in **Form view**. Resize the field widths in the subform so that all of the fields display in the subform, and then at the bottom of your screen, use the navigation area in the main form to navigate to the record that has **Cust # 105**. See Figure 6.47.

Both the form and the subform have their own navigation areas to assist you in locating specific records.

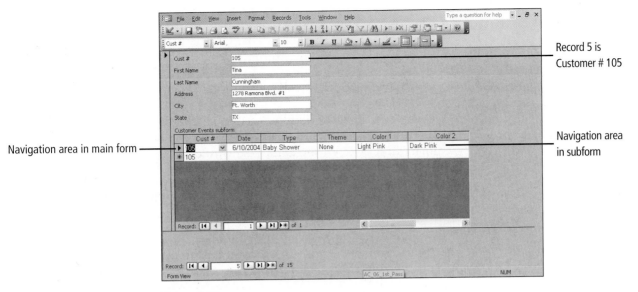

Navigation area in main form ⟶

Record 5 is
Customer # 105

Navigation area
in subform

Figure 6.47

2 In the subform, enter the data as shown in Figure 6.48 using the
down arrows to select from a list.

A relationship between the PP Customers table and the Customer
Events table exists. The field that ties the two tables together is the
Cust # field.

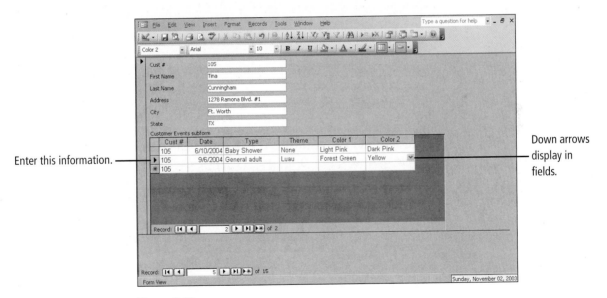

Enter this information. ⟶

Down arrows
display in
fields.

Figure 6.48

3 Display the **Page Setup** dialog box, click the **Page tab**, click **Landscape**, and then click **OK**. On the **File** menu, click **Print**, and in the **Print** dialog box, under **Print Range**, click **Selected Record(s)**. Click **OK**. Close the form and save your changes to the form and subform.

The subform name displays in the Database window. You can view the information contained in the subform either by opening the subform directly from the Database window or by opening the main form.

4 On the Objects bar, click **Tables**, and then open the **Customer Events** table and locate the information you just entered. See Figure 6.49.

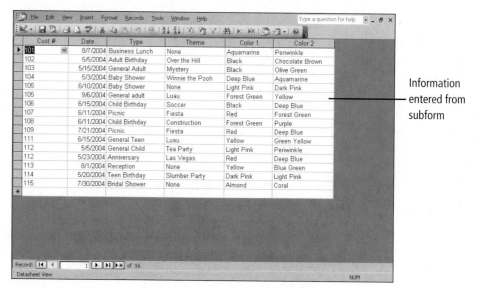

Information entered from subform

Figure 6.49

5 Close the **Customer Events** table. Close the database, and then close Access.

End You have completed Project 6B ──────────────

Summary

In this chapter, you practiced creating and modifying forms in Access using advanced techniques. You added fields to a form in Design view. You modified a form's properties using both the Formatting toolbar and the form's property sheet. You modified properties such as font properties, backgrounds, colors, and record sources. Additionally, you added user-friendly qualities to a form such as custom ControlTips, added status bar instructions, and customized the tab order.

You created a form in Design view and then modified its properties. Finally, you created a subform and added it to a main form. You practiced adding a record to the subform and viewed the updated record in the corresponding table.

In This Chapter You Practiced How To

- Add Fields to a Form
- Use Toolbar Buttons to Enhance a Form
- Use Form Control Properties
- Make a Form User-Friendly
- Create a Form in Design View
- Create a Subform

Matching

Match each term in the second column with its correct definition in the first column by writing the letter of the term on the blank line in front of the correct definition.

_____ **1.** The toolbar that contains buttons that allow you to change the way a control displays.

_____ **2.** The location that provides access to the properties of the controls on a form.

_____ **3.** The term used to describe two objects that are linked to each other.

_____ **4.** The control that contains the actual data from the corresponding table.

_____ **5.** The object where the data comes from between two linked objects.

_____ **6.** The horizontal bar at the bottom of the screen that displays information about the current condition of the program.

_____ **7.** The property sheet tab that contains properties for a control related to the manner in which the property displays.

_____ **8.** Descriptive text that temporarily displays when the mouse is pointed to a control in the form.

_____ **9.** The type of control that displays the field names.

_____ **10.** A graphical user interface object such as a text box or a check box that provides user control for a program.

_____ **11.** The characteristics that determine the appearance, structure, and behavior of a control.

_____ **12.** A form that is embedded within a main form.

_____ **13.** Used to select a portion of a form in order to perform section-level operations, such as adding background colors.

_____ **14.** Data in this kind of field is not derived from data contained in a table.

_____ **15.** In a one-to-many relationship, the form that contains the data from the table that corresponds to the *one* side of the relationship.

A Bound

B Control

C ControlTip

D Format

E Formatting

F Label control

G Main form

H Properties

I Property sheet

J Record source

K Section selector

L Status bar

M Subform

N Text box control

O Unbound

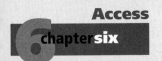
Fill in the Blank Write the correct answer in the space provided.

1. The control that lets you either type in text or choose from a list selection is a _____.

2. The properties for a control can be accessed by right-clicking the control, clicking the Properties button on the Formatting toolbar, or by _____ the control.

3. Each text box control on a form is bound, or linked to, a field in a _____.

4. In the property sheet, related properties are grouped together and can be accessed by clicking the appropriate _____.

5. The sequence in which fields are selected when the Tab key is pressed is referred to as the _____.

6. The Control Source property box is available in the property sheet on the _____ tab.

7. The control that contains a scrollable list of selections is a _____.

8. Creating a form using _____ provides additional flexibility in the form's construction over other methods of creating a form.

9. When adding a title to a form in the Form Header section, you should use a _____ control.

10. The small gray box located in a form's Design View where the two rulers meet is the _____.

Skill Assessments

Project 6C — Questionnaire

Objectives: *Add Fields to a Form and Use Toolbar buttons to Enhance a Form.*

In the following Skill Assessment, you will modify a form that is an interview questionnaire that customers of The Perfect Party fill out. You will add fields to the form and modify form properties. Your completed form will look similar to the one shown in Figure 6.50. You will rename the database as *6C_Questionnaire_Firstname_Lastname* in the folder you have created for this chapter.

Figure 6.50

1. Locate the file **a06C_Questionnaire** from your student files, and copy and paste the file to the Chapter 6 folder you created. Remove the Read-only property from the file and rename the file as **6C_Questionnaire_Firstname_Lastname** Start Access and open the database you just renamed.

2. Open the **Customer Questionnaire** form in **Form view** and examine the form structure.

(Project 6C–Questionnaire continues on the next page)

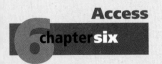
(Project 6C–Questionnaire continued)

3. Switch to **Design view**, maximize the window, and then view the controls in the form.

4. Display the **Toolbox** toolbar, click the **Label** button, draw a label control in the **Page Footer section**, and then using your own information, type **6C Questionnaire Firstname Lastname** into the **Page Footer control**.

5. On the Form Design toolbar, click the **Field List** button to display the list of fields in the **Customer Questionnaire** table. Alternatively, display the View menu and then click Field List.

6. If necessary, drag the field list to the right of your screen and expand it so that you can view all the fields in the list. Click the **Consultation?** field, drag into the form, position the small box under the left side of *What one special event do you plan this year?* and then release the mouse button.

7. If necessary, adjust the position of the **Consultation? text box control** and label control as shown in Figure 6.51.

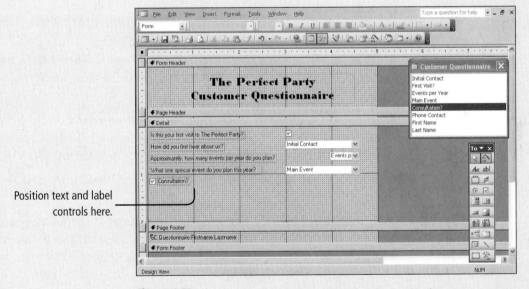

Position text and label controls here.

Figure 6.51

8. Select the **Events per Year** control and drag its left center sizing handle to the left to **3 inches on the horizontal ruler**. Then, using the technique you just practiced, add the **Phone Contact**, **First Name**, and **Last Name** fields to the **Customer Questionnaire** form and position them as shown in Figure 6.52. (Recall that the white box attached to the pointer indicates where the white label control will be placed, and that after you drop the field into the form, you can use Ctrl plus the arrow keys on your keyboard to nudge the control in small increments.)

(Project 6C–Questionnaire continues on the next page)

(Project 6C–Questionnaire continued)

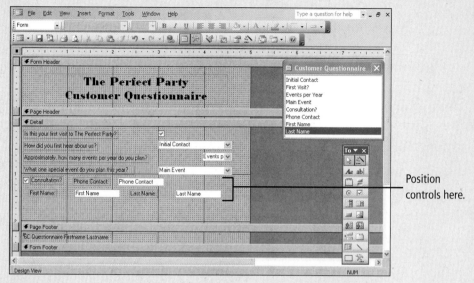

Position controls here.

Figure 6.52

9. Close the **Field List**, and then click once in the **Is this your first visit to The Perfect Party? label control**.

10. On the Formatting toolbar, click the **Font/Fore Color button arrow** and from the displayed color palette, in the third row, click the seventh color—**dark purple**.

11. Hold down Shift and select the remaining **label controls** on the form. Change the font color to the same dark purple color used in the previous step—the **Font/Fore Color** button will have retained this color.

12. Deselect the controls and then switch to **Form view** and view the changes to the form.

13. Switch to **Design view**. Click once in the **Initial Contact control** to select it. On the Formatting toolbar, click the **Fill/Back Color button arrow** and from the displayed color palette, in the fifth row, click the sixth color—**light blue**.

14. Hold down Shift and select the **five remaining controls** (Events per Year, Main Event, Phone Contact, First Name, Last Name), and apply the same blue color to those controls as you applied in Step 13.

15. Click to deselect all the controls, and then click once in the **Initial Contact control** to select it. On the Formatting toolbar, click the **Line/Border Color button arrow** and from the displayed palette, in the second row, click the seventh color—**blue**. The applied color is not immediately visible in Design view.

(Project 6C–Questionnaire continues on the next page)

(Project 6C–Questionnaire continued)

16. Select the **five remaining controls** (Events per Year, Main Event, Phone Contact, First Name, Last Name), and apply the same blue border color to those controls as you applied to the Initial Contact control in Step 15.

17. Switch to **Form view** and view the changes made to the form.

18. On the Formatting toolbar, click the **Print Preview** button to view your form as it will print, and then, on the Print Preview toolbar, click **Close**. On the **File** menu, click **Print**, and then click **OK**.

19. Close the form and save your changes. Close the database, and then close Access.

 You have completed Project 6C ———————————

Project 6D — Perfect Party Customers

Objectives: *Use Form Control Properties and Create a Form in Design View.*

In the following Skill Assessment, you will create a new form in Design view for customers of The Perfect Party. Additionally, you will modify properties for the form. Your completed form will look similar to Figure 6.53. You will rename and save your database as 6D_*PerfectPartyCustomers_Firstname_ Lastname.*

1. Locate the file **a06D_PerfectPartyCustomers** from your student files and copy and paste the file to the Chapter 6 folder you created. Remove the Read-only property from the file and rename the file as **6D_PerfectPartyCustomers_Firstname_Lastname** Start Access and open the database you just renamed.

2. On the Objects bar, click **Forms**, and then on the Database window toolbar, click the **New** button.

3. From the list of methods to create a form, be sure **Design View** is selected. To the right of *Choose the table or query where the object's data comes from*, click the **down arrow**, and then click **Perfect Party Customers.** Click **OK**.

4. **Maximize** the form. Display the **File** menu, click **Save As**, and in the **Save As** dialog box, under **Save Form 'Form1' To** type **Perfect Party Customers** and then click **OK**.

(Project 6D–Perfect Party Customers continues on the next page)

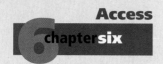

(Project 6D–Perfect Party Customers continued)

The Perfect Party Customers

Cust #:	201	First Name	Mary	Last Name	Martinez
Address	3293 Nyland Ave
City:	Dallas	State:	TX	Postal Code	75217
Phone:	214-555-0022	Initial Contact:

6D Perfect Party Customers Firstname Lastname

Figure 6.53

5. From the **View** menu, click **Page Header/Footer**. If necessary, display the Toolbox toolbar, click the **Label** button, and then draw a label control in the **Page Footer section** beginning at the upper left corner and extending down and to **3.5 inches on the horizontal ruler**. Using your own information, type **6D Perfect Party Customers Firstname Lastname** into the **Page Footer control**.

6. Expand the form to **6.5 inches on the horizontal ruler,** and then add all of the fields from the **Field List** to the form as shown in Figure 6.54.

(Project 6D–Perfect Party Customers continues on the next page)

(Project 6D–Perfect Party Customers continued)

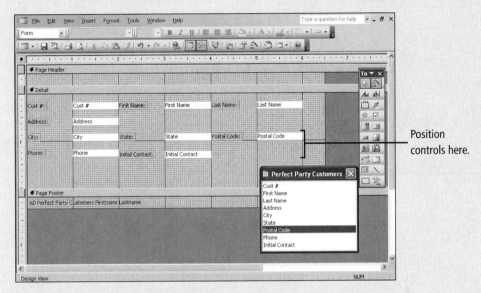

Figure 6.54

7. Display the **Edit** menu, click **Select All**, and then click the **Properties** button to display the Properties sheet.

8. Be sure the **Format tab** is selected, click in the **Font Name** property box, and then click the **down arrow** that displays.

9. From the list of available fonts, scroll as necessary, and then click **Lucida Sans**. Close the Properties sheet. Click in a blank area of the form to deselect the controls.

10. Hold down Shift, and then select all of the *label* controls. With all of the label controls selected, display the **Properties** sheet, and then click the **Format tab**. Click in the **Font Underline** property box, click the **down arrow** that displays, and then click **Yes**.

11. Close the Properties sheet. With all of the label controls still selected, right-click any *label* control, on the displayed shortcut menu, point to **Font/Fore Color**, and from the color palette, in the fifth row, click the last color—**white**.

12. Deselect the label controls by clicking a blank area of the form. Click the **Detail section selector**, and on the Formatting toolbar, click the **Fill/Back Color button arrow**. From the color palette, in the first row, click the seventh color—**dark blue**. Apply this same background color to the **Page Header section** and the **Page Footer section**.

13. Select the **Initial Contact label control**, and then stretch the right edge of this control slightly to the right so that the entire label displays. Select the **Page Footer control**, and then click the **Font/Fore Color** button, which should be white, to change the footer text to white.

(Project 6D–Perfect Party Customers continues on the next page)

(Project 6D–Perfect Party Customers continued)

14. From the **View** menu, click **Form Header/Footer,** and then expand the **Form Header section** down to approximately **0.5 inches on the vertical ruler**.

15. On the Toolbox toolbar, click the **Label** button, and then draw a label control in the **Form Header section** beginning at **1 inch on the horizontal ruler** to **6 inches on the horizontal ruler**, and in the label box, type **The Perfect Party Customers**

16. Click in a blank area of the form to deselect the label control and then click the **Form Header control** again to select it. Click the **Font/Fore Color** button to change the font color to **white**. On the Formatting toolbar, click the **Center** button.

17. On the Formatting toolbar, click the **Font Size button arrow**, and then click **14**.

18. Select the **Cust # text box control**. On the Form Design toolbar, click the **Properties** button, and then click the **Other tab**.

19. In the **Status Bar Text** property box, type **Enter the Customer #** and then close the Properties sheet.

20. Switch to **Form view**, and view the modifications you have made to the form.

21. Click once in the **Cust #** field in the form, and view the instruction in the status bar.

22. On the **File** menu, click **Print**, and in the **Print** dialog box, under **Print Range**, click **Selected Record(s)**, and then click **OK**.

23. Close the form and save your changes. Close the database, and then close Access.

 You have completed Project 6D ───────────────

Project 6E — Special Orders

Objectives: *Make a Form User-Friendly and Create a Subform.*

In the following Skill Assessment, you will modify the properties of an existing form and add a subform. Your completed form will look similar to Figure 6.55. You will rename and save your database as *6E_SpecialOrders_Firstname_Lastname.*

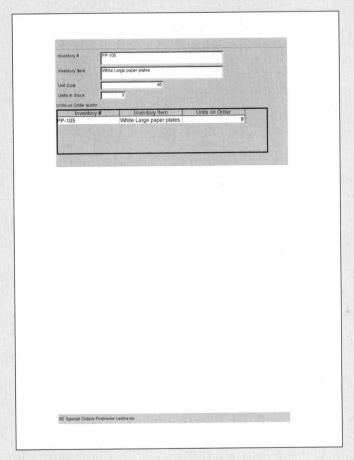

Figure 6.55

1. Locate the file **a06E_SpecialOrders** from your student files and copy and paste the file to the Chapter 6 folder you created. Remove the Read-only property from the file and rename the file as **6E_SpecialOrders_Firstname_Lastname** Start Access and open the database you just renamed.

2. On the Objects bar, click **Forms**. Open the **Inventory** form in **Form view** and examine the layout and data in the form. Switch to **Design view**, and then **maximize** the form on your screen.

(Project 6E–Special Orders continues on the next page)

(Project 6E–Special Orders continued)

3. From the **View** menu, click **Page Header/Footer**. If necessary, display the Toolbox toolbar, click the **Label** button, and then, beginning in the upper left corner of the **Page Footer section**, draw a control down and over to **3.5 inches on the horizontal ruler**. Using your own information, type **6E Special Orders Firstname Lastname** into the **Page Footer control** you just created.

4. Select the **Unit Cost label control**.

5. On the Formatting toolbar, click the **Properties** button, and then click the **Other tab**.

6. In the **ControlTip Text** property box, type **Cost for each inventory unit**

7. Leave the Properties sheet open, select the **Units in Stock label control**, and then in the **ControlTip Text** property box, type **Number of units currently in stock**

8. Close the Properties sheet. In the Toolbox, click the **Subform/Subreport** button. Starting at the left edge of the form at **1.5 inches on the vertical ruler**, draw a rectangle approximately one inch tall and four inches wide. Use the horizontal and vertical rulers to guide you, but do not be concerned about getting this measurement exact, because you will resize the subform in a later step.

9. In the first screen of the wizard, leave the default selection as *Use existing Tables and Queries*, and then click **Next**.

10. Under **Tables/Queries**, click the **down arrow**, and then click **Table: Units on Order**.

11. Click the **All Fields** button, and then click **Next**

12. Accept the default settings in this screen of the wizard, and then click **Next**.

13. In the final screen of the wizard, accept the default subform name and click **Finish**.

(Project 6E–Special Orders continues on the next page)

(Project 6E–Special Orders continued)

14. **Maximize** the form if necessary. As shown in Figure 6.56, resize the form and position the subform. Expand the right edge of the form as shown in Figure 6.56, and then expand the right edge of the subform.

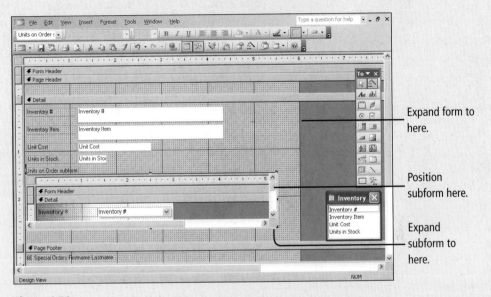

Expand form to here.

Position subform here.

Expand subform to here.

Figure 6.56

15. Switch to **Form view**. Navigate to record **PP-105**, examine the data in the subform and verify that there are 9 units on order for this record.

16. On the **File** menu, click **Print**, and in the **Print** dialog box, under **Print Range**, click **Selected Record(s)**, and then click **OK**.

17. Close the form and save your changes to the form and subform. Close the database, and then close Access.

End You have completed Project 6E

Project 6F—Customer Events

Objectives: *Make a Form User-Friendly and Create a Form in Design View.*

In the following Performance Assessment, you will create a form in Design view for The Perfect Party Customer Events. Your completed form will look similar to Figure 6.57. You will rename and save your database as *6F_CustomerEvents_Firstname_Lastname.*

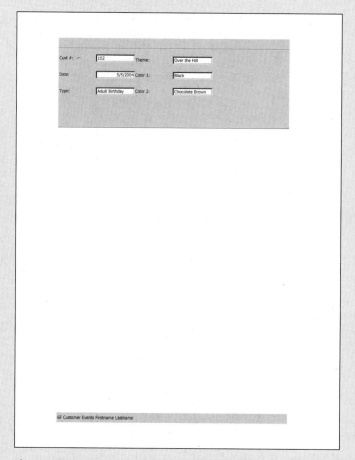

Figure 6.57

1. Locate the file **a06F_CustomerEvents** from your student files and copy and paste the file to the Chapter 6 folder you created. Remove the Read-only property from the file and rename the file as **6F_CustomerEvents_Firstname_Lastname** Start Access and open the database you just renamed.

2. On the Objects bar, click **Forms,** and then on the database window toolbar, click **New**. From the list of methods to create a form, be sure **Design View** is selected and select **Customer Events** as the table where the object's data comes from. Click **OK.**

(Project 6F–Customer Events continues on the next page)

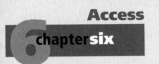
(Project 6F–Customer Events continued)

3. **Maximize** the form on your screen, and then save the form as **The Perfect Party Customer Events**

4. Add the **Page Header/Footer sections** to your form, draw a label control in the **Page Footer section**, and using your own information, type **6F Customer Events Firstname Lastname** into the form's **Page Footer section**.

5. Expand the right edge of the form to **6 inches on the horizontal ruler**. Expand the **Field List** as necessary to view all of the field names. Add all of the fields from the **Field List** to the form, dropping the text box controls on the vertical lines and positioning them as shown in Figure 6.58.

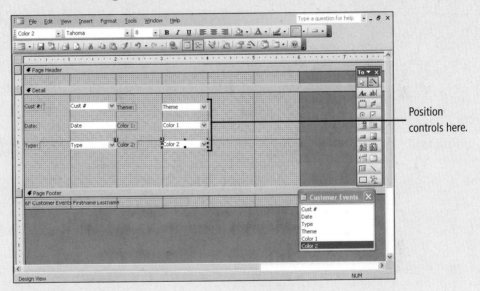

Figure 6.58

6. Right-click anywhere in a blank area of the **Detail section**, and from the displayed shortcut menu, click **Tab Order**.

7. In the **Tab Order** dialog box, position the pointer in the **selector** to the left of the **Theme** field until a black right-pointing arrow displays and then click. Point to the small selector box, and then drag up slightly to position this field as the first one in the list. Click **OK**.

8. Switch to **Form view** and notice that the **Theme** field is selected, because you made it first in the Tab order. Press Tab until you have moved through each field.

9. Be sure record 2 for Cust #102 is displayed. On the **File** menu, click **Print**, and in the **Print** dialog box, under **Print Range**, click **Selected Record(s)**, and then click **OK**.

10. Close the form and save your changes. Close the database, and then close Access.

End You have completed Project 6F

Project 6G—Customer Questionnaire

Objectives: *Use Toolbar Buttons to Enhance a Form and Use Form Control Properties.*

In the following Performance Assessment, you will modify an existing questionnaire form for new customers of The Perfect Party. Your completed form will look similar to Figure 6.59. You will rename and save your database as *6G_CustomerQuestionnaire_Firstname_Lastname*.

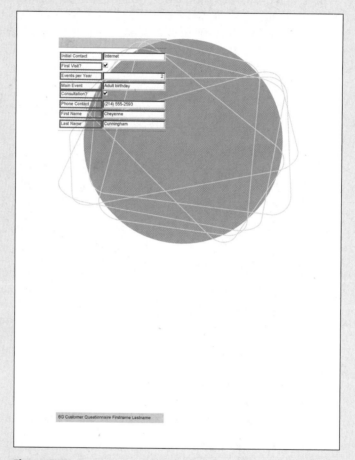

Figure 6.59

1. Locate the file **a06G_CustomerQuestionnaire** from your student files and copy and paste the file to the Chapter 6 folder you created. Remove the Read-only property from the file and rename the file as **6G_CustomerQuestionnaire_Firstname_Lastname** Start Access and open the database you just renamed.

2. Open the **Customer Questionnaire** form in **Design view** and **maximize** the form. Right-click a blank area of the form and from the **Fill/Back Color** palette, in the fifth row, click the last color—**white**.

(Project 6G–Customer Questionnaire continues on the next page)

(Project 6G–Customer Questionnaire continued)

3. Select all of the **label controls** on the form. On the Formatting toolbar, click the **Font/Fore Color button arrow** and from the displayed palette, in the first row, click the seventh color—**blue**.

4. With the label controls still selected, click the **Properties** button. On the **Format tab**, change the **Border Color** to **purple** (fourth row, seventh color). Change the **Border Width** to **2 pt**.

5. Leave the Properties sheet open. Click the **Form Selector** button (at the left end of the horizontal ruler), be sure the **Format tab** is displayed, click the **Picture** property box, and then click the **Build** button that displays. From the displayed **Insert Picture** dialog box, navigate to your student files and insert the file **a06G_ppbackground** as the background for this form.

6. In the Properties sheet, change the **Picture Size Mode** to **Zoom**, change the **Picture Alignment** to **Top Left**, and then close the Properties sheet.

7. Create a **Page Footer control** the approximate width of the form, and type **6G Customer Questionnaire Firstname Lastname** Switch to **Form view**.

8. On the **File** menu, click **Print**, and in the **Print** dialog box, under **Print Range**, click **Selected Record(s)**, and then click **OK**.

9. Close the form and save your changes. Close the database, and then close Access.

 End You have completed Project 6G ———————

Project 6H—Customer Orders

Objectives: *Add Fields to a Form and Create a Subform.*

In the following Performance Assessment, you will create a subform for the Customers Form that will include information about customer orders at The Perfect Party. Your completed form will look similar to Figure 6.60. You will rename and save your database as *6H_CustomerOrders_Firstname_Lastname*.

1. Locate the file **a06H_CustomerOrders** from your student files and copy and paste the file to the Chapter 6 folder you created. Remove the Read-only property from the file and rename the file as **6H_CustomerOrders Firstname_Lastname** Start Access and open the database you just renamed.

2. Open the **Customers Form** in **Design view**, and then **maximize** the form on your screen.

(Project 6H–Customer Orders continues on the next page)

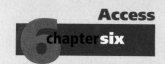

(Project 6H–Customer Orders continued)

Customer Order Form

Cust #	104		
First Name	Steven	Last Name	Bradley
Address	811 E. Santa Paula Pl. #335	Phone	972-555-0066
City	Irving	State	TX	Postal Code	75037

| Order # | Cust # | Item # | Item Name | Price |
| PP1001 | 104 | PP-102 | White Forks | $3.00 |

6H Customer Orders Firstname Lastname

Figure 6.60

3. In the **Toolbox**, click the **Subform/Subreport** button, and then draw a rectangle in the form approximately the width of the form beginning at **1.75 inches on the vertical ruler** down to **2.75 inches on the vertical ruler**, positioned directly under the **City**, **State**, and **Postal code controls**. In the Subform Wizard, use existing tables and queries, and then use all of the fields from the **Customer Orders** table in the subform. Accept the remaining defaults in the wizard.

4. The subform will display too small to use; therefore, **maximize** the form, and expand the subform to approximately the width of the main form.

5. Create a label control in the **Page Footer section** of the form, type **6H Customer Orders Firstname Lastname** and then switch to **Form view**. Resize the fields in the subform so that they fit in the viewable area of the subform. In the **main form**, navigate to **Cust # 104** and view the order information in the subform.

6. On the **File** menu, click **Page Setup**, and change the **Page Orientation** to **Landscape**. On the **File** menu, click **Print**, and in the **Print** dialog box, under **Print Range**, click **Selected Record(s)**, and then click **OK**.

7. Close the form and save your changes to the form and subform. Close the database, and then close Access.

 End You have completed Project 6H

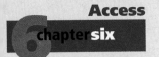
Project 6I—Inventory

Objectives: *Use Toolbar Buttons to Enhance a Form, Use Form Control Properties, Make a Form User-Friendly, and Create a Form in Design View.*

In the following Mastery Assessment, you will create a form in Design view for inventory at The Perfect Party. Your completed form will look like Figure 6.61. You will rename and save your database as *6I_Inventory_Firstname_Lastname*.

Inventory Form

Inventory #: PP-101
Inventory Item: White Napkins
Unit Cost: 3.25
Units in Stoc 4

6I Inventory Firstname Lastname

Figure 6.61

1. Locate the file **a06I_Inventory** from your student files and copy and paste the file to the Chapter 6 folder you created. Remove the Read-only property from the file and rename the file as **6I_Inventory_Firstname_Lastname** Start Access and open the database you just renamed.

(Project 6I–Inventory continues on the next page)

(Project 6I–Inventory continued)

2. On the Objects bar, click **Forms**. Using Figure 6.62 as your guide, from the database window toolbar, click **New** and create a new form in **Design View** using the data in the **Inventory** table. Save the form as **Inventory Form** and then add all four of the fields from the table to the form. Position the fields as shown in Figure 6.62. Recall that as you drag the field into the form, the white text box control will be positioned at the point where you drop the small box, and the gray label control box will be positioned to its left.

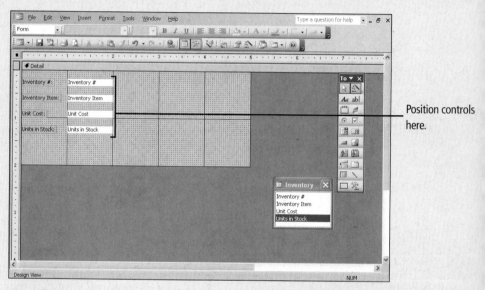

Figure 6.62

3. Change the font for the four **label controls** to **Times New Roman** and change the font size to **12**. Resize the label controls appropriately to accommodate the enlarged text.

4. Change the **background color** for the **label controls** to **white** and add a **1 pt. dark blue border** to the **label controls**. Change the **background color** for the **form** to **white**.

5. Add **ControlTip Text** to the **Unit Cost textbox control** that reads **Enter Cost per Unit**

(Project 6I–Inventory continues on the next page)

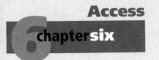

(Project 6I–Inventory continued)

6. Add a **Form Header section**, add a label that reads **Inventory Form** and then center the text in the control and change the font size to **14**. Apply **Bold** to the text in the Form Header. (Hint: Recall that you must deselect and then reselect the form header label for the purpose of applying formatting.)

7. Create a control the **Page Footer section** and type **6I Inventory Firstname Lastname**

8. Print only the first record of the form.

9. Close the form and save your changes. Close the database, and then close Access.

 End You have completed Project 6I

Project 6J — Orders and Events

Objectives: *Make a Form User-Friendly and Create a Subform.*

In the following Mastery Assessment, you will add a subform to an existing form. Your completed form will look similar to Figure 6.63. You will rename and save your database as *6J_OrdersEvents_Firstname_Lastname*.

1. Locate the file **a06J_OrdersEvents** from your student files and copy and paste the file to the Chapter 6 folder you created. Remove the Read-only property from the file and rename the file as **6J_OrdersEvents_Firstname_Lastname** Start Access and open the database you just renamed.

2. Using the **Customer Orders** form as the main form, add a **subform** using the **Customer Events** table. Include all of the fields from the table and accept the remaining defaults in the wizard.

3. The subform will display too small to use; therefore, expand the subform so that its left edge begins at the left edge of the main form and its right edge reaches to **7 inches on the horizontal ruler**.

4. In the **Page Footer section** of the main form, create a label control and type **6J OrdersEvents Firstname Lastname**

(Project 6J–Orders and Events continues on the next page)

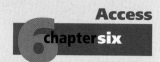

(Project 6J–Orders and Events continued)

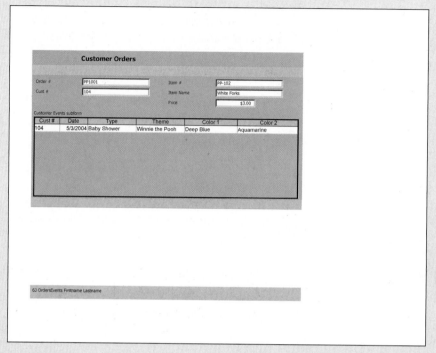

Figure 6.63

5. Switch to **Form view**. Resize the fields in the subform so that they display in the viewable area of the subform. In the **Page Setup** dialog box, change the page orientation to **Landscape**, and then print only the first record of the form.

6. Close the form and save your changes. Close the database, and then close Access.

End You have completed Project 6J

Project 6K — Calculated Control

Objective: *Add a Calculated Control to a Report Section.*

The owners of The Perfect Party want to know the value of their inventory. They have a report that lists each inventory item, its unit cost, and the number of units in stock. In the following Problem Solving exercise, you will add a calculated control to a report section to provide a total value of the inventory.

1. Locate the file **a06K_Calculated_Control** from your student files and copy and paste the file to the Chapter 6 folder you created. Remove the Read-only property from the file and rename the file as **6K_Calculated_Control_Firstname_Lastname** Start Access and open the database you just renamed.

2. On the Objects bar, click **Reports**, and then open the **Inventory** report in Report view. **Maximize** the window. Use the navigation bar at the bottom of the window to scroll to **page 2**, click the **Zoom** arrow, and then click **100%**. Scroll to view the bottom of the page, and notice that there is no total for the value of the inventory. Click the **View** button to open the **Design view** of the report and, if necessary, maximize the window.

3. On the Toolbox, click the **Text Box** button. At the bottom of the form, in the **Report Footer section**, create a text box the full height of the area beginning at **3 inches on the horizontal ruler** and dragging to **6 inches on the horizontal ruler**. Click in the box that indicates *Text* followed by a number, select and delete the text, and type **Total Value** Click in the **Unbound** box and type the formula **=Sum([Unit Cost]*[Units in Stock])**

4. Click in a blank area of the form, and then click to select the text box where you typed the formula. Right-click, click **Properties**, click the **Format tab**, click in the **Format** box, display the list, and then scroll the list and click **Currency**. Close the property sheet.

5. Expand the **Page Footer** area, create a label, and type **6K Calculated Control Firstname Lastname**

6. Switch to **Print Preview** and navigate to the second page. Scroll to view the bottom of the second page. The inventory value is totaled. Close the report, saving any changes. Close the database, and then close Access.

End You have completed Project 6K

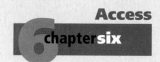

Project 6L — Customers

Objectives: *Import Structured Data Into a Table and Format a Query.*

In the following Problem Solving exercise, you will import data from an Excel spreadsheet into a table, create a query, and then format the query.

1. Locate the file **a06L_Import** from your student files and copy and paste the file to the Chapter 6 folder you created. Remove the Read-only property from the file and rename the file as **6L_Import Firstname_ Lastname** Start Access and open the database you just renamed.

2. From the **File** menu, point to **Get External Data**, and then click **Import**. In the displayed **Import** dialog box, navigate to your student files, change the **Files of type** at the bottom to **Microsoft Excel**, and then click the file **a06L_Excel_Data**. Click **Import**.

3. In the displayed wizard screen, select the **First Row Contains Column Headings** check box, and then click **Next**. Be sure the **In a New Table** option button is selected, and then click **Next**. Click **Next** two more times, and then under **Import to Table**, type **New Customers** Click **Finish**, and then click **OK**.

4. Open the **New Customers** table, and be sure that the data from the Excel spreadsheet was successfully imported. Close the table. On the Objects bar, click **Queries**, and then double-click **Create query in Design view**. Using the **New Customers** table, create a query that displays the **First Name**, **Last Name**, and **Phone** of all customers in **Dallas**. Do not display the **City** field. Save the query as **Dallas Customers Firstname Lastname**

5. Open your **Dallas Customers** query. Make the **Last Name** column the first column. From the **Format** menu, click **Font**, and then change the **Font** to **Bell MT**, the **Font style** to **Bold Italic**, and the **Size** to **12**. Resize the columns as necessary to display all the data. Sort the query alphabetically by **Last Name**.

6. Print the query, close and save your changes, close the database, and close Access.

 End You have completed Project 6L ——————————————

On the Internet

Locating Templates Online

Microsoft provides several templates that you can download and use to assist you in creating new databases, such as Order Management and Inventory Control. Go to **www.microsoft.com** and search for *templates*. Try to find some templates that would be helpful in a business that you have worked for, or the business of someone you know.

GO! with Help

Getting Help with PivotChart View

PivotChart view is a view that shows a graphical analysis of data in a datasheet or form. In PivotChart view, you can see different levels of detail or specify the layout by dragging fields and items or by showing and hiding items in the drop-down lists for fields.

1. Start Access. If necessary, from the **View** menu, click **Task Pane** to display the **Getting Started** task pane. On the task pane, to the right of *Getting Started*, click the **down arrow**. From the displayed list of available task panes, click **Help**.

2. Click in the **Search for** box, type **PivotChart view**

3. Press Enter, scroll the displayed list as necessary, and then click **Elements of a PivotTable or PivotChart view**. Maximize the Help screen. At the upper right, click Show All, and then scroll down to view the section beginning Elements of a PivotChart view.

(GO! with Help–Continues on the next page)

4. Read through each of the elements, and see if you can locate the various elements on the PivotChart view shown in Figure 6.64. If you would like to keep a copy of this information, click the **Print** button.

5. Click the **Close** button in the top right corner of the Help window to close the Help window, and then close Access.

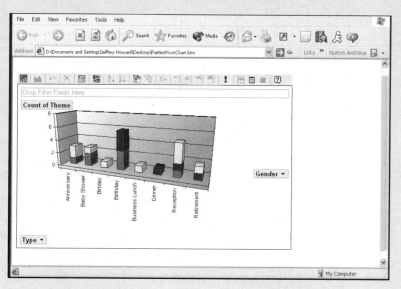

Figure 6.64

7 chapterseven

Advanced Reports and Queries

In this chapter, you will: complete these projects **and** practice these skills.

Project 7A **Customizing a Report**	**Objectives**
	• Create a Subreport
	• Group Data in a Report
	• Create Calculated Fields in a Report
	• Set Report and Report Section Properties
	• Create a Crosstab Report

Project 7B **Creating Queries**	**Objectives**
	• Create an Update Query
	• Create a Delete Query
	• Create Special Purpose Queries
	• Create Action Queries
	• View Queries in SQL

Greater Atlanta Job Fair

The Greater Atlanta Job Fair is a nonprofit organization supported by the Atlanta Chamber of Commerce and Atlanta City Colleges. The organization holds several targeted job fairs in the Atlanta area each year. Candidate registration is free and open to area residents and students enrolled in certificate or degree programs at any of the City Colleges. Employers pay a nominal fee to participate in the fairs. When candidates register for a fair, their resumes are scanned into an interactive, searchable database that is provided to the employers.

© Getty Images, Inc.

Advanced Reports and Queries

After you have entered data into the tables of your database, Access provides you with the tools to search, sort, update, and display your data in a variety of ways. You can display formatted information from one or more tables of a database in report form. You can also group information in a report and calculate results in a report. In this chapter, you will use advanced techniques to customize reports in Access.

Queries are usually thought of as a way to extract specific data from a database by asking questions and setting certain conditions. However, Access queries are also useful to add, update, or delete records from your database. In this chapter, you will create multiple types of queries.

Project 7A **Job Fair**

The Greater Atlanta Job Fair maintains a database to keep track of all the employers and candidates registered for the fair. The number of employers who exhibit at the fairs, and the number of candidates that attend, continues to grow. Thus, creating custom reports will be helpful in viewing the information in the database in a meaningful way.

In Activities 7.1 through 7.6, you will create and modify a report for Michael Augustino, Executive Director of the Greater Atlanta Job Fair, to view information from the Employers table and the Candidates table. You will customize the report using features available in Access. Your completed reports will look similar to Figure 7.1. You will save your database as *7A_Job_Fair_Firstname_Lastname*.

Employers Report

Employer Name	Address	City	State	ZIP	Fee Paid
A&G Consulting	107 Marguerite Drive S. #15	Roswell	GA	30077	$500.00

Industry	Position	# Openings	Ann Salary	Hours/week
11	Executive Assistant	5	$40,000.00	40
11	Senior Accounting Clerk	15	$35,000.00	40
	Total Salaries of Industry		$725,000.00	
14	Gift Shop Manager	5	$35,000.00	50
14	Catering Manager	3	$50,000.00	50
	Total Salaries of Industry		$325,000.00	
	Total Salaries		$1,050,000.00	

Affiliated Technologies	430 South Mountain Circle	Atlanta	GA	30301	$100.00

Atlanta Insurance Brokers	352 Piedmont Circle	Roswell	GA	30080	$800.00

Industry	Position	# Openings	Ann Salary	Hours/week
1	Actuary – Senior	3	$98,000.00	40
1	Actuary – Entry Level	5	$43,000.00	40
	Total Salaries of Industry		$509,000.00	
	Total Salaries		$509,000.00	

Saturday, March 13, 2004   7A Job Fair Firstname Lastname   Page 1 of 9

Job Openings by Employer_Crosstab

Industry	Average Ann Salary	GA	SC
Computer Science - Hardware	$105,000.00	$105,000.00	
Computer Science - Software	$71,500.00	$71,500.00	
Construction	$55,000.00	$55,000.00	
Environmental Technology	$57,500.00	$57,500.00	
Finance	$48,750.00	$52,500.00	$45,000.00
General Administration	$46,666.67	$37,500.00	$65,000.00
Health Care	$78,500.00	$78,500.00	
Heating/Air Conditioning	$48,000.00	$48,000.00	
Hotel & Food Service	$42,500.00	$42,500.00	
Insurance	$70,500.00	$70,500.00	
Medical Technology	$75,000.00		$75,000.00
Pharmaceutical	$50,000.00	$50,000.00	
Travel & Tourism	$28,000.00		$28,000.00

Saturday, March 13, 2004   7A Crosstab Firstname Lastname   Page 1 of 1

Figure 7.1
Project 7A—Job Fair

Objective 1
Create a Subreport

Reports can include information from more than one table in the database. For example, the Greater Atlanta Job Fair wants to create a report listing all the employer names (from the Employers table), and then under each employer name, list the job openings for which the employer will be recruiting at the Job Fair (from the Job Openings table). One way to accomplish this is by creating a **subreport**. A subreport is a report inserted into a control, and the control is then embedded in another report.

To create a subreport, the two tables must contain a one-to-many relationship. In your database, one employer can have many job openings, so a one-to-many relationship has been established between the Employers table and the Job Openings table. The main report will come from the *one* side of the one-to-many relationship—the Employers table—and the subreport will come from the *many* side of the relationship—the Job Openings table.

Activity 7.1 Embedding a Subreport in a Report

Recall that a subreport is a report inserted into a control, and then the control is embedded in another report. In this activity, you will embed a subreport into the existing *Employers Report*.

1 Create a new folder named Chapter 7 in the location where you will be storing your projects for this chapter. Locate the file **a07A_Job_Fair** from your student files, and copy and paste the file to the Chapter 7 folder you created. Remove the Read-only property from the file and rename the file as **7A_Job_Fair_Firstname_Lastname** Start Access and open the database you just renamed.

2 On the Objects bar, if necessary, click **Tables**. Take a moment to open and examine the data in each of the five tables in this database— **Candidates**, **Employers**, **Industries**, **Job Fair Sections**, and **Job Openings**.

3 On the Objects bar, click **Reports**, and then double-click the **Employers Report** to open it in **Print Preview**. If necessary, maximize ▣ the report window. Click the **Zoom arrow** and zoom to **100%**. Using the page navigation buttons in the lower left corner of the screen, take a moment to scroll through and examine the five pages of data presented in the report.

The Employers Report shows the Employer Name, Address, City, State, ZIP, and Fee Paid. This report was generated from the Employers table.

4 Switch to **Design view** and view the controls in the report. If necessary, maximize the window, and then expand the lower edge of the **Detail section** to slightly below **2 inches on the vertical ruler** as shown in Figure 7.2. This will give you space to work with the report.

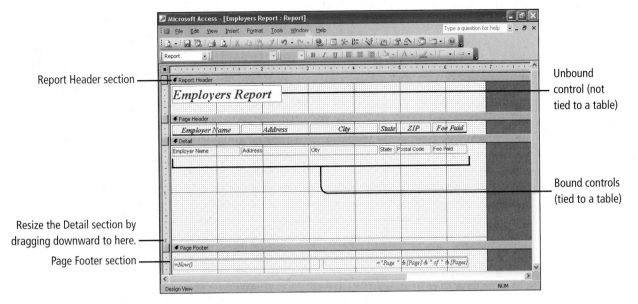

Report Header section ──

Unbound control (not tied to a table)

Bound controls (tied to a table)

Resize the Detail section by dragging downward to here. ──

Page Footer section ──

Figure 7.2

5 On your screen locate the **Report Header** and **Report Footer** sections.

This report has a ***Report Header*** section. The Report Header appears only once—at the beginning of a report. Use it for items such as a logo, report title, or print date. This report also has a ***Report Footer*** section. The Report Footer appears only once—at the end of the report. Use it to display items such as report totals. A report is not required to have a report header or a report footer; they are optional.

6 Locate the **Page Header** and **Page Footer** sections.

This report has a ***Page Header*** section. The Page Header appears at the top of every page. Use it for items such as column headings, as has been done in this report. This report also has a ***Page Footer*** section. The Page Footer appears at the bottom of every page. Use it for items such as page numbers. Page headers and footers are optional.

> **Note — Location of Report Headers and Footers in Relation to Page Headers and Footers**
>
> If a Page Header is included in your report, the Report Header prints before the Page Header on the first page of the report. If a Page Footer is included in your report, the Report Footer will print before the Page Footer on the last page of the report.

7 Locate the **Detail section** of the report.

Every report has a **Detail section**. The Detail section contains the main body of a report's data. This section is repeated for each record in the report's underlying record source. In Design view, you can see that this section usually contains **bound controls**—controls tied to a field in an underlying table or query, but can also contain **unbound controls**—controls that have no data source but that display information such as labels that identify a field's contents. See Figure 7.2.

8 In the **Page Footer** section, click to select the **=Now()** control on the left, and then drag its right center sizing handle to the left to approximately **2 inches on the horizontal ruler**. Click the **="Page"** control on the right, and then drag its left center sizing handle to the right to approximately **5.0 inches on the horizontal ruler**.

9 On the Toolbox toolbar, click the **Label** button [Aa]. Position the plus sign of your pointer just below the light gray bar in the **Page Footer section** at approximately **2.25 inches on the horizontal ruler**, and then drag down about a quarter of an inch and to the right to approximately **4.75 inches on the horizontal ruler**, as shown in Figure 7.3.

If you are not satisfied with your result, click the Undo button and begin again. An insertion point is blinking at the left edge of the label control.

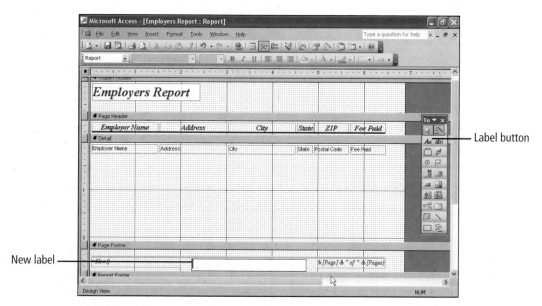

New label

Label button

Figure 7.3

10 In the label control you just created, using your own first and last name, type **7A Job Fair Firstname Lastname** Press [Enter]. Press [Ctrl] plus any of the directional arrow keys on your keyboard as necessary to nudge the control into the desired position.

11 On the Toolbox toolbar, click the **Subform/Subreport** button.

12 In the **Detail section** of the report, position the plus sign of your pointer at approximately **0.25 inch on the horizontal ruler** and at **0.5 inch on the vertical ruler** as shown in Figure 7.4.

Position your pointer here.

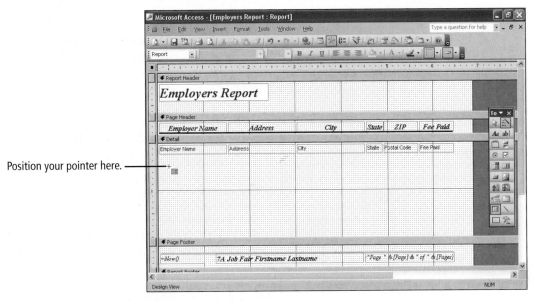

Figure 7.4

13 Click once to launch the SubReport Wizard. Be sure that the **Use existing Tables and Queries** option button is selected, and then click **Next**.

14 Click the **Tables/Queries arrow**, and from the displayed list, click **Table: Job Openings**. Under **Available Fields**, use the **One Field** button to move the fields **Industry**, **Position**, **# Openings**, **Ann Salary**, and **Hours/week** to the **Selected Fields** list as shown in Figure 7.5. Click **Next**.

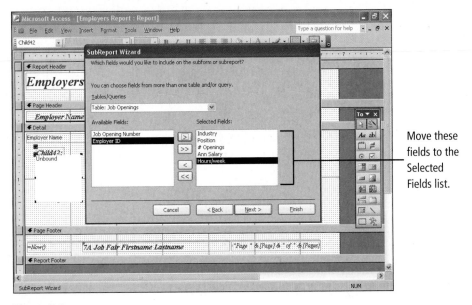

Move these fields to the Selected Fields list.

Figure 7.5

15 Be sure the **Choose from a list** option button is selected and that **Show Job Openings for each record in Employers using Employer ID** is selected.

Because a one-to-many relationship exists between the Employers table and the Job Openings table, you are able to list the current job openings for each employer below each employer name.

16 Click **Next**. Under **What name would you like for your subform or subreport?**, accept the default name *Job Openings subreport* and click **Finish**. If necessary, maximize the report window, and then compare your screen with Figure 7.6.

Job Openings subreport label ——

Job Openings subreport

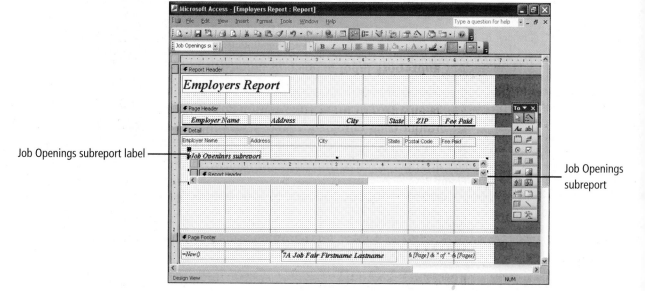

Figure 7.6

17 In the selected embedded report, position the mouse pointer over the lower center sizing handle to display the **Vertical Resize** pointer ⬍, and then drag down to approximately **2 inches on the vertical ruler**, as shown in Figure 7.7 (your fonts may differ from the figure).

This gives you a clear indication that another complete report is embedded in the main report, and will print below each employer's name in the main report.

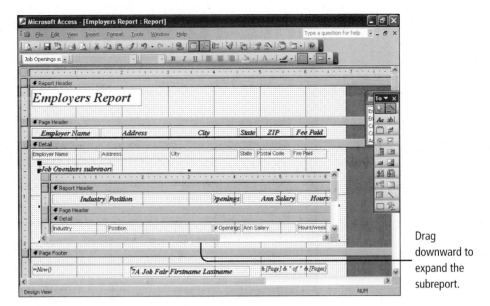

Drag downward to expand the subreport.

Figure 7.7

18 Switch to **Print preview** to view the **Employers Report** with the Job Openings subreport embedded in it. With the magnifying glass pointer positioned over the report, click to enlarge the report as necessary. Notice that the label *Job Openings subreport* repeats under each employer name. Notice also that the heading *# Openings* is slightly cut off at the beginning. Switch back to **Design view**.

19 In the **Detail section** of the main report, click the **Job Openings subreport label** to select it, and then press Delete.

Deleting the label will prevent it from printing above every subreport within the main report, which would be repetitious and unnecessary.

20 In the subreport, select the **Position label**, locate the horizontal ruler within the subreport, and then drag its right center sizing handle to **3 inches on the horizontal ruler**. Then, lengthen the left side of the **# Openings label** by approximately one-half inch, so that the *# Openings* is not cut off. Switch to **Print preview**, and then compare your screen with Figure 7.8.

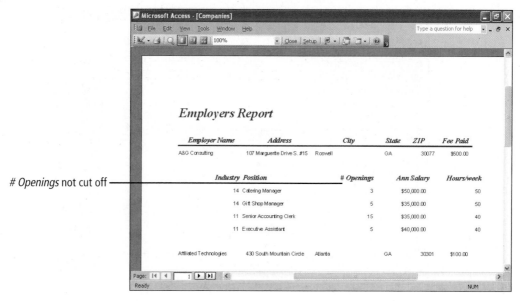

 # Openings not cut off —

Figure 7.8

21 Using the Page navigation buttons at the lower left corner of the screen, view each of the pages in the report, noticing the subreport inserted below each employer's name.

You can see that many employers have more than one opening, and some employers currently have no openings.

22 In the upper right corner of your screen, click the small **Close Window** button ☒ to close the **Employers Report**, and save your changes to the two objects. In the upper right corner of your screen, click the small **Restore Window** button ☐. Notice that on the list of reports, a new report is listed—**Job Openings subreport**—as shown in Figure 7.9.

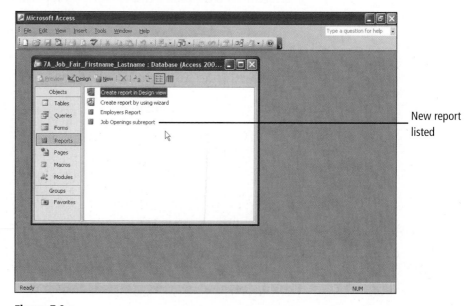

New report listed

Figure 7.9

23 Open the **Job Openings subreport**. Maximize and zoom as necessary to view the report.

The Job Openings subreport was generated by your responses in the Subreport Wizard. It contains a listing of all Job Openings.

24 **Close** the window, and then in the upper right corner, click the small **Restore Window** button to return the database window to a smaller size. Leave the database open for the next activity.

Objective 2
Group Data in a Report

When creating a report, you may need to group information and/or sort information to display the data in a specific format. Or, you may need to group the information before you can calculate a formula in your report. For example, Michael Augustino wants to calculate the total potential yearly income of all the jobs at the fair. This number is useful for advertising purposes, because it demonstrates how large an event the Greater Atlanta Job Fair has become.

Activity 7.2 Grouping Data in a Report

In this activity, you will group the fields in the Job Openings subreport so that jobs from the same industry are listed together.

1 Open the **Job Openings subreport**, switch to **Design view**, and maximize the report window.

2 On the Report Design toolbar, click the **Sorting and Grouping** button . See Figure 7.10.

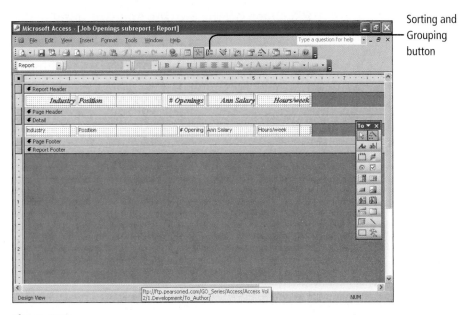

Figure 7.10

3 In the **Sorting and Grouping** dialog box, in the **Field/Expression** column, click the arrow in the first row. From the displayed list, click **Industry** and leave the sort order as **Ascending**. Under **Group Properties**, click the **Group Footer** box, click the arrow, and then click **Yes**. Click the **Keep Together** box, click the arrow, and click **Whole Group**. Compare your screen with Figure 7.11.

Within the Job Openings subreport, the jobs will be grouped by Industry, in Ascending order, and a Group Footer section will be created. You will need the Group Footer section to create a Calculated Field in the next activity.

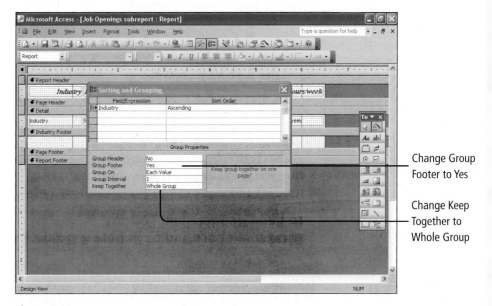

Change Group Footer to Yes

Change Keep Together to Whole Group

Figure 7.11

4 **Close** ✕ the **Sorting and Grouping** dialog box.

5 Switch to **Print preview**, and click on the report to zoom in.

Notice that the Job Openings are grouped in ascending order by industry number. See Figure 7.12.

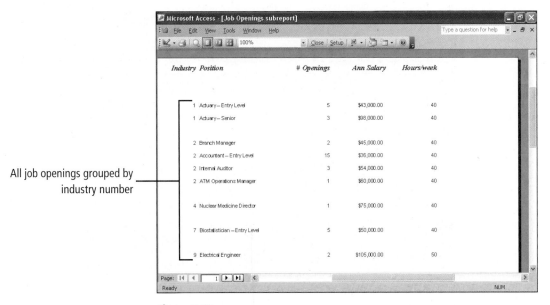

All job openings grouped by industry number

Figure 7.12

6 Switch to **Design view** and leave the report open for the next activity.

Objective 3
Create Calculated Fields in a Report

There are instances when it is useful to perform mathematical calculations and display the results in your report. For example, Michael Augustino wants to calculate the potential annual income of jobs within each industry, and then calculate the potential annual income of all the jobs at the fair. These numbers are useful in advertising the size and strength of the Greater Atlanta Job Fair.

Activity 7.3 Creating a Calculated Field for a Group

In this activity, you will create a calculated field to show the potential income available from all of the job openings within each industry.

1 Be sure the **Job Openings subreport** is open in **Design view**. On the Toolbox toolbar, click the **Text Box** button ![ab]. Locate the **Industry Footer section** of the report, position the plus sign of your pointer at the upper edge of the Industry Footer and at approximately **4.25 inches on the horizontal ruler**, and click. See Figure 7.13.

Recall that you created the Industry Footer section in a previous activity.

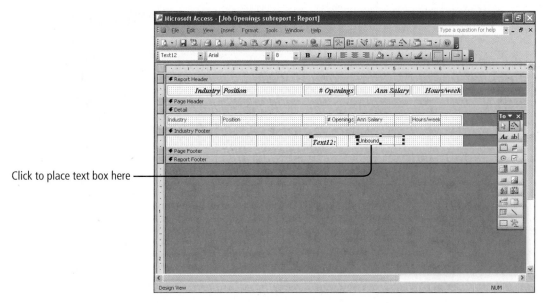

Figure 7.13

Click to place text box here

2 In the **Industry Footer** section, right-click on the **Text Label** you just created. From the shortcut menu, click **Properties**, and then click the **Format tab**. Click in the **Caption** box, delete the text and type **Total Salaries of Industry** See Figure 7.14.

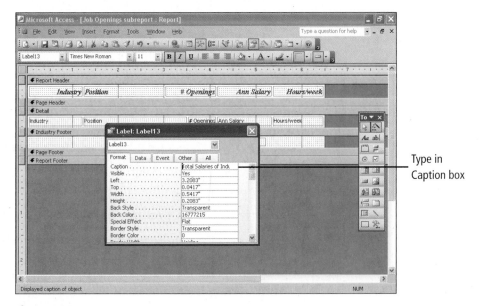

Type in Caption box

Figure 7.14

3 **Close** ☒ the property sheet.

4 With the label still selected, change the **Font Size** to **9**.

5 Lengthen the left side of the label to approximately **2.25 inches on the horizontal ruler** as shown in Figure 7.15.

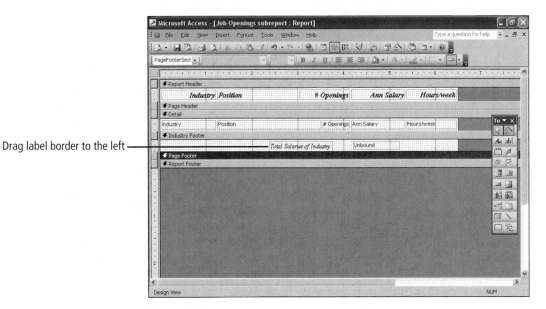

Drag label border to the left

Figure 7.15

6 Right-click the **Unbound control box**, click **Properties**, and then click the **Data tab**. See Figure 7.16.

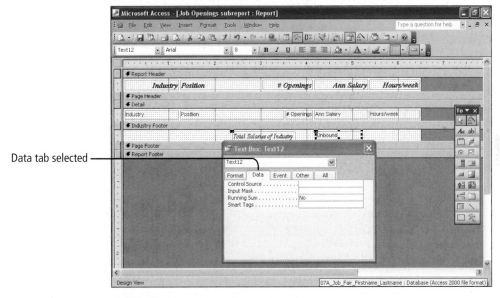

Data tab selected

Figure 7.16

7 Click in the **Control Source** box, and then click the **Build** button ... that displays.

8 In the displayed **Expression Builder** dialog box, at the insertion point type **=sum([# Openings]*[Ann Salary])** Compare your screen with Figure 7.17.

The equal sign indicates the beginning of a formula. First the number of openings for a position is multiplied by the Annual Salary of the position. Then, the formula calculates the sum of these salaries for the industry. When typing field names in a formula, a field name that contains blank spaces must be surrounded by square brackets [ ].

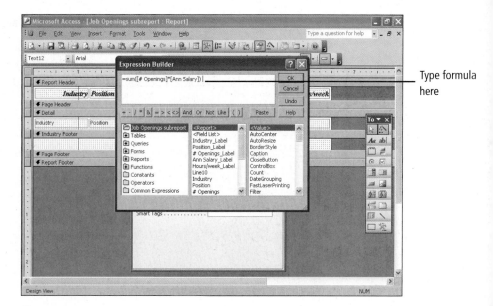

Type formula here

Figure 7.17

Another Way ── **To Enter a Formula**

Instead of typing field names in a formula, you can find the field names under the Report Field List in the expression builder and double-click on the field you want in your formula.

9 Click **OK** to insert the formula in the **Control Source** box. With the **Property sheet** still open, click the **Format tab**. Change the **Format** to **Currency** and the **Decimal Places** to **2**. See Figure 7.18.

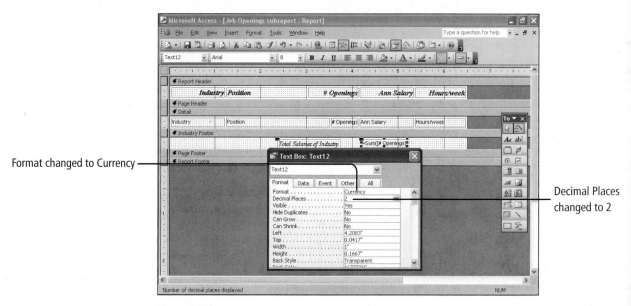

Format changed to Currency

Decimal Places changed to 2

Figure 7.18

10 **Close** ☒ the **Property sheet**. On the Toolbox toolbar, click the **Line** button ◿. Draw a line along the lower edge of the **Industry Footer** section by positioning the + sign on the left side of the report. Hold down (Shift) to maintain a straight, not jagged, line and drag the line across to the right side of the report—you will not see the line as you draw it, but after you release the mouse button it will be visible. Compare you screen with Figure 7.19.

The line will provide a visual separation between the different industries in your report.

Line will separate different industries

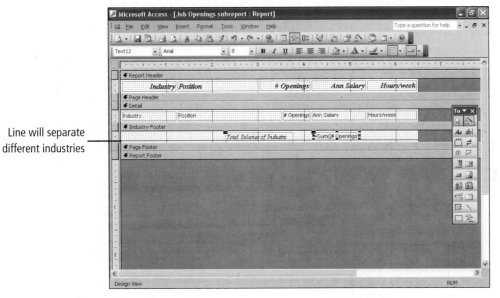

Figure 7.19

11 Switch to **Print preview** to view your updated report. Locate the subtotals of the total salaries by industry. Leave the subreport open for the next activity.

Note — Setting Margins on a Report

A subreport, when created, has margin settings smaller than a regular report so that it can easily fall into the main report at the location you indicate. However, if you decide to print the subreport, adjust the margins from the Page Setup dialog box.

Activity 7.4 Creating a Calculated Field for a Report

In the previous activity, you placed a formula in the Industry Footer section and it summed the total salaries by each industry—within a group. In this activity, you will place the same formula in the Report Footer section, which will sum the total salaries of all the job openings in the report. Recall that this number is useful for advertising how large the fair has become.

1 Switch to **Design view**. Drag the lower edge of the **Report Footer** section to expand its size as shown in Figure 7.20.

Resize Report Footer ——

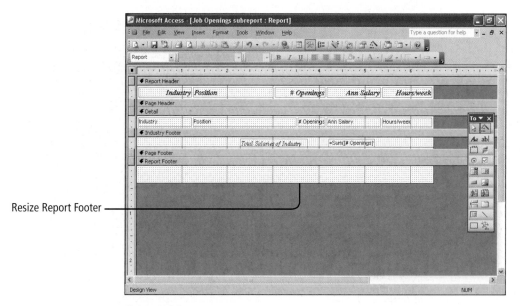

Figure 7.20

2 In the **Industry Footer** section, select the **unbound control box** containing the formula, and then on the Report Design toolbar, click the **Copy** button.

3 Click the **Report Footer section bar** to select the section, and then on the Report Design toolbar, click the **Paste** button to paste the formula in the Report Footer.

4 Drag the label and unbound control box to line up directly under the label and formula you created earlier in the Industry Footer section.

5 Select the text in the label and type **Total Salaries** and change the **Font Size** of the label to **10**. See Figure 7.21.

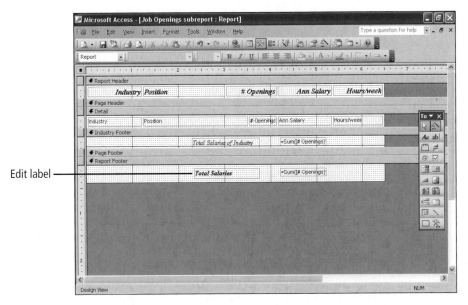

Edit label

Figure 7.21

6 Switch to **Print preview**. Navigate to the end of the report to see the Total Salaries of $6,441,000.00.

You can see that in advertising, using this large number of potential income would be quite effective.

7 In the upper right corner of your screen, click the small **Close Window** button ⊠ to close the **Job Openings subreport** and save your changes to the design. Open the **Employers Report**, and click on the report to magnify it.

8 Examine the **Employers Report** and notice that the embedded **Job Openings subreport** has been modified—the job openings are grouped and totaled by Employer.

9 Switch to **Design view** and leave the report open for the next exercise.

Objective 4
Set Report and Report Section Properties

In the previous activities, you worked with various sections of a report. Each section of a report has its own Property sheet, and thus each section can be modified separately.

Activity 7.5 Setting Report and Report Section Properties

Some of the most commonly used properties are located on the Format tab of the Property sheet. In this exercise you will change some of the properties on the Format tab to make your report display in a way that is more readable or useful.

1 With the **Employers Report** open in **Design view**, right-click the **Detail section bar**, and then from the shortcut menu, click **Properties**. Be sure the **Format tab** is selected as shown in Figure 7.22.

2 Click in the **Force New Page** box, click the arrow, and then from the displayed list, click **Before Section**. See Figure 7.22.

By forcing a new page before each section in the Detail section, each Employer and its accompanying list of Job Openings will display on a separate page. Because there are currently 25 employers, the result will be a 25-page report.

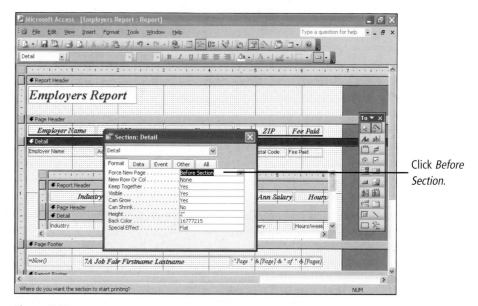

Figure 7.22

3 **Close** ⊠ the **Property sheet**, and switch to **Print preview**. Use the page navigation buttons in the lower left corner of the screen to scroll through the 25 pages of the report, and verify that each Employer has a separate page.

Notice that many employers do not currently have any job listings.

4 Switch to **Design view**, right-click on the **Detail bar**, and click **Properties**. On the **Format tab**, change the **Force New Page** property back to **None** and be sure the **Keep Together** property is set to **Yes**.

5 Click in the **Back Color** box and click the **Build** button ⊡ that displays. In the displayed **Color** dialog box, in the first row, click the second color—**light yellow**.

6 Click **OK** and close the **Property sheet**.

7 Switch to **Print preview** ▣ and navigate to **page 1**. Compare your screen with Figure 7.1.

8 From the **File** menu, click **Print**. Under **Print Range**, in the **From** box type **1** and in the **To** box type **1** so that only page 1 will print.

Click **OK**. **Close** ⊠ the report, saving the changes to the design.

Click the **Restore Window** button ▣ to return the Database window to its smaller size. Leave the database open for the next activity.

Objective 5
Create a Crosstab Report

A special type of query, called a **crosstab query**, performs calculations on data that is grouped by *two* types of information. For example, in the Greater Atlanta Job Fair database, if you want to compare a list of the salaries by industry and by state, you could use a crosstab query.

Activity 7.6 Creating a Report from a Crosstab Query

In this activity, you will create a report based on a crosstab query that has already been created.

1 On the Objects bar, click **Queries**, and then open the **Job Openings by Employer_Crosstab** query. Take a moment to study the information in the query. See Figure 7.23.

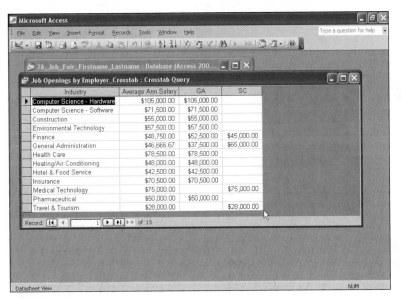

Figure 7.23

2 **Close** ☒ the query.

3 On the Objects bar, click **Reports**. Double-click the command icon **Create report by using wizard**.

4 Click the **Tables/Queries arrow**, and from the displayed list, click **Query: Job Openings by Employer_Crosstab**. Use the **All Fields** button ⊡ to move all the fields under **Selected Fields**. See Figure 7.24.

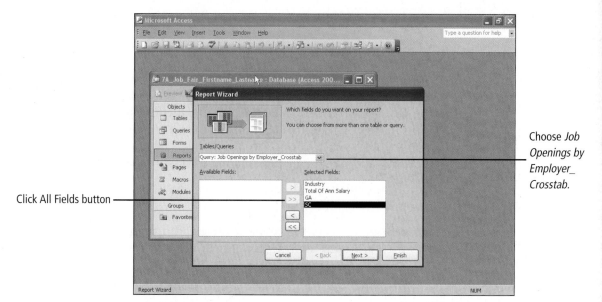

Choose *Job Openings by Employer_Crosstab*.

Click All Fields button

Figure 7.24

5 Click **Next**. No grouping levels will be added, so click **Next** again.

6 To sort the records within the report by Industry, click the arrow next to the **1** box. From the displayed list, click **Industry** and leave the sort order as **Ascending**. Click **Next**.

7 Under **Layout**, be sure the **Tabular** option button is selected, and under **Orientation**, be sure the **Portrait** option button is selected. Click **Next**. Click the **Corporate** style and click **Next**.

8 As the title for your report, accept the default **Job Openings by Employer_Crosstab**

9 Click **Finish** to view the report. Switch to **Design view**, and in the **Page Footer** section, select the **=Now()** control on the left. Drag its right center sizing handle to **2.0 inches on the horizontal ruler**. Select the **="Page"** control on the right, drag its left center sizing handle to **5 inches on the horizontal ruler**. On the Toolbox toolbar, click the **Label** button [Aa], and draw a label below the gray bar about one-quarter inch tall, from **2.25 inches on the horizontal ruler** to **4.75 inches on the horizontal ruler**. In the new label, type **7A Crosstab Firstname Lastname** Press [Enter], change the **Font Size** to **10**, and then nudge the control as necessary to line it up with the lower edge of the section.

10 Switch to **Print preview**.

11 From the **File** menu, click **Page Setup**. Click the **Margins tab**, and change the **Left margin** to **0.75** and the **Right margin** to **0.75**. From the **File** menu, click **Print**, and then click **OK**. **Close** [X] the report, save your changes, and then close the database.

End You have completed Project 7A

Project 7B **Job Fair Update**

As databases grow, you will find that entering new records into your database is only one part of maintaining your database. You will also need to update individual records, and occasionally you will need to update groups of records. Updating your database need not be time consuming. With the use of specific queries, the process of updating your database can be fast and efficient.

In Activities 7.7 through 7.14, you will use multiple queries to update the information in your database. Your results will look similar to those shown in Figure 7.25.

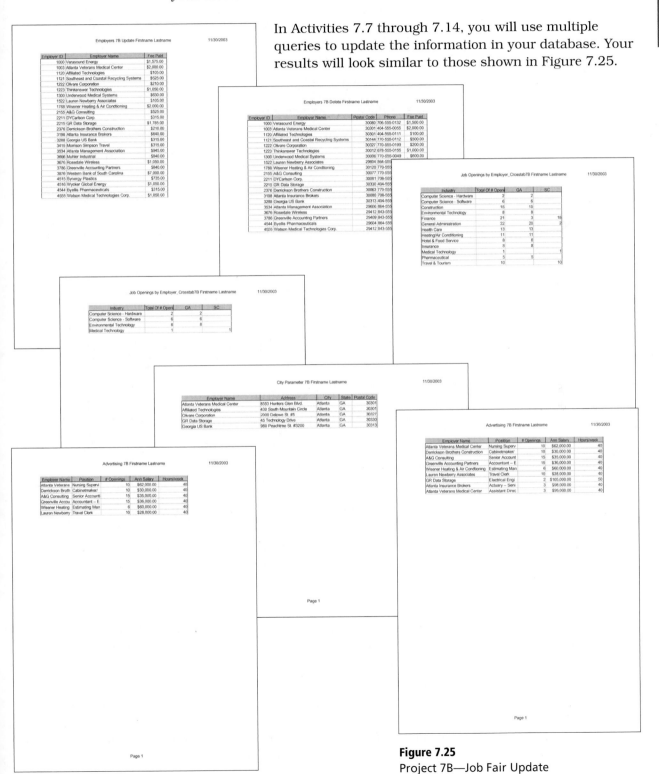

Figure 7.25
Project 7B—Job Fair Update

Objective 6
Create an Update Query

Recall that a *select query* retrieves and displays data from one or more tables based on *criteria* (conditions that identify specific records) that you specify. An *action query*, on the other hand, *changes* data in a table. One type of action query is an *update query*, which updates existing data. When a group of records in a table requires the same update, an update query is an efficient way to accomplish the task, rather than updating each record separately. For example, due to rising costs of conducting the Job Fairs, the Executive Director of the Greater Atlanta Job Fair has indicated that if an employer fee is currently less than $2,000, it should be increased by 5%.

Activity 7.7 Creating an Update Query

In this activity, you will create an update query to update each employer's Fee Paid by 5%—if the fee is currently less than $2,000.

1. Locate the database file **a07B_Job_Fair_Update** from your student files, and copy and paste the file to the Chapter 7 folder you created for this chapter. Remove the Read-only property from the file, and rename the file as **7B_Job_Fair_Update_Firstname_Lastname** Start Access and open the database you just renamed.

2. On the Objects bar, click **Tables**, right-click the **Employers** table, and then click **Copy**. Move your mouse pointer into the white area, right-click, and then click **Paste**. In the displayed **Paste Table As** dialog box, under **Table Name**, type Employers 7B Update Firstname Lastname and click **OK**. In this project, you will practice on copies of the original table.

3. Open your **Employers 7B Update** table. Drag across the gray column headings to select the columns **Contact**, **Contact Title**, and **Address**, display the **Format** menu, and then click **Hide Columns**.

4. Examine the numbers in the **Fee Paid** column, and notice that a number of them are less than $2,000. For example, the first Employer, **Verasound Energy**, has a fee of $1,500.00.

5. From the **Format** menu, click **Unhide Columns**. In the displayed **Unhide Columns** dialog box, select the **Contact**, **Contact Title**, and **Address** check boxes, and click **Close**. **Close** ⊠ the **Employers** table, and click **No** when asked if you want to save changes to the layout of the table.

   Recall that it is sometimes convenient to hide columns temporarily to get a better view of the table, rather than scrolling back and forth.

6. On the Objects bar, click **Queries**, and then on the database window toolbar, click the **New** button ⟦New⟧.

7. From the list of methods to create a new query, be sure **Design View** is selected, and then click **OK**. In the displayed **Show Table** dialog box, click the **Tables tab**, click to select your **Employers 7B Update** table, and then click **Add**. See Figure 7.26. **Close** the dialog box.

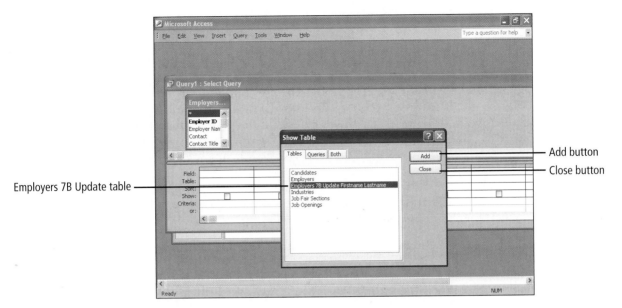

Employers 7B Update table

Add button
Close button

Figure 7.26

8 In the table area, scroll to the bottom of the table's field list and double-click the **Fee Paid** field to place it into to the design grid.

An Update query modifies an existing table or query; thus, you need only select the fields you want to change—in this case, the Fee Paid field. Recall that the query window has two parts: the *table area* (upper pane) and the *design grid* (lower pane).

9 Notice the name in the window's blue title bar—*Select Query*. See Figure 7.27. On the Query Design toolbar, click the **Query Type button arrow** , and then from the displayed list click **Update Query**.

The query type in the blue title bar changes to *Update Query*. When you create a new query, the default type is Select Query. For other types of queries, change the query type, and then set the criteria.

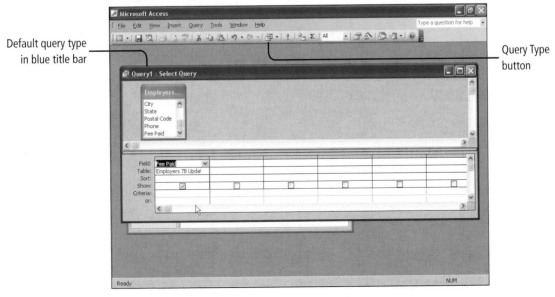

Default query type
in blue title bar

Query Type
button

Figure 7.27

To Change the Query Type

There are three ways to change the query type in Access. On the Query Design toolbar, click the Query Type button arrow and select from the displayed list, as you did in the previous step. Or, from the menu bar, click Query, and choose from the displayed menu. Finally, in the gray table area, right-click. On the displayed shortcut menu, point to Query Type, and then choose the type of query that you want.

10 In the design grid, in the **Update To** row, click in the first column and type **[Fee Paid]*1.05**

This formula will multiply the amount in the Fee Paid field by 1.05, an increase of 5 percent.

11 In the **Criteria** row, click in the first column and type **<2000**
See Figure 7.28.

Setting this criteria (condition) will apply the formula only to those records where the current value in the Fee Paid field is less than $2,000.

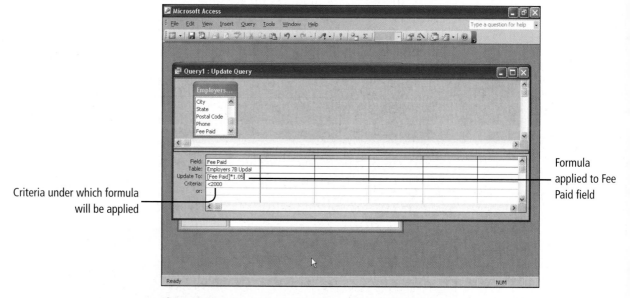

Criteria under which formula will be applied

Formula applied to Fee Paid field

Figure 7.28

12 On the Query Design toolbar, click the **Run** button.

As shown in Figure 7.29, a message displays indicating that this action will update 22 rows, which is 22 records. The Undo command cannot reverse this action. If you update a group of records by mistake, you must correct each record separately.

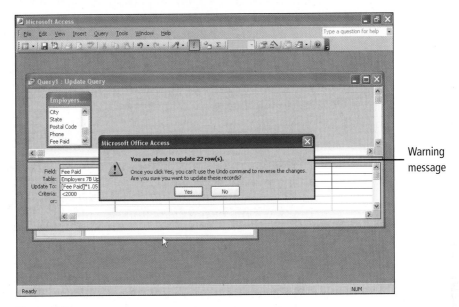

Warning message

Figure 7.29

13 Click **Yes**. **Close** the Update Query window, and then click **No** when asked to save the changes to the query.

The 22 records in the Employers table that met the criteria are updated. Because it is unlikely that you will raise the Employer fees in this manner again, it is not necessary to save the query.

14 On the Objects bar, click the **Tables** button, and then double-click your **Employers 7B Update** table to open it. Scroll all the way to the left, select the **Contact** column, hold down Shift, use the scroll bar to scroll all the way to the right, and select the **Phone** column. All the columns *except* **Employer ID**, **Employer Name**, and **Fee Paid** are selected. Display the **Format** menu and click **Hide Columns**.

Notice the updated fee amounts. For example, the fee for Verasound Energy has been raised to $1,575—an increase of 5 percent.

15 **Print** the table, display the **Format** menu, click **Unhide Columns**, and select the appropriate check boxes to unhide all the columns. Compare your printed table with Figure 7.25.

16 **Close** your **Employers 7B Update** table. Do not save the changes to the layout, so that the columns will not be hidden when you open the table again.

Objective 7
Create a Delete Query

A **delete query** is a type of action query that removes records from a table. When information becomes outdated or is no longer needed, the unneeded records should be deleted from your database. Assuming outdated records have a common criterion, perhaps a date, you can gather them together in a delete query, and then delete them all at once. This is much faster than deleting unneeded records one by one. For example, in the Job Fair database, the Executive Director needs to delete all the employers having the Postal Code of 29413 or 29423, because employers in these areas have decided they are not close enough to any of the Job Fair cities to justify exhibiting and paying for a booth.

Activity 7.8 Creating and Running a Delete Query

In this activity, you will create and run a delete query to delete, from the Employers table, employers having the 29413 or 29423 Postal Code. This is accomplished by first creating a select query containing the employers that have the Postal Code criteria, and then changing the query type to a Delete Query.

1 On the Objects bar, click **Tables**. Right-click the **Employers** table, and then click **Copy**. In the white area, right-click again, and then click **Paste**. Name the table **Employers 7B Delete Firstname Lastname** Recall that in this project, you will practice on copies of the original table.

2 On the Objects bar, click the **Queries** button, and then to the right, double-click **Create query in Design view**. Alternatively, on the Database window toolbar, click the New button and click OK.

3 In the **Show Table** dialog box, click the **Tables tab** if necessary, click your **Employers 7B Delete** table, and then click **Add**. Click **Close** to close the dialog box.

4 In the table area, use the vertical scroll bar to view all the fields in the table. Double-click the **Employer Name** field to add it to the first column of the design grid, and then double-click the **Postal Code** field to add it to the second column of the design grid.

5 In the **Criteria** row, click in the second (Postal Code) column and type **29413**

6 In **or** row, in the same column, type **29423** See Figure 7.30.

This action will cause the query to select only those Employers with a Postal Code of 29413 or 29423.

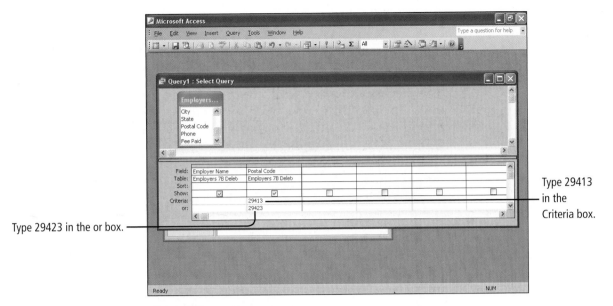

Figure 7.30

Type 29413 in the Criteria box.

Type 29423 in the or box.

7 Click the **Run** button ⊞.

The query displays five records that meet the criteria you specified.

8 Switch to **Design view**.

9 In the gray table area, right-click. From the displayed shortcut menu, point to **Query Type** as shown in Figure 7.31, and then click **Delete Query**.

This is another method to display the list of Query Types.

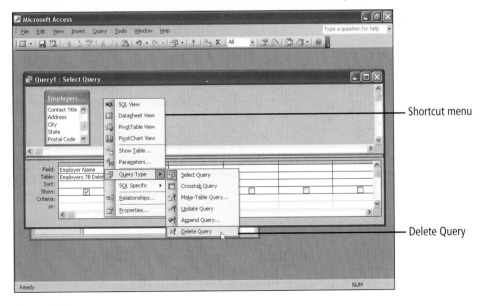

Shortcut menu

Delete Query

Figure 7.31

10 **Run** ![Run button] the query.

11 A warning message, as shown in Figure 7.32, displays indicating that 5 rows (records) will be deleted from the table.

This action cannot be reversed with the Undo command. If you delete records in error, you must enter each record again.

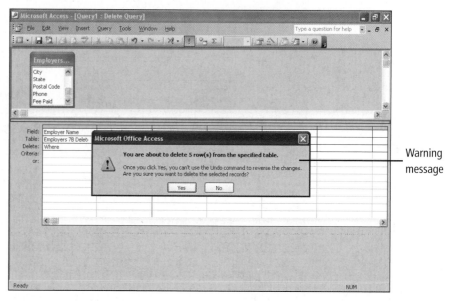

Warning message

Figure 7.32

Note — Check Your Relationships!

If you have created relationships between tables, running a delete query could also delete records from related tables. Before running a delete query, check the relationships between the table you are modifying and any other table. It is also a good idea to maintain a backup of your database so you can recover from any loss of data.

---

12 In the displayed warning message, click **Yes**. **Close** ![Close button] the query without saving changes, because it is unlikely that this query will be used again.

13 On the Objects bar, click **Tables**. Open your **Employers 7B Delete** table. Select the columns **Contact**, **Contact Title**, **Address**, **City**, and **State**. Display the **Format** menu and click **Hide Columns**. Notice that there are no records that have the Postal Code of 29413 or 29423. Compare your screen with Figure 7.33.

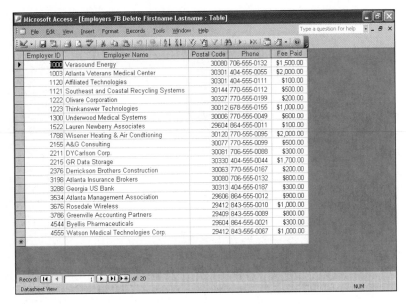

Figure 7.33

🔢 Print the table. **Close** ❎ the **Employers** table; do not save the changes to the layout.

Objective 8
Create Special Purpose Queries

A crosstab query is a query that groups summarized data by categories. A crosstab query always has a column heading, a row heading, and a summary field. Use a crosstab query when you want to summarize a large amount of data in a small space that is easy to read. For example, in the Job Fair database, Michael Augustino wants to summarize the number of job openings for each industry by state.

Activity 7.9 Creating a Crosstab Query

In this activity, you will create a crosstab query to summarize, by state, the number of job openings in each industry. Because a crosstab query usually contains information from more than one table in the database, you must first create a select query to include all the tables, and then create the crosstab query. A select query that combines the **Employers**, **Job Openings**, and **Industries** tables has already been created, and is named *Job Openings by Employer*.

🔢 On the Objects bar, click **Queries**. On the Database window toolbar, click the **New** button 🔲 New. In the **New Query** dialog box, click **Crosstab Query Wizard**. See Figure 7.34. Click **OK**.

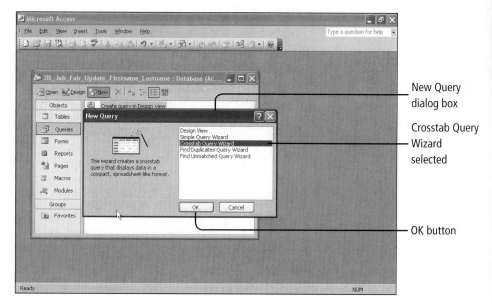

New Query
dialog box

Crosstab Query
Wizard
selected

OK button

Figure 7.34

2 In the first screen of the wizard, in which you select the table or query you want to use for your crosstab query, under **View**, click the **Queries** option button.

In the white box, the *Job Openings by Employer* query is selected. See Figure 7.35.

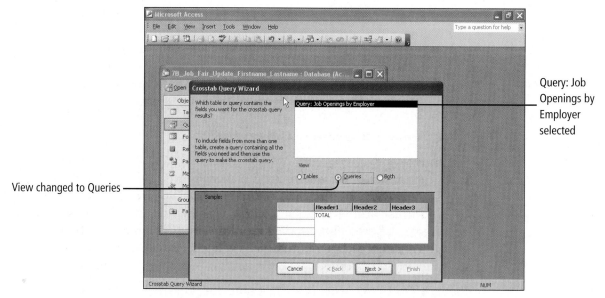

View changed to Queries

Query: Job
Openings by
Employer
selected

Figure 7.35

3 Click **Next**. Here you select the fields you want as row headings—up to three can be selected. Under **Available Fields**, use the **One Field** button 	 to move **Industry** under **Selected Fields**. See Figure 7.36.

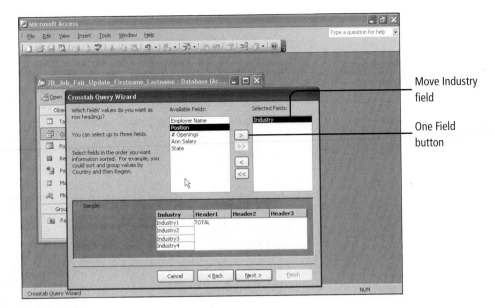

Move Industry field

One Field button

Figure 7.36

4 Click **Next**. Here you select a single field as the column heading. Click **State**.

5 Click **Next**. Here you indicate the number to be calculated for each column and row intersection. Under **Fields**, click **# Openings**, and then under **Functions**, click **Sum**. Under **Do you want to summarize each row?**, be sure that the **Yes, include row sums** check box is selected. See Figure 7.37.

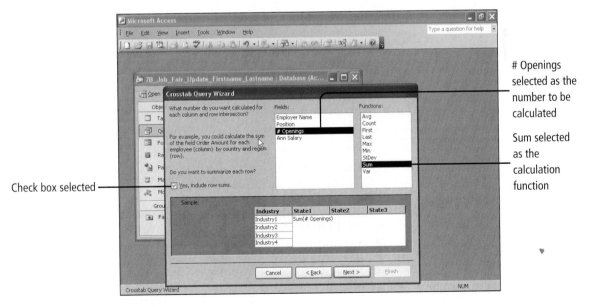

Openings selected as the number to be calculated

Sum selected as the calculation function

Check box selected

Figure 7.37

6 Click **Next**. In this screen, at the end of the proposed query name, click, and then type **7B Firstname Lastname** to add this to the query name. Click **Finish**. Compare your screen with Figure 7.38.

Recall that the purpose of the crosstab query was to summarize, by State, the number of job openings in each industry. Notice, for example, that in the Finance industry, there are a total of 21 jobs that will be advertised at the job fair—3 in Georgia and 18 in South Carolina.

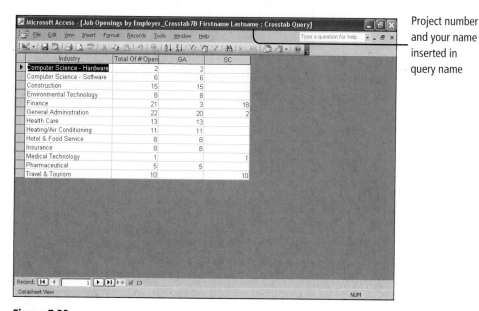

Project number and your name inserted in query name

Industry	Total Of # Open	GA	SC
Computer Science - Hardware	2	2	
Computer Science - Software	6	6	
Construction	15	15	
Environmental Technology	8	8	
Finance	21	3	18
General Administration	22	20	2
Health Care	13	13	
Heating/Air Conditioning	11	11	
Hotel & Food Service	8	8	
Insurance	8	8	
Medical Technology	1		1
Pharmaceutical	5	5	
Travel & Tourism	10		10

Figure 7.38

7 Print your crosstab query and compare your printed table with the one in Figure 7.25. Switch to **Design view**. Leave your query open in **Design view** for the next activity.

Activity 7.10 Adding Conditions to a Crosstab Query

After you have created a crosstab query, you can break down the information in the query even further. In this activity, you will add additional conditions to your query to display, by State, only the positions in the Computer and Technology industry.

1 Be sure your **Job Openings by Employer_Crosstab 7B** query is open in **Design view**. In the **Criteria** row, click in the **Industry** column and type **Computer*** See Figure 7.39.

The * is a wild card character, which can represent multiple characters, including spaces. Because the * comes after the word *Computer*, any industry starting with *Computer* will satisfy the condition.

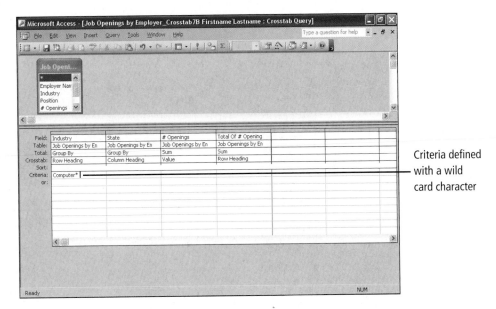

Figure 7.39

2 Switch to **Query view** and compare your screen with Figure 7.40.

Two industries, both beginning with *Computer*, display.

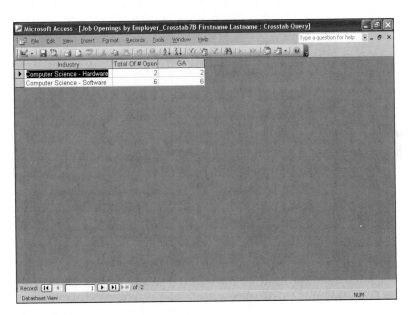

Figure 7.40

3 Switch to **Design view** and notice that the criteria row indicates *Like "Computer*"*.

4 In the **or** row, click in the **Industry** column and type ***Technology** See Figure 7.41.

This action will select any industry that begins with the word *Computer* or any industry that ends with the word *Technology*.

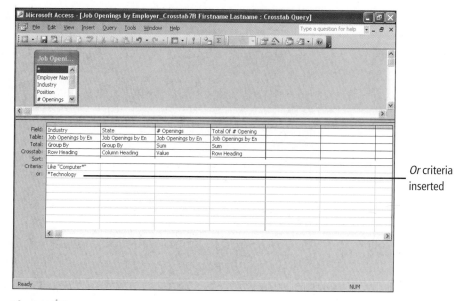

Figure 7.41

5 Switch to **Query view**.

Four different industries display, summarized by the total number of openings in each state. Each industry name either begins with *Computer* or ends with *Technology*.

6 Print, close, and save your query. Compare your printed query to Figure 7.25.

Activity 7.11 Creating a Parameter Query

A **parameter query** is a query that will prompt you for criteria before running the actual query. It can be a select query or an action query. For example, to find Employers in a specific city, you would create a select query and set the criteria to the specific city—creating a separate query for each city. But by using a parameter query, Access will prompt you for the city you want and then display the results based on the given parameter.

In this activity, you will create a parameter query to list Employers by city.

1 On the Objects bar, click **Tables**. Right-click the **Employers** table and click **Copy**. Right-click in the white area, click **Paste**, name the table **Employers 7B Parameter Firstname Lastname** and click **OK**.

2 On the Objects bar, click **Queries**. To the right, double-click the command icon **Create query in Design view**.

3 Add your **Employers 7B Parameter** table to the table area, and then close the **Show Table** dialog box.

4 In the field list, double-click **Employer Name**, **Address**, **City**, **State**, and **Postal Code** to add the fields to the design grid. See Figure 7.42.

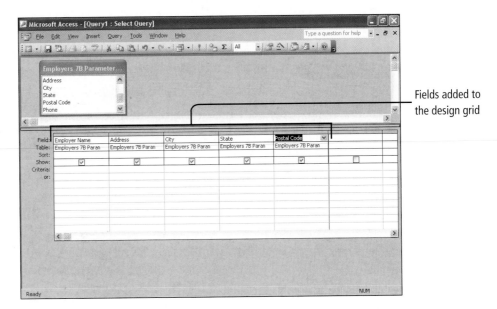

Fields added to the design grid

Figure 7.42

5 In the **Criteria** row, in the **City** column, type **[Enter a City]** and then compare your screen with Figure 7.43.

The brackets indicate a *parameter* rather than a specific criteria. When you run the query, the message *Enter a City* will display and allow you to type the name of a city. The city you type will be set as the criterion for the query. In this manner, you can reuse this query over and over without resetting specific criteria.

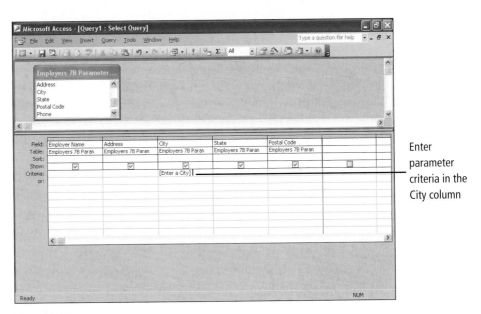

Enter parameter criteria in the City column

Figure 7.43

6 **Run** the query.

7 In the **Enter Parameter Value** dialog box, type **Greenville** as shown in Figure 7.44.

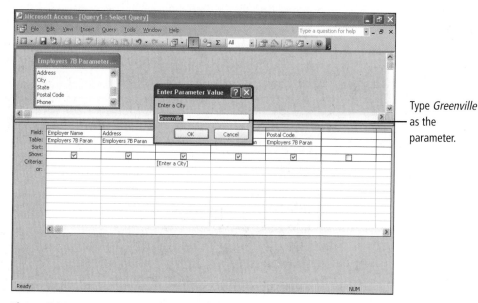

Type *Greenville* as the parameter.

Figure 7.44

8 Click **OK**.

Three employers, all located in Greenville, display.

9 Switch to **Design view** and **Run** the query again.

10 Type **Atlanta** as the parameter value, and then click **OK**.

Five employers, all located in Atlanta, display.

11 From the **File** menu, click **Save As**. In the **Save As** dialog box, type **City Parameter 7B Firstname Lastname** and then click **OK**. Display the **File** menu again, click **Page Setup**, and on the **Page tab**, change the **Orientation** to **Landscape**. Click **OK**, and then print the query.

Close the query. Compare your printed query to Figure 7.25.

Objective 9
Create Action Queries

An action query lets you change data in a table, or create a new table. A **make-table query** is an action query that creates a new table based on existing tables. Creating a new table can be useful if you need to back up a table, or if you need to create a custom table for a special purpose. For example, the Executive Director of the Greater Atlanta Job Fair wants to create a table for the purpose of gathering some information to be used in advertising the Job Fair. Creating a new table in this manner will not cause loss of data in or changes to the original table.

Activity 7.12 Creating a Make-Table Query

In this activity, you will use a make-table query to create a table listing all employers that have more than five job openings.

1 On the Objects bar, click **Queries**, and then to the right, double-click the command icon **Create query in Design view**.

2 Add the **Employers** table (the one without your name attached) and the **Job Openings** table to the table area, and then close the **Show Table** dialog box.

Notice that a one-to-many relationship exists between the two tables, because one employer can have many job openings.

3 From the **Employers** table, add the **Employer Name** field to the design grid, and from the **Job Openings** table, add the **Position**, **# Openings**, **Ann Salary**, and **Hours/week** fields to the design grid. See Figure 7.45.

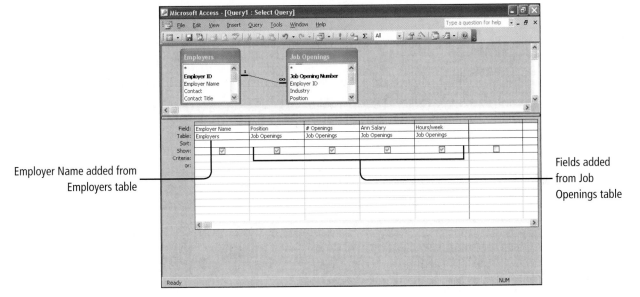

Employer Name added from Employers table

Fields added from Job Openings table

Figure 7.45

4 In the **Criteria** row, click in the **# Openings** column and type **>5**

5 On the menu bar, click **Query**, and then click **Make-Table Query**.

6 In the displayed **Make Table** dialog box, type **Advertising 7B Firstname Lastname** as shown in Figure 7.46.

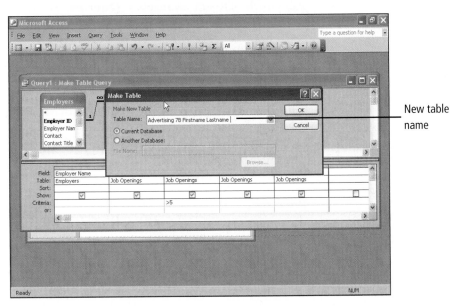

New table name

Figure 7.46

7 Click **OK**, and then **Run** 🔘 the query. When the message indicating *You are about to paste 6 row(s) into a new table* displays, click **Yes**.

8 **Close** ✖ the query and at the prompt, save the query as **Over 5 Openings 7B Firstname Lastname**

9 On the Objects bar, click **Tables**, and then double-click to open your **Advertising 7B** table.

Notice that all employers listed have more than 5 openings.

10 Print and then close your **Advertising** table. Compare your printed table to Figure 7.25.

Note — Using a Make-Table Query

A table created from a make-table query is not automatically updated when information from the original table or tables is modified. To keep the new table up to date, you must run the make-table query periodically to be sure your information is current.

Activity 7.13 Creating an Append Query

In the previous activity, you made a *new* table by copying information from other tables. An **append query** adds new records to an existing table by importing data from another Access database, from another program such as Microsoft Excel, or from a table in the same database. An append query can be limited by criteria.

Michael Augustino wants to add information to the Advertising table by gathering a list of employers that have numerous jobs at very high salaries. He feels that advertising this information will attract many good candidates to the job fairs. In this activity, you will add job openings with high annual salaries to the Advertising table that you created in the last activity by using an append query.

1 On the Objects bar, click **Queries**. To the right of the Objects bar, double-click **Create query in Design view**.

2 Add the **Employers** table (the one without your name) and the **Job Openings** table to the table area, and then close the **Show Table** dialog box.

3 From the **Employers** table, add the **Employer Name** field to the design grid, and from the **Job Openings** table, add **Position**, **# Openings**, **Ann Salary**, and **Hours/week** fields.

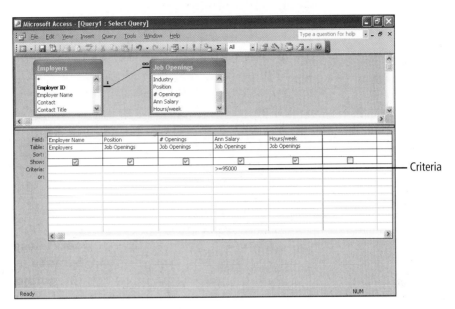

4 In the **Criteria** row, in the **Ann Salary** column, type **>=95000** as shown in Figure 7.47.

This criterion will limit the job openings displayed to those with an annual salary greater than or equal to $95,000.

Figure 7.47

5 In the gray table area, right-click, and from the displayed shortcut menu, point to **Query Type** and click **Append Query**.

6 In the displayed **Append** dialog box, click the **Table Name arrow**, and from the displayed list, click your **Advertising 7B** table. Click **OK**.

7 **Run** the query. In the warning message indicating *You are about to append 3 row(s)*, click **Yes**.

8 **Close** the query, and save it as **High Salaries 7B Firstname Lastname**

9 On the Objects bar, click **Tables**, and then open your **Advertising 7B** table. Locate the three records at the bottom of the table. This table now includes employers with more than five openings, and also, employers with job openings with salaries equal to or higher than $95,000.

10 Print and then close your **Advertising 7B** table. Compare your printed table to the one in Figure 7.25.

Objective 10
View Queries in SQL

In this project, you have created various types of queries. As you did so, Access was not directly interacting with your query. To run your query, Access must first translate the query you create in design view into an **SQL statement**. SQL is the commonly used term for **Structured Query Language**, which is a database sublanguage used in querying, updating, and managing relational databases in database programs such as Microsoft Access. Knowing a little about SQL can help you build more powerful queries than you could construct using only the design grid in Access.

Activity 7.14 Viewing Queries in SQL

In the following activity, you will look at a query in SQL view and look at a basic SQL statement.

1 On the Objects bar, click **Queries**, and then open the **Job Openings by Employer** query in **Design view**.

2 In the **Sort** row, under **Employer Name**, click in the box, click the arrow, and from the displayed list, click **Ascending**.

3 In the **Criteria** row, under **Ann Salary**, click in the box and type **<60000** as shown in Figure 7.48.

Two additional criteria are now added to the design grid, which will assist in viewing the four parts of a typical SQL statement.

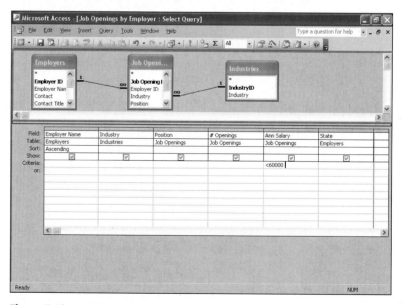

Figure 7.48

4 From the menu bar, click **View**, and then click **SQL View**.

When looking at an SQL statement, you will usually notice four parts: SELECT, FROM, WHERE, and ORDER BY. The SELECT statement lists the fields you want to display. The FROM statement lists the tables used in the query. WHERE indicates the selection criteria, and ORDER BY indicates how the information will be sorted.

While you are designing your queries in Design view, you can see that Access is hard at work translating your work into SQL statements.

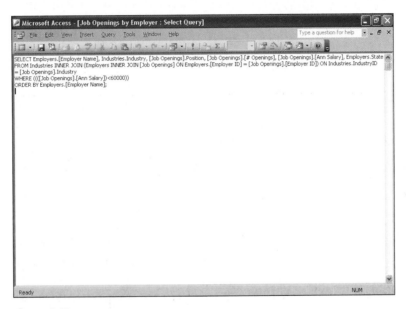

Figure 7.49

5 **Close** ☒ the query and save your changes.

End **You have completed Project 7B** ────────────────

Summary

Access provides a variety of ways to search, sort, update, and display data in your database. In this chapter, you practiced advanced techniques to customize reports. You created a subreport, in which a report is inserted into a control, and then the control is embedded in another report. Recall that to create a subreport, the two tables must have a one-to-many relationship established. You practiced how to group data in a report and create calculated fields in a report. Each section of a report has its own properties, and in this chapter you practiced modifying various properties of a report. Another type of advanced report, called a crosstab report, was created based on a crosstab query. A crosstab report displays calculated data grouped by two types of information.

In this chapter, you also conducted advanced queries. Whereas a select query retrieves and displays data from one or more tables based on criteria, action queries actually change data in tables. You practiced creating an update query, which is useful for updating a group of records at the same time. You practiced creating a delete query, which is an action query that removes records from tables. This is an efficient way to remove a group of records at one time. You also practiced creating a crosstab query, which is a query that groups summarized data by categories. A crosstab query always has a column heading, a row heading, and a summary field. Finally, you practiced creating a parameter query, a make-table query, and looked at an SQL statement. A parameter query prompts you for criteria before running the actual query. A make-table query is an action query that creates a new table. You saw that as you develop a query in design view, Access is actually building an SQL statement to carry out your query in structured query language.

In This Chapter You Practiced How To

- Create a Subreport
- Group Data in a Report
- Create Calculated Fields in a Report
- Set Report and Report Section Properties
- Create a Crosstab Report
- Create an Update Query
- Create a Delete Query
- Create Special Purpose Queries
- Create Action Queries
- View Queries in SQL

Concepts Assessments

Matching Match each term in the second column with its correct definition in the first column. Write the letter of the term on the blank line to the left of the correct definition.

____ **1.** An optional area in a report frequently used for a logo, report title, or print date, and that appears only once—at the beginning of the report.

____ **2.** An action query that creates a new table based on existing tables.

____ **3.** A query that adds new records to an existing table by importing data from another Access database, from another program such as Microsoft Excel, or from a table in the same database.

____ **4.** A database sublanguage used in querying, updating, and managing relational databases in database programs such as Microsoft Access.

____ **5.** A report generated from a crosstab query that displays calculated data grouped by two types of information.

____ **6.** An optional area in a report frequently used for column headings, and that appears at the top of every page in a report.

____ **7.** A query that changes data in a table.

____ **8.** A report inserted into a control, and the control is then embedded in another report.

____ **9.** A query that retrieves and displays data from one or more tables based on criteria that you specify.

____ **10.** A type of action query that removes records from a table.

____ **11.** Controls in a report that are tied to a field in an underlying table or query.

____ **12.** The acronym and commonly used term for structured query language.

____ **13.** A query that will prompt you for criteria before running the actual query.

____ **14.** A special type of query that performs calculations on data that is grouped by two types of information.

____ **15.** An optional area in a report useful for displaying report totals, and that appears only once—at the end of the report.

A Action query

B Append query

C Bound controls

D Crosstab query

E Crosstab report

F Delete query

G Make-table query

H Page header

I Parameter query

J Report footer

K Report header

L Select query

M SQL

N Structured Query Language

O Subreport

Fill in the Blank Write the correct answer in the space provided.

1. To create a subreport, the two tables involved must contain a _____ relationship.

2. In a subreport, the main report comes from the _____ side of the one-to-many relationship.

3. In a subreport, the embedded report comes from the _____ side of the one-to-many relationship.

4. An optional area in a report, frequently used for page numbers, and that appears at the bottom of every page of a report is a page _____.

5. Conditions that identify specific records in a query are called _____.

6. The area of a report that contains the main body of the report's data, and which is repeated for each record in the report's underlying record source is the _____ section.

7. A type of action query that replaces existing data is a(an) _____ query.

8. When you want to summarize a large amount of data in a small space, use a _____ query.

9. To run a query you create in design view, Access must first translate your query into an SQL _____.

10. Controls in a report that have no data source, but that display information such as labels that identify a field's contents are called _____ controls.

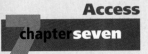
Project 7C—Industries Report

Objectives: *Create a Subreport and Create Calculated Fields in a Report.*

In the following Skill Assessment, you will create a subreport for Michael Augustino, Executive Director of the Greater Atlanta Job Fair, which will list each Industry, and then under each Industry, the number of candidates looking for a job in the industry. You will also calculate the number of candidates looking for jobs in each industry. Your completed report will look similar to the one shown in Figure 7.50. You will rename the database as *7C_Industries_Report_Firstname_Lastname* in the folder you have created for this chapter.

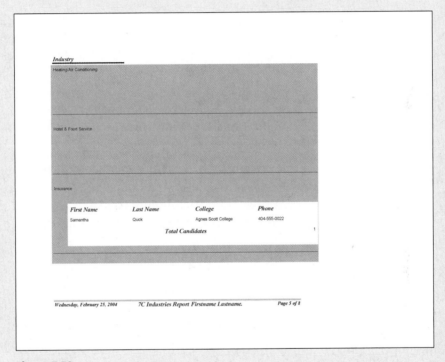

Figure 7.50

1. Locate the database file **a07C_Industries_Report** from your student files, and copy and paste the file to the Chapter 7 folder you created. Remove the Read-only property from the file and rename the file as **7C_Industries_Report_Firstname_Lastname** Start Access and open the database you just renamed.

2. On the Objects bar, click **Reports**, open the **Industries Report** in **Print preview**, **maximize** the report window, adjust the **Zoom** to **100%** so that you can view the data, and then examine the data in the report.

(Project 7C–Industries Report continues on the next page)

(Project 7C–Industries Report continued)

3. Switch to **Design view**. In the **Page Footer** section, click the control on the left, and then drag its right center sizing handle to the left to approximately **2 inches on the horizontal ruler**. Click the control on the right, and then drag its left center sizing handle to the right to approximately **5 inches on the horizontal ruler**.

4. On the Toolbox toolbar, click the **Label** button. In the **Page Footer section**, position the plus sign of your pointer just below the gray line at approximately **2.25 inches on the horizontal ruler**, and then drag down about a quarter of an inch and to the right to approximately **4.75 inches on the horizontal ruler**.

5. In the label control you just created, using your own first and last name, type **7C Industries Report Firstname Lastname** Then press Enter. Nudge the control as necessary. (Hint: Holding down Ctrl while pressing a directional key on your keyboard nudges in small precise increments.)

6. Position your mouse pointer at the top of the **Page Footer bar** until the double arrow mouse pointer displays, and then drag down to slightly below **1 inch on the vertical ruler**. This will expand the **Detail section** of the report.

7. On the Toolbox toolbar, click the **Subform/Subreport** button. Within the **Detail section**, position the plus sign attached to the mouse pointer at approximately **0.5 inch on the horizontal ruler** and at **0.5 inch on the vertical ruler** and click once.

8. In the first screen of the Subreport Wizard, be sure the **Use existing Tables and Queries** option button is selected, and then click **Next**.

9. Click the **Tables/Queries arrow**, and from the displayed list, click **Table: Candidates**. Under **Available Fields**, use the **One Field** button to move the **First Name**, **Last Name**, **College**, and **Phone** fields over to the **Selected Fields** list. Click **Next**.

10. Leave **Show Candidates for each record in Industries using IndustryID** selected and click **Next**. In the last screen of the wizard, accept the default report name by clicking **Finish**. **Maximize** the report window.

11. Click in the gray area to cancel any selections, and then click the **Candidates subreport label**. Press Delete. Recall that if this label is not deleted, it will repeat for every record in the report, which is repetitive and unnecessary. On the Toolbox toolbar, click the **Line** button, position the plus sign in the **Detail section** at the left edge and at **1.25 inches on the vertical ruler**, hold down Shift, and drag across to the right edge of the **Detail section**—you may not see the line until you release the mouse button. If you are not satisfied with your result, click **Undo** and begin again.

(Project 7C–Industries Report continues on the next page)

(Project 7C–Industries Report continued)

12. Right-click on the **Detail section bar**, from the shortcut menu point to **Fill/Back Color**, and then in the fifth row, click the sixth color— **light blue**.

13. In the upper right corner of your screen, click the small **Close Window** button to close the report, and then click **Yes** to save the changes to the design. Open the **Candidates subreport** and switch to **Design view**.

14. Drag the lower edge of the **Report Footer** down to **0.5 inch on the vertical ruler**. On the Toolbox toolbar, click the **Text Box** button. Position the plus sign of the pointer in the **Report Footer section** at approximately **4.75 inches on the horizontal ruler**, and then draw a text box approximately the same size as the *Phone* control directly above it.

15. Right-click the **Text Label** you just created and click **Properties**. Click the **Format tab**, and then change the **Caption** to Total Candidates Close the **Property sheet**. With the **Text Label** still selected, drag its left center sizing handle to the left to **2.5 inches on the horizontal ruler**.

16. Right-click the **Unbound control**, click **Properties**, and then click the **Data tab**. Click in the **Control Source** box and click the displayed **Build** button. In the **Expression Builder**, type =count([First Name]) Click **OK** and close the **property sheet**.

17. Click the small **Close Window** button to close the subreport, save your changes, and open the **Industries Report** in **Print preview**. From the **File** menu, click **Page Setup**. Click the **Page tab**, and under **Orientation**, click the **Landscape** option button. Click **OK**. From the **File** menu, click **Print**. Under **Print Range**, click in the **From** box and type **5** and then click in the **To** box and type **5** so that you print only page 5 of this report. Close the database, and then close Access.

End **You have completed Project 7C**

Project 7D—Zip Code

Objective: *Create an Update Query.*

In the following Skill Assessment, you will create an Update Query to update ZIP codes (also known as Postal Codes) in the Candidates table and the Employers table. You will rename and save your database as *7D_Zip_Code_Firstname_Lastname.* Your completed tables will look similar to Figure 7.51.

Candidates Firstname Lastname   12/1/2003

Title	College	First Name	Last Name	Address Line 1	Address Line 2	City	State	Postal Code
Ms.	Agnes Scott College	Samantha	Quck	124 Whitworth Drive	#352	Atlanta	GA	30103
Mr.	None	Walter	Perrie	2495 Sunset Drive		Conyers	GA	30012
Ms.	Central GA Technical College	Jacqui	Epps	653 Constitution Ave.	#D	Marietta	GA	30006
Ms.	Augusta Technical College	Kelley	Bondurant	179 Auburn Court		Cartersville	GA	30120
Mr.	Columbus State University	Taylor	Dunnahoo	189 Ventura Street		Atlanta	GA	30330
Ms.	East GA College	Lenesha	Barnett	2361 Bluebird Lane	#8	Smyrna	GA	30081
Mr.	Emory University	Daniel	Echols	2000 St. Luke Place		Atlanta	GA	30313
Mr.	GA Institute of Technology	Mauro	Calva	82 E. Ramona Blvd.		Atlanta	GA	30327
Mr.	GA Perimeter College	David	Feingold	1821 Alturas St.	#1442	Atlanta	GA	30103
Mr.	None	Byeong	Chang	2221 Flowers Road South		Roswell	GA	30077
Mr.	Gordon College	Bin	Wu	676 North St. Clair St.		Smyrna	GA	30081
Ms.	Emory University	Samira	Ahmed	3418 Longview Drive	#320	Marietta	GA	30063
Ms.	Central GA Technical College	Jessica	Pyun	1255 Miravista Street		Kennesaw	GA	30144
Mr.	Columbus State University	Phillip	Scroggs	1518 Orchard Place West		Kennesaw	GA	30152

Employers Firstname Lastname   3/13/2004

Employer Name	Address	City	State	Postal Code
Verasound Energy	1 Verasound Way	Smyrna	GA	30080
Atlanta Veterans Medical Center	8553 Hunters Glen Blvd.	Atlanta	GA	30103
Affiliated Technologies	430 South Mountain Circle	Atlanta	GA	30103
Southeast and Coastal Recycling Systems	698 Rosedale Circle SE, #550	Kennesaw	GA	30144
Olivare Corporation	2000 Delowe St. #5	Atlanta	GA	30327
Thinkanswer Technologies	898 Lakeview Drive	Conyers	GA	30012
Underwood Medical Systems	1558 McVie Plaza Drive	Marietta	GA	30006
Lauren Newberry Associates	527 Pelham Road	Greenville	SC	29604
Wisener Heating & Air Condtioning	862 Ingleside Way, #315	Cartersville	GA	30120
A&G Consulting	107 Marguerite Drive S. #15	Roswell	GA	30077
DYCarlson Corp.	511 King Street	Smyrna	GA	30081
GR Data Storage	45 Technology Drive	Atlanta	GA	30330
Derrickson Brothers Construction	2215 Lake Park Drive	Marietta	GA	30063
Atlanta Insurance Brokers	352 Piedmont Circle	Roswell	GA	30080
Georgia US Bank	980 Peachtree St. #3200	Atlanta	GA	30313
Morrison Simpson Travel	550 Lamboll St.	Charleston	SC	29423
Atlanta Management Association	151 Briarcreek Place	Greenville	SC	29606
Muhler Industrial	110 Harvard Road, #15	Charleston	SC	29423
Rosedale Wireless	5 Etiwan Ave., #200	Charleston	SC	29412
Greenville Accounting Partners	1631 Market St., #1520	Charleston	SC	29409
Western Bank of South Carolina	98 Montagu St.	Charleston	SC	29413
Synergy Plastics	103 Foxcroft Road	Charleston	SC	29423
Wycker Global Energy	642 Westchase Dr., #100	Charleston	SC	29413
Byellis Pharmaceuticals	9 Century Drive, #218	Greenville	SC	29604
Watson Medical Technologies Corp.	9822 Royal Palm Road	Charleston	SC	29412

Page 1

Figure 7.51

(Project 7D–Zip Code continues on the next page)

(Project 7D–Zip Code continued)

1. Locate the file **7D_Update_Zip_Code** from your student files, and copy and paste the file to the Chapter 7 folder you created. Remove the Read-only property from the file and rename the file **7D_Update_Zip Code_Firstname_Lastname** Start Access and open the database you just renamed.

2. On the Objects bar, click **Queries**, and to the right, double-click the command icon **Create query in Design view**. Add the **Candidates** table to the query, and then close the **Show Table** dialog box.

3. From the **Candidates** field list, double-click the **Postal Code** field to add it to the design grid.

4. On the Query Design toolbar, click the **Query Type button arrow**, and then from the displayed list, click **Update Query**.

5. In the **Criteria** row, under **Postal Code**, type **30301** and then in the **Update To** row in the same column type **30103** This will update any Postal Codes that are currently listed as 30301 to 30103, correcting errors that were made during data entry.

6. **Run** the query, and when the message indicates that you are about to update 2 rows, click **Yes**.

7. Close the query window without saving changes. On the Objects bar, click **Tables**, and then right-click the **Candidates** table. Click **Rename**, and then name the table **Candidates Firstname Lastname** Open the renamed table in **Datasheet view**. Select the first three columns of the table, display the **Format** menu, and then click **Hide Columns**. Use the same process to also hide the **Phone column**. From the **File** menu, click **Page Setup**. Click the **Page tab**, and under **Orientation**, click the **Landscape** option button. Click **OK**, and then on the Standard toolbar, click the **Print** button to print the table. Close the table and save the changes to the layout.

8. Rename the Employers table as **Employers Firstname Lastname** Using the steps above as your guide, update the **Postal Code** on the **Employers table** in the same manner, except that when preparing to print, hide the **Employer ID, Contact, Contact Title, Phone, and Fee Paid columns**.

End You have completed Project 7D ——————————————

Project 7E—Industry Fee

Objective: *Create a Crosstab Report.*

In the following Skill Assessment, you will create a crosstab query to show the fee collected from companies based on the industry type. Then you will create a crosstab report based on the query you created. Your completed report will look similar to Figure 7.52. You will rename and save your database as *7E_Industry_Fee_Firstname_Lastname*.

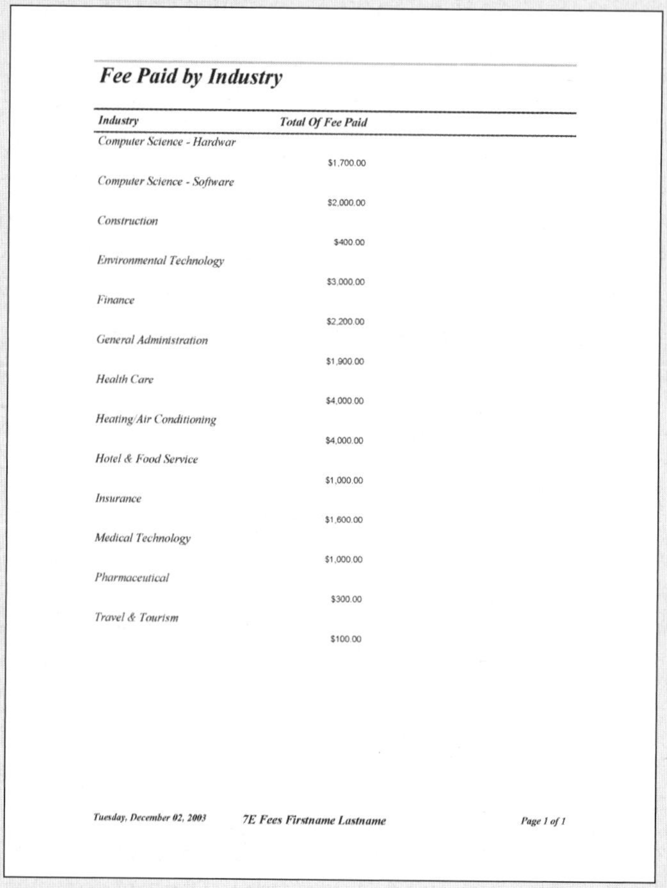

Fee Paid by Industry

Industry	Total Of Fee Paid
Computer Science - Hardwar	$1,700.00
Computer Science - Software	$2,000.00
Construction	$400.00
Environmental Technology	$3,000.00
Finance	$2,200.00
General Administration	$1,900.00
Health Care	$4,000.00
Heating/Air Conditioning	$4,000.00
Hotel & Food Service	$1,000.00
Insurance	$1,600.00
Medical Technology	$1,000.00
Pharmaceutical	$300.00
Travel & Tourism	$100.00

Tuesday, December 02, 2003   7E Fees Firstname Lastname   Page 1 of 1

Figure 7.52

1. Locate the file **7E_Industry_Fee** from your student files, and copy and paste the file to the Chapter 7 folder you created. Remove the Read-only property from the file and rename the file as **7E_Industry_Fee_Firstname_Lastname** Start Access and open the database you just renamed.

2. On the Objects bar, click **Queries**. On the Database window toolbar, click the **New** button, and then click **Crosstab Query Wizard**. Click **OK**.

(Project 7E–Industry Fee continues on the next page)

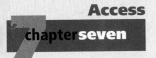
(Project 7E–Industry Fee continued)

3. Under **View**, click the **Queries** option button. In the white area, be sure that **Query: Job Openings by Employer** is selected, and then click **Next**.

4. Select **Industry** as the field value to use as the row heading, and move it the **Selected Fields** column. Click **Next**.

5. Select **Employer Name** as the field value to use as the column heading, and then click **Next**.

6. Select **Fee Paid** as the number to be calculated, and **Sum** as the calculation to perform. Click **Next**.

7. As the query name, type **Fee Paid by Industry Crosstab 7E Firstname Lastname** Be sure that the **View the query** option button is selected. Click **Finish**.

8. Examine and then **close** the Query. On the Objects bar, click **Reports**, and then on the Database window toolbar, click the **New** button. In the **New Report** dialog box, click **Report Wizard**. At the bottom of the dialog box, click the **Choose the table or query where the object's data comes from arrow**, and from the displayed list click your **Fee Paid by Industry_Crosstab 7E** query. Click **OK**.

9. Move **Industry** and **Total Of Fee Paid** to the **Selected Fields** list. Click **Next**.

10. For grouping levels, click the **Industry** field, and then click the **One Field** button. Click **Next**. To the right of the **1** box, be sure that **Ascending** displays. Click **Next**.

11. Leave the default setting for **Layout** as **Stepped** and the **Orientation** as **Portrait**. Click **Next**. Be sure the style is **Corporate** and click **Next**. Name the report **Fee Paid by Industry** Click **Finish**.

12. Switch to **Design view**. In the **Page Footer**, select the control on the left, and drag its right center sizing handle to **1.75 inches on the horizontal ruler**. Select the control on the right, and drag its left center sizing handle to **4.5 inches on the horizontal ruler**. On the Toolbox toolbar, click the **Label** button. Position your pointer even with the upper edge of the other controls and at **2 inches on the horizontal ruler**, and drag down about one quarter inch and to the right to **4.25 inches on the horizontal ruler**. Type **7E Fees Firstname Lastname** and then click outside to deselect the control. Select the control again and nudge the control as necessary to be in line with the other controls.

13. Switch to **Print preview**, print the report, close the report and save your changes, and close Access.

End You have completed Project 7E

Access
chapter seven

Performance Assessments

Project 7F — Job Openings

Objectives: *Create a Subreport and Create Calculated Fields in a Report.*

In the following Performance Assessment, you will embed a subreport in the Industry table to list the job openings within each industry. You will also calculate the number of job openings for each industry. Your completed report will look similar to Figure 7.53. You will rename and save your database as *7F_Job_Openings_Firstname_Lastname.*

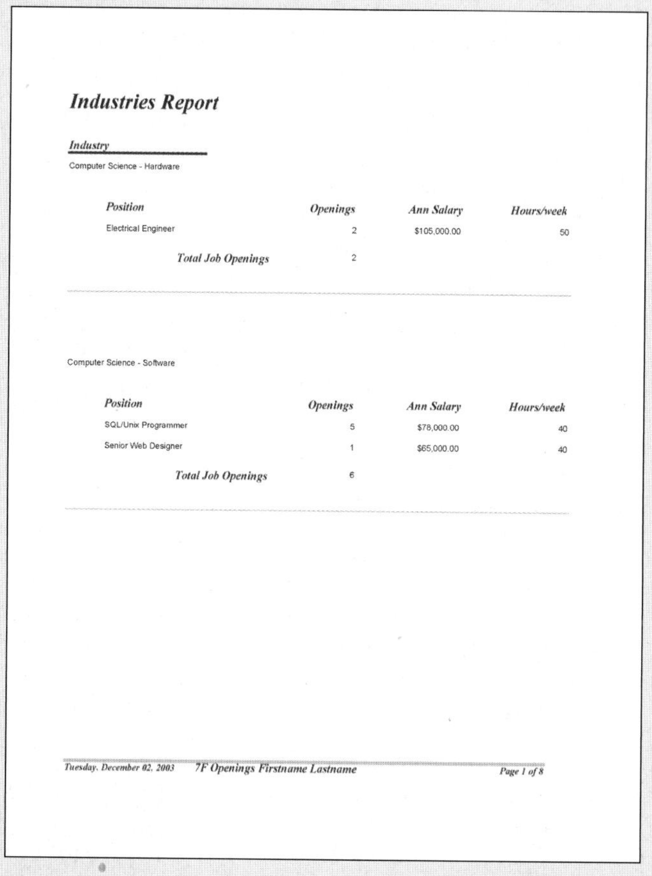

Industries Report

Industry
Computer Science - Hardware

Position	Openings	Ann Salary	Hours/week
Electrical Engineer	2	$105,000.00	50
Total Job Openings	2		

Computer Science - Software

Position	Openings	Ann Salary	Hours/week
SQL/Unix Programmer	5	$78,000.00	40
Senior Web Designer	1	$65,000.00	40
Total Job Openings	6		

Tuesday, December 02, 2003 7F Openings Firstname Lastname Page 1 of 8

Figure 7.53

1. Locate the database file **a07F_Job_Openings** from your student files, and copy and paste the file to the Chapter 7 folder you created. Remove the Read-only property from the file and rename the file as **7F_Job_Openings_Firstname_Lastname** Start Access and open the database you just renamed.
2. On the Objects bar, click **Reports**, and open the **Industries Report**. **Maximize** the report window, and then switch to **Design view**.
3. Expand the **Detail section** downward to slightly below **1 inch on the vertical ruler**. On the Toolbox toolbar, click the **Subform/Subreport** button, and insert the subreport in the **Detail section** at **0.5 inch on the horizontal ruler** and **0.5 inch on the vertical ruler**.

(Project 7F–Job Openings continues on the next page)

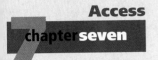

(Project 7F–Job Openings continued)

4. In the first screen of the wizard, use existing tables and queries, and in the second screen, select the **Job Openings Table**. Use **Position**, **# Openings**, **Ann Salary**, and **Hours/week** as the selected fields. Leave the name of the subreport as *Job Openings subreport*.

5. If necessary, maximize the report window. Click outside of the report to cancel any selections, and then select and delete the **Job Openings subreport label**. On the Toolbox toolbar, click the **Line** button, and then draw a line under the subreport at **1.25 inches** on the vertical ruler. As you drag across, hold down ⇧Shift to ensure a straight, not jagged, line. You may not see the line until you release the mouse button. If you are not satisfied with your result, click Undo and begin again.

6. In the **Page Footer** section, select the control on the left, and shorten its right side to **1.75 inches on the horizontal ruler**. Select the control on the right, and shorten its left side to **4.25 inches on the horizontal ruler**. On the Toolbox toolbar, click the **Label** button and create a label in the **Page Footer** section about one-quarter inch tall and from **1.75 inches on the horizontal ruler** to **4.25 inches on the horizontal ruler**. In the label, type **7F Openings Firstname Lastname** Deselect the label, select it again, and then nudge it as necessary to line up with the other controls in the **Page Footer section**. Click the small **Close Window** button, and save changes. Open the **Job Openings subreport** in **Design view**.

7. Expand the **Report Footer** to **0.5 inches on the vertical ruler**. On the Toolbox toolbar, click the **Text Box** button and insert a textbox in the **Report Footer** directly under the *# Openings* text box. Make the new text box the same approximate shape and size as the *# Openings* text box above.

8. Right-click on the **label** control you just inserted, display the **Property sheet**, and on the **Format tab**, change the **Caption** to **Total Job Openings** Close the **Property sheet**, and then drag the left center sizing handle of the label to **1 inch on the horizontal ruler** to accommodate the new caption.

9. Right-click on the **unbound control**, display the **Data tab** of the **Property sheet**, click in the **Control Source** box, and then click the **Build** button. In the Expression Builder, type **=sum([# Openings])** and then click **OK**. Close the **Property sheet**.

10. Click the **Close Window** button to close the subreport and save your changes to the design. Open the **Industries Report** in **Print preview**. From the **File** menu, click **Page Setup**, and change the **Left margin** and the **Right margin** to **0.5**.

11. From the **File** menu, click **Print**, and under **Print Range**, print only **page 1** of the report.

12. Close the report. Close the database, and then close Access.

 End You have completed Project 7F

Project 7G—Experienced Candidates

Objectives: *Create a Delete Query and Create Action Queries.*

In the following Performance Assessment, you will create a table using the Make-Table Query, and then use a Delete Query to remove unneeded records. Your completed table will look similar to Figure 7.54. You will rename and save your database as *7G_Experienced_Candidates_Firstname_Lastname*.

Title	First Name	Last Name	Address Line 1	Address Line 2	City	State	Postal Code	Phone
Ms.	Samantha	Quick	124 Whitworth	#352	Atlanta	GA	30301	404-555-0022
Mr.	Walter	Perrie	2495 Sunset Dr		Conyers	GA	30012	678-555-0186
Ms.	Kelley	Bondurant	179 Auburn Co		Cartersville	GA	30120	678-555-0066
Mr.	Taylor	Dunnahoo	189 Ventura St		Atlanta	GA	30330	770-555-0190
Ms.	Lenesha	Barnett	2361 Bluebird	#8	Smyrna	GA	30081	706-555-0183
Mr.	Mauro	Calva	82 E. Ramona		Atlanta	GA	30327	404-555-0096
Mr.	David	Feingold	1821 Alturas St	#1442	Atlanta	GA	30301	404-555-0101
Mr.	Byeong	Chang	2221 Flowers		Roswell	GA	30077	770-555-0066
Ms.	Samira	Ahmed	3418 Longview	#320	Marietta	GA	30063	770-555-0002
Ms.	Jessica	Pyun	1255 Miravista		Kennesaw	GA	30144	770-555-0003

Candidates with Experience 7G Firstname Lastname — 12/2/2003 — Page 1

Figure 7.54

1. Locate the database file **a07G_Experienced_Candidates** from your student files, and copy and paste the file to the Chapter 7 folder you created. Remove the Read-only property from the file and rename the file as **7G_Experienced_Candidates_Firstname_Lastname** Start Access and open the database you just renamed.

2. On the Objects bar, click **Queries**. Double-click the **Create query in Design view** command icon. Add the **Candidates** table to the table area, and close the dialog box.

3. In the field list, beginning with the first field, add all of the fields to the design grid.

4. On the Query Design toolbar, click the **Query Type button arrow**, and then click **Make-Table Query**. Name the new table **Candidates with Experience 7G Firstname Lastname Run** the query. You will add 14 records to the new table.

(Project 7G–Experienced Candidates continues on the next page)

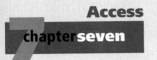
(Project 7G–Experienced Candidates continued)

5. **Close** the query and save it as **Query to Create Candidates Table**

6. To create a table that lists only those candidates with some experience, begin another new query in **Design view**. Add your **Candidates with Experience 7G** table to the table area and close the **Show Table** dialog box. To the design grid, add the fields **Experience?**, **First Name**, and **Last Name**.

7. In the **Criteria** row, under **Experience?** type **No**

8. **Run** the query. Four records will satisfy the criteria. These are the records to delete, because these candidates have no experience. In the Experience column, notice that the records indicate *0*. In Access, *0* means *no* or *false*.

9. Switch to **Design view** and change the **Query Type** to **Delete Query**. **Run** the query and confirm that you will delete 4 records from the table. **Close** the query without saving.

10. On the Objects bar, click **Tables**, and then open your **Candidates with Experience 7G** table in **Datasheet view**. You will see 10 records in your table. Select and hide the first three columns, and then hide the **College** column. From the **File** menu, click **Page Setup**, and change the **Orientation** to **Landscape**. On the **File** menu, click **Print**.

11. Close the table and save your changes. Close the database, and then close Access.

 You have completed Project 7G

Project 7H—Employers by City

Objective: *Create a Parameter Query.*

In the following Performance Assessment, you will create a parameter query for the Employers table for Michael Augustino, the Executive Director of the Greater Atlanta Job Fair. Mr. Augustino wants to be able to type in a city name and have all the employers located in the city display. Your completed query will look similar to Figure 7.55. You will rename and save your database as *7H_EmployersByCity_Firstname_Lastname*.

1. Locate the database file **a07H_EmployersByCity** from your student files, and copy and paste the file to the Chapter 7 folder you created. Remove the Read-only property from the file and rename the file as **7H_EmployersByCity_Firstname_Lastname** Start Access and open the database you just renamed.

(Project 7H–Employers by City continues on the next page)

(Project 7H–Employers by City continued)

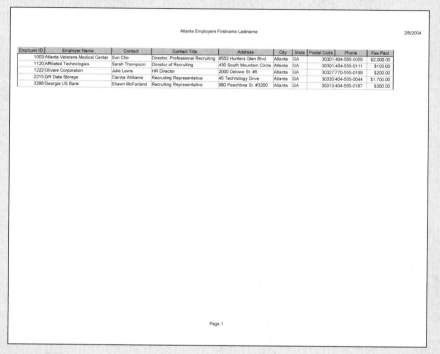

Figure 7.55

2. On the Objects bar, click **Queries**, and then double-click the command icon **Create query in Design view**. Add the **Employers** table to the query.

3. Add all of the fields from the **Employers** table to the design grid.

4. In the **Criteria** row, in the **City** column, type **[Enter the name of the City]**

5. **Run** the query and at the prompt type **Atlanta** as the city. In the resulting query, select all the columns, display the **Format** menu, and then change the **Font Size** to **8**. With the columns still selected, apply **Best Fit**. From the **File** menu, click **Save As**, and save the query as **Atlanta Employers Firstname Lastname** From the **File** menu, click **Page Setup**, and change the **Page Orientation** to **Landscape**. Change the **Left margin** and the **Right margin** to **0.25**. From the **File** menu, click **Print**, and click **OK**.

6. Close the query, close the database, and then close Access.

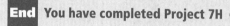
End You have completed Project 7H

Mastery Assessments

Project 7I—Job Fair Sections

Objectives: *Create a Subreport and Create Calculated Fields in a Report.*

The exhibit space at each of the Job Fairs is divided into sections, and each employer is assigned to a specific section. In the following Mastery Assessment, you will embed a subreport in the Job Fair Sections Report to list the employers and the sections they will occupy at the Job Fair. Your completed report will look similar to Figure 7.56. You will rename and save your database as *7I_JobFair_Sections_Firstname_Lastname*.

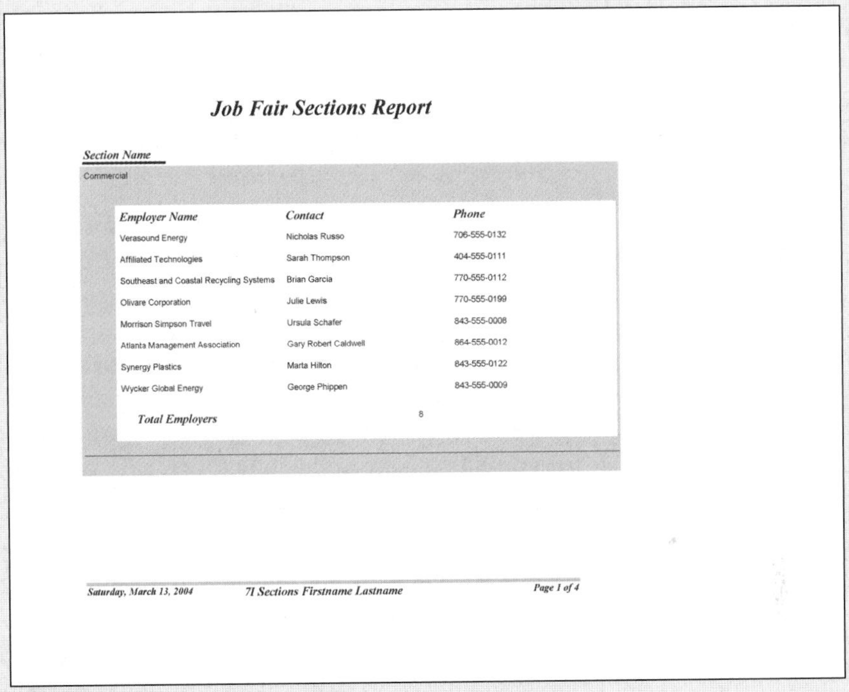

Job Fair Sections Report

Section Name
Commercial

Employer Name	*Contact*	*Phone*
Verasound Energy	Nicholas Russo	706-555-0132
Affiliated Technologies	Sarah Thompson	404-555-0111
Southeast and Coastal Recycling Systems	Brian Garcia	770-555-0112
Olivare Corporation	Julie Lewis	770-555-0199
Morrison Simpson Travel	Ursula Schafer	843-555-0008
Atlanta Management Association	Gary Robert Caldwell	864-555-0012
Synergy Plastics	Marta Hilton	843-555-0122
Wycker Global Energy	George Phippen	843-555-0009
Total Employers	8	

Saturday, March 13, 2004 *7I Sections Firstname Lastname* *Page 1 of 4*

Figure 7.56

1. Locate the file **a07I_JobFair_Sections** from your student files, and copy and paste the file to the Chapter 7 folder you created. Remove the Read-only property from the file and rename the file as **7I_JobFair_Sections_Firstname_Lastname** Start Access and open the database you just renamed.

2. On the Objects bar, click **Reports**, and then open the **Job Fair Sections Report** in **Design view**. Maximize the window.

3. Expand the **Detail section** by dragging its lower edge to slightly below **1 inch on the vertical ruler**. Insert a **Subreport** in the **Detail section** at approximately **0.5 inch on the horizontal and vertical ruler**. Use existing tables, and then select the **Employers** table and use **Employer Name**, **Contact**, **Contact Title**, and **Phone** fields as the **Selected Fields**.

(Project 7I–Job Fair Sections continues on the next page)

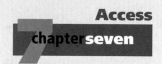
(Project 7I–Job Fair Sections continued)

4. Save the Subreport as **Employers Section Subreport**

5. Maximize the window, and then click in the gray area to cancel all selections. Then select and delete the **Employers Section Subreport label**. At **1.25 inches on the vertical ruler**, hold down Shift and draw a line across the report. In the **Detail section**, display the **Fill/Back Color** palette, and the fifth row, click the fourth color—**light green**.

6. In the **Page Footer** section, shorten the right side of the control on the left to **2 inches on the horizontal ruler**, and shorten the left side of the control on the right to **5 inches on the horizontal ruler**. Insert a new label control between the two shortened controls, and type **7I Sections Firstname Lastname** Nudge as necessary to align the new label.

7. Close the report, save the changes and open the **Employers Section Subreport** in **Design view**.

8. Expand the **Report Footer** to **0.5 inch on the vertical ruler**. In the **Report Footer** area, insert a **Text Box** at approximately **2 inches on the horizontal ruler** extending to **4 inches on the horizontal ruler**. Right-click the **label control**, display the **Property sheet**, and on the **Format tab**, change the **Caption** to **Total Employers** Select the **label control** and drag the left resizing handle to **0.5 inches** on the **horizontal ruler**. Right-click the **unbound control**, display the **Property sheet**, click the **Data tab**, and in the **Control Source** box, click the **Build** button. Use the count function to calculate the total number of Employers. Hint: =count([Employer Name])

9. Close the subreport and save the changes. Open the **Job Fair Sections Report** in Print preview. From the **File** menu, click **Page Setup**, and change the **Page Orientation** to **Landscape**. Use the page navigation buttons at the lower left of the screen to scroll through the pages of the report, and notice the names of each of the sections. From the **File** menu, click **Print**, and under **Print Range**, print from page **1** to **1** to print only the first page of the report.

10. Close the report, close the database, and then close Access.

End You have completed Project 7I

Project 7J — Exclusive Job Listings

Objective: *Create Action Queries.*

In the following Mastery Assessment, you will create a table using a Make-Table Query, and then you will add additional records using an Append Query. Your completed table will look similar to Figure 7.57. You will rename and save your database as *7J_Exclusive_JobListings_ Firstname_Lastname.*

Employer Name	Industry	Position	# Openings	Ann Salary	City	State
Thinkanswer Technologies	Computer Science - Software	SQL/Unix Programmer	5	$78,000.00	Conyers	GA
Atlanta Insurance Brokers	Insurance	Actuary – Entry Level	5	$43,000.00	Roswell	GA
Atlanta Veterans Medical Center	Health Care	Nursing Supervisor	10	$62,000.00	Atlanta	GA
A&G Consulting	Hotel & Food Service	Gift Shop Manager	5	$35,000.00	Roswell	GA
Derrickson Brothers Construction	Construction	Cabinetmaker/Carpenter	10	$30,000.00	Marietta	GA
Derrickson Brothers Construction	Construction	Civil Engineering Supervisor	5	$80,000.00	Marietta	GA
A&G Consulting	General Administration	Senior Accounting Clerk	15	$35,000.00	Roswell	GA
A&G Consulting	General Administration	Executive Assistant	5	$40,000.00	Roswell	GA
DYCarlson Corp.	Pharmaceutical	Biostatistician – Entry Level	5	$50,000.00	Smyrna	GA
Greenville Accounting Partners	Finance	Accountant – Entry Level	15	$36,000.00	Charleston	SC
Wisener Heating & Air Condtioning	Heating/Air Conditioning	Electrician – Entry Level	5	$36,000.00	Cartersville	GA
Wisener Heating & Air Condtioning	Heating/Air Conditioning	Estimating Manager	6	$60,000.00	Cartersville	GA
Lauren Newberry Associates	Travel & Tourism	Travel Clerk	10	$28,000.00	Greenville	SC
Verasound Energy	Environmental Technology	Petroleum Engineer – Mid Level	5	$70,000.00	Smyrna	GA
Thinkanswer Technologies	Computer Science - Software	SQL/Unix Programmer	5	$78,000.00	Conyers	GA
GR Data Storage	Computer Science - Hardware	Electrical Engineer	2	$105,000.00	Atlanta	GA
Atlanta Insurance Brokers	Insurance	Actuary – Senior	3	$98,000.00	Roswell	GA
Watson Medical Technologies Corp.	Medical Technology	Nuclear Medicine Director	1	$75,000.00	Charleston	SC
Atlanta Veterans Medical Center	Health Care	Assistant Director of Pharmacy	3	$95,000.00	Atlanta	GA
Derrickson Brothers Construction	Construction	Civil Engineering Supervisor	5	$80,000.00	Marietta	GA

7J Exclusive Jobs Firstname Lastname — 3/13/2004 — Page 1

Figure 7.57

1. Locate the database file **a07J_Exclusive_JobListings** from your student files, and copy and paste the file to the Chapter 7 folder you created. Remove the Read-only property from the file and rename the file as **7J_Exclusive_JobListings_Firstname_Lastname** Start Access and open the database you just renamed.

2. On the Objects bar, click **Queries**, and then double-click the command icon **Create query in Design view**. In the **Show Table** dialog box, click the **Queries tab**, and then add the **Job Openings by Employer** query to the table area.

3. Add all the fields to the design grid. In the **Criteria** row, in the **# Openings** column, type >=5

(Project 7J–Exclusive Job Listings continues on the next page)

(Project 7J–Exclusive Job Listings continued)

4. Change the type of query to a **Make-Table Query**. Name the table 7J Exclusive Jobs Firstname Lastname

5. **Run** the query, and when the message indicates that 14 row(s) will be added into a new table, click **Yes**.

6. Close the query, and save the query as **Job Listings** On the Objects bar, click **Tables**, and open your **7J Exclusive Jobs** table to view the 14 records. These employers all have 5 or more job openings. Close the table.

7. On the Objects bar, click **Queries**. Point to the **Job Listings** query and right-click. From the displayed shortcut menu, select **Design View**.

8. Delete >=5 from the **# Openings** criteria. In the **Criteria** row, in the **Ann Salary** column, type >=75000 Change the query type to **Append Query**. In the Append dialog box, click **OK**.

9. **Run** the Query. Click **Yes** to append 6 rows to the table.

10. Close the query and save the changes. Open your **7J Exclusive Jobs** table and notice that six records have been appended (added) to the end of the table. These records are for employers who have job openings with annual salaries equal to or greater than $75,000. Select all of the columns and apply **Best Fit**. Hide the **Postal Code**, **Phone**, and **Fee Paid** columns. On the **File** menu, click **Page Setup**, and change the **Page Orientation** to **Landscape**. Change the **Left** and **Right** margins to **0.75**. On the **File** menu, click **Print**. Close your table and save the changes. Close the database, and close Access.

End You have completed Project 7J ────────────────────

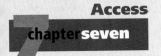

Problem Solving

Project 7K — Crosstab Choice

Objective: *Create a Crosstab Report.*

In the following Problem Solving exercise, you will create a crosstab query, and then create a new crosstab report for the query.

1. Locate the database file **a07K_CrosstabChoice** from your student files, and copy and paste the file to the Chapter 7 folder you created. Remove the Read-only property from the file and rename the file as **7K_CrosstabChoice_Firstname_Lastname** Start Access and open the database you just renamed.

2. Open the **Job Openings by Employer** query and examine all of the information in the query. Select three fields that would be useful to compare data in a crosstab query.

3. Create the crosstab query based on the fields you selected in the previous step. Be sure the information is displayed in an organized manner. Close the crosstab query you created.

4. Create a new report using the wizard to display the crosstab query in an attractive format.

5. Add your name in the page footer, and print the report.

6. Close the report, saving any changes. Close the database, and then close Access.

 You have completed Project 7K

Project 7L — Fee by Section

Objective: *Create a Subreport.*

In the following Problem Solving exercise, you will create a report with an embedded subreport.

1. Locate the file **a07L_FeeBySection** from your student files, and copy and paste the file to the Chapter 7 folder you created. Remove the Read-only property from the file and rename the file as **7L_FeeBySection_Firstname_Lastname** Start Access and open the database you just renamed.

2. Open the **Job Fair Sections** report and add a subreport based on the **Employers** table. Add the **Employer Name** and **Fee Paid** fields to the subreport.

3. Create a calculated field to sum the **Fees by Section** and also a calculated field to calculate the total amount of fees paid.

4. Add your name in the page footer. Print the report and close the report, saving any changes. Close the database, and then close Access.

 You have completed Project 7L

On the Internet

Getting More Information About Special Queries

The Microsoft Web page contains a variety of information about using special queries in Access. Got to the Microsoft site at www.microsoft.com and click Search. Search for Access queries and examine the information on queries. Print any information that is of interest to you.

GO! with Help

SQL-Specific Queries

In this chapter you viewed queries in SQL, and learned that as you create your queries in design view, Access is working in the background to create SQL statements to run your query. There are some query types, called **SQL-specific queries**, that cannot be created in the design grid; they must be created directly in SQL view. In this Help activity, you will use Help to learn about the four types of queries that are SQL-specific.

1. Start Access. In the *Type a question for help* box, type **SQL queries** and press Enter.

2. In the **Search Results** task pane, click **About SQL queries (MDB)**.

3. At the bottom of the Help window, click the link **SQL-specific queries**. Then click the link for each of the four types of SQL-specific queries—**union**, **pass-through**, **data-definition**, and **subquery**. Read the information for each of the query types.

4. Print the Help information if you want to keep a copy of it. Close the **Help** window, and then close Access.

8 chaptereight

Integrating Access with Other Office Applications

In this chapter, you will: complete these projects **and** practice these skills.

Project 8A **Using Access with Other Office Applications**	**Objectives** • Import Data from a Word Table • Use Mail Merge to Integrate Access and Word • Import from Excel • Add Hyperlinks to Word and Excel Files

Project 8B **Linking and Embedding Objects in Access**	**Objectives** • Link Database Objects to Office Files • Add a Chart to a Form • Add a Chart to a Report

University Medical Center

The University Medical Center (UMC) is a premier patient-care and research institution serving the metropolitan area of Orange Beach, Florida. UMC enhances the health and well being of the community through collaborative research and innovations in patient care, medications, and procedures. The center is particularly renowned for its state-of-the-art cancer diagnosis and treatment program and for its South-central Florida Cardiovascular Center. The pediatrics wing specializes in the care of high-risk newborns.

© Photosphere Images Ltd.

Integrating Access with Other Office Applications

When working with Access, information you want to use may be located in a file developed in another application. Fortunately, Access can import or link to the data in other applications so that you do not have to retype the data into your database. You can import data from a large variety of file formats. In this chapter, you will import data from both Microsoft Word and Microsoft Excel.

Rather than importing information from other applications into your database, you may choose to link your database to the original source so that you can view useful information. In this chapter, you will also link to information from an external source.

Project 8A **Medical Center**

For its popular program of public seminars, the University Medical Center Office of Public Affairs maintains a list of speakers, which is formatted as a Microsoft Word document. They also use Microsoft Excel to track the marketing expenses for the seminars. Finally, they have an Access database with a table containing the scheduled seminars and another table with the names and addresses of media contacts. Mike Martinez, the Director of Public Affairs, thinks it would be useful to bring the information from the Word and Excel files into the Access database.

In Activities 8.1 through 8.5, you will import and link information into an Access database from Word and Excel documents. You will use the information in the Media Contacts table to create a mail merge document in Microsoft Word. You will also create hyperlinks from a form in your database to Word and Excel files. You will save your database as *8A_Medical_Center_Firstname_Lastname*.

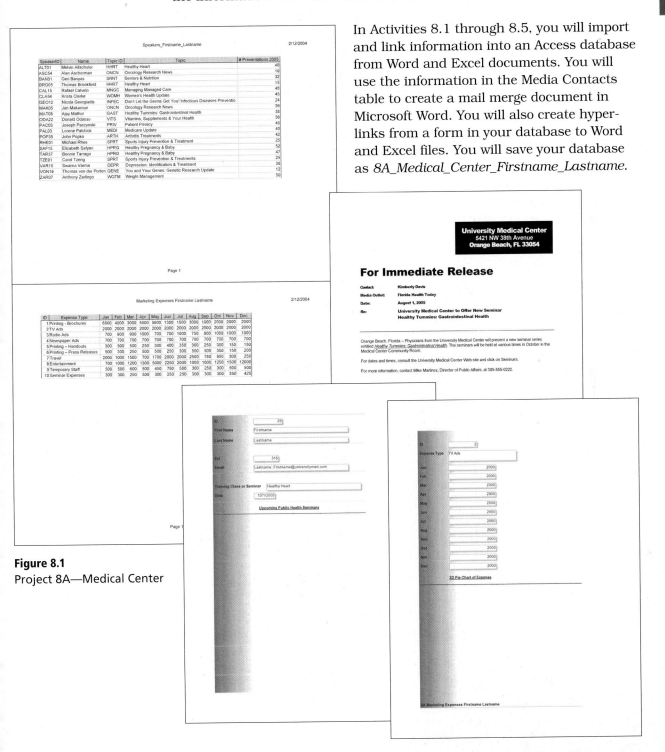

Figure 8.1
Project 8A—Medical Center

Objective 1
Import Data from a Word Table

When you create a database, you can type the records directly into a table. You can also **import** data from a variety of sources. To import means to copy data from a text file like Microsoft Word, a spreadsheet file like Microsoft Excel, or a database table from another Access database, and then insert it into an Access table. For example, the University Medical Center Office of Public Affairs wants to import the information regarding the seminar speakers into their Access database. Currently this information is in a Microsoft Word table.

Activity 8.1 Importing Data from a Word Table

In this activity, you will import information from a Word table and create a new table, named *Speakers*, in your database.

1 Start Microsoft Word. On the Standard toolbar, click **Open**, and from the student files that accompany this textbook, locate and open the Microsoft Word file **a08A_Speakers_Table**.

2 If necessary, click anywhere inside the table. On the menu bar, click **Table**, and then point to **Convert** as shown in Figure 8.2. Click **Table to Text**.

To import data from a Word table into an Access table, the data must first be converted to a **delimited text file**, which is a file containing data where individual field values are separated by a character, such as a comma or a tab. When you import this table into Access, you will choose the same delimiter character so that Access can separate the data into fields.

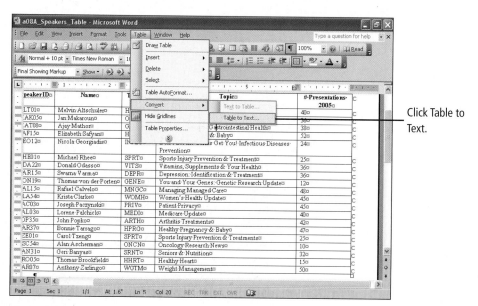

Click Table to Text.

Figure 8.2

3 In the displayed **Convert Table to Text** dialog box, be sure the **Tabs** option button is selected—this is the character you will use to separate the text into fields. Click **OK**. Click anywhere to deselect.

Note — Is the Show/Hide ¶ Button Turned On?

By turning on the Show/Hide ¶ button as shown in Figure 8.3, all of the tabs between the different fields and the extra paragraph mark at the end of the document will be displayed on the screen. If necessary, click the Show/Hide ¶ button to turn it on.

4 Hold down [Ctrl] and press [End] to move to the end of the document. Press [Bksp] once, and then compare your screen with Figure 8.3.

Deleting the extra blank line at the bottom of your file will prevent a blank record from being inserted into your new database table. Notice that Word will flag most proper names as spelling errors because they are not contained within Word's dictionary.

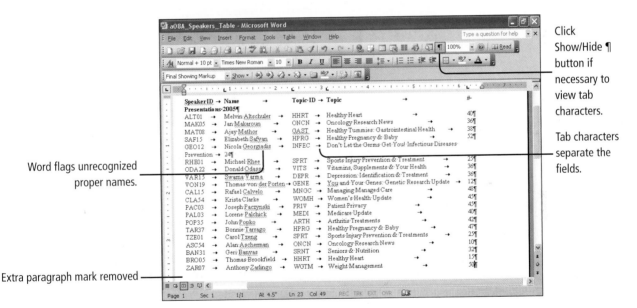

Click Show/Hide ¶ button if necessary to view tab characters.

Tab characters separate the fields.

Word flags unrecognized proper names.

Extra paragraph mark removed

Figure 8.3

5 From the **File** menu, click **Save As**, and then navigate to the location where you are storing your projects for this chapter, creating a new folder for Chapter 8 if you want to do so. At the bottom of the **Save As** dialog box, click the **Save as type arrow**, and from the displayed list, scroll as necessary and click **Plain Text**. In the **File name** box, type **8A_Speakers_Table_Firstname_Lastname** See Figure 8.4.

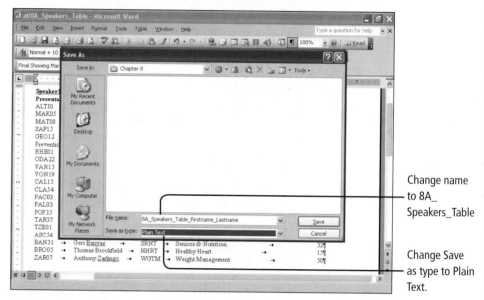

Figure 8.4

6 In the lower right corner of the dialog box, click **Save**. In the displayed **File Conversion** dialog box, accept the default settings and click **OK**. **Close** ☒ Microsoft Word.

7 Using **My Computer**, navigate to the student files that accompany this textbook and locate the Access database **a08A_Medical_Center**. Copy and paste the file to the Chapter 8 folder you created, and rename the file **8A_Medical_Center_Firstname_Lastname** Remove the Read-only property from the file. **Start** Access and open the database you just renamed.

8 On the Objects bar, click **Tables**. On the menu bar, click **File**, point to **Get External Data**, and on the submenu click **Import**. At the bottom of the displayed **Import** dialog box, click the **Files of type arrow**, and then scroll as necessary and click **Text Files**. Use the **Look in arrow** to navigate to your files for this chapter, and then click your **8A_Speakers_Table** text file as shown in Figure 8.5. In the lower right corner, click **Import**.

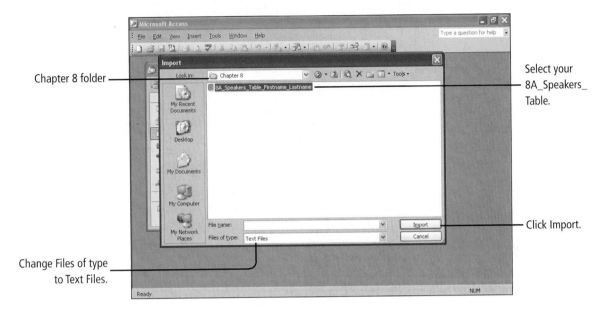

Chapter 8 folder

Select your 8A_Speakers_ Table.

Click Import.

Change Files of type to Text Files.

Figure 8.5

9 In the displayed first screen of the **Import Text Wizard**, be sure the **Delimited** option button is selected, and then click **Next**.

Here you indicate which type of character serves as the delimiter to separate the fields.

10 Under **Choose the delimiter that separates your fields**, be sure the **Tab** option button is selected, and then select the **First Row Contains Field Names** check box as shown in Figure 8.6.

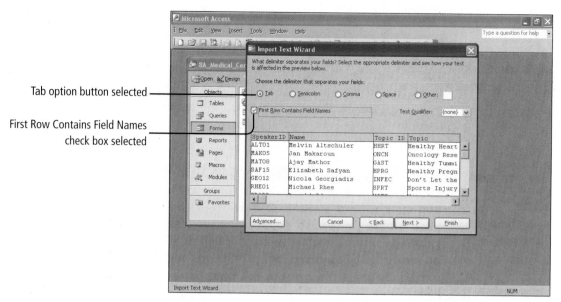

Tab option button selected

First Row Contains Field Names check box selected

Figure 8.6

11 Click **Next**. Here you will indicate where the imported data should be stored—either in a new table or in an existing table. Under **Where would you like to store your data**, be sure the **In a New Table** option button is selected, and then click **Next**.

In this wizard screen, you can specify information about each of the fields you are importing.

More Knowledge — Appending Data in an Existing Table

When importing data into Access, you can also add or update—append—data to the end of an existing table. This process of adding or updating is called *appending*.

12 Under **Field Options**, with **SpeakerID** displayed in the **Field Name** box, click the **Indexed arrow**, and then, as shown in Figure 8.7, click **Yes (No Duplicates)**.

Because the SpeakerID field will be used as the *primary key* in this new table, duplicates should *not* be allowed. Recall that a primary key is the field that uniquely identifies a record in a table.

Yes (No Duplicates) selected ——

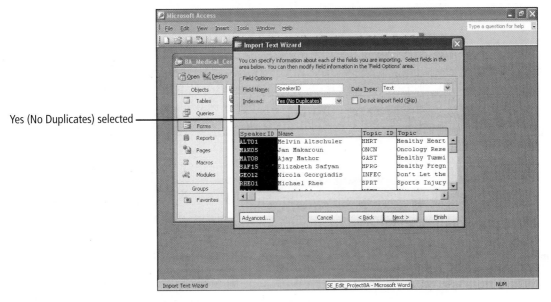

Figure 8.7

13 Click **Next**. Here you will define the field that will serve as the primary key. Click the **Choose my own primary key** option button and be sure that **SpeakerID** displays in the box to the right. Click **Next**. Here you name the new table that will be inserted into your database. In the **Import to Table** box, type **Speakers Firstname Lastname** and click **Finish**. If an error message displays (see the following Alert), click **OK**. In the message indicating that Access has finished importing, click **OK**.

The new table is added to your database.

Does an Error Message Display When You Click Finish?

If, when saving your Word document as a text file, you do not delete any extra blank lines at the end, one or more blank records will be inserted into your table and an error message displays after you click Finish. If you see the error message, click OK, and then click OK again. Then, open the new table, delete any empty records, display the table in Design view, and then set the appropriate field as the primary key.

14 Open your **Speakers** table in **Datasheet view**. In the column heading area, drag to select all of the columns, display the **Format** menu, and then click **Column Width**. In the **Column Width** dialog box, click the **Best Fit** button to resize all the columns to fit the data. Click anywhere to deselect, and then compare your completed table with Figure 8.8.

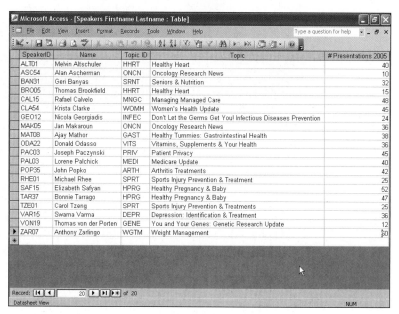

Figure 8.8

15 Display the **File** menu, click **Page Setup**, and then on the **Page tab**, change the **Orientation** to **Landscape**. Click **OK**. On the Database toolbar, click the **Print** button ⎙. **Close** ☒ your table and save the changes. Leave the database open for the next activity.

Objective 2
Use Mail Merge to Integrate Access and Word

Using Word's **mail merge** feature, letters or memos are created by combining (merging) two documents—a **main document** and a **data source**. The main document contains the text of the letter or memo. The data source—an Access table—contains the names and addresses of the individuals to whom the letter, memo, or other document is being sent.

The easiest way to perform a mail merge is to use the Mail Merge Wizard. Recall that a wizard asks you questions and, based on your answers, walks you step by step through a process.

Activity 8.2 Merging an Access Table with a Word Document

In this activity, you will send a Press Release memo to all the media contacts in your database announcing a new seminar that the Medical Center is conducting. You will create the memos by merging the individual names and addresses in the Media Contacts table with a memo created in Microsoft Word.

1 In the Database window, click the **Media Contacts** table to select it. On the Database toolbar, click the **OfficeLinks button arrow** 🔛 ▾, and from the displayed list, click **Merge It with Microsoft Office Word**.

2 In this first screen of the **Microsoft Word Mail Merge Wizard**, click the **Link your data to an existing Microsoft Word document** option button. Click **OK**. In the displayed dialog box, navigate to the student files that accompany this textbook, click the **a08A_Press_Release** Word document, and then click **Open**.

Microsoft Word opens with the memo on the left and the Mail Merge task pane on the right.

3 On the menu bar, click **View**, and then click **Header and Footer**. In the displayed Header and Footer toolbar, click the **Switch Between Header and Footer** button 🔁. As shown in Figure 8.9, with your insertion point positioned in the **Footer** box, type **8A Press Release Memo Firstname Lastname**

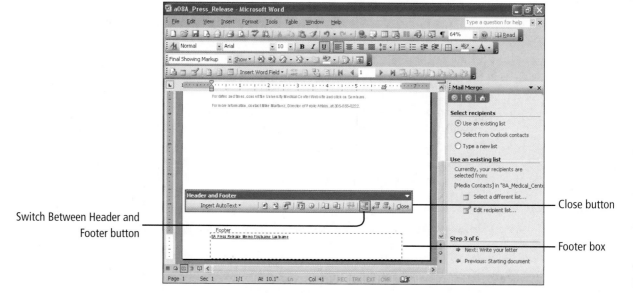

Switch Between Header and Footer button

Close button

Footer box

Figure 8.9

4 In the Header and Footer toolbar, click the **Close** button `Close`.

5 At the top of the **Mail Merge** task pane, under **Select recipients**, be sure the **Use an existing list** option button is selected. Compare your screen with Figure 8.10.

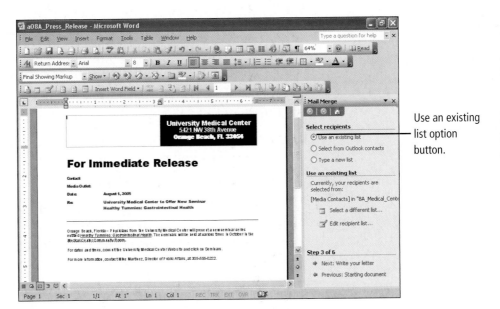

Use an existing list option button.

Figure 8.10

6 At the bottom of the task pane, click **Next: Write your letter**. In the displayed Press Release memo, click to move the insertion point to the right of the word *Contact:* and press Tab. In the **Mail Merge** task pane, click the **More items** button. In the displayed **Insert Merge Field** dialog box, under **Fields**, click **Contact**, and then click the **Insert** button. See Figure 8.11.

<<*Contact*>> displays. By merging the Word document with your Media Contacts table in Access, the field names in the table become available as merge fields in this dialog box.

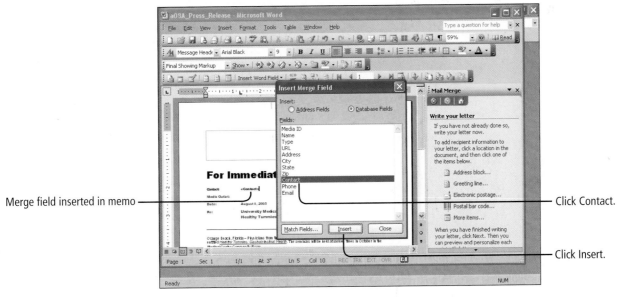

Merge field inserted in memo

Click Contact.

Click Insert.

Figure 8.11

7 At the bottom of the **Insert Merge Field** dialog box, click the **Close** button. In the memo, click to the right of *Media Outlet:* and press

[Tab]. On the task pane, click the **More items** button 🔲, click **Name**, click **Insert**, and then click **Close**.

8 At the bottom of the task pane, click **Next: preview your letters**.

9 At the top of the task pane, under **Preview your letters**, click the >> arrows to scroll through and view some of the memos.

You can see that for each record in the table, a memo has been created.

10 At the bottom of the task pane, under **Step 5 of 6**, click **Next: Complete the merge**. In the middle of the task pane, under **Merge**, click **Edit individual letters**. In the **Merge to New Document** dialog box, be sure the **All** option button is selected, and then click **OK**.

11 At the bottom of the Word window, notice that Word created a 20-page document—a one-page memo for each of the 20 media outlets in your Access table. See Figure 8.12.

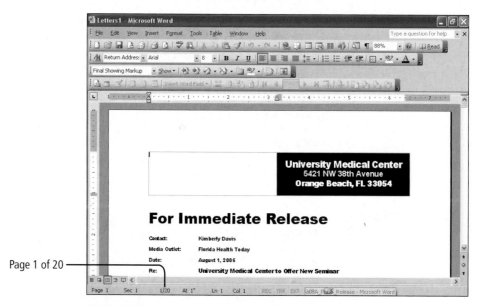

Page 1 of 20 ——

Figure 8.12

12 From the **File** menu, click **Save As**, navigate to the location where you are storing your files for this chapter, and then save the 20-page document as **8A_Press_Release_Memo_Firstname_Lastname**

13 From the **File** menu, click **Print**. Under **Page range**, click the **Pages** option button, and then type **1** as shown in Figure 8.13. Click **OK**. In the upper right corner of your screen, to the right of the *Type a question for help* box, click the small **Close Window** button ☒. Click the **Close Window** button ☒ again, and then click **No**. It is not necessary to save the original document. **Close** ☒ Word. Leave your database open for the next activity.

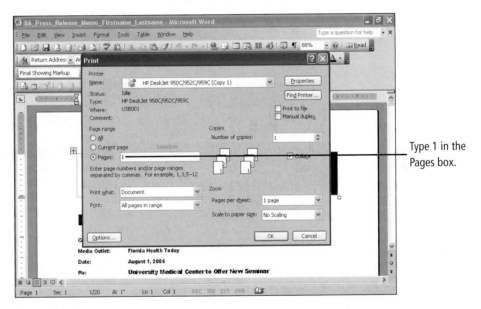

Type 1 in the Pages box.

Figure 8.13

More Knowledge — It's Not Always a "Mail" Merge

Even though the title says mail merge, you can also create form letters, e-mail messages, envelopes, labels, and directories by merging an Access table with Microsoft Word.

Objective 3
Import from Excel

The Office of Public Affairs keeps track of marketing expenses in an Excel worksheet. To use this information in an Access report, you can import the Excel spreadsheet data into your database.

Activity 8.3 Importing from Excel

In this activity, you will import an Excel worksheet containing the marketing expenses for the Office of Public Affairs into your database.

1 Be sure the **Tables** object is selected. From the **File** menu, point to **Get External Data**, and then on the submenu, click **Import**. At the bottom of the dialog box, change the **Files of type** to **Microsoft Excel**, navigate to the textbook's student files, and then select the Excel file **a08A_Marketing_Expenses**. See Figure 8.14.

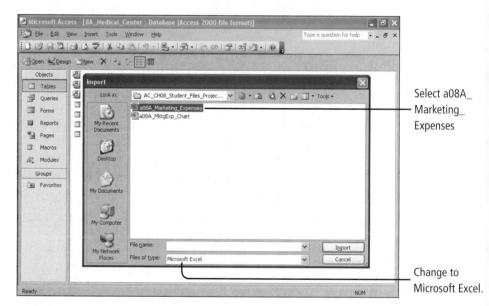

Select a08A_ Marketing_ Expenses

Change to Microsoft Excel.

Figure 8.14

2 In the lower right corner of the dialog box, click **Import**. In the **Import Spreadsheet Wizard**, be sure the **First Row Contains Column Headings** check box is selected, and then click **Next**. Be sure the **In a New Table** option button is selected, and then click **Next**. Click **Next** on this screen to accept the default setting. On the next screen, let Access add the primary key and click **Next**.

3 In the **Import to Table** box, type **Marketing Expenses Firstname Lastname** and click **Finish**. Click **OK** to acknowledge the *Finished importing* message.

4 Open your **Marketing Expenses** table in **Datasheet view**. Select all of the columns and apply **Best Fit**—either from the dialog box or by double-clicking on one of the selected column boundaries. Click anywhere in the datasheet to deselect.

5 From the **File** menu, click **Page Setup**, and on the **Page tab**, change the **Orientation** to **Landscape**. Click **OK**. On the Database toolbar, click the **Print** button 🖨. Close your table and save the changes.

Objective 4
Add Hyperlinks to Word and Excel Files

In the previous activities, you imported data from Word and Excel into your database. Sometimes you simply want to *view* a Word file or an Excel file while working in Access. For that purpose, you can create a hyperlink to a Word document or an Excel worksheet. A **hyperlink** is a pointer from one object to another. A hyperlink consists of colored or underlined text or a graphic that you click to go to a file, a location in a file, or a Web page. Hyperlinks provide a useful and convenient way to navigate between objects. When you are done viewing the information, you can close the file and return to your database.

Activity 8.4 Adding Hyperlinks from a Form to a Word Document

Employees at the Medical Center are eligible to attend the same seminars that are offered to the public. In this activity, you will enroll employees in seminars using an Access form. You will also create a hyperlink from the form to a Microsoft Word document that lists details about the seminars.

1 In the upper right corner of your screen, on the dark blue title bar, click the **Minimize** button 🗕 to minimize the Access application to a button on your taskbar.

2 Use **My Computer** to navigate to the student files that accompany this textbook. Locate the Microsoft Word file **a08A_Seminars**, and then copy and paste the file to the folder where you are saving your projects for this chapter. Remove the Read-only property from the file and then rename the file **8A_Seminars_Firstname_Lastname** Double-click your **8A_Seminars** document to open it in Word, and take a moment to examine the list of seminars.

3 Select the title text *Upcoming Public Health Seminars* by triple-clicking anywhere in the title or by dragging over the title, and then on the Standard toolbar, click the **Copy** button 📋. See Figure 8.15 and note that your screen may display the nonprinting Word characters (tabs, paragraph marks, and so forth) if your Word software is set to do so.

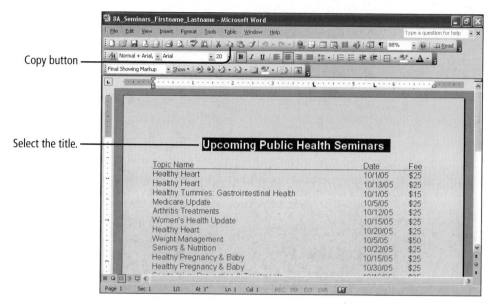

Copy button

Select the title.

Figure 8.15

4 In the upper right corner of the screen, in the dark blue title bar, click the **Minimize** button ▬ to minimize the Word application to a button on your taskbar.

5 On the taskbar, click the button representing your database to maximize it. On the Objects bar, click **Forms**, and then open the **Employee Training and Seminar Enrollments** form. Using the navigation arrows at the bottom of the form, scroll through the 27 records to familiarize yourself with the data.

The table to which this form is bound lists the information for employees who are enrolled in upcoming training courses. The form is also used to enroll employees in seminars.

6 Switch to **Design view** and **Maximize** ▣ the form on your screen. From the **Edit** menu, click **Paste as Hyperlink**.

The hyperlink is pasted into the form as a control, but it is pasted into the upper left corner, covering existing form controls.

7 Point to the pasted hyperlink until the Hand pointer 🖑 displays, and then drag to position the left edge at **1.5 inches on the horizontal ruler** and the bottom edge at **3 inches on the vertical ruler**. Compare your screen with Figure 8.16.

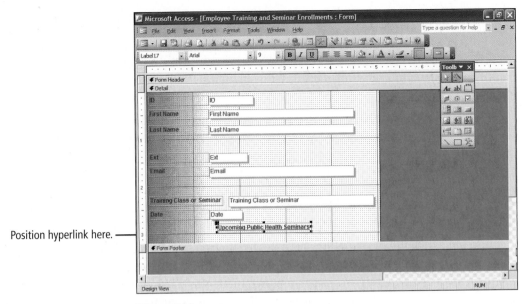

Position hyperlink here. —

Figure 8.16

8 Switch to **Form view** and examine the updated form. At the bottom of the form, click **Insert New Record** ▶✶. Using your own information and in the appropriate fields, type **Firstname** and **Lastname** and type **315** as your extension. For the email, use your name and type **Lastname_Firstname@universitymed.com**

9 Click the **Upcoming Public Health Seminars** hyperlink to view the flyer with the upcoming seminars and dates. If a message displays regarding hyperlinks that can be harmful to your computer, click **Yes** to continue.

10 **Minimize** ▬ Word and in the form, click in the **Training Class or Seminar** field. Type **Healthy Heart** and press Tab. Type **10/1/05**

11 From the **File** menu, click **Print**. Under **Print Range**, click the **Selected Record(s)** option button, and then click **OK**. Click the **Close Window** button ✕ to close the form and save your changes. To the right of the *Type a question for help* box, click the **Restore Window** button 🗗. Leave the database open for the next activity.

12 On the taskbar, click the button representing the Word document, and then **Close** ✕ Word.

Activity 8.5 Adding Hyperlinks from a Form to an Excel Worksheet

In this activity, you will create a hyperlink from an Access form to a Microsoft Excel file. The Excel file contains a 3-D pie chart indicating the percentage that each type of expense contributes to the total marketing expenses.

1 **Minimize** ▬ the Access window to a button on the taskbar. In **My Computer**, navigate to the student files, locate the Microsoft Excel file **a08A_MktgExp_Chart**, and copy and paste the file to the folder where you are storing your projects for this chapter. Remove the Read-only property, and rename the file **8A_MktgExp_Chart_ Firstname_Lastname** Open the file and examine the chart. **Close** the workbook and close Excel.

2 From the taskbar, restore the Access window. On the Objects bar, click **Forms**, and double-click **Create form by using wizard**. In the first screen of the wizard, click the **Tables/Queries arrow** and click your **Table: Marketing Expenses Firstname Lastname**. Click the

All Fields button 🔲 to move all the fields under **Selected Fields**. See Figure 8.17.

Select the Marketing Expenses table.

Move all the fields by clicking the All Fields button.

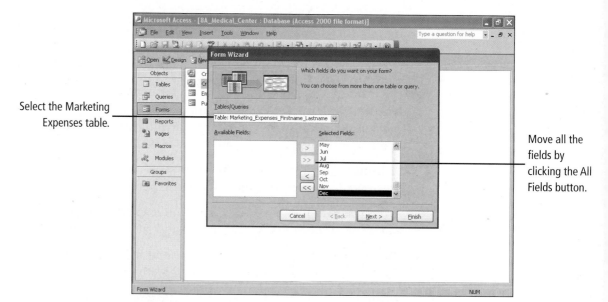

Figure 8.17

3 Click **Next**. Be sure the **Columnar** layout is selected and click **Next**. Click **Blends** as the style for the form and click **Next**.

4 Accept the default name **Marketing Expenses Firstname Lastname** and click **Finish**. Use the navigation buttons to scroll through the ten records representing the various types of marketing expenses.

5 Switch to **Design view** and **Maximize** 🔲 the window. Position your pointer over the upper edge of the **Form Footer bar** to display the double-headed pointer, and then drag toward the lower portion of the screen to **4.75 inches on the vertical ruler**. (Hint: Drag a little further than 4.75 inches and release the mouse button to view the mark, and then drag upward.) See Figure 8.18.

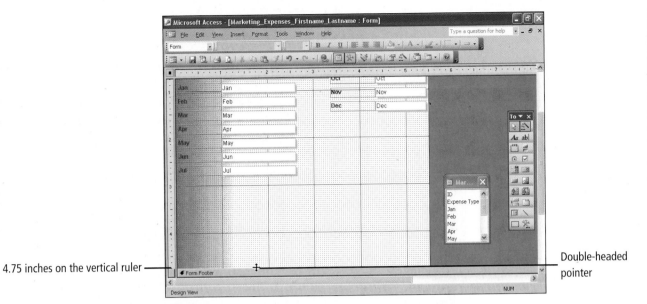

4.75 inches on the vertical ruler —

Double-headed pointer

Figure 8.18

6 At the top of the screen in the horizontal ruler, position the pointer over the **4.5-inch mark** to display a small black down arrow, and click once. All of the controls in the second column—**Aug** through **Dec**—are selected. Point to the selected controls until the Hand

pointer 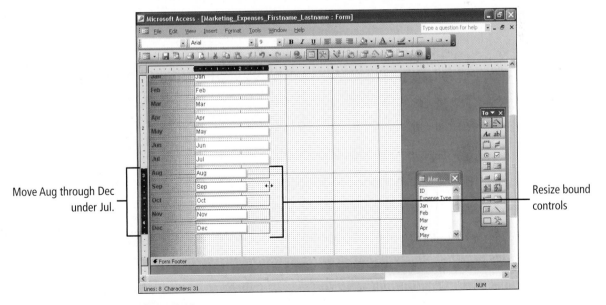 displays, and then drag the selected controls under the **Jan** through **Jul** labels and bound controls as shown in Figure 8.19. With the controls still selected, point to any of the controls to display

the Horizontal Resize pointer ↔ and resize the bound controls to match the Jan through Jul bound controls. See Figure 8.19.

Move Aug through Dec under Jul.

Resize bound controls

Figure 8.19

7 Click in a blank area of the form to deselect. From the **Insert** menu, click **Hyperlink**. Alternatively, on the Standard toolbar, click the Insert Hyperlink button . In the Link to bar, be sure **Existing File or Web Page** is selected. In the **Text to display** box, type **3D Pie Chart of Expenses** Click the **Look in arrow**, navigate to your chapter files, and then, as shown in Figure 8.20, click your file **8A_MktgExp_Chart_Firstname_Lastname**.

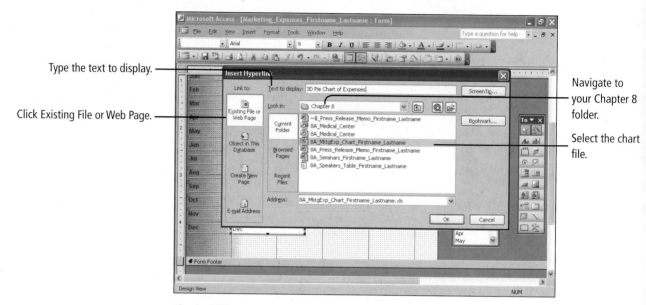

Type the text to display.

Click Existing File or Web Page.

Navigate to your Chapter 8 folder.

Select the chart file.

Figure 8.20

8 Click **OK**. Point to the hyperlink to display the Hand pointer and drag the hyperlink to the lower portion of the screen, positioning the left edge at **1 inch on the horizontal ruler** and directly below the December text box control. See Figure 8.21.

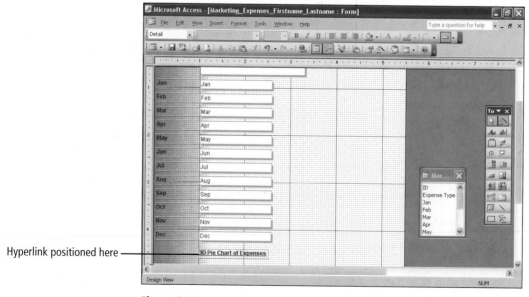

Hyperlink positioned here

Figure 8.21

9 From the **View** menu, click **Page Header/Footer**. In the **Page Footer** section, draw a label the approximate height of the area from the right edge to **3 inches on the horizontal ruler**. Type **8A Marketing Expenses Firstname Lastname** and click outside the label to deselect the control.

10 Switch to **Form View** and examine your updated form. Navigate to record **2**. At the bottom of the form, click the **3D Pie Chart of Expenses** hyperlink to view the Excel chart. If a warning message displays indicating that hyperlinks can be harmful to your computer, click **Yes** to continue. Notice that TV advertising accounts for 17% of the marketing expenses. **Close** ☒ Excel.

11 From the **File** menu, click **Print**. Under **Print Range**, click the **Selected Record(s)** option button, and then click **OK**. **Close** ☒ the form, save your changes, and then close the database and close Access.

End **You have completed Project 8A** ————————————————

Project 8B Medical Center Update

If you know you will use data only in Microsoft Access, use the import feature that you practiced in Project 8A. If, on the other hand, you want to use a table from another Access database, or information from some other program, and keep both data sources up to date within their own application, use the link feature.

In Activities 8.6 through 8.9, you will continue to import and link information and charts into your database from other sources. Your results will look similar to those shown in Figure 8.22. You will name your database *8B_Medical_Center_Update_Firstname_Lastname*.

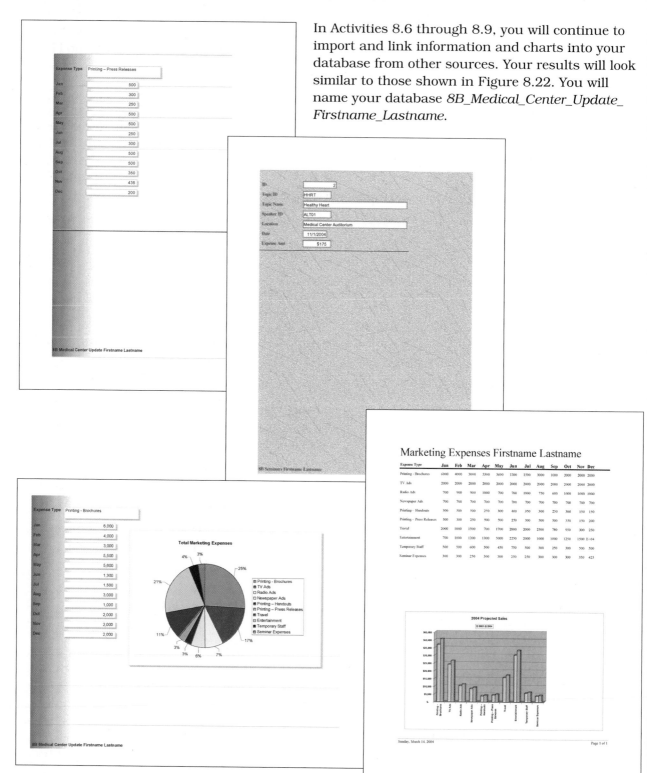

Figure 8.22

Objective 5
Link Database Objects to Office Files

When you *import* data into Access, the data is converted from its original format into an Access table. Changes you make to the data in the table are *not* made to the original file from which the data was imported—there is no connection between the two. Use the import feature when you want to move data into Access and no longer need to use the information in its original program.

There is also a method to connect to data from another program *without* importing it so that you can work with the data in both the original application and in an Access table. For example, when working in an environment where data is shared on a network, it is practical to **link** the data, rather than import it. When information is linked, the Access table will be updated automatically when the information in the original file is changed.

Activity 8.6 Linking a Form and an Excel Worksheet

Linking guarantees that the information in the ***external data source***—a file in a program other than Access—and the linked table in Access are always up to date. If you make changes to the linked table in Access, the file in the external data source is also changed. If you make changes to the file in the external data source, the Access table is also changed.

In this activity, you will create a table that is linked to an Excel spreadsheet. Then you will create a form in which changes can be made that are reflected both in the Access table and in the original file in the external data source. The worksheet contains the Marketing Expenses for the Medical Center, and it is important that both the file in the external data source and in the Access table are kept current.

1 Using **My Computer**, from the student files that accompany this textbook, locate the Excel spreadsheet **a08B_Marketing_Expenses**, copy and paste the file to the folder where you are storing your projects for this chapter, remove the Read-only property, and then rename the workbook **8B_Marketing Expenses_Firstname_Lastname** Start Excel, and open the workbook you just renamed.

2 In the Excel worksheet, locate cell **L7**, and notice that the expense amount for printing press releases in November is 150. **Close** ☒ Excel.

3 From the student files, locate the Access database **a08B_Medical_ Center_Update**, and then copy and paste the file to the folder where you are storing your projects for this chapter. Remove the Read-only property from the file, and rename the file as **8B_Medical_Center_ Update_Firstname_Lastname Start** Access and open the database you just renamed.

4 On the Objects bar, be sure **Tables** is selected. From the database window toolbar, click the **New** button, and in the **New Table** dialog box, click **Link Table**. See Figure 8.23.

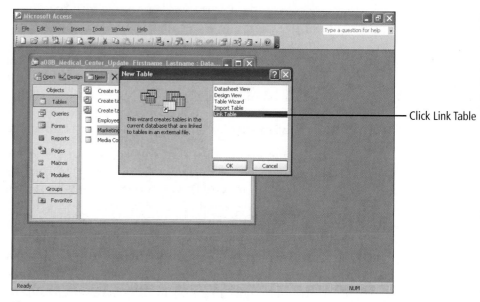

Click Link Table

Figure 8.23

5 Click **OK**. In the displayed **Link** dialog box, at the bottom, change the **Files of type** to **Microsoft Excel**, and then use the **Look in arrow** to navigate to your Excel file **8B_Marketing_Expenses_ Firstname_Lastname**. Select the file, and then in the lower right corner, click **Link**.

6 In the **Link Spreadsheet Wizard**, be sure the **First Row Contains Column Headings** check box is selected, and then click **Next**. Name the table **2004 Marketing Expenses Firstname Lastname** and click **Finish**. Click **OK** to acknowledge that the linking is finished.

Notice the icon to the left of your new table. The blue arrow indicates that the table is linked, and the Excel icon indicates that the link is to an Excel workbook. See Figure 8.24.

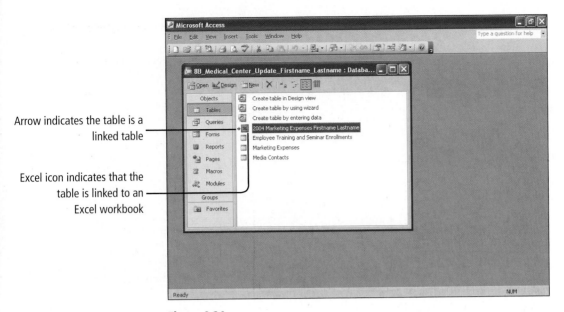

Arrow indicates the table is a linked table

Excel icon indicates that the table is linked to an Excel workbook

Figure 8.24

7 Open the new table in **Datasheet view**. Select all the columns and apply **Best Fit**, either by displaying the Column Width dialog box or by double-clicking a selected column boundary. Click anywhere to deselect. **Close** ✕ the table and save the changes.

8 On the Objects bar, click **Forms**, and then double-click **Create form by using wizard**. Click the **Tables/Queries arrow**, and then click your **Table: 2004 Marketing Expenses**. Move **all fields** over to the **Selected Fields** column, as shown in Figure 8.25.

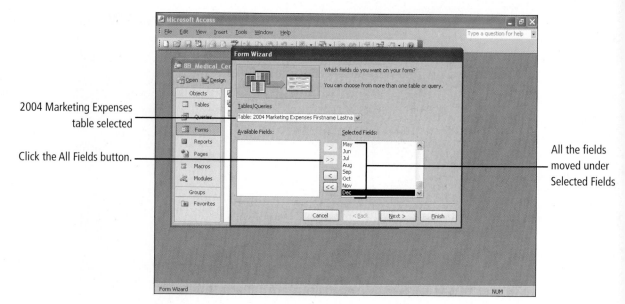

2004 Marketing Expenses table selected

Click the All Fields button.

All the fields moved under Selected Fields

Figure 8.25

9 Click **Next**. Click **Columnar** as the layout for the form and click **Next**. Click **Blends** as the style for the form and click **Next**. Leave the form name as **2004 Marketing Expenses Firstname Lastname** and click **Finish**. **Maximize** ▣ the form window and compare your screen with Figure 8.26.

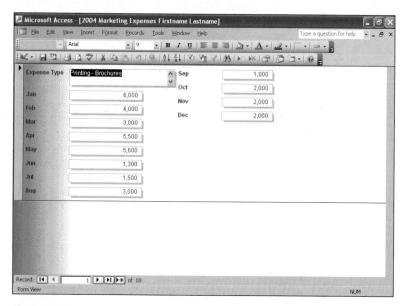

Figure 8.26

10 Switch to **Design view**. Position the pointer on the upper edge of the **Form Footer bar**, and when the double-headed arrow displays, drag downward to expand the **Detail section** to **5 inches on the vertical ruler**. (Hint: Drag a little further than 5 inches to view the mark, and then drag upward.) Position the pointer at approximately the **4.5-inch mark on the horizontal ruler** and click once to select all the controls in the second column. Using the technique you practiced in Project 8A, drag the group of controls under the first column, and widen to match the existing text box controls. See Figure 8.27.

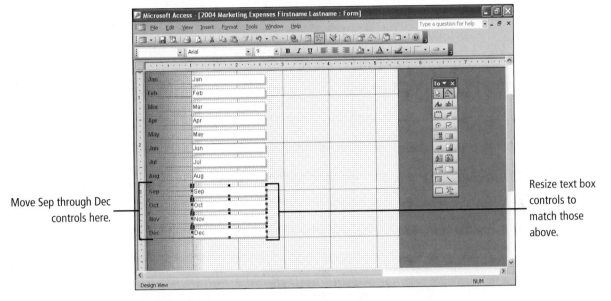

Move Sep through Dec controls here.

Resize text box controls to match those above.

Figure 8.27

11 From the **View** menu, click **Page Header/Footer**. In the **Page Footer section**, create a label the approximate height of the footer area, beginning at the left edge and extending to **3 inches on the horizontal ruler**. Type **8B Medical Center Update Firstname Lastname**

12 Switch to **Form View**. Navigate to record **6**, *Printing–Press Releases*, and change the amount spent in **Nov** from **150** to **435**

13 From the **File** menu, click **Print**. Under **Print Range**, click the **Selected Record(s)** option button, and then click **OK**. Click the **Close Window** button ✖ to close the form. Save the changes to the design.

14 Click the **Restore Window** button ⬜, and then **Minimize** ⬜ the Access window to a button on the taskbar. In **My Computer**, navigate to your files and open your Excel file **8B_Marketing_Expenses_ Firstname_Lastname**. Look at cell **L7**—the *Printing–Press Releases* expense for November—and notice that the amount has been updated to 435.

This is the advantage to linking. Changes made to the table in Access are automatically made to the worksheet in Excel because the two are linked.

15 **Close** ✖ Excel. Leave your **8B_Medical_Center_Update** database minimized as a button on the taskbar.

Activity 8.7 Linking Databases

The external data source to which an Access table is linked can be another Access database. After two tables in two separate Access databases are linked, you can update records in one table, and the record in the linked table will be automatically updated at the same time. The reverse is also true. When using the linked table, you may add records or change records, but you cannot change the structure of the table itself. You can change the structure of the table only from the original table.

1 Using **My Computer**, navigate to the student files and locate the Access database **a08B_Seminars**, copy and paste the file to the folder where you are storing your projects, remove the Read-only property from the file, and then rename the file as **8B_Seminars_ Firstname_Lastname** Open the database and open the **Seminars** table in **Datasheet view**. Examine record 2. See Figure 8.28.

Close ✖ the **Seminars** table, and then close your **8B_Seminars** database.

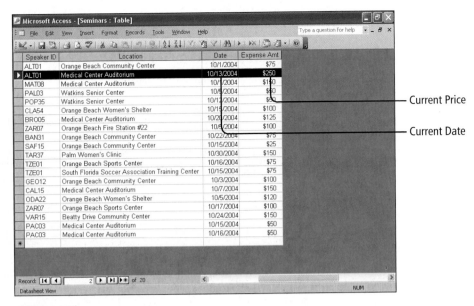

Figure 8.28

2 On the taskbar, click to restore your **8B_Medical_Center_Update** database. On the Objects bar, click **Tables**. On the database window toolbar, click the **New** button and from the **New Table** dialog box, click **Link Table**. Click **OK**.

3 At the bottom of the **Link** dialog box, change the **Files of type** to **Microsoft Office Access**, and then navigate to your projects folder for this chapter. Click your **8B_Seminars_Firstname_Lastname** Access database, and then in the lower right corner, click **Link**.

4 In the **Link Tables** dialog box, click the **Seminars** table, and then click **OK**.

The database window displays with the new table selected. The blue arrow indicates that the table is a linked table, and the Access icon indicates that the table is linked to another Access database.

5 Right-click on the **Seminars** table, click **Rename**, and rename the table **Seminars Firstname Lastname**

6 On the Objects bar, click **Forms**, and then double-click **Create form by using wizard**. Click the **Tables/Queries arrow**, click your **Table: Seminars**, and then move **all fields** over to the **Selected Fields** column as shown in Figure 8.29.

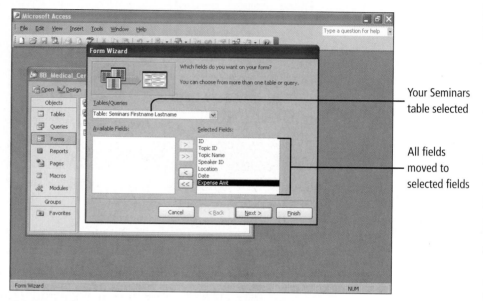

Your Seminars table selected

All fields moved to selected fields

Figure 8.29

7 Click **Next**. For the form layout, click **Columnar** and click **Next**. For the form style, click **Expedition** and click **Next**. Leave the form title as **Seminars Firstname Lastname**. Click **Finish**. When the form displays—this may take several seconds—**Maximize** the form window and compare your screen with Figure 8.30.

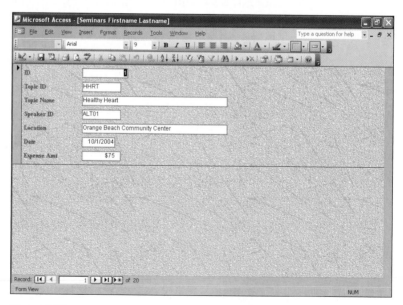

Figure 8.30

8 Switch to **Design view**. From the **View** menu, click **Page Header/Footer**. Create a label in the **Page Footer area**, beginning at the left edge, the approximate height of the footer area, and extending to **3 inches on the horizontal ruler**. Type 8B Seminars Firstname Lastname

9 Switch back to **Form view**. Navigate to record **2**, change the **Date** to **11/1/2004** and change the **Expense Amt** to **175**

10 From the **File** menu, click **Print**. Under **Print Range**, click the **Selected Record(s)** option button, and then click **OK**. **Close** ☒ the form window and save your changes. Click the **Restore Window** button ⧉, and then **Minimize** ▬ the database to a button on the taskbar.

11 Using **My Computer**, open your Access database **8B_Seminars_Firstname_Lastname**. Open the **Seminars** table in **Datasheet view**. Look at record 2, and notice that the record in this database was automatically updated when you changed the information in the other database.

12 **Close** ☒ the **Seminars** table, close the **8B_Seminars** database, and close Access. Redisplay your **8B_Medical_Center_Update** database, and leave the database open for the next activity.

More Knowledge — Object Linking and Embedding (OLE)

All Microsoft Office programs support *OLE*, which stands for *Object Linking and Embedding* and is pronounced *o-LAY*. OLE is a program-integration technology for sharing information between Office programs. Objects, for example, a Word table or an Excel chart, or some other form of information created in one Office program—the *source file*—can be linked to or *embedded* in another Office program—the *destination file*.

To embed means to insert, using a format that you specify, information from a source file in one program into a destination file in another program. An embedded object maintains the characteristics of the original application, but is not tied to the original file. For example, the object's information in the destination file does not change if you modify the information in the source file.

Objective 6
Add a Chart to a Form

A ***chart*** is a graphic representation of data. Data presented in a chart is easier to understand than a table of numbers. ***Column charts*** show comparisons among related numbers, ***pie charts*** show the contributions of parts to a whole, and ***line charts*** show trends over time.

Activity 8.8 Adding a Chart to a Form

Among the Microsoft Office programs, Excel is the best tool for producing a chart because it has a wide variety of charting types and options available. In this activity, you will insert a Microsoft Excel chart into an Access form—the 2004 Expenses form in your database.

1 On the Objects bar, click **Forms**. Double-click your **2004 Marketing Expenses** form to open it, **Maximize** [image] the form window, and then switch to **Design view**.

2 Resize the form by dragging the right border to **9.0 inches on the horizontal ruler**. At the bottom of the form, position the pointer on the upper edge of the **Page Footer bar**, and when the double-headed arrow displays, drag downward to expand the **Detail section** to **5.75 inches on the vertical ruler**.

3 From the **Insert** menu, click **Object**. On the left side of the dialog box, click the **Create from File** option button as shown in Figure 8.31.

Select Create from File. ————

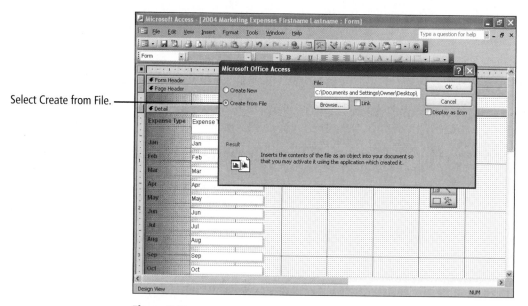

Figure 8.31

4 Click the **Browse** button. In the displayed **Browse** dialog box, navigate to the student files that accompany this textbook, select the Excel file **a08B_Pie_Chart_of_Marketing_Expenses**, and click **OK**. Because you will embed this file, *not* link it, in the displayed dialog box, be sure the Link check box is *not* selected. Click **OK**.

A copy of the Excel chart is embedded into your form. The chart is placed in the upper left of your form and will cover the fields in your form. Compare your form with Figure 8.32.

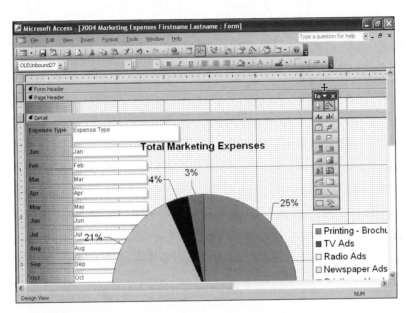

Figure 8.32

5 Scroll down and to the right so that you can see the bottom of the chart and position your mouse pointer over the lower right corner of the selected chart to display the Diagonal Resize pointer as shown in Figure 8.33.

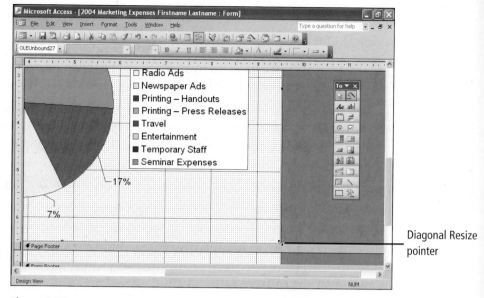

Figure 8.33

6 Drag up and to the left to **6 inches on the horizontal ruler** and **4 inches on the vertical ruler**, as shown in Figure 8.34.

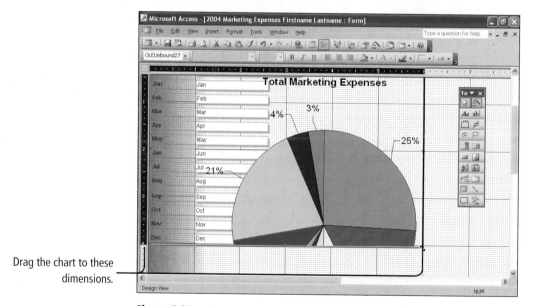

Drag the chart to these dimensions.

Figure 8.34

7 Point to the chart to display the Hand pointer 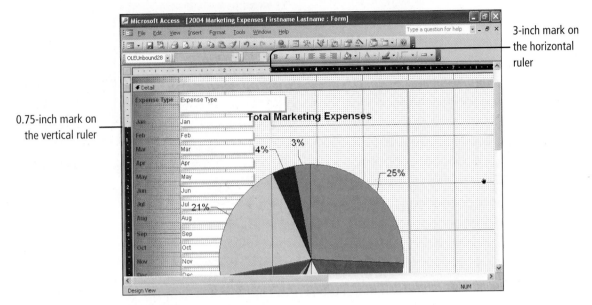 and drag so that the upper left corner of the chart is at the **3-inch mark on the horizontal ruler** and the upper edge is at the **0.75-inch mark on the vertical ruler**. See Figure 8.35.

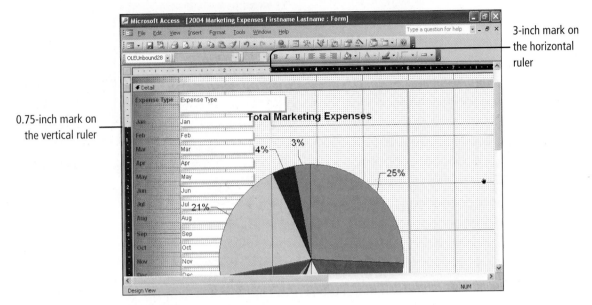

0.75-inch mark on the vertical ruler

3-inch mark on the horizontal ruler

Figure 8.35

8 Release the mouse button to reposition the chart, right-click on the chart, and from the displayed shortcut menu, click **Properties**. Be sure the **Format tab** is selected, click the **Size Mode** arrow, and then click **Zoom**. See Figure 8.36. **Close** ☒ the properties box.

The Zoom setting displays the picture in its entirety after sizing it to fill either the height or width of the area within the control. Using this setting will ensure that the image is not distorted.

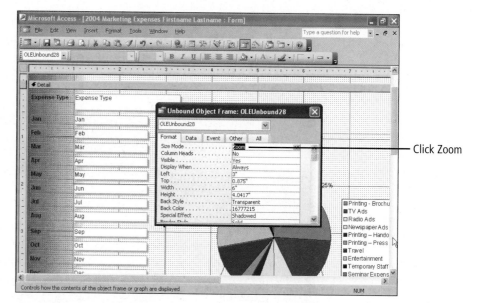

Click Zoom

Figure 8.36

9 Click in a blank area of the form to deselect the chart. Switch to **Form view**, and then scroll through all the records and view the embedded chart in each form. Then, navigate to record **1**.

The embedded chart shows the Total Marketing Expenses for the year by category. The chart can be used to compare the amount spent on each type of marketing expense to the total amount spent on marketing for the year.

10 From the **File** menu, display the **Page Setup** dialog box. On the **Margins tab**, change all four margin settings—**Top**, **Bottom**, **Left**, and **Right**—to **0.5**. On the **Page tab**, change the **Page Orientation** to **Landscape**. From the **File** menu, click **Print**. Under **Print Range**, click the **Selected Record(s)** option button, and then click **OK**.

Close ☒ the form and save your changes.

Objective 7
Add a Chart to a Report

Recall that a **report** is a database object that displays the fields and records from a table in an easy-to-read format suitable for printing. Reports are created to summarize information in a database in a professional-looking manner. Adding a chart to a report helps to summarize data by displaying the data in a graphical format.

Activity 8.9 Linking a Chart in a Report

In this activity, you will insert a Microsoft Excel chart into a report.

1 **Minimize** the database and, using **My Computer**, from your student files locate the Excel file **a08B_2004_Projected_Marketing_Expenses** and copy and paste it into your folder for this chapter. Remove the Read-only property, and then rename the file **8B_2004_Projected_Marketing_Expenses_Firstname_Lastname**

2 Close **My Computer** and restore your database. On the Objects bar, click **Reports**. Double-click **Create report by using wizard**. Select **Table: Marketing Expenses**. Move all the available fields over to the **Selected Fields** column. See Figure 8.37.

Choose the Marketing Expenses table.

Click to move all fields.

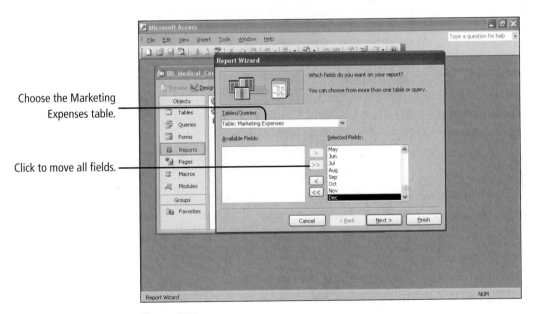

Figure 8.37

3 Click **Next** three times. For the **Layout** of your report, click **Tabular** and then click **Next**. For the **Style** of your report, click **Formal** and then click **Next**. Name the report **Marketing Expenses Firstname Lastname** and click **Finish**. Preview the report.

4 Switch to **Design view** and maximize the window if necessary. In the **Page Header section**, select the **ID label**, hold down Shift, and select the **ID bound control** in the **Detail section**. Press Delete. Hold down Shift and select both the **Expense Type label** and **Expense Type control**. Drag the left center sizing handle to the left edge of the form and the right center sizing handle to **1.25 inches on the horizontal ruler**. With the two controls still selected, change the **Font Size** to **8**. Hold down Shift and in the **Page Header section**, select the **Dec label**, and in the **Detail section**, select the **Dec bound control**. Drag the right center sizing handle of the selected controls to **6 inches on the horizontal ruler**.

5 Resize the **Report Header section** to **0.5 inches on the vertical ruler** by dragging the bottom of the Report Header section up slightly. Resize the **Page Footer section** down to **4 inches on the vertical ruler**. Hold down Shift and at the top of the **Page Footer section**, select the **black line** and then select the **two text boxes**.

With the Hand pointer ✋, drag the selected items to the bottom of the Page Footer section. See Figure 8.38.

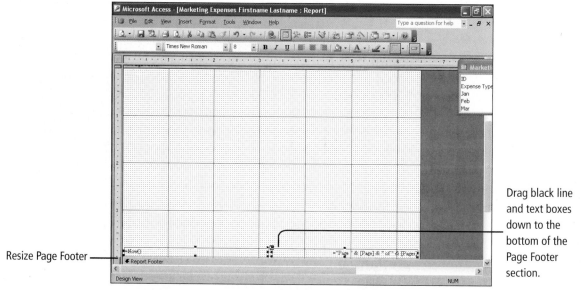

Resize Page Footer ——

Drag black line and text boxes down to the bottom of the Page Footer section.

Figure 8.38

6 Click the **Page Footer section bar** to select it. From the **Insert menu**, click **Object**. Click the **Create from File** option button. Click the **Browse** button, navigate to your folder for this chapter, select your **8B_2004_Projected_Marketing_Expenses** Excel file, and click **OK**. Because you want to link this file, in the displayed dialog box, select the **Link** check box. Click **OK**.

The chart from the Excel file is inserted into the Page Footer area, and the chart is linked to the Excel file. If, in the Excel spreadsheet, a change is made, that change will be reflected in this chart within the report the next time the report is opened.

7 Scroll down to view the bottom of the chart. In the lower right corner, point to the resizing handle to display the Diagonal Resize pointer and drag up and to the left to approximately **6 inches on the horizontal ruler** and **3.5 inches on the vertical ruler**. Right-click on the chart, and from the displayed shortcut menu, click **Properties**. Be sure the **Format tab** is selected, click the **Size Mode** arrow, and then click **Zoom**. In the **Left** box, type **0.25"** and press Enter. **Close** the property box.

8 Drag the bottom of the **Page Footer** section back up to **4 inches on the vertical ruler**. Drag the right edge of the form to **6.5 inches on the horizontal ruler**. See Figure 8.39.

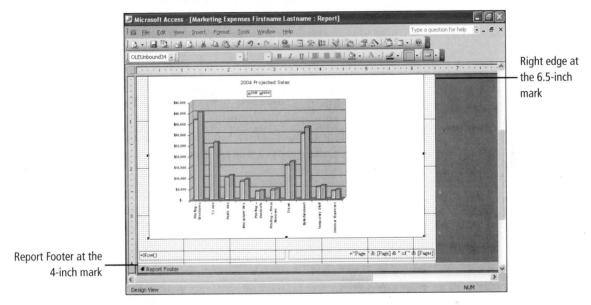

Report Footer at the 4-inch mark

Right edge at the 6.5-inch mark

Figure 8.39

9 Switch to **Report preview** to view your report.

10 From the **File** menu, click **Print**. Close the report, save changes, close the database, and then close Access.

End You have completed Project 8B

Summary

In this chapter, you integrated Access with other Office applications. Because information you want to use may be located in a file developed in another application, Access provides the ability to import or link to data located in other file formats. When you import, you copy data from a text file like Microsoft Word, a spreadsheet file like Microsoft Excel, or a database table from another Access database, and then insert it into an Access table. Importing is particularly convenient, because data does not have to be retyped into Access.

It is also useful to link your database to data in another application in a manner that, when data is updated in one file, it is automatically updated in the other. Linking guarantees that the information in the external data source and the linked table in Access are always up to date. You can also link to another Access database. After two tables in two separate Access databases are linked, you can update records in one table, and the record in the linked table will be automatically updated at the same time.

You practiced creating hyperlinks from Access to files in other applications. A hyperlink is a pointer from one object to another. Inserting a hyperlink provides a useful and convenient way to navigate between objects. When you are done viewing the information in the other application, you can close the file and return quickly to your database.

In this chapter, you practiced merging data from an Access table with Microsoft Word to create form letters. Using Word's mail merge feature, you can combine two documents—a main document created in Word and a data source created in Access—to create a mass mailing.

In This Chapter You Practiced How To

- Import Data from a Word Table
- Use Mail Merge to Integrate Access and Word
- Import from Excel
- Add Hyperlinks to Word and Excel Files
- Link Database Objects to Office Files
- Add a Chart to a Form
- Add a Chart to a Report

Concepts Assessments

Matching

Match each term in the second column with its correct definition in the first column by writing the letter of the term on the blank line in front of the correct definition.

_____ **1.** A graphic representation of data.

_____ **2.** A file in a program other than Access.

_____ **3.** A chart that shows trends over time.

_____ **4.** In a mail merge operation, the Word document that contains the text of the letter or memo.

_____ **5.** A database object that displays the fields and records from a table in an easy-to-read format suitable for printing. This object is created to summarize information in a database in a professional-looking manner.

_____ **6.** A chart that shows comparisons among related numbers.

_____ **7.** A file containing data where individual field values are separated by a character, such as a comma or a tab.

_____ **8.** To copy data from a text file like Microsoft Word, a spreadsheet file like Microsoft Excel, or a database table from another Access database, and then insert it into an Access table.

_____ **9.** To create a group of form letters by combining a main document created in Microsoft Word with a data source created in Access.

_____ **10.** In a database table, the field that uniquely identifies a record in a table.

_____ **11.** In a mail merge operation, the Access table that contains the names and addresses of the individuals to whom the document is being sent.

_____ **12.** A pointer from one object to another.

_____ **13.** The character, such as a comma or a tab, that separates individual field values in a converted text file.

_____ **14.** A chart that shows the contributions of parts to a whole.

_____ **15.** To insert information from an external source into an Access table in a way that, when the Access table is updated, the original file is also updated, and vice versa.

A Chart

B Column chart

C Data source

D Delimited text file

E Delimiter character

F External data source

G Hyperlink

H Import

I Line chart

J Link

K Mail merge

L Main document

M Pie chart

N Primary key

O Report

Fill in the Blank Write the correct answer in the space provided.

1. When saving a Word document as a text file for the purpose of importing the data into an Access table, be sure to delete any extra _____ lines at the end of the document so that empty records are not inserted.

2. To find the best fit for columns in a table without displaying a dialog box, select the columns, and then double-click any of the selected column _____.

3. The easiest way to perform a Mail Merge is to use the _____.

4. If you simply want to view a Word file or an Excel file while working in Access, create a _____ to the file.

5. A hyperlink consists of colored or _____ text or a graphic that you click to go to another location.

6. When you import data into Access, the data is converted from its original format into an Access _____.

7. When you want to move data into Access and no longer need to use the information in its original program, you should _____ rather than link the data.

8. When information is linked, any _____ in the original file are also made automatically in the Access table to which it is linked.

9. When tables from two separate Access databases are linked, you can add and change records in the linked table, but you cannot change the _____ of the table itself.

10. Among the Microsoft Office applications, _____ is probably the best suited for creating complex charts.

Project 8C—Updated Seminars

Objective: *Import Data from a Word Table.*

In the following Skill Assessment, you will import additional records from a Word table into your Seminars table in Access. Several new seminars, to be conducted in December, have been added to the schedule, and need to be included in the Access database. You will add (append) these records to the bottom of your Seminars table. Your completed table will look similar to Figure 8.40.

Topic ID	Topic Name	Speaker ID	Location	Date	Expense Amt
GAST	Healthy Tummies:Gastrointestinal Health	MAT08	Medical Center Auditorium	10/1/2005	$150
HHRT	Healthy Heart	ALT01	Orange Beach Community Center	10/1/2005	$75
INFEC	Don't Let the Germs Get You! Infectious Diseases Update	GEO12	Orange Beach Community Center	10/3/2005	$100
MEDI	Medicare Update	PAL03	Watkins Senior Center	10/5/2005	$50
WGTM	Weight Management	ZAR07	Orange Beach Fire Station #22	10/5/2005	$100
VITS	Vitamins, Supplements, & Your Health	ODA22	Orange Beach Women's Shelter	10/5/2005	$120
MNGC	Managing Managed Care	CAL15	Medical Center Auditorium	10/7/2005	$150
ARTH	Arthritis Treatments	POP35	Watkins Senior Center	10/12/2005	$50
HHRT	Healthy Heart	ALT01	Medical Center Auditorium	10/13/2005	$250
WOMH	Women's Health Update	CLA54	Orange Beach Women's Shelter	10/15/2005	$100
HPRG	Healthy Pregnancy & Baby	SAF15	Orange Beach Community Center	10/15/2005	$25
SPRT	Sports Injury Prevention & Treatments	TZE01	South Florida Soccer Association Training Center	10/15/2005	$75
PRIV	Patient Privacy	PAC03	Medical Center Auditorium	10/15/2005	$50
PRIV	Patient Privacy	PAC03	Medical Center Auditorium	10/16/2005	$50
SPRT	Sports Injury Prevention & Treatments	TZE01	Orange Beach Sports Center	10/16/2005	$75
WGTM	Weight Management	ZAR07	Orange Beach Sports Center	10/17/2005	$100
HHRT	Healthy Heart	BRO05	Medical Center Auditorium	10/20/2005	$125
SRNT	Seniors & Nutrition	BAN31	Orange Beach Community Center	10/22/2005	$75
DEPR	Depression: Identification & Treatment	VAR15	Beatty Drive Community Center	10/24/2005	$150
HPRG	Healthy Pregnancy & Baby	TAR37	Palm Women's Clinic	10/30/2005	$150
GAST	Healthy Tummies: Gastrointestinal Health	MAT08	Medical Center Auditorium	12/2/2005	$150
VITS	Vitamins, Supplements, & Your Health	ODA22	Kessler Community Center	12/6/2005	$120
MNGC	Managing Managed Care	CAL15	Medical Center Auditorium	12/8/2005	$150
HPRG	Healthy Pregnancy & Baby	SAF15	Midland Avenue Birthing Center	12/13/2005	$25
WOMH	Women's Health Update	CLA54	Orange Beach Women's Shelter	12/30/2005	$100

Seminars Firstname Lastname   3/14/2004

Page 1

Figure 8.40

1. Start Microsoft Word, and from the student files that accompany this textbook, locate and then open the Microsoft Word file **a08C_Updated_Seminars**.

2. If necessary, click anywhere inside the table. From the **Table** menu, point to **Convert**, and then click **Table to Text**.

3. In the displayed **Convert Table to Text** dialog box, be sure the **Tabs** option button is selected—this is the character you will use to separate the text into fields. Click **OK**. Click anywhere to deselect.

4. Hold down Ctrl and press End to move to the end of the document. Press Bksp once.

(Project 8C–Updated Seminars continues on the next page)

(Project 8C–Updated Seminars continued)

5. From the **File** menu, click **Save As**, and then navigate to the location where you are storing your projects for this chapter. At the bottom of the **Save As** dialog box, click the **Save as type arrow**, and from the displayed list, click **Plain Text**. In the **File name** box, type **8C_Updated_Seminars_Firstname_Lastname**

6. In the lower right corner of the dialog box, click **Save**. In the displayed **File Conversion** dialog box, accept the default settings and click **OK**. **Close** Microsoft Word.

7. From the student files, locate the Access file **a08C_Updated_Seminars**, and copy and paste the file to the Chapter 8 folder you created. Remove the Read-only property from the file and rename the file as **8C_Updated_Seminars_Firstname_Lastname** Start Access and open the database you just renamed.

8. Be sure the **Tables** object button is selected. Right-click on the **Seminars** table and rename the table **Seminars Firstname Lastname**

9. From the **File** menu, point to **Get External Data**, and on the submenu click **Import**. At the bottom of the displayed **Import** dialog box, click the **Files of type arrow**, and then click **Text Files**. Use the **Look in arrow** to navigate to your files for this chapter, click your **8C_Updated_Seminars text file**, and then click **Import**.

10. In this first screen of the **Import Text Wizard**, be sure the **Delimited** option button is selected, and then click **Next**.

11. Under **Choose the delimiter that separates your fields**, be sure the **Tab** option button is selected, and then be sure the **First Row Contains Field Names** check box is *not* selected.

12. Click **Next**. Under **Where would you like to store your data**, click the **In an Existing Table** option button, and then click the arrow to the right. From the displayed list, click your **Seminars Firstname Lastname** table, and then click **Next**. Recall that you are adding—appending—these records to an existing table, and that you must indicate the table to which you want to append the new records. Click **Finish**, and then click **OK** to acknowledge the message.

13. Open your **Seminars** table in **Datasheet view**. In the column heading area, drag to select all of the columns, display the **Format** menu, and then click **Column Width**. In the **Column Width** dialog box, click the **Best Fit** button to resize all the columns to fit the data. Click anywhere to deselect, and then click anywhere in the **Date** column.

(Project 8C–Updated Seminars continues on the next page)

(Project 8C–Updated Seminars continued)

14. On the toolbar, click the **Sort Ascending** button. The records are sorted chronologically by date, and you can see the new December seminars at the bottom of the table.

15. From the **File** menu, click **Page Setup**, and on the **Margins tab**, change the **Top**, **Bottom**, **Left**, and **Right** margins to **0.5 inches**. On the **Page tab**, change the **Orientation** to **Landscape**. Click **OK**. On the Table Datasheet toolbar, click the **Print** button. **Close** your table and save the changes. Close the database.

 End You have completed Project 8C ─────────────

Project 8D — Schedule

Objective: *Use Mail Merge to Integrate Access and Word.*

In the following Skill Assessment, you will create a mail merge document to create a directory of all of the media contacts that lists the contact name, organization, and phone numbers. You will rename and save your database as *8D_Schedule_Firstname_Lastname.* Your completed directory will look similar to Figure 8.41.

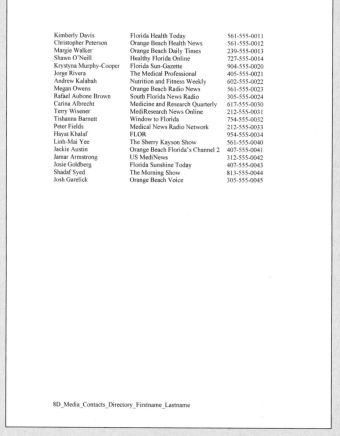

Kimberly Davis	Florida Health Today	561-555-0011
Christopher Peterson	Orange Beach Health News	561-555-0012
Margie Walker	Orange Beach Daily Times	239-555-0013
Shawn O'Neill	Healthy Florida Online	727-555-0014
Krystyna Murphy-Cooper	Florida Sun-Gazette	904-555-0020
Jorge Rivera	The Medical Professional	405-555-0021
Andrew Kalabah	Nutrition and Fitness Weekly	602-555-0022
Megan Owens	Orange Beach Radio News	561-555-0023
Rafael Aubone Brown	South Florida News Radio	305-555-0024
Carina Albrecht	Medicine and Research Quarterly	617-555-0030
Terry Wisener	MediResearch News Online	212-555-0031
Tishanna Barnett	Window to Florida	754-555-0032
Peter Fields	Medical News Radio Network	212-555-0033
Hayat Khalaf	FLOR	954-555-0034
Linh-Mai Yee	The Sherry Kayson Show	561-555-0040
Jackie Austin	Orange Beach Florida's Channel 2	407-555-0041
Jamar Armstrong	US MediNews	312-555-0042
Josie Goldberg	Florida Sunshine Today	407-555-0043
Shadaf Syed	The Morning Show	813-555-0044
Josh Garelick	Orange Beach Voice	305-555-0045

8D_Media_Contacts_Directory_Firstname_Lastname

Figure 8.41

1. From your student files, locate the database file **a08D_Schedule**, and then copy and paste the file where you are storing your projects for this chapter. Remove the Read-only property from the file and rename the file **8D_Schedule_Firstname_Lastname** Start Access and open the database you just renamed.

(Project 8D–Schedule continues on the next page)

(Project 8D – Schedule continued)

2. Be sure the **Tables** object is selected, and then click the **Media Contacts** table to select it. On the database toolbar, click the **OfficeLinks button arrow**, and from the displayed list, click **Merge It with Microsoft Office Word**.

3. In this first screen of the **Microsoft Word Mail Merge Wizard**, click the **Create a new document and then link the data to it** option button. Click **OK**. In the Word **Mail Merge** task pane, under **Select document type**, click the **Directory** option button. Selecting the *Directory* option creates a single document containing a catalog or printed list of addresses by merging your Access table with a specially formatted Word document.

4. At the bottom of the task pane, click **Next: Starting document**. At the top of the task pane, under **Select starting document**, be sure that the **Use the current document** option button is selected. At the bottom of the task pane, click **Next: Select recipients**.

5. At the top of the **Mail Merge** task pane, under **Select recipients**, be sure the **Use an existing list** option button is selected. Note that the term *recipients* is used, even though we are not actually creating letters, but rather a directory list.

6. At the bottom of the task pane, click **Next: Arrange your directory**. In the **horizontal ruler** at the top of the Word window, click directly on the ruler at the **2-inch mark**, and again at the **4.5-inch mark**. This will create a left tab at these two positions.

7. In the **Mail Merge** task pane, click the **More items** button. In the displayed **Insert Merge Field** dialog box, under **Fields**, click **Contact**, and then click the **Insert** button. At the bottom of the **Insert Merge Field** dialog box, click the **Close** button. Press [Tab]. On the task pane, click the **More items** button, click **Name**, click **Insert**, and then click **Close**. Press [Tab]. From the task pane, display the **Insert Merge Field** dialog box one more time, and insert the **Phone** field. Close the dialog box. Press [Enter].

8. At the bottom of the task pane, click **Next: Preview your directory**.

9. At the top of the task pane, under **Preview your directory**, click the >> arrows to scroll through and view the list of names.

10. At the bottom of the task pane, under **Step 5 of 6**, click **Next: Complete the merge**. In the middle of the task pane, under **Merge**, click **To New Document**. In the **Merge to New Document** dialog box, be sure the **All** option button is selected, and then click **OK**.

(Project 8D – Schedule continues on the next page)

(Project 8D–Schedule continued)

11. From the **File** menu, click **Save As**, navigate to the location where you are storing your files for this chapter, and then save the document as **8D_Media_Contacts_Directory_Firstname_Lastname**

12. On the menu bar, click **View**, and then click **Header and Footer**. In the displayed Header and Footer toolbar, click the **Switch Between Header and Footer** button. Then, on the same toolbar, click **Insert AutoText**, and from the displayed list, click **Filename**. This will place the name of your Word file in the footer. On the floating toolbar, click **Close**.

13. From the **File** menu, click **Print**, and then click **OK**. **Close** the document, saving your changes, and **Close** Word. It is not necessary to save the original document. **Close** your database and close Access.

 You have completed Project 8D ——————————————

Project 8E — Physicians

Objective: *Import from Excel.*

In the following Skill Assessment, you will import an Excel spreadsheet containing a list of the physicians at University Medical Center into your Access database. Your completed table will look similar to Figure 8.42. You will rename and save your database as *8E_Physicians_Firstname_Lastname*.

Phy Num	First Name	Last Name	Dept	Addr1	Addr2	City	State	Postal Code	Phone
PHY539	Sharon	Brougher	Pediatrics	2314 Highland Lake Road		Miami	FL	33145	305-555-0109
PHY148	Annette	Carpenter	Cardiology	28 Fairway Dr.		Miami	FL	33145	305-555-0067
PHY335	Michael	Franklin	Obstetrics	2600 Whisper Lake Lane		Winter Park	FL	32790	407-555-0076
PHY541	Robert	Gaines	Cardiology	200 N. Orlando Ave.	#1650	Coral Springs	FL	33077	954-555-0132
PHY353	Maria	Garcia	Dermatology	30 E. 46th St.		Miami	FL	33174	305-555-0078
PHY145	Jaleel	Hassan	Radiology	2230 Riverside Dr.		Coral Springs	FL	33077	954-555-0012
PHY889	Gregory	Ivanov	General Surgery	7865 Calibre Bend Ln		Hialeah	FL	33013	305-555-0054
PHY130	Nishan	Jibotian	General Surgery	76 Mahogany Key Circle		Miami	FL	33145	305-555-0112
PHY533	Laurene	Kormac	Neurology	1211 NW 87th Ave.		Miami	FL	33150	305-555-0113
PHY342	Paramjeet	Kumar	Radiology	2230 Camino Real	#A	Miami	FL	33143	305-555-0011
PHY451	Wendy	Lee	Psychiatry	2515 Main St.	#300	Hialeah	FL	33018	954-555-0087
PHY641	Vivian	Marsh	Pediatrics	3920 Casa Aloma Way		Miami	FL	33150	305-555-0123
PHY146	Joaquin	Pena	Pediatrics	875 Wood Run Court		Coral Springs	FL	33075	954-555-0122
PHY129	Deepa	Subramani	Geriatrics	1516 NW 67th St.	#1560	Miami	FL	33143	305-555-0111
PHY156	Louise	Tran	Obstetrics	38 111th Terrace	#1600	Coral Springs	FL	33065	954-555-0098
PHY545	Charles	Yang	Geriatrics	1350 Miami Lakeway		Hialeah	FL	33010	305-555-0089

Figure 8.42

1. From your student files, locate the Access database **a8E_Physicians**, and then copy and paste the file to the Chapter 8 folder you created. Remove the Read-only property from the file and rename the file as **8E_Physicians_Firstname_Lastname** Start Access and open the database you just renamed.

2. Be sure the **Tables** object is selected. From the **File** menu, point to **Get External Data**, and then on the submenu click **Import**. At the bottom of the dialog box, change the **Files of type** to **Microsoft Excel**, navigate to the student files that accompany this textbook, and then select the Excel file **a08E_Physicians**. In the lower right corner, click **Import**.

(Project 8E–Physicians continues on the next page)

(Project 8E–Physicians continued)

3. In the first screen of the wizard, be sure that the **Show Worksheets** option button is selected and that **Sheet 1** is selected, and then click **Next**. Be sure the **First Row Contains Column Headings** check box is selected, and then click **Next**. Store the data **In a New Table**, and then click **Next**. Under **Field Options**, click the **Indexed arrow**, and then click **Yes (No Duplicates)** because you will use the *Phy Num* (Physician Number) as a primary key. Click **Next**. Click **Choose my own primary key** and select **Phy Num** as the field to use for the primary key. Click **Next**.

4. In the **Import to Table** box, type **Physicians Firstname Lastname** and click **Finish**. Click **OK** to acknowledge the *Finished importing* message.

5. Open your **Physicians** table in **Datasheet view**. Select all of the columns and apply **Best Fit** by double-clicking on one of the selected column boundaries. Click anywhere to deselect. Click anywhere in the **Last Name** column, and then on the toolbar, click the **Sort Ascending** button.

6. From the **File** menu, click **Page Setup**, and on the **Page tab**, change the **Orientation** to **Landscape**. Click **OK**. On the Table Datasheet toolbar, click the **Print** button. Close your table and save the changes. Close the database and close Access.

End You have completed Project 8E ———————————

Performance Assessments

Project 8F — Physicians with Patients

Objective: *Add Hyperlinks to Word and Excel Files.*

In the following Performance Assessment, you will insert a hyperlink from an Access form to an Excel worksheet that contains a chart. Your completed form will look similar to Figure 8.43. You will rename and save your database as *8F_Physicians_with_Patients_Firstname_Lastname.*

Phy Num	PHY539
Dept	Pediatrics
Num Patients Seen	300
Average Hrs/ Patient	0.33
Total Patient Hours	99

Physicians with Patient

8F Physicians with Patients Firstname Lastname

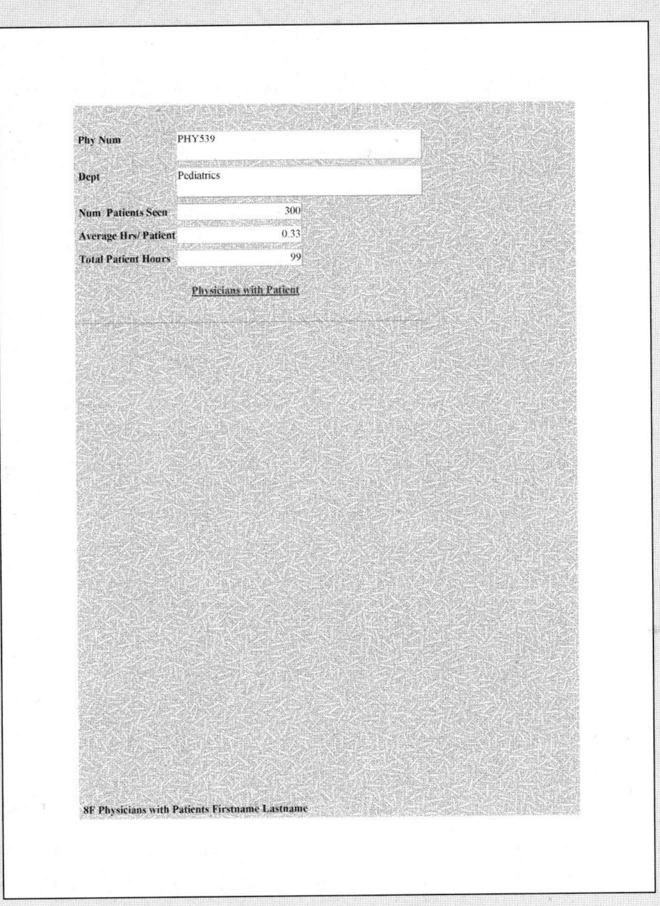

Figure 8.43

1. From your student files, locate the Access file **a08F_Physicians_with_Patients**, and then copy and paste the file to your projects folder for this chapter. Remove the Read-only property from the file and rename the file as **8F_Physicians_with_Patients_Firstname_Lastname** Start Access and open the database you just renamed.

(Project 8F–Physicians with Patients continues on the next page)

(Project 8F–Physicians with Patients continued)

2. **Minimize** your database to a button on the taskbar. In **My Computer**, navigate to your student files, locate the Microsoft Excel file **a08F_Physicians_Chart**, and then copy and paste the file to the folder where you are storing your projects for this chapter. Rename the file **8F_Physicians_Chart_Firstname_Lastname** Open the file and examine the chart. The chart compares the number of patients each physician has seen and the number of hours each physician spends with patients. **Close** Excel.

3. From the taskbar, restore your database. On the Objects bar, click **Forms**, and then double-click **Create form by using wizard**. In the first screen of the wizard, click the **Tables/Queries arrow** and click **Table: Physician Activity**. Move all the fields under **Selected Fields**.

4. Click **Next**. Be sure the **Columnar** layout is selected and click **Next**. Click **Ricepaper** as the style for the table and click **Next**. Name the form **Physicians Activity Firstname Lastname** and click **Finish**. Use the navigation buttons to scroll through the six records.

5. Switch to **Design view** and **Maximize** the form window. Resize the height of the **Detail section** to **2.5 inches on the vertical ruler**. From the **Insert** menu, click **Hyperlink**. In the Link to bar, be sure **Existing File or Web Page** is selected. In the **Text to display** box, type **Physicians with Patients** Click the **Look in arrow**, navigate to your files, and then click your Excel file **8F_Physicians_Chart_Firstname_Lastname**. Click **OK**.

6. Move the hyperlink to the lower portion of the screen, positioning the left edge at **1.5 inches on the horizontal ruler** and the top edge at **2 inches on the vertical ruler**.

7. From the **View** menu, click **Page Header/Footer**. In the **Page Footer** section, draw a label the approximate height of the footer area and three inches wide, and then type **8F Physicians with Patients Firstname Lastname** and click outside the label to deselect the control.

8. Switch to **Form View** and examine your updated form. Navigate to record **5**. At the bottom of the form, click the **Physicians with Patients** hyperlink to view the Excel chart. If a warning message displays indicating that hyperlinks can be harmful to your computer, click **Yes** to continue. **Close** Excel.

9. From the **File** menu, click **Print**. Under **Print Range**, click the **Selected Record(s)** option button, and then click **OK**. **Close** the form, save your changes, and then close the database and close Access.

End You have completed Project 8F

Project 8G — Hospital Staff

Objective: *Link Database Objects to Office Files.*

In the following Performance Assessment, you will create a form and link it to an Excel spreadsheet. Your completed form will look similar to Figure 8.44. You will rename and save your database as *8G_Hospital_Staff_Firstname_Lastname*.

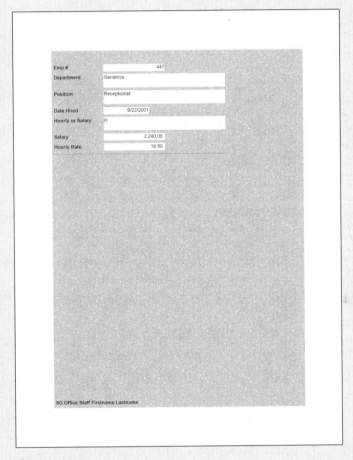

Emp #	447
Department	Geriatrics
Position	Receptionist
Date Hired	9/22/2001
Hourly or Salary	H
Salary	2,240.00
Hourly Rate	18.50

8G Office Staff Firstname Lastname

Figure 8.44

1. From the student files that accompany this textbook, locate the Excel spreadsheet **a08G_Office Staff**, copy and paste the file to the folder where you are storing your projects for this chapter, remove the Read-only property, and then rename the workbook **8G_Office_Staff_Firstname_Lastname** Start Excel and open the workbook you just renamed.

2. In the Excel worksheet, locate cell **G9**, and notice that the hourly rate for this staff member is 14.00. **Close** Excel.

(Project 8G–Hospital Staff continues on the next page)

(Project 8G–Hospital Staff continued)

3. From the student files, locate the Access database **a08G_Hospital_Staff**, and then copy and paste the file to the folder where you are storing your projects for this chapter. Remove the Read-only property from the file, and rename the file as **8G_Hospital_Staff_Firstname_Lastname** Start Access and open the database you just renamed.

4. On the Objects bar be sure **Tables** is selected. From the Database window toolbar, click the **New** button, and in the **New Table** dialog box, click **Link Table**.

5. Click **OK**. In the displayed **Link** dialog box, at the bottom, change the **Files of type** to **Microsoft Excel**, and then use the **Look in arrow** to navigate to your Excel file **8G_Office_Staff_Firstname_Lastname**. Select the file, and click **Link**.

6. In the **Link Spreadsheet Wizard**, be sure the **First Row Contains Column Headings** check box is selected, and then click **Next**. Name the table **Office Staff Firstname Lastname** and click **Finish**. Click **OK** to acknowledge that the linking is finished.

7. Open the new linked table in **Datasheet view**. Select all the columns and apply **Best Fit**. Click anywhere to deselect. **Close** the table and save the changes.

8. On the Objects bar, click **Forms**, and then double-click **Create form by using wizard**. As the table, use your **Office Staff** table, and then move all the fields over to the **Selected Fields** column.

9. Click **Next**. Click **Columnar** as the layout for the form, and in the next screen, click **SandStone** as the style for the form. On the last screen, accept the default name for the form and click **Finish**. **Maximize** the form window.

10. Switch to **Design view**. From the **View** menu, click **Page Header/Footer**. In the **Page Footer section**, create a label the approximate height of the footer area and three inches wide. Type **8G Office Staff Firstname Lastname**

11. Switch to **Form view**. Navigate to record **8**, *Emp # 447*, and change the hourly rate from 14.00 to **18.50**

12. From the **File** menu, click **Print**. Under **Print Range**, click the **Selected Record(s)** option button, and then click **OK**. Click the **Close Window** button to close the form. Save the changes to the design. **Close** Access.

13. In **My Computer**, navigate to your files and open your Excel file **8G_Office_Staff_Firstname_Lastname**. Look at cell **G9** and notice that the hourly rate has been updated to 18.50. **Close** Excel, and save any changes.

 End You have completed Project 8G

Project 8H — Billing

Objective: *Link a Chart in a Report.*

In the following Performance Assessment, you will insert and link a Microsoft Excel chart in an Access report. Your completed report will look similar to Figure 8.45. You will rename and save your database as *8H_Physicians_Billing_Firstname_Lastname*.

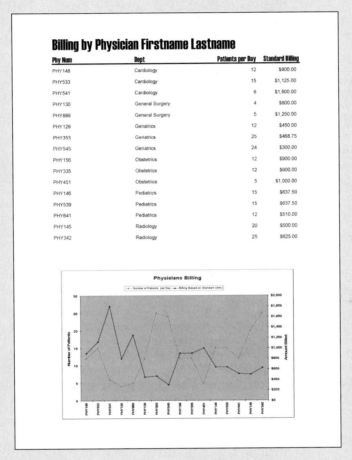

Figure 8.45

1. From the student files that accompany this textbook, locate the Excel file **a08H_Physicians_Billing**, copy and paste it into your chapter folder, and then remove the Read-only property. Rename the file **8H_Physicians_Billing_Firstname_Lastname** Open the file and examine the Excel chart. The chart shows the number of patients each physician had and how much the patients were billed. **Close** Excel.

(Project 8H–Billing continues on the next page)

(Project 8H–Billing continued)

2. From the student files, locate the Access database **a08H_Billing**, and then copy and paste the file to your chapter folder. Remove the Read-only property from the file, and rename the file as **8H_Billing_Firstname_Lastname** Start Access and open the database you just renamed.

3. On the Objects bar, click **Reports**. Double-click **Create report by using wizard**. Select the **Table: Billing by Physician**. Move the **Phy Num**, **Dept.**, **Patients per Day**, and **Standard Billing** fields over to the **Selected Fields** column and click **Next**. You will not add any grouping levels, so click **Next**, nor will you add a sort order, so click **Next** again. For the layout of your report, click **Tabular**, and for the **Orientation**, click **Portrait**, and then click **Next**.

4. For the report style, click **Compact**, and on the last screen, as the title for the report, type **Billing by Physician Firstname Lastname** and click **Finish**. Preview the report.

5. Switch to **Design view** and **Maximize** the report window. Decrease the size of the **Report Header section** to **0.5 inches on the vertical ruler**. Enlarge the **Page Footer section** to **4 inches on the vertical ruler**. At the top of the **Page Footer** section, hold down Shift and select the **line** and the **two text boxes**, and then press Delete to delete these three elements.

6. Click the **Page Footer section bar** to select the entire section. From the **Insert** menu, click **Object**. Click the **Create from File** option button. Browse to locate your Excel file **8H_Physicians_Billing_Firstname_Lastname**, select it and click **OK**. Select the **Link** check box and click **OK**.

7. Using the bottom right resize handle, resize the chart to approximately **6 inches wide** and **3.75 inches tall**. Right-click on the chart, click **Properties**, on the **Format tab** click the **Size Mode** arrow, and then click **Stretch**. For the **Left** type **0.25** Close the property box.

8. Reset the bottom of the **Page Footer section** to **4 inches on the vertical ruler**. Decrease the width of the entire form to **6.5 inches on the horizontal ruler**.

9. Switch to **Report preview**. From the **Page Setup** dialog box, change the **Top** and **Bottom margins** to **0.5 inch**. From the **File Menu**, click **Print**. Close the report, save changes, and close the database.

10. Close the database, and then close Access.

End You have completed Project 8H

Project 8I—Updated Staff

Objective: *Import Data from a Word Table.*

In the following Mastery Assessment, you will import records from a Word table in an Access database. The table contains records for members of the Facilities staff. Your completed table will look similar to Figure 8.46. You will rename and save your database as *8I_Updated_Staff_Firstname_Lastname.*

Facilities Staff Members Firstname Lastname   3/14/2004

ID	Classification	Last Name	First Name	Address	City	State	Postal Code	Phone	Emp Num
14	Laundry	Atkins	Jannelle	865 Middlebrook Rd.	Miami	FL	33143	305-555-0089	29
15	Laundry	Bennett	Jodie	76 Conch St.	Coral Springs	FL	33077	954-555-0002	15
7	Facilities Services	Bryant	Jeffery	1501 Bahia Dr.	Coral Springs	FL	33077	954-555-0000	24
8	Facilities Services	Carrasco	Tomas	1315 Sand Creek Way	Hialeah	FL	33013	305-555-0002	11
9	Facilities Services	Carter	Ted	20 S. 75th Ave.	Hialeah	FL	33013	954-555-0076	30
1	Housekeeping	Coronado	Linda	5368 Dahlia Dr.	Miami	FL	33143	305-555-0001	10
17	Maintenance	De La Hoya	Naomi	1042 Mancha Real Dr.	Winter Park	FL	32790	407-555-0103	27
2	Housekeeping	Diaz	Natalie	1078 Pine Crossing Cir.	Winter Park	FL	32790	407-555-0101	25
3	Housekeeping	Diaz	Phyllis	809 Miller Ave.	Miami	FL	33150	305-555-0004	13
18	Maintenance	Feinberg	Sid	8 Tropic Bay Ct.	Miami	FL	33150	305-555-0033	22
10	Facilities Services	Holcomb	Tyrone	3266 Osprey Links Dr.	Hialeah	FL	33010	305-555-0010	17
16	Laundry	Holmes	Jesus	8025 Valencia Village Way	Miami	FL	33145	305-555-0102	26
4	Housekeeping	Ludwig	Elizabeth	15002 Yellow Wood Cir.	Miami	FL	33150	305-555-0003	12
5	Housekeeping	Macias	Ida	8915 S. Fairlawn Dr.	Winter Park	FL	32790	407-555-0001	16
19	Maintenance	Martinez	Enrique	252 Conway St.	Ft. Lauderdale	FL	33345	754-555-0007	23
11	Facilities Services	Mauer	Vince	98510 Glen Cove Cir.	Coral Springs	FL	33075	954-555-0005	20
22	Facilities Services	Mayfield	James	1243 Egret Drive	Ft. Lauderdale	FL	33345	754-555-0110	30
12	Maintenance	Miller	Anthony	3650 Gatlin Ave.	Ft. Lauderdale	FL	33330	754-555-0001	14
13	Facilities Services	Shoenfeld	Edward	4210 Chalfont St.	Hialeah	FL	33010	305-555-0104	28
6	Housekeeping	Valencia	Josefina	9811 W. Fort Shea Ave.	Miami	FL	33174	305-555-0020	18
20	Maintenance	Vogan	Corey	4180 Robala Dr. East	Ft. Lauderdale	FL	33394	754-555-0008	21
21	Maintenance	Weber	Harry	1057 Kislin Pl.	Miami	FL	33150	305-555-0030	19

Page 1

Figure 8.46

1. From the student files, locate and then open the Microsoft Word file **a08I_Facilities_Staff**.

2. Click anywhere in the table. From the **Table** menu, convert the table to text using **Tabs** to separate the text. Press Ctrl + End to move to the end of the document, and press Bksp once to remove the blank line.

3. From the **File** menu, click **Save As**, and then navigate to the location where you are storing your projects for this chapter. Change the **Save as type** to **Plain Text**. In the **File name** box, type **8I_Facilities_Staff_Firstname_Lastname**

4. In the lower right corner of the dialog box, click **Save**. In the displayed **File Conversion** dialog box, accept the default settings and click **OK**. **Close** Microsoft Word.

(Project 8I–Updated Staff continues on the next page)

(Project 8I–Updated Staff continued)

5. From the student files, locate the database file **a08I_Updated_Staff**, and then copy and paste the file to your chapter folder. Remove the Read-only property from the file and rename the file as **8I_Updated_Staff_Firstname_Lastname** Start Access and open the database you just renamed.

6. On the Objects bar, click **Tables**. Import your text file **8I_Facilities_Staff**.

7. Be sure the **Delimited** option button is selected. Select **Tab** as the delimiter and indicate that the **First Row Contains Field Names**. Store the imported data in a new table. It is not necessary to index any fields; let Access choose the primary key. In the **Import to Table** box, type **Facilities Staff Members Firstname Lastname** Click **OK** to acknowledge the message box.

8. Open your **Facilities Staff Members** table. Apply **Best Fit** to the columns, and then sort the data alphabetically by **Last Name**.

9. From the **Page Setup** dialog box, change the **Top**, **Botton**, **Left**, and **Right** margins to **0.75 inch** and change the **Page Orientation** to **Landscape**. On the Table Datasheet toolbar, click the **Print** button. Close your table and save the changes. Close your database.

End You have completed Project 8I ——————————————

Project 8J — Medical Staff

Objective: *Link Database Objects to Office Files.*

In the following Mastery Assessment, you will create a form for a table, and then link it to an Excel spreadsheet. Your completed form will look similar to Figure 8.47. You will rename and save your database as *8J_Medical_Center_Staff_Firstname_Lastname.*

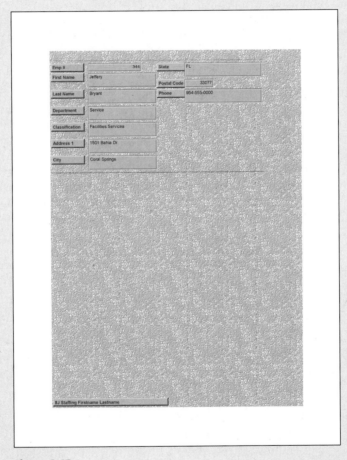

Figure 8.47

1. From the student files that accompany this textbook, locate the Excel file **a08J_Staffing**, copy and paste the file to your chapter folder, remove the Read-only property, and then rename the workbook **8J_Staffing_Firstname_Lastname** Start Excel and open the workbook you just renamed. Take a moment to examine the data, and then close Excel.

(Project 8J–Medical Staff continues on the next page)

(Project 8J–Medical Staff continued)

2. From the student files, locate the Access database **a08J_Medical_Center_Staff**, and then copy and paste the file to your chapter folder. Remove the Read-only property from the file and rename the file as **8J_Medical_Center_Staff_Firstname_Lastname** Start Access and open the database you just renamed.

3. On the Objects bar, be sure **Tables** is selected. From the Database window toolbar, click the **New** button, and in the **New Table** dialog box, click **Link Table**.

4. Click **OK**. Change the **Files of type** to **Microsoft Excel**, and then navigate to your Excel file **8J_Staffing_Firstname_Lastname**. Select the file, and click **Link**.

5. In the **Link Spreadsheet Wizard**, show the **Staffing** worksheet. Indicate that the **First Row Contains Column Headings**. Name the table **Staffing Firstname Lastname** and click **Finish**. Click **OK** to acknowledge that the linking is finished.

6. Open the new table in **Datasheet view**. Apply **Best Fit** to all the columns. **Close** the table and save the changes.

7. Create a new form using a wizard from your **Table: Staffing**. Move **all fields** over to the **Selected Fields** column. Use a **Columnar** layout for the form, and click **Stone** as the style for the form. Leave the form name as **Staffing Firstname Lastname**. **Maximize** the form window and switch to **Design view**. Shorten the left side of the bound controls in the second column to **1 inch on the horizontal ruler**, and then lengthen the label controls in the first column slightly so that none of the labels are cut off.

8. Insert page headers and footers, and in the **Page Footer section**, create a label the approximate height of the footer area and three inches wide. Type **8J Staffing Firstname Lastname**

9. Switch to **Form view** and navigate to record **42**. From the **File** menu, click **Print**. Under **Print Range**, click the **Selected Record(s)** option button, and then click **OK**. Close the form and save changes. Close the database and close Access.

End You have completed Project 8J ――――――――――――

Problem Solving

Project 8K — Friends and Family

Objective: *Import from Excel.*

In the following Problem Solving exercise, you will import an Excel spreadsheet into a new database.

1. Create an Excel spreadsheet with the names of ten of your friends and family members. Create a column for Firstname, Lastname, Address, City, State, ZIP Code, Phone, and E-mail address.

2. Import and Link the Excel worksheet into a new Access table.

3. Change the settings in the table to fit the columns and name the table **Classmates Firstname Lastname Print** the table. Save your database as **8K_Friends_Family_Firstname_Lastname**.

 You have completed Project 8K ———————————————

Project 8L — Classmates

Objective: *Use Mail Merge to Integrate Access and Word.*

In the following Problem Solving exercise, you will create envelopes in Microsoft Word using the Mail Merge wizard.

1. Open the Access database you created in Project 8K and select the Classmates table you imported from Excel.

2. Use the Mail Merge wizard in Microsoft Word to create an envelope for each of the classmates in the table. Put your name and address as the return address.

3. Print the first envelope. Save the ten envelopes as **8L_Friends_Family_Envelopes**.

 You have completed Project 8L ———————————————

On the Internet

Getting Information About OLE

The Microsoft Web site contains a variety of information about using OLE in Access. Go to the Microsoft site at www.microsoft.com and click **Search**. Search for **Access OLE** and examine the information. Print any information that would be helpful to you.

GO! with Help

Removing Links

In this chapter you worked with linking tables between databases. Once a link is created, it is possible to remove the link between the tables.

1. Start Access. In the *Type a question for help* box, type **remove links** and press Enter.

2. In the **Search Results** taskbar, click **Delete the link to a linked table in an Access database**.

3. At the top of the Help window, click **Show All** and read the information.

4. Print the Help information if you want to keep a copy of it. Close the **Help** window, and then close Access.

chapter four

Enhancing a Presentation with Graphic Elements

In this chapter, you will: complete this project **and** practice these skills.

Project 4A **Modifying a Presentation with Graphics**	**Objectives** • Draw and Format Lines • Create Basic Shapes and Text Boxes • Edit and Format Drawing Objects • Create and Format WordArt • Insert Images

The Perfect Party

The Perfect Party store, owned by two partners, provides a wide variety of party accessories including invitations, favors, banners and flags, balloons, piñatas, etc. Party planning services include both custom parties with pre-filled custom "goodie bags" and "parties in a box" that include everything needed to throw a theme party. Big sellers in this category are the Football and Luau themes. The owners are planning to open a second store and expand their party planning services to include catering.

© Getty Images, Inc.

Enhancing a Presentation with Graphic Elements

Clip art and other multimedia images in your presentations can add interest to a presentation and enliven the material. Images are most effective when used to help the audience understand a concept. Because not everyone will interpret a picture the same way, use key words to explain the concept that you want to convey.

With so much clip art from which to choose, it will be tempting to use pictures on every slide you create. Just remember that too many pictures can be distracting and may make the audience think you care more about the images than the message.

In this chapter you will work with graphic elements that you either create or obtain from another source and use PowerPoint's drawing tools to create presentations with graphic elements.

Project 4A **Party**

Microsoft Office PowerPoint 2003 provides a variety of tools for inserting graphic elements into your presentation. Graphic elements that you insert are easily sized, moved, and formatted. Thus, you can format graphics so that they coordinate with your presentation color scheme and design template.

In Activities 4.1 through 4.19, you will modify a presentation that The Perfect Party owners, Angie Nguyen and Gabriela Quinones, have created regarding the services they provide. The presentation will include graphic elements that you will draw using the Drawing toolbar, and pictures that you will insert using the Microsoft Office collections and your student files. Your completed project will look similar to Figure 4.1. You will name the file *4A_Party_ Firstname_Lastname.*

Figure 4.1
Project 4A—Party Presentation

Objective 1
Draw and Format Lines

Microsoft Office PowerPoint 2003 offers a variety of tools with which you can incorporate graphics into your presentations. You can insert graphics that were created in another program or you can create graphics—including shapes and lines—using the Drawing tools in PowerPoint.

Activity 4.1 Drawing Lines

In this activity, you will create a line—one of many **drawing objects** that you can create in PowerPoint. Drawing objects are graphics that include lines and shapes. Many of the techniques you will practice when creating lines can also be applied to other objects and to other drawing tasks in PowerPoint.

1 Start PowerPoint and from your student files, **Open** 📷 the file **p04A_Party**. This presentation contains four slides with the Balloons design template applied. Scroll through the presentation to familiarize yourself with each of the slides, and then on the **Outline/Slides** pane, click the **Close** button ⊠.

2 Check to see if the horizontal and vertical rulers are displayed at the top and left of your screen. If necessary, display the horizontal and vertical rulers by clicking the View menu, and then clicking Ruler.

The PowerPoint horizontal ruler displays above the Slide pane, and the vertical ruler displays to the left of the Slide pane. The PowerPoint rulers display measurements in inches, based on a distance from the center point of the slide. Notice that the center point displays as zero (0) on both the horizontal and vertical rulers. You will use the rulers throughout this chapter to position objects on your slides. See Figure 4.2.

Center point on horizontal ruler

Center point on vertical ruler

Figure 4.2

chapter **four**

3 Look at the lower portion of your PowerPoint window and determine if your Drawing toolbar displays above the status bar. If the toolbar is not displayed, from the View menu, point to Toolbars, and then click Drawing.

4 Display **Slide 2**. From the **Format** menu, click **Background**, and then, in the **Background** dialog box, select the **Omit background graphics from master** check box. Click **Apply**.

The balloon graphics no longer display on Slide 2, which will make it easier to draw your first object—a line.

5 On the Drawing toolbar, click the **Line** button. Move your mouse pointer into the presentation window and notice that it is in the shape of a **plus sign**. This is called the *crosshair pointer*. As you move the pointer in the presentation window, notice the *guides*—small vertical and horizontal lines—in the rulers. These guides visually indicate where you are drawing or positioning your object. For descriptions of the other buttons on the Drawing Toolbar, take a moment to study the table in Figure 4.3.

Buttons on the Drawing Toolbar

Button	Name	Description
Draw ▾	Draw	Displays a menu of controls for editing drawing objects including Group/Ungroup/Regroup, Order, Grid and Guides, Nudge, Align or Distribute, Rotate or Flip, Reroute Connectors, Edit Points, Change AutoShape, and Set AutoShape Defaults.
	Select Objects	Displays a tool used for selecting objects.
AutoShapes ▾	AutoShapes	Displays a menu of automatic shapes; includes Lines, Connectors, Basic Shapes, Block Arrows, Flowchart, Stars and Banners, Callouts, and Action Buttons.
	Line	Draws a line.
	Arrow	Draws an arrow.
	Rectangle	Draws a rectangle.
	Oval	Draws an oval.
	Text Box	Draws a text box.
	Insert WordArt	Opens the WordArt Gallery dialog box.
	Insert Diagram or Organization Chart	Opens the Diagram Gallery dialog box.
	Insert Clip Art	Opens the Clip Art task pane.
	Insert Picture	Opens the Insert Picture dialog box.
	Fill Color	Adds a color, pattern, or a fill effect to the inside of a selected drawing object.
	Line Color	Changes the color or pattern of a selected line.
	Font Color	Changes the color of selected text.
	Line Style	Formats line thickness and style.
	Dash Style	Formats line appearance to one of eight dashed options.
	Arrow Style	Changes arrowhead style to one of PowerPoint's preset arrow options.
	Shadow Style	Adds or changes the shadow of a selected drawing object.
	3-D Style	Adds or changes the 3-D effect of a selected drawing object.

Figure 4.3

6 Using the guides in the ruler to determine placement, position the crosshair pointer below the slide title at **3 inches to the left of zero on the horizontal ruler**, and at **2.5 inches above zero on the vertical ruler** so that the crosshair pointer is positioned below the letter *k* in *Making*. See Figure 4.4.

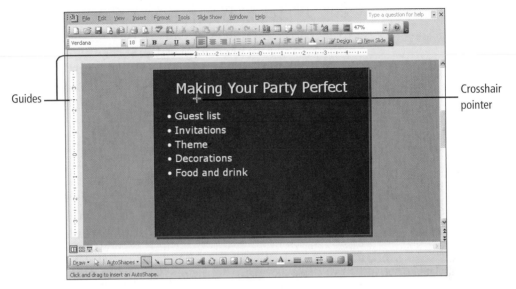

Guides

Crosshair pointer

Figure 4.4

7 Press and hold down Shift, and press and hold down the left mouse button. Holding down Shift ensures that you will draw a straight—not jagged—line. Drag your pointer to the right so that the line extends to the right edge of the slide. See Figure 4.5.

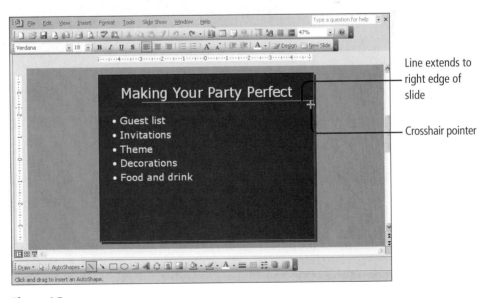

Line extends to right edge of slide

Crosshair pointer

Figure 4.5

8 Release the mouse button, and then release Shift. If you are not satisfied with your results, click the Undo button and begin again.

Releasing the mouse button prior to releasing Shift ensures that the line remains straight and will not revert to a jagged line. The small white circles at either end of the line are **sizing handles**. The sizing handles indicate that the line is currently selected.

9 Click anywhere on your slide so that the line is not selected. From the **File** menu, click **Save As**, and then navigate to the location where you are storing your projects for this chapter. Create a new folder for Chapter 4 if you want to do so. In the **File name** box type **4A_Party_Firstname_Lastname**

Activity 4.2 Changing Line Style

Lines add impact and visual interest to your presentations. The default line is a ¾ pt. solid line; however, you can format a line by changing both its color and its style. You can also apply a dash style to create a patterned line. To format a line or other object, you must first select it. An object is selected when you see the sizing handles at the edges of the object.

1 On **Slide 2**, move your pointer over the line to display the move pointer. Click the left mouse button.

The sizing handles display indicating that the line is selected.

2 On the Drawing toolbar, click the **Line Style** button. On the displayed list, click the **6 pt.** solid line style, as shown in Figure 4.6.

Figure 4.6

3 With the line still selected, move your pointer to the Drawing toolbar, and then click the **Dash Style** button ☰. On the displayed list, click the second dash style—**Round Dot**.

The Round Dot dash style is applied to the line.

4 With the line still selected, on the Drawing toolbar, click the **Dash Style** button ☰ again. On the displayed list, click the first style—**Solid**.

5 On the Standard toolbar, click the **Save** button 🖫.

Activity 4.3 Changing Line Color

The default line color is determined by the presentation's color scheme; however, the color is easily changed. You can choose a color from the template color scheme, from the Standard color honeycomb, or from the Custom color palette.

1 If necessary, select the line on **Slide 2** by moving the pointer over the line so that the move pointer ⊕ displays. Click the left mouse button so that the sizing handles are visible at both ends of the line.

2 On the Drawing toolbar, click the **Line Color arrow** ✏▾ to display the color scheme palette.

Alert!

Click the Arrow!

If you clicked the Line Color *button* instead of the Line Color *arrow*, the Line Color palette will not display and your line reflects the color of the Line Color button.

3 Click the fifth color in the color scheme—**teal**.

4 Point to the line so that the move pointer ⊕ displays. Press and hold down Ctrl.

The pointer displays with a plus sign attached to it. This pointer indicates that you can drag to *copy* the selected object. Recall that drag-and-drop is a feature that allows you to copy or move a selection. You can use drag-and-drop to duplicate your formatted line.

5 With Ctrl still pressed, press the left mouse button and drag the pointer down and to the left noticing the dashed line that displays. When the left edge of the dashed line aligns with the left edge of the slide at **2.5 inches below zero on the vertical ruler**, release the mouse button, and then release Ctrl to create a copy of the line. See Figure 4.7.

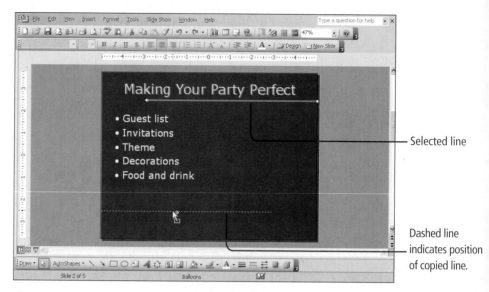

Selected line

Dashed line indicates position of copied line.

Figure 4.7

Alert!

Did You Move the Line?

If you released Ctrl before you released the left mouse button, your line was *moved* instead of copied. Click Undo and try again.

6️⃣ On the Standard toolbar, click the **Save** button 🖫.

Objective 2
Create Basic Shapes and Text Boxes

In addition to creating lines, you can draw a number of shapes. Shapes include circles and squares, rectangles and ovals, and a variety of special shapes found in the **AutoShapes** menu. AutoShapes include cubes, hearts, lightning bolts, arrows, stars, and flowchart elements.

Another type of drawing object is a **text box**, which is used to position text anywhere on a slide. As with all drawing objects, a text box can be moved and sized, and its colors can be changed. The same techniques that you used to draw and select lines can be applied to shapes and text boxes.

Activity 4.4 Creating Text Boxes

Slide layouts contain predefined placeholder positions. When you create a text box, you can *draw* a placeholder anywhere on the slide, and then if necessary, change its size and position.

1️⃣ If necessary, **open** 📂 your file **4A_Party_Firstname_Lastname**, and close the **Outline/Slides** pane.

2️⃣ Display **Slide 4**. On the Formatting toolbar, click the **New Slide** button.

A new slide is inserted as Slide 5 with the Title and Text layout.

3 In the **Slide Layout** task pane, under **Content Layouts**, click the first layout—**Blank**. On the task pane title bar, click the **Close** button ⊠.

The slide contains no placeholders.

4 On the Drawing toolbar, click the **Text Box** button 🔄, and then move your pointer into the slide.

The pointer displays as a vertical line with a small horizontal line near its lower end.

5 Using the guides in the ruler to assist with visual placement, position the pointer at **2 inches to the left of zero on the horizontal ruler** and at **2.5 inches below zero on the vertical ruler**. Press and hold down the left mouse button and drag down to **3 inches on the vertical ruler** and to the **right edge of the slide**. Release the left mouse button and compare your text box with Figure 4.8.

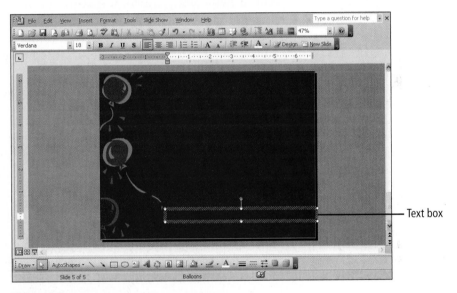

— Text box

Figure 4.8

6 With the insertion point positioned in the text box, type **At the Perfect Party, everyone has fun!**

7 Click on the outer edge of the text box so that its boundary box displays as a pattern of dots.

Recall that when a placeholder is selected in this manner, all of the text within the placeholder is also selected. This is also true for text boxes.

8 On the Formatting toolbar, click the **Font Size arrow** `32 ▾`, and then click **32**. On the Formatting toolbar, click the **Center** button 🔳.

The text box expands to accommodate the text size and the text is centered within the box.

9 On the Standard toolbar, click the **Save** button 🔳.

Activity 4.5 Drawing Ovals and Rectangles

In this activity, you will use the Rectangle and Oval buttons to draw basic shapes.

1 Display **Slide 3**. On the Drawing toolbar, click the **Rectangle** button ⬜.

Notice that the Rectangle button is highlighted and, as you move the pointer into the presentation, the crosshair pointer displays.

2 Position the pointer at **3 inches to the left of zero on the horizontal ruler** and at **2 inches above zero on the vertical ruler**. Drag down and to the right to create a rectangle that extends to **3 inches to the right of zero on the horizontal ruler** and to **2 inches below zero on the vertical ruler**.

A teal-colored rectangle is created. The inside color of an object is called the **_fill color_**. You can change the fill color to another solid color, a two-color pattern, a texture, or even fill it with a picture. The teal color currently displayed is the fill color for the color scheme associated with the Balloons design template. Thus, it is the default color applied to all filled objects in this presentation. See Figure 4.9.

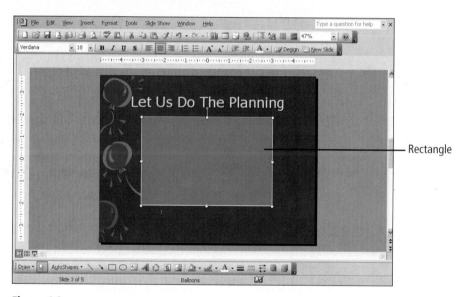

Figure 4.9

Note — Drawing Squares

You can draw a perfect square by pressing and holding down Shift while drawing a rectangle. Release the left mouse button before releasing Shift.

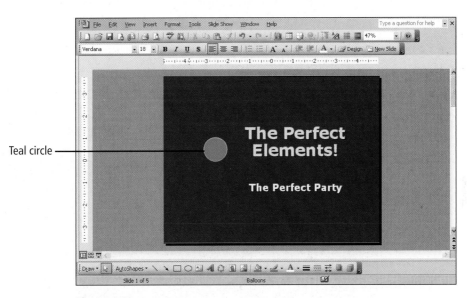

3 Display **Slide 1**. The background on this slide detracts from the text. Thus, you will turn off the background objects and use the Oval command to draw balloons. On the **Format** menu, click **Background**. In the **Background** dialog box, select the **Omit background graphics from master** check box, and then click **Apply**.

The background graphics are omitted, leaving a dark blue background.

4 On the Drawing toolbar, click the **Oval** button, and then move the pointer into the window to display the crosshair pointer.

5 Position the crosshair pointer at **3 inches to the left of zero on the horizontal ruler**, and at **1 inch above zero on the vertical ruler**. Hold down Shift, drag down and to the right to **2 inches to the left of zero on the horizontal ruler**, and **zero on the vertical ruler**, release the left mouse button, and then release the Shift key. Click outside of the circle to deselect, and then compare your slide with Figure 4.10.

A teal *circle* displays; this is the first of three balloons that you will draw. Holding down Shift ensures that you will draw a perfect circle rather than an oval.

Teal circle

Figure 4.10

Alert!

Does Your Circle Look Like an Oval?

Be sure to release Shift *after* you release the left mouse button. If your object looks like an oval instead of a circle, click Undo and try again.

6 Point to the circle so that the move pointer displays. Press and hold down Ctrl and drag the circle down and to the left as shown in Figure 4.11. Release the mouse button and then release Ctrl to duplicate the circle. Repeat the process to create the third circle as shown in Figure 4.11.

Your slide contains three circles. The placement of the circles need not be precise.

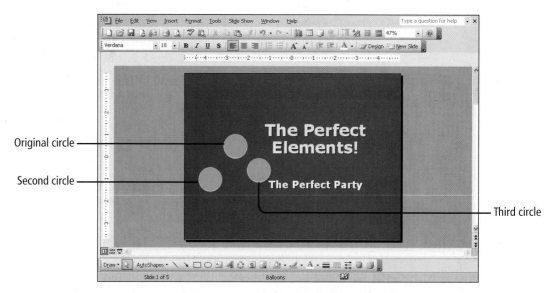

Original circle

Second circle

Third circle

Figure 4.11

7 On the Drawing toolbar, click the **Line** button ⬚. Press and hold down Shift, refer to Figure 4.12, and then draw a two-inch line that extends downward from the *center* circle. Release the left mouse button, and then release Shift.

A straight line displays.

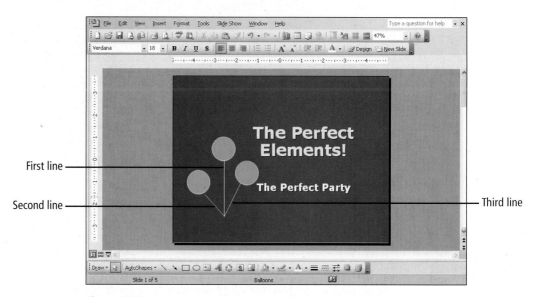

First line

Second line

Third line

Figure 4.12

8 On the Drawing toolbar, click the **Line** button ⬚. Press and hold down Shift, and then refer to Figure 4.12 to draw a line that extends from the circle closest to the left edge of the slide and that touches the first line you drew. Repeat the process to draw the third line.

Your slide contains three circles and three lines.

Note — Where Do You Draw the Line?

If you are having difficulty making the ends of your lines meet, first click Undo to remove the lines you drew. Then try this drawing technique. Draw the first line. Then, instead of drawing the second line starting at the circle and dragging down to meet the line, make your starting point the bottom of the first line. Then drag up to meet the circle.

9 On the Standard toolbar, click **Save** 🔲.

Activity 4.6 Creating and Customizing AutoShapes

In addition to ovals and rectangles, PowerPoint has a gallery of other interesting shapes called AutoShapes that you can place in a presentation. AutoShapes, which are accessed by clicking the AutoShapes button on the Drawing toolbar, are categorized into Lines, Connectors, Basic Shapes, Block Arrows, Flowchart, Stars & Banners, Callouts, Action Buttons, and More AutoShapes.

1 Display **Slide 5**. On the Drawing toolbar, click the **AutoShapes** button AutoShapes ▾. Point to each of the menu items to view a palette containing the shapes available in each category.

2 Point to **Stars and Banners** and then, in the second row, click the second shape—**16-Point Star**. See Figure 4.13.

Stars and Banners menu

AutoShapes button

16-Point Star

Figure 4.13

3 Position the crosshair pointer in the center of the slide—**at zero on the horizontal ruler** and **zero on the vertical ruler**. Click the left mouse button.

A 16-point star measuring 1 inch wide by 1 inch high displays in the center of the slide. When you are drawing an object, clicking the mouse button instead of dragging the mouse creates a 1-inch by 1-inch object.

4 If necessary, click the star to select it.

Notice that when the star is selected, a small yellow diamond displays in addition to the white sizing handles. This is the *adjustment handle*, which is used to adjust the appearance but not the size of an AutoShape, for example, the width of an arm on a star.

5 Point to the yellow adjustment handle until the pointer becomes an arrowhead. Press and hold down the left mouse button, and then drag toward the center of the star. When the pointer is approximately halfway to the center, as shown in Figure 4.14, release the left mouse button.

The points of the star are sharper. If you are not satisfied with your result, drag the adjustment handle again. Your result need not be precise.

Figure 4.14

More Knowledge — Have Some Fun with AutoShapes!

Many AutoShapes contain the adjustment handle, which allows you to customize the AutoShape. For example, the happy face found in the Basic Shapes menu can be changed to a sad face when the yellow diamond is dragged upward. Be creative!

---

6 Display **Slide 1**. On the Drawing toolbar, click the **AutoShapes** button `AutoShapes`, and then point to **Stars and Banners**. In the third row, click the first AutoShape—**Up Ribbon**.

7 Using Figure 4.15 as a guide, press and hold down the left mouse button and draw a small ribbon that overlaps the intersection of the balloon strings. Release the left mouse button to create a teal ribbon. As necessary to move your shape, point to display the move pointer and drag the shape to the desired position.

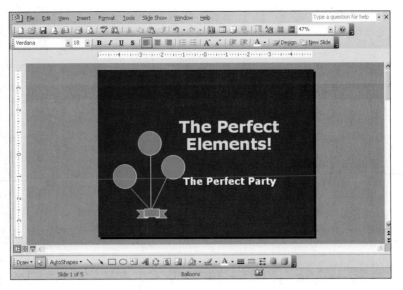

Figure 4.15

8 On the Standard toolbar, click **Save** [icon].

Objective 3
Edit and Format Drawing Objects

After they are created, drawing objects such as lines and shapes can be deleted, resized, and moved. Additionally, using the shortcut menu, text can be added to drawing objects.

Activity 4.7 Deleting and Changing a Drawing Object

To delete a drawing object, you must first select it. Recall that a drawing object is selected if the sizing handles display. In addition to deleting a selected object, you can change an object by applying a different AutoShape.

1 If necessary, **open** [icon] your file **4A_Party_Firstname_Lastname**.

2 Display **Slide 5**. Point to the star so that the move pointer [icon] displays. Click the left mouse button to select the star, and then press Delete.

The star is deleted from the slide.

3 Display **Slide 3**. Click the rectangle to select it. On the Drawing toolbar, click the **Draw** button [Draw ▾] to display the Draw menu. Point to **Change AutoShape**, and then point to **Basic Shapes**. In the fourth row, click the third shape—**Change Shape to Bevel**. See Figure 4.16.

The rectangle is converted to the bevel shape.

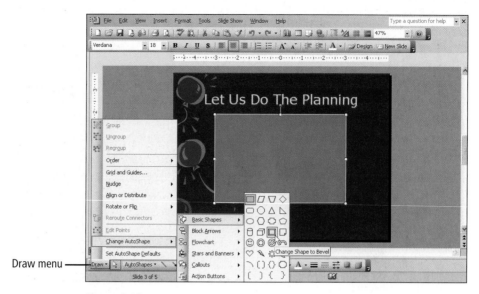

Draw menu

Figure 4.16

4 On the menu bar, click **Format**, and then click **Background**. In the **Background** dialog box, select the **Omit background graphics from master** check box, and then click **Apply**.

The balloons from the design template are removed from the slide.

5 **Save** the file.

Activity 4.8 Sizing a Drawing Object

You can change the size of a drawing object by dragging its sizing handle or by entering a measurement in the Format AutoShape dialog box. In this activity, you will change, or verify the size of, several of the shapes in your presentation.

1 If necessary, display **Slide 3**. Point to the bevel shape to display the move pointer ⊕, and then click to select it.

2 Point to the bottom center sizing handle to display the vertical resize pointer ↕. Press and hold down the left mouse button and drag up to **1.5 inches below zero on the vertical ruler**. Release the mouse button.

3 Point to the top center sizing handle to display the vertical resize pointer ↕. To resize the bevel, drag down to **1.5 inches above zero on the vertical ruler**.

4 Display **Slide 4**, and then click the bulleted list placeholder. Point to the bottom center sizing handle and drag up so that the bottom border is positioned at **2 inches below zero on the vertical ruler**.

5 Display **Slide 1**, and then click the **ribbon AutoShape** to select it. From the **Format** menu, click **AutoShape**. Alternatively, right-click, and on the shortcut menu, click Format AutoShape.

The Format AutoShape dialog box displays.

6 Click the **Size tab**.

In this dialog box, you can enter an exact width and height measurement. Under Scale, locate the Lock aspect ratio check box. When checked, this feature automatically adjusts the height proportionately if the width is adjusted, and vice versa.

7 Under **Scale**, if necessary, click to *clear* (remove the check mark from) the **Lock aspect ratio** check box. Under **Size and rotate**, select the entry in the **Height** box. Type **.25** and then press Tab to move the insertion point to the **Width** box. Type **1** and then compare your dialog box with Figure 4.17. Do not be concerned if the percentages under Scale do not match the Figure. Click **OK**.

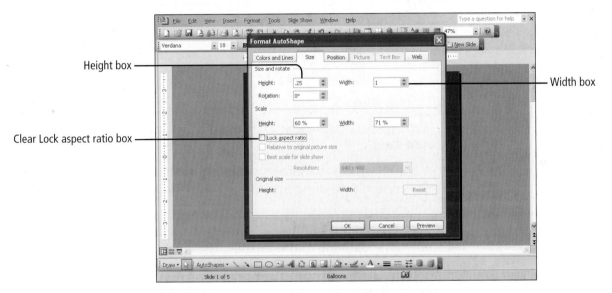

Height box ——

Width box

Clear Lock aspect ratio box ——

Figure 4.17

8 **Save** your file.

Activity 4.9 Moving a Drawing Object

An object can be positioned anywhere on a slide. You can move an object by dragging with the mouse, using the directional arrow keys on your keyboard to move it in small increments, or by entering a precise location in the Position box in the Format AutoShape dialog box. In this activity, you will reposition the ribbon shape on Slide 1 and the bevel shape on Slide 3.

1 Display **Slide 1**, and then select the ribbon. On your keyboard, press ← once, and notice that the object is nudged slightly to the left. As necessary, use the ← and/or → keys to nudge the ribbon so that the balloon strings touch the center of the ribbon.

You can use the directional arrow keys to move an object in all four directions in small increments.

2 Display **Slide 3**, and then point to the bevel so that the move pointer displays. Drag down so that the top edge of the shape is aligned at **1 inch above zero on the vertical ruler**.

3 Save 🖫 the file.

> ## Note — Experiment with the Size and Placement of Objects
>
> In this textbook, the size and position of the objects that you create have been determined for you. Sizing and positioning objects in a presentation takes time and practice. As you create your own presentations that contain objects, do not be surprised if you rearrange the objects many times. When creating your own presentations, experiment until you are satisfied with your results.

Activity 4.10 Adding Text to a Drawing Object

A drawing object adds visual interest to a presentation, but it also serves another purpose. Using the Add Text option on the shortcut menu, a shape can be used as a *container* for text. Text added to a drawing object can be formatted using the font formatting options.

1 Display **Slide 3**. Point to the bevel AutoShape until the move pointer ⊕ displays. Right-click to display the shortcut menu, and then click **Add Text**.

A boundary box composed of slash marks displays around the bevel object, and a flashing insertion point is positioned in the center of the bevel.

2 Type **Invitations** and then press Enter. Type **Decorations** and then press Enter. Type **Catering** and then click the outer edge of the shape so that its boundary displays as a pattern of dots.

Recall that a dotted pattern indicates that formatting will be applied to all of the text within a placeholder. The same is true of AutoShapes that contain text.

3 On the Formatting toolbar, click the **Font Size arrow** 32 ▾, click **32**, and then click the **Bold** button **B**.

4 Locate and point to the yellow adjustment handle to display the arrowhead pointer, and then using Figure 4.18 as a guide, drag up and to the left so that the bevel outline is very thin. Release the mouse button.

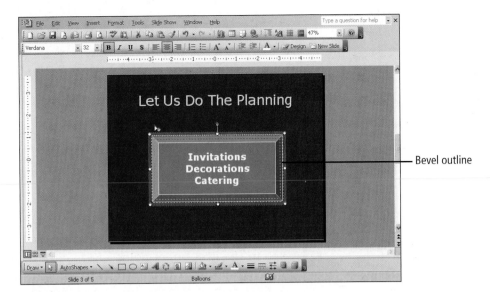

Bevel outline

Figure 4.18

More Knowledge — Wrapping Text in an AutoShape

Sometimes the text that you insert in an AutoShape does not wrap to the next line and extends outside the boundaries of the shape. To wrap text in an AutoShape or text box, display the Format menu, and then click AutoShape or Text Box. Click the Text Box tab, and then select the Word wrap text in AutoShape check box.

5 **Save** the file.

Activity 4.11 Changing the Fill Color and Line Color of an Object

Recall that the color of the inside of an object is called the fill color. You can change the fill color of an object or a placeholder to another solid color, a two-color pattern, a texture, or fill it with a picture. The techniques that you learned at the beginning of this chapter to change the color, the width, and the style of a *line* also apply to the *borders* of objects. Additionally, you can eliminate the border surrounding the object. In this activity you will change the fill and the line colors of several objects.

1 Display **Slide 4**, and then click in the bulleted list placeholder to select it.

2 On the Drawing toolbar, click the **Fill Color arrow** to display the design template's color scheme. Click the fifth color—**teal**.

Click outside the placeholder to deselect it and view the teal fill color.

Alert!

Is Your Placeholder a Different Color?

The Fill Color button reflects the most recently applied color. If you click the Fill Color button, the shape will fill with the color displayed. If this is not the desired color, click the Undo button.

3 Click the bulleted list placeholder again to select it. On the Drawing toolbar, click the **Line Color arrow** ![icon], and then click **More Line Colors**. In the **Colors** dialog box, click the **Standard tab**, and in the fourth row from the bottom of the color honeycomb, click the eighth color—**dark pink**. Click **OK**.

4 On the Drawing toolbar, click the **Line Style** button ![icon], and then click the **3 pt. solid line**.

5 On the Drawing toolbar, click the **Dash Style** button ![icon], and then click the second dash style—**Round Dot**.

Click outside the placeholder to deselect, and notice that the placeholder is bordered by a dark pink dotted line.

6 Click in the first bullet point—*Kids parties*. From the **Format** menu, click **Bullets and Numbering**, and then in the lower right corner of the **Bullets and Numbering** dialog box, click the **Picture** button. In the **Search text** box, type **ball** and then click **Go**. In the first row, click the **multicolored ball**, and then click **OK**.

The multicolored ball bullet is applied to the first bullet point.

7 Click in the *Adult parties* bullet point. Press [F4] to repeat the bullet format, and then click anywhere on the slide to deselect the placeholder. Compare your slide with Figure 4.19.

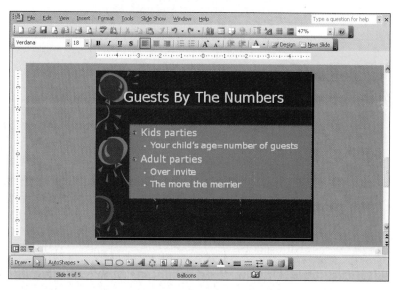

Figure 4.19

8 Display **Slide 5**. Point to the text box and right-click to display the shortcut menu. Click **Format Text Box**. Display the **Colors and Lines tab**, and under **Fill**, click the **Color arrow**. Notice that the slide color scheme displays, as does a palette of additional colors. In the slide color scheme, click the fifth color—**teal**.

9 Under **Line**, click the **Color arrow**. Below the palette, the custom colors that you have applied to the presentation display. Click the custom color—**dark pink**. Click the **Style arrow**, and then click the seventh style—**3 pt. solid line**. Compare your dialog box with Figure 4.20, and then click **OK**.

Using the Format Text Box dialog box, you applied all of the formatting necessary for the textbox—fill color, line color, and line style.

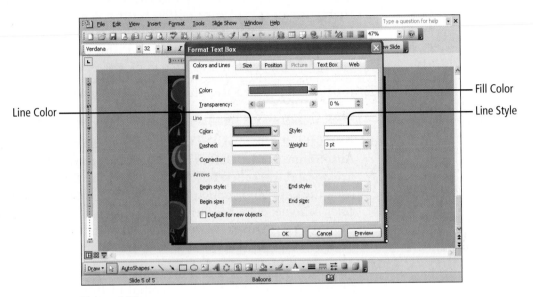

Figure 4.20

10 Display **Slide 3** and click the bevel AutoShape to select it. On the Drawing toolbar, click the **Fill Color arrow**, and then click **Fill Effects**.

Recall that the Fill Effects dialog box allows you to apply gradient fills, textures, pictures, and patterns to your backgrounds. You can use these same techniques to change the Fill Effect for an object.

11 Click the **Gradient tab**, and then under **Colors**, click the **One color** option button. Click the **Color 1 arrow**, and then click the fifth color—**teal**. Under **Shading styles**, click **From center**. Under **Variants**, click the first option, and then click **OK**. Click outside of the bevel to deselect and view the fill effect.

12 Display **Slide 1**, and then click the leftmost circle. On the Drawing toolbar, click the **Fill Color arrow**, and then click **Fill Effects**. Click the **Gradient tab**, and then click the **One color** option button. Click the **Color 1 arrow**, and then click **More Colors**. In the color honeycomb, in the third row from the bottom, click the third color—**yellow**. Click **OK**. Under **Shading styles**, click **From center**. Under **Variants**, click the first option, and then click **OK**.

A gradient fill is applied to the circle, giving it a 3-dimensional appearance so that it looks like a balloon.

13 If necessary, click the yellow circle. On the Drawing toolbar, click the **Line Color arrow**, and at the top of the menu, click **No Line**.

The line is removed from the circle.

14 Select the center circle. On the Drawing toolbar, click the **Fill Color arrow** , and then click **Fill Effects**. Click the **Gradient tab**, and then click the **One color** option button. Click the **Color 1 arrow**, and below the color scheme, in the custom colors palette, click **dark pink**. Under **Shading styles**, click **From center**. Under **Variants**, click the first option, and then click **OK**.

15 If necessary, select the pink circle. On the Drawing toolbar, click the **Line Color arrow** , and at the top of the menu, click **No Line**.

16 Select the third circle. On the menu bar, click **Format**, and then click **AutoShape**. In the **Colors and Lines tab**, under **Fill**, click the **Color arrow**, and then click **Fill Effects**. Click the **Gradient tab**, and then click the **One color** option button. Click the **Color 1 arrow**, and in the color scheme, click the fifth color—**teal**. Under **Shading styles**, click **From center**. Under **Variants**, click the first option, and then click **OK**. Under **Line**, click the **Color arrow**, and then click **No Line**. Click **OK**.

The circle is filled with a teal gradient. Fill color and Line color can be applied from the Drawing toolbar or from the Format AutoShape dialog box.

17 On **Slide 1**, select the ribbon shape. On the Drawing toolbar, click the **Fill Color arrow** , and then click the first custom color—**dark pink**. Click the **Line Color arrow** , and then click the first color—**dark blue**. Click outside to deselect the ribbon, and then compare your slide with Figure 4.21.

18 Save the file.

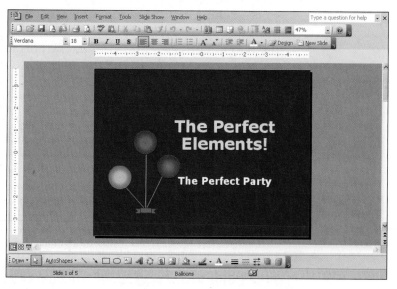

Figure 4.21

Objective 4
Create and Format WordArt

WordArt is a drawing tool used to transform text into graphic objects. It is best used for titles or short lines of text that you want to enhance and to which you want to draw the audience's attention. You can type your text in the WordArt dialog box, choose a texture or fill color and shadowing effect, and then pour the words into a WordArt shape. Once your WordArt is created, you can flip, stretch, rotate, and angle the words.

Activity 4.12 Inserting, Sizing, and Positioning WordArt

In this activity, you will insert, size, and position a WordArt object on Slide 3.

1 If necessary, **open** 📷 your file **4A_Party_Firstname_Lastname**.

2 Display **Slide 3**. On the Drawing toolbar, click the **Insert WordArt** button 4️⃣.

The WordArt Gallery dialog box displays the basic WordArt designs that you can apply to text. Here you can choose a design that resembles the type of WordArt that you want to apply. Later, you can redefine the color, shape, and shadowing for your selected WordArt design.

3 In the third row, click the first WordArt design. See Figure 4.22. Click **OK** to accept the design and open the **Edit WordArt Text** dialog box.

In the Edit WordArt Text dialog box, you will type the text that you want to enhance with the WordArt design. You can also change the font and font size.

Choose this design. —

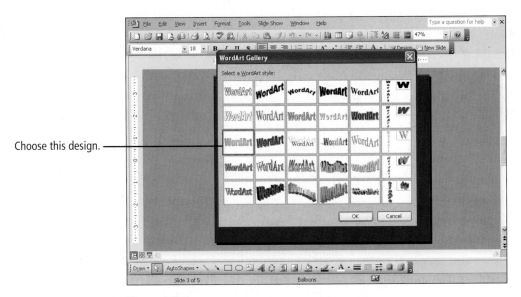

Figure 4.22

4 With the text *Your Text Here* selected, type **Come To The Perfect Party!** and then click **OK** to create the WordArt and return to the presentation.

The *Come To The Perfect Party!* WordArt displays in the center of the slide. Notice that the object is selected and displays sizing handles and a yellow adjustment handle. The WordArt toolbar also displays on your screen. See Figure 4.23.

Figure 4.23

5 To position the WordArt correctly, point to the WordArt object to display the move pointer ⊕. Press and hold down the left mouse button and drag the WordArt down, so that its bottom edge aligns with the lower edge of the slide. Release the mouse button.

Another Way — **To Size and Position a WordArt**

Use the Format WordArt Dialog Box

The Size and Position tabs of the Format WordArt dialog box contain the same sizing and positioning options that apply to drawing objects and AutoShapes.

6 To size the WordArt, point to the center top sizing handle to display the vertical resize pointer ↕. Drag the sizing handle up so that the top edge aligns at **2.5 inches below zero on the vertical ruler**. Click anywhere in the slide so that the WordArt object is not selected.

Notice that after the WordArt is deselected, the WordArt toolbar no longer displays.

7 Point to the WordArt to display the move pointer ⊕, and then click the left mouse button to select it.

The WordArt toolbar displays.

Is Your WordArt Toolbar Displayed?

If the WordArt toolbar does not display when the WordArt is selected, point to any displayed toolbar, right-click to display the toolbar list, and then click WordArt. Alternatively, on the menu bar, click View, point to Toolbars, and then click WordArt.

8 **Save** the file.

Activity 4.13 Changing the Shape and Design of WordArt

The design you choose from the WordArt Gallery dialog box is the basic design with which you work. In this activity, you will experiment with the *shape* of the design that you chose and then apply a different design from the gallery.

1 With the *Come To The Perfect Party!* WordArt object selected, move to the WordArt toolbar, and then click the **WordArt Shape** button to display a palette of shapes.

2 In the first row, click the fourth shape—**Triangle Down**. See Figure 4.24.

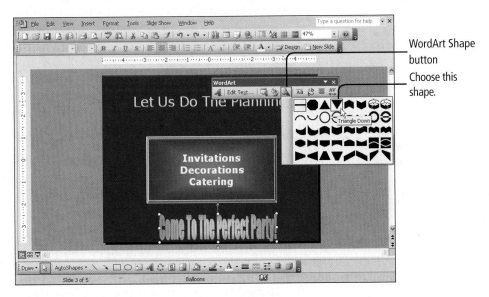

WordArt Shape button

Choose this shape.

Figure 4.24

3 Using the **WordArt Shape** button on the WordArt toolbar, apply several of the shapes. When you have finished experimenting with the shapes in the palette, in the first row, click the third shape—**Triangle Up**.

4 If necessary, select the WordArt. On the WordArt toolbar, click the **WordArt Gallery** button.

The WordArt Gallery dialog box displays. When a new design is chosen, the default color and shape of the design are applied, and any previous color and shape changes are removed.

5 In the second row, click the fourth design, and then click **OK**, to apply a new WordArt design.

6 On the Standard toolbar, click **Save**.

Activity 4.14 Changing the Fill Color of WordArt

After you choose a WordArt design from the gallery, you can easily change the default color using solid colors, gradient fills, and textures. Recall that a gradient fill is a color combination in which one color fades into another. In this activity, you will change the WordArt color by applying a gradient fill.

1 If necessary, point to the WordArt object and click to select it. If the WordArt toolbar is not displayed on your screen, point to a displayed toolbar, click the right mouse button to display the toolbar list, and then click WordArt.

2 On the WordArt toolbar, click **Format WordArt** 🎨. Click the **Colors and Lines tab**. Under **Fill**, click the **Color arrow**. Near the bottom of the color palette, click **Fill Effects**. Click the **Gradient tab**.

As with objects and backgrounds, notice that you can choose a One color gradient, a Two colors gradient, or a Preset gradient.

3 Under **Colors**, click the **Two colors** option button. Click the **Color 1 arrow** to display the color scheme, and then click the second color—**white**. Click the **Color 2 arrow**, and then click the fifth color—**teal**. Under **Shading styles**, click **Horizontal**. Under **Variants**, in the first row, click the second variant. Click **OK**, and then click **OK** again to apply the color change.

4 **Save** 💾 your presentation.

Activity 4.15 Formatting and Editing WordArt Text

In addition to changing the color and shape of WordArt, the text can be edited and the spacing, alignment, and direction of the text can be changed. In this activity, you will edit the text and change the spacing of your WordArt object.

1 Point to your WordArt to display the move pointer ✥, and then double-click. Alternatively, click the Edit Text button on the WordArt toolbar.

The Edit WordArt Text dialog box displays.

2 Select the text *Come To* and the space following it, and then press Delete. In the **Edit WordArt Text** dialog box, to the right of the Size box, click the **Bold** button **B**, and then click **OK**.

3 If necessary, select the **WordArt** object. On the WordArt toolbar, click the **WordArt Character Spacing** button ᴬⱽ↔, and from the displayed menu, click **Tight** and view the effect on the WordArt. Click the button again, and then click **Loose**. Click anywhere on your slide to deselect the WordArt object, and then compare your slide with Figure 4.25.

The characters are spaced less closely together than with the Tight spacing. The Character Spacing button adjusts the width of the individual letters in a WordArt.

Figure 4.25

4 Using Figure 4.25 as a guide, use the directional arrow keys on your keyboard to nudge the WordArt into the correct position on the slide. Then, click to deselect the WordArt object.

5 On the Standard toolbar, click **Save** 🖫.

Objective 5
Insert Images

One type of image that you can insert into your presentations is clip art. Clip art images—often called **clips**—can be purchased from software vendors. A clip is a single media file including art, sound, animation, or movies that you can use in a presentation. A collection of clip art images comes with your Microsoft Office software; additional images are available from the Microsoft Office Online Web site. Using the **Clip Organizer**, you can insert, view, and categorize the images that you want to use in your presentations. You can also insert digital images, including scanned photos or pictures taken with a digital camera. These images are composed of **pixels**—dots that help to determine the resolution of your computer screen.

Activity 4.16 Inserting Clip Art Using Content Layouts

In this activity, you will insert a clip art image on Slide 2 by using the Title, Text, and Clip Art slide layout.

1 If necessary, **Open** 📂 your file **4A_Party_Firstname_Lastname**.

2 Display **Slide 2**, which is currently formatted using the Title and Text layout. From the **Format** menu, click **Slide Layout**. In the **Slide Layout** task pane, scroll down and under **Other Layouts**, click **Title, Text, and Clip Art**. **Close** ⊠ the task pane.

The slide layout displays a bulleted list on the left and a placeholder on the right that allows you to add clip art. Notice also that the new layout moved the title placeholder partially below the teal line.

3 Click the title placeholder, and then point to the top center sizing handle. Drag down so that the top of the placeholder closely fits the title.

4 Point to an outer edge of the placeholder to display the move pointer ⊕ (do *not* point to a sizing handle) and drag up so that the bottom edge of the placeholder touches the teal line.

The title displays above the line.

5 Double-click the **Double click to add clip art** placeholder. See Figure 4.26.

The Select Picture dialog box displays, in which you can type a keyword to search for clips.

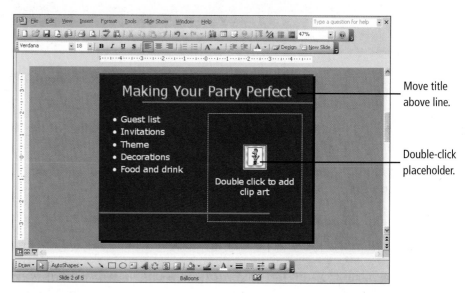

Figure 4.26

6 In the **Search text** box, type **celebration** and then click **Go**.

Several clips display matching the keyword Celebration.

More Knowledge — Get Your Clips Online!

Microsoft Office PowerPoint 2003 easily integrates with the Microsoft Office Online Web site where thousands of clips are stored. If your Internet connection is open when you search for clips, PowerPoint will include the online clips in your search results. To use this feature, connect to the Internet and then minimize your browser window. Click the Insert Clip Art button and type your keyword in the Search text box. Click Go, and then be amazed at the large number of clips to which you will have access!

7 Click the clip that contains a light blue and light green background with a mask, and then click **OK**. See Figure 4.27.

The mask clip is inserted and the placeholder no longer displays. You will size and move the image in a later activity.

Keyword Celebration

Click this picture.

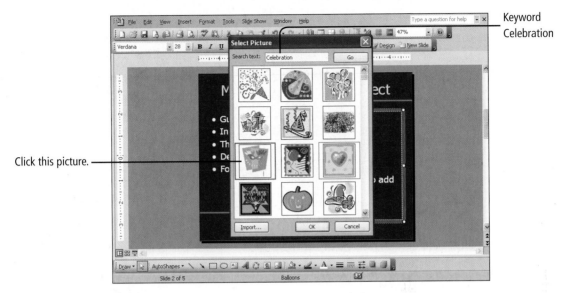

Figure 4.27

8 **Save** your presentation.

Activity 4.17 Inserting Clip Art Using the Drawing Toolbar

In this activity, you will add clip art to your presentation by using the Insert Clip Art button on the Drawing toolbar.

1 If possible, connect to the Internet, and then minimize your browser window.

Recall that connecting to the Internet before searching for clip art will give you access to the clips on the Microsoft Online Web site.

2 Display **Slide 5**. On the Drawing toolbar, click **Insert Clip Art** to display the **Clip Art** task pane.

3 In the **Search for** box, type **Hats and Balloons** to search for clips by keyword.

4 Click the **Search in arrow**.

A hierarchy of folders displays, indicating the *collections*—the categories into which your clips are organized. *My Collections* are clips that you have stored on your system. *Office Collections* are clips that are available with Microsoft Office 2003. *Web Collections* include clips from Microsoft Office Online. You can expand each of these collections to view their contents by clicking the plus sign to the left of each collection name.

5 If necessary, click to select the **Everywhere** check box. See Figure 4.28. The Search in box displays *All collections*.

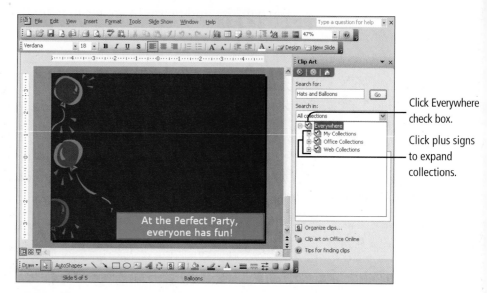

Click Everywhere check box.

Click plus signs to expand collections.

Figure 4.28

6 Click in an empty area of the task pane to close the **Search in** list. Then, click the **Results should be arrow** to display the types of *media*—Clip Art, Photographs, Movies, or Sounds—for which you can search. Click to *clear* the Photographs, Movies, and Sounds check boxes, and verify that the **Clip Art** check box is selected.

The task pane indicates that you will search *All collections* for *Clip Art* that matches the keywords *Hats and Balloons*. See Figure 4.29.

7 Click **Go**.

Keywords

All collections

Clip Art selected

Figure 4.29

8 Locate the picture of a party hat and balloon on a yellow and blue background. Point to the clip and notice that information regarding the image displays, including keywords, size, and image type.

9 Click the image to insert it into the center of your slide, and then **Close** ⊠ the task pane.

Another Way ── **To Insert Clip Art**

You can search for clips in collections without typing a keyword. For example, if you want to view all of the clips in the Animals collection, clear the Everywhere check box, click the Office Collections box, and then click the Animals check box. Click Go. Only the clips in the Animals collection will display.

10 **Save** 🖫 the file.

Activity 4.18 Sizing and Moving a Picture

Using the techniques you practiced to change the size of a drawing object, you can resize a clip art image. To maintain the original proportions of the image, use the corner sizing handles. You can also resize an image from the Format Picture dialog box, in which you can *lock the aspect ratio* in the Size tab of the Format Picture dialog box. This ensures that the image retains its original proportions.

1 Display **Slide 5** and click the clip art to select it. If necessary, right-click the clip art, and from the displayed shortcut menu, click Show Picture Toolbar to display the Picture toolbar. Point to the upper right sizing handle so that the diagonal resize pointer ⤢ displays. Drag up and to the right until the picture is approximately twice its original size.

2 Display **Slide 2**, and then right-click the mask image to display the shortcut menu. Click **Format Picture**, and then in the **Format Picture** dialog box, click the **Size tab**. Alternatively, you can click the image, and on the Format menu, click Format Picture.

3 Under **Scale**, verify that the **Lock aspect ratio** and **Relative to original picture size** check boxes are selected (checked).

Selecting these two options ensures that the image will maintain its original proportions based on the original size of the image.

4 Under **Scale** (*not* Under Size and rotate), select the value in the **Height** box, type **150** and then press Tab.

Notice that the Width box changes to 150%. When the Lock aspect ratio option is selected, the Width box is automatically adjusted when a Height percentage is changed. Compare your dialog box with Figure 4.30.

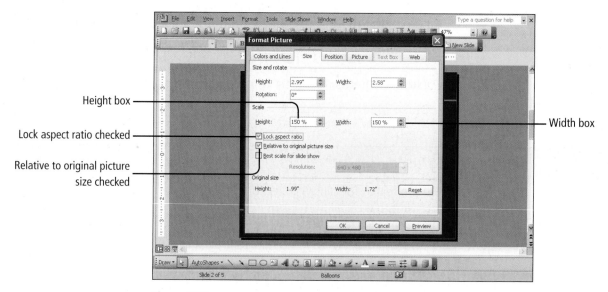

Height box

Lock aspect ratio checked

Relative to original picture size checked

Width box

Figure 4.30

5 Click **OK** to resize the picture.

6 To position the picture, point to the image to display the move pointer ⊕. Drag the picture down and to the right, noticing the dashed box that displays. Position the dashed box in the lower right corner of the slide, and then release the mouse button.

Another Way — **To Move Pictures Using the Format Picture Dialog Box**

In the Format Picture dialog box, from the Position tab, you can enter an exact location on the slide to position your pictures.

7 On the Standard toolbar, click **Save** 🔲.

Activity 4.19 Inserting Pictures from Files

In addition to clip art that is a part of the Microsoft Office collection of clips, you can insert clips that you have purchased from a software vendor, digital pictures that you have created in other software applications, and pictures from a digital camera or scanner. In this activity, you will insert a scanned picture on Slide 5.

1 Display **Slide 5** and click the picture of the party hat and balloon to select it. Press Delete.

2 On the Drawing toolbar, click the **Insert Picture** button 🖼 to display the **Insert Picture** dialog box.

This dialog box may display pictures or other folders that are saved on your system.

3 At the bottom of the dialog box, verify that *All Pictures* displays in the **Files of type** box. If it does not, click the **Files of type arrow**, and then click **All Pictures**.

4 Click the **Look in arrow** and navigate to your student files. Click the picture **p04A_Puppy**. Click **Insert**.

The picture is inserted in the center of the slide.

Another Way — **To Add a Picture Using a Content Layout**

You can change the slide layout to a text and content layout that allows you to insert objects such as clip art, pictures, and movie clips. A text and content layout is useful if you would like to place an image in a predefined location. For example, if you want to display a bulleted list on the left side of the slide and a picture on the right side, use a text and content layout. The inserted picture will be placed next to the bulleted list instead of in the middle of the slide.

---

5 Drag the picture to the right so that it is centered over the text box at the bottom of the slide. On the Drawing toolbar, click the **Line Color arrow** , and then click the fifth color—**teal**. Click the **Line Style** button, and then click the last line style.

6 From the **View** menu, click **Header and Footer**, and then click the **Notes and Handouts tab**. Create a footer for the notes and handouts that includes the date updated automatically and a footer with the text **4A Party-Firstname Lastname** Clear all other header and footer options, and then click **Apply to All**.

7 On the Standard toolbar, click the **Save** button. From the **File** menu, click **Print** to display the **Print** dialog box. In the **Print what** box, click the arrow, and then click **Handouts**. In the **Color/grayscale** box, click the arrow, and then click **Grayscale**. Under **Handouts**, click the **Slides per page arrow**, and then click **6**. Click the **Horizontal** option button. Click **OK**. Close the file and exit PowerPoint.

End You have completed Project 4A ——————————

Summary

In this chapter you practiced how to create and format objects using the Drawing toolbar. The objects that you practiced how to create included lines, ovals and rectangles, text boxes, AutoShapes, and WordArt. You can use the objects that you create to enhance your slides. Remember that an effective PowerPoint presentation keeps the audience focused on the message. Try not to clutter your slides with too many objects. The objects that you use should provide balance—conveying your ideas in a coherent manner.

In addition to creating objects, you practiced how to insert clip art and pictures. If you are using pictures that you obtained from a source such as the Internet, be sure that you have gained permission to use the pictures in your presentation. Copyright laws may restrict the use of pictures that you download from the Internet or that you scan from a book. Always use pictures appropriately, keeping your audience in mind.

As you work with pictures and objects, you will find that there are many ways that you can be creative with Microsoft Office PowerPoint 2003. You are only limited by your own imagination! Collaborate with a classmate or coworker to get a fresh perspective on your slides, and before you make a presentation, show it to someone else to see if the images that you are using accurately and professionally convey your message.

In This Chapter You Practiced How To

- Draw and Format Lines
- Create Basic Shapes and Text Boxes
- Edit and Format Drawing Objects
- Create and Format WordArt
- Insert Images

Matching

Match each term in the second column with its correct definition in the first column by writing the letter of the term on the blank line in front of the correct definition.

A AutoShapes

B Character spacing

C Clip

D Clip Organizer

E Collections

F Copyright

G Crosshair pointer

H Drawing Object

I Fill color

J Guides

K Media

L Pixels

M Sizing handles

N Text box

O WordArt

_____ **1.** Small circles at the edges of an object that are used to size the object.

_____ **2.** Small vertical and horizontal lines in the ruler that visually indicate where you are drawing or positioning an object.

_____ **3.** A single media file including art, sound, animation, or movies that you can use in a presentation.

_____ **4.** A PowerPoint feature with which you can insert, view, and categorize the images that you want to use in your presentations.

_____ **5.** Predefined drawing objects in PowerPoint used to draw lines, basic shapes, block arrows, flowcharts, stars and banners, and callouts.

_____ **6.** The dots that comprise and determine the resolution of a computer monitor.

_____ **7.** A type of graphic that includes lines, shapes, WordArt, text boxes, and AutoShapes.

_____ **8.** A drawing tool used to turn text into graphic objects.

_____ **9.** A drawing object that is used to position text anywhere on the slide.

_____ **10.** The mouse pointer when it is in the shape of a small plus sign used to draw the boundaries of a drawing image.

_____ **11.** A feature that adjusts the width of the individual letters in a WordArt.

_____ **12.** The inside color of an object.

_____ **13.** Categories into which clips are organized.

_____ **14.** A term that encompasses a variety of objects that can be inserted into a presentation—including clip art, pictures, sound, and movies.

_____ **15.** Laws that may restrict the use of images found in books and on the Internet.

Fill in the Blank Write the correct answer in the space provided.

1. By applying a _____ style to a line, you can create a patterned line.

2. The _____ diamond adjustment handle on an AutoShape is used to customize the AutoShape.

3. A _____ is a color combination in which one color fades into another.

4. The _____ option clears the fill color from an object.

5. Images are most effective when used to help the audience understand a _____.

6. To draw a perfect circle, click the Oval button and then press and hold down the _____ key while dragging the crosshair pointer.

7. The _____ check box maintains picture proportions while sizing an image using the Format Picture dialog box.

8. To draw a straight line, click the Line button and then press and hold down the _____ key while dragging the crosshair pointer.

9. When a line is drawn, the default line size is _____.

10. When an object is created, the fill color is determined by the _____ that is applied to the presentation.

Project 4B — Planning

Objectives: *Draw and Format Lines, Create Basic Shapes and Text Boxes, Edit and Format Drawing Objects, and Insert Images.*

In the following Skill Assessment, you will format a presentation regarding ideas for planning weddings and anniversaries. Your completed presentation will look similar to Figure 4.31. You will save your presentation as *4B_Planning_Firstname_Lastname.*

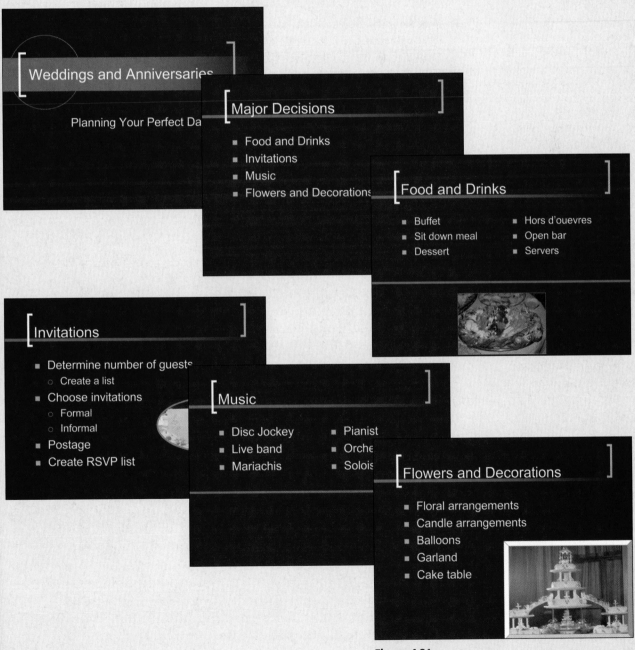

Figure 4.31

(Project 4B–Planning continues on the next page)

(Project 4B–Planning continued)

1. From your student files, open the file **p04B_Planning**. Save the file as **4B_Planning_Firstname_Lastname** Close the **Outline/Slides** pane, and then scroll through the presentation to familiarize yourself with the six slides.

2. Display **Slide 2**. On the Drawing toolbar, click the **Insert Picture** button. Navigate to your student files, and then click **p04B_Wedding**. Click **Insert**. Point to the picture to display the move pointer, and then drag the picture to the lower right corner of the slide.

3. If necessary, select the picture. On the Drawing toolbar, click the **Line Color arrow**, and then click the seventh color—**dark gold**. On the Drawing toolbar, click **Line Style**, and then click the last line style.

4. Display **Slide 3**. On the Drawing toolbar, click the **Line** button. Position the crosshair pointer at the left edge of the slide at **1 inch below zero on the vertical ruler**. Hold down ⇧Shift and drag to extend the line to the right edge of the slide. Release the mouse button, and then release ⇧Shift.

5. With the line selected, on the Drawing toolbar, click the **Line Color arrow**, and then click the sixth color—**orange**. On the Drawing toolbar, click **Line Style**, and then click the ninth style—**6 pt. solid** line.

6. On the Drawing toolbar, click the **Insert Picture** button. Navigate to your student files, and then click **p04B_Buffet**. Click **Insert**. The picture is inserted in the center of the slide.

7. Right-click the picture to display the shortcut menu. Click **Format Picture**. Click the **Size tab**, and then verify that the **Lock aspect ratio** and **Relative to original picture size** check boxes are selected. Under **Scale**, select the value in the **Height** box, type **85** and then click **OK**.

8. Drag the picture down so that its bottom edge is aligned with the bottom edge of the slide. On the Drawing toolbar, click the **Line Color arrow**, and then click the fifth color—**gold**. Click to deselect the picture.

9. Display **Slide 4**. On the Drawing toolbar, click the **Oval** button. Position the crosshair pointer at **1 inch to the right of zero on the horizontal ruler** and at **zero on the vertical ruler**. Drag down and to the right to extend the oval to the **right edge of the slide** at **2 inches below zero on the vertical ruler**.

10. If necessary, select the oval. On the Drawing toolbar, click the **Fill Color arrow**, and then click **Fill Effects**. Click the **Picture tab**. Click **Select Picture**, and then navigate to your student files. Click **p04B_Invitation**, click **Insert**, and then in the **Fill Effects** dialog box, click **OK** to fill the oval with the picture.

(Project 4B–Planning continues on the next page)

(Project 4B–Planning continued)

11. If necessary, select the oval. On the Drawing toolbar, click the **Line Color arrow**, and then click the seventh color—**dark gold**. On the Drawing toolbar, click **Line Style**, and then click the eighth style—**4½ pt. solid** line.

12. Display **Slide 6**. On the Drawing toolbar, click **AutoShapes**, and then point to **Basic Shapes**. In the fourth row, click the third shape—**Bevel**. Position the pointer at **zero on the horizontal and vertical rulers**. Drag down and to the right to extend the bevel to the lower right corner of the slide.

13. Point to the bevel's yellow adjustment handle. Press and hold down the left mouse button and drag up and to the left so that the bevel border is approximately half of its original size.

14. If necessary, select the bevel object. On the Drawing toolbar, click the **Fill Color arrow**, and then click **Fill Effects**. Click the **Picture tab**. Click **Select Picture**, and then navigate to your student files. Click **p04B_Cake**, click **Insert**, and then in the **Fill Effects** dialog box, click **OK** to fill the bevel with the picture. On the Drawing toolbar, click the **Line Color arrow**, and then click the seventh color—**dark gold**. Click to deselect the shape.

15. Display **Slide 3**, and click the orange line above the picture to select it. On the Standard toolbar, click **Copy**, and then display **Slide 5**. On the Standard toolbar, click **Paste** to copy the line to the same location as it was on **Slide 3**.

16. Display the **Header and Footer** dialog box, and then click the **Notes and Handouts tab**. Create a footer for the notes and handouts that includes the date updated automatically and a footer with the text **4B Planning-Firstname Lastname** Clear all other header and footer options, and then click **Apply to All**.

17. **Save** the file, and then print the presentation as **grayscale handouts**, **6** slides per page in **horizontal** order. **Close** the file.

End You have completed Project 4B

Project 4C — Investors

Objectives: *Draw and Format Lines, Create Basic Shapes and Text Boxes, Edit and Format Drawing Objects, and Insert Images.*

In the following Skill Assessment, you will format a presentation that the owners of The Perfect Party plan to make to a team of investors. Your completed presentation will look similar to Figure 4.32. You will save your presentation as *4C_Investors_Firstname_Lastname.*

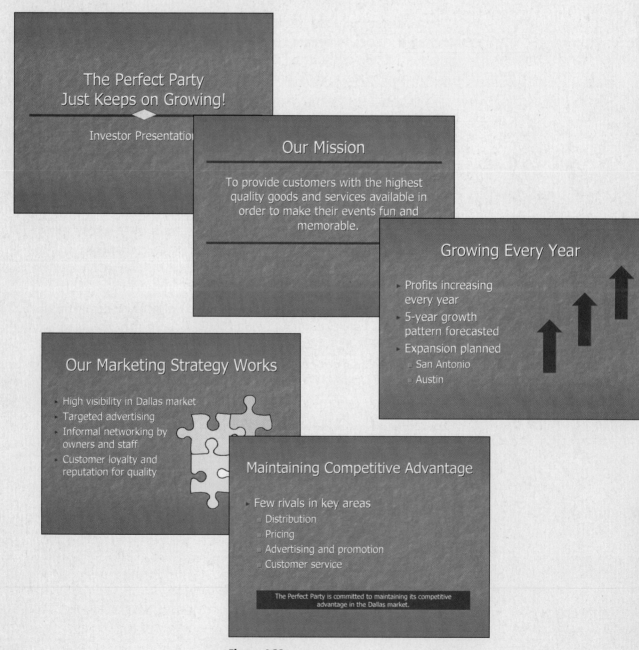

Figure 4.32

(Project 4C–Investors continues on the next page)

(Project 4C–Investors continued)

1. From your student files, open the file **p04C_Investors**. Save the file as **4C_Investors_Firstname_Lastname** and then scroll through the presentation to familiarize yourself with the slides.

2. On the Formatting toolbar, click the **Slide Design** button to display the **Slide Design** task pane. Apply the light blue **Textured** design template to the entire presentation. Close the **Slide Design** task pane.

3. Display **Slide 2**, and then display the **Slide Master** by holding down [Shift] and clicking the **Normal View** button. Recall that the Slide Master contains text, graphics, and formatting that is applied to *all* of the slides in the presentation.

4. In the bulleted list placeholder, click anywhere in the **Click to edit Master text styles** line. From the **Format** menu, click **Bullets and Numbering**. In the **Bulleted tab**, at the lower right corner, click the **Picture** button. In the **Search text** box, type **Triangles** and then click **Go**. Click the **blue, right-pointing triangle**, and then click **OK**.

5. Click anywhere in the **Second level** bullet point. From the **Format** menu, click **Bullets and Numbering**. In the **Bulleted tab**, click the **Color arrow**, and then change the color to the seventh color—**aqua**. Return the presentation to **Normal View**.

6. If necessary, display **Slide 2**. On the Drawing toolbar, click the **Line** button. Hold down [Shift], and then position the crosshair pointer at **4.5 inches to the left of zero on the horizontal ruler**, and at **2 inches above zero on the vertical ruler**. Drag to the right to **4.5 inches to the right of zero on the horizontal ruler**. Release the mouse button, and then release [Shift] to draw a line.

7. With the line selected, click the **Line Style** button, and then click the **6 pt. solid line**. Click the **Line Color arrow**, and then click the third color—**dark blue**.

8. Point to the line to display the move pointer. Hold down [Ctrl] to display the pointer with a plus sign attached to it, and then drag straight down to copy the line to **1 inch below zero on the vertical ruler**. Release the mouse button, and then release [Ctrl] to copy the line. If necessary, use the directional arrow keys on your keyboard to nudge the line so that it is centered on the slide.

9. Display **Slide 3**. On the Drawing toolbar, click **AutoShapes**, and then point to **Block Arrows**. In the first row, click the third shape—**Up Arrow**. Using the guides in the ruler to determine size and placement, position the crosshair pointer at **1 inch to the right of zero on the horizontal ruler** and at **2 inches below zero on the vertical ruler**. Drag up and to the right to **2 inches to the right of zero on the horizontal ruler** and to **zero on the vertical ruler**.

(Project 4C–Investors continues on the next page)

(Project 4C–Investors continued)

10. On the Drawing toolbar, click the **Fill Color arrow**, and then click the third color—**dark blue**. Click the **Line Color arrow**, and then click the fifth color—**teal**.

11. Point to the arrow shape, and hold down Ctrl to display the pointer with a plus sign attached to it, indicating that you can copy the arrow. Drag up approximately 1 inch and to the right approximately 1 inch, and then release the left mouse button to copy the arrow. Repeat the process to make a third copy of the arrow, with the third arrow approximately 1 inch up and to the right of the second arrow. Refer to Figure 4.33.

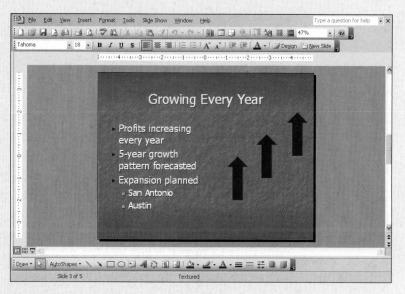

Figure 4.33

12. Display **Slide 4**, and then double-click the clip art placeholder to open the **Select Picture** dialog box. In the **Search text** box, type **Puzzle** and then click **Go**. Click the picture of four interlocking puzzle pieces, and then click **OK** to insert the image on **Slide 4**.

13. Display **Slide 5**, and then click in the bulleted list placeholder. Point to the bottom center sizing handle to display the vertical sizing pointer. Drag up so that the placeholder fits tightly to the text. Click anywhere on the slide so that the placeholder is deselected.

14. On the Drawing toolbar, click **Text Box**. Position the pointer at **4 inches to the left of zero on the horizontal ruler**, and at **2 inches below zero on the vertical ruler**. Drag down and to the right to **4 inches to the right of zero on the horizontal ruler** and to **3 inches below zero on the vertical ruler**. Type The Perfect Party is committed to maintaining its competitive advantage in the Dallas market.

(Project 4C–Investors continues on the next page)

(Project 4C–Investors continued)

15. **Center** the text in the text box. On the Drawing toolbar, click the **Fill Color arrow**, and then click the third color—**dark blue**.

16. Display **Slide 2**, and then select one of the lines that you drew. On the Standard toolbar, click **Copy**.

17. Display **Slide 1**, and then on the Standard toolbar, click **Paste**. Point to the copied line, press and hold down the left mouse button, and drag to move the line so that it is positioned at **zero on the vertical ruler** and is centered horizontally on the slide.

18. On the Drawing toolbar, click **AutoShapes**, and then point to **Basic Shapes**. In the first row, click the last shape—**Diamond**. Position the crosshair pointer at **0.5 inch to the left of zero on the horizontal ruler** and at **0.25 inch above zero on the vertical ruler**. Drag down and to the right to so that the right point of the diamond touches the line at **0.5 inch to the right of zero on the horizontal ruler**. Release the mouse button.

19. With the diamond selected, on the Drawing toolbar, click the **Fill Color arrow**, and then click **Fill Effects**. Click the **Texture tab**, and then in the third row, click the fourth texture—**Bouquet**. Click **OK**.

20. On the Drawing toolbar, click the **Line Color arrow**. Click the third color—**dark blue**. Click to deselect the shape.

21. Display the **Header and Footer** dialog box, and then click the **Notes and Handouts tab**. Create a footer for the notes and handouts that includes the date updated automatically and a footer with the text **4C Investors-Firstname Lastname** Clear all other header and footer options.

22. **Save** the file, display **Slide 1**, and then run the slide show. Then print the presentation as **grayscale handouts**, **6** slides per page in **horizontal** order. **Close** the file.

End You have completed Project 4C ——————————————————————

Project 4D—Fundraising

Objectives: *Draw and Format Lines, Create Basic Shapes and Text Boxes, Edit and Format Drawing Objects, and Insert Images.*

In the following Skill Assessment, you will format a presentation describing a new fundraising opportunity being offered by The Perfect Party. Your completed presentation will look similar to Figure 4.34. You will save your presentation as *4D_Fundraising_Firstname_Lastname.*

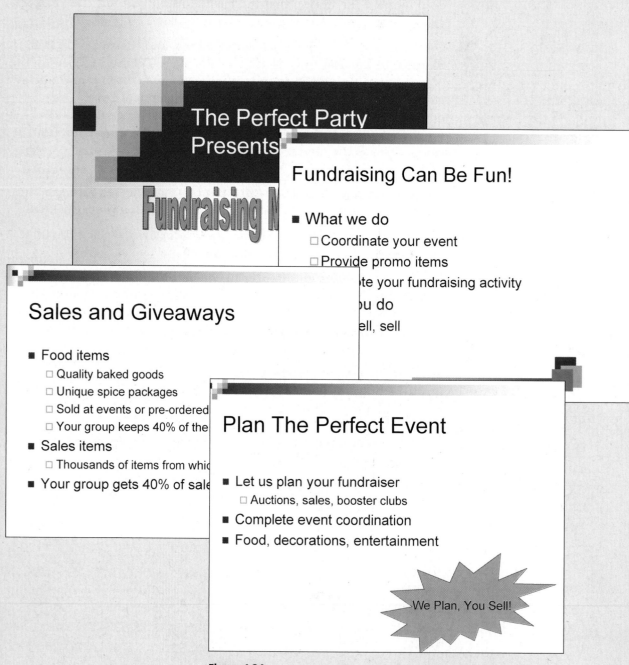

Figure 4.34

(Project 4D–Fundraising continues on the next page)

(Project 4D–Fundraising continued)

1. From your student files, open the file **p04D_Fundraising**. Save the file as **4D_Fundraising_Firstname_Lastname** Close the **Outline/Slides** pane, and then scroll through the presentation to familiarize yourself with the four slides.

2. On the Formatting toolbar, click the **Slide Design** button to display the **Slide Design** task pane. Apply the white and blue **Pixel** design template to the entire presentation. Close the **Slide Design** task pane.

3. Display **Slide 1**. On the Drawing toolbar, click the **Insert WordArt** button. In the WordArt Gallery, in the second row, click the third WordArt, and then click **OK**. In the **Edit WordArt Text** dialog box, type **Fundraising Made Fun!** and then click **OK**.

4. Point to the WordArt and right-click to display the shortcut menu. Click **Format WordArt**, and then click the **Size tab**. Under **Size and rotate**, select the value in the **Height** box. Type **1.5** and then press Tab to move the insertion point to the **Width** box. Type **6.5** and then click **OK**.

5. Point to the WordArt to display the move pointer, and then drag the WordArt down so that its top edge aligns just below the dark blue box containing the title. Click to deselect the WordArt.

6. Display **Slide 2**. Select the second, third, and fourth bullet points, and then on the Formatting toolbar, click **Increase Indent** to demote the selection to second-level bullet points. Select the last bullet point on the slide, and then demote it to a second-level bullet point.

7. On the Drawing toolbar, click the **Rectangle** button. Position the crosshair pointer at **1 inch to the left of zero on the horizontal ruler** and at **3 inches below zero on the vertical ruler**. Drag down and to the right to **4 inches to the right of zero on the horizontal ruler** and to **3.5 inches below zero on the vertical ruler** to create a rectangle.

8. With the rectangle selected, display the **Format** menu, and then click **AutoShape**. Under **Size and rotate**, select the value in the **Height** box, type **.25** and then press Tab to select the value in the **Width** box. Type **4.75** and then click **OK**.

9. With the rectangle selected, click the **Fill Color arrow**, and then click **Fill Effects**. In the **Gradient tab**, under **Colors**, click the **Two colors** option button. Click the **Color 1 arrow**, and in the color scheme palette, click the fifth color—**medium blue**. Click the **Color 2 arrow**, and in the color scheme palette, click the third color—**royal blue**. Under **Shading styles**, click **Vertical**, and under **Variants**, click the first variant in the first row. Click **OK**. Click the **Line Color arrow**, and then click **No Line**.

(Project 4D–Fundraising continues on the next page)

Skill Assessments (continued)

(Project 4D–Fundraising continued)

10. On the Drawing toolbar, click the **Rectangle** button. Position the pointer at **3 inches to the right of zero on the horizontal ruler** and at **2.5 inches below zero on the vertical ruler**. Click the left mouse button to create a one-inch square. Right-click the square to display the shortcut menu, and then click **Format AutoShape**. Under **Scale**, click to select the **Lock aspect ratio** check box. Under **Scale**, select the percentage value in the **Height** box, type **60** and then press Tab. Notice that the value in the **Width** box changes to 60. Click **OK**.

11. With the square selected, click the **Fill Color arrow**. Click the third color—**royal blue**. Click the **Line Color arrow**, and then click **No Line**.

12. If necessary, select the square. On the Standard toolbar, click **Copy**, and then click **Paste**. A copied square displays below and to the right of the original square. With the second square selected, click the **Fill Color arrow**. Click the fifth color—**light blue**. Press ↓ once to nudge the square down slightly.

13. With the second square selected, on the Standard toolbar, click **Copy**, and then click **Paste**. A third square displays below and to the right of the second square. With the third square selected, click the **Fill Color arrow**. Click the seventh color—**gray/blue**. Press ← five times to nudge the square to the left and press ↑ once to nudge the square up. Click outside of the slide to deselect, and then compare your slide with Figure 4.35. Make adjustments as necessary.

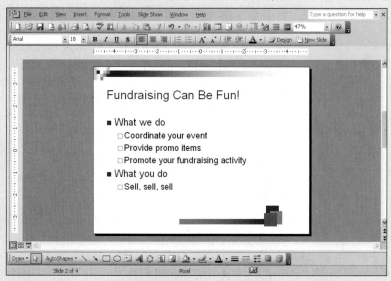

Figure 4.35

(Project 4D–Fundraising continues on the next page)

(Project 4D–Fundraising continued)

14. Display **Slide 4**. On the Drawing toolbar, click **AutoShapes**. Point to **Stars and Banners**, and then in the first row, click the second shape—**Explosion 2**. Position the crosshair pointer at **zero on the horizontal ruler** and at **1 inch below zero on the vertical ruler**. Drag down and to the right until the crosshair pointer is positioned in the lower right corner of the slide. Release the mouse button to create the explosion shape.

15. Point to the explosion and right-click. From the displayed shortcut menu, click **Add Text**. Type **We Plan, You Sell!** Select the text, and then change the **Font Size** to **24**.

16. Display the **Header and Footer** dialog box, and then click the **Notes and Handouts tab**. Create a footer for the notes and handouts that includes the date updated automatically and a footer with the text **4D Fundraising-Firstname Lastname** Clear all other header and footer options.

17. **Save** the file, display **Slide 1**, and then run the slide show. Then print the presentation as **grayscale handouts**, **4** slides per page in **horizontal** order. **Close** the file.

End **You have completed Project 4D** ——————————————

Project 4E — Menus

Objectives: *Insert and Format WordArt and Insert Images.*

In the following Performance Assessment, you will format a presentation regarding catering options available through The Perfect Party. Your completed presentation will look similar to the one shown in Figure 4.36. You will save your presentation as *4E_Menus_Firstname_Lastname.*

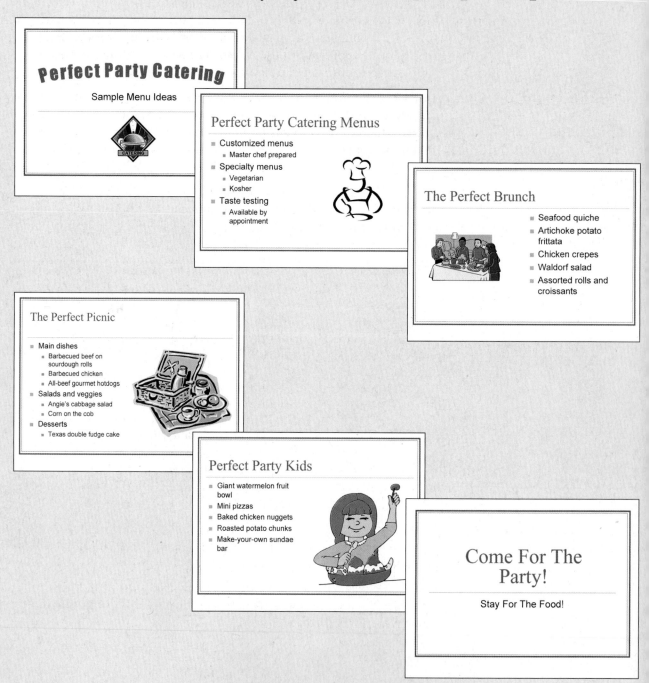

Figure 4.36

(Project 4E–Menus continues on the next page)

(Project 4E–Menus continued)

1. From your student files, open the file **p04E_Menus**. Save the file as **4E_Menus_Firstname_Lastname** Close the **Outline/Slides** pane, and then scroll through the presentation to familiarize yourself with the six slides.

2. Display **Slide 1** and on the Drawing toolbar, click **Insert WordArt**. In the third row, click the first WordArt design, and then click **OK**. Type **Perfect Party Catering** and then click **OK**. Size the WordArt by dragging its left and right center sizing handles so that it extends the length of the yellow line in the middle of the slide. Drag the WordArt up so that it is positioned just above the text *Sample Menu Ideas*.

3. On the WordArt toolbar, click **WordArt Shape**, and then in the second row, click the first shape, **Arch Up (Curve)**. Change the **WordArt Character Spacing** to **Loose**, and change the WordArt **Fill Color** to **red**.

4. If you do not have an Internet connection, go to the third sentence in Step 5. If you have an Internet connection, connect to the Internet and minimize your Internet browser window. On the Drawing toolbar, click **Insert Clip Art**. If necessary, click the Search in arrow and click Everywhere so that *All collections* displays in the Search in box.

5. In the **Search for** box, type **Catering** and then click **Go**. Insert the diamond-shaped picture with a person holding a covered dish. If you cannot access the Internet for this assignment, on the Drawing toolbar, click **Insert Picture** and navigate to your student files. Insert the picture **p04E_Catering**. Drag the picture down so that it is positioned below the yellow line.

6. On **Slides 2**, **3**, **4**, and **5**, read each slide and insert clip art images appropriate to the slide content. If possible, keep your Internet connection open so that you will have access to Microsoft clips online. Refer to Figure 4.36 for picture ideas. If you do not have access to the Internet, click once to select the appropriate placeholders on each slide, and use the **Insert Picture** command to insert the images from your student files (p04E_Chef, p04E_Brunch, p04E_Picnic, and p04E_Party_Kid).

7. Create a footer for the notes and handouts that includes the date updated automatically and a footer with the text **4E Menus-Firstname Lastname** Clear all other header and footer options.

8. **Save** the file, display **Slide 1**, and then run the slide show. Then print the presentation as **grayscale handouts**, **6** slides per page in **horizontal** order. **Close** the file.

End **You have completed Project 4E**

Project 4F—Inventory

Objectives: *Draw and Format Lines, Create Basic Shapes and Text Boxes, Edit and Format Drawing Objects, Create and Format WordArt, and Insert Images.*

In the following Performance Assessment, you will format a presentation for new employees regarding inventory procedures. Your completed presentation will look similar to the one shown in Figure 4.37. You will save your presentation as *4F_Inventory_Firstname_Lastname.*

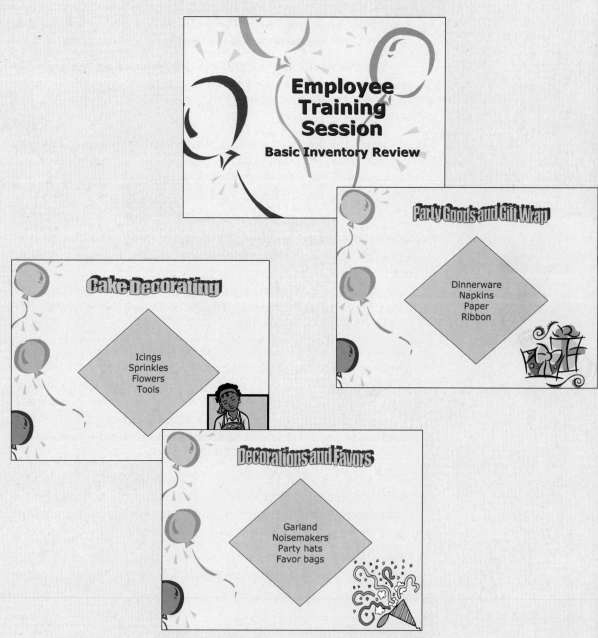

Figure 4.37

(Project 4F–Inventory continues on the next page)

(Project 4F–Inventory continued)

1. Start a new presentation based on the **Balloons** design template. Change the color scheme to the scheme with the light blue background and blue, aqua, and purple accents. In the title placeholder type **Employee Training Session** and in the subtitle placeholder type **Basic Inventory Review** and then save the file as **4F_Inventory_Firstname_Lastname**

2. Insert a new slide with the **Blank** slide layout, and then close the task pane. On the Drawing toolbar, click **Insert WordArt** and in the fourth row, double-click the fourth WordArt design. In the **Edit WordArt Text** dialog box, type **Party Goods and Gift Wrap** and then click **OK**.

3. With the WordArt selected, on the Drawing toolbar, click the **Fill Color arrow**, and then click the third color—**light blue**. Drag the WordArt up so that it becomes the title for the slide. Click to deselect the WordArt.

4. On the Drawing toolbar, click **AutoShapes**, point to **Basic Shapes**, and then in the first row, click the fourth shape—**Diamond**. Click anywhere on the slide to create a diamond that is 1 inch by 1 inch.

5. On the **Format** menu, click **AutoShape**. Click the **Size tab**. Under **Size and rotate**, change the AutoShape **Height** to **4.75** and its **Width** to **5.5** and then close the dialog box. Drag the diamond to position it in the center of the blank area of the slide. On the Drawing toolbar, click the **Fill Color arrow**, and then click the third color—**light blue**.

6. Right-click the **AutoShape**, and then on the shortcut menu, click **Add Text**. Type each of the following words on a separate line: **Dinnerware Napkins Paper Ribbon**

7. Select the text in the diamond and change the **Font Size** to **24**.

8. Display the presentation in **Slide Sorter View**. Select **Slide 2** and click **Copy**. Click to the right of **Slide 2** to position the blinking insertion line, and then click **Paste** twice to create two copies of the slide. Now you can edit the text on each of the new slides without having to re-create the slide elements.

9. Double-click **Slide 3** so that it displays in **Normal View**. Click to select the **WordArt** object, and then on the WordArt toolbar, click **Edit Text**. In the **Edit WordArt Text** dialog box, replace the existing text by typing **Cake Decorating** and then click **OK**.

10. Delete the text in the diamond and type on four separate lines: **Icings Sprinkles Flowers Tools**

11. Display **Slide 4** and edit the WordArt by typing **Decorations and Favors** in the **Edit WordArt Text** dialog box. Delete the text in the diamond and type on four separate lines: **Garland Noisemakers Party hats Favor bags**

(Project 4F–Inventory continues on the next page)

(Project 4F–Inventory continued)

12. If you do not have an Internet connection, move to the end of this step. If necessary, display **Slide 4** and open your Internet connection so that you have access to Microsoft Office Online. On the Drawing toolbar, click **Insert Clip Art**. In the **Search for** box, type **Confetti Party Hats** Insert the picture of the lavender hat with confetti and ribbon exploding. If you do not find the picture, on the Drawing toolbar click **Insert Picture**. Navigate to your student files and insert the file **p04F_Hat**

13. Move the picture to the lower right corner of your slide, and then point to the upper left sizing handle to display the diagonal resize pointer. Drag up until the sizing handle touches the diamond.

14. Display **Slide 3**, and verify that your Internet connection is still open. On the Drawing toolbar, click **Insert Clip Art**. In the **Search for** box, type **Cake Decorating** Insert the picture of the woman with the red hair ribbon decorating a cake. If you do not find the picture, on the Drawing toolbar click **Insert Picture**. Navigate to your student files and insert the picture **p04F_Decorating**

15. Move the picture to the lower right corner of your slide, and then point to the upper left sizing handle to display the diagonal resize pointer. Drag up until the sizing handle touches the diamond.

16. Display **Slide 2**. Repeat the process that you used on **Slides 3** and **4** for inserting and sizing a picture. Search for pictures matching the keyword **Presents** and insert a picture of your choice or navigate to your student files and insert the picture **p04F_Present** Position and size the image appropriately.

17. Create a footer for the notes and handouts that includes the date updated automatically and a footer with the text **4F Inventory-Firstname Lastname** Clear all other header and footer options.

18. **Save** the file, display **Slide 1**, and then run the slide show. Then print the presentation as **grayscale handouts**, **4** slides per page in **horizontal** order. **Close** the file.

End You have completed Project 4F

Project 4G — Convention

Objectives: *Draw and Format Lines, Create Basic Shapes and Text Boxes, Edit and Format Drawing Objects, Insert and Format WordArt, and Insert Images.*

In the following Performance Assessment, you will format a presentation regarding a partnership between The Perfect Party and the City Convention Center. The presentation describes event-planning services provided by the two organizations. Your completed presentation will look similar to the one shown in Figure 4.38. You will save your presentation as *4G_Convention_Firstname_Lastname.*

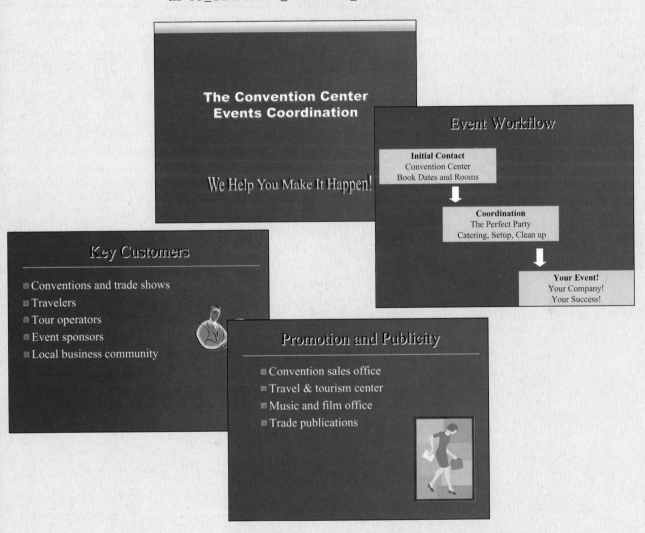

Figure 4.38

1. From your student files, open the file **p04G_Convention**. Scroll through the presentation to familiarize yourself with the slides, and if necessary, display the Ruler by clicking the View menu, and then clicking Ruler. Save the file as **4G_Convention_Firstname_Lastname** Close the **Outline/Slides** pane.

(Project 4G–Convention continues on the next page)

(Project 4G–Convention continued)

2. Display **Slide 1**, and then on the Drawing toolbar, click **Insert WordArt**. In the **WordArt Gallery** dialog box, in the fourth row, click the second WordArt. In the **Edit WordArt Text** dialog box, type **We Help You Make It Happen!** and then click **OK**.

3. On the WordArt toolbar, click **WordArt Shape**, and then in the fourth row, click the second shape—**Deflate**.

4. Move the WordArt so that its upper edge is positioned at approximately **2 inches below zero on the vertical ruler**.

5. On the Drawing toolbar, click the **Rectangle** button. Position the crosshair pointer in the **upper left corner of the slide** and drag down and to the right to draw a rectangle that extends **from the left edge of the slide** to the **right edge of the slide**, and down from the top edge of the slide approximately **0.5 inch**. A narrow rectangular band spans the width of the top edge of the slide.

6. With the rectangle selected, apply a two-color gradient fill effect. Click the **Color 1: arrow**, and then click **More Colors**. Click the **Standard tab**, and in the color honeycomb, in the eighth row, click the sixth color—**pale yellow**. Click **OK**.

7. Click the **Color 2: arrow**, and then click **More Colors**. Click the **Standard tab**, and in the color honeycomb, in the ninth row, click the seventh color—**light coral**. Click **OK**. Apply a **Horizontal** shading style, and under **Variants**, click the first sample in the first row. Click **OK**. On the Drawing toolbar, click the **Line Color arrow**, and then click **No Line**. The rectangular band contains colors similar to those in the WordArt object at the bottom of the slide.

8. Display **Slide 3**. On the Drawing toolbar, click the **Line** button, and then position the pointer at **4.5 inches to the left of zero on the horizontal ruler** and at **2.5 inches above zero on the vertical ruler**. Press and hold down [Shift], and then drag to the right to extend the line to **4.5 inches to the right of zero on the horizontal ruler**.

9. Click the **Line Style** button, and change the line style to **2¼ pt**. Click the **Line Color arrow**, and then in the custom color palette, click the light pink color.

10. Copy the line that you created, and then paste it to **Slide 4**. The line is duplicated in the same position as on **Slide 3**.

11. Display the **Slide Master** and click in the *Click to edit Master text styles* line. Change the bullet for this line to a picture bullet. In the **Picture Bullet** dialog box, type **nature** in the **Search text** box, and then click **Go**. Insert a lavender square bullet, and then return the presentation to Normal View.

(Project 4G–Convention continues on the next page)

(Project 4G–Convention continued)

12. Display **Slide 3**, and on the Drawing toolbar, click **Insert Clip Art**. In the **Clip Art** task pane, click in the **Search for** box, type **People** and then click **Go**. Insert the picture of the man wearing a brown suit working at a computer. Drag the picture to the right so that its left edge is aligned at approximately **2 inches to the right of zero on the horizontal ruler**.

13. Display **Slide 4** and insert the picture of the woman carrying a brief-case. Close the **Clip Art** task pane.

14. Drag the picture down and to the right so that its left edge aligns at **2 inches to the right of zero on the horizontal ruler** and its top edge aligns at **zero on the vertical ruler**.

15. Right-click the image to display the shortcut menu, and then click **Format Picture**. In the **Size tab**, verify that the **Lock aspect ratio** and **Relative to original picture size** boxes are selected (checked). Under **Scale**, click in the **Height** box, type **150** and then click **OK**.

16. If necessary, select the picture. Click the **Line Color arrow** and apply a **black** line. Change the **Line Style** to the last line style in the list—**6 pt. triple line**. This gives the picture a framed look.

17. Display **Slide 2**. Using Figure 4.39 as a guide, create the top text box, and type the text as shown. Select the entire text box by clicking its border to display a pattern of dots. Change the **Fill Color** to the seventh color—**light blue**, and change the **Font Color** to **black**. Center the text and apply bold as indicated. Copy the text box twice, type the text, and drag each new text box to its correct location on the slide.

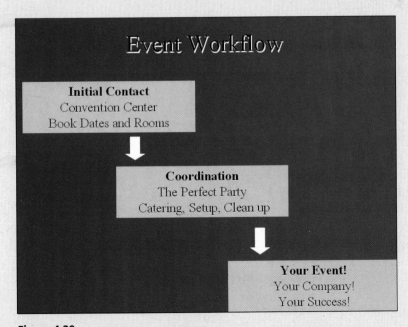

Figure 4.39

(Project 4G–Convention continues on the next page)

(Project 4G–Convention continued)

18. From the **AutoShapes** menu, point to **Block Arrows**, and then in the first row, click the fourth shape—**Down Arrow**. Draw the first arrow as shown, and then change its **Fill Color** to **white**. Copy the arrow and drag the new arrow to its correct location on the slide.

19. Create a footer for the notes and handouts that includes the date updated automatically and a footer with the text **4G Convention-Firstname Lastname** Clear all other header and footer options.

20. Save the file, display **Slide 1**, and run the slide show. Then print the presentation as **grayscale handouts**, **4** slides per page in **horizontal** order. **Close** the file.

 You have completed Project 4G ——————————————

Project 4H — Picnic

Objectives: *Draw and Format Lines, Create Basic Shapes and Text Boxes, Edit and Format Drawing Objects, Insert and Format WordArt, and Insert Images.*

In this Mastery Assessment, you will create a one-slide presentation to be used as a flyer announcing The Perfect Party annual employee picnic. Your completed presentation will look similar to the one shown in Figure 4.40. You will save your presentation as *4H_Picnic_Firstname_ Lastname.*

Figure 4.40

1. Start a new presentation and change the slide layout to **Blank**. Display the **Background** dialog box, and click the **Background fill arrow**. Click **Fill Effects**. Apply a two-color, yellow and white gradient fill background in which the shading style is yellow on top and white on the bottom.

2. Create a **WordArt** using the fifth WordArt in the second row. Type **Employee Picnic!** in the **Edit WordArt Text** dialog box. Use Figure 4.40 as a guide to determine size and placement.

3. Create a text box that includes the date information. Create a second text box that includes the location and time. Create a third text box that includes the text *Bring the family!* Change the **Font Size** to **44** for each of the text boxes, and use Figure 4.40 to determine placement.

(Project 4H–Picnic continues on the next page)

(Project 4H–Picnic continued)

4. Draw a line as shown in Figure 4.40 positioned under the *Bring the family!* text. Change the **Line Style** to **6 pt.** and change the **Line Color** to **red**.

5. Insert the clip art shown in Figure 4.40 by searching with the keyword *Picnic*. Recall that a wide variety of pictures are available to you if you first launch your Internet connection. If the picture is not available on your system, choose a similar picture or navigate to your student files and insert the picture **p04H_Picnic**.

6. Create a footer for the *slide* (not the Notes and Handouts) that includes the text **4H Picnic-Firstname Lastname** Clear all other header and footer options.

7. **Save** the file and then print the presentation as a **grayscale slide**. **Close** the file.

 You have completed Project 4H ─────────────────────────

Project 4I—Fiesta

Objectives: *Draw and Format Lines, Create Basic Shapes and Text Boxes, Edit and Format Drawing Objects, Insert and Format WordArt, and Insert Images.*

In this Mastery Assessment, you will format the title slide for the Fiesta! presentation used during the monthly company meeting highlighting employee news. Your completed presentation will look similar to the one shown in Figure 4.41. You will save your presentation as *4I_Fiesta_Firstname_Lastname*.

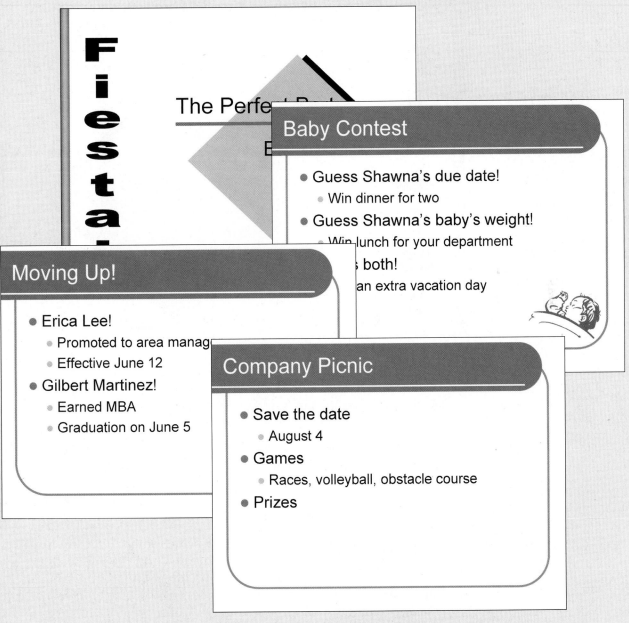

Figure 4.41

(**Project 4I**–Fiesta continues on the next page)

(Project 4I–Fiesta continued)

1. From your student files, open the file **p04I_Fiesta**. Save the file as 4I_Fiesta_Firstname_Lastname and then close the **Outline/Slides** pane.

2. On **Slide 1**, insert a **WordArt** object. In the **WordArt Gallery** dialog box, in the first row, click the last design, which displays a vertical WordArt. In the **Edit WordArt Text** dialog box, type **Fiesta!** Size and move the WordArt as shown in Figure 4.42, and continue to refer to Figure 4.42 as you format the remainder of Slide 1.

Figure 4.42

3. Along the left edge of the slide, from top to bottom, draw a narrow **Rectangle** that is approximately 0.25 inch wide. This forms a narrow band along the left edge of the slide.

4. Apply a two-color gradient fill effect to the rectangle. For the first color, choose the last color in the color scheme palette—**royal blue**. For the second color, choose the fifth color—**light blue**. Apply a **Vertical** shading style and choose the first variant in the second row. Change the **Line Color** to **No Line**.

5. From the **AutoShapes Basic Shapes** palette, insert a **Diamond**. Size the diamond so that it is **5.75 inches** in height by **6 inches** in width. Position the diamond so that its top point is at **2.5 inches above zero on the vertical ruler** and its right point touches the right edge of the slide. Change the **Fill Color** of the diamond to **black** and the **Line Color** to **No Line**.

(Project 4I–Fiesta continues on the next page)

(Project 4I–Fiesta continued)

6. Use **Copy and Paste** to duplicate the diamond AutoShape. If necessary, drag the diamond so you can see the copy. Change the **Fill Color** of the new diamond to the fifth color in the color scheme—**light blue**. Use the directional arrow keys to nudge the diamond to the left and up so that the black diamond appears to shadow the blue diamond.

7. **Add Text** to the blue diamond. (Hint: Use the shortcut menu.) Type **Employee** and then press Enter. Type **News** and then **right align** the text. Change the **Font Size** to **40**.

8. Draw a line that begins at **2 inches to the left of zero on the horizontal ruler** and at **0.5 inch above zero on the vertical ruler**. Extend the line to the right edge of the slide. Change the **Line Color** to the last color in the color palette—**blue**. Change the **Line Style** to a **6 pt. solid line**. The line should cut across the diamonds.

9. On the Drawing toolbar, click **Text Box** and then click just above the left edge of the blue line. Type **The Perfect Party** and then change the **Font Size** to **44 pt**. The *y* in *Party* should not extend into the black diamond. If it does, move the text box to the left.

10. Display **Slide 2**. From your student files, insert the picture **p04I_Baby**. Move the picture of the baby so that it is positioned in the lower right curve of the rounded rectangle.

11. Display **Slide 3**. Insert the **Explosion 1** AutoShape found in **Stars and Banners** so that it extends from **1 inch to the right of zero on the horizontal ruler** and **1 inch below zero on the horizontal ruler** to the lower right corner of the slide. **Add Text** to the explosion. Type **Congratulations!** and then change the **Font Size** to **24** and the **Font Color** to **White**. Change the explosion's **Fill Color** to the last color in the color scheme—**blue**.

12. Create a footer for the notes and handouts that includes the date updated automatically and a footer with the text **4I Fiesta-Firstname Lastname**. Clear all other header and footer options.

13. **Save** the file and run the slide show. Then print the presentation as **grayscale handouts**, **4** slides per page in **horizontal** order. **Close** the file.

End **You have completed Project 4I**

Problem Solving

Project 4J—Event

Objectives: *Draw and Format Lines, Create Basic Shapes and Text Boxes, Edit and Format Drawing Objects, and Insert Images.*

In this Problem Solving exercise, start a new presentation based on a design template. Think about a large event that might take place at your school or workplace. Create a presentation describing the attendees, the event purpose, and the activities. Some ideas include a new student or new employee orientation or a fundraiser. Create four to six slides that include at least two pictures and two lines or shapes. Create an appropriate footer for your notes and handouts and save your presentation as *4J_Event_Firstname_Lastname.* Print the presentation as handouts, 6 slides per page, in grayscale.

 End **You have completed Project 4J** ————————————————————

Project 4K—Activities

Objectives: *Draw and Format Lines, Create Basic Shapes and Text Boxes, Edit and Format Drawing Objects, and Insert Images.*

In this Problem Solving exercise, start a new presentation based on a design template. Create a presentation for a fiesta or auction that a city or nonprofit organization would conduct. Include in your presentation activities, volunteer committees, refreshments, and key organizing personnel. Create four to six slides that include a WordArt, pictures, and lines or shapes. Create an appropriate footer for your notes and handouts and save your presentation as *4K_Activities_Firstname_Lastname.* Print the presentation as handouts, 6 slides per page, in grayscale.

End **You have completed Project 4K** ————————————————————

On the Internet

Using Google to Find Clip Art

Connect to the Internet and type **www.google.com** to launch the Google search engine. Type **clip art** and then press Enter on your keyboard. Visit several of the clip art sites available on the Internet. Notice that some of the sites are free and some are not. Make a note of the sites that have clips that you think might be usable for presentations that you may create. If you are working in a classroom or lab, check with your instructor before downloading clips to your system.

GO! with Help

Organizing Media Clips with Clip Organizer

If you have media clips stored on your system, you can use the Clip Organizer to categorize them into collections. Use PowerPoint Help to learn how to organize your clips.

1. Click in the **Type a question for help** box, type **How do I use Clip Organizer?** and then press Enter.

2. Click **About the Clip Organizer**. Read the information and click each link that displays.

chapter five

Advanced Presentation Graphic Techniques

In this chapter, you will: complete these projects **and** practice these skills.

Project 5A **Creating a Recruitment Presentation**	**Objectives** • Enhance Objects with Visual Effects • Use the Draw Menu • Modify Pictures

Project 5B **Creating a Photo Album**	**Objective** • Create a Photo Album

Sensation! Park

Sensation! Park is a "family fun center" theme park designed for today's busy families. The park incorporates traditional amusement park rides and arcade games along with new and popular water rides, surf pools, laser tag, video games, and a racetrack for all ages. Situated on 100 acres, the park's mission is to provide a safe, clean, exciting environment where children and adults of all ages can find a game, ride, or event that suits their interests, or discover something completely new!

© Getty Images, Inc.

Advanced Presentation Graphic Techniques

In this chapter you will format objects by adding shadows and 3-D effects. You will also learn how to manipulate drawing objects by rotating, changing object order, creating groups, and by aligning and distributing selected objects.

In addition to formatting objects, you will practice a new method for creating presentations using the Photo Album feature. The Photo Album feature allows you to develop a presentation consisting primarily of scanned or digital pictures. Thus, the Photo Album feature in Microsoft PowerPoint 2003 provides a fun and easy way to show your pictures to your family, friends, and coworkers.

Project 5A **Application**

Microsoft Office PowerPoint 2003 provides a variety of methods for formatting and enhancing graphics and objects. You should carefully consider the formatting and colors that you apply to the objects in your presentations so that the objects blend with your presentation and help to convey your message. Your presentations will look more polished, and it will be apparent to your audience that you have spent considerable time creating a professional looking presentation.

In Activities 5.1 through 5.17, you will add visual effects to graphic objects in a presentation regarding job applications at Sensation! Park. Your completed presentation will look similar to Figure 5.1. You will save your presentation as *5A_Application_ Firstname_Lastname*.

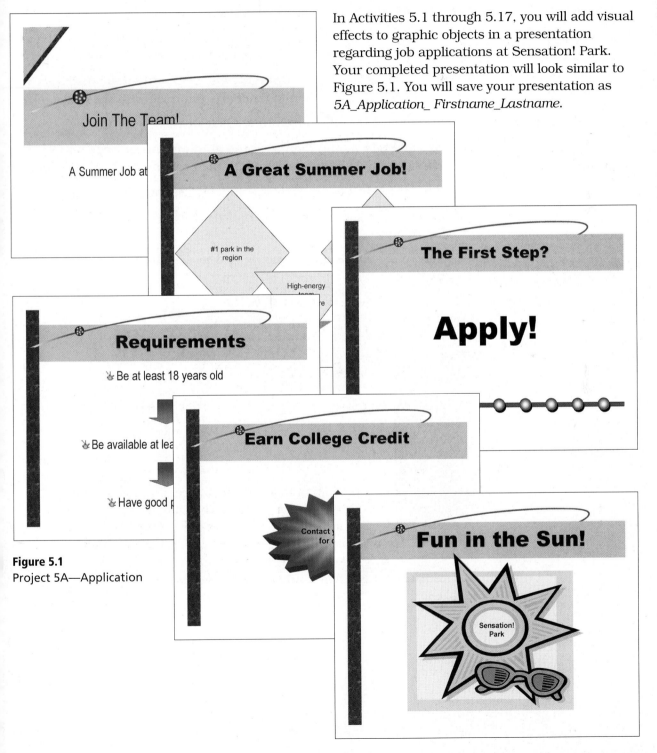

Figure 5.1
Project 5A—Application

Objective 1
Enhance Objects with Visual Effects

Recall that PowerPoint objects can include lines, shapes, and WordArt created using the PowerPoint Drawing toolbar. You can enhance an object by applying shadows or 3-D visual effects. After a shadow or 3-D effect has been applied to an object, you can change the shadow color and placement, and you can control the depth, lighting, and perspective of a 3-D effect.

Activity 5.1 Adding and Removing Shadows

PowerPoint provides options for 20 different shadow styles, so you have many ways to add impact to the drawing objects that you create.

1 From your student files, **Open** the file **p05A_Application**. Scroll through the presentation to familiarize yourself with the slides. If necessary, **Close** the Outline/Slides pane.

2 Display **Slide 2**, and then click the **diamond AutoShape on the left** side of the slide to select it. On the Drawing toolbar, click the **Shadow Style** button to display the Shadow Style palette.

3 In the first row, click the first shadow—**Shadow Style 1**. See Figure 5.2.

A green shadow is applied above and to the left of the diamond AutoShape.

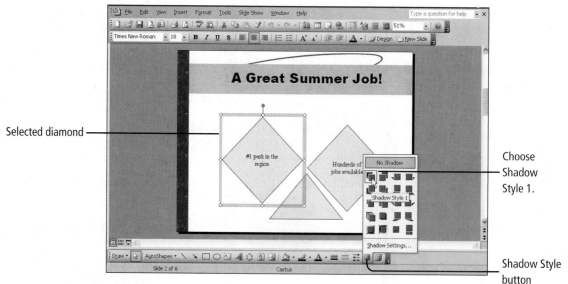

Selected diamond

Choose Shadow Style 1.

Shadow Style button

Figure 5.2

4 With the diamond still selected, display the **Shadow Style** 🔲 palette again and apply a different shadow. Take a moment to apply several different shadows to see the effect that each style has on the selected object. After you have seen the effect of several shadows, click the **Shadow Style** button again 🔲, and in the last row, click the third shadow—**Shadow Style 19**.

5 Select the **diamond on the right** side of the slide. On the Drawing toolbar, click **Shadow Style** 🔲, and in the first row, click the first shadow—**Shadow Style 1**.

6 To remove the shadow that you applied in the previous step, with the right diamond selected click **Shadow Style** 🔲. At the top of the Shadow palette, click **No Shadow**.

The shadow is removed from the diamond.

7 If necessary, select the **diamond on the right** side of the slide. Click **Shadow Style** 🔲, and in the last row, click the third shadow—**Shadow Style 19**.

8 On the menu bar, click the **File** menu, and then click **Save As**. Navigate to the location where you are storing your files for this chapter, creating a new folder for Chapter 5 if you want to do so. Save the file as **5A_Application_Firstname_Lastname**

Activity 5.2 Changing Shadow Settings

A shadow can be modified using the Shadow Settings toolbar. From the Shadow Settings toolbar, you can change shadow color, you can **nudge**—move in very small increments—the shadow up, down, left, or right, and you can toggle the shadow on and off.

1 Display **Slide 3**, and then in the lower left corner of the slide, click to select the small circle. On the Drawing toolbar, click the **Shadow Style** button 🔲, and then in the fourth row, click the second shadow—**Shadow Style 14**.

2 With the circle still selected, on the Drawing toolbar, click the **Shadow Style** button 🔲 again, and at the bottom of the Shadow Style palette, click **Shadow Settings**.

The Shadow Settings toolbar displays floating in your presentation window, or docked in the toolbar area of your presentation window. See Figure 5.3.

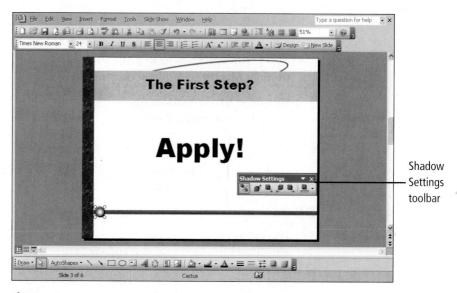

Shadow Settings toolbar

Figure 5.3

3 On the Shadow Settings toolbar, click **Nudge Shadow Down** 🔲.

The shadow moves down in a very small increment.

4 Click **Nudge Shadow Down** 🔲 twice more and notice the new position of the shadow.

5 With the circle still selected, on the Shadow Settings toolbar, click **Nudge Shadow Right** 🔲.

The shadow moves slightly to the right.

6 On the Shadow Settings toolbar, click the **Shadow Color button arrow** 🔲 ▾ to display the slide color scheme. Click the second color—**black**. Click anywhere on the slide to cancel the selection and notice the color and position of the shadow applied to the circle.

Alert! ── **Click the Shadow Color Arrow!**

If you click the Shadow Color *button*, as opposed to the Shadow Color *arrow*, the shadow color that displays in the button is applied to the selected slide object.

7 **Close** ❌ the Shadow Settings toolbar and **Save** 🔲 the file.

Activity 5.3 Adding 3-D Effects to an Object

When used effectively, applying 3-D effects to objects is a more dramatic method of adding visual impact than applying shadows. PowerPoint provides twenty 3-D effects, which add depth and **perspective** in a variety of directions. Perspective refers to the way in which a 3-D effect extends toward a single point.

1 Display **Slide 5**, and then click the **star** AutoShape in the center of the slide to select it.

2 On the Drawing toolbar, click the **3-D Style** button 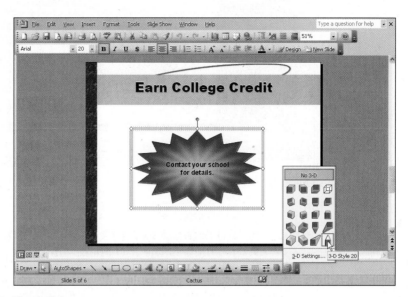.

3 In the last row of the 3-D Style palette, click the last style—**3-D Style 20**. See Figure 5.4.

Notice the 3-D effect applied to the shape.

Figure 5.4

4 With the star still selected, display the **3-D Style** palette again and apply a different 3-D effect. Take a moment to apply several different 3-D effects. After you have applied several of the effects, in the second row, click the third effect—**3-D Style 7**.

5 **Save** the file.

Activity 5.4 Changing 3-D Settings

A 3-D effect can be modified using the 3-D Settings toolbar. From this toolbar, you can change the angle in which the 3-D effect is tilted, increase or decrease the depth and direction of the effect, modify the intensity of the color using the lighting button, and change the color of the 3-D effect.

1 If necessary, select the star on **Slide 5**. On the Drawing toolbar, click the **3-D Style** button, and then click **3-D Settings** to display the 3-D Settings toolbar. See Figure 5.5.

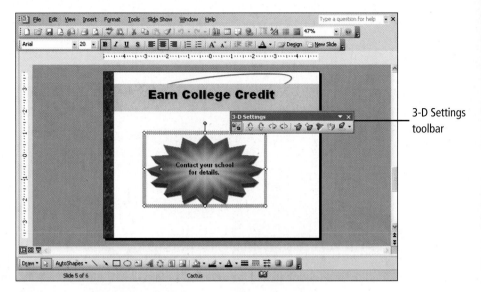

Figure 5.5

On the right side: 3-D Settings toolbar

2 On the 3-D Settings toolbar, click the **Tilt Down** button and notice the shape of the 3-D effect. On the 3-D Settings toolbar, click the **Tilt Up** button. On the 3-D Settings toolbar, click each of the four **Tilt** buttons several times and notice the effect on the object.

3 To reapply the original 3-D effect, select the star object, and then on the Drawing toolbar, click the **3-D Style** button. In the second row, click the third effect—**3-D Style 7**.

4 With the star AutoShape still selected, on the 3-D Settings toolbar click the **Depth** button. From the displayed palette, click **144 pt.** and notice that the 3-D effect is more dramatic.

5 On the 3-D Settings toolbar, click the **Direction** button. Apply several of the direction effects to the object.

6 At the bottom of the **Direction** palette, click **Parallel**.

Notice the difference in the shape of the object. Do not be concerned with the shape of your object, as you will reapply the original 3-D effect after experimenting with the 3-D settings.

More Knowledge — Changing the Surface and Lighting of a 3-D Effect

The Lighting button on the 3-D Settings toolbar modifies the color of a 3-D effect by making it lighter on one side or another, depending on the direction from which lighting is applied. The Surface button changes the surface of the 3-D object. For example, the Wire Frame option displays the object's outline as though it were made from wire.

7 On the 3-D Settings toolbar, click the **3-D Color button arrow** [icon], and then click the fifth color—**Beige**.

Notice that only the 3-D effect is changed, not the surface color of the object. Additionally, the color that you choose may not be the color that is displayed in the 3-D effect because the depth, direction, lighting, and surface settings applied to the object determine the variations in the 3-D color.

8 To reapply the original 3-D effect, select the star, and on the Drawing toolbar, click the **3-D Style** button [icon], and then in the second row, click the third effect—**3-D Style 7**.

9 On the 3-D Settings toolbar, click the **3-D Color button arrow** [icon], and then click **Automatic**.

The original 3-D settings are applied to the star.

10 On the 3-D Settings toolbar, click the **Close** button [X], and then on the Standard toolbar, click **Save** [icon].

Objective 2
Use the Draw Menu

The Draw menu, which is displayed from the Drawing toolbar, provides a variety of menu commands with which you can further customize the objects on your slides. For example, you can rotate or flip an object, you can align and distribute objects on your slides, and you can select several separate objects and group them so that they are treated as one object. When several objects are grouped, formatting can be applied to the entire group.

Activity 5.5 Flipping Objects

The Flip Vertical and Flip Horizontal commands create a mirror image of a selected drawing object by flipping it 180 degrees.

1 If necessary, **Open** [icon] your file **5A_Application_Firstname_Lastname**.

2 Display **Slide 2** and click the triangle so that it is selected.

3 On the Drawing toolbar, click the **Draw** button [Draw ▾], point to **Rotate or Flip**, and then click **Flip Vertical** so that the triangle is flipped 180 degrees.

Do not be concerned if the triangle overlaps the text in the diamonds—you will adjust the placement of the objects in a later activity.

4 Point to the triangle and right-click to display the shortcut menu. Click **Add Text**, and then type **High-energy team atmosphere**

5 Select the text that you just typed and change the **Font Size** [32 ▾] to **18**.

6 On the menu bar, click **Format**, and then click **AutoShape**. In the displayed **Format AutoShape** dialog box, click the **Text Box tab**, and then select the **Word wrap text in AutoShape** check box. Click **OK**.

The text wraps to three lines within the triangle.

7 On the Drawing toolbar, click the **Shadow Style** button 🔲, and in the last row, click the third shadow—**Shadow Style 19**. Click anywhere else on the slide, and then compare your slide with Figure 5.6.

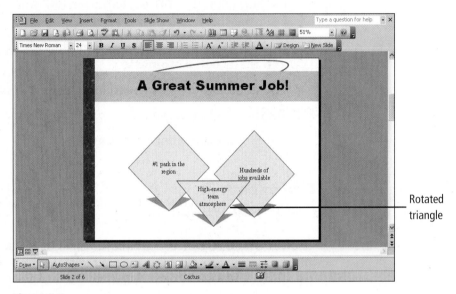

Rotated triangle

Figure 5.6

8 **Save** 🔲 the file.

Activity 5.6 Rotating Objects

The Rotate Left and Rotate Right commands rotate a selected object in 90-degree increments. In addition to these commands, you can rotate an object in any direction using the rotation handle.

1 Display **Slide 1**, and then in the upper left corner of the slide, click to select the **triangle**. Press and hold down Ctrl and press D to create a duplicate of the triangle.

2 On the Drawing toolbar, click the **Draw** button Draw ▾, point to **Rotate or Flip**, and then click **Rotate Right 90°**.

The triangle is rotated 90 degrees.

3 Display the **Draw** menu again, point to **Rotate or Flip**, and then click **Rotate Right 90°** again.

The triangle is rotated again, 90 degrees.

4 Point to the rotated triangle so that the move pointer ⊕ displays. Drag the triangle so that it fits into the lower right corner of the slide. Click anywhere on the slide so that the triangle is not selected, and then compare your slide with Figure 5.7.

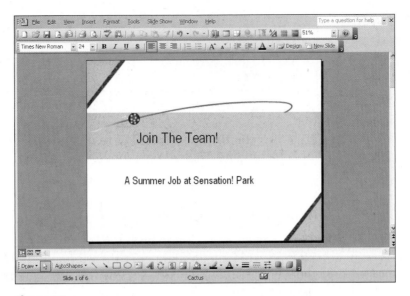

Figure 5.7

5 Display **Slide 3**, and then click in the word *Apply!*.

Notice that in addition to the white sizing handles, a small green circle is connected to the text box by a short line. This is the ***rotate handle***, which is used to rotate the object.

6 Move the pointer over the rotate handle and notice that the pointer displays as a curved arrow. See Figure 5.8.

Rotation pointer

Figure 5.8

7 Press and hold down the left mouse button so that the pointer displays as four curved arrows and a dotted box outlines the text box. Drag down and to the left to rotate the box at approximately a 45-degree angle. Release the mouse button.

8 Click the **Undo** button ⟲▾ to reverse the rotation and reset the object to its original position.

9 On the Standard toolbar, click **Save** 🖫.

Activity 5.7 Changing Object Order

When objects are created or inserted on a slide, they often overlap. For example, the master slide, and therefore, all of the slides except the title slide in your 5A_Application presentation, contain three major graphic elements—the green rectangle along the left edge of the slide, the gold rectangle near the top of the slide, and the green arc at the top of the slide. The element at the top of this stack (orderly pile) is the green rectangle, which overlaps the gold rectangle. The element at the bottom of the stack is the green arc, which is partially hidden by the gold rectangle.

The object created first is always at the *bottom* of a stack of objects, while the object created last is at the top of the stack of objects and may hide a part of the other objects in the stack. You can rearrange the objects using the Order options on the Draw menu. See the table in Figure 5.9 for a description of the commands on this menu.

The Order Menu

Command	Description
Bring to Front	Places the selected object in front of all other overlapping objects.
Send to Back	Places the selected object behind all other overlapping objects.
Bring Forward	Moves the selected object or group one object closer to the top of a stack of objects.
Send Backward	Moves the selected object or group one object closer to the bottom of a stack of objects.

Figure 5.9

In this activity, you will change the order of the graphic elements—the green rectangle, gold rectangle, and green arc—on the slide master so that the order of the elements will change on all of the slides in the presentation.

1 On the **View** menu, point to **Master**, and then click **Slide Master**. Verify that the slide master and not the title master displays (*Slide Master* is indicated in the status bar above the Start button). If necessary, drag the vertical scroll bar up to display the Slide Master.

2 On the left edge of the slide, click the **green rectangle** to select it.

3 On the Drawing toolbar, click the **Draw** button Draw ▾, and then point to **Order** to display the four Order commands. Click **Send to Back**.

The green rectangle is at the back of the stack of objects. Notice that the gold rectangle displays over the green rectangle.

4 With the green rectangle still selected, click the **Draw** button Draw ▾ again, point to **Order**, and then click **Bring to Front** to bring the green rectangle back to the front of the stack.

5 At the top of the slide, click the **green arc** to select it.

The arc may not appear to be selected because the sizing handles do not tightly enclose the arc. Compare your slide with Figure 5.10 to verify that you have selected the arc.

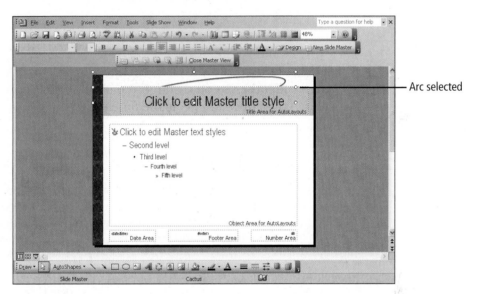

Arc selected

Figure 5.10

6 On the Drawing toolbar, click the **Draw** menu Draw ▾, and then point to **Order**. Click **Bring Forward**.

The portion of the arc that was behind the gold rectangle displays. A portion of the arc, however, is still behind the green rectangle.

7 Verify that the arc is still selected. On the Drawing toolbar, click the **Draw** button Draw ▾, and then point to **Order**. Click **Bring to Front**.

The portion of the arc that was behind the green rectangle displays. Compare your slide with Figure 5.11.

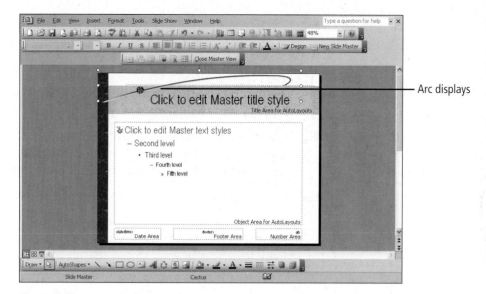

Figure 5.11

---

8 On the View buttons, click **Normal View** ⌨ to close the **Slide Master**. Scroll through the slides in the presentation and notice that the entire arc is visible on each of the slides.

More Knowledge — Floating the Order Menu

When you point to Order on the Draw menu, you can point to the dotted bar at the top of the Order menu and drag it to float the menu on your screen. The Order menu displays as a toolbar. It is a good idea to float the menu if you are going to use the Order menu extensively.

9 On the Standard toolbar, click the **Save** button 🖫.

Activity 5.8 Selecting Multiple Objects

You can format more than one object at a time by selecting multiple objects. In this activity, you will select multiple objects on Slides 2 and 4, and then format the text in the selections.

1 Display **Slide 4**, and then click anywhere in the first text box—*Be at least 18 years old.*

2 Press and hold down [Shift], and then click the second text box—*Be available at least 20 hours/week.*

Both text boxes are selected.

3 Press and hold down [Shift], and then click the third text box—*Have good people skills.*

All three text boxes are selected. See Figure 5.12.

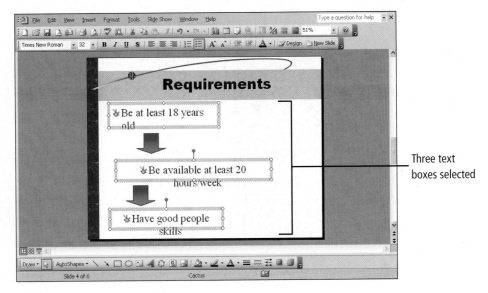

Three text boxes selected

Figure 5.12

4 On the Formatting toolbar, click the **Font button arrow** [Arial ▼], and then click **Arial Narrow**.

The text in each of the selected text boxes is formatted in Arial Narrow.

More Knowledge — Deselecting an Object

You can cancel the selection of an object in a group of selected objects by pressing and holding down Shift, and then clicking the object. The object that you click will no longer be selected, but all other objects remain selected.

5 Display **Slide 2**. On the Drawing toolbar, click the **Select Objects** button [⬚]. Move your pointer into the presentation window and notice that it displays as a left-pointing arrow.

To use the Select Objects pointer to select multiple objects, you must draw a rectangle that *completely* encloses the objects that you want to select. By default, the Select Objects button is on when you are working in PowerPoint.

6 Position the pointer just below the intersection of the gold and green rectangles. Hold down the left mouse button and drag down and to the right to draw a dashed box—**selection rectangle**—that extends to the bottom right corner of the slide. See Figure 5.13. Release the mouse button and notice that the two diamonds and the triangle are all selected.

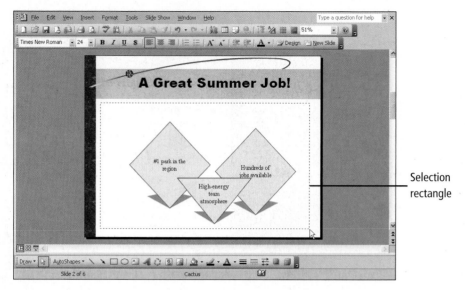

Selection rectangle

Figure 5.13

7 On the Formatting toolbar, click the **Font button arrow** [Arial ▼], and then click **Arial**.

The text in each of the selected text boxes is changed to Arial.

8 Click anywhere on the slide to cancel the selection.

More Knowledge — Combining Selection Techniques

You can combine two selection methods to select objects. For example, you can drag a selection rectangle to enclose some of the objects that you want to select. Then press and hold down [Shift] and click the remaining objects that you want to select.

9 On the Standard toolbar, click the **Save** button [■].

Activity 5.9 Using Grids and Guides to Position Objects

Recall that you can use the rulers to aid you with the placement of objects on a slide. PowerPoint provides two additional visual aids that you can use to precisely position objects—the **guides** and the **grid**. Guides are two lines that intersect at the horizontal and vertical center point on a slide. The guides do not print, and you can move the guides or create new ones. The grid is a series of horizontal and vertical intersecting gridlines, which you can use to visually align objects.

1 Display **Slide 5**. On the Drawing toolbar, click the **Draw** button [Draw ▼], and then click **Grid and Guides**. In the displayed **Grid and Guides** dialog box, under **Guide settings**, select the **Display drawing guides on screen** check box, and then click **OK**.

A horizontal and a vertical dashed line display, intersecting at the center point of the slide.

2 Point to the **star AutoShape** to display the move pointer ⊕, and then drag the star to the right so that its center point aligns with the vertical guide. See Figure 5.14. Release the mouse button.

The star is centered horizontally on the slide.

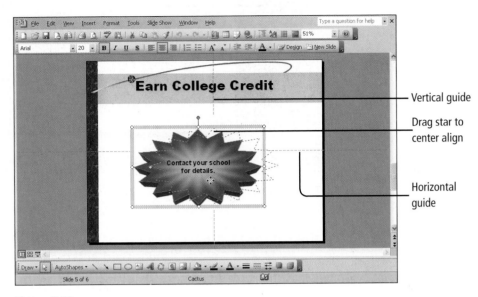

Figure 5.14

Is Your Star Centered?

It may take more than one try to center the star on your slide. You will know that the star is centered horizontally when the center sizing handles and the green rotate handle align with the vertical guide.

3 Display **Slide 2**. On the Drawing toolbar, click the **Draw** button **Draw ▾**, and then click **Grid and Guides**. Under **Guide settings**, clear the **Display drawing guides on screen** check box to turn the feature off.

4 Under **Grid settings**, select the **Display grid on screen** check box, and then click **OK.**

A series of horizontal and vertical dotted gridlines display on the slide, approximately 1 inch apart.

5 Click in the text in the diamond on the right side of the slide.

The selected diamond is slightly lower than the diamond on the left side of the slide. You will use the grid to align the two diamonds.

6 Drag the selected diamond up and to the right so that its top point aligns with the same gridline as the diamond on the left side of the slide and so that its left point aligns with the sixth vertical gridline.

7 Point to the left diamond and drag the diamond to the left so that its right point aligns with the fifth gridline. Compare your slide with Figure 5.15.

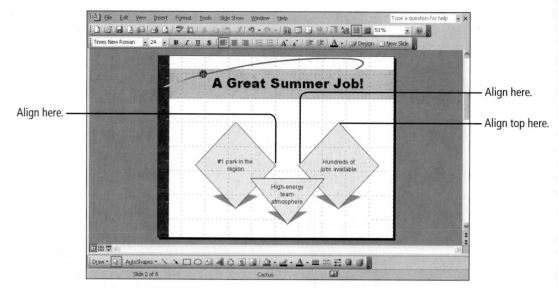

Align here.

Align here.

Align top here.

Figure 5.15

8 On the Drawing toolbar, click the **Draw** button Draw ▾ , and then click **Grid and Guides**. Under **Grid settings**, clear the **Display grid on screen** check box to turn the feature off. Click **OK**.

9 On the Standard toolbar, click the **Save** button 🖫 .

Activity 5.10 Grouping, Ungrouping, and Regrouping Objects

When objects are created on a slide, animation and formatting are applied individually to each object. Some slides may contain a group of objects that should be treated as one unit, rather than as several individual elements. For example, Slide 2 in your 5A_Application presentation contains three objects—two diamonds and a triangle. Each of these objects is currently formatted separately. If the three objects are *grouped*—treated as one object—they can be sized, moved, and formatted, all at one time. Alternatively, a grouped object can be *ungrouped*—treated as separate objects. In this activity, you will group the three objects on Slide 2, and then resize the entire group.

1 If necessary, display **Slide 2**. To select all three objects on the slide, click the diamond on the left side of the slide. Press and hold down [Shift] and click the diamond on the right side of the slide. Continue to press and hold down [Shift], and then click the triangle.

All three objects are selected.

Another Way ─ **To Select Objects**

You can select the objects by clicking Select Objects on the Drawing toolbar, and then pressing and holding down the left mouse button and dragging to draw a selection rectangle that encloses all three objects.

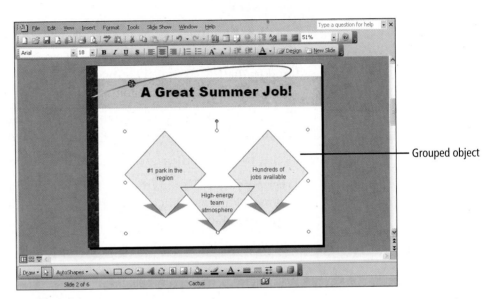

2 On the Drawing toolbar, click the **Draw** button Draw ▼, and then click **Group**.

Sizing handles enclose the entire group of objects, indicating that the three objects can now be treated as one single object. With the three objects treated as one object, the entire group can be moved and formatted together. See Figure 5.16.

Grouped object

Figure 5.16

3 Click anywhere on the slide so that the group is not selected.

4 Click anywhere above the text in the left diamond.

Notice that the diamond is not selected, but rather, the entire group is selected as indicated by the sizing handles enclosing the three objects.

5 Click the diamond again.

The entire group is still selected, but the diamond is surrounded by small circles that contain an x. Selecting an object in a group in this manner allows you to apply formatting to the selected object within the group.

6 With the left diamond selected within the group, on the Drawing toolbar, click the **Fill Color button arrow** ◇ ▼, and then click the last color—**Gray**.

The fill color of the selected diamond is changed to gray.

7 On the Standard toolbar, click **Undo** ↻ ▼.

8 Click any of the other objects in the group so that the entire group is selected. Do not be concerned if an individual object within the group is also selected. On the Drawing toolbar, click **Draw** Draw ▼, and then click **Ungroup**.

Each individual object in the group is selected, indicating that the objects are no longer grouped as one.

9 Click anywhere on the slide to deselect the three objects. Click one of the objects again. On the Drawing toolbar, click the **Draw** button Draw ▾, and then click **Regroup**.

When you click an object that was previously grouped, PowerPoint remembers the other objects in the group. The Regroup command reapplies the original grouping. The objects can be sized or formatted as a group.

10 Point to the upper left sizing handle so that the diagonal resize pointer ↖ displays. Press and hold down the left mouse button and drag up and to the left so that the crosshair pointer is positioned at the intersection of the green and gold rectangles. Release the mouse button.

The upper points of the diamonds almost touch the lower edge of the gold rectangle.

11 Point to the middle right sizing handle to display the horizontal resize pointer ↔ and drag to the right so that the right point of the diamond almost touches the right edge of the slide. Compare your slide with Figure 5.17.

All of the objects in the group are resized.

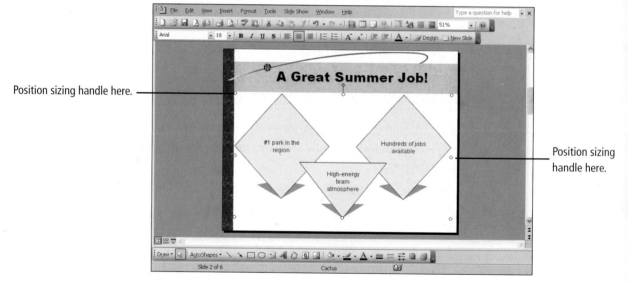

Position sizing handle here.

Position sizing handle here.

Figure 5.17

12 On the Standard toolbar, click the **Save** button 🖫.

Activity 5.11 Aligning Objects on a Slide

The vertical and horizontal rulers and the grids and guides provide visual methods for aligning objects on a slide. The Align or Distribute toolbar provides another method that is particularly useful for aligning multiple objects. Objects can be aligned horizontally or vertically, relative to the slide or relative to each other. For example, when an object is aligned relative to the slide, the edges of the slide determine the placement of the objects. In this activity, you will center align the objects on Slide 4 relative to the slide. On Slide 3, you will make several copies of the circle at the bottom of the slide, and then align the objects at the top, relative to the original circle.

1 Display **Slide 4**. On the Drawing toolbar, click the **Draw** button

Draw ▾ , and then point to **Align or Distribute**.

The Align or Distribute menu can be displayed as a floating toolbar. You will use the Align buttons extensively in this activity. Thus, it is a good idea to display the menu as a floating toolbar so that you can quickly access the commands.

2 Point to the dotted bar at the top of the **Align or Distribute** menu.

When you point to the bar, the ScreenTip *Drag to make this menu float* displays. See Figure 5.18.

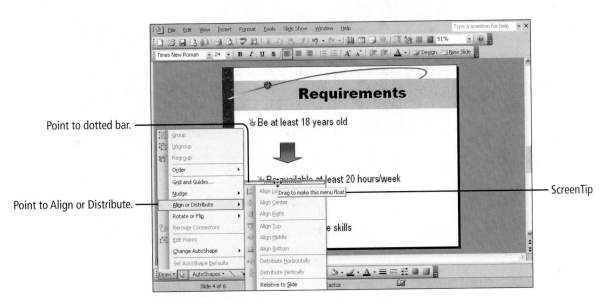

Point to dotted bar.

Point to Align or Distribute.

ScreenTip

Figure 5.18

3 Drag the menu onto the slide and release the mouse button to float the menu. Point to the **Align or Distribute** menu title bar and drag it up toward the Formatting toolbar at the top of your screen, until it is a ***docked toolbar***—a toolbar that snaps into place below the other toolbars or at the side of the window. Release the mouse button.

4 Position the pointer above and to the left of the first text box—*Be at least 18 years old*—so that the left-pointing selection arrow displays. Press and hold down the left mouse button and drag down and to the right to draw a selection rectangle that encloses the three text boxes and the two arrows. Release the mouse button. See Figure 5.19.

All of the objects are selected. If you did not fully enclose all of the objects, press and hold down [Shift] and click any of the text boxes or arrows that are not selected.

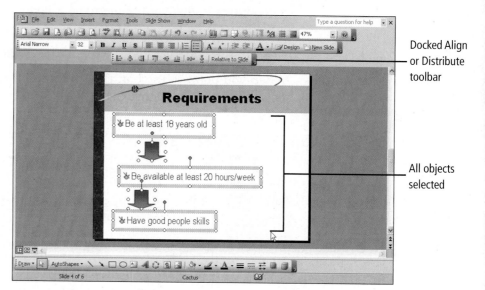

Figure 5.19

5 On the Align or Distribute toolbar, click the **Relative to Slide** button so that the button is highlighted.

When the Relative to Slide button is selected in this manner, the buttons on the toolbar will align the objects relative to the edges of the slide.

6 On the Align or Distribute toolbar, click the second button—**Align Center** [icon].

All of the objects are centered horizontally between the left and right edges of the slide.

7 Display **Slide 3**, and select the **circle** near the bottom left of the slide. Recall that a selected object can be duplicated by pressing and holding down Ctrl, and then pressing D. Make nine duplicates of the object by pressing and holding down Ctrl, and then pressing D nine times.

The duplicated circles display diagonally below and to the right of the original circle. Do not be concerned if some of the circles are off the slide. You will adjust placement in the next two steps.

8 Position the pointer above and to the left of the original circle. Press and hold down the left mouse button and drag down and to the right to create a selection rectangle that encloses all of the circles.

If you did not fully enclose all of the circles, press and hold down Shift and click any of the circles that are not selected. Compare your slide with Figure 5.20.

Selected circles —

Figure 5.20

9 On the Align or Distribute toolbar, click the **Relative to Slide** button to turn it off.

The feature is turned off because, when the circles are aligned, they should not align with the edge of the slide. Rather, they should align so that the top of each circle is even with the top of the original circle.

10 With the circles still selected, on the Align or Distribute toolbar, click the **Align Top** button .

All of the circles align with the top edge of the original circle, which was positioned highest on the slide.

11 On the Standard toolbar, click **Save** .

Activity 5.12 Distributing Objects on a Slide

In addition to aligning objects on a slide, you can **distribute**—evenly space—selected objects. Objects can be distributed relative to the slide—between the edges of the slide—or between the first and last objects in the selection.

1 If necessary, display **Slide 3**. If necessary, select the circles by drawing a selection rectangle that encloses all 10 circles.

2 On the Align or Distribute toolbar, click **Relative to Slide** to turn the feature on.

3 On the Align or Distribute toolbar, click the **Distribute Horizontally** button.

Notice that although Relative to Slide was turned on, the objects do not touch the edges of the slide. PowerPoint aligns the rightmost circle the same distance from the edge of the slide as the leftmost circle. Then, the circles in between are evenly distributed between the first and last circles in the selection. Click anywhere on the slide to cancel the selection. Compare your slide with Figure 5.21.

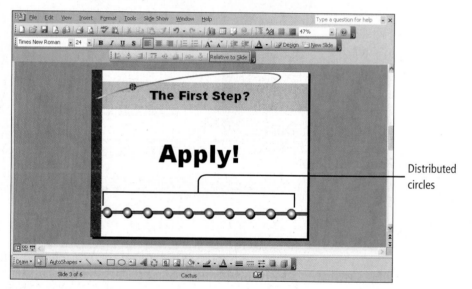

Distributed circles

Figure 5.21

4 On the menu bar, click the **View** menu, and then point to **Toolbars**. Click **Align or Distribute**.

The Align or Distribute toolbar is closed.

5 On the Standard toolbar, click the **Save** button.

Objective 3
Modify Pictures

Many of the pictures that you insert in a presentation can be modified using the Picture toolbar. The table in Figure 5.22 describes the buttons on the Picture toolbar.

The Picture Toolbar

Button	Button Name	Description
	Insert Picture	Inserts a picture that is stored on disk.
	Color	Converts the selected picture to grayscale, black and white, or to a watermark.
	More Contrast	Increases the intensity of the colors in the selected picture.
	Less Contrast	Decreases the intensity of the colors in the selected picture.
	More Brightness	Adds white to lighten the colors in the selected picture.
	Less Brightness	Adds black to darken the colors in the selected picture. The lower the brightness, the darker the color.
	Crop	Trims or restores a portion of a picture.
	Rotate Left 90°	Rotates a picture 90° to the left.
	Line Style	Sets a line width so that the picture appears to be framed.
	Compress Picture	Reduces resolution and discards cropped portions of a picture to reduce file size.
	Recolor Picture	Displays the Recolor Picture dialog box, in which you can change the fill and line colors of the selected picture.
	Format Picture	Displays the Format Picture dialog box, in which you can change the size, position, and other properties of the selected picture.
	Set Transparent Color	Sets a transparent color for the selected picture. This button works on all bitmaps and some, but not all, clip art.
	Reset Picture	Removes cropping from the selected picture and returns the size, color, brightness, and contrast to the original settings.

Figure 5.22

Activity 5.13 Modifying the Color of a Picture

The color button on the Picture toolbar provides several options for modifying the color of a picture.

1 If necessary, **Open** 📷 your file **5A_Application_Firstname_Lastname**.

2 Display **Slide 6**, and then click the sun picture to select it.

The Picture toolbar displays either docked in the toolbar area of your presentation window or floating in your presentation window. If the Picture toolbar does not display, click the View menu, point to Toolbars, and then click Picture.

3 On the Picture toolbar, click the **Color** button 🖼 to display the four color commands. See Figure 5.23. Click **Grayscale** to display the picture in varying shades of gray.

Color button ⎯⎯⎯⎯⎯⎯⎯⎯⎯⎯

Picture toolbar

Figure 5.23

4 On the Picture toolbar, click the **Color** button 🖼 again. Click **Black & White** to display the picture in all black and white.

If you are creating black and white transparencies, you may wish to choose this option so that you can see how the picture will display on the transparency film.

5 On the Picture toolbar, click the **Color** button 🖼 again. Click **Automatic** to return the picture to its original color. Click the **Color** button 🖼 again, and then click **Washout**.

Notice that the picture displays with very low contrast. The *Washout* feature is useful when you want to place text on top of a picture.

6 On the Picture toolbar, click the **Color** button 🖼 again, and then click **Automatic** to return the picture to its original color.

7 On the Standard toolbar, click the **Save** button 🖫 to save the file.

Activity 5.14 Adjusting Contrast and Brightness

When you apply the Washout format to a picture, the result is a picture with very low contrast. Sometimes the color of a picture may need to be adjusted only slightly so that the colors blend well with the overall color scheme of your presentation. Use the contrast and brightness buttons on the Picture toolbar to adjust the intensity of the colors in the picture.

1 If necessary, display **Slide 6** and click the sun picture to select it. On the Picture toolbar, click the **More Contrast** button ▣ several times.

Notice that the light pink color on the sunglasses lightens until it is almost white and the dark yellow lines on the sun fade out.

2 On the Picture toolbar, click the **Less Contrast** button ▣ several times.

The pink and dark yellow colors return slightly with each mouse click. After several clicks, the entire image begins to darken.

3 On the Picture toolbar, click the **More Brightness** button ▣ several times and notice the changes to the image, and then on the Picture toolbar, click the **Less Brightness** button ▣ several times.

Do not be concerned with the color in which your picture displays. You will reset the picture in a later activity.

4 On the Standard toolbar, click **Save** ▣.

Activity 5.15 Cropping a Picture

Cropping refers to trimming a portion of a picture so that the trimmed portion does not display. When the Crop button is activated, you can point to a sizing handle, and then drag to trim part of the picture. You can restore the picture by dragging with the crop tool in the opposite direction from which the picture was cropped. In this activity, you will crop the picture on Slide 6.

1 If necessary, display **Slide 6**, and then click the sun picture to select it. If necessary, drag the Picture toolbar away from the selected picture.

2 On the Picture toolbar, click the **Crop** button ▣.

The Crop button on the toolbar is selected. Crop lines at the corners and sides surround the picture. Move the pointer into the slide and notice that the crop tool is attached to the pointer.

3 Position the pointer inside the top left corner crop lines, just touching the lines.

The pointer takes on the shape of the corner crop lines.

4 Drag down and to the right, noticing the dashed box that displays.

The dashed box indicates the portion of the picture that will remain after you have finished cropping.

5 When the dashed box encloses the sunglasses in the lower right corner of the picture, release the mouse button to crop the picture. See Figure 5.24.

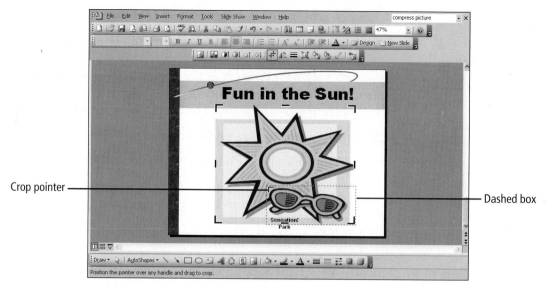

Crop pointer

Dashed box

Figure 5.24

6 On the Picture toolbar, click the **Crop** button ⊞ to toggle the **Crop** button off.

More Knowledge — Did You Crop Too Much?

You can restore a portion of a cropped picture by clicking the Crop button, and then dragging the crop lines back out toward their original location.

7 On the Standard toolbar, click the **Save** button ⊞.

Activity 5.16 Resetting a Picture

A picture can be restored to its original size and color using the Reset Picture command.

1 On **Slide 6**, if necessary, click the picture to select it.

2 On the Picture toolbar, click the **Reset Picture** button ⊞.

The original picture is restored, but is much smaller than it was prior to clicking the Reset Picture button. Reset Picture also restores the picture to its originally inserted dimensions. Thus, the picture must be resized.

3 Right-click the picture to display the shortcut menu, and then click **Format Picture**. Click the **Size tab**, and under **Scale**, verify that the **Lock aspect ratio** and **Relative to original picture size** check boxes are selected. Under **Scale**, in the **Height** box, delete the existing value, type **550** and then click **OK**.

4 Point to the center right sizing handle so that the horizontal resize pointer ↔ displays. Drag to the right until the dashed box aligns with the exclamation point in the title. See Figure 5.25. Release the mouse button.

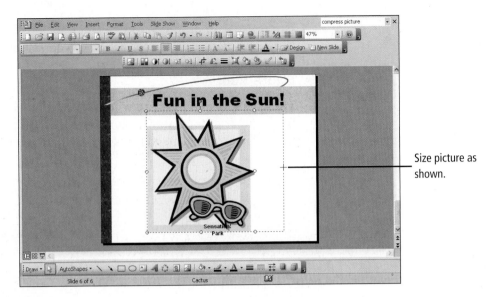

Size picture as shown.

Figure 5.25

5 On the Standard toolbar, click the **Save** button ⊞.

Activity 5.17 Recoloring a Picture

In this presentation, the color scheme consists primarily of gold, green, white, and black. Most clip art pictures can be recolored using the Recolor Picture feature so that the picture colors coordinate with the design template and slide color scheme.

> **Note** — Modifying Digital Pictures
>
> A picture that you have scanned or created with a digital camera cannot be recolored using PowerPoint, but must instead be modified using photo editing software.

1 If necessary, display **Slide 6**, and then click the picture to select it.

2 On the Picture toolbar, click **Recolor Picture** 🖼 to display the **Recolor Picture** dialog box.

  On the left side of the dialog box, the colors that comprise the picture are displayed in two columns. The first column displays the original color. The second column displays changes to the original color. Under Change, there are two option buttons—Colors and Fills. The Colors option allows you to change all of the colors in the picture. The Fills option allows you to change only the fill colors—the line colors remain unaffected.

3 In the second column of colors, under **New**, click the arrow to the right of the third color—**dark pink**—to display the color scheme. In the color scheme, click the sixth color—**gold**.

4 Under **New**, click the arrow to the right of the fifth color—**light pink**—to display the color scheme color palette. In the color scheme, click the seventh color—**dark tan**. Compare your dialog box with Figure 5.26.

The check boxes indicate whether or not a color has been changed from the original color. Look at the preview box in the Recolor Picture dialog box to see the effect of the two changed colors.

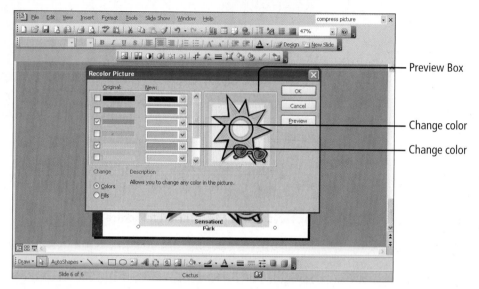

Figure 5.26

Note — Need More Colors?

You can choose additional colors by clicking the More Colors option below the color scheme.

---

5 Click **OK** to apply your color changes to the picture.

6 Point to the text box that contains the text *Sensation! Park*. Click to select the text box. Drag the text box to position it in the center of the sun, and click anywhere on the slide to deselect the text box. Compare your slide with Figure 5.27.

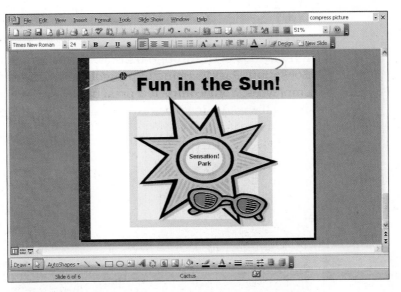

Figure 5.27

7 Display **Slide 1**, and then on the **View** buttons, click **Slide Show** 🖳 . Click the left mouse button to advance through the slide presentation. When the black slide displays, press Esc to end the slide show.

Note — Adding a Blank Slide

Some presenters prefer to end their presentations with a blank slide that displays the design template instead of the black slide.

8 On the **View** menu, click **Header and Footer**, and then click the **Notes and Handouts tab**. Create a footer for the notes and handouts that includes the date updated automatically and a footer with the text **5A Application-Firstname Lastname** Clear all other header and footer options, and then click **Apply to All**.

9 On the Standard toolbar, click the **Save** button 🖫 . From the **File** menu, click **Print** to display the **Print** dialog box. In the **Print what** box, click the arrow, and then click **Handouts**. In the **Color/grayscale** box, click the arrow, and then click **Grayscale**. Under **Handouts**, click the **Slides per page arrow**, and then click **6**. Click the **Horizontal** option button. Click **OK**. Close the file and close PowerPoint.

End You have completed Project 5A

Project 5B Album

In Activities 5.18 through 5.20, you will create a photo album that Sensation! Park is using to promote a whitewater rafting excursion for employees. Your completed presentation will look similar to Figure 5.28. You will save your presentation as *5B_Album_Firstname_Lastname.*

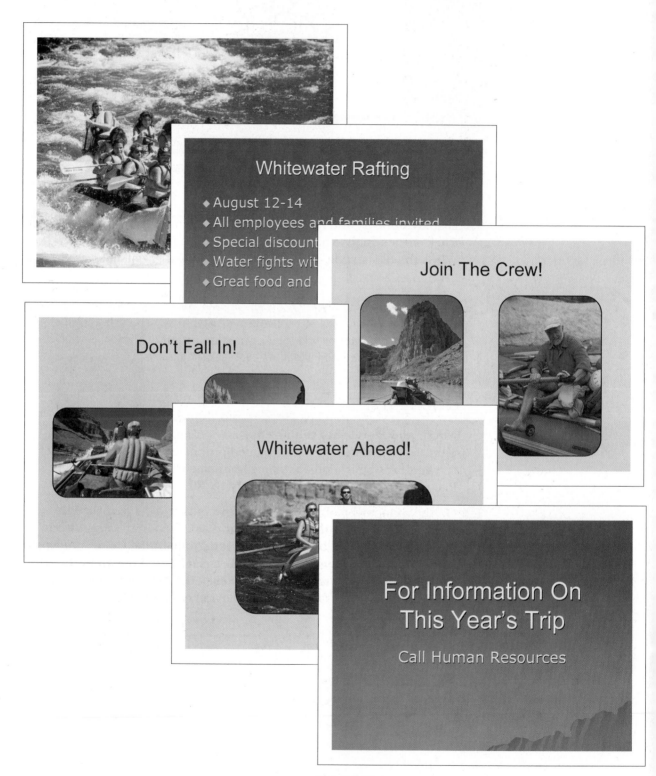

Figure 5.28
Project 5B—Album

Objective 4
Create a Photo Album

You can use Microsoft Office PowerPoint 2003 to create a *photo album*—a presentation composed of pictures. The pictures can be added all at once to your presentation photo album using a digital camera, scanner, files saved on disk, or a Web camera. You can format the photo album by adding captions, templates, textboxes, and frames.

Activity 5.18 Creating a Photo Album

In this activity, you will use the New Presentation task pane to create a photo album.

1 Start PowerPoint. From the **File** menu, click **New** to display the **New Presentation** task pane. Under **New**, click **Photo album**.

The Photo Album dialog box displays. Here you can choose the pictures that you want to add to the photo album, view a list of the pictures you have added, preview a picture, set picture options, move and format the pictures that you add, and choose a layout for your photo album.

2 Under **Insert picture from**, click **File/Disk** to open the **Insert New Pictures** dialog box.

In the Insert New Pictures dialog box, you can choose the pictures that you want to add to the photo album. You can add all of the pictures at one time, or you can add a few, and then add more later.

3 Navigate to the student files that accompany this textbook. Click **p05B_Raft1**, hold down Shift, and then click **p05B_Raft6**.

The pictures named *p05B_Raft1* through *p05B_Raft6* are selected. Recall that you can press Shift to select files that are contiguous (next to each other in the file list), or you can press Ctrl to select files that are not next to each other in the file list.

4 Click **Insert**.

The Photo Album dialog box displays and the filenames are listed under *Pictures in album*. A preview of one of the pictures displays in the Preview box. Notice that below the Preview box, the rotate, contrast, and brightness buttons display. These buttons work just as they do on the Picture toolbar and on the Draw menu, and can be used to format the picture displayed in the Preview box.

5 Under **Pictures in album**, click **p05B_Raft2**. Below the **Pictures in album** box are an up arrow and a down arrow. Click the **up arrow** until p05B_Raft2 moves to the first picture in the list. See Figure 5.29.

Using the up and down arrows, you can rearrange the pictures in the album.

Select file name

Click arrows to change order

Figure 5.29

6 Under **Pictures in album**, click **p05B_Raft6**. Under **Pictures in album**, click **Remove** to delete the picture from the list.

7 Under **Pictures in album**, use the **up** and **down arrows** to rearrange the pictures so that they are in numerical order, starting with picture p05B_Raft1 and ending with p05B_Raft5.

8 Under **Album Layout**, click the **Picture layout arrow**, and then click **1 picture**. Click the **Frame shape arrow**, and then click **Rectangle**.

The layout and frame shape that you selected is applied to every slide in the photo album.

More Knowledge — Adding Captions to Photo Albums

You can select the Captions below ALL pictures check box to add a caption below every picture in your presentation. By default, the caption includes the file name of the picture. You can type a new caption under the picture but you cannot delete a caption or move it as these actions result in deleting and moving the associated picture.

---

9 Compare your dialog box with Figure 5.30, and then click **Create**.

A new presentation is created with a title slide that includes the title *Photo Album*. A subtitle may display depending upon your system settings. Five additional slides display, each containing one framed picture.

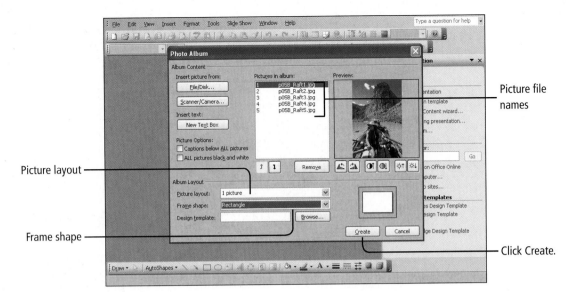

Picture file names

Picture layout

Frame shape

Click Create.

Figure 5.30

10 From the **File** menu, click **Save As**, and then save the file in your storage location for Chapter 5 as **5B_Album_Firstname_Lastname**

Activity 5.19 Modifying a Photo Album

Once a photo album is created, you can change the layout and frame shape, and you can add new pictures and text. When you modify the photo album, your changes affect the entire album. Thus, do not format your slides until you are finished using the Format Photo Album dialog box. Changes that you make to slide backgrounds, textboxes, and animation schemes will be lost if you make the changes prior to updating the photo album.

1 If necessary, click the **Normal View** button to display the **Outline/Slides** pane. Click the **Slides tab** to display the thumbnail images of the slides.

2 From the **Format** menu, click **Photo Album**. Under **Album Layout**, click the **Picture layout arrow**, and then click **2 pictures with title**. Click the **Frame shape arrow**, and then click **Rounded Rectangle**. Click **Update**.

Notice in the Outline/Slides pane that Slides 2 and 3 are reformatted to contain two images. Slide 4 contains only one image because only five pictures were inserted.

3 Display **Slide 2**. Click in the title placeholder and type **Join The Crew!** Display **Slide 3**. Click in the title placeholder and type **Don't Fall In!** Display **Slide 4**. Click in the title placeholder and type **Whitewater Ahead!**

4 In the **Outline/Slides** pane, select **Slides 2**, **3**, and **4**. From the **Format** menu, click **Background**. Click the **Background fill arrow**, and then in the color scheme, click the fifth color—**light blue**. Click **Apply**.

The light blue background is applied to Slides 2, 3, and 4.

5 Display **Slide 2**. Click the first picture, hold down Shift, and click the second picture.

With both pictures selected, you can apply formatting to both pictures at the same time.

6 On the Drawing toolbar, click the **Line Style** button ☰, and then click **2¼ pt**.

A 2¼ pt. black line is applied to the border of each picture.

7 Repeat the **Line Style** formatting to the pictures on **Slides 3** and **4**.

8 Display **Slide 4** and right-click the picture to display the shortcut menu. Click **Format AutoShape**.

The Format AutoShape dialog box displays. Because the picture is formatted within a rounded rectangle, it is treated as an AutoShape.

9 Click the **Size tab**. Under **Scale**, verify that the **Lock aspect ratio** and **Relative to original picture size** check boxes are selected (select them if necessary). Under **Scale**, change the value in the **Height** box to **160** and then click **OK** to resize the picture.

10 From the **View** menu, click **Grid and Guides**. Under **Guide settings**, select the **Display drawing guides on screen** check box, and then click **OK**. Move the picture, using the center sizing handles on each side as a visual guide to center the picture on the slide. Then, display the **View** menu again and turn off the guides by clearing the check box. Deselect the picture. Compare your slide with Figure 5.31.

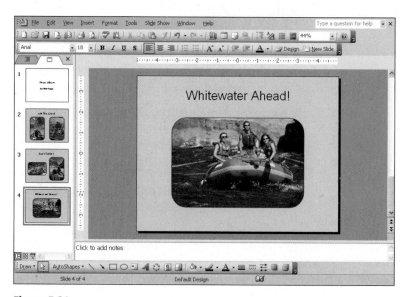

Figure 5.31

11 On the Formatting toolbar, click the **New Slide** button 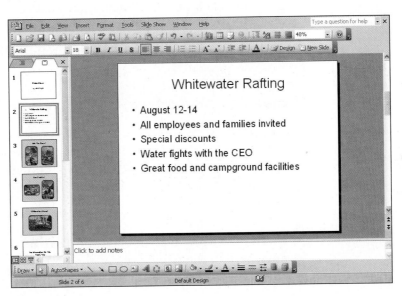. Under **Text Layouts**, click **Title Slide**. In the title placeholder type **For Information On This Year's Trip**

12 Click in the subtitle placeholder, and then type **Call Human Resources!**

13 Display **Slide 1**. On the Formatting toolbar, click the **New Slide** button , and then in the upper right corner of the **Slide Layout** task pane, click the **Close** button .

A slide with the Title and Text layout displays.

14 Type the text shown in Figure 5.32.

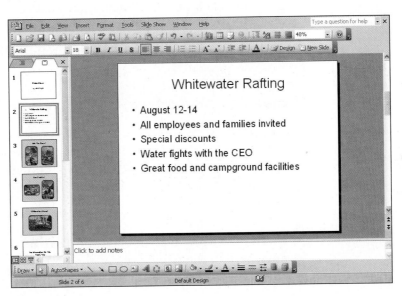

Figure 5.32

15 In the **Outline/Slides** pane, click **Slide 2**, hold down Ctrl, and then click **Slide 6** to select both slides. On the Formatting toolbar, click the **Slide Design** button to display the **Slide Design** task pane. Click the teal-colored **Cliff** design template.

The Cliff design template is applied to Slides 2 and 6.

16 Close the task pane, and then save the file.

Activity 5.20 Inserting a Picture as a Slide Background

You can insert a picture on a slide background so that the image fills the entire slide. In this activity, you will insert a picture on the background of Slide 1.

1 Display **Slide 1**. Select both placeholders on the slide. Press Delete to delete the text, and then press Delete again to remove the two placeholders.

2 From the **Format** menu, click **Background**. Click the **Background fill arrow**, and then click **Fill Effects**. In the **Fill Effects** dialog box, click the **Picture tab**, and then click **Select Picture**.

3 From the **Select Picture** dialog box, navigate to your student files, and then click **p05B_Album**. Click **Insert**. Click **OK**, and then click **Apply**.

The picture is inserted as the background fill on Slide 1.

More Knowledge — Overlaying Text on a Picture

When you insert a picture on a slide background, it is a good idea to choose a picture that has a solid area in which you can overlay a text box. For example, in the picture that you inserted on Slide 1, the lower right corner has a white area that provides good contrast for black text.

4 On the Drawing toolbar, click the **Text Box** button. Click anywhere in the white area at the bottom of the slide and type **Time For Another Sensational Trip!**

The text box may partially extend off the slide.

5 Select the text in the text box and change the **Font Size** 32 to **32**.

6 On the Formatting toolbar, click **Align Right**, and then size and move the text using the right middle sizing handle so that the box displays as shown in Figure 5.33.

Figure 5.33

Repositioned text box

7 On the menu bar, click **Slide Show**, and then click **Animation Schemes**. Under **Apply to selected slides**, scroll down until you see **Exciting**, and then click **Big title**. At the bottom of the task pane, click **Apply to All Slides**. If necessary, display Slide 1, and then at the bottom of the task pane, click Slide Show. Click the left mouse button to advance through the photo album.

8 On the **View** menu, click **Header and Footer**, and then click the **Notes and Handouts tab**. Create a footer for the notes and handouts that includes the date updated automatically and a footer with the text **5B Album-Firstname Lastname** Clear all other header and footer options, and then click **Apply to All**.

9 On the Standard toolbar, click the **Save** button . From the **File** menu, click **Print** to display the **Print** dialog box. In the **Print what** box, click the arrow, and then click **Handouts**. In the **Color/grayscale** box, click the arrow, and then click **Grayscale**. Under **Handouts**, click the **Slides per page arrow**, and then click **6**. Click the **Horizontal** option button, and then click **OK** to print the handouts. Close the file and close PowerPoint.

End You have completed Project 5B

Summary

In this chapter you practiced advanced graphic formatting techniques using the Drawing toolbar. You practiced adding shadows and 3-D effects and manipulating drawing objects by rotating, changing object order, creating groups, and by aligning and distributing selected objects. These minor formatting techniques can take your presentation from good to great! Take your time as you format your presentation but do not lose sight of the fact that accurate slides, your skills as a presenter, and your familiarity with the content are far more important than the objects that you include.

In addition to formatting objects, you practiced a new method for creating presentations that consists primarily of pictures that you have created with a digital camera or scanner. The Photo Album feature in Microsoft Office PowerPoint 2003 provides a fun and easy way to show your pictures to your family, friends, and coworkers. Using the Photo Album, you can quickly insert multiple pictures in a presentation and add captions, titles, and formats. Use the Photo Album for presentations in which pictures convey your message more appropriately and creatively than words.

This chapter helped you to see that there are many ways to enhance your presentations with AutoShapes and pictures. For example, arrows can be used to show process, and overlapping shapes make interesting backgrounds for pictures. Use your imagination and be creative! And don't be surprised if you find yourself spending many hours making your presentations look just right. Your audience will acknowledge and appreciate the time that you spend, thus making them more receptive to the message that you want to convey.

In This Chapter You Practiced How To

- Enhance Objects with Visual Effects
- Use the Draw Menu
- Modify Pictures
- Create a Photo Album

Concepts Assessments

Matching Match each term in the second column with its correct definition in the first column by writing the letter of the term on the blank line in front of the correct definition.

_____ 1. A command used to change the colors of a picture.

_____ 2. A command used to move a shadow in small increments.

_____ 3. A dashed box that is drawn using the Select Objects pointer and is used to enclose objects that you want to select.

_____ 4. Several objects that are treated as one object.

_____ 5. A command that separates a grouped object into individual objects.

_____ 6. A command that is used to trim a portion of a picture so that the trimmed portion does not display.

_____ 7. The way in which a 3-D effect extends toward a single point.

_____ 8. A format that displays a picture with very low contrast so that it can be displayed behind text.

_____ 9. The process of evenly spacing objects on a slide.

_____ 10. The process of lining up objects on a slide.

_____ 11. A series of horizontal and vertical intersecting gridlines, used to visually align objects.

_____ 12. A toolbar that snaps into place below the Standard and Formatting toolbars or at any side of the window.

_____ 13. A presentation comprised of pictures.

_____ 14. Lines that act as visual aids that intersect at the horizontal and vertical center point on a slide.

_____ 15. A command that reduces resolution and discards cropped portions of a picture to reduce file size.

A Align

B Compress picture

C Crop

D Distribute

E Docked toolbar

F Grid

G Grouped objects

H Guides

I Nudge

J Perspective

K Photo album

L Recolor

M Selection rectangle

N Ungroup

O Washout

Fill in the Blank Write the correct answer in the space provided.

1. The _____ command on the Draw menu allows you to rearrange the location of an object in a stack of objects.

2. The Flip Vertical and Flip Horizontal create a _____ image of an object.

3. When using the green rotate handle, press and hold down _____ to rotate the object in 15-degree increments.

4. The Rotate Left and Rotate Right commands rotate an object in _____ degree increments.

5. When the _____ option is applied, the edges of a slide determine how objects are aligned or distributed.

6. To select multiple objects, click the first object, and then press and hold down _____ and click the remaining objects that you want to select.

7. Some menus, such as the Align or Distribute menu, can be _____ so that the menu displays as a toolbar.

8. The _____ command restores a picture to its original size and color.

9. To insert a picture that fills the entire slide, use the _____ command on the Format menu.

10. To increase the intensity of the colors in a selected picture, click _____.

Skill Assessments

Project 5C—Summer

Objectives: *Enhance Objects with Visual Effects, Use the Draw Menu, and Modify Pictures.*

In the following Skill Assessment, you will format a presentation regarding a summer youth program at Sensation! Park. Your completed presentation will look similar to Figure 5.34. You will save your presentation as *5C_Summer_Firstname_Lastname.*

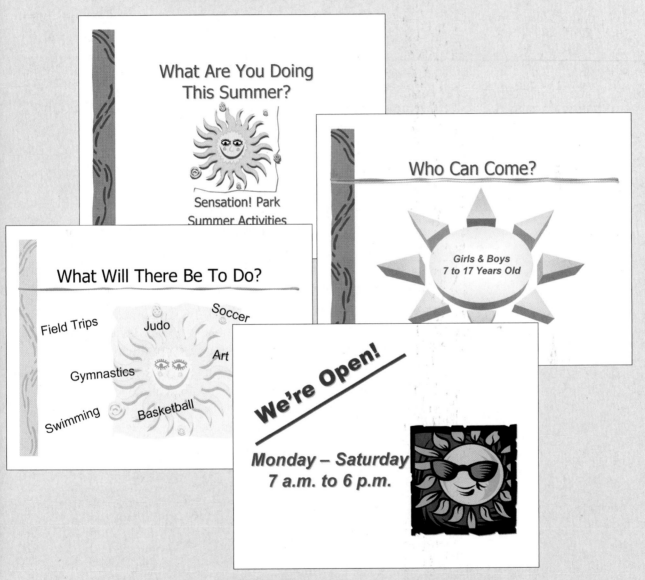

Figure 5.34

1. From your student files, open the file **p05C_Summer** in **Normal View**. Scroll through the presentation to familiarize yourself with the slides, and then close the **Outline/Slides** pane. Save the file in the location where you are storing your projects for this chapter as **5C_Summer_Firstname_Lastname**

(**Project 5C**–Summer continues on the next page)

(Project 5C–Summer continued)

2. On **Slide 2**, click the **sun** to select it. On the Drawing toolbar, click **Shadow Style**, and then click **No Shadow** to remove the shadow from the sun.

3. If necessary, select the sun again. On the Drawing toolbar, click **3-D Style**. In the second row, click the third effect—**3-D Style 7**.

4. Select the line under the title. On the Drawing toolbar, click **Shadow Style**, and then in the fourth row, click the second shadow—**Shadow Style 14**.

5. On the Drawing toolbar, click **Shadow Style**, and then click **Shadow Settings** to display the Shadow Settings toolbar. If necessary, select the line under the title, and then on the Shadow Settings toolbar, click the **Nudge Shadow Down** button four times to adjust the position of the shadow. Close the Shadow Settings toolbar.

6. Display **Slide 3,** and then select the picture of the sun. If the Picture toolbar does not display, click the **View** menu, point to Toolbars, and then click **Picture**.

7. On the Drawing toolbar, click the **Draw** menu, point to **Order**, and then click **Send to Back** to move the sun behind the text.

8. On the Picture toolbar, click the **Color** button to display the four color commands. Click the last command—**Washout**—to lighten the color of the sun so that the text displays more prominently.

9. If necessary, select the picture again. The sun almost disappears with the Washout effect. On the Picture toolbar, click **Less Brightness** three times so that the sun displays more prominently.

10. Display **Slide 4**. Click in the text *We're Open!* to display the text box boundaries. Move the pointer so that it is positioned over the green rotation handle. Drag to the left to rotate the text box so that its bottom edge is parallel with the line beneath it. Release the left mouse button, and then click anywhere on the slide to deselect.

11. Display **Slide 1**. On the **View** buttons, click **Slide Show**. Click the left mouse button to advance through the presentation.

12. Create a footer for the notes and handouts that includes the date updated automatically and a footer with the text **5C Summer-Firstname Lastname** Clear all other header and footer options.

13. **Save** the file, and then print the presentation as **handouts** in **grayscale**, **4** slides per page in **horizontal** order. Close the file.

End **You have completed Project 5C**

Skill Assessments (continued)

Project 5D—Enjoy

Objectives: *Use the Draw Menu, Modify Pictures, and Create a Photo Album.*

In the following Skill Assessment, you will create a presentation for the Sensation! Park Web site that illustrates a day at the park. Your completed presentation will look similar to Figure 5.35. You will save your presentation as *5D_Enjoy_Firstname_Lastname.*

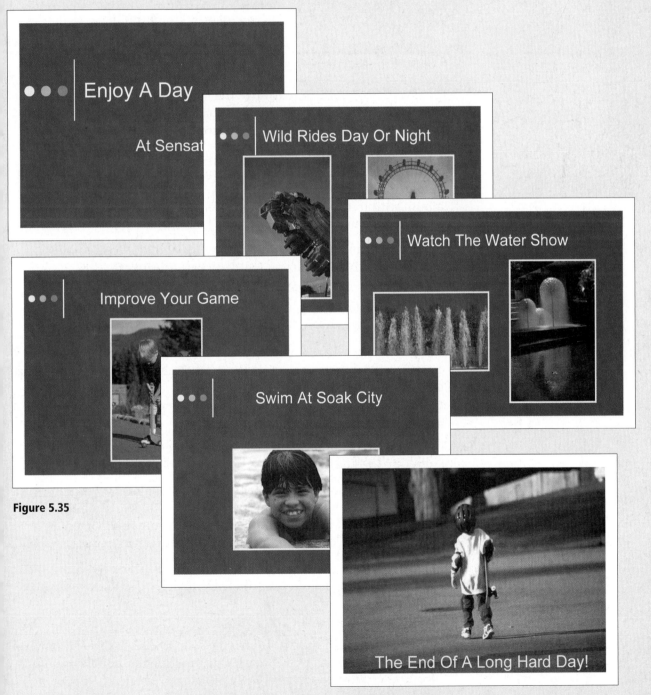

Figure 5.35

(Project 5D–Enjoy continues on the next page)

Skill Assessments (continued)

(Project 5D–Enjoy continued)

1. Start PowerPoint and on the **File** menu, click **New**. In the **New Presentation** task pane, click **Photo album**.

2. In the **Photo Album** dialog box, under **Insert Picture from**, click **File/Disk**. Navigate to your student files, and then click **p05D_Fountain**. Press and hold down Ctrl, and then click each of the following files so that a total of six files are selected: **p05D_Golf, p05D_Ride, p05D_Swim, p05D_Water, p05D_Wheel**. Click **Insert** to display the file names in the **Pictures in album** list.

3. To rearrange the list, under **Pictures in album**, click **p05D_Ride**. Below the list, click the **up arrow** until the file is listed as number 1. Click **p05D_Wheel**, and click the **up arrow** until the file is listed as number 2. Continue to rearrange the file names so that they are listed in the following order: **p05D_Ride, p05D_Wheel, p05d_Fountain, p05D_Water, p05D_Golf, p05D_Swim**.

4. Under **Album Layout**, click the **Picture layout arrow**, and then click **2 pictures with title**. If necessary, click the **Frame shape arrow**, and then click **Rectangle**. Click **Create** to create a photo album with four slides. Save the file in your storage location as **5D_Enjoy_Firstname_Lastname**

5. On **Slide 1**, select the text in the title placeholder, type **Enjoy A Day** and then on the Formatting toolbar, click **Align Left**.

6. In the subtitle placeholder, select the existing text, type **At Sensation! Park** and then on the Formatting toolbar, click **Align Right**. Select the text and change the **Font Size** to **44**.

7. On the Formatting toolbar, click the **Slide Design** button. In the **Slide Design** task pane, apply the white **Echo** template to the entire presentation. In the **Slide Design** task pane, click **Color Schemes**. Apply the color scheme with the **dark teal background** to the entire presentation. Close the task pane.

8. Display **Slide 2**. Click in the title placeholder, and then type **Wild Rides Day Or Night**

9. Click the picture of the Ferris wheel on the right side of the slide, noticing that the picture is quite dark. If the Picture toolbar does not display, click the **View** menu, point to **Toolbars**, and then click **Picture**. On the Picture toolbar, click the **More Brightness** button three times.

10. Display **Slide 3**. Click in the title placeholder, and then type **Watch The Water Show**

11. Display **Slide 4**. Click the picture of the boy in the pool on the right side of the slide, and then on the Standard toolbar, click the **Cut** button. On the Formatting toolbar, click **New Slide**, and in the **Slide Layout** task pane, under **Text Layouts**, click **Title Only**. Close the task pane.

(Project 5D–Enjoy continues on the next page)

(Project 5D–Enjoy continued)

12. On the Standard toolbar, click the **Paste** button to paste the swim picture to **Slide 5**. Point to the picture and right-click. From the short-cut menu, click **Format AutoShape**. Click the **Size tab**. Under **Scale**, in the **Height** box, delete the existing value and type **125** and verify that the **Lock aspect ratio** check box is selected. Click **OK**, and then save the file. The picture may display off the edge of the slide.

13. If necessary, click the picture of the boy to select it. On the Drawing toolbar, click the **Draw** menu, and then point to **Align or Distribute**. Click **Relative to Slide** so that the option is checked. Click the **Draw** menu again, and then point to **Align or Distribute**. Click **Align Center**. The picture is centered horizontally on the slide.

14. Click in the title placeholder. Type **Swim At Soak City** and then **center** the title.

15. Display **Slide 4**. Click in the title placeholder. Type **Improve Your Game** and then **center** the title. Use the same technique that you used in Step 13 to center the picture on the slide. Be sure that **Relative to Slide** is checked. **Save** the file.

16. Display **Slide 5**, and then on the Formatting toolbar, click **New Slide**. In the **Slide Layout** task pane, under **Content Layouts**, click **Blank**.

17. With the new slide displayed, from the **Format** menu, click **Background**. Click to select the **Omit background graphics from master** check box, and then click the **Background fill arrow**. Click **Fill Effects**, and then click the **Picture tab**. Click **Select Picture**, and then navigate to your student files. Click the file **p05D_Skateboard**, and then click **Insert**. Click **OK**, and then click **Apply** to apply the picture to the slide background.

18. On the Drawing toolbar, click **Text Box**. Click below the little boy's feet and type **The End Of A Long Hard Day!** Select the text, and then change the **Font Size** to **44**.

19. On the Drawing toolbar, click the **Draw** menu, and then click **Grid and Guides**. Under **Grid settings**, select the **Display grid on screen** check box. Click **OK**. Drag the text box to the left so that its left edge aligns with the first vertical gridline, and its top edge aligns just above the last horizontal gridline. On the Drawing toolbar, click the **Draw** menu, and then click **Grid and Guides**. Under **Grid settings**, clear the **Display grid on screen** check box. Click **OK** to turn off the grid. **Save** the file.

20. On the menu bar, click **Slide Show**, and then click **Animation Schemes**. Scroll to view the **Moderate** category, click **Compress**, and then click **Apply to All Slides**. Display **Slide 1**, and then at the bottom of the **Slide Design** task pane, click **Slide Show**, pressing the left mouse button to advance through the presentation.

(Project 5D–Enjoy continues on the next page)

(Project 5D–Enjoy continued)

21. Create a footer for the notes and handouts that includes the date updated automatically and a footer with the text **5D Enjoy-Firstname Lastname** Clear all other header and footer options.

22. **Save** the file, and then print the presentation as **grayscale handouts**, **6** slides per page in **horizontal** order. **Close** the file.

End You have completed Project 5D

Project 5E—Outreach

Objectives: *Enhance Objects with Visual Effects, Use the Draw Menu, and Modify Pictures.*

In the following Skill Assessment, you will format a presentation describing a youth foundation that Sensation! Park employees support through voluntary payroll contributions. Your completed presentation will look similar to Figure 5.36. You will save your presentation as *5E_Outreach_Firstname_Lastname.*

Figure 5.36

(Project 5E–Outreach continues on the next page)

(Project 5E–Outreach continued)

1. From your student files, open the file **p05E_Outreach**. Scroll through the presentation to familiarize yourself with the slides. If necessary, display the ruler and close the **Outline/Slides** pane. Save the file in your storage location as **5E_Outreach_Firstname_Lastname**

2. Display **Slide 1** and select the picture in the center of the slide. If necessary, display the Picture toolbar by clicking the View menu, pointing to Toolbars, and then clicking Picture.

3. On the Picture toolbar, click the **Recolor Picture** button. Scroll the list of colors and under **New**, click the arrow to the right of the second to last color—**light yellow**. In the color scheme, click the last color—**gray**. Click the arrow to the right of the third-to-last color—**gold**. In the color scheme, click the third color—**dark gray**. Click **OK**.

4. In the lower left corner of the slide, click the freeform line to the right of the heart and on the Drawing toolbar, click the **Shadow Style** button. Click **Shadow Style 13**. Leave the line selected.

5. Press Shift and click the heart so that both the line and the heart are selected. On the Drawing toolbar, click the **Draw** menu, and then click **Group** so that the heart and the freeform line are treated as one object. Press and hold down Ctrl and press D three times to duplicate the grouped object three times.

6. Position the left-pointing selection pointer above and to the left of the first heart, and then drag down and to the right to draw a selection rectangle that encloses the four hearts and lines so that all four groups are selected.

7. On the Drawing toolbar, click the **Draw** menu, point to **Align or Distribute**, and then point to the dotted bar at the top of the menu. Drag the menu to the lower right corner of the slide so that the **Align or Distribute** menu displays as a floating toolbar. Verify that **Relative to Slide** is turned *off* (not highlighted in orange), and then click the **Align Top** button so that the top of each group aligns with the top of the original group.

8. On the Align or Distribute toolbar, click **Relative to Slide** to turn the feature on, and then click the **Distribute Horizontally** button. Close the Align or Distribute toolbar.

9. Display **Slide 2**. On the Drawing toolbar, click **AutoShapes**. Point to **Stars and Banners**, and then click **4-Point Star**. Position the pointer at the top point of the black diamond, and then drag down and to the *left* to draw a star that extends to the bottom of the slide and to the left edge of the slide. Point to the center right sizing handle so that the horizontal resize pointer displays, and then drag so that the right point of the star extends to the right point of the diamond.

(Project 5E–Outreach continues on the next page)

(Project 5E–Outreach continued)

10. On the Drawing toolbar, click the **Fill Color button arrow**, and then click the sixth color in the color scheme—**blue**. On the Drawing toolbar, click the **Draw** menu, and then point to **Order**. Click **Send Backward** and compare your slide with Figure 5.37. **Save** the file.

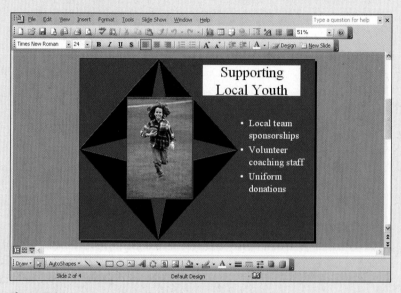

Figure 5.37

11. Display **Slide 3**. Select the bulleted list placeholder, and on the Drawing toolbar, click the **Fill Color button arrow**. In the custom color palette, click the second color—**light blue**. On the Drawing toolbar, click **3-D Style**, and apply **3-D Style 7**.

12. On the Drawing toolbar, click **3-D Style**, click **3-D Settings**, and then on the 3-D Settings toolbar, click the **Depth** button. Click **144 pt**. Click anywhere on the slide to deselect the text box and notice the 3-D setting. Leave the 3-D Settings toolbar open on your screen.

13. Display **Slide 4**, and then select the picture in the upper left corner of the slide. If necessary, display the Picture toolbar. Adjust the intensity of the colors by clicking the **More Contrast** button five times, and then clicking the **More Brightness** button five times.

14. Select the **explosion AutoShape**. On the Drawing toolbar, click the **3-D Style** button, and then apply **3-D Style 15**. On the **3-D Settings** toolbar, click **Depth**, and then click **288 pt.** On the same toolbar, click **Lighting**, and then click **Normal**. Click **Lighting** again, and then in the first row, click the second option. Close the 3-D Settings toolbar. **Save** the file.

(Project 5E–Outreach continues on the next page)

(Project 5E–Outreach continued)

15. Display **Slide 1**. On the menu bar, click **Slide Show**, and then click **Animation Schemes**. Under **Apply to selected slides**, scroll to view the **Exciting** category, click **Ellipse motion**, and then click **Apply to All Slides**. View the slide show, and then create a footer for the notes and handouts that includes the date updated automatically and a footer with the text **5E Outreach-Firstname Lastname** Clear all other header and footer options.

16. **Save** the file, and then print the presentation as **grayscale handouts**, **4** slides per page in **horizontal** order. **Close** the file.

End You have completed Project 5E ──────────────

Project 5F — Commitment

Objectives: *Enhance Objects with Visual Effects and Use the Draw Menu.*

In the following Performance Assessment, you will format a presentation that details the Sensation! Park mission statement and commitment to safety. Your completed presentation will look similar to the one shown in Figure 5.38. You will save your presentation as *5F_Commitment_Firstname_ Lastname.*

Figure 5.38

(Project 5F–Commitment continues on the next page)

(Project 5F–Commitment continued)

1. From your student files, open the file **p05F_Commitment**. Scroll through the presentation to familiarize yourself with the slides. Close the **Outline/Slides** pane. Save the file as **5F_Commitment_Firstname_ Lastname**

2. Display **Slide 2**. Click anywhere in the bulleted list placeholder and remove the bullet format from the paragraph. **Center** the text.

3. Select the narrow, light blue rectangle that displays to the left of the paragraph. Duplicate the rectangle using [Ctrl] + [D]. With the duplicated rectangle selected, click the **Draw** menu, and from the **Rotate or Flip** menu, rotate the rectangle 90° to the left or right. (In this instance, either one will have the same result.)

4. From the **Draw** menu, display the **Grid and Guides** dialog box, and then display the grid on the screen. Drag the rotated rectangle down so that its left edge aligns with the left edge of the slide and its top edge aligns with the second gridline from the bottom of the slide. Turn off the grid.

5. If necessary, select the rotated rectangle, and change its **Fill Color** to **red**. **Save** the file.

6. Display **Slide 3** and select the bulleted list placeholder. Resize the placeholder using the bottom center sizing handle so that the place-holder fits tightly to the text. On the **Draw** menu, point to **Align or Distribute**, and then turn on **Relative to Slide**. Display the **Draw** menu again, point to **Align or Distribute**, and click **Align Middle** to center the placeholder vertically on the slide.

7. Apply **3-D Style 12** to the bulleted list placeholder. Display the 3-D Settings toolbar, and then click the **Lighting** button. In the first row, apply the first lighting style, and then close the 3-D Settings toolbar. **Save** the file.

8. Display **Slide 4**. Select the two bulleted list text boxes (Hint: Use [Shift]), and then apply **Shadow Style 1**.

9. Select the upper right text box in which the first bulleted item is *Onsite trainers*. Drag the text box down and to the left so that the bottom edge of the dashed box aligns just below the word *handbook*, and its left edge aligns with the *d* in *and*. On the **Draw** menu, point to **Order**, and then click **Send to Back** so that the text in both text boxes displays. If the shadow in the lower text box overlaps the text in the upper text box, use the directional arrow keys to nudge the text boxes up or down so that all of the text displays.

(Project 5F–Commitment continues on the next page)

(Project 5F–Commitment continued)

10. Select the picture, and then on the Picture toolbar, click **More Brightness** twice. Drag the picture up and to the left so that it is positioned at the lower right intersection of the two text boxes. Apply **Shadow Style 5** to the picture, and then display the Shadow Settings toolbar and change the **Shadow Color** to the third color in the color scheme—**black**. Close the Shadow Settings toolbar, and then compare your slide with Figure 5.39. Save the file.

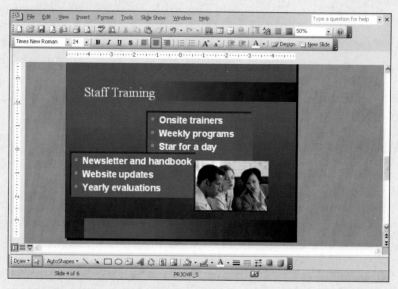

Figure 5.39

11. Display **Slide 5**. Use the **Select Objects** pointer to draw a selection rectangle that encloses the *Engineers*, *Maintenance*, and *Managers* text boxes. On the **Draw** menu, float the **Align or Distribute** menu into the upper right corner of your window so that it displays as a toolbar. If necessary, turn off Relative to Slide, and then click the Align Bottom button.

12. Click anywhere to deselect the three text boxes. Hold down [Shift], select the three down-pointing arrows that point from the *Engineers*, *Maintenance*, and *Managers* text boxes to the red arrow, and then click **Align Top**.

13. Select the three text boxes that contain the words *Morning*, *All Day*, and *Evening*. Be sure that you do *not* select the red arrow. Click **Distribute Horizontally** to center the *All Day* text box between the other two text boxes.

(Project 5F–Commitment continues on the next page)

(Project 5F–Commitment continued)

14. Draw a selection rectangle that encloses the bottom three text boxes—*Check equipment, Respond to calls, Research incidents.* Click **Align Top**, and then click anywhere on the slide to deselect the text boxes.

15. Using Shift to select multiple objects, select the **Engineers text box**, the **two black arrows below the text box**, and the **Check equipment text box.** Click **Align Center** so that all four objects are aligned relative to each other.

16. Select the **Maintenance text box**, the **two black arrows below the text box**, and the **Respond to calls text box.** Click **Align Center** so that all four objects are aligned relative to each other. Repeat this process for the **Managers text box**, the **two black arrows below the text box**, and the **Research incidents text box.** Close the Align or Distribute toolbar, and then click anywhere on the slide to cancel the selection. Compare your slide with Figure 5.40.

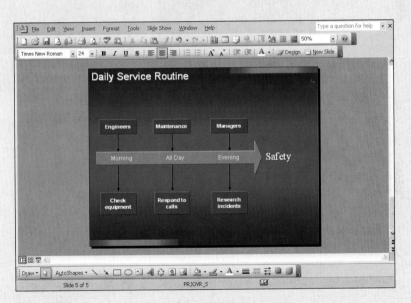

Figure 5.40

17. Save your presentation. Display **Slide 1**, and then view the slide show. Animation has been applied to this presentation with automatic timings on Slide 5.

18. Create a footer for the notes and handouts that includes the date updated automatically and a footer with the text **5F Commitment-Firstname Lastname** Clear all other header and footer options.

19. Save the file, and then print the presentation as **grayscale handouts, 6** slides per page in **horizontal** order. **Close** the file.

End You have completed Project 5F

Project 5G—Daycare

Objectives: *Enhance Objects with Visual Efects, Use the Draw Menu, and Modify Pictures.*

In the following Performance Assessment, you will format a presentation for the Human Resources Department at Sensation! Park that describes the new daycare program for the children of employees. Your completed presentation will look similar to the one shown in Figure 5.41. You will save your presentation as *5G_Daycare_Firstname_Lastname.*

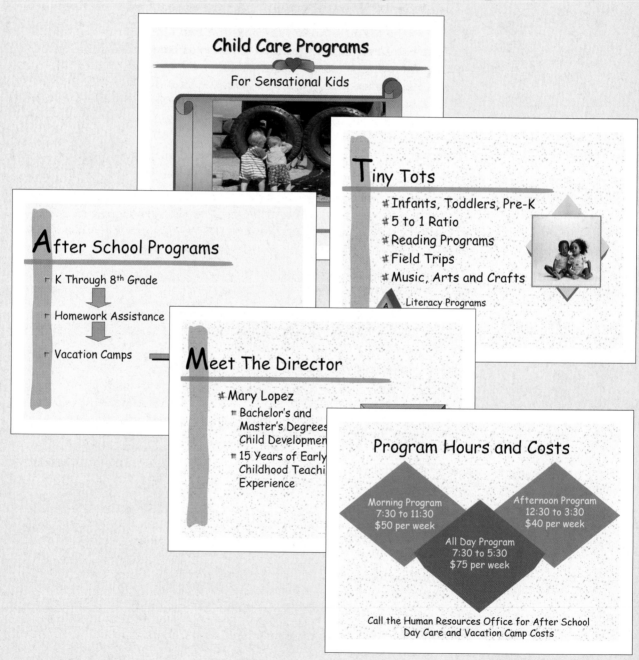

Figure 5.41

(Project 5G–Daycare continues on the next page)

(Project 5G–Daycare continued)

1. From your student files, open the presentation **p05G_Daycare**. Scroll through the presentation to familiarize yourself with the slides. Close the **Outline/Slides** pane. In your storage location for this chapter, save the file as **5G_Daycare_Firstname_Lastname**

2. If necessary, display the ruler. On **Slide 1**, below the title, select the three objects: the line, the heart, and the ribbon. From the **Draw** menu, **Group** the selection, and then use Ctrl + D to duplicate the selection. Drag the new group to **3 inches below zero on the vertical ruler** and maintain the same horizontal position.

3. From the **Draw** menu, display the **Align or Distribute** submenu, and then float the menu as a toolbar on your screen. If necessary, turn on Relative to Slide, and then select both of the grouped objects. On the Align or Distribute toolbar, click **Align Center**. Do *not* close the Align or Distribute toolbar, as you will use it again in a later step.

4. To enclose the picture within a scroll, on the **AutoShapes Stars and Banners** menu, click **Horizontal Scroll**. Begin the scroll at **4 inches to the left of zero on the horizontal ruler** and at **2 inches above zero on the vertical ruler**. Extend the scroll to **4 inches to the right of zero on the horizontal ruler** and to **3 inches below zero on the vertical ruler**. The picture is now hidden from view.

5. Apply a **One-color Gradient Fill Effect** to the AutoShape using the second-to-last color in the color scheme—**lavender**. Drag the scroll box in the **Dark/Light scale** ¾ of the way toward the light end of the scale. Apply a **Horizontal Shading style**, using the **first Variant in the second row**.

6. Apply **Shadow Style 1** to the AutoShape. From the Shadow Settings toolbar, change the shadow color to the third color in the color scheme—**burgundy**—verifying that **Semitransparent Shadow** is turned *off* (not highlighted). Close the Shadow Settings toolbar.

7. On the Drawing toolbar, display the **Draw** menu, and then use the **Order** command, **Send to Back**, so that the scroll displays behind the picture. **Save** the file.

8. Display **Slide 2** and select the **triangle** that contains the letter *A*. Apply **3-D Style 9**, and then bring the triangle to the front. Select the **square** and apply **3-D Style 3**. Select the **oval** and apply **3-D Style 11**. Drag the *Literacy Programs* text box up and to the left so that it is positioned above the oval and to the right of the triangle.

9. Select and then **Group** the triangle, rectangle, oval, and text box, and then drag the group so that the left edge of the gold rectangle touches the right edge of the long lavender rectangle.

(Project 5G–Daycare continues on the next page)

(Project 5G–Daycare continued)

10. Select the **diamond** on the right side of the slide and apply **3-D Style 7**, and then send the diamond to the back so that the picture of the two babies is on top of the diamond.

11. Select both the **diamond** and the **picture** and **Group** the two objects. Compare your slide with Figure 5.42.

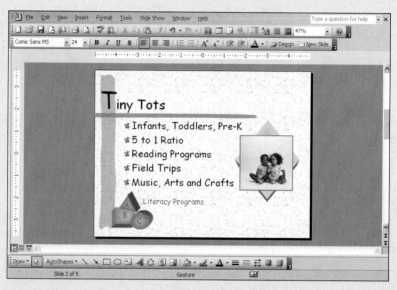

Figure 5.42

12. Display **Slide 3**, and then select the three bulleted text boxes. On the Align or Distribute toolbar, verify that **Relative to Slide** is turned *off*, then click **Align Left** so that all three text boxes align with the leftmost text box—*K Through 8th Grade*.

13. Select the two downward-pointing arrows, and on the Align or Distribute toolbar, click **Align Center**. Leave the Align or Distribute toolbar open. Select the **right-pointing arrow**, and then apply **Shadow Style 6**. Display the Shadow Settings toolbar, and then click **Nudge Shadow Up** twice. Change the **Shadow Color** to **Black**, verifying that **Semitransparent Shadow** is turned *off*. Close the Shadow Settings toolbar.

14. Select the picture, and from the Picture toolbar, change the **Color** to **Grayscale**, and then brighten the picture by clicking **More Brightness** twice. **Save** the file.

15. Display **Slide 4**. Draw a **Bevel AutoShape** that covers the picture on the right side of the slide. (Hint: Display the **Basic Shapes** palette from the **AutoShapes** menu.) Send the bevel to the back. Using Figure 5.43 as a guide, resize and position the bevel as necessary. **Save** the file.

(Project 5G–Daycare continues on the next page)

(Project 5G–Daycare continued)

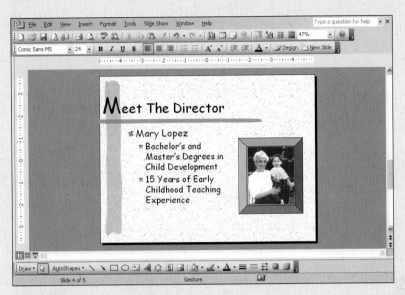

Figure 5.43

16. Display **Slide 5**, and then select the **diamonds** on the left and right sides of the slide. Use **Align Top** to align the two diamonds evenly. (Hint: Verify that **Relative to Slide** is turned *off.*)

17. Select the center diamond and apply **3-D Style 7**, and then display the 3-D Settings toolbar. Change the **Depth** of the 3-D effect to **144 pt**. Close the 3-D Settings toolbar.

18. Select the text box at the bottom of the slide, and then on the Align or Distribute toolbar, click **Relative to Slide** to turn the feature *on*. Click **Align Center** to center the text box between the left and right edges of the slide. Close the Align or Distribute toolbar.

19. Display **Slide 1**, and then view the slide show.

20. Create a footer for the notes and handouts that includes the date updated automatically and a footer with the text **5G Daycare-Firstname Lastname** Clear all other header and footer options.

21. **Save** the file, and then print the presentation as **grayscale handouts**, **6** slides per page in **horizontal** order. **Close** the file.

End You have completed Project 5G

Project 5H—Summary

Objectives: *Enhance Objects with Visual Effects, Use the Draw Menu, and Modify Pictures.*

In the following Performance Assessment, you will format a business summary presentation prepared by the Finance office at Sensation! Park. Your completed presentation will look similar to the one shown in Figure 5.44. You will save your presentation as *5H_Summary_Firstname_Lastname.*

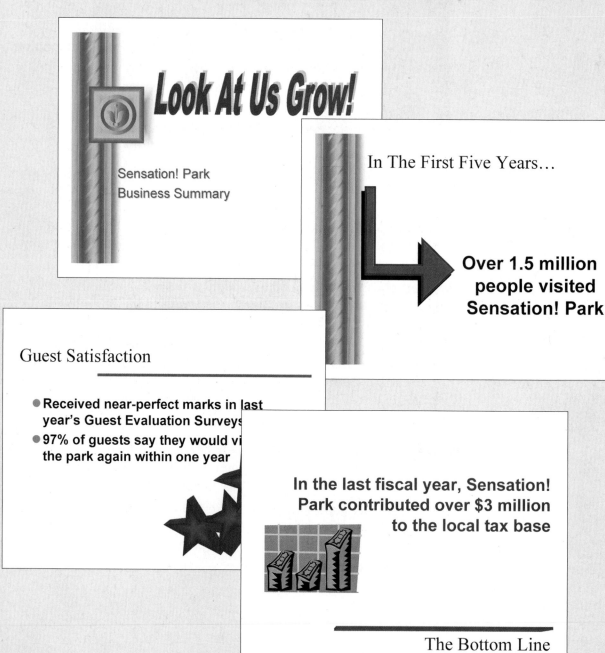

Figure 5.44

(Project 5H–Summary continues on the next page)

(Project 5H–Summary continued)

1. From your student files, **Open** the file **p05H_Summary**. Scroll through the presentation to familiarize yourself with the slides. Save the file as **5H_Summary_Firstname_Lastname**

2. Display **Slide 1**, select the WordArt graphic at the top of the slide, and then apply **Shadow Style 2**.

3. Display **Slide 2**, and then flip the arrow so that it is pointing toward the text box on the right side of the slide. Apply **Shadow Style 5** to the arrow. **Nudge** the **Shadow Down** five times, and **Nudge** the **Shadow Left** two times. Change the **Shadow Color** to **Black** and verify that **Semitransparent Shadow** is *off.* Close the Shadow Settings toolbar.

4. Display **Slide 3**, and then select and duplicate the star twice. Drag each star to position the stars approximately as shown in Figure 5.45.

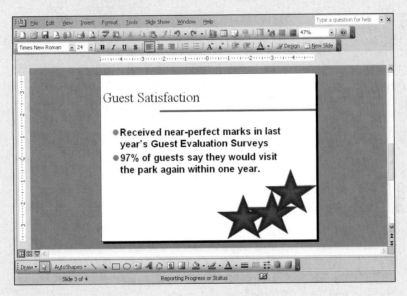

Figure 5.45

(Project 5H–Summary continues on the next page)

(Project 5H–Summary continued)

5. Select the original star and apply **3-D Style 9**. Select the center star and apply **3-D Style 13**. Select the third star and apply **3-D Style 11**. **Group** the three stars, and then **Rotate** the entire group approximately 15 degrees to the left. (Hint: Press and hold down Shift while rotating so that the object rotates in 15-degree increments.) Display the guides and nudge the group so that the leftmost point aligns with the vertical guide and the topmost point aligns just below the word *visit*. Turn off the guides.

6. Display **Slide 4** and crop the picture to eliminate the black lines to the left of and below the picture. **Recolor** the picture so that the yellow color is changed to the first custom color. **Recolor** the aqua color so that it is changed to the fifth color in the color scheme. **Recolor** the light green color so that it is changed to the seventh color in the color scheme.

7. Apply **3-D Style 16** to the line at the bottom of the slide. Change the **Depth** to **36 pt.** and the **Lighting** to the second option in the first row. Close the 3-D Settings toolbar.

8. Create a footer for the notes and handouts that includes the date updated automatically and a footer with the text **5H Summary-Firstname Lastname** Clear all other header and footer options.

9. **Save** the file, and then print the presentation as **grayscale handouts**, **4** slides per page in **horizontal** order. **Close** the file.

 You have completed Project 5H

Project 5I — Guests

Objectives: *Enhance Objects with Visual Effects, Use the Draw Menu, and Modify Pictures.*

In the following Mastery Assessment, you will create a presentation regarding customer service at Sensation! Park. Your completed presentation will look similar to the one shown in Figure 5.46. You will save your presentation as *5I_Guests_Firstname_Lastname.*

Figure 5.46

1. Start PowerPoint and create a new presentation based on the burgundy **Slit** design template. Save the presentation as **5I_Guests_Firstname_ Lastname** and then from your student files, open the presentation **p05I_Pictures**. This presentation contains one slide with a number of pictures that you will use in the 5I_Guests presentation.

2. Create the first slide as shown in Figure 5.47, copying and sizing the indicated picture from file **p05I_Pictures**. To create the frame for the picture, draw a **Rectangle** and apply **3-D Style 7**, changing the **Depth** to **144 pt**. Use the **Order** menu to stack the two objects correctly, and then **Group** the objects and position them on the slide as shown in Figure 5.47.

(Project 5I–Guests continues on the next page)

(Project 5I–Guests continued)

Figure 5.47

3. Insert a **New Slide** using the **Title Only** layout and create the slide shown in Figure 5.48, using the Times New Roman font for all of the text. Change **Fill** and **Line Colors** as shown and use text boxes to create the text along the outside of the bevel. Use the Align or Distribute toolbar to align the text boxes properly. When you have finished creating the objects, **Group** the bevel and the four text boxes and nudge the group to center it on the slide.

Figure 5.48

(Project 5I–Guests continues on the next page)

(Project 5I–Guests continued)

4. Insert a **New Slide**. Using the **Blank** layout, create the slide shown in Figure 5.49, and use the yellow diamond adjustment handle to modify the shape of the star. Change the *Guests* text to **Times New Roman**, **32 pt.**, and then **Shadow** the text. Apply the appropriate **3-D Style** to the star AutoShape and from the Align or Distribute toolbar, align the text boxes that surround the star. (Hint: Create the first text box, duplicate it, and then edit the text.) Use **Times New Roman**, **20 pt.** for all of the text boxes surrounding the star except for *The Star Team!*. Apply **Tahoma**, **32 pt.** to *The Star Team!* text box. When you have finished creating the objects, **Group** the star and the text boxes and nudge the group to center it on the slide. Change the **Background** slide color to the third color in the color scheme and **Omit the background graphics from master**.

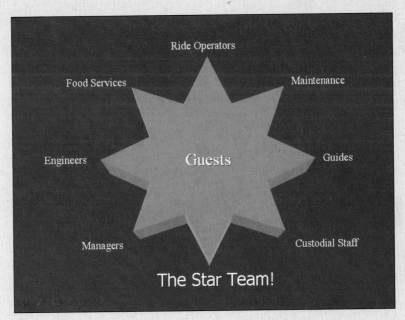

Figure 5.49

(Project 5I–Guests continues on the next page)

(Project 5I–Guests continued)

5. Insert a **New Slide**. Using the **Blank** layout, create the slide shown in Figure 5.50. **Copy** the pictures from presentation **p05I_Pictures** and arrange them as shown in the figure using the **Order** command and **Shadow Settings** as necessary. Adjust the contrast and brightness as necessary to brighten the pictures, and then draw and format the rectangle and text box as shown. Change the **Background** slide color to the third color in the color scheme and **Omit the background graphics from master**.

Figure 5.50

6. Apply an animation scheme of your choice, and then view the slide show.

7. Create a footer for the notes and handouts that includes the date updated automatically and a footer with the text **5I Guests-Firstname Lastname** Clear all other header and footer options.

8. **Save** the file, and then **print** the presentation as **grayscale handouts**, **4** slides per page in **horizontal** order. **Close** the file.

End   **You have completed Project 5I**

Project 5J—Boating

Objectives: *Create a Photo Album and Use the Draw Menu.*

In the following Mastery Assessment, you will create a photo album presentation to promote classes being offered by Sensation! Park at a local lake on safe boating, wakeboarding, and water skiing. Your completed presentation will look similar to the one shown in Figure 5.51. You will save your presentation as *5J_Boating_Firstname_Lastname.*

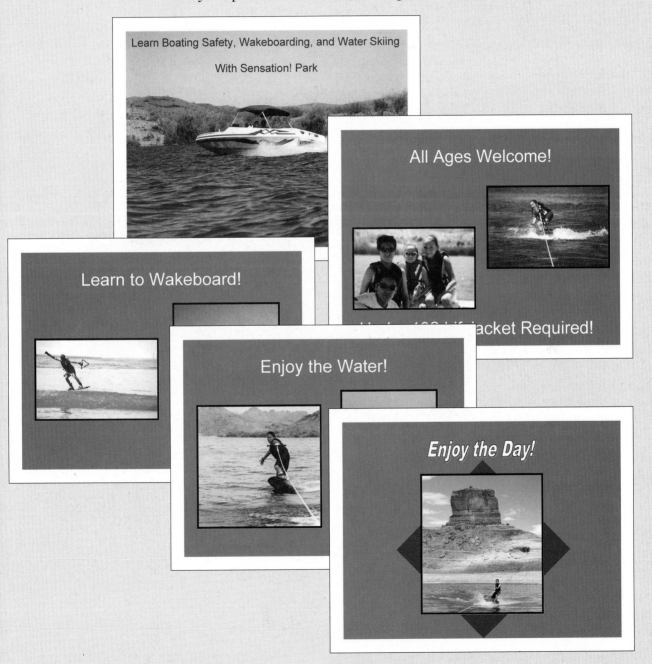

Figure 5.51

(**Project 5J**–Boating continues on the next page)

(Project 5J–Boating continued)

1. Create a new **Photo Album** and from your student files, insert the pictures **p05J_Lake2** through **p05J_Lake8**. A total of seven file names display in the **Pictures in album** list. Use the **2 pictures with title** option and a **Rectangle** frame shape. If necessary, rearrange the file names so that they are in numerical order, with **p05J_Lake2** first and **p05J_Lake8** last. After you create the Photo Album, scroll through each slide and adjust contrast and brightness as necessary.

2. **Save** the file as **5J_Boating_Firstname_Lastname** Display **Slide 1** and delete the two placeholders. Format the background with a fill effect using picture **p05J_Lake1**. (Hint: Do not use the Insert Picture command.) Create the text boxes shown in Figure 5.52.

Figure 5.52

3. Change the background color for **Slides 2** through **5** to **medium blue**—the third color in the second row of the Standard Colors honeycomb. Display **Slide 2**. Format the slide and create the text box at the bottom of the slide as shown in Figure 5.53.

(Project 5J–Boating continues on the next page)

(Project 5J–Boating continued)

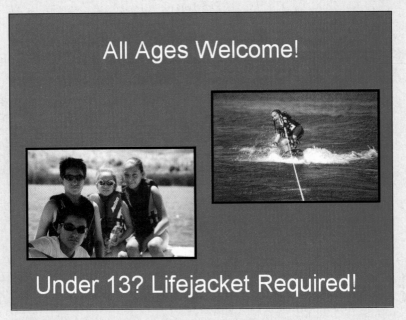

All Ages Welcome!

Under 13? Lifejacket Required!

Figure 5.53

4. On **Slide 3**, type the title **Learn to Wakeboard!** and on **Slide 4** type the title **Enjoy the Water!** Change the **Font Color** on both slides to **white**.

5. Display **Slide 5**. Replace the title placeholder with a **WordArt** using the first WordArt style in the second row. Type **Enjoy the Day!** in the **Edit WordArt Text** dialog box. Use the Align or Distribute toolbar to center the **WordArt** and picture on the slide.

6. Create a dark blue diamond and send it behind the picture, using Figure 5.54 as a guide.

(Project 5J–Boating continues on the next page)

(Project 5J–Boating continued)

Figure 5.54

7. Apply an **Animation Scheme** of your choice and view the slide show. Create a footer for the notes and handouts that includes the date updated automatically and a footer with the text **5J Boating- Firstname Lastname** Clear all other header and footer options.

8. **Save** the file, and then print the presentation as **grayscale handouts**, **6** slides per page in **horizontal** order. **Close** the file.

End You have completed Project 5J

Project 5K — Me

Objective: *Create a Photo Album.*

Create a new Photo Album presentation that you would like to show to your class that chronicles some of the important events in your life. Gather pictures, and check with your instructor to determine how you can get the pictures scanned. Arrange the pictures chronologically so that your classmates can watch you growing up! Create an appropriate footer for your notes and handouts and save your presentation as *5K_Me_Firstname_Lastname*. Print the presentation as handouts, 6 slides per page, in grayscale.

End **You have completed Project 5K** ─────────────────

Project 5L — Amusement Park

Objectives: *Enhance Objects with Visual Effects, Use the Draw Menu, and Modify Pictures.*

Start a new presentation based on a design template. Research your favorite amusement park and create a presentation that contains at least six slides explaining where the park is located, why you enjoy going there, and what your favorite rides and attractions are. Use shapes and pictures appropriately, applying shadows, 3-D settings, and groups as necessary. Create an appropriate footer for your notes and handouts and save your presentation as *5L_Amusement_Park_Firstname_Lastname*. Print the presentation as handouts, 6 slides per page, in grayscale.

End **You have completed Project 5L** ─────────────────

On the Internet

Exploring Presentation Templates Online

Connect to the Internet and go to the Microsoft Office Online Web site at **http://office.microsoft.com/templates/** and explore the presentation templates available for download from the site. If you are working in a classroom or lab, check with your instructor before downloading templates to your system.

GO! with Help

Setting Transparent Areas

Sometimes a picture that you have scanned may include a background color that you do not want visible on the slide. You can set transparent areas in a picture so that the background is not visible against the slide background.

1. Click in the **Type a question for help** box, type **How do I set transparent color?** and then press Enter.

2. Click **Create transparent areas in a picture**. Read the information and click each link that displays.

chaptersix

Delivering a Presentation

In this chapter, you will: complete this project **and** practice these skills.

Project 6A **Creating an Animated Presentation**	**Objectives**
	• Apply Slide Transitions
	• Apply Custom Animation Effects
	• Create Motion Paths
	• Insert Hyperlinks
	• Create Custom Shows
	• View a Slide Presentation

Lake Michigan City College

Lake Michigan City College is located along the lakefront of Chicago—one of the country's most exciting cities. The college serves its large and diverse student body and makes positive contributions to the community through relevant curricula, partnerships with businesses and nonprofit organizations, and learning experiences that allow students to be full participants in the global community. The college offers three associate degrees in 20 academic areas, adult education programs, and continuing education offerings on campus, at satellite locations, and online.

©Getty Images, Inc.

Delivering a Presentation

When you deliver a presentation, your credibility helps the audience believe what you say. The audience needs to know why you are qualified to speak on the topic and why they should believe you. Two keys to gaining credibility with your audience are honesty and accuracy. You should always be sure that everything you say in your presentation is truthful and accurate and that you disclose up front any conflicts of interest you may have. You also earn credibility with the audience through your credentials or knowledge of the subject. If someone else will be introducing you, ask him or her to mention your credentials, such as your degree or work experience. You can also briefly review your education or experience at the beginning of the presentation. Knowing you have first-hand knowledge of the topic gives the audience another reason to find you credible.

Project 6A **Learning**

In this chapter, you will animate presentation text and graphic elements and apply slide transitions so that you can deliver an effective presentation. You will insert hyperlinks and action buttons that take you to Web sites and to other slides within your presentation. You will also customize the delivery of a presentation by creating a custom show and by using onscreen navigation tools.

In Activities 6.1 through 6.19, you will format a presentation that describes the Lake Michigan City College Teaching and Learning Center. Your completed presentation will look similar to Figure 6.1. You will save the file as *6A_Learning_Firstname_Lastname*.

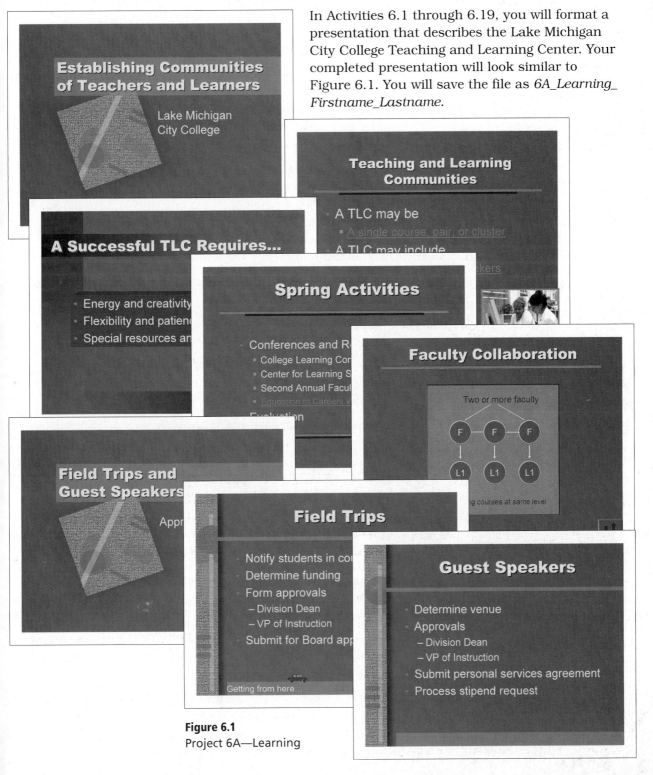

Figure 6.1
Project 6A—Learning

Objective 1
Apply Slide Transitions

Recall that a **slide transition** is a method of introducing a slide during an onscreen slide show. As you proceed through an onscreen slide show, transitions create flow from one slide to another. When you run a presentation that incorporates transitions, you can click the left mouse button or press Spacebar to advance from slide to slide, or you can set timed transitions in which the slides advance according to the amount of time that you have specified.

Activity 6.1 Applying Slide Transitions

It is usually best to choose one transition that works well with the majority of your slides. After viewing your presentation, you may decide that an individual slide layout looks best with a different transition; if so, apply a different transition to a single slide. Do not confuse your audience by applying a different transition to every slide in the presentation.

1 **Start** PowerPoint. From your student files, **Open** [icon] the file **p06A_Learning**. Scroll through the presentation to familiarize yourself with the slides. Using your own first and last name, save the file as **6A_Learning_Firstname_Lastname** creating a new folder for Chapter 6 if you want to do so. If necessary, display the **Outline/Slides pane** and click the **Slides tab**.

2 On the menu bar, click the **Slide Show** menu, and then click **Slide Transition**.

The Slide Transition task pane displays. The transitions are listed in alphabetical order under *Apply to selected slides*.

Another Way ——| **To Apply Transitions in Slide Sorter View**

When a presentation is displayed in Slide Sorter View, you can click the Slide Transition button on the Slide Sorter toolbar to open the Slide Transition task pane.

3 At the bottom of the **Slide Transition** task pane, verify that the **AutoPreview** check box is selected. Under **Apply to selected slides**, click **Blinds Horizontal** to apply this transition effect.

The transition is applied to the selected slide, and because AutoPreview is selected, the transition is played once so that you can see it. (If you missed the preview, click *Blinds Horizontal* again.)

4 In the task pane under **Modify transition**, click the **Speed arrow**, and then click **Medium**. If necessary, under **Advance slide**, select the **On mouse click** check box. See Figure 6.2.

The three Speed options—*Slow*, *Medium*, and *Fast*—control the speed with which the transition is applied. The *On mouse click* option requires that you click the left mouse button or press Spacebar to advance the slides during the slide show.

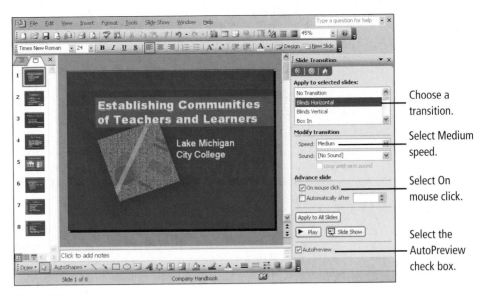

Choose a
transition.

Select Medium
speed.

Select On
mouse click.

Select the
AutoPreview
check box.

Figure 6.2

5 Under **Apply to selected slides**, click another transition effect, and under **Modify transition**, click the **Speed arrow** to view the transition at a different speed. Take a moment to apply several of the transitions to familiarize yourself with the types of slide transitions that are available.

6 After you have tried several of the transitions, under **Apply to selected slides**, scroll the list and click **Wipe Left**. Under **Modify transition**, if necessary, click the **Speed arrow**, and then click **Medium**. Near the bottom of the **Slide Transition** task pane, click **Apply to All Slides** to apply the transition to all of the slides in the presentation.

In the Slides tab, if it is wide enough, the *animation icon*—a small star—indicates that a transition has been applied. To view the small stars, if necessary, widen the Slides tab slightly by pointing to its right boundary (small line to the left of the vertical ruler) to display a double-headed pointer, and drag slightly to the right.

7 If necessary, display **Slide 1**. Near the bottom of the task pane, click the **Slide Show** button 🖳 Slide Show to start the onscreen slide show. Click the left mouse button to advance through the slides. When the black slide displays, click again to return the presentation to Normal View.

8 In the **Outline/Slides** pane, select **Slides 6**, **7**, and **8**. (Hint: Click Slide 6, hold down Shift, and then click Slide 8.) In the task pane, under **Apply to selected slides**, scroll the transition list, and then click **Wedge**.

The Wedge transition is applied to Slides 6, 7, and 8.

9 Display **Slide 1**, and then at the bottom of the task pane, click the **Slide Show** button ⬚ Slide Show to view the presentation. Continue to click the mouse button until the presentation returns to Normal View.

Notice that Slides 1 through 5 display the Wipe Left transition, while Slides 6 through 8 display the Wedge transition.

10 **Save** ⬚ the file.

More Knowledge — Adding Sound Effects to Transitions

You can add a sound that will play during the slide transition. Select a sound by clicking the Sound arrow and choosing a sound. Sounds can sometimes be distracting in a presentation, so be sure to apply sounds sparingly.

Activity 6.2 Advancing Slides Automatically in a Slide Show

When transitions are applied to a presentation, the *On mouse click* option allows the presenter to control when a slide moves off the screen. Alternatively, you can set the *Automatically after* option, which will move the slide off the screen after a specified amount of time has elapsed. In this activity, you will set an automatic timing for Slide 1.

1 Display **Slide 1**. If necessary, display the Slide Transition task pane by clicking the Slide Show menu, and then clicking Slide Transition.

2 In the task pane, under **Advance slide**, clear the **On mouse click** check box, and then select the **Automatically after** check box.

3 Click the **Automatically after up spin arrow** two times to set the slide transition to two seconds—indicated as *00:02*. Compare your task pane with Figure 6.3.

The 2-second transition is applied to Slide 1. When you run the slide show, the title slide will display for two seconds, and then Slide 2 will display automatically.

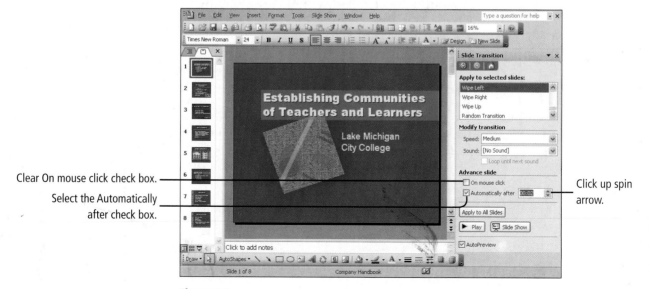

Clear On mouse click check box.

Select the Automatically after check box.

Click up spin arrow.

Figure 6.3

4 Near the bottom of the task pane, click the **Slide Show** button
![Slide Show] but do not click the mouse button when the title slide
displays. Instead, wait for **Slide 2** to display, and then continue to
click the mouse button to view the remaining slides and to return
the presentation to Normal View.

5 **Save** ![save] the file.

Alert!

Setting Automatic Slide Transitions

For most slides in your presentation, it is best to use the *On mouse click*
option. Unless your timing is perfect when you are making the presentation,
you may be discussing Slide 2, and your presentation may have already
advanced to Slide 4! Use the automatic option carefully, and only if you are
sure that the slide will transition when you are ready for it to do so.

Objective 2
Apply Custom Animation Effects

Animation effects are used to introduce individual slide elements so
that the slide can progress one element at a time. When used correctly,
animation effects focus the audience's attention on a single element,
providing the speaker with an opportunity to emphasize an important
point using the slide element as an effective visual aid.

Activity 6.3 Adding Entrance Effects

Entrance effects are animations that bring a slide element onto the
screen. In this activity, you will apply entrance effects to elements on
Slides 2 and 3.

1 If necessary, open your file **6A_Learning_Firstname_Lastname**, and
then display **Slide 2**. From the **Slide Show** menu, click **Custom
Animation** to display the **Custom Animation** task pane.
Alternatively, if the task pane is open, click the Other Task Panes
arrow, and then click Custom Animation.

2 Click the bulleted list placeholder. At the top of the **Custom
Animation** task pane, click the **Add Effect** button ![Add Effect], and
then point to **Entrance**.

A list of the most recently used animation effects displays. At the
bottom of the list, the *More Effects* option displays.

3 Click **More Effects** to display the **Add Entrance Effect** dialog box.
Scroll through the list to view the names listed under *Basic*, *Subtle*,
Moderate, and *Exciting* entrance effects.

4 Point to the title bar on the **Add Entrance Effect** dialog box, and
then drag the dialog box to the right so that it covers the task pane.
Be sure that the **Add Entrance Effect** vertical scroll bar is visible.

With the dialog box no longer blocking the slide, you will be able to
view the entrance effects that you apply.

5 At the bottom of the **Add Entrance Effect** dialog box, if necessary, click to select the **Preview Effect** check box. Click several of the effects in each of the four categories to view the animation.

6 Under **Moderate**, click **Center Revolve**, and then click **OK**.

Notice that the numbers *1* and *2* display to the left of the bulleted list placeholder, indicating the order in which the bulleted points will display. For example, the first bullet point and its subordinate bullet are both numbered *1*. Thus, both will display at the same time. In the task pane, the ***custom animation list*** indicates that an animation effect has been applied to the selected item. The custom animation list displays the animation sequences for a slide, including the first few words of the animated text. The mouse image next to item 1 in the custom animation list indicates that the animation will display the bulleted list placeholder text when the left mouse button is clicked. Below item 1, a button with two downward-pointing arrows displays. This is the *Click to expand contents* button. See Figure 6.4.

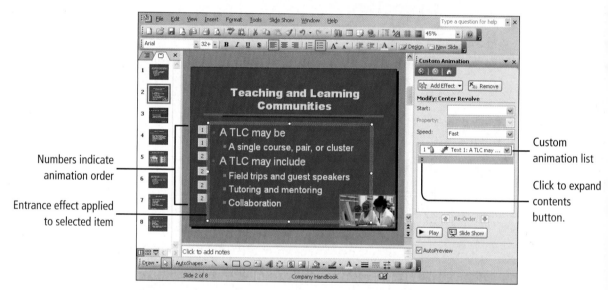

Numbers indicate animation order

Entrance effect applied to selected item

Custom animation list

Click to expand contents button.

Figure 6.4

7 Click to select the picture in the lower right corner of the slide.

The Picture toolbar may display floating in your window, or it may be docked in the toolbar area of your window.

8 If the Picture toolbar is floating on your screen, double-click its title bar to dock it in the toolbar area of your window, or click its **Close** button so that it does not display.

9 In the **Custom Animation** task pane, click the **Add Effect** button [Add Effect ▾], and then point to **Entrance**. Click **More Effects** to display the **Add Entrance Effect** dialog box. Under **Basic**, click **Dissolve In**, and then click **OK**.

The task pane displays item number 3 in the custom animation list, displaying the file name of the inserted picture. In this case, the file name is *Connection*. Additionally, the name of the applied animation displays near the top of the task pane preceded by the word *Modify*.

10 In the **Custom Animation list**, between **items 1** and **3**, click the **Click to expand contents** button to display items 1 and 2. If necessary, scroll the Custom Animation list up to view items 1 and 2.

The expanded list displays the contents of the first, second, and third animated elements, indicating the order in which the elements will display. See Figure 6.5.

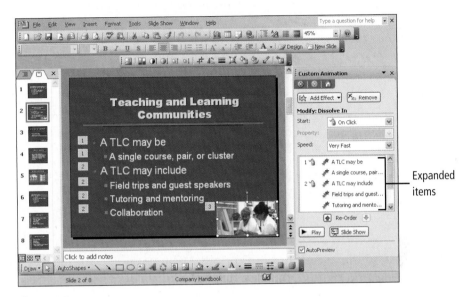

Expanded items

Figure 6.5

11 At the bottom of the task pane, click the **Play** button [▶ Play].

For the active slide only, the slide transition and each animation display. Additionally, the task pane indicates the number of seconds that elapse with each animation. This is a good way to test the animations you have applied to a single slide without switching to Slide Show View.

Alert!

If You Blinked, You Missed It!

If you did not notice the timing of the slide displaying in the task pane, click the Play button again and watch the task pane instead of the slide!

12 **Save** [🖫] the file, and then display **Slide 3**.

13 Click to select the title placeholder. In the **Custom Animation** task pane, click the **Add Effect** button [☆ Add Effect ▼], and then point to **Entrance**. Click **More Effects** to display the **Add Entrance Effect** dialog box. Under **Basic**, click **Strips**, and then click **OK**.

14 In the **Custom Animation** task pane, click the **Direction arrow**, and then click **Right Down**. Click the **Speed arrow**, and then click **Fast**.

15 Click the bulleted list placeholder. In the **Custom Animation** task pane, click the **Add Effect** button [★ Add Effect ▾], and then point to **Entrance**. Click **More Effects** to display the **Add Entrance Effect** dialog box. Under **Basic**, click **Peek In**, and then click **OK**.

Notice in the slide that the numbers 2 through 5 display. The 2 refers to the animation applied to the 3-D placeholder containing the text. The numbers 3 through 5 refer to the bulleted points.

16 Click the text box at the lower right edge of the slide. In the **Custom Animation** task pane, click the **Add Effect** button [★ Add Effect ▾], and then point to **Entrance**. In the displayed list, click **Strips**.

The Strips animation was recently applied and should display in the animation list when you point to Entrance Effect. If Strips does not display in the list, click More Effects. Under Basic, click Strips, and then click OK.

17 In the **Custom Animation** task pane, click the **Speed arrow**, and then click **Fast**.

Notice that the Custom Animation list displays items 1, 2, and 6. Items 3, 4, and 5 are part of the item 2 animation sequence.

18 In the **Custom Animation** list, under **item 2**, click the **Click to expand contents** button.

Notice that all of the animated items display and that items 3, 4, and 5 match the numbering on the slide in the Slide pane. Recall that by expanding the Custom Animation list, you can view all of the animations that you have applied to the slide. After the list is expanded, the *Click to expand contents* button name changes to *Click to hide contents*.

19 In the **Custom Animation** list, under **item 5**, click the **Click to hide contents** button so that the list collapses.

20 Display **Slide 1**, and then in the **Custom Animation** task pane, click the **Slide Show** button [🖥 Slide Show]. Recall that the first slide will advance automatically after two seconds. When **Slide 2** displays, click the mouse button to advance through the remainder of the presentation, and to observe the various animations.

21 **Save** [💾] the file.

Activity 6.4 Setting Effect Options

After animation is applied, you can set *effect options*. Using effect options, you can change the direction of the effect and play a sound when an animation takes place. Effect options also allow you to control the levels of text that display. For example, you can animate text by first-level paragraphs, so that first-level bullet points and their subordinate text display all at once. Or, you can animate text by second-, third-, fourth-, or fifth-level paragraphs so that each bullet on the slide, regardless of level, displays individually. Finally, you can use the effect options to control how text displays when the next animation sequence occurs. For example, after you have discussed a bullet point, you can click the mouse button to display the next point and dim the previous point, thus keeping the audience focused on the new bullet point.

1 Display **Slide 4**, and then click in the bulleted list placeholder. If necessary, display the Custom Animation task pane by clicking the Slide Show menu, and then clicking Custom Animation.

2 To display the **Add Entrance Effects** dialog box, in the **Custom Animation** task pane, click **Add Effect**, and then point to **Entrance**. Click **More Effects**, and then under **Basic**, click **Blinds**. Click **OK**.

In the Custom Animation list, notice that item 1 is selected and a downward-pointing arrow displays to the right of the item.

3 In the **Custom Animation** list, click the **item 1 arrow**, and then click **Effect Options**. See Figure 6.6.

The Blinds dialog box displays. When you click the Effect Options command, the dialog box that displays is named according to the applied animation.

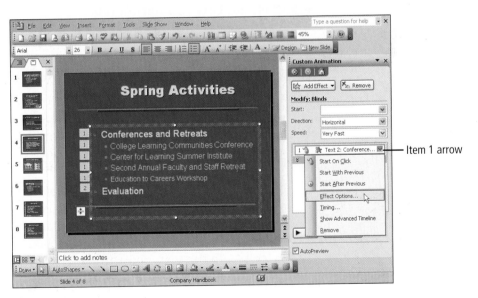

Figure 6.6

4 Click the **Effect tab**. Under **Enhancements**, click the **After animation arrow**.

Use the After Animation options to choose how the text will display after it is animated and you click the mouse button. The default—*Don't Dim*—keeps the text onscreen without any changes. You can dim the text by choosing a color that blends with the slide background, or you can hide the text so that it does not display at all.

5 In the **second row** of colors, click the **first color**. See Figure 6.7.

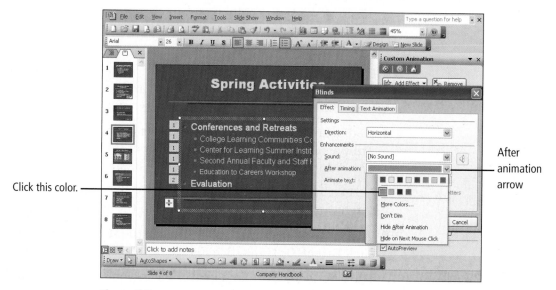

Click this color.

After animation arrow

Figure 6.7

6 Click the **Text Animation tab**.

Here you can indicate the levels by which the text should display when it is animated.

7 Click the **Group text arrow**, and then click **By 2nd level paragraphs**. Click **OK**.

When the mouse is clicked during the slide show, each bullet point will display individually.

8 Display **Slide 3**, and then click the bulleted list placeholder.

Recall that when the bulleted list displays in the slide show, the 3-D placeholder in which it is contained also contains animation. Because a 3-D style has been applied to the placeholder, it is treated as a drawing object. Thus, PowerPoint applied the animation to the object as well as to the text. You can use the Effects Options command to turn off the shape's animation.

9 In the **Custom Animation** list, click **item 2**, and then click the **item 2 arrow**. From the displayed list, click **Effect Options**. In the **Peek In** dialog box, click the **Text Animation tab**, and then click to clear the **Animate attached shape** check box. See Figure 6.8. Click **OK**.

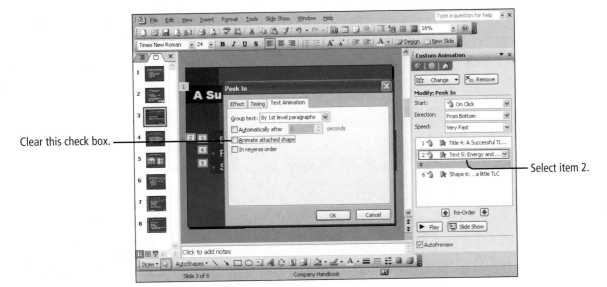

Clear this check box.

Select item 2.

Figure 6.8

10 Display **Slide 1**, and then in the task pane, click the **Slide Show** button [Slide Show]. View the presentation until **Slide 5** displays, and then press [Esc] to end the show.

As you view the slide show, notice that on Slide 3, the 3-D rectangle containing the bulleted list displays when the slide displays. Notice on Slide 4 that each bullet dims when the next bullet is displayed. In order for Slide 5 to display, the *Evaluation* bullet point must dim, and then you must click the mouse button again. Since *Evaluation* is the last item on the slide, it is not necessary for it to dim. To create a smoother transition, you can turn the dim option off for the *Evaluation* bullet point.

11 Display **Slide 4**. In the **Custom Animation** list, click the **Click to expand contents** button.

Items 1 through 6 display in the list.

12 Click **item 6**, and then click the **item 6 arrow**. Click **Effect Options**. Click the **After animation arrow**, and then click **Don't Dim**. Click **OK**. Click the **Play** button [▶ Play] to play the individual slide as it will display in the onscreen slide show, and then notice that *Evaluation* does not dim.

13 **Save** [💾] the file.

Activity 6.5 Adding Emphasis Effects

Emphasis effects are animations that draw attention to a slide element that is currently displayed. In this activity, you will add an emphasis effect to the title on Slide 1.

1 Display **Slide 1**, and if necessary, display the **Custom Animation** task pane.

2 Click the title placeholder. In the **Custom Animation** task pane, click the **Add Effect** button [⭐ Add Effect ▼], and then point to **Emphasis**. Click **More Effects**, and if necessary, drag the **Add Emphasis Effect** dialog box to the right so that you can view the slide. Click several of the emphasis effects to view the animation.

3 Under **Subtle**, click **Brush on Underline**, and then click **OK**. At the bottom of the task pane, click the **Play** button [▶ Play] to view the animation you have applied to the slide.

4 Save [💾] the file.

Activity 6.6 Adding Exit Effects

Exit effects are animations that move a slide element off the screen and are most commonly used when the presenter wants another slide element to take its place. In this activity, you will add entrance and exit effects to Slide 5.

1 Display **Slide 5**. Click in the red area on the left side of the slide to select the grouped object. In the **Custom Animation** task pane, click the **Add Effect** button [⭐ Add Effect ▼], and then point to **Entrance**. Click **More Effects**, and then under **Basic**, click **Fly In**. Click **OK**.

The Fly In effect is applied to the object. The default direction for the Fly In effect is *From Bottom.*

2 In the **Custom Animation** task pane, click the **Direction arrow**, and then click **From Left**.

3 With the object on the left side of the slide still selected, in the **Custom Animation** task pane, click the **Add Effect** button [⭐ Add Effect ▼], and then point to **Exit**. Click **More Effects**, and then under **Basic**, click **Fly Out**. Click **OK**. If necessary, click the Direction arrow, and then click To Bottom.

Notice that in the Custom Animation list, item 2 displays three red stars and item 1 displays three green stars. The green stars indicate an entrance effect, whereas the red stars indicate an exit effect.

4 Click in the red area on the right side of the slide to select the grouped object. In the task pane, click the **Add Effect** button [⭐ Add Effect ▼], and then point to **Entrance**. Click **More Effects**, and then under **Basic**, click **Fly In**. Click **OK**. Click the **Direction arrow**, and then click **From Left**.

Three items display in the custom animation list. See Figure 6.9.

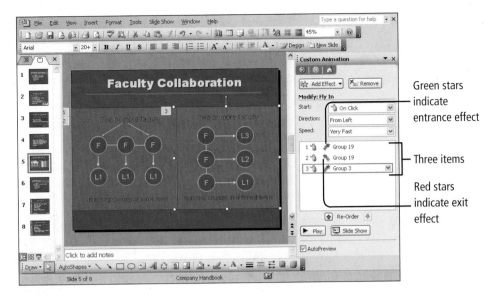

Green stars
indicate
entrance effect

Three items

Red stars
indicate exit
effect

Figure 6.9

5 In the task pane, click the **Play** button [▶ Play].

Notice that after the first grouped object exits the slide, the second one enters. When you view this animation, consider the placement of the two objects as they enter and exit. The layout for this slide would improve if both grouped objects displayed in the center of the slide. To achieve this effect, you will align the objects using the Align or Distribute commands.

6 Select both objects by clicking the first object, and then holding down [Shift] and clicking the second object. On the Drawing toolbar, click the **Draw** button [Draw ▾], point to **Align or Distribute**, and then check to see if a check mark displays to the left of **Relative to Slide**. If necessary, click so that a check mark displays to the left of the command.

7 On the Drawing toolbar, click the **Draw** button [Draw ▾] again, point to **Align or Distribute**, and then click **Align Center**.

The objects are stacked, one behind the other, with the *Two or more faculty teaching courses at same level* object on top.

8 In the task pane, click the **Play** button [▶ Play], and notice the improved animation effects.

9 **Save** [💾] the file.

Activity 6.7 Changing Animation Order

The order in which animation is applied to slide elements is the order in which slide elements are displayed. In the Custom Animation task pane, you can change the order in which slide elements are animated.

1 Display **Slide 2**, and then click in the title placeholder to select it. In the **Custom Animation** task pane, click the **Add Effect** button ⟨Add Effect ▾⟩, point to **Entrance**, and then click **More Effects** to display the **Add Entrance Effect** dialog box. Under **Moderate**, click **Ascend**, and then click **OK**. Click anywhere on the slide to deselect the title placeholder.

2 Click to select the grouped lines below the title placeholder. In the **Custom Animation** task pane, click **Add Effect**, point to **Entrance**, and then click **More Effects**. Under **Moderate**, click **Stretch**, and then click **OK**. If necessary, click the Direction arrow, and then click Across.

3 In the task pane, click the **Play** button ⟨▶ Play⟩.

The title and the grouped lines below it are the last items to be animated on the slide. The slide would display more appropriately if the title displayed first, immediately followed by the red and black grouped lines. In the Custom Animation list, notice that above item 3, the *Click to hide contents* button displays two up pointing arrows.

4 Click the **Click to hide contents** button to collapse **items 1** and **2** so that the detail does not show.

5 In the **Custom Animation** list, click **item 4** so that it is selected.

Notice that in the slide pane, the number 4 next to the title placeholder is highlighted and bordered, indicating the slide element animation to be modified.

6 Below the **Custom Animation** list, click the **Re-Order up arrow** to move **item 4** up to the **item 3** position in the list. Continue to click the **up arrow** until the title item displays as **item 1** and the **Re-Order up arrow** is dimmed and no longer available. See Figure 6.10.

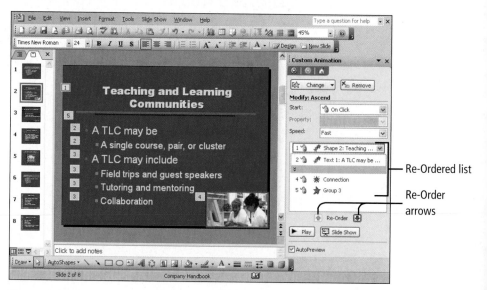

Figure 6.10

7 In the **Custom Animation** list, click **item 5** so that it is selected.

Notice that in the Slide pane, the number 5 next to the grouped lines is highlighted and bordered.

8 Point to **item 5** and notice that an up and down pointing arrow displays.

The up and down pointing arrow shape of your mouse pointer indicates that you can move the item to another location in the list, thus changing the slide animation sequence.

9 While pointing to **item 5**, press and hold down the left mouse button and drag up, noticing that while you drag, a black line displays. When the black line displays between **items 1** and **2**, release the mouse button. See Figure 6.11.

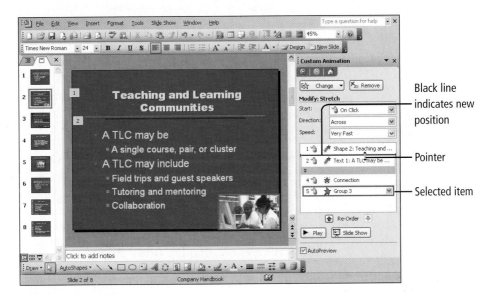

Figure 6.11

10 In the task pane, click the **Play** button [▶ Play], and notice that the animations display in the following order: title, line, bulleted list, picture. If your slide does not display in this order, compare your **Custom Animation** list with Figure 6.12, and make adjustments to the animation sequence as necessary.

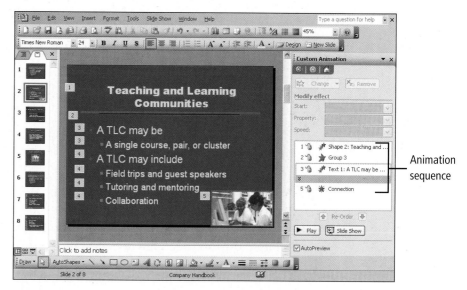

Figure 6.12

11 Save 🖫 the file.

Activity 6.8 Setting Animation Timing

Recall that as you view a slide presentation, you can click the left mouse button to advance through the slide transitions and animations. There may be occasions when you want to advance the animations either at the same time as the previous animation, or immediately following the previous animation without clicking the mouse button. In this activity you will set automatic animation on Slides 2, 3, and 5.

1 If necessary, display **Slide 2**, and display the **Custom Animation** task pane.

Every object on this slide is animated. It is a good idea to have an animated slide title display immediately after the slide transitions onto the screen, without the presenter having to remember to click the mouse button to display the title.

2 In the **Custom Animation** list, click **item 1** to select it. Click the **item 1 arrow** and from the displayed menu, click **Start After Previous**. See Figure 6.13.

The Start After Previous option begins the animation sequence for the selected slide element immediately after the completion of the previous animation or transition. In this instance, the previous animation is the slide transition. Thus, the slide will transition onto the screen and the slide title will immediately display with the *Ascend* entrance effect. Notice that the items are renumbered, beginning with zero. The title is treated as a zero because it displays immediately upon completion of the transition.

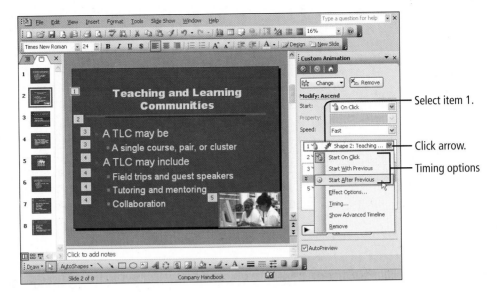

Select item 1.

Click arrow.

Timing options

Figure 6.13

3 In the **Custom Animation** list, click **item 1—Group 3**—so that it is selected. Click the **item 1 arrow**, and from the displayed menu, click **Start With Previous**.

The Start With Previous option begins the animation sequence at the same time as the item preceding it in the Custom Animation list. Thus, the line and title animations will occur at the same time. The grouped line is no longer numbered, and is treated as part of the zero animation sequence.

Alert!

Did You Choose the Right Item?

Be sure that you chose item 1, which is the second item in the list. If you inadvertently chose item 0, the first item in the list, click Undo, and then repeat Step 3.

4 On the slide, click the **picture**.

Notice that when the slide element is selected, the corresponding custom animation list item is selected and the animation information displays.

5 In the **Custom Animation** task pane, under **Modify: Dissolve In**, click the **Start arrow**. Click **After Previous**.

The Start arrow displays a menu that provides the same Start options as the item arrow. You may use either method to change the way in which an animation sequence begins.

6 At the bottom of the task pane, click the **Slide Show** button ▣ Slide Show , and wait for the title and line to display. After the title and line display, click the mouse button to display the first group of bullets points, and then click again to display the second group of bullet points. Press [Esc] after the picture displays to end the slide show.

7 Display **Slide 5**.

Recall that in this slide, the first grouped object displays and then exits the slide. Then, the second grouped object displays. To smoothly animate the exit of the first object and the entrance of the second object, you will apply the *Start With Previous* timing option to the second grouped item so that it enters the slide as the first grouped object exits the slide.

8 In the **Custom Animation** list, click **item 3** to select it. Click the **item 3 arrow**, and from the displayed menu, click **Start With Previous**.

9 In the task pane, click the **Slide Show** button ▣ Slide Show . Click the left mouse button to view the animation, noticing the change in animation as the exit and entrance effects start simultaneously—the first red grouped object exits toward the bottom as the second red grouped object enters from the left. Press [Esc] to end the slide show.

10 Display **Slide 3**, and then click the title placeholder.

11 In the **Custom Animation** list, click **item 1**, and then click the **item 1 arrow**. Click **Timing**. In the displayed dialog box, click the **Start arrow**, and then click **After Previous**.

The Strips dialog box displays, indicating that Strips is the animation effect applied to the selection. Recall that by default, the Start After Previous setting displays the animated element immediately after the preceding animation or transition. There are several options in the Strips dialog box Timing tab. You can set the amount of time that must elapse after the previous event ends and before the new animation begins; you can set the speed of the selected animation; you also can indicate how many times, if any, you would like the animation to repeat.

12 Click the **Delay up spin arrow** one time to set the **Delay** at **0.5** seconds, as shown in Figure 6.14. Click **OK**.

The 0.5 Delay setting instructs PowerPoint to display the animated graphic ½ second after the previous event—the slide transition.

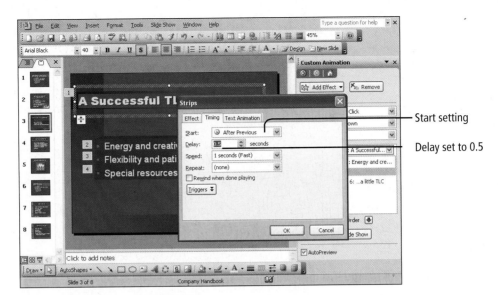

Figure 6.14

Start setting

Delay set to 0.5

13 Display **Slide 1**, and then run the **Slide Show**. Recall that on **Slide 1**, you do not need to click because the slide will transition after 2 seconds. On **Slide 2**, wait for the title and line to display, and then click the mouse button to view the first bullet point. Click to display the second bullet, and then notice that the picture displays automatically. Click to display **Slide 3** and wait for the title to display. Continue to click and view the slide. As you click through **Slide 4**, notice that each bullet point with the exception of the last one dims. On **Slide 5**, notice the improvement to the animation sequence as the second grouped object seems to push the first grouped object off the slide. Continue to view the remainder of the presentation.

14 **Save** the file.

Activity 6.9 Changing and Removing Animation Effects

After animation is applied, you can change the effect or remove it. Using the Change command in the Custom Animation task pane ensures that you are *changing* the effect, not adding a new effect. If you add an effect that you do not need, you can use the Remove command in the Custom Animation task pane to delete the animation from the slide.

1 Display **Slide 1**, and then click the title placeholder. In the **Custom Animation** task pane, click the **Remove** button.

The item is removed from the Custom Animation list and the number *1* is removed from the slide. Thus, the emphasis animation effect is removed from the title.

2 Display **Slide 4**. In the **Custom Animation** list, scroll as necessary to locate and then click the **Click to hide contents** button to collapse the list. Then, click **item 1** to select it.

When you click an item in the Custom Animation list, the Add Effect button changes to the Change button. See Figure 6.15.

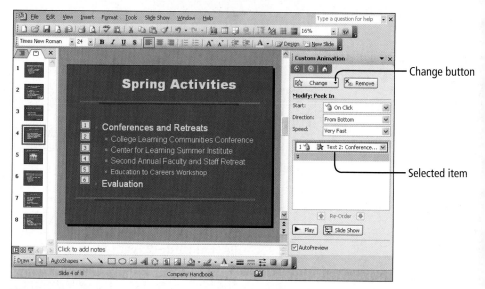

Figure 6.15

Alert!

Changing an Animation Effect

To activate the Change button, you must click the item in the Custom Animation list. If instead you select the item on the slide, the Change button is not activated and you will *add* a new effect rather than *change* an existing effect.

3 In the **Custom Animation** task pane, click the **Change** button [Change], point to **Entrance**, and then click **More Effects**. Under **Basic**, click **Peek In**, and then click **OK**.

4 Display **Slide 1**, and then view the slide show.

On Slide 1, the Brush on underline emphasis effect no longer displays and on Slide 4, the bulleted list is animated with the Peek In animation.

5 **Save** [ ] the file.

Objective 3
Create Motion Paths

In addition to entrance, emphasis, and exit animation effects, you can create a *motion path*—a path that a specified object or text will follow as part of an animation sequence. For example, you can create a customized entrance or exit path for text, or you can draw an invisible path for a graphic to follow.

Activity 6.10 Creating a Motion Path

When you create a motion path, you can use a preset path or you can create a path that you draw using your pointer. In this activity, you will use a preset motion path on Slide 7.

1 If necessary, open your file **6A_Learning_Firstname_Lastname** and display **Slide 7**. From the **Slide Show** menu, click **Custom Animation** to display the **Custom Animation** task pane. In the **Custom Animation** task pane, click the **Slide Show** button [Slide Show].

Notice that the picture of the car bounces up and down and looks as though it is being driven. The car is an animated file with the extension *.gif*.

2 After you have viewed the car, press (Esc) to end the slide show.

3 At the bottom of the slide, click the **Getting from here** text box. In the **Custom Animation** task pane, click the **Add Effect** button [Add Effect ▾], and then point to **Entrance**. If displayed in the animation list, click **Fly In**. Otherwise, click **More Effects**, and under **Basic**, click **Fly In**. Click **OK**.

4 Under **Modify: Fly In**, click the **Start arrow**, and then click **After Previous** to begin the animation immediately after the slide transition.

5 Deselect the text box, and then click the **car**. In the **Custom Animation** task pane, click the **Add Effect** button, and then point to **Entrance**. To display the **Add Entrance Effect** dialog box, click **More Effects**, and then under **Basic**, click **Appear**. Click **OK**. Under **Modify: Appear**, click the **Start arrow**, and then click **After Previous** to begin the animation immediately after the *Getting from here* text box displays.

6 With the car still selected, in the **Custom Animation** task pane, click the **Add Effect** button, and then point to **Motion Paths**. Click **More Motion Paths**. If necessary, point to the Add Motion Path title bar and drag to the right so that the slide is visible.

7 Take a few moments to click several of the paths and view the animations. After you have viewed several animations, under **Lines & Curves**, click **Bounce Right**. Click **OK**.

A green arrowhead displays on the car and a dashed line indicates the bouncing motion path that you chose. Notice that the path disappears off the slide.

8 To the right of the slide, drag the vertical scroll box down very slightly so that the entire motion path, ending in a red arrowhead, displays. See Figure 6.16.

The red arrowhead indicates the point on the slide to which the animated graphic will move.

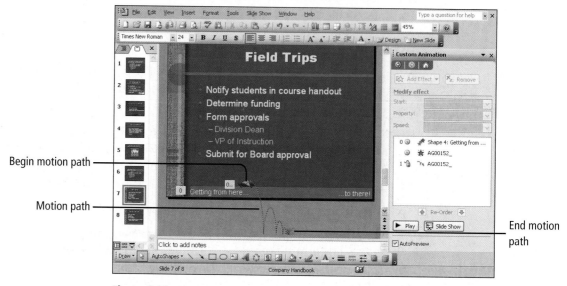

Begin motion path

Motion path

End motion path

Figure 6.16

Alert!

Did You Scroll Too Far?

If you scrolled too far, you may have inadvertently displayed Slide 8. Scroll up a little to display Slide 7 and the entire motion path.

---

9 If necessary, in the **Custom Animation** list, click **item 1** so that the motion path is selected. Under **Modify: Bounce Right**, click the **Start arrow**, and then click **After Previous** so that the motion path animation sequence begins as soon as the car appears.

10 **Save** the file.

Activity 6.11 Modifying a Motion Path

After you create a motion path, you can modify its start or end position, or the path itself.

1 If necessary, point to the motion path to display the move pointer ⊕, and then click the left mouse button to select it.

Sizing handles surround the motion path, indicating that it is selected.

2 Point to the lower right sizing handle below the red triangle to display the diagonal resize pointer . Press and hold down the left mouse button and drag up and to the right so that the crosshair pointer is positioned to the left of the word *to* in *to there*. See Figure 6.17. Release the mouse button.

The new motion path displays.

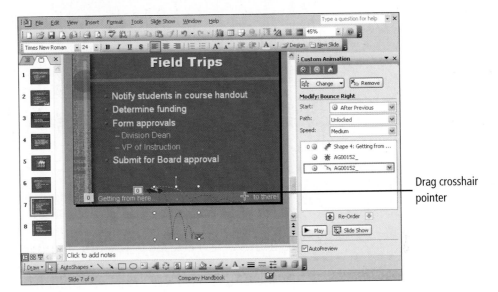

Drag crosshair pointer

Figure 6.17

3 In the **Custom Animation** task pane, click the **Play** button .

Notice the car as it drives across the slide. The path is somewhat flat because of the adjustment made in Step 2. You can edit the path using the Edit Points feature.

4 Point to the path to display the move pointer , and then click the right mouse button to display the shortcut menu. Click **Edit Points**.

Black squares indicate the points on the line that you can move to edit the motion path.

5 Point to the fourth black square so that the pointer displays as a square with four small arrowheads. Press and hold down the left mouse button and drag up about ½ inch. Release the mouse button and compare your motion path with Figure 6.18.

The motion path is modified and a blue line dissects the edited point. White handles are attached to both ends of the blue line, providing additional editing points.

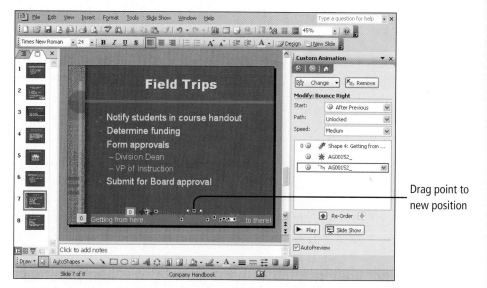

Figure 6.18

Drag point to new position

6 At the bottom of the slide, click to select the **to there!** text box. In the **Custom Animation** task pane, click the **Add Effect** button, and then point to **Entrance**. If displayed in the animation list, click **Fly In.** Otherwise, click **More Effects**, and under **Basic**, click **Fly In** and click **OK**. Under **Modify: Fly In**, click the **Start arrow**, and then click **After Previous** to begin the animation immediately after the motion path animation sequence ends.

7 Click the bulleted list placeholder. In the **Custom Animation** task pane, click the **Add Effect** button [Add Effect ▾], and then point to **Entrance**. If displayed in the animation list, click **Blinds**. Otherwise, click **More Effects**, and under **Basic**, click **Blinds**, and then click **OK**.

8 In the **Custom Animation** task pane, click the **Slide Show** button [Slide Show], and then view the animations on **Slide 7**. When the animation on **Slide 7** is complete, press [Esc] to end the slide show.

9 **Close** the task pane, and then **Save** [💾] the file.

Objective 4
Insert Hyperlinks

A **hyperlink** is a button, text, or image that when selected, activates another information resource. Provide hyperlinks in a PowerPoint presentation to give the speaker easy access to related information. You can insert a hyperlink that goes to another slide in the current presentation, to another presentation, to a file created in another application such as Word or Excel, to a Web page, or to an email address.

Activity 6.12 Inserting a Hyperlink to a Web Page

Information on the World Wide Web is viewed with a **browser**, software that lets you view and navigate on the Web. A hyperlink can be created that launches your Web browser and connects to a Web page. In this activity, you will create a hyperlink on Slide 4 that connects to the Web site for the Illinois Education to Careers Web site.

1 If necessary, open your file **6A_Learning_Firstname_Lastname**. Display **Slide 4**, and then select the text **Education to Careers Workshop**.

2 On the Standard toolbar, click the **Insert Hyperlink** button to open the **Insert Hyperlink** dialog box.

In this dialog box you can enter a Web address to launch a Web browser that displays a Web page during the PowerPoint presentation. The insertion point is blinking in the Address box near the bottom of the dialog box.

3 In the **Link to bar**, click **Existing File or Web Page**, and then in the **Address** box, type **www.illinois.gov/learning/lifelong.cfm** See Figure 6.19.

This is the **URL**—Uniform Resource Locator—for the State of Illinois Lifelong Learning Web page.

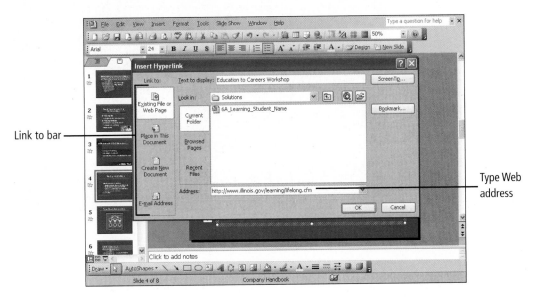

Figure 6.19

4 In the upper right corner of the **Insert Hyperlink** dialog box, click **ScreenTip**.

In the Set Hyperlink ScreenTip dialog box, you can type the ScreenTip that you want to display when you point to the hyperlink during the slide show.

5 Type **Illinois Lifelong Learning Initiative** and then click **OK**. In the **Insert Hyperlink** dialog box, click **OK**, and then click anywhere on the slide to cancel the selection.

Notice that the hyperlink text is underlined. During the slide show, you can click the hyperlink, and your Internet connection will launch and the Web site will display.

Alert!

Connecting to the Internet

Check with your instructor to see if your browser will launch during an onscreen slide show. In some network environments, it may be necessary to launch your Internet connection before you view the slide show.

6 To test your hyperlink, click the **Slide Show** button ⬚, and then click the left mouse button until the hyperlink bullet point displays.

Point to the hyperlink text so that the Link Select pointer ⬚ displays, and then click the left mouse button to launch your browser and access the Web page. See Figure 6.20.

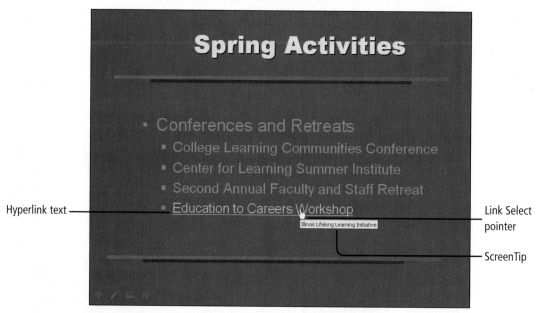

Hyperlink text —

Link Select pointer

ScreenTip

Figure 6.20

7 After you have viewed the Web page, close your browser to return to the slide presentation. Press [Esc] to end the presentation.

8 **Save** 🖫 the file.

More Knowledge — Removing and Editing a Hyperlink

You can remove or edit a hyperlink by pointing to it and then clicking the right mouse button to display the shortcut menu. Click Remove Hyperlink or Edit Hyperlink.

Activity 6.13 Inserting a Hyperlink to a Slide

When you are delivering a presentation, your presentation can contain a slide that displays only if you want it to. For example, you may anticipate that the audience will have a question about a topic in your slide. You can create a slide that addresses the topic and insert a hyperlink to the slide. If an audience member asks about the topic, you can link to and display the slide. In this activity, you will create a hyperlink on Slide 2 that displays Slide 5.

1 Display **Slide 2**, and then select the text **A single course, pair, or cluster**.

2 On the Standard toolbar, click the **Insert Hyperlink** button 🔗 to open the **Insert Hyperlink** dialog box.

In addition to creating a hyperlink to a Web site, you can use this dialog box to create a hyperlink to another slide within the presentation.

3 Under **Link to**, click **Place in This Document**.

When Place in This Document is selected, you can choose to link to the first or last slides, the next or previous slides, or you can choose a specific slide in the presentation.

4 Under **Select a place in this document**, click **5. Faculty Collaboration**. See Figure 6.21. Click **OK**.

A hyperlink is created as indicated by the underlined text. During the slide show, if the hyperlink is clicked, Slide 5 will display. In the next activity, you will create a link from Slide 5 back to Slide 2.

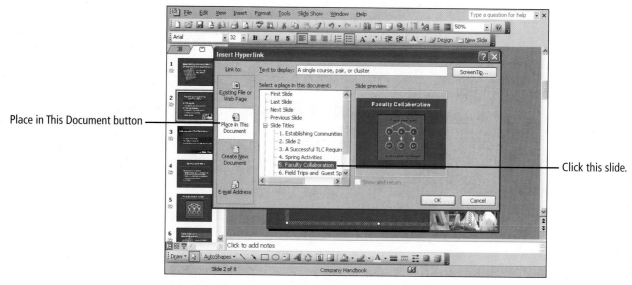

Place in This Document button

Click this slide.

Figure 6.21

5 Save 🖫 the file.

Activity 6.14 Creating an Action Button to Link to Another Slide

An *action button* is a type of hyperlink created using the AutoShapes menu on the Drawing toolbar. During a slide presentation, you can click an action button to execute the action that has been assigned to the button. For example, you can create an action button that opens another PowerPoint presentation, that opens a file from another application such as Word or Excel, that launches a browser and opens a Web page, or that displays another slide in your presentation. In this activity, you will create an action button on Slide 5 that returns the presentation to Slide 2.

1 Display **Slide 5**. Check to see if the horizontal and vertical rulers are displayed on your screen. If necessary, display the ruler by clicking the View menu, and then clicking Ruler.

After this slide is displayed during the slide show, the presentation must resume on Slide 2. You can create an action button that will return the presentation to Slide 2, thus allowing the presenter to continue the slide show.

2 On the Drawing toolbar, click **AutoShapes** AutoShapes ▾ , and then point to **Action Buttons**. In the **Action Buttons** palette, in the third row, click the first button—**Action Button: Return**.

Another Way — **To Create Action Buttons**

You can create an action button by clicking the Slide Show menu, pointing to Action Buttons, and then clicking the button that you want to create.

3 Move the pointer into the presentation window and notice the crosshair pointer that displays. Recall that the crosshair pointer is used to draw an object. Position the pointer at **4 inches to the right of zero on the horizontal ruler** and at **3 inches below zero on the vertical ruler**. Press and hold down the left mouse button and drag the pointer down and to the right so that the shape extends to the lower right corner of the slide. Release the mouse button.

An action button is created in the lower right corner of the slide and the Action Settings dialog box displays. In the Action Settings dialog box, you can indicate the action that takes place when the action button is clicked during a slide presentation. You can choose to link to another slide within the presentation, to another presentation, to a Web site, or to a file created in another application.

4 If necessary, click the **Mouse Click tab**.

The Mouse Click tab sets the action button options so that the action button is activated when it is clicked during a slide presentation.

5 Click the **Hyperlink to arrow**, and then scroll through the list to view the various locations to which you can create a hyperlink. Click **Last Slide Viewed**, as shown in Figure 6.22, and then click **OK**.

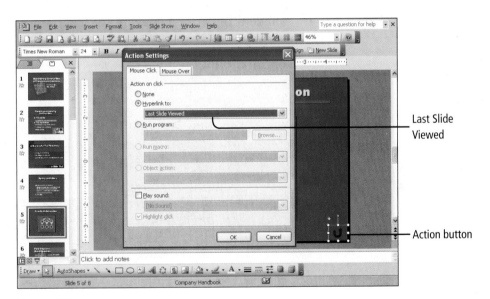

Figure 6.22

6 **Save** ⊞ the file.

More Knowledge — Using the Mouse Over Options

The Mouse Over tab contains the same options as the Mouse Click tab. When action buttons are created using the Mouse Over tab, the action button is activated when you move the pointer over it, rather than when the action button is clicked. Be careful when using this option, as you may move the pointer over an action button during the presentation and inadvertently activate the hyperlink.

Activity 6.15 Hiding a Slide

In this presentation, Slide 5 should not display unless the action button on Slide 2 is clicked. Thus, Slide 5 must be formatted as a **hidden slide**. A hidden slide displays when the action button to which it is linked is clicked during an onscreen presentation. Hidden slides are useful because they allow you to create a slide that you can display only if necessary. For example, questions may arise during the presentation or clarification may be needed on a certain point. If the speaker can anticipate some of these questions, a hidden slide can be prepared, and then displayed only when necessary. In this activity, you will hide Slide 5.

1 Display **Slide 5**. On the menu bar, click **Slide Show**, and then click **Hide Slide**.

Notice that in the Outline/Slides pane, the number 5 displays with a diagonal line through it, indicating that the slide is hidden.

2 Display the presentation in **Slide Sorter View**.

In Slide Sorter View, notice the animation icon below each slide, indicating that a transition has been applied. Under Slide 1, notice that 00:02 displays next to the star, indicating that the slide will transition automatically after 2 seconds. The Slide 5 number is boxed and the box contains a diagonal line through the number. A slide number displayed in this manner indicates that the slide is hidden. See Figure 6.23.

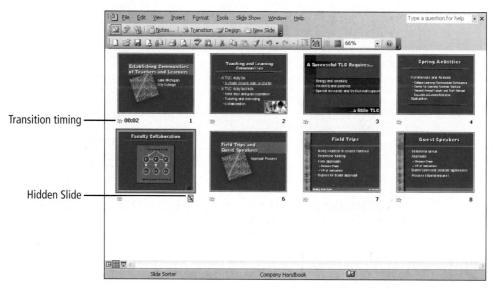

Figure 6.23

3 Click **Slide 2**, and then from the **View** buttons, click the **Slide Show** button. Click once to display the first bullet point. Click the **A single course, pair, or cluster** hyperlink to display **Slide 5**.

4 When **Slide 5** displays, click to display the first grouped item. Click the mouse again to display the second grouped item. Then, point to the **action button** in the lower right corner of the slide to display the Link Select pointer 🖑, and then click the **action button**.

The presentation returns to Slide 2. Notice that the hyperlink is dimmed, indicating that during the slide presentation, it has been clicked.

5 Continue to view the remainder of the slide show, and on **Slide 4**, click the hyperlink to launch your browser and open the Web page. Close the browser window to return to **Slide 4**, and then click two more times.

Notice that Slide 5 does not display because it is a hidden slide. The presentation jumps to Slide 6.

6 Press [Esc] to end the slide show, and then return the presentation to **Normal View** 🖳.

7 **Save** 🖫 the file.

Note — Showing a Hidden Slide

You can unhide a slide by selecting the slide, displaying the Slide Show menu, and then clicking Hide Slide. In Slide Sorter View, you can also click the Hide Slide button on the Slide Sorter toolbar. The Hide Slide button is a toggle button that turns the Hide Slide option on and off.

Objective 5
Create Custom Shows

When you deliver a presentation to more than one audience at different times, you may want to customize your presentation. You can create a *custom show*—a presentation within a presentation in which you group several slides to be shown to a particular audience. For example, in the 6A_Learning presentation, the first five slides are relevant for every audience to whom it is shown. The last three slides are relevant only to faculty and a custom show can be created so that when faculty members view the presentation, the presenter can show the last three slides and then return to the main presentation.

Activity 6.16 Creating a Custom Show

In this activity, you will create a custom show using Slides 6, 7, and 8.

1 If necessary, open your file **6A_Learning_Firstname_Lastname**.

2 On the menu bar, click **Slide Show**, and then click **Custom Shows**. In the **Custom Shows** dialog box, click **New**.

The Define Custom Show dialog box displays. In this dialog box, you can name your custom show and add and remove slides in the show.

3 In the **Slide show name** box, the name *Custom Show 1* is high-lighted. Type **Trips and Speakers**

4 Under **Slides in presentation**, click **Slide 6**. Press and hold down ⇧Shift, and then click **Slide 8**.

Slides 6, 7, and 8 are selected.

5 Click **Add**, and then compare your dialog box with Figure 6.24. Click **OK**.

The Custom Shows dialog box displays and the name *Trips and Speakers* displays in the Custom shows list.

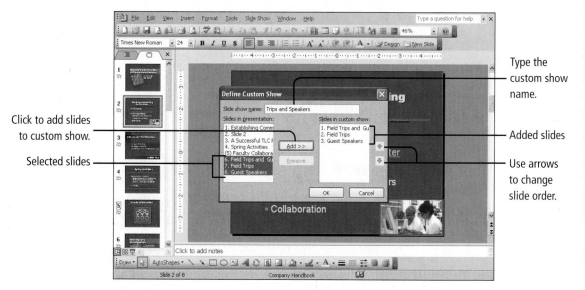

Figure 6.24

6 **Close** the **Custom Shows** dialog box, and then **Save** 🔲 the file.

Activity 6.17 Creating a Hyperlink to a Custom Show

You can create a hyperlink to a custom show from any slide within the presentation. When you create a hyperlink to a custom show, you can instruct PowerPoint to return to the slide that contains the hyperlink.

1 Display **Slide 2**. Select the text **Field trips and guest speakers**.

2 On the Standard toolbar, click the **Insert Hyperlink** button 🔲 to display the **Insert Hyperlink** dialog box.

3 Under **Link to**, click **Place in This Document**. Scroll the **Select a place in this document list** so that the last item—*Custom Shows*—displays. Click **Trips and Speakers**, and then click to select the **Show and return** check box, as shown in Figure 6.25. Click **OK**.

When the *Show and return* check box is selected, the presentation, when viewed, will return to Slide 2 after the three slides in the custom show have been viewed.

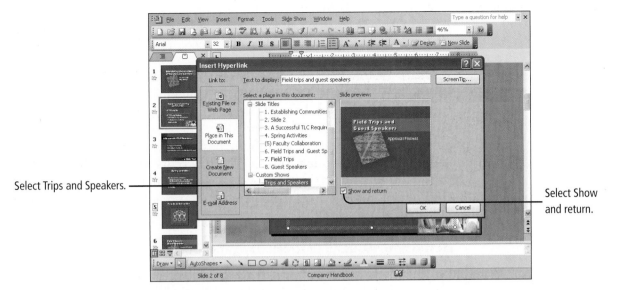

Select Trips and Speakers.

Select Show and return.

Figure 6.25

☐4 In the **Outline/Slides** pane, select **Slides 6**, **7**, and **8**. Display the **Slide Show** menu, and then click **Hide Slide**.

Hiding the three slides in the custom show prevents the slides from being viewed after Slide 4 displays. The Outline/Slides pane indicates that a total of four slides are hidden—Slides 5 through 8.

☐5 Display **Slide 2**, and then from the **View** buttons, click the **Slide Show** button 🖵. Click to advance the animations, and then click the **Field trips and guest speakers** hyperlink to display the custom show. On the **Field Trips** slide, do not click the mouse button until the car and text boxes display. After you have viewed the custom show and the presentation returns to **Slide 2**—*Teaching and Learning Communities*—continue to view the remaining slides.

Notice that the presentation ends after Slide 4 because Slides 5 through 8 are hidden. When the black slide displays, click again to return the presentation to Normal View.

☐6 **Save** 🖫 the file.

Objective 6
View a Slide Presentation

You can start a slide presentation on any slide by displaying the slide with which you want to begin and then clicking the Slide Show button. Once the slide presentation is running, you can move backward and forward within the presentation using slide show navigation tools. For example, an audience member may have a question that pertains to a slide that was previously shown. You can redisplay that slide during the presentation using the slide show navigation tools. Additionally, you can use the pointer as a pen and make annotations to your slides while the presentation is running.

Activity 6.18 Using Onscreen Navigation Tools

In this activity you will use the onscreen navigation tools to view the slides in a different order than the order in which they were created.

1 If necessary, open your file **6A_Learning_Firstname_Lastname** and display **Slide 1**. Before you begin the slide show, read Steps 2 through 8 so that you are familiar with the steps that you will follow.

2 Click the **Slide Show** button ⬚ to begin the slide presentation.

Recall that on the first slide, the transition is set to run automatically and you need not click the left mouse button until Slide 2 displays.

3 When the title on **Slide 2** displays, move your pointer into the slide and notice that in the lower left corner, four buttons display.

When you move the pointer onscreen, the buttons display for approximately three seconds. The left and right pointing arrows move the presentation backward or forward one slide, the pen activates the annotation pointer, which you will use in the next activity, and the slide button displays the shortcut menu. See Figure 6.26.

Next slide arrow ——

Slide menu ——

Annotation pointer ——

Previous slide arrow ——

Figure 6.26

4 In the lower left corner of the screen, click the third button—the **Slide**—and then point to **Go to Slide** to display the list of slides in the presentation.

You can display any slide in the presentation by clicking a slide in the list. Notice that the hidden slide numbers are in parentheses in the list.

5 Click **Slide 4 Spring Activities**. See Figure 6.27.

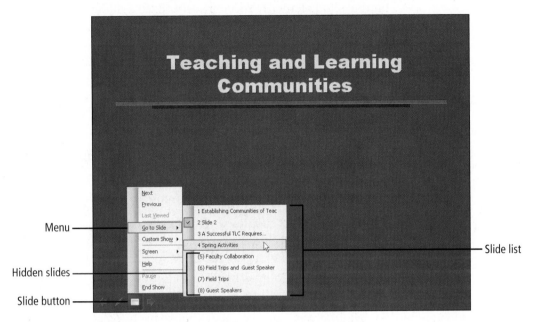

Figure 6.27

6 With **Slide 4** displayed, on your keyboard, press B.

Your system appears to have shut off! During a meeting, it may be desirable to pause a presentation so that a discussion can be held without the distraction of the presentation visuals. Rather than turning off the projection system or ending the slide show, you can display the slide as a black screen, and then redisplay the same slide when you are ready to resume the presentation.

7 To redisplay the slide, on your keyboard, press B.

8 Press Esc to end the show.

To Display the White Screen

If you prefer to display a white screen instead of a black screen, press the W key on your keyboard. Press the W key again to redisplay the presentation.

Activity 6.19 Using the Pen to Annotate a Presentation

When making a presentation, you may want to draw attention to a particular slide element. You can *annotate* a slide by using the pointer as a pen, and then by writing on the slide. The annotations that you create are not permanently stored on the slide. They are automatically erased when the next slide element displays, and you have the option to erase the annotations *before* displaying the next slide element. The default pen color is the same as the Text and Lines Scheme Color in the template color palette. Thus, the default pen color will vary from presentation to presentation.

1 Display **Slide 1**, and then click the **Slide Show** button ▯.

Recall that automatic timings have been set for this slide and that Slide 2 will display after two seconds.

2 When **Slide 2** displays, click twice to display the bullets on the slide, and then move your pointer into the slide so that the four slide show buttons display in the lower left corner of the slide. Click the second button—the **pen**—to display a menu.

Notice that you can choose a Ballpoint Pen, Felt Tip Pen, or a Highlighter. You can also choose an Ink Color.

To Display the Pen

You can press and hold down Ctrl and press P to display the pen pointer.

3 Click **Felt Tip Pen**. See Figure 6.28.

The pointer displays as a small white diamond, indicating that you can use it to draw on the slide.

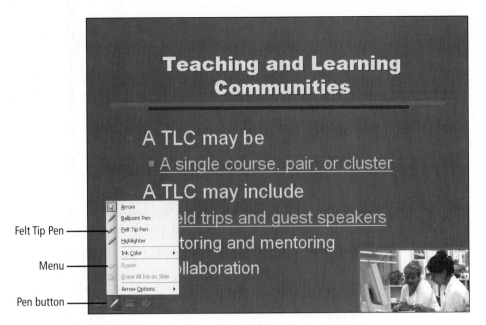

Felt Tip Pen

Menu

Pen button

Figure 6.28

4 Position the pointer above or below the word *Collaboration*, and then press and hold down the left mouse button and drag to draw a circle around the word. Release the mouse button. See Figure 6.29.

By using the pen in this manner, you are drawing attention to an important concept on the slide. After you draw the circle, the pen pointer still displays. To continue advancing through the presentation, you must redisplay the arrow pointer.

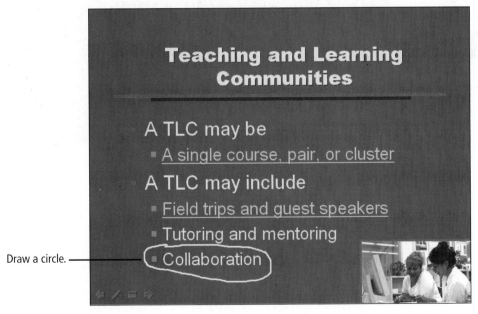

Draw a circle.

Figure 6.29

More Knowledge — Can You Draw a Circle?

Do not be concerned if your circle does not look like the figure. Drawing with your pointer takes some practice and when your presentation is over, you will be given the option whether or not to keep your annotations. If you keep the annotations, they display as objects on your slides.

5 Press Esc to restore the arrow pointer, and then click the mouse button to display **Slide 3**.

On this slide, you will change the pen color and use the highlighter to draw attention to important points.

6 Move your pointer onto the screen. In the lower left corner of the slide, click the **pen**, and then point to **Ink Color**. In the third row of the large palette, click the first color—**red**. See Figure 6.30.

Notice that the pointer displays as a red diamond, indicating the selected ink color.

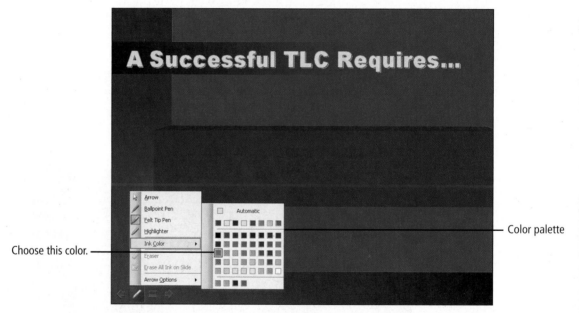

Choose this color.

Color palette

Figure 6.30

7 Move your pointer under the word **Requires** and drag to draw two lines to underscore the word, thus emphasizing its importance.

8 Press and hold down Ctrl and press A to restore the arrow pointer. Click to display the three bullet points in the center of the slide.

9 Move your pointer onto the screen. In the lower left corner of the slide, click the **pen**, and then click **Highlighter**. In the second bullet point, drag to highlight the word **Flexibility**.

After you have used an annotation tool to draw attention to something on your slide, you can erase the annotations that you made.

10 Press E.

The annotations on Slide 3 are erased. Recall that you also created an annotation on Slide 2. Because Slide 2 is not the current slide, the annotation is still included.

11 Press Esc to turn off the **Highlighter**, and then press Esc to end the slide show. A warning box asks if you would like to keep your ink annotations. Click **Discard**.

All the annotations in your presentation are erased.

12 Display **Slide 1**, and then view your slide presentation. Click each hyperlink to display the hidden slide, custom show, and Web page.

13 On the **View** menu, click **Header and Footer**, and then click the **Notes and Handouts tab**. Create a footer for the notes and handouts that includes the date updated automatically and a footer with the text **6A Learning-Firstname Lastname** Clear all other header and footer options, and then click **Apply to All**.

14 **Save** 🖫 the file. From the **File** menu, click **Print** to display the **Print** dialog box. Click the **Print what arrow**, and then click **Handouts**. Click the **Color/grayscale arrow**, and then click **Grayscale**. Under **Handouts**, click the **Slides per page arrow**, and then click **4**. Click the **Horizontal** option button. Click **OK**. Two pages, each containing four slides, will print. Hidden slides will print on a handouts page. **Close** the file and exit PowerPoint.

End **You have completed Project 6A** ━━━━━━━━━━━━━

Summary

In this chapter, you practiced how to animate presentation text and graphic elements and how to apply slide transitions in order to effectively deliver a presentation. Transitions and animations make your presentations interesting and can help to keep your audience focused on the information that you are discussing. You also learned how to use onscreen navigation tools so that you can display slides in a different order if your audience raises questions. The onscreen navigation and the annotation tools provide two methods for customizing your presentations so that you can be responsive to the needs of your audience.

The use of a custom show is another technique that you practiced in this chapter that allows you to customize your presentation. Custom shows allow you to create a basic presentation suitable for a wide variety of audiences, but which is also adaptable to specific audiences. Developing an understanding of the demographics of your audience will help you to anticipate the types of questions that they may have and will facilitate the creation of a custom show. Your audience will recognize that you have taken the time to address their questions, and your credibility as a presenter will increase.

As you develop your presentations, be sure to take advantage of the many resources available to you on the Internet. By accessing the World Wide Web during a presentation, you expose your audience to a wide variety of information that will potentially expand their understanding of your topic. Be sure that the Web sites that you use are pertinent and appropriate. Thoroughly explore the sites that you want to use in your presentations so that you do not accidentally stumble onto a portion of the site that is not relevant to your topic. Check all addresses to be sure they are current and you can still access them. You will want to do this even on the day of your presentation, as Web addresses can change frequently. Furthermore, if you want to use the Web during a presentation, verify ahead of time that the system you will be using has access to the Internet. Finally, when you arrive at your presentation location, rehearse the presentation to be sure that all of your transitions and animations run correctly, and that your hyperlinks to the Internet launch smoothly and quickly.

In This Chapter You Practiced How To

- Apply Slide Transitions
- Apply Custom Animation Effects
- Create Motion Paths
- Insert Hyperlinks
- Create Custom Shows
- View a Slide Presentation

Concepts Assessments

Matching   Match each term in the second column with its correct definition in the first column by writing the letter of the term on the blank line in front of the correct definition.

_____ **1.** Effects used to introduce individual slide elements so that the slide can progress one element at a time.

_____ **2.** A list that displays the animation sequences for a slide.

_____ **3.** Software that lets you view and navigate on the Web.

_____ **4.** A type of hyperlink created using the AutoShapes menu on the Drawing toolbar.

_____ **5.** Options that allow you to modify animations, including changing the direction of an effect and playing a sound when an animation takes place.

_____ **6.** A feature that allows you to write on a slide during a slide show by using the pointer as a pen.

_____ **7.** An animation path that a specified object or text will follow as part of an animation sequence.

_____ **8.** A slide that does not display unless the action button to which it is linked is clicked during an onscreen presentation.

_____ **9.** A method of introducing a slide during an onscreen slide show.

_____ **10.** A button, text, or image that, when selected, activates another information resource.

_____ **11.** Animations that move a slide element off the screen.

_____ **12.** Animations that bring a slide element onto the screen.

_____ **13.** Animations that draw attention to a slide element that is currently displayed.

_____ **14.** The abbreviation for Uniform Resource Locator.

_____ **15.** A presentation within a presentation in which several slides are grouped to be shown to a particular audience.

A Action button

B Animation effects

C Annotate

D Browser

E Custom animation list

F Custom Show

G Effect options

H Emphasis effects

I Entrance effects

J Exit effects

K Hidden slide

L Hyperlink

M Motion path

N Transition

O URL

Fill in the Blank Write the correct answer in the space provided.

1. _____ means the audience has reason to believe what you say.

2. Two keys to gaining credibility with your audience are _____ and _____.

3. To advance slides during a slide show, click _____ or press _____.

4. Red stars in the custom animation list indicate an _____ effect.

5. To keep the audience focused on one bullet at a time, you can _____ the bullets that you have already discussed.

6. You can use the _____ buttons in the Custom Animation task pane to rearrange the animation sequence for a slide.

7. To display animations without clicking the left mouse button, you can set the Start option to _____ or _____.

8. To edit a hyperlink, point to the hyperlink and click the _____ mouse button.

9. You can display the pen pointer during a slide show by pressing _____ + _____.

10. Green stars in the custom animation list indicate an _____ effect.

Project 6B — Adults

Objectives: *Apply Slide Transitions, Apply Custom Animation Effects, and Insert Hyperlinks.*

In the following Skill Assessment, you will format a presentation regarding the Adult Education program at Lake Michigan City College. Your completed presentation will look similar to Figure 6.31. You will save your presentation as *6B_Adults_Firstname_Lastname*.

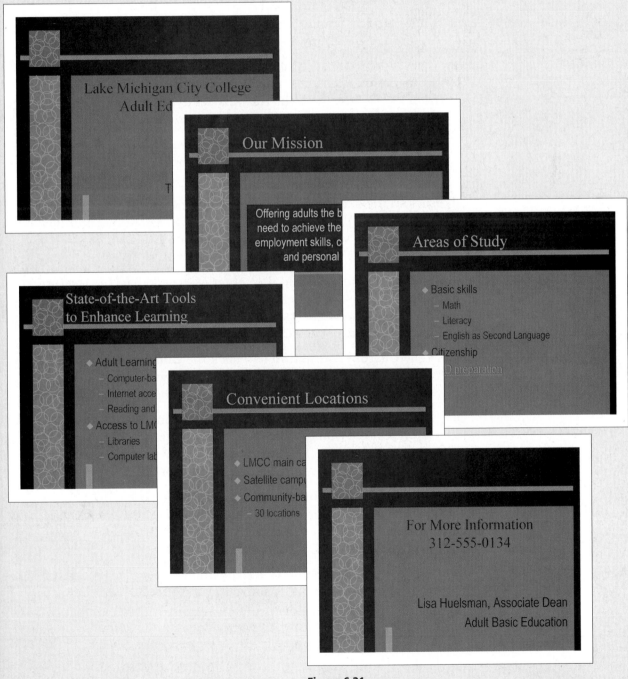

Figure 6.31

(Project 6B–Adults continues on the next page)

(Project 6B–Adults continued)

1. From your student files, open the file **p06B_Adults** in **Normal View** with the slide thumbnails displayed in the **Outline/Slides** pane. Scroll through the presentation to familiarize yourself with the slides. **Save** the file as **6B_Adults_Firstname_Lastname**

2. On the **Slide Show** menu, click **Slide Transition** to display the **Slide Transition** task pane. Under **Apply to selected slides**, click the **Box Out** transition.

3. Under **Modify transition**, click the **Speed arrow**, and then click **Medium**. Click **Apply to All Slides**.

4. If necessary, display **Slide 1**. Under **Advance slide**, clear the **On mouse click** check box, and then click to select the **Automatically after** check box. Click the **Automatically after up spin arrow** three times to apply a three-second delay before **Slide 2** displays.

5. Display **Slide 2**. Click the **Other Task Panes arrow** to display the task panes list, and then click **Custom Animation** to display the **Custom Animation** task pane.

6. Click in the slide title placeholder. In the **Custom Animation** task pane, click the **Add Effect** button, point to **Entrance**, and then click **More Effects** to display the **Add Entrance Effect** dialog box. Under **Moderate**, click **Ease In**, and then click **OK**.

7. Click in the paragraph in the center of the slide. In the **Custom Animation** task pane, click **Add Effect**, point to **Entrance**, and then click **More Effects** to display the **Add Entrance Effect** dialog box. Under **Moderate**, click **Compress**, and then click **OK**.

8. In the **Custom Animation** list, click the **Click to expand contents** button. Click **item 3**, click the **item 3 arrow**, and then click **Start After Previous**. Click **Save** to save the changes you have made.

9. Display **Slide 3**. Select the text of the last bullet point—**GED preparation**. On the Standard toolbar, click the **Insert Hyperlink** button. In the **Link to bar**, click **Existing File or Web Page**, and then in the Address box type **www.acenet.edu/calec/ged/**

10. In the upper right corner of the **Insert Hyperlink** dialog box, click the **ScreenTip** button. In the **ScreenTip text** box, type **American Council on Education** and then click **OK**. In the **Insert Hyperlink** dialog box, click **OK** to create the hyperlink.

11. Display **Slide 4**, and then click the bulleted list placeholder. In the **Custom Animation** task pane, click **Add Effect**, point to **Entrance**, and then click **Compress**. If Compress does not display in the list, click **More Effects** to display the **Add Entrance Effect** dialog box, and then under **Moderate**, click **Compress**. Click **OK**.

(Project 6B–Adults continues on the next page)

(Project 6B–Adults continued)

12. Click the **picture**. In the **Custom Animation** task pane, click **Add Effect**, point to **Entrance**, and then click **More Effects**. Under **Subtle**, click **Faded Zoom**. Click **OK**.

13. Click in the title placeholder. In the **Custom Animation** task pane, click **Add Effect**, point to **Emphasis**, and then click **More Effects**. Under **Exciting**, click **Bold Reveal**, and then click **OK**.

14. In the **Custom Animation** list, click to select **item 4**—the title. The title should be the first animated element to display. Click the **Re-Order up arrow** until the title is **item 1**. Click the **item 1 arrow**, and then click **Start After Previous** so that the title emphasis effect displays immediately after the slide transitions onto the screen.

15. Display **Slide 1**, and then view the slide show. Click the hyperlink on **Slide 3**, and then close your browser to return to the presentation. Continue to view the remainder of the presentation.

16. Create a footer for the notes and handouts that includes the date updated automatically and a footer with the text **6B Adults-Firstname Lastname** Clear all other header and footer options and click **Apply to All**.

17. **Save** the file, and then print the presentation as **grayscale handouts**, **6** slides per page in **horizontal** order. **Close** the file.

 End **You have completed Project 6B**

Project 6C—Alumni

Objectives: *Apply Slide Transitions, Apply Custom Animation Effects, and Insert Hyperlinks.*

In the following Skill Assessment, you will format a presentation that provides information about the alumni association, its purpose, and its benefits. Your completed presentation will look similar to Figure 6.32. You will save your presentation as *6C_Alumni_Firstname_Lastname*.

1. From your student files, open the file **p06C_Alumni** in **Normal View** with the slide thumbnails displayed in the **Outline/Slides** pane. Scroll through the presentation to familiarize yourself with the slides. **Save** the file as **6C_Alumni_Firstname_Lastname**

2. From the **Slide Show** menu, click **Slide Transition** to display the **Slide Transition** task pane. Under **Apply to selected slides**, click the **Shape Diamond** transition. Under **Modify transition**, click the **Speed arrow**, and then click **Medium**. Click **Apply to All Slides**.

(Project 6C–Alumni continues on the next page)

(Project 6C–Alumni continued)

Figure 6.32

3. Display **Slide 2**. This slide will be used as a table of contents for the presentation, using the three bullet points as hyperlinks to the other slides. Select the text of the first bullet point—**Develop alumni networking opportunities**. On the Standard toolbar, click the **Insert Hyperlink** button.

(Project 6C–Alumni continues on the next page)

(Project 6C–Alumni continued)

4. Under **Link to**, click **Place in This Document**. Under **Select a place in this document**, under **Slide Titles**, click **Slide 3. Networking**. Click **OK**.

5. Select the text of the second bullet point—**Strengthen college and community ties**. On the Standard toolbar, click the **Insert Hyperlink** button. Under **Link to**, click **Place in This Document**. Under **Select a place in this document**, under **Slide Titles**, click **Slide 4. Strengthen Ties to the Community**. Click **OK**.

6. Select the text of the third bullet point—**Provide benefits to alumni**. On the Standard toolbar, click the **Insert Hyperlink** button. Under **Link to**, click **Place in This Document**. Under **Select a place in this document**, under **Slide Titles**, click **Slide 5. Alumni Association Member Benefits**. Click **OK**.

7. Click anywhere on the slide to deselect the placeholder and notice that the hyperlink text is almost the same color as the background. Because the text is formatted according to the color scheme hyperlink color, you must edit the color scheme.

8. Click the **Other Task Panes arrow**, and then click **Slide Design–Color Schemes**. Near the bottom of the task pane, click **Edit Color Schemes**, and in the displayed **Edit Color Scheme** dialog box, click the **Custom tab**. Under **Scheme colors**, click the seventh color—**Accent and hyperlink**—and then click **Change Color**. In the Standard colors honeycomb, in the second-to-last row, click the third color—**orange**. Click **OK**, and then click **Apply**.

9. Display **Slide 3**. Click in the title placeholder, and then click the **Other Task Panes arrow**. Click **Custom Animation**. In the **Custom Animation** task pane, click the **Add Effect** button, point to **Entrance**, and then click **More Effects**. Under **Basic**, click **Peek In**, and then click **OK**. Under **Modify Peek In**, click the **Direction arrow**, and then click **From Left**. Click the **Start arrow**, and then click **After Previous** to start the animation after the slide transitions onto the screen.

10. Click the **picture** to the right of the title and apply the same animation—**Peek In**—changing the direction to **From Right**. Click the **Start arrow**, and then click **With Previous** to start the title and picture animations at the same time.

11. Select the bulleted list placeholder, and apply the **Peek In** entrance effect.

(Project 6C–Alumni continues on the next page)

(Project 6C–Alumni continued)

12. Display **Slide 4**. Select the bulleted list placeholder, and apply the **Peek In** entrance effect. In the **Custom Animation** list, click the **item 1 arrow**, and then click **Effect Options**. In the displayed dialog box, click the **Effect tab**. Under **Enhancements**, click the **After animation arrow**, and then click the sixth color—**blue**—so that the bullet points dim to blue after they display. Click **OK**.

13. Select the third bullet point—**Financial support of college programs**. On the Standard toolbar, click the **Insert Hyperlink** button. Under **Link to**, click **Existing File or Web Page**. In the **Address** box type **http://new.ccc.edu/aboutccc/grants** and then click the **ScreenTip** button. In the **ScreenTip text** box type **Grants Newsletter** and then click **OK**. Click **OK** again to create the hyperlink.

14. Display **Slide 5** and select the bulleted list placeholder. Apply the **Peek In** entrance effect. In the **Custom Animation** list, click the **item 1 arrow**, and then click **Timing**. In the displayed dialog box, click the **Text Animation tab**, and then click the **Group text arrow**. Click **By 2nd level paragraphs**, and then click **OK**.

15. With **Slide 5** still displayed, on the Drawing toolbar, click **AutoShapes**. Point to **Action Buttons**, and then in the third row, click the first button—**Action Button: Return**. In the lower right corner of the slide, draw a small action button that is approximately ½ inch by ½ inch. In the **Action Settings** dialog box, verify that under **Hyperlink to**, **Last Slide Viewed** displays, and then click **OK**. With the action button still selected, on the Drawing toolbar, click the **Fill Color button arrow**, and then click the seventh color in the color scheme—**orange**.

16. If necessary, select the action button, and then on the Standard toolbar, click **Copy**. Display **Slide 3**, and on the Standard toolbar, click **Paste**. Display **Slide 4** and click the **Paste** button again. When you view these slides during the slide show, you can click the hyperlink on each slide to return to **Slide 2**.

17. Select **Slides 3**, **4**, and **5**. On the **Slide Show** menu, click **Hide Slide**.

18. Display **Slide 1**, and then view the slide show. Click the hyperlinks on **Slide 2**, and remember to click the return action buttons on **Slides 3**, **4**, and **5**. Test your hyperlink on **Slide 4** that launches the browser. After you view the Web site, close your browser window, and then continue to view the presentation.

19. Create a footer for the notes and handouts that includes the date updated automatically and a footer with the text **6C Alumni-Firstname Lastname** Clear all other header and footer options.

20. **Save** the file, and then print the presentation as **grayscale handouts**, **6** slides per page in **horizontal** order. **Close** the file.

 End You have completed Project 6C

Project 6D — Student Services

Objectives: *Apply Slide Transitions, Apply Custom Animation Effects, Create Motion Paths, Insert Hyperlinks, Create Custom Shows, and View a Slide Presentation.*

In the following Skill Assessment, you will format a presentation describing Student Services programs at LMCC. Your completed presentation will look similar to Figure 6.33. You will save your presentation as *6D_Student_Services_Firstname_Lastname.*

1. From your student files, open the file **p06D_Student_Services** in **Normal View** with the slide thumbnails displayed in the **Outline/Slides** pane. Scroll through the presentation to familiarize yourself with the slides. **Save** the file as **6D_Student_ Services_Firstname_Lastname**

2. On the menu bar, click **Slide Show**, and then click **Slide Transition**. Under **Apply to selected slides**, click **Uncover Right**, and then click **Apply to All Slides**.

3. Select **Slides 7**, **8**, and **9**. In the **Slide Transition** task pane, under **Apply to selected slides**, click **Split Vertical Out**.

4. Display **Slide 1**. In the **Slide Transition** task pane, under **Advance slide**, clear the **On mouse click** check box, and then click to select the **Automatically after** check box. Click the **up spin arrow** twice.

5. Display **Slide 3**. Click the **Other Task Panes arrow**, and then click **Custom Animation**. In the **Custom Animation** list, click **item 1**. At the top of the task pane, click **Change**, point to **Entrance**, and then click **More Effects**. Under **Moderate**, click **Ascend**, and then click **OK**.

6. Display **Slide 4** and in the lower left corner, click the small picture of the girl. In the task pane, click **Add Effect**, and then point to **Motion Paths**. Click **More Motion Paths**, and then under **Lines & Curves**, click **Right**. Click **OK**.

7. Click the motion path so that a sizing handle displays on both ends. Point to the **right sizing handle** to display the diagonal resize pointer. Press and hold down the left mouse button and drag to the right until the crosshair pointer is positioned in front of the doors of the school building. Release the mouse button to modify the motion path.

8. In the task pane, under **Modify: Right**, click the **Speed arrow**, and then click **Very Slow**. Click the **Start arrow**, and then click **With Previous**. Click **Play** to view the animation.

(Project 6D–Student Services continues on the next page)

(Project 6D–Student Services continued)

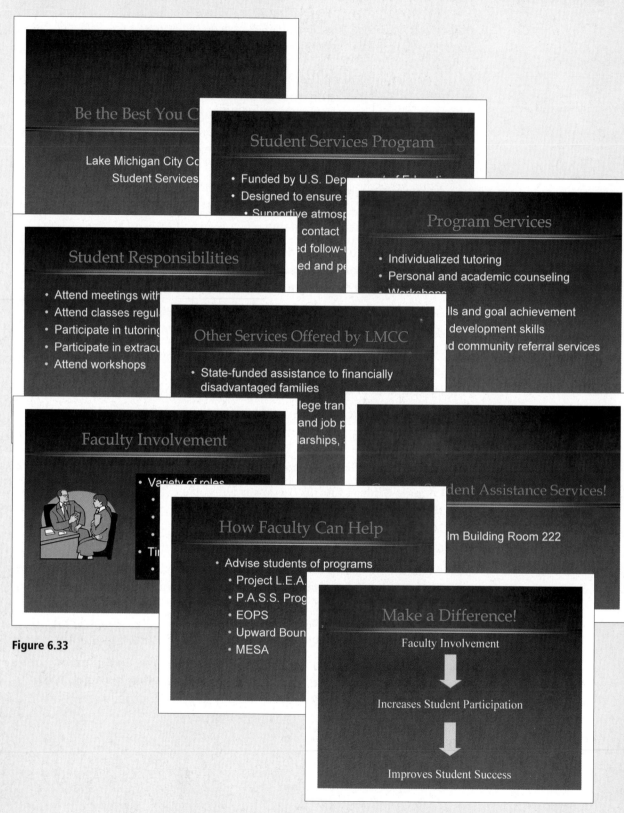

Figure 6.33

(Project 6D–Student Services continues on the next page)

(Project 6D–Student Services continued)

9. On the menu bar, click **Slide Show**, and then click **Custom Shows**. In the **Custom Shows** dialog box, click **New**. In the **Define Custom Show** dialog box, in the **Slide show name** box type **Faculty** In the **Slides in presentation list**, click **Slide 7**. Press and hold down Shift, and click **Slide 9** so that **Slides 7**, **8**, and **9** are selected. Click **Add**, and then click **OK** to create the custom show. Click **Close**.

10. Display **Slide 5** and click the picture of the graduate. On the Standard toolbar, click the **Insert Hyperlink** button. Under **Link to**, click **Place in This Document**. Scroll the **Select a place in this document** list, and under **Custom Shows**, click **Faculty**. Select the **Show and return** check box, and then click **OK** to create a hyperlink from the graduate picture.

11. Select **Slides 7**, **8**, and **9**. On the **Slide Show** menu, click **Hide Slide**.

12. Display **Slide 9**. Move the pointer to the left edge of the slide and below the title so that the left pointing white selection arrow displays. Press and hold down the left mouse button and drag down and to the right to draw a dashed selection rectangle that encloses the three text boxes and two arrows. Each of the objects is selected. If any of the objects are not selected, press Shift and click to select those objects.

13. On the **Draw** menu, point to **Align or Distribute**, and then check to see if **Relative to Slide** has a check mark indicating that it is active. If it is active, click outside the menu; if it is not, click to select it. Be sure the three text boxes and two arrows are still selected, and, if necessary, draw the selection rectangle again to select them. On the **Draw** menu, point to **Align or Distribute** again, and then click **Align Center** so that all of the objects are horizontally centered on the slide.

14. Select the first text box—**Faculty Involvement**. In the **Custom Animation** task pane, click the **Add Effect** button. Point to **Entrance**, and then click **More Effects**. Under **Basic**, click **Blinds**, and then click **OK**.

15. Select the **first arrow**. In the **Custom Animation** task pane, click the **Add Effect** button. Point to **Entrance**, and then click **More Effects**. Under **Moderate**, click **Stretch**, and then click **OK**. In the task pane, under **Modify Stretch**, click the **Direction arrow**, and then click **From Top**.

16. Click the second text box—**Increases Student Participation**. In the **Custom Animation** task pane, click the **Add Effect** button. Point to **Entrance**, and in the list, click **Blinds**.

(Project 6D–Student Services continues on the next page)

(Project 6D–Student Services continued)

17. Select the **second arrow**. In the **Custom Animation** task pane, click the **Add Effect** button. Point to **Entrance**, and in the list, click **Stretch**. In the task pane, under **Modify Stretch**, click the **Direction arrow**, and then click **From Top**.

18. Click the third text box—**Improves Student Success**. In the **Custom Animation** task pane, click the **Add Effect** button. Point to **Entrance**, and in the list, click **Blinds**.

19. Each of the effects that you applied should start immediately after the preceding animation. You can apply the start timing for all of the animations at one time. In the **Custom Animation** list, click **item 1**. Press and hold down Shift, and then click **item 5**, being careful not to accidentally move any of the items in the list.

20. Under **Modify selected effects**, click the **Start arrow**, and then click **After Previous**. Click the **Speed arrow**, and then click **Fast**.

21. Display **Slide 1** and view the slide show. Recall that **Slide 1** will advance automatically after three seconds and that on **Slide 4** the motion path will begin after the last bullet displays. Do not click the mouse button to display the next slide until the motion path is finished. On **Slide 5**, click the picture of the graduate to view the custom show. Practice using the pen and highlighter as you view the presentation but be sure to discard your annotations.

22. Create a footer for the notes and handouts that includes the date updated automatically and a footer with the text **6D Student Services-Firstname Lastname** Clear all other header and footer options.

23. **Save** the file, and then print the presentation as **grayscale handouts**, **3** slides per page. **Close** the file.

End **You have completed Project 6D**

Performance Assessments

Project 6E—Online

Objectives: *Apply Slide Transitions, Apply Custom Animation Effects, Insert Hyperlinks, Create Custom Shows, and View a Slide Presentation.*

In the following Performance Assessment, you will format a presentation regarding online services that is shown to students attending orientation at LMCC. Your completed presentation will look similar to the one shown in Figure 6.34. You will save your presentation as *6E_Online_Firstname_Lastname*.

1. From your student files, open the file **p06E_Online**. Scroll through the presentation to familiarize yourself with the slides. **Save** the file as **6E_Online_Firstname_Lastname**

2. Display the **Slide Transition** task pane. Apply to all slides the **Wheel Clockwise, 2 Spokes** transition and change the speed to **Medium**. Advance **Slide 1** automatically after 2 seconds.

3. Display **Slide 2**, and then display the **Custom Animation** task pane. Select the title placeholder, and in the **Add Entrance Effect** dialog box, under **Exciting**, apply the **Thread** animation. **Start** the animation **After Previous**. In the **Custom Animation** list, click the **item 1 arrow**, and then click **Timing**. Change the **Delay** to **1** second.

4. On **Slide 2**, select the text box at the bottom of the slide and apply the **Thread** animation. **Start** the animation **After Previous** and change the **Timing** so that the **Delay** is set at **1** second.

5. Display **Slide 3** and select the title placeholder. Display the **Add Emphasis Effect** dialog box and under **Moderate**, click **Flicker**, and then click **OK**. In the task pane, click the **Start arrow**, and then click **After Previous** and change the **Timing** so that the **Delay** is set at **1** second.

6. Select the bulleted list placeholder, and in the **Add Entrance Effect** dialog box, under **Moderate**, apply the **Rise Up** animation.

7. Display **Slide 4** and to the bulleted list placeholder, apply the **Rise Up** entrance effect. Change the **Effect Options** so that the **Text Animation** is grouped **By 2nd level paragraphs**.

8. Create a new **Custom Show** named **Financial Aid**. Add **Slides 7** and **8** to the custom show. After you create the show, display **Slide 3**. Select the last bullet point—**Access financial aid information**. Insert a **hyperlink** that links to a **Place in This Document**, the **Financial Aid** custom show. In the **Insert Hyperlink** dialog box, select the **Show and return** check box.

9. Select **Slides 7** and **8** and hide the slides.

10. Display **Slide 8** and select the third bullet point—**Stafford Loans**. Insert a **hyperlink** to the Web address **www.staffordloan.com**

(Project 6E–Online continues on the next page)

(Project 6E–Online continued)

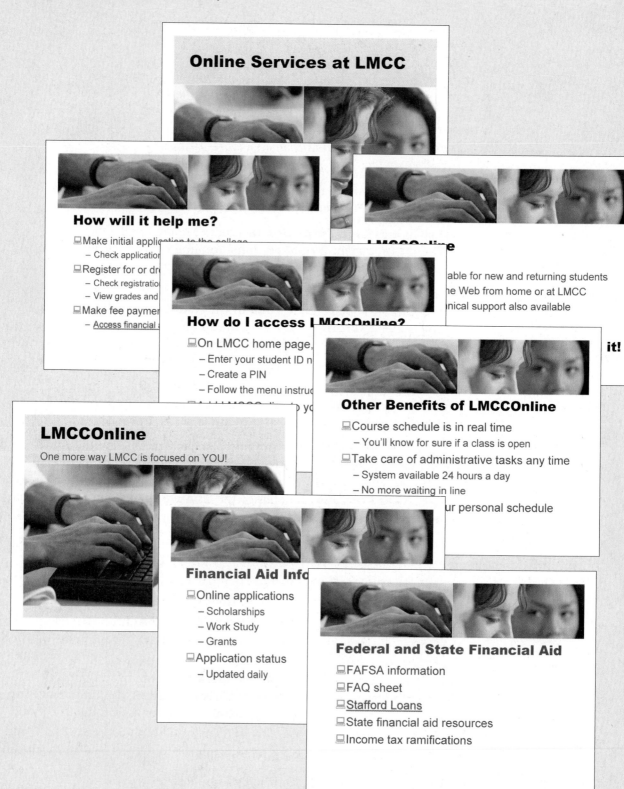

Figure 6.34
(Project 6E–Online continues on the next page)

(Project 6E–Online continued)

11. Display **Slide 1** and view the slide show. Recall that there are automatic timings on **Slides 1**, **2**, and **3**. Click each hyperlink to view the custom show and the Web site. After you have viewed the Web site, close the browser window and view the remainder of the presentation. Practice using the highlighter and the pen, and then discard your annotations.

12. Create a footer for the notes and handouts that includes the date updated automatically and a footer with the text **6E Online-Firstname Lastname** Clear all other header and footer options.

13. **Save** the file, and then print the presentation as **grayscale handouts**, **4** slides per page in **horizontal** order. **Close** the file.

End You have completed Project 6E

Project 6F—Athletics

Objectives: *Apply Slide Transitions, Apply Custom Animation Effects, and Create Motion Paths.*

In the following Performance Assessment you will format a presentation by the Athletic department at LMCC for students at a local high school who are interested in attending summer sports camps at the college. Your completed presentation will look similar to the one shown in Figure 6.35. You will save your presentation as *6F_Athletics_Firstname_Lastname.*

1. From your student files, open the file **p06F_Athletics**. Scroll through the presentation to familiarize yourself with the slides. **Save** the file as **6F_Athletics_Firstname_Lastname**

2. Display the **Slide Transition** task pane. Click the **Split Vertical Out** transition, change the speed to **Slow,** and then click **Apply to All Slides**.

3. Display **Slide 2**, and then display the **Custom Animation** task pane. Select the *Women's Athletics* text box, and display the **Add Entrance Effect** dialog box. Under **Moderate**, apply the **Zoom** animation. Click the **item 1 arrow**, and then click **Effect Options**. In the **Text Animation tab**, group the text **As one object**.

4. Select the *Men's Athletics* text box and apply the same animation and effect options as you did to the *Women's Athletics* text box. After you apply the animation and effect options, change the **Start** setting to **With Previous**.

(Project 6F–Athletics continues on the next page)

Performance Assessments (continued)

(Project 6F–Athletics continued)

Figure 6.35

5. Select the *Meet the LMCC Lancers!* title, and then display the **Add Emphasis Effect** dialog box. Under **Exciting**, apply the **Style Emphasis**. Click the **item 2 arrow**, click **Timing**, and then in the **Timing tab**, change **Start** to **After Previous** and change **Duration** to **1 second (Fast)**.

6. Display **Slide 3**. Select the picture and apply the **Dissolve In** entrance effect. Change the **Start** option to **After Previous**. Select the bulleted list placeholder and apply the **Zoom** entrance effect. **Re-Order** the effects so that the bulleted list placeholder displays first (before the picture displays).

(Project 6F–Athletics continues on the next page)

(Project 6F–Athletics continued)

7. Display **Slide 4**. Select the **Soccer** text box, and then apply the **Zoom** entrance effect. Select the **soccer ball picture**, and then apply the **Appear** entrance effect. With the soccer ball still selected, display the **Add Motion Path** dialog box. Under **Lines & Curves**, apply the **Bounce Right** motion path. The motion path ends where the baseball displays on the slide.

8. Select the **Baseball** text box and apply the **Zoom** entrance effect. Select the **baseball picture**, and apply the **Appear** entrance effect. With the baseball still selected, apply the **Bounce Right** motion path. Notice that the path ends near the bottom of the slide.

9. Point to the baseball's motion path and click to select it. Point to the lower right sizing handle below the red arrowhead to display the diagonal resize pointer. Press and hold down the left mouse button and drag up and to the right so that the crosshair pointer is positioned on the volleyball. Release the mouse button to edit the motion path.

10. Select the **Volleyball** text box, and apply the **Zoom** entrance effect. Select the **volleyball picture**, and apply the **Appear** entrance effect. With the volleyball still selected, display the **Add Motion Path** dialog box. Under **Lines & Curves**, apply the **Zigzag** motion path.

11. Point to the volleyball's motion path and click to select it. Point to the upper right sizing handle above the red arrowhead to display the diagonal resize pointer. Press and hold down the left mouse button and drag up and to the left so that the crosshair pointer is positioned to the left of the golf ball. Release the mouse button to edit the motion path.

12. Select the **Golf** text box, and apply the **Zoom** entrance effect. Select the **golf ball picture**, and apply the **Appear** entrance effect. With the golf ball still selected, apply the **Bounce Right** motion path. The ball will bounce off the slide.

13. In the task pane, select all of the items in the list. (Hint: Use , and be sure that you do not inadvertently move any of the list items.) Change the **Start** option for every item to **After Previous**.

14. Display **Slide 1** and view the slide show, but on **Slide 4**, do not click the mouse button because the animations will begin immediately.

15. Create a footer for the notes and handouts that includes the date updated automatically and a footer with the text **6F Athletics-Firstname Lastname** Clear all other header and footer options.

16. **Save** the file, and then print the presentation as **grayscale handouts**, **6** slides per page in **horizontal** order. **Close** the file.

End You have completed Project 6F

Project 6G — Distance Education

Objectives: *Apply Slide Transitions, Apply Custom Animation Effects, and View a Slide Presentation.*

In the following Performance Assessment, you will format a presentation that will be made by a faculty member to the Board of Trustees regarding the development of distance education programs at LMCC. Your completed presentation will look similar to the one shown in Figure 6.36. You will save your presentation as *6G__Distance_Education_Firstname_Lastname*.

1. From your student files, open the file **p06G_Distance_Education**. Scroll through the presentation to familiarize yourself with the slides. **Save** the file as **6G_Distance_Education_Firstname_Lastname**

2. Display the **Slide Transition** task pane and apply the **Strips Right-Down** transition to all of the slides in the presentation.

3. Display **Slide 2**. Select the bulleted list placeholder, and then display the **Custom Animation** task pane. In the **Add Entrance Effect** dialog box, apply the **Wipe** effect. In the task pane, change the **Direction** to **From Left**. Click anywhere on the slide to cancel the selection.

4. The picture on the right side of the slide consists of two objects—the **picture** and the **yellow text box**. Use ⇧Shift to select both objects, and then from the **Draw** menu, click **Group** to group the two objects.

5. Select the grouped object and apply the **Spinner** entrance effect. In the **Custom Animation** list, under **item 1**, click the **Click to expand contents** button. Click **item 3**, and then click the **Re-Order up arrow** four times so that *Group 3* becomes item 2. Change the **item 2 Start** option to **After Previous**. Click **Play** and notice that the object displays after the ITV Courses bullet point.

6. Display **Slide 3**, and then apply the **Wipe** effect to the bulleted list. Change the **Direction** to **From Left**.

7. Display **Slide 4**. Select the **large yellow arrow**, hold down ⇧Shift, and then select the four text boxes that are in the center of the arrow—**1998, 2001, 2004, Projection**. From the **Draw** menu, **Group** the five items, and then apply the **Stretch** entrance effect. Change the **Direction** to **From Left**, and then change the **Start** option to **After Previous**.

8. Select the **Course Handouts Online** text box and apply the **Blinds** entrance effect. Select the **white arrow** below the *Course Handouts Online* text box and apply the **Stretch** entrance effect. Change the **Direction** to **From Top**. Change the white arrow's **Start** option to **After Previous**.

(Project 6G–Distance Education continues on the next page)

(Project 6G–Distance Education continued)

Figure 6.36

9. Select the **First Hybrid Courses** text box and apply the **Blinds** entrance effect. Select the **white arrow** above the *First Hybrid Courses* text box and apply the **Stretch** entrance effect. Change the **Direction** to **From Bottom**. Change the **white arrow's Start** option to **After Previous**.

(Project 6G–Distance Education continues on the next page)

(Project 6G–Distance Education continued)

10. Select the **First Fully Online Courses** text box, and then repeat the formatting from Step 8.

11. Select the **Online Degree Programs** text box, and then repeat the formatting from Step 9.

12. Display **Slide 5**. Click anywhere on a blank area of the slide, and then press Ctrl + A to select all of the objects on the slide. Point to the boundary box that surrounds the word *Policy* in the center of the slide, hold down Shift and click the boundary box so that all of the objects *except* the *Policy* text box are selected. From the **Draw** menu, **Group** the items, and then apply the **Spinner** entrance effect. Change the **Start** option to **After Previous**, and change the **Speed** to **Fast**.

13. Double-click the word **Policy** to select it, and then add the **Flicker** emphasis effect. Change the **Timing** for the Policy item to **After Previous** and change the **Repeat** option to **Until End of Slide**. (Hint: Use the Flicker dialog box.) In the task pane, click **Play** to view the animation sequence. The Policy text should flicker several times. If the entire box flickers, remove the emphasis effect, and then be sure that you select the Policy *text*, not the text box.

14. Display **Slide 6**, and then apply the **Wipe** entrance effect to the bulleted list placeholder. Change the **Direction** to **From Left**. Change the **Effect Options** so that **After animation**, the bullets dim to the last color in the color scheme—**red**.

15. Display **Slide 7**. Apply the **Dissolve In** entrance effect to the picture, and change the **Start** option to **After Previous**. Apply the **Wipe** entrance effect to the bulleted list placeholder. Change the **Direction** to **From Left**.

16. Display **Slide 8**. The subtitle consists of two separate text boxes. Click the top text box—**The Classroom is Open**. Display the **Add Entrance Effect** dialog box and apply the **Fly In** animation. With the text box still selected, apply the **Fly Out** exit effect, and then change the **Direction** to **To Left**.

17. Select the lower text box—**Imagine the Possibilities**—and then apply the **Fly In** entrance effect. Change the **Start** option to **After Previous** so that the animation begins with the previous text box flying out.

18. Display **Slide 1**, and then view the slide show. Practice using the pen and highlighter, and then discard your annotations when the slide show is complete.

19. Create a footer for the notes and handouts that includes the date updated automatically and a footer with the text **6G Distance Education-Firstname Lastname** Clear all other header and footer options.

20. **Save** the file, and then print the presentation as **grayscale handouts**, **4** slides per page in **horizontal** order. **Close** the file.

 You have completed Project 6G

Project 6H—Activities

Objectives: *Apply Slide Transitions, Apply Custom Animation Effects, Create Motion Paths, Insert Hyperlinks, and Create Custom Shows.*

In the following Mastery Assessment, you will format a presentation that the Student Affairs office has created regarding student activities. Your completed presentation will look similar to the one shown in Figure 6.37. You will save your presentation as *6H_Activities_Firstname_Lastname*.

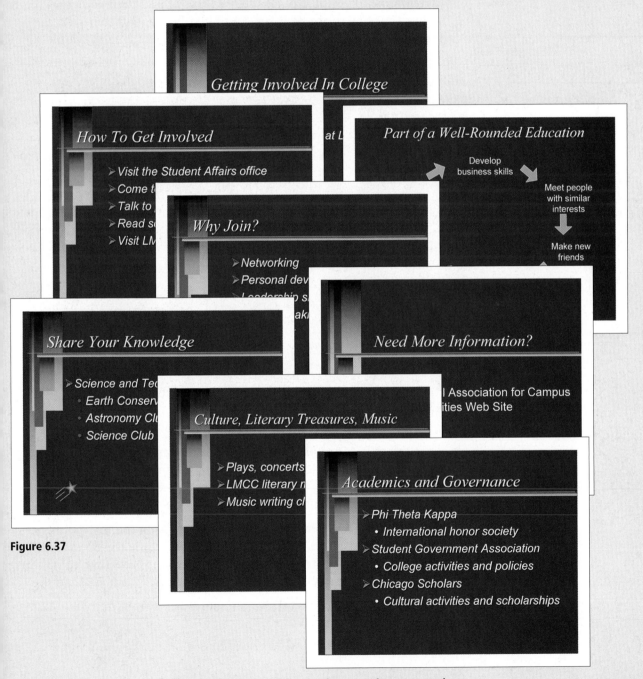

Figure 6.37

(Project 6H–Activities continues on the next page)

(Project 6H–Activities continued)

1. From your student files, open the file **p06H_Activities**. Scroll through the presentation to familiarize yourself with the slides. **Save** the file as 6H_Activities_Firstname_Lastname

2. Insert a **New Slide** after **Slide 1** with the **Title Only** layout. Omit the background graphics from the slide, and then create the slide shown in Figure 6.38. You will create six text boxes with text formatted in **Arial**, **24 pt**. Create the arrows using the **AutoShapes**, **Block Arrows** menu. (Hint: Create the first arrow, and then copy and rotate it five times.) **Group** the arrows and text boxes, and then add the **Pinwheel** entrance effect, so that it displays after the previous animation.

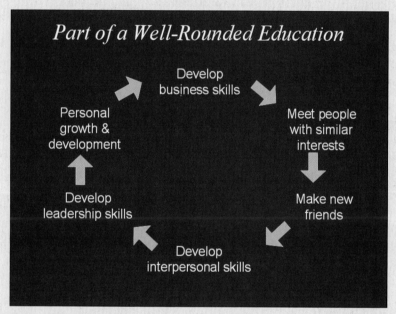

Figure 6.38

3. On **Slides 3**, **4**, and **8**, apply the **Glide** entrance effect to the bulleted list placeholders. (Hint: You must apply the animation to each individual slide.) Change the **Speed** to **Fast**, and dim the bullet points to the sixth color in the color scheme—**lavender**.

4. Display **Slide 5**. Create an **Action Button** using the last button in the first row—**Action Button: Information**. Draw the action button in the lower right corner of the slide. Click the **Hyperlink to** option button, and then click the **Hyperlink to arrow**. Click **URL**. In the URL box, type **www.naca.org**

(Project 6H–Activities continues on the next page)

(Project 6H–Activities continued)

5. Display **Slide 6** and apply the **Arc Up Motion Path** to the star in the lower left corner of the slide. Select the motion path and drag its center top sizing handle up so that it touches the line below the title. Drag the lower right sizing handle to the right so that the red arrow-head is positioned in the middle of the graphic on the right side of the slide. (Hint: Be sure that when you drag the lower right sizing handle, the diagonal arrow displays.) Change the **Start** option to **After Previous**.

6. Display **Slide 7**. Apply the **Glide** entrance effect to the bulleted list placeholder, and change the **Speed** to **Fast**. Apply the **Transparency** emphasis effect to the picture. Set the **Duration** to **Until Next Click**. Change the animation sequence order so that **item 3**—the picture emphasis effect—becomes **item 1**.

7. Apply the **Wheel Clockwise, 3 Spokes** transition to the entire presentation.

8. Create a **Custom Show** named **Clubs** using **Slides 6**, **7**, and **8**, and then **Hide Slides 6**, **7**, and **8**.

9. Display **Slide 4** and create the **Action Button: Forward or Next** in the lower right corner of the slide. Use the action button to create a hyperlink to the **Clubs Custom Show**, and select the **Show and return** check box so that when the custom show is complete, the presentation returns to **Slide 4**.

10. View the presentation, testing all hyperlinks. Create a footer for the notes and handouts that includes the date updated automatically and a footer with the text **6H Activities-Firstname Lastname** Clear all other header and footer options.

11. **Save** the file, and then print the presentation as **grayscale handouts**, **4** slides per page in **horizontal** order. **Close** the file.

 End **You have completed Project 6H** ───────────────

Project 6I—Certificate

Objectives: *Apply Slide Transitions, Apply Custom Animation Effects, and View a Slide Presentation.*

In the following Mastery Assessment, you will format a presentation that faculty members in the Computer Technology Department have created to inform students about a new certificate program. Your completed presentation will look similar to the one shown in Figure 6.39. You will save your presentation as *6I_Certificate_Firstname_Lastname.*

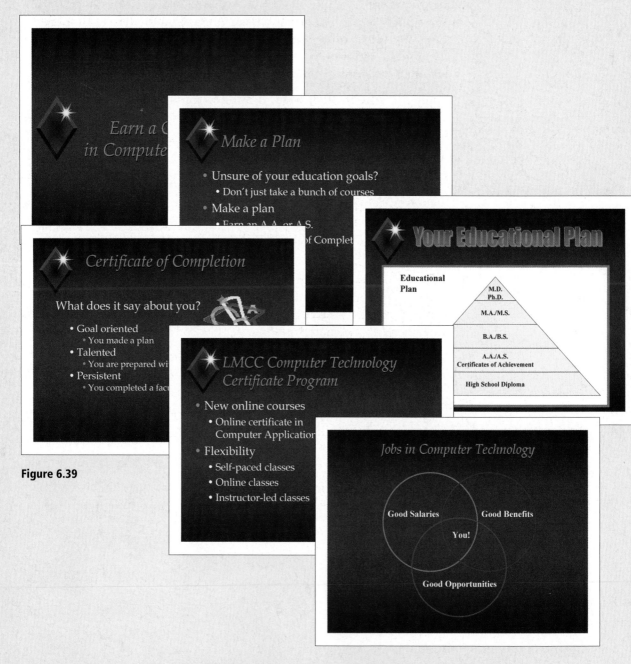

Figure 6.39

(Project 6I–Certificate continues on the next page)

(Project 6I–Certificate continued)

1. From your student files, open the file **p06I_Certificate**. Scroll through the presentation to familiarize yourself with the slides. **Save** the file as **6I_Certificate_Firstname_Lastname**

2. On **Slide 1**, apply the **Grow With Color** emphasis effect to the title. Change the **Start** option to **After Previous**.

3. On **Slides 2**, **4**, and **5**, apply the **Curve Up** entrance effect to the bulleted list placeholders.

4. Display **Slide 3**. The title on this slide is a WordArt object. In the **WordArt Gallery**, change the style to the second style in the third row. Change the **WordArt Shape** to a straight line—**Plain Text**. Apply the **Fly In** entrance effect to the WordArt object, so that it flies in from the top of the slide as soon as the slide displays.

5. Select the **pyramid** on **Slide 3** and create a border around the object by applying a **pink**, **6 pt. solid line** to it. Apply the **Box** entrance effect, and change the **Direction** to **Out**.

6. At the end of the presentation, insert a new **Slide 6** with the **Title Only** layout and create the slide shown in Figure 6.40. Draw the first circle, and then duplicate it twice. Create four text boxes and position them as shown in the figure, using **Times New Roman**, **24 pt.** Use the **Align or Distribute** toolbar to align the text boxes and circles as necessary. **Group** the three circles and four text boxes, and then apply the **Boomerang** entrance effect.

(Project 6I–Certificate continues on the next page)

(Project 6I–Certificate continued)

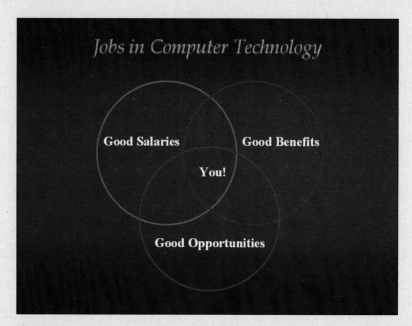

Figure 6.40

7. Apply the **Cover Left** transition to the entire presentation, and then view the slide show. Practice using the pen and the highlighter, and then discard the annotations.

8. Create a footer for the notes and handouts that includes the date updated automatically and a footer with the text **6I Certificate-Firstname Lastname** Clear all other header and footer options.

9. **Save** the file, and then print the presentation as **grayscale handouts**, **6** slides per page in **horizontal** order. **Close** the file.

End You have completed Project 6I

Project 6J — Organization

Objectives: *Apply Slide Transitions, Apply Custom Animation Effects, and Insert Hyperlinks.*

Work with a partner to research an organization on your campus. Attend at least one meeting of the organization and interview the officers and faculty advisor to discover the organization's mission, bylaws, and presence on campus. Create a presentation with six slides describing the organization, governance structure, and activities. Include information such as fees, meeting schedules, and recruitment strategies. If possible find an Internet site that contains information about a regional chapter for the organization, and then create a hyperlink to the Web site. Format the presentation appropriately using pictures and objects to help convey your message. Apply transitions and effects, create an appropriate footer for your notes and handouts, and save your file as *6J_Organization_Firstname_Lastname.* Print the presentation as handouts, 6 slides per page, in grayscale.

End You have completed Project 6J ──────────────────

Project 6K — Career

Objectives: *Apply Slide Transitions, Apply Custom Animation Effects, and Create Custom Shows.*

Start a new presentation based on a design template. Research a career that you are interested in pursuing. Create a presentation that contains at least eight slides describing the career, the education and experience necessary to be successful, the types of opportunities for advancement, and the job outlook for the next five years. Within the eight slides in your presentation, create a custom show that contains two slides. The first slide should describe the reasons that you are interested in this career, and the second slide should describe the skills and personality traits you have that you feel will help you to be successful in this career. Use the techniques that you have learned throughout this textbook to format the presentation, including shapes, pictures, groups, animations, and transitions. Create an appropriate footer for your notes and handouts and save your presentation as *6K_Career_Firstname_Lastname.* Print the presentation as handouts, 4 slides per page, in grayscale.

End You have completed Project 6K ──────────────────

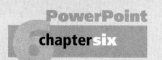
On the Internet

Financial Aid Information

Connect to the Internet and go to the FAFSA Web site, the government site for information on Financial Aid at **www.fafsa.ed.gov** Explore the site to find out the types of financial aid available and the documentation necessary for filling out the forms.

GO! with Help

Rehearsing Slide Timings

You can create a presentation that is self-running without a presenter. This type of presentation may require that you set timings for each slide. Use Microsoft Office PowerPoint Help to learn how to rehearse timings.

1. In the **Type a question for help** box, type **How do I rehearse timings?** and then press ⏎.

2. In the **Search Results** task pane, click **About Delivering presentations**, and then click **On-screen presentations**. Scroll down and read the information about **Self-running presentations**. Read the information and click each link that displays.

3. In the **Search Results** task pane, click **Set timings for a slide show**, and then click **Record timings while you rehearse**. Read the Help information and read the Tip.

7 chapterseven

Presenting Information Using Tables, Charts, and Diagrams

In this chapter, you will: complete these projects **and** practice these skills.

Project 7A **Presenting Data with Tables and Diagrams**	**Objectives** • Create a Table • Create and Format Diagrams • Create and Format Organization Charts

Project 7B **Presenting Data with Charts**	**Objectives** • Create and Modify a Column Chart • Create and Modify a Pie Chart

Oceana Palm Grill

Oceana Palm Grill is a chain of 25 upscale, casual, full-service restaurants based in Austin, Texas. The company opened its first restaurant in 1975 and now operates 25 outlets in the Austin and Dallas areas. Plans call for 15 additional restaurants to be opened in California and Oregon by 2008. These ambitious plans will require the company to bring in new investors, develop new menus, and recruit new employees, all while adhering to the company's strict quality guidelines and maintaining its reputation for excellent service.

© Getty Images, Inc.

Presenting Information Using Tables, Charts, and Diagrams

Charts and graphs can help an audience understand numeric data and trends just as clip art can help illustrate a concept. Microsoft Office PowerPoint 2003 allows you to create a number of chart types easily and quickly. The data that you are presenting should determine the type of chart that you create. Line, bar, column, and pie charts are commonly used in PowerPoint presentations to display information based on spreadsheet data. Regardless of the type of chart that you create, always be sure that the data is accurate. Inaccurate data results in a misinterpreted chart.

There are other types of charts and diagrams that you can create using Microsoft Office PowerPoint 2003. One type of chart that you can create is an organizational chart, sometimes called an "org chart." An organizational chart presents a picture of the relationships among people in an organization. You can also create a variety of diagrams to show the flow of a process, the steps toward a goal, or the relationships among elements.

Project 7A **System**

In this chapter you will present information using tables, charts, and diagrams. Because they are highly visual, using a table or chart to present your data makes it easy for your audience to grasp a concept quickly. Thus, charts, diagrams, and tables are an engaging and effective alternative for presenting data.

In Activities 7.1 through 7.12, you will create a presentation that the Oceana Palm Grill Information Technology Division has created regarding a new inventory and financial system for the restaurants. Your completed presentation will look similar to Figure 7.1. You will save your presentation as *7A_System_Firstname_Lastname*.

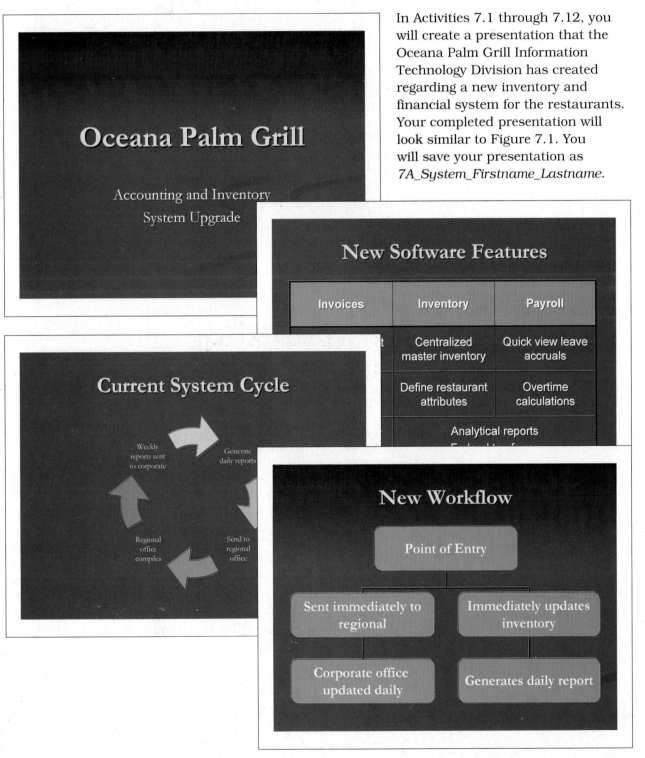

Figure 7.1
Project 7A—System

Objective 1
Create a Table

A **_table_** is a format for information that organizes and presents text and numbers in columns and rows. The intersection of a column and a row in a table is a **_cell_**. You can insert a table by applying a table slide layout, by clicking the Insert Table button on the Standard toolbar, or by drawing a table using the Draw Table command. To enter text in a table, click inside a cell and type. If the text you type is longer than the cell, the text wraps to the next line.

A table created in PowerPoint is inserted as an object and can be layered in a stack with other objects. A table can also be sized by dragging a sizing handle and moved when dragged to a new position on the slide.

Activity 7.1 Creating a Table

In this activity, you will create a table by inserting a new slide that is formatted with the Table slide layout.

1 Start PowerPoint and begin a new presentation using the blue, **Stream** design template. In the title placeholder, type **Oceana Palm Grill** In the subtitle placeholder, type **Accounting and Inventory** and then press Enter. Type **System Upgrade** and then using your own first and last name, save the file in your storage location as **7A_System_Firstname_Lastname** creating a new folder for Chapter 7 if you want to do so. **Close** the Outline/Slides pane.

2 On the Formatting toolbar, click the **New Slide** button [New Slide], and then in the **Slide Layout** task pane under **Other Layouts**, click **Title and Table** to create a new slide with the Title and Table layout. Close the task pane, and then click in the title placeholder and type **New Software Features**

3 Point to the table placeholder, and then double-click to open the **Insert Table** dialog box. In this dialog box, enter the number of rows and columns for the table that you want to create. Click the **Number of columns up spin arrow** once to create **3 columns**. Click the **Number of rows up spin arrow** once to create **3 rows**. See Figure 7.2. Click **OK** to create the table.

A table displays with three columns of equal size and three rows of equal size. The table placeholder determines the initial size of the table. The gridlines that outline the table cells are, by default, a 1 pt. single line in the Text and lines color scheme color. In this presentation, the Text and lines scheme color is white. Notice that the Tables and Borders toolbar displays either floating in your presentation window or docked in the toolbar area of your window.

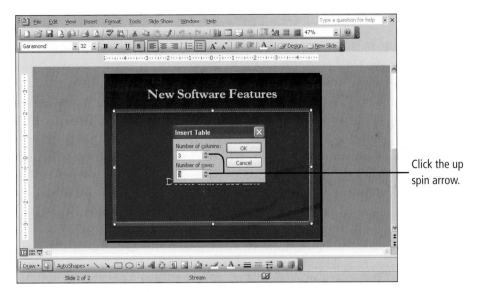

Click the up
spin arrow.

Figure 7.2

Another Way ─┐ **To Create a Table**

You can insert a table on any slide by clicking the Insert Table button on the Standard toolbar. When the Insert Table dialog box displays, type a number in the Number of rows and Number of columns boxes.

4 Recall that a floating toolbar can be docked in the toolbar area of your presentation window. If the Tables and Borders toolbar is floating in your presentation window, point to its title bar, and then drag the toolbar so that it docks below the Formatting toolbar. The table in Figure 7.3 describes the buttons on the Tables and Borders toolbar.

The Tables and Borders Toolbar

Button	Button Name	Description
	Draw Table	Draws lines in a table or changes the format of existing lines in a table.
	Eraser	Removes a table cell line and merges the contents of the adjacent cells.
	Border Style	Changes the style of a selected line.
	Border Width	Changes the thickness of a border.
	Border Color	Changes the color of a border.
	Borders	Adds or removes a border around the selected cells.
	Fill Color	Adds, modifies, or removes the fill color or fill effect from the selected cells.
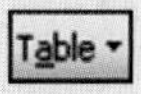	Table	Activates the Table menu.
	Merge Cells	Combines the contents of selected adjacent cells into a single cell.
	Split Cell	Splits the selected cells into the number of rows and columns that you specify.
	Align Top	Aligns text with the top of the table cell.
	Center Vertically	Aligns text centered between the top and bottom of the table cell.
	Align Bottom	Aligns text with the bottom of the table cell.
	Distribute Rows Evenly	Creates rows of equal height within a selection.
	Distribute Columns Evenly	Creates columns of equal width within a selection.

Figure 7.3

5 If necessary, click to position the insertion point in the first cell of the table. Type **Invoices** and then press Tab. The insertion point moves to the second cell in the first row. Type **Inventory** and then press Tab. Type **Payroll** and then press Tab to move the insertion point to the first cell in the second row. Continue to enter the text in the table as shown in Figure 7.4, pressing Tab to move from cell to cell. Let the text wrap within the cells; do *not* press Enter.

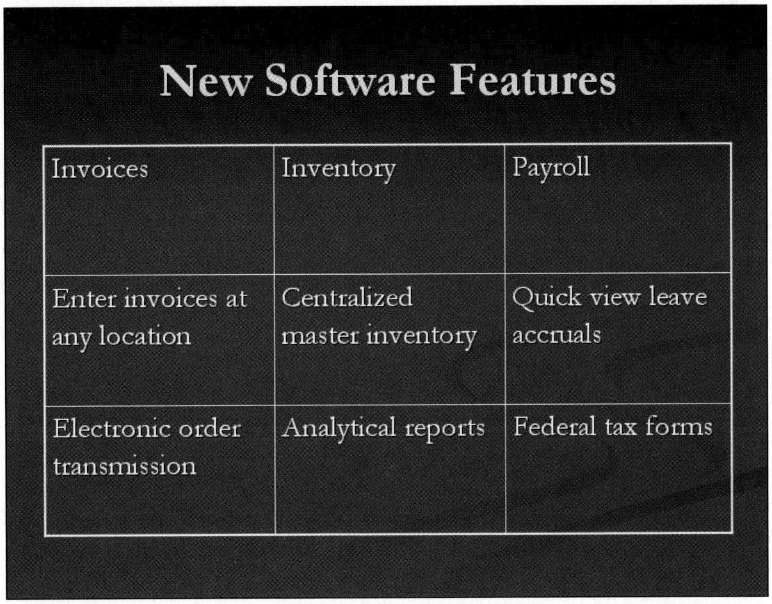

New Software Features

Invoices	Inventory	Payroll
Enter invoices at any location	Centralized master inventory	Quick view leave accruals
Electronic order transmission	Analytical reports	Federal tax forms

Figure 7.4

Did You Add an Extra Row?

When you enter the text in the last cell, do *not* press [Tab], as this action creates a new row. If you inadvertently add a new row at the bottom of the table, click Undo.

6 Point to the first cell in the first row that contains the word *Invoices*, and then drag to the right until all three of the cells in the first row are selected. On the Formatting toolbar, click **Bold** **B**.

7 On the Tables and Borders toolbar, click the **Table** button **Table ▾**, and then click **Select Table**.

A pattern of dots surrounds the outside border of the table. This indicates that the entire table is selected and any formatting that is applied will be applied to all of the text within the table. You can use the Table button on the Tables and Borders toolbar to select various table elements, and to modify and format your table. The table in Figure 7.5 describes other methods that you can use to navigate in a table.

Navigating in a Table

Pressing this key:	Results in:
[Enter]	Inserts a new line within a cell.
[Delete] or [Bksp]	Deletes text within a cell.
[Tab]	Moves insertion point one cell forward.
[Shift] + [Tab]	Moves insertion point one cell backward.
[Tab] in the last cell of a table	Inserts a new row.

Figure 7.5

8 On the Formatting toolbar, click the **Font Size arrow** `32 ▼`, and then click **24**. Click the **Font arrow** `Arial ▼`, and then click **Arial**.

9 **Save** 🖫 the file.

Activity 7.2 Inserting and Deleting Rows and Columns

When the insertion point is positioned in the last cell of the table, recall that you can add a new row to a table by pressing the `Tab` key. To insert a new row in the middle of a table, to insert a column, or to delete rows or columns, you must use either the Table menu on the Tables and Borders toolbar or the shortcut menu.

1 If necessary, display the rulers by clicking the View menu, and then clicking Ruler.

2 Click anywhere in the third row of the table. On the Tables and Borders toolbar, click **Table** `Table ▼` to display the Table menu. Click **Insert Rows Above** to insert a new third row.

Notice that the table expands and the last row may move off of the slide.

More Knowledge — Inserting Multiple Rows and Columns

To insert multiple rows, select the number of rows that you want to insert. Then, on the Tables and Borders toolbar, click Table, and click Insert Rows Above or Insert Rows Below.

---

3 Click in the first cell of the row that you just inserted. Type **Audit trail** and then press `Tab`. Type **Define restaurant attributes** and then press `Tab`. Type **Overtime calculations**

4 On the Standard toolbar, click the **Zoom arrow** `74% ▼`, and then click **33%** to view the entire slide, including the portion of the table that has extended below the edge of the slide.

5 Point to the table's lower middle sizing handle so that the vertical resize pointer `↕` displays. Drag upward so that the guide is positioned at **3 inches below zero on the vertical ruler**.

Notice that the table rows and columns have been resized proportionately.

6 On the Standard toolbar, click the **Zoom arrow** `74% ▼`, and then click **Fit**.

The slide size is increased to fit the window.

7 Position the pointer above the second column, at the top edge of the pattern of dots, until a downward-pointing black arrow displays (several pointer shapes may display before you see the black arrow). Press and hold down the left mouse button and drag to the right to select the second and third columns. See Figure 7.6.

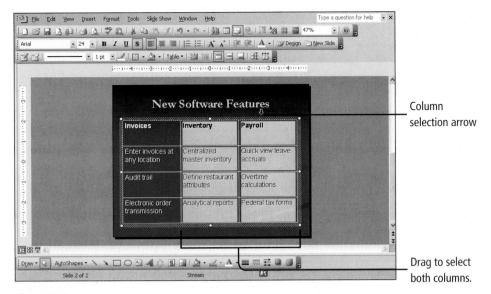

Column selection arrow

Drag to select both columns.

Figure 7.6

Another Way — **Selecting Table Columns**

An easy way to select columns in a table is to first drag to select the first cell—or cells—of the columns. Then, on the Tables and Borders toolbar, click the Table menu and click Select Column.

---

8 On the Tables and Borders toolbar, click **Table** Table ▾ , and then click **Insert Columns to the Left**.

Two new columns are inserted and the table extends outside of the slide boundary.

9 If necessary, select the two columns that you just inserted by positioning the pointer above the first inserted column so that the downward pointing black arrow displays. Press and hold down the left mouse button and drag to the right to select the second column that you inserted. On the Tables and Borders toolbar, click **Table** Table ▾ , and then click **Delete Columns**.

Another Way — **To Delete Columns or Rows**

You can delete a column or row by right-clicking to display the shortcut menu, and then clicking Delete Columns or Delete Rows.

---

10 **Save** 🖫 the file.

Activity 7.3 Drawing and Erasing Table Lines

The ***Draw Table*** command activates the pencil pointer and is used to draw rows and columns in a new or existing table. You can draw the outside, rectangular border of the table first, and then create the rows and columns by drawing lines within the rectangular border. After you draw a table, you may decide that some of the lines are not necessary. To remove lines in a table, use the ***Eraser*** button on the Tables and Borders toolbar. Erasing lines in a table merges two separate cells into one cell.

1 On the Tables and Borders toolbar, click **Draw Table** 📝 so that the pointer displays as a pencil.

2 In the first table cell, position the pencil pointer below the letter *I* in the word *Invoices*—at the approximate midpoint in the cell. Press and hold down the left mouse button and drag the pointer to the right so that a dashed line extends from the left edge of the table to the right edge of the table. See Figure 7.7. Release the mouse button to draw the line.

By using the Draw Table pencil pointer in this manner, the original cells are split and a new row is created.

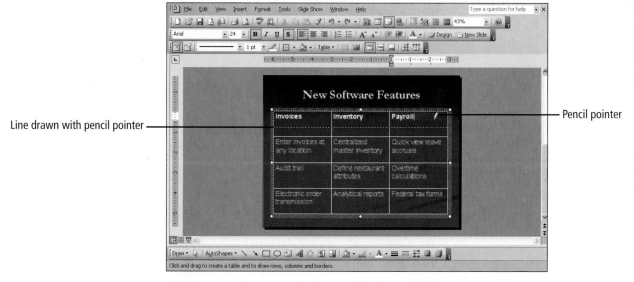

Figure 7.7

3 On the Tables and Borders toolbar, click **Eraser** 📝 to display the pointer as a small eraser. Position the eraser over the line that you drew in the previous step. Press and hold down the left mouse button and drag to the right. Notice that as you drag the pointer, the line is selected. Continue to drag the Eraser pointer to the right until the entire line is selected across all three cells. Release the mouse button to erase the line.

4 With the Eraser pointer still active, click the vertical line that separates the last two cells of the table—between *Analytical reports* and *Federal tax forms*.

The line is erased and the two cells are merged into one cell, indicating that the two listed items are part of both the *Inventory* and *Payroll* software options.

5 On the Tables and Borders toolbar, click **Eraser** ⌨ to turn off the Eraser pointer. Alternatively, press [Esc] to turn off the Eraser.

6 If necessary, delete any extra blank lines that display in the merged cell. Compare your table with Figure 7.8.

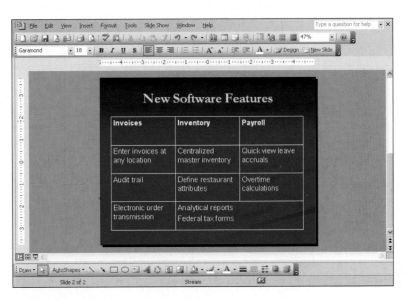

Figure 7.8

7 **Save** 💾 the file.

Another Way ── **To Merge and Split Cells**

Instead of the Eraser and Draw Table pointers, you can use the Merge Cells and Split Cells buttons on the Tables and Borders toolbar to merge multiple cells into one cell or to create new cells in a table.

Activity 7.4 Changing Text Alignment

Within a table, ***horizontal alignment*** refers to the placement of the text between the left and right edges of the cell. ***Vertical alignment*** refers to the placement of the text between the top and bottom edges of the cell. You can change horizontal alignment by clicking the Align Left, Center, or Align Right alignment buttons on the Formatting toolbar. You can change vertical alignment by clicking the Align Top, Center Vertically, and Align Bottom buttons on the Tables and Borders toolbar. When text is entered into a table, the text aligns, by default, at the top left edge of the cell. To change horizontal or vertical text alignment, first select the cells to which you want to apply the alignment change.

1 If necessary, click anywhere in the table so that the Tables and Borders toolbar displays. On the Tables and Borders toolbar, click

Table `Table ▾`, and then click **Select Table**.

2 On the Formatting toolbar, click **Center** [icon] to center align all of the text within each table cell.

3 With the entire table still selected, as indicated by the pattern of dots surrounding the table, move to the Tables and Borders toolbar, and then click **Center Vertically** [icon]. Compare your table with Figure 7.9.

The text is centered between the top and bottom edges of each cell. Alignment changes can be applied to individual cells, to entire rows or columns, or to an entire table.

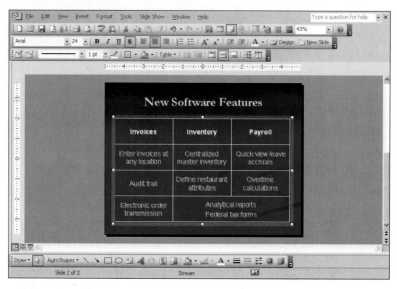

Figure 7.9

4 **Save** [icon] the file.

Activity 7.5 Modifying Borders and Shading

Recall that in a table, the default border style is a 1 pt. single line in the Text and lines color scheme. You can change the border style and color using the buttons on the Tables and Borders toolbar. You can also apply shading to any of the cells in a table by choosing a shading color from the template color scheme, or from the custom or standard color palettes.

1 Click anywhere in the table so that the Tables and Borders toolbar displays.

2 If necessary, on the Tables and Borders toolbar, click **Table** [Table ▾], and then click **Select Table**.

By selecting the entire table, you can change the borders for all of the cells at one time.

3 On the Tables and Borders toolbar, click **Border Color** [icon], and then click the third color in the color scheme—**black**.

Notice that the Draw Table pencil pointer becomes active.

4 On the Tables and Borders toolbar, click the **Borders button arrow** to display the Borders palette. See Figure 7.10.

The Borders palette contains buttons to apply borders to the top, bottom, left, and right of a selection. You can also use the Borders palette to create diagonal borders, or to clear the borders from a selection.

Borders palette —

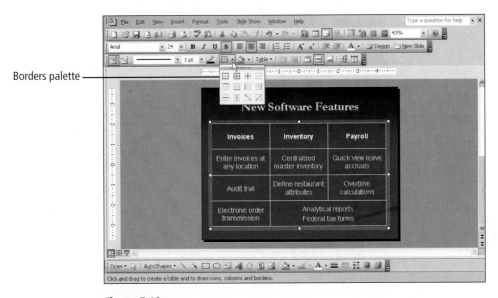

Figure 7.10

Alert!

Using the Borders Button

The Borders button and its ScreenTip reflect its most recent use. Clicking the button will apply the border indicated in the ScreenTip to your selection. The result of clicking the Borders button arrow, however, will always display the Borders palette, from which you can choose any of the border styles.

5 Point to each button in the Borders palette to read the ScreenTip and to familiarize yourself with the buttons. In the third row, click the third button—**Diagonal Down Border**.

Diagonal lines cut through each cell in the table.

6 If necessary, select the entire table by moving to the Tables and Borders toolbar, and then clicking Table . Click Select Table. On the Tables and Borders toolbar, click the **Borders button arrow** to display the Borders palette. In the first row, click the last button, **No Border**, to remove all of the borders from the table.

7 On the Tables and Borders toolbar, click the **Borders button arrow** . In the first row, click the second button—**All Borders**—to apply borders to the entire table.

8 On the Tables and Borders toolbar, click the **Border Width arrow** ⌈1 pt ▾⌋, and then click **3 pt**. On the Tables and Borders toolbar, click the **Borders button arrow** ⌈⊞ ▾⌋, and then click **Outside Borders** to apply the 3 pt. border to the outside of the table.

The Draw Table pencil pointer is still active.

9 In the first cell in the first row, point to the line that forms the cell's lower border, and then press and hold down the left mouse button. Notice that the border under the first cell displays as a dashed line. This indicates that the line is selected. Drag the Draw Table pencil pointer over the entire line, from the left edge of the table to the right edge of the table so that the entire line displays as a dashed line. See Figure 7.11. Release the mouse button.

The line is drawn as a 3 pt. black line; the current border width and style remain with the pencil pointer.

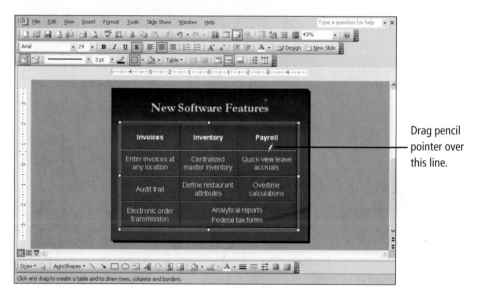

Drag pencil pointer over this line.

Figure 7.11

10 Click the **Draw Table** button ⌈◭⌋ to turn off the Draw Table pointer.

11 Point to the first cell in the first row of the table and drag the pointer to the right to select all three cells in the first row of the table.

12 On the Tables and Borders toolbar, click the **Fill Color button arrow** ⌈◇ ▾⌋ to display the color scheme. Click the fifth color, **blue**, to apply the blue color to the first row of cells. Click anywhere on the slide to cancel the selection.

13 On the menu bar, click the **Format** menu, and then click **Background**. Click to place a check mark in the **Omit background graphics from master** check box. Click **Apply**.

14 **Save** ⌈▣⌋ the file.

Objective 2
Create and Format Diagrams

Microsoft Office PowerPoint 2003 has six predefined *diagrams* that can be used to illustrate a concept or relationship. In the following activities, you will use the diagram feature to create a cycle diagram illustrating the weekly inventory reporting cycle at the local, regional, and corporate Oceana Palm Grill locations.

Activity 7.6 Creating a Continuous Cycle Diagram

A cycle diagram illustrates a continuous process—a sequence of actions that loops through the same cycle on an ongoing basis.

1 If necessary, open your file **7A_System_Firstname_Lastname** and display **Slide 2**.

2 On the Formatting toolbar, click **New Slide** [New Slide], and then in the **Slide Layout** task pane under **Other Layouts**, click **Title and Diagram or Organization Chart**. **Close** the task pane.

A new slide displays containing a title placeholder and a content placeholder.

3 Double-click the content placeholder to display the **Diagram Gallery** dialog box. See Figure 7.12.

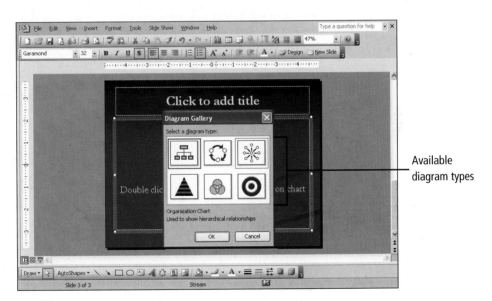

Available
diagram types

Figure 7.12

4 In the **Diagram Gallery** dialog box, click on each diagram and read the description that explains the purpose of the diagram. The table in Figure 7.13 summarizes the purpose of each diagram.

Description of Diagrams

Diagram Name	Icon	Purpose
Organization Chart		To show hierarchical relationships.
Cycle		To show a process with a continuous cycle.
Radial		To show relationships of a core element.
Pyramid		To show foundation-based relationships.
Venn		To show areas of overlap between elements.
Target		To show steps toward a goal.

Figure 7.13

5 In the first row, click the **Cycle Diagram** button and then click **OK**.

A cycle diagram with three arrows and three text boxes displays and the Diagram toolbar is either docked or is floating on the screen. The text box in the upper right area of the placeholder is selected. See Figure 7.14.

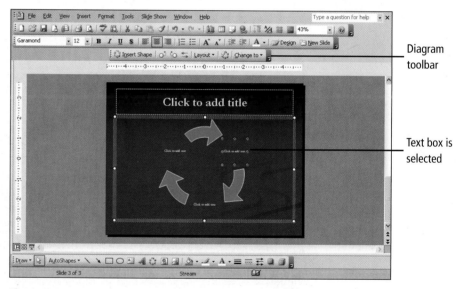

Diagram toolbar

Text box is selected

Figure 7.14

6 Type **Generate daily reports**

The text displays in the selected text box.

7 In the text box at the bottom of the diagram, click on the words *Click to add text* and type **Regional office compiles**

8 In the text box at the left of the diagram, click on the words *Click to add text* and in the text box type **Send to regional office** and then click outside of the placeholder to deselect it. Compare your diagram with Figure 7.15.

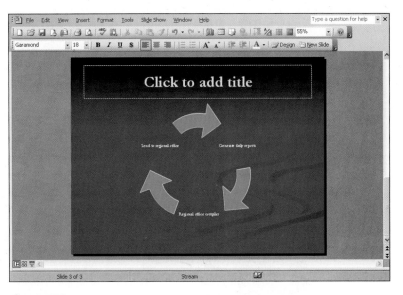

Figure 7.15

9 Click in the title placeholder and type **Current System Cycle**

10 **Save** 🔲 the file.

Activity 7.7 Formatting a Diagram

There is a selection of preformatted styles that can be applied to a diagram.

1 Select the diagram to display the Diagram toolbar—a pattern of dots surrounds the entire placeholder to indicate it is selected. On the

Diagram toolbar, click the **Reverse Diagram** button 🔲.

The arrows reverse direction and the boxes rotate counterclockwise one position. See Figure 7.16.

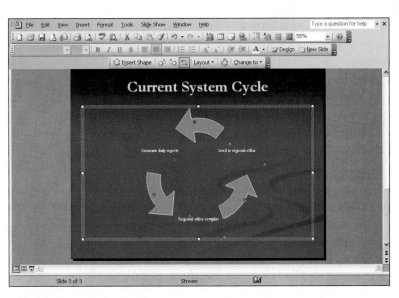

Figure 7.16

2 On the Diagram toolbar, click the **Reverse Diagram** button 🔲 again to return the diagram to its original configuration.

3 On the Diagram toolbar, click the **AutoFormat** button ⟳.

The Diagram Style Gallery dialog box displays. There are ten different styles that can be used for this diagram.

4 In the **Diagram Style Gallery** dialog box, under **Select a Diagram Style**, click on each style to see the style displayed in the preview window. After reviewing the style selections, click **Shaded**. See Figure 7.17.

Shaded style selected ────

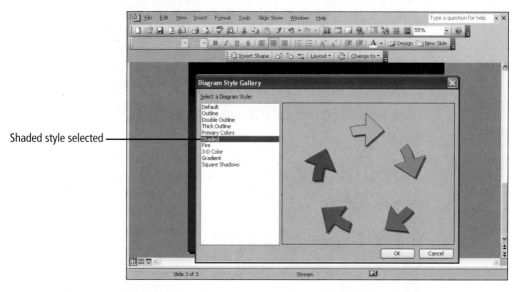

Figure 7.17

5 In the lower right corner of the dialog box, click **OK**.

The new style is applied to the diagram.

6 **Save** 🖫 the file.

Activity 7.8 Inserting and Moving a Shape

If the diagram does not have enough shapes to illustrate the concept or display the relationship, you can add more shapes. In a cycle diagram, the shape is inserted to the right of the shape that you select. You can also move the text boxes forward and backward in the diagram. Moving a text box does not affect the shapes. When you move a text box, the diagram shapes remain in place.

1 Click on the text *Send to regional office* to select the text box.

2 On the Diagram toolbar, click the **Insert Shape** button ⬚ Insert Shape ▾.

An arrow and text box are inserted, and the insertion point is blinking in the inserted text box.

3 Type **Weekly reports sent to corporate**

4 Click the **Send to regional office** text box to select it, and then on the Diagram toolbar, click the **Move Shape Backward** button ⟲.

To move a shape, first select it, and then click the Move Shape Forward or Move Shape Backward buttons. Each time you click one of these two directional buttons, the selected shape moves one position forward or back.

5 Press Shift and click on the text in each of the text boxes so that all four text boxes are selected. From the **Format** menu, click **AutoShape**, and then click the **Text Box tab**. Click the **Word wrap text in AutoShape** check box so that it is selected, and then click **OK**. On the Formatting toolbar, click the **Font Size arrow** 32 ▾, and then click **16**.

6 From the **Format** menu, click **Background**, and then select the **Omit background graphics from master** check box. Click **Apply**, click outside of the slide to deselect, and then compare your diagram with Figure 7.18.

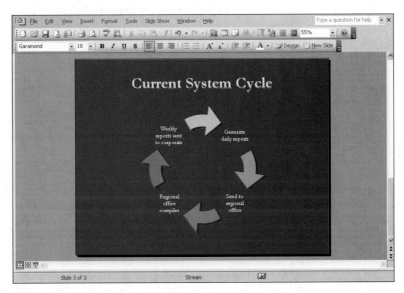

Figure 7.18

7 Formatting for the diagram is complete. On the Standard toolbar, click the **Save** button 🖫.

Objective 3
Create and Format Organization Charts

Organization charts show a graphical representation of the relationships among individuals in an organization. They show the levels of management and they outline to whom each person in the organization reports. They can also be used to show workflow within an organization.

Activity 7.9 Creating an Organization Chart

An organization chart consists of boxes that often include job titles and employee names, or job actions. Lines that indicate reporting levels or workflow connect these boxes. In this activity, you will create an organization chart that demonstrates the improved workflow of the new software system.

1 If necessary, open your file **7A_System_Firstname_Lastname** and display **Slide 3**. On the Formatting toolbar, click the **New Slide** button ![New Slide], and then in the task pane under **Other Layouts**, click **Title and Diagram or Organization Chart**. **Close** the task pane.

2 Click in the title placeholder and type **New Workflow**

3 Double-click the content placeholder to display the **Diagram Gallery** dialog box. The **Organization Chart** is selected. Click **OK**.

The slide displays a simple organization chart that includes two levels in the hierarchy—a superior position box at the top and three subordinate position boxes below. The text boxes are filled with the design template Fills scheme color, and the Organization Chart toolbar floats on the screen. The superior box is selected. See Figure 7.19.

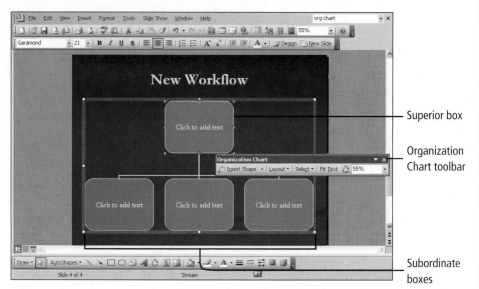

Figure 7.19

4 If necessary, drag the Organization Chart toolbar so that it is docked below the Formatting toolbar.

5 Press and hold down Shift and click each of the boxes in the organization chart so that they are all selected—check to be sure that you did not deselect the top box. On the menu bar, click **Format**, and then click **AutoShape**. Click the **Text Box tab**, and then select the **Word wrap text in AutoShape** check box. Click **OK**, and then click anywhere on the slide to deselect the boxes.

By selecting the Word wrap text in AutoShape check box, text that you type that extends outside the organization chart boxes will wrap to the next line.

6 Click in the box at the top of the organization chart and type **Point of Entry**

7 In the second row of boxes, click in the left most text box and type **Sent immediately to regional**

8 Click in the center box and type **Immediately updates inventory**

9 Click in the last box, and then click its outer edge so that the small circles containing x's surround the box. See Figure 7.20.

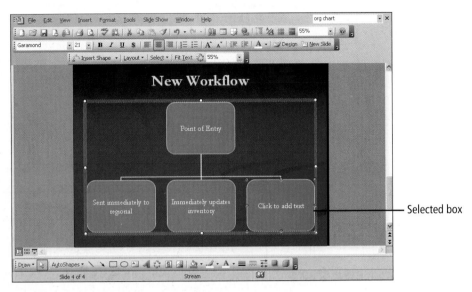

Selected box

Figure 7.20

10 Press Delete.

The box is deleted and the three remaining boxes are resized.

11 Save 🖫 the file.

Activity 7.10 Adding Organization Chart Elements

In this activity you will add two subordinate boxes to complete the workflow chart.

1 Click anywhere in the *Sent immediately to regional* box. On the Organization Chart toolbar, click the **Insert Shape** button 🔲 Insert Shape ▾ .

When you click the Insert Shape button, a subordinate box is inserted below the selected box.

2 Click in the box that you just inserted and type **Corporate office updated daily**

3 Click after the word *office* and press Enter to move the words *updated daily* to the second line.

Note — Wrapping Text

Recall that in the Text Box tab of the Format AutoShape dialog box, the Word wrap text in AutoShape check box will wrap the text to the next line. However, if the check box is selected in this instance, only the word *daily* wraps to the next line, giving the box an unbalanced appearance.

---

4 If necessary, click in the *Corporate office updated daily* box. On the Organization Chart toolbar, click the **Insert Shape button arrow** [Insert Shape ▼] to display the three shape options, and then click **Coworker**. See Figure 7.21.

A new box is inserted on the same level as the selected box. When you click the Insert Shape button arrow, you can choose which of the three types of boxes that you would like to insert.

Click the arrow. ——

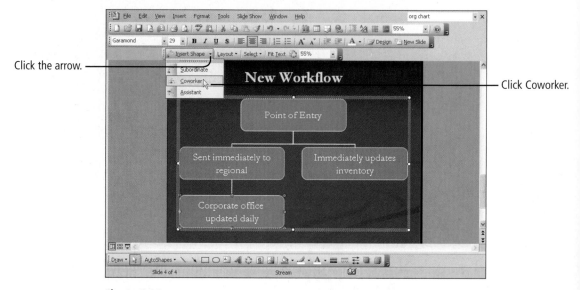

—— Click Coworker.

Figure 7.21

5 On the Standard toolbar, click **Undo** [↺ ▼] to remove the box that you inserted.

6 Click the *Immediately updates inventory* box, and then click the **Insert Shape** button [Insert Shape ▼] to insert a box below the selected box. Click in the new box and type **Generates daily report**

7 **Save** [💾] the file.

Activity 7.11 Changing the Organization Chart Layout

Organization charts are composed of branches and levels. A ***branch*** refers to boxes connected vertically and a ***level*** refers to boxes connected horizontally. You can change the way in which the branches and levels display by changing the organization chart layout.

1 Click the **Point of Entry** box, and then on the Organization Chart toolbar, click the **Layout** button [Layout ▼]. Be sure that the **Auto Layout** button is highlighted, and then click **Left Hanging**.

Each of the four boxes displays below and to the left of the Point of Entry box. Notice that there are still two boxes connected to the Point of Entry box and each of those boxes has a subordinate box.

2 With the **Point of Entry** box still selected, click the **Layout** button Layout ▾ . Click **Standard** to change the organization chart back to the default.

3 **Save** 🖫 the file.

Activity 7.12 Formatting an Organization Chart

After you have created an organization chart, you can format the chart by changing the fill colors and border styles and colors for the text boxes. You can also change the style and color for the lines that connect the boxes.

1 Click in the **Point of Entry** box, and then on the Organization Chart toolbar, click the **Select** button Select ▾ . Click **Branch**. See Figure 7.22.

All of the boxes in the organization chart are selected because they are all connected vertically to the highest-level box.

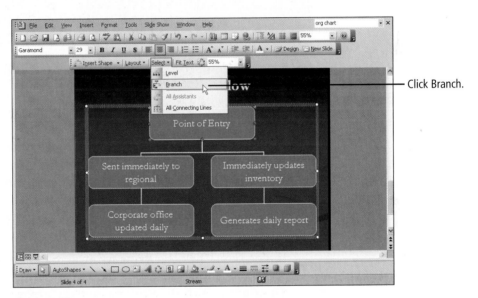

— Click Branch.

Figure 7.22

2 On the Formatting toolbar, click the **Bold** button **B** .

Bold is applied to the text in each box.

3 With all of the boxes still selected, on the Drawing toolbar, click the **Line Color button arrow** ✏▾ , and then click the third color—**black**.

Click the **Shadow Style** button ▦ , and then in the fourth row, click the second shadow—**Shadow Style 14**.

Each box is bordered and shadowed.

4 On the Organization Chart toolbar, click the **Select** button Select ▾ , and then click **All Connecting Lines**.

Each of the connector lines is selected.

5 On the Drawing toolbar, click the **Line Color button arrow** 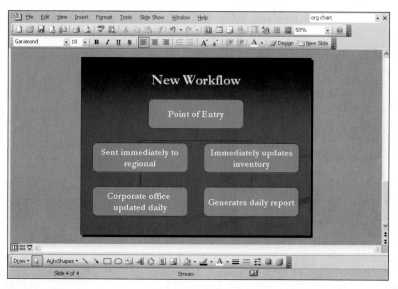, and then click the third color—**black**. Click anywhere on the slide so that the organization chart is not selected.

All of the connector lines are black. Compare your chart with Figure 7.23.

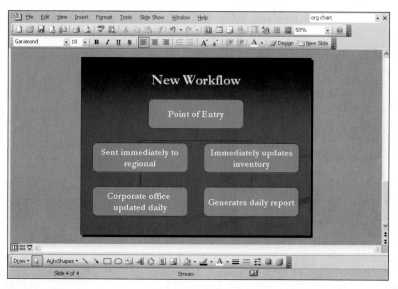

Figure 7.23

6 On the **View** menu, click **Header and Footer**, and then click the **Notes and Handouts tab**. Create a header for the notes and handouts that includes the date updated automatically and a footer with the text **7A System-Firstname Lastname** Clear all other header and footer options, and then click **Apply to All**.

7 **Save** the file. From the **File** menu, click **Print** to display the **Print** dialog box. Click the **Print what arrow**, and then click **Handouts**. Click the **Color/grayscale arrow**, and then click **Grayscale**. Under **Handouts**, click the **Slides per page arrow**, and then click **4**. Click the **Horizontal** option button. Click **OK**. Close the file and exit PowerPoint.

End You have completed Project 7A

Project 7B **Chart**

A chart visually represents numerical information. There are a number of charts that you can create to present different types of information. For example, you can use a bar or column chart to compare data, you can use a line chart to show trends over time, and you can create a pie chart to show percentage of parts to a whole.

In Activities 7.13 through 7.19, you will format a presentation that contains a column chart and a pie chart. Your completed presentation will look similar to Figure 7.24. You will save your presentation as *7B_Chart_ Firstname_Lastname.*

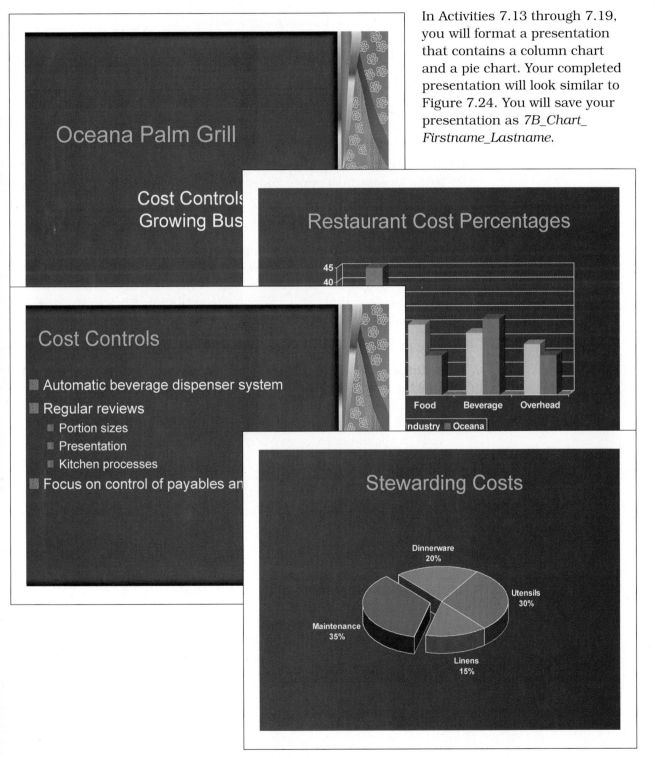

Figure 7.24
Project 7B—Chart

Objective 4
Create and Modify a Column Chart

To create a chart, you can change the layout of the slide to a Title and Chart layout, and then double-click the chart placeholder to activate *Microsoft Graph*. Microsoft Graph is a *shared application*, available to all of the applications in the Microsoft Office suite. When you create a chart using Microsoft Graph, the Microsoft Graph toolbar and menus replace the PowerPoint toolbars and menus.

Activity 7.13 Creating a Column Chart

In this activity you will create a column chart that compares industry cost percentages to Oceana Palm Grill cost percentages.

1 From your student files, **Open** the file **p07B_Chart**. In your storage location for this chapter, save the file as **7B_Chart_Firstname_Lastname**

2 On the Formatting toolbar, click **New Slide** New Slide, and then in the **Slide Layout** task pane, under **Other Layouts**, click **Title and Chart**. **Close** the task pane.

A new Slide 2 is created.

3 From the **Format** menu, click **Background**. Select the **Omit background graphics from master** check box, and then click **Apply** so that the graphic on the right side of the slide does not interfere with the chart that you will create on this slide. Click in the title placeholder and type **Restaurant Cost Percentages**

4 Double-click the chart placeholder to activate Microsoft Graph.

A *datasheet* window displays containing data from which a sample chart is generated. The default chart that is created is a 3-D Column chart displayed on the slide. The datasheet consists of columns and rows that intersect to form cells. You can enter your data into the cells in the datasheet and Microsoft Graph will update the chart. In addition to the datasheet and sample chart that display, the Standard and Formatting toolbars include additional Microsoft Graph buttons and the menu bar displays with options that can be used to format and edit the chart. See Figure 7.25.

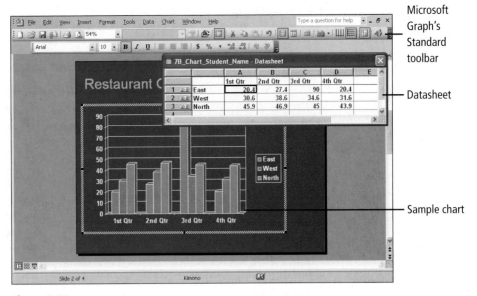

Microsoft Graph's Standard toolbar

Datasheet

Sample chart

Figure 7.25

Alert!

Are Your Toolbars Sharing One Row?

If the Standard and Formatting toolbars are sharing one row, you may not be able to view the additional Microsoft Graph buttons on the Standard toolbar. To separate the toolbars, on the Formatting or Standard toolbar, click the Toolbar Options button ▌, and then click show Buttons on Two Rows.

---

5 In the **Datasheet**, click in the cell that contains the text *1st Qtr.* Type **Industry** and then press Tab to move the insertion point to the cell that contains the text *2nd Qtr.* Type **Oceana**

6 Click in the cell that contains the word *East.* Type **Labor** and then press Enter.

The insertion point moves down one cell.

7 Type **Food** and then press Enter. Type **Beverage** and then press Enter. Type **Overhead** and then press Enter.

The labels for the datasheet are complete. Notice that the *Labor* row does not display and that the sample values must be changed. Additionally, the *3rd* and *4th Qtr* columns must be deleted.

8 At the top of the datasheet, point to the gray box containing the letter *C*. Press and hold down the left mouse button and drag to the right to select **columns C and D**. Point anywhere in the selected columns, right-click to display the shortcut menu as shown in Figure 7.26, and then click **Delete**.

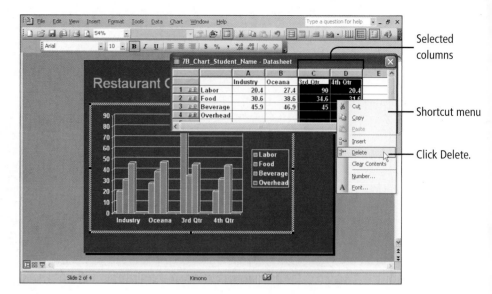

Selected columns

Shortcut menu

Click Delete.

Figure 7.26

9 Press and hold down Ctrl, and then press Home to move the insertion point to the cell containing the value 20.4. Type **35** and then press Enter. Continue to replace the data in the datasheet with the numbers shown in Figure 7.27.

Notice that as you type each number, the bars in the chart are updated to reflect the new data. When you are finished entering the data, a chart comparing four sets of data—*Labor, Food, Beverage,* and *Overhead*—for two of the categories *Industry* and *Oceana* is created. The data is charted according to the rows of data so that the column headings display at the bottom of the chart, identifying the categories you are comparing.

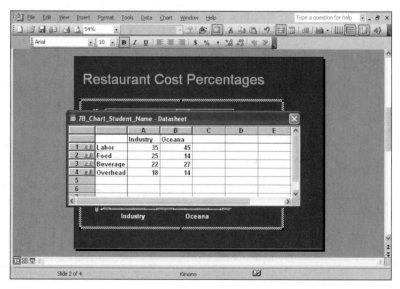

Figure 7.27

10 On the Chart toolbar, click **By Column** ▥.

The chart is rearranged so that the data is charted with the row headings displaying at the bottom of the chart.

More Knowledge — Expanding Column Width in a Datasheet

When you enter text in a datasheet, the column may not be wide enough to accommodate the text. You can widen a column by clicking anywhere in the column, clicking the Format menu, and then clicking Column Width. In the Column width dialog box, you can enter a number or you can click Best Fit. Best Fit widens the column to accommodate the text in the cell in which the insertion point is positioned.

11 On the datasheet title bar, click **Close** ✕.

The datasheet window is closed.

12 Click anywhere on the slide outside of the chart placeholder.

The chart displays within the PowerPoint window and the Microsoft Graph toolbars are closed.

13 **Save** 🖫 the file.

Activity 7.14 Modifying Chart Options

When a chart is created, a **data marker**, such as a bar, a line, or a pie slice, represents a single value in the datasheet. When a column chart is created, a **legend** displays to the right of the chart to identify each data series. The Chart Options command allows you to modify the legend by changing its placement. You can also add a chart title, or a title to the **value axis** or to the **category axis**. In a column chart, the value axis is the vertical axis and contains the incremental data values. The category axis is the horizontal axis and contains the names of the categories that are being charted. In this activity, you will move the legend so that it displays below the chart, and you will add a value axis title to the chart.

1 Point to the chart, and then double-click to activate Microsoft Graph.

The Microsoft Graph toolbars and menu bar display.

2 To change the placement of the legend, on the menu bar click **Chart**, and then click **Chart Options**. Click the **Legend tab**, and then click **Bottom**.

3 To add a value-axis title, click the **Titles tab**, and then click in the **Value (Z) axis box**. Type **Percentage** and then click **OK**. Click in the upper left corner of the chart placeholder so that the *Percentage* title is not selected, and then compare your slide with Figure 7.28.

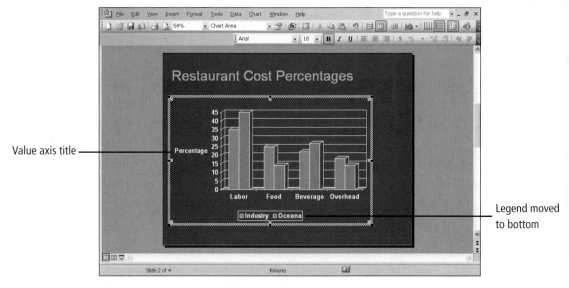

Value axis title

Legend moved
to bottom

Figure 7.28

4 Save 🖫 the file.

Activity 7.15 Formatting Chart Elements

When a chart is displayed in Microsoft Graph, various chart elements can be modified and formatted. These chart elements include the legend, plot area, chart walls, chart area, titles, data markers, and the category and value axes. Figure 7.29 identifies the location of each of these chart elements.

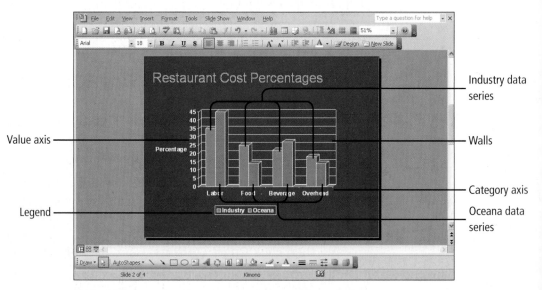

Value axis

Legend

Industry data
series

Walls

Category axis

Oceana data
series

Figure 7.29

1 If necessary, double-click the chart to activate Microsoft Graph and close the datasheet. Point anywhere on the chart and notice the ScreenTip that displays.

As you move your pointer around within a chart, a ScreenTip displays indicating the area of the chart to which you are pointing. When the ScreenTip for the chart element that you want to format displays, you can click the left mouse button to select the chart element. Then you can access the context-sensitive Format menu. Recall that a menu command or button that is context-sensitive *changes* based on what is selected. In this manner, Microsoft Graph attempts to anticipate which commands to make available to you.

2 Click the value axis title *Percentage* to select it. On the menu bar, click **Format**, and then click **Selected Axis Title**. Click the **Alignment tab**.

In this dialog box, you can change the text orientation so that it displays vertically.

Another Way ── **To Format a Chart Element**

You can access the Format command for any chart element by double-clicking the chart element that you want to format. Or you can right-click the element and from the shortcut menu, click Format Element Name.

---

3 Under **Orientation**, point to the red diamond. Press and hold down the left mouse button and drag up so that the red diamond is at the top of the Orientation box, and *90* displays in the **Degrees** box. See Figure 7.30. Click **OK** and notice that the title displays vertically.

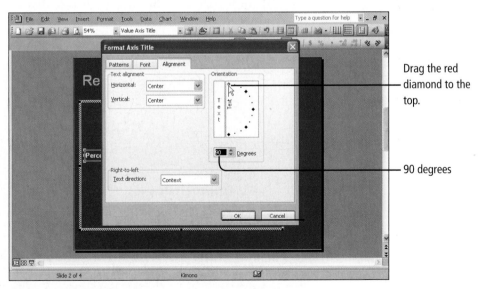

Drag the red diamond to the top.

90 degrees

Figure 7.30

4 Point to the lavender column data marker in the **Labor** category so that the ScreenTip *Series "Industry" Point "Labor" Value: 35* displays. See Figure 7.31, and then click the left mouse button.

Notice that all of the lavender column data markers are selected, indicating that the formatting that you choose will be applied to all of the selected data markers.

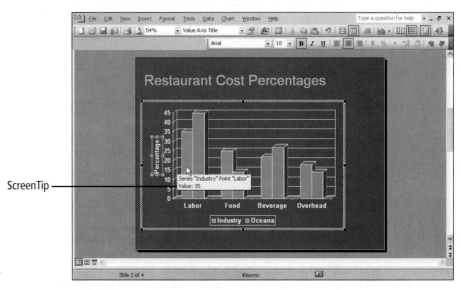

Figure 7.31

5 On the menu bar, click **Format**, and then click **Selected Data Series**. If necessary, click the **Patterns tab**. Under **Area**, in the fourth row, click the second color—**gold**. Under **Border**, click **None**. Compare your dialog box with Figure 7.32, and then click **OK**.

The first data marker in each series displays in gold, as does the Industry series in the legend.

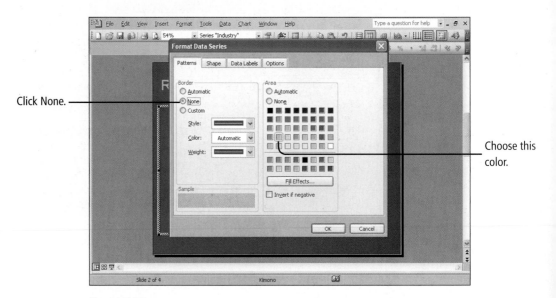

Figure 7.32

6 Point to the dark pink data marker in the **Labor** category so that the ScreenTip *Series "Oceana" Point "Labor" Value: 45* displays, and then click the left mouse button to select all of the dark pink data markers. On the menu bar, click **Format**, and then click **Selected Data Series**. Under **Border**, click **None**, and then click **OK**.

The border is removed from each of the selected data markers.

7 Double-click the legend to open the **Format Legend** dialog box. Click the **Patterns tab**, and then under **Border**, select the **Shadow** check box. Click **OK**.

8 Click anywhere on the slide outside of the chart placeholder to close Microsoft Graph and return to PowerPoint. Click in the title placeholder, and on the Formatting toolbar, click the **Center** button ▤.

Notice that the slide title and the chart are positioned on the left side of the slide. To center the title and chart, use the Align or Distribute command.

9 Click the title placeholder, and then press and hold down Shift and click the chart so that both objects are selected. On the Drawing toolbar, click the **Draw** menu, and then point to **Align or Distribute**. Click **Relative to Slide** so that it is selected.

10 On the Drawing toolbar, click the **Draw** menu, and then point to **Align or Distribute**. Click **Align Center**.

The title and chart are centered on the slide.

11 Click outside of the chart to deselect. **Save** ▤ the file.

Activity 7.16 Animating a Chart

A chart can be introduced in a slide show all at one time, or by data series, or by category.

1 Display **Slide 2**, and then click once on the chart to select it.

2 On the menu bar, click **Slide Show**, and then click **Custom Animation** to display the Custom Animation task pane. Click **Add Effect**, and then point to **Entrance**. Click **More Effects**, and then under **Basic**, click **Split**. Click **OK**.

3 In the **custom animation list**, click the **item 1 arrow**, and then click **Effect Options**. Click the **Chart Animation tab**.

In this dialog box, you can modify how the chart elements display. The default setting—*As one object*—will display the entire chart at one time.

4 Click the **Group chart arrow**, and then click **By category**. If necessary, click to select the Animate grid and legend check box so that the grid and legend display after the slide is introduced. Click the **Timing tab**, and then click the **Start arrow**. Click **After Previous**, and then click **OK**.

View the animation and notice that the data markers display by categories, from the left to the right.

5 Close the task pane, and then **Save** ▤ the file.

Objective 5
Create and Modify a Pie Chart

A pie chart is used to illustrate percentages or proportions, and includes only one series of data. Many of the formatting options that you applied to a 3-D Column chart are also available in a 3-D Pie chart. For example, you can change the color of a data marker, and you can add and format titles. Pie charts usually do not contain a legend. Instead, data labels are usually displayed next to the individual pie slices that identify the slice and the amount that the slice represents.

Activity 7.17 Changing the Chart Type

After you create a chart, you may change your mind and decide to use a different chart type. It is not necessary to recreate the chart. In this activity, you will change a line chart to a pie chart.

1 If necessary, **Open** 📇 your file **7B_Chart_Firstname_Lastname**, and display **Slide 4**.

Slide 4 contains a line chart with the various types of stewarding costs for the Oceana Palm Grill. Recall that a line chart is better suited to show trends over time. The data in this chart shows the amount that each cost contributes to the total cost, and thus would be easier to interpret if formatted as a pie chart.

2 Double-click the chart to open Microsoft Graph. Close ❌ the datasheet.

3 On the Chart toolbar, click the **Chart Type button arrow** 📊▾. In the fifth row, click the second chart—**3-D Pie Chart**. See Figure 7.33.

A 3-D Pie chart displays. The chart plot area is surrounded by a solid white border.

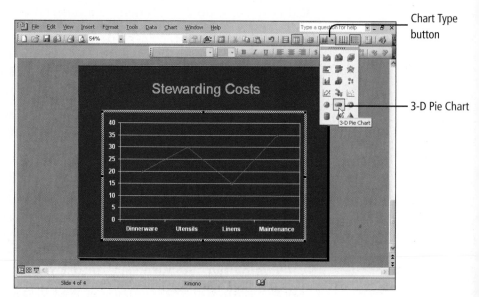

Figure 7.33

4 Point slightly inside the white plot area border so that the ScreenTip *Plot Area* displays. Double-click to display the **Format Plot Area** dialog box. Alternatively, click the Plot Area once to select it, click the Format menu, and then click Selected Plot Area.

5 Under **Border**, click **None**, and then click **OK**.

The white border is removed from the plot area.

6 **Save** 🖫 the file.

Activity 7.18 Adding Data Labels

A well-constructed pie chart does not include a legend. Instead, *data labels* that align next to each pie slice are used to identify each slice. The data labels in a pie chart may include a label and a percentage or a value. Percentages represent the proportion of each slice to the whole amount of the pie. Values are the actual numbers entered in the datasheet. In this activity, you will add a label and percentage data labels to the pie chart.

1 If Microsoft Graph is not active, double-click the pie chart to activate it now.

2 On the menu bar, click **Chart**, and then click **Chart Options**. Click the **Data Labels tab**. Under **Label Contains**, click to select the **Category name** and **Percentage** check boxes. If necessary, *clear* the Legend key and Show leader lines check boxes. Click the **Legend tab**, and then clear the **Show legend** check box. Click **OK**.

Each slice of the pie is identified by category name and the associated percentage displays. One or more of your labels may wrap to two lines.

3 Point to one of the data labels and click the left mouse button.

Notice that sizing handles surround each set of data labels, indicating that all of the labels are selected. With all of the labels selected, you can apply formatting that affects every label. See Figure 7.34.

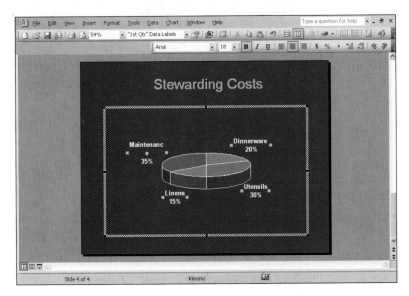

Figure 7.34

Selecting Data Labels

If all of the data labels are not selected, you may have inadvertently double-clicked one of the labels. Click on another chart element, and then try again.

4 On the Formatting toolbar, click the **Font Size arrow** `32 ▾`, and then click **16**.

All of the data labels are resized.

5 **Save** 💾 the file.

Activity 7.19 Rotating, Elevating, and Exploding a 3-D Pie Chart

A 3-D Pie chart can be rotated and elevated to change the way in which the chart is viewed. Additionally, the slices of a 3-D Pie chart can be pulled out from the chart—**exploded**—to draw attention to the exploded piece.

1 If necessary, double-click the chart to display the chart menu and toolbars.

2 On the menu bar, click **Chart**, and then click **3-D View**. In the **Elevation** box, type **30** Press ⊤ab to move the insertion point to the **Rotation** box. Type **320** and then click **OK**.

Notice that the *Linens* slice is rotated to the front of the chart, and that the chart appears to be tilted forward.

3 Click once on the chart so that a sizing handle displays on each slice of the pie. Point to the Maintenance slice, and then click the left mouse button to select only that slice.

Opening the Format Data Point Dialog Box

In a pie chart, you *cannot* double-click a slice to select it. Doing so opens the Format Data Point dialog box. You must first click to select the entire pie, and then click the individual slice that you want to select.

4 Point to the **Maintenance** slice, and press and hold down the left mouse button. Drag the pointer a small distance to the left to explode the slice from the rest of the pie. See Figure 7.35. Release the mouse button.

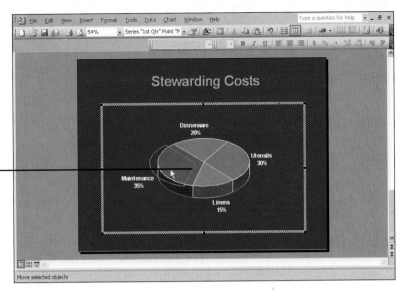

Drag to explode the slice.

Figure 7.35

5 Click anywhere outside of the slide to return to PowerPoint. On the menu bar, click the **Slide Show** menu, and then click **Slide Transition**. In the task pane, under **Apply to selected slides**, click **Box In**. Under **Modify transition**, click the **Speed arrow**, and then click **Slow**. Click **Apply to All Slides**. Close the task pane, and then display **Slide 1**. Click **Slide Show** 🖵 to view your slide presentation.

6 On the **View** menu, click **Header and Footer**, and then click the **Notes and Handouts tab**. Create a header for the notes and handouts that includes the date updated automatically and a footer with the text **7B Chart-Firstname Lastname** Clear all other header and footer options, and then click **Apply to All**.

7 **Save** 🖫 the file. From the **File** menu, click **Print** to display the **Print** dialog box. Click the **Print what arrow**, and then click **Handouts**. Click the **Color/grayscale arrow**, and then click **Grayscale**. Under **Handouts**, click the **Slides per page arrow**, and then click **4**. Click the **Horizontal** option button. Click **OK**. Close the file and exit PowerPoint.

End **You have completed Project 7B** ──────────

Summary

In this chapter, you practiced how to develop charts, graphs, and diagrams, which can help an audience understand numeric data and trends just as clip art can help illustrate a concept. As you saw, PowerPoint lets you create a number of chart types easily and quickly.

You practiced how to develop line charts, which show changes over time, or trends. You practiced column charts, which are used to show comparisons among various types of data. Pie charts show proportions—the parts of a whole. Organizational charts show the relationships among people in an organization and are also used to show work organization. Managers may create draft charts to view possible new structures just as they would create draft documents before publishing a final version.

Within PowerPoint, you can insert diagrams. For example, a Venn diagram shows areas of overlap between and among elements. You practiced inserting a cycle diagram, which shows a process that has a continuous cycle. Other types of diagrams include a pyramid, which demonstrates foundation-based relationships; a target diagram, which shows steps toward a goal; and a radial diagram, which shows relationships of elements to a core element.

In This Chapter You Practiced How To

- Create a Table
- Create and Format Diagrams
- Create and Format Organization Charts
- Create and Modify a Column Chart
- Create and Modify a Pie Chart

Concepts Assessments

Matching Match each term in the second column with its correct definition in the first column by writing the letter of the term on the blank line in front of the correct definition.

_____ **1.** The intersection of a column and a row in a table or datasheet.

_____ **2.** A spreadsheet containing data from which a sample chart is generated.

_____ **3.** A chart element consisting of a box that defines the patterns and colors that are assigned to the data series or categories in a chart.

_____ **4.** A chart that presents a picture of the relationships of people in an organization.

_____ **5.** A format for information that organizes and presents text and numbers in columns and rows.

_____ **6.** Text used to identify the labels, values, or percentages in a chart and that display above or next to a data marker.

_____ **7.** A type of diagram that illustrates a continuous process.

_____ **8.** A shared application used to create graphs.

_____ **9.** A software application available to other applications in the Microsoft Office suite including PowerPoint, Word, Excel, and Access.

_____ **10.** A marker such as a bar, a line, or a pie slice that represents a single value in the datasheet.

_____ **11.** In a column or bar chart, the vertical axis that contains incremental data values.

_____ **12.** In a column or bar chart, the horizontal axis that contains the names of the categories that are being charted.

_____ **13.** The placement of text between the top and bottom edges in a table.

_____ **14.** A command that activates a special pencil-shaped pointer to draw rows and columns in a new or existing table.

_____ **15.** A type of chart used to illustrate a concept or relationship.

A Category axis

B Cell

C Cycle diagram

D Data labels

E Data marker

F Datasheet

G Diagram

H Draw Table

I Legend

J Microsoft Graph

K Organization chart

L Shared application

M Table

N Value axis

O Vertical alignment

Fill in the Blank Write the correct answer in the space provided.

1. A type of diagram used to show foundation-based relationships is a _____ diagram.

2. To draw rows and columns in a table, click the _____ button on the Tables and Borders toolbar.

3. In a column chart, the horizontal axis containing the names of the categories that are being charted is the _____.

4. In a column chart, the vertical axis containing the incremental data values is the _____.

5. To remove lines in a table, and to merge two separate cells into one cell, click the _____ button or the _____ button on the Tables and Borders toolbar.

6. To show trends over time, use a _____ chart.

7. The two types of charts that can be used effectively to show comparisons are a _____ chart or a _____ chart.

8. To show percentages or proportions, use a _____ chart.

9. When entering text in a table, press the _____ key to move from cell to cell.

10. A type of diagram used to show overlap of elements is a _____ diagram.

Project 7C—Acquisition

Objectives: *Create a Table and Create and Format Diagrams.*

In the following Skill Assessment, you will format a presentation regarding research that the Oceana Palm Grill Finance Department is conducting on the acquisition of another restaurant chain. Your completed presentation will look similar to Figure 7.36. You will save your presentation as *7C_Acquisition_Firstname_Lastname.*

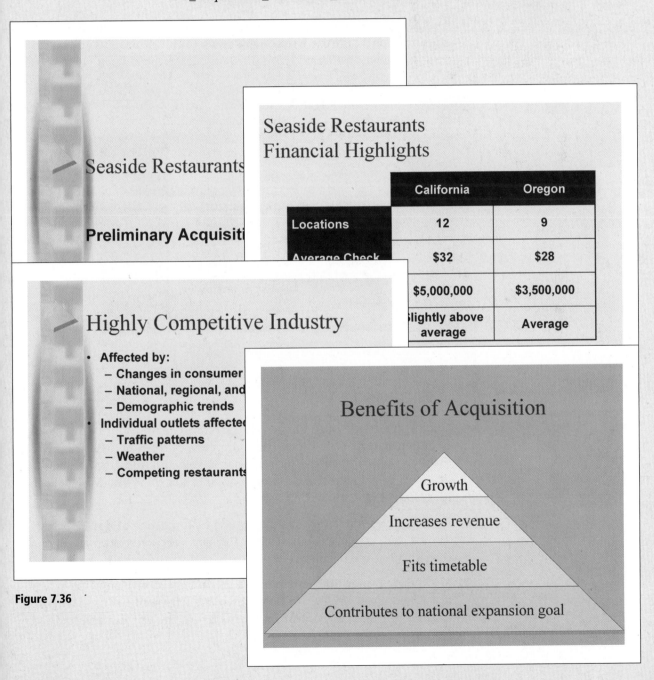

Figure 7.36

(Project 7C–Acquisition continues on the next page)

(Project 7C–Acquisition continued)

1. From your student files, open the file **p07C_Acquisition**. **Save** the file in your storage location as 7C_Acquisition_Firstname_Lastname

2. On the Formatting toolbar, click the **New Slide** button. In the task pane, under **Other Layouts**, click **Title and Table** to create a new Slide 2. Close the task pane.

3. Click in the title placeholder, type **Seaside Restaurants** and then press Enter. Type **Financial Highlights**

4. Double-click the table placeholder, and increase the **Number of columns** to **3** and the **Number of rows** to **5**. Click **OK**. Type the table text as shown in Figure 7.37, pressing Tab to move from cell to cell.

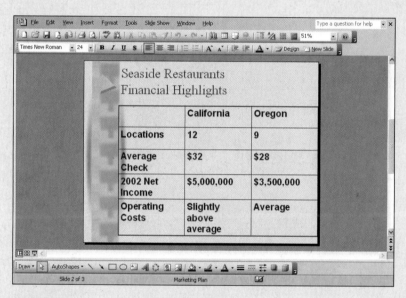

Figure 7.37

5. Click the outside edge of the table so that the boundary box displays as a pattern of dots. Recall that when the pattern of dots displays, all of the text within the placeholder is selected and can be formatted at one time. On the Formatting toolbar, click the **Font Size arrow**, and then click **24**.

6. With the boundary box still displayed as a pattern of dots, on the Tables and Borders toolbar, click **Center Vertically** so that all of the text in the table is centered vertically within the cells.

7. Move the pointer above **column 2** so that the down-pointing black arrow displays. Press and hold down the left mouse button and drag to the right to select **columns 2 and 3**. On the Formatting toolbar, click **Center**.

(Project 7C–Acquisition continues on the next page)

(Project 7C–Acquisition continued)

8. On the Tables and Borders toolbar, click the **Eraser** button. Point to the line above the blank, upper left cell and click to erase the line. In the same cell, point to the line at the left edge of the cell and click to erase the line. The upper left blank cell no longer displays. Press Esc to turn off the Eraser.

9. Select the cells that contain the text *California* and *Oregon*. On the Tables and Borders toolbar, click the **Fill Color button arrow**. Click the second color—**dark blue**. With the cells still selected, on the Formatting toolbar, click the **Font Color button arrow**. Click the first color—**light blue**.

10. Select the four cells in the first column. Apply the same **Fill Color** and **Font Color** as you did to the *California* and *Oregon* cells.

11. On the **Format** menu, click **Background**. Click **Omit background graphics from master**, and then click **Apply** so that the graphic on the left side of the slide does not display.

12. Point to the table border so that the move pointer displays, and then drag the table to the left and visually center it on the slide. Point to the title placeholder so that the move pointer displays, and then drag the title to the left so that its left edge touches the left edge of the slide. **Save** the file.

13. Display **Slide 3**. On the Formatting toolbar, click the **New Slide** button. In the task pane, under **Other Layouts**, click **Title and Diagram or Organization Chart**. Close the task pane. Click in the title placeholder and type **Benefits of Acquisition**

14. On the **Format** menu, click **Background**. Click **Omit background graphics from master**, and then click **Apply** so that the graphic on the left side of the slide does not display.

15. Double-click the diagram placeholder, and then click the **Pyramid Diagram**. Click **OK** to create the pyramid diagram. Zoom in as necessary to view the text that you type. With the shape at the top of the pyramid selected, press Enter twice, and then type **Growth**

16. Click in the middle shape and type **Fits timetable** and then click in the last shape and type **Contributes to national expansion goal**

17. Click in the top shape, and on the Diagram toolbar, click **Insert Shape**. Type **Increases revenue**

18. Click the diagram boundary box so that a pattern of dots displays. On the Formatting toolbar, click the **Font Size arrow**, and then click **24**. Notice that the text extends outside of the diagram.

(Project 7C–Acquisition continues on the next page)

(Project 7C–Acquisition continued)

19. On the Diagram toolbar, click the **Layout** button, and then click **Fit Diagram to Contents**. Notice that the boundary box tightly encloses the diagram; now you can expand the diagram using the sizing handles.

20. Drag the left and the right center sizing handles so that the diagram boundary box extends to the left and the right edges of the slide. Drag the bottom center sizing handle down so that the diagram boundary box extends to the bottom of the slide.

21. On the Diagram toolbar, click the **AutoFormat** button. Click **Shaded**, and then click **OK**.

22. Click in the title placeholder and drag the center left sizing handle so that it extends to the left edge of the slide. **Center** the title. On the **Format** menu, click **Background**, and then click the **Background Fill arrow**. Click the last color—**blue**. Click **Apply**.

23. On the menu bar, click **Slide Show**, and then click **Slide Transition**. Apply the **Wheel Clockwise, 4 Spokes** transition to all of the slides. Display **Slide 1** and view the slide show.

24. Create a header and footer for the notes and handouts that includes the date updated automatically and a footer with the text **7C Acquisition-Firstname Lastname** Clear all other header and footer options and click **Apply to All**.

25. **Save** the file, and then print the presentation as **grayscale handouts**, **4** slides per page in **horizontal** order. Close the file.

 End You have completed Project 7C ——————————————

Skill Assessments (continued)

Project 7D—Pension

Objectives: *Create and Format Organization Charts and Create and Modify a Pie Chart.*

In the following Skill Assessment, you will format a presentation that provides information about the Oceana Palm Grill pension plan. Your completed presentation will look similar to Figure 7.38. You will save your presentation as *7D_Pension_Firstname_Lastname.*

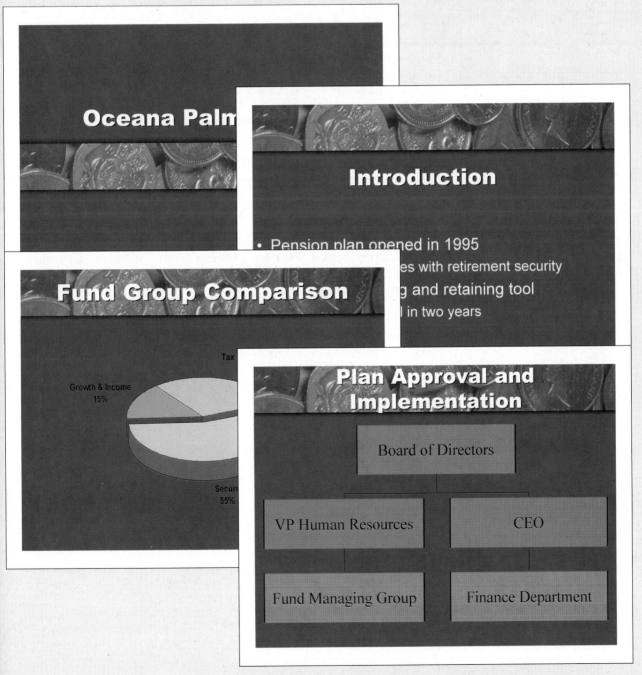

Figure 7.38

(Project 7D–Pension continues on the next page)

(Project 7D–Pension continued)

1. From your student files, open the file **p07D_Pension**. **Save** the file as 7D_Pension_Firstname_Lastname

2. Display **Slide 2**. On the Formatting toolbar, click the **New Slide** button. In the task pane, under **Other Layouts**, click **Title and Chart**. Close the task pane. Click in the title placeholder and type **Fund Group Comparison**

3. Double-click the chart placeholder to open the datasheet. In the displayed datasheet, click in the *East* cell, type **Secure** and then press Enter to move down one cell. Type **Growth & Income** and then press Enter. Notice that all of the text does not display in the cell. Click in the *Growth & Income* cell, from the **Format** menu click **Column Width**, and then click **Best Fit**.

4. Click in the *North* cell, type **Tax Protection** and then click in the *1st Qtr* cell. Type **Percent** and then press Enter. Type **55** and then press Enter. Type **15** and then press Enter. Type **30**

5. In the gray column heading boxes at the top of the datasheet, point to the letter **B**. Press and hold down the mouse button and drag to the right to select **columns B**, **C**, and **D**. Press Delete, and then close the datasheet.

6. On the Chart toolbar, click **By Column** so that the data series is charted by columns rather than rows. On the Chart toolbar, click the **Chart Type button arrow**, and then in the fifth row, click the second chart—**3-D Pie Chart**—to change the chart type.

7. The pie chart that you created includes a legend, although a pie chart usually uses data labels rather than a legend. Click the legend to select it. Press Delete to remove the legend from the chart. Alternatively, on the Standard toolbar, click the Legend button to turn the legend off.

8. To identify each slice of the pie, from the **Chart** menu, click **Chart Options**, and then click the **Data Labels tab**. Under **Label Contains**, click **Category name** and **Percentage**. Clear the **Show leader lines** check box, and then click **OK**. The data labels identify each slice.

9. Click on one of the data labels so that all three of the data labels are selected. Change the **Font** to **Arial Narrow**.

10. Point to the thin black line border that surrounds the chart so that the *Plot Area* ScreenTip displays. Double-click to open the **Format Plot Area** dialog box. Under **Border**, click **None**, and then click **OK**.

11. Click once on the chart so that all three pie slices are selected, then click the largest slice—**Secure**—so that sizing handles surround only the *Secure* slice. Point to the selected slice, and then drag the slice slightly away from the pie so that the slice is exploded.

(Project 7D–Pension continues on the next page)

(Project 7D–Pension continued)

12. From the menu bar, display the **Chart** menu, and then click **3-D View**. Click in the **Elevation** box, and then type **30** Click in the **Rotation** box, and then type **70** to rotate the chart so that the *Secure* slice displays at the front of the chart. Click **OK**.

13. Click in the gray area outside the slide to deselect it and close Microsoft Graph. On the Formatting toolbar, click **New Slide**. In the task pane, under **Other Layouts**, click **Title and Diagram or Organization Chart**. Close the task pane. Click in the title placeholder, and then type **Plan Approval and Implementation**

14. Double-click the diagram placeholder, and then click **OK** to create an organization chart. Type **Board of Directors** and then click in the center box in the second row. Type **CEO** and then click in the box to the left of the CEO box. Type **VP Human Resources** and then click in the box to the right of the CEO box. Click on the outside border of the box and press ⌈Delete⌉ to remove the box from the organization chart.

15. Click the **VP Human Resources** box, and then on the Organization Chart toolbar, click **Insert Shape** to insert a subordinate box. Click in the new box, and then type **Fund Managing Group**

16. Click the **CEO** box, and then on the Organization Chart toolbar, click **Insert Shape** to insert a subordinate box. Click in the new box, and then type **Finance Department**

17. On the Organization Chart toolbar, click the **Autoformat** button. As the diagram style, click **Bookend Fills**, and then click **OK**.

18. Create a header and footer for the notes and handouts that includes the date updated automatically and a footer with the text **7D Pension-Firstname Lastname** Clear all other header and footer options and click **Apply to All**.

19. Display **Slide 1**, and then view the slide show. **Save** the file, and then print the presentation as **grayscale handouts**, **4** slides per page in **horizontal** order. Close the file.

End You have completed Project 7D ——————————————

Project 7E—Brunch

Objectives: *Create a Table and Create and Modify a Column Chart.*

In the following Skill Assessment, you will format a presentation that describes a new brunch menu. Your completed presentation will look similar to Figure 7.39. You will save your presentation as *7E_Brunch_Firstname_Lastname.*

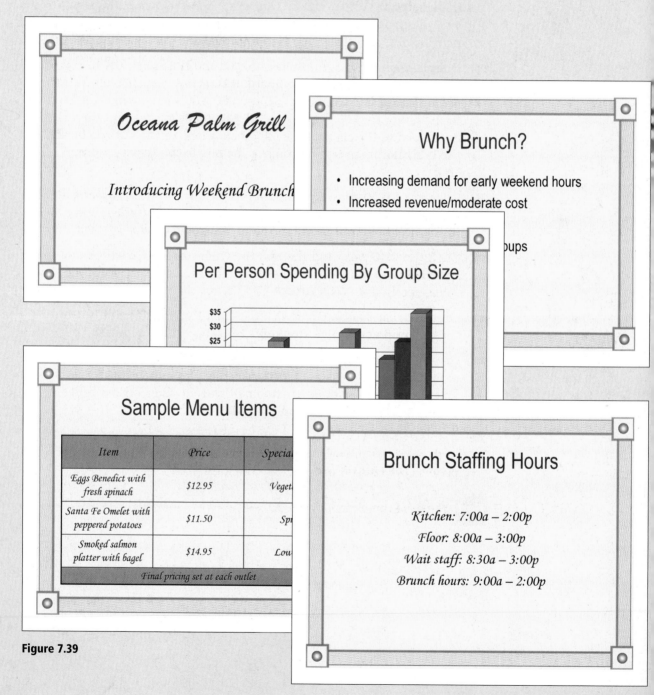

Figure 7.39

(Project 7E–Brunch continues on the next page)

(Project 7E–Brunch continued)

1. From your student files, open the file **p07E_Brunch**. Scroll through the presentation to familiarize yourself with the slides. **Save** the file as **7E_Brunch_Firstname_Lastname**

2. Display **Slide 2**, and on the Formatting toolbar, click **New Slide**. In the task pane, under **Other Layouts**, click **Title and Chart**. Close the task pane. Click in the title placeholder and type **Per Person Spending By Group Size**

3. Double-click the chart placeholder to open Microsoft Graph. Click the gray, **column D** heading box, and then press Delete. Create the datasheet (shown at an enlarged size) in Figure 7.40, and then close the datasheet by clicking the red close button in the datasheet toolbar.

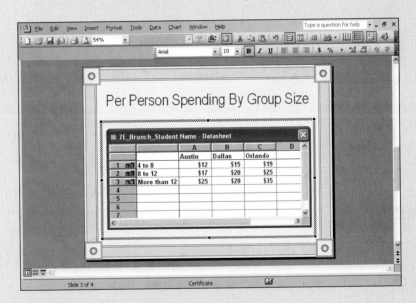

Figure 7.40

4. From the **Chart** menu, click **Chart Options**. Click the **Legend tab**, under **Placement** click the **Bottom** option button, and then click **OK** to move the legend to the bottom of the chart.

5. Click anywhere outside of the chart placeholder to close the Microsoft Graph toolbars and menu and return to PowerPoint.

6. On the Formatting toolbar, click the **New Slide** button. In the task pane, under **Other Layouts**, click **Title and Table**. Close the task pane. Click in the title placeholder and type **Sample Menu Items**

(Project 7E–Brunch continues on the next page)

(Project 7E–Brunch continued)

7. Double-click the table placeholder, and then click the up arrows to increase the **Number of columns** to **3** and the **Number of rows** to **4**. Click **OK**. Type the table information in Figure 7.41, pressing Tab to move from cell to cell.

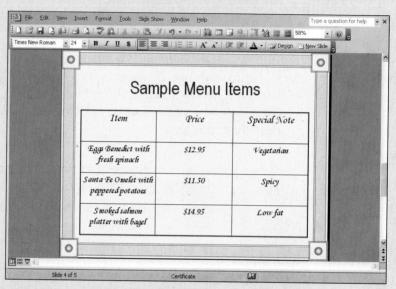

Figure 7.41

8. Click the table's boundary box so that it displays as a pattern of dots. On the Tables and Borders toolbar, click **Center Vertically**. On the Formatting toolbar, click the **Font Size arrow**, and then click **24**.

9. On the Tables and Borders toolbar, click the **Draw Table** button to display the pencil pointer. In the last row, position the pointer below the word *platter*. Drag to the right to draw a line that extends to the right edge of the table to create a new row. Press Esc to turn off the **Draw Table** pointer.

10. Select the three cells in the new row. On the Tables and Borders toolbar, click the **Merge Cells** button. Type **Final pricing set at each outlet**

11. Point to the bottom center sizing handle so that the vertical sizing pointer displays. Drag up about one-half inch to resize the table.

12. Select **rows 1 through 4**. On the Tables and Borders toolbar, click the **Distribute Rows Evenly** button to make the four rows equal in height.

(Project 7E–Brunch continues on the next page)

(Project 7E–Brunch continued)

13. Select the first row. On the Tables and Borders toolbar, click the **Fill Color button arrow**. Click the seventh color—**dark gold**. Click in the last row, and then press ⟨F4⟩ to repeat the gold fill color.

14. On the menu bar, display the **Slide Show** menu, and then click **Slide Transition**. In the task pane, under **Apply to selected slides**, click **Split Vertical In**. Under **Modify transition**, click the **Speed arrow**, and then click **Medium**. Click **Apply to All Slides**. Display **Slide 1**, and then view the slide show. Close the task pane.

15. Create a header and footer for the notes and handouts that includes the date updated automatically and a footer with the text **7E Brunch-Firstname Lastname** Clear all other header and footer options and click **Apply to All**.

16. **Save** the file, and then print the presentation as **grayscale handouts**, **6** slides per page in **horizontal** order. Close the file.

 You have completed Project 7E ————————————

Performance Assessments

Project 7F—Chefs

Objectives: *Create a Table and Create and Format Organization Charts.*

In the following Performance Assessment, you will format a presentation regarding the responsibilities of the various chefs at Oceana Palm Grill. Your completed presentation will look similar to the one shown in Figure 7.42. You will save your presentation as *7F_Chefs_Firstname_Lastname.*

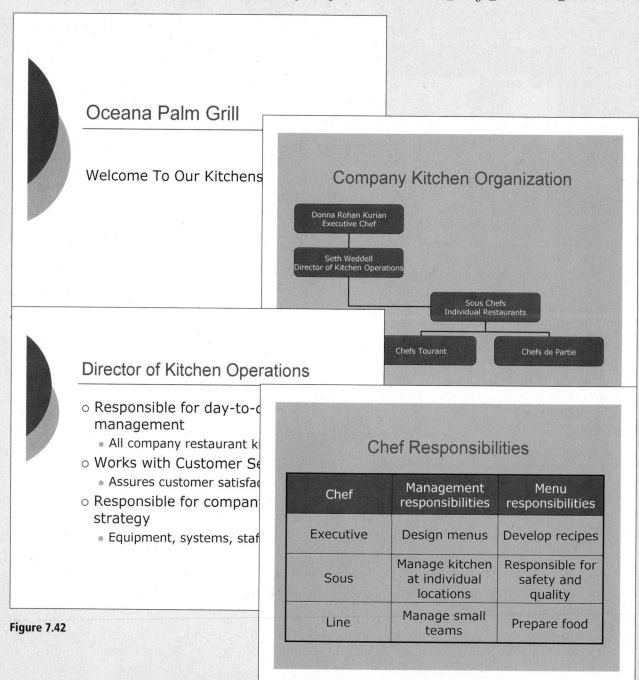

Figure 7.42

(Project 7F–Chefs continues on the next page)

(Project 7F–Chefs continued)

1. From your student files, open the file **p07F_Chefs**. Apply the white and teal **Eclipse** design template to the presentation. **Save** the file as **7F_Chefs_Firstname_Lastname**

2. Display **Slide 1**, insert a **New Slide** with the **Title and Diagram or Organization Chart** layout, and then create an organization chart. Close the task pane. Click in the title placeholder and type **Company Kitchen Organization**

3. In the top most box, type **Donna Rohan Kurian** and then press Enter. Type **Executive Chef**

4. Click in the center box in the second row. Type **Seth Weddell** and then press Enter. Type **Director of Kitchen Operations** and then delete the two remaining boxes in the organization chart.

5. Click the organization chart's boundary box so that a pattern of dots displays. Change the **Font Size** to **24**.

6. Click the bottom box, and then on the Organization Chart toolbar, click **Insert Shape**. With the center box still selected, on the Organization Chart toolbar, click **Layout**, and then click **Right Hanging**.

7. Click in the new box and type **Sous Chefs** and press Enter. Type **Individual Restaurants**

8. Insert two **Subordinate** shapes below the *Sous Chefs* shape. With the *Sous Chefs* box selected, on the Organization Chart toolbar, click **Layout**, and then click **Standard**.

9. Click in the box on the left, type **Chefs Tourant** and then click in the box on the right. Type **Chefs de Partie**

10. Click the top box in the organization chart. On the Organization Chart toolbar, click **Select**, and then click **Branch** so that all of the boxes are selected. On the Drawing toolbar, click the **Fill Color button arrow**, and then click the seventh color—**dark teal**. On the Drawing toolbar, click the **Font Color button arrow**, and then click the first color—**white**.

11. Omit the background graphics from the master so that the two half circles on the left side of the slide do not display. Change the background to the sixth color in the color scheme—**light aqua**, and apply the change to the current slide only.

12. Point to the center left sizing handle so that the horizontal sizing pointer displays, and then drag to the left about one-half inch to resize the organization chart. On the Organization Chart toolbar, click **Fit Text** to make the font size larger.

13. Click outside of the chart to close the toolbar. Display **Slide 3**, and then insert a **New Slide** with the **Title and Table** layout. Omit the background graphics from the master for this slide, and then in the title placeholder type **Chef Responsibilities**

(Project 7F–Chefs continues on the next page)

(Project 7F–Chefs continued)

14. Size the title placeholder by dragging the center left and right sizing handles so that they extend to the left and right edges of the slide. Center the title.

15. Create a table with **3 columns** and **4 rows**. Drag the center left sizing handle to the left about 1 inch. First, type the table text shown in Figure 7.43, and then after you type the text, select the entire table and center the text vertically and horizontally within the cells as shown in the table.

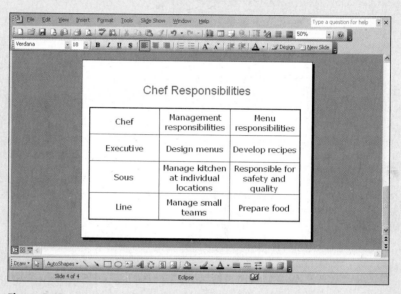

Figure 7.43

16. Select the first row of the table and change the **Fill Color** to the seventh color—**dark teal**. With the first row still selected, change the **Font Color** to the first color—**white**.

17. On the **Format** menu, click **Background**, and then change the background fill color to the sixth color in the color scheme—**light aqua**.

18. Display **Slide 1**, and then apply the **Compress** animation scheme to the entire presentation. View the slide show.

19. Create a header and footer for the notes and handouts that includes the date updated automatically and a footer with the text **7F Chefs-Firstname Lastname** Clear all other header and footer options and click **Apply to All**.

20. **Save** the file, and then print the presentation as **grayscale handouts**, **4** slides per page in **horizontal** order. Close the file.

 You have completed Project 7F ——————

Project 7G—Summary

Objectives: *Create and Format Diagrams and Create and Modify a Column Chart.*

In the following Performance Assessment you will format the Oceana Palm Grill annual summary presentation. Your completed presentation will look similar to the one shown in Figure 7.44. You will save your presentation as *7G_Summary_Firstname_Lastname.*

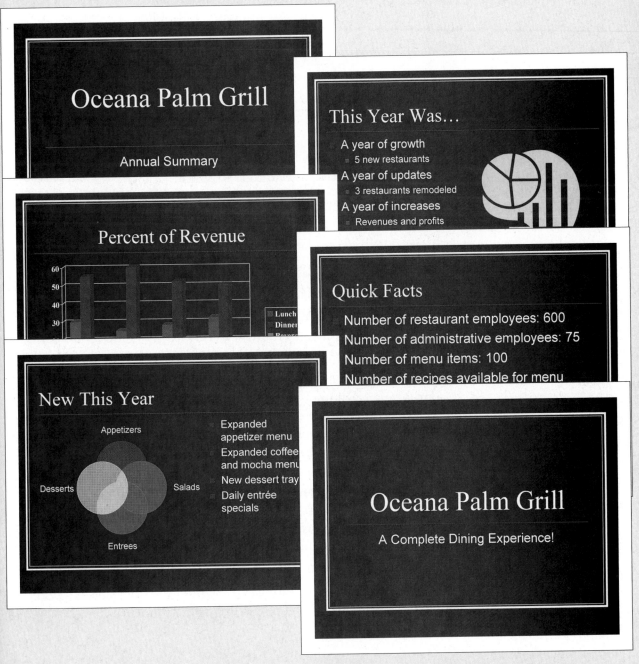

Figure 7.44

(Project 7G–Summary continues on the next page)

(Project 7G–Summary continued)

1. From your student files, open the file **p07G_Summary**. Apply the black **Refined** design template to the presentation. **Save** the file as 7G_Summary_Firstname_Lastname

2. Display **Slide 2** and insert a **New Slide** with the **Title and Chart** layout. In the title placeholder type **Percent of Revenue** and then **Center** the title.

3. Double-click the chart placeholder, and then create the datasheet (shown at an enlarged size) in Figure 7.45. Close the datasheet.

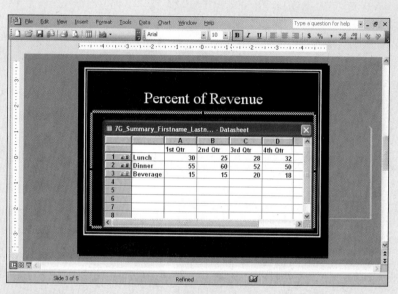

Figure 7.45

4. In the **1st Qtr** category, click the lavender column marker so that all four lavender column markers are selected. On the **Format** menu, click **Selected Data Series**. In the **Patterns tab**, change the **Border** to **None**. Repeat this process for the red and the green column markers so that none of the column markers are bordered.

5. Click outside of the chart area to return to PowerPoint, and then display the **Custom Animation** task pane. Select the chart, and then add the **Blinds Entrance Effect**. In the **custom animation list**, click the **item 1 arrow**, and then click **Effect Options**. Click the **Timing tab**, and change the **Start** option to **After previous**. Click the **Chart Animation tab**, and then change the **Group chart** option to **By category**. Click **OK**.

(Project 7G–Summary continues on the next page)

Project 7G–Summary continued)

6. Display **Slide 4** and insert a **New Slide**. Under **Text and Content Layouts**, click the **Title, Content and Text** layout. In the title placeholder, type **New This Year** and then in the bulleted list placeholder, type the text in Figure 7.46. Close the task pane.

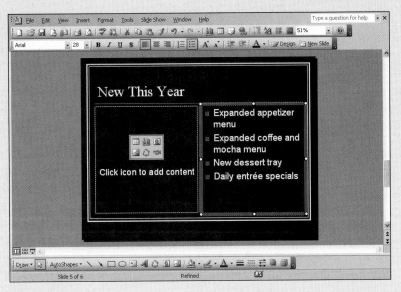

Figure 7.46

7. Select the text in the bulleted list, and then change the **Font Size** to **24**. Drag the center left sizing handle of the bulleted list placeholder to the right about one-half inch. The word *specials* in the last bullet point wraps to another line. If it does not wrap, drag the sizing handle again until it does.

8. Click in the content placeholder to select it, and then drag the center right sizing handle to the right until it almost touches the red, square bullets.

9. In the content placeholder, within the small graphic, in the second row, click the second icon—**Insert Diagram or Organization Chart**. In the second row, click the second diagram, **Venn Diagram**, and then click **OK**.

10. Insert another shape in the diagram so that there are four circles. Above the circle at the top of the diagram, click in the *Click to add text* box. (Hint: The text box border does not display because it is the same color as the slide background.) Type **Appetizers**

(Project 7G–Summary continues on the next page)

(Project 7G–Summary continued)

11. Click the right most text box, type **Salads** and then click the bottom text box. Type **Entrees** and then click the left most text box. Type **Desserts**

12. Hold down and click each of the text boxes so that all four text boxes are selected. Change the **Font Size** to **20**. Click outside the slide to view your changes.

13. Display the **Slide Transition** task pane, and then apply the **Wipe Right** transition to the entire presentation. Display **Slide 1**, and then view the slide show.

14. Create a header and footer for the notes and handouts that includes the date updated automatically and a footer with the text **7G Summary-Firstname Lastname** Clear all other header and footer options and click **Apply to All**.

15. **Save** the file, and then print the presentation as **grayscale handouts**, **6** slides per page in **horizontal** order. Close the file.

End You have completed Project 7G

Project 7H — Recruiting

Objective: *Create and Modify a Pie Chart.*

In the following Performance Assessment, you will format a presentation regarding an online recruiting plan developed by the Oceana Palm Grill Human Resources department. Your completed presentation will look similar to the one shown in Figure 7.47. You will save your presentation as *7H_Recruiting_Firstname_Lastname.*

The Wired Work Force

Online Recruiting Plan

Need For Online Recruiting

- Growing numbers of job seekers look online
- Low unemployment necessitates enhanced recruiting methods
- Cost savings over traditional ~ting methods

Recruiting Costs

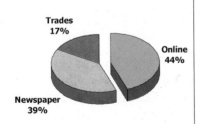

Trades
17%

Online
44%

Newspaper
39%

Online Recruiting Advantages

- Access to more qualified applicants
- Increased diversity of applicant pools
- Online application process
  - Automated database
- Easily maintained and updated

Figure 7.47
(Project 7H–Recruiting continues on the next page)

(Project 7H–Recruiting continued)

1. From your student files, open the file **p07H_Recruiting**. **Save** the file as **7H_Recruiting_Firstname_Lastname**

2. Display **Slide 2**, and then insert a **New Slide** with the **Title and Chart** layout. In the title placeholder, type **Recruiting Costs** and then **Center** the title. Close the task pane.

3. Double-click the chart placeholder and create the datasheet shown in Figure 7.48, which has been enlarged for viewing. Delete any unnecessary columns. Close the datasheet, and then on the Chart toolbar, click the **By Column** button to have the columns on the datasheet represent the data series.

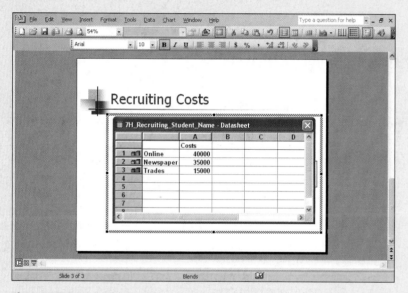

Figure 7.48

4. On the Chart toolbar, click the **Chart Type button arrow**, and then change the chart to a **3-D Pie Chart**. Select and delete the legend.

5. Point to the border surrounding the chart so that the *Plot Area* ScreenTip displays. Double-click the border to display the **Format Plot Area** dialog box, and then format the **Plot Area** so that the border surrounding the plot area does *not* display.

6. Double-click the chart to display the **Format Data Series** dialog box, and then add **Data Labels** to the chart that display the **Category name** and the **Percentage**. Do not display the leader lines.

(Project 7H–Recruiting continues on the next page)

(Project 7H–Recruiting continued)

7. From the **Chart** menu, click **3-D View**, and then change the **Elevation** to **35**. **Explode** the *Online* slice.

8. Click anywhere outside of the chart to return to PowerPoint, and then drag the chart to center it under the title. Apply **Custom Animation** to the chart, using the **Compress Entrance Effect**. Display **Slide 1**, and then view the slide show.

9. Create a header and footer for the notes and handouts that includes the date updated automatically and a footer with the text **7H Recruiting-Firstname Lastname** Clear all other header and footer options and click **Apply to All**.

10. **Save** the file, and then print the presentation as **grayscale handouts**, **4** slides per page in **horizontal** order. Close the file.

End You have completed Project 7H ———————————————

Project 7I — Certification

Objective: *Create a Table.*

In the following Mastery Assessment, you will format a presentation regarding a food safety training program at Oceana Palm Grill. Your completed presentation will look similar to the one shown in Figure 7.49. You will save your presentation as *7I_Certification_Firstname_Lastname*.

Oceana Palm Grill
Employee Food Safety
Training

Introduction to Government

Some Government Resources

- FDA food code
  - Best practices
    - Retail and food service industries
- National Agricultural Library Manager tool kit
  - Training program in safety

Food Safety Training

Program	Description	Offered by
Certified Food Protection Professional (CFPP)	Geared to the foodservice professional; class work, independent study, or online courses	Dietary Managers Association
Certified Food Safety Manager (CFSM)	Measure understanding of food safety and ability to protect the public	National Registry of Food Safety Professionals
Certified Professional Food Manager (CPFM)	Tests knowledge of food protection and ability to	Certified Food Management

Certified Professionals Nationwide

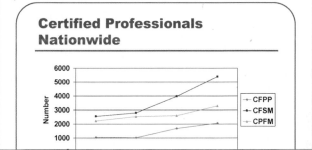

Gateway to U.S.
Government

Food Safety Information

Oceana Palm Grill employees
are encouraged to seek
additional food safety training

See your general manager
for details

Figure 7.49
(**Project 7I**–Certification continues on the next page)

(Project 7I–Certification continued)

1. From your student files, open the file **p07I_Certification**. Scroll through the presentation to familiarize yourself with the slides. **Save** the file as 7I_Certification_Firstname_Lastname

2. Display **Slide 2** and insert a **New Slide** with the **Title and Table** layout. In the title placeholder, type **Food Safety Training** and then **Center** the title.

3. Double-click the table placeholder and create the table in Figure 7.50 as follows: Create three rows, and before you begin to type, draw the narrow top row. Then, select all the cells and change the **Font Size** to **18**. After you type the text, distribute rows 2, 3, and 4 evenly and widen the table as needed.

Food Safety Training

Program	Description	Offered by
Certified Food Protection Professional (CFPP)	Geared to the foodservice professional; class work, independent study, or online courses	Dietary Managers Association
Certified Food Safety Manager (CFSM)	Measure understanding of food safety and ability to protect the public	National Registry of Food Safety Professionals
Certified Professional Food Manager (CPFM)	Tests knowledge of food protection and ability to organize and supervise employees	Certified Food Management Association

Figure 7.50

4. Insert a **New Slide 4** with the **Title and Chart** layout. In the title placeholder, type **Certified Professionals Nationwide** and then create the chart using the datasheet in Figure 7.51. Close the datasheet.

(Project 7I–Certification continues on the next page)

(Project 7I–Certification continued)

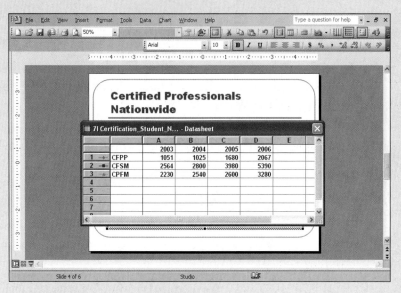

Figure 7.51

5. Change the chart to a **Line** chart. From the **Chart Options** dialog box, add the value axis title **Number** and add the category axis title **Year**

6. Display **Slide 5**. Click in the subtitle placeholder and type **Food Safety Information** Select the text and create a **hyperlink** to the www.FoodSafety.gov Web site.

7. Apply the **Split Horizontal Out** slide transition and change the **Speed** to **Medium**. Apply the transition to all of the slides in the presentation.

8. On **Slide 2**, select the **bulleted list** and apply the **Blinds Horizontal** entrance effect. On **Slide 3**, select the **table** and apply the **Blinds Horizontal** entrance effect. On **Slide 4**, select the **chart** and apply the **Box** entrance effect. Change the **Speed** to **Fast**, and change the **Start** option to **After Previous**.

9. Display **Slide 1** and view the slide show, testing the hyperlink on **Slide 5**. Create a header and footer for the notes and handouts that includes the date updated automatically and a footer with the text **7I Certification-Firstname Lastname** Clear all other header and footer options.

10. **Save** the file, and then print the presentation as **grayscale handouts**, **6** slides per page in **horizontal** order. Close the file.

End You have completed Project 7I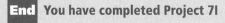

Project 7J — Service

Objectives: *Create and Format Diagrams and Create and Format Organization Charts.*

In the following Mastery Assessment, you will format a presentation regarding customer service at the Oceana Palm Grill corporate office. Your completed presentation will look similar to the one shown in Figure 7.52. You will save your presentation as *7J_Service_Firstname_Lastname.*

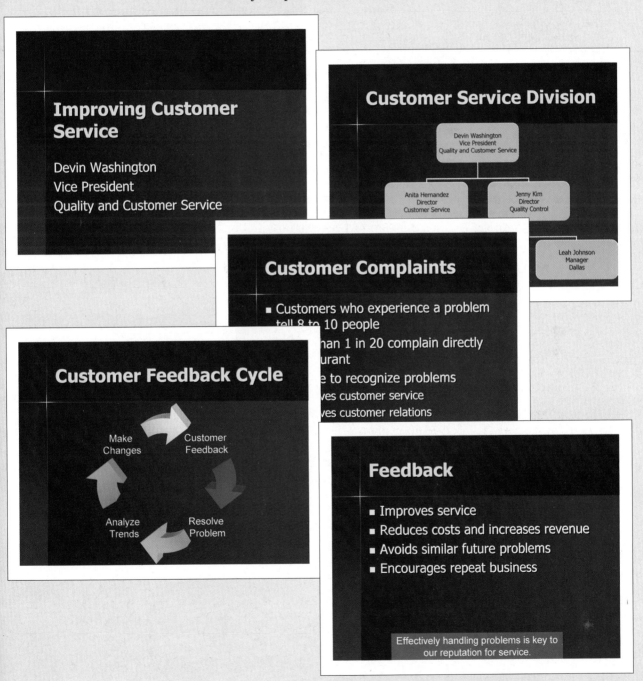

Figure 7.52

(**Project 7J**–Service continues on the next page)

(Project 7J–Service continued)

1. Start a new presentation based on the blue, **Shimmer** design template. On **Slide 1**, click in the title placeholder. Type **Improving Customer Service** and then in the subtitle placeholder type **Devin Washington** and press Enter. Type **Vice President** and then press Enter. Type **Quality and Customer Service** and then save the file as 7J_Service_Firstname_Lastname

2. Create **Slides 2** and **3** by typing the outline text (shown wider) in Figure 7.53.

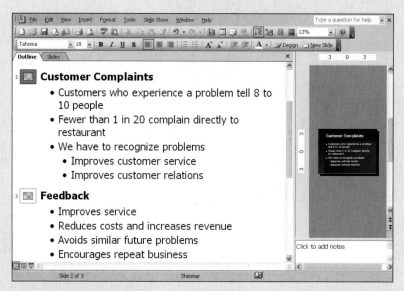

Figure 7.53

3. Display **Slide 3** and insert a **New Slide** with the **Title and Diagram or Organization Chart** layout. Create the slide shown in Figure 7.54. Resize the diagram so that the placeholder's left, right, and bottom edges extend to the edges of the slide. (Hint: Use the **Fit Text** option so that the text fits within the boxes.)

(Project 7J–Service continues on the next page)

(Project 7J–Service continued)

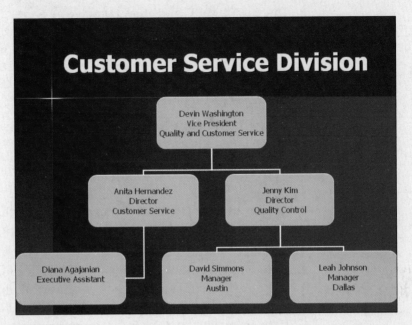

Figure 7.54

4. Insert a **New Slide** with the **Title and Organization Chart or Diagram** layout. Create the slide shown in Figure 7.55, pressing ⟨Enter⟩ after the first word in each text box.

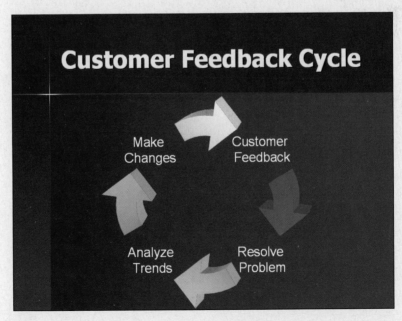

Figure 7.55

(Project 7J–Service continues on the next page)

(Project 7J–Service continued)

5. Display **Slide 3**, and then display the **Ruler**. Create a **text box** that extends from **3 inches to the left of zero** and **3 inches below zero** to **3 inches to the right of zero** and to the **bottom of the slide**. Type **Effectively handling problems is key to our reputation for service.** Change the **Fill Color** to the sixth color—**blue**—and change the **Font Color** to the second color—**white**. Change the **Font Size** to **24**.

6. Apply the **Shape Circle** slide transition to the entire presentation and change the **Speed** to **Medium**.

7. Rearrange the slides so that the slide with the organization chart is **Slide 2**, and the slide with the cycle diagram is **Slide 4**.

8. Create a footer for the notes and handouts that includes the date updated automatically and a footer with the text **7J Service-Firstname Lastname** Clear all other header and footer options.

9. **Save** the file, and then print the presentation as **grayscale handouts**, **6** slides per page in **horizontal** order. Close the file.

End You have completed Project 7J

Problem Solving

Project 7K — Restaurant

Objectives: *Create a Table, Create and Format Organization Charts, and Create and Modify a Column Chart.*

Work with a partner to research a large restaurant chain. Create a presentation with six slides that includes one or two slides that describe the restaurant, a slide with a table layout that contains a sample menu, a slide with a column chart that indicates the number of restaurants in various states or cities and if possible, a slide with a company organization chart. On one of your slides, create a hyperlink to the restaurant's Web site. If appropriate, include pictures that illustrate the menu or the restaurant theme. Apply transitions and effects, create an appropriate footer for your notes and handouts, and save your file as *7K_Restaurant_Firstname_Lastname*. Print the presentation as handouts, 6 slides per page, in grayscale.

End You have completed Project 7K

Project 7L — Process

Objectives: *Create a Table and Create and Format Diagrams.*

Research a process at your school such as registering for classes, creating an education plan, or applying for financial aid. Create a presentation that contains at least six slides describing the process, the forms, and the people or departments with whom you will come into contact as you complete the process. Illustrate the process using at least one diagram and a table. Use the techniques that you have learned throughout this textbook to format the presentation, including shapes, pictures, groups, animations, and transitions. Create an appropriate footer for your notes and handouts and save your presentation as *7L_Process_Firstname_Lastname*. Print the presentation as handouts, 6 slides per page, in grayscale.

End You have completed Project 7L

On the Internet

United States Census Bureau

Connect to the Internet and go to the Web site of the United States Census Bureau at http://www.census.gov/. Click **Your Gateway to Census 2000**, and then click **State and County Quick Facts**. Click your state, and then explore the census data tables regarding people, businesses, and geography.

GO! with Help

Inserting an Excel Chart

You can create a chart in Microsoft Excel and link or embed the chart in a PowerPoint presentation. Use Microsoft Office PowerPoint Help to learn how to insert an Excel chart in your presentations.

1. Click in the **Type a question for help** box, type **How do I insert an Excel chart?** and then press Enter.

2. In the **Search Results** task pane, click **Link or embed an Excel chart**. Read the information and click each link that displays.

8 chaptereight

Customizing a Presentation for Web Viewing

In this chapter, you will: complete this project **and** practice these skills.

Project 8A Customizing a Presentation for Web Viewing	Objectives
	• Create a Design Template • Enhance a Presentation with Sound • Modify a Presentation Using Research and Comparison Tools • Share Files with Other Users • Format a Presentation for Web Viewing

The Greater Atlanta Job Fair

The Greater Atlanta Job Fair is a nonprofit organization supported by the Atlanta Chamber of Commerce and Atlanta City Colleges. The organization holds several targeted job fairs in the Atlanta area each year. Candidate registration is free and open to area residents and students enrolled in certificate or degree programs at any of the City Colleges. Employers pay a nominal fee to participate in the fairs. When candidates register for a fair, their resumes are scanned into an interactive, searchable database that is provided to the employers.

© Getty Images, Inc.

Customizing a Presentation for Web Viewing

Microsoft Office PowerPoint 2003 makes it possible to make a presentation available without a presenter. Such self-running presentations are often used on Web sites, in information kiosks in public places like shopping malls, and at exhibition booths at trade shows. Information in a self-running show must be more carefully prepared and more clearly outlined than a presentation given by a speaker, because the audience must be able to understand the information from the slides alone.

PowerPoint allows you to insert audio and video clips that can help the audience understand the information. This combination of video, text, and graphics is known as **multimedia**. Multimedia presentations are becoming more common as the software necessary to produce them becomes more affordable and widely available. The guidelines for using multimedia in your presentations are much the same as the guidelines for any presentation: Tailor the presentation to your audience, do not overuse sound and video, and be sure the clips are relevant to the information. Focus the presentation on the ideas, and use the multimedia elements to enhance the audience's understanding.

Project 8A **Information**

In Activities 8.1 through 8.14, you will create a presentation describing the Greater Atlanta Job Fair. Your completed presentation will look similar to Figure 8.1. You will save your presentation as *8A_Information_Firstname_ Lastname*. You will also create a three-page Word document (not pictured) containing copies of the presentation slides, which you will save as a Word file named *8A_Word_Firstname_Lastname*.

Figure 8.1
Project 8A—Information

Objective 1
Create a Design Template

Microsoft Office PowerPoint 2003 includes a number of professionally designed templates that you can apply to your presentations. You can modify any template by changing the design elements on the slide master such as the background graphics, the color scheme, or the font selections. After you have modified the template, you can save it as a new template so that you can use the same formatting in another presentation.

In addition to creating a template based on an existing presentation, you can create a new template by applying text or graphics, color schemes, backgrounds, and other elements to a blank presentation. When you design a template in PowerPoint, apply the background formatting and graphics to the Slide and Title Masters, then modify other elements such as the slide color scheme and font selections.

Activity 8.1 Creating and Saving a Design Template

A background in PowerPoint can consist of a solid color, a gradient fill, a texture, or a picture. The background may also contain graphic elements applied to the Slide Master. In this activity, you will open an existing presentation and format the Slide Master. Then you will save the presentation as a design template. By default, templates that you create are saved in a Templates folder and display in the Slide Design task pane. You can save a template to another location; just remember to navigate to the appropriate template location when you are ready to apply it to a presentation.

1 Start PowerPoint, and then from your student files, **Open** the file **p08A_Atlanta**.

This presentation contains one slide based on the Default Design template. The slide has been formatted to include five rectangles—two blue and three teal green—and a diamond with a gradient fill. These six objects form the graphic design of the slide, and have been grouped as a single object.

2 Point to one of the teal rectangles so that the move pointer displays, and then click the left mouse button.

Notice that sizing handles surround the entire slide, indicating that the objects have been grouped and are selected.

3 On the Standard toolbar, click **Copy**.

4 On the **View** buttons, point to **Normal View**, and then press and hold down Shift so that the ScreenTip *Slide Master View* displays. Click the left mouse button to display the Slide Master.

5 On the Standard toolbar, click **Paste** to copy the grouped objects to the Slide Master.

Recall that in addition to the objects on the Slide Master, a slide background can include a fill color or effect.

6 On the menu bar, click **Format**, and then click **Background**. Click the **Background fill arrow**, and then in the color scheme, click the sixth color—**blue**. Click **Apply**.

7 Click in the title placeholder, and then on the Formatting toolbar, click the **Font arrow** Arial . Click **Arial Rounded MT Bold**.

8 In the bulleted list placeholder, click in the line that contains the first level bullet—**Click to edit Master text styles**. On the menu bar, click the **Format** menu, and then click **Bullets and Numbering**. Click the **Picture** button to open the **Picture Bullet** dialog box. In the **Search text** box type **square** and then click **Go**.

Several square bullets display.

9 Click the teal bullet shown in Figure 8.2, and then click **OK**.

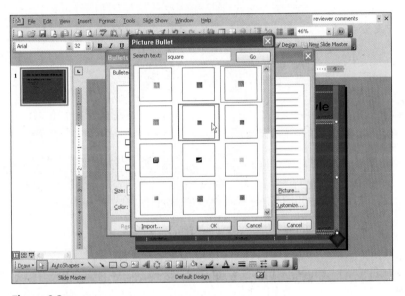

Figure 8.2

10 In the bulleted list placeholder, click the **Second level** line. From the **Format** menu, click **Bullets and Numbering**. In the first row, click the last bullet—the **square**. Click the **Color arrow**, and then click the seventh color—**teal**. Click **OK**.

The second level bullet is formatted as a teal square. In addition to Slide Master formatting, a custom template may include changes to the slide color scheme.

Alert!

Displaying the Square Bullet in the Bullets and Numbering Dialog Box

If the square bullet does not display in the Bullets and Numbering dialog box, click the last bullet style in the first row, and then in the lower left corner of the dialog box, click Reset. Then change the bullet color.

11 On the Formatting toolbar, click the **Slide Design** button 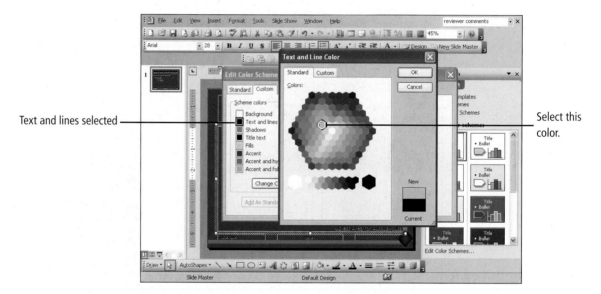 to display the **Slide Design** task pane. In the task pane, click **Color Schemes**. At the bottom of the task pane, click **Edit Color Schemes**. If necessary, click the **Custom tab**, and then under **Scheme colors**, click the black **Text and lines** box. Click **Change Color** to display the color honeycomb. In the sixth row, click the fifth color—**light aqua**. See Figure 8.3. Click **OK**, and then click **Apply**. Close the **Slide Design** task pane.

Notice that all of the text in the bulleted list placeholder is formatted in light aqua.

Text and lines selected ⎯⎯⎯⎯⎯⎯

Select this color.

Figure 8.3

12 To save the file as a template, move to the menu bar, and then click **File**. From the menu, click **Save As**. At the bottom of the **Save As** dialog box, click the **Save as type arrow**, and then scroll the list. Click **Design Template**. Notice that the Save in box displays the *Templates* folder name. In the **File name box**, type **8A_Template_ Firstname_Lastname** Click the **Save in arrow**, and then navigate to the location where you are storing your projects for this chapter, creating a new folder for Chapter 8 if you want to do so. Compare your dialog box with Figure 8.4, and then click **Save**. Leave the file open for the next activity.

You will continue to format the template in the next activity.

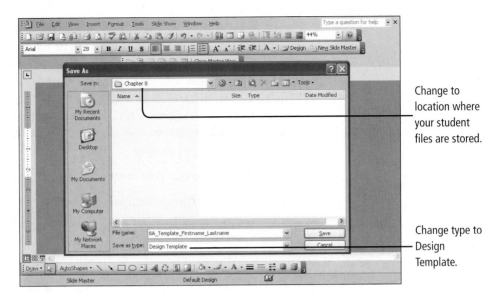

Change to location where your student files are stored.

Change type to Design Template.

Figure 8.4

Activity 8.2 Adding a Master Slide to a Template

In this activity, you will use the Slide Master View toolbar to add a Title Master to your design template.

1 If necessary, display the slide master. The Slide Master View toolbar displays floating on your screen or docked in the toolbar area of your window. On the Slide Master View toolbar, click the **Insert New Title Master** button.

The Title Master displays. Although the file was saved as a design template type, the Default Design name is still applied. Notice that in the Status bar, the *Default Design* template name also displays.

2 On the Slide Master View toolbar, click the **Rename Master** button. In the displayed **Master name** box, type **8A Template** as shown in Figure 8.5, and then click **Rename**.

The name *8A Template* displays in the Status bar.

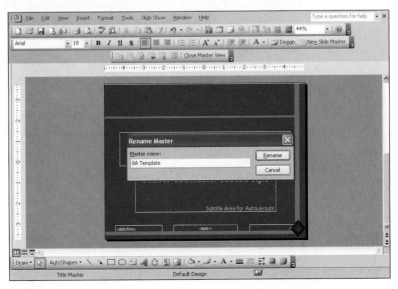

Figure 8.5

3 If necessary, display the title master (the vertical scroll bar is all the way to the bottom). From the **Format** menu, click **Background**, and then click the **Background fill arrow**. Click **Fill Effects**, and then in the **Gradient tab**, click **One color**. Drag the slider in the **Dark/Light** bar to the right so that it is approximately three-fourths of the way to the **Light** end of the scale. Under **Shading styles**, click **Vertical**, and under **Variants**, in the first row, click the second option. Click **OK**, and then click **Apply**.

A shaded background is applied to the title master.

4 Click on any of the rectangles on the slide so that the group of objects is selected. On the Drawing toolbar, click the **Draw** menu, and then click **Ungroup**.

All of the drawing objects on the title master are selected, but each is selected separately.

5 Click in the gray area outside the slide to deselect the objects, and then click the horizontal teal rectangle above the title placeholder. Press Delete.

The horizontal rectangle is deleted from the title slide master.

6 Move the pointer to the right of the vertical teal rectangle so that the move pointer displays between the teal rectangle and the right edge of the slide. See Figure 8.6. Click to select the royal blue rectangle on the right edge of the slide, and then drag the selected blue rectangle to the left edge of the slide.

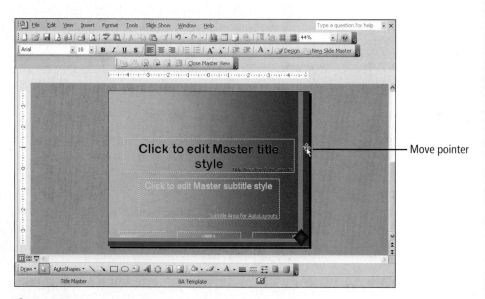

Figure 8.6

7 Select the vertical teal rectangle on the right side of the slide and drag to the left so that it aligns with the right edge of the blue rectangle and with the top edge of the slide.

8 Select the teal rectangle at the bottom of the slide, hold down Shift, and select the blue rectangle at the bottom of the slide so that both rectangles are selected. Release Shift, and then drag the two rectangles up so that the bottom of the blue rectangle touches the top of the title placeholder.

9 Click anywhere on the slide so that the two rectangles are deselected. Then, select the teal rectangle that you just moved and drag to the right so that its right edge touches the right edge of the slide.

10 Select the vertical teal rectangle, and then point to the bottom right sizing handle and drag straight down slightly so that the rectangle extends from the top to the bottom of the slide.

11 Point to the diamond in the lower right corner of the slide, and then drag the diamond so that it is positioned at the intersection of the horizontal and vertical rectangles. Click anywhere on the slide to deselect the diamond, and then compare your slide with Figure 8.7.

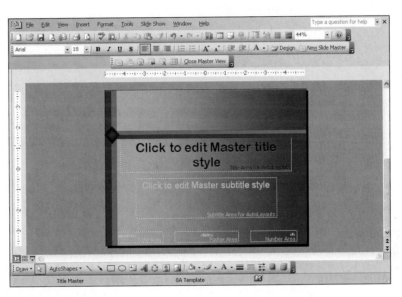

Figure 8.7

12 Drag the title placeholder toward the top of the slide so that its bottom and left edges touch the teal rectangles. If necessary, with the placeholder selected, hold down Ctrl and press the directional arrow keys on your keyboard to nudge the placeholder into a precise position.

13 Select the **subtitle placeholder**, and then drag it so that its right edge touches the right edge of the slide.

14 **Save** and **Close** the file.

Activity 8.3 Modifying a Design Template

Your template contains graphics, a color scheme, and a gradient fill background. After you have created a template, you can modify it by adding additional formatting, text, or graphics. To modify an existing template, you must first open the file as a template.

1 On the Standard toolbar, click **Open** 📂, and then click the **Files of type arrow**. Click **Design Templates**. Navigate to your storage location, and then double-click your **8A_Template_Firstname_Lastname** file.

The title master displays.

2 Click in the title placeholder. On the Formatting toolbar, click the **Font Color button arrow** 🔲, and then click the second color— **aqua**. On the Formatting toolbar, click the **Font Size arrow** 32 🔲, and then click **40**. On the Formatting toolbar, click the **Shadow** button 🔲.

3 Click in the subtitle placeholder, and then press F4 to repeat the Shadow formatting.

4 In the vertical scroll bar, move the scroll box to the top to display the slide master. Click in the title placeholder, and then click the **Font Color button arrow** 🔲. Click the second color—**aqua**. On the Formatting toolbar, click the **Shadow** button 🔲.

5 Click the outer edge of the bulleted list placeholder so that its boundary displays as a pattern of dots, indicating that formatting will be applied to the entire placeholder. Press F4 to repeat the Shadow formatting.

Your template design is complete, and because it is saved as a template, it can be used over and over for creating presentations.

6 Click **Save** 💾 to save the changes you have made to the template, and then **Close** ❎ the template file.

Activity 8.4 Applying a Custom Template to a Presentation

In this activity, you will apply the template that you created to an existing presentation.

1 From the student files that accompany this textbook, **Open** 📂 the file **p08A_Information**. If necessary to view the file list, click the Files of type arrow and click All PowerPoint presentations. From the **File** menu, click **Save As**, navigate to the location where you are storing your files for this chapter, and then save the file as **8A_Information_Firstname_Lastname**

Alert!

Displaying the Correct File Type

When you display your student files, p08A_Information may not display because the Files of type box may be displaying Design Templates. If that is the case, click the Files of type arrow, and then click All PowerPoint Presentations.

2 On the Formatting toolbar, click the **Slide Design** button [Design]. At the bottom of the task pane, click **Browse**, and then navigate to the folder where you are storing your projects for this chapter. Click the file name **8A_Template_Firstname_Lastname**, and in the displayed **Apply Design Template** dialog box, click **Apply**.

The entire presentation is formatted with the template that you created.

3 **Close** the **Slide Design** task pane, and then **Save** [💾] the file.

Objective 2
Enhance a Presentation with Sound

The PowerPoint Clip Gallery provides a variety of sound files that you can insert into your presentations. In addition to the sounds available in the Microsoft Clip Gallery, you can record your own sound files using special recording software or the Windows Sound Recorder. You can also create movie clips with a digital video camera. Each of these types of files can be inserted into your presentations.

Activity 8.5 Inserting a Sound File

In this activity, you will insert a sound file on Slide 1 from the PowerPoint Clip Gallery. The sound file that you insert will begin playing on Slide 1. Many presenters use projection systems to display the first slide of a presentation while audience members are gathering in the room. As audience members settle in and find seats, this is a good time to include a music sound file. If you are creating a presentation for independent viewing at a computer, you might decide to instruct PowerPoint to continue playing the sound file throughout the entire presentation.

1 If necessary, **Open** [📂] your file **8A_Information_Firstname_Lastname**.

2 Display **Slide 1**. On the menu bar, click **Insert**, and then point to **Movies and Sounds**. Click **Sound from Clip Organizer** to display the **Clip Art** task pane.

3 In the task pane, click in the **Search for** box. Type **Symphony** and then click **Go**. Click the first sound file—**Beethoven's Symphony No. 9**. (If your search found no results, read the Alert box following Figure 8.8.)

A message displays asking how you want the sound to start in the slide show. If you click Automatically, the sound clip plays when the slide is displayed in the slide show. If you click When Clicked, you must click the clip to play it during the slide show. See Figure 8.8.

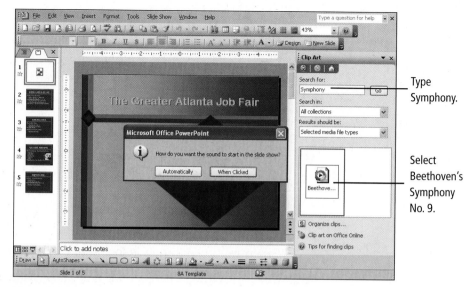

Type Symphony.

Select Beethoven's Symphony No. 9.

Figure 8.8

Inserting a Sound File

If the *symphony* search does not return any results, you can insert a recorded sound file. On the menu bar, click the Insert menu, and then point to Movies and Sounds. Click Sound from File, and then in the Insert Sound dialog box, navigate to your student files. Click p08A_Beethoven, and then click OK to insert the sound.

4 Click **Automatically**.

A small sound icon displays in the center of the slide. Do not be concerned with the placement of the sound icon, as you will hide it in a later activity.

5 **Save** the file.

More Knowledge — Playing Music from a CD

You can play a track from a CD in a slide presentation. Insert the CD into your CD/DVD drive, and, if necessary, close the Windows Media Player. On the PowerPoint menu bar, click the Insert menu, point to Movies and Sounds, and then click Play CD Audio Track. In the displayed dialog box, type the starting and ending tracks that you want to play, and then enter the start and end times.

Activity 8.6 Setting Multimedia Animation Options

The Multimedia Settings tab in the Custom Animation task pane includes options to control sound files during a presentation. These controls include pausing or continuing the slide show while the sound plays, looping the sound so that it begins again after it has finished playing, and hiding the sound icon during the slide presentation.

1 Display **Slide 1**, and then if necessary, click the megaphone sound icon to select it. In the task pane, click the **Other Task Panes arrow** ▼, and then click **Custom Animation**.

Notice that the Beethoven's Symphony sound file is listed in the Custom Animation list. When the sound was inserted and you chose *Automatically*, the After Previous animation option was applied to the sound so that it will begin to play as soon as the slide displays.

2 In the task pane, in the **Custom Animation list**, click the **item 0 arrow**, and then click **Effect Options**.

The Play Sound dialog box displays. In this Effect tab, you can set start and stop options for the sound that you inserted. In the Timing tab, you can change when the sound begins to play and you can instruct PowerPoint to repeat the sound. In the Sound Settings tab, you can adjust the volume and you can hide the icon during the slide show.

3 In the center section of the **Effect tab**, under **Stop playing**, click **After current slide** so that the music plays until Slide 2 is displayed.

4 Click the **Sound Settings tab**. Under **Display options**, click to select the **Hide sound icon during slide show** check box. See Figure 8.9, and then click **OK**.

Select check box ——

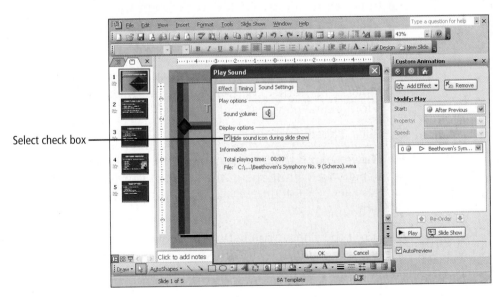

Figure 8.9

5 At the bottom of the task pane, click **Slide Show**.

If you have speakers or headphones attached to your computer, notice that on Slide 1, the music plays, but the megaphone does not display.

6 Click the mouse button to display Slide 2 and notice that the music stops. Press [Esc] to end the slide show, and then **Save** ▣ the file.

Objective 3
Modify a Presentation Using Research and Comparison Tools

Microsoft Office PowerPoint 2003 allows you to send a presentation to other people so that they can review it and make changes and add comments. After a presentation is reviewed, you can compare it to the original presentation, review the comments and changes, and then accept or reject the changes. You can also use a variety of research tools to modify your presentation. For example, you can use the Thesaurus to find words with similar meanings, and you can use the Translation option to translate words or short phrases using the bilingual dictionaries. If you are connected to the Internet, you can translate an entire presentation.

Activity 8.7 Using the Thesaurus

The Thesaurus allows you to look up *synonyms*—words with similar meanings, and insert them into your presentation.

1 If necessary, **Open** 🗁 your file **8A_Information_Firstname_Lastname**. Display **Slide 5**.

2 In the slide title, select the words **Sign Up**.

3 Point to the selected text and right-click. At the bottom of the short-cut menu, point to **Synonyms**.

A list of synonyms displays. You can click a word from this list to replace the phrase *Sign Up* or you can click Thesaurus to view additional synonyms.

4 Click **Thesaurus**.

The Research task pane displays. In the Thesaurus list, the words in bold are definitions of the selected word or phrase and indicate the part of speech to which the word belongs, for example, a verb or noun.

5 Scroll the Thesaurus list until the words under **join** display. Point to **register**, and then click the arrow. As shown in Figure 8.10, click **Insert**.

The word *Register* replaces the phrase *Sign Up*.

6 **Close** the task pane and **Save** ▣ the file.

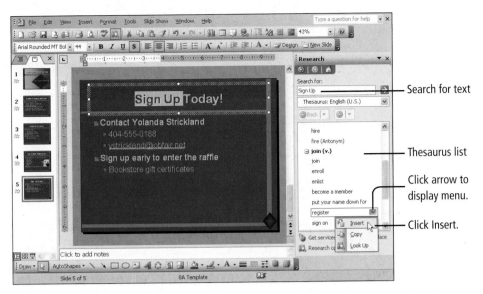

Search for text

Thesaurus list

Click arrow to display menu.

Click Insert.

Figure 8.10

Alert!

Using the Thesaurus

When you point to a word in the Thesaurus, you can click its arrow and then insert the word. If you click the word instead of pointing to it, the word becomes the new *Search for* text and the synonyms that display are based on the word that you clicked. If you want to return to the original word, under Search for, click the Back button arrow.

Activity 8.8 Saving a Presentation for Review

To send a presentation to reviewers, you must save it with a different file name, and change the file type to Presentation for Review. When a presentation is saved for review, you can either email or send the file by Microsoft Outlook to the reviewers, post it to a network server where reviewers can access it, or you can save it to disks and distribute the disks to the reviewers.

1 If necessary, **Open** your file **8A_Information_Firstname_ Lastname**. Display **Slide 1** and close the **Outline/Slides** pane.

2 From the **File** menu, click **Save As**. Navigate to your storage location, and in the **File name** box, type **8A_Review_Firstname_Lastname** and then click the **Save as type arrow**. Click **Presentation for Review**. See Figure 8.11. Click **Save**.

Notice that the title bar retains the original file name *8A_Information_Firstname_Lastname*.

3 **Close** the file.

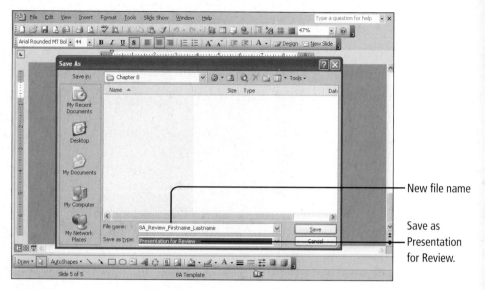

New file name

Save as Presentation for Review.

Figure 8.11

Activity 8.9 Inserting Comments and Editing a Presentation for Review

When you receive a presentation that you are going to review, open the presentation, and then edit it. While you are reviewing the presentation, you may also add **comments** that function as electronic sticky notes within your presentation. After you edit the reviewed file, you must save it and then you can send it by email or Microsoft Outlook to the originator, post it to a network server, or return the disk on which it was saved.

1 From your storage location, **Open** [icon] your file **8A_Review_ Firstname_Lastname**.

A Microsoft Office PowerPoint box displays asking if you want to merge changes in 8A_Review_Firstname_Lastname back into 8A_Information_Firstname_Lastname. If you click Yes, then PowerPoint will open 8A_Information and merge your changes. Because you have not yet made changes to the file, you do not want to merge the two files at this time.

2 Click **No**.

3 On **Slide 1**, select the title text. On the Formatting toolbar, click the **Font Color arrow** [icon], and then click the fourth color—**black**. Select the subtitle text, and change the **Font Color** to **black**.

4 Display **Slide 2**. Click in front of the word **Internships**, and then press [Enter] to create a new bullet. Press [↑] or click in the blank line created when you pressed [Enter] to position the insertion point in the blank line. Type **Variety of job opportunities** and then click in the last bullet point. On the Formatting toolbar, click the **Increase Indent** button [icon] to demote the bullet point.

5 Display **Slide 3**. Select the word **October**, and then type **November**

6 Display **Slide 4**. From the menu bar, display the **Insert** menu, and then click **Comment**.

A comment opens displaying the user information in the General tab of the Options dialog box and the current date. An insertion point is blinking in the comment indicating that you can type. In the upper left corner of the slide, a button displays the name and initials of the person entered in the User Information section of the Options dialog box in the General tab. This information is followed by the number of the comment. Comments are numbered sequentially in the order in which they are entered.

7 Type **I think the last bullet should be deleted since many of this year's employers are traveling as much as 200 miles to attend.** See Figure 8.12.

Comment button ─

Type comment text

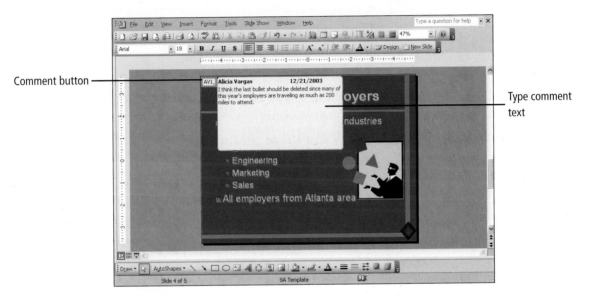

Figure 8.12

8 Click anywhere on the slide to close the comment.

The comment no longer displays.

9 In the upper right corner of the slide, click the **comment button** to open the comment.

When the comment is open, you can view it but you cannot change it. To change the comment you must use the Edit Comment command.

10 Point to the comment button, and then right-click to display the shortcut menu. Click **Edit Comment**. See Figure 8.13.

Right-click comment button. —

Click Edit Comment. —

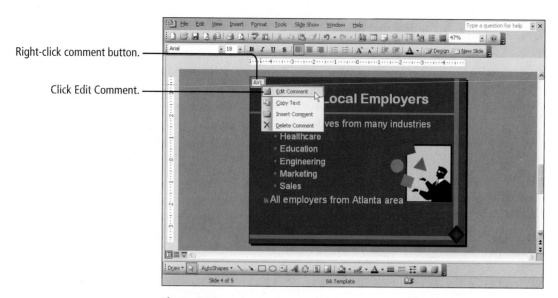

Figure 8.13

11 Change *200* to **100** and then click anywhere on the slide to close the comment.

12 **Save** 🖫 and **Close** ☒ the file.

More Knowledge — Deleting a Comment

You can delete a comment by clicking on the comment and then pressing ⌊Delete⌋. You can also delete a comment by right-clicking on the comment to display the shortcut menu, and then clicking Delete Comment.

Activity 8.10 Comparing and Merging Presentations

PowerPoint 2003 can compare the changes between the original and reviewed files. You can choose to accept or reject the changes that reviewers have made. If more than one person has reviewed the document, you can view reviewer changes individually, or all at one time. To compare presentations, you must first open the original presentation, and then use the Compare and Merge Presentations feature on the Tools menu to open the Revisions task pane and view each revision.

1 From the folder where you are storing your projects for this chapter,

Open 📂 your file **8A_Information_Firstname_Lastname**.

2 From the **Tools** menu, click **Compare and Merge Presentations** to open the **Choose Files to Merge with Current Presentation** dialog box.

In this dialog box, you may choose the presentation that you want to compare. You can choose multiple reviewed presentations by using the ⌊Shift⌋ and ⌊Ctrl⌋ keys to select each presentation that you want to merge.

3 Click **8A_Review_Firstname_Lastname**, and then in the lower right corner, click **Merge**.

The Reviewing toolbar and the Revisions task pane display. See Figure 8.14. The List tab displays the revisions suggested by each reviewer. When you click the Reviewer list box arrow, you can choose the reviewer whose changes you want to view or you can choose All Reviewers to view all reviewers' changes simultaneously. The slide and the Revisions task pane display *Change markers*—icons that designate a change made by a reviewer. The Gallery tab displays the slide miniatures of the current slide for each reviewer. When you click the slide miniature, all changes made by that reviewer are applied to the original presentation. You can use either the Revisions task pane or the Reviewing toolbar to accept or reject reviewer changes. Since you are only viewing changes made by one reviewer, it is easier to use the toolbar.

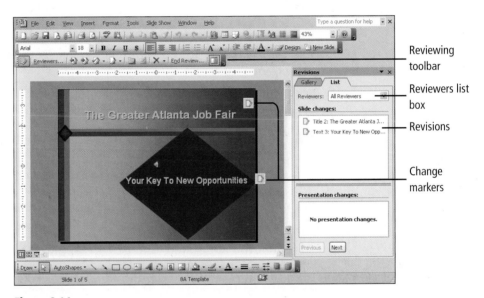

Figure 8.14

4 **Close** the **Revisions** task pane, and if necessary, display **Slide 1**.

5 Click the change marker that is displayed next to the title placeholder.

A check box, a description of the change—in this case a font color change—and the reviewer name display. When you select the check box, the suggested change is displayed on the slide, indicating to PowerPoint that you want to accept the change.

6 Click the check box. See Figure 8.15.

The title displays in black and a check mark displays on the change marker.

Click the check box. ——

Description of change

Change marker

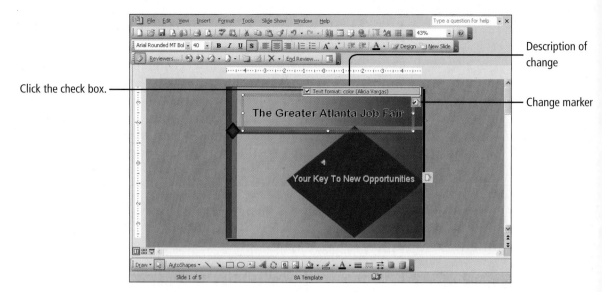

Figure 8.15

7 On the Reviewing toolbar, click **Next Item** to activate the subtitle change marker.

8 Click the check box and notice that the blue diamond does not provide enough contrast for the black text.

9 Click the check box again to reject the formatting change.

10 On the Reviewing toolbar, click **Next Item** to display the revisions on Slide 2.

11 On the Reviewing toolbar, click the **Apply button arrow**, and then click **Apply All Changes to the Current Slide**. See Figure 8.16.

All of the suggested changes are applied to the slide.

Click the arrow. ——

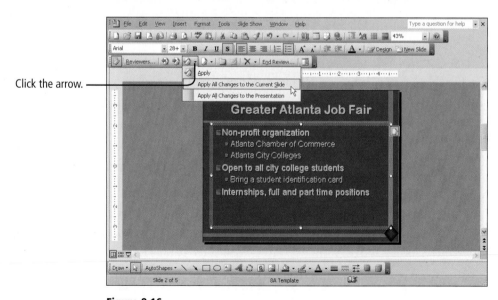

Figure 8.16

12 On the Reviewing toolbar, click **Next Item** 🔛 to display the revisions on Slide 3. Leave the check boxes blank so that none of the changes on this slide are accepted.

13 On the Reviewing toolbar, click **Next Item** 🔛 to display the comment on Slide 4.

When you are comparing and merging a presentation, you can read comments and then delete them.

14 Press Delete to delete the comment. Select the last bullet point on the slide, and then press Delete.

15 On the Reviewing toolbar, click **Next Item** 🔛. An alert displays indicating that you have reached the end of the presentation. Click **Cancel**.

16 On the Reviewing toolbar, click **End Review**. Read the displayed alert box, and then click **Yes** to end the review session. Scroll through the presentation and notice that the change markers no longer display and the changes that you accepted have been applied.

17 **Save** 🖫 the file.

Objective 4
Share Files with Other Users

In addition to the compare and merge feature, you can share PowerPoint files with other users by exporting the files to another application such as Microsoft Office Word 2003, and by packaging the files to a CD. The Package for CD feature in Microsoft Office PowerPoint 2003 allows you to copy your presentations to a CD, to a network or hard disk location, or to a removable disk. The Microsoft Office **PowerPoint Viewer** is included when you package a presentation. The Viewer is a program that will run the presentation on another computer even if PowerPoint is not installed.

Activity 8.11 Packaging a Presentation

In this activity, you will go through the process necessary to package a presentation. The amount of disk space required for the PowerPoint Viewer is approximately 3 megabytes. Thus, you will not complete the final steps of the packaging process unless you have access to a rewritable CD or DVD drive.

1 If necessary, **Open** 📄 your file **8A_Information_Firstname_Lastname**.

2 On the menu bar, click **File**, and then click **Package for CD**.

In the Package for CD dialog box, you can give the CD to which you are copying files a name, you can add files to the CD in addition to the currently opened file, and you can access the Package for CD options. You can also specify whether you want to copy the files to a CD or to another folder location, such as a zip disk, a network drive, or a hard drive. See Figure 8.17.

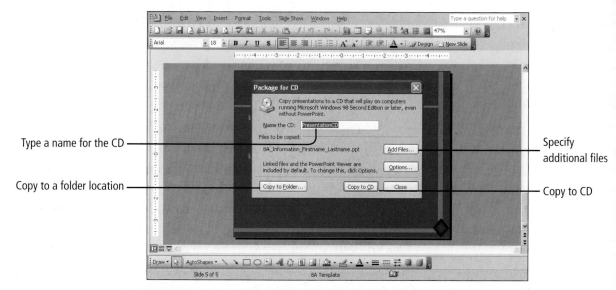

Type a name for the CD ——————

Copy to a folder location ——————

Specify additional files

Copy to CD

Figure 8.17

3 If you have access to a rewritable CD or DVD drive, insert a rewritable CD into the drive, and then click **Copy to CD**. If you do not have access to a rewritable drive, click **Close**, and then skip Step 4.

If you can write to a CD or DVD, PowerPoint will copy the files to the CD. When it is done copying the files, a Microsoft Office PowerPoint question box displays asking if you would like to copy to another CD.

4 Click **No**, and then click **Close**.

The files are copied to a CD. If you insert the CD in another computer, the presentation slide show will launch immediately.

More Knowledge — Package for CD Options

In the Package for CD dialog box, you can click the Options button to display the Options dialog box. In the Options dialog box, you can choose the order in which presentations are played when the CD is inserted into a computer. By default, when the CD is inserted into a computer, the PowerPoint Viewer launches. In the Options dialog box you can indicate whether the Viewer plays all presentations automatically, plays only the first presentation, or whether the user can select which presentation to view. You can also choose not to play the CD automatically.

In addition to Viewer options, you can choose whether or not to include linked files that contain graphics and multimedia, and you can choose to embed TrueType fonts. By embedding TrueType fonts, the correct font will display in your presentation even if it is not available on the system from which you are viewing the presentation. You can also add a password to password protect your files.

Activity 8.12 Exporting a Presentation to Microsoft Word

When you export a presentation to Microsoft Word, you can choose to
display the slides in a table with notes or blank lines below or to the
right of the image of the slide. For example, you may want to print two
slides per page with blank lines to the right of each slide. In PowerPoint,
you can either print two slides per page with no lines, or you can print
three slides per page with blank lines. By exporting the presentation to
Microsoft Word, you can manipulate the layout so that handouts fit the
needs of your audience. You can also send the outline version of a presentation to Microsoft Word.

1 If necessary, **Open** your file **8A_Information_Firstname_
Lastname**.

2 From the **File** menu, point to **Send To**, and then click **Microsoft
Office Word**. See Figure 8.18.

The Send To Microsoft Office Word dialog box displays, in which you
can specify the layout for the presentation in Word.

Point to Send To.

Click Microsoft
Office Word.

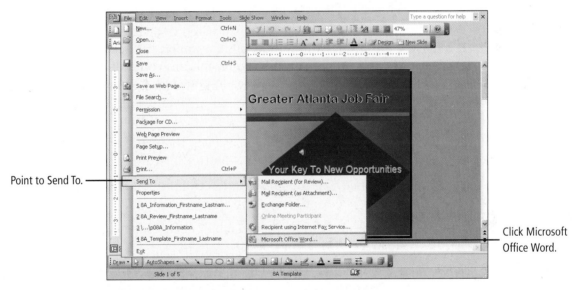

Figure 8.18

3 Click **Blank lines next to slides**, and then under **Add slides to
Microsoft Office Word document**, click **Paste**. See Figure 8.19.

The Paste option creates an *embedded object*. An object embedded
in Word is one in which a link is established between the object and
its source application. Thus, while the object displays in Word, you
can right-click to display a shortcut menu that includes some of the
PowerPoint features. The *Paste link* command creates a link in
which changes to the slide in the source application, PowerPoint, can
be updated in the destination application, Word.

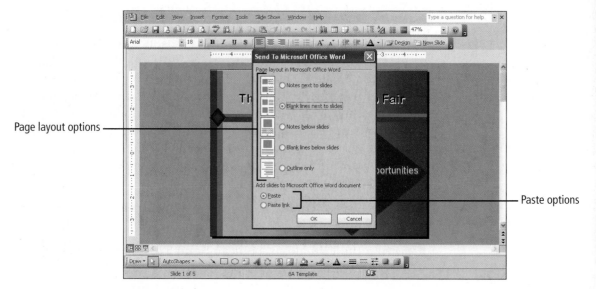

Page layout options

Paste options

Figure 8.19

4 Click **OK**.

A three-column table is created in Microsoft Office Word. The first column contains the slide number, the second column contains the slide image, and the third column contains the blank lines. If you are familiar with Microsoft Office Word, you can change the page orientation and margins, modify the table properties, or delete the lines and add text to the third column.

5 On the Standard toolbar, click the **Print Preview** button 🔍 to view how the presentation will print in Word.

Notice that the presentation will print similar to the *Handouts, 3 slides per page* option in PowerPoint.

6 On the Print Preview toolbar, click **Close** to return to Microsoft Office Word.

7 On the menu bar, click **File**, and then click **Page Setup**. In the **Margins tab**, under **Orientation**, click **Landscape** as shown in Figure 8.20, and then click **OK**.

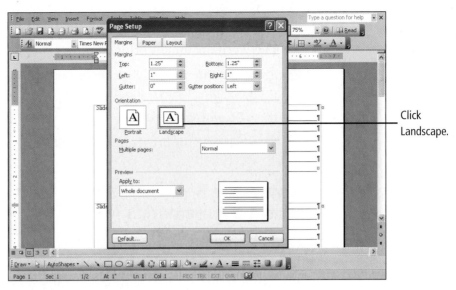

Figure 8.20

Click Landscape.

8 On the Standard toolbar, click the **Print Preview** button 🔍 to view how the presentation will print in Word.

Notice that in the Landscape orientation, the presentation will print two slides per page. This format is not available in PowerPoint.

9 On the Print Preview toolbar, click **Close** to return to Microsoft Office Word.

10 From the **View** menu, click **Header and Footer**. In the displayed Header and Footer toolbar, click the **Switch Between Header and Footer** button 🔲 to move the insertion point to the footer text box.

11 Type **8A Word-Firstname Lastname** using your own first and last name. See Figure 8.21. On the Header and Footer toolbar, click **Close**.

Your name will print at the bottom of every page.

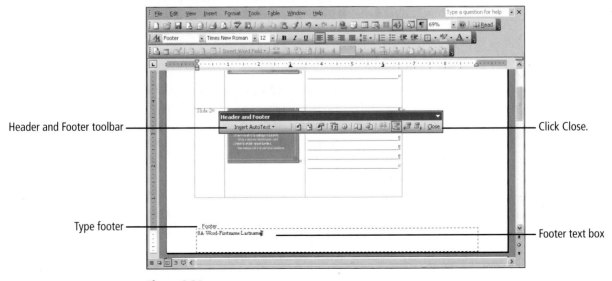

Header and Footer toolbar ⎯⎯

Click Close.

Type footer ⎯⎯

Footer text box

Figure 8.21

12 On the Standard toolbar, click the **Print** button 🖨️.

The Word document prints on three pages.

13 From the **File** menu, click **Save As**, and then navigate to your projects folder. **Save** the file as **8A_Word_Firstname_Lastname** and then **Close** ☒ Word.

Your PowerPoint presentation displays.

Objective 5
Format a Presentation for Web Viewing

A presentation created in Microsoft Office PowerPoint 2003 can be saved as a Web page and posted to a company *intranet* or to the World Wide Web. An intranet is an organization's internal network. Information on the World Wide Web is viewed with a *browser*—software that lets you view and navigate on the Web. Web browsers can read *Hypertext Markup Language* (also known as *HTML*), which is the language that indicates how Web browsers should display page elements.

You do not need to know how to code a presentation in HTML to be able to create a presentation for viewing on the Web. When you access the Save as Web Page command from the File menu, PowerPoint automatically saves the presentation with the associated HTML codes. Anyone can view your presentation on the Web, even if PowerPoint is not installed on the viewer's system.

Activity 8.13 Viewing a Presentation in Web Page Preview

Before you save a presentation as a Web page, you should preview it in your browser to make sure that the slides display as you intended. On the File menu, the Web Page Preview command allows you to preview the current presentation in your browser so that you can see how it will look before you save it as a Web page.

1 If necessary, **Open** 📂 your file **8A_Information_Firstname_ Lastname** and display **Slide 1**.

2 On the menu bar, click **File**, and then click **Web Page Preview**. If necessary, **Maximize** ⬜ the browser window.

Your browser launches and the first slide of your presentation displays in the browser window. Notice that the outline frame to the left of the slide contains the slide titles. To view a particular slide, click a slide title in the outline frame. You can turn the outline off by clicking the Outline button below the outline frame. Below the slide is a *navigation bar*. The navigation bar contains two arrows that allow you to move forward and backward through the presentation one slide at a time. The Full Screen Slide Show button allows you to view the presentation as a slide show. See Figure 8.22.

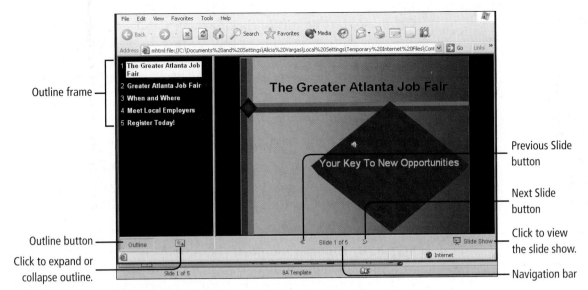

Outline frame

Outline button

Click to expand or collapse outline.

Previous Slide button

Next Slide button

Click to view the slide show.

Navigation bar

Figure 8.22

▣3 In the Outline frame, point to the slide title *When and Where* so that the title displays in yellow and the Link Select pointer ⬚ displays. Click the left mouse button to display **Slide 3**.

▣4 On the navigation bar, click the **Previous Slide arrow** twice to display **Slide 1**.

▣5 If you have headphones or speakers attached to your system, adjust the volume to a level that is comfortable for you. At the far right edge of the navigation bar, click **Slide Show** to view the slide show as it would appear on the Web. When Slide 1 displays, click the megaphone to play the sound file. Then click the left mouse button to proceed through the presentation.

As you view the slide show in the browser, you may notice minor differences from when you viewed the presentation in PowerPoint. For example, on Slide 1, the sound icon is *not* hidden and the music does not play until you click the sound icon. There are a small number of features that are not supported by all browsers when a presentation is viewed as a Web page. This is an example of one of these features. When you have finished viewing the presentation and the black slide displays, click the left mouse button to return to Slide 1.

▣6 On the browser title bar, click **Close** ☒ to return to PowerPoint.

Activity 8.14 Publishing a Presentation to the Web

Saving a presentation for viewing on the Web is known as *publishing*. When you publish a presentation to the Web, recall that the file is saved in HTML format. A presentation saved in HTML format is saved with the .htm extension and PowerPoint encapsulates all of the elements in the presentation, including text, graphics, media files, and transitions and animations within the file. Thus, the file is larger than a standard PowerPoint file. When you save a presentation in HTML format, you can open it in PowerPoint and make editing and formatting changes just as if it were a standard PowerPoint file.

1 From the **File** menu, click **Save as Web Page**, and then navigate to your storage location for this chapter. In the **File name** box, change the file name to **8A_Information_Web_Firstname_Lastname** and then click the **Change Title** button to display the **Set Page Title** dialog box.

In the Set Page Title dialog box, you can enter the title that will display in the browser title bar.

2 Type **Greater Atlanta Job Fair** and then click **OK**.

3 Click **Publish** to display the **Publish as Web Page** dialog box.

Under *Publish what*, you can choose to publish the entire presentation or you can choose to publish only the slides that you select.

4 Under **Publish what?**, be sure that **Complete presentation** is selected.

5 Under **Browser support**, choose the browser that is closest to your system configuration.

Alert!	**Web Page File Sizes**
	Recall that a presentation saved as a Web page will be larger than a standard presentation file. If your Web page does not fit on your disk, click Cancel.

6 Click **Publish** to create the HTML file, and then **Close** ☒ the file. Save your changes if prompted to do so.

7 On the Standard toolbar, click **Open** 📂.

Notice that the file list includes the file *8A_Information_Web_ Firstname_Lastname*. The Web page file name displays with an icon that contains a frame. This icon indicates that the file is saved as a Web page. See Figure 8.23. You can open the file and make changes to it just as you would any other PowerPoint presentation, and then view the file as a Web page. After you have saved a file as a Web page, it can be posted to a Web server and viewed on the Internet.

PowerPoint Web page icon ——

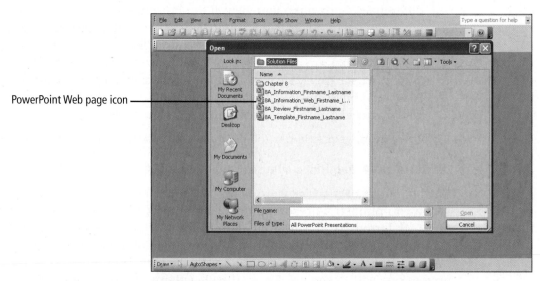

Figure 8.23

8 Click **Cancel**, and then close PowerPoint.

End You have completed Project 8A

Summary

In this chapter you practiced how to create and save a custom design template. When modifying the slide master with graphics that include AutoShapes, logos, or other images, you are limited only by your own imagination. A custom template can include changes to the color scheme, text, and background colors or fills. If you do not want to use one of the templates provided by Microsoft Office PowerPoint, design your own—keeping in mind the basic presentation design tips that you have learned throughout this text. Keep your template and colors appropriate to your audience, provide enough contrast between text and backgrounds, and do not clutter your background with unnecessary objects.

You also practiced in this chapter how to share your presentations with others. Teamwork is an essential skill in today's workplace. Thus, collaborating with other people using the Compare and Merge feature is a useful tool when a presentation is created and modified by a team. Whether you are the presentation creator or reviewer, you can use the reviewing tools to improve the presentation and to get feedback from others who may have a different perspective on the topic that you are presenting. In addition to the reviewing tools, you practiced how to share your presentations with others by creating a file that can be viewed on the World Wide Web. As you create presentations for viewing on the Internet, be sensitive to the diversity of your viewers. Keep your presentations appropriate and professional, and research the guidelines on accessibility so that people with disabilities can access your Web presentations easily and thoroughly.

Throughout this text you practiced how to create simple, text-based presentations, and you learned how to create complex presentations that include graphics, multimedia, and animation. Have fun with what you learned, develop presentations that are creative yet professional, explore the resources on the Microsoft Office Web site, and most importantly, practice your presentation skills. Remember that even the best PowerPoint presentation is no substitute for a well-prepared presenter who knows the topic and can deliver a presentation with confidence and credibility.

In This Chapter You Practiced How To

- Create a Design Template
- Enhance a Presentation with Sound
- Modify a Presentation Using Research and Comparison Tools
- Share Files with Other Users
- Format a Presentation for Web Viewing

Matching

Match each term in the second column with its correct definition in the first column by writing the letter of the term on the blank line in front of the correct definition.

_____ **1.** A pasted object in which a link is established between the object and its source application.

_____ **2.** The language used to code and store presentations that are viewed on the Web.

_____ **3.** A combination of video, text, and graphics used in a presentation.

_____ **4.** Software that allows you to view and navigate on the Web.

_____ **5.** In the browser window, a bar that displays below the slide and that allows you to move forward and backward through the presentation one slide at a time.

_____ **6.** Icons that designate a change made by a reviewer.

_____ **7.** A program that will run a PowerPoint slide show on another computer even if PowerPoint is not installed.

_____ **8.** Electronic notes that usually contain reviewer questions or thoughts.

_____ **9.** A commonly used abbreviation for Hypertext Markup Language.

_____ **10.** The term used to describe a company's internal network.

A Browser

B Change markers

C Comments

D Embedded object

E HTML

F Hypertext Markup Language

G Intranet

H Multimedia

I Navigation bar

J PowerPoint Viewer

Concepts Assessments (continued)

Fill in the Blank Write the correct answer in the space provided.

1. A presentation can be saved as a _____ that can be applied to other presentations that you create.

2. The command that creates a link in which changes to the source application are updated in the destination application is called _____.

3. A command that allows you to preview the current presentation as a Web page is _____.

4. The Windows _____ software can be used to record sound files that you can insert in a presentation.

5. A PowerPoint feature in which you can search for words with similar meanings is called the _____.

6. When you _____ a presentation to Microsoft Word, you can choose to display the slides in a table with notes or blank lines below or to the right of the image of the slide.

7. Saving a presentation for viewing on the Web is also known as _____.

8. The Set Page Title dialog box allows you to enter a title that displays in the _____ title bar.

9. The _____ option in the Publish as Web Page dialog box allows you to optimize the presentation for the different types of browsers that your audience may use when viewing your Web presentation.

10. The _____ feature allows you to combine, accept, or reject reviewers' comments and revisions to your presentation.

Project 8B — Success

Objective: *Modify a Presentation Using Research and Comparison Tools.*

In the following Skill Assessment, you will format a candidate seminar presentation regarding important skills and attitudes that will help attendees at the Greater Atlanta Job Fair learn to be successful in a career. Your completed presentation will look similar to Figure 8.24. You will save your presentation as *8B_Success_Firstname_Lastname.*

1. From your student files, open the file **p08B_Success**. Scroll through the presentation to familiarize yourself with the slides, and then **Save** the file as **8B_Success_Firstname_Lastname**

2. From the **Slide Show** menu, click **Slide Transition** to display the **Slide Transition** task pane. Under **Apply to selected slides**, click the **Strips Left-Up** transition.

3. Under **Modify transition**, click the **Speed arrow**, and then click **Slow**. Click **Apply to All Slides**. **Save** the file.

4. To save the presentation for review, on the **File** menu, click **Save As**. In the **File name** box type **8B_Review_Firstname_Lastname** and then click the **Save as type arrow**. Click **Presentation for Review**, and then click **Save**.

5. On the Standard toolbar, click the **Open** button. Double-click to open your **8B_Review_Firstname_Lastname** file. If the Microsoft Office PowerPoint question box displays, click **No**.

6. Display **Slide 2**, and then select the word **Explain**. Point to the selection and right-click to display the shortcut menu. Point to **Synonyms**, and then click **Thesaurus**. In the **Research** task pane, under **give details (v.)**, point to **describe**, and then click the arrow. On the displayed menu, click **Insert** to change the word.

7. Display **Slide 5**, and then in the second bullet, right-click the word **whine** to display the shortcut menu. Point to **Synonyms**, and then click **complain** to replace the word. **Close** the Research task pane.

8. Display **Slide 6**, and then click anywhere in the text box at the bottom of the slide—*Companies change, jobs change. Be ready for it.* From the **Slide Show** menu, click **Custom Animation**. In the **Custom Animation** task pane, click **Add Effect**. Point to **Entrance**, and then click **Fly In**. **Close** the task pane.

9. On the menu bar, click **Insert**, and then click **Comment**. In the comment box type **I think the two bullets under Be observant should be deleted.**

10. **Save** and **Close** the file.

(Project 8B—Success continues on the next page)

(Project 8B–Success continued)

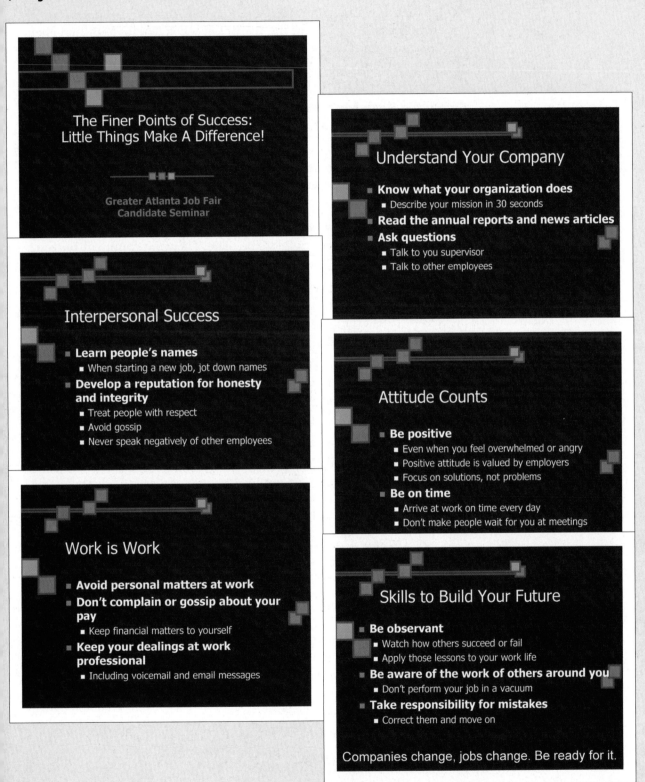

Figure 8.24

(Project 8B–Success continues on the next page)

(Project 8B–Success continued)

11. If necessary, open your file **8B_Success_Firstname_Lastname** and display **Slide 1**. On the menu bar, click **Tools**, and then click **Compare and Merge Presentations**. In the **Choose Files to Merge with Current Presentation** dialog box, double-click your **8B_Review_Firstname_Lastname** file.

12. On the **Reviewing** toolbar, click the **Next Item** button to display **Slide 2**. Click the **All changes to Text 2** check box to accept the changes to this slide.

13. On the **Reviewing** toolbar, click the **Next Item** button to display **Slide 5**. Click the **All changes to Text 2** check box to accept the changes to this slide.

14. On the **Reviewing** toolbar, click the **Next Item** button to display **Slide 6**. At the lower right of the slide, click the comment button, and then press Delete to delete the comment.

15. On the **Reviewing** toolbar, click the **Next Item** button. Do *not* click the Animation settings check box; thus you will reject, rather than accept, this change. On the **Reviewing** toolbar, click **End Review**. In the Microsoft Office PowerPoint question box, click **Yes**.

16. Create a header and footer for the notes and handouts that includes the date updated automatically and a footer with the text **8B Success-Firstname Lastname** Clear all other header and footer options and click **Apply to All**.

17. View the slide show. **Save** the file, and then print the presentation as **grayscale handouts**, **6** slides per page in **horizontal** order. Close the file.

End You have completed Project 8B ────────────────

Project 8C—Jobs

Objective: *Create a Design Template.*

In the following Skill Assessment, you will create a template and format a presentation that provides information about various types of administrative positions. Your completed presentation will look similar to Figure 8.25. You will save your presentation as *8C_Jobs_Firstname_Lastname.*

1. On the Standard toolbar, click **New** to start a new blank PowerPoint presentation. Press Shift, and then click the **Normal View** button to display the slide master.

(Project 8C–Jobs continues on the next page)

(Project 8C–Jobs continued)

The Right Job for You in Administration

Greater Atlanta Job Fair

Administrative Assistant

- Manage and organize information and schedules
  - Make and manage travel arrangements
- Use computers
  - Send email, create spreadsheets, and manage databases
- Varied duties depending upon company

Accounting Clerk

- Perform accounting clerical work
- Use spreadsheets or specialized accounting software
  - Record debits and credits
  - Perform variety of calculations
- Other duties
  - Balance accounts, prepare purchase orders

Customer Service Representative

- **Provide information on products or services**
  - Answer questions and resolve problems
  - Interact with customers via phone or computers
  - Use email and fax to send/receive information
- **Technological developments provide efficient customer service**
  - Representatives need higher level of technical skills

Human Resources Representative

- Represent organization to current and prospective employees
  - Manage recruiting, interviewing, and benefits
  - Develop diversity and professional development activities
- Maintain confidential employee information
  - Database and human resource software

Legal Assistant

- Research and assistance
  - Cases, closings, hearings, and meetings
  - Manage and organize information
  - Prepare written reports
- Computer skills essential for researching legal databases
  - Internet and CD

Figure 8.25

(Project 8C–Jobs continues on the next page)

(Project 8C–Jobs continued)

2. From the **Format** menu, click **Background**. Click the **Background fill arrow**, and then click **Fill Effects**. In the **Gradient tab**, click **One color**. Click the **Color 1 arrow**, and in the color scheme palette, click the sixth color—**blue**. Drag the slider in the **Dark/Light** bar approximately three-fourths of the way toward the **Light** end of the scale. Under **Shading styles**, click **Diagonal down**, and under **Variants**, in the second row click the first variant. Click **OK**, and then click **Apply** to create the template background color.

3. Click in the title placeholder, and then on the Drawing toolbar, click the **Font Color arrow**. Click the first color—**white**—so that when the template is applied to a presentation, the title of every slide will display in white.

4. In the Bulleted list placeholder, click in the *Click to edit Master text styles* line. On the menu bar, click **Format**, and then click **Bullets and Numbering**. Click the **Color arrow**, and then click **More Colors**. In the second to last row of the color honeycomb, click the eighth (last) color—**dark red**—and then click **OK** twice to change the bullet color to dark red.

5. On the Formatting toolbar, click the **Slide Design** button. In the task pane, click **Color Schemes**, and then at the bottom of the task pane, click **Edit Color Schemes**. In the **Custom tab**, click the light aqua **Fills** box. Click **Change Color**, and then click the **Standard tab** to display the color honeycomb. In the third to last row of the color honeycomb, click the third color—**yellow**—and then click **OK**. Click the teal **Accent and hyperlink** box. Click **Change Color** to display the color honeycomb. In the fourth row of the color honeycomb, click the seventh color—**medium blue**—and then click **OK**. The color scheme changes are complete. Click **Apply**.

6. On the Slide Master View toolbar, click the **Insert New Title Master** button to create a title master. Click in the title placeholder, and then on the Drawing toolbar, click the **Font Color arrow**. Click the second color—**black**.

7. All formatting for the template is complete. From the **File** menu, click **Save As**. In the File name box, type **8C_Template_Firstname_Lastname** Click the **Save as type arrow**, and then click **Design Template**. Click the **Save in arrow**, and then navigate to the location where you are storing your files for this chapter. Click **Save**. Close the template.

8. From the student files, if necessary, change the Files of type to All PowerPoint Presentations, and then open the presentation **p08C_Jobs**. If necessary, display the **Slide Design** task pane, and in the task pane, click **Design Templates**. At the bottom of the task pane, click **Browse**. Navigate to your chapter folder. Click the template that you just created—**8C_Template_Firstname_Lastname**—and then click **Apply**.

(Project 8C–Jobs continues on the next page)

(Project 8C–Jobs continued)

9. From the **Slide Show** menu, click **Slide Transition** to display the **Slide Transition** task pane. Under **Apply to selected slides**, click the **Blinds Vertical** transition.

10. Under **Modify transition**, click the **Speed arrow**, and then click **Medium**. Click **Apply to All Slides**.

11. Create a footer for the notes and handouts that includes the date updated automatically and a footer with the text **8C Jobs-Firstname Lastname** Clear all other header and footer options and click **Apply to All**.

12. Display **Slide 1**, and then view the slide show. **Save** the file as **8C_Jobs_Firstname_Lastname** in your chapter folder, and then print the presentation as **grayscale handouts**, **6** slides per page in **horizontal** order. Close the file.

 End You have completed Project 8C ──────────────

Project 8D — Job Fair

Objectives: *Enhance a Presentation with Sound, Share Files with Other Users, and Format a Presentation for Web Viewing.*

In the following Skill Assessment, you will animate a presentation and publish it for Web viewing. You will also export the presentation to Microsoft Word. Your completed presentation will look similar to Figure 8.26. You will save your presentation as *8D_Job_Fair_Firstname_Lastname.*

1. From the student files, open the file **p08D_Job_Fair**. Scroll through the presentation to familiarize yourself with the slides.

2. On **Slide 1**, display the **Insert** menu, and then point to **Movies and Sounds**. Click **Sound from File**, and then navigate to the student files that accompany this textbook. Click **p08D_Fair**, and then click **OK**. Click **Automatically** so that the clip plays when you run the slide show.

3. Select the **sound icon**, and then from the **Slide Show** menu, click **Custom Animation**. In the **Custom Animation list**, click the **item 0 arrow**. Click **Effect Options**. In the **Effect tab**, under **Stop playing**, click the **After** option button, and then in the **slides** box, type 6

4. Click the **Timing tab**, and then click the **Repeat arrow**. Click **2**. Select the **Rewind when done playing** check box so that when the music is finished, it starts over and repeats itself until the end of the slide show.

(Project 8D–Job Fair continues on the next page)

(Project 8D–Job Fair continued)

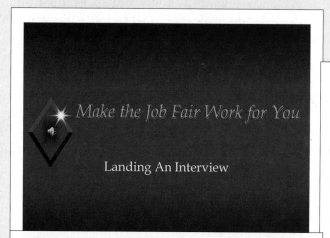

Make the Job Fair Work for You

Landing An Interview

Setting The Stage
- Dress for a job interview
  - You will be meeting HR representatives and hiring managers
- Bring writing materials
  - You want to be able to take notes quickly
- Carry plenty of copies of your resume
  - Use a brief case or portfolio

Keep Your Focus
- Review the exhibitors list
- Choose a few target companies
  - Do background research on those companies
- At the fair
  - Focus your energies on those companies
  - Wander around after visiting target companies

Know What's Available

The Job Fair Company List
- Outlines available positions for each company
- Use the fair kiosks to check for updates
- Apply for positions for which you are qualified

Don't be discouraged by the number of other job seekers – you only need one job!

Make The Most Of Each Meeting

- Introduce yourself to company representatives
  - Be upbeat
  - Project energy and confidence
- Prepare a two minutes or less statement
  - Include your background and qualifications
- Ask questions about the company
  - Listen to what they have to say

Follow Up!
- Note the name of each person you meet
  - Ask for business cards
- Follow up with each company
  - Send a letter or email to the person you met
  - Tell them about your interest in their company
  - Briefly discuss your qualifications
  - Include a copy of your resume

Figure 8.26

(Project 8D–Job Fair continues on the next page)

(Project 8D–Job Fair continued)

5. Click the **Sound Settings tab**. Under **Display options**, select the **Hide sound icon during slide show** check box. Click **OK**. Point to the sound icon so that the move pointer displays, and then drag the sound icon so that it is centered in the diamond on the left side of the slide.

6. Click the **Other Task Panes arrow**, and then click **Slide Transition**. Click the **Box In** transition, and then change the speed to **Medium**. Click **Apply to All Slides**, and then close the task pane. View the slide show, and read the information on each slide. Notice that the sound plays until the end of the presentation.

7. This presentation will be printed in landscape orientation with two slides per page using Microsoft Office Word. From the **File** menu, point to **Send To**, and then click **Microsoft Office Word**.

8. Click **Blank lines next to slides**, and then click **OK** to send the presentation to Word.

9. On the Word menu bar, click **View**, and then click **Header and Footer**. On the Header and Footer toolbar, click the **Switch Between Header and Footer** button, and then in the **Footer** text box, type **8D Job Fair-Firstname Lastname** On the Header and Footer toolbar, click **Close**.

10. On the menu bar, click **File**. Click **Page Setup**, and then on the **Margins tab**, click **Landscape**. Click **OK**.

11. Display the **File** menu, click **Save As**, and then navigate to your student files. Save the file as **8D_Job_Fair_Firstname_Lastname**

12. On the Standard toolbar, click **Print**. Close the file and close Word. Your PowerPoint presentation displays.

13. On the **File** menu, click **Save as Web Page**. Navigate to your storage location, in the **File name** box type **8D_Job_Fair_Firstname_Lastname** and then click **Change Title**. Type **Getting the Most from the Job Fair** and then click **OK**. In the **Save As** dialog box, click **Save** to save the presentation as a Web page.

14. From the **File** menu, click **Web Page Preview**. Maximize the browser window if necessary, and then in the lower right corner of the browser window, click **Slide Show**, and then view the presentation. Do not be concerned if the music stops after the first slide. **Close** the browser window, and then close the file.

End **You have completed Project 8D** ———————————

Project 8E — Interview

Objectives: *Create a Design Template, Format a Presentation for Web Viewing, and Share Files with Other Users.*

In the following Performance Assessment you will format a presentation for the Web regarding successful interviewing skills. Your completed presentation will look similar to the one shown in Figure 8.27. You will save your presentation as *8E_Interview_Firstname_Lastname*.

1. Start a new blank PowerPoint presentation based on the **Default Design template**. Display the **slide master**. If necessary, close the Getting Started task pane.

2. From the **Format** menu, click **Background**. Change the background to a textured fill effect using the last texture in the first row— **Stationery**.

3. If necessary display the ruler. Draw a line that begins at **2 inches above zero on the vertical ruler** and that extends from the left edge of the slide to **2 inches to the right of zero on the horizontal ruler**. Change the **Line Style** to **4½ pt.**, and then click the **Line Color arrow**. Click **More Line Colors** and in the color honeycomb, in the last row, click the sixth color—**dark red**.

4. Use Ctrl + D to duplicate the line. Drag the duplicated line to the right edge of the slide and positioned at **3 inches below zero on the vertical ruler**.

5. In the lower right corner of the slide master, click in the **Number Area** placeholder and then press Delete. On the Drawing toolbar, click **Text Box**, and then in the lower right corner, below the red line and to the right of the Footer Area text box, click once. Type **Interview Skills** and then change the **Font Size** to **24**. Apply **Italic** and drag the text box so that its lower right corner touches the lower right corner of the slide.

6. Click in the **Click to edit Master text styles** line. Display the **Bullets and Numbering** dialog box. Change the bullet color to the same **dark red** that you used for the lines that you drew. Change the **Second level** bullet color to **dark red** also.

7. Display the **Slide Transition** task pane. Apply the **Wheel Clockwise, 2 Spokes** transition and change the speed to **Medium**. By applying the transition to the master, all slides will contain the transition.

8. On the Slide Master toolbar, click **Insert New Title Master**. The formatting applied to the slide master is also applied to the title master. Delete the *Interview Skills* text box in the lower right corner of the slide, and then delete the line in the lower right area of the slide.

(**Project 8E**–Interview continues on the next page)

(Project 8E–Interview continued)

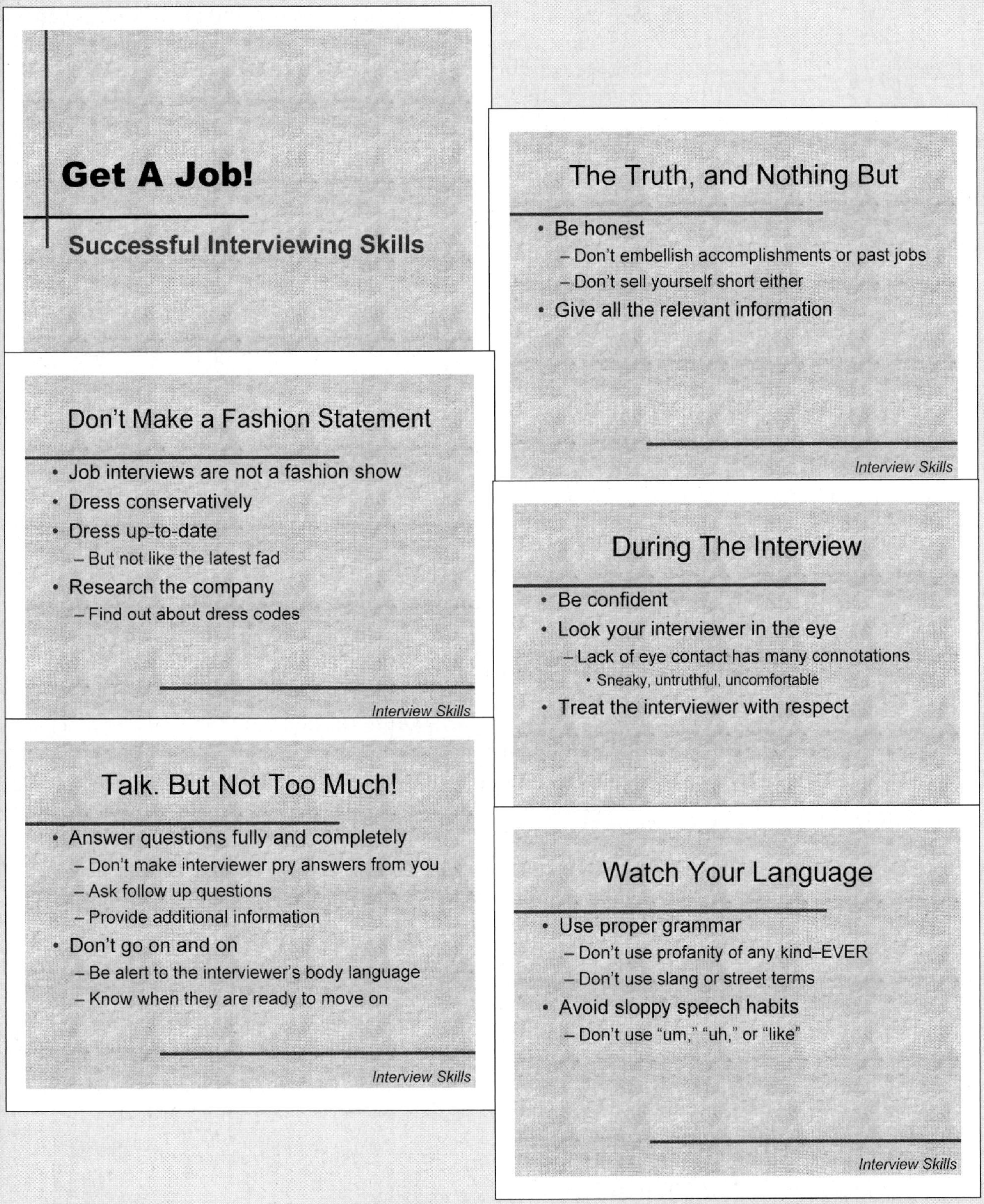

Get A Job!

Successful Interviewing Skills

Don't Make a Fashion Statement

- Job interviews are not a fashion show
- Dress conservatively
- Dress up-to-date
  - But not like the latest fad
- Research the company
  - Find out about dress codes

Interview Skills

Talk. But Not Too Much!

- Answer questions fully and completely
  - Don't make interviewer pry answers from you
  - Ask follow up questions
  - Provide additional information
- Don't go on and on
  - Be alert to the interviewer's body language
  - Know when they are ready to move on

Interview Skills

The Truth, and Nothing But

- Be honest
  - Don't embellish accomplishments or past jobs
  - Don't sell yourself short either
- Give all the relevant information

Interview Skills

During The Interview

- Be confident
- Look your interviewer in the eye
  - Lack of eye contact has many connotations
    - Sneaky, untruthful, uncomfortable
- Treat the interviewer with respect

Watch Your Language

- Use proper grammar
  - Don't use profanity of any kind–EVER
  - Don't use slang or street terms
- Avoid sloppy speech habits
  - Don't use "um," "uh," or "like"

Interview Skills

Figure 8.27

(Project 8E–Interview continues on the next page)

(Project 8E–Interview continued)

9. Select and drag the remaining line so that it is positioned between the title and subtitle placeholders, and so that its left edge touches the left edge of the slide. Shorten the line so that it extends only to **zero on the horizontal ruler**. Change the line color to **black**.

10. Draw a **line** that begins at the **top of the slide** and at **4.5 inches** the left of zero on the horizontal ruler, and that extends to **1 in** **below zero on the vertical ruler**. Change the **Line Style** to **4½ pt** and change the **Line Color** to **dark red**.

11. Select the title placeholder, and then change the **Font** to **Arial Bla** and the **Font Size** to **54**. Change the alignment to **Align Left**.

12. Click in the subtitle placeholder. Change the **Font Size** to **40**, and then change the **Font Color** to **dark red**. Apply **Bold**, and then siz the placeholder so that it is the same width as the title placeholder.

13. **Save** as a **Design Template**, navigate to your storage location, an name the file **8E_Template_Firstname_Lastname** Close the template.

14. From the student files, open **p08E_Interview**. Apply the **8E_Template_Firstname_Lastname** design template to your pre-sentation. (Hint: Display the Slide Design task pane and use the Browse command to navigate to your student files.)

15. Display **Slide 1** and view the slide show.

16. Send the presentation to **Microsoft Office Word** using the **Blank lines next to slides** option. In Microsoft Office Word, click the **Vie** menu, and then click **Header and Footer**. Click the **Switch Between Header and Footer** button, and in the footer type **8E Interview Skills-Firstname Lastname** and then **close** the Header and Footer toolbar. **Save** the document in your chapter folder as **8E_Interview_Skills_ Firstname_Lastname** and then **Print** and docu-ment. Close Microsoft Word to return to your presentation.

17. **Save** the file as a **Web Page** with the name **8E_Interview_Firstname_ Lastname** in the location where you store your student files. Close the file.

End You have completed Project 8E ─────────────────

Project 8F—Leaving

Objectives: *Modify a Presentation Using Research and Comparison Tools and Enhance a Presentation with Sound.*

In the following Performance Assessment, you will modify a presentation for the Greater Atlanta Job Fair regarding tips for leaving a job. This presentation will be self-running, meaning that viewers may come and see the presentation as it continually runs on a kiosk computer. Your completed presentation will look similar to the one shown in Figure 8.28. You will save your presentation as *8F_Leaving_Firstname_Lastname*.

1. From your student files, open the file **p08F_Leaving**. Scroll through the presentation to familiarize yourself with the slides. In your chapter folder, save the file as **8F_Leaving_Firstname_Lastname**

2. Display the **Slide Transition** task pane, and apply the **Split Vertical In** transition. Change the **Speed** to **Medium**. Clear the **On mouse click** check box, and then change the transition to advance **Automatically after 5** seconds. Click **Apply to All Slides**.

3. Display **Slide 1**, and then from the student files, **Insert** the **Sound from File—p08F_Tips**. Play the sound **Automatically**. Display the **Custom Animation** task pane, and then in the **Custom Animation list**, click the **item 0 arrow**. Change the **Effect Options** to **Stop playing After 6 slides**. Change the **Timing** to **Repeat 2** times and to **Rewind when done playing**. Change the **Sound Settings** by selecting the **Hide sound icon during slide show**.

4. Display **Slide 2**. In the third bullet, select the word **great**, and then use the **Thesaurus** to replace it with the word **terrific**. Display **Slide 5** and use the **Thesaurus** to change the word **Prospective** to **Potential**. Correct capitalization if necessary.

5. View the slide show. You do not need to click the mouse button to advance the slides; just wait for the slide to transition to the next slide.

6. Create a header and footer for the notes and handouts that includes the date updated automatically and a footer with the text **8F Leaving-Firstname Lastname** Clear all other header and footer options.

7. **Save** the file, and then print the presentation as **grayscale handouts**, **6** slides per page in **horizontal** order. Close the file.

(Project 8F–Leaving continues on the next page)

(Project 8F–Leaving continued)

Making a Smooth Move: Tips for Leaving a Job

Candidate Seminar

Be Prepared for Change

- Keep your resume and cover letter current
  - Update experience and education
  - Update new skills
- Keep your contacts current
  - Periodically contact possible references
  - Expand your professional network

Reason For Leaving

- Your reason should be positive
  - Avoid negative comments about company
- Consistency is important
  - Potential employers should get a consistent reason
  - Consider discussing reasons with your boss

No Matter Why You Leave A Job

- You need to be prepared
  - Layoffs can happen at any time
  - You could be offered a great new job today
- Make your exit with style and grace

Finances First

- Get the facts about finances
  - Continuing health insurance
  - Payment for unused vacation time
  - Final paycheck

Pack it Up!

- Computer safety
  - Always keep personal files to a minimum
  - Delete personal files and email
- Pack your personal belongings
- Say goodbye without drama or negativity
  - You may be coworkers again someday

Figure 8.28

End You have completed Project 8F

Project 8G — Resume

Objectives: *Modify a Presentation Using Research and Comparison Tools and Share Files with Other Users.*

In the following Performance Assessment, you will format a presentation that includes guidelines for developing a resume. Your completed presentation will look similar to the one shown in Figure 8.29. You will save your presentation as *8G_Resume_Firstname_Lastname.*

1. From your student files, open the file **p08G_Resume**. Scroll through the presentation to familiarize yourself with the slides. Save the file as **8G_Resume_Firstname_Lastname** in your projects folder for this chapter.

2. Display the **Slide Transition** task pane and apply the **Uncover Left** transition at **Medium** speed to all of the slides in the presentation.

3. Display **Slide 2**. Select the bulleted list placeholder, and then display the **Custom Animation** task pane. In the **Add Entrance Effect** dialog box, apply the **Wipe** effect. In the task pane, change the **Direction** to **From Left**. Click anywhere on the slide to cancel the selection.

4. Select the picture and apply the **Box** entrance effect. Change the **Start** option to **After Previous**.

5. Display **Slide 3**, and then apply the **Wipe** entrance effect to the bulleted list. Change the **Direction** to **From Left**. Add the **Wipe From Left** entrance effect to the bulleted lists on **Slides 4, 5**, and **6**. On the Standard toolbar, click the **Save** button.

6. From the **File** menu, click **Save As** and then save the file in your storage location as a **Presentation for Review** with the name **8G_Review_Firstname_Lastname Close** the review file.

7. Reopen your **8G_Review_Firstname_Lastname** file and in the Microsoft Office PowerPoint question box, click **No**.

8. On **Slide 1**, insert the following **Comment: Should we include information on cover letters also?**

9. Display **Slide 2** and in the second bullet, delete the words **at the most**. Display **Slide 3**. In the bullet point *Begin sentences with power word or phrase*, change **word** to **words** and **phrase** to **phrases** Display **Slide 4**. At the end of the last bullet point, type a comma, and then press Space. Then, type the text **and addresses**

10. Display **Slide 5**. In the second bullet point, change **words** to **keywords**

11. **Save** and close the file. Open the **8G_Resume_Firstname_Lastname** file. Be sure that **Slide 1** is displayed.

12. **Compare and merge** the **8G_Resume_Firstname_Lastname** and the **8G_Review_Firstname_Lastname** presentations, applying all of the changes to the presentation. View and delete the comment on **Slide 1**, and then end the review. **Save** the file.

(Project 8G–Resume continues on the next page)

(Project 8G–Resume continued)

Create a Resume Employers Want to See!

Greater Atlanta Job Fair
Candidate Seminar

Summarize Your Expertise

- Describe what you can do
  - Two or three sentences
- Briefly outline your career focus
- What to include
  - Industries in which you've worked
  - Your education

Focus on Achievements

- Describe your accomplishments
  - Don't use job description
  - Outline your achievements, creativity, skills
- Use Power Words
  - Begin sentences with power words or phrases
    - Facilitate, implement, develop, manage, create, coordinate, etc.

Proof Your Work

- Proofread
  - Ask someone else to proof application package
  - Spelling errors, typos, poor grammar
    - May keep you from getting the interview
  - Software spell check won't catch every error
- Accuracy is critical
  - Dates, phone numbers, and addresses

Make Your Resume Database Friendly

- Resumes are scanned into electronic databases
- Use keywords related to job
  - Employers often search databases for keywords
- Use a sans serif font such as Arial
  - Easily recognized by software
- Keep it simple
  - Don't use boxes, columns, or different fonts

Customize Each Resume

- Specific to employer and job opening
  - Change keywords to match job description
  - Highlight skills necessary for job
- Rearrange education and experience
  - Depending upon which is most relevant to job

Figure 8.29

13. Send the presentation to Microsoft Office Word as **Blank lines next to slides**. When the presentation displays in Word, change the **Page Setup** to **Landscape**. In Word, create a **footer** with the text **8G Word Resume-Firstname Lastname** and then print the document. **Save** the file as **8G_Word_Resume_Firstname_Lastname** and then close and exit Word and PowerPoint.

 You have completed Project 8G

Project 8H — Skills

Objectives: *Create a Design Template and Enhance a Presentation with Sound.*

In the following Mastery Assessment you will create and apply a template to a presentation regarding interpersonal skills that employers look for in potential employees. Your completed presentation will look similar to the one shown in Figure 8.30. You will save your presentation as *8H_Skills_Firstname_Lastname.*

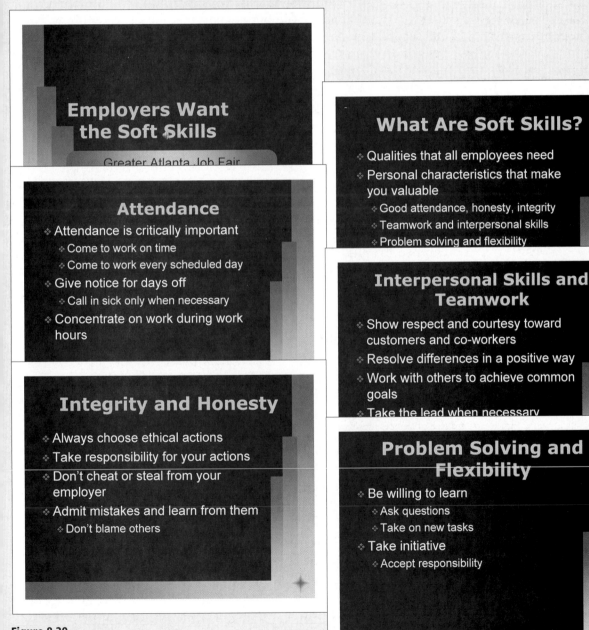

Figure 8.30

(**Project 8H**–Skills continues on the next page)

(Project 8H–Skills continued)

1. Start a new blank presentation and display the slide master. If necessary, close the task pane.

2. Select the **Master title placeholder**. Change the title **Font** to **Verdana** and apply **Bold**. Change the **Font Color** to the fifth color in the color scheme—**light aqua**. Change the **Font Color** for all of the bulleted list text to **white**. Apply a **black background** to the slide.

3. Select the **first level bullet**, display the **Bullets and Numbering** dialog box, and change the bullet character to the second bullet in the second row—four dots forming a diamond shape. Display the color honeycomb for the bullets, and in the third row, click the second color—**teal**. In the Bullets and Numbering dialog box, change the **Size** to **75%**. Repeat the bullet formatting for the **Second level** bullet. Change the color of the **Third level** bullet to **teal**.

4. Using a **One color gradient fill** effect in **light aqua** (from the color scheme), create the four rectangles shown in Figure 8.31. Apply horizontal fill effects to the three vertical rectangles using the second variant in the first row, and apply a vertical fill effect to the horizontal rectangle. Remove the line from around the rectangles. (Hint: Recall that you can use Ctrl + D to duplicate a shape, and then resize, reformat, rotate, and reposition as necessary. Recall also that you can use Ctrl plus the directional keys on your keyboard to nudge a shape into a precise location.)

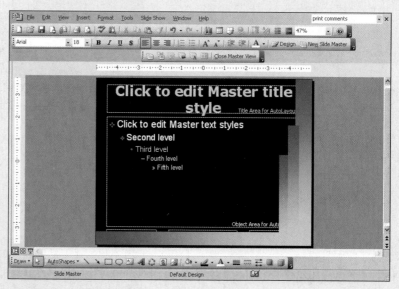

Figure 8.31

(Project 8H–Skills continues on the next page)

(Project 8H–Skills continued)

5. Create a **Plaque AutoShape** found in the **Basic Shapes** menu. Click in the lower right corner of the slide to create a 1-inch by 1-inch plaque. Apply a **One color gradient fill effect** in **light aqua** using the **From center Shading style**. Select the **second Variant**. Change the **Line Color** to **No Line**. Use the yellow adjustment handle to drag inward and change the shape of the AutoShape, and then position the object as shown in Figure 8.32.

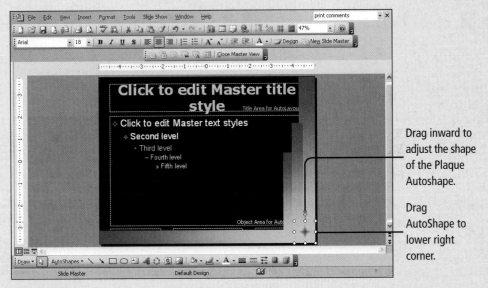

Drag inward to adjust the shape of the Plaque Autoshape.

Drag AutoShape to lower right corner.

Figure 8.32

6. Insert a new title master. Select the subtitle placeholder and from the **Draw** menu, change the AutoShape to a **Rounded Rectangle**, found in the **Basic Shapes** menu.

7. Delete the rectangles and plaque AutoShape from the title master, and then create the objects and size the placeholders as shown in Figure 8.33.

(Project 8H–Skills continues on the next page)

(Project 8H–Skills continued)

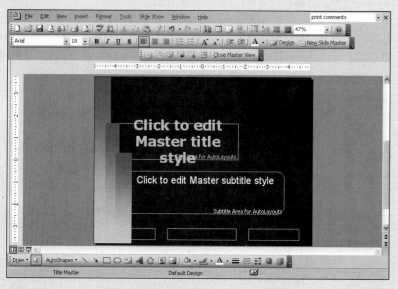

Figure 8.33

8. Select the subtitle placeholder, and then apply a **One color gradient fill effect** in **light aqua** using the **Vertical Shading** style. Select the second **Variant** in the second row. Change the **Font Color** to **black**.

9. **Save** the file as a **Design Template** in the location where you store your project files. Name the template **8H_Template_Firstname_Lastname** and then close the template file.

10. From your student files, **Open** the file **p08H_Skills** and apply the design template that you just created to the presentation. **Save** the file as **8H_Skills_Firstname_Lastname**

11. On **Slide 1**, adjust the size and placement of the title placeholder so that it displays as shown in Figure 8.34.

(Project 8H–Skills continues on the next page)

(Project 8H–Skills continued)

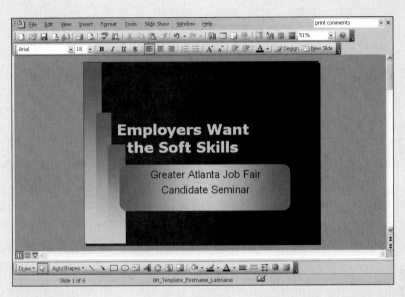

Figure 8.34

12. Insert the **p08H_Music** sound file so that it plays **Automatically**. Use the **Custom Animation Effect Options** to hide the icon during the slide show, and **Stop playing** the sound file **After 6 slides**.

13. Apply the **Box In** slide transition at **Medium Speed** to all of the slides. View the slide show.

14. Create a header and footer for the notes and handouts that includes the date updated automatically and a footer with the text **8H Skills-Firstname Lastname** Clear all other header and footer options.

15. **Save** the file, and then print the presentation as **grayscale handouts**, **6** slides per page in **horizontal** order. **Close** the file.

End **You have completed Project 8H**

Project 8I — Benefits

Objectives: *Modify a Presentation Using Research and Comparison Tools, Share Files with Other Users, and Format a Presentation for Web Viewing.*

In the following Mastery Assessment, you will modify a presentation for the Greater Atlanta Job Fair Web site that describes typical employee benefits. Your completed presentation will look similar to the one shown in Figure 8.35. You will save your presentation as *8I_Benefits_Firstname_Lastname*.

1. From the student files, open the file **p08I_Benefits**. Scroll through the presentation to familiarize yourself with the slides. Apply the white **Echo** template, and then in your projects folder for this chapter, **Save** the file as 8I_Benefits_Firstname_Lastname

2. On **Slides 2** through **5**, apply a **light aqua Fill Color** and **Shadow Style 6** to each of the bulleted list placeholders. You will adjust the size of the placeholders on Slide 3 later.

3. Display the slide master and change the **Second level** bullet to the third color scheme color—**periwinkle**. Change the **Third level** bullet to **white**.

(Project 8I–Benefits continues on the next page)

(Project 8I–Benefits continued)

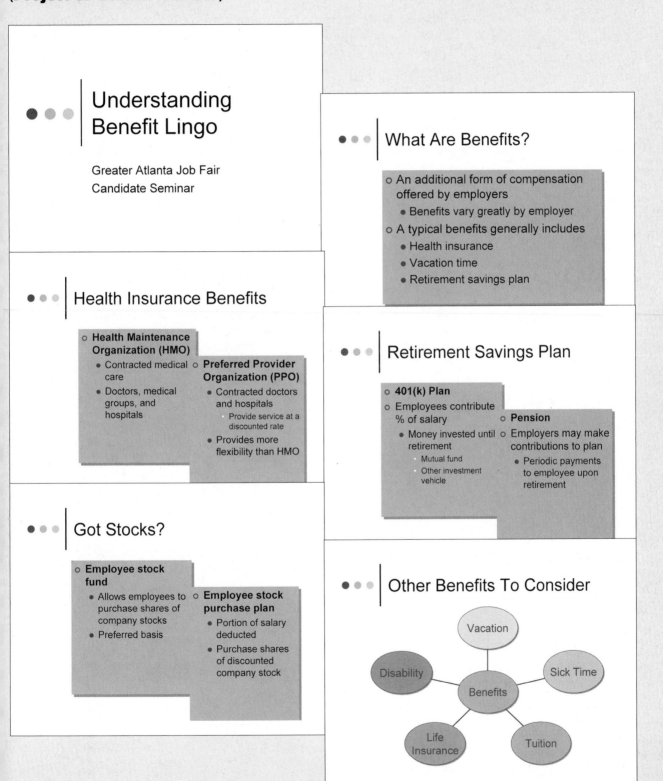

Understanding Benefit Lingo

Greater Atlanta Job Fair
Candidate Seminar

What Are Benefits?

- o An additional form of compensation offered by employers
  - Benefits vary greatly by employer
- o A typical benefits generally includes
  - Health insurance
  - Vacation time
  - Retirement savings plan

Health Insurance Benefits

- o **Health Maintenance Organization (HMO)**
  - Contracted medical care
  - Doctors, medical groups, and hospitals
- o **Preferred Provider Organization (PPO)**
  - Contracted doctors and hospitals
    - Provide service at a discounted rate
  - Provides more flexibility than HMO

Retirement Savings Plan

- o **401(k) Plan**
- o Employees contribute % of salary
  - Money invested until retirement
    - Mutual fund
    - Other investment vehicle
- o **Pension**
- o Employers may make contributions to plan
  - Periodic payments to employee upon retirement

Got Stocks?

- o **Employee stock fund**
  - Allows employees to purchase shares of company stocks
  - Preferred basis
- o **Employee stock purchase plan**
  - Portion of salary deducted
  - Purchase shares of discounted company stock

Other Benefits To Consider

Vacation

Disability

Sick Time

Benefits

Life Insurance

Tuition

Figure 8.35

(Project 8I–Benefits continues on the next page)

(Project 8I–Benefits continued)

4. Display **Slide 3**. Apply **Bold** to the first bullet point in each place-holder. Adjust the size and placement of the two bulleted list placeholders as shown in Figure 8.36, changing font sizes as necessary. (Hint: Try font size 26 for the first level bullet and use smaller sizes for the second and third level bullets.)

Figure 8.36

5. Display **Slide 4**. Apply **Bold** to the first bullet point in each place-holder. Adjust the size of the placeholders so that the second bullet point in each placeholder displays on two lines. Then, position the placeholders similar to the placement on Slide 3.

6. Display **Slide 5**. Apply **Bold** to the first bullet point in each place-holder. Adjust the size of the placeholder on the left side of the slide so that the second bullet point displays on three lines. Then, position the placeholders similar to the placement on Slide 3.

(Project 8I–Benefits continues on the next page)

(Project 8I–Benefits continued)

7. Insert a new slide and create the **Radial Diagram** and title shown in Figure 8.37. To size the diagram as shown in the figure, first change the **Layout** to **Fit Diagram to Contents**. Change the diagram text **Font Size** to **24**. Apply the **Shaded AutoFormat**.

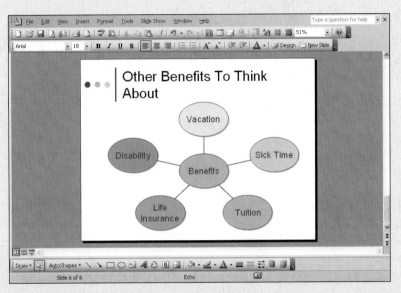

Figure 8.37

8. Apply the **Split Horizontal Out** transition at **Medium Speed** to the entire presentation, and then view the slide show. **Save** the file.

9. **Save** the **Presentation for Review** with the name **8I_Review_ Firstname_Lastname** Practice using the pen and the highlighter, and then discard the annotations.

10. Open the **8I_Review_Firstname_Lastname** presentation and answer **No** to the Microsoft Office PowerPoint question box. On **Slide 1**, delete the text *Candidate Seminar*.

(Project 8I–Benefits continues on the next page)

(Project 8I–Benefits continued)

11. On **Slides 3** and **4**, delete the word *Your* in the title. Display **Slide 5**. Use the **Change Case** command to change the words **stock purchase plan** to lowercase. Display **Slide 6**. Use the **Thesaurus** to change the words **Think About** to **Consider**. If necessary, capitalize the word. **Save** and **close** the file.

12. **Compare and merge** the **8I_Review_Firstname_Lastname** and **8I_Benefits_Firstname_Lastname** files.

13. On **Slide 1**, do not apply the change. Apply all of the other changes made to the presentation, and then **Save** the file.

14. Send the presentation to Microsoft Office Word in the **Blank lines next to slides** format. Create a **footer** with the text **8I Benefits Document-Firstname Lastname** and change the **Page Layout** to **Landscape**. **Save** the file as 8I_Benefits_Document_Firstname_ Lastname and then **Print**. Close the file and exit Word.

15. Use the **Web Page Preview** command to view the file as a Web page. Then, publish the PowerPoint presentation as a Web page with the file name **8I_Benefits_Web_Firstname_Lastname** Close the file.

 You have completed Project 8I ———————————————

Problem Solving

Project 8J — Company

Objectives: *Modify a Presentation Using Research and Comparison Tools and Format a Presentation for Web Viewing.*

In this Problem Solving exercise, work in a team of two or three people to create a presentation on an organization of your choice. Create a presentation with eight slides describing the organization and its products or services. Include information such as the types of careers available with the company, the benefits, and promotional opportunities. Include in the presentation a hyperlink to the company's Web site, and objects such as clip art, tables, and charts that appropriately display information about the company. Use the compare and merge feature to share the presentation for review with team members. Apply transitions and effects, and create an appropriate footer for your notes and handouts. Save your file as a Web page with the name *8J_Company_Firstname_Lastname*. Print the presentation as handouts, 4 slides per page, in grayscale.

End You have completed Project 8J ————————————————

Project 8K — Template

Objectives: *Create a Design Template and Share Files with Other Users.*

In this Problem Solving exercise, create an original design template using background fill effects and shapes, text, or graphics on the slide master. Create a color scheme and change fonts as necessary. Save your template as *8K_Template_Firstname_Lastname*. Apply your template to one of the student files in this chapter. Then, send the presentation to Microsoft Office Word and change the orientation to Landscape. Create an appropriate header for your document and save your document as *8K_Template_Firstname_Lastname*. Print the document.

End You have completed Project 8K ————————————————

On the Internet

Online Presentations

Connect to the Internet and launch a search engine such as www.google.com or www.yahoo.com. Conduct a search on the words *computer based presentations*. The search will return information on many companies that produce computer-based presentations and computer-based training. Click on some of the links to these companies and see if any of them present examples of their work.

GO! with Help

Managing Multiple Masters

A presentation in which more than one design template is applied contains multiple slide and title masters. Use Microsoft Office PowerPoint Help to learn more about working with multiple masters.

1. Click in the **Type a question for help** box, type **How do I manage multiple masters?** and then press Enter.

2. In the **Search Results** task pane, click **Allow or prevent multiple masters in a presentation**. Read the information and click each link that displays.

3. In the **Search Results** task pane, click **About the slide master**, and then scroll to the bottom of the Help window. Click **Making changes to multiple slide masters**. Read the Help information, and then close the Help window.

Task Guides

Each book in the *GO! Series* is designed to be kept beside your computer as a handy reference, even after you have completed all the activities. Any time you need to recall a sequence of steps or a shortcut needed to achieve a result, look up the general category in the alphabetized listing that follows and then find your task. To review how to perform a task, turn to the page number listed in the second column to locate the step-by-step exercise or other detailed description. Additional entries without page numbers describe tasks that are closely related to those presented in the chapters.

Word 2003

Word Task	Page	Mouse	Menu Bar	Shortcut Menu	Shortcut Keys
Character style, create for selected character(s)	1286	Apply formatting and then click New Style; in Style type box, click Character			
Chart, add title	1256		Activate chart, Chart | Chart Options | Titles tab	Activate chart; right-click chart area, Chart Options | Titles tab	
Chart, center	1262	▤ on Formatting toolbar	Format | Paragraph | Indents and Spacing tab, Alignment		Ctrl + E
Chart, change type	1258	▨▾ on Graph Standard toolbar	Select chart, Chart | Chart Type	Select chart; right-click chart area, Chart Type	
Chart, close datasheet	1260	✕ on datasheet title bar ▦ on Standard toolbar when the datasheet is open	View | Datasheet	Activate chart; right-click, Datasheet	
Chart, create from table	1254		Activate table, Insert | Picture | Chart		
Chart, display datasheet	1254		Activate chart, View | Datasheet		
Chart, edit	1254	Double-click chart	Activate chart, Edit | Chart Object | Edit	Double-click chart; right-click chart, Chart Object | Edit	
Chart, format text	1260	▨ on Graph Standard toolbar	Activate chart, Format | Selected <object>	Activate chart; right-click text, Format <object>	
Chart, graph by column	1258	▥ on Graph Standard toolbar	Activate chart, Data | Series in Columns		
Chart, graph by row	1258	▤ on Graph Standard toolbar	Activate chart, Data | Series in Rows		

Word Task	Page	Mouse	Menu Bar	Shortcut Menu	Shortcut Keys
Chart, resize	1262	Drag a selection handle	Activate chart, Format | Object | Size tab	Double-click chart; right-click chart, Format Object	
Chart, select	1256	Click chart			
Command, repeat	1303				`F4`
Comment, delete		[icon] on Reviewing toolbar		Right-click comment balloon or comment in reviewing pane, and then click Delete Comment	
Comment, insert	1354	[icon] on Reviewing toolbar	Insert | Comment		`Alt` + `Ctrl` + `M`
Comment, modify	1359	Click in comment balloon or in reviewing pane, edit text			
Comment, read in reviewing pane	1357	[icon] on Reviewing toolbar; click in text that has a comment, and then read in reviewing pane			
Crop image	1449	[icon] on Picture toolbar			
Document, accept merge changes	1374	[icon] on Reviewing toolbar			
Document, attach to email message	1371		File | Send To | Mail Recipient (as Attachment)		
Document, reject merge changes	1374	[icon] on Reviewing toolbar			
Document, save in another format	1369		File | Save As; change *Save as type* to another format		
Documents, compare and merge	1374		Tools | Compare and Merge Documents		
Drop cap, create	1265		Format | Drop Cap		
Email, document as attachment	1371		File | Send To | Mail Recipient (as Attachment)		
Excel chart, edit embedded chart	1491		Double-click embedded chart; make changes	Right-click embedded chart; Chart Object; Edit	
Excel chart, embed	1486	[icon] on Excel Standard toolbar; [icon] on Word Standard toolbar	Edit | Copy (in Excel); Edit | Paste (or Paste Special) in Word	Right-click chart in Excel; Copy | right-click in Word; Paste	`Ctrl` + `C` in Excel; `Ctrl` + `V` in Word
Excel chart, link to	1495		Edit | Copy (in Excel); Edit | Paste Special (in Word); Paste link		
Excel chart, modify linked chart	1497		Change the data (in Excel); Edit | Update Link (in Word)	Change the data (in Excel); right-click the chart (in Word); Update Link (if necessary)	`F9`

Word Task	Page	Mouse	Menu Bar	Shortcut Menu	Shortcut Keys
Excel data, embed	1489		Edit | Copy (in Excel); Edit | Paste Special (in Word)		
Excel worksheet, edit embedded worksheet	1491		Double-click embedded worksheet; make changes	Right-click embedded worksheet; Worksheet Object; Edit	
File, view properties	1349		File | Properties		
Form letter, set up mail merge	1515	on Mail Merge toolbar; Letters	Tools | Letters and Mailings | Mail Merge; Letters in task pane		
Form letters, merge to Word document	1526	on Mail Merge toolbar			
Form letters, print	1525	on Mail Merge toolbar; on Standard toolbar	File | Print in merged document		Ctrl + P
Format, paragraph	1280		Format | Paragraph	Paragraph	
Hide/Show, space between pages (Print Layout View)	1291	Point between pages to display Hide/Show White Space pointer, and then click	Tools | Options | View tab, White Space between pages		
Image, brightness	1453	and on Picture toolbar	Format | Picture | Picture tab; Brightness	Format Picture | Picture tab; Brightness	
Image, contrast	1453	and on Picture toolbar	Format | Picture | Picture tab; Contrast	Format Picture | Picture tab; Contrast	
Image, crop	1449	on Picture toolbar			
Image, resize	1452	Drag a sizing handle	Format | Picture | Size tab; set Height and Width	Format Picture | Size tab; set Height and Width	
Image, rotate	1449	on Picture toolbar; Drag rotate handle	Format | Picture | Size tab; Rotation	Format Picture | Size tab; Rotation	
Image, scale	1452		Format | Picture | Size tab; set Scale options	Format Picture | Size tab; set Scale options	
Image, wrapping style	1453	on Picture toolbar	Format | Picture | Layout tab	Format Picture | Layout tab	
Labels, create with mail merge	1506, 1508		Tools | Letters and Mailings | Mail Merge; Labels in task pane		
Labels, edit after mail merge	1512	Click in label; edit text			
Labels, preview after merge	1513	on the Standard toolbar			

Word Task	Page	Mouse	Menu Bar	Shortcut Menu	Shortcut Keys
Labels, print after merge	1513	In the Mail Merge task pane, click Print			
List style, create for selected list	1283	Apply formatting, and then click New Style button in Styles and Formatting task pane; in Style type box, click List			
Mail merge, display toolbar	1515		View | Toolbars | Mail Merge	Right-click toolbar; Mail Merge	
Mail merge, edit merged labels	1512	Click in label; edit text			
Mail merge, edit recipients	1518	▨ on Mail Merge toolbar; clear check box to remove recipient; click Edit to change data			
Mail merge, form letters to Word document	1526	▨ on Mail Merge toolbar			
Mail merge, highlight merged fields	1523	▤ on Mail Merge toolbar			
Mail merge, insert merge fields	1520	▤ on Mail Merge toolbar			
Mail merge, open data source	1518	▤ on Mail Merge toolbar			
Mail merge, preview merged data	1523	ABC on Mail Merge toolbar; navigate using ◀◀ , ◀ , [1] , ▶ , and ▶▶			
Mail merge, set up form letter	1515	▨ on Mail Merge toolbar; Letters	Tools | Letters and Mailings | Mail Merge; Letters in task pane		
Mail merge, set up labels	1506, 1508	▨ on Mail Merge toolbar; Labels	Tools | Letters and Mailings | Mail Merge; Labels in task pane		
Mail merge, sort recipients	1518	▨ on Mail Merge toolbar; click a column heading			
Markup, show/hide	1360	Final Showing Markup ▾ on Reviewing toolbar	View | Markup		
Memo, create from template	1342	Click On my computer on New Document task pane, and then click Memos tab	File | New, On my computer, click Memos tab		

Word Task	Page	Mouse	Menu Bar	Shortcut Menu	Shortcut Keys
Memo, replace placeholder text	1344	Click in a placeholder and then type			
Merge, accept changes	1374	⬜▾ on Reviewing toolbar			
Merge, documents	1374		Tools | Compare and Merge Documents		
Merge, reject changes	1374	⬜▾ on Reviewing toolbar			
Object, insert	1444		Insert | Object | Create New tab		
Object, modify	1446		Format | Object	Format Object	
Outline entry, collapse	1306	⬜ on Outlining toolbar Double-click Collapse indicator			
Outline entry, demote	1299	⬜ on Outlining toolbar		Increase Indent	Tab or Alt + Shift + →
Outline entry, expand	1306	⬜ on Outlining toolbar Double-click Expand indicator			
Outline entry, move down	1306	⬜ on Outlining toolbar			In Outline View, drag Expand/ Collapse button down
Outline entry, move up	1306	⬜ on Outlining toolbar			In Outline View, drag Expand/ Collapse button up
Outline entry, promote	1299	⬜ on Outlining toolbar		Decrease Indent	Shift + Tab or Alt + Shift + ←
Outline, set numbering	1296		Format | Bullets and Numbering | Outline Numbered tab	Bullets and Numbering | Outline Numbered tab	
Paragraph style, create for selected paragraph	1280	Apply formatting, and then click New Style button in Styles and Formatting task pane Normal ▾ on Formatting toolbar; type a new name and then press Enter			
Paragraph, format	1280		Format | Paragraph	Paragraph	
PowerPoint presentation, link to	1499		Insert | Object | Create from File tab; Browse for file; select Link to file		

Word Task	Page	Mouse	Menu Bar	Shortcut Menu	Shortcut Keys
Print, document properties	1351		File | Print; click Print what, and then click Document properties		
Print, form letters	1525	on Mail Merge toolbar on Standard toolbar	File | Print in merged document		Ctrl + P
Resize image	1452	Drag a sizing handle	Format | Picture | Size tab; set Height and Width	Format Picture | Size tab; set Height and Width	
Reviewing pane, show/hide	1357	on Reviewing toolbar			Alt + Shift + C (hide only)
Rotate image	1449	on Picture toolbar Drag rotate handle	Format Picture | Size tab; Rotation	Format Picture | Size tab; Rotation	
Save, document in another format	1369		File | Save As; change *Save as type* to another format		
Scale image	1452		Format | Picture | Size tab; set Scale options	Format Picture | Size tab; set Scale options	
Statistics, view properties	1349		File | Properties | Statistics tab		
Style area, display (Normal View)	1274		Tools | Options | View tab, Style area width (increase)		
Style area, hide (Normal View)	1274	Drag style area's vertical border to left edge of window	Tools | Options | View tab, Style area width (set to 0)		
Style, apply	1274, 1277, 1283	Normal on Formatting toolbar Click Style in Styles and Formatting task pane			
Style, clear	1279	Normal on Formatting toolbar, and then click Clear Formatting Click Clear Formatting in Styles and Formatting task pane			
Style, modify	1289	In Styles and Formatting task pane, point to style, click arrow, and then click Modify		Right-click style in Styles and Formatting task pane, and then click Modify	
Styles and Formatting task pane, display/hide	1274	on Formatting toolbar	Format | Styles and Formatting		Ctrl + F1, then choose Styles and Formatting
Summary, view or edit properties	1349, 1351		File | Properties | Summary tab		

Word Task	Page	Mouse	Menu Bar	Shortcut Menu	Shortcut Keys
Table style, apply	1409	Normal [icon] on Formatting toolbar; [icon] on Formatting toolbar; click style name in task pane	Format | Styles and Formatting; select style name		Ctrl + Shift + S, ↑ or ↓ to display style, then Enter
Table style, create	1406	[icon] on Formatting toolbar; New Style, then click Style type arrow and select Table	Format | Styles and Formatting; New Style, then in Style type list, select Table		
Table, add caption	1429		Insert | Reference | Caption		
Table, add lines	1436	[icon] on Tables and Borders toolbar	Table | Draw Table		
Table, add row at end	1427, 1504	Position insertion point in last row; [icon] arrow on Tables and Borders toolbar, Insert Rows Below	Table | Insert | Rows Below		Tab in last cell
Table, AutoFormat	1431	[icon] on Tables and Borders toolbar	Table | Table AutoFormat		
Table, delete	1262		Click in table, Table | Delete | Table		
Table, distribute columns evenly	1439	[icon] on Tables and Borders toolbar			
Table, draw	1434	[icon] on Tables and Borders toolbar	Table | Draw Table		
Table, fit text in cell	1424		Table | Table Properties | Cell tab; select Options, then select Fit text	Right-click in cell; Table Properties; click Cell tab, click Options, then click Fit text	
Table, insert formula	1427		Table | Formula		
Table, line style	1434	[icon] on Tables and Borders toolbar	Table | Table Properties | Table tab; Borders and Shading, Borders tab; Style	Right-click in cell; Borders and Shading, Borders tab; Style	
Table, merge selected cells	1411	[icon] on Tables and Borders toolbar	Table | Merge Cells	Right-click in selected cells; Merge Cells	
Table, remove lines	1436	[icon] on Tables and Borders toolbar			
Table, select	1254	Click table move handle in Print Layout View	Table | Select | Table		Alt + 5
Table, shading color	1441	[icon] on Tables and Borders toolbar	Table | Table Properties | Table tab; Borders and Shading, Shading tab	Right-click in cell; Borders and Shading, Shading tab	

Word Task	Page	Mouse	Menu Bar	Shortcut Menu	Shortcut Keys
Table, sort	1425	⬆ (ascending) or ⬇ (descending) on Tables and Borders toolbar	Table | Sort		
Table, text alignment	1418	on Tables and Borders toolbar	Table | Table Properties | Cell tab	Right-click in cell, Cell Alignment	
Table, text direction	1416, 1439	on Tables and Borders toolbar		Right-click in cell, Text Direction	
Table, wrap text around	1422		Table | Table Properties | Table tab; select Around	Right-click in cell; Table Properties; click Table tab, then click Around	
Template, find on Web	1342	Click Templates on Office Online on New Document task pane	File | New, Templates on Office Online		
Template, use to create document	1342	Click On my computer on New Document task pane	File | New, On my computer		
Text, character spacing	1270		Format | Font | Character Spacing tab	Font | Character Spacing tab	
Text, drop cap	1265		Format | Drop Cap		
Text, shadow effect	1267		Format | Font | Font tab, Shadow	Font | Font tab, Shadow	
Text, small caps effect	1267		Format | Font | Font tab, Small Caps	Font | Font tab, Small Caps	Ctrl + Shift + K
Track changes, accept change	1365	on Reviewing toolbar			
Track changes, locate next change	1363	on Reviewing toolbar			
Track changes, reject change	1365	on Reviewing toolbar			
Track changes, reviewers	1363	Show ▾ on Reviewing toolbar; click Reviewers and then click All Reviewers or a reviewer's name			
Track changes, show settings	1363	Show ▾ on Reviewing toolbar			
Track changes, show/hide markup	1360	Final Showing Markup ▾ on Reviewing toolbar	View | Markup		
Track changes, turn on/off	1360	Show ▾ on Reviewing toolbar	Tools | Track Changes	Right-click a tracked change, and then click Track Changes	Ctrl + Shift + E

Word Task	Page	Mouse	Menu Bar	Shortcut Menu	Shortcut Keys
Window, remove split	1293	Double-click split bar between panes Drag split bar up	Window | Remove Split		
Window, split	1293	Drag split box (above vertical scroll bar)	Window | Split		
Word count, check	1352	`<Click Recount to view>` on Word Count toolbar	Tools | Word Count View | Toolbars | Word Count		Ctrl + Shift + G, and then Enter

Excel 2003

Excel Task	Page	Mouse	Menu Bar	Shortcut Menu	Shortcut Keys
Arrange, view of workbooks	1726		Window | Arrange		
Arrow style, change	1759	Click line or arrow on Drawing toolbar			
Arrow, draw	1759	on Drawing toolbar			
Auditing, circle invalid data	1850	on Formula Auditing toolbar			
Auditing, clear validation circles	1850	on Formula Auditing toolbar			
Auditing, error checking	1847	on Formula Auditing toolbar	Tools | Formula Auditing | Trace Error		
Auditing, remove all arrows	1837	on Formula Auditing toolbar	Tools | Formula Auditing | Remove All Arrows		
Auditing, remove dependent arrows	1837	on Formula Auditing toolbar			
AutoFilter, apply or remove	1733		Data | Filter | AutoFilter		
AutoFilter, custom (including *and* and *or*)	1903		Data | Filter | AutoFilter; select Custom in column's drop-down list; select settings		
AutoFilter, enable	1900		Data | Filter | AutoFilter		
AutoFilter, remove	1904		Data | Filter | AutoFilter		
AutoFormat, apply	1751		Format | AutoFormat		
Calculated field, add to data table	1914		Insert | Columns; enter formula in column; copy formula to other cells in column		
Chart, 3-D View options	1666	Drag corner(s) where walls or floor intersect	Click blank area in chart, Chart | 3-D View	Right-click blank area in chart, 3-D View	
Chart, add axis title	1642	Click in title text box, edit	Click blank area in chart, Chart | Chart Options | Titles tab	Right-click blank area in chart, Chart Options | Titles tab	
Chart, add data labels	1661		Click blank area in chart, Chart | Chart Options | Data Labels tab	Right-click blank area in chart, Chart Options | Data Labels tab	

Excel Task	Page	Mouse	Menu Bar	Shortcut Menu	Shortcut Keys
Chart, align axis title	1642	Click axis title, [icon] on Chart toolbar, then click Alignment tab Double-click axis title, then click Alignment tab	Click axis title, Format | Selected Axis Title | Alignment tab	Right-click axis title, Format Axis Title | Alignment tab	Select axis title, Ctrl + 1
Chart, change data display (axis)	1641	[icon] or [icon] on Chart toolbar	Click blank area in chart, Chart | Source Data | Data Range tab, Rows or Columns	Right-click blank area in chart, Source Data | Data Range tab, Rows or Columns	
Chart, change type	1659	Click arrow on [icon] ▾ on Chart toolbar	Click blank area in chart, Chart | Chart Type	Right-click blank area in chart, Chart Type	
Chart, create	1632	[icon]	Insert | Chart		
Chart, create in existing worksheet	1648	[icon]; in Chart Location step, under *Place chart*, click As object in	Insert | Chart; in Chart Location step, under *Place chart*, click As object in		
Chart, create in new worksheet	1632, 1657	[icon]; in Chart Location step, under *Place chart*, click As new sheet	Insert | Chart; in Chart Location step, under *Place chart*, click As new sheet		
Chart, edit chart title	1646, 1651	Click in title text box, edit	Click blank area in chart, Chart | Chart Options | Titles tab	Right-click blank area in chart, Chart Options | Titles tab	
Chart, edit source data	1646	Click worksheet cell, edit Drag data point on chart			
Chart, edit source data range	1641		Click blank area in chart, Chart | Source Data | Data Range tab	Right-click blank area in chart, Source Data | Data Range tab	
Chart, explode pie slice	1667	Click pie chart, click a slice, drag slice away from center of pie			
Chart, format axis label	1644	Click axis, [icon] on Chart toolbar [Chart Area ▾] arrow on Chart toolbar, click Category Axis or Value Axis Double-click axis	Click axis, Format | Selected Axis	Right-click axis label, Format Axis	Select axis title, Ctrl + 1
Chart, format axis title	1642	Click axis title, [icon] on Chart toolbar, then click Font tab Double-click axis title, then click Font tab	Click axis title, Format | Selected Axis Title | Font tab	Right-click axis title, Format Axis Title | Font tab	Select axis title, Ctrl + 1
Chart, format chart title	1645	Click chart title, [icon] on Chart toolbar, then click Font tab Double-click chart title, then click Font tab	Click chart title, Format | Selected Chart Title | Font tab	Right-click chart title, Format Chart Title | Font tab	Select chart title, Ctrl + 1

Excel Task	Page	Mouse	Menu Bar	Shortcut Menu	Shortcut Keys
Chart, format data labels	1661	Double-click a data label, click Font tab Click a data label, 🖼 on Chart toolbar, click Font tab	Select data label, Format | Selected Data Labels | Font tab	Right-click data label, Format Data Labels | Font tab	Select data label, Ctrl + 1
Chart, format data point	1664	Click data point twice; double-click data point	Click data point twice, Format | Selected Data Point	Click data point twice; right-click data point, Format Data Point	Select data point, Ctrl + 1
Chart, format data series	1654	Double-click a data marker, click Patterns tab	Click data series, Format | Selected Data Series | Patterns tab	Right-click data series, Format Data Series | Patterns tab	Select data series, Ctrl + 1
Chart, format legend	1660	Click legend, 🖼 on Chart toolbar, then click Font tab Double-click legend, then click Font tab	Click legend, Format | Selected Legend | Font tab	Right-click legend, Format Legend | Font tab	Select legend, Ctrl + 1
Chart, format plot area	1654	Double-click plot area Click plot area, 🖼 on Chart toolbar	Click plot area, Format | Selected Plot Area	Right-click plot area, Format Plot Area	Select plot area, Ctrl + 1
Chart, legend placement	1660	Drag legend text box	Click blank area in chart, Chart | Chart Options | Legend tab	Right-click blank area in chart, Chart Options | Legend tab	
Chart, move	1650	Click blank area in chart, drag chart area			
Chart, move data label	1661	Click data label, drag			
Chart, print chart only	1647	Click blank area in chart, 🖼 on Standard toolbar	Click blank area in chart, File | Print		Click blank area in chart, Ctrl + P
Chart, print on same page with worksheet	1656	Click a cell (to deselect chart), 🖼 on Standard toolbar	Click a cell (to deselect chart), File | Print		Click a cell (to deselect chart), Ctrl + P
Chart, print preview of chart only	1647	Click blank area in chart, 🖼 on Standard toolbar	File | Print Preview File | Print, Preview		
Chart, print preview on same page with worksheet	1656	Click a cell (to deselect chart), 🖼 on Standard toolbar	Click a cell (to deselect chart), File | Print Preview		
Chart, remove legend	1651	🖼 on Chart toolbar	Click blank area in chart, Chart | Chart Options | Legend tab, clear Show legend	Right-click blank area in chart, Chart Options | Legend tab, clear Show legend	Select legend, Delete

Excel Task	Page	Mouse	Menu Bar	Shortcut Menu	Shortcut Keys
Chart, scale value axis	1652	Double-click value axis (or value), click Scale tab Click value axis, [icon] on Chart toolbar, then click Scale tab	Click axis, Format | Selected Axis | Scale tab	Right-click axis, Format Axis | Scale tab	Select axis, Ctrl + 1
Chart, select and modify chart object	1642	Chart Area ▾ arrow on Chart toolbar, click object name, then click [icon] on Chart toolbar Double-click object		Right-click object, Format <object>	
Chart, size	1650	Click blank area in chart, drag a selection handle			
Chart, snap to grid	1650	Alt + drag chart area			
Columns, hide/ unhide	1725		Format | Hide or Unhide	Right-click column heading, Hide or Unhide	
Conditional format, apply	1832		Format | Conditional Formatting		
Countif function, use	1723	fx, click Statistical category, click COUNTIF function	Insert | Function, click Statistical category, click COUNTIF function		Shift + F3
Data form, edit data	1897		Data | Form; find record; type in form field(s)		
Data form, enter data	1892		Data | Form; type in form fields		
Data form, find data	1895		Data | Form; click Criteria; enter criteria; click Find Next		
Data table, group and outline	1915		Select rows or columns to group; Data | Group and Outline | Group		
Data table, hide outline detail	1915	In outline bar, click Level buttons and/or Hide Detail buttons	Select rows or columns to hide; Data | Group and Outline | Hide Detail		
Data, display using AutoFilter	1900		Data | Filter | AutoFilter; select criteria from column's drop-down list		
Data, display using AutoFilter criteria for multiple fields	1902		Data | Filter | AutoFilter; select criteria in multiple columns		
Data, extract	1908		Name the range for the filtered results: *Extract*; define criteria; select cell in data table; Data | Filter | Advanced Filter; select Copy to another location		

Excel Task	Page	Mouse	Menu Bar	Shortcut Menu	Shortcut Keys
DAVERAGE database function, use	1919	f_x on Formula Bar, click *Database* category; click DAVERAGE function	Insert | Function; select *Database* category; select DAVERAGE function		Shift + F3
DCOUNT database function, use	1924	f_x on Formula Bar, click *Database* category; click DCOUNT function	Insert | Function; select *Database* category; select DCOUNT function		Shift + F3
Dependents, trace	1837, 1843	on Formula Auditing toolbar	Tools | Formula Auditing | Trace Dependents		
DGET database function, use	1926	f_x on Formula Bar, click *Database* category; click DGET function	Insert | Function; select *Database* category; select DGET function		Shift + F3
Diagram, change style	1673	on Diagram toolbar			
Diagram, create	1669		Insert | Diagram, select diagram type		
Diagram, insert shape	1672	Insert Shape on Diagram toolbar		Right-click a shape, Insert Shape	
Diagram, move shape	1672	or on Diagram toolbar			
Draw, arrow	1759	on Drawing toolbar			
Draw, text box	1759	on Drawing toolbar			
DSUM database function, use	1922	f_x on Formula Bar, click *Database* category; click DSUM function	Insert | Function; select *Database* category; select DSUM function		Shift + F3
Error checking formulas	1847	on Formula Auditing toolbar	Tools | Formula Auditing | Trace Error		
Error checking, enable	1837		Tools | Options | Error Checking tab; select Enable background error checking		
External data, display toolbar	1886		View | Toolbars | External Data	Right-click any toolbar, click External Data	
Filter, Advanced	1905		Data | Filter | Advanced Filter		
Filter, custom AutoFilter (including *and* and *or*)	1903		Data | Filter | AutoFilter; select Custom in column's drop-down list; select settings		
Filter, data	1733		Data | Filter | AutoFilter		
Filter, show all data	1902		Data | Filter | Show All		

Excel Task	Page	Mouse	Menu Bar	Shortcut Menu	Shortcut Keys
Find, text	1719		Edit | Find		Ctrl + F
Format, apply AutoFormat	1751		Format | AutoFormat		
Formula auditing mode	1837		Tools | Formula Auditing | Formula Auditing Mode		Ctrl + '
Formula auditing, display toolbar	1837		View | Toolbars | Formula Auditing	Right-click any toolbar, click Formula Auditing	
Formula, create using range name	1567	Type = followed by formula, replacing range reference with range name			
Formula, evaluate	1837	[fx] on Formula Auditing toolbar	Tools | Formula Auditing | Evaluate Formula		
Formula, trace error	1837, 1845	on Formula Auditing toolbar	Tools | Formula Auditing | Trace Error		
Freeze/unfreeze, panes	1716		Window | Freeze/Unfreeze Panes		
Function, average	1580	[fx], click Statistical category, click AVERAGE function	Insert | Function, click Statistical category, click AVERAGE function		Shift + F3
Function, count	1580	[fx], click Statistical category, click COUNT function	Insert | Function, click Statistical category, click COUNT function		Shift + F3
Function, countif	1723	[fx], click Statistical category, click COUNTIF function	Insert | Function, click Statistical category, click COUNTIF function		Shift + F3
Function, date	1584	[fx], click Date & Time category, click DATE function	Insert | Function, click Date & Time category, click DATE function		Shift + F3
Function, future value	1587	[fx], click Financial category, click FV function	Insert | Function, click Financial category, click FV function		Shift + F3
Function, if	1594	[fx], click Logical category, click IF function	Insert | Function, click Logical category, click IF function		Shift + F3
Function, insert	1572 thru 1594, 1723	[fx], click category, click function [fx] on Formula Bar	Insert | Function, click category, click function Insert | Function		Shift + F3
Function, maximum	1578	[fx], click Statistical category, click MAX function	Insert | Function, click Statistical category, click MAX function		Shift + F3

Excel Task	Page	Mouse	Menu Bar	Shortcut Menu	Shortcut Keys
Function, median	1572	fx, click Statistical category, click MEDIAN function	Insert | Function, click Statistical category, click MEDIAN function		Shift + F3
Function, minimum	1576	fx, click Statistical category, click MIN function	Insert | Function, click Statistical category, click MIN function		Shift + F3
Function, now	1584	fx, click Date & Time category, click NOW function	Insert | Function, click Date & Time category, click NOW function		Shift + F3
Function, payment	1590	fx, click Financial category, click PMT function	Insert | Function, click Financial category, click PMT function		Shift + F3
Go to, specified cell	1722		Edit | Go To		F5 Ctrl + G
Goal seek	1767		Tools | Goal Seek		
Hide/unhide, columns	1725		Format | Hide or Unhide	Right-click column letter; Hide or Unhide	
HLOOKUP function, use	1828	fx on Formula Bar, click *Lookup & Reference* category; click HLOOKUP function	Insert | Function; select *Lookup & Reference* category; select HLOOKUP function		Shift + F3
Horizontal lookup, create using Paste Special	1826	Select range; on Standard toolbar; click a cell; Edit | Paste Special; Transpose	Select range; Edit | Copy; select a cell; Edit | Paste Special; Transpose	Select range; right-click; Copy; right-click a cell; Paste Special; Transpose	
Hyperlink, insert	1740	on Standard toolbar	Insert | Hyperlink	Right-click selection, Hyperlink	Ctrl + K
Hyperlink, modify	1742	on Standard toolbar	Insert | Hyperlink	Right-click hyperlink, Edit Hyperlink	Ctrl + K
Image, brightness	1805	Select image; and on Picture toolbar	Format | Picture | Picture tab; drag brightness slider or enter percentage	Right-click image; Format Picture | Picture tab; drag brightness slider or enter percentage	Select image; Ctrl + 1; Picture tab
Image, contrast	1805	Select image; and on Picture toolbar	Format | Picture | Picture tab; drag contrast slider or enter percentage	Right-click image; Format Picture | Picture tab; drag contrast slider or enter percentage	Select image; Ctrl + 1; Picture tab
Image, crop	1805	Select image; on Picture toolbar; drag corners of image			
Image, insert	1805	on Picture or Drawing toolbars	Insert | Picture | From File		

Excel Task	Page	Mouse	Menu Bar	Shortcut Menu	Shortcut Keys
Image, modify	1805	Select image; use Picture toolbar buttons Double-click image; select formatting options	Format | Picture	Right-click image; Format Picture	Select image; Ctrl + 1
Import data, from Access database	1886		Data | Import External Data | Import Data Data | Import External Data | New Database Query; select MS Access Database		
Import data, from external source	1886		Data | Import External Data | Import Data		
Import data, from Word table	1886	Select Word table; ▢ on Standard toolbar; click an Excel cell; ▢▾ on Standard toolbar	Select Word table; Edit | Copy; select an Excel cell; Edit | Paste	Select Word table; right-click; Copy; right-click an Excel cell; Paste	In Word, Ctrl + C; in Excel, Ctrl + V
Insert, hyperlink	1740	▢ on Standard toolbar	Insert | Hyperlink	Right-click selection, Hyperlink	Ctrl + K
Line color, change	1759	▢▾ on Drawing toolbar			
Look up, supporting information	1762	▢ on Standard toolbar	Tools | Research	Look Up	Alt + click
Lookup table, create	1823		Select range; Data | Sort; sort by the column that will be used for lookup		
Name, range	1558	Select cells, type name in Name box on Formula Bar, press Enter	Select cells, Insert | Name | Define		Ctrl + F3
Normal View, return to	1735		View | Normal		
Outline, group data table	1915		Select rows or columns to group; Data | Group and Outline | Group		
Outline, hide detail	1915	In outline bar, click Level buttons and/or Hide Detail buttons	Select rows or columns to hide; Data | Group and Outline | Hide Detail		
Outline, worksheet	1915		Data | Group and Outline | Settings		
Panes, freeze/unfreeze	1716		Window | Freeze/Unfreeze Panes		
Picture, brightness	1805	Select image; ▢ and ▢ on Picture toolbar	Format | Picture | Picture tab; drag brightness slider or enter percentage	Right-click image; Format Picture | Picture tab; drag brightness slider or enter percentage	Select picture; Ctrl + 1; Picture tab

Excel Task	Page	Mouse	Menu Bar	Shortcut Menu	Shortcut Keys
Picture, contrast	1805	Select image; and on Picture toolbar	Format | Picture | Picture tab; drag contrast slider or enter percentage	Right-click image; Format Picture | Picture tab; drag contrast slider or enter percentage	Select picture; Ctrl + 1; Picture tab
Picture, crop	1805	Select image; on Picture toolbar; drag corners of image			
Picture, insert	1805	on Picture or Drawing toolbars	Insert | Picture | From File		
Picture, modify	1805	Select image; use Picture toolbar buttons Double-click image; select formatting options	Format | Picture	Right-click image; Format Picture	Select picture; Ctrl + 1
Precedents, trace	1837	on Formula Auditing toolbar	Tools | Formula Auditing | Trace Precedents		
Preview, as Web page	1743		File | Web Page Preview		
Preview, page breaks	1735	on Standard toolbar, Page Break Preview	View | Page Break Preview File | Print Preview, click Page Break Preview		
Print area, clear	1599		Select range, File | Print Area | Clear Print Area		
Print area, set	1599		Select range, File | Print Area | Set Print Area File | Page Setup | Sheet tab		
Print, preview multiple sheets	1567	Select sheet tabs, on Standard toolbar	Select sheet tabs, File | Print Preview Select sheet tabs, File | Print, Preview		
Protection, disable for worksheet	1820		Tools | Protection | Unprotect Sheet		
Protection, enable for worksheet	1815		Tools | Protection | Protect Sheet		
Protection, enable or disable for workbook	1815		Tools | Protection | Protect Workbook or Unprotect Workbook		
Protection, unlock cell(s)	1815		Select cells to unlock; Format | Cells | Protection tab; deselect Locked check box	Right-click selected cells; Format Cells | Protection tab; deselect Locked check box	Select cells to unlock; Ctrl + 1; Protection tab; deselect Locked check box

Excel Task	Page	Mouse	Menu Bar	Shortcut Menu	Shortcut Keys
Range, create name using row or column label	1566		Select cells, Insert | Name | Create		
Range, define name	1558	Select cells, type name in Name Box on Formula Bar, press Enter	Select cells, Insert | Name | Define		Ctrl + F3
Range, delete name	1565		Insert | Name | Define, Delete		Ctrl + F3, Delete
Range, modify reference	1564		Insert | Name | Define, Refers to		Ctrl + F3
Range, select named range	1558	Click Name Box arrow, click range name	Edit | Go To, click range name		Ctrl + G
Repeat row/column headings	1738		File | Page Setup | Sheet tab		
Replace, text	1719		Edit | Replace Edit | Find | Replace tab		Ctrl + H
Research	1762	[icon] on Standard toolbar	Tools | Research	Look Up	Alt + click
Save, as comma separated values	1746		File | Save As, click Save as type, select CSV (Comma delimited)		
Save, as text file	1747		File | Save As, click Save as type, select Text (Tab delimited)		
Save, as Web page	1743		File | Save as Web Page		
Select, nonadjacent ranges	1657	Select first range, Ctrl + select remaining ranges			
Sort table, ascending order	1888	Click a cell in the column to sort by; [icon] on Standard toolbar; click Ascending	Data | Sort; select column; Ascending		
Sort table, descending order	1888	Click a cell in the column to sort by; [icon] on Standard toolbar; click Descending	Data | Sort; select column; Descending		
Sort table, multiple columns	1889		Data | Sort; select primary and secondary sort column(s) and order		
Sort table, undo effects	1891	[icon] on Standard toolbar	Edit | Undo Sort		Ctrl + Z
Sort, ascending	1730	[icon] on Standard toolbar	Data | Sort, Ascending		
Sort, descending	1730	[icon] on Standard toolbar	Data | Sort, Descending		

Excel Task	Page	Mouse	Menu Bar	Shortcut Menu	Shortcut Keys
Split, worksheet (or remove split)	1726		Window | Split or Remove Split		
Style, apply	1753		Format | Style, select a name		
Style, create	1753		Format | Style, type a name, Modify		Alt + ′
Style, modify	1757		Format | Style, select a name, Modify		
Styles, use in another workbook	1756		Format | Style, Merge		
Subtotals, apply to a data table	1912		Click in data table; Data | Subtotals		
Subtotals, remove	1912		Click in data table; Data | Subtotals | Remove All		
Template, create	1798		Enter text and formulas in worksheet; File | Save As; Save as type: Template; Save		
Template, enter formula	1802	Type = followed by formula			
Template, format	1800		Select ranges; Format | Cells	Right-click range; Format Cells	
Template, save file as	1803		File | Save As; Save as type: Template; Save		
Template, use custom	1818		File | New; select On my computer in task pane; select General tab; select template		
Template, use to create workbook	1710		File | New | On my computer (in task pane) | Spreadsheet Solutions tab		
Text box, draw	1759	[icon] on Drawing toolbar			
Text, find	1719		Edit | Find		Ctrl + F
Text, replace	1719		Edit | Replace; Edit | Find | Replace tab		Ctrl + H
Transpose, rows and columns	1826	Select range; [icon] on Standard toolbar; click a cell; Edit | Paste Special; Transpose	Select range; Edit | Copy; select a cell; Edit | Paste Special; Transpose	Select range; right-click; Copy; right-click a cell; Paste Special; Transpose	
Validation list, create	1830		Data | Validation | Settings tab		
Validation message, create ScreenTip	1830		Data | Validation | Input Message tab		

Excel Task	Page	Mouse	Menu Bar	Shortcut Menu	Shortcut Keys
Validation message, create warning message	1830		Data | Validation | Error Alert tab		
View, return to normal	1735		View | Normal		
VLOOKUP function, use	1824	[fx] on Formula Bar, click *Lookup & Reference* category; click VLOOKUP function	Insert | Function; select *Lookup & Reference* category; select VLOOKUP function		Shift + F3
Web page, preview	1743		File | Web Page Preview		
Web page, save as	1743		File | Save as Web Page		
WordArt Gallery, open	1810	[icon] on WordArt toolbar [icon] on Drawing toolbar			
WordArt, edit text	1810	[Edit Text...] on WordArt toolbar Double-click object		Right-click object; Edit Text	
WordArt, format	1810	Select object; [icon] on WordArt toolbar	Select object; Format | WordArt	Right-click object; Format WordArt	Select object; Ctrl + 1
WordArt, insert	1810	[icon] on the WordArt or Drawing toolbars	Insert | Picture | WordArt		
WordArt, resize	1810	Select object; drag sizing handles	Select object; Format | WordArt | Size tab	Right-click object; Format WordArt | Size tab	Select object; Ctrl + 1; Size tab
WordArt, rotate	1810	Select object; drag rotation handle	Select object; Format | WordArt | Size tab; Rotation	Right-click object; Format WordArt | Size tab; Rotation	Select object; Ctrl + 1; Size tab; Rotation
Workbook, arrange multiple	1726		Window | Arrange		
Workbook, maximize	1726	[icon] in workbook title bar			
Worksheet, delete	1675		Edit | Delete Sheet	Right-click sheet tab, Delete	
Worksheet, format sheet tab	1676		Format | Sheet | Tab Color	Right-click sheet tab, Tab Color	
Worksheet, hide	1679		Format | Sheet | Hide		
Worksheet, insert	1675		Insert | Worksheet	Right-click sheet tab, Insert	
Worksheet, move	1676	Drag sheet tab to new location in sheet tab row	Edit | Move or Copy sheet	Right-click sheet tab, Move or Copy	

Excel Task	Page	Mouse	Menu Bar	Shortcut Menu	Shortcut Keys
Worksheet, protect	1815		Tools | Protection | Protect Sheet		
Worksheet, select multiple (group)	1675	Click first worksheet tab, Ctrl + click other tab(s)			
Worksheet, split or remove split	1726		Window | Split or Remove Split		

Access 2003

Access Task	Page	Mouse	Menu Bar	Shortcut Menu	Shortcut Keys
Action query, create	2184	[icon] on Query Design toolbar; click one of the action query types	Query	*Action Query type*	Right-click Query window; Query Type	*Action Query type*	
Analyze, performance	2050		Tools	Analyze	Performance		
Analyze, table	2047		Tools	Analyze	Table		
Append query, create	2186	Create query; [icon] on Query Design toolbar; click Append Query	Create query; Query	Append Query	Right-click Query window; Query Type	Append Query	
Best fit, apply to table columns	2214	Select columns; double-click border between column headings	Format	Column Width, Best Fit		
Calculated field, create for group in report	2159	[abl] in Toolbox; click in group footer; click Control Source box; [...]			
Calculated field, create in report	2164	[abl] in Toolbox; click in report footer; click Control Source box; [...] Click group footer's calculated field; [icon] on Report Design toolbar; click Report Footer section bar; [icon] on Report Design toolbar			
ControlTip, add to form	2101	Display property sheet, click Other tab, then enter value in ControlTip Text box			
Crosstab query, add conditions	2180		In Query Design view, enter condition(s) in Criteria row		
Crosstab query, create	2177	[New] in Database window; click Crosstab Query Wizard	Insert	Query; select Crosstab Query Wizard		
Data access page, add new record	1995	[icon] on Navigation bar			
Data access page, browse records	1993	First [icon], Previous [icon], Next [icon], and Last [icon] on Navigation bar			

Access Task	Page	Mouse	Menu Bar	Shortcut Menu	Shortcut Keys
Data access page, create with Page Wizard	1990	On Objects bar, click Pages; click [New], Page Wizard OR double-click *Create data access page by using wizard*	Insert | Page, Page Wizard		
Data access page, delete record	1993	[>X] on Navigation bar			
Data access page, filter records in Page view or Web page preview	1993	Click in filter field, [icon] on Navigation bar			
Data access page, open in Design view	1993	Click data access page name then [Design]		Right-click data access page name; click Design View	
Data access page, open in Page view	1993	Click data access page name then [Open] Double-click data access page name		Right-click data access page name; click Open	
Data access page, remove filter	1993	[filter icon] on Navigation bar			
Data access page, save record	1995	[icon] on Navigation bar			
Data access page, sort records in Page view or Web page preview	1993	Click in sort field, [A↓Z] or [Z↓A] on Navigation bar			
Data access page, switch to Design view	1993	[icon ▾]	View | Design View		
Data access page, switch to Page view	1993	[icon ▾]	View | Page View	Right-click data access page title bar; click Page View	
Data access page, view in browser (Web page preview)	1993	Click arrow on [icon ▾] or [icon ▾], click Web Page Preview	File | Web Page Preview	Right-click data access page name; click Web Page Preview	
Data type, change	1958	In Table Design view, click a field's Data Type box, then select from drop-down list			
Database, compact	2056		Tools | Database Utilities | Compact and Repair Database		
Database, convert from previous version of Access	1997		Tools | Database Utilities | Convert Database | (choose a format)		

Access Task	Page	Mouse	Menu Bar	Shortcut Menu	Shortcut Keys
Database, encode/decode	2054		Tools | Security | Encode/Decode Database		
Database, protect with password	2051		Tools | Security | Set Database Password		
Database, remove password	2051		Tools | Security | Unset Database Password		
Database, repair	2056		Tools | Database Utilities | Compact and Repair Database		
Database, replicate	2057		Tools | Replication | Create Replica		
Delete query, create	2174	Create query; [icon] on Query Design toolbar; click Delete Query	Create query; Query | Delete Query	Right-click Query window; Query Type | Delete Query	
Delete, record in data access page	1993	[icon] on Navigation bar			
Encode/decode, database	2054		Tools | Security | Encode/Decode Database		
Enforce referential integrity	2031		In Relationship window, Relationship | Edit Relationship, select Enforce Referential Integrity check box	In Relationship window, right-click relationship line, click Edit Relationship, select Enforce Referential Integrity check box	
Excel chart, insert in Access form	2244		In form Design view, Insert | Object; select Create from File; browse and select Excel file		
Excel chart, link to Access report	2249		In report Design view, Insert | Object; select Create from File; browse and select Excel file; click Link check box		
Excel, import worksheet data in Access	2226		Files | Get External Data | Import; select Excel file; click Import and follow wizard steps		
Expression Builder, use	1976	Type an expression or use the buttons to insert characters into the expression			
Field, add to form	2084	In Design view, drag field from field list to form			
Field, change size	1962	In Table Design view, click field name; click Field Size box, enter number			
Field, create input mask	1972	In Table Design view, click field name; type input mask characters in Input Mask box			

Access Task	Page	Mouse	Menu Bar	Shortcut Menu	Shortcut Keys
Field, create input mask using wizard	1970	In Table Design view, click field name; click Input Mask box, click [...] button		In Table Design view, click field name; right-click Input Mask box, then click Build	
Field, create lookup using wizard	1980	In Table Design view, click a field's Data Type box, then select Lookup Wizard			
Field, create validation text	1978	In Table Design view, click field name; type text message in Validation Text box			
Field, format	1967	In Table Design view, click field name; click Format box, then click down arrow and select a format			
Field, format in lowercase	1965	In Table Design view, click field name; click Format box, type < followed by letter mask character (L or ?)			
Field, format in uppercase	1965	In Table Design view, click field name; click Format box, type > followed by letter mask character (L or ?)			
Field, require entry	1974	In Table Design view, click field name; click Required box, then click down arrow and select Yes			
Field, set default value	1964	In Table Design view, click field name; click Default Value box, type value			
Field, validate using Expression Builder	1976	In Table Design view, click field name; click Validation Rule box, click [...] button		In Table Design view, click field name; right-click Validation Rule box, then click Build	
Filter, by form	1987	In Table Datasheet view, [icon], type text (use wildcard) or select from field's drop-down list, then [icon]	In Table Datasheet view, Records | Filter | Filter By Form; type or select text; Filter | Apply Filter/Sort	In Table Datasheet view, right-click field, right-click any field, click Filter By Form; right-click in table, Apply Filter/Sort	
Filter, by selection	1985	In Table Datasheet view, click in field that has the value, [icon]	In Table Datasheet view, click in field that has the value, Records | Filter | Filter By Selection	In Table Datasheet view, right-click field, click Filter By Selection	
Filter, by selection in data access page	1993	Click in filter field, [icon] on Navigation bar			
Filter, remove	1985	[icon] on Table Datasheet toolbar	In Table Datasheet view, Records | Remove Filter/Sort	In Table Datasheet view, right-click field, right-click any field, click Remove Filter/Sort	

Access Task	Page	Mouse	Menu Bar	Shortcut Menu	Shortcut Keys
Filter, remove in data access page	1993	▽ on Navigation bar			
Find, value in column	1982	Click in column to be searched; 🔍 on Table Datasheet toolbar	Select column; Edit | Find	Right-click column heading, then click Find	[Ctrl] + [F]
Find, value in table	1984	🔍 on Table Datasheet toolbar; click Look in box, select table name	Select column; Edit | Find	Right-click any column heading, then click Find	[Ctrl] + [F]
Form, add combo box	2102	📇 on Toolbox in Design view			
Form, add custom ControlTip	2101	Display property sheet, click Other tab, then enter value in ControlTip Text box			
Form, add field	2084	In Design view, drag field from field list to form			
Form, add record using subform	2118	Display record in form, add record to related subform			
Form, add status bar instructions	2099	Display property sheet, click Other tab, then enter value in Status Bar Text box			
Form, add subform	2116	In Design view, 📇 on Toolbox			
Form, add title	2114	In Design view, add a label 𝐴𝑎 on Toolbox to Form Header section	View | Form Header/Footer, add a label	Form Header/Footer, add a label	
Form, apply border to control	2091	In Design view, click control, ▭ arrow on Formatting toolbar, then click a border width			
Form, change background color	2089	In Design view, click a Section selector, 🎨 on Formatting toolbar, then click a color		Right-click a Section selector, Fill/Back Color arrow, then click a color	
Form, change background color of control	2089	In Design view, click control, 🎨 arrow on Formatting toolbar, then click a color		Right-click control, Fill/Back Color arrow, then click a color	
Form, change background to picture	2113	Double-click form selector, click Format tab, Picture box, 🖼		Right-click form title bar, Properties | Format tab, Picture box, Build button	
Form, change font color	2087	In Design view, click control, 𝐀 arrow on Formatting toolbar, then click a color		Right-click control, Font/Fore Color arrow, then click a color	

Access Task	Page	Mouse	Menu Bar	Shortcut Menu	Shortcut Keys
Form, change tab order	2107		View | Tab Order	Tab Order	
Form, create in Design view	2110	On Objects bar, click Forms, then click ☐ New, Design View Double-click *Create form in Design View*	Insert | Form, Design View		
Form, insert Excel chart	2244		In form Design view, Insert | Object; select Create from File; browse and select Excel file		
Form, insert hyperlink to a Word document	2227	In Word, select text to be destination of hyperlink, click ☐; in Access form Design view, click Edit | Paste as Hyperlink	In Word, select text to be destination of hyperlink, click Edit | Copy	In Word, right-click selected text; click Copy; in Access form Design view, click Edit | Paste as Hyperlink	In Word, select text; Ctrl + C
Form, insert hyperlink to an Excel worksheet	2230	☐ on Form Design toolbar; select the Excel file	In form Design view, Insert | Hyperlink; select the Excel file		Ctrl + K
Form, link to an Excel worksheet	2235	Click Tables in Objects bar; click ☐ New; click Link Table; select Excel file and click Link; follow wizard steps	Insert | Table; click Link Table; select Excel file and click Link; follow wizard steps	Right-click Tables in Objects bar; Link Tables; select Excel file and click Link; follow wizard steps	
Form, select multiple controls	2087	Shift + click each control In Design view, drag to draw a box around fields or drag in a ruler			
Form, use Format Painter to format control	2091	☐ on Standard toolbar (double-click to apply repeatedly)			Ctrl + Shift + C and Ctrl + Shift + V
Hyperlink to Excel, insert in Access form	2230	☐ on Form Design toolbar; select the Excel file	In form Design view, Insert | Hyperlink; select the Excel file		Ctrl + K
Hyperlink to Word, insert in Access form	2227	In Word, select text to be destination of hyperlink, click ☐; in Access form Design view, click Edit | Paste as Hyperlink	In Word, select text to be destination of hyperlink, click Edit | Copy	In Word, right-click selected text; click Copy; in Access form Design view, click Edit | Paste as Hyperlink	In Word, select text; Ctrl + C
Import, data from a Word table	2214		In Word: Table | Convert | Table to Text; save as a plain text file; in Access: Files | Get External Data | Import; select the text file; click Import and follow wizard steps		

Access Task	Page	Mouse	Menu Bar	Shortcut Menu	Shortcut Keys
Import, data from an Excel worksheet	2226		Files | Get External Data | Import; select Excel file; click Import and follow wizard steps		
Index field, create with duplicates	2025	In Table Design view, click Indexed box, select Yes (Duplicates OK)			
Index field, create without duplicates	2024	In Table Design view, click Indexed box, select Yes (No Duplicates)			
Indexes, display	2025	in Table Design view	In Table Design view, View | Indexes	Right-click table title bar in Design View, Indexes	
Input mask, create	1970	In Table Design view, click field name; click Input Mask box, click ... button		In Table Design view, click field name; right-click Input Mask box, then click Build	
Input mask, create in Design view	1972	In Table Design view, click field name; type input mask characters in Input Mask box			
Link databases	2240	Click Tables in Objects bar; click New; click Link Table; select database file and click Link; follow wizard steps	Insert | Table; click Link Table; select database file and click Link; follow wizard steps	Right-click Tables in Objects bar; Link Tables; select database file and click Link; follow wizard steps	
Link form and Excel worksheet	2235	Click Tables in Objects bar; click New; click Link Table; select Excel file and click Link; follow wizard steps	Insert | Table; click Link Table; select Excel file and click Link; follow wizard steps	Right-click Tables in Objects bar; Link Tables; select Excel file and click Link; follow wizard steps	
Lookup Wizard, use for field lookup	1980	In Table Design view, click a field's Data Type box, then select Lookup Wizard			
Mail merge, insert merge field	2221	In Mail Merge task pane or on Mail Merge toolbar, click ; click a field and then click Insert			
Make-table query, create	2184	Create query; on Query Design toolbar; click Make-Table Query	Create query; Query | Make-Table Query	Right-click Query window; Query Type | Make-Table Query	
Merge, Access table with a Word document	2221	on Database toolbar; click Merge It with Microsoft Office Word; follow wizard and task pane steps	Tools | Office Links | Merge It with Microsoft Office Word; follow wizard and task pane steps		
Minimize, Access window	2227	in title bar		Right-click title bar; Minimize	

Access Task	Page	Mouse	Menu Bar	Shortcut Menu	Shortcut Keys
Parameter query, create	2182		In Query Design view, enter condition(s) in Criteria row within [ ]		
Performance, analyze	2050		Tools | Analyze | Performance		
Picture from file, insert in field	1958	Data type must be OLE object; in Table Datasheet view, Insert | Object, Create from File, Browse; locate and double-click picture file		Data type must be OLE object; right-click field in Table Datasheet View, then click Insert Object; click Create from File, then click Browse; locate and double-click picture file	
Picture, view OLE object in table	1958	In Table Datasheet view, double-click Package in field		In Table Datasheet view, right-click Package in field; Package Object | Activate Contents	
Print relationships	2034	Display Relationships report, 🖨	In Relationships window, File | Print Relationships	Right-click Relationships report, Print	
Property sheet, display in Design view	2094	🗗 on Form Design toolbar Double-click control or section of form	View | Properties	Properties	Alt + Enter
Property sheet, set format properties	2094, 2097	🗗 on Form Design toolbar, click Format tab, select property, enter value	View | Properties | Format tab, select property, enter value	Properties | Format tab, select property, enter value	Alt + Enter, Format tab, select property, enter value
Query, create action query	2184	🗗 ▾ on Query Design toolbar; click one of the action query types	Query | *Action Query type*	Right-click Query window; Query Type | *Action Query type*	
Query, create append query	2186	Create query; 🗗 ▾ on Query Design toolbar; click Append Query	Create query; Query | Append Query	Right-click Query window; Query Type | Append Query	
Query, create crosstab query	2177	🗐 New in Database window; click Crosstab Query Wizard	Insert | Query; select Crosstab Query Wizard		
Query, create delete query	2174	Create query; 🗗 ▾ on Query Design toolbar; click Delete Query	Create query; Query | Delete Query	Right-click Query window; Query Type | Delete Query	
Query, create Find Duplicates	2043	🗐 ▾, Query, Find Duplicates Query Wizard On Objects bar, click Queries; click New 🗐 New; click find Duplicates Query Wizard	Insert | Query, Find Duplicates Query Wizard		

Access Task	Page	Mouse	Menu Bar	Shortcut Menu	Shortcut Keys
Query, create Find Unmatched	2045	[icon] , Query, Find Unmatched Query Wizard On Objects bar, click Queries; click New [New]; click Find Unmatched Query Wizard	Insert | Query, Find Unmatched Query Wizard		
Query, create make-table query	2184	Create query; [icon] on Query Design toolbar; click Make-Table Query	Create query; Query | Make-Table Query	Right-click Query window; Query Type | Make-Table Query	
Query, create parameter query	2182		In Query Design view, enter condition(s) in Criteria row within [ ]		
Query, create update query	2170	Create query; [icon] on Query Design toolbar; click Update Query	Create query; Query | Update Query	Right-click Query window; Query Type | Update Query	
Query, run	2170, 2174, 2182, 2184	[icon]	Query | Run		
Query, view in SQL	2188		Open Query; View | SQL View	Right-click Query window; SQL View	
Record, insert in data access page	1995	[icon] on Navigation bar			
Record, search in column	1982	Click in column to be searched; [icon] on Table Datasheet toolbar	Select column; Edit | Find	Right-click column heading, then click Find	Ctrl + F
Record, search table to find record	1984	[icon] on Table Datasheet toolbar; click Look in box, select table name	Select column; Edit | Find; click Look in box, select table name	Right-click any column heading, then click Find; click Look in box, select table name	Ctrl + F
Records, browse in data access page	1993	First [icon], Previous [icon], Next [icon], and Last [icon] on Navigation bar			
Records, find duplicates	2043	[icon] , Query, Find Duplicates Query Wizard	Insert | Query, Find Duplicates Query Wizard		
Records, find unmatched	2045	[icon] , Query, Find Unmatched Query Wizard	Insert | Query, Find Unmatched Query Wizard		
Referential integrity, enforce	2031		Relationships | Edit Relationships	Right-click relationship line, Edit Relationships	
Relationship, edit	2031, 2034, 2037	Double-click relationship line	Relationships | Edit Relationship	Right-click relationship line, Edit Relationship	

Access Task	Page	Mouse	Menu Bar	Shortcut Menu	Shortcut Keys
Relationship, establish	2031, 2034, 2037	Drag a field from one table to a related field in another table	Relationships | Edit Relationship	Right-click relationship line, Edit Relationship	
Relationships, display content of table	2026	Drag border of table window			
Relationships, display window	2026	⊞ on Database toolbar	Tools | Relationships	Right-click Database window, Relationships	
Relationships, hide table	2026		Relationships | Hide Table	Right-click table, Hide Table	
Relationships, print	2034	Display Relationships report, 🖨	File | Print Relationships	Right-click Relationships report, Print	
Relationships, show all	2026	▦ in Relationships window	Relationships | Show All	Right-click Relationships window, Show All	
Relationships, show table	2034	⊞ in Relationships window	Relationships | Show Table	Right-click Relationships window, Show Table	
Report, create from crosstab query	2167	Click Reports in Objects bar; double-click *Create report by using wizard*; click a query in the Tables/Queries list; complete the wizard steps. 🗋 New in Database window; click Report Wizard; click a query in the Tables/Queries list; complete the wizard steps	Insert | Report; select Report Wizard; select a query in the Tables/Queries list; complete the wizard steps		
Report, create subreport	2150	▦ in Toolbox; click in Detail section in Design view; follow the wizard steps			
Report, group data	2157	▦ on Report Design toolbar	View | Sorting and Grouping	Right-click report in Design view; Sorting and Grouping	
Report, link to an Excel chart	2249		In report Design view, Insert | Object; select Create from File; browse and select Excel file; click Link check box		
Report, set margins	2159	Setup on Print Preview toolbar	File | Page Setup | Margins tab		
Report, set properties (Design view)	2165	▦ on Report Design toolbar	View | Properties	Right-click section heading bar; Properties	Alt + Enter
Save, record in data access page	1995	🖫 on Navigation bar			

Access Task	Page	Mouse	Menu Bar	Shortcut Menu	Shortcut Keys
Security, remove password	2051		Tools | Security | Unset Database Password		
Security, set database password	2051		Tools | Security | Set Database Password		
Sort, records in data access page	1993	Click in sort field, [↑] or [↓] on Navigation bar			
SQL, view query	2188		Open Query; View | SQL View	Right-click Query window; SQL View	
Status bar, add instructions to form	2099	Display property sheet, click Other tab, then enter value in Status Bar Text box			
Subform, add record	2118	Display record in form, add record to related subform			
Subform, add to form	2116	In Design view, [▦] on Toolbox			
Subreport, embed in report	2150	[▦] on Toolbox; click in Detail section in Design view; follow the wizard steps			
Table, analyze	2047		Tools | Analyze | Table		
Update query, create	2170	Create query; [▦ ▾] on Query Design toolbar; click Update Query	Create query; Query | Update Query	Right-click Query window; Query Type | Update Query	
Word, import data into Access	2214		In Word: Table | Convert | Table to Text; save as a plain text file; in Access: Files | Get External Data | Import; select the text file; click Import and follow wizard steps		
Word, mail merge with Access table	2221	[▦ ▾] on Database toolbar; click Merge It with Microsoft Office Word; follow wizard and task pane steps	Tools | Office Links | Merge It with Microsoft Office Word; follow wizard and task pane steps		

PowerPoint 2003

PowerPoint Task	Page	Mouse	Menu Bar	Shortcut Menu	Shortcut Keys
3-D style, add to object	2346	⬚ on Drawing toolbar			
3-D style, change color	2347	⬚ ▾ arrow on 3-D Settings toolbar			
3-D style, change depth	2347	⬚ on 3-D Settings toolbar			
3-D style, change direction	2347	⬚ on 3-D Settings toolbar			
3-D style, change lighting	2347	⬚ on 3-D Settings toolbar			
3-D style, change settings	2347	⬚ on Drawing toolbar, then click 3-D Settings			
3-D style, change surface	2347	⬚ on 3-D Settings toolbar			
3-D style, change tilt	2347	Click a tilt setting on 3-D Settings toolbar			
Action button, create	2442	AutoShapes ▾ on Drawing toolbar, then click Action Buttons	Slide Show | Action Buttons		
Align, objects	2361	Draw ▾ on Drawing toolbar; click Align or Distribute, then click an alignment option			
Align, objects relative to slide	2361	Draw ▾ on Drawing toolbar; click Align or Distribute, then click Relative to Slide			
Animation, add to slide	2419		Slide Show | Custom Animation	Right-click slide, then click Custom Animation	
Animation, change effect	2433	Click item in Custom Animation task pane, then click ☆ Change ▾			
Animation, change order	2428	Click item in Custom Animation task pane, then click up or down Re-Order button Drag item in custom animation list			

PowerPoint Task	Page	Mouse	Menu Bar	Shortcut Menu	Shortcut Keys
Animation, change timing	2430	In Custom Animation task pane, click item in list; click item's arrow, then click Timing		In Custom Animation Task Pane, right-click item in list, then click Timing	
Animation, play in Normal View	2419	▶ Play in Custom Animation task pane			
Animation, remove effect	2433	Click item in Custom Animation task pane, then click ✗ Remove		In Custom Animation Task Pane, right-click item in list, then click Remove	
Annotation pen, turn on or off	2450	In Slide Show view, click Pen button in lower left corner; click Ballpoint Pen, Felt Tip Pen, or Highlighter		Right-click slide in Slide Show View; Pointer Options | Ballpoint Pen or Felt Tip Pen or Highlighter	Ctrl + P (activates pen) Ctrl + A or Esc (turns off pen)
Annotations, erase	2450	End show, then click Discard when prompted		Right-click slide in Slide Show View; Pointer Options | Eraser	
AutoShape, change	2291	Draw ▾ on Drawing toolbar, then click Change AutoShape; click button on palette			
AutoShape, clear line	2295	Click arrow on 🖊 ▾ on Drawing toolbar, then click No Line	Format | AutoShape, Colors and Lines tab	Format AutoShape | Colors and Lines tab	
AutoShape, copy	2283	📋 and 📋 on Standard toolbar	Edit | Copy and then Edit | Paste	Right-click image, Copy, then right-click at new location and click Paste	Ctrl + drag Ctrl + X and Ctrl + V
AutoShape, customize	2289	Drag yellow diamond on selected shape			
AutoShape, draw	2289	AutoShapes ▾ on Drawing toolbar, then click a category; click button on palette then drag on slide	Insert | Picture | AutoShapes		
AutoShape, rotate	2299	Drag green circle rotation handle on selected shape			
AutoShape, size	2292	Drag sizing handle(s) Double-click shape, then click Size tab	Format | AutoShape | Size tab	Format AutoShape | Size tab	
AutoShape, wrap text	2294		Format | AutoShape | Text Box tab, then Word wrap text in AutoShape	Format AutoShape | Text Box tab	
Chart options, modify	2511		Chart | Chart Options	Right-click chart area or plot area; click Chart Options	

PowerPoint Task	Page	Mouse	Menu Bar	Shortcut Menu	Shortcut Keys
Chart, add data labels	2517		Chart | Chart Options | Data Labels tab	Right-click chart area or plot area; click Chart Options | Data Labels tab	
Chart, animate	2515		Slide Show | Custom Animation; click Add Effect in the Custom Animation task pane; click Entrance and then click an effect. In the custom animation list, click the effect's arrow, and then click Effect Options; click the Chart Animation tab		
Chart, change type	2516	on MS Graph Standard toolbar	Chart | Chart Type	Right-click chart area or plot area; click Chart Type	
Chart, explode 3-D pie	2518	Click slice twice to select it; drag slice away from the pie			
Chart, format selected element	2512	Double-click chart element	Format | Selected <element>	Right-click chart element; click Format <element>	
Chart, rotate or elevate 3-D pie	2518		Chart | 3-D View	Right-click chart area or plot area; click 3-D View	
Circle, draw	2286	on Drawing toolbar, then press Shift and drag on slide	Insert | Picture | AutoShapes		
Clip art, insert	2303, 2305	on Drawing toolbar or on Content layout; search for and click clip	Insert | Picture | Clip Art		Ctrl + F1, then choose Clip Art
		in task pane, then click Clip Art; search for and click clip	Insert | Picture | From File		
Clip art, search for	2305	In Clip Art task pane, type keyword(s) in Search for box, select collection(s), and/or select media file types, then click Go			
Column chart, arrange data by column	2508	on MS Graph Standard toolbar	Data | Series in Columns		
Column chart, change datasheet column width	2508	Drag right border of column heading	Format | Column Width	Right-click column heading; click Column Width	
Column chart, create	2508	on Standard toolbar or on slide content layout	Insert | Chart		
Comment, delete	2568	on Reviewing toolbar		Right-click comment icon; choose Delete Comment	Click comment, Delete
Comment, edit	2568	on Reviewing toolbar Double-click comment icon		Right-click comment icon; choose Edit Comment	

PowerPoint Task	Page	Mouse	Menu Bar	Shortcut Menu	Shortcut Keys
Comment, insert	2568	[icon] on Reviewing toolbar	Insert | Comment		
Custom animation, add to slide	2419		Slide Show | Custom Animation	Right-click slide, then click Custom Animation	
Custom animation, change speed or direction	2419	Click Speed or Direction arrow in Custom Animation task pane			
Custom animation, create motion path for selected object	2435	[Add Effect] in Custom Animation task pane; click Motion Paths	Slide Show | Custom Animation; click Add Effect, Motion Paths		
Custom animation, modify motion path	2436	Click path, drag sizing handle		Right-click path, then click Edit Points	
Custom show, create	2445		Slide Show | Custom Shows | New		
Custom show, hyperlink to	2446	[icon] on Standard toolbar; click Place in This Document, then click custom show name	Select text or object; Slide Show | Action Settings, Hyperlink to, Custom Show	Right-click selected text or object, click Hyperlink; click Place in This Document, then click custom show name	
Dash style, change	2282	[icon] on Drawing toolbar	Format | AutoShape, Colors and Lines tab	Format AutoShape | Colors and Lines tab	
Design template, apply custom	2562	In Slide Design task pane, click Browse; locate and click template name; click Apply			
Design template, create and save	2556		Format the slide master and title master as desired; File | Save As; in Save as type list, click Design Template		
Design template, insert new title master	2559	[icon] on Slide Master View toolbar	In Slide Master view, Insert | New Title Master		
Design template, modify	2562	Open template, make changes to slide master and/or title master			
Design template, open custom	2559	[icon] on Standard toolbar; in Files of type list, click Design Templates; navigate to folder	File | Open; in Files of type list, click Design Templates; navigate to folder		
Design template, rename master	2559	[icon] on Slide Master View toolbar	In Slide Master view, Edit | Rename Master		
Diagram, create	2497	[icon] on Drawing toolbar or on slide content layout	Insert | Diagram		
Diagram, format	2499	[icon] on Diagram toolbar			

PowerPoint Task	Page	Mouse	Menu Bar	Shortcut Menu	Shortcut Keys
Diagram, insert shape	2500	**Insert Shape** on Diagram toolbar		Right-click diagram; click Insert Shape	
Diagram, move shape	2500	(backward) or (forward) on Diagram toolbar			
Diagram, reverse	2499	on Diagram toolbar			
Distribute, objects	2364	**Draw ▾** on Drawing toolbar; click Align or Distribute, then click Distribute Horizontally or Distribute Vertically			
Distribute, objects relative to slide	2364	**Draw ▾** on Drawing toolbar; click Align or Distribute, then click Relative to Slide			
Draw, AutoShape	2289	**AutoShapes ▾** on Drawing toolbar, then click a category; click button on palette and then drag on slide	Insert | Picture | AutoShapes		
Draw, circle	2286	on Drawing toolbar, then press Shift and drag on slide	Insert | Picture | AutoShapes		
Draw, oval	2286	on Drawing toolbar, then drag on slide	Insert | Picture | AutoShapes		
Draw, rectangle	2286	on Drawing toolbar, then drag on slide			
		AutoShapes ▾ on Drawing toolbar, then click Basic Shapes; click button on palette, then drag on slide	Insert | Picture | AutoShapes		
Draw, square	2286	on Drawing toolbar, then press Shift and drag on slide	Insert | Picture | AutoShapes		
Draw, text box	2284	on Drawing toolbar, then drag on slide	Insert | Text Box		
Drawing object, add text	2294	Select shape, then type		Add Text	
Drawing object, change fill color	2295	On Drawing toolbar, click arrow on , then click color or option	Format | AutoShape, Colors and Lines tab	Format AutoShape | Colors and Lines tab	
Drawing object, change fill effect	2295	On Drawing toolbar, click arrow on , then click Fill Effects	Format | AutoShape, Colors and Lines tab	Format AutoShape | Colors and Lines tab	

PowerPoint Task	Page	Mouse	Menu Bar	Shortcut Menu	Shortcut Keys
Drawing object, delete	2291		Edit	Clear	Right-click object, Cut	Delete
Drawing object, move	2293	Drag object [icons] and [icon] on Standard toolbar	Edit	Cut and then Edit	Paste	Right-click object, Cut, then right-click at new location and choose Paste	Ctrl + X and Ctrl + V
Duplicate, object	2350		Edit	Duplicate		Ctrl + D
Effect option, add	2423	In Custom Animation task pane, click item in list; click item's arrow, then click Effect Options		In Custom Animation Task Pane, right-click item in list, then click Effect Options	
Emphasis effect, add to selected object	2425	[☆ Add Effect ▼] in Custom Animation task pane; click Emphasis	Slide Show	Custom Animation; click Add Effect, Emphasis		
Entrance effect, add to selected object	2419	[☆ Add Effect ▼] in Custom Animation task pane; click Entrance	Slide Show	Custom Animation; click Add Effect, Entrance		
Exit effect, add to selected object	2426	[☆ Add Effect ▼] in Custom Animation task pane; click Exit	Slide Show	Custom Animation; click Add Effect, Exit		
Export, presentation to Microsoft Word	2575		File	Send To	Microsoft Word		
Fill color, clear	2295	Click arrow on [icon ▼] on Drawing toolbar, then click No Fill	Format	AutoShape, Colors and Lines tab	Format AutoShape	Colors and Lines tab	
Flip, object	2349	[Draw ▼] on Drawing toolbar; click Rotate or Flip, then click a flip option			
Float, Order menu (and other Draw submenus)	2352	Drag dotted bar at top of menu			
Graphics, omit from slide background	2494		Format	Background; choose *Omit background graphics from master* check box	Right-click slide; click Background; click *Omit background graphics from master* check box	
Grid, turn on/off	2356	[Draw ▼] on Drawing toolbar; click Grid and Guides, Display grid on screen	View	Grid and Guides, Display grid on screen		
Group, selected objects	2358	[Draw ▼] on Drawing toolbar, then click Group		Right-click objects, Grouping	Group	Ctrl + Shift + G
Guides, turn on/off	2356	[Draw ▼] on Drawing toolbar; click Grid and Guides, Display drawing guides on screen	View	Grid and Guides, Display drawing guides onscreen		

PowerPoint Task	Page	Mouse	Menu Bar	Shortcut Menu	Shortcut Keys
de/unhide slide	2444	[icon] on Slide Sorter toolbar	Slide Show | Hide Slide		
yperlink, insert	2439, 2441	[icon] on Standard toolbar	Select text or object; Insert | Hyperlink Select text or object; Slide Show | Action Settings, Hyperlink to	Right-click selected text or object, then click Hyperlink	
ne, change color	2283, 2295	On Drawing toolbar, click arrow on [icon], then click color or option	Format | AutoShape, Colors and Lines tab	Format AutoShape | Colors and Lines tab	
ne, change ash style	2282	[icon] on Drawing toolbar	Format | AutoShape, Colors and Lines tab	Format AutoShape | Colors and Lines tab	
ne, change style	2282	[icon] on Drawing toolbar	Format | AutoShape, Colors and Lines tab	Format AutoShape | Colors and Lines tab	
ne, draw	2278	[icon] on Drawing toolbar, then drag on slide [AutoShapes] on Drawing toolbar, then click Lines; click button on palette and then drag on slide	Insert | Picture | AutoShapes		
Merge, resentations	2570		Tools | Compare and Merge Presentations		
Motion path, create or selected object	2435	[Add Effect] in Custom Animation task pane; click Motion Paths	Slide Show | Custom Animation; click Add Effect, Motion Paths		
Motion path, modify	2436	Click path, drag sizing handle		Right-click path, then click Edit Points	
Move, drawing bject	2293	Drag object [icon] and [icon] on Standard toolbar	Edit | Cut and then Edit | Paste	Right-click object, Cut, then right-click at new location and choose Paste	Ctrl + X and Ctrl + V
Move, object orward or ackward	2352	[Draw] on Drawing toolbar; click Order, then click an order option		Right-click object; click Order, then click an order option	
Multimedia, set animation options	2565	Select media icon on slide; in Custom Animation task pane, click item's arrow, select Effect Options			
Music, playing rom CD	2563		Insert | Movies and Sounds | Play CD Audio Track		
Navigation, use during slide show	2448	Click Slide button in lower left corner; click Go to Slide, then click a slide title		Right-click slide in Slide Show View; Go to Slide | slide title	

PowerPoint Task	Page	Mouse	Menu Bar	Shortcut Menu	Shortcut Ke
Objects, select multiple	2354	Click an object; press Shift while clicking other objects; [arrow icon] on Drawing toolbar; draw rectangle around multiple objects			Shift + click
Order, change object	2352	Draw ▼ on Drawing toolbar; click Order, then click an order option		Right-click object; click Order, then click an order option	
Organization chart, change layout	2504	Layout ▼ on Organization Chart toolbar; click a layout		Right-click a shape; click Layout; click a layout	
Organization chart, create	2501	[icon] on Drawing toolbar or on slide content layout	Insert	Diagram; select the first diagram type		
Organization chart, format selected element	2505	Click button(s) on Formatting toolbar and Drawing toolbar	Format	AutoShape	Colors and Lines tab	Right-click selected element; click Format AutoShape	Colors and Lines tab	
Organization chart, insert shape	2503	Insert Shape ▼ arrow on Organization Chart toolbar; click Subordinate, Coworker, or Assistant		Right-click shape; click Subordinate, Coworker, or Assistant	
Organization chart, select a level or branch	2505	Select ▼ on Organization Chart toolbar; click Level or Branch		Right-click a shape; click Select; click Level or Branch	
Organization chart, select all assistants or connecting lines	2505	Select ▼ on Organization Chart toolbar; click All Assistants or All Connecting Lines		Right-click a shape; click Select; click All Assistants or All Connecting Lines	
Organization chart, wrap text in shape	2501		Format	AutoShape	Text Box tab; choose *Word wrap text in AutoShape* check box	Right-click shape; click Format AutoShape; click Text Box tab and then choose *Word wrap text in AutoShape* check box	
Oval, draw	2286	[oval icon] on Drawing toolbar, then drag on slide	Insert	Picture	AutoShapes		
Package presentation	2573		File	Package for CD		
Photo album, add captions	2373		Format	Photo Album, click Captions below ALL pictures		
Photo album, create	2373	Click Photo Album in New Presentation task pane	Insert	Picture	New Photo Album; File	New	Photo Album		
Photo album, modify	2375		Format	Photo Album		

PowerPoint Task	Page	Mouse	Menu Bar	Shortcut Menu	Shortcut Keys
Picture, adjust brightness	2367	▨ or ▨ on Picture toolbar	Format	Picture	Picture tab, Brightness	Format Picture	Picture tab, Brightness	
Picture, adjust contrast	2367	▨ or ▨ on Picture toolbar	Format	Picture	Picture tab, Contrast	Format Picture	Picture tab, Contrast	
Picture, crop	2367	▨ on Picture toolbar, then drag crop corners			
Picture, insert	2308	▨ on Drawing toolbar or on Content layout	Insert	Picture	From File		
Picture, insert as slide background	2378		Format	Background; click Background fill arrow, then click Fill Effects	Picture tab; click Select Picture	Right-click slide or slide icon, then click Background; click Background fill arrow, then click Fill Effects	Picture tab; click Select Picture	
Picture, modify color	2366	▨ on Picture toolbar	Format	Picture	Picture tab, Color	Format Picture	Picture tab, Color	
Picture, move	2307	Drag picture	Edit	Cut and then Edit	Paste	Right-click picture, Cut, then right-click at new location and choose Paste	
		▨ and ▨ on Standard toolbar	Format	Picture	Position tab	Right-click picture, Format Picture	Position tab	Ctrl + X and Ctrl + V
			Double-click picture, then click Position tab		
Picture, recolor	2369	▨ on Picture toolbar	Format	Picture	Picture tab, Recolor	Format Picture	Picture tab, Recolor	
Picture, reset original size and color	2368	▨ on Picture toolbar	Format	Picture	Picture tab, Reset	Format Picture	Picture tab, Reset	
Picture, resize	2368	Drag a sizing handle	Format	Picture	Size tab	Format Picture	Size tab	
Picture, return to original color	2366	▨ on Picture toolbar, then click Automatic	Format	Picture	Picture tab, Color, Automatic	Format Picture	Picture tab, Color, Automatic	
Picture, size	2307	Drag sizing handle	Format	Picture	Size tab	Right-click picture, Format Picture	Size tab	
		▨ on Picture toolbar			
		Double-click picture, then click Size tab			
Picture, washout color	2366	▨ on Picture toolbar, then click Washout	Format	Picture	Picture tab, Color, Washout	Format Picture	Picture tab, Color, Washout	
Presentation, package for CD	2573		File	Package for CD		

PowerPoint Task	Page	Mouse	Menu Bar	Shortcut Menu	Shortcut Keys
Presentations, compare and merge	2570		Tools | Compare and Merge Presentations		
Publish presentation to Web	2578		File | Save As Web Page		
Rectangle, draw	2286	▢ on Drawing toolbar, then drag on slide AutoShapes ▾ on Drawing toolbar, then click Basic Shapes; click button on palette and then drag on slide	Insert | Picture | AutoShapes		
Regroup, ungrouped objects	2358	Draw ▾ on Drawing toolbar, then click Regroup		Right-click objects, Grouping | Regroup	
Review, apply all changes on slide by one reviewer	2570	In Revisions task pane, click Gallery tab; point to slide and click arrow; click Apply All Changes By This Reviewer			
Review, apply change(s)	2570	◇ ▾ on Reviewing toolbar Click check box in change marker			
Review, end	2570	Click End Review on Reviewing toolbar			
Review, next item in merged presentation	2570	⇥ on Reviewing toolbar			
Review, save presentation for	2567		File | Save As; in Save as type list, click Presentation for Review		
Rotate, 15° increments	2350	Press Shift while dragging green rotation handle			
Rotate, object	2350	Drag green rotation handle Draw ▾ on Drawing toolbar; click Rotate or Flip, then click a rotate option			
Ruler, display or hide	2278		View | Ruler		
Save, presentation as Web page	2578		File | Save As Web Page		
Save, presentation for review	2567		File | Save As; in Save as type list, click Presentation for Review		
Select, multiple objects	2354	Click an object; press Shift while clicking other objects			

PowerPoint Task	Page	Mouse	Menu Bar	Shortcut Menu	Shortcut Keys
Shadow, add to selected object	2344	▣ on Drawing toolbar			
Shadow, change color	2345	▣ ▾ arrow on Shadow Settings toolbar			
Shadow, change settings	2345	▣ on Drawing toolbar, then click Shadow Settings			
Shadow, nudge position	2345	Click a nudge setting on Settings toolbar			
Shadow, remove from selected object	2344	▣ on Drawing toolbar, then click No Shadow			
Slide show, activate starting with current slide	2416	▣ in lower-left corner of PowerPoint window ▣ Slide Show in Slide Transition or Custom Animation task pane			Shift + F5
Slide show, blank screen	2448			Right-click slide in Slide Show View; Screen | Black Screen or White Screen	B or W
Slide, add transition	2416	▣ Transition on Slide Sorter toolbar	Slide Show | Slide Transition	Right-click slide, then click Slide Transition	
Slide, advance automatically	2418	Click Automatically after in Slide Transition task pane; set time			
Slide, insert picture as background	2378		Format | Background; click Background fill arrow, then click Fill Effects | Picture tab; click Select Picture	Right-click slide or slide icon, then click Background; click Background fill arrow, then click Fill Effects | Picture tab; click Select Picture	
Sound, hide icon during slide show	2565	Select sound icon; in Custom Animation task pane, click item's arrow, select Effect Options; click Hide sound icon during slide show	Click sound icon; Edit | Sound Object; click Hide sound icon during slide show	Right-click sound icon; click Hide sound icon during slide show	
Sound, insert from CD	2563		Insert | Movies and Sounds | Play CD Audio Track		
Sound, insert from file	2563		Insert | Movies and Sounds | Sound from File		
Square, draw	2286	▣ on Drawing toolbar, then press Shift and drag on slide	Insert | Picture | AutoShapes		
Synonym, find for text	2566	▣ on Standard toolbar; in Research task pane, select Thesaurus in drop-down list	Tools | Thesaurus	Right-click word or selected text; point to Synonyms; select from list or click Thesaurus	Alt + click a word or selected phrase

PowerPoint Task	Page	Mouse	Menu Bar	Shortcut Menu	Shortcut Keys
Table, apply border	2494	on Tables and Borders toolbar			
Table, center text horizontally	2493	on Formatting toolbar			
Table, center text vertically	2493	on Tables and Borders toolbar			
Table, change border	2494	(arrow) on Tables and Borders toolbar			
Table, change border color	2494	on Tables and Borders toolbar			
Table, create	2486	on Standard toolbar	Insert | Table		
Table, delete row(s) or column(s)	2490	Table ▾ on Tables and Borders toolbar; Delete Rows or Delete Columns		Right-click row(s); choose Delete Rows	
Table, draw	2492	on Tables and Borders toolbar			
Table, erase line	2492	on Tables and Borders toolbar; click line or drag			
Table, insert column	2490	Table ▾ on Tables and Borders toolbar; Insert Columns to the Left or Insert Columns to the Right			
Table, insert row	2490	Table ▾ on Tables and Borders toolbar; Insert Rows Above or Insert Rows Below		Right-click row(s); click Insert Rows	Tab in last cell of table
Table, merge cells	2492	on Tables and Borders toolbar			
Table, move insertion point	2486	Click a cell			Tab or Shift + Tab; arrow keys
Table, select	2486	Table ▾ on Tables and Borders toolbar; Select Table Click table border		Right-click inside table; choose Select Table	
Table, split cell	2492	on Tables and Borders toolbar			
Tables and Borders toolbar, display	2486	on Standard toolbar	View | Toolbars | Tables and Borders	Right-click any toolbar; click Tables and Borders	

PowerPoint Task	Page	Mouse	Menu Bar	Shortcut Menu	Shortcut Keys
Text box, draw	2284	[A] on Drawing toolbar, then drag on slide	Insert | Text Box | Horizontal or Vertical		
Text box, wrap text	2294		Format | Text Box | Text Box tab, then Word wrap text in AutoShape	Format Text Box | Text Box tab	
Thesaurus, use	2566	[icon] on Standard toolbar; in Research task pane, select Thesaurus in drop-down list	Tools | Thesaurus	Right-click word or selected text; point to Synonyms; select from list or click Thesaurus	Alt + click a word or selected phrase
Title master, insert new	2559	[icon] on Slide Master View toolbar	In Slide Master view, Insert | New Title Master		
Toolbar, hide docked	2361		View | Toolbars, click toolbar name	Right-click toolbar, click toolbar name	
Transition, add sound	2416	Click Sound in Slide Transition task pane			
Transition, add to slide	2416	[Transition] on Slide Sorter toolbar	Slide Show | Slide Transition	Right-click slide, then click Slide Transition	
Transition, advance slide automatically	2418	Click Automatically after in Slide Transition task pane; set time			
Transition, change speed	2416	Click Speed in Slide Transition task pane			
Ungroup, objects	2358	[Draw ▾] on Drawing toolbar, then click Ungroup		Right-click objects, Grouping | Ungroup	Ctrl + Shift + H
Washout, picture color	2366	[icon] on Picture toolbar, then click Washout	Format | Picture | Picture tab, Color, Washout	Format Picture | Picture tab, Color, Washout	
Web Page Preview, activate	2578		File | Web Page Preview		
Web Page Preview, expand or collapse outline	2578	Click Expand/Collapse Outline button			
WordArt, change design	2301	[icon] on WordArt toolbar			
WordArt, change fill color	2302	[icon] on WordArt toolbar, then click Colors and Lines tab	Format | WordArt, Colors and Lines tab	Format WordArt | Colors and Lines tab	
WordArt, change shape	2299	[A] on WordArt toolbar			
WordArt, character spacing	2302	[AV ↔] on WordArt toolbar			

PowerPoint Task	Page	Mouse	Menu Bar	Shortcut Menu	Shortcut Keys
WordArt, display toolbar	2299	Click the WordArt toolbar	View | Toolbars | WordArt		
WordArt, edit/format text	2302	Double-click WordArt Edit Text... on WordArt toolbar		Edit Text	
WordArt, format	2299	on WordArt toolbar	Format | WordArt	Format WordArt	
WordArt, insert	2299	on Drawing toolbar	Insert | Picture | WordArt		
WordArt, position	2299	Drag WordArt on WordArt toolbar, then click Position tab	Format | WordArt | Position tab	Format WordArt | Position tab	

Glossary

Action button A type of hyperlink created using the AutoShapes menu on the Drawing toolbar.

Action query A query that changes data in a table.

Active Area The area of the worksheet that contains data or has contained data—it does not include any empty cells that have not been used in the worksheet.

Adjustment handle Displays at the left of an image and can be used to adjust the appearance, but not the size, of a WordArt or AutoShape.

Adobe Acrobat Reader A free program that is used to open Portable Document Format (PDF) files.

Advanced filter Limits the records that display based on comparison criteria.

Animation effects A command that introduces individual slide elements so that the slide can progress one element at a time.

Animation icon A small star that displays next to the slide in the Slides tab of the Outline/Slides pane, or below the slide in the Slide Sorter View, indicating that a transition has been applied.

Annotate The process of using the pointer as a pen and then writing on the slide during a slide show.

Annuity A sum of money payable in a lump sum or as a series of equal annual payments.

Append query A query that adds new records to an existing table by importing data from another Access database, from another program such as Microsoft Excel, or from a table in the same database.

Arguments Specified values that are used in a function to perform a calculation.

Ascending When sorting data, a sort in alphabetical order (A–Z) or numerical order from lowest to highest.

Aspect ratio Proportional relationship of the height and width of an image.

Auditing The process of examining a worksheet for errors in formulas.

AutoFilter A command in Excel that assists in filtering a range by placing AutoFilter arrows to the right of column labels from which you can display a list of possible data that can be used to restrict the records that are displayed.

AutoFormat A formatting command that provides a selection of predefined formats that can be applied to cells on a worksheet.

AutoShapes Drawing objects that include lines, basic shapes, arrows, stars, and flowchart elements.

Binary Pertains to a numbering system that uses two digits; Access databases are binary, meaning they are constructed of mostly unreadable characters.

Body text Text in the Outline View that does not use a heading style.

Bound Linked.

Bound controls Controls in a report that are tied to a field in an underlying table or query.

Branch In an organization chart, refers to boxes connected vertically.

Brightness The light-to-dark ratio of an image. Increasing the brightness lightens both the dark areas and the light areas in an image. Decreasing the brightness darkens both the dark areas and the light areas in an image.

Browser Software that allows you to view and navigate on the Web.

Bulk mailing A reduced-rate mailing that is sorted by ZIP code when processed by the U.S. Postal Service.

Caption A title that can be added to a table or figure.

Caret When moving a worksheet, the tiny triangle that displays to indicate the new location where the worksheet will be positioned.

Category (x) axis The horizontal axis along the bottom of a chart that displays labels containing the names of the categories that are being charted.

Cell The intersection of a column and a row in a table or datasheet.

Change markers Icons that designate a change made by a reviewer.

Character style Style that contains a set of instructions for changing a group of formatting characteristics, such as font and font size, for text only. All changes are applied together.

Chart A graphic representation of data used to display comparisons, change over time, contributions to the whole, or some other relationship that is easier to understand with a picture.

Chart area The part of the chart that displays the chart graphic.

Chart objects The elements that make up a chart.

Chart sheet A separate worksheet in which a chart fills the entire page in landscape orientation.

Chart sub-type Variations on a standard chart type.

Chart Wizard An Excel tool that walks you through four steps in creating a chart.

Clip Organizer A feature used to categorize pictures.

Collapse button An open minus symbol to the left of a heading in an outline indicating that no text or lower-level headings are associated with the heading.

Collapsed Subordinate headings and text associated with a heading are hidden.

Collections Categories in which clips are organized.

Column chart A graph with vertical columns that is used to make comparisons among related numbers.

Combo box A control that allows the user to either type the information in the field or choose a selection from a predefined list; a combo box combines the features of a textbox and a list box.

Comma delimited file Also known as a comma separated value (CSV) file, a type of file format in which each field is separated by a comma. This type of file may be readily exchanged with database programs.

Comma separated value (CSV) A file format in which each cell is separated by a comma and an end-of-paragraph mark at the end of each row. Excel files can be saved in this format for transferring information to other programs.

Comments Electronic notes that usually contain reviewer questions or thoughts. By default, comments do not print.

Compacting Reduces the size of a file and removes deleted objects from the database.

Comparison operators Symbols such as the equal sign (=), the greater than sign (>), or the less than sign (<), used singly or in combination, to compare two values. When two values are compared using these operators, the result is a logical value of either TRUE or FALSE.

Compound criteria When two criteria are placed on the same row in a criteria range, both conditions must be met for the records to be included in the results.

Compound filter A filter that requires that more than one condition be met for a record to be included in the results.

Conditional Format Any formatting characteristic that is applied to cells when the value in that cell meets a specified condition.

Conditional test A test performed by using an equation to compare two values (or two functions or two formulas).

Constant information The information that does not change from letter to letter in a form letter created using Mail Merge.

Contrast The differentiation between light and dark. When you increase contrast, the dark areas get darker and the light areas get lighter. Decreasing the contrast brightens the dark areas and darkens the light areas.

ControlTip Displays when a user pauses the mouse pointer over a control in a form.

COUNTIF The Excel function that sums the number of occurrences in a given range that match a condition value. This function has two arguments: the range and the condition.

Criteria A value or condition that must be matched.

Criteria range An area on your worksheet that is named criteria, and in which conditions are set that must be matched when the database is filtered. This area consists of at least three blank rows above or below the data and contains the column labels and at least one blank row separating it from the data table.

Crop To trim part of a picture or clip art image using the crop tool without resizing the image.

Crop handle Brackets that display at the corners and sides of an image when the crop tool is activated and which are used to assist you in cropping the image.

Crosshair pointer The shape of the pointer when drawing an object.

Crosstab query A special type of query that performs calculations on data that is grouped by two types of information.

Crosstab report A report generated from a crosstab query that displays calculated data grouped by two types of information.

Custom animation list A list that displays the animation sequences for a slide.

Custom chart Advanced charts that can include your own features.

Custom show A presentation within a presentation in which several slides are grouped to be shown to a particular audience.

Data Facts about people, events, things, or ideas.

Data labels Labels used to identify the labels, values, or percentages and that display above or next to a data marker.

Data marker A marker such as a bar, a line, or a pie slice that represents a single value, a data series, or a data point in the datasheet.

Data point A single value in a worksheet represented by a data marker in a chart.

Data series A group of related data points.

Data source 1. A list of variable information that is merged with a main document to create customized form letters or labels. 2. In a mail merge operation, the Access table that contains the names and addresses of the individuals to whom the document is being sent.

Database A collection of data related to a particular topic or purpose.

Datasheet A spreadsheet containing data from which a chart is generated.

Delete query A type of action query that removes records from a table.

Delimited text file A file containing data for which individual field values are separated by a character, such as a comma or a tab.

Delimiter character The character, such as a comma or a tab, that separates individual field values in a converted text file.

Dependent cell A cell that uses the value in a selected cell. It can contain a value or a formula.

Design Master A copy of the original database that is created when a database is replicated and is the only copy to which structural changes can be made.

Destination file A file in which an object from another Office file is linked or embedded.

Detail data The subtotal rows or columns that are totaled by summary data.

Detail section The area of a report that contains the main body of the report's data and which is repeated for each record in the report's underlying record source.

Diagram A tool used to graphically illustrate a concept or relationship.

Distribute A command that evenly spaces selected objects.

Distribute columns evenly Formats columns so that their widths are equal within the boundaries that you select.

Distribute rows evenly Formats rows so that their heights are equal within the boundaries that you select.

Docked toolbar A toolbar that snaps into place below the Standard and Formatting toolbars or at the side of the window.

Document properties Statistics and related information about a document, including file size and location, author, title, and subject.

Draw Table The command used to draw rows and columns in a table.

Drawing objects Shapes such as lines, arrows, rectangles, and circles that can be drawn for the purpose of adding information or to illustrate an idea.

Drawing tools Buttons that are used to draw objects such as lines, arrows, rectangles, circles, and text boxes.

Drop cap The first letter (or letters) of a paragraph, enlarged and either embedded in the text or placed in the left margin.

Dropped Drop cap position embedded in the text, rather than in the margin.

Editing time How many minutes the document has been open. Editing time is not an exact measurement of actual time on task.

Effect options Options that allow you to modify animations, including changing the direction of an effect and playing a sound when an animation takes place.

Elevation The angle at which a chart is titled on the screen.

Embed To insert an object from another program. The object maintains the characteristics of the original application, but is not tied to the original file.

Embedded chart A chart that is inserted into the same worksheet that contains the data used to create the chart.

Embedded object An object contained in a source file and inserted into a destination file or an object that is placed in the database object; used with the OLE data type. Once embedded, the object becomes part of the destination file. Changes you make to the embedded object are reflected in the destination file but not the source file.

Emphasis effects Animations that draw attention to a slide element that is currently displayed.

Encode Scrambling a file so the file is unreadable.

Entrance effects Animations that bring a slide element onto the screen.

Eraser The command used to remove lines in a table, and that merges two separate cells into one cell.

Exclusive use Exclusive use means that nobody else can have the database open at that time.

Exit effects Animations that move a slide element off the screen.

Expand button An open plus symbol to the left of a heading in an outline indicating that there is text associated with the heading. If double-clicked, it acts as an on/off button to display subordinate text.

Explode A feature used for 3-D pie charts in which one or more pie pieces is pulled away from the center of the chart.

Expression Combination of functions, field values, constants, and operators that bring about a result.

Expression builder A feature used to create formulas (expressions) in query criteria, form and report properties, and table validation rules.

External data source A file in a program other than Access.

Extract range An area on your worksheet that is defined as the location to display records that match specified conditions. This area consists of a row of database column labels and at least one empty row, and it can be defined using the Name Box.

Field A category of data, such as name, employee number, or social security number, that has been included in a record. Fields are stored in columns.

Field Properties Pane that is in the lower portion of the table window in Design view where individual characteristics for a field can be set.

Fill color The inside color of an object.

Filter The process of limiting the records displayed by establishing restrictions that require the displayed records to match specified conditions.

Filter By Form Allows you to locate records by typing the desired values into one or more fields on a blank form.

Filter By Selection Allows you to locate records based on data in a field.

Find A command that is used to search and locate specific data each time it occurs.

Flat file database A database that stores different types of information in one table and usually contains data about one particular item in multiple places.

Font descenders The lower parts of letters, such as *y* and *p*, that extend slightly below the line of text.

Foreign key In a relationship, the field in the second table that is linked to the primary key in the first table; the field on the many side of a one-to-many relationship.

Form letter A letter containing constant information (a fixed message) that can be merged with an address list to create customized letters.

Form selector Used to select the entire form to perform form-level operations.

Freeze Panes The Excel command that enables you to select one or more rows or columns and freeze (lock) them into place. This is frequently used to keep column and row headings visible while scrolling a large worksheet.

Function A predefined formula that performs calculations by using specific values, called arguments, in a particular order or structure.

Function name The word is used to label a function, and which indicates the type of calculation that will be performed, for example, SUM or AVERAGE.

Function syntax The proper format of typing the equal sign, the function name, and the arguments when constructing a function.

Future value (FV) An Excel function that calculates future value—the value of an investment at the end of a specified period of time—based on periodic, constant payments and a constant interest rate.

Goal Seek A what-if analysis tool that can help you answer questions. It is used to find the input needed in one cell in order to arrive at the desired result in another cell.

Grayscale Displays all colors as shades of gray.

Grid A series of horizontal and vertical intersecting gridlines, used to visually align objects.

Group A command that treats several objects as one so that they can be sized, moved, and formatted.

Guides 1. Vertical and horizontal lines in the rulers used to visually indicate the position of an object. 2. Lines that act as visual aides that intersect at the horizontal and vertical center point on a slide.

Hidden slide A slide that displays when the hyperlink to which it is linked is clicked during an onscreen presentation.

HLOOKUP An Excel function that looks up values that are displayed horizontally in a row.

HTML Abbreviation for Hypertext Markup Language.

Hyperlink A button, text, or image that, when selected, activates another information resource, such as another location in a worksheet, another file, or a Web page on the Internet or on your organization's intranet.

Hypertext Markup Language A programming language that indicates how Web browsers should display page elements.

Import To copy data from another Access database or from a file created in another program—such as Microsoft Word or Microsoft Excel—and then insert it into an Access table.

In margin Drop cap position with the letter in the margin, rather than embedded in the text.

Index A special list that is created in Access to speed up searches and sorting.

Information Data that has been organized in a useful manner.

Input mask Field property that determines the data that can be entered, how the data displays, and how the data is stored.

Intranet A privately owned Web-based network used by companies and organizations to share information internally.

Junction table The third table in a many-to-many relationship.

Label control The field name attached to a text box control in a form or report; can also be a text description in a form or report.

Labels Column and row headings used in a chart to describe the values in the chart.

Leader line In a chart, a line that connects a data label with its data marker.

Legend 1. A chart element that identifies each data marker. 2. A key that identifies a data series by color.

Level In an organization chart, refers to boxes connected horizontally.

Line chart A chart that shows trends over time.

Link 1. To insert an object from another program that maintains a connection to the file that contains the original information. 2. To insert information from an external source into an Access table in a way that, when the Access table is updated, the original file is also updated, and vice versa.

Linked Objects that have only a link in the database object to an external file, such as a graphic; used with the OLE data type.

Linked object An object that is created in a source file and inserted into a destination file, while maintaining a connection between the two files. The linked object in the destination file can be updated when the source file is updated.

List In Excel, related information that is stored in contiguous rows and columns; also referred to as a table.

List box A control that displays a scrollable list of selections.

List style Formats font style, font size, alignment, and bullet or number characteristics in lists.

Locked A condition applied to cells that prevents the user from accidentally overwriting them. This is frequently used to preserve built-in formulas or data that should not be changed.

Logical operator A mathematical symbol that tests the relationship between the two elements of a conditional test, for example, greater than (>), less than (<), or equal (=).

Logical test Any value or expression that can be evaluated as true or false.

Lookup field Allows you to display a list of values from a field in another table.

Mail Merge A feature that joins a main document and a data source to create customized form letters or labels.

Main document In a mail merge operation, the Word document that contains the text of the letter or memo.

Main form The form that contains a subform.

Major sort 1. The first sort of a multi-column sort performed on a table of data; also known as the primary sort. 2. The term used for the first sort in a multiple-field sort. In Excel, the value that is placed in the Sort by box.

Make-table query An action query that creates a new table based on existing tables.

Many-to-many A relationship that involves two tables that each have a one-to-many relationship to a third table, called a junction table.

Media A variety of objects that include art, photographs, movies, or sounds.

Median Within a set of values, the value below and above which there are an equal number of values; the value that falls in the middle of a ranked set of values.

Merge field A placeholder that you insert within a document.

Microsoft Graph A subprogram built into Microsoft Office that is used to create charts.

Minor sort 1. The second or third column that is sorted on in a multi-column sort; also known as a secondary sort. 2. The second or third sort in a multiple-field sort. In Excel, the values that are placed in the Then by boxes.

Motion path An animation path that a specified object or text will follow as part of an animation sequence.

Multimedia A combination of video, text, and graphics used in a presentation or Web page.

Navigation bar An area of the browser window that contains buttons that allow you to move forward and a backward through the presentation one slide at a time.

Normal The default style that is applied to new worksheets. In Excel, the Normal style includes Arial 10-point font.

Normal template The template on which most documents are based, which contains the default Word document settings.

Nper Within an Excel function, the total number of payment periods in a loan over a specific span of time.

Nudge A command that moves an object in very small increments.

Object A portion of a document, such as a range of data from Excel, an Excel chart, or a PowerPoint slide or presentation. Objects can be copied and moved to another document or another application.

Object Linking and Embedding (OLE) A program-integration technology for sharing information, such as Word documents, spreadsheets, and graphics, among Office programs.

One-to-many A relationship between two tables where one record in the first table corresponds to many records in the second table.

One-to-one A relationship that requires that for every record in one table, there can be only one matching record in the other table.

Optimize Improve performance by increasing efficiency.

Organization chart A chart that presents a picture of the relationships in an organization.

Outline 1. A gray bar at the left side of a data table that visually represents levels of summary information that can be displayed or hidden. It displays when data is summarized with subtotals. 2. A list of topics for an oral or written report that visually indicates the order in which the information will be discussed, as well as the relationship of the topics to each other and to the total report.

Page footer An optional area in a report frequently used for page numbers, which appears at the bottom of every page in a report.

Page header An optional area in a report frequently used for column headings, which appears at the top of every page in a report.

Pages The database object that enables users to view information contained in a database from the Internet or a company intranet.

Pane A portion of a worksheet window bounded by and separated from other portions by vertical or horizontal bars.

Paragraph style Style that contains a set of instructions for changing a group of formatting characteristics in a paragraph, such as font, font size, line spacing, and indentation. All changes are applied together.

Parameter query A query that will prompt you for criteria before running the actual query.

Password Any combination of numbers, letters, or symbols up to fifteen characters long that is applied to a file to prevent others from gaining access or changing the file. A password should be known only to the person who uses the password.

Paste link A command that creates a link in which changes to the source application are updated in the destination application.

Paste Special Enables you to copy information from one location and paste it in another location using a different format. In Excel, it enables you to paste just one particular characteristic of a cell, reverse rows and columns, or to copy and include in a formula information from another cell.

Perspective The way in which a 3-D effect extends toward a single point.

Photo album A presentation composed of pictures.

Pie chart A graph in the shape of a pie that is used to show the contribution of each part to the whole.

Pixels The dots that comprise and determine the resolution of a computer monitor.

Placeholder text In a document created using a template, text that can be replaced but not edited.

Plot To represent numbers graphically on a chart.

Plot area 1. The area on the chart bounded by the category axis (x-axis) and the value axis (y-axis) that includes the data series. 2. The portion of a chart occupied by the chart graphic—a pie or columns. It does not include the title or legend areas.

Pmt Within an Excel function, such as the FV (Future Value) function, the payment that will be made in each annual period.

PMT function An Excel function that calculates the payment for a loan based on constant payments and a constant interest rate. The structure for the function is *PMT(rate, number of periods, present value, future value, type)*.

Portable Document Format (PDF) A standard document format that enables the document to be opened on different computers using different operating systems. PDF files can be opened with Adobe Acrobat Reader, a free program.

Postal bar code A bar code based on the ZIP code that allows addresses to be scanned and sorted electronically by the U.S. Postal Service.

PowerPoint Viewer A program that will run a PowerPoint slide show on another computer even if PowerPoint is not installed.

Precedent cells The cells used in a formula.

Primary key In a database table, the field that uniquely identifies a record in a table.

Primary sort The first sort of a multi-column sort performed on a table of data; also known as the major sort.

Properties Characteristics that determine the appearance, structure, and behavior of a control as well as the characteristics of the text or data it contains.

Property sheet Where users can view a control's properties.

Protection A worksheet condition that is invoked to make cells inaccessible unless they have been specifically unlocked. Individuals entering data cannot change areas of the worksheet that are protected and thus cannot alter important formulas and formats built into the template.

Pv Within an Excel function, the value that represents the amount an annuity is worth now; also referred to as the present value.

Query To ask a question. When applied to a database, it implies a process of restricting records through the use of criteria conditions that will display only those records that answer a question you might have about the data.

Range name A specific name given to a range of cells that can then be used to refer to the range in a function or formula.

Record All of the data about one item in a database. Records are stored in rows.

Record source Between two bound objects, the record source is the object from which the actual data comes.

Referential integrity A set of rules that Access uses to ensure that the data between related fields is valid.

Relational database A database that contains several tables that are related, or connected, to each other by common fields.

Relationship The connection between two fields in separate tables within a relational database.

Relationship line The line that connects two related objects in the Relationships window.

Relationships window The location where relationships can be viewed, created, and modified.

Replace A command that finds specific data and then replaces it with data that you specify.

Replica A copy of a database created so that multiple users can edit it.

Replica set Consists of the Design master and any replicas of a database when a database is replicated.

Report A database object that displays the fields and records from a table in an easy-to-read format suitable for printing and useful for summarizing information in a database in a professional-looking manner.

Report footer An optional area in a report useful for displaying report totals and which appears only once—at the end of the report.

Report header An optional area in a report frequently used for a logo, report title, or print date, and which appears only once—at the beginning of the report.

Research A feature that can be used to look up information in an encyclopedia, dictionary, thesaurus, or other reference tool using the MSN Learning and Research Web site.

Reviewing pane An area at the bottom of the screen that displays comments and tracked changes.

Rich Text Format (RTF) A universal document format that can be read by nearly all word processing programs.

Rotate handle A small green circle that is connected to an object by a short line and is used to rotate the object to any angle.

Salutation Part of a letter that begins with *Dear* and that can be customized for each individual.

Scale 1. The range of numbers in the data series that controls the minimum, maximum, and incremental values on the value axis of a chart. 2. To resize an image, keeping the same image proportions.

Scale to fit An Excel feature that enables you to control the number of pages that are required to print a worksheet. The font, rows, and columns are resized to force the worksheet into a selected number of pages.

Secondary sort The second or third column that is sorted on in a multi-column sort; also known as a minor sort.

Section selectors Used to select entire sections of a form to perform section-level operations, such as adding background colors.

Select query A query that retrieves and displays data from one or more tables based on criteria that you specify.

Selection handles Small black boxes surrounding an object to indicate the object is selected and can be modified or moved; also referred to as sizing handles.

Selection rectangle A dashed box that is drawn using the Select Objects pointer and is used to enclose objects that you wish to select.

Shared application A software application available to all of the applications in the Microsoft Office suite, including PowerPoint, Word, Excel, and Access.

Sizing handles Small white circles around an object that indicate that an object is selected.

Slide transition A method of introducing a slide during an onscreen slide show.

Sort A command used to organize table data numerically or alphabetically.

Source file The file in which an Office object is created.

Split box The short gray bar at the top of the vertical scroll bar that can be dragged to split the screen and as a result display two different parts of the document.

SQL The acronym and commonly used term for structured query language.

Standard chart type Fourteen predefined chart designs that are available in the Excel Chart Wizard.

Standardization The procedure whereby all forms created within the organization will have a uniform appearance and the data is organized in the same manner.

Status bar The horizontal bar at the bottom of the screen directly above the task bar.

Structured query language A database sublanguage used in querying, updating, and managing relational databases in database programs such as Microsoft Access.

Style 1. A set of formatting characteristics that is stored in one shortcut command. All formatting characteristics, such as font, font size, and indentation, are applied together. 2. A format designed by the user that can be applied to cells in multiple worksheets or other workbooks.

Subform A form that is embedded within another form (the main form).

Subreport A report inserted into a control; the control is then embedded in another report.

Synchronization The process of merging the replicas with the Design Master database.

Synonyms Words with similar meanings.

Syntax The arrangement of the elements in a function.

Tab delimited file A text file in which a tab character is used to separate the cell contents in rows. Excel files can be saved in this format for transferring information to various database or other types of programs.

Tab order The order in which the fields on a form are selected when the Tab key is pressed.

Table A format for information that organizes and presents text and numbers in columns and rows; also referred to as a list.

Table array A defined range of cells in another part of a workbook that can be searched to find a corresponding value.

Table move handle A four-way arrow that displays near the upper left corner of a table, and enables you to move the table by dragging the handle.

Table style Formats border type and style, shading, cell alignment, and fonts in a table.

Template 1. A workbook used as a pattern for creating other workbooks. Templates are preformatted and have built-in formulas for calculating totals based on the data that is entered. 2. Predefined document structures defining the basic document settings, such as font, margins, and available styles.

Text box 1. A drawing object that is used to position text anywhere on a slide. 2. A drawing object container into which you can type or insert text that is not constrained by the dimension of a cell.

Topic marker A small open square symbol to the left of body text in an outline.

Tracer arrow Shows the relationship between the active cell and its related cells. Tracer arrows are blue when pointing from a cell that provides data to another cell.

Track Changes A feature in Word that provides a visual indication of deletions, insertions, and formatting changes in a document.

Transpose To switch copied data between columns and rows.

Type Within an Excel function, a value that represents the timing of the payment, whether it will be paid at the beginning of each period (indicated by a 1) or at the end of the period (indicated by a 0).

Unbound controls Controls in a report that have no data source, but that display information such as labels that identify a field's contents.

Ungroup A command that returns a grouped object into separate objects.

Unlock The act of removing the default locked condition from cells that you want accessible for use.

Update query A type of action query that replaces existing data.

URL The abbreviation for Uniform Resource Locator.

Validation list A list of values that are acceptable for a group of cells. Anything not on the list would be considered invalid.

Validation rule An expression that precisely defines the information that will be accepted in a field.

Validation text Displays the correct format for a field that has a validation rule.

Value (y) axis The vertical line on the left side of the chart that displays the numeric scale for numbers in the selected data.

Variable information The information, such as name and address, that varies from letter to letter in a form letter created using Mail Merge.

VLOOKUP An Excel function that looks up values that are displayed vertically in a column.

Washout A color condition that creates a faded image, sometimes called a watermark, that can be placed in the background.

Wildcard A symbol that is used to help search a field when you are uncertain of the exact value, or when you want to widen a search to include more records. The asterisk (*) is a wildcard that can be used before or after a string of characters to search for any records that contain the specified string of characters.

Wizard template A step-by-step program that asks you questions and then sets up a document based on your answers.

WordArt A drawing tool used to transform text into graphic objects, such as logos or headings.

Worksheet In Excel, a set of cells that are identified by row and column headings. An Excel spreadsheet can contain more than one worksheet.

Index

Browse dialog box (Access), 2245
browsers, 2439, 2578
    viewing data access pages,
        1989, 1993–1995
Build button (Access)
    Back Color box, 2166
    Control Source box, 2161
    Field Properties box, 1964,
        1967–1968, 1976–1977
    Properties sheet, 2114
built-in styles. *See* styles
bulk mailing rates, 1519
Bullets and Numbering dialog box
    PowerPoint, 2296, 2557
    Word, 1283, 1296–1297
buttons. *See also* action
    buttons; toolbars
By Column button
    Chart toolbar
        Excel, 1638, 1641
        PowerPoint, 2511
    Standard toolbar (Word), 1259
By Row button (Chart toolbar,
    Excel), 1638, 1641–1642

C

C, input mask character, 1974
calculated fields, 1914–1915
    crosstab query, 2179
    groups, 2159–2163
    reports, 2164–2165
calculations
    order of operations, 1597. *See
        also* formulas; functions
    Word, 1427, 1494–1495, 1497
capital letters in input
    masks, 1970
Caption box (Change Icon dialog
    box, Word), 1500
Caption dialog box (Word),
    1429–1430
Captions below ALL pictures
    check box (PowerPoint), 2374
captions in tables, 1425,
    1429–1430
cascade, 2034
Cascade Delete Related Records
    check box, 2034, 2037–2038
Cascade Update Related Fields
    check box, 2033, 2037–2038
case sensitive passwords, 2053
category axes (charts)
    Excel, 1634, 1637, 1639, 1641
    PowerPoint, 2511–2512
    Word, 1255
CDs
    adding audio tracks to
        presentations, 2564
    packaging presentations,
        2573–2574
cell location indicators,
    1409–1410
Cell Options dialog box
    (Word), 1424

cells, 2486. *See also* tables
    active, 1711
    aligning, 1274
        text, 1418–1419, 2493–2494
    applying styles, 1754, 1758
    conditional formatting,
        1832–1835
    counting cells meeting a
        condition, 1723–1724
    creating, 2493
    dependent, 1844
    embedding Excel charts in
        Word, 1486–1491
    finding blank, 1722–1723
    going to specified, 1722–1723
    labeling, 1489
    locked, 1710–1711, 1713
    merging, 2492–2493
    precedent cells, 1841
    printing selected, 1599
    ranges. *See* ranges
    removing borders, 2492–2493
    shading, 1832,
        1834–1835, 2496
    specifying as function
        arguments, 1588–1591
    text
        aligning, 2493–2494
        entering, 2488–2489
        fitting in cells, 1424
    Word tables
        aligning text, 1418–1419
        fitting text, 1424
        formatting, 1441–1442
        merging, 1411, 1413–1414
        *summing numbers,
            1427, 1429*
Center button
    (Formatting toolbar)
    Access, 2115
    Excel, 1752, 1887
    PowerPoint, 2285,
        2493–2494, 2515
    Word, 1264, 1344, 1410, 1414,
        1440, 1502
Center Vertically button (Tables
    and Borders toolbar,
    PowerPoint), 2488, 2493–2494
centering
    charts, 1262–1265
        embedded charts, 1656
    columns, 1752
    objects, 2356–2358
    text, 1410, 1414
        in merged cells, 1758
Change AutoShape command
    (Draw menu, PowerPoint), 2291
Change button (Custom
    Animation task pane,
    PowerPoint), 2434
Change Icon dialog box (Word),
    1445, 1500
change markers, 2571
Change Text Direction button
    (Word), 1412, 1416–1417, 1440

changes
    accepting/rejecting,
        1365–1367, 1374–1376
    displaying, 1363
    locating, 1363–1365
    tracking, 1360–1362
changing text direction, 1416
characters
    counting, 1352
    readable, 2054
    spacing, modifying, 1270–127?
    styles, 1252, 1274
        *creating/applying,
            1286–1288*
Chart menu commands
    Excel, 1637
        3-D View, 1666
        Chart Options, 1642, 1661
        Chart Type, 1660
        Source Data, 1642
    PowerPoint
        3-D View, 2518
        Chart Options, 2511, 2517
        Word, Chart Options, 1256
Chart Object command (shortcu?
    menu, Word), 1491
Chart Objects button arrow
    (Chart toolbar, Excel),
    1637–1638, 1640, 1644, 165?
Chart Options dialog box
    Excel
        Data Labels tab, 1661
        Titles tab, 1642–1643
    PowerPoint
        Data Labels tab, 2517
        Legend tab, 2511, 2517
        Titles tab, 2511
    Word, Titles tab, 1256
Chart toolbar
    Excel, 1491–1492, 1637
        Angle Clockwise button, 16?
        *Angle Counterclockwise
            button, 1638*
        By Column button, 1638
        *By Row button, 1638,
            1641–1642*
        *Chart Objects arrow, 1640,
            1644, 1654*
        *Chart Objects button,
            1638, 1640*
        *Chart Type button arrow,
            1638, 1659, 2516*
        Data Table button, 1638
        displaying, 1637–1638
        Format Object button, 1644
        *Format Selected Object
            button, 1638*
        Legend button, 1638
    PowerPoint, By Column
        button, 2511
Chart Type button arrow
    Chart toolbar
        Excel, 1638, 1659
        PowerPoint, 2516
    Standard toolbar (Word), 125?

Hyperlink command (Insert menu, Access), 2232
Hyperlink data type, 1959, 1962
hyperlinks, 2227, 2439. *See also* **Web pages**
　action buttons, 2442–2443
　adding to worksheets, 1735, 1740
　editing, 2441
　from form
　　to Excel worksheet, 2230–2233
　　to Word document, 2227–2229
　linking to
　　custom shows, 2446–2447
　　hidden slides, 2444–2445
　　slides, 2441–2442
　　Web pages, 2439–2440
　modifying, 1742–1743
　removing, 2441
Hypertext Markup Language (HTML), 2578

I

icons
　Access, 1518
　changing colors, 1447
　PDF file, 1444–1446
Idea (Performance Analyzer), 2051
IF function, 1594–1597
images, 2303. *See also* **pictures**
　adding to text and content layouts, 2309
　adjusting
　　brightness, 1454–1455, 2365, 2367
　　color, 1453, 2365–2366
　　contrast, 1454–1455, 2365, 2367
　bitmap files, 2308
　clip art
　　collections, 2305
　　placeholders, 2304
　cropping
　　Excel, 1808
　　PowerPoint, 2367–2368
　　Word, 1449–1450
　digital images, 2308
　grayscale image color, 1453–1454
　inserting, 2305–2307
　media types, 2306
　modifying, 2365–2367
　moving, 2308
　overlaying text, 2378
　photo albums, 2373–2376
　Picture toolbar, 2365–2366
　purchased images, 2308
　recoloring, 2369–2370
　resetting to original, 2368–2369

　resizing, 1452–1453, 2307–2308
　restoring cropped areas, 2368
　rotating, 1450–1451
　searching for clips, 2304–2307
　slide backgrounds, 2378
　WordArt. *See* WordArt
Import Data dialog box (Excel), 1886
Import dialog box (Access), 2217, 2226
Import External Data command (Data menu, Excel)
Import Spreadsheet Wizard (Access), 2226
Import Text Wizard (Access), 2217–2218
Import to Table box (Access), 2219, 2227
importing
　Access databases to Excel, 1886–1887
　data
　　from Excel worksheet, 2226–2227
　　from Word tables, 2214–2217, 2219–2220
　　vs. linking, 2235
inactive sheet, tab color, 1677
Increase Indent button (Formatting toolbar, Word), 1284, 1299–1300
increasing space between characters, 1270
indents, 1274
index field in tables, 2024
Indexed arrow, 2219
Indexes dialog box (Access), 2025
indexing fields
　with duplicates, 2025
　without duplicates, 2024–2025
infinity sign (∞) on relationship line, 2029
information, 1348, 1884. *See also* **data**
　finding and replacing, 1716, 1719–1721, 1728–1730
　finding with Research tool, 1762–1764
Ink Color command (pen menu, PowerPoint), 2452
Input Mask Properties box, 1967–1972
input masks, 1967
　characters used, 1970, 1974
　numeric, 1972
　vs. field formats, 1972
Insert Address Block button (Word), 1516, 1521
Insert Address Block dialog box (Word), 1510–1511
Insert AutoText button (Header and Footer toolbar, Word), 1272, 1310, 1370, 1420, 1432, 1442

Insert button
　PowerPoint, 2223
　Word, 1521
Insert Clip Art button (Drawing toolbar, PowerPoint), 2280, 2304–2305
Insert Clip Art task pane (PowerPoint), 2305–2307
Insert Columns to the Left command (Table menu, PowerPoint), 2491
Insert command (Table menu, Word), 1427
Insert Comment button (Reviewing toolbar, Word), 135
Insert company name check box (Word), 1510
Insert Diagram or Organization Chart button (Drawing toolbar, PowerPoint), 2280
Insert dialog box (Excel), 1675, 1920
Insert Function button (Formula Bar, Excel), 1572, 1576, 1586, 1595, 1824, 1828, 1920
Insert Function dialog box (Excel), 1572–1573
　AVERAGE function, 1580
　COUNT function, 1580
　COUNTIF function, 1723
　DATE function, 1584
　FV function, 1587, 1767
　HLOOKUP function, 1828
　IF function, 1595
　MAX function, 1578
　MEDIAN function, 1573
　MIN function, 1577–1578
　NOW function, 1586
　PMT function, 1590
　VLOOKUP function, 1824
Insert Greeting Line button (Word), 1516
Insert Hyperlink button (Standard toolbar)
　Access, 2232
　PowerPoint, 2441
Insert Hyperlink dialog box
　Excel, 1740
　PowerPoint, 2439–2441
Insert menu commands
　Access
　Excel
　　Columns, 1759, 1762, 1914
　　Diagram, 1669
　　Function, 1572–1573, 1584, 1587, 1590, 1824, 1828, 1920
　　Name, Create, 1566, 1830
　　Name, Define, 1560
　　Picture, From File, 1806
　　Picture, WordArt, 1810
　　Worksheet, 1675

PowerPoint
Comment, 2569
Hyperlink, 2232
Movies and Sounds,
2563–2564
Word
Object, 1444, 1499
Picture, 1449
Picture, Chart, 1255
Reference, 1429–1430
Insert Merge Field dialog box
Access, 2223–2224
Word, 1521
Insert Merge Fields button
(Word), 1516, 1520–1522
Insert New Pictures dialog box
(PowerPoint), 2373
Insert New Record (Access), 2229
Insert New Title Master button
(Slide Master View toolbar,
PowerPoint), 2559
Insert Object dialog box
(Access), 1961
Insert Picture button
(PowerPoint)
Drawing toolbar, 2280, 2308
Picture toolbar, 2365
Insert Picture dialog box
Access, 2114
Excel, 1806
PowerPoint, 2280, 2308
Insert Picture From File button
(Picture toolbar, Excel),
1807, 1813
Insert Rows Above command
(Table menu, PowerPoint), 2490
Insert Rows Below command
(Table menu, PowerPoint), 2490
Insert Rows button (Word), 1427
Insert Shape button arrow
Excel, Diagram toolbar, 1673
PowerPoint
Diagram toolbar, 2500
Organization Chart toolbar,
2503–2504
Insert Table button
(Standard toolbar)
PowerPoint, 2487
Word, 1412
Insert Table dialog box
(PowerPoint), 2486–2487
Insert Word Field button
(Word), 1516
Insert WordArt button
PowerPoint Drawing toolbar,
2280, 2299
Excel WordArt toolbar, 1813
Insert WordArt dialog box
(PowerPoint), 2280
Inserting. *See also* embedding

merge fields in document,
1520–1522
objects in documents,
1444–1446
shapes in diagrams,
1672–1673
supporting information, 1764
table rows and columns,
2490–2491
worksheets, 1675
**instructions added to status bar,
2099–2100**
interest rates. *See also* **financial
functions**
future value of investment,
1587–1588
Goal Seek tool, 1767–1769
monthly loan payments,
1590–1591
Internet
accessing templates, 1343, 1355
hyperlinks. *See* hyperlinks
searching for clip art, 2304
**intersections, formula error
notations, 1839**
intranets, 1989, 2578
investments. *See also* **financial
functions**
future value of investments,
1587–1588
Goal Seek tool, 1767–1769
ISNA function, 1833–1834
Italic button (Formatting toolbar)
Excel, 1661
Word, 1281, 1408–1409

J-K

**joined tables, creating queries,
2040–2041**
junction tables, 2037–2039

Keep Together box, 2158
Keep Together property, 2166
**Key area (Performance
Analyzer), 2051**
keyboard shortcuts
Excel
Copy, 1764
Define Name dialog box, 1564
Find, 1719–1720
*Find and Replace dialog
box, 1728*
Go To, 1722, 1739
Paste, 1764
*toggling between formulas and
worksheet numbers, 1570*
PowerPoint
black screen, 2449
duplicating objects, 2363
pen pointer, 2450
restoring arrow pointer, 2453
rotating objects, 2352
white screen, 2450

L

**L, input mask character,
1970, 1974**
**Label button (Toolbox toolbar,
Access), 2085, 2114,
2152, 2168**
**label controls, in Design view of
forms, 2084–2085**
**Label Options dialog box (Word),
1506–1507**
Label products arrow, 1506
labels, 1506, 1632
axis labels, 1644–1645
data labels, 1634, 1639,
1661–1663
editing, 1512–1513
header rows, 1732
naming ranges, 1566–1567
previewing, 1512
and printing, 1513–1515
template labels, 1798–1799
tick mark labels, 1639
using Mail Merge Wizard,
1506–1508
large worksheets. *See
also* **worksheets**
column references, 1718
counting cells meeting a
condition, 1723–1724
filtering data, 1716, 1733–1735
finding and replacing
information, 1716,
1719–1721, 1728–1730
freezing and unfreezing panes,
1716, 1718–1719
going to specified cells,
1722–1723
hiding and unhiding
columns, 1725
splitting and unsplitting
worksheets, 1726–1730
Last Record button
Access, 1994
Word, 1516, 1524
Last Slide Viewed option, 2443
**launching applications from
slides, 2442–2443**
**Layout button (Organization
Chart toolbar, PowerPoint),
2504–2505**
layouts, text and content, 2309
leader lines, 1663
**Legend button (Chart toolbar,
Excel), 1638**
**legends, charts, 1255, 1637,
1639, 1641**
deleting, 1651
formatting
Excel, 1660
PowerPoint, 2515
moving, 1660–1661
positioning, 2511–2512

ail programs, 1372
ailing labels, 1503
ain document, 1504, 1520. *See also* documents
  linking with data source, 1522
  mail merge, 2221
  merging to/with
    data source, 1518
    records, 1523
    Word document, 1526–1527
ain document setup button
(Word), 1516–1517
ain form, 2116–2120
ajor sorts, 1732, 1890. *See also* sorting, data
ake-Table Query, 2184–2186
anagement levels. *See* organization charts
any-to-many relationship
(Access), 2037–2039
argins
  complex tables, 1435
  reports, 2163
  setting, 2248
aster, Slide Master command
(View menu, PowerPoint), 2352
aster Name dialog box
(PowerPoint), 2559
aster Slides
  adding to templates, 2559
  arranging slide elements, 2560–2561
  formatting, 2560
  Slide Master, 2556–2558
  Title Master, 2559–2560
atch box, 1984
atch Fields button (Word), 1516
atch Fields dialog box (Word), 1510–1511
AX function, 1578–1579
aximize button (Access), 2228
easurements, tick marks in charts, 1639
edia field, 1995
edia types, clip art, 2306. *See also* clip art
EDIAN function, 1573, 1576
edium Date format, 1966–1967
emo data type, 1962
emos
  creating, using templates, 1342–1344, 1355
  customizing, 1344, 1346–1347
enus, docking as toolbars, 2361–2362
erge and Center button
(Formatting toolbar, Excel), 1558, 1758
erge Cells button (Tables and Borders toolbar)
  PowerPoint, 2488, 2493
  Word, 1412–1414

merge fields, inserting in document, 1520–1522
Merge Styles dialog box
(Excel), 1756
Merge to E-mail button
(Word), 1516
Merge to Fax button (Word), 1516
Merge to New Document button
(Word), 1516, 1526
Merge to New Document dialog
box (Word), 1526
Merge to Printer button (Word), 1516, 1525
Merge to Printer dialog box
(Word), 1514, 1525
merging
  applying styles to merged cells, 1758
  cells, 1411, 1413–1414
  documents, 1373–1374
    accepting/rejecting changes, 1374–1376
    types of, 1373
  form letters to document, 1526–1527
  letters with records, 1523
  reviewed presentations, 2571–2572. *See also* reviewing presentations
  styles, merging with other workbooks, 1756
  table cells, 2492–2493
  table with Word document, 2221–2225
messages
  blank records in tables, 2220
  database conversion, 1998
  earlier version of Access, 1997
  email. *See* email, attachments
  exclusive use, 2052
  hyperlinks harmful to computer, 2229, 2233
  invalid value, 1959–1960
  record search complete, 1984
  validation, 1831–1832
  warning
    data integrity rules, 1975–1976
    field size changed, 1963–1964
    validation rule violation, 1977
Microsoft Graph
  PowerPoint, 2508–2509
  Word, 1254
    Formatting toolbar, 1258
    Standard toolbar, 1258
Microsoft Access. *See* Access
Microsoft Excel. *See* Excel
Microsoft PowerPoint. *See* PowerPoint
Microsoft Word. *See* Word

MIN function, 1577–1578
Minimize button, 2227
minor sorts, 1732, 1890. *See also* sorting, data
minus sign (-)
  collapse indicator, 2027
  order of operations, 1597
Misspelling the Name
option, 1847
Modify Style dialog box (Word), 1289–1290
modifying
  document windows, 1291–1292
  images and pictures, 1449
  new styles, 1280–1283
  outlines, in Outline View, 1306–1310
  styles, 1289–1291
monitors, screen
resolutions, 1717
monthly payments. *See also* financial functions
  calculating, 1590–1591
  Goal Seek tool, 1767–1769
months
  DATE function, 1584–1585
  NOW function, 1586
  serial values of dates, 1585–1586
More Brightness button
(Picture toolbar)
  Excel, 1807, 1809
  PowerPoint, 2365
  Word, 1454–1455
More Contrast button
(Picture toolbar)
  Excel, 1807
  PowerPoint, 2365, 2367
  Word, 1454
More items button (Access), 2223–2224
motion paths, 2435
  creating, 2435–2436
  editing points, 2437–2438
  resizing, 2437
mouse clicks
  advancing transitions, 2417–2419, 2426
  links. *See* hyperlinks
mouse pointers. *See* pointers
Move Down button (Outlining
toolbar, Word), 1306
move pointer, 1423
Move Shape Backward button
(Diagram toolbar)
  Excel, 1673
  PowerPoint, 2500
Move Shape Forward button
(Diagram toolbar)
  Excel, 1673
  PowerPoint, 2500